PowerWeb
FOR REAL ESTATE

PowerWeb included with this book
Online Resources for Improved Course Performance

Access to PowerWeb gives you:

Dynamic!

- Study tips with self-quizzes
- Links to related sites for this course

Easy to use!

- Current readings from *Annual Editions*
- Weekly Updates

On the Web!

- Current News
- Web research guide

To access this site, go to your text's Online Learning Center or:

http://www.dushkin.com/powerweb/

See other side for your special code and details.

The McGraw-Hill/Irwin Series in Finance, Insurance and Real Estate

Stephen A., Ross
Franco Modigliani Professor of
Finace and Economics
Sloan School of Management
Massachusetts Institute of Technology
Consulting Editor

FINANCIAL MANAGEMENT

Adair
Excel Applications for Corporate Finance
First Edition

Benninga and Sarig
Corporate Finance: A Valuation Approach

Block and Hirt
Foundations of Financial Management
Eleventh Edition

Brealey and Myers
Principles of Corporate Finance
Seventh Edition

Brealey, Myers and Marcus
Fundamentals of Corporate Finance
Fourth Edition

Brooks
FinGame Online 4.0

Bruner
**Case Studies in Finance: Managing
for Corporate Value Creation**
Fourth Edition

Chew
**The New Corporate Finance:
Where Theory Meets Practice**
Third Edition

Chew and Gillan
**Corporate Governance at the Crossroads:
A Book of Readings**
First Edition

DeMello
Cases in Finance

Grinblatt and Titman
Financial Markets and Corporate Strategy
Second Edition

Helfert
**Techniques of Financial Analysis:
A Guide to Value Creation**
Eleventh Edition

Higgins
Analysis for Financial Management
Seventh Edition

Kester, Ruback, and Tufano
Case Problems in Finance
Twelfth Edition

Ross, Westerfield and Jaffe
Corporate Finance
Seventh Edition

Ross, Westerfield and Jordan
Essentials of Corporate Finance
Fourth Edition

Ross, Westerfield and Jordan
Fundamentals of Corporate Finance
Sixth Edition

Smith
The Modern Theory of Corporate Finance
Second Edition

White
**Financial Analysis with an Electronic
Calculator**
Fifth Edition

INVESTMENTS

Bodie, Kane and Marcus
Essentials of Investments
Fifth Edition

Bodie, Kane and Marcus
Investments
Sixth Edition

Cohen, Zinbarg and Zeikel
**Investment Analysis and Portfolio
Management**
Fifth Edition

Corrado and Jordan
**Fundamentals of Investments: Valuation
and Management**
Third Edition

Farrell
**Portfolio Management: Theory and
Applications**
Second Edition

Hirt and Block
Fundamentals of Investment Management
Seventh Edition

FINANCIAL INSTITUTIONS AND MARKETS

Cornett and Saunders
**Fundamentals of Financial Institutions
Management**

Rose and Hudgins
Commercial Bank Management
Sixth Edition

Rose
**Money and Capital Markets: Financial
Institutions and Instruments in a Global
Marketplace**
Eighth Edition

Santomero and Babbel
**Financial Markets, Instruments,
and Institutions**
Second Edition

Saunders and Cornett
**Financial Institutions Management:
A Risk Management Approach**
Fourth Edition

Saunders and Cornett
**Financial Markets and Institutions: A
Modern Perspective**
Second Edition

INTERNATIONAL FINANCE

Beim and Calomiris
Emerging Financial Markets

Eun and Resnick
International Financial Management
Third Edition

Levich
**International Financial Markets:
Prices and Policies**
Second Edition

REAL ESTATE

Brueggeman and Fisher
Real Estate Finance and Investments
Twelfth Edition

Corgel, Ling and Smith
**Real Estate Perspectives: An Introduction
to Real Estate**
Fourth Edition

Ling and Archer
Real Estate Principles: A Value Approach
First Edition

FINANCIAL PLANNING AND INSURANCE

Allen, Melone, Rosenbloom and Mahoney
**Pension Planning: Pension, Profit-Sharing,
and Other Deferred Compensation Plans**
Ninth Edition

Crawford
Life and Health Insurance Law
Eighth Edition (LOMA)

Harrington and Niehaus
Risk Management and Insurance
Second Edition

Hirsch
Casualty Claim Practice
Sixth Edition

Kapoor, Dlabay and Hughes
Personal Finance
Seventh Edition

Williams, Smith and Young
Risk Management and Insurance
Eighth Edition

Real Estate Principles

A Value Approach

David C. Ling
University of Florida

Wayne R. Archer
University of Florida

 **McGraw-Hill Irwin**

Boston   Burr Ridge, IL   Dubuque, IA   Madison, WI   New York   San Francisco   St. Louis
Bangkok   Bogotá   Caracas   Kuala Lumpur   Lisbon   London   Madrid   Mexico City
Milan   Montreal   New Delhi   Santiago   Seoul   Singapore   Sydney   Taipei   Toronto

McGraw-Hill
Irwin

REAL ESTATE PRINCIPLES: A VALUE APPROACH

Published by McGraw-Hill/Irwin, a business unit of The McGraw-Hill Companies, Inc., 1221 Avenue of the Americas, New York, NY, 10020. Copyright © 2005 by The McGraw-Hill Companies, Inc. All rights reserved. No part of this publication may be reproduced or distributed in any form or by any means, or stored in a database or retrieval system, without the prior written consent of The McGraw-Hill Companies, Inc., including, but not limited to, in any network or other electronic storage or transmission, or broadcast for distance learning. Some ancillaries, including electronic and print components, may not be available to customers outside the United States.

This book is printed on acid-free paper

2 3 4 5 6 7 8 9 0 DOW/DOW 0 9 8 7 6 5 4

ISBN 0-07-282463-8

Vice president and editor-in-chief: *Robin J. Zwettler*
Publisher: *Stephen M. Patterson*
Developmental editor: *Jennifer V. Rizzi*
Executive marketing manager: *Rhonda Seelinger*
Media producer: *Kai Chiang*
Senior project manager: *Kari Geltemeyer*
Senior production supervisor: *Sesha Bolisetty*
Director of design BR: *Keith J. McPherson*
Photo research coordinator: *Kathy Shive*
Supplement producer: *Lynn Bluhm*
Senior digital content specialist: *Brian Nacik*
Cover design: *Kami Carter*
Cover credits: *Upper left, Museum of Modern Art, Nice, France; © gettyimages, Taxi; Jerry Driendl. Second from left, Chrysler Building, New York, New York; © gettyimages, Stone; Joseph Pobereskin. Center, Transamerica Building, San Francisco, California; © Larry Fisher/Masterfile. Second from upper right, Petronas Twin Towers, Kuala Lumpur, Malaysia; © gettyimages, Taxi; Josef Beck. Upper right, Wrigley Building, Chicago, Illinois; © gettyimages, Photodisc; Hisham F. Ibrahim. Bottom left, Guggenheim Museum, New York, New York; © gettyimages, Stone; Hiroyuki Matsumoto. Second from bottom left, Hancock Building, Chicago, Illinois; © gettyimages, Stone; Mark Segal. Second from bottom right, Trump Tower, New York, New York 1986; © gettyimages, Stone; Ernst Haas. Bottom right, Flatiron Building, New York, New York; © Tsuyoi/Masterfile.*
Typeface: *10/12 Times Roman*
Compositor: *Carlisle Communications, Ltd.*
Printer: *R. R. Donnelley*

Library of Congress Cataloging-in-Publication Data

Ling, David C.
    Real estate principles : a value approach / David C. Ling, Wayne R. Archer.
       p. cm. — (The McGraw-Hill/Irwin series in finance, insurance, and real estate)
    Includes index.
    ISBN 0-07-282463-8 (alk. paper)
    1. Real estate business—United States. I. Archer, Wayne R. II. Title. III. Series.
HD255.L56 2005
  333.33'2—dc22
                                              2003066494

www.mhhe.com

Dedications

To my wife, Lucy, for her patience and understanding during the preparation of this book and to our children, Alex, Sarah, and Rebecca, who really tried to understand what Dad was doing locked in his study for the better part of a year.

—DCL

To my wife, Penny, who matched our efforts in this book with an equal measure of her devotion, support and assistance; to our Stephen, John and Jennifer, who generously supported me with enthusiasm and tools for the task, and to my mother and Penny's mother, who always kept the faith that I would do something useful with my "typewriter."

—WRA

About the Authors

DAVID C. LING

David C. Ling is the William D. Hussey Professor of Real Estate and Director of graduate real estate programs at the University of Florida. Professor Ling received an MBA (1977) in finance and a Ph.D. (1984) in real estate and finance from The Ohio State University. Prior to moving to the University of Florida in 1989, Ling was a professor of real estate at Southern Methodist University and has taught at the Swedish School of Economics. His academic and professional publications have included articles on housing policy and economics, mortgage markets and pricing, private commercial real estate investments, publicly traded real estate companies, and performance evaluation.

During 2000 Professor Ling served as President of the American Real Estate and Urban Economics Association (AREUEA) and is currently a co-editor of *Real Estate Economics.* Professor Ling also serves on numerous editorial boards including the *Journal of Real Estate Finance and Economics,* the *Journal of Housing Economics, Journal of Property Research,* and *The Journal of Real Estate Research.*

Professor Ling has provided research and consulting services to several state and national organizations including the Federal National Mortgage Association, the National Association of Home Builders, the National Association of Realtors, the Florida Association of Realtors, and the CCIM Institute. He is a Fellow of the Homer Hoyt Institute, a faculty member of the Weimer School of Advanced Studies in Real Estate, and a Distinguished Fellow of The National Association of Industrial and Office Properties.

Additional information on Professor Ling is available at *http://www.cba.ufl.edu/fire/faculty.*

WAYNE R. ARCHER

Wayne R. Archer is professor of real estate and the Wachovia Fellow at the Warrington College of Business, University of Florida. He was director of the Center for Real Estate Studies from 1999 to 2003. He received a Masters in economics from Wichita State University (1968) and a Ph.D. in economics from Indiana University (1974). He has been a faculty member at the University of Florida since 1971. From 1979 through 1981 he served as a visiting researcher at the Federal Home Loan Bank Board and Federal Savings and Loan Insurance Corporation. His research publications include articles on office markets, house price indices, mortgage prepayment, mortgage pricing, and mortgage default risk.

Professor Archer is a member of the American Real Estate and Urban Economics Association, where he has served on the board of directors, and also is a member of the American Real Estate Society. He serves on the editorial board of *Real Estate Economics.* He is a Fellow of the Homer Hoyt Institute.

Professor Archer has worked in industry education throughout his academic career, including service as the educational consultant to the Florida Real Estate Commission from 1985 to 1999. Among additional roles, he served as a regular faculty member in programs of the Mortgage Bankers Association of America, in the Institute of Financial Education affiliated with the U.S. League of Savings and Loan Associations, and, more recently, with Freddie Mac. In addition, he has provided consulting services to industry and government from time to time throughout his career.

Additional information on Professor Archer is available at *http://www.cba.ufl.edu/fire/faculty.*

Preface

The study and practice of real estate draws on a multitude of disciplines including architecture, urban and regional planning, building construction, urban economics, law, and finance. This diversity of perspectives presents a challenge to the instructor of a real estate principles course. Depending on their backgrounds and training and on the interests of the students, some instructors may choose to emphasize the legal concepts that define and limit the potential value of real estate. Other instructors may focus more on licensing and brokerage issues (popular topics with many students) or on the investment decision making process. Still others may feel that real estate market and feasibility analysis should be the core topics in a principles class. In short, one of the difficulties in teaching an introductory real estate course is that there appear to be too many "principles." The critical question thus becomes: What framework should be used to teach these principles?

Although the subject of real estate can be studied from many perspectives, we have adopted the value perspective as our unifying theme. Why? Because value is central to virtually all real estate decision making including whether and how to lease, buy, or mortgage a property acquisition, whether to renovate, refinance, demolish, or expand a property, and when and how to divest (sell, trade, or abandon) a property. The ubiquitous reference in real estate to "improving a property" reflects this theme. "Improvement" in this context is another expression for adding value. Thus, whether a person enters the business of real estate in a direct way (e.g., development and ownership), becomes involved in a real estate service business (e.g., brokerage, property management, consulting, appraisal), or simply owns a home, he or she must continually make investment valuation decisions or advise others on their decisions. The decision for homeownership is a particularly important example of real estate value decisions. Homeownership is a beneficial choice for most households, for some time in their lives. But it is not the right choice for all households at all times, as seems to be implied at times by public discussion. If the household needs high mobility, or cash for school, or if the residence acquired is in a declining area, the value of homeownership could be negative. The key to making sound investment decisions is to understand how property values are created, maintained, increased, or destroyed.

Once value is established as the central theme, all other concepts and principles of real estate analysis can be built around it. Legal considerations, financing requirements and alternatives, income and property tax considerations, and local market conditions all are important primarily in the context of how they affect the value of the property. For example, in Part II students will study growth management and land use regulations. Although these concepts have great interest from a political and public policy perspective, they are important from a real estate view primarily because of their potential effects on property rents and values. Similarly, the "imperfections" in real estate markets discussed in Part II—such as the lack of adequate data, the large dollar value of properties, and the immobility of land and structures—are of interest for their effects on market values. Even the major valuation "techniques" discussed in Parts III and V, such as income capitalization and discounted cash flow models are presented here not as being ends unto themselves, but as tools to help determine value. Our objective is to provide the reader with a framework and a set of valuation and decision making tools that can be used in a variety of situations.

Real estate is a richly complex world where the decision maker is variously confronted with inadequate information for value determinations, and with too much information of the wrong kind. Our goal in the theme of this book is to direct the student toward an oriented and focused view concerning real estate value so that he or she has a better chance to ask the right questions and seek the right information when faced with the complexities of real-world real estate decisions.

Intended Audience

Real Estate Principles is designed for use in an introductory real estate course at both the undergraduate and graduate levels. In terms of background or prerequisites, some familiarity with basic economics and business finance principles is helpful and will allow the instructor to move more quickly through some of the material (especially Parts I, IV, V, and VII). However, the book is designed to be largely self-contained. As a result, students with different backgrounds will find the text accessible. Chapters 21-23 in Part VII (Advanced Topics) are largely designed for instructors who wish to emphasize commercial real estate investment topics.

Organization

Before the student can understand valuation and the investment decision-making process, the basic nature of real estate markets must be understood and the tools of financial analysis mastered. Part I of the book provides an overview of real estate and real estate markets and illustrates by example the value perspective in real estate decisions. For a diversity of cases, we consider in Chapter 2 the basic elements of real estate decisions: namely, determining value and comparing it to cost. In Chapter 3 we also introduce the basics of risk, compound interest, and present value that are essential to any valuation and investment decision.

For upper division undergraduate students who have had basic economics and business finance courses, Chapters 2 and 3 of Part I may contain substantial review. For others, these chapters contain new concepts that will require study and practice to master. In either case, however, the importance of these initial chapters cannot be overstated because they underlie the valuation and decision making focus of the remainder of the book. Even students who have previously studied finance or accounting should not take Chapters 2 and 3 lightly. It has been our experience that these basic valuation and decision-making concepts are rarely integrated into one's thinking the first time around and their application to real estate valuation questions presents new challenges.

Although we recommend that the material be covered in the order presented in the text, Parts II through VI can generally be covered in any order, depending on the preferences of the instructor and the primary focus of the course. For example, instructors who prefer to cover legal issues first may choose to assign Chapters 4 and 18-20 immediately following Chapter 1. Those who prefer to cover the investment material first can elect to move directly to Chapters 16 and 17 (and perhaps one or more of the Advanced Topics Chapters) immediately after Chapter 3.

Regardless of the emphasis placed on the various chapters and materials, we believe strongly that an introductory course in real estate should be as substantive and challenging as beginning courses in fields such as accounting, economics, and finance. The course should go beyond definitions and the discussion of current professional practice. Moreover, its focus should be on real estate principles and decision tools, not simply the current rules and practice for transactions that are so important to real estate sales licensing and brokerage. A general approach that recognizes the relationships among valuation and investment decision making, urban development and redevelopment, and the flow of scarce investment capital, determined by the framework of legal, social, and economic systems, should be the goal for real estate education.

Main Features

We have included many pedagogical features in this text that will be valuable learning tools for your students. This overview walks through some of the most important elements:

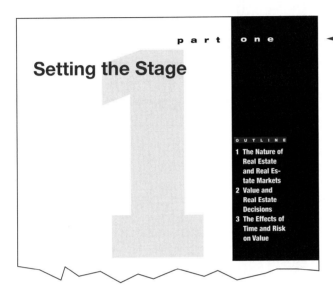

Part Openers

As an indicator, this one page opener outlines each chapter within its part.

Learning Objectives

Each chapter begins with a summary of the objectives of the chapter and describes the material to be covered, providing students with an overview of the concepts they should understand after reading the chapter.

Main Features

Chapter Outlines

On each chapter opener, a highlighted chapter outline can be found in the margin. Each outline lists the chapter headings and subheadings for a quick reference for both professors and students.

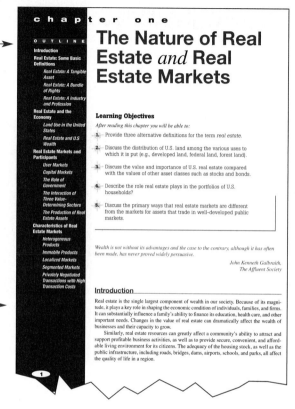

The Nature of Real Estate *and* Real Estate Markets

Learning Objectives

After reading this chapter you will be able to:

1. Provide three alternative definitions for the term *real estate*.

2. Discuss the distribution of U.S. land among the various uses to which it is put (e.g., developed land, federal land, forest land).

3. Discuss the value and importance of U.S. real estate compared with the values of other asset classes such as stocks and bonds.

4. Describe the role real estate plays in the portfolios of U.S. households?

5. Discuss the primary ways that real estate markets are different from the markets for assets that trade in well-developed public markets.

Wealth is not without its advantages and the case to the contrary, although it has often been made, has never proved widely persuasive.

John Kenneth Galbraith,
The Affluent Society

Introduction

Real estate is the single largest component of wealth in our society. Because of its magnitude, it plays a key role in shaping the economic condition of individuals, families, and firms. It can substantially influence a family's ability to finance its education, health care, and other important needs. Changes in the value of real estate can dramatically affect the wealth of businesses and their capacity to grow.

Similarly, real estate resources can greatly affect a community's ability to attract and support profitable business activities, as well as to provide secure, convenient, and affordable living environment for its citizens. The adequacy of the housing stock, as well as the public infrastructure, including roads, bridges, dams, airports, schools, and parks, all affect the quality of life in a region.

1

Chapter Introductions

The first section of each chapter describes the purpose of reading each chapter, and provides links between the different concepts.

Real Estate: Some Basic Definitions

It is important at the outset that we define the term *real estate*, as well as some closely related terms that are used throughout this book. When people think of real estate, they often think of the homes in their community or the business of buying and selling houses. This is probably because the personal investment that most households make in their home represents their primary involvement in the real estate market. Of course, real estate includes not only our homes, but also our places of work, commerce, worship, government, education, recreation, and entertainment—our physical environments, natural and built. In addition, it includes a wide range of business and institutional activities associated with the development, purchase, use, and sale of land and buildings.

Real estate is property. The term **property** refers to anything that can be owned, or possessed. Property can be a tangible asset or an intangible asset. **Tangible assets** are *physical* things, such as automobiles, clothing, land, or buildings. **Intangible assets** are *nonphysical* and include contractual rights (e.g., mortgage and lease agreements), financial claims (e.g., stocks and bonds), interests, patents, or trademarks.

The term real estate is used in three fundamental ways. First, its most common use is to identify the tangible assets of land and buildings. Second, it is used to denote the "bundle" of rights that are associated with the ownership and use of the physical assets. Finally, the term real estate may be used when referring to the industry or business activities related to acquisition, operation, and disposition of the physical assets.

Key Terms

Key terms are indicated in bold within the text for easy reference. A list of key terms from each chapter plus page references can be found in the end-of-chapter material. The glossary contains the definitions of all key terms.

Industry Issues

Industry Issues

5-1

A Redevelopment Where Everybody Wins

On the northeast border of Texas is the proud town of Marshall, population 24,000, in a county of about 60,000, and one of the oldest cities in the state. For a century its life revolved around the Texas and Pacific Railroad, and cotton production, followed later by oil and lumber. A center for production of fine railcars a century ago, it also is a town of well-built historic homes. But in the mid-1990s Marshall, like so many small cities in the United States, found itself with a struggling local economy. Its orientation to oil production and lumber gave it a ticket on the train of high unemployment and slow growth. Symptomatic of the economic challenges was the town's shopping center, the Marshall Mall, a 195,000-square-foot center built in 1980. By 1995 the anchor tenant, Kmart, occupying a third of the space, had closed, leaving 61,000 feet of darkness. The unemployment rate in the county was over 8 percent at that time, and the Marshall Mall, owned by a major life insurance company, was for sale for a small fraction of replacement cost.

Enter a thoughtful and enterprising development group. They learned about the mall, and also found that Blue Cross/Blue Shield of Texas was undertaking a program of regional decentralization. While working with the local economic development agency and submitting a proposal to BCBS for a regional processing center, the development group acquired the mall and set about to allow Kmart to buy out its lease. It worked. Kmart moved out, BCBS moved in. The mall came back to life, and rents began to flow. In 2003 the Marshall Mall is generating over three times as much net cash flow, and has increased its value probably fourfold. But Marshall Mall's recovery may be the minor story. BCBS has brought over 500 new jobs to the economic base of Marshall, along with a healthy economic base multiplier effect that may easily have doubled the number of new jobs. BCBS is now the city of Marshall's second largest private employer. Marshall's unemployment rate relative to the rest of Texas is the best it has been in years, and many more people are able to find jobs in their hometown.

Source: Kelley Bergstrom, Marshall Mall L.L.C., Kelley Bergstrom Investment Management, L.L.C.

These boxes, located in almost all chapters, feature current and interesting real-world applications of the concepts discussed in the chapters.

Career Focus

Career Focus

Real Estate Appraisers

Real estate appraisal practices are typically focused on either residential or commercial appraisal. Residential appraisers focus on single-family homes and small residential rental properties. Most of this work deals with appraisals for mortgage lending purposes or for corporate relocation firms.

National appraisal standards are set by the Appraisal Standards Board in Washington, D.C. All 50 states require real estate appraisers to be licensed or certified. Certification is at two levels, residential and general. These qualification levels are based on a combination of education, tests, and experience. The activities of "licensed appraisers" are limited to residential properties valued up to $1 million and nonresidential properties up to $250,000. Licensed appraisers must have at least 2,000 hours of appraisal experience over a two-year period and 90 hours of approved appraisal education. In addition, they must pass a uniform state examination. Finally, they must complete a minimum of 14 classroom hours of approved continuing education each year for license renewal.

"Certified residential appraisers" are allowed to appraise all types of residential property plus nonresidential property up to a value of $250,000. The minimum education requirement for a certified residential appraiser is 120 hours (although a college degree may largely substitute in some states). The experience requirement is 2,500 hours over a two-year period. Uniform state exams for certification are more rigorous than state licensing exams. Again, 14 hours of continuing education are required each year to maintain certification.

The "certified general appraiser" is permitted to value any types of real estate, including large commercial properties. The experience requirement is 3,000 hours of appraising over 30 months, half of which must be with nonresidential property. The certified general appraiser must complete 180 hours of appraisal education. Again, there is a required state exam, and required continuing education of 14 hours a year.

Many appraisers go beyond certification to obtain trade association designations. These designations signal to potential clients that the appraiser has obtained even more education and/or professional experience in the field than is required for state certification. The Appraisal Institute (www.appraisalinstitute.org) offers the residential SRA designation and the prestigious MAI designation for commercial appraisers.

Sources: *Information on Career Paths in Commercial Real Estate*, University of Cincinnati, www.cba.uc.edu/getreal and *Career Opportunities*, Washington State University, www.cbe.wsu.edu/~fire/real_estate

These boxed readings provide students with valuable information on the many different career options available to them, and what those positions entail.

Main Features

Website Annotations

Websites are called out in the margins in every chapter and include a notation of what can be found by visiting them.

Exhibit 8-9 Summary of Cost Approach

	Estimated reproduction cost of structure
−	Accrued depreciation
=	Depreciated cost of building improvements
+	Estimated value of site
=	Indicated market value by the cost approach

termed *accrued depreciation*. After the appraiser has estimated the building's value by subtracting all elements of accrued depreciation from the building's cost, the value of the land (and permanent improvements to the land) is estimated separately and added to the depreciated cost of the building. The general steps of the cost approach are outlined in Exhibit 8-9.

Estimating Cost. For appraisal purposes, there are two possible types of construction costs: reproduction costs and replacement costs. The **reproduction cost** of a building is the cost to construct the building today, replicating it in exact detail. This includes any outdated functional aspects of the building such as poor room arrangement, better-than-necessary fixtures, or inadequate equipment. It also includes the cost of any outmoded materials such as surface wiring, steel window frames, and steel plumbing.

www.marshallswift.com
Leading cost estimator for the appraisal industry.

In contrast, **replacement cost** is the money required to construct a building of *equal utility*.[7] This includes the use of modern construction techniques, materials, and design and represents the cost of a building for which some or all outdated aspects are eliminated.

www.rsmeans.com
Provider of cost estimation services.

In estimating cost, appraisers tend to rely on builders' cost figures to maintain comparative cost data on a square-foot or cubic-foot basis for various types of properties, and to use cost estimating services. In addition to builders, several private companies, such as Marshall and Swift, are in the business of proving detailed cost estimates.

The theoretical base for the cost approach is reproduction cost. However, reproduction cost is often difficult to estimate because the building may include materials that are no longer available or no longer permitted by current construction standards. As a result, replacement cost is often used since it is easier to obtain.

Concept Check

Every major section contains one or more questions for review. This feature helps students test their understanding of the material before moving on to the next section. Solutions to each concept check are provided at the end of each chapter so students can check their answers.

Concept Check

5.7 Cost efficiencies that arise in a city due to concentration of an industry are called _____ whereas cost efficiencies arising from the concentration of multiple industries are called _____ .

Concept Check

5.10 Why is it that in a simple bid-rent model a person who commutes on foot will outbid one who commutes by car for the closest space to downtown?

Explore the Web

Found in every chapter, these boxes contain Internet activities that weave the web, real data, and practical applications with concepts found in the chapters.

Explore The Web

To examine the recent stock market performance of Equity Residential Properties (EQR), go to the NAREIT website (www.nareit.com). Click on "Investing in REITs," then on "REIT Performance Information." Retrieve information on EQR. What was EQR's total return in the last month? The last year? The last five years? How do these returns compare to other publicly traded apartment REITs?

Online Learning Center (OLC) available at www.mhhe.com/lingarcher1e

This website follows the text chapter-by-chapter with digital supplementary content specific to this book. As you read the book, instructors can go online to access the password-protected Instructor's Manual and PowerPoint, and students can take self-grading quizzes, review material, and work through interactive exercises.

Real Estate Online

As part of this OLC, instructors and students will also have free access to Real Estate Online, found on the opening page of the website. Real Estate Online is an exclusive web tool from McGraw-Hill/Irwin. For each of the 24 key real estate topics, students can complete challenging exercises and discussion questions that draw upon recent articles, company reports, government data, and other Web-based resources. Some topics include: valuation methods, lease analysis, acquisition, risk analysis and cycles and trends. For instructors, there are also password-protected teaching notes to assist with classroom integration of the material.

Chapter One

www.cba.uc.edu/getreal
www.census.gov
www.nrcs.usda.gov
www.bea.doc.gov
www.federalreserve.gov
www.bloomberg.com
www.jblevy.com
www.uli.org
www.marshallswift.com
www.prea.org
www.loopnet.com
www.hud.gov

Chapter Two

www.fool.com
www.hud.gov/buying/index.cfm
www.houseandhome.msn.com
www.hud.gov
www.houseandhome.msn.com/improve/checklists/
    setpriorities.asp
www.uli.org
www.appraisalinstitute.org
www.freddiemac.com/homebuyers/library
www.houseandhome.msn.com

Chapter Three

www.rerc.com

Chapter Four

www.rentlaw.com
www.r6.fws.gov/pwf/r6pwf8b.htm
www.mechlien.com/lien_links.htm
www.firstam.com/landsakes/html/email/042202fed.html
www.megalaw.com/top/condo.php
www.keln.org/bibs/barnes.html
www.firstam.com/title-ca/sanjoaquin/html/cust/2195.html
www.arda.org
www.epa.gov/region5/water/cwa.htm

Chapter Five

www.stats.indiana.edu/uspr/a/us_profile_frame.html
www.census.gov/prod/
www.ccdb.html
www.census.gov
www.terrafly.fiu.edu

Chapter Six

www.sustainable.doe.gov/landuse/luintro.shtml
www.plannersweb.com/sprawl/home.html
www.planning.org
www.planetizen.com/sites
www.smartgrowth.net/links/sg_links.fst.html
www.law.cornell.edu/topics/land_use.html
www.realtor.org/libweb.nsf/pages/fg805
www.epa.gov/epahome/laws.htm
www.epa.gov/asbestos
www.epa.gov/swerust1/mtbe/
www.epa.gov/iag/radon/pubs/consguid.html
www.moldupdate.com
www.tamu.edu
www.statetaxcentral.com/

Chapter Seven

www.uli.org
www.census.gov
www.census.gov/epcd/cbp/view/cbpview.html
www.terrafly.com
www.bis.gov
www.orlandoairports.net
www.bls.gov
www.grubb-ellis.com/
www.cbre.com/research/market+reports/
    us+vacancy+reports/default.htm
www.cushmanwakefield.com/us/markets/
    us.cfm.world_id=1
www.gsd.harvard.edu/pbcote/GIS/
    web_resources.html
www.gisportal.com
www.retailtraffic.com
www.cluster1.claritas.com
www.census.gov

(continued on inside back cover)

Assume you expect to pay off the loan at the end of six more years (72 months), leaving 108 months at payoff. Following our earlier method, we compute the balance at payoff as the present value of the 108 remaining payments. This gives a balance of $66,065.42.[15] Now we have the necessary information to compute the present value of the loan, prepaid. Discounting at the current loan interest rate of 6 percent, our computation is:

72	6 ÷ 12	$860.09	$66,065.42
n	i	PV	PMT	FV

−$98,037.87

Thus, the present value of the existing loan, prepaid at the end of six years, is $98,030.87.

Calculator Keystrokes

Found in applicable chapters, calculator keys are shown with values to help guide students through numerical calculations.

Exhibit 10-3 Mortgage versus Deed of Trust

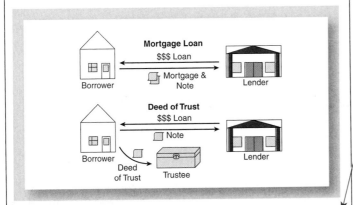

Figures & Tables

This text makes extensive use of real data and presents them in various exhibits. Explanations in the narrative, examples, and end-of-chapter problems will refer to many of these exhibits.

Exhibit 13-5 Consolidation in the Top 20 Home Mortgage Lenders

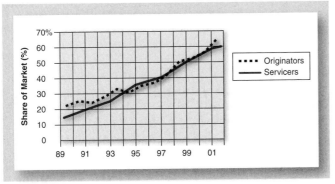

Source: The *2002 Mortgage Market Statistical Annual,* vol 1. Inside Mortgage Finance Publications Inc. Bethesda, Md. 2002.

End-of-Chapter Features

Chapter Summary

Each chapter ends with a short section that highlights the important points of the chapter. This provides a handy study tool for students when they review the chapter.

Summary

Homebuyers have a number of choices when deciding where to obtain mortgage financing. Altogether, depository institutions such as thrifts, credit unions, and commercial banks have diminished as a source of home loans, largely due to the drastic decline of thrifts. Still, thrifts account for perhaps 15 percent of home mortgage loans (specializing in ARMS), and depositories account for over 40 percent of all conventional one- to four-family residential mortgage originations being made. Mortgage banking companies account for almost all of the remaining originations. Their increasing role is evidence of a larger shift from "portfolio" lending to reliance on the secondary market and securitization.

More than half of all residential mortgage loans originated in the United States are now sold into the secondary mortgage market. The largest purchasers of residential mortgages in this market are Fannie Mae and Freddie Mac. These government-sponsored enterprises (GSEs) also are the largest issuers of residential mortgage-backed securities (MBSs), which are written against pools of mortgages purchased from primary market originators.

In developing and facilitating the secondary market in residential mortgages, Fannie Mae and Freddie Mac have developed standardized documents and procedures for loans submitted to them for purchase. This has brought wide conformity to the primary, as well as the secondary, mortgage market. Because of this standardization, investors today are much better able to buy and sell mortgages and MBSs because the risk return characteristics of these securities are more easily analyzed. The increased standardization and liquidity provided by the GSEs has greatly improved mortgage market efficiency.

www.mhhe.com/lingarch

List of Key Terms

A list of the bold key terms in the text with page references is included for easy reference at the end of each chapter.

Key Terms

Affordable housing loan 349	Forward commitment 335	Pipeline risk 333
Automated underwriting 347	Government National Mortgage	PITI 346
Collateral 346	Association (GNMA) 339	Portfolio lenders 332
Commercial banks 331	Housing expense ratio 346	Risk-weighted assets 329
Conduits 340	Interest rate risk 334	Savings and loan associations
Credit scoring 346	Loan servicing 336	(S&Ls) 327
Credit unions 331	Loan underwriting 346	Savings banks 327
Disintermediation 328	Mortgage bankers 332	Standby forward commitment 335
Fallout risk 334	Mortgage brokers 332	Total debt ratio 346
Financial intermediaries 327	Mortgage pipeline 334	Warehousing 331

End-of-Chapter Features

Test Problems

Answer the following multiple choice problems:

1. Mortgage banking companies:
   a. Collect monthly payments and forward them to the mortgage investor.
   b. Arrange home loan originations, but do not make the actual loans.
   c. Make home loans and fund them permanently.
   d. None of the above.

2. In recent years, the mortgage banking industry has experienced:
   a. Decline.
   b. Decentralization.
   c. Limited consolidation.
   d. Rapid consolidation.

3. Currently, which type of financial institution in the primary mortgage market provides the most funds for the residential (owner-occupied) housing market?
   a. Life insurance companies.
   b. Savings and loan associations.
   c. Credit unions.
   d. Commercial banks

4. For all except very high loan-to-value conventional home loans, the standard payment ratios for underwriting are:
   a. 28 percent and 36 percent.
   b. 25 percent and 33 percent.
   c. 29 percent and 41 percent.
   d. 33 percent and 56 percent.

5. The numerator of the standard housing expense (front-end) ratio in home loan underwriting includes:
   a. Monthly principal and interest.
   b. Monthly principal, interest, and property taxes.
   c. Monthly principal, interest, property taxes, and hazard insurance.
   d. All of these plus monthly obligations extending 10 months or more.

6. The most profitable activity of residential mortgage bankers is typically:
   a. Loan origination.
   b. Loan servicing.
   c. Loan sales in the secondary market.
   d. Loan brokerage activities.

7. Potential subprime borrowers include persons who:
   a. Are creditworthy but want a 100 percent or higher LTV loan.
   b. Are credit-impaired.
   c. Persons with no documentation of their income.
   d. All of these.

8. Savings banks are now virtually indistinguishable from:
   a. Credit unions.
   b. Savings and loan associations.
   c. Commercial banks.
   d. Mortgage bankers.

9. The reduced importance of certain institutions in the primary mortgage market has been largely offset by an expanded role for others. Which two are these?
   a. Commercial bankers; savings and loan associations.
   b. Mortgage bankers; commercial banks.
   c. Commercial banks; mortgage bankers.
   d. Savings and loans associations; mortgage bankers.

10. *Warehousing* refers to:
    a. Short-term loans made by mortgage bankers to commercial banks.
    b. Short-term loans made by commercial banks to mortgage bankers.
    c. Long-term loans made by commercial banks to mortgage bankers.
    d. Short-term loans to finance the construction of industrial warehouses.

Study Questions

1. What is the primary purpose of the risk-based capital requirements that Congress enacted as part of the Financial Institutions Reform, Recovery, and Enforcement Act (FIRREA)?

2. Explain what is meant by *forward commitments* and *standby forward commitments*. Which part of the mortgage banker's pipeline is often hedged with forward commitments? With standby forward commitments? Why?

3. Describe the basic activities of Fannie Mae in the secondary mortgage market. How are these activities financed?

4. Explain the importance of Fannie Mae and Freddie Mac to the housing finance system in the United States.

5. Describe the activities mortgage bankers often engage in to generate income.

6. Describe the mechanics of warehouse financing, in mortgage banking.

7. Explain how affordable housing loans differ from standard home loans.

8. List three "clients" for subprime home mortgage loans.

9. You have just signed a contract to purchase your dream house. The price is $120,000 and you have applied for a $100,000, 30-year, 5.5 percent loan. Annual property taxes are expected to be $2,000. Hazard insurance will cost $400 per year. Your car payment is $400, with 36 months left. Your monthly gross income is $5,000. Calculate:
   a. The monthly payment of principal and interest (PI).
   b. One-twelfth of annual property tax payments and hazard insurance payments.
   c. Monthly PITI (principal, interest, taxes, and insurance).
   d. The housing expense (front-end) ratio.
   e. The total obligations (back-end) ratio.

10. Contrast automated underwriting with

Test Problems

Because solving problems is so critical to a student's learning, approximately 10 multiple-choice problems are provided per chapter to help students master important chapter concepts.

Study Questions

Each chapter contains 10 to 20 study questions that ask students to apply the concepts they have learned to real situations and problems to reinforce chapter concepts.

End-of-Chapter Features

Solutions to Concept Checks

Located at the end of each chapter, answers to each concept check question are provided to help the student understand the concepts and the reasoning behind them.

Explore the Web

These boxes are not only in the text but also in the end-of-chapter material. In every chapter, these boxes contain Internet activities that weave the Web, real data, and practical applications with concepts found in the chapters.

Additional Readings & Websites

Each chapter is followed by a list of books and articles to which interested students can refer to for additional information and research.

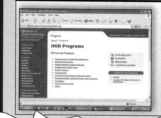

Solutions To Concept Checks

1. A major determinant between real and personal property is whether or not the property is movable or permanently affixed to the land.
2. Tangible assets are physical assets such as land, automobiles, and buildings. Intangible assets are nonphysical, including patents, financial claims, or contractual agreements. Real estate is a tangible asset, but a bundle of intangible rights is also associated with the ownership and use of the property.
3. About 43 percent of the U.S. housing stock is financed with home mortgage debt.
4. The four capital market quadrants include private equity, private debt, public equity, and public debt. The private equity market includes transactions of real property between individuals, firms, and institutions. Private debt includes the trading of home mortgages. Investors trade real estate companies such as equity REITs in the public equity market. Mortgage-backed securities are traded in the public debt markets.
5. Commercial real estate rental rates are determined in user markets while investors' required rates of return are determined in the capital market.
6. First, real estate is a heterogeneous product distinguished by its age, building design, and location. Second, real estate is immobile, and therefore location and its accessibility are important. Third, real estate is a localized, segmented market due to local competition and the heterogeneous nature of the product. Finally, real estate transactions have high transfer costs and deals are privately negotiated.

www.mhhe.com/lingarcher1e

Explore The Web

The government affects real estate in many ways. At the federal level, many housing programs exist. Go to www.hud.gov, and explore the different housing programs available. Give a brief overview of five of the programs you find on this site.

Additional Reading

Substantial portions of the following books are devoted to residential mortgage financing:

Brueggeman, William B., and Jeffrey D. Fisher. *Real Estate Finance and Investments*, 11th ed. New York: McGraw-Hill Irwin, 2002.

Clauretie, T. M., and G. S. Sirmans. *Real Estate Finance: Theory and Practice*, 4th ed. Cincinnati, OH: South-Western Publishing, 2002.

Fabozzi, Frank J., and Franco Modigliano. *Mortgage and Mortgage-Backed Securities Markets*. Cambridge: Harvard Business School Press, 1992.

Lederman, J. *The Handbook of Mortgage-Banking: Trends, Opportunities, and Strategies*, 2nd ed. New York: McGraw-Hill, 1993.

Weicher, J. C. *The Home Equity Lending Industry: Refinancing Mortgages Borrowers with Impaired Credit*. Indianapolis: Hudson Institute, 1997.

Wiedemer, John P. *Real Estate Finance*, 9th ed. Cincinnati, OH: South-Western Publishing 2001.

Supplements

For Instructors

The **Instructor's Resource CD-ROM** contains the following assets:

Instructor's Manual, *prepared by Shiawee Yang, Northeastern University*
Developed to clearly outline the chapter material as well as provide extra teaching support, the first section contains an Instructor Outline that follows the material, as well as containing teaching experiences, and covers what typical students know and do not know. Other sections include: learning objectives, lecture notes, and suggested solutions to end-of-chapter problems and questions.

Test Bank, *prepared by Charles Delaney, Baylor University*
With almost 1,000 multiple-choice questions and problems in Microsoft Word format, this Test Bank provides a variety of question levels to meet any instructor's testing needs.

Computerized Test Bank
Available in Windows format, this software provides you with the Test Bank in electronic form. The keyword search option lets you browse through the question bank for problems containing a specific word or phrase. Password protection is available for saved tests or for the entire database. Questions can be added, modified, or deleted.

PowerPoint Presentation, *prepared by Wayne R. Archer and David C. Ling*
Prepared by the authors, more than 500 full-color slides of images and tables from the text, lecture outlines and additional examples are available with this product.

Online Support

Online Learning Center (OLC)
www.mhhe.com/lingarcher1e.

This website follows the text chapter-by-chapter with digital supplementary content specific to this book. The Instructor's Manual and PowerPoint Presentation are available to the instructor in the password-protected Instructor's Center.

As students read the book, they can go online to the Student Center to take self-grading quizzes, review material, and work through interactive exercises, created by Dr. Greg Smersh, University of North Florida.

Real Estate Online
As part of this OLC, instructors and students will also have access to Real Estate Online, found on the opening page of the text website. Real Estate Online is an exclusive Web tool from McGraw-Hill/Irwin. For each of the 24 key real estate topics, students complete challenging exercises and discussion questions, prepared by Dr. Greg Smersh, University of North Florida, that draw on recent articles, company reports, government data, and other Web-based resources. Some topics include: valuation methods, lease analysis, acquisition, risk analysis, and cycles and trends. For instructors, there are also password-protected teaching notes to assist with classroom integration of the material.

Business Around the World
Located on the homepage of the OLC and on the Real Estate Online homepage, this product is an exclusive McGraw-Hill/Irwin global business resource, providing real-time links for researching and exploring business online, country by country. Online resources for business news, analysis, general facts, and guidelines on conducting business in the country or countries that interest you.

Acknowledgments

We take this opportunity to thank those individuals who helped us prepare this first edition of *Real Estate Principles*. A special debt of gratitude goes to Dr. Halbert Smith, Director of the Center for Real Estate Studies and Professor Emeritus at the University of Florida. Professor Smith has been a long time mentor and colleague to us both. His book titled *Real Estate* and *Urban Development* (Irwin 1981), coauthored with Tschappat and Racster, has significantly influenced our approach to the teaching of real estate principles over the last twenty years. Many of the ideas first put forth in *Real Estate and Urban Development* can be found in this text. Dr. Smith served as Contributing Editor on this project, providing detailed comments and suggestions during each phase of the book's development.

Our good friend and colleague, Dean Gatzlaff was to have joined us in the creation of this book, but found it to be infeasible. We are grateful to him for his substantial contribution in providing initial drafts of Chapters 1, 6, 8 and 9.

We are grateful to the following individuals for their thoughtful reviews and suggestions for the first edition of this text:

Paul Asabere,
  Temple University
Steven Bourassa,
  University of Louisville
Jay Butler,
  Arizona State University
Jon Crunkleton,
  Old Dominion University
Charles Delaney,
  Baylor University
David Downs,
  Virginia Commonwealth University

Steven Ott,
  University of North Carolina—Charlotte
Marion Sillah,
  South Carolina State University
Neil Waller,
  Clemson University
Alex Wilson,
  California State University—Long Beach
Alan Ziobrowski,
  Georgia State University

Special thanks go to Penny Archer for extensive Internet research leading to most of the photos and a large portion of the Industry Issues material in the text and to the graduate students in our 2003 summer and fall real estate courses who provided numerous suggestions and corrections on the manuscript.

We would especially like to thank Professor Shiawee Yang, Northeastern University, for authoring the Instructor's Manual, Professor Chuck Delaney, Baylor University, for authoring the Instructor's Test Bank, and to Dr. Greg Smersh, University of North Florida, for creating both the Online Self-Study Questions and Real Estate Online, which can be found on the book website, *www.mhhe.com/lingarcher1e*. Nicholas Kastanias contributed significantly to the development of the glossary and to the solutions for the end of chapter problems. We are confident that users of the book will find these ancillary materials to be first rate.

Finally, we are grateful to Steve Patterson, Publisher at McGraw-Hill, for encouraging us to undertake this project and for his help in developing the book's theme and target market. A special debt of gratitude also goes to Jennifer Rizzi, our Developmental Editor at McGraw-Hill, who devoted substantial energy to this project.

We are also grateful to the rest of the talented staff at McGraw-Hill who worked on the book: Rhonda Seelinger, Executive Marketing Manager; Kari Geltemeyer, Project Manager; Sesha Bolisetty, Production Supervisor; Keith McPherson, Design Director; Lynn Bluhm, Supplements Producer; and Kathy Shive, Photo Coordinator.

David C. Ling

Wayne R. Archer

Brief Contents

Contents

Contents

Real Estate Principles

A Value Approach

Setting the Stage

chapter one

The Nature of Real Estate *and* Real Estate Markets

Learning Objectives

After reading this chapter you will be able to:

1. Provide three alternative definitions for the term *real estate.*

2. Discuss the distribution of U.S. land among the various uses to which it is put (e.g., developed land, federal land, forest land).

3. Discuss the value and importance of U.S. real estate compared with the values of other asset classes such as stocks and bonds.

4. Describe the role real estate plays in the portfolios of U.S. households.

5. Discuss the primary ways that real estate markets are different from the markets for assets that trade in well-developed public markets.

Wealth is not without its advantages and the case to the contrary, although it has often been made, has never proved widely persuasive.

John Kenneth Galbraith,
The Affluent Society

Introduction

Real estate is the single largest component of wealth in our society. Because of its magnitude, it plays a key role in shaping the economic condition of individuals, families, and firms. It can substantially influence a family's ability to finance its education, health care, and other important needs. Changes in the value of real estate can dramatically affect the wealth of businesses and their capacity to grow.

Similarly, real estate resources can greatly affect a community's ability to attract and support profitable business activities, as well as to provide secure, convenient, and affordable living environments for its citizens. The adequacy of the housing stock, as well as the public infrastructure, including roads, bridges, dams, airports, schools, and parks, all affect the quality of life in a region.

Real estate has been estimated to represent approximately one-half of the world's total economic wealth.[1] In addition, it is often viewed as an important symbol of strength, stability, and independence. Consider, for example, the symbolic importance of structures such as the Sears Tower in Chicago to Sears, Roebuck and Company, Saint Peter's Basilica in Rome to the Roman Catholic Church, or the buildings of the Forbidden City in Beijing to the Chinese people (see also, Industry Issues 1-1). It is not surprising that real estate has been at the center of many regional disputes. It has been, and continues to be, a vital resource.

The prominence of real estate means that decisions about it also are important. For the individual, the firm, and the region, better decisions about the creation and use of real estate assets will bring greater productivity, greater wealth, and a better set of choices for life.

This book is about making informed decisions concerning real estate. We will show that virtually all decisions about the acquisition, disposition, or improvement of real estate depend on some assessment of the real estate's value. These decisions, which we refer to as investment decisions, involve comparing the resulting value of an action to its immediate cost. If the value exceeds the cost, the action should be pursued. The breadth and importance of these investment decisions in real estate are hard to overstate, and are the subject of Chapter 2.

As a beginning, we first look at the different uses of the term *real estate*. This is followed by a discussion of land use in the United States and real estate's contribution to U.S. and household wealth. The chapter finishes with a discussion of the real estate market, its participants, and the characteristics that make real estate assets unique.

Real Estate: Some Basic Definitions

It is important at the outset that we define the term *real estate,* as well as some closely related terms that are used throughout this book. When people think of real estate, they often think of the homes in their community or the business of buying and selling houses. This is probably because the personal investment that most households make in their home represents their primary involvement in the real estate market. Of course, real estate includes not only our homes, but also our places of work, commerce, worship, government, education, recreation, and entertainment—our physical environments, natural and built. In addition, it includes a wide range of business and institutional activities associated with the development, purchase, use, and sale of land and buildings.

Real estate is property. The term **property** refers to anything that can be owned, or possessed. Property can be a tangible asset or an intangible asset. **Tangible assets** are *physical* things, such as automobiles, clothing, land, or buildings. **Intangible assets** are *nonphysical* and include contractual rights (e.g., mortgage and lease agreements), financial claims (e.g., stocks and bonds), interests, patents, or trademarks.

The term *real estate* is used in three fundamental ways. First, its most common use is to identify the tangible assets of land and buildings. Second, it is used to denote the "bundle" of rights that are associated with the ownership and use of the physical assets. Finally, the term real estate may be used when referring to the industry or business activities related to the acquisition, operation, and disposition of the physical assets.

Real Estate: A Tangible Asset

Viewed purely as a tangible asset, real estate constitutes the physical components of location and space. In this context, **real estate** is defined as the land and its permanent improvements. **Improvements *on* the land** include any fixed structures such as buildings, fences, walls, and decks. **Improvements *to* the land** include the components necessary to make the land suitable for building construction or other uses. These improvements are

---

1. Estimate by Ibbotson & Associates, 1991.

1-1

Skyscrapers: A Shift in Development Trends

A t least 10 super-tall buildings have been completed in the last decade (see listing below). They are in cities such as Hong Kong and Shanghai in China and Dubai on the Arabian Peninsula. Currently, the world's tallest building—the twin Petronas Towers at 1,483 feet—is in Kuala Lumpur, Malaysia. Tall structures are as old as civilization, from the Pyramids in Egypt to the cathedrals of medieval Europe. Historians attribute this phenomenon in part to religious and spiritual motives—the desire to build to the sky. In modern times, however, the motive has been largely economic. The skyscraper era began in the United States in the late 19th century when the technology of steel-framed construction and safe elevators made it possible. It started in Chicago, although New York evolved into the leading skyscraper city during the 20th century.

World's Tallest Buildings: 2002 and 1992

2002 Rank	1992* Rank	Building	City, Country	Height (feet)	Year Built
1		Petronas Tower I	Kuala Lumpur, Malaysia	1,483	1998
1		Petronas Tower II	Kaula Lumpur, Malaysia	1,483	1998
3	1	Sears Tower	Chicago, US	1,450	1974
4		Jin Mao Tower	Shanghai, China	1,381	1998
5		Two Int'l Fin. Ctr.	Hong Kong, China	1,352	2003
6		CITIC Plaza	Guangzhou, China	1,283	1997
7		Shun Hing Square	Shenzhen, China	1,260	1996
8	2	Empire State Bldg.	New York City, US	1,250	1931
9	3	Central Plaza	Hong Kong, China	1,227	1992
10	4	Bank of China Tower	Hong Kong, China	1,204	1990
11		Emirates Office Tower	Dubai, United Arab Emirates	1,165	2000
12		The Center	Hong Kong, China	1,148	1998
13		Tuntex Sky Tower	Kaohsiung, Taiwan	1,142	1997
14	5	Aon Center	Chicago, US	1,135	1973
15	6	John Hancock Center	Chicago, US	1,129	1969
16		Burj Al Arab	Dubai, United Arab Emirates	1,053	1999
17	7	Chrysler Building	New York City, US	1,047	1930
18	8	Bank of America Plaza	Atlanta, US	1,024	1992
19	9	Library Tower	Los Angeles, US	1,017	1990
20		Menara Telecom	Kuala Lumpur, Malaysia	1,017	2000

*The Twin Towers of the World Trade Center in New York ranked second in 1992. The proposed replacement to the W.T.C., designed by Daniel Libeskind, will have a height of 1,776 feet.

The rising value of land in densely settled cities has been the economic incentive to build up rather than out. "Everything is always built in response to the market," said Atlanta architect Thomas Ventulett. "The height of a building is related to the value of the property, and that is due to the size and density of the city." In a market economy, the prospective return on this type of building might not be enough to make it worthwhile in a given location.

The shift of skyscraper development to the Far East has been a reflection of other trends, especially that region's emergence onto the global economic scene. The region's spectacular buildings are symbols of pride among nations that see themselves with new roles in the 21st century. A return on investment is less of an impediment in nations not wedded to market economics, such as China.

Source: Tom Walker, "Skyscrapers: A Shift in Development Trends," *Atlanta Journal-Constitution*, May 5, 2002; www.skyscrapers.com, October 2002.

often referred to as infrastructure, and consist of the streets, walkways, storm water drainage systems, and other systems such as water, sewer, electric, and telephone utilities that may be required for land use. Subject to legal and practical limits, it should be noted that real estate includes not only the surface of the earth, but also the area above and below the surface.

In practice the term **land** may include more than simply the earth; it may also include the improvements *to* the land. For example, the term *land* is often used to refer to a building site, or lot, and includes the infrastructure but not any structures. In contrast, land is also commonly used to refer to a larger area that does not include *any* improvements. This is sometimes identified as **raw land.** These distinctions may seem unimportant, but they become especially important when the value of land is considered.

Tangible assets include both real property and personal property. In professional practice and throughout this book, the terms **real property** and real estate are treated as interchangeable. **Personal property** refers to things that are movable and not permanently affixed to the land. For example, a motor home is personal property, while a custom "site-built" house is real property. A mobile home may be real or personal property, depending on how it is secured to the land and legally recognized by the jurisdiction (e.g., city, county, or state) in which it is located.

Concept Check

1.1   What distinguishes real property from personal property?

Real Estate: A Bundle of Rights

Although real estate is a tangible asset, it can also be viewed as a "bundle" of intangible rights associated with the ownership and use of the physical characteristics of space and location. These rights are to the *services,* or benefits, that real estate provides its users. For example, real property provides the owner rights to shelter, security, and privacy, as well as a location that facilitates business or residential activities. This concept of real property as rights is extremely important to understanding real estate, and is the subject of Chapter 4.

The bundle of property rights may be limited in numerous ways. It typically is reduced by land use restrictions (see Chapter 6). Also, the rights can be divided and distributed among multiple owners and nonowners. For example, an apartment owner divides his full interest in the property when he leases an apartment unit and grants to a tenant the right to occupy and control access to the unit. Similarly, the tenant may further divide (i.e., subdivide) his interests by subleasing the apartment to another. As another example, an owner may purchase a property that has a utility access granted through a portion of the property. Thus, real estate can also be viewed as a bundle of rights inherent in the ownership of real property.

The value of a real estate bundle of rights is a function of the property's physical, locational, and legal characteristics. The physical characteristics include the age, size, design, and construction quality of the structure, as well as the size, shape, and other natural features of the land. For residential property, the locational characteristics include convenience and access to places of employment, schools, shopping, health care facilities and other places important to households. The location characteristics of commercial properties may involve visibility, access to customers, suppliers, and employees, or the availability of reliable data and communications infrastructure. The physical and location characteristics required to provide valued real estate services vary by property type.

One of the exciting things about pursuing a career in real estate is that many options are available. Career paths can accommodate white-collar executives working for corporations, banks, advisory firms, or in the mortgage industry; analytical personality types working in real estate appraisal or consulting jobs; sales people working in brokerage, leasing, or property management; or entrepreneurs interested in developing new properties or in renovation of historical buildings. Career opportunities also exist in the public sector with employers like the Department of Housing and Urban Development (HUD), the General Service Administration (GSA), the Bureau of Reclamation,

Career Opportunities in Real Estate

the U.S. Postal Service, and with the numerous county tax assessors, to name just a few.

As you familiarize yourself with the material presented in this book, the type of work associated with the job opportunities listed above will become increasingly clear. However, it is important that you begin to read some of the real estate articles that appear in newspapers, magazines, and journals. You should also begin searching for and book marking interesting real estate websites. To get started, we suggest you take a look at the University of Cincinnati's Real Jobs website (www.real-jobs.com), where you can post your resume, search for real estate jobs, and read descriptions of available job opportunities—all free of charge.

Source: Information on Career Paths in Commercial Real Estate, University of Cincinnati, www.cba.uc.edu/getreal

Concept Check

1.2   What is the difference between tangible and intangible assets? Does the ownership of "real estate" involve tangible assets, intangible assets, or both?

Real Estate: An Industry and Profession

The term *real estate* frequently is used to refer to the industry activities associated with evaluating, producing, acquiring, managing, and selling real property assets. Real estate professions vary widely and include (1) real estate brokerage, leasing, and property management services, (2) appraisal and consulting services, (3) site selection, acquisition, and property development, (4) construction, (5) mortgage finance and securitization, (6) corporate and institutional real estate investment, and (7) government activities such as planning, land use regulation, environmental protection, and taxation.

Real estate business opportunities in areas such as brokerage, leasing, appraisal, construction, and consulting often offer entrepreneurial-minded individuals the ability to observe and understand local real estate markets in addition to receiving above average compensation. These types of positions allow individuals the opportunity to have their fingers on the "pulse" of the market, often enabling them to directly participate in real estate investment activities.

Real estate professionals involved in a wide range of activities can be found in small consulting firms, as well as with the larger accounting firms, corporate users, insurance companies, financial institutions, real estate investment firms, and pension fund advisories. Companies such as restaurant groups and retailers seeking to expand, often require the services of "in-house" site acquisition analysts, construction managers, and facility managers.

Finally, the activities of state and federal government units such as departments for transportation, commerce, planning, housing, and environmental protection, and local government agencies such as planning and property tax offices necessitate the employment of real estate research analysts and professionals. This includes the activities of government-sponsored enterprises (GSEs) such as Fannie Mae and Freddie Mac.

Explore The Web

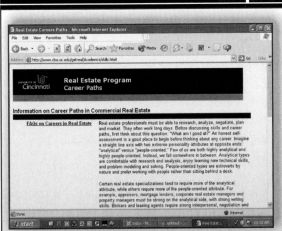

For answers to frequently asked questions on careers in real estate, visit the real estate program site at the University of Cincinnati: www.cba.uc.edu/getreal. Which real estate career appears to be the most structured in terms of time and pay? Which seems to require the least amount of time "behind a desk?" Which appears to be the most entrepreneurial?

Real Estate and the Economy

www.census.gov

Numerous construction statistics

Real estate generates nearly a third of United States gross domestic product (GDP), creates jobs for nearly 9 million Americans, and is the source for 70 percent of local government revenues.[2] The total contribution of the housing sector alone approaches 20 percent of GDP.[3] Because of the significant influence of real estate on the nation's economy, investors on Wall Street closely monitor real estate construction, construction permit activity, and real estate sales figures. Housing starts and sales are widely viewed as leading economic indicators.

Land Use in the United States

The United States represents about 6 percent of the earth's land area, or approximately 2.3 billion acres (3.5 million square miles). To give a sense of scale to an acre, a football field, not including the end zone areas, is slightly more than one acre (1.1 acres). More precisely, an **acre** is defined as 43,560 square feet, or about 209 feet square; there are 640 acres in one square mile. The size of a single-family residential lot is typically between one-fifth and four-fifths of an acre.

Approximately 40 percent of U.S. land is owned by federal, state, and local governments, with the remaining 60 percent in private ownership. According to the 1997 National Resources Inventory Report, developed land represents approximately 5.0 percent of the land in the continental United States (see Exhibit 1-1). Developed land consists of residential, industrial, commercial, and institutional land uses, including roads, railways, rights-of-ways, construction sites, utility sites, sanitary landfills, and other land uses of similar purpose. Undeveloped land in the United States is divided in approximately equal shares among federal lands (23 percent), cropland and Conservation Reserve Program (CRP) land (21 percent), range land (21 percent), and forest land (21 percent).[4]

2. National Policy Agenda 2002: America's Real Estate (Washington, DC: Real Estate Roundtable, 2002).

3. The State of the Nation's Housing (Cambridge, MA: Joint Center for Housing Studies of Harvard University, 2002).

4. CRP land is a federal program established under the Food Security Act of 1985 to assist private landowners in converting highly erodible cropland to vegetative cover.

There are more than five million people in the United States employed in identifiable real estate fields such as title insurance, construction, mortgage banking, property management, real estate appraisal, brokerage and leasing, and real estate development. In addition, many are engaged in corporate real estate and in real estate lending in commercial banks, savings and loans, and insurance companies where their jobs are not included in the real estate sector. In addition, real estate is used by its owners as collateral to obtain mortgages and other financial assets. As important as the field of real estate might be, it is also worth recognizing how interesting work in this field is. Real estate professionals are tied to the development of our society in a very direct way and participate in decisions that will shape the way we live for centuries. Work in real estate is personally rewarding, ever-changing, and challenging.

Source: Careers in Finance, Bentley College, www.careers-in-finance.com/re.htm

Exhibit 1-1 Land Use and Land Use Change in the United States

Land use	1982 Land use (000s of acres)	% of total	1997 Land use (000s of acres)	% of total
Developed land	73,246	4	98,252	5
Water areas and federal land	448,198	23	452,118	23
Crop land	420,954	22	376,998	19
CRP land			32,696	2
Pasture land	132,006	7	119,992	6
Range land	416,740	21	405,977	21
Forest land	403,338	21	406,955	21
Other rural land	49,648	2	51,142	3
Totals	1,944,130	100.0	1,944,130	100.0

Source: U.S. Department of Agriculture, 1997 National Resources Inventory, Revised 2000, http://www.nrcs.usda.gov/technical/NRI/1997/summary_report/report.pdf. Note that Alaska and the District of Columbia are not included in the tabulated figures.

www.nrcs.usda.gov

U.S. Department of Agriculture Resources include comprehensive information on trends for land use and development

During the past 15 years overall land use changes have been relatively minor. Most notable, however, is the increase of developed land from 73 million acres in 1982 to almost 100 million acres in 1997. Although only a small portion of the total land area in the United States, the amount of developed land has increased 34 percent over the 15-year period. Although the availability of land is not currently a problem in the United States, changes in its use are routinely monitored.

Real Estate and U.S. Wealth

The value of real estate plays an important role in the wealth of the United States. We estimate that the total market value of nongovernment-owned real estate is approximately $22 trillion. This estimate includes owner-occupied housing, investible commercial real estate, real estate held by non-real estate corporations, and land. This constitutes the single largest asset class in the United States as shown in Exhibit 1-2. In comparison, the total value of publicly traded corporate equities (i.e., stocks) in September 2002 was approximately, $13.3 trillion. As of September 2002, the value of outstanding real estate mortgage debt (an intangible asset) was approximately $7.7 trillion. This is larger than the existing stock of both corporate and government debt and the total value of pension fund reserves.

www.bea.doc.gov

U.S. Department of Commerce site contains vast amounts of National and International Economic data

Exhibit 1-2 Aggregate Market Values of Selected Asset Categories

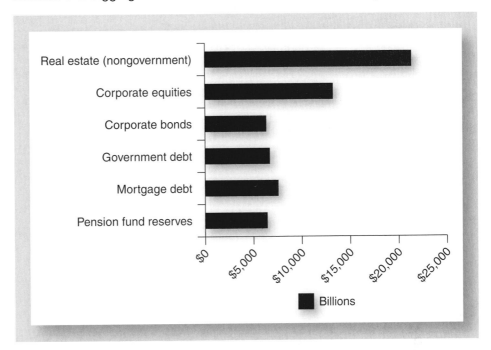

Note: Real estate (nongovernment) includes developed land. It does not include farmland, water areas, and other rural lands. Government debt includes all federal, state, and local government liabilities.

Sources: Flow of Funds Accounts of the United States, Federal Reserve, (September 2002, various tables). The value of nongovernment real estate is the authors' estimate based on the reproduction cost of private residential and nonresidential structures reported in the *Survey of Current Business,* U.S. Department of Commerce (September 2002, P70–71, Tables 1, 3 and 11).

As reported by the U.S. Federal Reserve Board, housing represents the single largest asset category in the net worth portfolios of households (see Exhibit 1-3). On average, it represents approximately 28 percent of U.S. household wealth. This compares with household holdings of corporate stock and mutual fund shares of 21 percent. Housing's 28 percent share in the typical household's portfolio also dominates deposits and money market funds (11 percent), pension asset (12 percent), and equity invested in noncorporate businesses (11 percent). Moreover, the 28 percent housing share understates the importance of real estate for some households because direct investments in private commercial real estate assets (e.g., apartments, office buildings) are not included as household assets in Exhibit 1-3. Finally, note that 70 percent of household liabilities are home mortgages.

By year-end 2002, U.S. households had accumulated approximately $7.3 trillion in housing equity (market value minus mortgage debt). This represents, on average, about 54 percent of the value of their real estate and about 19 percent of their net worth. As a percentage of total household wealth, housing diminished slightly during the 1990s as corporate stock values increased rapidly. Beginning in 2000, however, stock values declined sharply. This trend can be seen in Exhibit 1-4, and highlights the important role real estate plays in the diversification of household wealth.

Concept Check

1.3   According to Exhibit 1-3, U.S. households own $13.5 trillion in real estate. Assume, for simplicity, that this amount does not include rental real estate. On average, what percent of the value of the U.S. housing stock is financed with home mortgage debt?

www.federalreserve.gov

U.S. Federal Reserve System site contains extensive information on U.S. Banking System and Economy

Exhibit 1-3 U.S. Household Wealth*

Asset/liability category	Year-End 2002 ($ in billions)	% of total
Tangible assets		
Housing	$13,527	28%
Consumer durables	3,066	6
Nonprofit tangible assets	1,443	3
Financial assets		
Deposits & money market funds	5,234	11
Government & corporate bonds	2,388	5
Stocks & mutual fund shares	9,948	21
Pension assets (Excluding stocks)	6,004	12
Other securities	1,422	3
Noncorporate business equity	6,069	11
Total assets	48,101	100.0
Home mortgages (including lines of credit)	6,219	70
Other debt	2,708	30
Total liabilities	8,927	100.0
Net worth	$39,174	
Owners' equity in real estate	$ 7,308	
Owners' equity as percent of real estate and net worth	54	19

Source: *This sector consists of individual households and nonprofit organizations. Nonprofits account for about 6 percent of the sector's financial assets. Flow of Funds Accounts of the United States, Federal Reserve (June 2003, Table B.100 and L.100) http://www.federalreserve.gov/releases/Z1/Current/z1.pdf

Exhibit 1-4 Selected Household Assets as a Percentage of Total Assets

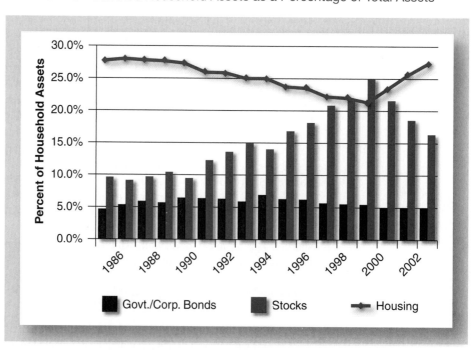

Source: Flow of Funds Accounts of the United States, Federal Reserve, (Various Years, Table B.100)

Real Estate Markets and Participants

In the United States and many other countries, market competition serves to distribute resources (i.e., goods, services, and capital) among the various users. The market's forces of demand and supply interact within the economy to determine the price at which goods, capital, and services are exchanged and to whom they are allocated. Real estate resources are allocated among its various users—individuals, households, businesses, and institutions—in the real estate market. Real estate values derive from the interaction of three different sectors in the economy: the "real" world, or user markets; the "financial" world, or capital markets; and government. A discussion of each sector in this process is presented below.

User Markets

Real estate **user markets** are characterized by competition among users for physical location and space. As we will explain in Chapter 5, this competition determines who gains the use of each parcel of land and how much they must bid for its use. The primary participants in user markets are the potential occupants, both owner occupants and tenants, or renters. Ultimately, the demand for real estate derives from the need that these individuals, firms, and institutions have for convenient access to other locations, as well as for shelter to accommodate their activities. Based on the financial positions of households and firms and their operational needs, they decide either to own and occupy property, or to lease property from others. Thus, about two-thirds of U.S. households own their home, and many businesses own their property, while most prime commercial real estate located in the central business districts of U.S. cities is leased.

Capital Markets

www.bloomberg.com
www.jblevy.com

Two private firms that provide data on interest rates and bond yields

The **capital markets** serve to allocate financial resources among households and firms requiring funds. Participants in the capital markets invest in stocks, bonds, mutual funds, private business enterprises, mortgage contracts, real estate, and other opportunities with the expectation of receiving a financial return on their investment. Funds flow from investors to the investment opportunities yielding the highest expected return (i.e., the greatest benefit), considering risk. Thus, real estate competes with a diverse menu of other investment opportunities available in the capital market.

The capital markets can be divided into two broad categories: equity interests and debt interests. We commonly view the equity participants as the "owners." Equity investors in real estate expect to receive a return on their investment through periodic rent and price appreciation.[5] The debt participants, the "lenders," hold claims to the interest on borrowed funds that are secured by individuals, businesses, and property. The equity and debt interests can each be divided further into private and public market components. The primary participants in each of the four capital market categories—private equity, public equity, private debt, and public debt—are outlined in Exhibit 1-5. (The capital sources of real estate finance are discussed further in Chapters 13 and 15.)

Concept Check

1.4 Assets based on real estate are traded in each of the four capital market quadrants. List the four quadrants and at least one real estate asset that trades in each.

---

5. Investors who occupy their own properties "receive" the rent they would have paid to others had the property been leased from another investor. This is termed "implicit" rent.

Exhibit 1-5 Real Estate Capital Market Participants

	Private Markets (directly held)	Public Markets (indirectly held)
Equity/owners	Individuals, firms, and institutions	Investors in publicly traded real estate companies and equity REITs
Debt/lenders	Banks, insurance companies, private lenders	Investors in mortgage-backed securities and mortgage REITs

The Role of Government

Government affects real estate markets in a host of ways. Local government has perhaps the largest influence on real estate. It affects the supply and cost of real estate through zoning codes and other land use regulations, fees on new land development, and building codes that restrict methods of construction. Further, local government affects rental rates in user markets through property taxes. Finally, it profoundly affects the supply and quality of real estate by its provision of roads, bridges, mass transit, utilities, flood control, schools, social services, and other infrastructure of the community. (The influence of local government through land use controls, property tax policy, and services is expanded upon in Chapter 6.)

State government has perhaps the least effect on real estate, although it still is important. Through licensing of professionals and agents, states constrain entry into real estate–related occupations. (See Chapter 19.) Through statewide building codes, they can affect building design and cost. Through disclosure laws and fair housing laws, states affect the operation of housing markets. In addition, states typically set the basic framework of requirements for local government land use controls, and even intervene in the realm of land use controls for special purposes such as protection of environmentally sensitive lands. Finally, states affect the provision of public services important to a community, including schools, transportation systems, social services, law enforcement, and others.

The national government influences real estate in many ways. Income tax policy can greatly affect the value of real estate, and therefore the incentive to invest in it. (The extensive effect of income taxes on real estate value is detailed in Chapter 22.) Housing subsidy programs can have enormous effects on the level and type of housing construction. Federal flood insurance programs can influence development in coastal and wetlands regions. Federal financial reporting and disclosure requirements, and government-related financial agencies such as the Federal Reserve System, the Federal Deposit Insurance Corporation (FDIC), and Fannie Mae and Freddie Mac all have profound effects on the operation of the real estate capital markets. (See Chapter 13 for details of the government in mortgage markets.) Further, consumer protection laws affect few aspects of household activity more than they impact housing purchases and financing. (See Chapters 10 and 20.) In addition, laws protecting the environment and endangered species have significantly affected the use of real estate. Finally, national fair housing laws and other civil rights legislation are very important influences on housing markets.

The Interaction of Three Value-Determining Sectors

The interaction of the three value-determining sectors is illustrated in Exhibit 1-6. In user markets, households and firms compete for the currently available supply of locations and space (left-hand side of Exhibit 1-6). This competition determines the level of rental income for each submarket and property, and determines how reliable or uncertain the income is.[6] Capital markets provide the financial resources necessary for the de-

www.uli.org

The Urban Land Institute Influential U.S. organization for those engaged in development and land use planning

---

6. This applies to owner-occupied residences as well as to actual rental property. For an owner-occupied residence the rent is in actual housing services rather than dollars. It sometimes is referred to as implicit rent.

Exhibit 1-6 User Markets, Capital Markets, Government and Real Estate Values

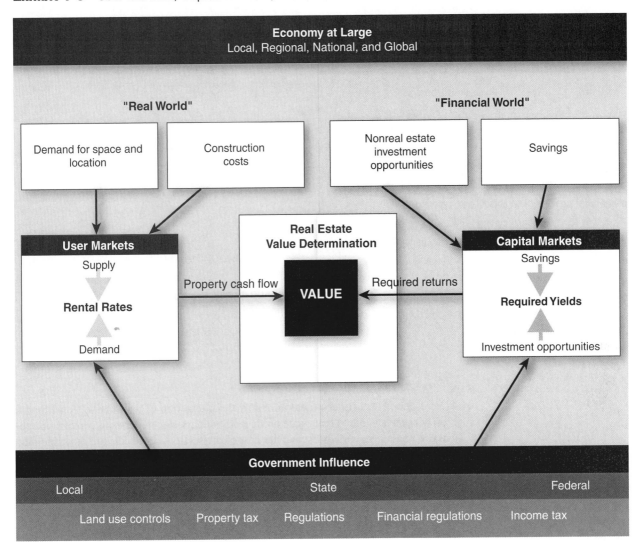

velopment and acquisition of real estate assets (right-hand side of Exhibit 1-6). Within the capital markets, the returns investors require for a broad range of available investment opportunities, including real estate, are determined. Finally, in the interaction between user and capital markets the expected rental income becomes transformed to value through "discounting," which is the process of converting expected future cash flows into present value. Discounting incorporates the opportunity cost of waiting for the uncertain cash flows (center panel of Exhibit 1-6). (Discounting is the subject of Chapter 3.) As noted above, government influences on this value-determining process are numerous, ranging from local government land use controls and property taxes, to federal government income tax policy.

Our view is that good decision making requires an understanding of how real estate values are determined. Thus, value is the unifying theme of this book. This allows for an integrated framework for the study of real estate because all of the concepts and principles discussed in this text—such as legal considerations, local market conditions, interest rates, and local land use controls and regulations—are important primarily in the context of how they affect real estate values.

Industry Issues

1-2

The Amazing U.S. Housing Market—Even as the U.S. economy slumped during the early 2000s, the national housing market remained buoyant. Sales of new and existing homes did in fact slow immediately after September 11, 2001, but the pullback was brief and 2001 ended on a strong note as annual sales of new and existing single-family homes reached an all-time high of 6.2 million units. This record was eclipsed again in 2002 as total single-family home sales reached 6.6 million units. The boom in home sales has kept builders busy. Starts of single-family homes and the total value of single-family construction activity both reached historic highs in 2001, only to be exceeded again in 2002. Housing's resilience during the 2001–2002 economic downturn reflects the ongoing

Source: Adapted from *The State of the Nation's Housing* (Cambridge, MA: Joint Center for Housing Studies of Harvard University, 2002). Photo from *The Economist,* March 30–April 5, 2002.

demand of the baby boomers and their parents for high-quality housing, as well as 40-year lows in mortgage interest rates. Many have argued that the strong performance of housing during this downturn significantly softened the severity of the recession, as suggested by the cover page of *The Economist* shown above.

The Production of Real Estate Assets

The real estate values (prices) determined by the interaction of user markets and capital markets become a guide to real estate producers (builders, developers and conversion specialists). When market prices exceed the cost of production, producers are more inclined to build, thereby simultaneously adding to the supply of space and to the stock of investable real estate assets.

Real estate production historically has been a volatile process because real estate prices and costs tend to be volatile. The increase in supply by producers tends to lower rents in the user markets and to lower property values (prices), which reduces the feasibility of additional new construction. Thus, building booms and slumps often characterize real estate production, as discussed in Chapter 7. To compound the volatility further, real estate values also can be affected by shocks to the capital markets. For example, if interest rates rise, property values will generally fall, again rendering construction less profitable. Finally, construction costs can be very volatile. Organized labor disputes in cities such as New York or Boston, or unexpected events causing shortages in lumber or other building materials, can severely damage the financial viability of a major real estate development. (Real estate development is treated further in Chapter 24.)

Concept Check

1.5 In what market are rental rates for commercial real estate assets determined? In what market are investors' required rates of return determined?

Characteristics of Real Estate Markets

Real estate assets and markets are unique when compared to other goods. The two primary characteristics of real estate assets are their heterogeneity and immobility. Because of these two factors, the market for buying, selling, and leasing real estate tends to be localized and highly segmented, with privately negotiated transactions and high transaction costs.

www.marshallswift.com

Private firm that tracks
construction costs

Heterogeneous Products

Real estate tends to be heterogeneous, meaning that each property has unique features. An example of a relatively homogeneous product is gasoline. Although it is possible to purchase different grades of gasoline (e.g., octane levels), a gallon of gasoline received from a particular pump cannot be distinguished from the next gallon.

For real estate, however, age, building design, and especially location combine to give each property distinctive characteristics. Even in residential neighborhoods with very similar houses, the locations differ. Corner lots have different locational features than interior lots; their access to parks and transportation routes may differ, and the traffic patterns within the neighborhood create differences. These differences create variation in values. Locational differences are particularly critical for retail properties. Drastic value differences may result between retail properties opposite each other on different sides of the same street, depending on whether the property is on the "going-home" or the "going-to-work" side. Most food outlets, drugstores, clothing stores, and service centers prefer to be on the going-home side of the street. Even within a single shopping center there are important differences in location for a retail establishment depending on the need of the establishment for exposure to shoppers.

Immobile Products

Real estate is location, and it is immobile. Although it is sometimes physically possible to move a building from one location to another, this is generally not financially feasible. The vast majority of structures removed from the land are demolished rather than moved.

Another term for location is access. For households it is access to school, shopping, entertainment, and places of employment. For commercial properties it may be access to customers, the labor force, or suppliers. The nuances of access are fundamental to real estate value, as we discuss in Chapter 5.

Localized Markets

Real estate markets tend to be localized. By this we mean that the potential users of a property, and competing sites, generally lie within a short distance of each other. For example, competing apartment properties may lie within 15 minutes, or less, in driving time from each other, while competing properties of single-family residences may tend to be within a single elementary school district or even within a small number of similar subdivisions. Users of commercial property may be more "footloose"—that is, they do not depend so heavily on access to a particular location. Thus, commercial property users may search a wide range of alternative markets within a single metropolitan area or even among different metropolitan areas.

Segmented Markets

www.prea.org

Pension Real Estate Association

Real estate markets tend to be highly segmented due to the heterogeneous nature of the products. Households that search for single-family detached units in the market will generally not consider other residential product types such as an attached townhouse unit or condominium. In addition, real estate is segmented by product price. The same holds true, although to a lesser extent, in the commercial property market. Commercial property markets are segmented by both users and investors. Larger, more valuable commercial properties, generally well over $10 million, are often referred to as **investment-grade properties,** or **institutional-grade real estate.** This is the segment of the property market targeted by institutional investors such as pension funds and foreign investors. Individual private investors typically do not compete directly with institutional investors for properties.

Privately Negotiated Transactions with High Transaction Costs

Transactions involving directly held real estate generally are privately negotiated between the buyer and seller. The negotiation process can be lengthy, and the final transaction price is not always readily observable. Because real estate assets are highly heterogeneous and transaction prices are not widely available, the time and effort involved in searching, pricing, and evaluating alternative properties is substantial. Transaction costs include both search costs (e.g., time) and actual costs. Thus, the transaction costs involved in the transfer of directly owned real estate from one owner to another are high compared to other goods. In addition, real estate agents, mortgage brokers, attorneys, and others may be involved in the transaction due to the considerable value of the investment. These services tend to increase transaction costs.

Concept Check

1.6   Identify three ways in which real estate markets differ from the market for publicly traded stocks.

Summary

We began this chapter by looking at the different uses of the term *real estate*. This was followed by a discussion of land use in the United States and the contribution of real estate to U.S. and household wealth, and a discussion of the real estate market.

The term *real estate* is used in three fundamental ways: (1) to identify the tangible assets of land and buildings, (2) to denote the "bundle" of rights associated with the ownership and use of the physical assets, and (3) to refer to the industry, or business activities, related to the acquisition, operation, and disposition of the physical assets. Viewed as a tangible asset, real estate constitutes the physical components of location and space. In this context, real estate is defined as the land and any built improvements permanently affixed on, or to, the land. The bundle of intangible rights, or interests, associated with the ownership and use of the physical characteristics of space and location constitute the services that real estate provides to its users.

Real estate generates nearly a third of United States gross domestic product (GDP), creates jobs for nearly nine million Americans, and is the source for 70 percent of local government revenues. The total contribution of the housing sector alone approaches 20 percent of GDP. Real estate construction, construction permit activity, and real estate sales figures are closely watched by investors on Wall Street because of the effect real estate has on the nation's economy. Real estate also represents a significant share of our accumulated national wealth. The total value of nongovernment-owned real estate in the U.S. is estimated to be $22 trillion. Approximately $12 trillion of this represents the value of owner-occupied housing. Real estate represents approximately 28 percent of U.S. household wealth and is the single largest asset category of households.

Real estate market activity is influenced by the activities and conditions that take place in three sectors of a market economy: (1) the user market, (2) the financial or capital market, and (3) the government sector. Real estate users compete in the market for location and space. Among the users are both renters and owners. The financial resources to acquire real estate assets are allocated in the capital market; hence, the equity (ownership) and debt investors are capital market participants. Government influences the activities of each of the participant groups through regulations, provisions of services and infrastructure, taxes, and various subsidies.

Two primary characteristics of real estate assets distinguish them from others: heterogeneity and immobility. Because of these two factors, the market for evaluating, producing, buying, selling, leasing, and managing real estate tends to be localized, highly segmented, and involves privately negotiated transactions with relatively high transaction costs.

Key Terms

Acre 7	Intangible assets 3	Raw land 5
Capital market 11	Investment-grade property 15	Real property 5
Improvements on the land 3	Land 5	Tangible assets 3
Improvements to the land 3	Personal property 5	User markets 11
Institutional-grade real estate 15	Property 3	

Test Problems

1. A market where tenants negotiate rent and other terms with property owners or their managers is referred to as a:
   a. Rental market
   b. User market
   c. Housing market
   d. Capital market

2. The market in which required rates of return on available investment opportunities are determined is referred to as the:
   a. Rental market
   b. User market
   c. Housing market
   d. Capital market

3. The actions of local, state, and federal governments affect real estate values
   a. Primarily through user markets
   b. Primarily through the capital market
   c. Primarily through their taxation policies
   d. All of the above

4. What portion of households own their house?
   a. Approximately one-third
   b. Approximately two-thirds
   c. Approximately one-half
   d. Approximately one-quarter

5. Of the following asset categories, which has the greatest aggregate market value?
   a. Corporate equities
   b. Mortgage debt
   c. Government debt
   d. Nongovernment real estate

6. Storm water drainage systems are best described as:
   a. Tangible assets
   b. Improvements to the land
   c. Intangible assets
   d. Improvements on the land

7. What is the single largest asset category in the portfolio of a typical U.S. household?
   a. Real estate
   b. Consumer durables
   c. Stocks
   d. Bonds

8. Real estate markets differ from other asset classes by having all of the following characteristics except:
   a. Local market
   b. High transaction costs
   c. Segmented market
   d. Homogeneous product

9. Which of the following is *not* important to the location of commercial properties?
   a. Access to customers
   b. Visibility
   c. Access to schools
   d. Availability of communications infrastructure

www.mhhe.com/lingarcher1e

Study Questions

1. The term *real estate* can be used in three fundamental ways. List these three alternative uses or definitions.

2. The United States represents about 6 percent of the earth's land surface, or approximately 2.3 billion acres. Who owns this land? What is the distribution of this land among the various uses (e.g., developed land, federal land, forest land)?

3. Describe the value of U.S. real estate by comparing it to the values of other asset classes (e.g., stocks, bonds).

4. How much of the wealth of a typical U.S. household is tied up in real estate? How does this compare to the role that assets and investments play in the portfolios of U.S. households?

5. Real estate assets and markets are unique when compared to other assets or markets. Discuss the primary ways that real estate markets are different from the markets for other assets that trade in well-developed public markets.

6. Explain the role of government in real estate at the federal, state, and local level. Which has the most significant impact on real estate markets?

7. Identify and describe the interaction of the three economic sectors that affect real estate value.

8. Real estate production is a volatile process determined by the interaction of the user and capital markets. What signals do real estate producers use to manage this process? What other factors affect the volatility of real estate production?

Solutions To Concept Checks

1. A major determinant between real and personal property is whether or not the property is movable or permanently affixed to the land.

2. Tangible assets are physical assets such as land, automobiles, and buildings. Intangible assets are nonphysical, including patents, financial claims, or contractual agreements. Real estate is a tangible asset, but a bundle of intangible rights is also associated with the ownership and use of the property.

3. About 43 percent of the U.S. housing stock is financed with home mortgage debt.

4. The four capital market quadrants include private equity, private debt, public equity, and public debt. The private equity market includes transactions of real property between individuals, firms, and institutions. Private debt includes the trading of home mortgages. Investors trade real estate companies such as equity REITs in the public equity market. Mortgage-backed securities are traded in the public debt markets.

5. Commercial real estate rental rates are determined in user markets while investors' required rates of return are determined in the capital market.

6. First, real estate is a heterogeneous product distinguished by its age, building design, and location. Second, real estate is immobile, and therefore location and its accessibility are important. Third, real estate is a localized, segmented market due to local competition and the heterogeneous nature of the product. Finally, real estate transactions have high transfer costs and deals are privately negotiated.

Explore The Web

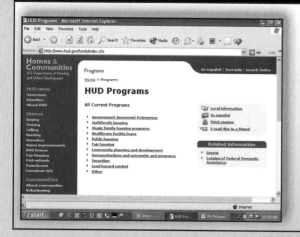

The government affects real estate in many ways. At the federal level, many housing programs exist. Go to www.hud.gov, and explore the different housing programs available. Give a brief overview of five of the programs you find on this site.

Additional Readings

Appraisal Institute, *Dictionary of Real Estate Appraisal.* 4th ed. Chicago: Appraisal Institute, 2002.

Edwards, K. W. *Your Successful Real Estate Career.* 3rd ed. New York: AMACOM, 2003.

Evans, M., and R. Mendenhall. *Opportunities in Real Estate Careers,* Rev. 2nd ed. New York: McGraw-Hill/Contemporary Books, March 27, 2002.

Friedman, J. P., and J. C. Harris. *Real Estate Handbook.* 5th ed. Hauppauge, NY: Barron's Educational Series, 2001.

Janik, C., and R. Rejnis. *Real Estate Careers: 25 Growing Opportunities.* New York: John Wiley, 1994.

Masi, M. *Real Estate Career Starter: Launch a Lucrative and Fulfilling Career.* New York: LearningExpress, 1998.

Rowh, M. *Careers in Real Estate.* New York: McGraw-Hill/Contemporary Books, 2002.

Vault Career Guide to Real Estate. New York: Vault Reports, 2003.

www.mhhe.com/lingarcher1e

Value *and* Real Estate Decisions

Learning Objectives

After reading this chapter you will be able to:

1. List two components of a real estate investment decision.

2. Distinguish between investment and non-investment decisions.

3. List three steps in analyzing incremental investment decisions.

4. Identify two effects of debt financing upon the cash flows of an incremental investment.

5. List two low risk types of real estate investment and two high-risk types.

6. List four strategies for managing investment risk.

7. List four characteristics of an individual (or household) that affect the desirability of investing directly in rental single-family homes.

8. State the difference between investment analysis and appraisal for an investment property.

Introduction

The subject of real estate can be studied from many perspectives. Especially valuable, as we will argue in this chapter, is a value perspective. The point, in short, is that value is central to virtually all real estate decision making. This chapter illustrates by example what is meant by real estate decisions and how a value perspective applies. For a diversity of cases, we consider the basic elements of real estate decisions—namely, determining value and comparing it to cost.

Real estate decisions often involve more than simply dollars or cash flows. Thus, we also discuss nonmonetary influences on value. Real estate decisions often involve an incremental change in an existing situation or asset, so analysis of incremental decisions is explored. The availability of debt financing can affect value, so the impact of debt financing on real estate decisions is outlined.

Investment Risk can be defined as the possibility that future cash flows or nonmonetary costs and benefits will differ from what was expected when the investment was undertaken. Risk considerations permeate real estate investment decisions and complicate the valuation process. Thus, we provide an introduction to real estate risk and distinguish among different categories of risk, such as risky costs and risky future benefits. We also discuss how these risks vary across types of real estate decisions. In addition, we explore strategies for managing value risk. Real estate value cannot prudently be considered apart from the characteristics, needs, and capacities of the owner, or investor. Thus, we also discuss these factors as part of a portfolio perspective on real estate value. Finally, we highlight the difference between investment valuation and another important, closely related perspective, real estate appraisal.[1]

The Idea of Investment

We often speak of some sacrifice that we make as an "investment in the future." Parents give up their time and resources now so that their children may go to college later. Students (sometimes) give up concerts, parties, or other recreation to improve their academic outcomes later. In both cases the individuals are judging that the value of what is gained exceeds the immediate cost being paid. It is in this sense that we use the term **investment.** Any decision that involves significant costs now for the sake of future benefits requires a judgment about the value of the future benefits. We refer to such a decision as an *investment decision* and the value of the expected future benefits as *investment value.* The importance of this concept is that every investment decision involves the same two elements: the initial costs and the value of the future benefits. Making good investment decisions is important because, by their nature, they cannot be undone easily or without cost. There are more of these investment decisions than one commonly thinks, as we will show below.

Concept Check

2.1 What are the two basic elements of an investment decision?

www.fool.com

Sensible advice on many investment type decisions.

Not every decision is worth treating as an investment. Decisions such as what music CD to listen to, what flavor of ice cream to choose, what to wear for the day, or how to organize an immediate work task lack one or more components of the investment value problem. For example, these decisions commonly lack a significant cost at the time they are made. Moreover, the time horizon is very short, and the decision can be reevaluated and revised very quickly, so one is not forced to live with the choice over a long time.

But many decisions in daily life do involve an investment. The decision to purchase an expensive television set or stereo certainly is an investment. There are significant costs up front, typically the benefits are spread over several years, and the choice cannot be "undone" (after some days) without significant costs. Similarly, purchasing expensive furniture or clothing is an investment. So also is the decision to upgrade a computer, replace a car, or change apartments. The choice to attend a college or university is a major life investment, as is the choice among schools and programs of study. Selecting a certain college course, to the exclusion of another, is an investment. The decision to change jobs can be a

---

1. In addition to this chapter, the treatment of risk and uncertainty in real estate is a subject of Chapters 1, 5, 7, 16, 21, 23, and 24.

major investment, especially as one progresses further along a career path and perhaps also takes on increasing family and personal responsibilities. A commitment to fair, honest, and generous business practices is understood by wise businesspersons to be an investment in future business relationships. In all of the cases above, the immediate cost of an action must be weighed against the (investment) value of future resulting benefits.

Concept Check

2.2   Why is choosing which college course to take arguably an investment whereas choosing which sporting event to watch on a Saturday afternoon is not an investment?

Investment Value in Real Estate

The world of real estate is rich with investment decisions, but not all of these truly concern real estate. True real estate decisions are about acquiring, financing, using, improving, and disposing of actual real estate assets (land and its permanent structures). In contrast to these decisions are management or operational choices that coincidentally arise from involvement with real estate. For example, a residential real estate brokerage company must make a host of decisions about operating the business—personnel recruitment and compensation, marketing methods and strategies, equipment decisions, and organizational decisions. But these decisions are not really about real estate. Rather, they are the kind of decisions that *any* organization must make to reach its goals, and are not our concern here. This book is about the investment valuation of real estate assets.

Concept Check

2.3   Which of these is a real estate investment decision, and why? (1) The decision to replace an air conditioner. (2) The decision to change telephone service.

Investment Value and Time

Real estate investment decisions, like all investment decisions, involve present costs and the value of future benefits (usually quantified as cash flows), as depicted in Exhibit 2-1. However, in finding the value of future benefits we cannot simply add them up. A moment's thought makes it clear that benefits 10 years from now, for example, are not as valuable as the same benefits received immediately. So we must have a way of converting future benefits to their equivalent value in immediate cash. The generally accepted method for doing this conversion is known as **discounting.** This procedure is fundamental to good investment valuation when a long time horizon is involved, such as in real estate. Discounting is explained in depth in Chapter 3. Suffice it to say now that the value of future benefits from a real estate investment must be equated through discounting to an equivalent current (present) value, which can then be compared to the immediate cost.

Concept Check

2.4   Why must we discount the future benefits of a real estate investment?

Exhibit 2-1   The Cash Flows of a Real Estate Investment

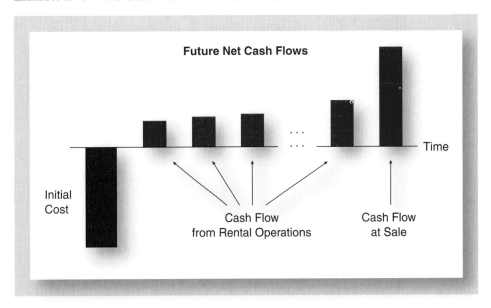

Investment Value and Nonmonetary Effects

Even if the costs and benefits of an investment are nonmonetary, the decision problem is still to weigh the costs against the value of the benefits. Perhaps the main example of a **nonmonetary** real estate investment is the choice of a home. A home satisfies many needs beyond simple physical shelter, and many of these benefits are very difficult to quantify. The location of a home determines access to places of work, to recreation and sports opportunities, to places of worship, to community and commercial services, and to the social network of the household. Perhaps above all, for families with children, the location of a residence determines the schools and social environment to which children have access (see Industry Issues 2-1). In addition, the immediate neighborhood of a home determines the surroundings the household experiences, including the level of crime, pollution, noise, traffic, and the image or aura of the neighborhood. Under these complex circumstances, homebuyers or renters typically will not be able to measure *explicitly* the future benefits of a dwelling. But they will still judge whether the value of the "package" of expected benefits exceeds its cost. Indeed, buyers and renters likely will compare cost to the value of the benefit "package" among several dwellings, seeking to find the one that is affordable and offers them the greatest net difference.

For example, suppose a family searching for a home has narrowed the choice to two residences. The houses are very similar and affordable, and each seems to be at least worth the seller's asking price to the family. Dwelling A is $140,000, but is in a struggling public school district, while dwelling B is $160,000, but is in an exceptionally successful public school district. Having children, the family could conceivably have several reactions to the choice. If the family places high value on access to good public schools, it may regard choice B as superior, judging that the incremental value of the superior schools is greater than the $20,000 house price differential. On the other hand, the family may already have determined that the children will not attend public school, making the difference in school district largely irrelevant, and making choice A the more attractive of the two. A third possibility is that, based on a careful assessment of the school situation, the family judges the difference in schools to be transitory, reducing the value of the superior school district and thus the value advantage of the more expensive house. The point is that each time a household makes a choice of a residence, it implicitly makes value comparisons and value judgments, even though the values are not measured explicitly. Thus, the purchase of a residence involves an investment valuation.

Industry Issues

2-1

Nonmonetary Factors in Real Estate Value:
Are Housing Values Sensitive to Elementary School Quality? And How!

The most recent evidence that homebuyers care about the quality of elementary schools is exemplified by the findings of Dr. David Figlio and Maurice Lucas in a study sponsored by the prestigious National Bureau of Economic Research.* Figlio and Lucas examined the relationship of house price changes to local elementary school "report cards" based on standardized statewide achievement tests. They found that a grade of A can add as much as 14 percent to the value of above-median-size homes. Figlio and Lucas's study is not the first to show that standardized test grades of a local elementary school affect house values. What Figlio and Lucas added to the findings is the discovery of an effect of the "report card" above and beyond the direct impact of test scores.

*David N. Figlio and Maurice E. Lucas, "What's In a Grade? School Report Cards and House Prices," National Bureau of Economic Research Working Paper 8019.

Local P.S. 196 Report Card

___ A. $20,000 more value
___ B. $2,000 more value
___ C. $2,000 less value
___ D. $10,000 less value

For questions regarding this report see your local property appraiser.

When a large part of the costs or benefits of a real estate investment valuation are non-financial, as with a residence choice, estimating the value of the benefits requires many kinds of information. For a residence, important information will include accessibility to the locations and services critical to the needs of the household, any trends or changes occurring in the immediate and surrounding neighborhoods, prospective changes in roads or land uses in the area, school quality, school district boundaries, restrictive covenants for the subdivision, flood zone status of the property, crime rates in the area, and other information about factors affecting the "package" of nonfinancial benefits from a prospective residence. (The nature and characteristics of location in real estate are the subject of Chapter 5.) Part of the role of a knowledgeable real estate agent can be to assist in obtaining this information. There are, however, limits to how much one can rely on the advice of a real estate agent because of the legal nature of the agency function. (These limits are discussed in Chapter 19.)

Concept Check

2.5 What are two classes of benefits (costs) for a real estate investment? Give an example of each.

Incremental Investment Value

Frequently, real estate investment decisions involve incremental changes in existing real estate. For example, a homeowner may consider installing more insulation, double pane windows, or a more efficient heating and cooling system in order to reduce utility costs. In such cases the future benefits are the projected reductions in utility bills, while the cost is the price of immediate installation or conversion. So the investment analysis involves the following steps:

1. Obtain reliable information on the resulting reductions in utility costs. One must be very careful in this step to obtain realistic estimates. Most utility companies can be quite helpful in verifying the credibility of savings estimates provided by a vendor, or in referring one to agencies that can assist.

2. Obtain credible estimates of installation costs. In many instances, multiple estimates are desirable because different vendors may be able to offer different ideas about the most cost-effective configuration of equipment to install. As an example, the authors have seen estimates for plumbing projects that vary by a factor of three simply because of different ideas about how to make incremental changes in the plumbing system.

3. Compare the incremental value to the incremental costs involved. This will be done by discounting the stream of future utility cost savings to a present value. If the value of the discounted benefits exceeds the immediate cost, the project is a good investment.

Incremental real estate investment decisions are quite common. For homeowners, there may be incremental decisions regarding additions to an existing residence, upgrading landscaping, remodeling bathrooms, remodeling a kitchen, or rewiring. In most cases, the cost of such home improvements can be quantified within a useful range. Obviously, what is more difficult is to quantify the value of the resulting benefits. Nevertheless, countless households do make such improvements, having judged the nonmonetary value of the improvement project to exceed its estimated cost.

Owners of income-producing real estate also make incremental investment decisions. Income-producing property includes apartments and other rental residential, retail, office, hospitality, industrial, and many types of specialty properties. (Investment decisions for income-producing property are the subject of Chapter 16.) The most extensive example would be expansion of a property by adding an additional building. Less extensive incremental investments might include rewiring an office building to support modern electronics and communications, refurbishing a lobby, painting, relandscaping, improving parking areas, installing additional lighting, installing additional security systems and devices, installing more efficient heating or cooling systems, adding insulation, and replacing furnishings. Many incremental investment decisions for income-producing property are made as part of property management, which we discuss in Chapter 17.

Explore The Web

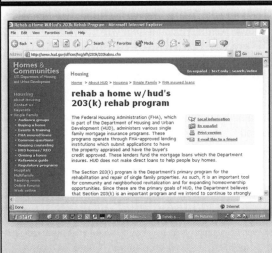

An exciting and rewarding challenge in real estate investment can be to purchase a home that is a "fixer-upper," one needing significant repairs. Many new investors have obtained their start by this means, obtaining a wealth of experience (not all serene), capped off with a rewarding increase in the value of the dwelling. The U.S. Department of Housing and Urban Development has sought to encourage such investment adventures by providing special home financing programs through the Federal Housing Administration (FHA). Go to the HUD website (www.hud.gov). Once there, go to "Homes" and select "Home Improvements," then "about HUD's rehabilitation." Find out why normal financing poses problems for serious "fixer-uppers." Then find what kind of houses and what kinds of repairs are eligible for this 203(k) financing.

With income-producing real estate, the measure of benefits is much simpler than with homes. The central benefit criterion is how the investment affects rental net income (income after expenses), and therefore value, and this can come about through several avenues. For example, an additional building would be expected to provide more space to rent and greater future net revenue. Many other improvements might make the property more beneficial to tenants, making them more willing to accept rent increases and perhaps less likely to move. Others may reduce operating expenses. For example, investments in improved fire safety or improved security may reduce the annual cost of hazard and liability insurance.

Concept Check

2.6 The distinguishing aspect of an incremental investment decision is that it involves comparing cost to the _____ in discounted net income or net benefits.

All of these kinds of incremental investments for income-producing properties have in common the objective of increasing net income. Thus, step 1 in the analysis of incremental investments for commercial real estate focuses on estimating the resulting increases in net revenue. Step 2 seeks to estimate the cost of the improvement, as in any investment analysis. Step 3 of the analysis converts the projected net revenue changes to incremental present value so that they can be compared to their cost. If an analysis of the proposed investment shows that the value of net revenue increases exceed cost, then the owner is made better off (wealthier) by engaging in the project. It is important to note that many public utility companies and government agencies have programs to aid or subsidize the costs of qualified property improvements (for an example, see the nearby Explore the Web).

houseandhome.msn.
com/improve/checklists/
setpriorities.aspx

Home Improvement Advice

Incremental Investment Value with Financing

In thinking about incremental investment value, one important aspect is how the investment is financed. (The effect of financing on value for homes is discussed in Chapter 12 and for income-producing property in Chapter 14). For example, suppose a homeowner is considering a new air-conditioning and heating system to reduce utility costs. Perhaps the replacement system costs $2,000 and the homeowner will finance 75 percent of the cost with a home equity mortgage loan. Then it is important to account for the effect of the loan on the investment outcome. The first effect is that the investment cost now is $500 instead of $2,000. But offsetting this advantage, in whole or in part, is that the savings in utility costs now go partially to repay the loan, thus reducing the future net benefit for the first few years, and therefore reducing the incremental value. Usually such a loan will enhance the attractiveness of the investment, but it must be evaluated on a case-by-case basis.

Concept Check

2.7 When financing is considered in an incremental investment decision, what two changes result in the numbers used?

Investment Value and Risk

Cash flows are said to be risky if their arrival time or if their amount can vary from what was expected when the asset was purchased. If there were no risk in costs and benefits, real estate investment valuations would be quite simple. Any accountant, financial analyst, or other person with training in basic present value analysis (such as presented in Chapter 3) could find the correct answers to real estate investment questions. Sometimes real estate in-

Exhibit 2-2 The Spectrum of Risk in Investments

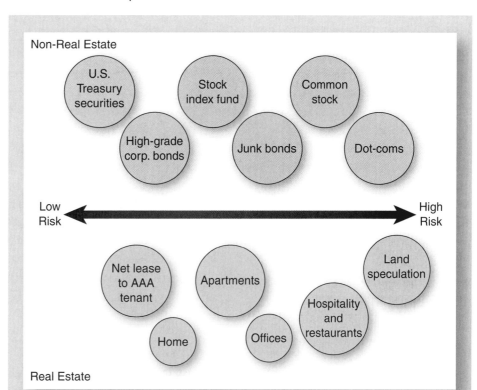

vestment decisions do approach certainty. For example, suppose you are contemplating investing in a warehouse, fully occupied through a long-term lease by a high-quality company such as General Electric. Moreover, GE is responsible for paying all of the property's operating expenses. This type of lease is referred to as a "net" lease.[2] In this case the net revenue to the owner is highly certain, much like the income from a high-quality bond. If the cost of acquisition also is certain, then a simple comparison of the value of the discounted cash flows to the cost is easily done and is a reliable guide to decisions.

But an investment with such certainty as the warehouse example is a rarity in real estate and perhaps even more rare in most other realms of business investment. As suggested in Exhibit 2-2, there is a wide spectrum of cash flow risk (uncertainty) in the investment world, ranging from very high quality bonds (e.g., U.S. Treasury bonds or private bonds rated AAA) to dot-com type equities (stocks) with extreme uncertainty. Real estate investments also present a range of risk possibilities, though perhaps not quite as broad as the entire investment spectrum. The lowest risk level in real estate is investment in properties like the warehouse example, involving a financially strong tenant committed to a long-term net lease. Among the highest risk levels of real estate investment is raw land held for speculation because it faces both extreme market uncertainty and regulatory uncertainty. (See Chapter 24 for the risks of land development.)

While real estate investments generally are less risky than the typical business investment, they still have significant uncertainty. Even within a rather safe class of properties such as personal residences, there is a range of value predictability. For standard single-family homes—three bedroom, two baths, two-car garage, in an urban setting—value tends to be quite predictable. But for residences having unusual locations or designs, value can be quite uncertain. Also relatively uncertain in value are many condominium

---

2. Leasees are discussed in more detail in later chapters (see, for example, Chapters 17 and 21).

Career Focus

The Real Estate Entrepreneur

Real estate may be one of the last bastions of the free-enterprising entrepreneur who buys properties in hope that they will rise in value. Since World War II some of the wealthiest persons in the world have been real estate entrepreneurs. Sometimes these persons purchase property purely as a speculator, taking the risk that the market for the property will improve. A more common role of the entrepreneur is to buy land, change its use, and then sell it. In this role the entrepreneur undertakes extremely complex and risky challenges, but enjoys the prospect of large wealth and the thrill of creating communities. The role of entrepreneur requires exceptional capacities. First, one must be willing to ride a financial roller coaster. Most entrepreneurs have been wealthy several times, losing much of their wealth between the peaks. The entrepreneur must thrive on complicated challenges and surprises. They must have exceptional confidence in their goals and in themselves. They must be comfortable working with limited information, and with uncertainty. They must be savvy and skilled in negotiating with others, who frequently have motives to frustrate the entrepreneur's goals or to capture the value of the entrepreneur's efforts. They must earn the confidence and loyalty of lenders, contractors, partners and others on whom they must depend. They must be farsighted and patient, able to wait until the timing is right. They must be capable of organizing and controlling an organization that is operating under stress. Finally, they need a sense of humor, to be able to chuckle at the many times their efforts lead to naught.

Source: Based partly on material from *Careers in Finance,* Bentley College, www.careers-in-finance.com/re.htm

---

apartments, partly because they sometimes become caught up in speculative rental investment activity. (For a discussion of the condominium form of real estate ownership, see Chapter 4.)

A major factor in all real estate cash flow uncertainty is **liquidity,** the ability to sell quickly for fair market value. Less liquidity means more value uncertainty. While there is variation in real estate markets, most tend to be illiquid. The time horizon for marketing ownership interests in real estate, except for certain classes of properties such as standard single-family residences, can be many months, even years. Particularly for the larger and more specialized properties, and for undeveloped land, there may be few prospective buyers, or no prospective buyers at a given time. For example, after Congress enacted the Tax Reform Act of 1986, which diminished many tax incentives for apartment investment, a sale of an apartment property became a rare event for several years. Consistent with this pattern, even among single-family residences, the largest homes tend to be much less liquid than more typical ones. As a consequence, they also have more value uncertainty.

Concept Check

2.8   When does it matter whether an asset is liquid or illiquid?

Four reference cases of cash flow risk or uncertainty can be thought of in real estate investment, as suggested in Exhibit 2-3:

1. No risk (all costs and future cash flows can be predicted with certainty).
2. Uncertainty only in immediate costs.
3. Uncertainty only in the value of future cash flow.
4. Uncertainty in both the immediate costs and value of the future cash flows.

Below we explore examples of each case that involves uncertainty.

Exhibit 2-3 Four Combinations of Investment Risk

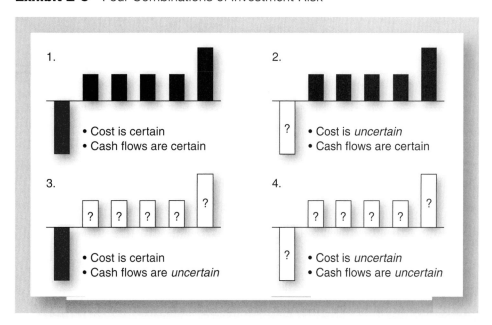

www.uli.org

Urban Land Institute offers a wealth of information about properties, design, and development.

Uncertainty of Costs

Uncertainty of costs also is characteristic, for example, of renovation and urban redevelopment. In renovation of an aged building, it often is impossible to know the true condition of the structure until it is partially dismantled. Experienced renovators understand that old walls, floors, and ceilings can mask costly surprises in structural damage, decay, or design deficiencies. Similarly, when land is cleared in urban redevelopment, there may be surprises in the condition of the underlying utility infrastructure—gas lines, water lines, and sewer and drainage systems. Further, there is the threat in many instances of prior soil contamination, which can require costly mitigation. By contrast, one of the attractions of new development and new construction is that no preexisting structures or utilities can harbor such costly surprises.

Uncertainty of cost also is characteristic of innovative or unique structures. There seem to be few ways for construction costs to be under budget, and many ways for them to exceed it. It is very common for cost overruns to occur whenever a structure is constructed that has not been, in large measure, built before.

The point of the examples above is that the degree of cost uncertainty varies in real estate investment decisions. In some cases, such as the acquisition of a new home or some other newly constructed structure, the buyer can be protected by both the newness of the structure and by builder warranties. Most purchases of structures, however, entail at least some degree of cost uncertainty due to possible structural deficiencies.

In undertaking investments with cost risk, investors must be prepared. They must have adequate capital, suitable temperament, requisite knowledge and skill, sufficient organization and personnel, and sufficient flexibility of time.

Uncertainty in investment cost can be mitigated in a number of ways. First, an investor, recognizing that some kinds of investments will inherently have cost uncertainty, can avoid them. For example, the investor can avoid renovation projects, redevelopment projects, or projects involving construction of innovative structures. Another strategy for managing cost risk is to employ individuals and companies with extensive, successful experience in the type of investment contemplated. If one wants to invest in risky projects, perhaps a compromise between these strategies is to begin with small projects having risky costs so as to develop gradually the capacity to manage such investments.

Exhibit 2-4 The Spectrum of Cost Uncertainty

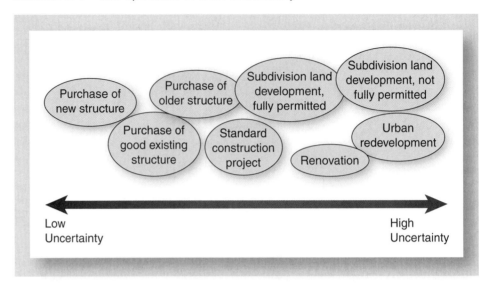

Uncertainty of real estate investment costs depends, of course, on the nature of the investment. As suggested in Exhibit 2-4, this risk ranges widely across investments from being a very small factor in newly constructed buildings to a dominating factor in such undertakings as renovation, redevelopment, and development of raw land when all of the regulatory permits are not in hand.

Uncertainty of Value

The value of an investment is dependent on the certainty of the future cash flows. This certainty can vary widely across the spectrum of real estate investments.

In no case is the uncertainty of future income greater than with "raw" land held for development. To begin, the value of the land usually is dependent on future urban growth to create market potential that presently does not exist. But this risk historically has been amplified by the uncertainty of land use regulation. If, for example, the land is included within a designated "urban service boundary," the permits for development of the land are likely to be expedited by the local planning authority, and demand for the land will be enhanced.[3] If, on the other hand, the land is excluded from the urban service boundary, obtaining permits for development could be difficult or impossible, and the market potential would be diverted elsewhere. If an investor "wins" this uncertain game of land speculation, the value of the land involved can increase many fold. But the risks can be severe and unforgiving.

Uncertainty of cash flows also varies across existing properties. Many investors believe that standard types of **industrial property** (e.g., warehouses and light manufacturing) tend to have reliable cash flows. Others point to "normal" **multifamily property** (e.g., apartments) as having steady cash flows since every individual must live somewhere. Especially interesting in the realm of multifamily has been investment in subsidized apartments for low-income households. Since waiting lists exist for most such properties, vacancy often has been nonexistent. Toward the other extreme, office property markets have been cyclical, creating volatility in occupancy and rental rate growth. At the top of the spectrum in cash flow uncertainty may be **hospitality property.** Hotels, motels, and many types of restaurants have experienced great volatility. Further, even in a stable mar-

---

3. An urban service boundary designates an area within which local government gives priority in establishing development infrastructure such as roads, sewers, and utilities.

ket these types of properties seem inherently vulnerable to competition from new entrants in the market. Note that in hotels and motels occupancy is unusually short, and the cost to the customer of "moving" is often essentially nothing.

Concept Check

2.9   List four theoretical cases of uncertainty in a real estate investment. Which case does each of the following fit? (1) Purchase and resale of raw land. (2) Construction of a warehouse for the U.S. government for a predetermined price. (3) Development of residential subdivision lots for sale to builders. (4) Purchase of a warehouse leased to General Electric on a 50-year net lease.

Managing Risk

Several strategies can be pursued to mitigate the uncertainty of future cash flows. To begin, prudent real estate investors will make the study of real estate markets a constant part of their activity. Seldom in real estate is there a source of market information and analysis sufficiently reliable to substitute completely for the investor's own efforts. The reason for this is that real estate markets are vulnerable to the **agency problem** and **adverse selection;** that is, if an investor relies in an uninformed manner on advisers or agents for investment advice there may be an incentive for the advisers to "shortchange" the investor. The adviser may have incentive to filter the investment opportunities available, keeping the more promising ones and offering the investor the less promising ones. Because it is inherently difficult to evaluate the adviser's behavior, this propensity to present the client with an "adverse" selection of investments may not be apparent for years, if ever. The investor must be sufficiently knowledgeable to guard against such behavior.

   Agency risk is common in real estate. Many decisions depend on other persons for "input" or efforts that are difficult to evaluate. This occurs in obtaining construction work, an appraisal, a market or feasibility study, brokerage services, property management, and investment advice. When the quality of such service is unverifiable and provided by someone who does not bear the cost of error or failure, there is incentive to "shortchange" the client. The greatest cure for this problem is for the provider to be sensitive to business reputation. Thus, in using real estate services it is wise to know the reputation of the providers and to be sure they believe their reputation is at stake in the current assignment.

Concept Check

2.10   The problem of agency arises in real estate investment when an agent or advisor has _____ that the investor lacks. This may result in adverse selection where the advisor claims _____ investment opportunities, leaving the investor with _____ ones.

   The investor also can manage cash flow risk by exercising investment patience. The greatest single cash flow uncertainty for most real estate investments is the sale price at the end of the investor's **holding period.** For this reason, real estate has been argued to be strictly a long-term investment. If a property has an uncertain resale price, but steady cash flow, selling it after a short time sacrifices its "safe" value (the regular income) and magnifies its uncertain value ("price risk"). By contrast, holding it for, say, 10 years of cash flow before selling will magnify the effect of the safe cash flow and diminish the effect of the price uncertainty. This works because later cash flows have less effect on value, an effect that becomes clearer when one understands the ideas of discounting and present value presented in Chapter 3.

2-2
A Case of Extreme Real Estate Risk

Jensen Beach—[The developer of the Villas of Pinecrest Lakes] gambled when he built a $3 million cluster of luxury apartment buildings about four years ago, ignoring a lawsuit filed by nearby homeowners alleging the buildings violated Martin County's growth rules. The Florida Supreme Court has proven just how risky that gamble was. The state's highest court sided with a controversial ruling requiring five apartment buildings in the Villas of Pinecrest Lakes to be demolished, according to an order lawyers received. By agreeing not to hear the developer's appeal, the court upheld the 4th District Court of Appeal's decision that the buildings are illegal, primarily because they were built too close to neighboring single-family homes in the Pinecrest Lakes development.

Source: Sarah Eisenhauer, "Jensen Villas Must be Razed," *Palm Beach Post,* June 7, 2002

Update: Within six months the Villas of Pinecrest Lakes were all demolished.

[The developer] argued throughout the seven-year legal fight that his buildings should be allowed to stay because he had permission from the county commission to build. . .

In [the plaintiff's] first victory in the case, [the judge] ruled in 1999 that the buildings violated Martin County's growth-management plan and must come down. He said the apartments weren't compatible with the single-family homes and violated a county policy that calls for "tiering," or gradually increasing densities between neighborhoods. The Martin County Commission approved the apartments by a 3–2 vote in 1995, prompting a lawsuit from the homeowners association less than a month later. Several residents argued throughout the approval process that the plans didn't comply with the county's rules for growth. . .

The Villas model office was closed late Thursday when [a prospect] arrived hoping to rent an apartment in the complex for her daughter. "There are so few apartments out here and these are the nicest ones I know in the area," she said.

This risk effect of a short holding period is important, for example, in the decision for home ownership. It provides an incentive for households to rent if they expect to move in a short time. If the need to move arises quickly, the "thinness" of real estate markets can put the homeowner in a troublesome position of either selling a house at a discount to true market value or "carrying" a vacant house for a significant period of time and bearing the monthly costs of two residences. From a strictly financial perspective, this can easily result in a net loss from owning the house, adding significantly to the overall cost of ownership. The large costs of a real estate transaction (i.e., purchase) add to the penalty of short-term home ownership. Fees and other costs of purchasing a home commonly exceed 5 percent of the price (see Chapter 20).

Concept Check

2.11 What effect does an investor's holding period usually have upon the riskiness of a real estate investment?

Exhibit 2-5 The Spectrum of Cash Flow Uncertainty

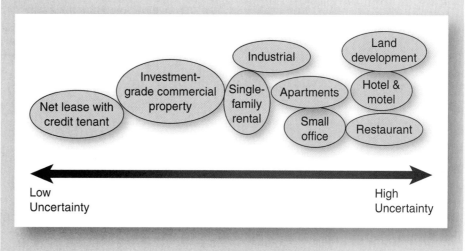

There are other strategies to reduce cash flow risk. Investment in existing properties enables one to be able to see a "track record" of performance for the property in recent times. This is likely one reason that large institutional investors tend to concentrate investment in properties that are relatively new and fully occupied by "quality" tenants.

As with uncertainty of investment costs, the uncertainty of net cash flows, in reality, ranges across different types of investments. This variance is suggested in Exhibit 2-5. On one extreme is our earlier example of the property occupied by a "credit" tenant on a net lease. At the other extreme would be the cash flows from land development. Between these extremes lie the vast majority of developed properties with, for example, the rents and sale price of a single-family dwelling at a modest-risk level, and the cash flows and value of a motel or restaurant at a high-risk level.

Revisiting Three Investment Risk Scenarios

Let us return to the three common risk combinations in real estate investment. The first possibility, again, is uncertainty of immediate investment costs but certainty of future cash flows and value. Pure examples of this case might be "custom" homebuilding, or building a presold, or **turnkey,** commercial building for a financially strong corporation.[4] The entire risk is in keeping construction costs and the construction schedule under control. The second possibility is certainty of cost but uncertainty of value. Investing in an existing property for the purpose of leasing it to unknown future tenants is an example of this case. The third possibility would be the combination of both uncertainty of cost and uncertainty of value. The classification of actual projects within these categories often is less than clear. Still, it is helpful to recognize that projects can have different degrees of risks between costs and value because the methods of managing risk between the two categories are very different.

Risk, Investment Value, and Investment Yield

We have suggested above that risk affects value. As a further example, suppose you have the opportunity to purchase a vacant residential lot that you are told should sell in one year for $50,000 (above any transactions costs). Suppose you also can buy a number of U.S.

4. Custom homebuilding is the practice of building homes for buyers who have already committed to a purchase contract. This is in contrast to "speculative" building where construction of the home begins before it has been sold.

Treasury securities that will pay no coupon (interest) income, but will mature in one year to pay $50,000. It is not hard to determine which of these choices would bring the highest price. While the Treasury securities would bring a price well above $45,000, the lot may not bring a price of even $40,000. The main difference, of course, is the perceived uncertainty of the final sale price. The "sale price" (and sale date) of the Treasury securities is absolutely certain, whereas the sale price (and sale date) of the lot is quite uncertain. As a result, the residential lot is worth less to the average risk-avoiding investor than the extremely safe Treasuries. In short, riskiness reduces value.

There is a corollary story to the value effect of risk. Assume that the market price for the Treasury securities above is exactly $48,000, and the market price for the lot is exactly $40,000. We then could ask how much the invested money "grows" for each investment. For the Treasuries the invested money grows by $2,000, which is 4.17 percent of the original $48,000 investment. But for the residential lot the investment is expected to grow by $10,000, which is 25 percent of the original $40,000 investment. We refer to this growth in the invested dollars as the **investment yield.** What happened to create this difference in yield? It derived from the risk-adjusted valuation by the potential investors. The risk adjustment to value has an opposite effect on yield: The high-valued (safe) investment results in a low yield, and the low-valued (risky) investment results in a high investment yield. The expected investment yield for the safe investment is 4.17 percent, while the expected investment yield for the risky investment is 25 percent. Determining required investment yields on risky real estate investments is one of the most important, and difficult, steps in the valuation/decision-making process, which we discuss in detail in Chapter 3.

Concept Check

2.12   What effect does riskiness have on the price that investors are willing to pay for real estate?

Concept Check

2.13   What is the expected growth rate in invested money normally called? How is this expected growth rate normally affected by riskiness of the investment cash flows?

A Portfolio Perspective on Real Estate Investment

Most of the focus of this text is on individual properties and individual real estate transactions. But one does not own real estate in isolation from other possessions and pursuits. For example, owning rental houses may be a good investment for a person with financial liquidity, a stable job, low expected mobility, and the time and skill to manage the properties. But it can be risky and unrewarding for a person with low financial liquidity, a changing job outlook, a time-intensive job, or the need to be able to relocate upon short notice. For similar reasons, home ownership makes good investment sense to most households at some point in their life, but not to all households at all times.

Viewing real estate investments in the context of the owner's other assets and the owner's overall situation may be thought of as a **portfolio perspective** on real estate investment—that is, the real estate investment is valued in the context of all the other assets and characteristics of the investor's portfolio, including human capital (i.e., personal capacities or needs). (A more complete analysis of risk in a portfolio context is the subject of Chapter 23.) From the examples above, it should be clear that this portfolio perspective can be very important to consider in any real estate decision. As further examples, the desirability of investment in home improvements can depend on the needs and expectations of the household. A family with children about to leave home certainly views the addition of a swimming pool or another bedroom differently than a family with young children. A household that is mobile and expects to move within a few years also will view a home expansion differently from a household that expects to remain in the house for a longer time. Similarly, a mobile family is more likely than a nonmobile family to place greater value on a residence that is easily resalable.

The portfolio perspective is important in commercial real estate as well. For example, a person who expects to move frequently is less likely to be comfortable investing in local rental properties because of unfamiliarity with the local market and the risk of managing property at a long distance. This person might find investment in real estate through a publicly traded real estate investment trust (REIT) a much more satisfactory option. (REITs are discussed in Chapters 15 and 23.) In addition, the knowledge and experience of the investor can be very important in determining what is a good real estate investment. For example, persons familiar with industrial and manufacturing activity may want to restrict investment to industrial properties because they have a better chance of detecting, assessing, and mitigating risks in that sphere.

Concept Check

2.14   A portfolio approach to making real estate decisions involves valuing a prospective real estate opportunity in the context of one's other _____ and one's _____ _____ .

Investment Value and Appraisal

So far we have considered the value of a real estate asset to a particular individual, which we have called **investment value.** But often we need to know what value a real estate asset may have to an unknown typical investor or purchaser; that is, we need to know the most probable selling price. This is essential, for example, in determining the financial feasibility of a development project. It also is important for an owner in determining whether an asset should be held or sold (market price exceeds investor's present value), and it is critical to lenders who are concerned with the possibility of needing to sell a property if the borrower fails to pay back the loan. (The risk of loan default is discussed in Chapter 10.) Further, it can be necessary in incremental investment decisions to know how much an improvement to a property affects its future market price in order to estimate its full future benefits. The problem in real estate is that, because of scarce transactions, markets seldom reveal prices easily.

www.appraisalinstitute.
org

Professional appraisal
organization

The solution to this problem is called appraisal. **Appraisal** provides an estimate of the most probable selling price of a property. It differs from the investment perspective in that it seeks to reveal what some "typical," unidentified investor is likely to pay for a property rather than what value the property has to a specific owner. But in predicting the probable price to this nameless investor, **appraised value** really is a form of generalized investment valuation, which also provides a crucial element in making individual investment decisions. (The methods and details of appraisal are discussed in Chapters 8 and 9.)

Concept Check

2.15   While investment value is value of a real estate asset to _____ , appraisal is the estimated value of the asset to _____ .

T he appraiser always has been a central figure in the real estate community. The job of the appraiser is described by the principal appraisal organization, the Appraisal Institute, as follows:

Real estate appraisers are problem solvers. Basically, they assemble and interpret a diversity of information regarding a specific property and develop a value estimate. . . Appraisals may be required for just about any type of property, including single-family homes, apartment buildings and condominiums, office buildings, shopping centers, industrial sites, and farms. The reasons for performing a real estate appraisal are just as varied. An appraisal may be required for mortgage lending, tax assessments, negotiations between buyers and sellers, government acquisition for public use, and for mergers or acquisitions. Appraisers may be employed by financial institutions, government agencies, or real estate services corporations or organizations. Many real estate appraisers are in business for themselves and work independently. . . .Much of their work is accomplished away from the office, inspecting property, researching official records and deeds, and interviewing informed sources. Appraisers who accept assignments in a number of states or abroad may travel extensively.

Source: http://www.appraisalinstitute.org/resources/ap_careers.asp

Summary

The purpose of this chapter is to illustrate typical real estate decisions and discuss how a value perspective applies to those decisions. Investment decisions relate costs incurred now to the value of benefits resulting in the future. These are decisions that, once made, cannot be reversed without cost. Analysis of such decisions involve two elements: the initial costs and the value of the stream of future benefits. Decisions such as selecting a residence involve nonmonetary costs and benefits which, while challenging to incorporate into the investment value equation, are no less important and relevant to the investment decision. The best means of treating nonmonetary costs and benefits is to obtain as much information about them as possible so that their influence is considered at least intuitively in the ultimate decision.

Many investment decisions are about incremental change in an existing situation or asset. However, the basic investment analysis remains the same. The incremental costs are weighed against the value of the incremental benefits. Debt financing can affect investment decisions. It is accounted for by lessening the initial cash outlay or cost, and by reducing the net benefits to account for the necessary expenditures for debt repayment.

Risk and uncertainty are omnipresent in real estate decisions and must be accounted for in informed decision making. Cost uncertainty varies greatly across types of real estate. It is least in the acquisition of newly completed structures and greatest in undeveloped, unpermitted raw land. Uncertainty of future benefits also varies greatly across types of real estate investments. It is low, for example, with properties occupied by financially strong tenants under a net lease or with single-family residences, and high with hospitality properties and raw land, among others.

Investors in real estate use a number of strategies to manage risk. These include studying real estate markets, gaining experience with the type of investment of interest, employing experienced help and advice, selecting investments that are relatively liquid or marketable, and opting for properties with lower risk. Finally, allowing for a longer holding period reduces the effect of selling price risk inherent in real estate investment. The riskiness and investment value of a real estate investment depends in important ways on the characteristics, needs and capacities of the investor. Characteristics such as experience, financial depth, personality, interests, locational stability, and others affect the relative desirability of real estate investments. Considering these issues is part of a larger "portfolio perspective" in real estate investment.

An important final distinction is the difference between investment valuation and appraisal. While investment value estimates the value of an investment to a specific individual, appraisal estimates the value (i.e., its probable selling price) of the same investment to a typical individual.

Key Terms

Adverse selection 31
Agency problem 31
Appraisal 35
Appraised value 35
Discounting 22
Holding period 31
Hospitality property 30

Incremental real estate investment
    decisions 25
Industrial property 30
Investment 21
Investment risk 21
Investment value 35
Investment yield 34

Liquidity 28
Multifamily property 30
Nonmonetary 23
Portfolio perspective 34
Turnkey 33

Test Problems

1. Which of these is the best example of an investment decision, based on the criteria identified in this chapter?
   a. Choice among similarly priced hotels for a vacation to New York City.
   b. Choice among similarly priced airlines for a trip to Europe.
   c. Decision whether or not to purchase a high definition television (HDTV) or stay with a conventional TV at $500 lower cost.
   d. Choice between colors for a custom-ordered car.
   e. Choice of guests for a party.

2. Examples of incremental investment decisions include:
   a. Adding space to a structure.
   b. Giving a retail building a new front.
   c. Improving heating or cooling efficiency in a building.
   d. All except c.
   e. All of the above.

3. The effect of selecting a residence upon such matters as lifestyle and relations with others outside the household are described as:
   a. Irrelevant to an investment decision.
   b. Pecuniary costs or benefits.
   c. Nonmonetary costs or benefits.
   d. Risk elements to be addressed through discounting.
   e. Too little to consider in the normal case.

4. Of these real estate investments, the riskiest is:
   a. Property "net-leased" to a financially strong corporation.
   b. A single-family residence.
   c. An office building.
   d. A retail center.
   e. Raw land.

5. Of these real estate investments, the one with the greatest cost uncertainty is a:
   a. New single-family residence.
   b. Subdivision development with all permits granted.
   c. Subdivision development with permits not yet granted.
   d. Standard construction project.
   e. Purchase of an older structure.

6. As the level of perceived risk increases
   a. Values and expected returns increase
   b. Values and expected returns decrease
   c. Values increase and expected returns decrease
   d. Values decrease and expected returns increase
   e. Values decrease but expected returns are unaffected.

7. The most liquid form of real estate is:
   a. Raw land.
   b. Wetlands.
   c. Office buildings.
   d. Standard single-family residences.
   e. Specialty single-family residences.

8. The type of real estate that tends to have the highest cash flow uncertainty is:
   a. Industrial.
   b. Office.
   c. Single family residential.
   d. Apartments.
   e. Hotels and motels.

9. Which of these strategies in real estate investment would tend to increase risk?
   a. Study real estate markets.
   b. Select typical size properties.
   c. Select typical design of properties.
   d. Invest for a short term (short holding period).
   e. Select lower-risk property types.

10. Which of these is the correct statement about the relationship of investment analysis and appraisal?
    a. Investment analysis estimates value to a specific investor while appraisal estimates value to a typical investor.
    b. Investment analysis estimates value to a typical investor while appraisal estimates value to a specific investor.
    c. Both estimate value to a typical investor, but one is less costly to do.
    d. Both estimate value to a specific investor, but one is less costly to do.
    e. Appraisal is completely unrelated to investment, and can contribute nothing to investment analysis.

Study Questions

1. Buying a home is not about return on investment. It is about family or household security, opportunity, and other irreplaceable intangibles. As a person who understands the meaning of investment, how would you answer this assertion?

2. Many banks pitch home equity loans as a way to finance a vacation. Is using the equity in one's house to finance a vacation a good investment decision? Why? Why not?

3. It is common for parents to purchase a residence for their child to live in while going to college, often reasoning that apartment rent is a complete waste when the money could be used to build up owner equity. What are some arguments for such an investment? Against it?

4. Raw land at the edge of urban development that lacks the necessary permits for development is, in general, the most risky kind of real estate investment. Defend or refute this assertion.

5. An appraisal of a property estimates the value to a typical investor, that is, the probable selling price. Why might this be a misleading indicator to a specific investor for the investment value?

6. You are contemplating replacing your conventional hot water and heating system with a solar hot water heating system at a cost of $4,000. How should you define the potential benefits that you need to estimate? Are there any risk or other considerations that should be examined?

Explore The Web

Go to the Web page of Freddie Mac Homebuyers: *http://www.freddiemac.com/homebuyers/library* Browse the site. Then select "Rent" or "Buy" and go down the page to the calculator.

Can you figure out why each calculator entry is relevant to the question of rent or buy?

Go to the Web page of Microsoft Network House and Home: *http://houseandhome.msn.com* Choose calculators, and then "Rent" or "Buy."

Compare results with the Freddie Mac calculator. Does one seem more realistic than the other?

Solutions To Concept Checks

1. The two basic elements of an investment decision are the initial costs and the value of future benefits.

2. While choosing a college course will have significant upfront costs and the benefits are spread out over time, choosing which football game to watch does not involve an investment decision because it lacks initial cost and the time period is very short.

3. Real estate decisions are about acquiring, financing, using, improving, and disposing of actual real estate assets. Therefore, the decision to replace the air conditioner would be a real estate investment decision. Its replacement is directly related to the value of the real estate.

4. We must discount the cash flow of a real estate investment because a dollar in the future has less value than a dollar today. The present value of the future benefits can then be compared to the initial cost of the investment.

5. A real estate investment has monetary and nonmonetary costs and benefits. One of the costs involved is the initial purchase price of the property. Nonmonetary costs can include time expended, or stress. Nonmonetary benefits include the effects of the surrounding area on the property and access to places like work or school.

6. The distinguishing aspect of an incremental investment decision is that it involves comparing cost to the increase in discounted net income or net benefits.

7. When using financing in an incremental investment decision, the initial cash cost is reduced. Furthermore, because the loan must be repaid, the future net benefits are reduced, thus reducing incremental value.

8. The liquidity of an asset matters if the investor may need to sell in a short period of time. If the investor will never need to dispose of the asset quickly then he or she is not affected by illiquidity.

9. Four theoretical cases of uncertainty are no uncertainty, uncertainty only in immediate costs, uncertainty only in the value of future cash flow, and uncertainty in both the immediate costs and the value of future cash flow. Some examples are as follows. (1) the purchase and resale of raw land involves uncertainty only in the value of future cash flow. (2) The construction of a warehouse for the U.S. government for a predetermined price has uncertainty only in immediate costs. (3) The development of residential subdivision lots for sale to builders has uncertainty of immediate costs and value of future cash flow. (4) The purchase of a warehouse leased to General Electric on a 50-year net lease involves no uncertainty about the immediate costs.

10. The problem of agency arises in real estate investment when an agent or advisor has information that the investor lacks. This may result in adverse selection where the advisor acquires promising investment opportunities, leaving the investor with "adverse" ones.

11. If a property has an uncertain resale price, but steady cash flow, selling it after a short time sacrifices its "safe" value (the regular income) and magnifies its uncertain value (price risk). However, long holding periods will magnify the effect of the safe cash flow, and reduce the effect of uncertainty in price. Therefore, longer holding periods in real estate are less risky than shorter holding periods.

12. Higher risk assets will command a lower price than an asset with low risk, all else being equal.

13. The expected growth rate in invested money is called investment yield. A low-risk investment results in a low investment yield, and a risky investment results in a high yield.

14. A portfolio approach to making real estate decisions involves valuing a prospective real estate opportunity in the context of one's other assets and overall situation.

15. While investment value is value of a real estate asset to a specific individual, appraisal is the estimated value of the asset to a "typical" individual.

Additional Readings

Brueggeman, William B., and Jeffrey D. Fisher. *Real Estate Finance and Investments,* 11th ed. New York: McGraw-Hill/Irwin, 2001.

Cruikshank, J. L., and W. J. Poorvu. *The Real Estate Game: The Intelligent Guide to Decision-Making and Investment.* New York: Free Press, 1999.

Friedman, Jack P. *Keys to Investing in Real Estate.* Hauppauge, NY, Barron's Educational Series, 2000.

Tanzer, M. *Real Estate Investments and How to Make Them,* 3rd edition. Upper Saddle River, NJ, Prentice Hall Press, February 1997.

Tompos, A. W. *Analyzing Investment Properties,* 2nd edition. Cincinnati, OH: South-Western College Pub, 2001.

Wolfe, Tom. *A Man in Full.* New York: Farrar, Straus and Giroux, 1998.

chapter three

The Effects of Time *and* Risk on Value

Learning Objectives

After reading this chapter you will be able to:

1. Explain why future cash flows must be converted (discounted) into present values.

2. Perform basic time-value-of-money calculations using a financial calculator.

3. Explain the importance of risk in the valuation process.

4. Explain and use the internal rate of return decision rule.

5. Explain and use the net present value decision rule.

Introduction

Any decision about real estate involves the commitment of resources over time, usually a number of years. For example, owners must repeatedly determine how much to spend on property maintenance and repair. Decisions also must be made periodically about rehabilitation, modernization, expansion, conversion of the property to another use, or demolition of the existing improvements. Further, an owner may repeatedly face the decision of whether to continue holding or to sell. Even the decision to abandon real estate involves an investment decision.

As emphasized in Chapter 2, each of these real estate decisions involves comparing the immediate cost of an action against the value of the future resulting benefits (usually quantified as cash flows). However, the valuation of future benefits is complicated by two factors. First, even if their timing and magnitude can be known with certainty, the future benefits of a proposed investment cannot simply be added up to determine their value to investors because the value of future benefits declines with time into the future.

Consider, for example, what happens when investors walk away from the settlement table after purchasing real estate. Their balance of cash (or equivalent valuables) is reduced by the required down payment on the property. Why will investors sacrifice assets to acquire property? Because they expect the present value of the benefits from future cash flows to exceed the burden of the initial down payment. Clearly, the timing of these future cash flows matters. For example, if investors must wait, say, 20 years for a series of annual cash flows to begin, they would surely value them less than if the same series of cash flows were to begin immediately after the acquisition of the property. What they

40

are willing to pay at the closing table must decline accordingly. That is, future cash flows must be "discounted" for time before they can be compared to current cash inflows and outflows.

The second complication associated with real estate valuation is that value assessments are based on *expected* cash flows, but what actually happens is seldom, if ever, exactly what the investor expected. **Risk** is the possibility that actual outcomes will vary from what was expected when the asset was purchased. Because most investors are risk averse, the relationship between risk and return is positive: The more risk investors face when undertaking an investment, the greater the rate of return they should expect (require). When valuing real estate, adjusting for risk introduces an important complication.

This chapter discusses standard techniques for quantifying the effects of time and risk on value. These **time-value-of-money (TVM)** techniques are not unique to real estate valuation and decision making. They are widely used by finance professionals to calculate mortgage payments, determine values for stocks and bonds, calculate insurance premiums, and decide whether potential capital expenditures are profitable enough to commit investment capital. Nonfinance professionals also find an understanding of TVM concepts extremely beneficial. Armed with such an understanding, individuals can apply TVM procedures to compare costs on alternative loans, determine whether an existing mortgage loan should be refinanced, calculate the future value of a retirement fund (given estimates of annual contributions to the fund), decide whether a car leasing plan is preferred to a bank loan, and calculate the returns their investments have earned in the past. In short, an understanding of TVM techniques is necessary for informed valuation assessments and decision making.

The emphasis in the current chapter is on asset valuation techniques; we do not discuss the factors that actually contribute to the value of the real estate, such as location, building design, and the existing supply of competing properties. These determinates of future cash flows are discussed in detail in later chapters (see, especially, Chapters 4–7).

The Time Value of Money

Money is an economic good. Like other economic goods, such as televisions and automobiles, people prefer to have more, rather than less, money—that is, the magnitude of the cash flows matters. Moreover, investors prefer to have the money *now* rather than later. If money is received later, for example, next week instead of today, it isn't worth as much to those receiving it, and an adjustment is required. This adjustment is called **discounting.** Understanding how to adjust cash flows received at different times is the essence of the time-value-of-money problem.

Assume an investor with $100 to invest is considering three alternatives, each covering 10 years. These plans are as follows:

Plan A: The investor receives $10 at the end of the first year, plus the original $100 at the end of year 10, and no other returns.

Plan B: The investor receives $1 at the end of each year for 10 years, plus the original $100 at the end of 10 years, and no other returns.

Plan C: The investor receives $10 at the end of the 10th year of the plan, plus the original $100, and no other returns.

Each plan returns the investor's $100, plus $10 of interest over the 10-year period. Which plan should the investor prefer?

Answer: The investor should choose Plan A. Why? Because money can be put to one of two possible uses when it is received. First, the investor may spend the money, for example, by taking a friend to a movie. Second, the investor may invest the money. With Plan A, the investor has the greatest opportunity to spend the money or to earn interest on the money throughout the 10-year period by spending or reinvesting the $10 received at the end of year 1. Ten dollars invested for nine years will accumulate more interest than the 10 yearly investments of $1 each he or she would receive in Plan B. Therefore, investors who plan to reinvest their returns prefer earlier returns to later returns because of the opportunity to earn interest. Investors who consume their money returns have the same time preferences for early returns. Would you want to wait 10 years to take your friend to a movie, as you would with Plan C?

The Timeline

Panel A of Exhibit 3-1 presents a timeline, which is simply an aid for visualizing the time pattern of money returns. The line is broken into time points and time intervals, or periods, beginning on the left with the present, time point 0, and ending on the right with the terminal time point, N. Annual time periods are typically used in evaluating single-property investments, but sometimes monthly periods are appropriate (e.g., when analyzing mortgage or lease payments).

All money *inflows* are placed on top of the line, and all *outflows* of money (e.g., the time 0 investment) go beneath the line, corresponding to the time point at which they occur. The inflows and outflows from the investment decision involving the three alternative plans are shown in panel B of Exhibit 3-1. Note that the $100 investment is located beneath the line at time 0, and the three sets of inflows are located on top of the line beginning at time point 1. All future inflows and outflows are assumed to occur at the end of the period in which they are received or paid, respectively.

Exhibit 3-1   The Timeline

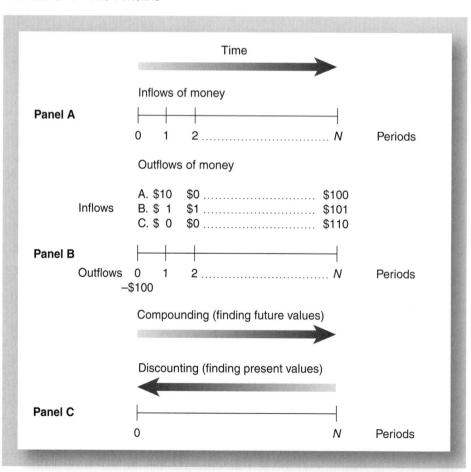

Terminology

The following are common terms used in applying time-value-of-money concepts:

Future value (*FV*)—the value of money in some period beyond time zero. "Calculating a future value" means converting cash invested in the current period (or some prior period) into what it will be worth at some future date.

Present value (*PV*)—the value of future cash flows at time zero. "Taking the present value of inflows" means converting future cash flows in present value (i.e., at time zero).

Lump sum—a one-time receipt or expenditure occurring in a given period. In panel B of Exhibit 3-1, the $10 received in year 1 under Plan A is an example of a lump sum, as is the $110 received in the 10th period under Plan C.

Ordinary annuity (*A*)—a common amount of money received at the end of every period (i.e., a series of equal lump sums). The series of $1 annual cash flows under Plan B is an example of an annuity.

Compounding—calculation of future values, as shown in panel C of Exhibit 3-1.

Discounting—calculation of present values, as shown in panel C of Exhibit 3-1.

Equations, Calculators, and Spreadsheets

Various mathematical equations can be used to adjust for differences in the timing of cash flows. However, most analysts employ a financial calculator or use "spreadsheet" programs, such as Microsoft's EXCEL, that are loaded on their personal computers. Both calculators and spreadsheet software contain internal programs that provide solutions to common TVM calculations.

There are four basic time-value-of-money adjustments. Exhibit 3-2 lists these adjustments and their associated mathematical equations. In the equations for monthly adjustments, the annual interest rate is divided by 12 to obtain the monthly interest rate, and the number of years (*n*) is multiplied by 12 to obtain the total number of monthly periods. If interest on an investment is earned (compounded) daily, the annual interest rate is divided by 365 to obtain the daily interest rate, and the number of years (*n*) is multiplied by 365 to determine the number of daily periods.

Through the manipulation of the financial functions of handheld calculators, any problem that may be solved with the TVM equations may be solved with a calculator—and usually much faster and more accurately. Financial calculators, which have the

Exhibit 3-2   Equations for Time-Value-of-Money Adjustments

Operation	Symbols	Equation for Annual Adjustment (n = number of years) (r = annual interest rate)	Equation for Monthly Adjustment (r = annual interest rate)
Future value of a lump sum	FV	$(1 + r)^n$	$(1 + r/12)^{12n}$
Future value of annuity	FV_A	$\dfrac{(1 + r)^n - 1}{r}$	$\dfrac{(1 + r/12)^{12n} - 1}{r/12}$
Present value of a lump sum	PV	$\dfrac{1}{(1 + r)^n}$	$\dfrac{1}{(1 + r/12)^{12n}}$
Present value of annuity	PV_A	$\dfrac{1 - [1/(1 + r)^n]}{r}$	$\dfrac{1 - [1/(1 + r/12)^{12n}]}{r/12}$

Career Focus

Real estate professionals must constantly update their knowledge and skill set. They must constantly strive to stay abreast of business trends, and think about issues—tax laws, new highway routes, technology, or existing and proposed zoning regulations—affecting their clients, business, and investments. Beyond a general knowledge of business, economics, and, increasingly, a global market

Real Estate Career

perspective, employers expect neophyte real estate professionals to be computer literate and adept at using spreadsheets, database analysis, word processing, graphical analysis, and mapping software. Employers also expect new employees to communicate well and to be comfortable making oral presentations. Negotiation skills are also an important aspect of the real estate industry.

Source: Information on Career Paths in Commercial Real Estate, University of Cincinnati, www.cba.uc.edu/getreal

necessary formulas preprogrammed into their computational algorithms, are merely a more efficient option than equations for making TVM adjustments. Although financial calculators vary, all have five basic keys (or registers):

N—the number of compounding (or discounting) periods. If the cash flows from a real estate investment are received, say, annually for 5 years, then $N = 5$. If they are received monthly for 5 years, then $N = 60$.

I—the periodic (usually monthly or annual) interest rate. If the cash flows are received or invested annually, I is the annual interest rate. If the cash flows occur at monthly intervals, I equals the annual rate divided by 12.

PV—the lump sum amount invested in time zero. In real estate this is often the required cash down payment. PV may also be the discounted present value of future cash flows at time zero.

PMT—the periodic level payment or receipt (annuity). This may be a fixed monthly mortgage payment or a lease payment. The cash inflows on income-producing properties are generally not fixed-level amounts.

FV—the lump sum cash flow or the future value of an investment. In real estate, FV may be the cash flows netted from the sale of a property at the end of an N year holding period.

Once a student becomes comfortable with the basic operations of his or her calculator, the key to solving time-value-of-money problems is knowing what, if anything, to enter into each of these five registers. In the problems that follow, and throughout the text, the basic keystrokes needed to solve a TVM problem are identified without specifying the exact sequence of keystrokes necessary to solve the problem on a particular calculator.

Spreadsheet programs such as EXCEL have significantly increased the use of personal computers in the analysis of real estate decisions. The Appendix discusses how to solve basic time-value-of-money problems using an EXCEL spreadsheet.

Compounding Operations

The first two time-value-of-money (TVM) operations are used for calculating future values resulting from the compounding of interest. Compound interest means the investor earns interest on the principal amount invested plus interest on accumulated interest.

Future Value of a Lump Sum. Suppose an investor deposits $1,000 today in an interest-bearing account at a local bank. The account pays 5 percent interest compounded annually, and the investor expects to withdraw the original principal, plus accumulated interest, at the end of five years. Panel A of Exhibit 3-3 provides a timeline demonstration of the cash inflows and outflows for this problem.

Exhibit 3-3 Timeline Demonstration for Compounding Problems

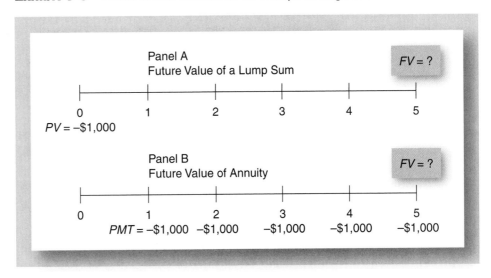

To solve this problem, the present value (*PV*) amount of $1,000 invested at time zero is converted to a future value (*FV*) at the end of five years. The conversion is made by multiplying the *PV* by the future value interest factor (*FVF*) for the specified interest rate and time period. Because the interest rate is 5 percent and the period is five years, the equation for conversion of a present value into a future value is

$$FV = PV \times FVF \text{ (5\%, five years)}$$
$$= \$1,000 \times 1.276282$$
$$= \$1,276.28$$

The *FVF* of 1.276282 is the solution to the future value of a lump sum equation in Exhibit 3-2, at 5 percent for five years. It reveals that a dollar invested today at 5 percent for five years will grow (compound) to $1.276282 at the end of five years (assuming annual compounding). Therefore, $1,000 invested today will grow to $1,276.28 in five years. The calculator keystrokes required to solve this problem are

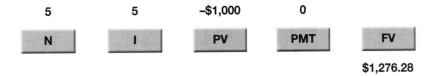

$1,276.28

The $1,000 lump sum investment is entered as a negative number, consistent with it being an outflow (i.e., cash paid) from the perspective of the investor. Solving using a calculator requires the user to enter *N, I, PV,* and *PMT* (the "knowns"); pressing the *FV* key (the "unknown") produces the $1,276.28 solution. If the interest rate is 10 percent, then $1,000 invested today will grow to $1,610.51 in five years. The conversion equation and calculator keystrokes are

$$FV = PV \times FVF \text{ (10\%, five years)}$$
$$= \$1,000 \times 1.610510$$
$$= \$1,610.51$$

5	10	–$1,000	0	
N	I	PV	PMT	FV

$1,610.51

Note that if any four of the five required inputs are known, the fifth can be determined. For example, assume the future value of $1,610.51 is known and that *I*, the annual interest rate, is unknown. Entering $1,610.51 in the *FV* register (along with *N* = 5, *PV* = −$1,000, and *PMT* = 0) and pressing the *I* key will produce the answer of 10 percent.

Concept Check

3.1 You have agreed to purchase a piece of real estate today for $15,000. You expect to hold the property for eight years and then sell it. You expect the property to increase in value 15 percent per year, compounded annually. For how much should you be able to sell the property in eight years?

A Note of Caution. It is important when learning TVM techniques that students be able to match their answers to those provided in the text or in other materials. Therefore, throughout this chapter we will generally provide answers that include both dollars and cents in order to avoid rounding errors that may be confusing. In practice, however, professionals rarely display digits to the right of the decimal. In fact, in many cases industry professionals will round TVM calculations to the nearest one hundred dollar amount or even to the nearest one thousand dollar amount. Why? Because although TVM calculations are mathematically precise, the outcomes are based on a set of assumptions that may not be accurate. Displaying results with digits to the right of the decimal point may convey a sense of accuracy that does not exist is some cases.

The Power of Compounding. To illustrate the power of compounding, we examine more closely the rate of growth in the above $1,000 investment. Exhibit 3-4 shows the amounts to which the lump sum investment will grow if interest is compounded (paid) annually and the investor does not withdraw any of the $1,000 initial investment or any of the interest earnings. With annual compounding, the value of the investment remains unchanged throughout the year. At the end of the year, the accumulated investment value increases by the interest rate associated with the period (10 percent in this case).

If the investor withdraws the investment after one year, the accumulated investment value will be $1,100, which represents the initial $1,000 investment plus $100 of interest income. If the investment is withdrawn after five years, the accumulated investment value will be $1,611, which is equal to the $1,000 investment plus $611 in interest income. By the end of year 30, the value of the investment will have grown to $17,449. Note that the average annual interest earned by the investor increases as the length of time increases. This is because interest is being earned on an increasingly larger investment. Thus, the greater the length of time an investment is allowed to compound, the greater the power of compounding! The growth in the initial $1,000 investment with annual compounding at

Exhibit 3-4 The Power of Compounding

| | $1,000 INVESTMENT AT 10% WITH ANNUAL COMPOUNDING | | |
End of Year	Investment Value	Total Interest Earned	Average Annual Interest Earned
1	$1,100	$100	$100
5	1,611	611	122
10	2,594	1,594	159
20	6,727	5,727	286
30	17,449	16,449	548

Exhibit 3-5 Power of Compounding

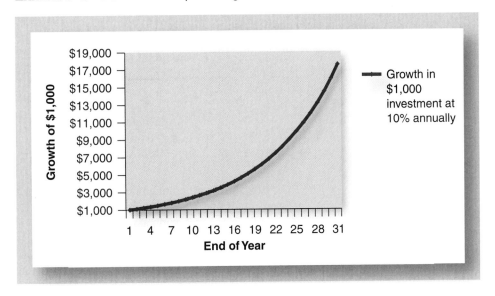

10 percent is displayed graphically in Exhibit 3-5. Note that the line is curved with its slope increasing as the length of the investment holding period increases.

This example assumes annual compounding of interest. However, banks and other borrowers often pay interest more frequently, such as monthly or even daily. Exhibit 3-6 compares accumulated investment values for the $1,000 investment, assuming monthly and daily compounding to accumulated values assuming annual compounding. For a five-year investment, a $1,000 investment will accumulate to $1,645 with monthly compounding compared with $1,611 with annual compounding. With daily compounding of interest, the investment value will grow to $1,649 in five years. Note that the effects of more frequent compounding are more pronounced as the investment time horizon increases. Unless otherwise specified, we will assume that the frequency of compounding equals the frequency with which the payments are made or received. Thus, for example, if cash flows are received annually, we will assume annual compounding.

Concept Check

3.2   Assume $1,000 is invested for 10 years. The annual interest rate is 10 percent, but the interest will be compounded quarterly. What is *N*? What is the periodic (i.e. quarterly) interest rate? What will be the accumulated *FV* in 10 years?

Exhibit 3-6 Accumulated Future Value of an Initial $1,000 Lump Sum Investment at 10% with Varying Compounding Periods

End of Year	Annual Compounding	Monthly Compounding	Daily Compounding
1	$1,100	$1,105	$1,105
5	1,611	1,645	1,649
10	2,594	2,707	2,718
20	6,727	7,328	7,387
30	17,449	19,837	20,077

Future Value of Annuity. Now assume the investor plans to deposit $1,000 at the end of *each* year in a 5 percent annually compounded account and wants to know how much these deposits will be worth at the end of five years. As shown in panel B of Exhibit 3-3, solving this problem involves finding the future value of the annuity. Future value factors for annuities (FVF_A) are used to convert the $1,000 annuity (i.e., cash flows occurring at the end of each period) to future values. The conversion equation and calculator keystrokes are

$$FV_A = \text{Annuity} \times FVF_A \text{ (5 percent, five years)}$$
$$= \$1,000 \times 5.525631$$
$$= \$5,525.63$$

The FVF_A of 5.525631 is the solution to the future value of an annuity equation in Exhibit 3-2 at 5 percent for five years. It reveals that one dollar invested at the end of each year for five years at 5 percent will compound to $5.52563 at the end of five years. Thus, $1,000 invested each year for five years will grow to $5,525.63. The calculator keystrokes required to solve this future value of an annuity problem are

5	5	0	−$1,000	
N	I	PV	PMT	FV

$5,525.63

Future value is again the unknown. Note that when finding the future value of a series of level payments (deposits), the level deposit amount is entered as a negative number in the *PMT* register and the *PV* register contains a zero amount (or is empty). This tells the calculator that the amount will be deposited *every* year for N years. Recall that when finding the future value of a lump sum, the one-time deposit is entered in the *PV* register—the *PMT* register contains a zero or is empty.

Finally, assume the investor is instead considering making monthly deposits of $83.33 ($1,000 ÷ 12) for five years. N in this case is 60 (5 × 12) and I, the monthly interest rate, is equal to 0.41667 percent (5 percent/12). The conversion equation is

$$FV_A = \text{Annuity} \times FVF_A \text{ (5 percent/12, 60 months)}$$
$$= \$83.33 \times 68.006083$$
$$= \$5,666.95$$

The corresponding keystrokes are

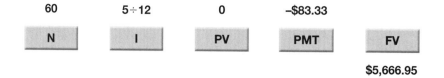

60	5÷12	0	−$83.33	
N	I	PV	PMT	FV

$5,666.95

In this example, the investor will deposit a total of $1,000 per year regardless of whether payments are made monthly or annually. However, if payments of $83.33 are made monthly, the investor will accumulate $5,666.95 at the end of five years compared with $5,525.63 with annual deposits. Why is there a $141.32 difference in future values if total deposits over the five-year period are the same with both strategies? Notice that the initial deposit occurs at the end of month 1 in the monthly compounding scenario whereas it occurs at the end of *year* 1 in the annual case. Thus, the monthly deposits begin to accumulate interest 11 months earlier than the annual case. The message is that one should select the compounding interval that best reflects what is actually occurring.

Concept Check

3.3   You purchase a parcel of land today for $50,000. For how much will you have to sell the property in 15 years to earn a 10 percent annual return on both your initial $50,000 outlay and the expected annual payment of $1,000 for property taxes and insurance? Assume these funds could be invested at comparable risk to earn a 10 percent annual return.

Future Value of an Annuity Due.   What if the investor plans to deposit $1,000 at the *beginning* of each year for five years? These situations are referred to as "future value of an annuity due" problems. Because the initial and subsequent $1,000 annual payments are shifted forward a year, the average amount deposited over the five-year period will be greater; thus, the total amount of interest earned over the five-year period will increase. Financial calculators readily permit the user to specify that cash flows will be invested or received at the beginning of each period ("begin mode") instead of the end ("end mode"). The future value of this annuity due is $5,801.91, or $276.28 greater than the $5,525.63 accumulated value assuming year-end deposits. What is the relationship between the standard future value result and the annuity-due result? Note that the $5,801.91 annuity due solution can be obtained by multiplying the solution to the regular annuity problem by 1 plus the periodic interest rate [i.e., $5,801.91 = $5,525.63 × (1 + 0.05)].

Concept Check

3.4   Assume the owner of a 10-unit apartment building will deposit $2,000 per year, or $200 per unit, in an interest-bearing reserve account. These funds will be used to refurbish the apartments at the end of five years. If the deposits are made at the beginning of each year and will earn 5 percent interest, compounded annually, what will be the accumulated value of the reserve account at the end of five years?

Discounting Operations

The third and fourth basic TVM operations are used to convert future dollar amounts into present values. The concept underlying these operations is extremely important for investment analysis because converting future dollar amounts into present values is the cornerstone of asset valuation.

Present Value of a Lump Sum.   This operation is used to calculate the present value of future lump sum (i.e., one-time) receipts. Consequently, it is useful for discounting future cash flows, positive or negative, back to the present.

Assume the investor has been offered an investment opportunity that is expected to provide a $1,276.28 cash inflow at the end of five years, as shown in panel A of Exhibit 3-7. Assume also that the investor is able to earn 5 percent, compounded annually, on similar investments. More specifically, the 5 percent discount rate can be thought of as an **opportunity cost**—that is, the return the investor is forgoing on an alternative investment of equal risk in order to invest in the current opportunity.

How much can the investor pay today for this $1,276.28 future lump sum receipt and still earn a 5 percent return on the investment? This problem calls for the conversion of an uncertain future lump sum receipt into a present value. The conversion equation is

$$PV = FV \times PVF \text{ (5\%, five years)}$$
$$= \$1,276.28 \times 0.783526$$
$$= \$1,000.00$$

Exhibit 3-7 Timeline Demonstration for Discounting Problems

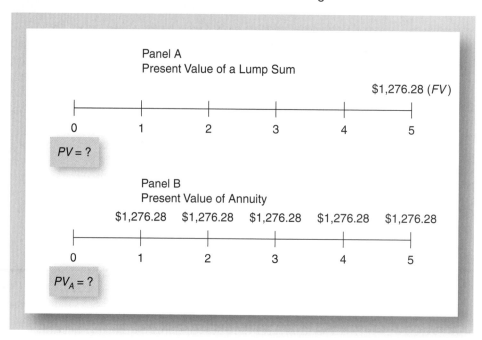

The investor should be willing to pay up to $1,000 today for the right to receive $1,276.28 in five years if he or she can earn a 5 percent annual return on similar investments. The corresponding calculator keystrokes are

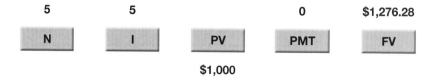

A calculator should produce a result of −$1,000 with these inputs. Present values are shown as negative amounts (if the future value is entered as a positive amount) because calculators require a matching of inflows (+) with outflows (−) to perform TVM calculations.

Another interpretation of this result is that the investor is exactly indifferent between having $1,000 today and having (owning) the right to receive $1,276.28 five years from today. How can this be? Why doesn't the investor prefer the larger amount?

Concept Check

3.5 You are considering the purchase of some raw land. If the property is expected to be worth $50,000 in 15 years, what is the present value of this investment? Assume there will be no intermittent cash inflows or outflows and that the investor expects to earn a 10 percent annual return on such investments.

Present Value as a Point of Indifference. To understand why investors are indifferent between having $1,000 today and having the right to receive $1,276.28 five years from today, recall the future value of a lump sum problem depicted in panel A of Exhibit 3-3. If they invest a lump sum of $1,000 at 5 percent they will accumulate $1,276.28 at the end of five years. Thus, investors can either (1) purchase today, for $1,000, the right to receive $1,276.28 at the end of five years or (2) invest the $1,000 elsewhere at 5 percent. The second option will also yield $1,276.28 in five years; thus, investors have a "take it or leave it" attitude toward the first option because they can replicate the $1,276.28 payoff on their own by simply investing the $1,000 at 5 percent. The present value of the $1,000 is the only value that makes investors indifferent between the two options, assuming a 5 percent required annual rate of return.

What if investors could purchase the right to receive $1,276.28 in five years for $900 today? Would they be happy to undertake this investment? Given that we know they are indifferent to the investment opportunity if the asking price is $1,000, clearly investors would be happy to invest at a price of $900. Why? If investors were to invest the $900 at 5 percent annually, they would accumulate $1,148.65 at the end of five years, which is less than the promised payoff of $1,276.28. Because they cannot replicate the $1,276.28 payoff by investing $900 in an alternative investment, they would be happy to pay $900 today for this investment opportunity. By paying $900 today for an investment worth $1,000 to them, investors' current wealth would increase by $100.

Why would investors not be willing to pay more than $1,000—say, $1,100—for the right to receive $1,276.28 in five years? Because if they were to invest the $1,100 at 5 percent, they would accumulate $1,403.91 by the end of five years. That is, they could do better with an alternative investment. Investors should reject this investment opportunity at any price greater than $1,000 because they could more than replicate the $1,276.28 payoff on their own.

The first discounting operation can be used to find the present value of multiple lump sums. For example, in the above problem, there may have been an additional lump sum of $2,000 at the end of year 7 in addition to the $1,276.28 at the end of year 5. The value of this additional lump sum is $1,421.36 and was found by entering $2,000 as *FV,* 7 as *N,* 5 as the interest rate, and then solving for *PV.* The result of this operation is added to the previous result (i.e., $1,000) to obtain a total value of $2,421.36 for the investment opportunity. Once individual cash flow amounts are "brought back" to time zero, they may be added or subtracted to determine the total present value of the investment package.

Concept Check

3.6   Assume the owner of an apartment complex follows a strict schedule for replacing carpeting. She currently projects she will spend $10,000 at the end of three years and $12,000 at the end of six years to replace the carpeting in all units. What is the total present value of these expected expenditures assuming a 7 percent annual rate of return?

Present Value of Annuity. Now suppose investors are confronted with an opportunity to receive $1,276.28 at the end of *every* year for five years, as shown in Exhibit 3-7, panel B. Investors requiring a 5 percent return need to know the maximum amount to pay for this annuity and still earn their required 5 percent return. Two options are available for converting the annuity to a present value. One is to find the present value of five separate lump sum amounts, one for each year, then sum the results. The less time-consuming option is to calculate the present value of an annuity (PV_A). The conversion equation and calculator keystrokes for this alternative operation are

$$PV_A = Annuity \times PVF_A \,(5\%, 5 \text{ years})$$
$$= \$1,276.28 \times 4.329477$$
$$= \$5,525.62$$

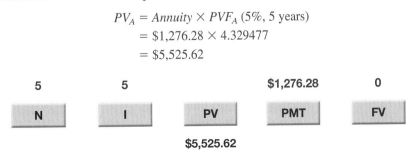

$5,525.62

Note that because the cash flows will be received *every* year over the five-year period, the annuity amount is entered into the *PMT* register. There is no lump sum (*FV*) amount.

What if the payments are to be received at the *beginning* of each year? The present value of this annuity due is $5,801.91 and is calculated by using your calculator's "begin mode" or by multiplying the present value of the regular annuity by an additional year's worth of interest [i.e., $5,801.90 = $5,525.62 × (1 + 0.05)].

Concept Check

3.7   You have just purchased 100 shares of stock in a publicly traded real estate company that invests in apartment complexes throughout the United States. The company is expected to pay quarterly dividends of $1.50 per share. If you expect the stock will be worth $75 per share at the end of the five years, what is the value of the stock to you today if your required rate of return on an annual basis is 14 percent?

A Commercial Property Example. The following example demonstrates that the expected cash flows from direct investments in commercial properties typically come from two sources:

1. Rental operations
2. Eventual sale of the property

Both cash flow components must generally be considered when estimating value.

Consider a small warehouse building that is leased to a high-quality tenant on a long-term basis. The property is expected to produce $10,000 in income from rental operations each year for five years. The expected sale of the property at the end of the fifth year will generate an additional (lump sum) net cash flow of $100,000. Assume the investor requires a 10 percent annual return on investments of similar risk. The equation to convert these uncertain future cash flows into a present value is

$$PV = \text{Annuity} \times PVF_A \,(10\%, 5 \text{ years}) + FV \times PVF \,(10\%, 5 \text{ years})$$
$$= (\$10,000 \times 3.790787) + (\$100,000 \times 0.620921)$$
$$= \$37,908 + \$62,092$$
$$= \$100,000$$

The first term on the right-hand side of the conversion equation represents the valuation of the annual rental income (i.e., the annuity), while the second term represents the valuation of the future lump sum sale proceeds. The total present value of the cash flow components can also be determined with the following keystrokes:

Note that the $10,000 annual annuity is entered into the *PMT* register and the lump sum sale proceeds are entered in the *FV* register. Also note that 62 percent of the total $100,000 present value is contributed by the expected cash flow from the sale of the property in five years. With longer expected holding periods this percentage generally decreases. However, future sale proceeds are an extremely important determinant of current property values.

3.8 What is the maximum price you should pay today for the right to receive $10,000 per year for 20 years from a piece of rental real estate if the series of rental payments is discounted at a 10 percent annual rate? Assume the property will be worth $50,000 at the end of the 20-year period.

Uneven Cash Flows. Typically, the annual (periodic) cash flows from owning and operating commercial real estate assets are not expected to be constant over time. Consider the following investment opportunity in a small apartment building named Lee Vista. The total net cash flow from owning and operating Lee Vista is estimated to be $48,000 in year 1, growing to $54,025 in year 5. The estimated selling price in year 5 is $560,000. These uncertain future cash flows must be converted into a lump sum present value. One approach to solving this problem is to find the present value of the separate annual cash flow amounts, then sum the results. This approach is depicted in Exhibit 3-8. The total present value of the potential investment is $464,480 assuming a 14 percent expected investment yield. The calculator keystrokes that would be used to solve for the present value of the cash flow in, say, year 3, which equals $34,372, are

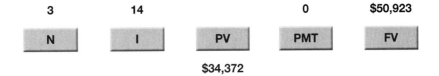

$34,372

An alternative, and usually preferred, approach to solving present value problems when the periodic future cash flows are uneven is to use the cash flow ("CF_j") key available on most financial calculators. In this example, 0 would be entered as CF_0, 48,000 would be entered as CF_1, 49,440 as CF_2, 50,923 as CF_3, 52,451 as CF_4, and 614,025 as CF_5. The investor would then solve for present value by pressing the appropriate key (which, for example, is the shift "NPV" key on the Hewlett Packard 10B). The calculations that appear in Exhibit 3-8 can also be performed with Microsoft's EXCEL, as is demonstrated in the Appendix.

Two final points concerning discounting should be stressed. First, the present value of future cash flows is inversely related to the level of the interest rate used for discounting. This concept is reinforced by calculations displayed in Exhibit 3-9, which show the present values of a lump sum receipt of $1,000 for periods that extend from 1 to 20 years and for two interest rates, 5 percent and 10 percent. When the interest rate is 5 percent, the present value of the right to receive $1,000 in five years is $784. However, if the interest rate

Exhibit 3-8 Present Value of Series of Uneven Cash Flows: Lee Vista Apartments

Year	Annual CF	CF From Sale	Total CF	PVF @ 14%	Present Value
1	$48,000		$ 48,000	0.877193	$ 42,105
2	49,440		49,440	0.769468	38,042
3	50,923		50,923	0.674972	34,372
4	52,451		52,451	0.592080	31,055
5	54,025	$560,000	614,025	0.519369	318,905
Total present value =					$464,480

Exhibit 3-9 PV of $1,000 Lump Sum Payment

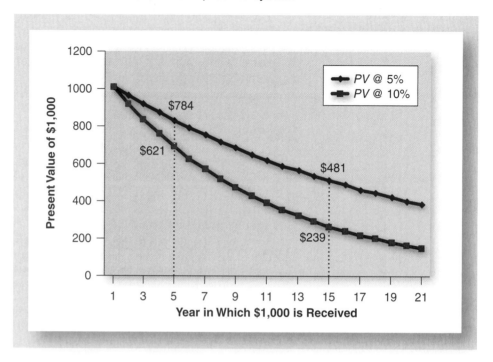

rises to 10 percent, this present value declines to $621, a reduction of $163. This relation between interest rates and present value actually makes a lot of sense. If an investment is expected to produce a fixed set of cash flows, the only way that expected returns can change is if the market price (present value) changes. For example, if higher returns are required, perhaps because of an increase in perceived risk, market values will decline. This inverse relation between interest rates and present values explains, for example, why mortgage amounts move inversely to changes in market interest rates. That is, the higher the interest rate, the smaller the mortgage the borrower can obtain, given the same monthly payments. Conversely, with lower interest rates, borrowers can obtain larger mortgage loans with the same monthly payments.

A second important concept is also revealed by examination of Exhibit 3-9. The present value of long-term cash flows is more sensitive to changes in discount rates than securities with shorter-term cash flows. Recall that the present value of $1,000 to be received in five years is $163 lower when an interest rate of 10 percent is used instead of 5 percent. Now consider the present values for $1,000 to be received in 15 years. When the interest rate is 5 percent, the present value equals $481, but if the interest rate increases to 10 percent, the present value falls to $239, a $242 decline (versus a $163 decline in year 5). The conclusion, of course, is that the present value of long-term cash flows is more sensitive to interest rate changes than shorter-term cash flows.

Yields and Internal Rates of Return

To this point we have explored (1) how to determine future values when the amounts to be invested are known (i.e., compounding) and (2) how to determine present values when the future values are known or assumed (i.e., discounting). These TVM concepts can be used to determine rates of return on real estate investments—an extremely important extension.

Consider the future value of a lump sum problem examined earlier in which we determined that if $1,000 is invested today for five years in an account that pays 5 percent interest, compounded annually, the balance of the account at the end of five years will be

$1,276.28. Hence, making this investment is equivalent to earning a rate of return of 5 percent. This rate of return is usually referred to as the **investment yield** or the **internal rate of return** *(IRR).*

Recall also the present value of an annuity problem in which investors were presented with an opportunity to receive $1,276.28 at the end of every year for five years. If investors believe they should earn a 5 percent return on such investments, the present value of the future cash flows is $5,525.62. What yield or *IRR* will investors earn if they purchase this investment opportunity for $5,525.62? It should be clear that investors will earn a 5 percent internal rate of return on their $5,525.61 investment. The calculator keystrokes are

5.00%

Because the periodic cash flows from owning and renting real estate assets are generally not expected to be constant over time, the above calculator solution procedure will not work. Instead, investors must use a spreadsheet program or use the cash flow ("CF$_j$") key on their financial calculators. For example, assume the Lee Vista investment opportunity depicted in Exhibit 3-8 is purchased by the investor for $464,480. This now becomes a problem in which the immediate cost is known, but the future cash flows are uncertain. Given the expected annual cash flows, what is the internal rate of return on this investment? To solve this problem $-464,480$ would be entered as CF_0, 48,000 would be entered as CF_1, 49,440 as CF_2, 50,923 as CF_3, 52,451 as CF_4, and 614,025 as CF_5. The investor would then solve for the *IRR* by pushing the appropriate key (which is the "shift IRR/YR" key on a Hewlett Packard 10B). This would return a solution of 14 percent.

The internal rate of return is an indispensable tool widely used in real estate investment and finance. It captures the return on an investment, expressed as a compound rate of interest, over the entire investment holding period. The calculated (or "going-in") *IRR* can be compared to the investor's required *IRR* on similar projects of equivalent risk. If the going-in *IRR* exceeds the investor's required rate of return, the investment should be undertaken.

If the going-in *IRR* is less than the investor's required rate of return, the investment should be forgone and another opportunity pursued.[1]

A Final Note on Terminology. Throughout the book we will use the terms *investment yield* and *internal rate of return* interchangeably. If the calculation is based on expected cash flows, we will use the terms *expected investment yield* or *going-in IRR* to differentiate the results from historical (i.e. realized) yields and *IRR*s. In the real estate appraisal business, the *IRR* is often referred to as the "total yield." This convention reflects the fact that income-producing properties generally provide a "current yield" in the form of current income relative to the required investment and an "appreciation yield" that results from appreciation in the market value of the asset. By referring to the return as a total yield, the investor is making it clear that the measured return includes both the current income and appreciation components.

Concept Check

3.9   Assume a $400,000 investment in a small shopping center is expected to produce the following annual cash flows over a five-year holding period: CF_1, 37,000; CF_2, 38,100; CF_3, 39,253; CF_4, 40,431; and CF_5, 504,000. What is the going-in *IRR* on this investment?

Determining Required Returns

It is clear from the TVM problems above that the present value of an investment opportunity is a function of:

1. The magnitude of the expected future cash flows.
2. The timing of the expected future cash flows.
3. The interest (discount) rate used to convert the expected future cash flows into present value.

To complete our discussion of TVM calculations, we need to give some more attention to the interest rate used to convert uncertain future cash flows into a present value. Fundamentally, the discount rate can be thought of as the investor's required internal rate of return (*IRR*).

Consider again the expected cash flows from investing in the Lee Vista apartment complex displayed in Exhibit 3-8. When discounted at 14 percent, these uncertain cash flows have a total present value of $464,480. However, when discounted at 12 percent the value increases to $500,264, which is a 7.7 percent increase. If the required *IRR* is 10 percent, present value increases 16.2 percent to $539,841. When discounted at 16 percent and 18 percent, respectively, the present value falls 7.0 percent and 13.3 percent, respectively, relative to the use of 14 percent as the required yield. Clearly, even small changes in the assumed rate of discount can significantly affect the estimated value of the risky future cash flows and, therefore, the ultimate decision.

So, from where do required *IRR*s/yields come? A good place to begin is to recall that the discount rate is meant to reflect the investor's opportunity cost of investing in the subject investment. That is, the appropriate discount rate is the yield the investor could typically earn on other investments of *similar risk*. As "other investments" are traded in the capital market (see Exhibit 1–6), it should be clear that discount rates come from the capital market where investors buy and sell real estate, stocks, bonds, and other assets.

---

1. The IRR has some inherent assumptions that make its use as an investment criterion problematic in some situations. These issues are discussed in Chapter 16.

Exhibit 3-10   The Effect of Discount Rates on Present Values

Y	Annual CF	CF From	Total CF	PVF @ 10%	PVF @ 12%	PVF @ 14%	PVF @ 16%	PVF @ 18%
1	$48,000		$ 48,000	$ 43,636	$ 42,857	$ 42,105	$ 41,379	$ 40,678
2	49,440		49,440	40,860	39,413	38,042	36,742	35,507
3	50,923		50,923	38,259	36,246	34,372	32,624	30,993
4	52,451		52,451	35,825	33,334	31,055	28,968	27,054
5	54,025	$560,000	614,025	381,261	348,414	318,905	292,345	269,396
Total present value =				$539,841	$500,264	$464,480	$432,059	$402,628
% change in PV from 14%				16.2%	7.7%		−7.0%	−13.3%

But how, exactly, do investors determine the specific discount rate to use in a TVM calculation? To address this question consider the following representation of an investor's required yield:

$$E(R_j) = R_f + RP_j$$

where

$E(R_j)$ is the expected or required *IRR* on the jth investment
R_f is the current yield available on a risk-free Treasury security of comparable maturity
RP_j is the required risk premium

As an example, assume potential investors in downtown Chicago office buildings are currently requiring an 11 percent going-in *IRR* on their expected 10-year investments. Also assume that U.S. Treasury bonds with remaining maturities of 10 years are currently priced to yield a 5 percent *IRR* to investors. The 11 percent expected yield is therefore composed of a 5 percent compensation for time, as measured by the 5 percent risk-free rate, and a 6 percent risk premium. Recall that risk is the possibility that actual returns will vary from what was expected at acquisition. Thus, the 6 percent risk premium reflects the extent to which Chicago investors believe actual returns are likely to vary from expectations.

Investors struggling to determine their required investment yields on a potential investment frequently find themselves asking the following question: "What rate of return are other investors requiring on similar investments?" Although attitudes toward risk—and therefore required risk premiums—vary across investors, the ability to abstract this information from other investors is very useful in determining the investor's required risk premium and *IRR*.

The Real Estate Research Corporation (RERC) regularly surveys the before-tax real estate return expectations of a representative sample of pension funds and life insurance company investors. Published quarterly in the *Real Estate Report,* this survey provides insights into the required returns and risk adjustments used by institutional investors when making real estate acquisitions. As such, this and other similar surveys (formal and informal) provide valuable information to individual investors.

Portions of tables from various issues of the *Real Estate Report* are reproduced in Exhibit 3-11. The mean required yield for first quarter 2003 investments in all property types was 11.2 percent. The spread over 10-year U.S. Treasury securities was 7.3 percentage points, or 730 basis points (one basis point equals 0.01 percent). Note that although the required real estate return in the first quarter of 2003 is the lowest in 10 years, required real estate *IRR*s have varied little. However, yields on 10-year Treasury securities have displayed substantially more volatility. As a result, spreads over Treasuries have varied from 4.5 percentage points in 1995 to a high of 7.3 percentage points in the first quarter of 2003.

Exhibit 3-11 Required Returns on Investment-Grade Properties vs. Comparable Treasury Securities, 1993–2003

	1Q93	1Q95	1Q97	1Q99	1Q01	1Q02	1Q03
Required real estate return	12.2%	11.6%	11.5%	11.4%	11.5%	11.8%	11.2%
Return on 10-year Treasuries	6.0	7.1	6.6	5.0	5.1	5.0	3.9
Spread over Treasuries	6.2	4.5	4.9	6.4	6.4	6.8	7.3

Source: Various issues of the *Real Estate Report* Real Estate Research Corporation, Chicago.

Although useful in helping investors quantify required risk premiums and returns, it is important to understand that the required yields reported by RERC represent broad averages across many properties and local markets. Thus, they should not be directly applied to specific properties without adjustments for the physical characteristics of the subject property and the specific market in which the subject property is located.

It is also important to emphasize that the going-in *IRR*s reported by RERC are for existing properties that are large (values in excess of $10 million), relatively new, located in a major metropolitan areas, and fully leased. Such properties, often referred to as **investment-grade properties,** are the lowest risk real estate investments available. Yet as can be seen in Exhibit 3-11, investment grade assets still require substantial risk premiums relative to risk-free Treasury securities. Generally, properties that are less than investment grade are even more risky because of their smaller size, advanced age, location in a small or transient market, lack of tenants or even improvements, or some combination of these and other shortcomings.

If the 7.3 percent average risk premium for investment grade properties reported by RERC in 2003 represents the minimum risk premium required on commercial real estate assets, what are typical risk premiums for noninvestment-grade properties? At the high end of the real estate risk spectrum are investments in raw (i.e., undeveloped) land. To induce individuals to forgo less risky projects and to invest in raw land, property markets must generally provide such investors with going-in *IRR*s in excess of 30 percent. Thus, real estate discount rates range from 10 to 11 percent to rates in excess of 30 percent. In the end, the specification of the required *IRR* is a subjective process that relies heavily on the experience and expertise of the investor.[2]

Comparing Investment Values to Acquistion Costs

We have emphasized in both Chapter 2 and the current chapter that real estate decision making fundamentally involves comparing the costs of various decisions, including the decision to purchase a property, to the benefits that the decision would produce. In the present chapter, we show that benefits (cash flows) to be received in the future must be discounted (converted) into present values in order to make rational, wealth-enhancing, decisions. These conversions of future cash flows into present values are simply direct applications of time-value-of-money concepts.

Take the case of a real estate investor who wants to purchase a small apartment building to add to her portfolio at year-end 2004. Numerous potential investments have been

---

2. The subjectivity of the discount rate specification is perceived by some to be a weakness of real estate TVM valuation techniques. At a minimum, it has frequently left investors asking whether more objective quantitative models for specifying the discount rate are available. Formal asset pricing models, developed initially for the valuation of stocks, are able to quantify required risk premiums in an objective fashion. Unfortunately, as is discussed in Chapter 23, these techniques are difficult, if not impossible, to apply to the valuation of individual real estate properties.

Exhibit 3-12 Cash Flows from Two Alternative Apartment Investment Opportunities

	Lee Vista		Colony Park	
Year-End	Estimated Cash Flows from Operations	Estimated Sale Proceeds	Estimated Cash Flows from Operations	Estimated Sale Proceeds
2005	$48,000		$56,000	
2006	49,440		57,400	
2007	50,923		58,835	
2008	52,451		60,306	
2009	54,025	$560,000	61,814	$597,000

Exhibit 3-13 Present Value Calculations for Alternative Apartment Investment Opportunities

		Lee Vista		Colony Park	
Year	PVF @ 14%	Total Cash Flows	Present Value	Total Cash Flows	Present Value
2005	0.877193	$ 48,000	$ 48,105	$ 56,000	$ 49,123
2006	0.769468	49,440	38,042	57,400	44,167
2007	0.674972	50,923	34,372	58,835	39,712
2008	0.592080	52,451	31,055	60,306	35,706
2009	0.519369	614,025	318,905	658,814	342,167
Total present value =			$464,480		$510,875

screened and two properties have been identified as potentially worthy of acquisition: The first is Lee Vista, the apartment complex discussed earlier in the chapter. The second investment opportunity is Colony Park Apartments. The investor estimates the expected cash flows from annual operations for each property during the next five years. She also estimates the net proceeds from the sale of each complex at the end of the fifth year (2009). Exhibit 3-12 displays these cash flow estimates.[3]

To find the present value of both properties, the projected cash flows from operations and the sale proceeds must be converted into present value. The investor estimates that her required *IRR* on investments of this type is 14 percent. The annual present value conversions are found in Exhibit 3-13. The present value of the Lee Vista investment opportunity is $464,480, while the present value of the Colony Park alternative is $510,875. Given its *PV* of $510,875, Colony Park may appear to be a superior investment because of its higher present value. However, one important consideration has been omitted—the asking price of each property.

The **net present value** (*NPV*) of an investment alternative is defined as the difference between the present value of the cash inflows (PV_{in}) and the present value of the cash outflows (PV_{out}). In symbols,

$$NPV = PV_{in} - PV_{out}$$

---

3. Analyses of this kind most frequently use a 10-year time horizon; a 5-year period is used here for simplicity.

If, for example, the year-end 2004 acquisition prices are $425,000 for Lee Vista and $540,000 for Colony Park, the *NPVs* of the two opportunities are:

$$NPV \text{ (Lee Vista)} \quad = \$464,480 - \$425,000 = \$39,480$$
$$NPV \text{ (Colony Park)} = \$510,875 - \$540,000 = -\$29,125$$

The *NPV* simply compares the costs (PV_{out}) with the benefits (PV_{in}) of investment opportunities. This measure is interpreted using the following very simple, but very important, decision rule: If the *NPV* is greater than zero, the property should be purchased, assuming the investor has adequate resources, because it increases the investor's wealth. If the calculated *NPV* is negative, the investment should be rejected. If the *NPV* equals zero, the investor is indifferent. A negative *NPV* means the investor expects to earn a return less than her required investment yield for such an investment.

Concept Check

3.10   Does a zero *NPV* imply that the investor's expected yield/*IRR* is equal to zero?

Now that the asking price has been incorporated into the analysis, a different picture emerges concerning the investor's two apartment property alternatives. Although the Colony Park cash flows from annual operations and from the sale of the property have a higher present value, the cost of the property is sufficiently high to make the *NPV* negative. Lee Vista is the only acceptable property because of its positive *NPV*. The going-in *IRRs* for Lee Vista and Colony Park are 16.5 percent and 12.5 percent, respectively. Given a required yield of 14 percent, Lee Vista would be accepted, while Colony Park would be rejected. Note also that use of *IRR* as the decision-making criterion produces the same accept/reject signals as *NPV*.

Summary

Commercial real estate developers, investors, appraisers, and managers are continually making decisions about committing funds to real estate. These decisions typically involve significant costs now in exchange for uncertain future benefits. The costs and benefits frequently, although not always, assume the form of cash flows (i.e., money) to the investor/owner. The primary purpose of this chapter is to examine how the timing and riskiness of cash inflows and outflows affect the value of real estate assets and, thus, the decision-making process.

There are four fundamental time-value-of-money (TVM) calculations: (1) finding the future value of a lump sum investment, (2) finding the future value of a series of level payments, (3) finding the present value of a future lump sum payment, and (4) finding the present value of a series of level payments. This chapter introduces these basic TVM calculations and demonstrates how they are solved using handheld calculators (spreadsheet solutions using EXCEL are demonstrated in an Appendix).

TVM concepts are the cornerstone of real estate valuation techniques. The prices at which real estate assets and other securities trade are based on the discounted present value of each asset's future cash flows. This does not mean that all market participants make explicit present value calculations before they buy or sell an asset. Indeed, many investors have no knowledge of TVM. But many investors, traders, and portfolio managers do have a good understanding of TVM and base their real estate decisions (e.g., buy, sell, renovate) on a comparison of the costs and the present value of the asset's expected future cash flows when discounted at the appropriate (equivalent risk) opportunity cost.

Solving TVM problems can involve a significant amount of "number crunching." Although these quantitative valuation tools are of fundamental importance, decisions makers should not put total reliance on the quantitative information—the "numbers"—provided by TVM calculations. As discussed in Chapter 2, many real estate decisions involve costs and benefits that are difficult, if not impossible, to quantify in terms of monetary cash flows. In such situations, the owner (or potential owner) must collect and rely upon, in whole or in part, qualitative information. This qualitative information, in the form of appraiser, lender, and investor interpretations and judgments, plays a significant role in real estate decision making. Therefore, quantitative information used in value estimation should be viewed in many situations as merely one important input into the real estate decision-making process. Judgment and interpretations also are important inputs.

Key Terms

Compounding 43
Discounting 41
Future value 43
Internal rate of return 55
Investment grade properties 58

Investment yield 55
Lump sum 43
Net present value 59
Opportunity cost 49
Ordinary annuity 43

Present value 43
Risk 41
Time value of money 41

Test Problems

Answer the following multiple choice questions:

1. How much will a $50 deposit made today be worth in 20 years if interest is compounded annually at a rate of 10 percent?
   a. $150.00   d. $336.38
   b. $286.37   e. $2,863.75
   c. $309.59

2. How much would you pay for the right to receive $80 at the end of 10 years if you can earn 15 percent interest?
   a. $19.15   d. $38.82
   b. $19.77   e. $70.65
   c. $38.48

3. How much would you pay to receive $50 in one year and $60 in the second year if you can earn 15 percent interest?
   a. $88.85   d. $107.91
   b. $89.41   e. $110.00
   c. $98.43

4. What amount invested at the end of each year at 10 percent annually will grow to $10,000 at the end of five years?
   a. $1,489.07   d. $1,809.75
   b. $1,637.97   e. $2,000.00
   c. $1,723.57

5. How much would you pay for the right to receive nothing a year for the next 10 years and $300 a year for the following 10 years if you can earn 15 percent interest?
   a. $372.17   d. $600.88
   b. $427.99   e. $1,505.63
   c. $546.25

6. What is the present value of $500 received at the end of each of the next three years and $1,000 received at the end of the fourth year, assuming a required rate of return of 15 percent?
   a. $900.51   d. $1,784.36
   b. $1,035.59   e. $2,049.06
   c. $1,713.37

7. If a landowner purchased a vacant lot six years ago for $25,000, assuming no income or holding costs during the interim period, what price would the landowner need to receive today to yield a 10 percent annual return?
   a. $40,262.75   c. $44,289.03
   b. $41,132.72   d. $64,843.563

8. What is the present value of the following series of cash flows discounted at 12 percent: $40,000 now; $50,000 at the end of the first year; $0 at the end of the second year; $60,000 at the end of the third year; and $70,000 at the end of the fourth year?
   a. $165,857   c. $168,555
   b. $167,534   d. $171,836

9. Assume a property is priced at $5,000 and has the following income stream:

Year	Cash Flow
1	$ 1,000
2	−2,000
3	3,000
4	3,000

Would an investor with a required rate of return of 15 percent be wise to invest at the current price?
   a. No, because the project has a net present value of −$1,139.15.
   b. No, because the project has a net present value of −$1,954.91.
   c. Yes, because the project has a net present value of $1,069.66.
   d. Yes, because the project has a net present value of $1,954.91.
   e. An investor would be indifferent between purchasing and not purchasing the above property at the stated price.

www.mhhe.com/lingarcher1e

Study Questions

1. Dr. Bob Jackson owns a parcel of land that a local farmer has offered to rent for the next 10 years. The farmer has offered to pay $20,000 today or an annuity of $3,200 at the end of each of the next 10 years. Which payment method should Dr. Jackson accept if his required rate of return is 10 percent?

2. You are able to buy an investment for $1,000 that gives you the right to receive $438 in each of the next three years. What is the internal rate of return on this investment?

3. Calculate the present value of the income stream given below assuming discount rates of 8 percent and 20 percent.

Year	Income
1	$3,000
2	4,000
3	6,000
4	1,000

4. Calculate the IRR and the *NPV* for the following investment opportunities. Assume a 16 percent discount rate for the NPV calculations.

	Project 1		Project 2
Year	Cash Flow	Year	Cash Flow
0	−$10,000	0	−$10,000
1	1,000	1	1,000
2	2,000	2	12,000
3	12,000	3	1,800

5. How much would you pay for an investment that provides $1,000 at the end of the first year if your required rate of return is 10 percent? Now compute how much you would pay at 8 percent and 12 percent rates of return.

6. Your grandmother gives you $10,000 to be invested in one of three opportunities: real estate, bonds, or zero coupon bonds. If you invest the entire $10,000 in one of these opportunities with the cash flows shown below, which investment offers the highest NPV? Assume an 11 percent discount rate is appropriate for all three investments.

Investment	Year 1	Year 2	Year 3	Year 4	Year 5
Real estate	$1,300	$1,300	$1,300	$1,300	$ 9,000
Bond	1,000	1,000	1,000	1,000	11,000
Zero coupon	0	0	0	0	18,000

7. If you purchase a parcel of land today for $25,000, and you expect it to appreciate 10 percent per year in value, how much will your land be worth 10 years from now?

8. If you deposit $1 at the end of each of the next 10 years and these deposits earn interest at 10 percent, what will the series of deposits be worth at the end of the 10th year.

9. If you deposit $50 per month in a savings and loan association at 10 percent interest, how much will you have in your account at the end of the 12th year?

10. If your parents purchased an endowment policy of $10,000 for you and the policy will mature in 12 years, how much is it worth today, discounted at 15 percent?

11. A family trust will convey property to you in 15 years. If the property is expected to be worth $50,000 when you receive it, what is the present value of your interest, discounted at 10 percent?

12. You want to buy a house for which the owner is asking $625,000. The only problem is that the house is leased to someone else with five years remaining on the lease. However, you like the house and believe it will be a good investment. How much should you pay for the house today if you could strike a bargain with the owner under which she would continue receiving all rental payments until the end of the leasehold, at which time you would obtain title and possession of the property? You believe the property will be worth the same in five years as it is worth today and that this future value should be discounted at a 10 percent annual rate.

13. If someone pays you $1 a year for 20 years, what is the value of the series of future payments discounted at 10 percent annually?

14. You are at retirement age and one of your benefit options is to accept an annual annuity of $7,500 for 15 years. What lump sum settlement, if paid today, would have the same present value as the $7,500 annual annuity? Assume a 10 percent discount rate.

15. What *monthly* deposit is required to accumulate $10,000 in eight years if the deposits are compounded at an annual rate of 8 percent?

16. You are thinking about purchasing some vacant land. You expect to be able to sell the land 10 years from now for $500,000. What is the most you can pay for the land today if your required rate of return is 15 percent? What is the expected (annualized) return on this investment over the 10-year holding period if you purchase the land for $170,000?

17. You are considering the purchase of a small income-producing property for $150,000 that is expected to produce the following net cash flows.

End of Year	Cash Flow
1	$50,000
2	50,000
3	50,000
4	50,000

Assume your required internal rate of return on similar investments is 11 percent. What is the net present value of this investment opportunity? What is the going-in internal rate of return on this investment?

Explore The Web

Real Estate Research Corporation (RERC) was one of the first and continues to be one of the most recognized commercial real estate research, valuation, and consulting firms in the nation. For the last 70 years RERC's real estate research, publications, market studies, property valuations, investment criteria, and trends analysis have been widely used by real estate practitioners. Published quarterly, RERC's *Real Estate Report* is a rich source of information on the expectations of institutional investors, including their required internal rates of return on investments in various property types and metropolitan areas. Go to RERC's home page (www.rerc.com). Follow the research link to the RERC Data Center and view the products offered by RERC. Then find a *sample* of one of the standard reports (full access requires a membership fee) for a metropolitan area. What is contained in this standard metro report? What are the required *IRR*s (referred to by RERC as before-tax yields) for the various property types?

Solutions To Concept Checks

1. $45,885.34
2. $N = 40$ (4×10), $I = 2.5\%$ ($10\% \div 4$), the accumulated *FV* in 10 years is $2,685.06
3. $240,634.89
4. $11,603.83
5. $N = 15$, $I = 10$, $FV = 50,000$; $PV = $11,969.60
6. *PV* of $10,000 expenditure is $8,162.98. *PV* of $12,000 expenditure is $7,999.10. Total present value is $16,159.09.
7. $N = 20$, $I = 3.5\%$ ($14\% \div 4$), $PMT = 1.5$, $FV = 75$; $PV = $59.01 per share
8. $N = 20$, $I = 10$, $PMT = 10,000$, $FV = 50,000$; $PV = $92,567.82.
9. Going-in *IRR* is 12.20%.
10. A zero *NPV* does not mean the investor's yield/*IRR* is zero. What it does mean is that the expected yield/*IRR* is equal to the investor's required yield/*IRR*.

Additional Readings

Coleman, D. S.; L. L. Coleman; L. L. Crawford; and G. Gaines. *Real Estate Math: Explanations, Problems, Solutions.* 5th ed. Chicago: Real Estate Education Company, 1997.

Fernandez, R.; G. V. Karels; and A. J. Prakash. *Financial, Commercial, and Mortgage Mathematics and Their Applications.* Westport, CT: Greenwood Publishing Group, 1987.

Tamper, R., and W. L. Ventola. *Mastering Real Estate Mathematics.* 7th ed. Chicago: Dearborn Publishing, 2002.

Appendix   Solving Time-Value-of-Money Problems Using EXCEL

Solving time-value-of-money (TVM) problems can be accomplished quickly and accurately with the aid of computer spreadsheet packages such as EXCEL. The following EXCEL-based examples are designed to guide you through the process of solving the four basic time-value functions introduced in this chapter.

The Basic Layout

After opening EXCEL, you should see a grid of cells with each column labeled alphabetically and each row labeled numerically. A cell is identified as the intersection of a column and a row, such as B4.

www.mhhe.com/lingarcher1e

	A	B	C
1			
2			
3			
4			
5			
6			

Above this grid is a series of pull-down menus, which can be activated by clicking on the desired menu title (FILE, EDIT, VIEW, INSERT, FORMAT, TOOLS, DATA, WINDOW, or HELP), and a set of toolbars containing pictorial shortcut keys known as icons. These icons are designed to simplify the processing and formatting of information contained within your spreadsheet. Throughout the following examples, we will provide instructions using both the pull-down menus and shortcut icons.

Getting Started

Recall from the chapter that each TVM operation employs the same five pieces of information: number of periods (N), periodic interest rate (I), present value (PV), periodic payment (PMT), and future value (FV). Given any four of these inputs, you should be able to solve for the fifth, unknown, quantity. Because all time-value operations incorporate this same set of information, one easy way to solve many problems quickly is to develop a spreadsheet template that incorporates this information. Enter each of the five input labels in column A as shown.

	A	B	C
1	Number of periods (N) =		
2	Periodic rate (I) =		
3	Periodic value (PV) =		
4	Periodic payment (PMT) =		
5	Future value		
6			

Values for each of these components then may be entered in column B and referenced in formulas to solve for the unknown factor. The primary advantage of using this method is the ability to alter one or more of the inputs and let the computer automatically recalculate the new solution. This spreadsheet template now can be used to solve four problems that were previously solved in the chapter using a calculator.

Future Value of a Lump Sum

Suppose an investor deposits $1,000 today in an interest-bearing account at a local bank. The account pays 5 percent compounded annually, and the investor expects to withdraw the principal plus compound interest at the end of five years. How much will the investor accumulate by the end of the fifth year?

To solve the problem, the present value (*PV*) amount of $1,000 must be converted to a future value (*FV*) occurring at the end of five years. To do this, enter the given information into the input section of your time-value template as shown.

	A	B	C
1	Number of periods (*N*) =	5	
2	Periodic rate (*I*) =	5%	
3	Present value (*PV*) =	−1,000	
4	Periodic payment (*PMT*) =	0	
5	Future value		
6			
7	Future value =	1,276.28	

The future value answer is $1,276.28. This cell is shaded to indicate that it is a solution rather than an input assumption. To replicate this answer, first move the cursor to cell B7. This is the cell where the answer is to be displayed. To calculate the future value, activate the INSERT pull-down menu and select the Function option. Alternatively, clicking the function wizard icon $\boxed{\text{fx}}$ produces the same result. A menu of available options should now appear, and you should select the financial function category and the *FV* (future value) function name. Click the "Next>" button to continue. A window should appear guiding you through the calculation. Specifically, for this example, at the *rate* prompt enter B2 specifying the cell containing the requested information. Similarly, at the *nper* prompt enter B1, at the *pmt* prompt enter B4, and at the *pv* prompt enter B3. The *type* prompt allows you to specify when the cash flows occur: 1 indicates that they occur at the beginning of each period, while 0 signifies that they occur at the end of each period. For this example, enter 0. Click on the "Finish" button to close the function wizard. The future value of $1,276.28 should now be displayed in cell B7.

Future Value of a Series of Level Payments

Now assume the investor plans to deposit $1,000 at the end of each year in a 5 percent, annually compounded account and wants to know how much these deposits will be worth at the end of five years.

To solve the problem, the future value (*FV*) of the annual annuity payment must be calculated. To do this, first clear all information from your spreadsheet template except the input section labels. Then, enter the new assumption information into the input section of your time value template as shown.

	A	B	C
1	Number of periods (*N*) =	5	
2	Periodic rate (*I*) =	5%	
3	Present value (*PV*) =	0	
4	Periodic payment (*PMT*) =	−1,000	
5	Future value		
6			
7	Future value of annuity =	5,525.63	

The future value of the annuity solution in cell B7 is $5,525.63 and is calculated as follows. First, move the cursor to cell B7 where your new answer is to be displayed. To calculate the future value, activate the INSERT pull-down menu and select the Function option (or activate the function wizard icon). You should once again select the financial function category, the *FV* (future value) function name, and click the "Next>" button to continue. As before, a window should appear guiding you through the calculation. For this example, enter B2 at the *rate* prompt, B1 at the *nper* prompt, B4 at the *pmt* prompt, B3 at the *pv* prompt, and 0 at the *type* prompt. Click on the "Finish" button to close the function wizard. The future value of $5,525.63 should now be displayed in cell B7.

Present Value of a Lump Sum

Assume an investor has been offered an investment opportunity that will provide a $1,276.28 payment at the end of five years. If the investor is able to earn 5 percent on other investments (i.e., 5 percent is the required rate of return on investments of this type), how much can he or she pay today for this $1,276.28 future lump sum receipt and still earn 5 percent?

This problem calls for the conversion of a future amount to a present value. Once again, clear your spreadsheet of all information except the input section labels and enter the new information provided as shown.

	A	B	C
1	Number of periods (*N*) =	5	
2	Periodic rate (*I*) =	5%	
3	Present value (*PV*) =		
4	Periodic payment (*PMT*) =	0	
5	Future value (*FV*) =	1,276.28	
6			
7	Present value =	−1,000	

The present value of the future $1,276.28 lump sum cash flow is $1,000. To produce this solution, move the cursor to cell B7. Activate the function wizard, select the financial function category, and choose the *PV* (present value) function name. Click on "Next>" to continue. At the *rate* prompt enter B2, at the *nper* prompt enter B1, at the *pmt* prompt enter B4, at the *fv* prompt enter B5, and at the *type* prompt enter 0. Click on the "Finish" button to close the function wizard. The present value of the lump sum payment, equal to $1,000, should now be displayed in cell B7. It is calculated as a negative number because the future value amount is entered as a positive number.

Present Value of an Annuity

Suppose an investor is confronted with an opportunity to receive $1,276.28 at the end of every year for five years. The investor, who requires a 5 percent return, needs to know the maximum amount he or she can pay for this annuity and still earn the required 5 percent return.

This problem requires the conversion of a series of future payments to a present value. First, clear your time-value template of old and extraneous information and enter the new data as shown.

	A	B	C
1	Number of periods (N) =	5	
2	Periodic rate (I) =	5%	
3	Present value (PV) =		
4	Periodic payment (PMT) =	1,276.28	
5	Future value (FV) =	0	
6			
7	Present value of annuity =	5,525.62	

The present value of an annuity of $1,276.28 per year is $5,525.62. To calculate, position the cursor in cell B7, activate the function wizard, select the financial function category, and highlight the PV (present value) function name, click on the "Next>" button to continue, and fill in the appropriate references in the space provided (i.e., $rate$ = B2, $nper$ = B1, pmt = B4, fv = B5, and $type$ = 0). Click on the "Finish" button to close the function wizard. The present value solution of $5,525.62 should now be displayed in cell B7.

Present Value of Uneven Cash Flows

Typically, the annual cash flows from operating a commercial real estate investment are not expected to be constant over time. There are many other examples of uneven cash flows in investment analysis such as mortgage investments with adjustable interest rates and payments, floating rate corporate bonds, and leases with varying rental payments, to name a few. If the number of periodic payments is relatively small (perhaps less than 10), solving the present value problem with the "CFj" key of your financial calculator is quite efficient. However, as the number of (uneven) payments increases, or if you wish to frequently redo the present value calculation with different discount rate assumptions, it may be more efficient and less prone to error to use EXCEL. The solution to the uneven cash flow problem that was presented in Exhibit 3-8 is reproduced below in the form of an EXCEL spreadsheet. The question is: What formulas underlie the results presented in this table?

	A	B	C	D	E	F
1				**Exhibit 3-8**		
2				**Present Value of Series of Uneven Cash Flows**		
3	Year	Annual CF	CF From Sale	Total CF	PVF @ 14%	Present Value
4	1	$48,000		$48,000	0.877193	$42,105
5	2	49,440		49,440	0.769468	38,042
6	3	50,923		50,923	0.674972	34,372
7	4	52,451		52,451	0.592080	31,055
8	5	54,025	560,000	614,025	0.519369	318,905
9					Total present value =	$464,480

To address this question, the above spreadsheet is reproduced below. However, what appears in each cell of this spreadsheet are the actual inputs. If the cell is to produce simple text, then all that needs to be entered is the text. If numbers are to be included that require no calculation, they can be entered directly into the cell. This is the case for the numbers entered in the "Year" column and the "Annual CF" column. In the remaining cells, calculations are performed and the formulas or EXCEL functions (the "inputs") are displayed instead of the outputs.

	A	B	C	D	E	F
1			Exhibit 3-8			
2			Present Value of Series of Uneven Cash Flows			
3	Year	Annual CF	CF From Sale	Total CF	PVF @ 14%	Present Value
4	1	$48,000		=B4	=1/(1.14)	=D4*E4
5	2	49,440		=B5	=1/(1.14)^2	=D5*E5
6	3	50,923		=B6	=1/(1.14)^3	=D6*E6
7	4	52,451		=B7	=1/(1.14)^4	=D7*E7
8	5	54,025	560,000	=B8+C8	=1/(1.14)^5	=D8*E8
9					Total present value =	=sum(F4:F8)

Conclusion

Spreadsheet users should be aware that the examples provided in this appendix barely scratch the surface of computing power available within these packages. As you become more familiar with EXCEL, we encourage you to investigate the wide range of computing options available within the software.

Sources *and* Limitations *to* Value: Market Research

Legal Foundations *to* Value

Learning Objectives

After reading this chapter you will be able to:

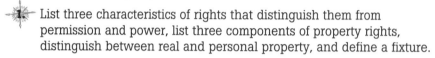 **1.** List three characteristics of rights that distinguish them from permission and power, list three components of property rights, distinguish between real and personal property, and define a fixture.

2. State the distinguishing characteristic of an estate, list three types of freehold estates, and distinguish a freehold estate from a leasehold.

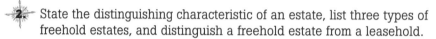 **3.** Define an easement, distinguish it from a license, distinguish two basic types of easements, and identify four examples of each.

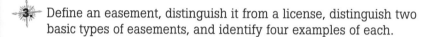 **4.** Define a restrictive covenant, state who can enforce it and how, and list five ways that restrictive covenants can become unenforceable.

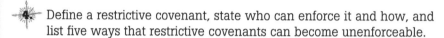 **5.** List one type of general lien and three types of specific liens, list two factors that determine priority among liens, and state the significance of priority.

6. List the features that distinguish these forms of ownership: estate in severalty, tenancy in common, joint tenancy, tenancy by the entireties, condominium and cooperative.

7. Distinguish between the provisions of dower, elective share, and community property for distribution of property between husband and wife.

8. List three common levels of timeshare claims, and identify what is most important to evaluate in a timeshare plan.

Introduction

When we purchase real estate, it is not so much the ground and bricks that we acquire but rights to do certain things with them. This understanding opens the window to a wealth of questions and possibilities. The diversity of the possible claims (rights) to land is rich, with important implications for value. In fact, no estimate of value is meaningful until we know what rights are involved. This chapter provides a tour of these possible claims on real estate, to some of their uses, and to some of the resulting effects on value.

Exhibit 4-2 Real Property: Rights in Three Dimensions

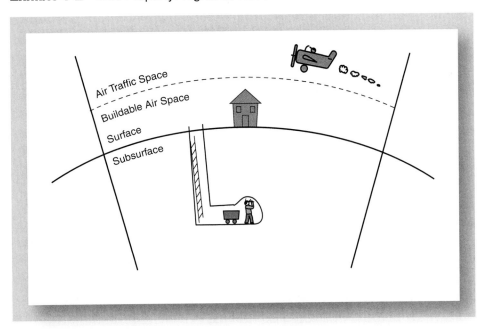

Exhibit 4-3 "Groundless" Building Stories: The Use of Air Rights

In New York City the MetLife Building towers 59 floors above the railroad right-of-ways entering Grand Central Station.

In Chicago the "New East Side" is a cluster of world-class buildings built on air rights above a former railroad yard.

Real Property and Personal Property: The Problem of Fixtures

An enduring problem is the distinction between personal property and real property. Consider these questions relating to this problem: On a construction site, when do building materials cease to be the personal property of the contractor and become part of the "land and its permanent structures" (real property)? If a valuable antique chandelier is hung in a new home, is it then part of the real property? Are custom draperies real property? What about removable shutters or storm windows? What about a kitchen range or refrigerator? This ambiguity between personal property and real property has long been recognized, and rules have evolved in the common law tradition to help sort it out.[2]

2. Common law is the body of traditional law derived from the ancient courts of England, constantly evolving through new court rulings, or case law.

4-1

Which of these poses a greater challenge to property rights?

SANTA CLARITA, California (AP)—A developer trying to get a 400-year-old oak tree out of the way of a road-widening project turned up the heat on the treesitter trying to protect it, charging him with trespassing and shooing away his supporters. Private security guards, accompanied by California Highway Patrol officers and Los Angeles County sheriff's deputies, served tree-sitter John Quigley with a trespassing lawsuit on Thursday. Supporters sleeping below the tree were ordered to clear the area, and a chain-link fence and "No Trespassing" signs went up around the oak.

Bill Rattazzi, president of the Los Angeles division of John Laing Homes, said no attempt was made to remove or arrest Quigley. "These actions were taken to stabilize the situation and allow the issue to be decided in the courts in an orderly manner," he said.

Laing, which owns the property on which the tree grows, wants it out of the way to widen a road that would serve the proposed 21,600-home Newhall Ranch development north of Los Angeles. The company has offered to relocate the tree, but Quigley, who has been tree-sitting for over 70 days, and other

Update: The California developer summarily relocated the 400-year-old oak.

environmentalists don't believe it can survive being moved . . .

In a ruling the timber industry hopes will have widespread implications, a federal judge has approved logging of pockets of old-growth forest frequented by the northern spotted owl even though the bird is protected under the Endangered Species Act. U.S. District Judge Michael Hogan last week lifted a temporary ban on a timber company's plans to clear-cut a 94-acre stand in Oregon's Coast Range not far from the nest of a pair of spotted owls. The ruling marks the first time a federal judge has interpreted a landmark 1995 U.S. Supreme Court ruling in a way that requires the government to show logging on private land would directly harm owls before it could prevent the cut, said Chris West of the Northwest Forestry Association, a timber industry group.

"(Judge Hogan) said the fact that you're cutting habitat doesn't prove there will be harm to the species," West said. Hogan's ruling deals with a 1995 U.S. Supreme Court ruling in a case from Sweet Home, Ore. The court in that case ruled 6–3 that the government has the obligation to protect plants and animals under the Endangered Species Act, even on private property.

Update: Large portions of the forests of Oregon remain subject to logging bans to protect the northern spotted owl.

Tree protester sued for trespassing

Source: CNN.com/us, January 10, 2003.

U.S. judge permits limited logging of Oregon owl habitat
By ROBERT McCLURE
SEATTLE POST-INTELLIGENCER REPORTER

The legal question is whether an object has become a fixture. A **fixture** is defined as an object that formerly was personal property but has been converted to real property. Thus, fixtures are a special class of real property. Four rules have evolved over time for determining whether an object has become a fixture:

1. **The manner of attachment:** The question in this rule is whether removal of the object results in damage to the property. Clearly, for example, removal of vinyl floor covering would damage a building. But a court may regard removal of wire connecting a dwelling to cable service as being damage as well.[3]

2. **The character of the article and manner of adaptation:** Under this rule, items that have been custom designed or custom fitted tend to be regarded as fixtures. Examples might include window screens, storm windows, church pews, custom bookshelves, custom draperies, or custom security systems.

3. **The intention of the parties:** This rule refers not to the private intention of the parties but to the facts of the situation and the intention that an observer would reasonably conclude from them. A major example would be kitchen appliances: If a kitchen range or refrigerator is in a single-family residence being sold, it normally is expected to remain with the seller. On the other hand, if the appliances are furnishings in a rental apartment building they normally would be expected to remain with the building. Thus, the rule of intention would treat the appliances as personal property in the single-family residence case, and as fixtures in the apartment case.

4. **Relation of the parties:** For landlord and tenant relationships, special versions of the rule of intention have evolved in determining fixtures:
   a. Trade fixtures, which are items installed by a commercial tenant to conduct its business, are always considered personal property of the tenant unless they are abandoned at termination of the lease. Thus, despite the fact that wall treatments, wall display cases, floor display cases, and so forth are usually custom fitted, and usually "injure" the facility when removed, they still are regarded as property of the tenant.
   b. Agriculture fixtures, such as fences, also are considered property of the tenant. Anything that is installed by the tenant remains personal property.
   c. Residential tenants also tend to be given the same protection. Any item installed in the residence by the tenant is regarded as the tenant's personal property, at least until it is abandoned.

The rule of intention is the most recent, and dominant, rule. That is, if there is ambiguity based on application of the other rules, the rule of intention generally will take precedence.

There is a very practical importance to the fixture issue for property value. A contract for the sale of real estate applies only to real property unless personal property involved is explicitly included. Frequently when property is purchased, including personal residences, there are items on the property that may or may not be fixtures. Thus, who owns them after sale of the property may not be clear. In any real estate transaction, it is important for both parties involved to carefully review the property with this issue in mind, and to draw up the contract so that there is no ambiguity regarding disposition of these items. The value of the property exchanged can depend heavily on what items are included.

Concept Check

4.3 Is a fixture real or personal property? What is the dominant rule for determining whether something is a fixture? Under the "rule of intention," identify two possible results for the example of kitchen appliances.

3. *T-V Transmission, Inc.* v. *County Board of Equalization,* 338 N.W. 2nd 752 (Neb. 1983).

The Real Property Bundle of Rights

The owner of real property holds a bundle of rights that is complex. As noted above, this bundle is some combination of the right of exclusive possession, use (enjoyment), and disposition. But this bundle can be dismantled in many ways, creating lesser bundles, held by different individuals. These bundles of rights are referred to as **interests.** The value of the property will tend to vary with the completeness of the interest. Below, we examine the possible variation in the bundle.

Possessory Interests (Estates)

Interests in real property that include possession are called **estates.** These can range from the complete bundle of potential rights (fee simple absolute) to a claim that is little more than "squatter's rights" (tenancy at sufferance). In between are a variety of bundles, differing by the combination of other rights included. The range of estates is displayed in Exhibit 4-4. The most complete estate, the fee simple absolute, is singled out, as are the weakest, tenancy at will and tenancy at sufferance. Each possible estate is discussed below.

Concept Check

4.4   When is a real property interest an estate?

Exhibit 4-4   Estates

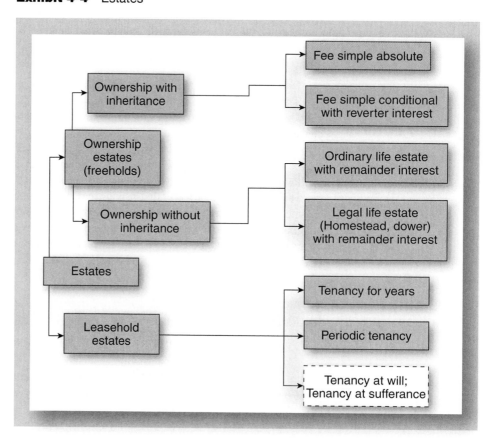

Ownership Estates (Freeholds or Titled Interests). The more substantial or complete estates are those that are indefinite in length. These are the titled interests we commonly think of as ownership. In the common law term, they are **freeholds.** They can differ by variations in the right of disposition.

Fee Simple Absolute. **Fee simple absolute** is the most complete bundle of rights possible, and has the greatest value. Subject to the limitations imposed by government or by prior owners, all possible rights of exclusive possession, use and enjoyment, and disposition are possessed by the owner. This is the traditional concept of landownership. It is this interest that is intended when persons of the real estate world refer to owning or holding the "fee."

Fee Simple Conditional. In a **fee simple conditional,** ownership is subject to a condition or trigger event. In this case the owner's bundle of rights is complete unless the trigger event occurs, which may cause ownership to revert to a previous owner (or his or her heirs). This uncertain interest held by the previous owner (or heirs) is called a **reverter** interest. For example, an owner could convey a small apartment building to a university, but require that the property be used for a scholarship dormitory for women students. As long as the university uses the property for this purpose, it may enjoy all the rights of a fee simple owner. However, if it ever allows men students to occupy the house, the previous owner or the owner's heirs can bring suit to recover the property. The resulting uncertainty that this kind of condition creates can, of course, greatly reduce the value of ownership.

Ordinary Life Estate and Remainder. In an **ordinary life estate** the rights of disposition of the fee simple absolute are unbundled and separated completely. For example, suppose an older homeowner lives adjacent to an expanding university, and the university would like to acquire her residence for future university use. Suppose also that she is willing to sell, but is not interested in moving. A possible solution is for the university to purchase a **remainder estate** while the owner retains a life estate. In this arrangement the homeowner retains all rights of exclusive possession, use, and enjoyment for her lifetime while the university gains the right of disposition. The owner is compensated either through additional income or a tax deduction (if the remainder is donated) and simplifies the eventual settlement of her estate, while assuring the continued right to occupy her home. At the time of her death the life estate and remainder estate are rejoined, becoming a complete fee simple absolute owned by the university.[4]

Legal Life Estate. **Legal life estates** are created by the action of law. In Florida, for example, a family residence that is declared a homestead carries the possibility of becoming subject to a life estate. If a family having minor children occupies a homestead residence, and if one spouse dies, Florida's homestead law gives the surviving spouse a life estate and gives the children "vested remainder" interests in the residence. While intended to protect the surviving family, this law can create as many problems as it solves. If the surviving spouse needs to sell the residence to relocate, a trustee must be created to act on behalf of the minor children to convey their interests in the sale. Thus, additional legal costs and delays are likely to result.[5]

Other Life Estates. Life estates also can arise out of a marriage. In the English common law tradition a right known as dower automatically gave a widow a life estate in one-third of the real property of her decedent husband. Today, however, dower generally has been displaced, as discussed later in this chapter.

---

4. While rare, and normally inadvisable, the life estate could be tied to the life of someone other than the owner.

5. For this reason, families in Florida are advised to acquire their primary personal residence by the special joint ownership known as tenancy by the entirety (discussed later in this chapter).

Concept Check

4.5   Name three ways that a life estate can arise. What companion estate is
automatically created with the life estate?

Leasehold (Nonownership) Estates.   Leasehold interests are possessory interests, and are
therefore estates. They differ from freehold estates in three respects: (1) They are limited in
time. (2) They have no meaningful right of disposition because they are limited in time.
(3) They are not titled interests. Essentially, they are a temporary conveyance of the rights
of exclusion, use, and enjoyment, but not the right of disposition.

Tenancy for Years (Estate for Years).   A **tenancy for years** is a leasehold interest for a specific period of time. It may be for a few days, or for hundreds of years, state law permitting.
Until recently the relationship between landlord and tenant was governed entirely by the
terms of the lease. However, as explained below, changing social needs have altered this.
While all leases should be put in writing, this is especially true for the lease conveying a
tenancy for years because the lease may be the only tangible evidence of the landlord-tenant
understanding. If the term is for more than one year (a year and a day, or more) the lease
must be in writing to be enforceable. (This requirement results from the Statue of Frauds,
discussed in Chapter 18.)

Periodic Tenancy.   Any lease that has no definite term at the start is a **periodic tenancy.** In
sharp contrast to the tenancy for years, the lease conveying the periodic tenancy usually is
oral and, hence, is rather informal. While simpler and quicker, this carries more risk of landlord and tenant misunderstanding. The length of the period is implied by the payment period. Every state has specified requirements for notification prior to terminating a periodic
tenancy, with both landlord and tenant subject to the same requirements. Generally, the
minimum notice period is one-half the payment period, and begins the day after actual notification, running to the end of the last day of the rental period.[6] While periodic tenancy
conveyed by an oral lease is common between individual landlords and tenants, it is less
common where the landlord has multiple tenants. The use of written rental contracts is a superior practice that reduces risk for both parties, thus adding to the value of the property.

Tenancy at Will.   Sometimes at the end of a lease there is a short period of time when it suits
both landlord and tenant for occupancy to continue. For example, this might occur if the
building is being sold or renovated in the near future. If there is agreement that the tenant will
stay until either landlord or tenant gives notice, the tenancy is known as a **tenancy at will.**[7]

Tenancy at Sufferance.   A **tenancy at sufferance** occurs when a tenant that is supposed to
vacate does not, but continues to pay rent, and the landlord accepts it. This tenancy, at least
until the landlord accepts rental payment, differs from trespassing only in that the tenant
previously occupied the property under a legitimate leasehold interest.

Changing Leasehold Concepts.   Dramatic change has occurred in leasehold law in recent
decades. Until around 1970, the law of leasehold estates had evolved little from the English
common law tradition of rural leaseholds. In that setting, the obligation of the landlord was
little more than to get off the land and leave the tenant alone. In an urban setting of residential apartments, this treatment of landlord-tenant relations was woefully inadequate. As a result, states have enacted elaborate residential landlord-tenant laws that take great strides in

---

6. In Florida, for example, the periods for notification are as follows: for year-to-year, three months; for a
quarterly, 45 days; for a monthly period, 15 days; for a weekly period, 7 days.

7. The use of the term here is derived from common law usage. In some states, such as Florida, "tenancy at
will" has been redefined to be a periodic tenancy that is conveyed by a written lease.

defining the rights and obligations of both parties under a residential lease. The laws address such matters as obligations for care and repair of the premises, rights of entry, handling of deposits, notification requirements, and many other matters. In short, something of a revolution has taken place in residential leasehold law. During the last few decades, it has gone from the common law tradition of agrarian relationships formed in preindustrial England to viewing residential tenancy as the providing of services. (More about modern statutory landlord-tenant relationships is available on the website in the margin, and in Chapters 17 and 21.)

www.rentlaw.com

Landlord-tenant law with state links

Concept Check

4.6 In contrast to the traditional English common law notion of landlord and tenant relationships, modern society has come to regard a residential lease as a contract for _____.

Nonpossessory Interests

Bundles of real property rights that do not include possession are particularly varied and interesting, and can affect the value of real estate significantly. We consider three quite different classes of nonpossessory interests: easements, restrictive covenants, and liens.

Easements. An **easement** is the right to use land for a specific and limited purpose. The purpose can range from very passive, such as access to a view, to virtually exclusive possession of the land, such as a street right-of-way or railroad right-of-way. A rich variation of applications lies between these extremes, as we show below.

Concept Check

4.7 What is the basic definition of an easement?

Easements Appurtenant. **Easements appurtenant** have two distinguishing features. First, the easement appurtenant involves a relationship between two parcels of land. The **dominant parcel** benefits from the easement while the **servient parcel** is constrained or diminished by the easement. Second, the easement appurtenant "runs with the land"; that is, it becomes a permanent and inseparable feature of both parcels involved.

Easements appurtenant are of two types: affirmative and negative. The examples below clarify this difference.

Affirmative Easements Appurtenant. Affirmative easements give the dominant parcel some intrusive use of the servient parcel. There are many examples:

1. An easement of access across one parcel to another.
2. A drainage easement for storm water from one parcel across another.
3. Access across a parcel for sewer service.
4. A common wall easement requiring the wall of one townhouse to support the floors, roof, and structure of an adjacent one.
5. A common drive easement where owners of adjoining lots must permit each other to use a driveway lying on their shared property line.

Negative Easements Appurtenant. Negative easements allow no intrusion onto the servient parcel. One example of a negative easement appurtenant is a sunlight easement that restricts the configuration of adjacent buildings so as to assure access to direct sunlight. Another example, the scenic easement, has been used to restrict construction on adjacent parcels so as to preserve a valued view.

www.r6.fws.gov/pwf/
r6pwf8b.htm

Conservation easements

Easements in Gross. An **easement in gross** is the right to use land for a specific, limited purpose unrelated to any adjacent parcel. While there is one or more servient parcels, there is no dominant parcel. Further, the easement in gross, unlike the easement appurtenant, is transferable to another owner without transfer of any parcel of land. Examples of easements in gross can include rights-of-way for roads, railroads, irrigation water, communication and electrical cables, gas lines, billboards, access for timber or crop harvesting, or for mineral or oil extraction. Not surprisingly, easements in gross are sometimes referred to as commercial easements, although noncommercial versions also exist. Noncommercial examples might be access for recreation purposes—fishing, hunting, boating, or snowmobiling—granted by a landowner to friends or family members. More recently, conservation easements have become an important tool to preserve wetlands, open spaces and well fields for a community's water supply.

One significant issue with a commercial easement in gross is whether it is exclusive or nonexclusive. The owner of an exclusive easement in gross holds all the easement rights, in effect, and can extend them to others, thus giving additional persons access to the easement and potentially increasing the usage burden on the servient land. If the easement is not exclusive, the owner of the easement cannot extend his rights to others. This prevents proliferation in use of the easement and preserves more of the value of the servient parcel.

Implications of Easements. In any locality, urban or rural, a variety of easements are usually present. This adds challenges to the task of determining what bundle of rights is available to an owner of the land and what value the property has. This problem is suggested in Exhibit 4-5. Examine the diagram and see if you can identify at least six potential easements in the picture.

Exhibit 4-5 How Many Easements Are In This Scene?

The easements suggested in this exhibit include the following: On parcels A and C is a common driveway easement. On parcel C is an implied easement of access in favor of parcel B. Parcel E appears to have an involuntary driveway easement known as an easement by prescription (see Chapter 18). On parcel F is an implied easement of access to extract oil. Associated with the power lines and the roadside electric lines are easements to permit the installation and maintenance of the lines. With the road sign is an easement to permit installation and maintenance of the sign.

Concept Check

4.8 What is the basic difference between an easement appurtenant and an easement in gross?

License. An important distinction both practically and conceptually is the difference between an easement and a **license.** Whereas an easement is the *right* to use another's land for a specific and limited purpose, a license is *permission* to do so. Unlike an easement, the license is revocable by the grantor. A license to use land is not uncommon. Examples might be permission for the various recreational uses of land noted above. A license is regarded as terminated if the land is sold, or if the grantor dies. Licenses can be *granted orally,* whereas easements, being an interest in land, cannot.

The imposition by easements upon an ownership or leasehold estate can vary from only a minor effect to virtually complete displacement of the estate. As a result, the concept of easement can be confusing. Exhibit 4-6 displays the basic differences in rights for ownership estates, leasehold estates, and easements.

Restrictive Covenants (Deed Restrictions). **Restrictive covenants** impose limits on the uses of land. As their name suggests, they can be created when land is conveyed to a new owner by placing a restrictive clause in the deed that conveys the property. (Deeds are discussed in Chapter 18.) For example, it was not uncommon in the past to place a restriction in a deed prohibiting the new owner from certain activities on the property, such as the sale of alcoholic beverages. A much more common use of the restrictive covenant today is to control the character of land use in a subdivision. At the creation of a residential subdivision, a developer usually records in the associated public documents a series of restrictions on the use of the lots in order to improve the perceived quality, stability, and value of the lots. (These recorded documents are also discussed in Chapter 18.) Examples of residential subdivision restrictions include:

Setback line and/or height restriction for houses.
Minimum floor area.

Exhibit 4-6 Variation of Rights in Real Property Interests

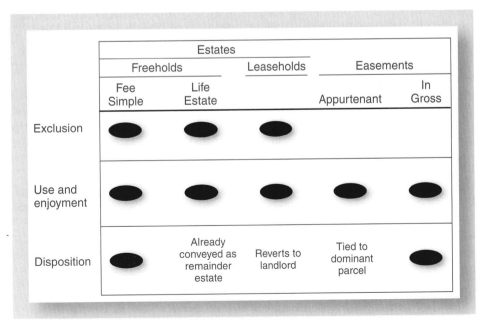

Search the Web under "deed restrictions" for numerous actual examples.

No freestanding garage.
No freestanding utility building.
No chain-link fences.
No recreational vehicles or boats parked in view of the street.
No garage door facing the street.
Required architectural review of new structures or major additions.
No external antennae, satellite dishes, or clotheslines.
No habitual parking of cars in the driveway.
Requirement to use professional lawn service.

Restrictive covenants are strictly private; that is, they can only be enforced by those who hold a legal interest in the property. In the case of an isolated **deed restriction,** the owner who created the restriction or that owner's heirs are the only persons who can enforce the restriction. They would do so by suing for an injunction against a violation. Such individual restrictions usually must be enforced promptly. For example, if a seller of property created a restriction that the property must be used for residential purposes, and the seller seeks to enforce the restriction only after a commercial establishment has been created and is operating, the courts may be unwilling to uphold the restriction. Court decisions concerning enforcement seem to reflect the common law tradition that property should be productive, with less restriction being better. When restrictions are ambiguous, the court is likely to interpret in favor of the current owner.

Enforcement of subdivisionwide restrictions is similar to enforcement of an isolated deed restriction. However, by a doctrine of rights known as "equitable servitude," subdivisionwide restrictions are deemed to serve the interest of all owners present and future in the subdivision lots, as well as others with interests in the land, such as mortgage lenders, and even renters. Any of these "parties at interest" can sue for injunction against violation of a restriction.

Whether the restriction is in an isolated deed or part of a general set of subdivision restrictions, the courts have been reluctant to maintain them for an unreasonably long time. Even in states where no time limit exists, courts may refuse to enforce restrictions due to changing neighborhood character, abandonment (neglect of enforcement), and changing public policy. In most states it is difficult to maintain individual restrictive covenants for more than a few decades, and several states have enacted time limits of 20 years or so.[8]

Concept Check

4.9 Who can enforce a restrictive covenant? How is it done?

Liens. A **lien** is an interest in real property that serves as security for an obligation. It is useful to think of two types: general liens and specific liens. A **general lien** arises out of actions unrelated to ownership of the property. A **specific lien** derives directly from events related to a property. Specific liens include property tax and assessment liens, mortgages, and mechanics' liens.

General Liens. The most prominent example of a general lien arises from a court judgment. If a property owner is successfully sued for damages for any reason, the court, in

---

8. Restrictive covenants, in effect, are a removal of some of the rights of use and enjoyment from property. Whether these covenants actually are real property interests has been questioned; that they tend to be more fragile and less durable than other real property interests may give credence to this question. Nevertheless, for some years after their creation, it is practical to regard restrictive covenants as amounting to negative property interests that cannot be altered.

awarding the damages, normally will **attach** (place a lien on) available real property of the defendant as security for payment of the damage award.

Property Tax and Property Assessment Liens. Every real property owner is subject to property tax as a primary means of supporting local government. Since local government services are a benefit to property owners, the governments are able to exercise an automatic **property tax lien** on the benefiting properties to assure payment of property taxes. Similarly, when a local government makes improvements in a neighborhood, such as street paving or utility installations, adjacent properties that receive the primary benefit will be charged a "fair share" assessment, usually based on the street frontage (front footage of each lot). This fair share assessment is secured with an automatic **assessment lien.** One of the important aspects of the property tax liens and assessment liens is their priority; they are automatically superior to any other lien.

Mortgages. A **mortgage** is an interest in property as security for a debt. Mortgage liens exist for a high percentage of all properties. Because of their central importance in real estate, they are discussed at length in Chapter 10. A property can have multiple mortgages, which are ordered in priority by the date of their creation. (This order can be changed by use of a subordination agreement, discussed in Chapter 10.) Later mortgages are referred to as junior mortgages, or they are identified by order of creation as a second mortgage, third mortgage, and so forth.

www.mechlien.com/ lien_links.htm

Information on mechanics liens for all 50 states, with current developments.

Mechanics' Liens. **Mechanics' liens** arise from construction and other improvements to real estate. If a property owner defaults on a construction contract, it is not realistic to expect the contractor to recover the materials and services used to improve the real estate. The solution is the mechanics' lien. Following completion of a contract, a contractor has a period of time (determined by each state) to file for a lien on the property improved. Since the priority of private liens depends upon when they were created, a major question with mechanics' liens is when they are deemed to be created. The answer differs, with some states treating the date that construction starts as the beginning of the lien, while other states use the date the construction contract was signed.

Mortgage lenders must be very attentive to the potential for mechanics' liens. They must carefully account for any possible mechanics' lien and assure that it is resolved with a waiver so that it does not preempt the priority of the mortgage.

Concept Check

4.10 What is generally the determinant of lien priority? What lien always preempts this order?

Consequences of Liens. Several aspects of liens need to be understood. First, all liens are security interests that can lead to sale of the property to compensate the creditor or taxing authority in the event of default. The priority, after tax and assessment liens, is by chronology among all private liens. Lien priority is significant because of the "all or nothing" treatment of creditors in the event of a property sale. Creditors receive no relief until all liens senior to theirs have been fully satisfied.

The difference between general and specific liens is important in most states. Designation of a principal residence as a homestead usually creates automatic protection of the residence from general liens, up to some limit.[9] So, while the homestead is subject to

9. The amount of homestead value protected from general liens ranges between roughly $10,000 and $60,000, with the exceptions of Missouri ($8,000) and Connecticut ($75,000). Florida and Texas, on the other hand, have no limits to the protection.

Exhibit 4-7 Three Levels of Liens on a Personal Residence

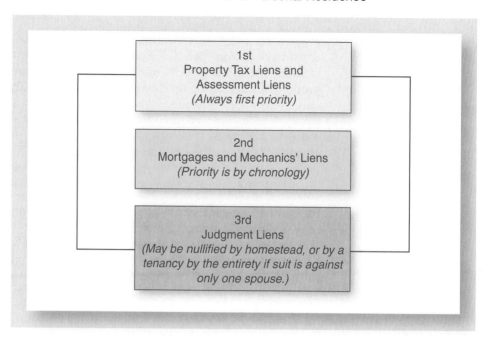

property tax liens and mortgages or mechanics' liens, it would be protected from a judgment awarded for general debts.[10] The priority of liens for a personal residence are summarized in Exhibit 4-7.

Forms of Co-Ownership

Real estate often is owned by a group of persons; that is, more than one person holds precisely the same "bundle of rights," and the interests of the owners cannot be physically or otherwise separated. Imagine, for example, three unrelated persons who jointly purchase an ordinary house to live in, making equal contributions to the purchase price (the contributions would not need to be equal). While each may have an appointed bedroom, in large measure all must share the same space and rights of use. This indivisibility is the nature of true co-ownership that we are focusing on here; only if the owners vacate the house and rent it out can they truly divide up the "fruits" of the property by dividing up the rental income. Co-ownership can occur in a variety of ways, with significant variation in how the bundle of rights is jointly held. The variety of co-ownership forms are displayed in Exhibit 4-8, and each form is discussed on the following pages.

Indirect Co-Ownership through a Single Entity

In Chapter 15 we will present several business entities through which multiple persons can form a business organization: partnership, limited partnership, limited liability company, Subchapter S corporation, standard C corporation and real estate investment trust (REIT).

10. In Florida and Texas, the homestead also is protected from bankruptcy sale. The protection of homesteads in these two states is quite controversial. An all-too-common practice is for a wealthy person to move to Florida, acquire an extremely valuable homestead residence, and then declare bankruptcy on prior obligations. The effect is to be able to transfer considerable wealth out of the reach of creditors. Kenneth Lay, former C.E.O. of Enron, is reputed to live in a Texas residence valued at close to seven million dollars. Scott Sullivan, the former C.F.O. at WorldCom who is charged with massive accounting fraud has a personal residence in Florida estimated to be worth $15 million.

Exhibit 4-8 Forms of Co-Ownership

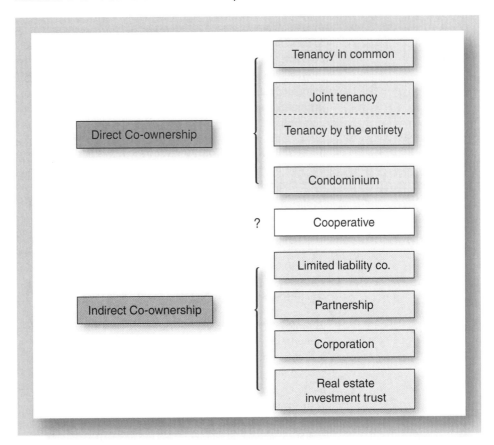

Any of these business entities can acquire real estate, acting as a single artificial "person." It is this artificial entity that owns the property rather than the individuals themselves. In these cases the co-ownership, in legal substance, is no different than a true single-person owner.

Direct Co-Ownership

In contrast to single entity ownership are several forms of direct co-ownership. Unlike ownership through a business organization that holds title to property, each direct co-owner holds a titled interest in the property. In effect, each owner holds a freehold estate, but without exclusive possession with respect to the other co-owners. The forms of direct co-ownership differ in how they can be created, and the rights of disposition each owner enjoys.

Tenancy in Common. The **tenancy in common** is the "normal" form of direct co-ownership and is as close to the fee simple absolute estate as is possible. Each co-owner retains full rights of disposition and is free to mortgage, or to convey his or her ownership share to a new owner (in whole or in part), who receives exactly the same set of shared rights. While the owners' interests may differ in relative size, they are otherwise indistinguishable. No owner can use the property in a way that preempts the ability of the other owners to similarly enjoy the property. Tenancy in common is the "default" form of co-ownership in that it results unless there is explicit provision for another form, or unless the property is being acquired by a husband and wife. A common occurrence of this form of ownership is in the disposition of an estate to the heirs.

Tenancy in Common as a Business Ownership Form. Tenancy in common sometimes occurs, by default, as a joint ownership form for income-producing property. It is most likely to result from settlement of an estate. Other than requiring no special legal action, it appears to have no advantages over other business entities, and may carry disadvantages. First, all co-owners may bear personal liability in judgments against the property. Second, spousal interests in the property (discussed below) will be governed by the state where the property is located rather than the state or states of residence of the co-owners. Third, tax and legal implications of tenancy in common may be less widely understood than for standard business entities.

Joint Tenancy. In a **joint tenancy** the rights of disposition are severely restricted. Only the heirs of the last surviving owner have any claim to the property as inheritance. Although each owner holds a titled interest in the property, in the eyes of the law a joint tenancy effectively has a single owner—the *last* one to remain alive. If one of the owners dies, the law recognizes no event, so his heirs have no claim on the property. This provision is called, oddly, the "right of survivorship." Since the interest of the last surviving owner automatically becomes a single owner estate, his heirs regain normal rights of inheritance. Historically, joint tenancy was used as a device to prevent otherwise legitimate heirs from making claim to the property.[11] For this reason, it has been regarded as somewhat less than beneficial to society and has been made difficult to establish and maintain.

Tenancy by the Entirety. **Tenancy by the entirety** is a form of joint tenancy for husband and wife. In some states it occurs automatically when property is conveyed to a husband and wife jointly. In other states it must be created explicitly. Tenancy by the entireties is of special interest in states with homestead rights. In Florida, for example, a homestead automatically implies, at the death of one spouse, that a surviving spouse will share ownership with any surviving minor children. The surviving spouse receives a life estate in the homestead while minor children share vested remainder interests.[12] However, if the homestead residence is held as a tenancy by the entireties, the law recognizes no event at the death of one spouse, and the survivor obtains a single-owner estate. Thus, it is possible to dispose of the property as needed without additional delays and legal expense.

Perhaps because tenancy by the entirety is regarded as more socially constructive than joint tenancy, it is easier to create and less fragile. In general, neither husband nor wife alone can pledge the property held in tenancy by the entireties. It follows that the property cannot be foreclosed in the event of default on an obligation of only one spouse or the other, nor can it be attached in a judgment against one spouse alone.

www.firstam.com/ landsakes/html/email/ 042202fed.html

Tenancy by the entirety and spousal debt

Concept Check

4.11   The most common and least specialized form of direct co-ownership is _____

Condominium. **Condominium** is a form of ownership combining single person ownership with tenancy in common. Specifically, the owner holds a fee simple interest, as an individual owner, to a certain space (such as an apartment). Joint, and inseparable, with this estate, the owner is a tenant in common in the "community" elements (e.g., building shell, floors, halls, elevators, stairwells, driveways, and other common areas) of the property.[13]

---

11. Joint tenancy could be used, for example, by a group of men to jointly acquire a hunting lodge, clubhouse, or other recreational retreat, and prevent wives and children from gaining ownership in it.

12. This compels the surviving spouse to appoint a trustee for the children in any effort to dispose of the homestead, which often is necessary.

13. Some states allow ownership of the common areas through an owner corporation instead of through tenancy in common. This may be preferable, where possible, because rules and procedures for corporate governance are well established.

Condominium is an ancient concept but became enabled in the United States only as recently as the 1960s when every state adopted condominium laws. Condominium ownership is most common in apartment buildings, but also is used for townhouses, cluster homes, parking lots, recreational vehicle camping sites, marinas, offices, and even hotels. An important feature of a condominium is that each owner can mortgage his or her interest independently of other owners.

Condominium ownership is well established and undoubtedly will increase in use with a rising population and urban density. However, those purchasing a condominium must realize that it entails a cost in ownership complexity, together with restrictions on owner discretion that follow from living in close proximity to others. Even the simplest condominium necessitates creation and management of an owner association. This association is a minigovernment that must maintain all common areas and structures, make and enforce **condominium bylaws,** and levy and collect owner assessments. There must be an effective transfer of control from the original developer to the owner association. There also must be orderly and fair procedures for association meetings, elections, a budgeting process, and revision of bylaws pertaining to such matters as pets, parking, guests, exterior decorating, noise, and use of common facilities. The association must assure a program of property and liability insurance that is adequate for both the common facilities and for unit owners. There also must be adequate accounting, control, and reporting systems.

The condominium is created through a master deed or **condominium declaration.** In this document are three-dimensional descriptions of the space occupied by each unit, a description of the common facilities and areas, a determination of the proportion of common areas associated with each unit, provision for expansion of the property, if needed, and numerous fundamental rules. These basic rules may include restrictions on the presence of minor children or other age restrictions. They will define basic rights, procedures and restrictions in leasing units, and provisions for dealing with destruction of the facilities. Most importantly, they will set the framework to create and enforce bylaws, and to levy and collect assessments.

It is very important in considering the purchase of a condominium to carefully examine the declaration and bylaws. Condominiums have an unfortunate history of owners failing to understand the restrictions involved. All too often, this gives rise to conflicts among owners and to litigation, as exemplified in Industry Issues 4-2.

www.megalaw.com/top/ condo.php

Condominium law

Concept Check

4.12 The organization and rules of a condominium are very important because it serves as a small-scale _____ . What are the two most important documents of a condominium?

Cooperative. A **cooperative** actually is not a form of true direct co-ownership, but rather is a proprietary corporation. Just as with a partnership, limited liability company (LLC), or standard corporation, the cooperative owns real estate as a single owner. The unique aspect is that each owner of the corporation holds a "proprietary lease" for some designated space.[14] Historically, this form of ownership has been used for apartment buildings, with each of the co-owners having a proprietary lease to one apartment unit. Before states adopted laws enabling condominiums in the United States following World War II, the cooperative enabled individuals to own their residence where it might otherwise not have been possible, such as in high-density cities like New York City. The arrangement has at least one major limitation: Because the corporation owns the property, occupants cannot obtain mortgage financing without placing all other owners at risk for the debt. By contrast,

---

14. A proprietory lease is of indefinite length, and requires the owner-tenant to make contributions for maintenance expenses, but does not require rent payments.

Industry Issues

Let Condo Bylaws be Bylaws?

SHELTON, Conn.—More than a year after the terror attacks, the red, white, and blue still blazes out from mailboxes, car windows, and front porches all over this middle-class Fairfield County town. But here at the Sunwood Condominiums, Arthur and Jane Buchanan have reluctantly taken the American flag from its rod on the front of their home and packed it away. Mrs. Buchanan said all their other possessions would soon follow. Last Friday the Buchanans put their unit up for sale to protest the Sunwood Condominium Association's crackdown on outdoor decorations, which forbids flagflying except on six days each year. "We got the letter and when my husband was reading it, he said, 'O.K., I'll take it down. But we're moving,' " Mrs. Buchanan recalled.

Mr. Buchanan, a retired Bridgeport police captain, said the inconvenience of uprooting himself at 75 was nothing compared with the letter's demand. "Nobody's going to tell me where I can put up my flag," he said. "I was in Korea for 13 months, and a lot of my friends who died there would turn over in their graves if

they thought I'd put up with that." The flag fight is a twist on similar battles being fought around the nation as homeowners' associations—often prodded by residents—try to maintain a uniformity of style to keep up property values and keep the peace. But in the patriotic fervor that followed Sept. 11, the battle here has been unusually fierce.

The dispute started on Oct. 8, when owners of the 168 Sunwood units got a letter from the association board, citing the complex's bylaws and ordering them to remove all unapproved items attached to their units' exteriors or placed in a common area. The list of forbidden articles included hose racks, nonconforming light fixtures, statues, lawn furniture and "flags or other banners."

The letter said the American flag could be displayed only on Presidents' Day, Memorial Day, Flag Day, Independence Day, Sept. 11 and Veterans Day.

"Basically, we're asking those who are flying them to remove torn and tattered flags," said Mr. Lupo the association president.

Said Maxine Baena, "All the board did was ask them to clean it up. That's the difference between living in a house or a condo. In a condo, you give up some rights."

Source: "Condo Flag Ban Has a Family Packing" *New York Times,* November 1, 2002.

---

owners in a condominium can mortgage their property without putting other owners at risk. Perhaps due to this difference, the cooperative has been much less widely used than the condominium in recent decades.

Ownership Interests from Marriage. All of the legal traditions that have descended to the United States—English common law, the French Napoleonic code (Louisiana), and Spanish traditional law—provide for spousal rights to property in a marriage. While these rights have carried to the United States, virtually every state has modified them to better fit our modern, nonagricultural society.

Dower/Curtesy. The common law provision of **dower** gave a wife a one-third life estate in all of the real property of a decedent husband that was ever owned by him during the marriage, provided that the wife did not join in conveying the property to a new owner. Curtesy was a similar common law provision for husbands. Dower and curtesy are poor solutions to the needs of surviving spouses in an industrial, mobile society because they ignore personal property wealth (stocks and bonds), and because they created only a (non-marketable) life estate. From the concept, only the notion of a one-third spousal share survives in most states.

http://www.keln.org/bibs/barnes.html

Offers information on the status of elective share in each state as of 1996.

Elective Share. Recognizing the limitations of dower and curtesy, most states in the United States have replaced them with a modern substitute. The most common provision, adopted by more than 25 states, is **elective share,** which gives a surviving spouse a share of most of the wealth of the decedent. The most common share is one-third. The surviving spouse must elect to take the share within some time limit, usually no later than nine months after the death or six months after the conclusion of probate, whichever is later.[15] Elective share applies to both real and personal property of the decedent, though not all elective share laws have been effective in actually encompassing the bulk of the decedent's wealth.[16]

www.firstam.com/
title-ca/sanjoaquin/html/
cust/2195.html

Comparison of Tenancy in
common, joint tenancy and
community property

Community Property. In nine states, mainly of Spanish tradition, the automatic right of husband and wife in property of each other is known as **community property.**[17] Community property gives a spouse a one-half claim on all property acquired "from the fruits of the marriage." Thus, if either spouse should independently acquire property during the marriage, it is likely to be regarded by courts as community property. Excluded from this is property that the husband or wife acquired prior to the marriage, or gifts or inheritance received during the marriage, all of which is **separate property.** In some states, community property also includes any rents, royalties, or profits from separate property.[18] In all community property states, business income or earned income from separate assets is still treated as community property. Some community property states, including Arizona, California and Texas, have advanced the traditional concept by adding a right of survivorship. As with tenancy by the entirety, at the death of one spouse, the survivor automatically becomes the sole owner of the property, without probate and tax complications.

The notion of community property is widely regarded as more equitable than the marital property tradition of English common law, and appears to be influencing marital property law in an increasing number of states.

Implications of Ownership from Marriage. Two main forms of marital property rights— elective share and community property—are summarized in Exhibit 4-9. All of the special property rights created from marriage have a clear implication for real estate transactions. A purchaser of real estate always must be sure that any current or previous spouse of a seller joins in the conveyance of a property. Otherwise, there is high risk that the spouse will have latent ownership claims that are not conveyed to the buyer.

Exhibit 4-9 Two Main Forms of Marital Property Rights

	Elective Share	Community Property
Mainly used in:	English heritage states	Spanish/French heritage states
Spousal share:	One-third	One-half
How triggered:	Explicit declaration	Automatic
Wealth coverage:	Varies up to all wealth	All wealth created in the marriage
Number of states:	About 25	Nine states, with influence on more

15. Probate is the legal process of authenticating the will and administering distribution of the estate in accordance with it.

16. The most recent version of elective share is represented by the Uniform Probate Code (UPC). This model law has been adopted (and adapted), in whole or in part, by a growing minority of states. The UPC version of elective share represents a very extensive effort to apply elective share to all wealth of a decedent, whether real or personal, movable or immovable. The details and progress of the Uniform Probate Code can be monitored on a variety of legal-oriented websites.

17. Community property states include Arizona, California, Idaho, Louisiana, Nevada, New Mexico, Texas, Washington, and Wisconsin. In the French civil law tradition of Louisiana, the community property tradition exists, approximately, under the term *usufruct.* In Wisconsin, community property was created when the state adopted a model law in 1986 known as the Uniform Marital Property Act.

18. These states include Idaho, Louisiana, and Texas.

Explore The Web

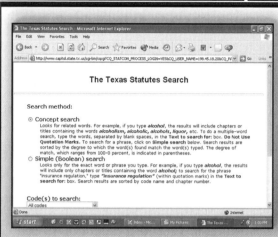

Select a state of interest to you. (The example is for Texas.) Using your favorite Internet search engine enter "*your state statutes.*" The statutes of virtually all states are online and searchable, although all have different search formats. For your state, find out what you can about:

1. The meaning of homestead with respect to protection against liens and automatic (vested) interests for members of a family.
2. Whether the state has tenancy by the entirety.
3. Whether the state has elective share, and, if so, what the share is, and what wealth is covered by it.
4. When mechanics' liens become effective (contract signing? start of construction?)

Concept Check

4.13   Two types of co-ownership interest between spouses that occur automatically for any marriage are _____ or _____ depending on the state.

Timeshare

In **timesharing,** multiple individuals have use of property but, unlike traditional forms of co-ownership, the interests are not simultaneous. Rather, the estate is divided into separate time intervals. This concept has been used almost exclusively for resorts. Commonly the time interval is in weekly units per year, although it can be for other periods. The term *time-sharing* covers a variety of legal arrangements with varying levels of property rights and varying degrees of user flexibility or options.

Timeshare Rights.   A timeshare contract may convey any level of real property interest. The buyer may acquire a "slice" of a true fee simple interest (usually as a partial condo-minium owner). However, the buyer often acquires a leasehold interest for a fixed number of years (tenancy for years). Thus, at the end of the term the buyer's interest is extinguished. Finally, it is possible that the buyer only acquires a license for partial use. In this case, the buyer may not be able to transfer the license. Moreover, it is revocable. Thus, the buyers of a timeshare need to examine carefully what legal interest they are getting.

Timeshare Plans.   A very common form of timeshare plan involves "floating time intervals" (spanning a period of perhaps three or four months) and multiple resort properties. A buyer purchases a certain quantity of "points," which are used annually to bid for a particular site and time unit within the set of resorts and the designated floating time interval.

Concept Check

4.14   What are three levels (qualities) of property rights found in timeshare arrangements?

History of Timeshare. While timeshare began in the 1960s in the French Alps, and is found in many international resort locations, the predominant single market is in the United States. The largest concentrations of timeshare properties are beach resorts, followed by mountain and lake resorts. Not surprisingly, timeshare properties in the United States are concentrated in Florida, Hawaii, California, Colorado, North Carolina, Arizona, and Nevada, in roughly that order.[19]

The early history of timeshare in the United States was tainted by misrepresentations and failures to perform. Two major changes may have altered the industry in more recent times. First, Florida and other states have enacted laws regulating the industry and requiring extensive and strict disclosures for the sale of timeshares. Second, the industry appears to have become more concentrated in larger, more experienced, and financially stronger hospitality companies.

Nevertheless, even industry representatives offer cautions to those interested in purchasing a timeshare. First, it should never be considered a financial investment. (The strict financial yield on a timeshare has rarely, if ever, been positive.) Rather, it should be regarded as a purchase of long-term resort services. This implies another critical point. What a timeshare buyer really is purchasing is the ability of the management company to deliver the expected resort services. Thus, it is the capacity of that company to perform and endure that the buyer must evaluate foremost.

www.arda.org/

Time-share industry organization

Rights Related to Water

As population and economic expansion exert ever-growing demands on the water supply, rights to water become increasingly important, as reported in Industry Issues 4-3. Rights to water are a component of real property, and a particularly complex one. To sort them out, several questions must be considered:

1. Who owns the land under a body of water? (This is especially important for mineral, oil, and gas rights that may be involved.)
2. Who controls use of land under a body of water?
3. Who has the right to use the surface of a body of water?
4. Who has the right to use the water itself (to alter the character of the water by consumption, degradation, use in irrigation, and so on)?
5. Who has the right to use groundwater?

In addition, questions arise concerning ownership of coastal shorelines. Especially interesting are questions of ownership of the massive amount of coastal tidewater estuaries since some are extremely rich in petroleum and other mineral resources. Since an orderly answer to these issues may be beyond the scope of this book, further discussion is deferred to the appendix to this chapter.

Rights to Oil, Gas, and Minerals

Rights to the subsurface include rights to minerals. **Mineral rights,** including, oil, gas, coal, and other substances that are mined can be separated from land ownership. When this occurs, the owner of the mineral rights also receives an implied easement to retrieve the minerals, which implies the right to disturb the surface as necessary (e.g., building roads, erecting mining equipment, opening mine shafts, drilling wells, creating storage tanks, and other drastic alterations of the terrain). States differ on several aspects of mineral rights. For example, in some states mining companies are deemed to own not only the minerals but the

19. An industry trade organization for timeshare, American Resort Development Association, provides descriptive information about the industry and its offerings.

Industry Issues

Water Rights Create a Torrent of Legal Disputes

The Colorado River, as it shapes the border between Arizona and California, is not the raging cataract of the Grand Canyon. It's not the vast impoundment of Lake Powell or Lake Mead. The lower Colorado, in contrast, meanders along the Fort Yuma Indian Reservation. But it's critical to the Quechan tribe there.

The U.S. Supreme Court ruled that the Quechan could pursue their claim to increased water rights. The court also supported claims to the Colorado on four other tribal reservations. The ruling raises the competition between the states and the tribes for the most valuable resource in the Southwest: water.

The states of Arizona and California, the Coachella Valley Water District, and the Metropolitan Water District of Southern California all argued against additional water rights for disputed boundary lands on the Fort Yuma Reservation. Justice Ruth Bader Ginsburg wrote the tribes could proceed because the "water rights were effective as of the time each reservation was created."

Chief Justice William Rehnquist disagreed: "A major purpose of this litigation, from its inception to the present day, has been to provide the necessary assurance to States of the Southwest and to various private interests, of the amount of water they can anticipate to receive from the Colorado River system." Rehnquist is a former Arizona resident, as is Justice Sandra Day

O'Connor, who joined his dissent. The Colorado flows faster than the legal system. The Supreme Court, which has "original jurisdiction" over disputes between states, has been dealing with these recurring tribal claims over the Colorado since 1952.

A legal water battle over the Potomac River traces back further. In 1632, King Charles I of England granted ownership of the Potomac to Maryland—shoreline to shoreline. Where rivers separate states, the border more commonly lies at midstream. The Supreme Court last month agreed to consider Virginia's complaint that Maryland has restricted access to the Potomac. Both states, as well as West Virginia, draw water from the river.

- Go west. The Republican River—no political affiliation—winds out of Colorado and into Kansas and Nebraska. The Supreme Court must referee Kansas's claim that Nebraska has violated a 1943 agreement by diverting the Republican's flow into thousands of wells to irrigate the Cornhuskers' crops.

- Go south. Georgia, Alabama, and Florida have a compact to share the resources of the Apalachicola-Chattahoochee-Flint basin. But the states cannot agree on how to implement it.

There, too, development has helped create the dilemma. The water demands of sprawling urban centers such as Atlanta are on the increase. As a result, Florida worries the Apalachicola will be severely depleted by the time it reaches the oyster beds at its mouth. The Georgia-Alabama-Florida dispute is not on the Supreme Court's horizon yet, but it could flow that way.

Source: Charles Bierbauer, "Water Rights Create a Torrent of Legal Disputes," cnn.com lawcenter-news analysis June 26, 2000.

---

space the minerals occupied before they were removed. Regarding oil and gas rights, some states deem oil and gas to be owned just like any other mineral. These states are referred to as ownership states. But other states, recognizing that oil and gas can flow due to drilling, hold that the substance is not owned until it is removed from the earth. These states are known as "law of capture" states. Traditionally, all states followed a **rule of capture** whereby the owner of an oil or gas well could claim all that is pumped from it, regardless of whether the oil or gas migrated from adjacent property. However, because methods of so-called secondary recovery have enabled well owners today to recover oil and gas from such an extensive surrounding area, the law of capture has been curtailed in some states. Today every oil-producing state has evolved its own considerable statutory law pertaining to oil and gas rights.

Summary

Owning real property is a matter of having rights. These can include the rights of exclusive possession, of use (enjoyment), and of disposition. Rights are claims that organized government is obligated to enforce; they are nonrevocable and they are enduring. Real property is rights in land and its permanent structures, while personal property is rights to any other object or to intellectual matters. Government can reduce the bundle of rights called real property through its police power. However, if the exercise of police power goes too far, it becomes a "taking," which requires just compensation.

Bundles of real property that include the right of exclusive possession are called estates. Estates are either titled (freehold) or untitled (leasehold) interests. Freeholds are indefinite in length, allowing the right of disposition, while leaseholds have a definite ending, thus no right of disposition. The most complete estate is the fee simple absolute, which is the common notion of ownership.

Three important nonpossessory interests in real property are restrictive covenants, easements, and liens. Restrictive covenants are created in a deed or in subdivision declarations, and can impose a wide variety of restrictions on land use. An easement is the right to use land for a specific, limited purpose. The easement appurtenant involves the relationship between a dominant parcel and a servient parcel, and "runs with the land." The easement in gross often involves a right-of-way (e.g., road, pipeline, power line) and can be conveyed separately from the landownership. A lien is an interest in property as security for an obligation.

Co-ownership is the simultaneous ownership of essentially the same set of rights by multiple persons. The most flexible and robust co-ownership is tenancy in common, which has rights of disposition the same as individual ownership. A joint tenancy gives no rights of inheritance to any but the last surviving co-owner. A tenancy by the entireties is a marital form of joint tenancy. Condominium combines individual ownership of a space (unit) with tenancy in common ownership of the related common facilities. Cooperative is a special form of corporation, which gives each shareholder a "proprietary" (indefinite) lease to one unit in the structure (usually an apartment). Marriage usually creates automatic co-ownership interests. The most important of these are elective share and community property. In recent years, property also has been conveyed to multiple owners through timeshare interests, which range from true ownership to no more than a license.

Key Terms

Assessment lien 83

Attach 83

Community property 89

Condominium 86

Condominium bylaws 87

Condominium declaration 87

Cooperative 87

Deed restriction (restrictive covenants) 81

Dominant parcel 79

Dower 88

Easement 79

Easement appurtenant 79

Easement in gross 80

Elective share 88

Estate 76

Fee simple absolute 77

Fee simple conditional 77

Fixture 75

Freehold 77

General lien 82

Interest 76

Joint tenancy 86

Leasehold 78

Legal life estate 77

License 81

Lien 82

Mechanics' lien 83

Mineral rights 91

Mortgage 83

Ordinary life estate 77

Periodic tenancy 78

Personal property 72

Personal rights 72

Property rights 72

Property tax lien 83

Real property 72

Remainder estate 77

Reverter 77

Rule of capture 92

Tenancy at sufferance 78

Tenancy at will 78

Tenancy by the entireties 86

Tenancy for years 78

Tenancy in common 85

Timesharing 90

Separate property 89

Servient parcel 79

Specific lien 82

Test Problems

1. Which of the following is *not* a form of property right?
   a. Lien
   b. Easement
   c. Leasehold
   d. License
   e. Mineral rights
2. Which of these easements is most likely to be an easement in gross?
   a. Common wall easement
   b. Driveway easement
   c. Drainage easement
   d. Power line easement
   e. Sunlight easement
3. Rules used by courts to determine whether something is a fixture include all *except:*
   a. Intention of the parties
   b. Manner of attachment
   c. Law of capture
   d. Character of the article and manner of adaptation
   e. Relation of the parties
4. Which of these is a titled estate?
   a. Fee simple absolute
   b. Fee simple conditional
   c. Conventional life estate
   d. Legal life estate
   e. All of these
5. Which of these forms of co-ownership could best be described as "normal ownership," except that multiple owners share identically in one bundle of rights?
   a. Tenancy in common
   b. Joint tenancy
   c. Tenancy by the entireties
   d. Condominium
   e. Estate in severalty

6. Which of these marriage-related forms of co-ownership gives each spouse a one-half interest in any property that is "fruits of the marriage"?
   a. Dower
   b. Curtesy
   c. Community property
   d. Elective share
   e. Tenancy by the entireties
7. Which of these liens has the highest priority?
   a. First mortgage lien
   b. Mechanics' lien
   c. Property tax lien
   d. Second mortgage lien
   e. Unable to say because it depends strictly on which was created first
8. Restrictive covenants for a subdivision usually can be enforced by:
   a. Subdivision residents
   b. Lenders with mortgage loans in the subdivision
   c. Local government
   d. *a* and *b*, but not *c*
   e. All three, *a, b,* and *c*
9. Timeshare programs can involve which of the following claims or interests?
   a. Fee simple ownership
   b. Leasehold interest
   c. License
   d. Condominium
   e. All of these are possible
10. Every condominium buyer needs to know the details of which document(s):
    a. Condominium declaration
    b. Bylaws
    c. Proprietary lease
    d. *a* and *b*, but not *c*
    e. All three, *a, b,* and *c*

Study Questions

1. Explain how rights differ from power or force, and from permission.
2. A developer of a subdivision wants to preserve the open space and natural habitat that runs along the back portion of a series of large lots in the proposed subdivision. He is debating whether to use restrictive covenants to accomplish this or to create a habitat easement on the same space. What are the pros and cons of each choice?
3. Why are restrictive covenants a good idea for a subdivision? Can they have any detrimental effects on the subdivision or its residents? For example, are there any listed in the chapter that might have questionable effects on the value of a residence?
4. The traditional common law concept of landlord-tenant relationship was that the landlord's obligation was simply to stay

off the property and the tenant's obligation was to pay the rent. Explain why this is an obsolete arrangement for apartment residents in an urban society.
5. A friend has an elderly mother who lives in a house adjacent to her church. The church is growing, and would welcome the opportunity to obtain her house for its use. She would like to support the needs of her church, but she doesn't want to move and feels strongly about owning her own home. On the other hand, your friend knows that she will not be able to remain in the house many more years, and will be faced with moving and selling within a few years. What options can you suggest as possible plans to explore?
6. A friend has owned and operated a small recreational vehicle camp on a lake in Daytona Beach, Florida. It is close to the

ocean and close to the Daytona Speedway, home of the Daytona 500 and a host of other prominent races. The occupants are very loyal, making reservations far in advance, and returning year after year. She is asking your thoughts on whether to continue the camp as a short-term rental operation, to convert it and sell the parking spaces as condominium parking spaces, or to convert to condominium timeshare lots. What thoughts would you offer?

7. In the United States the bundle of rights called real property seems to have gotten smaller in recent decades. Explain what has caused this. Why is it good? Why is it bad?

Explore The Web

Choose two states of interest to you. Similar to the problem in the chapter, use your favorite search engine and enter "*your state* statutes." For the two states you have chosen, compare and contrast the statutes on issues such as:

1. Timeshare laws.
2. Laws pertaining to property obtained during marriage.
3. Laws regarding tenant-landlord relationships.

Solutions to Concepts Checks

1. Rights are claims or demands that our government is obligated to enforce, whereas claims that are obtained by threat or force are not honored or supported by the government. Rights differ from permission in that rights are nonrevocable and permission is revocable. Finally, rights are enduring. They do not end.

2. The three components of property rights are exclusive possession, use (enjoyment), and disposition.

3. A fixture is defined as an object that formerly was personal property but has converted to real property. Although there are four rules used to determine whether something is a fixture, the dominant rule is the intention of the parties. For example, a kitchen appliance in a single-family residence is expected to remain with the seller when the residence is sold. On the other hand, if the appliances are furnishings in a rental apartment building, they normally would be expected to remain with the building. Thus, the rule of intention would treat the appliances as personal property in the single-family residence case, and as fixtures in the apartment case.

4. Real property interests that include possession are called estates.

5. Life estates can be created by private agreement, by action of law such as through homestead, and through marriage. Each life estate is coupled with a remainder estate.

6. In modern U.S. law, a residential leasehold has come to be regarded as a contract for services.

7. An easement is the right to use land for a specific and limited purpose.

8. The major difference between the easement appurtenant and an easement in gross is that the easement appurtenant involves a dominant parcel constraining a servient parcel, while the easement in gross is an inseparable feature of both parcels. Also, the easement appurtenant "runs with the land" and the easement in gross can be transferred without the transfer of any parcel.

9. Restrictive covenants are strictly private and can only be enforced by those holding a legal interest in the property. They would be enforced by filing suit for an injunction against a violation.

10. The lien priority is generally determined by the order in which they were created. However, property tax and assessment liens are always superior to any other liens.

11. The most common and least specialized form of direct co-ownership is tenancy in common.

12. Organization and rules are very important to a condominium because it serves as a small-scale government. The two most important documents for a condominium are the declaration and bylaws.

13. Two types of co-ownership between spouses, depending on the state, are elective share and community property.

14. The three levels of property rights in timeshare arrangements are a part of a fee simple interest, a leasehold interest for a tenancy for years, or a license for partial use of the timeshare.

Additional Readings

The following real estate law texts offer excellent additional material on many of the subjects in this chapter:

Jennings, Marianne, *Real Estate Law,* 6th ed., Cincinnati, OH: West, 2002.

Portman, J., and M. Stewart. *Every Tenant's Legal Guide,* 3rd ed. Berkeley, CA: Nolo Press, 2002.

Siedel, George J., III, Robert J. Aalberts, Janis K. Cheezem, *Real Estate Law,* 5th ed. Mason, OH: Thomson, 2003.

Real Estate Law: Leading Real Estate Lawyers Reveal the Secrets to the Art & Science of Real Estate Law. Boston, Mass. Aspatore Books, 2003.

Werner, Raymond J., *Real Estate Law,* 11th ed. Cincinnati, OH: South-Western, 2002.

Appendix Property Rights Relating to Water

Discussion in the text ennumerates several questions regarding rights to flowing water, ground water and coastal waters. These questions and cases are displayed in Exhibits 4-A and 4-B. Each situation is discussed below.

Navigability Status of the Water

The first three issues above—who owns the submerged land, who controls it, and who controls the water surface—depend on the navigability status of the water body in question. Three levels of navigability are important:

- Nonnavigable
- Intrastate navigable
- Interstate navigable

Navigability, according to the U.S. Supreme Court, depends on whether the body of water may be considered as part of, or susceptible to being part of a "highway for commerce." While the highway of commerce notion has been dominant in determining navigability, a few states recently have given less weight to commercial uses and more to public recreational usage in determining whether water is navigable. Determination of whether a body of water is intrastate or interstate navigable depends on whether the highway for commerce links more than one state so as to support interstate commerce.

Nonnavigable Bodies of Water

For nonnavigable bodies of water, the first three questions are answered as follows:

1. Land under the body of water is owned by the adjacent (**riparian**) landowners.[1] On a river, the riparian owners own to the middle of the river. On a lake the owners own a "slice of the pie" extending to the center of the lake.
2. Control of the submerged land is by the riparian landowners.
3. Control of the water surface is by the riparian landowners, but they share control of the entire surface jointly.

Exhibit 4-A Ownership and Control of Water Bodies and Riparian Land

Classification of Water Body	Ownership of Submerged Land?	Control of Submerged Land?	Control of Surface Water?
Nonnavigable	Riparian Land Owners	Riparian Land Owners	Riparian Land Owners, jointly*
Intrastate navigable	State	State	State
Interstate navigable	State	U.S. Army Corps of Engineers	U.S. Army Corps of Engineers

*Owners jointly share control of entire water surface.

1. Riparian land is land adjacent to a river or lake. Some restrict riparian to refer to land adjacent to nonnavigable streams or lakes.

Intrastate Navigable Bodies of Water

For intrastate navigable bodies of water, the state becomes the controlling entity:

1. Submerged land belongs to the state.
2. Control of the submerged land also is by the state.
3. Control of the surface use also is by the state.

Interstate Navigable Bodies of Water

For interstate navigable waters both the state and the U.S. Army Corps of Engineers become important:

1. Submerged lands belong to the state.
2. Control of the submerged lands is by the U.S. Army Corps of Engineers in accordance with the Clean Water Act of 1972.[2]
3. Control of the surface use also is by the U.S. Army Corps of Engineers.

Ocean Shorelines

For ocean shorelines the questions about land ownership, land control, and surface use have different answers that depend on the tide level. In general, land above the mean high tide level is owned and controlled by the adjacent landowners. Land between the mean high tide and mean low tide is owned and controlled by the state as a public trust.[3] Land below the mean low tide level is owned and controlled by the government of the United States.

Use of the Water Itself

www.epa.gov/region5/ water/cwa.htm

Clean Water Act: see numerous valuable references under "doctrine of prior appropriation"

In the United States there are two very different traditions concerning the use of water. The first, found in states with a history of relatively high rainfall and ample flowing water, is the doctrine of reasonable use. The other tradition, in states with scarce flowing water, is the doctrine of prior appropriation. The doctrine of **prior appropriation** is the simpler of the two. It simply gives all rights of use to the first person that claims them. Any subsequent party can make no claim for the water. While this prior appropriation sometimes is tempered by the reservation of water rights for matters of public interest, it generally is strictly interpreted, making water rights a most precious asset in the "prior appropriation" states.[4]

Exhibit 4-B Ownership and Control of Ocean Shoreline

Zone	Normal Owner
Above mean high tide?	Adjacent landowners
Between mean high and mean low tides?	State
Below mean low tide?	Government of the U.S.

2. Passed in 1972, the Clean Water Act established a national objective to restore and maintain the chemical, physical, and biological integrity of the nation's surface waters so that "fishable and swimmable" water would be achieved. The act assigned sweeping power to the U.S. Army Corps of Engineers to regulate not only interstate navigable waters, but much of the watershed of the rivers involved.

3. By the doctrine of public trust, some states have been held to own all tidewater land, regardless of the extent to which private owners may have used, developed, and paid taxes on the lands. This issue has enormous implications for mineral rights, for example, with oil rights in tidal marsh areas.

4. Prior appropriation states include Alaska, Arizona, Colorado, Idaho, Montana, Nevada, New Mexico, Utah, and Wyoming.

www.mhhe.com/lingarcher1e

In **"reasonable use"** states a riparian owner can use water as long as the use does not unreasonably interfere with use of it by other riparian owners. Courts have considered a number of issues in sorting out the meaning of reasonable use, including desirability of the use, suitability of the use, and risks or harm that may result.

Ten states have adopted a blend of the prior appropriation doctrine and the reasonable use doctrine. Usually, these approaches restrict riparian use to a level that prevailed at some reference date in the past.[5] As water becomes increasingly scarce in many of the "reasonable use" states, one might expect new blends of the doctrines to emerge.

Use of Groundwater

Rights to the use of groundwater follow the rights to the use of flowing water. That is, in "prior appropriation" states, rights to groundwater are by prior appropriation as well. However, not all "reasonable use" states distribute groundwater by the reasonable use doctrine. A few follow an absolute ownership rule whereby the landowner can extract water without limit.

5. These blend states include California, Kansas, Mississippi, Nebraska, North Dakota, Oklahoma, Oregon, South Dakota, Texas, and Washington.

chapter five

Market Determinants *of* Value

Learning Objectives

After reading this chapter you will be able to:

1. Explain the role of transportation modes and natural resources in the location and evolution of cities.

2. Define economic base activities, distinguish them from secondary activities, and explain the role of both in the growth or decline of a city.

3. Identify supply factors influencing the growth of a city.

4. Demonstrate how demand for access influences the value of urban land and determines the patterns of location of activities within a city.

5. Explain what effects evolving transportation technology, evolving communications technology and changing production and retailing methods have had on urban form.

6. Distinguish between "convenience goods" and "comparison goods" in their urban location patterns.

7. Define industry economies of scale and agglomeration economies of scale, and offer examples of each.

Introduction

To determine the value of a property, the most difficult and critical part of the task is to evaluate the market for the property in order to estimate its future cash flows. Some stories from real estate experience help to make this case.

Market Misjudgments In Real Estate

In the early 1970s most downtowns of the United States witnessed the completion of office buildings that set new records in size, height, and cost. Unfortunately, many of the very buildings that defined new skylines for U.S. cities also defined new levels of financial loss because they fell far short in occupancy. In Atlanta, Miami, Minneapolis, and many other cities, the largest building on the downtown skyline was also the largest economic disaster. On the island of Manhattan, alone, the office market became so overbuilt that the resulting value of the new structures fell to approximately a billion dollars below their cost of construction. What is most intriguing about this office market disaster of the mid-1970s was its repetition in even larger terms little more than a decade later. By the end of the 1980s the average occupancy of major office buildings across the United States was falling toward a devastating 80 percent after a new building boom added more than 30 percent to an already ample supply.

The problem of market misjudgment is not limited to office buildings. In St. Louis the Pruitt-Igoe public housing project was completed in 1954 and heralded worldwide as a model for a generation of postwar public housing projects that followed. Unfortunately, this 33-building complex for 10,000 occupants was found to be ill-designed for the needs of the occupants and uninhabitable, setting a pattern for similar projects in the years that followed when it was completely demolished and replaced. In 1962 Robert Simon launched the new community of Reston, Virginia, in suburban Washington, D.C., which was heralded by architects and planners of the Western world as a model example of a new town. By 1967 he had lost control of the struggling community due to inadequate prospects for cash flow. In 1971 Walt Disney World in Orlando, Florida, opened to its first year with sensational success, receiving some 12 million visitors. Nearby, at the intersection of I-4 and the Florida Turnpike, sometimes referred to as the "bull's-eye" of Florida real estate, Gulf Oil Company's development subsidiary launched Florida Center, another in its series of "new communities," as it had done many times throughout the world. Only this time Gulf was building for the local market rather than its own employees. But the local market never came, and the project collapsed with gigantic financial losses. About the same time, the residential condominium was discovered in Florida and elsewhere. In the first half of the 1970s, close to a quarter million condominium units were launched. But the market turned out to want far fewer than that number. Thousands of units were either never completed or, in some cases, torn down shortly after being constructed to make the land available for more viable uses.

These stories are only some of the more spectacular examples of market misjudgments in real estate. Virtually every community has its album of stories of landowners, large and small, who built their dream project, only to have it die financially for lack of an adequate market. Frequently, the developer disappears from the industry and little attention is ever again paid to the failure.

Market misjudgments in real estate too often are enduring and disastrous because the commitment is large, permanent, and immobile. Further, many developers have learned through bitter and financially devastating experience that if the market they had counted on is not there when their project is completed, it is beyond their power to create it.

Minimizing Market Errors

How, as a real estate investor, does one prevent market disaster? As with any business venture, there rarely is a sure protection against market misjudgment; this risk simply "comes with the territory." However, there are important ways to manage the market risk in real estate. One way, as noted in Chapter 2, is to avoid real estate investments that have a high market risk. For example, one can avoid any kind of land development where the end user is not already "locked in." And one can avoid any investment where there is a prospect of major change in the users or tenants of the property. More generally, however, investors in real estate must become students of urban land use and urban real estate markets. Most properties will need new tenants or users from time to time, and the investor wants to be reasonably sure they will appear. This assurance depends, first of all, on the property being in a supportive market environment. Lacking this, little or nothing can save most real estate investments.

What does a real estate investor need to know about urban markets? First, it is valuable to recognize the fundamental forces that create these markets, which are the same forces that create and shape cities. In addition, it is valuable to understand what brings change to the shape of cities, and how this change takes place. Further, it is important to understand the variations among types of urban land uses—especially variations in their patterns of location—and variations in their relationships to other land uses, which we refer to as **linkages.**

In this chapter we first consider why cities exist, and examine the demand for access as the "gravity" that holds a city together. Then we consider factors that cause continuing change in this demand for access, thereby changing the ultimate shape and character of a city, bringing change to real estate markets. Next, we use the idea of demand for access to see how various land uses may compete with each other for locations in the city, how the outcome is determined, and how the result determines the topography of value for urban land. But there are important variations among land use types in how they need to arrange themselves across the urban landscape—some clustering close together, for example, and others dispersing evenly. We examine the causes and the variation in these patterns. Further, there are hierarchies in the resulting network of land uses, which we explore. Finally, we consider how the matrix of land uses within a city create markets in the traditional economic sense, with both demand and supply emerging from this matrix of land uses.

Concept Check

5.1   The demand for access between one urban activity and others is referred to as the activity's _____ .

Probably the best-known adage in real estate is that the three most important things about real estate are location, location, and location. The old saying survives because there is more than a little truth in it. But what does it really mean? This chapter might be thought of, in large part, as studying the many meanings of urban location.

The Creation, Growth, and Decline of Cities

Economic activity—production and exchange—brings people together. Traveling to the location of production or exchange requires time and cost whether it is commuting to work at a factory, traveling to a management meeting, calling on a customer, going shopping, or going to a show, concert, or sporting event. And time is valuable. Therefore, it is no surprise that human settlement has long tended to cluster so that people can gather more quickly and efficiently.

Where Cities Occur

The interesting question was where did these clusters occur, and economists have noted several answers. For example, preindustrial communities often centered around a religious institution or a fortress as the most important social and organizational entity in an agrarian society. But some of these towns grew into preindustrial cities, propelled by trade and exchange. And the most compelling locations for such cities were the intersections of different modes of transportation. Thus, many of the oldest cities were seaports where land travel and ocean travel interfaced. Still other great cities developed at the mouth of rivers where river transit intersected with oceans, such as New Orleans at the mouth of the Mississippi; New York at the mouth of the Hudson; Hamburg, Germany, at the mouth of the Elbe; and Rotterdam, the Netherlands, at the mouth of the Rhine. Yet other cities emerged at the intersection of rivers or trails, such as St. Louis, Missouri, at the confluence of the Ohio, Missouri, and Mississippi rivers; and St. Joseph, Missouri, where the Oregon Trail launched from the Missouri River. In the industrial age, the intersection of rail transportation with seaports or with other rail lines became locations for cities, as with Atlanta, Minneapolis, Chicago, and St. Louis. Historical changes in transportation modes have brought changing fortunes to many cities. New Orleans and Baltimore, for example, were equal in size, and second only to New York City in 1840. But their relative fortunes faded with the coming of the railroad, and New Orleans idled for most of a century before the discovery of oil nearby, the "rebirth" of the South, and other factors gave it new momentum.

Concept Check

5.2   The "gravity" that draws economic activity into forming cities is the need for

_____ .

Still other cities were born of mining and resource extraction. A number of American cities, for example, were propelled by coal and iron ore extraction, and then became efficient centers for heavy manufacturing. Other cities were propelled by the extraction of oil and gas. Thus, Houston and neighboring cities stretching as far east as New Orleans have become the world's largest concentration of petrochemical industries.

Concept Check

5.3   Historically, cities tended to form at the intersection of _____ .

In many cases the driving activity for a city has changed through time. Many of the great modern cities result from the good fortune of being in a location that became important for a chain of functions, or core activities, through time. Often, as one core activity declined, another emerged, sustaining the growth of the city from one era to another. Hence, Minneapolis, Chicago, and other major cities of the middle United States evolved core functions far beyond the agriculture-based economy that first brought them to maturity; Detroit went from fur and agricultural trade to iron industry and manufacturing, and then to automobiles; and Pittsburgh, Pennsylvania, transcended its original role as a river trade center with the birth of the iron and steel industries, which it then transcended to become a much more diversified center of commerce, manufacturing, research and health care.

Other cities struggled with the erosion of their economic base in recent decades. Duluth, Minnesota has mitigated the decline of its historic iron ore base through growth in tourism, general commerce and more diversified Great Lakes shipping. Youngstown, Ohio, awaits new direction after the devastating loss of its coal and steel mill base, and the city of Detroit similarly searches for its new directions after the decline of its central city automobile plants.

The Economic Base of a City

The birth of every city resulted from some function that it served for the economic world at large. The great trade cities, for example, provided an interface among multiple continents. In the industrial world, manufacturing cities serve the markets of an entire continent, if not worldwide, and resource extraction cities frequently ship to worldwide markets. University cities serve entire states, nations, or the world. Likewise, medical cities serve far more than the needs of a local population. Recognizing this, economists focus on the **economic base** of a city to understand it. The economic base is that set of economic activities that a city provides for the world beyond its boundaries (thus, often called its export base). The economic base of a city determines its growth or decline.

Concept Check

5.4   The theory underlying the concept of economic base is that cities exist to serve

_____ .

The Economic Base Multiplier. The concept of economic base is extremely useful. As one better understands the economic base of a city and therefore what it offers, or can offer, to the larger world, one has a better basis to understand its potential for future growth, or decline. Thus, for example, many cities heavily oriented toward Cold War defense production faced a time of stagnation following the fall of the Berlin Wall, and cities centered on supporting agriculture have faced decline for many decades as farms and farm populations have diminished in number. On the other hand, cities oriented to medical services such as Chapel Hill and Durham, North Carolina, or Rochester, Minnesota have seen strong growth in recent decades due to increased demand for medical services as average real household income rises with economic growth, as medical advancements occur, and as the population ages. Similarly, many university cities have experienced strong growth due to the expansion of university age population and the growing importance in modern economies of higher education. In short, it is imperative for persons considering real estate investments or real estate careers to be aware of the economic base of cities they are contemplating. This gives them a much better chance to understand the city's real estate character, and its potential for the future.

A city's economic base drives local economic activity and land use through a multiplier process. As suggested in Exhibit 5-1, base (export) activities and services bring money into a city, which then is respent and recirculated within the city. Since most of this recirculation occurs through paychecks or commissions, employment is a particularly important measure of multiplier impact.

Several factors affect the size or power of the base multiplier. For example, as cities become larger, they tend to "take in more of their own linen"; that is, they tend to provide more of their own local goods and services. Thus, for example, a small town seldom will have a large regional shopping mall, and will have a limited array of furniture stores, automobile dealerships, medical specialists, and business services. Therefore, residents will tend to make frequent trips to the "big city" for shopping and other services, spending income outside of their local community. However, as cities grow, they become capable of supporting a larger share of household and business services locally. Further, more isolated cities tend to recirculate more base income locally. As the cost of traveling to alternative cities is greater, residents become more willing to accept the goods and services available locally. As base firms and households respend a larger share of their initial income, their

Exhibit 5-1   The Economic Base Multiplier

5. Total community income is the sum of export dollars plus respent dollars

1. "Exports" bring dollars into the community

2. Most is respent on local goods and services

4. Some "leaks" into savings

Savings

3. Some "leaks" through outside expenditures

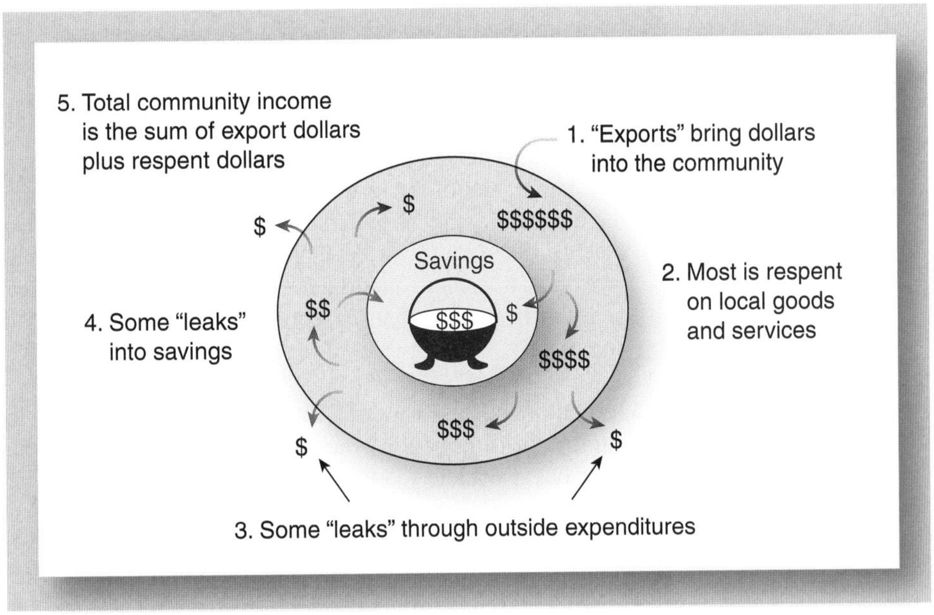

impact on the local community is greater. But as more of the money "leaks" out through expenditures elsewhere, the impact is less. Thus, for example, tourism in cities such as Orlando, Florida, or Las Vegas, Nevada is a rather high impact or high multiplier economic base activity. It is very labor intensive, and a large share of the money brought into a community through tourism goes to food and hospitality services that must be locally produced, by local labor. Even some of the ubiquitous screen-printed T-shirts may be created locally in the tourist city! On the other hand, most of the other necessary souvenirs are likely to come from China or another low-wage country, creating a "leakage" in the local tourism multiplier.

Another relatively high multiplier activity may be retirement. In Florida and other Sun Belt states, persons who have retired from colder climates bring their retirement income to the locality, purchasing local housing and a wide range of local services. In contrast to tourism and retirement, computer assembly may have a lower economic base multiplier. For example, many of the components for U.S.-bound computers tend to be manufactured in the Third World, then shipped to a U.S. city for final assembly. Thus, many of the dollars that might flow to the city of final assembly actually bypass it to flow elsewhere in the world. In short, economic base activities are those that bring money into a city to recirculate, producing additional income and employment. The impact of a base activity, per dollar of base income, varies, depending on how much of the base income finally recirculates within the local economy.

Concept Check

5.5   The size of an economic base multiplier depends on the amount of "_____" from the local economy.

Base and Local Economic Activity. In contrast to base activities are **local economic activities** (sometimes called secondary activities). Activities in a city that serve the local businesses and households are recirculating the income derived through base activities. Most urban land use is for local activities—retail centers, government and public land uses, medical offices, business service establishments, restaurants, automotive services, and so forth. The importance of this is that the creation of a new secondary activity facility, such as a new neighborhood shopping center, adds little to the economic activity of a city (except temporarily, through construction). Rather, it will compete with existing facilities for the total business derived from export activity. On the other hand, a new regional office center, a new manufacturing center, a new state government office center, or other new export activity will bring a true increase in export derived dollars, adding still more to secondary activity through the multiplier process.

In summary, persons involved in real estate need to be aware of the economic base in any community of interest. They must learn not only what the current economic base of the community is, but understand any important future economic base activity that may emerge. Then they can better judge the long-term prospects of the city for economic growth and business opportunities. Further, they will understand better how to assess the near-term impact of changes, either positive or negative, as businesses open or close in the community.

www.stats.indiana.edu/ uspr/a/us_profile_frame. html

Extremely accessible data, on population, income and employment for every U.S. County.

Indicators of the Economic Base. To quickly examine a local economic base, a growing number of information sources is available. Always important are data from a local chamber of commerce or government agency concerning the major employers, what they produce, and how many persons they employ locally. The most useful economic summary data on local economies is increasingly available on websites. For example, at www. stats.indiana.edu one can obtain a large portion of the available summary data on local pop-

5-1

A Redevelopment Where Everybody Wins

On the northeast border of Texas is the proud town of Marshall, population 24,000, in a county of about 60,000, and one of the oldest cities in the state. For a century its life revolved around the Texas and Pacific Railroad, and cotton production, followed later by oil and lumber. A center for production of fine railcars a century ago, it also is a town of well-built historic homes. But in the mid-1990s Marshall, like so many small cities in the United States, found itself with a struggling local economy. Its orientation to oil production and lumber gave it a ticket on the train of high unemployment and slow growth. Symptomatic of the economic challenges was the town's shopping center, the Marshall Mall, a 195,000-square-foot center built in 1980. By 1995 the anchor tenant, Kmart, occupying a third of the space, had closed, leaving 61,000 feet of darkness. The unemployment rate in the county was over 8 percent at that time, and the Marshall Mall, owned by a major life insurance company, was for sale for a small fraction of replacement cost.

Enter a thoughtful and enterprising development group. They learned about the mall, and also found that Blue Cross/Blue Shield of Texas was undertaking a program of regional decentralization. While working with the local economic development agency and submitting a proposal to BCBS for a regional processing center, the development group acquired the mall and set about to allow Kmart to buy out its lease. It worked. Kmart moved out, BCBS moved in. The mall came back to life, and rents began to flow. In 2003 the Marshall Mall is generating over three times as much net cash flow, and has increased its value probably fourfold. But Marshall Mall's recovery may be the minor story. BCBS has brought over 500 new jobs to the economic base of Marshall, along with a healthy economic base multiplier effect that may easily have doubled the number of new jobs. BCBS is now the city of Marshall's second largest private employer. Marshall's unemployment rate relative to the rest of Texas is the best it has been in years, and many more people are able to find jobs in their hometown.

Source: Kelley Bergstrom, Marshall Mall L.L.C., Kelley Bergstrom Investment Management, L.L.C.

www.census.gov/prod/ www/ccdb.html

County and City Data Book: data on a wide range of items for cities and counties.

ulation, income, and employment for any county in the United States.[1] Many other types of local data are available from the *County and City Data Book* produced by the U.S. Bureau of Census and also available through the Web.[2] A review of employer and summary economic data puts one in a position to ask informed questions about the local economic base and its future. In addition, most cities have public economic development authorities whose officials can respond to questions about the local economic base. Thus, with a modest amount of time and effort, one can gain an understanding of a city and its future opportunities for economic growth, new business opportunities, and real estate investments.

1. This website sets new standards for accessibility of data at the county level. Not only does it provide data from most available standard sources but it allows the user to specify a remarkable variety of useful display formats. For summary employment and population reports at the county level, few other sites should be necessary as data sources.

2. The *County and City Data Book* is downloadable in pdf format. While it is less convenient than the Indiana website, it provides a much wider range of county level data on housing, health, crime, businesses, government, and a host of other subjects.

One quick indicator of a community's economic base is called a **location quotient.** The underlying idea is that a community has some normal pattern of employment distribution, and excessive concentrations of employment in a particular industry must indicate that the community is producing surpluses for export in that industry. The location quotient is intended to identify such concentrations, and works as follows:

1. Compute the percentage of total employment in a given industry—for example, education—for the local community. Suppose this is 20 percent.
2. Compute the percentage in education employment for a reference population (often percentage employment for the entire United States is used). Suppose this is 9 percent.
3. Compute the location quotient, the ratio of the local to reference percentage. (20 ÷ 9 = 2.22)

In this case the 2.2 indicates that the concentration of education employment in the local community is 2.2 times normal, suggesting that education must be an export industry. By calculating location quotients for all industries, one can gain quick clues about the economic base of a local community. The primary database for these computations is the U.S. Census, which is readily available on the Web (See Explore the Web).

Explore The Web

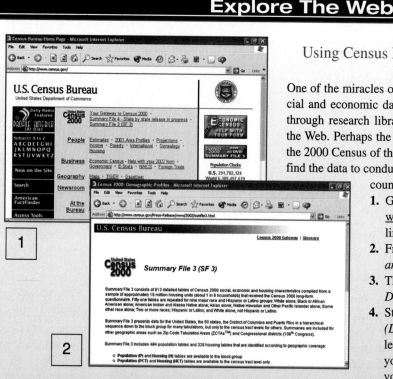

Using Census Data to Analyze a Community Economic Base

One of the miracles of the Web is that most of the nation's social and economic data, which previously was available only through research libraries, now is instantly available through the Web. Perhaps the most dramatic of these new resources is the 2000 Census of the United States. In this exercise, you will find the data to conduct a detailed economic base analysis of a county using location quotients.

1. Go first to the main U.S. Census website: www.census.gov. There select the third line entry, *Summary File 3 (SF3)*.
2. From there select *Data: Access to all tables and maps in American FactFinder.*
3. Then, at the top of the right-hand list, select *Detailed Tables.*
4. Staying with the default selection method *(List),* select *County* as your geographic level. You will then be prompted to select your state and county. Add the county of your choice to the selection box at the lower left. Now go back to the initial selection and choose *Nation,* and add this to the selection box as well. (This gives you a basis for comparing your county.)
5. Now click on *"Next"*. You are now offered dozens of tables of data from the 2000 Census. Scroll down to Table P49, and select.
6. Click *"Add,"* and *"Show Table."* You are looking at the raw data for your county and for the United States (by male and female separately) which can enable you to quickly compute location quotients. You simply find the percentage that each count is of the total employment (top of table). Then compute the ratio of county percentage to the U.S. percentage. For example, if the sum of male and female employment in finance, insurance, real estate and rental and leasing is 5 percent of the total in the county, but is 7 percent nationally, then the location coefficient is 5 ÷ 7 = .71, indicating a less than normal local concentration in that field.

Resources of a City: The Supply Side of Urban Growth

The analysis of a city's economic base is largely preoccupied with what the external world wants from the city, which is largely a question of external demand. The other side of the question is: What can a city offer to the world? This is a supply-side question. It is a longer-run issue because, while world markets for a city's base output can vary quite rapidly in the short run, a city's mix of output capacities changes slowly.

Labor Force Characteristics. The supply potential of a city depends on a diversity of factors. Certainly the nature of its available labor force is important. For example, when commercial aviation was born during the 1920s, Wichita, Kansas, was a small agricultural and oil city, not unlike many others across the Great Plains of the United States. A handful of local business leaders recognized the future of the aviation industry and that the small, often struggling farms of the region offered an abundant source of highly skilled, well-educated mechanics with a strong work ethic. They encouraged and financially supported the birth of several aircraft manufacturers, including two "barnstorming" aircraft designers of the era, Clyde Cessna and Walter Beech. In the next 70 years, Beech Aircraft, Cessna Aircraft, and other aircraft companies, were born and prospered in the area. Wichita became

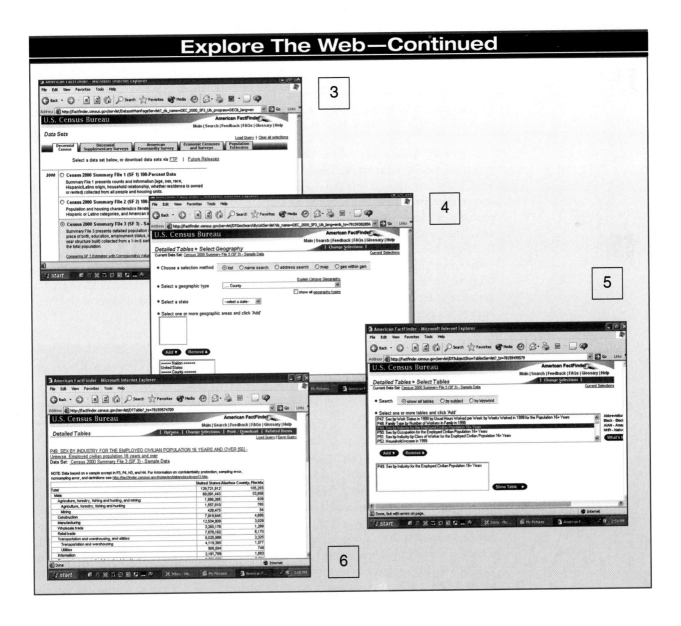

lanners develop land use plans to provide for growth and revitalization of communities, while helping local officials make decisions ranging from broad urban problems to new community infrastructure. They may participate in decisions on alternative public transportation system plans, resource development, and protection of ecologically sensitive regions. Planners also may be involved with drafting legislation concerning local community issues.

Urban and regional planners often confer with land developers, civic leaders, and public officials. They may function as mediators in community disputes and present alternatives

Urban and Regional Planners

acceptable to opposing parties. Planners may prepare material for community relations programs, speak at civic meetings, and appear before legislative committees and elected officials to explain and defend their proposals. Planners rely heavily on sophisticated computer-based databases and analytical tools, including geographical information systems (GISs).

Most entry-level jobs in federal, state, and local government agencies require a master's degree in urban or regional planning, urban design, geography, or a similar course of study. Planners must be able to think in terms of spatial relationships and visualize the effects of their plans and designs. They should be flexible and able to reconcile different viewpoints and to make constructive policy recommendations. The ability to communicate effectively, both orally and in writing, is necessary for anyone interested in this field.

Source: Summarized from *The Occupational Outlook Handbook* (current edition) from the U.S. Department of Labor, Bureau of Labor Statistics. http://stats.bls.gov/oco/ See this Web publication for many more details.

recognized as the world's leading center for light commercial aviation production. Legions of other plant and company location decisions attest to the importance that companies give to the character of the available labor force in selecting a location.

Quality of Life and Leadership. The existing labor force is not the only factor in the local growth equation. Increasingly, knowledge-intensive firms are sensitive to quality of life issues. They want to be where the characteristics of the community are attractive to current and prospective employees in terms of schools, recreational opportunities, cultural environment, housing, commuting, and other aspects of daily living. Further, companies are concerned with the business leadership and environment. Sophisticated firms recognize that their "cost of doing business" can depend on the support of local leadership and government in assuring, for example, roads, utilities, effective airport service, reasonable taxation, and compatible land use controls. The aircraft story in Wichita attests to the importance of business leadership. Central to the story was the support of the core business leaders who staked large amounts of money on the aircraft industry.

Concept Check

5.6   The customary analysis of a city's economic base tends to focus on _____ which tends to be a short-term phenomenon.

Industry Economies of Scale. Economists have long recognized that the growth of an industry within a city can create special resources and cost advantages for that industry. This phenomenon is called **industry economies of scale.** In Wichita, for example, the establishment of Beech and Cessna created an infrastructure of management and production knowledge, parts venders, a strong aeronautical engineering program at the local university, and other resources. Such resulting resources apparently were material in attracting other aircraft companies to the city. Thus, formerly Seattle-based Boeing placed it largest plant outside the state of Washington in Wichita, and Lear Jet was launched in the city several decades after the beginning of Beech and Cessna. More familiar examples of where industry economies of scale have propelled city growth include the automobile industry in Detroit, the motion picture industry in the Los Angeles area, the petrochemical industry in the Houston area, and, more recently, the computer and software industry in "Silicon Valley" in the San Francisco–San Jose region of California, and the computer industry in Austin, Texas.

Agglomeration Economies. As cities grow, they develop additional productive resources. Important examples include improved transportation terminals such as airline service and shipping terminals, specialized nonfinancial business services (e.g., in communications, technical support, and advertising), and more specialized financial services. Some observers point to cities with a Federal Reserve Bank as having a level of advancement and specialization in the field of financial services that other cities find difficult to match. These cities tend to host a diverse range of financial information providers and financial consulting firms such as money management firms that are much less common in other cities. The emergence of specialized resources in response to demand from multiple industries is referred to as **agglomeration economies.** This phenomenon is perhaps the distinctive economic feature of very large cities. New York, for example, has served historically as a birthplace for complex industries, hosting the creation of a wide array of innovations in electronics, publications, communications, finance, and other fields. This birthing role has been possible because highly specialized resources necessary for development of innovations are readily available in the region, sustained by the occasional needs of a vast array of different industries.[3]

An important effect of agglomeration economies in real estate is upon market risk. Both for real estate investments and for real estate careers, it may be that larger cities, with greater diversity of the economic base, and more advanced development of agglomeration economies, have greater capacity to withstand industry downturns. An example might be Los Angeles following the end of the Cold War. While Los Angeles was a major production center for military electronics, aircraft, and other material, and felt the severe effects of reduced military production, it has rebounded, riding the tide of other industries. One particular effect of agglomeration economies in real estate is that it causes institutional investors to favor real estate investments in large urban markets. This appears to be due to better transportation and information access for these cities, and the greater likelihood of successful retenanting if the current tenants are lost. Thus, perceived agglomeration economies directly impact the investment policies of major real estate investors.

Concept Check

5.7 Cost efficiencies that arise in a city due to concentration of an industry are called _____ whereas cost efficiencies arising from the concentration of multiple industries are called _____ .

The Shape of a City

We have said that the central force creating cities is the demand for proximity. The cost of distance works as an "economic gravity," forever offering gains in efficiency for production and exchange through proximity, and forever shaping urban form. While we will consider a variety of other influences that differentiate the tapestry of urban land use, all are subject to this demand for proximity.

Demand for Proximity and Bid-Rent Curves

To explore the effects of demand for proximity, it is helpful to construct a logical model. Known as a **bid-rent model** by land economists and geographers, this simplified story of how land users bid for location is remarkably helpful in revealing the influences on the way density of land use is determined, how competing urban land uses sort out their locations, how urban land value is determined, and why land use change occurs.

3. Ray, Vernon, *Metropolis 1985.* (Garden City, NY: Doubleday, 1963), pp. 99–118.

Exhibit 5-2   A Simple Bid-Rent Curve

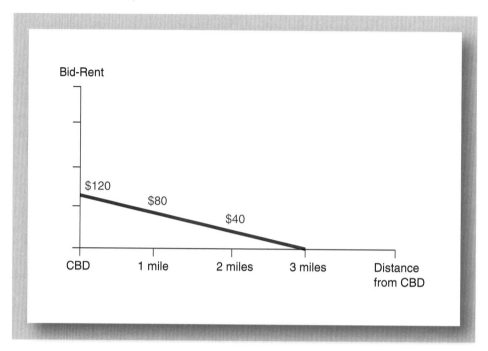

Imagine a one-dimensional world that exists along a single street, as in Exhibit 5-2. Suppose that all employment and exchange takes place at point zero, the central business district (CBD), and that each household must select a place to live along the street, where all housing spaces have identical physical features. For convenience, we will assume that each residential lot is 100 feet wide and that, initially, households live in what amount to identical motor homes (large recreational vehicles, or "RVs") that can be moved costlessly from one lot to another. (Thus, we only need to be concerned with paying rent for the lot, rather than for a lot and house.) Further, we will assume the lots are not owned by households, so that households must pay rent for a space. We will allow households to live on both sides of our simple street.

Suppose that each household contains one person, who is employed and completes one round-trip daily to the downtown. Suppose further that each person earns $20 an hour, and assume initially that all transportation is by car, at an average rate of 20 miles per hour. Finally, suppose that there are 318 households working downtown and seeking housing locations and they all make competitive bids for locations up to the amount that leaves them indifferent between winning and losing.

The principal question is this: What will households bid for the various residential lots in this simple world? The answer lies in recognizing that by living closer to the downtown, households reduce their time cost of commuting. The idea is that time saved from commuting can be used to earn money. From our assumptions, then, we can compute the cost of daily travel as $1.00 per mile ($20 per hour ÷ 20 miles per hour). Thus, a one-mile round-trip commute costs $2.00 per day in time given up. If each person works five days a week, 48 weeks a year, then they will spend 20 days a month, on average, commuting.

Using our assumptions, we now can consider how much households will bid for various locations on our urban street. With 318 households located on lots on both sides of the street, the farthest household from downtown commutes exactly three miles.[4] The cost of commuting from this lot will be $120 a month ($1 per mile × 3 miles × 2 directions × 20 days per month). Thus, this household will be willing to pay $120 per month more in rent

---

4. A mile is 5,280 feet. The midpoint of the most remote lot is located $50 + 158 \times 100 = 15,850$ feet from the center of downtown, whereas three miles is 15,840 feet.

to live downtown. (Remember, for simplicity, we assume there are no lifestyle or environmental differences in the two locations.) More generally, consider the choices of any commuter on any of the lots. By the logic above, we conclude that each commuter will be willing to bid $40 per month per mile to move closer to downtown than he or she currently lives.

Concept Check

5.8   The economic incentive that gives rise to bid-rent curves is the desire to reduce

_____ .

Notice that our simple model of land rent implies several things about the patterns of rent in our city. First, beginning from the edge of settlement, rent for lots increases at a rate of $40 per mile as one moves closer to downtown. As shown in Exhibit 5-2, we can think of this rent level as forming a line (or curve) that runs from zero at the border of the city to $120 downtown. But we also can see what might change this "bid-rent" curve. If individuals earn more than $20 an hour, then they have a higher time cost. This means that they will bid still more per month per mile to be closer to the central business district (CBD). If, for example, they earn $30 an hour, then commuting costs $1.50 per mile, workers will pay $60 per month per mile to move closer to the CBD ($1.50 × 2 directions × 20 days), and the most remote commuter will pay $180 to move downtown. On the other hand, suppose that average travel speed increases from 20 miles per hour to 30. Then less time is required to commute one mile, and being closer is less valuable. At 30 miles per hour, our commuter will only bid $26.67 per month per mile to move closer to downtown ($20 per hour ÷ 30 miles per hour × 2 directions × 20 days per month), and the most remote commuter will pay only $80 to move downtown. Finally, if more households arrive, this growth will push the edge of settlement farther out, causing bidding to begin at a greater distance from the CBD. This raises the bid-rent curve at every point.

Bid-Rent Curves with Multiple Types of Households. This simple bid-rent model enables us to think systematically about the factors that affect land value in a city, but it also can reveal how various land uses compete for space and sort themselves out on the urban map. Suppose that 106 of the households in our simple model are without cars, and people must walk to work. Suppose further they can walk, on average, at three miles an hour. From these assumptions, the cost of commuting for a walker is $266.67 per mile per month ($20 per hour ÷ 3 miles per hour × 2 directions × 20 days). In our original model, a driver living one mile from downtown is willing to bid $80 to be at that location rather than at the edge of the city. However, a walker is willing to bid far more, and will preempt the location. Since every walker will outbid every driver, all of the walkers will live in the first mile adjacent to the CBD. The most remote walker will simply outbid drivers, paying $80 per month in rent. But, just as drivers compete with each other, the walkers will bid against each other to live still closer. Since they are willing to pay $266.67 more to move the last mile to downtown, the bid-rent at the city center, determined by the walkers, is $346.67 ($80 + $266.67). The case with both walkers and drivers reveals how two different land uses with different intensities of need for access will get sorted out on the urban map. The workers with more costly commutes will command the closer locations and will bid against each other to set a higher level of rent. The resulting rent topography, or rent gradient, is shown in Exhibit 5-3.

Concept Check

5.9   How does each of these affect the *slope* of a bid-rent curve: Faster travel, more frequent trips, more commuters (think carefully!), higher-density housing (again, think carefully!), higher hourly wage rate.

Exhibit 5-3   Rent Gradient with Drivers and Walkers

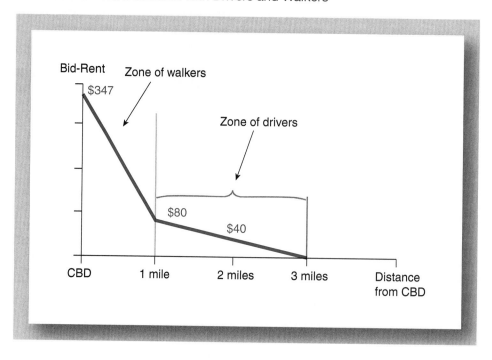

To further illustrate the model, suppose 26 of the households are medical doctors with incomes of $200 per hour. Assume the doctors have their offices in their homes and commute by car to a CBD hospital. Commuting to the hospital then costs each doctor $400 per month per mile ($200 ÷ 20 miles per hour × 2 directions × 20 days). Thus, all of the doctors will outbid every other household for the closest lots, and the closest lots to the CBD become medical office/residences rather than strictly residences. Bid-rent for the closest lot to downtown now becomes approximately $380.[5]

Concept Check

5.10   Why is it that in a simple bid-rent model a person who commutes on foot will outbid one who commutes by car for the closest space to downtown?

From this example, it is apparent how land users with the highest cost of commuting to downtown will bid the closest land away from other users, followed by the group having the second highest cost of commuting, and so forth. Thus, different land uses occupy different "zones" along the distance from the center, with rent at any point determined by the combined bidding of all current and lower intensity (i.e., lower commuting cost) land users. The resulting rent gradient for our three example groups is shown in Exhibit 5-4.

Effect on Development Intensity. Not only does the bidding among various groups of commuters establish a rent gradient and sort out different zones of users along the curve, it also affects the density of land use. Since the locational rent increases with proximity

---

5. This assumes that there now are 26 doctors, and 292 other commuters, of which 80 walk and 212 drive. Drivers, starting from three miles from downtown bid rents up from zero to $80. Walkers dominate bids for the next three-quarters of a mile (40 lots ÷ 52.8 lots per mile), bidding rent from just over $80 up to $282.00 (approximately ($266.67 ÷ 52.8 lots per mile × 40 lots) + $80). Finally, doctors dominate the closest quarter-mile, bidding rent from just over $282 to about $380 for the first lot adjacent to the downtown.

Exhibit 5-4 Rent Gradient with Drivers, Walkers, and Medical Offices

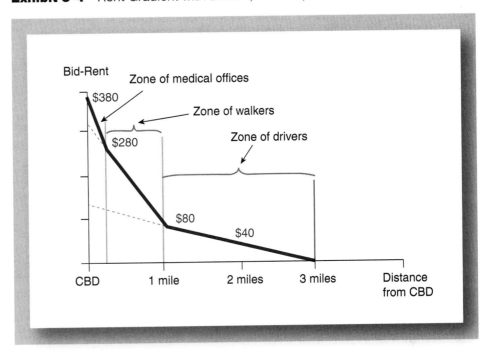

to the CBD, so also does the incentive to build upward on the lot to allow multiple tenants. Even though the cost of building structures increases with density (structure height), higher locational rent justifies the additional cost per unit in order to capture multiple tenants. The effect rapidly becomes too complex for a simple numerical example. However, note that the profits from capturing multiple tenants increase as the lot is closer to the CBD. Thus, higher construction costs per unit are justified, and density of land use, through smaller lots and higher buildings, tends to increase with proximity to the downtown.

Multiple City Centers. Modern cities have multiple centers, with different core activities. We can expand our bid-rent model to represent this. Suppose our city has both a central business district and a medical center, including related physicians' offices and support services (e.g., laboratories, equipment venders), located just over a mile from the downtown. For simplicity, we assume that all nonmedical activities are in the CBD, while all medical-related activities are centered around the hospital. In this case, the pattern of rent gradients and land use zones would be as shown in Exhibit 5-5. As before, the rent gradient will extend from the downtown to the perimeter of land use, with multiple zones of land use differentiated by cost of commuting. But preempting part of this curve will be curves extending in either direction from the hospital. These curves also will have multiple segments representing the bidding of hospital-oriented groups with different costs of commuting. Presumably physicians' offices will have the highest cost of commuting to the hospital due to high opportunity cost and frequent needs to commute. The supporting laboratories, medical equipment vendors, and other medical services will probably be second while the homes of persons employed at the medical center might be third. To the extent the households commuting to the medical center have higher wages (opportunity cost of time) or they commute more frequently than commuters to the downtown, they will bid residential space away from CBD-oriented commuters. Thus, the pattern of Exhibit 5-5 results. At every location on our line, the land use is determined by bidding among multiple potential land users. The highest bidder at each location determines both the land use and, through interaction with all other bidders, the level and slope of the rent gradient.

Exhibit 5-5 Rent Gradient with Medical Center

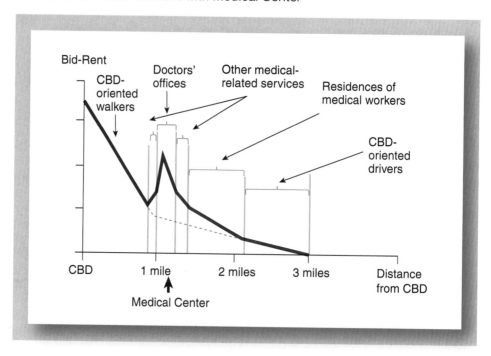

The bid-rent model also helps to understand land use changes. As a particular center grows, it generates more bidders for proximity. So, at the perimeter of the center, land is bid away from land uses oriented to elsewhere in the city.

Bid-Rent Curves, Urban Land Uses, and Land Value Contours

While bid-rent curves give a powerful means of understanding the forces in determining urban land uses and land values, they cannot capture all of the influences on land use. Whereas bid-rent curves are based on one dimension of access need (the single-person commute), both households and businesses have multiple needs for access. Real estate analysts often refer to such needs for access as linkages, the important spatial connections between one urban land use and others. Restated, then, the problem with our bid-rent model is that it is based on only one linkage, the commuting linkage, whereas urban land uses involve many linkages. For example, a household may involve two or more working persons, each with different commuting linkages. In addition, the household has linkages to schools, friends, shopping, and other points of destination. In reality, all of these linkages enter into the household's bid for a location. In short, the bid-rent "equation" for a household or business may be more complex than can be accounted for in a simple graphical model. But the bid-rent model still reveals the fundamental relationships that are the urban economic "gravity" creating, shaping, and sustaining cities.

Changing Transportation, Changing Technology, and Changing Urban Form

Analysts have long recognized that cities are made up of a tapestry of different land uses. Through bid-rent curves we have seen the dynamics of how this tapestry is composed and how it can change. But transportation modes and production technology are the dominant factors in determining the number and location of nuclei within a city. As transportation modes and production technology have changed, so has our notion of urban form.

Exhibit 5-6 Early 20th-Century Models of Urban Form

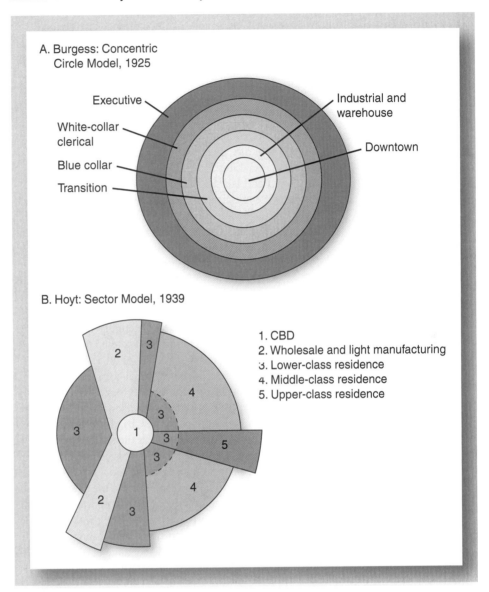

A. Burgess: Concentric
   Circle Model, 1925

Executive

White-collar
clerical

Blue collar

Transition

Industrial and
warehouse

Downtown

B. Hoyt: Sector Model, 1939

1. CBD
2. Wholesale and light manufacturing
3. Lower-class residence
4. Middle-class residence
5. Upper-class residence

Concentric Ring Model of Urban Form. In 1925 E. W. Burgess offered a **concentric ring model** of urban form, as depicted in Exhibit 5-6, panel A.[6] In the center circle is the CBD. Adjacent to it is a zone of transition which contains warehousing and other industrial land uses. This is followed by a ring of lower-income residential land use, followed by a ring of middle- and upper-income land use. In broad terms, it is easy to see a correspondence between this early model of land use and the notion of bid-rent curves. Each ring represents a different level of commuting cost to the CBD. The only puzzling aspect of the model is why lower-income residential land use is closer to the CBD than higher-income land use. Economists have long contemplated this apparent anomaly. They have offered as an explanation that higher-income households want sufficiently larger residential lots so that as they move closer to the city the rise in land prices more than offsets their savings in travel cost. There probably are dynamic reasons as well for the closer-in location of lower-income

6. E. W. Burgess, "The Growth of the City: An Introduction to a Research Project," in *The City,* ed. R. E. Park et al. (Chicago: University of Chicago Press, 1925).

housing. Rapidly changing transportation systems and technology may cause housing design to change, rendering older housing obsolete. Then higher-income households will tend to leave older houses, allowing them to "filter down" to lower-income households. Meanwhile, the most available locations to build new housing are at the perimeter of the city, causing higher-income households to move further from the CBD.

While the concentric ring model of urban form seems inappropriate today, it can be largely explained by the transportation and production technologies of its day. In 1923 less than half of U.S. households had acquired Ford's miraculous Model-T (the only affordable car), and most of these had been purchased within the last five years. Railroads were at their zenith in the economy and were the primary means of transportation. Chicago, where Burgess formulated the concentric model, was centered on the main railroad station, Union Station (see Exhibit 5–7). Large parts of the downtown, including most of the modern-day park areas and lakeside office building complexes of the city, were railroad switchyards. Business communication was limited to few and rudimentary telephone systems, with no ability to transmit documents or graphical information except by physical means. Thus, for transportation and communication reasons, production, management offices, and rail stations had to be in close proximity. The elevator, made practical by Elisha Otis in the mid-19th century, became the means of facilitating the necessary close proximity. Management offices, production facilities, and warehousing were constructed vertically, packed close together in the center of the city around the railroad facilities.

Sector Model of Urban Form. Roughly a decade after the concentric ring model of Burgess was published, Homer Hoyt studied data on residential rents from 1878 to 1928 for 142 cities in the United States.[7] He found a seemingly different pattern, shown in panel B of Exhibit 5-6, characterized by radial corridors or wedges, particularly for higher-income residential land use. In addition, he found that middle-income housing tended to be in wedges adjacent to the high-income corridors. Low-income housing, on the other hand, tended to be in areas opposite the CBD from the high-income corridor, typically adjacent to industrial areas. This is known as the **sector model** of urban form.

The difference between the Burgess concentric ring model and the Hoyt sector model tends to be overstated. A close examination of the diagrams from the two researchers shows some apparent evidence corresponding to the alternate theory in both cases. However, there is little question about the sector patterns reported by Hoyt. Furthermore, inspections of residential rental rate patterns during the 1990s in Moscow, Russia, for example, show a very strong pattern of wedges or corridors that strongly coincide with the Hoyt model. Thus, the sector pattern appears to span a wide range of time and cultures, probably shaped by the nature of the prevailing urban transportation system.[8]

Concept Check

5.11 The Burgess concentric model of urban form was conceived in an era when the dominant form of transportation was by _____ and the principal method of moving goods within factories was by _____ .

In American cities, it is generally conceded that the sector model was a good characterization of urban patterns when Hoyt did his analysis using pre-1930 data. However, it also is accepted that this model is no longer as valid. Two trends, at least, have served to

7. Homer Hoyt, *The Structure and Growth of Residential Neighborhoods in American Cities* (Washington DC, Federal Housing Administration, 1939).

8. Until the dissolution of the USSR in 1991, there were few automobiles in Moscow. Automobile transportation was probably similar to that of the United States in the early 1920s. Urban commuting and other personal travel was by bus or by the highly developed subway system.

weaken the sector pattern. First, in the last 70 years heavy manufacturing and industrial pollution have diminished, reducing the environmental differential across areas of the city and dependence on rail access. Second, the motor vehicle rapidly replaced fixed rail transit in intraurban use after 1920.

A Multinuclei City. By 1945 departure from a single-center city was clear. In that year Harris and Ullman, in a landmark study, coined the term **multinuclei city.**[9] The motor vehicle, combined with new technologies of production, had released the city from its absolute ties to the CBD. Since 1945 continued advances in motor vehicles, along with waves of other technological innovations, have continued to propel urban activity away from the CBD, as we describe below.

Concept Check

5.12 The radial or "pie slice" pattern in the Hoyt sector model of urban form probably can be explained by the dominance of _____ for intra-urban transportation at the time the model was formulated.

Technological Change in the 20th Century. Since 1930 technological changes have occurred on numerous fronts to propel employment centers out of the CBD. First, of course, was the transportation revolution, which was accompanied by a revolution in manufacturing organization and products, propelled especially by World War II. In the years following the war modern air-conditioning and fluorescent lighting were introduced, enabling new forms of urban structures. This was accompanied by the rapid evolution of self-service retailing technology that resulted in the emergence of modern shopping facilities. Finally, the most recent chapter of change has been the revolution in data processing and electronic communication.

The Urban Transportation Revolution. The most obvious aspect of the transportation revolution was the rise of the automobile. As late as 1920 there was roughly one car for every 13 persons, and few highways. But 10 years later there was approximately one car for every five persons, approaching one per household. Further, by 1930 numerous state and federal laws had been enacted to support construction of roads for automobiles, including gasoline taxes to fund construction. By 1940 nearly half of the roads and highways in the United States had hard surfaces of some sort to support motor vehicle usage.

The emergence of the truck and bus have been at least as important as the car for the effect on urban form. The bus enabled the creation of lateral as well as radial passenger routes, with flexibility of routes to accommodate change. In the truck-oriented world of today, it is perhaps hard to appreciate the growth, not only in the number of trucks since 1920, but also in their design and capacity. Whereas the passenger capacity of cars has changed relatively little since 1920, the capacity and variety of trucks has grown manyfold. In short, the transformation of the United States into a motor vehicle society largely took place in the period from 1920 to 1940. It continued to accelerate after World War II with the increase in the number of vehicles and the construction of the Interstate Highway System, tollways, and other express highways. The impact on future urban form was profoundly affected by both the car and the truck, and continues to respond to the completion of new roadway systems in recent decades.

The Production Revolution. Simultaneous with, and driven by, the motor vehicle revolution came the emergence of assembly lines. Increasingly, the efficient layout of assembly lines was horizontal, particularly as automation advanced. Thus, the older factories of the

---

9. C. D. Harris and E. L. Ullman, "The Nature of Cities," *Annals, American Academy of Political and Social Science* 242 (1945), pp 7–17.

central city became obsolete. With trucks, cars, and highways, it now was possible to relocate production away from central railroad yards to areas where horizontal buildings and large parking lots were feasible. In numerous cities the movement of manufacturing to the suburbs was accelerated by the emergence of new industries such as the aircraft industry, especially during World War II. In the postwar era, flexibility in location was further advanced by the trend in the economy away from heavy manufacturing and toward services. Thus, there was increasing recognition of the growth of "footloose" industries that were not tied to rail lines, ports, or natural resources.

Concept Check

5.13   One of the most profound forces bringing about urban change in the United States is that whereas cars were a novelty in 1915, most households owned one by about

_____ .

Air Conditioning, Lighting, and New Forms of Retailing and Offices. Parallel with advances in production technology came changes that altered retailing and offices. First, during the 1930s fluorescent lighting became effective, enabling both retail facilities and office buildings to operate for the first time without direct sunlight. Coupled with this was the emergence of air-conditioning, making it possible to eliminate window ventilation. For both retailing and office facilities, these technological advances propelled radical changes toward much larger floor plans for structures, hastening the obsolescence of traditional downtown structures and enabling the creation of modern, horizontal retailing facilities. Thus, the technology became available for the supermarket and the modern shopping center, adding another large thrust to the migration of employment to suburban nuclei following World War II.

Advances in Data Processing and Communications. One challenge that was posed by the migration of production out of the central city was separation of management from the production processes for the first time. When production was downtown, management could be at the production site and still maintain the necessary interface with banks and other external sources of financing, as well as other contacts important to the firm. This challenge was mitigated, first by the evolution of reliable and efficient telephone service, then by the emergence of high-speed data processing and reporting, then further by the growth of electronic data and document transmission, and in the present by wireless technology. As a result, it has become increasingly feasible to separate production processes from central management, further weakening a vast array of traditional intrafirm linkages and further enabling new spatial arrangements of production. Web-based information systems, e-mail and cellular phones may have reduced the cost of distance still further in recent years, with effects that are not yet clear.

Concept Check

5.14   The demand for space for horizontal factories was greatly accelerated in the 1920s by development of _____ production.

Combined Effects on Urban Form.   The transportation and technology changes of the last 80 years obviously have had profound effects on urban form. Not the least of these is that most urban employment is now outside the CBD. Whereas, in 1920, the largest percentage of all types of employment was in the CBD, today even the most centralized remaining function—office employment—is largely outside the CBD. In Houston, for example with a relatively strong central city remaining, only about 20 percent of major office space is located in the CBD. Every other kind of urban activity is even less concentrated downtown. An important point about this is that it is easy to underestimate how long it takes the urban environment to adapt to new transportation and technology. For example, many downtown streets were laid out in the preautomobile era, and office buildings still exist that were built during the 1930s. While the process of adaptation in central cities has been greatly accelerated in many places by urban renewal programs, many aspects of the process are slow. The full impact of opening a new interstate highway can take decades, and its effect can be so gradual that naïve observers perceive existing arrangements to be a steady state when, in fact, they are being impacted by slow but inexorable change.

Concept Check

5.15   Modern office structures and retail facilities were not possible before the
development of _____ and _____ .

The dramatic change in North American cities during the 20th century is suggested by two pairs of photos in Exhibit 5-7. The first pair, of Jacksonville, Florida, are particularly representative. In the 1955 view, virtually every type of urban land use is still concentrated in the downtown. Just out of view to the left is a major element in creating the scene, the large Florida East Coast Railroad Depot. In 1985, little else remains downtown but office functions and government. By then, the (out of view) railroad station also is out of service and awaiting new use as a convention center. Meanwhile, in the perimeter of the newer photo is evidence of the interstate highway system, symbol of the new era.

The Chicago photos are less dramatic in showing the relocation of urban activities because Chicago's downtown is one of the few that has not fully succumbed to motor vehicles. Nevertheless, it dramatizes the change from dependency on rail transportation. The photos reveal that Chicago's CBD once was formed between railroad stations and the related marshaling yards. In the later photo, the extent of change is such that the rail yards are totally replaced with the high-rise offices, apartments, and hotels of the "New East Side," at the top of the parks and the formerly dominating railroad tracks are barely detectable in the photo.

Differing Location Patterns of Urban Land Uses

The models of urban form that we have considered recognize the qualitatively different types of land uses—residential, industrial, educational, medical, and other. Within some of these types of land use there are polar patterns of location among competitors. On one extreme are so-called central place activities. The other extreme is agglomeration activity.

Convenience "Goods" and Central Place Patterns

Some types of urban services and products are **convenience activities,** meaning that users seek to obtain the good or service from the closest available source. Examples typically include bakeries, delicatessens, hair salons and barbershops, supermarkets, fast-food restaurants, copy shops, dry cleaners, coffee boutiques, and many others. Providers of this type of "good" are compelled to disperse fairly evenly across the urban landscape.

The logic works as follows. Consider, for example, a convenience-type grocery store (a "quickshop") serving surrounding single-family residential areas. As a customer moves farther away from the store, the customer will patronize it less, perhaps tending to make a few, planned trips to a full-line supermarket instead of many, spontaneous trips to the quickshop. If there are multiple, virtually identical quickshops at the same location, they will compete for the same available market. So, even if the market at that location were large

Exhibit 5-7   The Transformation of American Downtowns Jacksonville, Florida

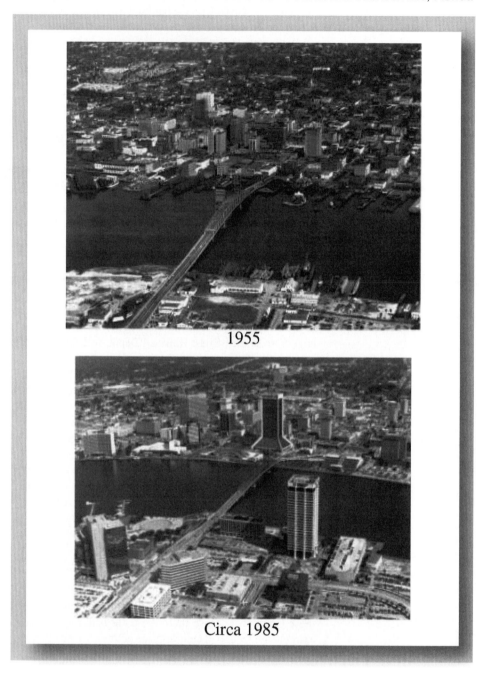

1955

Circa 1985

enough to support multiple quickshops, the profit-maximizing strategy for each competitor is to separate from the others in order to capture a larger share of the market. In summary, the nature of "convenience" shopping creates the tendency for competitors to disperse over the region of potential customer units (households) to the point where each establishment is equidistant from any other, and they are separated by the minimum distance that allows sufficient customers to support each establishment.

The resulting pattern of establishment locations is suggested in Exhibit 5-8. If the influence of transportation routes and constraints such as turning barriers were ignored, and if the density of customers were even, the resulting pattern of locations and markets would be a "honeycomb" of hexagonal markets with an establishment at the center of each cell

Exhibit 5-7 Continued The Transformation of American Downtowns
Chicago, Illinois

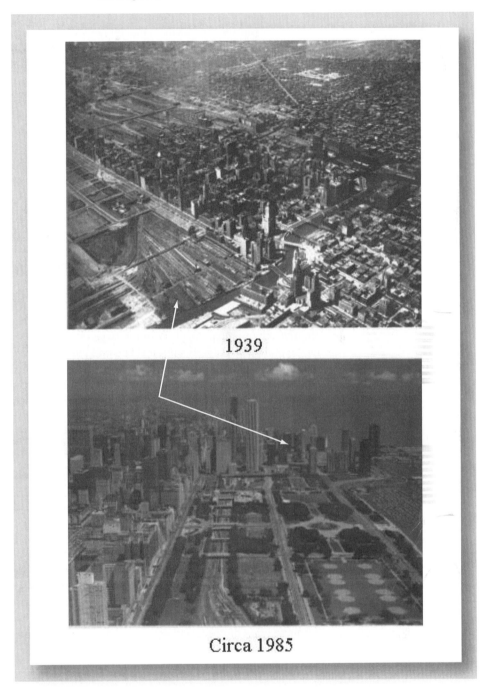

1939

Circa 1985

in the honeycomb. Naturally, this pattern is distorted by variations in customer concentrations, travel routes, turning limitations, and variation in travel times, but the basic idea remains compelling.

At some level of geography most urban goods and services have a **central place pattern.** For example, even though regional shopping malls are driven by a phenomenon that is the polar opposite of convenience shopping, a large metropolitan area will have numerous regional malls. In relation to each other, they tend to locate in a central place pattern.

Exhibit 5-8   Idealized Location Pattern of Convenience Goods and Services

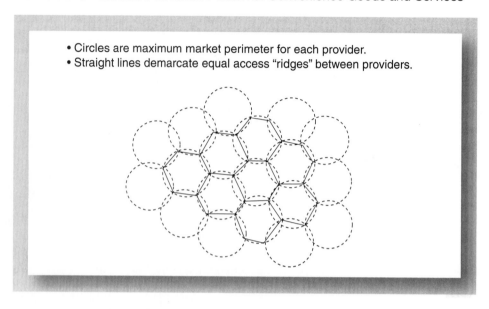

- Circles are maximum market perimeter for each provider.
- Straight lines demarcate equal access "ridges" between providers.

Geographers have studied central place patterns extensively, and have noted that there are hierarchies among them. Within a large city, regional malls and large discount stores may represent a relatively high-level central place function, while sandwich shops or hair salons may represent low-level ones. The difference in hierarchy is by area or population required for a viable market. The important features of all central place activities is that they tend to be evenly dispersed, and serve some minimum population as a threshold market.

Concept Check

5.16   The essential feature of a convenience good or central place activity is that households, in acquiring it, go to the _____ source.

Comparison Goods and Clustering

The opposite of central place location patterns is clustering. In retailing this occurs with shopping or **comparison activities** ("goods"). Examples include apparel stores like those within a regional mall, car dealers, club districts, and other types of businesses where customers typically wish to go from one competitor to another in the course of a single trip. For these types of goods and services, the optimal location pattern is to cluster, and shopping malls are a major example of the phenomenon.[10]

Industry Economies of Scale and Clustering

In addition to the comparison behavior of customers, other forms of clustering also result from the industry economies of scale discussed earlier; that is, by clustering, firms engaged in the same kind of activity may create mutual efficiencies. For example, clustered suburban office buildings appear to be increasingly attractive to many office tenants. One reason for this may be the supporting services that tend to result when many offices cluster in the

---

10. Regional malls and so-called festival shopping centers exemplify the comparison activity. In contrast, neighborhood shopping centers anchored by a supermarket, and "power centers" anchored by discount stores are primarily convenience good centers.

Industry Issues

5-2

W al-Mart continues to single-handedly change the face of suburban retailing. The company that challenged, and came to dominate an already mature industry of discount stores in the past, has launched a new attack on established forms of discount stores and supermarkets. From an insignificant place in the rankings of supermarkets, Wal-Mart has risen to take over the position of number one food retailer in the nation in 2002 with more than a 17 percent market share (combining all Wal-Mart related food stores). This has left second place Kroger well behind with a market share of 12 percent. What is most remarkable is how Wal-Mart is

It's a bird, it's a plane, it's a Supercenter!

winning this food fight: with Supercenters. It built its first 140,000-square-foot-plus Supercenter in 1988. At the end of 2002, it had opened over 1,250 Supercenters and is projected by 2006 to have opened nearly 2,000 of them. Wal-Mart will then have 700 more Supercenters than it has standard discount stores. Supercenters accounted in 2002 for nearly half of Wal-Mart food sales. Analysts quoted in industry media predict that by 2006 Wal-Mart will account for one-fourth of all food sales, largely through Supercenters.* As a result, it is estimated that at least one in 18 existing supermarkets will be forced to close.

The raging success of the Supercenter flies in the face of conventional retail wisdom. Few believed in the past that shoppers would combine food purchases with shopping for other retail goods. The success of this unorthodox approach spells trouble not only for existing neighborhood shopping centers anchored by weaker supermarkets, but it also spells the demise of many conventional discounters, including a large number of existing Wal-Marts.

*Progressive Grocer, December 1, 2002, p. 36.

same location, including travel agencies, car rentals, office supplies, computer services and support, restaurants, health clubs, day care, and many other kinds of business and employee services. In addition, a highly visible and well-planned cluster of buildings may afford office tenants an attractive setting that has image or advertising value, or value as a pleasant environment for employees.

Concept Check

5.17 The location tendency of comparison activities is to _____ whereas the location tendency of convenience activities is to _____ .

Another interesting example of industry economies of scale is the typical large research university. Most graduate school and research oriented universities have many different colleges, with separate administrations, separate students, separate curricula, and separate facilities. Thus, it may be less than obvious why the university exists as a total unit. Indeed, it is not uncommon for political leaders to suggest that various professional schools be pulled away from a major state university and relocated to their favorite urban center.

The explanation for the multicollege university lies in industry economies of scale. For example, even schools as diverse as medicine, engineering, and law share a multitude of

Community Development Specialist

ommunity development is the economic, physical, and social revitalization of a community led by the people who live in that community. Community developers work in community-based organizations; banks; city, state and federal government; foundations; real estate development companies; social service agencies; job training and placement organizations; investment firms; and think tanks. Community developers do things with, not to or for, the community.

They transform a brownfield into a neighborhood shopping center, creatively finance low-cost mortgages, shape public policy, develop community health centers, build housing to shelter battered women and their families, train residents for well-paying jobs, start new local businesses, organize tenants to convert their apartments to cooperative ownership, create a joint venture with developers to develop a local supermarket, counsel families to move off welfare, assist farm workers to build their own houses, create new enterprises with community youth.*

Community development specialist describes a very diverse range of roles and settings, ranging from large central cities, to rural United States, to developing countries. The common thread is that such positions are needed anywhere that development by the private sector is less than what the community needs. Jobs in this emerging field appear to require at least an undergraduate degree. Many require business and real estate training, though many more seem primarily to demand organizational and communication skills.

*(Quoted from Paul C. Brophy and Alice Shabecoff, *A Guide to Careers in Community Development* (Washington DC: Island Press, 2001.)

---

common supporting services that are enhanced and refined through joint utilization by multiple schools. These include advanced library services, advanced technical and computer expertise, administrative support services, classroom and pedagogical support services, and editorial and publishing services. A second aspect of industry economies within the university is in advanced education curricula. Many degree programs depend on courses provided by one or more other schools because it is too costly, or even impossible, to maintain the expertise for the needed courses internally. A third form of agglomeration comes in interdisciplinary research and development. In many universities, for example, engineering schools have joined with medical schools to produce an amazing array of materials suitable to replace or supplement components of the human body, as well as to produce equipment for medical and rehabilitative needs.

The university, like other activities in the economy, has felt the recent dramatic advancements in electronic communication and document transmission. But while this has reduced the need for proximity is some ways, it has enhanced it in others. For example, as electronic-based distance learning has grown, so has the need for common studios, equipment, and expertise necessary for delivering such programs. Further, internationalization has created additional common needs among schools of the university relating to foreign languages and translation, international travel arrangements, and provisions for international students and visitors. Thus, as some multicollege "industry economies" diminish, others seem to evolve.

The Role of Urban Analysis in Real Estate Decisions

It is reasonable to ask how the broad ideas about urban land use we have presented in this chapter really help with particular real estate decisions. In answer, it is the larger urban relationships that give meaning to the notion of location—that is, the most important meaning of location is location within a matrix of urban activities. Several points follow from this proposition. First, the location of a parcel is about its linkages or access to various nodes within the urban matrix. Second, the nature of this location depends on the type of land use being considered. For example, a weak location for a central place or convenience activity may be a strong location for a comparison shopping activity. Similarly, a weak location for

www.terrafly.fiu.edu

An elaborate, nationwide
system of aerial photos, linked
together so as to permit one to
"fly" over any location in the
U.S. (see footnote)

a retail activity may be a strong location for warehouses. And a good location for student apartments may be a poor location for residential condominiums because of differences in linkage needs between the types of occupants.

Another point is that cities do not grow evenly. Rather, some nodes of activity grow faster, while some may decline. So the growth potential for a site, and the appreciation potential of a site, depends on where it is with respect to growing and declining nodes within the city. In short, the location quality of a particular site cannot be evaluated except as part of the larger urban matrix.[11]

Finally, the story of urban evolution recounted here punctuates the importance of urban change. In real estate analysis one must look not only to the current urban matrix but also to where changes in technology, transportation systems, and the economic base are leading this network of relationships in the future. The good location of one decade can become the declining location of the next as new arterials, new intersections, new employment centers, and new forms of retailing emerge.

11. To look at urban form and composition, few media are more useful than aerial photos. The website www.terrafly.fiu.edu is a particularly interesting source. A jointly sponsored project of Florida International University, NASA, the United States Geological Survey, and the National Science Foundation, "terrafly" simulates flying over virtually any location in the United States at the altitude of the user's choice.

Summary

History is replete with real estate ventures that failed due to an inadequate market for the project. While market risk is inherent in any business, many real estate failures could have been avoided through more thoughtful and careful assessment of market potential for the intended project.

To understand real estate markets requires an understanding of the urban economies that generate those markets. One must understand the economic base of a city—those activities that bring income into a city—and what is happening to it. One also must understand the subsectors or clusters within a city to be able to distinguish areas of high growth from areas of slow growth or decline. Further, one must understand differing locational needs among urban land uses, such as the need of convenience "goods" for dispersed locations as opposed to the need of "comparison" goods to cluster. One must be aware of the importance of industry and agglomeration economies as factors that strengthen and stabilize urban markets, or leave less stable markets in their absence.

Urban form and urban real estate markets have never ceased to be impacted by change. It is important to recognize the dominant patterns of change and the steady, yet profound, pressures they exert on land use. The real estate analyst must understand the long periods over which such changes occur, and must understand which land uses are favored and which are diminished by the forces of change. Especially important has been change in transportation systems, causing whole areas of cities to expand or decline drastically. But also important are changes in production and distribution technology, bringing the need for new kinds of structures and real estate developments. Finally, the revolutions in communications technology have been loosening spatial bonds through much of the 20th century and undoubtedly will continue to impact urban form for years to come.

Within the urban matrix are diverse types of activities with different locational needs with respect to competitors. Convenience activities seek to disperse uniformly over the urban landscape while comparison activities seek to cluster with competitors. Industry economies of scale may draw a cluster of complementary activities together at a single urban node, such as a medical center or major university.

www.mhhe.com/lingarcher1e

Key Terms

Agglomeration economies 109
Bid-rent model 109
Central place pattern 121
Concentric ring model 115
Convenience activities 119

Comparison activities 122
Economic base 102
Industry economies of scale 108
Linkages 100
Local economic activities 104

Location quotient 106
Multinuclei city 117
Sector model 116

Test Problems

1. The "gravity" that draws economic activity into clusters is:
   a. Common laws and regulations.
   b. Common language.
   c. Demand for access or proximity.
   d. Cost of land.
   e. Streets.

2. Spatial or distance relationships that are important to a land use are called its:
   a. Linkages.
   b. Agglomerations.
   c. Facets.
   d. Dimensions.
   e. Attractions.

3. Cities have tended to grow where:
   a. Transportation modes intersect or change.
   b. Transportation is uninterrupted.
   c. People are concentrated.
   d. Where there is ample land and energy.
   e. Where there is demand for economic goods.

4. The economic base multiplier of a city tends to be greater if the city is:
   a. Larger.
   b. Older.
   c. Less isolated from other cities.
   d. Newer.
   e. Less diversified.

5. The best example of a base economic activity would be a:
   a. Supermarket.
   b. Department store.
   c. Fire department.
   d. Large apartment complex.
   e. Regional sales office.

6. Important supply factors affecting a city's growth or growth potential include all of the following *except* the:
   a. Unemployment rate.
   b. Business leadership.

   c. Presence of any industry economies of scale.
   d. Labor force characteristics.
   e. Education system.

7. Which of these are true about agglomeration economies?
   a. They result from demand created by multiple industries.
   b. They create a readily available supply of highly specialized goods and labor.
   c. They tend to reduce risks in real estate.
   d. They occur in larger cities.
   e. All of the above.

8. Which of these influences will decrease the level of a bid-rent curve at the center of the city?
   a. Faster travel time.
   b. Higher average wage rate.
   c. Increased number of trips per household.
   d. Larger number of households bidding.
   e. None of these.

9. In a system of bid-rent curves, assuming that households are identical except for the feature noted, which of these prospective bidders will bid successfully for the sites nearest to the CBD?
   a. Households with the greatest number of commuting workers.
   b. Households with the lowest income.
   c. Households with superior means of transportation.
   d. Households that arrive in the city last.
   e. Households requiring more land.

10. A large university is an example of what kind of economic phenomenon?
    a. Convenience activity.
    b. Comparison activity.
    c. Industry economies of scale.
    d. Secondary or local economic activity.
    e. Quality of life activity.

Study Questions

1. List five major economic base activities for your city of residence.

2. Find the historical population figures for your community for the 20th century. Create a chart with 10-year intervals. Determine the most rapid periods of growth, and try to discover what caused them. (One source of the necessary population numbers is the U.S. Census home page www.census.gov.

Look in the right-hand column to find *State & County Quick-Facts,* and select your state and county. At the top of the large table of current information that appears, click on "Browse more datasets. . ." Then look down the page for the heading "Historical Population Counts").

3. On the U.S. Census website, use the approach shown in the chapter in Explore the Web to access the SF3 detailed census

Year	Total Population	Total Employment	Basic Employment	Nonbasic Employment
2000	50,000	25,000	6,250*	18,750
2001	53,000	26,500	6,625	19,875
2002	57,000	28,500	7,125	21,375
2003	65,000	32,500	8,125	24,375
2004	70,000	35,000	8,750	26,250
2005	?	?	9,000*	?

*Estimated from surveys

tables for 2000. For your county, and for your state find the distribution of income for all households. Graph the distributions using percentage for each income interval. Which is higher, county or state?

4. Identify at least five locational attributes that you believe are important in the location of a fast-food restaurant. Compare notes with someone in the industry such as a local restaurant manager or owner.

5. Perfect Population Projections Inc. (PPP) has entered into a contract with the city of Popular, Pennsylvania, to project the future population of the city. In recent years, Popular has become a desirable place to live and work, as indicated by the table above.

The contract states that PPP must project Popular's population for the year 2005 using both a simple linear method and an economic base analysis. The ratio of population to total employment is 2.0833.

Your help is needed!

Explore The Web

Go to the U.S. Census home page, www.census.gov. In the righthand column find *State & County QuickFacts*. Select a county of interest (perhaps your county of residence). From the initial table, find the following information from the 2000 census:

   a. Mean travel time to work.

   b. Mean value of owner-occupied residences.

   c. Number of households.

   d. Percent of housing units in multiunit structures.

At the top of the table, click on "Browse more data sets for. . ." Then, under Census 2000, click on "Economic Characteristics" (note that you need Adobe Acrobat Reader, a downloadable program free from Adobe and a host of other sources.) This brings up a four-page profile of your county. Within the four pages find the following:

   e. For all households and for families, find the income interval with the largest number of households. What is the percentage concentration in each case?

   f. For industry of employment, which category, other than retail, has the largest percentage of persons?

   g. For housing units, which unit age interval has the largest concentration of housing units? What is the percentage?

   h. For owner-occupied units, what value range has the largest concentration?

   i. For what percent of housing units did the householder (principal occupant) move in between the beginning of 1999 and March 2000?

Returning to the Browsing page, under Census 1990, click on "General Population" and "Housing Characteristics." Find:

   j. The number of owner-occupied housing units with a value below $50,000.

   k. The population age interval with the largest concentration of persons.

Click on "1990 Census, Labor force and employment characteristics."

   l. Find the industry category, other than retail, with the largest number of employed persons.

www.mhhe.com/lingarcher1e

Solutions to Concept Checks

1. The demand for access between one urban activity and others is referred to as the activity's linkages.

2. The "gravity" that draws economic activity into forming cities is the need for access.

3. Historically, cities tended to form at the intersection of different modes of transportation.

4. The theory underlying the concept of economic base is that cities exist to serve the economic world at large.

5. The size of an economic base multiplier depends on the amount of "leakage" from the local economy.

6. The customary analysis of a city's economic base tends to focus on external demand, which tends to be a short-term phenomenon.

7. Cost efficiencies that arise in a city due to concentration of an industry are called industry economies of scale, whereas cost efficiencies arising from the concentration of multiple industries are called agglomeration economies.

8. The economic incentive that gives rise to bid-rent curves is the desire to reduce commuting time.

9. Faster travel results in less value to be close to the CBD, and a lesser slope of the bid-rent curve. More trips make being close to the CBD more valuable, and a steeper slope. More commuters will cause a higher curve with the same slope. Higher-density housing (since it doesn't change travel cost) leaves the slope unchanged, but can allow the curve to be at a lower level since it enables the most remote bidder to live closer to the CBD. A higher hourly wage will cause the proximity to the CBD to be more valuable, thus an increase in the slope.

10. A person who commutes on foot will always outbid a person who commutes by car for space near downtown because the pedestrian commuter's cost of traveling is far greater.

11. The Burgess concentric model of urban form was conceived in an era when the dominant form of transportation was by railway and the principal method of moving goods within factories was by elevator.

12. The radial or "pie slice" pattern in the Hoyt sector model of urban form probably can be explained by the dominance of the streetcar (fixed-rail transit) for intraurban transportation at the time the model was formulated.

13. One of the most profound forces bringing change in urban form in the United States is the automobile. Whereas cars were a novelty in 1915, most households owned one by about 1930.

14. The demand for space for horizontal factories was greatly accelerated in the 1920s by the development of assembly-line production.

15. Modern office structures and retail facilities were not possible before the development of air-conditioning and fluorescent lighting.

16. The essential feature of a convenience good or central place activity is that households, in acquiring it, go to the closest source.

17. The location tendency of comparison activities is to cluster whereas the location tendency of convenience activities is to disperse.

Additional Readings

Books on real estate markets include the following:

Clapp, John M. *Handbook for Real Estate Market Analysis.* Upper Saddle River, NJ: Prentice Hall, 1987.

DiPasquale, Denise, and William C. Wheaton, *Urban Economics and Real Estate Markets.* Upper Saddle River, NJ: Prentice Hall, 1996.

Geltner, David, and Norman G. Miller. *Commercial Real Estate Analysis and Investments.* Upper Saddle River, NJ: Prentice Hall, 2001. (See Part II.)

Kibert, C. J., and A. Wilson. *Reshaping the Built Environment: Ecology, Ethics, and Economics.* Washington, DC: Island Press, 1999.

Thrall, Grant I. *Business Geography and New Real Estate Market Analysis.* New York: Oxford University Press, 2002.

For exposure to geographic information systems in many variations and levels, visit the website of ESRI: www.ESRI.com (ESRI is a principal provider of GIS systems).

chapter six

Government Controls *and* Real Estate Markets

Learning Objectives

After reading this chapter you will be able to:

1. Cite three reasons why the market system may not operate to maximize the net social benefits of land use.

2. Identify the principal provisions typically contained in state planning and growth management legislation.

3. Describe eight elements of traditional zoning and identify other traditional land use controls.

4. Identify three possible adverse effects of traditional zoning.

5. Explain the "revolution" in scope, focus and extent of land use controls that occurred during the 1970s.

6. Identify four tools of land use control widely adopted since 1970, and contrast *new urbanism* with traditional land use.

7. Identify the major types of environmental hazards and the steps real estate investors should take to protect against them.

8. Describe eminent domain and explain the current concern with its use for *public purpose.*

9. Explain how property tax is computed. Discuss three possible deficiencies with the property tax system.

Introduction

Most of the real property in the United States is privately owned. (See Chapter 1 for U.S. property ownership statistics.) If real estate markets worked well, this should allow market forces to determine land uses quite effectively. Unregulated competitive bidding would bring about the most productive use of each parcel, and the price paid for the parcel would exactly reflect its usefulness, much as described in Chapter 5. But this does not completely happen for several reasons. One of the reasons is because of **externalities:** the unintended and unaccounted consequences of one land user upon others. For example, the creation of a shopping center on a site may cause harm to neighbors through traffic congestion, noise, increased storm runoff across neighboring land, "light pollution," or other visual or environmental degradation. Another problem that arises is that buyers of property suffer from incomplete information. Once a structure is built it is very difficult, often impossible, to determine the sturdiness and safety of the structure. Still another kind of problem that arises in a totally private land market is locational monopoly. For example, when land is needed for roads certain specific parcels are needed, for which there is no substitute. The owner of these critical locations, in effect, has a monopoly on the supply, and can extract unreasonable prices from other tax-paying citizens.

In summary, an unregulated private market for land would be fraught with problems resulting from externalities, from incomplete information, and from locational monopolies. These kinds of problems have persuaded most observers and most communities that government must intervene in the use of land to mitigate the resulting distortions in the markets for land use.

In this chapter we survey three basic powers of government that limit private property use and affect property value. We first discuss the government's right to regulate land use and set minimum standards for safe construction through its broad police powers. Second, we look at the power of government to acquire private property for the benefit of the public using its power of eminent domain. Finally, we examine the right of government to tax property. All of these government interventions can have profound effect on the value of private property.

The Power of Government to Regulate Land Use

The authority of state and local governments to regulate land use and enforce property standards is vested in its police power.[1] This power establishes the right of government to enact laws to protect the general health, welfare, and safety of the public. In the United States, almost all county and city governments use some combination of planning, zoning, building codes, and other restrictions to regulate the use of land and set property standards within their jurisdiction.

Concept Check

6.1   What constitutional power enables state and local government to regulate land use?

Monopolies, Externalities, and Other Market Distortions

Monopolies. Monopolies misallocate resources by overpricing goods and services at the expense of some, and producing less output than is efficient from society's view. Monopoly pricing in the real estate market by owners is less common than often perceived since most land uses have near-substitutes that effectively offer competition. However, city transportation, water, and sewer systems represent natural monopolies because it would be costly to establish competition. Competitive systems would require the duplication of costly capital investments (e.g., roadways, water distribution, and storm water drainage systems). It is generally in the interest of the community to either regulate these services as monopolies or own them outright.

Another form of potential land monopoly is the holdout. For example, land must be acquired for most large public projects such as roads. When assembly of multiple private parcels is involved, one or more land holders can "hold hostage" the entire project by

---

1. Police power is largely reserved to the states, and derives from the Constitution and U.S. Supreme Court interpretations of it.

refusing to sell at a reasonable price, thus extracting wealth from other citizens. Thus, it is deemed necessary for governments to have the capacity to require the sale of land to the government at a reasonable price. This power of eminent domain is discussed below.

Concept Check

6.2   Name two examples of monopoly affecting local land use.

Externalities. Externalities can be either positive or negative. Examples of positive externalities are the beneficial effects on property value from exceptional vistas, nearby parks and recreation facilities, quality neighborhood schools, quality architecture, attractive commercial areas, well-kept landscapes and so forth. In a strictly private market the producers of these community benefits are unrewarded for their value to other property owners, and therefore provide less than is desirable from the viewpoint of the community as a whole. Under-provision of positive externalities is an argument for government intervention to encourage more. Negative externalities, unaccounted negative effects of a land use on the value of surrounding properties, have the opposite result. The perpetrator of the externalities has too little incentive to curtail the offending activity, and produces an excess from the perspective of the community as a whole. This overproduction of negative externalities is an argument for government intervention to reduce their output.

There are many examples of *negative* externalities in land use: A factory may spew smoke or other emissions on surrounding properties; shopping centers and other businesses frequently generate a wide range of externalities, as noted above; building additional housing units in an area often brings increased traffic congestion, crowding of schools and hastening of the disappearance of natural areas; public assistance facilities such as homeless shelters are regarded apprehensively by neighbors; increased neighborhood crime can result from poorly managed low-income apartments, and college fraternity houses may host loud parties, producing unwanted noise for neighbors. While each of these land uses produces a good or service that benefits some, the property values of others may be diminished. In an unregulated private market the "victims" of these effects are likely to have no voice in the builder's or developer's decisions, no way to call the "perpetrator" to account for the damage, and are never "made whole" for the harm they suffer.

Congestion. One major form of urban land use externalities is congestion. Congestion occurs when an individual uses a system (such as roads) near capacity and slows the performance of the entire system for all users. For example, when drivers enter a congested freeway they are well aware of the delay for themselves, but they usually feel little guilt for incrementally slowing down many other drivers on the freeway. We generally think of congestion in terms of highway traffic, but it can be present in many other services such as water, telephone, Internet services, the court system and public schools.[2]

Urban Sprawl. Externalities are a major argument cited by critics of "urban sprawl." If one defines urban sprawl as development taking place in rural areas well beyond the urban fringe ("leapfrog" development), then the argument is as follows. Such development can enable builders to offer lower prices than buyers can obtain within developed areas, but

---

2. Another example of congestion is the downloading of MP3 music files by students using dorm Internet facilities. The downloading activity uses a substantial portion of the bandwidth available to all users of the Internet system, and substantially slows its performance. Students download the files because their benefit of receiving the music is greater than the slow service (cost) they individually experience. However, the cost of slowing the entire system is substantial because it is experienced by all students and, if considered, may be greater than the aggregate benefits to "downloaders" in the dorm "society." If the aggregate costs are greater than the aggregate benefits, and if all costs are considered, the downloaders would not choose to download the music. Accessing MP3 files, in this case, is considered to be a congestible good.

http://www.sustainable.
doe.gov/landuse/luintro.
shtml

Covers urban sprawl and
related issues.

http://www.plannersweb.
com/sprawl/home.html

Another gateway to discussion
on urban sprawl.

only because the builder is not bearing the full cost of development. Typically, the cost of extending community services—road improvements, new schools or more school buses, additional utilities, extended police and fire protection—are not accounted for in the prices or property taxes paid by the developers and subsequent property buyers. Thus, the costs are shared by the entire community and, it is argued, other taxpayers must subsidize the leapfrog development at the urban fringe.

The costs and benefits of sprawl and congestion are controversial and require careful thought. There are reasons to doubt that government planning always improves these problems. For example, it is unlikely that planners and officials can accurately anticipate the market and forecast the most efficient locations for future land use. Government regulations may go beyond correcting misallocations, resulting in new misallocations and inequities. Rebuilding utilities and streets, and assembling parcels of land for central city redevelopment may be more costly than providing services to suburban development.

Despite the risks of errors in the efforts, it is generally conceded that development must be managed by the community. Providing adequate services such as streets, parks, storm drainage, water, and waste treatment represent substantial investments of the community. The cost of expanding these systems is greatly affected by the degree to which it can be accomplished in an orderly and compact fashion. Therefore, government planning and regulation are often justified to increase market efficiencies.

Concept Check

6.3   List three examples of negative externalities in local land use.

Incomplete Information.   After a structure is built it is impractical even for a building expert, let alone others, to fully assess the quality of the construction and the safety hazards it may harbor. This problem was broadly recognized by the early 20th century, and building codes were widely adopted as a remedy. Building codes remain an important protection against safety hazards. In similar fashion, subdivision regulations ensure minimum street design standards for traffic safety, adequate provision for fire hydrants and firefighting access, and other matters of safety and health.

Concept Check

6.4   Identify the most universal example of incomplete information in real estate, and what solution is widely implemented as a remedy.

Information and Value Stability.   Homes are the largest single asset of most households, as we noted in Chapter 1. Uncertainty in the value of the home could pose a significant risk. In unregulated real estate markets, homeowners may become apprehensive about possible adverse changes in nearby land uses. The apprehension alone could adversely affect values. Thus homeowners may be willing to accept the constraints of community land use regulation to reduce the risk of unexpected, harmful changes in surrounding land use. It has been argued that the main motivation for traditional residential zoning was precisely to attain such value stability.

Counterarguments to Land Use Controls.   While the arguments presented above for market distortions are widely recognized, their importance is not universally accepted. The value of zoning, in particular, as a corrective to market distortions has been questioned by many who examine the experience of Houston, Texas, where zoning does not exist. (See Industry Issues 6-1.) There, land use control is largely through private means, including restrictive covenants, easements, and owner associations (all discussed in Chapter 4).

Industry Issues

Houston Says No to Zoning

"Zoning goes down for third time" read the morning headline of the *Houston Post* last November 3. As they had in 1948 and 1962, Houstonians voted once more to remain America's largest city without a zoning ordinance . . . Hispanics and low-income blacks voted overwhelmingly, 58 percent and 71 percent, against a measure touted as the way to "save" their neighborhoods. In a low-turnout referendum, only 10 percent of the city's registered voters gave their nod to zoning . . .

Exaggerated Risks

[Zoning] supporters said that homes unprotected by zoning risk a loss in property value if a business or apartment locates nearby . . . [but] within Houston are two small, independent cities, Bellaire and West University, with zoning. Between 1970 and 1980 home prices in Bellaire and West University climbed more slowly than in many Houston communities, including those lacking private neighborhood restrictions against businesses and apartments . . . [Another concern] is that single-family neighborhoods without zoning are likely to be overrun by businesses and apartments. In the Houston Heights, a century-old neighborhood of 300 blocks, only about 5 percent of the residential blocks have private restrictions . . . Yet single-family homes occupy almost 86 percent of the lots on interior streets. Businesses take up 7 percent; industrial uses, less than 2 percent; apartments, less than 2 percent; churches and schools, 4 percent . . .

Source: Excerpts from an essay by James D. Saltzman, *The Freeman* 44, no. 8 (August 1994). *The Freeman* is a publication of the Foundation for Economic Education, Inc. The complete essay, with extensive references is available at: http://www.libertyhaven.com/ personalfreedomissues/freespeechorcivilliberties/houstonzoning.html

The Houston Way

Under the Houston system, heavy industry voluntarily locates on large tracts near rail lines or highways; apartments and stores seek thoroughfares; gas stations vie for busy intersections . . . Businesses that thrive amidst homes often serve strong local demand. "Shade-tree" mechanics appear in low-income neighborhoods to service old cars owners cannot afford to replace. "Mom and pop" grocery stores supply those who have no cars . . . In locations with stable demand for single-family homes, healthy real estate values are likely to prohibit many "noxious" uses—like junkyards and machine repair shops—that want cheap land. Without realizing it, the homeowners have "zoned out" such uses through their own free choices. As zoning expert Bernard Siegan says, "The most effective of restrictions [is] competition." . . . Even without zoning, homebuyers wanting control over the development of land in their neighborhood have a choice called "deed restrictions." . . . most homes in Houston built since World War II have such renewable restrictions.

The Houston Advantage

Without zoning, Houston ranks consistently as the leader among major American cities for housing affordability. "It's more affordable here than any other large city in the nation," said University of Houston economist Barton Smith. According to Smith, one reason for this affordability is Houston's lack of zoning. And a federal report in 1991 cited zoning as a leading cause for the shortage of affordable housing in America.

The greatest beneficiaries of Houston's abstention from zoning are not the rich, greedy developers as zoning proponents would claim . . . As one Houston reporter recalls: "Because there were a handful of neighborhoods where there were no significant barriers to home businesses, the bust [of the 1980s] became an opportunity instead of a devastation. Time and time again I saw the unemployed become entrepreneurs." Time and time again in Houston's Hispanic neighborhoods, entrepreneurs also emerge from homes.

---

http://www.planning.org/

Website of the leading organization of urban planners.

Some critics of land use controls conclude that whatever market distortions exist in land use are outweighed by the detrimental effects of zoning. For example, it is often argued that zoning restricts the supply of modestly priced housing. At the same time, excessively low zoning density may contribute to urban sprawl. Further, if a zoning plan conflicts with the natural economic land use pattern, it can cause inefficient distortions in land use. For example, it may force household services such as grocery stores, delicatessens, or hair salons to be excessively distant from residential neighborhoods.

Concept Check

6.5   List five issues that may be addressed in a community land use plan.

Public Planning for Land Use Control

The theory of public planning is that directing land uses from a community perspective is the best means of correcting market failure. Incompatible land uses are more efficiently separated, both congestion and environmental effects are more completely incorporated into the land use and development decision process, and buyers are best protected from incomplete information about structures.

Comprehensive Planning

A **comprehensive plan** is a general guide to a community's future growth and development. In its most complete form, it involves projecting a community's future population growth, its requirements for water and other natural resources, its physical characteristics (e.g., existing development and soil conditions), its need for public services (e.g., schools and utilities), and its need for various types of land use (e.g., single-family residential and office), financial resources, and political constraints. Thus, a comprehensive plan attempts to guide future growth and development to accommodate the various needs of the community. Many communities and some states have developed detailed plans to "manage" growth, particularly those communities and states experiencing rapid growth. (See Industry Issues 6-2.) An enormous variety of material concerning planning methods, resources and issues is on the Internet. (See Explore the Web.)

Growth management laws at the state level may require local jurisdictions to plan for and meet certain requirements.[3] In their most extensive form these laws may require that:

1. Local jurisdictions (counties and cities) must have comprehensive plans submitted and approved by a state agency.
2. Proposals for large-scale developments must be accompanied by **economic and environmental impact statements** (studies) that analyze the project's effect on surrounding

Explore The Web

Go the the Planetizen website http://www.planetizen.com/sites/. From there you find many prominent websites relevant to planning and land use controls. Find an interesting website on the following subjects:

1. A directory.
2. A reseach and data site.

---

3. Twenty-three U.S. states currently have enacted laws requiring some form of land use planning at the local government level. James Schwab, *Summary of U.S. State Planning Laws, July 2002.* (Tampa, FL: Institute for Business and Home Safety).

Industry Issues

Limits on Growth through Local Land Use Controls: The Case of Petaluma, California

During the past three decades, several communities in the United States have instituted provisions in their land use and zoning regulations to limit growth. These communities include Ramapo, New York; Boca Raton, Florida; and Boulder, Colorado. One of the most interesting court cases involving limits on growth occurred in Petaluma, California. This rapidly growing community north of San Francisco instituted a number of

provisions to control its growth during the early 1970s. One of these measures placed a cap on the number of housing units that could be provided in the city in any year (approximately 6 percent of the total stock, or about 500 units).

The Construction Industry Association of Sonoma County [builders] challenged the regulation, asserting it violated the constitutional right to travel. The federal district court agreed with the builders and struck down the regulation. The court of appeals overturned the ruling, thus allowing the plan to stand as a legitimate use of the city's police power. The U.S. Supreme Court refused to hear the case, so the ruling of the court of appeals stands.

Source: *Construction Industry Association of Sonoma County v. City of Petaluma,* 275 F. Supp. 574 (1974); *Construction Industry Association of Sonoma County v. City of Petaluma,* 522 F. 2nd 897 (9th cir. 1975).

---

areas. They usually must show that existing infrastructure will handle the added burdens or demonstrate how the burdens will be accommodated. They must also show that the environment will not be significantly degraded. (Industry Issues 6-3 illustrates how an Oregon county worked out an agreement with a major employer to cope with the costs of growth.)

3. Further development at the local level must be prohibited unless adequate infrastructure, schools, police and fire protection, and social services are in place when development commences (termed the **concurrency** requirement).

4. Local governments must include an **affordable housing allocation** in their comprehensive plans. This type of requirement means local governments must encourage or mandate a "reasonable and fair" component of new housing construction for lower-income families.

Additionally, state laws may *permit* local communities to use the following techniques to manage growth and new development:

1. Establish **urban service areas.** For these areas, boundaries are delineated around a community within which the local government plans to provide public services and facilities, and beyond which urban development is discouraged or prohibited. Boundaries are usually designed to accommodate growth for 10 to 20 years with the intended result that the community can provide more efficient services and that rural land and natural resources will be protected from development.

2. Establish **extraterritorial jurisdiction.** Some states give local governments the power to plan and control urban development outside their boundaries until annexation can occur.

Concept Check

6.6   In a sentence, explain these terms:

1. Economic and environmental impact statement
2. Concurrency
3. Affordable housing allocation
4. Urban service area
5. Extraterritorial jurisdiction.

Industry Issues

6-3

W hen officials of Washington County, Oregon, negotiated a package of tax incentives to keep the state's largest private employer in Oregon, they agreed to give Intel $200 million in property tax breaks over the next 15 years. In return, Intel agreed to invest up to $12.5 billion in new equipment and plant upgrades over that period.

Fighting the Costs of Growth, a County Gets Intel to Limit Jobs

But in an unusual arrangement that the county asked for, the company agreed to pay a "growth impact fee" if it exceeds a ceiling of 1,000 new manufacturing jobs in addition to the 4,000 it already provides in the county. The amount of the fee will be $1,000 per excess worker per year, if it surpasses the new job limit.

County officials say they are thrilled to keep the existing jobs here but are not really interested in a major expansion, which would put new strains on schools, roads, utilities, and many other services in the area.

Source: *New York Times on the Web,* June 9, 1999. www.nytimes.com

Challenges in Public Land Use Planning

Public land use planning faces serious challenges on a number of fronts. The entire concept of modern land use planning is extremely new, being the outgrowth of what some have called the revolution in land use controls of the last three decades. Thus, planning has little data to work from concerning the true extent of various externalities or the effect of various remedies. Further, the very notion of what constitutes "best practice" in land use remains in evolution.

The "Revolution in Land Use Controls." As late as the mid-1960s public interest in land use controls was minimal. While land use plans existed, virtually none had the force of law. While building codes were well established for public safety, the zoning laws that existed had the limited purpose of protecting the value and stability of single-family subdivisions. Laws protecting the environment or water quality were virtually nonexistent.

This perspective was radically changed with the arrival of the environmental movement of the late 1960s. There was growing recognition of disasters such as *The Silent Spring,* wherein species were reported to be eliminated through insecticides.[4] This was followed by such stories as the Love Canal (see Industry Issues 6-5), all of which led to a radical change in the conception of the world at large. Perceptions of the environment as an endless and cost-less resource was replaced almost overnight by the notion of "spaceship earth."

Concept Check

6.7 Explain what launched the "revolution in land use controls" about 1970.

Conflicting Notions of Best Practice. While land use planning gained enormous momentum with the birth of the environmental movement, it was compelled to go forward with only rudimentary intellectual foundation. Even basic notions of what constitutes best practice in land use planning are debated. For example, in basic street layouts, many U.S. planners of recent decades favored hierarchies built around cul-de-sacs.[5] Many of these same planners favored complete "containment" of nonresidential land uses in designated centers. In recent years, however, both of these tenets have been challenged.

4. Rachel Carson, *The Silent Spring* (Boston: Houghton Mifflin, 1962; Mariner Books, 2002).

5. Reid Ewing, *Best Development Practices* (Chicago: Planners Press, American Planning Association, 1996).

Exhibit 6-1 New Urbanism Integrates Multiple Types of Land Uses and Restores Spaces for Community Life

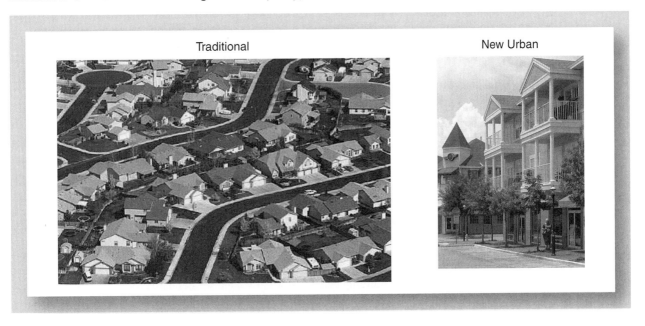

Traditional   New Urban

A growing number of urban planners believe the social problems plaguing urban areas (e.g., crime, poverty, isolation, and congestion) have resulted, at least in part, from incorrect assumptions about the way people want to live and relate to work, recreation, and other people. They contend that neighbors have become isolated because the layout and design of newer neighborhoods and homes do not foster interpersonal contact.

One of the major remedies these planners have advocated is termed **new urbanism,** or **smart growth.** Some of the tenets of this school of planning are that houses should be constructed closer to the street, and they should have front porches to encourage outdoor conversations with neighbors. Local streets should be narrowed to "calm" traffic and traditional grid street patterns should prevail. Public transportation should be an integral design element of the community. A mix of land uses (e.g., residential and commercial) should be encouraged (1) to provide job opportunities for residents (2) to decrease commuting, and (3) to encourage 24-hour presence of people in the community. While some early indications show positive results, a careful analysis and judgment as to the efficacy of new urbanism will take considerably more time, perhaps 10 or 20 years.

http://smartgrowth.net/
links/sg_links_fst.html

A site hosted by the Urban Land Institute regarding "smart growth" and new urbanism.

Concept Check

6.8 Identify two divergent views in recent planning theory concerning the best practice in street layouts and in the relationship between residential and commercial land use.

Zoning and Other Tools of Public Land Use Control

The comprehensive plan is usually general in nature. Its implementation must be through a variety of specific land use regulations. As noted before, these regulations grow out of the police powers of government to make laws to assure the health, safety and welfare of citizens. In this section we look at the more established and conventional kinds of land use regulations, which remain the "work horses" of land use control. These include building codes, zoning, and subdivision regulations. We also consider the administration of these regulations through appointed commissions and site plan review.

Building Codes

Building codes were the earliest use of police power to regulate land use. By the turn of the 20th century it was well accepted that, in the urban environment, design and materials of structures were an important concern for public safety. Certainly after the Chicago fire of 1871, which destroyed about one-third of the value of the city and left some 100,000 persons homeless, it was not hard to recognize the need for fire safety in urban construction.

Modern building codes set standards for numerous aspects of construction. Specifications for fire safety are paramount. These include the requirement of fire resistant materials for both structures and interior finishes, requirements for safety of electrical systems, gas lines, gas using appliances, adequate fire alarm systems, and requirements for accessible and safe emergency exits. Minimum specifications for structural strength and integrity also are important. Structural standards have been elevated in recent years in coastal states due to experience with Hurricane Andrew in 1992, which destroyed over 25,000 homes in South Florida and Louisiana, and damaged over 100,000. Building codes also address standards for safety, health and sanitation. They require designs of stairways, elevators and other aspects of the structure to be safe for normal use, and they require water pipes, fixtures and sanitary plumbing to meet minimum requirements of integrity and durability. Similarly, codes set standards for ventilating and air conditioning systems. Finally, building codes historically have set standards for access to air and sunlight, with minimum requirements for window size and openings. Because of the need for standardization in construction to control costs, building codes generally have been applied at the state, and even regional level (such as the Southern Standard Building Code adopted in many states of the South), though local areas sometimes exercise the right to impose still stricter standards.

Zoning

Zoning ordinances have been the main approach to land use regulation in the United States since the 1920s. A zoning ordinance contains several important elements:

1. A land use classification list, with such categories as single family residential, multi-family residential, commercial and industrial. Each of these categories is subdivided into multiple subcategories according to local needs. For example, single family classifications are differentiated by minimum lot size, while multi-family classifications are differentiated by maximum residential units per acre.
2. A map showing the zoning classification of all areas within the municipality or county involved.
3. Minimum front, rear, and side setback requirements from the boundaries of a lot.
4. Building bulk limits, including size, height, "footprint," and placement on the lot. (For office buildings, maximum floor/area ratios often limit the floor space per square foot of lot.)
5. Minimum lot dimensions.
6. Provision for special use districts (discussed below).
7. A zoning board or commission appointed to oversee the administration of the ordinance and to make recommendations regarding rezoning requests or changes in the ordinance offered by the zoning and planning staff.
8. A zoning adjustment board appointed to review hardship cases.

Historically, there has been a definite hierarchy in the classifications of zoning with the lowest density single family being at the top. Early approaches to zoning used *cumulative* classifications of land uses where the highest order classification (single family homes) could be placed in any lower order, but not vice versa. However, this is a questionable approach to zoning since it permits, for example, residential areas adjacent to oil refineries or chemical plants with potentially dire consequences in case of fire or explosion. Thus, the trend in more modern practice has been to require *exclusive* categories where there is complete separation between at least some of the classifications.

A number of land uses are classified in the zoning ordinance but have no predesignated locations on the zoning map. These may include service stations, churches, hospitals, private schools, cemeteries, or clubs. Instead, a landowner must petition to be granted one of these *special use* classifications, and the petition is then considered in a public hearing.

Usually when a zoning ordinance is revised some of the earlier land uses then fall outside the new zoning classification. These are called **non-conforming uses;** they may continue to exist, despite the change in classification, provided that they never are discontinued (temporary interruption is tolerated) and the structure is not destroyed or substantially altered (it can be repaired but not improved or replaced). Some courts will allow certain non-conforming uses to be "amortized" away over a period of years. For example, a zoning authority can require a billboard that is a non-conforming use to be discontinued after, say, five years.

A zoning ordinance must provide some relief mechanism for cases where the regulations impose exceptional hardship and loss of value. This relief is called a **variance.** For example if setback requirements render a lot too narrow to build on, it may be reasonable to waive a setback line by a small amount in order to make the land usable and restore its value. Variances are to be used only if three conditions are met:

1. The owner must show true hardship in terms of inability to use the lot as zoned.
2. The condition must be unique to the lot and not a condition common to other parcels in the vicinity.
3. The variance must not materially change the character of the neighborhood.

Concept Check

6.9   List three apects of land use typically restricted by zoning, in addition to type of land use.

Legality of Zoning. As mentioned earlier, zoning is an exercise of police power—the right of a government to enact and enforce laws to protect the health and welfare of its citizens. Increasingly, numerous and severe land use regulations have led some observers to contend that land is becoming more of a public resource than private property. For this reason, both zoning laws and their specific applications have been attacked on constitutional and applied grounds. Indeed, zoning laws have been attacked in courts as confiscation of property without compensation—an act prohibited by the U.S. Constitution (see Industry Issues 6-4).

Although some zoning laws have been declared unconstitutional, most have met constitutional tests, and zoning as a general practice has been legally acceptable in the United States for over 75 years. The general thrust of court decisions is that zoning is constitutional and will be upheld when zoning ordinances are reasonable, are based on a comprehensive plan, and provide for all types of housing. Courts have overturned zoning ordinances that tend to exclude lower income groups by large lot size, or that do not adequately provide low- and moderate-income housing. This is termed **exclusionary zoning.**

Concept Check

6.10   List three requirements of the courts for zoning to be a legitimate use of police powers.

Subdivision Regulations

Along with zoning, virtually every local government has adopted regulations that govern the creation of subdivisions. The purpose of these regulations is to promote the proper arrangement and coordination of streets in relation to existing or planned streets and to

Industry Issues

The Landmark Decision on the Legality of Land Use and Zoning Regulations

The Ambler Realty Company intended to sell the 68-acre tract of land it owned in the village of Euclid, Ohio, to an industrial developer. However, in 1922 Euclid enacted a land use–zoning ordinance that set aside part of this tract for residential development, ostensibly reducing its value by 75 percent. Ambler Realty sued Euclid, claiming the ordinance resulted in a "taking" of Ambler's property without payment of just compensation, as prescribed by the U.S. Constitution.

Source: *Village of Euclid, Ohio v. Ambler Realty Co.* 272 U.S. 365, 47 S. Ct. 1/4, 71 L. Ed. 303 (1926).

The District Court agreed with Ambler Realty, but in a landmark decision, the U.S. Supreme Court ruled that Euclid was not taking any part of the tract for a public purpose and that this ordinance was a legitimate use of the village's police power to control land uses.

This Supreme Court ruling has withstood the test of time in that it has served as an important precedent in virtually all subsequent disputes involving the question of a "taking." The ruling legitimized both land use controls as a police power exercise and the separation of land uses into districts and zones for land use control.

---

assure coordination of subdivisions with the local comprehensive plan. The regulations provide guidelines for the layout of lots, for adequate and convenient provision of open spaces, utilities, recreation, and access for service and emergency vehicles. The standards imposed by the ordinance also assure adequate provision of water, drainage, sewer, and other sanitary facilities.

The developer who is subdividing will present a preliminary site plan in a public meeting where local officials, including utility officials, emergency service officials, school officials, transportation officials and others have the opportunity to comment on the plan and challenge any aspects of it that concern them. One very practical reason for the review by a variety of officials is that roadways and utilities in subdivisions usually are **dedicated** to the local government, meaning that they become the property and responsibility of the local government to maintain.

Zoning and Planning Administration

Property owners frequently wish to have the zoning classification of their property changed. A developer, for example, may want to construct a residential subdivision on land currently zoned for agriculture, or an apartment building owner may wish to increase the size of the project to accommodate more units. The planning and zoning commission, and staff, normally reviews all such rezoning requests.

In considering rezoning requests, they will use the following criteria:

1. Will the new zoning be compatible with the comprehensive plan?
2. Should the comprehensive plan be modified?
3. What effect will the new zoning have on surrounding land uses and on the larger community?

A request for rezoning that is consistent with the comprehensive plan is more likely to be approved than one that is not. If the request is inconsistent with the plan, the question becomes whether the comprehensive plan should be modified, and the planning and zoning commission, with staff, must turn to the third question, how does the proposal affect the larger community? They will form a recommendation on the zoning and any related change on the comprehensive plan. Both of these will go before the elected governing body for final action.

A second appointed board for administration of the zoning ordinance is the board of adjustment. This board is charged with reviewing petitions for variances. They must determine whether the three conditions for relief, noted above, are met. If so, they will grant the variance. Unlike the zoning and planning commission that makes recommendations to the elected governing body, determinations of the board of adjustment are final, and can only be appealed in court.

Site Plan Review. Besides overseeing the comprehensive plan and zoning, the planning and zoning commission usually wears yet another hat as a site plan review board. Site plans arise both from proposed subdivisions and from proposed apartment, commercial and industrial projects. As noted above, site plan reviews involve a diversity of potential commentators, including the public. It is a particularly complex and uncertain process from a developer's point of view, as discussed at length in Chapter 24. The review can involve a great diversity of concerns, perspectives and voices. It typically is an open and informal process, thus leaving ample room for the unexpected, for misunderstandings and clashes in views. Developers often point to the site plan review process as one of the riskiest points in the development process.

Concept Check

6.11   In a sentence, define each of these:
1. Nonconforming use
2. Variance
3. Exclusionary zoning

Modern Tools of Land Use Control

Planned Unit Developments. Traditional zoning has been criticized on several fronts. It has been accused of being oblivious to the effect of land use on traffic and environmental systems. At the same time it is accused of being far too rigid, forcing uniform patterns and density of development where variation would be much better. The planned unit development concept has emerged to address these concerns. In the **planned unit development (PUD),** traditional requirements, such as setback requirements (distance of buildings from lot lines) and floor-area ratios (FAR, the total building square footage divided by the lot square footage), are allowed to vary in some areas in exchange for larger areas of open space and nature preservation, public facilities, and attractive layouts and designs. PUDs often integrate residential and commercial development.

http://www.law.cornell.edu/topics/land_use.html

Website for land use law.

Concept Check

6.12   Identify four differences between a PUD and traditional zoning.

Performance Standards. Traditional zoning fails to address concerns for urban systems such as traffic, watershed, green space, air quality, or other aspects of the environment. A **performance standard** can fill this void. For example, storm runoff can be controlled by requiring that runoff from a parcel of land be no greater after development than before. Tree canopy can be preserved by requiring permits to remove trees of a certain size or character. Local emission and noise limits can be adopted for industrial and commercial activity. Further, traffic generation limits can be made a part of the development permission process. An important attraction of performance standards is their ability to offer a more flexible substitute to the traditional separation of land uses. Thus, rather than prohibiting industrial use in a commercial area or commercial use in a residential area, the use may be allowed if it meets relevant performance standards.

Land Planner

The role of land planners is to create actual site plans for subdivision development. In that capacity they must account for the characteristics of the site, including topography, soils, drainage and floodplains, possible environmental hazards, possible endangered species, and other natural factors. In addition, they must have a thorough knowledge of all land use and development regulations affecting the site. Finally, they must understand the requirements of the target market to which the final product is being directed as well as the goals, schedule, and budget requirements of the client. They must be able to integrate the character of the site, the pertinent regulatory guidelines and constraints, and the demands of the market into a creative and attractive site solution—and still fit the time and budgetary requirements of the client. Further, the planner often will need to represent the client in meetings with public officials, lenders, and others.

Usually working as a private consultant, the land planner commonly has a civil engineering, urban planning, or landscape architecture degree, but not always. Specific tools of value to the site planner include a strong capacity in geographic information systems, computer-aided design and drafting (CADD), and presentation graphics software.

Concept Check

6.13 List three examples of land use performance standards.

http://www.realtor.org/libweb.nsf/pages/fg805

Extensive material on impact fees.

Impact Fees. The primary means that economists advocate to "internalize" externalities is by charging compensating fees. Thus, if development imposes externality costs on the community at large, the developer should pay an **impact fee** commensurate with the externalities. This concept is growing in acceptance and a wide range of development impact fees can be found. (See Industry Issues 6-3.)

Growth Restrictions. Under the rationale that growth can impose broad externalities on a community, some local governments have successfully imposed restrictions on overall growth. In the extreme, a temporary **growth moratorium,** or prohibition of development, has occurred. (See Industry Issues 6-2.) This may be justified because of an immediate need to forestall a public health, safety, or welfare problem. Such problems may include the lack of sewage treatment capacity or intense traffic congestion. The moratorium might be imposed for one to three years to allow time for the problem to be resolved.

www.epa.gov/epahome/laws.htm

An overview of all major U.S. environmental laws

Environmental Hazards

State and federal control of land uses has increased greatly over the past 20 years due in part to an increased awareness of environmental hazards. The following is a partial list of federal environmental control laws:

Clean Air Act, 1970	Gave EPA authority to set National Ambient Air Quality Standards.
Clean Water Act, 1972–1977	Gave EPA authority to control discharges of pollutants into waters of the United States.
Safe Drinking Water Act, 1974	Gave EPA authority to implement quality standards for drinking water.
Resource Conservation and Recovery Act, 1976	Gave EPA "cradle-to-grave" authority over handling of hazardous waste.
Toxic Substances Control Act, 1976	Gave EPA authority to monitor and control 75,000 industrial chemicals, and new ones that are created.
Comprehensive Environmental Response Compensation and Liability Act (CERCLA), 1980	Established the "Superfund," and gave EPA authority to clean up abandoned or uncontrolled toxic sites.

Industry Issues

Love Canal and the Establishment of the EPA Superfund

n 1978 President Carter declared a state of emergency for the Love Canal area of Niagara Falls, New York, when toxic materials migrated to the surface and other areas through contaminated groundwater. The scope of the problem and its national attention ultimately led to the passage of the Comprehensive Environmental Response, Compensation, and Liability Act (CERCLA) in 1980. The act established the "Superfund" to finance emergency responses and cleanups of abandoned and unregulated waste dumps.

William Love began excavation on a canal in 1892 to divert water from the Niagara River for a hydroelectric power project that was never completed. Beginning in 1942 the partially completed canal was used as a landfill by Hooker Chemicals and Plastics (now Occidental Chemical Corporation) for the disposal of over 21,000 tons of various chemicals. Dumping ceased in 1952,

and in 1953 the landfill was covered and deeded to the Niagara Falls Board of Education. Subsequently, the area near the covered landfill was extensively developed, including the construction of an elementary school and numerous homes. Problems with odors and residues, first reported in the 1960s, increased during the 1970s as the water table rose, bringing contaminated groundwater to the surface. In 1976 chemicals were found to be leaking at the site.

More than 900 families were evacuated from affected areas and over 200 homes closest to the canal demolished. In 1988 some areas near the site were declared habitable for residential use. Since 1995 Occidental Corp. has paid over $250 million to the state and federal governments to reimburse cleanup costs and natural resource damages, and to property owners. In compliance with a 1991 order from the U.S. Environmental Protection Agency, the company is required to manage and prevent the spread of pollution from the site.

Source: U.S. Environmental Protection Agency, Fact Sheet, EPA ID# NYD000606947; *New York Times*, July 20, 1999, section B, p. 7.

Environmental hazards are regulated by federal, state, and local agencies such as the federal Environmental Protection Agency (EPA), the U.S. Department of Housing and Urban Development, state environmental protection agencies, local departments of environmental quality, local building and fire departments, and property lenders and loan insurers.

The scope and intensity of environmental regulation means property owners are subject to huge dollar amounts of potential liability if environmental hazards are found on their properties. For example, under the "Superfund" legislation (Comprehensive Environmental Response Compensation and Liability Act of 1980 and subsequent amendments), property owners must clean up many kinds of toxic wastes if they knew or had any reason to know the property was contaminated when they purchased it (see Industry Issues 6-5). Lenders who acquire impacted property through forecloseure also may be subject to this cleanup requirement. (Foreclosure is discussed in Chapter 10.) Furthermore, some courts have required owners to clean up toxic wastes on their properties, even if they were *unaware* of its existence when they bought the property.

Types of Hazardous Materials

Several types of hazardous materials are often present in properties, and these materials are a major concern of property owners, prospective buyers, lenders, and the public. These hazardous materials are sometimes termed **toxic waste.**[6] A partial list of toxic waste includes the following materials, substances, and gases: asbestos, fiberglass, polychlorinated biphenyls (PCBs), leaking underground storage tanks (LUSTs), radon and the most recent culprit, mold.

6. David A. Smith, "Investor Topics: Investor Protection against Environmental Risks," *Real Estate Review* 19, no. 2 (Summer 1989), pp. 14–19.

Asbestos and Fiberglass. Asbestos has been a major problem in buildings constructed before the early 1970s. It was the primary material used for insulation and was considered ideal until its health hazards were discovered. If released into the air, the tiny fibers can enter the lungs and reduce breathing capacity. Other forms of asbestos, such as vinyl asbestos tile (often used in kitchens and bathrooms) and jacketed asbestos insulation around hot-water tanks and pipes (if sealed airtight) do not present this problem.

Nevertheless, asbestos in all forms has caused a virtual panic, and costly asbestos removal programs for public buildings (especially schools) and some private buildings have been undertaken. More recently, however, several studies have suggested asbestos is not as big a problem as originally believed. The only time serious health risks are created is when asbestos is ripped out of walls and thus released into the air. It seems likely that reevaluation of the asbestos problem will result in less-stringent removal requirements and greater reliance on sealing, encapsulation, and fusion of the asbestos where it exists.

PCBs. Polychlorinated biphenyls (PCBs) typically were used in electrical equipment, such as transformers, capacitors, and fluorescent lights. When broken, such equipment releases PCBs into the ground or air, and exposure to PCBs can cause cancer and other health problems. Fortunately, removal and disposal is relatively simple and most of the PCB threat has been eliminated.

LUSTs. Leaking underground storage tanks (LUSTs) are potentially a huge problem for real estate investors. While the underground tanks in service stations are the largest source of such sludge, many others exist as well. Septic tanks and oil tanks of abandoned houses are but two examples. Many industrial firms have stored fuel or buried wastes in underground receptacles, and these sites are often unmapped and forgotten.

Radon. Radon is a naturally occurring radioactive gas found in soils containing uranium, granite, shale, and phosphate. These rocks and soils are common and are constantly generating radon. It can enter buildings through openings in the floor. If radon gas accumulates in sufficient quantities in a building, the chances of contracting lung cancer are increased significantly. Mitigation usually involves either increasing ventilation or sealing floor and foundation cracks. It can be moderately costly and time consuming.

Mold. Mold has been around forever, but now it's being called "the new asbestos." With recent jury verdicts in the millions of dollars and many people running scared, a debate has emerged as to whether mold is one of the major health crises of the decade or junk science that has propelled plaintiff attorneys in a feeding frenzy. The problem is that science has yet to catch up with case law. While judges and juries have been convinced by anecdotal arguments of cause and effect, various scientists and medical experts claim there are still no credible, peer-reviewed studies or clear environmental standards on mold. The potential risk to homeowners and investors is significant because mold caused by water from excessive humidity, leaks, condensation, or flooding is a maintenance issue for the property owner, like termite or mildew prevention, and is not covered by standard insurance policies.[7]

Implications for Real Estate Investors

Purchasers, owners, and lenders must be aware of potential environmental hazards on real estate. To protect themselves, both legally and economically, prospective buyers and lenders should require environmental risk assessments from qualified environmental consultants. Also, buyers of new properties should require confirmation from the developer

---

http://www.epa.gov/asbestos/

U.S. Environmental Protection Agency coverage of asbestos issues.

http://www.epa.gov/swerust1/mtbe/

U.S. Environmental Protection Agency coverage of LUSTs.

http://www.epa.gov/iaq/radon/pubs/consguid.html

Consumer guide to radon.

www.moldupdate.com

Provides mold information for insurers.

www.tamu.edu

The website of the Texas A&M Real Estate Center, provides numerous articles about the effect of mold on real estate.

---

7. Numerous sources of updated information on mold and its implications for homeowners, investors, and insurers are now available. Visit, for example, www.moldupdate.com, a site provided by the National Association of Mutual Insurance Companies; www.naiop.org, the website of the National Association of Industrial and Office Realtors; and recenter.tamu.edu, the website of the Texas A&M Real Estate Center.

that there are no toxic wastes that could be harmful to the property. Freddie Mac and Fannie Mae now require environmental assessments before they will purchase a loan.

The initial standard environmental assessment is known as a *Phase I EVA* (Environmental Value Assessment). It is based largely on a sampling of air and water sources, a search of property records, and a visual inspection of the property. It determines whether there is a reasonable basis to suspect the presence of an environmental risk in the use of the property.[8] If evidence of toxicity is found, more invasive and costly studies will be necessary.

This report, together with written representation from the developer or current owner, constitutes a set of documentary protections for investors. They are particularly necessary because liability insurance to cover toxic wastes cannot be purchased. The risk can only be minimized or shifted to the seller through documentary provisions.

Concept Check

6.14   Why must investors in real estate be concerned with environmental hazards when they acquire property?

The Government's Power of Eminent Domain

Eminent domain is the right of government to acquire private property, without the owner's consent, for public use in exchange for just compensation. The legal procedure involved is called **condemnation.** The power of eminent domain arises from practical necessity of governments to provide basic public services. Federal, state, and local government agencies generally use their rights to take title to real property, or portions of real property, when constructing highways, schools, fire and police stations, and other public facilities.[9]

8. Albert R. Wilson, "The Environmental Opinion: Basis for an Impaired Value Opinion," *Appraisal Journal,* 62, no. 3 (July 1994), pp. 410–23.

9. While the Fifth Amendment gives the federal government the right to "take" private property, the right is also made available to states by the due process clause of the Fourteenth Amendment and confirmed in state constitutions and statutes. Governments may also delegate their power of eminent domain to nongovernmental agencies such as public utilities.

Industry Issues

Is Eminent Domain Out of Control?

Atlantic City, N.J.—An elderly widow whose home was being condemned so Donald Trump could expand one of his casinos hit the jackpot Monday when a judge threw out the cases against her and two other property owners.

In a decision that could prove important throughout the country, Superior Court Judge Richard Williams said the state's plan to seize the land under the government's power of eminent domain was flawed because it set no limits on what Trump could do once he got the property.

Source: Trump loses fight to seize widow's Atlantic City home. reviewjournal.com. *Las Vegas Review Journal,* Tuesday, July 21, 1998
Note: The attempted use of eminent domain for inappropriate private purposes (commonly successfully) is a concern in many circles. See, for example: Dana Berliner, "Public Power, Private Gain," http://www.castlecoalition.com/

Trump had said the land would be used at his Trump Plaza Hotel & Casino for a park, a parking lot, and a limousine waiting area that would add green space, provide jobs, and relieve traffic congestion. As the case ground on, Trump expanded without the three disputed parcels, adding green space around them. Lawyers for Vera Coking, restaurateurs Clare and Vincent Sabatini, and jewelry store owner Josef Banin said the plan was a ruse to allow Trump to avoid paying market value for the land. They had predicted Trump would get control of the property and use it for more casino space.

"I believe in justice. I didn't believe before, but I do now," said the 70-ish Coking, who battled casino companies that have sought her home for more than 16 years.

But Coking is now willing to sell. She wants at least $1.2 million.

"David beat two Goliaths," said her attorney, Glenn Zeitz. "We were up against a strongly funded government agency and one of the most wealthy, powerful individuals in the country."

Public Use

Courts have interpreted the term *public use* broadly, and successful challenges to whether a taking is for a valid public use are rare.[10] The concept of **public use** has evolved to one no longer requiring actual physical use by the condemning agency. It has been expanded by the courts to include instances when there is a clear "public benefit," or **public purpose.** Thus, property for civic centers, cultural centers, trade facilities, and sports facilities may be deemed public uses. In a 1954 ruling, the U.S. Supreme Court further expanded the definition of public benefits to allow for the condemnation of blighted areas for aesthetic benefit.[11] The Michigan Supreme Court later ruled (1981) that the government's power of eminent domain could be used to acquire property to revitalize the manufacturing facilities of the General Motors Corporation on the theory that it provided substantial economic benefit to the public.[12] These cases open the door to a considerable array of arguable uses and apparent abuses as local governments seek to replace low value land uses with higher value uses producing greater tax revenue. (See Industry Issues 6-6.)

Concept Check

6.15 Explain what change has occurred over the last half-century in the use of eminent domain.

Just Compensation

Just compensation is the market value of the property, if completely taken, or the total value of all financial loss if partially taken. The value of a property is based on its highest and best use at the time it is condemned, not necessarily its current use. Just compensation

---

10. Most successful challenges to the government's exercise of its eminent domain rights occur due to technical violations (e.g., improper notification).

11. See *Berman v. Parker,* 348 U.S. 26, 75 S. Ct. 98, 99 L. Ed. 27 (1954).

12. See *Poletown Neighborhood Council v. City of Detroit,* 410 Mich. 616, 304 N.W. 2d 455 (1981).

is the amount that restores the property owner to a financial position equivalent to that existing before the property was taken.

Inverse Condemnation and Regulatory Takings

At times, government activities may result in "taking" a portion of an owner's property rights without using condemnation. New public projects or regulatory provisions may substantially restrict the use of private property and diminish its value. In these cases, a property owner may seek compensation under a concept called inverse condemnation. **Inverse condemnation** is an action, initiated by a property owner against the government, to recover the loss in property value attributed to government activity. Since 1922 an opinion of the U.S. Supreme Court has influenced cases in which the right of compensation for property owners, resulting from zoning and other regulations, has been questioned. In ruling that restrictions on coal mining where surface subsidence could threaten dwellings did not constitute a taking, the Court stated, "The general rule at least is, that while property may be regulated to a certain extent, if regulation goes too far it will be recognized as a taking."[13] This is referred to as a **regulatory taking.** Nevertheless, a 1987 study pointed out that the limitation of property rights by zoning must be severe before the courts grant compensation to property owners. The authors concluded that in eminent domain takings, compensation is almost always expected and required; yet courts usually have refused to compensate owners whose rights have been limited or taken by zoning laws.[14] More recent decisions by the U.S. Supreme Court, however, have shifted the legal doctrine more toward the side of property owners.[15] (See Industry Issues 6-7.)

Concept Check

6.16   Explain the difference between condemnation and inverse condemnation.

The Power of Government to Tax Real Property

In the previous sections of this chapter, we first discussed the power of government to regulate property use through planning, zoning, and building code administration. We then looked at the government's power to acquire private property for public benefit through the eminent domain process. In this section, we look at the power of government to tax real property owners.

For most local governments, real estate taxes represent the largest single source of revenue. Counties, cities, school districts, and other special taxing jurisdictions, such as urban service districts, transit authorities, and water management districts, may levy real property taxes. Most property taxes are **ad valorem taxes;** they are applied in relation to the value of the property.[16] Ad valorem property taxes are charged to property owners by each taxing jurisdiction in which the property is located. Although ad valorem property tax rates vary, they are typically levied at rates between 1.0 and 4.0 percent of a property's market value.[17]

13. See *Pennsylvania Coal Company v. Mahon* (260 U.S. 393, 43 S. Ct. 158, 67 L. Ed. 322 (1922).

14. Jerry T. Ferguson and Robert H. Plattner, "Can Property Owners Get Compensation for 'Takings' by Zoning Laws?" *Real Estate Review* 16, no. 4 (Winter 1987), pp. 72–75.

15. See *First English Evangelical Lutheran Church of Glendale v. County of Los Angeles,* 482 U.S. 304, 107 S. Ct. 2378, 96 L. Ed. 2d 250 (1987), *Lucas v. South Carolina Coastal Council,* No. 505 U.S. 1003, 112 S. Ct. 2886 (1992), and *Dolan v. City of Tigard,* 854 P. 2d 437 (Ore. 1993), reversed, 114 S. Ct. 2309 (1994).

16. The Latin term *ad valorem* is defined as "according, or in proportion, to value."

17. Property tax rates vary considerably due to the number and types of taxing authorities, the different costs of services, and the statutory tax policies of each jurisdiction. While all properties in a single jurisdiction are generally taxed at the same rate, some jurisdictions tax properties of different types, classes, and values at different rates.

6-7

Lucas v. South Carolina Coastal Council

n June 1992 the Supreme Court had an opportunity to revisit this issue in the case of *Lucas v. South Carolina Coastal Council,* 112 S.Ct. 2886 (1992). In that case, developer David Lucas purchased two vacant lots in the Wild Dunes subdivision on the Isle of Palms, a barrier island a few miles south of Charleston, South Carolina. The lots had been flooded in the past, and emergency sandbagging and shore protection were needed in 1983 to defend neighboring homes from erosion. Between 1957 and 1963, the property was underwater. During Hurricane Hugo, the lots were covered by four feet of water.

In July 1988 South Carolina enacted the Beachfront Management Act (S.C. Code Sec. 48–39–250 et seq.) in response to the requirements of the 1980 amendments to the federal Coastal Zone Management Act (CZMA, 16 U.S.C. Sec. 1451 et seq.). The federal statute directed the states to "prevent or significantly reduce threats to life and the destruction of property by eliminating development and redevelopment in high-hazard areas." To regulate development, the South Carolina legislature established "baselines" back from the sand dunes. Most construction or rebuilding of damaged structures seaward of the baseline was prohibited by the act. Lucas, whose lots fell between the baseline and the sea, sued the state for "taking" the use and value of his property, claiming that the regulation constituted a compensable taking under the Fifth Amendment to the U.S. Constitution. The trial court awarded Lucas $1.2 million for the lots. On appeal, the state supreme court ruled that Lucas could not be compensated because building on the lots would be hazardous to the public and the environment. Lucas appealed the decision to the U.S. Supreme Court.

In his appeal, Lucas contended that, because the South Carolina statute deprived him of all economic uses of his property, he must be compensated under the Fifth Amendment, even if the land use regulation was enacted to prevent serious harm. On June 29, 1992, the U.S. Supreme Court reversed the decision by the state supreme court and sent the case back to the South Carolina courts to determine whether the state statute deprived Lucas of his Fifth Amendment right to compensation. The Supreme Court held, by a six to three vote, that regulations that deny a property owner all economic use of land—regardless of the public interest in prevention of harm to the public health, safety, and welfare—violate a property owner's right to compensation under the Fifth Amendment. Thus, when government regulations prohibit previously legal land uses and have the effect of extinguishing all economic value of the property, compensation is owed.

While the Lucas case was being argued before the state supreme court but before the court issued its opinion, the state legislature amended the Beachfront Management Act. The amendment will allow Lucas to gain permits from the Coastal Council after a showing of special circumstances. On remand from the U.S. Supreme Court, the South Carolina Supreme Court concluded that nothing in common law prevented Lucas from developing the lots in the manner he intended. The most recent trial date in the South Carolina Superior Circuit Court was vacated and the parties were able to negotiate a settlement. The state purchased both of Lucas's lots for $1.575 million.

Update: Soon after acquiring the lots, the state sold them for private development, and at least one house (5,000 square feet) now stands on the lots.

Source: Excerpt from Carolynne C. White, JD, and Gerald G. Alberts, MA, National Conference of State Legislatures, *State Legislative Report* 18, no. 9 (September 1993)

In general, property tax revenues are used by governments to finance the public services they provide their constituencies. For example, tax revenues pay for police and fire protection, schools, streets, curbs, sewers, street lighting, parks, and a number of social services. The value of the services provided is capitalized (i.e., captured) in the prices buyers are willing to pay for the properties served. In other words, properties that are occupied by users benefiting from the public services are worth more than they would be without the services. Nevertheless, property taxes may be levied unequally or the revenues misallocated.

Mechanics of the Property Tax

Although property taxes are typically collected through a single county office, several tax jurisdictions within the county where the property is located may levy taxes. A property owner, for example, may pay property taxes to support the budgets of a county, a city, a school district, and a special taxing district (e.g., a downtown redevelopment area). Estimating a particular property owner's total tax liability requires a general understanding of how tax rates are determined.

Determining a Jurisdiction's Budget and Tax Rate

A jurisdiction's **tax rate** is established by evaluating both its budget and the value of its **tax base.** The budget of each jurisdiction with taxing authority is determined by estimating all proposed expenditures of each unit within the jurisdiction. For example, police and fire services, judicial services, public works and engineering, community development, planning and environmental management offices, facilities and information management, parks and recreation, and various social service departments may be included in the budget of a single municipality. The jurisdiction's administrative staff reviews and aggregates the budgets of the individual units and then estimates revenues to be obtained from *nontax* sources. These include license fees, inspection fees, garbage removal fees, fines, intergovernmental transfers (e.g., when a city sells fire protection services to the county), and profits from subsidiary operations (e.g., when a city owns a utility company that earns a profit).

The proposed budget, including projected expenditures and nontax revenues, is then presented to the elected governing board of the jurisdiction (e.g., a city council, county commission, or school board) for approval. Since the tax base—which consists of the taxable value of all the jurisdiction's properties—is known, budget approval implies the adoption of a tax rate sufficient to support the budget.

The basic formula for determining the tax rate is

$$R_T = (E_B - I_O) \div (V_T - V_X)$$

where R_T denotes the tax rate; E_B, the budgeted expenditures; I_O, the income from sources other than property tax; V_T, the total assessed value of all properties; and V_X, the value of property exemptions.

As an example, consider a community's budget, which forecasts expenditures for the coming year of $65 million. Tax income from nonproperty sources is forecast to be $25 million, and the community contains properties with a total assessed value of $2.5 billion. The total value of properties exempt from the property tax is $500 million. Thus, the tax base is $2.0 billion. The tax rate would be established by the following calculation:

$$R_T = (\$65,000,000 - \$25,000,000) \div (\$2,500,000,000 - \$500,000,000)$$
$$R_T = 0.020, \text{ or } 2.0 \text{ percent.}$$

In other words, 2 percent of the taxable value of all properties in the community is required in taxes to pay for the community's expenditures during the coming year. Instead of percentages, however, tax rates are usually stated in **mills,** or dollars per $1,000 of value. Converted to mills, the tax rate, or **millage rate,** for the above community would be 20 mills (i.e., $20 of tax per $1,000 of value).

Concept Check

6.17 With the following information, compute the property tax rate for the community. Total budget expenditures: $40 million, Total nonproperty tax income: $5 million, Total taxable value: $1 billion, Total exemptions: $250 million.

Tax-Exempt Properties

Most communities contain a number of **tax-exempt properties.** Such properties include government-owned properties and others exempted by state law or the state constitution. This category typically includes universities, schools, hospitals, places of worship, and other property of religious organizations. Exempt properties lower the tax base of the community, thus raising the taxes of other property owners.

Homestead and Other Exemptions

Some states allow property owners to deduct a specified amount from their assessed valuations before calculating their property tax bills. The largest of these deductions is the **homestead exemption.** In homestead states, if the property owner occupies a home as the family's principal residence and has claimed residency within the state, the property may be regarded as the family's homestead. In Florida, for example, homeowners may apply for the homestead tax exemption on their principal residences.[18] If they qualify, $25,000 will be deducted from the assessed valuation before their taxes are calculated. Many states also allow property tax exemptions for agricultural and historical property, and for disabled persons, veterans, widows, and the blind. The value of all such exemptions must be subtracted from the total assessed value of properties in calculating a community's tax base.

Calculating Tax Liability

The **tax assessor** (or county property appraiser) appraises all taxable properties in a jurisdiction for property tax assessment. The value for taxation, or **assessed value,** is always related to market value; some states specify that the assessed value must be calculated as a certain percentage of market value, such as 50 percent or 80 percent. Today, however, many states require that assessed values be 100 percent of market values as defined in the law or as interpreted by a state agency, such as the department of revenue. For example, assessed value may be defined or interpreted as market value less the costs of making a property ready for sale, less a normal real estate commission. Thus, the assessed value, while nominally representing 100 percent of market value, may be perhaps 85 or 90 percent of market value, assuming that the market value is estimated accurately by the property tax assessor (or property appraiser). After the property value for tax purposes is determined, the tax rate is multiplied by the **taxable value,** the assessed value less any applicable exemptions, to determine the amount of tax owed.

For example, consider a property appraised for $150,000 in a state that requires tax assessments to be 90 percent of market value. Assume the owner qualifies for a $25,000 homestead exemption. Thus, the taxable value is found to be $110,000.

Market value	$150,000
Assessed value	$135,000 $= (0.90 \times MV)$
Less: Exemptions	$-25,000$
Taxable value	$110,000

Now assume the taxing authorities in the jurisdiction where the property is located have established their tax rates to be the following:

Taxing Authority	**Property Tax Calculation**	
	Millage Rate	**Taxes Levied**
County	8.58	$943.80
City	3.20	$352.00
School district	9.86	$1,084.60
Water management district	0.05	$5.50
Total	21.69	$2,385.90

18. To qualify for a homestead exemption in Florida, the law requires applicants to have legal and equitable title to the property and be residing on the property as of January 1 of the tax year the exemption is to apply. Proof of residency may be offered in the form of a Florida driver's license, voter registration, or vehicle registration and tag number.

The property owner's tax bill would be $110,000 \times 0.02169 = \$2,385.90$, or $\$110 \times 21.69$ mills. If the property owner did not qualify for the homestead exemption, the tax liability would be $\$135,000 \times 0.02169 = \$2,928.15$. Thus, the value of the homestead exemption in terms of property taxes saved is $\$2,928.15 - \$2,385.90 = \$542.25$, or $0.02169 \times \$25,000 = \$542.25$.

A property owner's **effective tax rate** is an important calculation for comparison purposes. It is defined as the amount of tax paid (or owed) divided by the market value of the property. The effective tax rate for this property is 1.59 percent ($\$2,385.90 \div \$150,000$). Because assessment ratios and millage rates can vary, taxes among properties and among taxing jurisdictions are best compared on an effective rate basis.

Concept Check

6.18   Given the following data, compute taxable value: Market value: 100,000 Assessment percentage: 85 percent. Exemption: 10,000. 1.) With a tax rate of 25 mills, what is the amount of the property tax? 2.) What is the effective property tax rate?

Special Assessments

In contrast to ad valorem property taxes levied to finance services that benefit the general community, **special assessments** are levied to pay for specific improvements that benefit a particular, or limited, area. They are commonly used to finance streets, storm water systems, sidewalks, and other area improvements. Special assessments are applied as pro rata charges, not ad valorem, to cover the cost of the improvement, and are levied directly on the properties benefited. For example, the cost of constructing new sidewalks in a subdivision may be shared equally by all the parcels located in the subdivision, or perhaps relative to the size of their lot frontages. In many areas, the use of special assessments has become a popular tool of elected officials to pay for community services and capital improvements while holding down the more politically sensitive tax rates.

Nonpayment of Property Taxes

Foreclosure for nonpayment of property taxes takes several forms among various states. Typically, lists of delinquent taxpayers are published in a newspaper of general circulation, and the delinquents are given a grace period to pay the taxes plus interest and penalties. The right to pay unpaid taxes, plus interest and penalties, before public sale and to reclaim full title to the property, like overdue mortgage payments (see Chapter 10), is known as the *equity right of redemption*. If the taxes are not paid, the properties may be sold at public auction, with the proceeds first used to pay back taxes.[19]

http://www.
statetaxcentral.com/

Coverage and links to tax programs of all states.

Concept Check

6.19   In a sentence, explain each of these terms:
1.   Ad valorem
2.   Pro rata
3.   Special assessments
4.   Exemption

---

19. In some states, the original owner has a period of time (up to two years) after the sale to pay all back taxes, interest, and penalties and to reclaim the property. This right is known as the *statutory right of redemption.*

Criticisms of the Property Tax

The property tax is subject to three major criticisms: (1) It is regressive. (2) It varies among geographic areas. (3) It is poorly administered.

Property Taxation Is Regressive. This criticism holds that the property tax of lower-income households is higher than that of higher-income households, *as a percentage of their respective incomes.* Higher-income households tend to occupy housing that is proportionately less valuable than lower-income households. For example, households with $500,000 annual incomes might own houses averaging $1 million in value (twice the size of their incomes), whereas $75,000 households might have houses averaging $225,000 in value (three times their incomes). Thus, the lower-income households would pay at a higher rate when evaluated as a percentage of their respective incomes. However, whether this constitutes regressive taxation depends on how the resulting public services are distributed across income levels. "Regressive" property taxes may be appropriate if, as evidence indicates, lower-income households use more police protection, fire protection, public schools, and public health services.[20]

Property Tax Rates Vary among Geographic Areas. Because of the local nature of the property tax and its administration, the incidence of the tax may vary from property to property, county to county, and state to state. To reduce inconsistency among counties, most states have undertaken programs to equalize the percentage of tax appraisals to market value. In these states, the tax rolls for each county must be submitted to a state agency for testing and approval. A number of states have enacted constitutional provisions or laws to limit property taxes. The most famous of these (because it was the first) was Proposition 13, enacted in 1978 in California, which limited the property tax rate to 1 percent of property values.

The Property Tax Is Poorly Administered. In many states, county tax assessors or appraisers are elected officials. Special qualifications are not required; therefore the *quality* and *uniformity* of assessing procedures are likely to be less than ideal. In addition, political supporters and large financial contributors may be able to exert considerable influence for favorable appraisals.

To promote education and competence in tax assessing, the International Association of Assessing Officials (IAAO) sponsors courses and other educational programs for members. Many assessors also take courses and seminars sponsored by the leading professional appraisal organizations. And state departments of revenue require that assessors follow prescribed procedures and adhere to minimum appraisal standards.

Concent Check

16.20   List three criticisms of the property tax.

---

20. D. Netzer, *Economics of the Property Tax* (Washington, DC, Brookings Institution, 1966), pp. 45–62.

Summary

This chapter surveys three basic powers of government: its right to regulate land use, its right to take private property for public use, and its right to tax property. The power of federal, state, and local governments to regulate land use through planning, zoning, building codes, and other means is vested in their police power. Communities use these tools to limit the negative effects of noncompetitive market conditions such as externalities, monopolies, congestion, sprawl, and incomplete structure information to increase market efficiency and equity.

Planning is the process of developing guidelines for controlling growth and development. Zoning assigns specific permitted uses to individual parcels of land to carry out the comprehensive plan. States and local jurisdictions experiencing rapid growth have adopted a wide variety of measures to manage such growth. Some states pass laws requiring cities and counties to develop comprehensive plans, require economic and environmental impact statements in large development proposals, prohibit new development unless concurrency provisions are met, and require an allocation of affordable housing in new residential developments. Additionally, some states give local communities the right to establish urban service areas, plan and control urban development outside their boundaries, limit new developments on the basis of objective criteria, and impose development moratoriums. Though lawsuits have challenged zoning and growth management from a variety of standpoints, courts generally have upheld its validity when it is reasonable, nonexclusionary, and comprehensive.

Environmental hazards have become an important consideration in land use regulation in recent years. Asbestos, fiberglass, PCBs, LUSTs, lead paint, radon gas, and mold are some of the most common threats. Real estate investors face large risks from these hazards because owners can be required to clean them up. They must protect themselves by having environmental inspections and by requiring written statements of indemnification from developers and previous owners.

The power of government to acquire private property for public use in exchange for just compensation is referred to as eminent domain. Courts have interpreted the term *public use* broadly to include property taken for a public purpose. Just compensation is the market value of the property. Courts have generally ruled that regulations that limit property rights do not need to be compensated; however, if regulation goes "too far" it will be recognized as a taking and subject to compensation.

The power of government to tax real property owners is the principal source of revenue for local governments. The tax is levied on the value of all property in the taxing jurisdiction, less exempt property. A property's value for tax purposes is usually equal to, or a direct function of, its market value.

Key Terms

Ad valorem taxes 147

Affordable housing allocation 135

Assessed value 150

Comprehensive plan 134

Concurrency 135

Condemnation 145

Dedicated (property) 140

Economic and environmental impact statements 134

Effective tax rate 151

Eminent domain 145

Exclusionary zoning 139

Externalities 129

Extraterritorial jurisdiction 135

Growth moratorium 142

Homestead exemption 150

Impact fee 142

Inverse condemnation 147

Just compensation 146

Mills 149

Millage rate 149

New urbanism 137

Non-conforming use 139

Performance standard 141

Planned unit development (PUD) 141

Public purpose 146

Public use 146

Regulatory taking 147

Smart growth 137

Special assessments 151

Taxable value 150

Tax assessor 150

Tax base 149

Tax-exempt properties 149

Tax rate 149

Toxic waste 143

Urban service area 135

Variance 139

www.mhhe.com/lingarcher1e

Test Problems

Answer the following multiple choice problems.

1. Zoning is an exercise of which type of general limitation on property rights?
   a. Eminent domain.
   b. Taxation.
   c. Police power.
   d. Escheat.
   e. All of the above.

2. A comprehensive plan usually deals with which of the following elements?
   a. Land uses.
   b. Population.
   c. Public services.
   d. Natural resources.
   e. All of the above.

3. Property taxes are the principal source of revenue for:
   a. The federal government.
   b. School districts.
   c. Local governments.
   d. State governments.
   e. Both local governments and school districts.

4. The authority for approving site plans for large projects ultimately rests with the:
   a. City council or commission.
   b. Mayor or city manager.
   c. Planning board or commission.
   d. Planning board or commission staff.
   e. Zoning review board.

5. The most accurate conclusion about the regressivity of the property tax is that it is:
   a. Regressive.
   b. Not regressive.
   c. Based on ability to pay.
   d. Regressive, but when benefits are considered, the net result is not regressive.
   e. Not regressive until the benefits are considered.

6. Traditional land use controls (pre-1970) include:
   a. Zoning.
   b. Building codes.
   c. Subdivision regulations.
   d. a and b, but not c.
   e. All three: a, b, and c.

7. Radon gas is:
   a. A naturally occurring result of geologic activity.
   b. A relatively recent phenomenon caused by the earth's warming.
   c. Important only in the western United States.
   d. Controllable by soil treatment.
   e. Regarded as a nuisance but not a health hazard.

8. *New urbanism* is a term used to describe:
   a. Growth management laws enacted by state governments.
   b. Improvement of transportation systems to encourage dispersion of a city's population.
   c. The requirement that infrastructure be available concurrently with new development.
   d. The theory that residential and commercial uses should be integrated, streets and parking should discourage through traffic, and housing should be built close to the street.
   e. The trend for the construction of self-sufficient "new towns."

9. Elements of traditional zoning include all *except:*
   a. Performance standards.
   b. Setback requirements.
   c. Bulk limits.
   d. Land use categories.
   e. Provision for special use districts.

10. Externalities in land use include all *except:*
    a. Leap-frog development
    b. Increase storm runoff from paving.
    c. Traffic congestion.
    d. Inability to judge the quality of a structure, once built.
    e. Noise created by a land use.

Study Questions

1. Assume that you own a small apartment building close to a major commercial street and a service station. You learn that there has been a major leak of underground storage tanks from the service station, and the gasoline has spread onto and below the surface of your property. Discuss sources of value loss to your property from the contamination.

2. A local businessman has applied for a permit to construct a bar that will feature "adult dancing" in a commercially zoned area across the street from your residential subdivision. As an owner of a $120,000 house within the subdivision, would you favor or oppose this development? What effect do you think it could have on the value of your property? If you were opposed, how could you fight approval of the permit?

3. A medium-size city has proposed to build a "greenway" along a creek that flows through the center of the city. The city wants to clear a strip about 50 feet wide and construct a paved path for bicycles and foot traffic (walkers and joggers). Proponents claim that it would be a highly desirable recreational facility for the community, while a very vocal and insistent group of opponents claims that it would degrade the environment and open properties along the creek to undesirable users and influences.

   Identify some specific positive and negative aspects of the proposal. Would you be in favor of the proposal, if you lived in the city? Would it make a difference if you lived along the creek?

4. The main argument traditionally advanced in favor of zoning is that it protects property values. Do you believe this contention? If so, how does zoning protect property values? If you do not believe the contention, why not?

5. Do you believe that the owners of properties contaminated by events that occur on another property (e.g., gasoline leakage or spills) should be responsible for cleaning up their properties? Why or why not? If not, who should pay for the cleanup?

6. The property tax has been criticized as an unfair base for financing public schools. Areas that have high property values are able to pay for better schools than areas having lower property values. Thus, there is an inequality of educational opportunities that tends to perpetuate educational and social disadvantages for those who live in low-income areas.

   a. Do you agree or disagree?

   b. How could school financing be modified to provide more equal funding among all regions of a state?

7. A property owner who owes 8 mills in school taxes, 10 mills in city taxes, and 5 mills in county taxes and who qualifies for a $25,000 homestead exemption would owe how much tax on a property assessed at $80,000?

Explore The Web

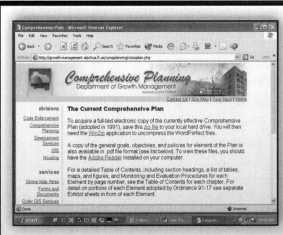

Go to your county's Internet home page. Locate your county's comprehensive plan and summarize one of its basic elements.

Solutions to Concept Checks

1. State and local governments are granted police power by the Constitution to regulate land use.

2. Examples of monopolies that affect local land use are transportation, water, and sewer systems.

3. Examples of negative externalities that affect local land use are excessive smoke, congestion, debris, noise, and excessive storm runoff.

4. The most universal example of incomplete information in real estate is the assessment of the quality of construction and the safety hazards that may exist in a structure. Building codes have been adopted to remedy the problem.

5. A community land use plan should address the community's future population growth, its requirements for water and other natural resources, its physical characteristics, its need for public services, and its need for various types of land use, financial resources, and political constraints.

6. Economic and environmental impact statements analyze a development project's effect on the surrounding areas. Concurrency is the requirement that infrastructure be available in an area before development takes place. Affordable housing allocation is a requirement that encourages or mandates a "reasonable and fair" component of new housing construction for lower-income families. An urban service area delineates a boundary around a community where local government plans are set to provide for public services and urban development is discouraged outside the urban service area. Extraterritorial jurisdiction allows local governments to plan and control urban development outside their boundaries until annexation can occur.

7. An environmental revolution in the late 1960s launched the revolution in land use controls about 1970. Environmental events such as publication of *Silent Spring,* the Love Canal incident, and the concept of spaceship earth all contributed to the land use control revolution.

8. Traditional planning of street layout is built through a hierarchy of cul-de-sacs. Additionally, traditional planning favors complete containment of nonresidential land uses in designated areas. On the other hand, the new urbanism planning allows for grid pattern, narrow streets, and a mix of land uses within the same area.

9. In addition to type of land use, zoning typically imposes setback requirements, building height limits, building floor area limits as a ratio to land area.

10. Three requirements for zoning to be a legitimate use of police power are that the ordinances are reasonable, based on a comprehensive plan, and provide for all types of housing.

11. Nonconforming land use is one that has previously been allowed on a parcel of land but which would no longer be permitted due to a change in the zoning ordinance. A variance is the change in the requirements of an existing zoning ordinance due to a hardship condition. Exclusionary zoning tends to exclude lower-income groups.

12. A PUD can differ from traditional zoning by: allowing mixed uses, not imposing uniform setbacks, allowing variable density, and incorporating open spaces and nature preservation along with structures.

13. Some examples of performance standards include requiring storm water runoff to be no greater than before the development of the parcel, requiring permits before cutting down trees, and enforcing local emission and noise limits.

14. Investors in real estate must be concerned with environmental hazards when they acquire a property because they will ultimately be responsible for any hazard found on the site, which may be a costly cleanup.

15. In the last half century, the use of eminent domain has come to include public benefit as a public use. Therefore, the public does not need to use the property, but only to benefit from its taking.

16. Condemnation is the legal procedure of the government acquiring private property through eminent domain. Inverse condemnation is an action, initiated by property owners against the government, to recover the loss in their property's value attributed to government activity.

17. The tax rate is 4.67 percent.

18. The amount of property tax equals $1,875. The effective tax rate is 1.875 percent.

19. Ad valorem taxes are based upon the value of the property. Pro rata charges are used for special assessments, where owners pay a fair share for the assessment, usually based on street front footage. Special assessments are taxes specifically levied for a certain purpose that benefits a limited area. Exemptions are a specified deduction from a property's assessed value before calculating property tax bills.

20. Criticisms of property taxes include that they are regressive, vary by geographical area, and are poorly administered.

Additional Readings

The following books contain expanded examples and discussions of government regulation and real estate markets:

Collier, Nathan S. *Construction Funding: The Process of Real Estate Development, Appraisal, and Finance.* New York: John Wiley, 2002.

Downs, A. *Urban Affairs and Urban Policy.* Cheltenham U.K. Edward Elgar Publication, 1998.

Miles, Mike E., Gayle Berens, and Marc A. Weiss. *Real Estate Development: Principles and Practices,* 3rd ed. Washington, DC: Urban Land Institute, 2000.

Russ, Thomas H., *Redeveloping Brownfields: Landscape Architects, Planners, Developers.* New York: McGraw-Hill, 2000.

Schilling, Joseph M., Christine Gaspar, and Nadejda Mishkovsky. *Beyond Fences: Brownfields and the Challenges of Land Use Controls.* Washington, DC: International City/County Management Association, 2000.

Schiffman, Irving. *Alternative Techniques for Managing Growth,* 2nd ed. Berkeley: University of California, Institute of Governmental Studies Press, 1999.

Gitelman, Mortan and Robert R. Wright. *Land Use in a Nutshell,* 4th ed. St. Paul, MN: West Group, 2002.

The following text is an excellent introduction to the field of urban planning:

Levy, John M. *Contemporary Urban Planning,* 5th ed. Upper Saddle River, NJ: Prentice Hall, 1999.

The following article discusses the U.S. Supreme Court decisions that make it more difficult for condemners to take or limit property rights without paying just compensation to the owner.

Epstein, Paul C. "Dedications and Exactions: The Supreme Court Levels the Playing Field." *Appraisal Journal* 63, no. 4 (October 1995), pp. 453–56.

The author of the following article presents appraisal methodology and case studies dealing with the valuation of contaminated properties:

Patchin, Peter J. "Contaminated Properties and the Sales Comparison Approach." *Appraisal Journal* 62, no. 3 (July 1994), pp. 402–409.

This article reports on a study of regulatory policies, often achieved through zoning ordinances, used by state and local governments to encourage or mandate the production of affordable housing units. The authors conclude that these programs have been effective, but by themselves are inadequate to meet the needs for affordable housing.

Smith, Marc T., Charles J. Delaney, and Thomas Liou. "Inclusionary Housing Programs: Issues and Outcomes." *Real Estate Law Journal* 25, no. 2 (Fall 1996), pp. 155–71.

The following newsletter of the Lincoln Institute of Land Policy provides news, articles, and summaries of studies undertaken by the Institute. Most of the articles and studies pertain to topics covered in this chapter.

Lincoln Institute of Land Policy. *Land Lines* (newsletter). 113 Brattle Street, Cambridge, MA 02138-3400. www.lincolninst.edu

Forecasting Ownership Benefits *and* Value:
Market Research

Learning Objectives

After reading this chapter you will be able to:

1. Define market segmentation and give three examples for real estate markets.

2. Identify the sequence of steps in the cycle of real estate market research.

3. Identify five questions for writing a "market-defining story."

4. Locate data sources on the Internet for county, MSA, and census tract level household demographics, detailed local employment, and the composition of business by county.

5. Identify at least two applications in real estate market research for geographic information systems.

6. Explain what role psychographics can have in real estate market research.

7. Identify at least two possible applications of survey research in real estate market research.

Introduction

In Chapter 5 we examined cities. We considered the influences that created them and caused their decline or growth. Further, we examined the forces that determine a city's form, resulting in a matrix or network that we know as the urban spatial economy. It remains, however, to relate the urban economic matrix to the value of a specific property. This chapter is about bridging that gap through real estate market research. The objective here is to construct a plausible relationship between the patterns and forces at work within the urban matrix and the cash flows to an individual property that give value to its owner.

We first note the neglected challenge of real estate market research: market segmentation. Our argument is that segmentation must be adequately recognized to do successful market research, but the challenge of market research is made especially difficult by market segmentation because it leaves little to rely on as constant. For this reason real estate market research must be understood not as a form but as a process. We outline that process and demonstrate it through three cases. Then we consider the challenge that real estate market cycles pose for market research. Finally, we discuss three tools applicable to real estate market research: geographical information systems (GIS), psychographics, and survey research.

Market Research: The Weak Link of Real Estate Valuation

Chapter 5 opened with numerous examples of real estate market "disasters." The message of this chapter is that one cannot value real estate without understanding its urban context. This context certainly includes the urban economic relationships discussed in that chapter, but it also includes land use controls that may constrain the use of a site or dampen or accentuate the effects of economic forces.

But there is still more to the puzzle of market research. Not only do land uses vary by the set of linkages important to them, but they vary by nonlocational requirements as well. For example, the features required of a housing unit depend heavily upon the income level of the target household. The land use density, the size of the dwelling, the mix of rooms, and a host of other factors may differ between low-income and high-income housing. And the difference is not merely a matter of scale. Lower-income households do not merely demand a smaller pool in their backyard, nor do they simply demand a smaller country club in their neighborhood than wealthy households. Instead, they typically look for completely different means of meeting their leisure and social needs. In addition, the housing decisions of lower-income households are likely to be more sensitive to the type of financing available than higher-income households.

But these qualitative differences in housing preference are not by income level alone. Single persons or working couples certainly have different housing preferences than families with children, and retired households have different preferences than working households.

In nonresidential realms, differing real estate needs among firms can become even more important. For example, some analysts believe that markets of neighborhood shopping centers and "power centers" have a winner-take-all character that enable only shopping facilities with a market-dominating anchor tenant to have long-term viability.[1] If so, the value of a center with a "winning" anchor tenant is likely to reflect that advantage. Office buildings have their own set of nonlocational features that differentiate properties, including floor plate size, amount and character of parking, provisions for electronics and communications systems, adequacy of common areas, available amenities and services, nature of existing tenants, and other factors.

Concept Check

7.1 List three kinds of factors that affect the value of an urban property.

Often these nonlocational aspects of properties dominate the selection decisions of renters or buyers. Unfortunately, real estate market analysis often has inadequately recognized both the locational and nonlocational nuances of intended markets. When a senior official of one disaster described in Chapter 5 was asked about the market analysis for his project, he simply replied, with all too much credibility, "Market analyses are useless!"

---

1. "Power centers" are shopping centers dominated by such "big box" retailers as discount stores, or "category killers" such as Circuit City or Best Buy, and Lowes or Home Depot.

Market Segmentation

The nuances in the preferences or needs of market subgroups are generally termed **market segmentation.** The notion of market segmentation, long established in the realm of marketing for beverages, cars, and most retail goods, has been much slower to penetrate the analysis of real estate markets. Appraisers, for example, seldom acknowledge it in their work, though it presumably can be fundamental in determining the selection of comparables, a critical step in most appraisal work, as discussed in Chapter 8.

The importance of market segmentation is this: To the extent that it exists in a market, market analysis should focus on the relevant market segments for the property involved. This point has a profound corollary: Most data about most real estate are irrelevant to a given market study. A second corollary, demonstrated in the examples below, is that the most important data for a given market study often are not readily available, and must be approximated by creative use of other data. It is not far off the mark to say that *effective real estate market research is largely a matter of excluding the irrelevant.*[2]

A problem with market segmentation is that it is an empirical notion; that is, its most significant facets are not known without actually researching the relevant markets. Moreover, the important facets of market segmentation may vary with market type and location. Thus, the challenge in real estate market research is to recognize market segmentation in a manageable but effective manner. This is a primary goal of the approach to market analysis elaborated below.

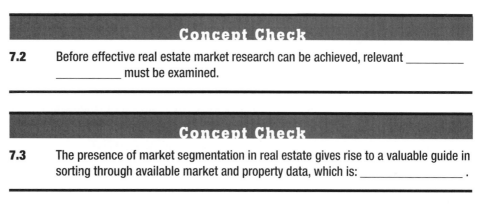

Concept Check

7.2   Before effective real estate market research can be achieved, relevant _____ _____ must be examined.

Concept Check

7.3   The presence of market segmentation in real estate gives rise to a valuable guide in sorting through available market and property data, which is: _____ .

Real Estate Market Research as Storytelling

Unfortunately, our ideas about real estate market segmentation have a sobering implication for market research: Little can be said, in general, about how to do it. Indeed, it is best thought of as a process of discovery rather than a particular formula or format. Where this process leads can depend on the particular type of property involved and the particular market context. Among other implications, this arguably makes market research the most creative and challenging aspect of real estate analysis. The process is suggested in Exhibit 7-1. It begins by tentatively defining the market "story" involved. This is followed by collection of *relevant* data to examine the market and test the initial definitions. Then comes an initial evaluation of results, or market assessment. Frequently this may be followed by the refinement of the market definitions and further collection of *relevant* data. Sometimes at this point, very specifically focused survey research may become important. This iterative process may continue through multiple rounds until further refinements will yield no additional useful information.

Concept Check

7.4   Rather than approaching real estate market research as a form or formula, the conditional nature of the task makes it a _____ .

_____

2. This was a point frequently made by the brilliant real estate academic and analyst James Graaskamp. (See footnote 14.)

Exhibit 7-1   The Cycle of Market Research

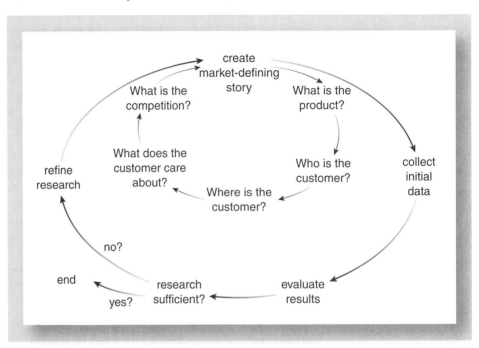

The Beginning Point: A Market-Defining Story

The crucial beginning point of the market research process is to construct a market defining "story." This story needs to answer the following questions:

1. What is the real estate product under consideration?
2. Who are the customers (target market)?
3. Where are the customers? (What is the market area?)
4. What do the customers care about? (What aspects of the product?)
5. Who are the competitors?

We argue that an important beginning of any real estate market research should be to actually *write* a page or more story of this nature. The discipline of writing it cannot help but clarify the researcher's understanding of the market involved. Further, because market research is, after all, the researcher's story of what is happening and will happen, it is important to the ultimate user to understand the writer's underlying assumptions. The more difficult it is to write this story, the more important it is to do it. Below, we will show examples of such stories.

Important help in writing a market-defining story can come from industry literature. Clues about potential market segmentation can come from information on various types of properties and their characteristics. A particularly rich source is the list of publications from the Urban Land Institute.[3] Other good sources are listed at the end of this chapter.[4]

www.uli.org

The single richest source of written material and other resources on real estate design and development.

Concept Check

7.5   It is recommended that the first step in evaluating any property is to write:

---

3. More recent examples of ULI publications include Adrienne Schmitz and Deborah L. Brett, *Real Estate Market Analysis,* (2001) and Richard Peiser and Anne B. Frej, *Professional Real Estate Development: The ULI Guide to the Business,* 2nd ed. (2003). Many older publications of ULI are excellent as well.

4. In addition to descriptive information, the literature mentioned contains a voluminous amount of material on methods and formats for market research in real estate. While we agree with the potential value of much of this material, we simply caution that its relevance depends altogether on the nature of the case involved—hence our focus on defining the market at the outset.

Initial Collection of Data

The market-defining story should serve to identify the needed data in the analysis. It also should identify as irrelevant a vast amount of commonly available data. However, little can be said in advance about which is which. For this reason we simply show examples of what data are relevant in the three "stories" that follow, and what data are at hand in each case.

The initial story that one constructs may be as much fiction as reality. However, it gives one something to focus on, to test, and to verify. Thus, as one collects relevant data, one remains wary of evidence that compels a refinement of the story. It may be possible to find clues to whether one's story is on the mark or in need of revision, as we will show later.

First Analysis

With initial data in hand, one makes a first attempt to draw conclusions about the market questions. Commonly the critical questions will be about **market parameters,** that is, key numbers that characterize the current condition and trend in the market. For rental markets these typically include current occupancy rate, future occupancy rates and rental rate growth. For buyer markets they include current and projected sales rates. Thus, one will ask what range of these critical parameters appears to be consistent with the data that have been assembled. For example, with subdivision or condominium projects, the critical question will concern how many units will sell (at a given price) in each month, quarter, or year of the study horizon, that is, the period covered by the study. For an operating property such as apartments, rental offices, or rental retail, the critical questions will be about projected occupancy level and rental rate growth over the study horizon. If the initial efforts have been successful, the analyst will be able to identify boundaries (never a single number) for these critical parameters.

Refining the Research

In some cases, the initial projections will answer the question at hand, and the analysis is complete. However, if the "story" is unconvincing or the range of projected parameters is too wide to answer the question at hand, the analysis will need to be refined.

After the first analysis, the analyst will better understand what factors are important to the market projections. He or she may need to modify the market-defining story or collect additional data from the marketplace about demand or supply. Still more iterations of data collection and analysis may occur, so long as these are cost effective in narrowing the forecast range for the critical parameters. However, it may also become clear that the forecast range of parameters is too broad to answer the critical question and that additional research will not help. This would suggest that the property is highly risky, with very uncertain value.

A Reverse to Conventional Market Research

An important point about our "story" approach to market research is that it starts at the property and moves outward—that is, our initial step is to characterize the property and its specific market, whereas the conventional approach to market analysis is to move from general to specific. While conventional market analysis starts with national or world conditions and works down by steps to the property, our story approach first seeks to define the property and its market in order to identify a stronger bridge outward to the macro conditions. We know better what macro conditions to be concerned about if we have established a clearer understanding of our target market and the factors that drive it.

Below, we apply our story approach to three diverse cases. The first two dramatically illustrate the significance of recognizing market segmentation, revealing real cases where a small amount of market segmentation analysis could have prevented unmitigated real estate disasters. The final case is one where the end remains open. It is an application to an apartment feasibility problem, and is a more standard example. Even so, it illustrates that seemingly standard real estate market analysis can have surprising twists that lead to much more revealing analysis.

Concept Check

7.6   Whereas real estate market research traditionally starts with a _____ perspective, the approach argued here begins with _____ .

Three Examples of Market Research

Market Research Example 1: Elysian Forest, a Planned Unit Development

Some years ago in a small college community, University City, the first planned unit development, Elysian Forest, was introduced by a large national developer. As discussed in Chapter 6, a planned unit development (PUD) is a residential development that differs from traditional residential subdivisions in several respects. First, it allows for variable density, encompassing some blend of detached single family, attached single family, townhouses and apartments. Second, it typically has smaller individual lots, often without side-yards, but includes a variety of common areas and recreation facilities. Elysian Forest was a bold, innovative and sophisticated project for the city, and with 900 units, was of unprecedented scale.

In Exhibit 7-2 are basic dimensions of the local housing market and of Elysian Forest. Features that distinguished the houses of Elysian Forest include the following:

1. The lots of Elysian Forest averaged less than half the size of typical single family lots prevailing for University City housing at the time, with most of the lots planned for zero-lot-line cluster homes or townhouses. (See Exhibits 7-3 and 7-4)
2. The housing units of Elysian Forest were in a price range between the 70th and 92nd percentile of the University City Sales distribution. (That is, only 30 percent of all local sales were at prices above the Elysian Forest minimum price, while 8 percent of all local sales were at prices still higher than those of Elysian Forest.)[5]
3. As a planned unit development, 15 to 20 percent of the land in Elysian Forest was reserved for open space and recreation areas in place of buildable lots.
4. Linkages of Elysian Forest were of average quality with respect to work commuting, school access, shopping and distance to "preferred" neighborhoods. Schools serving the neighborhood were good, as were most of the schools in the city.
5. Topography and other features of the site were satisfactory, but not distinguished.

Exhibit 7-2   Characteristics of Elysian Forest and the University City Housing Market

	Projected Sales of Elysian Forest				
Year	1	2	3	4	5
Patio Homes, Townhouses, Condos and Small-lot Single Family	88	212	236	260	104
	Estimated Sales in the University City Housing Market				
Year	1	2	3	4	5
All Sales	1,500	1,500	1,550	1,600	1,700
New Units	500	600	850	900	1,100

5. One of the most valuable types of information about local housing markets is the volume of sales, by price. Unfortunately, in too many cases, neither local real estate organizations nor local governments bother to report this data, even though it is easily compiled from property transaction records.

Exhibit 7-3 Elysian Forest and Its Competition

Elysian Forest: Two Cluster Homes with Common Wall

The Competitive Standard: Two "Parade of Homes" of the Time

Exhibit 7-4 Example Patio Home Cluster of Elysian Forest

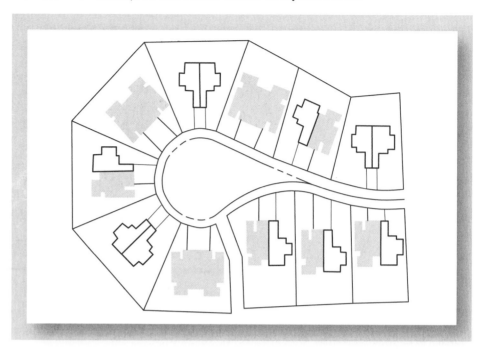

Typical Cluster plan.

The Market Defining Story. Since Elysian Forest was very different from the customary housing stock of University City at the time of its introduction, careful attention to the market defining story seems important. We approach the story using the five questions listed earlier:

1. *What is the product?* We have noted that it is mostly cluster homes and townhouses built at relatively high density. The project is relatively "high end" since the lowest price unit is higher than 70 percent of the house prices transacted in the University City market. The prices projected for Elysian Forest compare to about 22 percent of the residences being sold at the time in University City.

2. *Who are the customers?* We must ask about the buyer income range, and about the types of households likely to be interested in Elysian Forest. Remembering that the units are relatively small, with a high cost per square foot of floor space, it becomes clear that a buyer can get much more house and yard by purchasing from the more conventional stock of houses in University City, such as shown in Exhibit 7-3. Further, the city is relatively small, with low density, and has a tradition of large private yards and houses. As a tentative story, we assume that families with children and pets are likely to prefer the more conventional residences where they can obtain more space and more distance from neighbors for the money. Adopting this assumption for the moment, we conclude that the primary market segment for Elysian Forest is an upper income range representing 22 percent of the housing market in terms of price, and is comprised of households that are not traditional "full-nest" families.[6] Thus, the market might include childless couples, "empty nesters," retired couples, single adults, and possibly single parents.

3. *Where are the customers?* There are multiple possible market segments. With University City's fairly young population, most retirement buyers are likely to come from out-

---

6. Families with husband, wife and children at home.

of the current decade), data similar to the "long-form" data of the decennial census used here will become available on an annual basis through the American Community Survey.[9]

Concept Check

7.8 Data from the U.S. Census is durable for a number of years, even with changing population counts, so long as one is using the data to obtain _____ .

Market Research Example 2: Palm Grove Office Complex

A second example of a market analysis problem illustrates the importance of a market-defining story in a nonresidential context. Again in University City, a developer proposed the Palm Grove office complex, an innovative project for the city in both scale and type of buildings. The project proposed two four-floor "glass blocks," each with 40,000 square feet of space, or 10,000-square-foot floor plates. While a few buildings of similar magnitude existed in the city, they were built by and for the users, and no office building of the scale proposed ever had been built on a speculative basis.[10]

While the location is on a major arterial, the site poses some concerns. It is surrounded by housing, a car dealer, a high school, and a few small "strip" offices. It is distant from any other office centers.

The Market-Defining Story. Once again we construct our market-defining story as answers to the series of questions identified previously:

1. *What is the product?* The structures are general-purpose office space, modern, but of modest quality (i.e., they lack distinguishing architecture, landscaping, or other notable features), in a location lacking strong positive supporting amenities and where the average distance to employee parking is approximately 75 yards. The structures are not designed with special facilities that might serve laboratories or medical offices.

2. *Who is the customer?* As a starting point in identifying the Palm Grove market segment, it is useful to compare the building design to the predominant stock of office buildings in University City. A drive down any of the main arteries of the city reveals that, apart from some medical offices near hospitals and some government offices, the typical office buildings are smaller than the proposed complex—say, 1,200 to 4,000 square feet, with two floors at most—with very close access to surface parking, and usually with high visibility from the street. This stock contrasts with Palm Grove where the floors are 10,000 square feet, parking is several hundred feet from the office, and three floors require an elevator ride. The design suggests that the proposed buildings are best suited to organizations that require the larger floor plates. If we suppose that office firms typically want 150 square feet of space per employee, then firms with, say, 25 or more employees would be the best candidates for the proposed office buildings. (The existing style of buildings should be satisfactory for fewer than this number of employees.)

    For general-purpose office buildings such as proposed for Palm Grove, likely categories of firms include the following:

    - Finance and insurance, except depository institutions such as banks and credit unions.
    - Nonresidential real estate brokerage and management firms.

---

9. Refer to the website of the U.S. Bureau of the Census for updates on the plans and progress for the American Community Survey: www.census.gov.

10. Speculative building is constructing for unknown buyers or tenants.

- Engineering and consulting.
- Accounting.
- Computer services and programming.
- Management consulting.
- Market and public opinion research.

Types of office firms unlikely to be interested in Palm Grove would include medical offices because of the distance from hospitals and the absence of special plumbing. Law offices also would have little interest due to the distance from the courtrooms (five miles away). Residential real estate firms do not concentrate their employees in a large single office, and they want maximum street access. Social service organizations might use the larger floor plates, but they might reduce the attractiveness of the property for nonsocial service businesses, and would not pay premium rents. Thus, they would be last-resort tenants in the view of the owner.

3. *Where are the customers?* The market could possibly be among firms relocating to University City, but the flow of such firms with 25 or more employees is small and quite uncertain. Thus, we assume that most of the prospective tenants are local.

4. *What do the customers (tenants) care about for Palm Grove?* The business community of University City, apart from higher education and medical activity, is small and local in character. Thus, a very large portion of the business community provides services to households and other small businesses. The linkages of the site appear satisfactory for many of these users with the possible exception of the isolation of the site from any comparable offices. In addition, several building features, which we already have alluded to, appear to be concerns for local service tenants.

5. *Who is the competition?* For occupants needing space of, say, 4,000 square feet or less (those with under 25 employees), existing single-floor office buildings and "build-to-suit" space is very competitive. Because of convenient access and parking, the competitive space appears to hold significant advantages for most of these firms.

Initial "Story." The outcome of our tour through the market defining questions is this: We are looking for general-purpose office tenants with 25 or more employees. We believe that they must already be within the city.

Initial Data Collection. In assessing the market potential for the building, one approach might be to canvass the business community in search of office-based businesses that have 25 or more employees. Lists of chamber of commerce members or lists of firms from a local economic development authority usually include the number of employees, and would assist with this effort. A virtue of this approach to market research is that it also could serve to actually market the buildings since the firms identified are the most likely tenants. However, as a preliminary approach, we can examine published data on local business patterns. Such information is instantly available over the Internet from the U. S. Bureau of the Census in *County Business Patterns,* an annual county-level survey of firms by industry and number of employees.

http://www.census.gov/ epcd/cbp/view/cbpview. html.

County Business Patterns

Initial Analysis. Examination of *County Business Patterns* reveals the number of firms by size for detailed categories of all of the prospective market segment groups listed. The important result is that at the actual launch of the project in University City, the total number of firms in the office categories identified with more than 20 employees was less than 10. In short, University City is revealed to be a city of predominantly very small office firms, and there was little prospect of finding enough tenants from a total of less than 10 to successfully fill the buildings.

The history of the project is that only one of the two buildings was built, and it has spent much of its life more than half vacant. Obviously, it was a financial disaster that could have been predicted with a few minutes of thoughtful examination of the relevant market segments and the use of freely available government data.

7.9   A local source for local employers and their size usually is from the _____
        or _____ . A national source for county level data on firms and their size
        is _____ .

Market Research Example 3: Plane Vista Apartments

Orlando International Airport in Florida was the 16th busiest airport in the United States in 2002, and has been among the most rapidly growing. Immediately to the north of the airport is an area of business and apartment development, much of which has been created since 1995. The owners of Plane Vista apartments, in that area, are considering adding a second phase to increase the total apartment complex from 500 to 900 units. Before committing to the expansion, they want to determine the market potential over the next five years. Thus, they wish to conduct a market analysis for the expansion.

The Market-Defining Story. The existing apartment complex appears standard in terms of its mix by unit size and number of bedrooms. Its quality, design, and amenities are very competitive among high-quality apartment complexes in the area. It does not appear targeted to any special demographic group such as singles, students, retired persons, or military. The breadth of its appeal is suggested by its unusually large variation in floor plans. The only aspect of the complex that might give it special appeal to younger working people is its large weight room and large indoor gymnasium for basketball and volleyball. It seems reasonable to expect the second phase to be even more competitive because its design may be able to benefit from experience of the initial phase in "fine-tuning" for the market. In short, the first phase of Plane Vista appears targeted to a fairly broad market range at the high-quality end of the spectrum.

   One possible concern is the nature of the location. First, the site (see Exhibit 7-9) is near the perimeter of development for Orlando. Thus, in a soft market it could be forced to give up unusually high concessions relative to competitors that are closer to central Orlando. A second concern is with the amenities in the area. As an essential part of getting acquainted with the property, we visit and inspect the neighborhood. We observe that the area surrounding Plane Vista probably compares weakly to many other areas of Orlando in terms of amenities such as recreation, entertainment, or scenic areas. (The lakes in the area appear to be largely privatized.) Further, we do not detect any special schools in the area, and suspect that the location is a weak competitor for students at the rapidly growing University of Central Florida, 15 miles to the northeast. Thus, it appears that households generally would choose the area purely as a cost-effective choice for commuting access to jobs. In short, we suspect that the location, at best, offers no premium advantage to households relative to other locations in Orlando. At worst, it might suffer a deduction in rent because of its location at the edge of the market, and might be particularly vulnerable in a market downturn.

   With these impressions, we begin the process of writing a market-defining story, using our sequence of questions, as before:

1. *What is the product?* To reiterate, it is a fairly standard, broad appeal, high-quality apartment complex. It may be slightly pitched to young working households, given the generous athletic facilities. It may be slightly remote relative to other competitive apartment complexes, a point that needs to be examined more closely.

2. *Who are the customers?* We will initially assume that the customers come from the broad spectrum of working renter households, restricted perhaps to the upper third of the renter household income range.

3. *Where are the customers?* At first inspection, the existing apartments seem to be integrated into the broader metro, higher rent apartment market, suggesting that customers will be persons working in much of central, south, and eastside Orlando. Note that initially we are assuming that commuting time has little significance in the choice of apartment location within Orlando.

http://terrafly.com

Provides aerial photo coverage for most areas of the United States.

Exhibit 7-9   The Location of Plane Vista Orlando, Florida

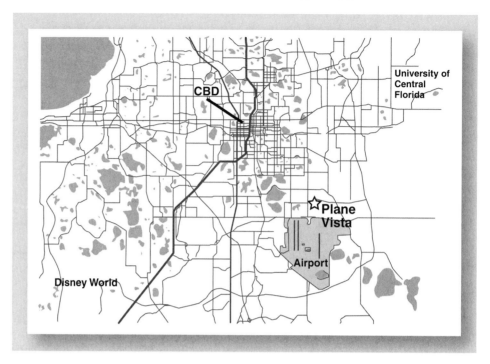

4. *What aspects of the product are customers sensitive to?* For brevity, we bypass this question. Because the owners have experience operating a successful apartment complex adjacent to the target site, we can assume that they will incorporate a sophisticated answer to this question in any proposed designs.

5. *Who is the competition?* The competition appears to be other similar, new or emerging, high-quality apartment complexes in central, south, and eastside Orlando.

Initial Data Collection. Our initial story is that prospects of Plane Vista, Phase II will parallel those of the general, high-end apartment market in Orlando, with possible focus on central, south, and east Orlando. But with Plane Vista lying somewhat on the edge of the city, we want to see what portion of competitors have an access advantage to central Orlando. Thus, we begin data collection by examining the pattern of relatively new apartment complexes in the Orlando area, as shown in Exhibit 7-10.

However, in examining the distribution of apartment complexes in Exhibit 7-10, we immediately see a rather sharp discrepancy between our initial market story and the actual data. We assumed that Plane Vista is part of the larger Orlando apartment market, yet the map shows that it is rather far removed from most other recently built apartments. This compels us to reevaluate our market-defining story. We must ask why this isolation exists. Is it because of restrictions on apartment supply, which could be positive, or because of demand factors?

To examine the pattern of demand, we look for information on the location of jobs. We have assumed in our market-defining story that demand for the apartments in Plane Vista is driven by jobs. We find that data on job locations are not available publicly or even privately. So, given the perceived importance of our question, we set about to create an approximation of work location patterns. We obtain the database of the county property appraiser which includes property parcel boundaries, structure size, and land use by some 200 categories. We obtain this database in a GIS (geographic information systems) format so that we can map various land uses.[11] We will use nonresidential building space as a proxy for job locations.

---

11. The GIS property parcel data base was provided by KeyInSites of Orlando, Florida.

Exhibit 7-10 Locations of Recently Built Apartments

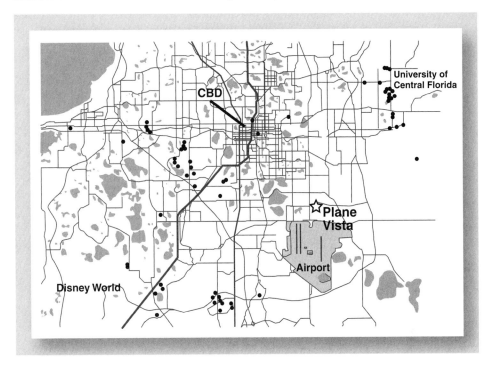

Because we know that space per worker varies greatly by industry, we want to account for this as best we can. So, from the U.S. Bureau of Labor Statistics website, we first obtain county employment data by industry that correspond as closely as possible to the land use groups in the property database. (See Explore the Web.) Next, for about 20 major land use/industry groups, we divide the total enclosed building space from our property data by the total employment in the associated industry. This yields us, by industry, a crude measure of space per employee, which we will refer to as a space requirement factor. Then, again by industry, we can use our space requirement factor to approximate the locational distribution of jobs. We divide the enclosed building space of each of 43,000 business and government properties by its industry space requirement factor, which results in an approximation of the number of jobs at that property. For example, if our space requirement factor for an industry is 400 square feet per worker, and if a particular property classified in that industry is reported to have 7,000 square feet of enclosed building space, we will approximate the job count as 17.5 jobs (7,000 ÷ 400) at that property.

We use GIS to display this approximation of job locations as shown in Exhibit 7-11. The results reveal an unexpected pattern. We find that, like the distribution of newer apartments shown in Exhibit 7-10, the distribution of jobs also suggests a clustering of jobs at the airport. We note that a line of jobs extends from the airport northward. But to the west we see several lakes, and what turns out to be large areas of single-family residential development with very limited east-west access. We also note that the airport is both an employment center and a barrier on the south of the area we are interested in. To the east we find little or no development. Thus, on at least three sides the area of interest is somewhat isolated.

www.bls.gov

Source of virtually all detailed employment data for the U.S., for states, counties and MSAs. Also the source of household expenditure information.

Concept Check

7.10 The location pattern of jobs in a city can be approximated by examining the location patterns of _____ .

Exhibit 7-11 Where People Work in Orlando

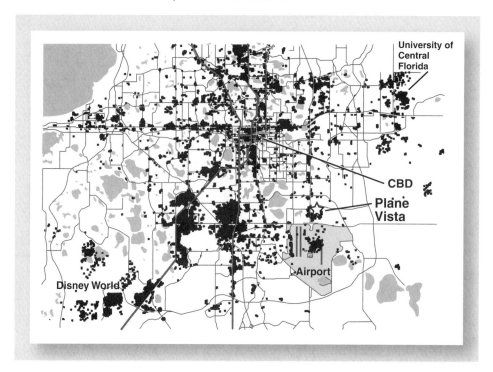

A Revised Market-Defining Story. We conclude that our original story wherein Plane Vista apartments is viewed as part of the larger Orlando apartment market is faulty. Rather, we now find as a more plausible story that Plane Vista apartments are located on an "island" of employment focused on the airport. We begin to suspect, given the nature of the location as discussed above, that as many as 75 percent of residents on "airport island" work on the island. We adopt the notion of airport island as our revised story. But since we concluded earlier that demand for our apartments is driven by jobs, we now are compelled to ask what the job outlook is for airport island.

Data Collection, Round Two. We first want to understand the current employment on airport island. Helpful information to give us a base picture would be the total employment on the "island" and the percentage of that employment at any large employers; we naturally suspect that the airport is the largest employer. Lacking actual data on jobs by location, we return to our GIS proxy for jobs. By designating the island area, shown in Exhibit 7-12, we quickly obtain from GIS the total proxied employment on the island, which is about 25,000. Then we contact the airport directly, and are informed that the airport has approximately 15,000 badges issued to on-site workers of all kinds. Further, we learn that the total has increased by approximately 2,000 in the last three years. We conclude that the airport accounts for about 60 percent of the employment on airport island, and that its employment has grown at least 5 percent annually over the last three years, despite declines in air traffic. We also find that the latest projections for air traffic assume a complete recovery by 2004 from declines since the year 2000. Since these projections are very recent, we tentatively accept them. This leads us to conclude that airport-related jobs are most likely to continue growing at their current rate of 5 percent.

Our next most important question is what is happening to other employment on airport island? Through inquiries at the metropolitan economic development agency, we learn that at least two firms are relocating to airport island, north of the airport, in the near future. One is a medical equipment firm, serving a national market, which will employ over 450 persons. The other is thought to be a more local firm, expected to employ 100.

http://www.
orlandoairports.net

Orlando International Airport

Explore The Web

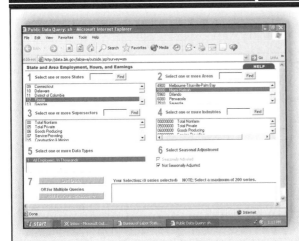

Tapping the Master Sources of Employment Data

1. Go to the U.S. Bureau of Labor Statistics (www.bls.gov).
   - Once there, select from the menu across the top: "Get Detailed Statistics."
   - Then read down the left-hand column to "Employment, Hours, and Earnings . . . (State and Metro Area)" and select the icon for one-screen customized tables.
   - From the sequence of menus, select a state and city (MSA) of interest to you.
   - Select "Total Nonfarm Employment," then click on "Get Data."
   - What is the latest annual count? How much has it changed from the previous year?
   - How far back does the data series go?

2. Now return to the "Get Detailed Statistics" page.
   - Read down the menu to "State and County Employment . . ."
   - Again select the icon for one-screen customized tables.
   - For a county within your MSA of interest, find the employment in residential property management and non-residential property management (North American Industry Classification System, or NAICS, codes 531311 and 531312)
   - Find the employment in two other industry categories that interest you.

Exhibit 7-12 "Airport Island" Job Locations

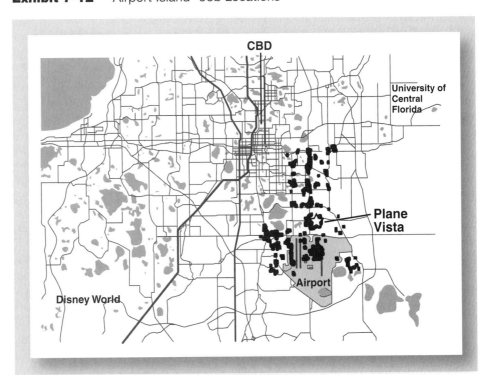

In summary, the most likely projection for employment growth on the island, with airport growth and other known expansions combined is 1,300 (750 + 550) from a base of 25,000, or 5.2 percent.

We also are concerned with the outlook "off the island." While we doubt that a strong market off the island could assist our market greatly, we suspect that a weak market, with growing vacancies and concessions, could drain many renters from the island. We are re-assured when we discover that job growth prospects for Orlando at large are reported to be between 2 and 4 percent a year over the next two years, giving it an active recovery.[12]

Finally, we are concerned with any growth in the supply of competing apartments. A check of building permit applications, supported by conversations with permitting officials, indicates no other projects on the horizon for the island, and few elsewhere.

A Final Market Assessment. We are prepared to draw conclusions about projected occupancy and rental rate growth for Plane Vista, Phases I and II. We first start with the assumption that in a stable market apartment rental rates should be expected to grow, on average, at the rate of general inflation. Plane Vista and its neighbors are averaging about 90 percent occupancy. Over the next two years, we expect to see at least 1,300 new jobs on our island, and more likely, given the positive outlook for Orlando and the airport, we could reasonably expect to see that number of jobs added each of the next two years.

Thus, we judge that the 24-month projection of job growth on the island is between 650 and 1,300 per year, which translates to a growth rate range between 2.5 percent and 5 percent per year. After two years, the airport will have added a fourth runway, is expected to continue strong growth, and the addition of a second terminal may be under way. Therefore, we believe that there is reason for job growth on the island to continue at least as strong for the remainder of our five-year horizon. Thus, we assume the same range of job growth for the entire projection period.

We believe that demand for apartments is proportionate to job growth. Using data from local apartment market experts, we construct an inventory of apartments on airport island which, by price range and vintage, are competitors or near competitors (including Plane Vista, Phase I). We believe this includes about 3,500 units. In 2002, a year during which job growth for the Orlando MSA was below 1.5 percent and falling interest rates were drawing significant numbers of apartment renters into homebuying, the absorption of new apartment units for the Orlando MSA was 4.5 percent of the total stock.[13] We believe that our island should see a minimum of that amount given that its job growth exceeds the Orlando metropolitan area. Our judgment is that the absorption of new units on the island should follow expected job growth in a manner similar to metro Orlando. Thus, if island job growth is half again greater than that of metro Orlando, apartment absorption can be half again greater as well. Since our projected job growth for the island is 2.5 to 5 percent, compared to 2.5 percent for Orlando, we believe that island absorption can be between 4.5 and 9.0 percent. This yields between 150 and 300 units a year. Thus, if Plane Vista, Phase II, comes on line in two years, the market should have seen net absorption by then of 300 to 600 units. Since both phases of Plane Vista are relatively competitive, the worst-case scenario would result in occupancy in two years' time falling from 91 to 90 percent for the 3,800 units in the market segment. However, this effect would most likely be concentrated in other, less competitive complexes.

We must translate our projections to the occupancy and rental rate growth for Plane Vista. We assume that Plane Vista will be fully operative in two years; we are concerned with projecting rental rate growth and occupancy for Phase I and II combined for the immediate five-year horizon. Exhibit 7-13 contains our projections.

Note that we have not explained every aspect of deriving the numbers presented. A market analysis never will. The number of variables involved in determining the projection

12. Metropolitan projections of employment and population normally are known by local economic development agencies, though the sources of the forecasts may vary.

13. All Orlando apartment data used here are courtesy of Charles Wayne Consulting Inc., Orlando, Florida.

Exhibit 7-13 Projections of Rental Rate Growth and Occupancy for Plane Vista, Phases I and II

(Projection Date: January, 2004)					
	2004	**2005**	**2006***	**2007**	**2008**
Total units	500	500	900	900	900
Occupancy	90%	91–93%	90–93%	91–95%	92–95%†
Rental rate growth	0%	1–2%	2–3%	2–4%	2–4%‡

*Initial Year of Phase II

†Occupancy projections assume that demand growth is 150 to 300 units per year, with an initial base demand of 3,500 units in the relevant market segments.

‡It is assumed that continued strong growth of employment will bring a new supply of apartments into the market, limiting further occupancy and rental rate gains.

of occupancy and the parameters of rental rate growth is beyond any formal analysis. Thus, at some point the analyst must make a judgment leap to the final projections. The objective of market analysis is to make that leap as controlled and understandable as is reasonably possible. It should be spelled out to the point that other reasonably knowledgeable analysts know whether they agree or disagree with the final leap of judgment.

Reassessment of Market-Defining Story. The core of our market-defining story is that demand for new and high-quality apartment units on our airport island is driven by job growth on the island. We have assumed this accounts for 75 percent of island apartment demand. If our results depend critically on the 75 percent assumption, we could test it easily. Our clients could survey their tenants to determine what area of Orlando they work in. The question is whether it is cost-effective to test the assumption. The answer seems to depend on the projected job growth rate for metro Orlando. If we believe that growth is at least 2.5 percent, then our minimum projected growth of apartment demand will be achieved regardless of the percent of tenants working on our island, and we may be comfortable with our unverified assumption. More significant may be our assumptions about airport employment growth. We may wish to pursue multiple additional sources of information regarding airport expansion and employment growth to better understand the influences and prospects.

A Perspective on Our Final Results. It is important to understand the role of projections such as in Exhibit 7-13. The late James Graaskamp often asserted that when one buys real estate, what one is buying is a set of assumptions about the future.[14] The projections in Exhibit 7-13 are an example of such assumptions. When translated into cash flow projections they will determine the estimated value of the property. The process of turning assumptions about the future of a property into cash flow projections and estimates of value is developed in detail beginning with Chapter 9. The subject continues through much the remainder of the book.

Some Final Notes on the Process of Market Research

By the approach that we advocate for market research, the format, organization, and content of the presentation will always be somewhat unique. (There still may be many common elements.) Further, the same assignment will be executed somewhat differently by

---

14. Professor Graaskamp was a revered teacher at the University of Wisconsin and an acclaimed industry guru. Few have offered more insightful observation on real estate analysis.

different analysts. This will occur, in part, because different analysts will form different market-defining stories. Is one analysis the correct one? In short—not that we will ever know. There will always be more than one answer to questions as complex as those involved in market research. Some answers will be more compelling than others, but no human will know the "correct" one. No doubt the thoughtful reader could see possible changes or alternatives in our analysis for Plane Vista. No doubt some of these ideas would improve our analysis. It is always in the nature of business and markets that decision makers are dealing with uncertainty. Successful market research is a dialogue between researcher and client that serves to articulate and reduce this uncertainty but never to eliminate it.

Improving One's Capacity in Real Estate Market Research

Real estate market research is a blend of knowledge, skill, and inspiration. There are ways to increase one's effectiveness in the task. First, an effective real estate analyst needs to study real estate firsthand. There probably is no substitute for the habit of observing real estate persistently. This includes looking for what is successful, and asking why, but perhaps more importantly it includes finding the unsuccessful ventures, and asking why. Discussing both extremes with "experts" or other thoughtful observers can be revealing about the actual properties as well as how views ("stories") can differ among experts.

Another means of improving real estate market analysis is careful observation of a subject property. One very successful real estate expert suggested the following exercise in studying any urban property: Go to the property of interest in time for the morning commuting hour and find a place on or near it where you can remain for some time. Then observe the traffic coming to the property and to surrounding properties for perhaps 30 minutes to an hour. Ask yourself whether any surrounding properties interact, or should interact, with the subject property. Finally, peruse the neighborhood around the site. It can be remarkable what insights you can take away from that effort concerning the market context of the property. A closely related suggestion in evaluating a property is to stand at the site and look away from it in all directions. Consider what clues that perspective yields about what the property can (and cannot) be used for.

Market Projections and Real Estate Cycles

http://www.grubb-ellis.com/

See research—Quarterly Trend Reports for nonresidential cycles.

http://www.cbre.com/ Research/Market+Reports/ US+Vacancy+Reports/ default.htm

CB Richard Ellis office and industrial market vacancy reports.

http://www. cushmanwakefield.com/us/ markets/us.cfm?world_ id=1

Cushman Wakefield office and industrial market reports.

A major challenge in forecasting real estate market parameters, and therefore in predicting value, is the presence of real estate cycles. For example, Exhibit 7-14 portrays apartment vacancy rates for the Orlando MSA and for the United States. In the national vacancy pattern since 1970, note the peaks in 1974, 1988, and projected for 2003. Notice that Orlando vacancy patterns have tended to follow movements of the national vacancy level, but with far greater amplitude. A graph of vacancy cycles for office, retail, and hotel/motel properties would show that they are even more extreme.

If real estate markets were perfectly correcting, cycles would not occur. Indeed, an incentive for self-correction exists. Builders and developers watch real estate values, and when the market value of their product exceeds its construction cost, it is profitable for them to build. The resulting increase in supply eventually causes occupancy levels to decline, therefore causing real rental rates to decline, lowering market values. Thus, the market value of the product eventually falls below construction cost, causing further building to become unprofitable, so builders cease to build. With supply thus curtailed, the market value of the product will begin to rise once more, and the cycle continues.

If this natural correction process were instantaneous, there would be no cycles, but it is not. Development of subdivisions, apartments, offices, or other commercial structures can have a lead time of two years or more. Note in Exhibit 7-14 that the local Orlando vacancy rate frequently has changed radically within a two-year interval. Thus, what appears to be a favorable market when the builder commits to build may turn out quite differently,

Exhibit 7-14 Apartment Vacancy Rates

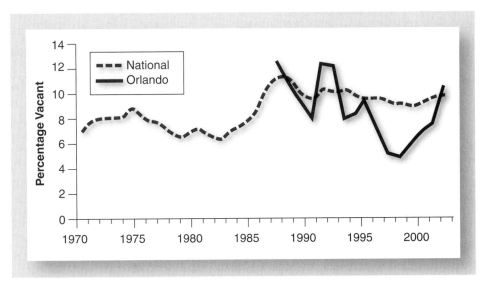

Sources: *Current Population Survey/Housing Vacancy Survey,* Series H-111, U.S. Bureau of the Census, Charles Wayne Consulting, Inc., Orlando.

particularly if numerous builders make the same decision at the same time. In general, the longer the construction lead-time, the greater the amplitude of real estate cycles. But there is another contributor to cycles as well. Real estate cycles might eventually fade out, except for the presence of business cycles. The economy has never been without ups and downs in employment and in business income, and therefore in demand for real estate.

Concept Check

7.11 The amplitude or volatility of the real estate cycle tends to be greater for a property type, as its _____ is _____ .

The sobering implication of real estate cycles is that effective market forecasts must account for them. Unfortunately, it is not easy to do so. Generally, the best that can be done is to monitor good information about the business outlook and be well informed about the construction "pipeline." Knowing about all relevant building permits issued reveals the maximum amount of building that can occur during the immediate construction "gestation" period (some permits will not be used). But, it does not reveal what additional permits will be issued in the days ahead. Thus, the investigation of the construction pipeline ideally goes beyond existing permits to judgments about probable additional projects seeking permits.

An important aspect of assessing a real estate project is how vulnerable it will be to future cycles. For example, an all-too-common pattern with new apartments is that the project built at the "end of the line" in commuting distance, is the most vulnerable to vacancy in a down cycle.

Concept Check

7.12 A key indicator in attempting to evaluate where a property is in the real estate cycle is to carefully examine and evaluate _____ .

Most real estate development projects and many real estate appraisal assignments require supporting market research. Development projects usually also require an economic and financial feasibility analysis. This type of research may be offered by a variety of firms, including sophisticated appraisal firms, accounting/consulting firms, or firms devoted exclusively to market research and market consulting. While the type of firm can vary, the qualifications of the researchers will be similar. They usually will have a degree in economic geography, economics, or a closely related field. Often they will have an MBA or master's degree in economics, real estate, or geography.

Market and Feasibility Analysis for Real Estate

With the exception of the real estate practices of large accounting firms, the firms providing market research and feasibility analysis are structured similarly to appraisal firms and tend to be compensated in the same manner. They will be paid on a fee basis rather than a commission. Real estate researchers may need to be familiar with several kinds of quantitative tools, including a general knowledge of computers, geographic information systems (GIS), multivariate statistical analysis, and database management. Like all real estate consulting and advisory services, the typical market researcher works out of the office a substantial portion of the time, in contact with other persons of the real estate industry.

Some Tools of Market Research

Numerous skills, data, and technologies can be useful in real estate market research. Geographic Information Systems technology (GIS) is becoming increasingly recognized for its extreme power to process and display spatial (location-specific) data. Another tool of value in real estate is psychographics, a high-tech approach to analysis of market segmentation. Finally, a tool that can be very valuable in many contexts is survey research.

http://www.gsd.harvard.edu/~pbcote/GIS/web_resources.html

A Harvard University compilation of GIS websites.

http://www.gisportal.com/

A commercial site with vast, well-organized links to the world of GIS.

Geographical Information Systems (GIS)

Geographical information systems (GIS) are computer software systems that enable one to manipulate and "map" information with great flexibility and speed. GIS offers benefits at several levels in real estate research. Most obviously, it can produce quality maps and displays with unprecedented efficiency. But more importantly, it can make feasible new avenues of real estate market research. Note that without GIS tools, our analysis of the market for Plane Vista would have been impossible. Our effort to approximate job locations required us to identify and obtain data from more than 43,000 specific parcels of land in central Orlando from a total of several hundred thousand parcels in Orange County, Florida.

GIS can be a powerful facilitator in identifying market opportunities. If researchers can translate market segmentation features to a geographically coded database, then they can use GIS to quickly determine the locational patterns of that market segment, and compare them with the locational patterns of competitors. Thus, they can conduct a sophisticated form of "gap" analysis, searching for untapped market opportunities. This is far more difficult, if not infeasible, using conventional tables and charts.

For example, suppose a major grocery chain is considering a site for a shopping center (with a grocery store and other retail uses) in Columbia, South Carolina. Exhibit 7-15 shows a GIS map of the metropolitan area with the selected site, Dentsville Square Shopping Center. The map depicts highways, population density by census tract, and existing grocery stores in the Columbia area. By selecting any given grocery store, detailed data can be available about its size, owner, and volume of business. Additionally, the GIS can be used to calculate detailed information for a market area (such as a two-mile or five-mile radius) around Dentsville Square. This information might include the number of persons, number of households, median household income, estimated annual retail expenditures, daily traffic counts, and the total and vacant square footage of other retail properties. Thus, by having a GIS program and the appropriate data, an analyst can quickly and easily determine whether the site meets basic criteria and should be investigated further.

Industry Issues

7-1

The Urban Frontier of Retail

The Home Depot Inc. boasts more than 900 stores throughout the United States, Canada, and Puerto Rico, and even has a location in South America. Now the company is on the verge of establishing itself in a new frontier: Manhattan.

Home Depot's management sees tremendous untapped potential in Manhattan. "They're an overlooked market," says a Home Depot spokesman. Overlooked, at least so far, by other home improvement chains. The Home Depot already has about a half-dozen stores in inner-city locations in Boston, Pittsburgh, and Chicago. The Manhattan site, however, is a major departure for the chain. With skyrocketing land values and operating costs, Manhattan is the most densely settled urban locale in the country. For it to work as a retail location, companies must be creative. For Home Depot, that means tearing down an abandoned factory building in low-income East Harlem. In its place will rise an urban two-story Home Depot, with a uniquely tailored layout. Its product line will be customized to meet the needs of apartment dwellers, their landlords, and contractors. "You have to look at the bridges and see what gets carried in—lumber and grout," says the spokesman. "There's old housing stock with a lot of character that needs a lot of care."

Densely populated urban sites are looking better and better to national retailers, according to one retail specialist. "It's a trend that's been in play for a while, but it's accelerated recently," he says. As downtown districts revitalize, national chains hoping for continuing growth are following their customers to Main Street. Higher costs are offset by sales per square foot that can triple the average—simply from foot traffic. Hence, Home Depot's new Manhattan focus. As goes Home Depot, so have already gone a number of chain stores—with more following fast.

What retailers should look for in a site, says one expert, is one not only with good demographics, but good "psychographics"— the shopping style or mentality of the people. In cities, psychographics may not measure the same people as demographics do. For example, cities welcome huge numbers of tourists, but they also have their own local "destination" shopping spots, which vary according to each category or subcategory of shopper. "You need to know who's shopping in Santa Monica on a Saturday and on a Monday," he points out.

Source: Excerpts from Laurie Joan Aron, "Downtown Goes Shopping," *Location Strategies*, June 12, 2002 (Reed Business Information)

Exhibit 7-15 Population Density and Grocery Stores: Columbia, South Carolina

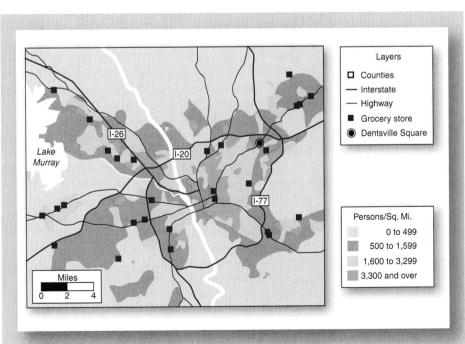

Concept Check

7.13   GIS is a uniquely powerful tool for assisting retailers or service providers in the task of _____ .

Psychographics

http://cluster1.claritas. com/claritas/Default. jsp?main=3&submenu= seg&subcat=segprizm#1

A particularly transparent example of "psychographic" market segmentation. The Claritas PRIZM system describes 62 household market segments.

Psychographics is a tool for sophisticated determination of market segmentation. One description of psychographics is that it "seeks to describe the human characteristics of consumers that may have bearing on their response to products, packaging, advertising, and public relations efforts. Such variables may span a spectrum from self-concept and lifestyle to attitudes, interests, and opinions, as well as perceptions of product attributes."[15] The idea of psychographics is to relate a consumer's activities, interests, opinions, and values—especially as they relate to product choices—to a consumer's demographics. Through the application of complex multivariate analysis, an analyst seeks to develop one or more equations that can use observable demographics, (e.g., as in the census data used in this chapter) to distinguish various market segments. Firms providing this kind of research claim to identify several dozen market segments for consumer behavior. In real estate, psychographics has been applied primarily to retailing and consumer services. Both Industry Issues features of this chapter demonstrate settings where psychographics apply.

Concept Check

7.14   Psychographics are of potential interest to real estate market researchers to refine the identification and use of _____ .

Survey Research

Survey research has been applied to real estate markets at many levels. Perhaps one of the most useful is at the project design level. For example, a development team for a coastal condominium arranged for some of their sales staff to contact and interview owners of existing condominiums in the target area concerning what they liked and disliked about their units. From these interviews, the developers were able to identify some design features that enabled them to create a project distinctly more successful than others in the area. One of the authors conducted a survey of restaurant preferences among students, which succeeded in identifying a very promising chain of restaurants not represented in the local area. The chain subsequently entered the community successfully. Builders often use interviews or questionnaires to obtain helpful clues in designing for a local market. For this purpose, the opinions of those rejecting a builder's product are frequently the most informative. Another potential use of survey research is to identify target markets for advertising and market assessment. In the case of Plane Vista, for example, a survey of where residents work could help confirm our assumptions concerning where the demand for Plane Vista comes from, and it also could help identify effective project marketing channels.

A word of caution regarding survey research: While simple survey research is not difficult, it can be fraught with abortive errors. Thus, it is wise to prepare carefully and to pretest any questionnaire at least one time. If possible, obtain the guidance of an experienced survey researcher. A little advice in formulating questions, designing a questionnaire format, selecting a sampling method, and administering the survey can reduce time and cost enormously, and can avoid the all-to-common misfortune of getting uninterpretable results.

15. B. Gunter and A. Furnham, *Consumer Profiles: An Introduction to Psychographics.* (New York: Routledge, 1992).

Industry Issues

7-2

Psychographic Research Comes to Real Estate

At (Ronald Reagan) Washington National Airport, Westfield fine-tuned the new business of airport retail management. "This kind of airport retail is a business that didn't exist a few years ago," says the president of the Los Angeles–based Westfield Corp. Inc., which developed and now manages National Airport's 31,200 square feet of retail space . . . "it's a whole new world."

At National Airport, it's a spectacular new world. The one-million-square foot National Hall runs north and south, with three boarding piers jutting east. Along the west wall of the concourse, 23 retail shops open toward the glass wall. Fifteen retail shops, kiosks, and carts run along the east side of the concourse and into the piers . . . Westfield brought a number of retail firsts to National Hall. Shops developed by high-profile organizations exclusively for the facility include National Zoo, Smithsonian, and National Geographic. In addition, six national retailers—Waldenbooks, Brookstone, Victoria's Secret, Gymboree, Easy Spirit, and Travel 2000—have touched down at National with their first airport stores. Managing an airport mall is challenging. Airport demographics, for example, reverse the classic 60-to-40 percent women-to-men ratio of a mall market, and the airport shoppers have higher income. The psychographics of airport retail prospects differ from shopping centers as well. "People don't go to airports to shop," a Westfield official says. "They go to travel. So we were looking for retailers offering impulse merchandise rather than destination purchases." What does that mean? "People just don't take off their pants in an airport," says the official. "So the type of apparel we have here doesn't need to be tried on. Most of it is outerwear. Westfield provides specialized customer service training for employees. One of the key training points is speed of service, the official says. "In a shopping center, you train people to show a lot of options," she explains. "Here, we train people to ask a lot of questions fast, narrow the choices, and present one or two options."

Source: Exerpts from Michael Fickes, "High Flying Retail," *Retail Traffic,* October 1, 1997.

Concept Check

7.15 Survey research can be especially valuable in real estate during project _____ .

Summary

Real estate market research seeks to relate the cash flow prospects of a property to the economic and social forces of its urban context. It must account for the effects of the urban economic matrix, but also the effect of land use controls. It must recognize both locational and nonlocational market segmentation.

Because of market segmentation and the variation in property context, little can be said, in general, about the form of effective real estate market research. It is a process rather than a formula. We have presented it as a process of constructing, verifying, and quantifying a story. The process begins with constructing the market-defining story. This is followed by initial data collection and then initial analysis or evaluation. From that point, one determines whether a conclusion can be reached or whether the research should be refined. The goal of the research is to determine a plausible range for critical cash flow parameters for the subject property. For rental property these parameters are projected rental rate growth and vacancy rates. For a subdivision or condominium project the critical parameters are sales rates.

A market analysis never will explain its conclusions completely. The number of variables involved in determining the projection of occupancy and rental rate growth parameters is beyond any formal analysis. Thus, at some point the analyst makes a judgment leap to the final projections. The objective of market analysis is to make that leap as controlled and understandable as is reasonably possible. It should be spelled out to the point that other reasonably knowledgeable analysts know whether they agree or disagree with the final leap of judgment.

Key Terms

Geographic information systems (GIS) 180

Market parameters 161
Market segmentation 159

Psychographics 182
Metropolitan statistical area (MSA) 166

Test Problems

1. Factors that affect housing market segmentation include all except:
   a. Household income.
   b. Household age.
   c. Household size.
   d. Household unemployment status.
   e. Household lifestyle.

2. The process of creating a market-defining story includes all of these questions except:
   a. What is the product?
   b. Who is the customer?
   c. Where is the customer?
   d. What is the price?
   e. What is the competition?

3. The cycle of real estate market research starts with:
   a. Creating a market-defining story.
   b. Assessing the national market.
   c. Collecting market data.
   d. Posing preliminary conclusions.
   e. Testing the current market condition.

4. Features of an office building that may be important to one market segment or another include:
   a. Floor plate size.
   b. Character and amount of parking.
   c. Nature of other tenants.
   d. Provision for electronics and communication systems.
   e. All of the above.

5. A strong assertion about the large amount of data seemingly available for real estate market research is that most of it is:
   a. Inaccurate.
   b. Too costly.
   c. Irrelevant to a given analysis.
   d. Too detailed.
   e. Too old.

6. The approach to real estate market research advocated in this chapter starts with the:

   a. National economy.
   b. Local economy.
   c. Relevant industry market.
   d. Region.
   e. Nature of the property.

7. A powerful tool for managing, manipulating, and displaying location-specific data is:
   a. Statistical regression analysis.
   b. Development cash flow software.
   c. Psychographics.
   d. Geographic information systems.
   e. Database management software.

8. A very sophisticated, data intensive, and statistically intensive method of examining market segmentation is known as:
   a. Regression analysis.
   b. Discriminant analysis.
   c. Survey research.
   d. Psychographic research.
   e. Cluster analysis.

9. Causes of real estate cycles include:
   a. Business cycles.
   b. Long real estate "gestation" periods.
   c. Weather cycles.
   d. Both *a* and *b*, but not *c*.
   e. All three, *a*, *b*, and *c*.

10. Data used in the market research cases in this chapter that are publicly available over the Internet include all of the following except:
   a. Detailed data of the U.S. decennial census.
   b. Data from *County Business Patterns* (U.S. Bureau of the Census).
   c. National apartment vacancy rates from the U.S. *Current Population Survey*.
   d. Data on job location from the National Transportation Board.
   e. Data from the U.S. Bureau of Labor Statistics.

Study Questions

1. On the U.S. census website, use the approach shown in Explore the Web, Chapter 5, to access the SF3 detailed census tables for 2000. For your county, find the distribution of reported house values for owner-occupied residences.

2. If you were looking for an apartment at this time, what are six non-locational requirements that you would consider important?

3. Select a site in your city that is in a mixed-use or nonresidential area, and either is vacant or appears to be ready for change (e.g., structure partially used or vacant, or in need of refurbishing). Go to the site during the morning commuting period of a business day. Situate yourself at or near the site and observe the activity at and around the site. Pay particular attention to why people pass the site—where they are coming from and where they are going. Note any nearby land uses or pedestrian flows that could potentially involve the site. Then explore the area around the site for a block or so in each direction, and record on a simple map the main patterns of traffic flow and the broad variations in land uses. Finally, after at least one observation session of 30 minutes, record your main impressions and thoughts concerning the potential use of the site. (*Hint:* A good way to select a site might be to go to a commercial real estate/broker or appraiser and ask him or her about a site this professional finds intriguing. This will give you an interesting industry contact, and another perspective on the problem.)

4. Select a property of interest to you or to an industry contact, and one for which market research would be interesting. Examine the property and collect available information about it. Then write a market-defining story for the property using the questions from the chapter as a guide.

5. University City is a town of more than 200,000 persons, with over 50,000 university and community college students. It has over 30,000 apartment units which, with one or two exceptions, are garden apartments with a maximum of three floors. Except for buildings within or immediately adjacent to the university medical center, the football stadium, and two graduate student dorms, only two other buildings in the University City exceed five floors. A developer proposes to introduce two 24-story apartment buildings halfway between the downtown and the university, which are about 1.5 miles apart. One tower would be targeted to undergraduate students and the other to graduate students. The downtown consists of little more than government offices, mostly local and county. What questions should the developer ask in order to create a "market defining story" for the twin towers?

Explore The Web

Go to the U.S. census home page, www.census.gov. In the right-hand column find "State & County Quick-Facts." Select a county of interest (perhaps your county of residence). From the initial table, find the following information from the 2000 census:

1. Mean travel time to work.
2. Mean value of owner-occupied residences.
3. Number of households.
4. Percent of housing units in multiunit structures.

At the top of the table, click on "Browse more data sets for . . ." Then, under "Census 2000," click on "Economic Characteristics." (Note that you need Adobe Acrobat Reader, a downloadable program free from Adobe, and a host of other sources.) This brings up a four-page profile of your county.

Within the four pages find the following:

5. For both all households and for families, find the income interval with the largest number of households. What is the percentage of concentration in each case?
6. For industry of employment, which category, other than retail, has the largest percentage of persons?
7. For housing units, which unit age interval has the largest concentration of housing units? What is the percentage?
8. For owner-occupied units, what value range has the largest concentration?
9. What is the percent of housing units into which the householder (principal occupant) moved between the beginning of 1999 and March of 2000?

Solutions to Concept Checks

1. Three kinds of factors affecting the value of an urban property are locational characteristics, land use controls, and nonlocational characteristics.
2. Before effective real estate market research can be achieved, relevant market segmentation must be examined.
3. The presence of market segmentation in real estate gives rise to valuable advice in sorting through available market and property data: *Exclude the irrelevant.*
4. Rather than approaching real estate market research as a form or formula, the conditional nature of the task makes it a process of discovery.
5. It is recommended that the first step in evaluating any property is to write a market-defining story.
6. Whereas real estate market research traditionally starts with a national or global perspective, the approach argued here begins with the property.

7. The primary data source for information on household characteristics is the U.S. decennial census.

8. Data from the U.S. census is durable for a number of years, even with changing population counts, so long as one is using the data to obtain ratios or percentages for a characteristic of the population.

9. A local source for local employers and their size is usually the chamber of commerce or a local economic development agency. A national source for county-level data on firms and their size is *County Business Patterns*.

10. The location pattern of jobs in a city can be approximated by examining the location patterns of nonresidential buildings.

11. The amplitude or volatility of the real estate cycle tends to be greater for a property type, as its "gestation" or construction lead-time is longer.

12. A key indicator in attempting to evaluate the place of a property in the real estate cycle is to carefully examine and evaluate relevant building permits.

13. GIS is a uniquely powerful tool for assisting retailers or service providers in the task of site selection.

14. Psychographics are of potential interest to real estate market researchers to refine the identification and use of market segmentation.

15. Survey research can be especially valuable in real estate during project design.

Additional Readings

Books on real estate markets and market analysis include the following:

Clapp, John M. *Handbook for Real Estate Market Analysis.* Upper Saddle River, NJ: Prentice Hall, 1987.

DiPasquale, Denise, and William C. Wheaton. *Urban Economics and Real Estate Markets.* Upper Saddle River, NJ: Prentice Hall, 1996.

Fanning, Stephen F., Terry V. Grissom, and Thomas D. Pearson. *Market Analysis for Valuation Appraisals.* Chicago: Appraisal Institute, 1994.

Geltner, David, and Norman G. Miller. *Commercial Real Estate Analysis and Investments.* Upper Saddle River, NJ: Prentice Hall, 2001. (See Part II.)

Schmitz, Adrienne, and Deborah L. Brett. *Real Estate Market Analysis: A Case Study Approach.* Washington DC: Urban Land Institute, 2001.

Thrall, Grant I. *Business Geography and New Real Estate Market Analysis.* New York: Oxford University Press, 2002.

The article below is a position paper adopted by the Joint Valuation/Research Subcommittees of the National Council of Real Estate Investment Fiduciaries (NCREIF) on the role, purpose, and procedures for market analysis in appraisals:

Wincott, D. Richard, and Glenn R. Mueller. "Market Analysis in the Appraisal Process." *Appraisal Journal* 63, no. 1 (January 1995), pp. 27–32.

The following article presents a structure for market analysis. It also suggests nine specific improvements to the customary practice of real estate market analysis:

Malizia, Emil E., and Robin A Howarth. "Clarifying the Structure and Advancing the Practice of Real Estate Market Analysis." *Appraisal Journal* 63, no 1. (January 1995), pp. 60–68.

For exposure to geographic information systems in many variations and levels, visit the website of ESRI: www.ESRI.com. (ESRI is a principal provider of GIS systems.)

Market Valuation *and* Appraisal

3

Valuation Using the Sales Comparison *and* Cost Approaches

Learning Objectives

After reading this chapter you will be able to:

1. Explain why the sales comparison and cost approaches are important methods of appraisal.

2. Explain the steps involved in applying the sales comparison approach.

3. Make adjustments in the proper sequence in the sales comparison approach.

4. Explain the steps involved in applying the cost approach.

5. Define the three primary types of accrued depreciation.

6. Reconcile three or more final adjusted sale prices in the sales comparison approach into an indicated value, or two or more indicated values into a final estimate of value.

7. Interpret the results of a simple multivariate regression model.

Introduction

This chapter and the one immediately following are focused on estimating the market value of real estate. Understanding the market value of a property is vital to potential purchasers and sellers, to owners contemplating renovations and improvements, to a judge attempting to determine the appropriate division of assets in a divorce, to lenders contemplating a mortgage loan on a property, to government officials when estimating the costs of acquiring the right-of-way to construct a highway, or to anyone needing an estimate of a property's current market value.

Why must the market value of real estate be estimated? Cannot values simply be observed in the marketplace? Consider the value of Camden Property Trust (CPT), a public company that trades on the New York Stock Exchange (NYSE). At the close of trading on May 6, 2003, CPT was selling for $35.09 a share. There may have been some investors who felt that CPT was worth more, or less, than $35.09 a share at that time, but the consensus among those actively buying and selling CPT was that $35.09 was a fair price.

What are some of the characteristics of the NYSE that permit us to conclude that $35.09 was the fair market value of a share of CPT stock at the closing of the exchange on May 6, 2003? First, there are many active buyers and sellers of CPT on the NYSE, and the trading activities of any one buyer or seller are not likely to affect CPT's stock price. Second, many transactions of CPT occur each hour; thus, market prices are revealed almost instantaneously. Third, each share of CPT's common stock is *exactly* alike; thus, any one share is a perfect substitute for another. In addition, shares of CPT's stock can be taken anywhere—unlike real estate assets. Thus, the location of the seller or the share offered for sale has no bearing on the price potential buyers are willing to pay.

Contrast these characteristics of the New York Stock Exchange to a typical real estate market. First, unlike stocks, no two properties are exactly alike. Even if the physical attributes of two properties are similar, their different locations render them less than perfect substitutes. Second, transactions of similar properties occur infrequently, resulting in a scarcity of comparable price data. The physical immobility of real estate also has an important implication for the valuation of real estate. Since a parcel of real estate cannot be moved from its location, its value is subject to the effects of economic, social, or political developments emanating from the regional, community, and neighborhood levels.

The unique characteristics of real estate markets, including those discussed above, significantly complicate the estimation of market value. Nevertheless, for many real estate decisions it is sufficient to rely on *informal* methods of appraising the value of real estate assets. Informal appraisal is a common part of our lives. Whenever we make purchases of goods or services, we generally perform an informal appraisal to determine if the prices are reasonable. We do this by comparing one product and its price to competing products.

Informal appraisal methods also are used frequently in real estate. These informal methods include discussions with neighbors, friends, and local real estate sales professionals, as well as the collection of readily available data (e.g., newspaper articles). However, the complexity and large dollar value of many real estate decisions dictate that homeowners, lenders, judges, and other decision makers base their decisions on a *formal* appraisal, which is an estimate of value reached by the methodical collection and analysis of relevant market data.

Concept Check

8.1   List several types of real estate decisions that often require formal real estate appraisals.

www.appraisalinstitute. org

The Appraisal Institute is the primary industry professional organization for real estate appraisers in the United States.

www.rics.org

The Royal Institute of Chartered Surveyors is the largest professional association of appraisers (valuers) outside the United States.

The focus of this chapter is on the formal approaches to real estate valuation used by trained and licensed professionals who are in the business of providing opinions of value for a fee. An **appraisal** is an unbiased written estimate of the fair market value of a property, usually referred to as the **subject property,** at a particular time. The **appraisal report** is the document the appraiser submits to the client and contains the appraiser's final estimate of value, the data upon which the estimate is based, and the calculations used to arrive at the estimate. The licensing and certification of real estate appraisers is the subject of this chapter's Career Focus.

We next discuss the relationships among market value, investment value, and transaction prices. This is followed by an overview of the real estate appraisal process, including the three conventional approaches used to estimate the market value of real estate. We then focus on the two methods (approaches) that provide a means for estimating a property's market value without directly considering the property's income-producing potential: the sales comparison approach and the cost approach. The income approach to valuation is the focus of Chapter 9.

Career Focus

Real Estate Appraisers

Real estate appraisal practices are typically focused on either residential or commercial appraisal. Residential appraisers focus on single-family homes and small residential rental properties. Most of this work deals with appraisals for mortgage lending purposes or for corporate relocation firms.

National appraisal standards are set by the Appraisal Standards Board in Washington, D.C. All 50 states require real estate appraisers to be licensed or certified. Certification is at two levels, residential and general. These qualification levels are based on a combination of education, tests, and experience. The activities of "licensed appraisers" are limited to residential properties valued up to $1 million and nonresidential properties up to $250,000. Licensed appraisers must have at least 2,000 hours of appraisal experience over a two-year period and 90 hours of approved appraisal education. In addition, they must pass a uniform state examination. Finally, they must complete a minimum of 14 classroom hours of approved continuing education each year for license renewal.

Sources: *Information on Career Paths in Commercial Real Estate,* University of Cincinnati, www.cba.uc.edu/getreal and *Career Opportunities,* Washington State University, www.cbe.wsu.edu/~fire/real_estate

"Certified residential appraisers" are allowed to appraise all types of residential property plus nonresidential property up to a value of $250,000. The minimum education requirement for a certified residential appraiser is 120 hours (although a college degree may largely substitute in some states). The experience requirement is 2,500 hours over a two-year period. Uniform state exams for certification are more rigorous than state licensing exams. Again, 14 hours of continuing education are required each year to maintain certification.

The "certified general appraiser" is permitted to value any types of real estate, including large commercial properties. The experience requirement is 3,000 hours of appraising over 30 months, half of which must be with nonresidential property. The certified general appraiser must complete 180 hours of appraisal education. Again, there is a required state exam, and required continuing education of 14 hours a year.

Many appraisers go beyond certification to obtain trade association designations. These designations signal to potential clients that the appraiser has obtained even more education and/or professional experience in the field than is required for state certification. The Appraisal Institute (www.appraisalinstitute.org) offers the residential SRA designation and the prestigious MAI designation for commercial appraisers.

---

www.iaao.org

International Association of Assessment Officers;

www.masterappraiser.org,

National Association of Master Appraisers

Market Value, Investment Value, and Transaction Prices

Before discussing the framework for estimating the market value of real estate, it is important to distinguish among the concepts of market value, investment value, and transaction price. Real estate appraisers generally define the **market value** of a property as its most probable selling price, assuming "normal" sale conditions.[1] Alternatively, it can be viewed as the value the typical (imaginary) participant would place on a property. The concept of market value rests upon the presence of willing buyers and sellers freely bidding in competition with one another. It is the result of the interacting forces of supply and demand. If real estate markets were perfectly competitive, market value would equal the most recent transaction price. There would be no need for value estimates.[2] As discussed above, the problem of market value estimation arises because of the existence of imperfections in the real estate market.

---

1. In professional appraisal practice, market value definitions may vary as to the precise motivations, terms, and conditions specified.

2. Students may note that the definition of market value adopted by appraisers is similar, but not identical, to the definition of value under perfect competition. The sale conditions defined by appraisers differ from the conditions in a perfect market. The real world dictates a compromise between the theoretically pure concept of market value under perfect market conditions and the necessity to make decisions and settle disputes based on appraised value estimates.

In contrast to market value, **investment value** is the value a *particular* investor places on a property. Investment value, discussed in detail in Chapter 16, is useful to buyers and sellers for making investment decisions. It is based on the unique expectations of the individual investor, not the market in general. It may differ between a buyer and a seller. A buyer's investment value is the *maximum* that he or she would be willing to pay for a particular property. The seller's investment value is the *minimum* he or she would be willing to accept. Investment values generally differ from market values because individual investors have different expectations regarding the future desirability of a property, different capabilities for obtaining financing, different tax situations, and different return requirements. Although the methods used to estimate investment value and market value are similar, analysts who determine investment value apply the expectations, requirements, and assumptions of a particular investor, not the market.

Finally, **transaction prices** are the prices we observe on sold properties. They are different, but related, to the concepts of market value and investment value. We observe a transaction only when the investment value of the buyer exceeds the investment value of the seller. If the seller's minimum investment value exceeds the buyer's maximum investment value, the sale will not occur. Thus, the transaction price must lie between the buyer's and the seller's investment values. Real estate appraisers and analysts observe these transaction prices and use them as factual evidence in making inferences and estimating the market value of similar properties.

In summary, market value is an estimate of the most probable selling price in a competitive market. Market value can be estimated from observed transaction prices of similar properties. These transaction prices are negotiated in an imperfect market between buyers and sellers, each having his or her own investment value of the property. Investment value and market value thus are linked through the competitive market process that determines transaction prices.[3]

Concept Check

8.2 Assume a house is listed for sale for which you would be willing to pay up to $200,000. The seller has put the property on the market with an asking price of $180,000. List some possible reasons why your investment value exceeds that of the seller. Will the price you pay be closer to $200,000 or $180,000? Explain.

The Appraisal Process

www.appraisalfoundation.org

Contains links to USPAP information.

How do real estate appraisers do their job? Professional appraisal groups have long supported strict standards of ethics and practice among their members. In 1987 nine leading appraisal groups jointly promulgated uniform appraisal standards, now recognized by professional appraisal organizations throughout North America. Maintained by the Appraisal Foundation, the **Uniform Standards of Professional Appraisal Practice (USPAP)** are required and followed by all states and federal regulatory agencies. USPAP imposes both ethical obligations and minimum appraisal standards that must be followed by all professional appraisers.

To comply with USPAP, real estate appraisers follow a general framework, or process. As outlined in Exhibit 8-1, this process consists of (1) defining the problem, (2) selecting and collecting data, (3) identifying the highest and best use, (4) applying the three valuation

---

3. Market and investment values are but two kinds of value of concern to the real estate analyst. Other values that sometimes must be estimated include the assessed value, the value assigned to property for ad valorem taxation; insurable value, the value of the insurable portion under the provisions of an insurance contract; going-concern value, the value of a property that includes the value of the associated businesses occupying the property; use value, the value of a property for a specific use; and others.

approaches, (5) reconciling the indicated values that result from the multiple approaches to valuation, and (6) preparing the appraisal report for submission to the client. Although the details of each of these steps are beyond the scope of this text, a brief description follows.

Definition of the Problem

In the first step, definition of the problem, the analyst identifies the property (i.e., the subject property) and the property rights to be valued, the type of value to be estimated and the date of the estimate, and any limitations of the analysis. Most appraisal assignments focus on estimating the current market value of a property under the assumption that the owner(s) will hold full (i.e., fee simple) title to the property. (The various forms of ownership, or estates, in real estate, including fee simple absolute ownership, are discussed in detail in Chapter 4.) However, lesser interests (estates) in property can be the subject of an appraisal. Moreover, a large portion of commercial property appraisals are completed subject to the leasehold interests of tenants, as we will show in Chapter 9. Other appraisal problems may involve retrospective or prospective value estimates required for insurance, taxation, or other purposes.

Exhibit 8-1 The Appraisal Process

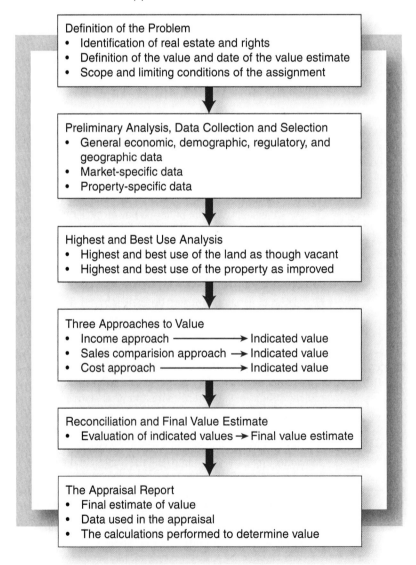

Data Selection and Collection

General data must be gathered concerning the market context of the "subject" property. These data include information on economic, demographic, regulatory, and geographic factors that are important to consider. This information often includes such items as the expected rates of return on alternative investments (i.e., stocks, bonds, and real estate), population and employment trends, existing and future land use data, and flood zone data. Additionally, property-specific data must be gathered. This normally includes transaction information, rental rates, vacancy rates, expense rates, lease provisions, and information on the physical characteristics of both the subject property and comparable properties.

Highest and Best Use Concepts

The concept of highest and best use is central to the estimation of market value, primarily because it serves as the foundation for identifying comparable properties. The **highest and best use** of a property is defined as that use found to be (1) legally permissible, (2) physically possible, (3) financially feasible, and (4) maximally productive (i.e., yielding the greatest benefit to an owner). The principal idea is that the market value of a property is a function of its most productive use. Property is always valued at its highest and best use. To make this concept workable in "real-world" situations, the analyst visualizes highest and best use in two separate circumstances: the highest and best use of land as though vacant, and the highest and best use of a property as improved.

Highest and Best Use of the Land as Though Vacant. Land, improved or not, is always valued as though vacant and available for development to its highest and best use. The value attributed to the land is the total value of the property less the value of any improvements (e.g., the building) . Identification of the highest and best use of land as though vacant helps the analyst identify the appropriate comparable data with which to value the land.

Highest and Best Use of the Property as Improved. When a separate value of the land is not necessary, the analyst focuses on the highest and best use of the property as it is currently developed. Again, this analysis helps the appraiser identify the appropriate comparable data to select in valuing the property. In addition, it may help to determine whether the existing improvement should be retained, modified, or demolished. The appraiser must decide whether the value estimate should be reached under the assumption that the improvement will remain, or with the assumption that the improvements are torn down, or put to another use.

Concept Check

8.3   You estimate that the value of an existing single-family home is $450,000. However, local zoning regulations would permit a four-unit rental housing structure to be built. The estimated value of the rental structure is $600,000 upon completion, but the construction costs total $300,000, including the demolition costs of the existing house. What is the property's highest and best use?

Three Conventional Approaches to Estimating Market Value

There are three conventional approaches for estimating the market value of real estate: the income approach, the sales comparison approach, and the cost approach. Generally, all three approaches must be used in a formal appraisal. Although we discuss the approaches separately in this and the following chapter, each approach is, in principle, related to the other two. The three approaches can be regarded as different methods of seeking the same final objective: an estimate of market value.

The sales comparison approach is applicable to almost all one- to four-family residential properties and even to some types of income-producing properties where enough comparable sales are available. This approach has the additional advantage of being easily understood by buyers and sellers. They usually can follow the procedures and check the data to determine whether they agree with the appraiser's value estimate.

The income approach, presented in Chapter 9, is the dominant approach when estimating the value of any income-producing type of property. It assumes a property's value is determined solely by its expected future cash flows. Thus, the income approach is less appropriate as the value of a property depends more on nonmonetary (or partially monetary) future benefits, as with owner-occupied homes, public auditoriums, public arenas, or public marinas.

The cost approach is necessary when good comparable sales or good income data are absent. It is most commonly used for specialty properties such as education facilities, places of worship, or special-purpose government properties—parks, monuments, bridges, or courthouses, for example. The cost approach involves estimating the cost of the property new, and then subtracting accrued depreciation. As the subject structure is older, the amount of depreciation is greater. This renders the estimate of value by the cost approach increasingly uncertain because, as discussed below, estimating depreciation is very difficult.

There is a clear order of preference for methods of appraisal. An appraiser always prefers to estimate value directly from the market, that is, from actual sales of comparable properties. That way the appraiser can rely on the value judgments of actual buyers and sellers, whereas other methods only simulate these judgments. Often, however, adequate sales comparables are not available. In this case, an appraiser simulates market judgment for income-producing properties through a discounted cash flow approach. If there are no comparable sales and there is no income to measure, as a last resort the appraiser must turn to the cost method.

Reconciliation and a Final Estimate of Market Value

Whenever possible, each of the three approaches is applied to establish alternative "indicators" of market value. For example, all three may be applied in estimating the value of a rented single-family home. In this case, the appraisal process will result in three value indicators. In assigning a final (single) estimate of market value, the appraiser weighs the relative reliability of value indicators for the property being valued—a procedure referred to as **reconciliation.** A simple average of the indicated values is seldom applied. Rather, more weight is generally given the most applicable method and most reliable data. When applying this last step, the analyst needs to understand clearly the relationship among the three approaches and be able to discern which approach is most appropriate in a given situation.

The Appraisal Report

The sixth and final step in the appraisal process is reporting the appraisal opinion or conclusion. Appraisers spend a significant portion of their time preparing written appraisal reports. The content of these must meet the requirements of one of the reporting options defined in USPAP. The narrative appraisal report is the longest and most formal of the appraisal formats and contains a step-by-step description of the facts and methods used to determine value. Narrative reports are typical in appraisals performed for government agencies and in estimating the value of major investment properties. Shorter "form" reports are often used for real estate loan appraisals; one- to five-page "letter" reports may also be appropriate in certain circumstances. Experienced appraisers understand that report writing is one of the most important functions performed by those undertaking the appraisal process. (See Industry Issues 8-1.)

Industry Issues

8-1

Pressure to Produce Favorable Appraisals Puts Appraisers in Tough Spot

Source: Excerpted from "Shaky Foundation: Rising Home Prices Cast Appraisers in Harsh Light," *The Wall Street Journal*, John Hechinger December 13, 2002.

Federal regulations require some form of appraisal for virtually every residential real estate loan to protect lenders and homeowners against overextending themselves. Unlike mortgage loan brokers and real estate sales agents, appraisers get paid whether the deal gets done or not, and the fee—typically $250 to $500—isn't a percentage of the price. A good appraisal requires hours of legwork, visiting a property to check its condition, and coming up with at least three comparable sales.

The appraisal profession first organized in the 1930s. In the 1980s, when appraisers came under fire for valuations that supported shaky loans made by savings and loan institutions, Congress passed a law establishing state licensing requirements for appraisers, including course work and continuing education. But Congress hadn't reckoned on a major shift in the residential mortgage business: Few of the people involved in making mortgage loans these days have a long-term interest in them. Traditionally, the majority of residential lenders held their loans as long-term investments, giving the lenders a strong incentive to find fair appraisals to protect their interests.

Today, many appraisers are picked by independent mortgage brokers, who are paid per transaction and have little stake in the long-term health of the loans. Many lenders also have lost a long-term interest in their loans, because they sell them off to investors. Appraisers increasingly fear that if they don't go along with the higher valuations sought by brokers, their business will dry up. More than 7,000 appraisers have signed a petition saying they have been subjected to customer pressure and calling on regulators to forbid the practice.

Traditional Sales Comparison Approach

The sales comparison approach is a general method for appraising all types of properties and involves comparing the subject property with **comparable properties** (i.e., similar properties) that have sold recently. No adjustments to the sale prices of the comparable properties would be needed if the site, building, and location characteristics of the comparable properties were *identical* to the subject property, and if the transactional details were the same. The real estate market, however, is imperfect; no two properties are exactly alike, and various aspects of transactions may vary greatly. Therefore, to estimate the market value of the subject property, appraisers make explicit adjustments—additions and subtractions—to and from the sale prices of comparable properties. The result of this adjustment procedure is a **final adjusted sale price** for each comparable property. The appraiser then evaluates and reconciles the final adjusted sale prices of the comparable properties into a single **indicated value** for the subject property. The fundamental steps of the sales comparison approach are outlined in Exhibit 8-2.

Exhibit 8-2   Steps in the Sales Comparison Approach

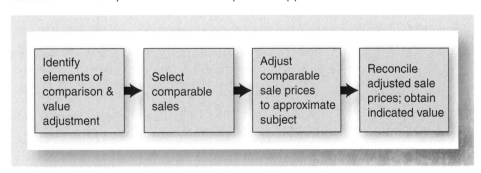

Comparable Sales Data

The selection of representative property sales data is crucial to the sales comparison approach. The appraiser's objective is to identify property sales that are similar to the subject property and reflect the general pricing preferences (values) of the *typical* buyer in the market. When appraising detached single-family homes and attached townhomes and condominiums, an appraiser will often begin by identifying recent sales located in the subject property's immediate neighborhood. Such properties are generally influenced by common economic, demographic, geographic, and regulatory factors. However, there seldom are enough comparable sales transactions in the subject's neighborhood. This forces an appraiser to expand the search area. When appraising commercial real estate, it is almost always necessary to search beyond the immediate area for comparable sale transactions. In doing so, an appraiser must take care to ensure that selected comparables truly compete with the subject property for buyers or tenants. This is where real estate appraisal is "more art than science"; identifying truly comparable (i.e., substitute) properties is a subjective process that requires skill, experience, and extensive knowledge of the area's real estate market.

In addition to determining whether the comparable sales are truly substitutes for the subject property, it is important that the sales represent **arm's-length** transactions; that is, a fairly negotiated transaction that occurred under typical market conditions. Properties that are sold under unusual conditions (e.g., as part of estate auctions, foreclosure proceedings, special low-interest financing programs, or commingled business transactions) are generally avoided. (Mortgage default and foreclosure are discussed in Chapter 10.) Assuming the transactions are representative, the comparable properties are selected to be as physically similar to the subject property as possible, to minimize the number and size of any necessary price adjustments.

Concept Check

8.4   Assume you are appraising a single-family home. Recently, a home directly across the street was sold by the owners to their daughter. Why should the appraiser exclude this transaction from the set of comparable sales? If included, what kind of adjustment probably needs to be made?

Once the comparable sales have been investigated, the next step is to collect the required data on each comparable transaction. Generally, information on the property's physical characteristics, legal status, and exact location are required.

There is no specific number of comparables that is right for every appraisal. If the comparables sales are very similar, three sales are considered adequate for most appraisal assignments. However, if the sales are less comparable or the appraiser has concerns about the reliability of the information obtained about the sales, a larger number is usually desirable.

Sources of Market Data

The appraiser generally must search a variety of sources to obtain the necessary information on the subject and comparable properties. These sources include public records, multiple listing services, and private companies.

Public Records. The public records collected by cities and counties include copies of most local deeds that transfer the ownership or other interests in real estate. (Deeds and other issues associated with acquiring and disposing of ownership interest in real estate are discussed in Chapter 18.) The local (usually county) property tax assessor is a major public source of information including records of sale prices, for appraisers. In addition to showing the assessed value (for property tax purposes) of the subject and comparable properties, the assessor's records also show the name(s) and address of the current owner(s). The tax assessor's office may also be able to provide maps and information on permitted uses for every parcel of real estate in the county.

Multiple Listing Services. The local board of Realtors usually sponsors and maintains a multiple listing service (MLS). All properties listed for sale by MLS members are combined and listed in this easily accessible database. When listed properties are sold, the sale price is added to the record. Thus, MLSs are a potential rich source of current price trends in a local market.

realestate.yahoo.com/ realestate/homevalues.

Provides sale price information for specific properties as well as aggregate data for the industry.

www.cswcasa.com

Website of Case Shiller Weiss, a leader in the provision of home price and characteristic information, as well as automated valuation models (AVMs).

Private Data Services. In recent years, the number of private, for profit, data vendors has increased dramatically. Some vendors specialize in only one local market, some have regional or even national platforms. In some areas, local appraisers have formed data cooperatives. Title insurance companies are another potential source of valuable data. Regardless of the source, most of these data can be delivered electronically to the appraiser's desktop or laptop computer. The days of appraisers searching for papers and documents in physical locations is giving way to electronic distribution by means of the Web.

Adjustments to Comparable Property Transaction Prices

Appraisers must consider numerous **adjustments,** when employing the sales comparison approach. These adjustments are divided into two categories: transactional adjustments and property adjustments. The goal of these adjustments is to convert each comparable sale into an approximation of the subject property. If the comparable property is inferior to the subject property with respect to any of these items, the comparable property's sale price would be adjusted upward. Conversely, if the comparable property is superior to the subject property along any important dimension, the comparable property's sale price would be adjusted downward. The most common required adjustments are listed below.

Transactional Adjustments	**Property Adjustments**
1. Conditions of sale	4. Location
2. Financing terms	5. Physical characteristics
3. Market conditions	6. Legal characteristics
	7. Use
	8. Nonrealty items (personal property)

The first three, labeled **transactional adjustments,** concern the nature and terms of the deal. These potential influences on the bargaining position or motivation of buyer, seller, or both can have an overall effect on the price being negotiated, regardless of the detailed features of the property. The five **property adjustments** recognize that the locational, physical, and legal differences between properties, plus the ways that the properties are used and the presence or absence of personal property, all can add or subtract incrementally to a base value, much like the effect of options on the price of a car. Each of these types of adjustments is briefly explained below.

Conditions of Sale. A forced sale or a desperation purchase can cause unequal bargaining power between buyers and sellers. More commonly, personal relationships may cause a transaction price to be lower than market value, as when a parent "sells" real estate to a son or daughter. Appraisal analysts must check each comparable sale to ensure that it truly was an arm's-length transaction between buyers and sellers who have relatively equal bargaining power. Rarely is it possible to know how much a transaction that is not arm's length should be adjusted so that it is usable. Therefore, it normally is rejected from the analysis.

Financing Terms. Occasionally, properties are sold with nonmarket financing. For example, a lender may participate in a government-sponsored low-income (or first-time) home-buyer program and grant below-market interest rate loans to buyers. Favorable financing may allow buyers to pay a somewhat higher purchase price. Thus, the possibility of non-market financing must always be considered. When detected, we recommend that the property not be used as a comparable sale. However, if the number of comparable sale transactions is extremely limited, compelling the appraiser to include the transaction, the transaction price of the comparable property must be adjusted accordingly (usually downward) when such financing occurs.

Market Conditions. The transaction prices of comparable properties are historical data. That is, the transactions may have taken place yesterday, last month, or several months ago. In using transaction data to determine the *current* value of the subject property, it is important to recognize that general market conditions may have changed since the transaction occurred. Changes in **market conditions** result from general price inflation (or deflation) or changes in local conditions of supply and demand.

The value movements attributed to changes in market conditions are best estimated by tracking the prices of individual properties as they sell repeatedly over time. This general method is known as **repeat-sale analysis.** For example, consider three comparable properties that all sold recently (assumed to be today) and at some time during the past 24 months (see Exhibit 8-3). By dividing the average monthly price increase of each property by its respective initial sale price (SP_1), it is determined that prices of comparable properties have increased, on average, about 0.32 percent per month.[4]

Appraisers can use this rate to adjust the **normal sale prices** of comparable properties for the number of months since they were sold. The result is the **market-adjusted normal sale price.** For example, if a comparable property sold 10 months ago for $100,000, assuming an arm's-length transaction under normal financing conditions, the adjustment would be $100,000 × (0.0032 × 10) = $3,200, and the market-adjusted normal sale price would equal $103,200. If insufficient repeat-sale data are available, an appraiser may be forced to use other information to infer recent price changes, such as recent changes in median sale prices.

Concept Check

8.5   Assume an analysis of recent sale prices indicate that properties in the subject's market have declined, on average, 1/4 of a percent each month over the last two years. If the comparable property sold 12 months ago, what adjustment is required?

Exhibit 8-3   Repeat-Sale Analysis for Market Conditions Adjustment

Property	Date of Previous Sale	Price at Previous Sale (SP_1)	Price Today (SP_2)	Change per Month (SP_2-SP_1)/mos.	Monthly Rate of Increase (% of SP_1)
A	12 mos. ago	$191,000	$197,900	$575	0.30%
B	18 mos. ago	158,600	167,000	467	0.29
C	24 mos. ago	148,900	162,000	546	0.37
	Average monthly rate of increase =				0.32%

4. Students may note that this is not the compounded monthly rate, but rather a linear rate of increase. This rate is commonly used in practice to estimate changes over short time periods.

Exhibit 8-4 Paired-Sales Analysis for Location Adjustment

Pair	Property	Neighborhood	Recent Sale Price	Difference	Difference as a % of B
	1-a	Center Place	$183,500		
1	1-b	Distant Grove	175,900	7,600	4.3%
	2-a	Center Place	200,000		
2	2-b	Distant Grove	192,500	7,500	3.9
	3-a	Center Place	202,900		
3	3-b	Distant Grove	194,700	8,200	4.2
				Average =	4.1%

Location. The primacy of location in real estate valuation is discussed extensively in Chapters 5 to 7. A location adjustment is required when the location of a comparable property is either superior or inferior to the location of the subject property, which is almost always the case. When the subject and comparable properties are located in different neighborhoods, an appraiser must quantify the required location adjustment by somehow comparing the prices of similar properties, some of which are in the subject property's neighborhood and some in the comparable property's neighborhood. Ideally the appraiser would like to use a method of comparison known as **paired sales analysis,** which is demonstrated in Exhibit 8-4. One property in each pair of "nearly-identical" properties is in the subject property's neighborhood (Center Place), while the other property is in the comparable property's neighborhood (Distant Grove). As calculated in Exhibit 8-4, houses in Center Place sell for an average of 4.1 percent more than otherwise similar houses in Distant Grove.

Available sales information seldom permits the paired sales analysis shown above; a pair of sold properties with only one differing feature is seldom to be found. As a result, appraisers have long had to rely on more intuitive, creative, and diverse methods to ascertain appropriate feature adjustments. However, help in estimating feature adjustments is available today. The rapid growth of electronic data retrieval and use of computers has put sophisticated electronic data analysis within the reach of almost all appraisers. It now is possible for virtually any appraiser to conduct sales comparison valuation by multivariate regression analysis (MRA), as demonstrated in the last section of this chapter. One of the major contributions of MRA is to estimate and implement feature adjustments in an objective manner.

Physical Characteristics. Adjustments for physical characteristics are intended to capture the dimensions in which a comparable property differs physically from the subject property. These include differences such as lot size, structure size, desirability of the floor plan, architectural style, condition, type of construction, materials, and the presence or absence of various features such as a garage, fireplace, built-in appliances, bookshelves, carpet, swimming pool, or patio. Ideally, appraisers would like to use the paired sales technique to estimate the value of a particular characteristic by comparing the sale prices of pairs of recently sold properties that are similar in all respects, except for the characteristic of interest. Again, it is seldom possible, and the appraiser must rely on more eclectic techniques or, nowadays, on multivariate regression analysis (MRA).

Legal Characteristics. Potentially, a sale price adjustment must be made if the legal estate, or bundle of rights, of a comparable property differs from those of the subject property. (Legal estates are discussed in Chapter 4). In reality, however, the amount of the required adjustment is almost impossible to measure from the market. Thus, a property having a legal estate different than that of the subject property should generally be eliminated as a comparable, even if physically very similar.

Concept Check

8.6   Assume the interest conveyed from seller to buyer is a fee simple estate. A similar property in the neighborhood that recently sold conveyed title under the condition that the property not be sold for three years. What adjustment is required?

Use. Two properties located in the same market can be physically similar, but their *uses* may differ, requiring either an adjustment or elimination of the property as a comparable. For example, an appraiser may be valuing an older single-family residence near the center of a medium-size city. One of the comparable properties is a similar house next door. However, this comparable is used for law offices. Although existing zoning (see Chapter 6) permits the subject to be used as an office building, its value depends on its anticipated highest and best use. If the appraiser believes the highest and best use is as a single-family residence, he cannot use the law offices as a comparable sale. Note that the decision depends on the *anticipated* use of the subject at its highest and best use, not its historic or current use.

Nonrealty Items. Sometimes the sale price of either the subject property or one of the comparable properties will contain items of personal property, such as furniture, equipment, rugs, fireplace equipment, and TVs. The price of the comparable must therefore be adjusted to reflect either the presence or lack of these **nonrealty items.** In doing so, it is the current market value of these items that is used as the adjustment, not their original cost or today's replacement cost.

Types of Adjustments

Appraisers use two types of adjustments: dollars and percentages. If the dollar difference is estimated, the appraiser simply adds it to, or subtracts it from, the price of the comparable property. Some adjustments (e.g., financing and physical characteristics) usually are made in dollars, whereas adjustments for market conditions and location are more typically made in percentage terms.

Sequence of Adjustments

In accordance with the practice recommended by the Appraisal Institute, appraisers should make adjustments to comparable sale prices in the *sequence* presented in Exhibit 8-5. Adjustments 1 and 2 are applied to the *transaction price,* adjustment 3 to the *normal sale price,* and adjustments 4 to 8 to the *market-adjusted normal sale price.* The sequence would make no difference if all adjustments are either dollar adjustments or percentage adjustments, but with mixed adjustments the sequence matters. We caution that two of the recommended adjustments generally should not be used; namely, for legal characteristics and for use. As we have noted above, we believe they are too difficult to do correctly, and comparables which differ from the subject by these characteristics should simply be set aside.

Example 8-1   2380 Appletree Court

To illustrate the sales comparison approach, assume transaction data from three comparable properties are used in valuing the subject property—a single-family residence located at 2380 Appletree Court, in the Parkway Estates neighborhood. The relevant characteristics, termed the **elements of comparison,** used to compare and adjust the property prices, are summarized in Exhibit 8-6, the market data grid.

Exhibit 8-5   Sequence of Adjustments to Sale Price of Comparable

---

Transaction Price of Comparable Property

   1. +/− Conditions of sale
   2. +/− Financing terms

= Normal Sale Price

   3. +/− Market conditions

= Market-Adjusted Normal Sale Price

   4. +/− Location
   5. +/− Physical characteristics
   6. +/− Legal characteristics
   7. +/− Use
   8. +/− Nonrealty items

= Final Adjusted Sale Price of Comparable

We can see from the location line on the market data grid that the comparable properties are in the subject property's neighborhood. Two sold within the last three months, while the third sold four months ago. Their prices range from $157,100 to $169,900. Note that the conditions of sale, financing terms, legal characteristics, use, and several of the physical features of the subject are identical to the comparable properties. Thus, no adjustment will be necessary for these elements. However, adjustments are necessary for differences in several characteristics that, in the opinion of the appraiser, materially affected the comparable transaction prices. The amount of the adjustment for each item has been estimated by the appraiser and is shown in the list below:

- Market conditions: 0.3 percent per month.
- Lot size: $100,000 per acre.
- Construction quality: No adjustment if all siding. $1,500 adjustment if brick front with remainder siding; $3,000 adjustment if all brick.
- Age: $1,250 per year.
- Living area: $48.00 per square foot.
- Porch, patio, deck area: $16.00 per square foot.
- Pool area: $7,000.
- Bath: $4,000.

The individual adjustments are shown, following the recommended sequence, in Exhibit 8-7. For example, Comparable Sales 2 and 3 require an adjustment for market conditions because they sold in earlier months. The adjustment for Comparable 2 is calculated as $167,200 × 0.003 per mo. × 3 mos. = $1,504.80, and Comparable 3 as $157,100 × 0.003 per mo. × 4 mos. = $1,885.20. However, these estimates suggest a degree of precision in the estimate that is unintended and the adjustments are rounded to $1,500 and $1,900.

The individual adjustments for the various differences in physical characteristics are shown next. For example, the subject does not have a pool although Comparable Sales 2 and 3 do. Therefore, the estimated value of the pool ($7,000) is *subtracted* from the market-adjusted normal sale price of the comparable sales 2 and 3. The adjustments are made for all items that differ, resulting in a *final adjusted sale price* for each of the comparable properties.

It is extremely important to emphasize that required adjustments, such as those detailed in Exhibit 8-7, are subjective and therefore require significant experience as well as constant attention to market transactions, trends, and conditions.

Exhibit 8-6 Sale Comparison Approach: Market Data Grid for 2380 Appletree Court

Element of Comparison	Subject	Comparable Sale 1	Comparable Sale 2	Comparable Sale 3
Transaction price	————	$169,900	$167,200	$157,100
Conditions of sale	Arm's length	Same	Same	Same
Financing terms	Conventional	Conventional	Conventional	Conventional
Sale (value) date	Today	This month	3 mos. ago	4 mos. ago
Location	Parkway Estates	Parkway Estates	Parkway Estates	Parkway Estates
Site size	0.5 acres +/−	0.5 Acres +/−	0.45 Acres +/−	0.48 Acres +/−
Construction quality	Siding	Siding/brick	Siding	Brick
Effective age	3 yrs.	6 yrs.	10 yrs.	15 yrs.
Living area	1,960 sq.ft.	2,060 sq.ft.	2,077 sq.ft.	1,818 sq.ft.
Number of baths	2.5 baths	2.5 baths	2.5 baths	3.0 baths
Garage spaces	2-car	2-car	2-car	2-car
Porch, patio, deck	None	None	None	200 sq.ft.
Pool, fence, etc.	None	None	Pool	Pool
Legal characteristics	Fee simple	Same	Same	Same
Use	Single-family	Same	Same	Same
Nonrealty items	None	None	None	None

Exhibit 8-7 Sale Comparison Approach: Adjustment Grid for 2380 Appletree Court

Element of Comparison	Subject	Comparable Sale 1	Comparable Sale 2	Comparable Sale 3
Transaction price	————	$169,900	$167,200	$157,100
+/− Conditions of sale	Arm's length	0	0	0
+/− Financing terms	Conventional	0	0	0
= Normal sale price	————	$169,900	$167,200	$157,100
+/− Market conditions	Today	0	+1,500	+1,900
= Market-adjusted normal sale price		$169,900	$168,700	$159,000
+/− Location	Suburban	0	0	0
Physical characteristics				
+/− Site	0.5 acres	0	+5,000	+2,000
+/− Construction quality	Siding/good	−1,500	0	−3,000
+/− Effective age	3 years	+3,750	+8,750	+15,000
+/− Living area	1,960 sq.ft.	−4,800	−5,600	+6,800
+/− Bath	2.5	0	0	−2,000
+/− Porch, patio, deck	None	0	0	−3,200
+/− Fence, pool, etc.	None	0	−7,000	−7,000
= Final adjusted sale price		$167,350	$169,850	$167,600

Concept Check

8.7 Explain the difference, sequentially, between the normal sale price, the market adjusted normal sale price, and the final adjusted sale price.

A Note on Selection of Comparables and Adjustments

The steps of the sales comparison approach involve both selection of comparables and the execution of adjustments. While both steps can be important in the procedure, the authors have observed that more and greater errors in appraisal have resulted from careless selection of comparables than from poor adjustments. Unless the adjustments are unusually large, say, greater than 10 percent of a sale price, the first order of investigation in evaluating an appraisal is to assure that the comparables used are reasonable.

Reconciliation to an Indicated Value Estimate

The final step in obtaining an indicated value of the subject property from the sales comparison approach is to reconcile the final adjusted sale prices of the comparable properties. In this step an appraiser considers which, if any, of the comparable properties are better indicators of the subject property's value. More complete data, fewer and smaller adjustments, and more recent transactions probably would cause the appraiser to consider the adjusted sale prices of some comparable properties to be better indicators of value than others. In this case, Comparable 1 was weighted more heavily (60 percent) than the other two (20 percent each) because the appraiser believed that Comparable 1 was very similar to the subject property, required few adjustments, and represented the best indicator of value. As shown in Exhibit 8-8, reconciliation is a weighting process. The weighted average price is rounded to obtain the *indicated value* from the sales comparison approach of $167,900.

In professional practice, appraisers seldom explicitly identify the weights given to each comparable. They apply the weights implicitly in rendering their professional opinion of value. The weights are detailed here only to describe the process.

Cost Approach

Market forces compel construction costs to approximate the market value of newly constructed properties. When the cost to produce a property is less than its completed market value, developers have an incentive to construct additional properties, which tends to reduce market values.[5] When the cost to produce a property exceeds its market value, developers have the incentive to stop or slow construction, which tends to increase market values. Thus, construction costs and market values differ, but are always pressured toward each other by the actions of market participants.

The cost approach to valuation assumes the market value of a *new* building is similar to the cost of constructing it today. For an existing property, the appraiser identifies and measures reductions in the value from today's reproduction cost. These reductions are

Exhibit 8-8 Reconciliation of Adjusted Final Sale Prices

Source	Final Adjusted Sale Price		Weight (%)		Weighted Price
Comparable Sale 1	167,350	×	60%	=	$100,410
Comparable Sale 2	169,850	×	20	=	33,970
Comparable Sale 3	167,600	×	20	=	33,520
Indicated Value (using the sales comparison approach)				=	$167,900

5. The costs, as described here, include all outlays required to acquire the land, develop it, and construct the building improvements. The costs include the direct material and labor costs, as well as all indirect overhead, design, permit, financing, marketing, and entrepreneurial costs.

Exhibit 8-9 Summary of Cost Approach

−	Estimated reproduction cost of structure
	Accrued depreciation
=	Depreciated cost of building improvements
+	Estimated value of site
=	Indicated market value by the cost approach

termed *accrued depreciation*. After the appraiser has estimated the building's value by subtracting all elements of accrued depreciation from the building's cost, the value of the land (and permanent improvements to the land) is estimated separately and added to the depreciated cost of the building. The general steps of the cost approach are outlined in Exhibit 8-9.

Estimating Cost. For appraisal purposes, there are two possible types of construction costs: reproduction costs and replacement costs. The **reproduction cost** of a building is the cost to construct the building today, replicating it in exact detail. This includes any outdated functional aspects of the building such as poor room arrangement, better-than-necessary fixtures, or inadequate equipment. It also includes the cost of any outmoded materials such as surface wiring, steel window frames, and steel plumbing.

In contrast, **replacement cost** is the money required to construct a building of *equal utility*.[6] This includes the use of modern construction techniques, materials, and design and represents the cost of a building for which some or all outdated aspects are eliminated.

In estimating cost, appraisers tend to rely on builders' cost figures to maintain comparative cost data on a square-foot or cubic-foot basis for various types of properties, and to use cost estimating services. In addition to builders, several private companies, such as Marshall and Swift, are in the business of proving detailed cost estimates.

The theoretical base for the cost approach is reproduction cost. However, reproduction cost is often difficult to estimate because the building may include materials that are no longer available or no longer permitted by current construction standards. As a result, replacement cost is often used since it is easier to obtain.

www.marshallswift.com

Leading cost estimator for the appraisal industry.

www.rsmeans.com

Provider of cost estimation services.

Concept Check

8.8 Distinguish between reproduction cost and replacement cost. Which is generally greater?

Accrued Depreciation

Accrued depreciation is the difference between the market value of a building (or improvement) and its cost.[7] These differences generally occur over time and are attributed to three elements: physical deterioration, functional obsolescence, and external obsolescence.

Physical deterioration represents the loss in value of an improvement over time associated with the aging and decay of its physical condition. This occurs in both short-lived items (e.g., carpeting, roofing materials, appliances) and long-lived items (e.g., roof framing, windows, doors, stairs, foundation).

---

6. The term *utility* means satisfaction. Therefore, a building of equal utility is a building that provides satisfaction equal to that of the building being appraised as if it were new.

7. It is important to note that the appraisal concept of depreciation differs substantially from the accounting concept used for income tax calculation. The appraisal term is associated with *actual* reductions in market value, while the term used in calculating taxable income deals with *allowable* reductions to a property's book value, or depreciable basis.

Functional obsolescence represents the loss in value of an improvement associated with a loss in useful capacity. It is "a loss in value within a structure due to changes in tastes, preferences, technical innovations, or market standards."[8] Similar to physical deterioration, functional obsolescence tends to be associated with the passage of time; however, a direct relationship between age and functional obsolescence is not required. Newer building materials, construction techniques, and designs, coupled with changing consumer tastes and preferences, generally make older buildings less desirable and thus not as valuable as newer buildings. For example, a new home without a master bathroom suite may be deemed to be functionally obsolete in some markets. Examples of curable functional obsolescence include outdated fixtures, too few electrical outlets, lack of bookcases, too-high ceilings, and lack of insulation. Examples of functional obsolescence that cannot be fixed include a poor exterior design or interior floor plan, outdated plumbing, and a poor electrical system. The use of replacement cost, rather than reproduction cost, eliminates the need to estimate some forms of functional obsolescence.

Finally, **external obsolescence** reflects the loss in value due to influences *external to the physical improvement* that affect value. Noxious odors, unpleasant sights, and increased traffic due to more intensive uses (e.g., commercial and industrial) introduced into a residential neighborhood are examples of this external obsolescence. External obsolescence can also result from a deterioration in the demand for properties in a particular submarket.

Example 8-2   2380 Appletree Court

To estimate the value of 2380 Appletree Court using the cost approach, an appraiser estimates the current cost of the improvements, the total accrued depreciation, and the value of the site (and any site improvements). The appraiser's estimates are shown in Exhibit 8-10.

The cost estimate is based on information supplied by a cost estimating service and data obtained from local building contractors. The living area of the dwelling is estimated at a cost of $121,520 (1,960 sq. ft. $\times$ $62 per sq. ft). To that is added the cost of the garage ($8,800) and appliances ($2,400), resulting in a total improvement cost of $132,720. Physical depreciation is estimated at 5 percent of the total improvement costs ($6,636 = $132,720 $\times$ 0.05). The appraiser concludes that the property has not suffered any functional or external obsolescence. This results in a depreciated value of $126,084. The site value is estimated to be $40,000. Landscaping and other miscellaneous site improvements are estimated to have a current value of $4,000. Thus, the indicated value using the cost approach is $170,084, rounded to $170,000. Declines in value associated with accrued depreciation are difficult to estimate in practice. This explains why the other methods of valuation are relied upon more in most appraisal assignments.

Exhibit 8-10   Smith Residence: Cost Approach Summary

Reproduction cost of improvement		
Living area (conditioned space)	$121,520	
Garage area	8,800	
Appliances, porch, patio areas	2,400	$132,720
Less: Depreciation of improvement		
Physical deterioration	6,636	
Functional obsolescence	0	
External obsolescence	0	−6,636
Depreciated value of improvements		$126,084
Plus: Value of the site		40,000
Plus: Depreciated Value of site improvement		4,000
Indicated value by cost approach		$170,084

8. Dennis S. Tosh, Jr., *Handbook of Real Estate Terms* (Englewood, NJ: Prentice Hall, 1990), p. 208.

Concept Check

8.9   Of the three basic steps in the cost approach to valuation: estimate reproduction cost, estimate accrued depreciation, and estimate site value, which is generally the most difficult and why?

Final Reconciliation

In determining the final estimate of market value, an appraiser considers and weighs the reliability of the indicated values, and the relevance of the approaches to the valuation of the subject property. In the Appletree Court example, the appraiser has produced estimated market values using the sales comparison approach and the cost approach of $167,900, and $170,000, respectively. The appraiser has determined that owing to the reliability of the comparable sales data and the applicability of the approach to residential properties, the sales comparison approach yields the most reliable indicator of value—all weight is placed on this approach in reconciling the value indicators. Thus, the final estimate of value of the residence located at 2380 Appletree Court is $167,900.

The appraisal of a residence, as described using the Appletree Court example, is generally required to obtain financing when purchasing a property. Lenders ask appraisers to submit their value opinion by completing a Uniform Residential Appraisal Report (URAR) form. This form report has been developed by Fannie Mae and Freddie Mac in order to standardize the underwriting of loans that are to be purchased in the secondary mortgage market (discussed in Chapter 13). A sample URAR is shown for the Appletree Court property in Exhibit 8-11.

Multivariate Regression Analysis

Multivariate regression analysis (MRA) is a statistical procedure applied to examine the relationship between a dependent variable and multiple independent, "explanatory," variables. For example, it can be applied to examine the relationship between the sale prices of properties (the dependent variable) and the characteristics of the properties, such as square footage, age, and location (the independent variables). Reliable application of the procedure requires detailed data on a substantial number of property sales (i.e., generally more than 30 or 40 sample observations are required).

While the computational tools for applying multivariate regression analysis (MRA) in the appraisal of real estate have been used for many years, the availability of adequate property-specific data has been a major constraint. With the ongoing development of electronic databases by state and county government offices, brokerage associations, and lenders, this deficiency has substantially diminished in recent years. For example, the enormous data banks of Fannie Mae and Freddie Mac cover millions of transactions in which these secondary mortgage market organizations are involved. These data are now stored in digital form and are regularly used in property analysis. The models and procedures that will govern the application of these data sources are currently being developed and will undoubtedly lead to major changes in the scope of the residential appraisal function and in the way that residential appraisals (and appraisals of other property types, as well) are conducted. Today, the vast majority of appraisals of one- to four-family residences are completed because they are required for a homebuyer to obtain a loan from a lending institution. However, many of these appraisals may be completed by computer-aided modeling and multivariate regression analysis (see Industry Issues 8-2.)

Exhibit 8-11

UNIFORM RESIDENTIAL APPRAISAL REPORT
File No. R2003-100

Property Description

Property Address 2380 Appletree Court	City Orlando	State FL Zip Code 32855
Legal Description Lot 10, Block B, Parkway Estates, Plat Book 245, Page 34		County Orange
Assessor's Parcel No. T34SR26E-59-B-0100	Tax Year 2002 R.E. Taxes $ 2,520	Special Assessments $ 0.00
Borrower Jacob Jones	Current Owner Jacob Jones	Occupant: ☒ Owner ☐ Tenant ☐ Vacant

Property rights appraised ☒ Fee Simple ☐ Leasehold Project Type ☐ PUD ☐ Condominium (HUD/VA only) HOA $ 30.00 /Mo.
Neighborhood or Project Name Parkway Estates Map Reference 34-26 Census Tract 38.04
Sale Price $ N/A Date of Sale N/A Description and $ amount of loan charges/concessions to be paid by seller Refinance
Lender/Client Bank of Florida Address 15760 N. Main, Orlando, Fl.
Appraiser Jerry McGuire Address 1535 Centre Point Office, Orlando, FL 32801

NEIGHBORHOOD

Location	☐ Urban ☒ Suburban ☐ Rural	Predominant occupancy	Single family housing	Present land use %	Land use change
Built up	☒ Over 75% ☐ 25-75% ☐ Under 25%		PRICE $(000) AGE (yrs)	One family 80	☒ Not likely ☐ Likely
Growth rate	☐ Rapid ☒ Stable ☐ Slow	☒ Owner	100 Low New	2-4 family 5	☐ In process
Property values	☒ Increasing ☐ Stable ☐ Declining	☐ Tenant	220 High 30	Multi-family 5	To:
Demand/supply	☐ Shortage ☒ In balance ☐ Over supply	☐ Vacant (0-5%)	Predominant	Commercial 5	
Marketing time	☐ Under 3 mos. ☒ 3-6 mos. ☐ Over 6 mos.	☐ Vac. (over 5%)	140-160 10	Vacant 5	

Note: Race and the racial composition of the neighborhood are not appraisal factors.

Neighborhood boundaries and characteristics: The subject neighborhood is bounded to the north by Red Lake Road, to the east by Shamrock Way, to the south by Dodd Road, and to the west by Aloma Ave.

Factors that affect the marketability of the properties in the neighborhood (proximity to employment and amenities, employment stability, appeal to market, etc.): The subject is located approximately 10 miles northeast of the Orlando downtown area and is composed primarily of owner-occupied, single-family, detached homes. The subject is located convenient to centers of employment and public schools. Shopping, banking, restaurants and other commercial facilities are located on the major highways surrounding the area, but do not adversely affect the subject's value.

Market conditions in the subject neighborhood (including support for the above conclusions related to the trend of property values, demand/supply, and marketing time -- such as data on competitive properties for sale in the neighborhood, description of the prevalence of sales and financing concessions, etc.): This is an established residential area. The area appears to be stable with moderately increasing property values. Most homes in the area, when placed on the market, sell within six months. Market interest rates are at competitive levels. Sales and financing concessions are uncommon.

PUD
Project Information for PUDs (If applicable) - - Is the developer/builder in control of the Home Owners' Association (HOA)? ☐ Yes ☐ No
Approximate total number of units in the subject project N/A Approximate total number of units for sale in the subject project N/A
Describe common elements and recreational facilities: N/A

SITE

Dimensions 110 x 180 x 98 x 210 Topography Level
Site area 21,345 +/- square feet Corner Lot ☐ Yes ☒ No Size Typical for area
Specific zoning classification and description Residential (R-1) Shape Rectangular
Zoning compliance ☒ Legal ☐ Legal nonconforming (Grandfathered use) ☐ Illegal ☐ No zoning Drainage No apparent problems
Highest & best use as improved: ☒ Present use ☐ Other use (explain) View Residential properties
Landscaping Typical for area

Utilities	Public	Other	Off-site Improvements	Type	Public	Private	
Electricity	☒		Street	Asphalt	☒		Driveway Surface Concrete
Gas	☒		Curb/gutter	Concrete			Apparent easements None apparent
Water	☒		Sidewalk	Concrete			FEMA Special Flood Hazard Area ☐ Yes ☒ No
Sanitary sewer	☒		Street lights	Low Pressure Sodium	☒		FEMA Zone C Map Date 11/19/99
Storm sewer	☒		Alley	None			FEMA Map No. 12077-C-0400-E

Comments (apparent adverse easements, encroachments, special assessments, slide areas, illegal or legal nonconforming zoning use, etc.): The site is typical for the area. No adverse easements, encroachments or conditions were observed.

DESCRIPTION OF IMPROVEMENTS

GENERAL DESCRIPTION		EXTERIOR DESCRIPTION		FOUNDATION		BASEMENT		INSULATION	
No. of Units	One	Foundation	Concrete	Slab	Yes	Area Sq. Ft. N/A		Roof	☐
No. of Stories	One	Exterior Walls	Siding (Hardy)	Crawl Space	No	% Finished N/A		Ceiling	☒
Type (Det./Att.)	Detached	Roof Surface	Comp.shingle	Basement	No	Ceiling N/A		Walls	☒
Design (Style)	Traditional	Gutters & Dwnspts.	None	Sump Pump	No	Walls N/A		Floor	☐
Existing/Proposed	Existing	Window Type	Alum./thermal	Dampness	None apparent	Floor N/A		None	☐
Age (Yrs.)	3	Storm/Screens	Screens	Settlement	None apparent	Outside Entry N/A		Unknown	☐
Effective Age (Yrs.)	3	Manufactured House	No	Infestation	None apparent				

ROOMS	Foyer	Living	Dining	Kitchen	Den	Family Rm.	Rec. Rm.	Bedrooms	# Baths	Laundry	Other	Area Sq. Ft.
Basement												N/A
Level 1	Area	1	1	1		1		3	2.5	Area		1,960
Level 2												

Finished area above grade contains: 7 Rooms; 3 Bedroom(s); 2.5 Bath(s); 1,960 Square Feet of Gross Living Area

INTERIOR	Materials/Condition	HEATING		KITCHEN EQUIP.		ATTIC		AMENITIES		CAR STORAGE:	
Floors	Carpet/Vinyl/Good	Type	Ht. pump	Refrigerator ☒		None		Fireplace(s) # One ☒		None ☐	
Walls	Drywall/Good	Fuel	Electric	Range/Oven ☒		Stairs	☐	Patio None		Garage	# of cars
Trim/Finish	Wood/Good	Condition	Good	Disposal ☒		Drop Stair	☒	Deck None		Attached 2-car	
Bath Floor	Ceramic/Good	COOLING		Dishwasher ☒		Scuttle	☒	Porch None		Detached	
Bath Wainscot	Ceramic/Good	Central	Yes	Fan/Hood ☒		Floor	☐	Fence None		Built-In	
Doors	Hollow core wd/Gd	Other	Clg.Fans	Microwave ☒		Heated	☐	Pool No Pool		Carport	
		Condition	Good	Washer/Dryer ☒		Finished	☐			Driveway	

Additional features (special energy efficient items, etc.): The additional features include crown molding, 9-foot ceilings, and a bay window.

COMMENTS

Condition of the improvements, depreciation (physical, functional, and external), repairs needed, quality of construction, remodeling/additions, etc.: The subject appears to be in good to excellent condition. The subject has been well maintained and there are no apparent signs of deferred maintenance. No elements of functional or external obsolescence were observed at inspection.

Adverse environmental conditions (such as, but not limited to, hazardous wastes, toxic substances, etc.) present in the improvements, on the site, or in the immediate vicinity of the subject property.: There were no apparent adverse conditions observed at inspection.

Freddie Mac Form 70 6/93 PAGE 1 OF 2 Fannie Mae Form 1004 6/93

Exhibit 8-11—continued

UNIFORM RESIDENTIAL APPRAISAL REPORT

Valuation Section   File No. R2003-100

COST APPROACH

ESTIMATED SITE VALUE .... = $	40,000
ESTIMATED REPRODUCTION COST-NEW-OF IMPROVEMENTS:	
Dwelling 1,960 Sq. Ft. @ $ 62 = $	121,520
_____ Sq. Ft. @ $ _____ =	
Appliances =	2,400
Garage/Carport 440 Sq. Ft. @ $ 20 =	8,800
Total Estimated Cost New .... = $	132,720
Less Physical Functional External	
Depreciation 6,636 = $	6,636
Depreciated Value of Improvements = $	126,084
"As-is" Value of Site Improvements = $	4,000
INDICATED VALUE BY COST APPROACH = $	170,084

Comments on Cost Approach (such as, source of cost estimate, site value, square foot calculation and for HUD, VA and FmHA, the estimated remaining economic life of the property):

The cost approach estimate is based on information supplied by the Marshall & Swift cost service and data obtained from local building contractors. The estimate of land value is derived using the sale comparison approach from vacant land sales in the area. The size of the subject's site, 0.5 acres, is typical of the subdivision

The estimated remaining economic life : 57 years.

The estimated remaining physical life: 57 years.

SALES COMPARISON ANALYSIS

ITEM	SUBJECT	COMPARABLE NO. 1	+(−)$ Adjust.	COMPARABLE NO. 2	+(−)$ Adjust.	COMPARABLE NO. 3	+(−)$ Adjust.
Address	2380 Appletree Court Orlando	2043 Appletree Court Orlando		4207 E. Park Trail Orlando		4470 E. Park Trail Orlando	
Proximity to Subject		Approx. 3 blocks south		Approx. 1 block east		Approx. 3 blocks east	
Sales Price	$ N/A	$ 169,900		$ 167,200		$ 157,100	
Price/Gross Living Area	$ ⌀	$ 82.48 ⌀		$ 80.50 ⌀		$ 86.41 ⌀	
Data and/or Verification Source	Inspection	MLS & Public Records		MLS & Public Records		MLS & Public Records	
VALUE ADJUSTMENTS	DESCRIPTION	DESCRIPTION		DESCRIPTION		DESCRIPTION	
Sales or Financing Concessions		Conventional Typical		Conventional Typical		Conventional Typical	
Date of Sale/Time		09/03		06/03	+1,500	05/03	+1,900
Location	Suburban/Avg.	Suburban/Avg.		Suburban/Avg.		Suburban/Avg.	
Leasehold/Fee Simple	Fee Simple	Fee Simple		Fee Simple		Fee Simple	
Site	.5-Acres +/-	.5-Acres +/-		.45-Acres +/-	+5,000	.4-Acres +/-	+2,000
View	Residential/Avg.	Residential/Avg.		Residential/Avg.		Residential/Avg.	
Design and Appeal	Traditional/Avg.	Traditional/Avg.		Traditional/Avg.		Traditional/Avg.	
Quality of Construction	Wood Siding	Brick - 1 side	-1,500	Wood Siding		Brick - 1 side	-3,000
Age	A3/E3	A6/E6	+3,750	A15/E10	+8,750	A15/E15	+15,000
Condition	Good - Excellent	Good -Excellent		Good - Excellent		Good - Excellent	
Above Grade Room Count	Total 7 Bdrms 3 Baths 2.5	Total 6 Bdrms 3 Baths 2.5		Total 7 Bdrms 4 Baths 2.5		Total 7 Bdrms 3 Baths 3	-2,000
Gross Living Area	1,960 Sq. Ft.	2,060 Sq. Ft.	-4,800	2,077 Sq. Ft.	-5,600	1,818 Sq. Ft.	+6,800
Basement & Finished Rooms Below Grade	None None	None None		None None		None None	
Functional Utility	Average	Average		Average		Average	
Heating/Cooling	Central	Central		Central		Central	
Energy Efficient Items	Average	Average		Average		Average	
Garage/Carport	Garage (2)	Garage (2)		Garage (2)		Garage (2)	
Porch, Patio, Deck, Fireplace(s), etc.	FP (1)	FP (1)		FP (1)		FP(1)Porch/Deck	-3,200
Fence, Pool, etc.	No Pool	No Pool		Pool	-7,000	Pool	-7,000
Net Adj. (total)		☐+ ☒− $	2,550	☒+ ☐− $	2,650	☒+ ☐− $	10,500
Adjusted Sales Price of Comparable		Net 1.5 % Gross 5.9 % $	167,350	Net 1.6 % Gross 16.7 % $	169,850	Net 6.7 % Gross 26.0 % $	167,600

Comments on Sales Comparison (including the subject property's compatibility to the neighborhood, etc.):

The sample of comparable sales is taken from the subject's general area. Other sales were reviewed, and the sample data selected is comparable in terms of size, location, age, and condition. All sales occurred within the last three months.

ITEM	SUBJECT	COMPARABLE NO. 1	COMPARABLE NO. 2	COMPARABLE NO. 3
Date, Price and Data Source, for prior sales within year of appraisal	N/A	N/A	N/A	N/A

Analysis of any current agreement of sale, option, or listing of subject property and analysis of any prior sales of subject and comparables within one year of the date of appraisal: Prior sales of the comparable properties selected occurred more than one year ago. The subject property was not listed for sale.

INDICATED VALUE BY SALES COMPARISON APPROACH	$	167,900
INDICATED VALUE BY INCOME APPROACH (if Applicable) Estimated Market Rent $ N/A /Mo. x Gross Rent Multiplier N/A = $		N/A

RECONCILIATION

This appraisal is made ☒ "as is" ☐ subject to the repairs, alterations, inspections or conditions listed below ☐ subject to completion per plans & specifications.

Conditions of Appraisal: The subject has not been listed, sold, or changed ownership within the last 12 months. This is a summary report as per USPAP.

Final Reconciliation: The value estimate is supported by the sales comparison approach and the cost approach. However, the sales comparison approach best reflects the preferences of the buyers and sellers. Homes in the subject neighborhood are not typically leased, therefore, the income approach is not relevant to our analysis.

The purpose of this appraisal is to estimate the market value of the real property that is the subject of this report, based on the above conditions and the certification, contingent and limiting conditions, and market value definition that are stated in the attached Freddie Mac Form 439/FNMA form 1004B (Revised 6/93).

I (WE) ESTIMATE THE MARKET VALUE, AS DEFINED, OF THE REAL PROPERTY THAT IS THE SUBJECT OF THIS REPORT, AS OF September 15, 2003 (WHICH IS THE DATE OF INSPECTION AND THE EFFECTIVE DATE OF THIS REPORT) TO BE $ 167,900

APPRAISER:	SUPERVISORY APPRAISER (ONLY IF REQUIRED):	
Signature	Signature	☒ Did ☐ Did Not
Name Jerry McGuire	Name	Inspect Property
Date Report Signed September 15, 2003	Date Report Signed	
State Certification # St.Cert.REA RD 013019 State FL	State Certification # State	
Or State License # State	Or State License # State	

Freddie Mac Form 70 6/93   PAGE 2 OF 2   Fannie Mae Form 1004 6-93

Form UA2 — "TOTAL for Windows" appraisal software by a la mode, inc. — 1-800-ALAMODE

Industry Issues

Sources: Excerpted from "Computerized Appraisals Catch On Despite Flaws," *Real Estate Journal* (The Wall Street Journal Online): http://homes.wsj.com; and "Online Automated Valuation Models," Appraisal Network: www.appraisal-network.com/avm.htm

8-2 Computerized Appraisals Catch on Despite Flaws

The traditional home appraisal—long disparaged by lenders and homebuyers as taking too much time and costing too much money—could be going the way of the one-car garage. Instead of the usual visit from an appraiser who examines every nook and cranny, some lenders are turning to automated valuation models (AVMs) that use statistical models to compute appraisal values in a matter of seconds. The systems work by mining databases that contain sales prices of homes in a given neighborhood, and comparing those properties with the one that is being appraised. The information is limited to factual data, such as how big the house is, the number of rooms and bedrooms, age of the house, and the size of the lot. Some databases are collecting information from appraisal reports, where a property's physical characteristics are verified by a real human being.

Details as to the level of updates, remodeling, overall level of appeal are not typically available with raw data. This would require a "qualitative analysis" based on reasoning and most of the models (the way databases do the search) typically don't have the ability to make such judgments. The key to any AVM is to use your judgment, just like an appraiser does with raw data. At least drive by the comparables to see if they are similar or verify the data with one of the market participants (e.g., buyer, seller, broker).

AVMs are generating significant controversy. Many of the nation's 85,000 real estate appraisers worry that automation could put them out of work, and they contend the systems aren't always accurate.

MRA is particularly applicable to residential properties. In general, it can be employed whenever a relatively large numbers of transactions of similar properties and their characteristic data can be found. The equation estimated by the linear multivariate regression takes the following general form:

$$Y = \beta_0 + \beta_1 x_1 + \beta_2 x_2 + \beta_3 x_3 + \ldots + \beta_n x_n + e$$

where Y denotes the **dependent variable** to be "explained" (typically price in an appraisal context); each x denotes an independent "explanatory" variable, such as square footage of the improvements, age, and lot size. The βs, the estimated model coefficients, are estimated by the regression method. The model's error term, ε, captures the variance in prices that is unexplained by the **independent variables.**

Example 8-3   2380 Appletree Court

The appraiser has identified sufficient data to estimate the market value of the 2380 Appletree Court example using regression analysis. The accuracy of the data was verified and 30 sales observations from Parkway Estates and a few other competing neighborhoods were entered into an EXCEL spreadsheet. The sales data are listed in rows 6 to 35 in Exhibit 8-12.

For each "comparable" property sale the appraiser listed the sale price (the dependent variable in column B of the spreadsheet), and the independent "explanatory" variables (in columns G through J). The property's size, age, number of baths, construction quality, patio/deck square footage, lot size, sale date (months from today), are entered as independent variables. In addition, a categorical variable is set equal to 1 if the property had a pool, otherwise it is set to zero.

The multivariable regression procedure was run by first selecting the "tools" button on the standard EXCEL menu, then choosing "data analysis," and then "regression." The regression procedure requires the analyst to specify (block) the Y column observations and the X column observations, and then select a location on the spreadsheet for the results. The regression results are shown in Exhibit 8-12, to the right of the data (columns L to P).

Exhibit 8-12 2380 Appletree Court: Estimation of Value Using Multivariate Regression Analysis

REGRESSION DATA

Independent variable (Y) = Sale price; Dependent variables: X1 to X8, as noted

Obs. No.	Sale Price ($)	Size (sq.ft.)	Age (years)	Baths (number)	Quality (rating)	Deck (sq.ft.)	Lot Size (acres)	Sale Date (mos.)	Pool (y=1; n=0)
	Y	X1	X2	X3	X4	X5	X6	X7	X8
1	160000	1890	10	2	1	100	0.50	5	0
2	169900	2060	6	2.5	0	0	0.52	0	0
3	171000	2135	3	2.5	1	0	0.48	0	0
4	171000	2102	15	1.5	1	200	0.51	6	1
5	190300	2077	2	2.5	0	100	0.50	20	0
6	167260	2186	11	2	2	200	0.44	1	0
7	157800	1935	9	3	1	200	0.40	13	0
8	171550	1970	12	2	1	100	0.55	18	0
9	177900	1912	2	2.5	1	100	0.54	17	0
10	157100	1818	15	3	2	200	0.48	4	1
11	184750	2110	2	1.5	1	200	0.45	19	0
12	159750	1966	15	3	0	100	0.47	17	0
13	168000	1963	12	3.5	2	0	0.58	10	0
14	173750	1969	8	1.5	0	0	0.50	16	0
15	178300	2104	3	3	1	100	0.42	13	0
16	187300	2006	8	2.5	2	0	0.52	13	1
17	175000	1898	6	3.5	1	200	0.44	12	0
18	178800	2128	2	2	0	100	0.45	13	0
19	185000	1941	11	3.5	1	200	0.57	14	0
20	177300	1933	6	3.5	0	0	0.55	18	0
21	164700	1829	14	3.5	0	0	0.52	12	0
22	167200	2077	15	2.5	2	0	0.46	5	1
23	188000	1978	2	2.5	2	100	0.59	20	0
24	180800	2014	11	3.5	2	0	0.56	4	0
25	175000	1802	2	3	2	200	0.46	17	0
26	157275	1998	12	2	0	100	0.46	16	0
27	165400	2022	8	2.5	2	0	0.42	17	0
28	175800	1892	2	2	2	100	0.48	16	0
29	171500	1966	3	2.5	0	0	0.46	22	0
30	169400	2057	0	2.5	1	200	0.37	3	0
Mean	172561	1991	8	3	1	93	0.49	12	0.13
Subject Property		1960	3	2.5	0	0	0.50	0	0

Indicated Value of the Subject Using Regression Analysis: **167820**

SUMMARY OUTPUT

Regression Statistics

Multiple R	0.914
R Square	0.835
Adjusted R Sq	0.772
Standard Erro	4450.251
Observations	30

ANOVA

	df	SS	MS	F
Regression	8	2099486635	2.62E+08	13.2512
Residual	21	415899349.1	19804731	
Total	29	2515385984		

	Coefficients	Standard Error	t Stat	P-value
Intercept	14855.22	26882.33	0.55	0.586
X Variable 1	48.00	10.54	4.56	0.000
X Variable 2	-1259.36	212.19	-5.93	0.000
X Variable 3	3959.06	1613.90	2.45	0.023
X Variable 4	1530.00	1204.56	1.27	0.218
X Variable 5	15.74	11.15	1.41	0.173
X Variable 6	105513.91	17302.57	6.10	0.000
X Variable 7	516.08	151.95	3.40	0.003
X Variable 8	7127.56	3114.39	2.29	0.033

Indicated Value of Components from Regression (rounded)

Structure =	$ 48 per sq.ft.
Age of Bldg =	$ -1,260 decrease per year, or 0.8% per year
Baths =	$ 4,000 per bath
Quality =	$ 1,500 per construction rating
Deck =	$ 16 per sq. ft. for deck area
Lot =	$ 100,000 per acre
Sale Date =	$ 500 per mo., or 0.3% per month
Pool =	$ 7,000 per pool

Interpreting the Regression Results

The **R-square statistic (R^2)** measures how well the regression model fits the data. It compares the observed sale price of each property with the estimated sale price computed by the regression model, showing that the model in this case can explain 83.5 percent (0.835) of the variations in the observed sale prices (see "Regression Statistics"). The **standard error (SE)** statistic measures the likely amount of error in an estimate using the model. Thus, for an estimate of market value of $172,561 (the average price in this market), the standard error is expected to be $4,450, or about 2.6 percent ($4,450 ÷ $172,561). The standard error will be used later to establish a confidence interval around the value estimate.

Estimation of the **coefficients, β,** represents a primary advantage of regression analysis. The estimated β coefficients represent the marginal or incremental contribution of each respective characteristic variable to the predicted value (market value), or the "implicit" price of the component. For example, the value of each additional square foot (variable 1) is estimated to be $48 (rounded). In addition, each additional year of age (variable 2) decreases the value of the mean residence by approximately $1,260 (rounded). The indicated value of each housing characteristic is listed in the lower-right-hand corner of Exhibit 8-12. Finally, the **intercept (β_o)** estimate of $14,855 is the base value estimate, assuming the value of all the explanatory variables are set equal to zero.

Concept Check

8.10 What does the *R*-square statistic measure?

Regression analysis is a variant of the sales comparison approach. With both approaches, appraisers look to the market for evidence on market pricing. In the sales comparison approach, the adjustments are estimated—somewhat qualitatively—from comparable sales. With regression analysis, the appraiser is able to quantify the value of any feature, controlling for the nature of other features. In Exhibit 8-12, we see that a pool (variable X8) adds, on average, $7,127 to the value of homes in the regression sample. Similarly, $48 is the estimated market price for each square foot of living space (variable X1) in the sample. Total market value is the sum of the value of all the property's physical and location characteristics.

To estimate the market value of the subject property, we list the estimated coefficients of the regression equation.

$$V_o = 14,855 + 48x_1 - 1,259x_2 + 3,959x_3 + 1,530x_4 + 15.74x_5 + 105,514x_6 + 516x_7 + 7128x_8$$

The estimated value of the subject property is calculated by inserting in the appropriate x-values ($x_1 = 1,960$ sq.ft.; $x_2 = 3$ years; $x_3 = 2.5$ baths; $x_4 = 0$; $x_5 = 0$; $x_6 = 0.5$ acres; $x_7 = 0$ and $x_8 = 0$). Thus, the indicated market value using MRA is approximately $167,800. (Recall that the final value estimate using the sales comparison approach was $167,900.)

We can use the standard error (SE) to give us an approximation of the variability of sale prices for similar residences. For example, we can say that approximately 68 percent of the properties having the subject property's features will have sale prices of within $4,450 of $167,820 (one standard error of the mean), and 95 percent within $8,900 (two standard errors of the mean). Thus, a major advantage of using MRA is that it provides a basis for establishing a confidence interval around the predicted value.

Concept Check

8.11 Objectivity is a major advantage of MRA in the estimation of market values. Objectivity, or the lack of qualitative inputs to the valuation process, is also a major disadvantage of MRA. Explain.

Explore The Web

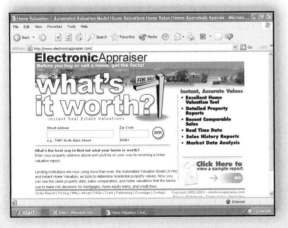

The Emergence of Online Appraisal Tools

Numerous private firms are now offering online automated valuation models (AVMs) and/or comparable sales reports for borrowers, lenders, and other participants in the single-family residential market interested in homes values. The Appraisal Network (www.appraisal-network.com) provides a list of companies that have developed online valuation resources, including AVMs based on multiple regression analysis. One of the authors paid $29.50 to have his home appraised online by the "Electronic Appraiser" (www. electronicappraiser.com). Just prior to this, the author's home had been appraised by a traditional fee appraiser for the purposes of a mortgage refinancing. The online AVM returned a value estimate 7 percent greater than the traditional appraiser's estimate.

Search the Appraisal Network website for an AVM model available for use free of charge. Use this website to obtain an estimate of market value for a relative's (or your) home. If you are unable to find a free AVM service, and you are not willing to pay the required $30–$50 fee charged by most companies, go to Yahoo real estate— http://list.realestate.yahoo.com/re/homevalues. Once there, type in a street address and zip code for a property. Although this site will not provide a regression-based estimate of market value, it will provide comparable sales information on up to 20 comparable properties to help you analyze in seconds the value of your home or other homes. Results include price, square footage, bedrooms, and year built (where available). Type in the information for your parents' home and surprise them with your market knowledge!

Summary

Appraisal is the process of estimating the market value of real estate. The process involves the systematic comparison of the sale prices of a subject property and several comparable properties. Professional appraisers use three general methods, or approaches: sales comparison, cost, and income (the topic of Chapter 9). Multivariate regression analysis can be used directly as a variant of the sales comparison approach or as a component of one of the other approaches (e.g., estimating market rents to be used in the income approach).

Appraising one- to four-family residential properties has been an important activity for many appraisers, and the most applicable method for these appraisals has been the traditional sales comparison approach. However, the appraisal of small residential properties is becoming increasingly computerized, and the traditional sales comparison approach is being augmented, if not replaced, by computer-aided analyses. Nevertheless, the sales comparison approach will continue to be important in the appraisal of residential properties. Appraisers adjust the sale price of each comparable property to reflect differences between it and the subject property for each element. They follow a sequence of adjustments calculated either as percentages or dollar amounts.

In the cost approach, the appraiser subtracts the building's accrued depreciation from its current reproduction cost. Three types of accrued depreciation may exist: physical deterioration, functional obsolescence, and external obsolescence. Reproduction cost of the building less accrued depreciation equals the building's indicated value. The estimated site value (plus the current value of site improvements) is then added to obtain the indicated property value by the cost approach.

Key Terms

Adjustments 197
Accrued depreciation 204
Appraisal 189
Appraisal report 189
Arm's-length transaction 196
Coefficients 210
Comparable properties 195
Dependent variable 209
Elements of comparison 200
External obsolescence 205
Final adjusted sale price 195
Functional obsolescence 205
Highest and best use 193

Independent variables 209
Indicated value 195
Intercept 210
Investment value 191
Market conditions 198
Market-adjusted normal sale price 198
Market value 190
Multivariate regression analysis (MRA) 206
Nonrealty items 200
Normal sale price 198
Paired sales analysis 199
Physical deterioration 204

Property adjustments 197
R square statistic (R^2) 210
Reconciliation 194
Repeat-sale analysis 198
Replacement cost 204
Reproduction cost 204
Standard error (SE) 210
Subject property 189
Transactional adjustments 197
Transaction price 191
Uniform Standards of Professional Appraisal Practice (USPAP) 191

Test Problems

Answer the following multiple choice problems:

1. The final price for each comparable property reached after all adjustments have been made is termed the:
   a. Final estimate of value.
   b. Final adjusted sale price.
   c. Market value.
   d. Indicated value.
   e. Replacement value.

2. The final price from each appraisal approach is termed the:
   a. Final estimate of value.
   b. Final adjusted sale price.
   c. Market value.
   d. Indicated value.
   e. Replacement value.

3. The final price after reconciliation of the answers obtained from two or more approaches is termed the:
   a. Final estimate of value.
   b. Final adjusted sale price.
   c. Market value.
   d. Indicated value.
   e. Replacement value.

4. A new house in good condition that has a poor floor plan would suffer from which type of accrued depreciation?
   a. Curable physical deterioration.
   b. Incurable physical deterioration.
   c. Curable functional obsolescence.
   d. Incurable functional obsolescence.
   e. External obsolescence.

5. To reflect a change in market conditions between the date on which a comparable property sold and the date of appraisal of a subject property, which type of adjustment is made?
   a. Conditions of sale.
   b. Market conditions.
   c. Location.
   d. Financing terms.
   e. Unit.

6. The R-square statistic
   a. Measures how well the regression model fits the data.
   b. Represents the incremental contribution of each explanatory variable to the predicted property value.
   c. Is the base value estimate, assuming the explanatory variables are set equal to zero.
   d. Measures how well the regression model fits the data.
   e. Measures the likely amount of error in an estimate using the model.

7. In appraising a single-family home, you find a comparable property very similar to the subject property. One important difference, however, concerns the financing. The comparable property sold one month ago for $120,000 and was financed with an 80 percent, 30-year mortgage at 5.0 percent interest. Current market financing terms are 80 percent, 30-year mortgages at 7 percent interest. The monthly payments on the market financing would be approximately $639, while the monthly payments on the special 5.0 percent financing are approximately $431. Assume the borrower's opportunity cost rate is 7 percent. The approximate present value of the payment savings on the nonmarket financing is _____, and this amount should _____ to the transaction price of the comparable
   a. $38,564, added.
   b. $38,564, subtracted.

   c. $17,613, added.
   d. $17,613, subtracted.

8. You find two properties that have sold twice within the last two years. Property A sold 22 months ago for $98,500; it sold last week for $108,000. Property B sold 20 months ago for $105,000; it sold yesterday for $113,500. What is the average monthly rate of increase in sale prices?
   a. 0.42%.
   b. 4.20%.
   c. 0.84%.
   d. 8.87%.

9. A comparable property sold 10 months ago for $100,000. This sale price is adjusted to a normal sale price of $98,500. If the appropriate adjustment for market conditions is 0.30% per month, what would be the market-adjusted normal sale price of the comparable property?
   a. $98,795.
   b. $101,455.
   c. $103,600.
   d. $103,000.

10. A comparable property sold six months ago for $150,000. The adjustments for the various elements of comparison have been calculated as follows:
    Location: −5 percent.
    Market conditions: +8 percent.
    Physical characteristics: +$12,500.
    Financing terms: −$2,600.
    Conditions of sale: None.
    Legal characteristics: None.
    Use: None.
    Nonrealty items: −$3,000.
    What is the comparable property's final adjusted sale price?
    a. $160,732.
    b. $164,400.
    c. $169,600.
    d. $162,500.
    e. $163,232.

Study Questions

1. What is the theoretical basis for the direct sales comparison approach to market valuation?

2. What main difficulty would you foresee in attempting to estimate the value of a 30-year-old property by means of the cost approach?

3. The cost approach to market valuation does not work well in markets that are overbuilt. Explain why.

4. What is meant by functional obsolescence? Could a new building suffer from functional obsolescence?

5. Why is an estimate of the developer's fair market profit included in the cost estimate?

6. Reproduction cost has been estimated as $350,000 for a property with a 70-year economic life. The current effective age of the property is 15 years. The value of the land is estimated to be $55,000. What is the estimated market value of the property using the cost approach, assuming no external or functional obsolescence?

7. What is an appraisal report?

8. You have performed a multiple regression analysis in order to estimate the value of a single-family home. You have collected data on 43 properties for five independent variables and their prices. A summary of the regression output follows.

Multiple Regression Output Summary

Variable Number	Variable Name	beta Coefficient	Standard Error
X_1	Square feet livable area/100	0.664	0.16
X_2	Effective age (years)	21.68	0.64
X_3	Quality of location (rank)	4.38	0.94
X_4	Quality of construction (rank)	3.68	1.62
X_5	Lot size (square feet/100)	2.84	2.04

Dependent variable	Price/$1,000
Intercept	9.16
R^2	0.890
Standard error	8.74

a. Which variable appears to have the least explanatory power? Why?

b. Explain the meaning of the intercept, R^2, and standard error.

c. Calculate the estimated value of the property under appraisal. It contains 2,000 square feet of livable area, has an effective age of 10 years, has a location ranking of 4, a quality-of-construction ranking of 3, and a lot size of 12,500 square feet.

d. What would be the 95 percent confidence interval?

Explore The Web

Find out who hires appraisers, what types of career opportunities are available to appraisers, and capabilities and skills that appraisers should have. Also determine which universities have specialized graduate programs emphasizing appraisal. On the World Wide Web go to http://www.appraisalinstitute.org. Select "Careers" to pursue the answers to these questions.

Also, in the Yellow Pages of your telephone book look under "Real Estate Appraisers" to find the names of two appraisers in your area who hold MAI or SRA designations. Then from the home page of the "Appraisal Institute" select "Find an Appraiser." Enter the information about each appraiser's name and address to obtain more information about the person's background and specialties.

Solutions to Concept Checks

1. A few examples of real estate decisions that require an appraisal are owners who are contemplating renovations and improvements, a judge attempting to determine the appropriate division of assets in a divorce, lenders contemplating a mortgage loan on a property, government officials estimating the costs of acquiring the right-of way to construct roadways, or local tax officials determining the appropriate tax on a property.

2. An investor may value a property more than market value because individual investors have different expectations regarding the future desirability of a property, different capabilities for obtaining financing, different tax situations, and different return requirements. The price paid for the home should be closer to $180,000. Although an investor may be willing to pay $200,000, this house and, presumably other close substitutes, are available at $180,000. Although willing, investors should not pay more than market value.

3. The highest and best use of the property as though vacant is the four-unit rental housing structure, which is valued at $600,000 compared with $450,000 for the single-family home. However, the highest and best use of the property as improved is the single-family home. After subtracting the demolition costs, the four-unit rental structure's value is only $300,000, which is less than the single-family home value of $450,000.

4. Under these circumstances, an appraiser would typically exclude the sale because the sale was not at arm's length. More than likely, the daughter paid a price below market value. If included, an upward adjustment of the comparable sale price would be required.

5. The comparable sale price should be adjusted downward by three percent to find the value of the subject property.

6. Although a similar property in the neighborhood sold recently, it is very difficult to measure the value of the condition that the property is never to be sold again. Therefore, this property should be dropped as a comparable. If retained, an upward adjustment should be made to the comparable sale price.

7. To find the normal sale price, one must adjust for the conditions of sale and financing terms. Then, market conditions are adjusted to find the market adjusted normal sale price. Last, the final adjusted sale price is found by adjusting for location, physical characteristics, legal characteristics, use, and nonrealty items.

8. The reproduction cost of a building is the cost to construct the building today, replicating it in exact detail. The replacement cost is the money required to construct a building of equal utility. The reproduction cost is generally greater than the replacement cost.

9. Estimating accrued depreciation is generally the most difficult step in the cost approach because it is very difficult to quantify the dollar value of physical depreciation and often even more difficult to quantify the dollar value of functional and external obsolescence.

10. The R-square statistic measures how well the model fits the data. In particular, it measures the percentage of the variation in the dependent variable (house price in this context) that is explained by the independent variables (e.g., age, square footage of house, number of baths).

11. An advantage of using multivariate regression analysis is that the data tell the researcher what the dollar value of individual adjustments should be—subjectivity is removed. However, it is very difficult to measure, or even observe, all the factors that may affect house prices. Thus, all regression models are misspecified to some degree and appraisers are not able to use their vast knowledge base to make subjective adjustments.

Additional Readings

The following books contain expanded examples and discussions of real estate valuation and appraisal:

Appraisal Institute. *The Appraisal of Real Estate,* 13th ed. Chicago, American Institute of Real Estate Appraisers, 2001.

Betts, R. M., and S. J. Ely. *Basic Real Estate Appraisal,* 5th ed. Mason, OH: South-Western, 2000.

Betts, R. M., and D. J. McKenzie. *Essentials of Real Estate Economics,* 4th ed. Mason, OH: South-Western, 2001.

Lusht, Kenneth L. *Real Estate Valuation: Principles and Applications.* New York: McGraw-Hill, 1997.

Rayburn, W. B., and D. S. Tosh. *Uniform Standards of Professional Appraisal Practice,* 10th ed. Chicago: Dearborn Trade, 2003.

Smith, H. C., L. C. Root, and J. D. Belloit. *Real Estate Apraisal,* 3rd ed. Upper Saddle River, NJ: Prentice Hall, 1995.

Williams, M. R., W. L. Ventola, and W. L. Ventola, Jr. *How to Use the Uniform Residential Appraisal Report,* 2nd ed. Chicago: Dearborn Trade, 1993.

The following journals contain numerous articles on real estate valuation and appraisal:

The Appraisal Journal, published quarterly by the Appraisal Institute, Chicago.
Real Estate Review, published quarterly by Warren, Gorham and Lamont, Boston.
Real Estate Issues, published three times annually by the American Society of Real Estate Counselors, Chicago.

The following special issue of the *Journal of Real Estate Research* is devoted to articles reporting on research in real estate appraisal:

Grissom, Terry V., and Halbert C. Smith, eds. *Journal of Real Estate Research* 5, no. 1 (Spring 1991).

The following article discusses the application of linear regression analysis to economic variables in the sales comparison and income capitalization approaches:

Kincheloe, Stephen C. "Linear Regression Analysis of Economic Variables in the Sales Comparison and Income Approaches." *Appraisal Journal* 61, no. 4 (October 1993), pp. 576–85.

www.mhhe.com/lingarcher1e

chapter nine

Valuation Using the Income Approach

Learning Objectives

After reading this chapter you will be able to:

1. Explain the difference between direct capitalization and discounted cash flow (DCF) models of property valuation.

2. Distinguish between operating expenses and capital expenditures.

3. Explain the general relationship between discount rates and capitalization rates.

4. Calculate the overall capitalization rate by direct market extraction, mortgage-equity rate analysis, and the constant growth formula given appropriate data.

5. Describe a gross income multiplier (*GIM*) approach to valuation and demonstrate its use, given appropriate data.

6. Explain the difference between levered and unlevered cash flows.

7. Develop a 10-year net cash flow forecast (pro forma), including the expected cash flows from sale, given appropriate data.

8. Estimate an indicated market value by DCF analysis using the overall discount rate, or using the discount rate on equity and the mortgage terms.

Introduction

In Chapter 8 we introduced the formal appraisal process, including the three conventional approaches to estimating the market value of real estate assets: the sales comparison approach, the cost approach, and the income approach. The chapter then focused on two approaches—the sales comparison and cost approaches—that provide a method for estimating a property's market value without directly considering the property's income-producing potential.

In this chapter we turn our attention to the income approach to valuation. The rationale for the income approach is straightforward: Common among commercial property owners is the anticipation that they will receive cash flows from the property in the form of income from rental operations and price appreciation. The value of a property is therefore a function of the income stream it is expected to produce. Although the sales comparison and cost approaches to valuation discussed in Chapter 8 can be, and are, used to estimate the value of commercial property, they are most applicable to the valuation of non-income-producing property.

In the income approach, appraisers first estimate the periodic income the property is expected to generate and then convert the income forecast into a value estimate. The process of converting periodic income into a value estimate is referred to as **income capitalization.**

Because the income approach is based on the premise that a property's market value is a function of the income it is expected to produce, the first step is to estimate "income." The measure of income generally sought is annual **net operating income (*NOI*)**, which is equal to expected annual rental income, net of vacancies, minus operating and capital expenses. In most cases, however, the property owner or investor does not pocket the full amount of *NOI*. Why? Because if the owner has made use of borrowed funds to help finance the investment, a portion of the *NOI* will be payable, usually on a monthly basis, to the mortgage lender(s). In addition, the U.S. government (and most states) will collect a portion of the property's annual *NOI* in the form of income taxes. Nevertheless, because *NOI* measures the overall income-producing ability of a property, it is considered the fundamental determinate of market value.

9.1   If a commercial property is performing well, what other parties, in addition to the owner(s), also benefit from this performance?

The second step in the income approach is to convert (i.e., capitalize) the *NOI* forecast into an estimate of property value. There are many models or techniques available to the appraiser for income capitalization. However, these models can be divided into two categories: (1) direct capitalization models and (2) discounted cash flow models.

Direct Capitalization versus Discounted Cash Flow

With direct capitalization models, value estimates are based on a ratio or multiple of expected first year *NOI*. It is essential that the ratios used to value the subject property are based on data from sales of comparable properties. Direct capitalization is analogous to the use of price-earning (PE) ratios to value common stocks. For example, if publicly traded apartment REITs (real estate investment trusts) are, on average, currently trading at 11 times expected earning over the next 12 months, this PE ratio can be multiplied by the expected earnings of the subject REIT to approximate market value. For example, if Camden Property Trust, an apartment REIT, is expected to produce earnings of $2.80 per share during the next 12 months, then a defensible estimate of Camden's stock market value is $30.80 ($2.80 × 11) per share. Similarly, if properties similar to the subject property are, on average, currently selling for 12 times first-year *NOI,* then a reasonable estimate of the subject's market value is obtained by multiplying the subject's expected first-year *NOI* times 12.

Discounted cash flow (DCF) valuation models differ from direct capitalization models in several important ways. First, the appraiser must select the investment holding period that is typical of investors who might purchase the subject property. Second, the appraiser must make explicit forecasts of the property's net income for each year of the expected holding period, not just a single year. This forecast must include the net income produced by a sale of the property at the end of the expected holding period. Third, the appraiser must select the appropriate yield, or required internal rate of return, at which to discount all future cash flows. The requirements of DCF analysis place a much greater analytical burden on the appraiser because forecasts of future cash flows cannot be explicitly abstracted from past sales of comparable properties. Critics of DCF models argue that future cash flow projections not supported by market evidence can result in flawed value estimates.

While residential appraisers focus on single-family homes and small residential rental properties, commercial property appraisers deal primarily with more complex apartment properties, shopping centers, office buildings, industrial properties, hotel/motel properties, subdivisions, vacant land, and special-purpose properties such as restaurants, car washes, branch banks, and so forth. Most commercial real estate appraisers work for a variety of clients on a fee basis; that is, the

Commercial Real Estate Appraisers

appraiser and client negotiate a fee that is paid upon the completion of the appraisal. Because the fee is generally fixed, the appraiser must do an accurate job of estimating the costs his or her firm will incur in the process of producing the appraisal. Often, clients solicit bids from multiple appraisers. This competition generally prevents appraisers from "padding" their fees. Some firms involved in mortgage lending and property acquisitions hire internal staff appraisers to produce value opinions or to examine the work performed by external fee appraisers.

For more information about commercial appraisal and consulting, see the websites of the Appraisal Institute (www.appraisalinstitute.org) and the Counselors of Real Estate (CRE) (www.cre.org).

Sources: Information on Career Paths in Commercial Real Estate, University of Cincinnati, www.cba.uc.edu/getreal and Career Opportunities, Washington State University, www.cbe.wsu.edu/~fire/real_estate

www.appraisalinstitute.
org/publications/
periodicals/ano/
default.asp

Appraisal Institute's free online news service provides coverage of industry trends and regulatory developments.

Concept Check

9.2 List three important ways in which DCF valuation models differ from direct capitalization models.

The chapter proceeds as follows. First, we discuss how the appraiser estimates the expected annualized net operating income of the subject property—either for a single year or for each year of an expected holding period. We then discuss, in turn, direct capitalization models and discounted cash flow models of market value.

Estimating Net Operating Income

Net operating income (*NOI*) is calculated by deducting from the property's rental income all expenses associated with operating and maintaining the property. As discussed above, *NOI* focuses on the income produced by the property after operating expenses, but before mortgage payments and the payment of income taxes. These latter expenses are personal and unique to each owner and not directly related to the property's basic income-producing ability, although, as we shall see in Chapters 16 and 22, mortgage financing and income taxes are important considerations in the investment decision.

In estimating the expected *NOI* of an existing property, appraisers and analysts rely on (1) the experience of similar properties in the market and (2) the historic experience of the subject property. The current owners may not be renting the subject property at the going market rate, and its current expenses may differ from market averages. Thus, an appraiser must evaluate all income and expense items in terms of current market conditions. These items are then placed in a **reconstructed operating statement** format (see Exhibit 9-1), which shows the appraiser's estimate of stabilized income and expenses. By "stabilized" we mean under current economic conditions, but adjusted to show current market rents, average vacancy and collection losses, and normal operating and capital expenses for this type of property in this location and market. The reconstructed operating statement excludes some types of expenses (e.g., tax depreciation and mortgage payments) that usually are included in the accounting statements furnished to the appraiser by the current owner.

Furthermore, appraisers generally estimate income and expenses for the *next* calendar year, rather than using figures from a previous calendar or tax year. Information obtained for comparable properties also must be reformulated to be consistent with the reconstructed operating statement of the subject property.

Concept Check

9.3   What is "stabilized" net income?

To show how the analyst estimates the cash flows from owning an existing commercial property, suppose the appraiser's assignment is to determine the market value of a small suburban office building, called Centre Point. The basic assumptions for Centre Point are listed in Exhibit 9-2.[1] Unfamiliar terms are discussed below.

Exhibit 9-1   Reconstructed Operating Statement

	PGI	Potential gross income
−	VC	Vacancy & collection loss
+	MI	Miscellaneous income
=	EGI	Effective gross income
−	OE	Operating expenses
−	CAPX	Capital expenditures*
=	NOI	Net operating income

*Traditionally, appraisers have included in their estimates of *NOI* a "reserve for replacement" of capital items. However, in the real estate investment community, expected capital expenditures are increasingly being referred to in cash flow forecasts as "capital expenditures" or "capital costs." To be consistent with the current treatment in the investment community, and to avoid changing terminology as we progress through the text, we will refer to these anticipated expenses as capital expenditures or "CAPX."

Exhibit 9-2   Property Assumptions for Centre Point Office Building

- Property consists of 9 office suites, 4 on the first floor and 5 on the second.
- Contract rents: 6 suites at $1,800 per month and 3 at $1,400 per month.
- Annual market rent increases: 3% per year
- Vacancy and collection losses: 10% per year
- Operating expenses: 40% of effective gross income each year
- Capital expenditures: 5% of effective gross income each year
- Expected holding period: 5 years

1. The remainder of this chapter focuses on the analysis of existing commercial properties. Existing properties provide analysts with historical information on rents and operating expenses to evaluate. Market rents and expenses are established by evaluating the rents and operating expenses of the subject property with that of comparable properties. The valuation of proposed properties (i.e., new development) is the focus of Chapter 24.

Potential Gross Income

The starting point in calculating NOI is to estimate **potential gross income (*PGI*)**. *PGI* is the total annual rental income the property would produce assuming 100 percent occupancy and no collection losses (in other words, assuming tenants always pay their full rent on time). Although rents are generally received from tenants on a monthly basis and operating expenses are incurred during each month, as a matter of practice most appraisers and investment analysts estimate property cash flows on an annual basis.[2] *PGI* is the estimated rent per unit (or per square foot) for each year multiplied by the number of units (or square feet) available for rent. Appraisers estimate *PGI* by examining the terms of any existing leases and the present tenant(s), if any. From this examination they decide whether to estimate *PGI* based on contract rents or market rents. **Market rent** is the rental income the property would most probably command if placed for lease on the open market as of the effective date of the appraisal. **Contract rent** refers to the actual rent being paid under contractual commitments between owners and tenants. Generally, *PGI* is based on market rent. However, if the property is subject to long-term leases to financially reliable tenants at rates above or below market, the estimation of *PGI* will include the contract rent of these leases.

Concept Check

9.4   Distinguish between contract rent and market rent.

Example 9-1   Centre Point

The Centre Point Office Building has four 1,000-square-foot, first-floor suites with long-term leases, each renting for $1,800 per month, or $1.80 per square foot. The second floor contains five 800-square-foot suites, two of which rent for $1,800 per month ($2.25 per square foot) and three renting for $1,400 ($1.75 per square foot), all under short-term leases. Therefore, potential gross income in the first year of operations—assuming the property is purchased on the effective date of the appraisal—is estimated to be $180,000. This *PGI* is calculated as follows:

First Floor		
1,000 sq.ft. suites: 4 × $1,800 × 12 months	$86,400	
Second Floor		
800 sq.ft. suites: 2 × $1,800 × 12 months	43,200	
800 sq.ft. suites: 3 × $1,400 × 12 months	50,400	93,600
Potential gross income (*PGI*) =		$180,000

The average per square foot per month rental rate of the five second-floor units is $1.95.

The analyst should gather rental data on similar properties in the same market to judge whether the contract rents are equal to market rents. For example, to determine market rental rates for the second-floor units of Centre Point, the analyst should obtain data on second-floor units in similar buildings. When possible, this market rent survey should be limited to properties of the same general age, design, services, and amenities as the subject property. Thus, if the comparable rents obtained from the survey are as shown in Exhibit 9-3, market rents of the 800 square-foot, second-floor units are estimated as:

$$\$1.94 \times 800 \text{ sq. ft.} \times 5 \text{ units} = \$ 7,760 \text{ per month, and}$$
$$\$7,760 \times 12 \text{ mos.} = \$93,120 \text{ per year}$$

2. To the degree that appraisers replicate the decision making practice of investment analysts, this method produces valid estimates of market value.

Exhibit 9-3 Market Rents for Comparable Second-Floor Units

	Comparable			
	1	2	3	Average
Rent per month	$1,620	$1,540	$1,680	
Sq. ft. per unit	790	810	900	833
Rent per sq. ft. per month	$ 2.05	$ 1.90	$ 1.87	$1.94

www.reis.com

REIS, a for-profit firm, provides rent comparable information for 80 metro areas.

In this case, data from the comparable properties imply that the indicated market rent of $93,120 for the second-floor units is very similar to the current contract rents of $93,600. This suggests that the current contract rents are consistent with market rents and that normal increases should be expected in the future.

It should be noted that office, retail, and industrial tenants most commonly occupy their space under leases ranging from three to five years. However, tenants of more specialized properties such as restaurants, department stores, and freestanding drugstores often sign leases of 10 years or more. An additional complication is that appraisers encounter numerous lease types. The straight lease is one in which the monthly rent remains fixed over the entire lease term. The step-up (or "graduated") lease establishes a schedule of rental rate increases over the term of the lease. In other leases, rental rate increases are not prespecified, but instead are tied (i.e., indexed) to the general rate of inflation. Finally, in some retail leases the total rent collected is a function of tenant sales. Clearly, the existing lease structure of the subject and comparable properties can significantly complicate the appraisal. An extended discussion of commercial leases and leasing strategies is provided in Chapter 21.

www.cpnrenet.com

Commercial Property News Online, an excellent source of news and data on commercial real estate.

Effective Gross Income

It is nearly impossible to realize a property's full potential income. Even if there is no excess supply of space for lease, there will always be a few premature vacancies, some rental income will be lost when tenants vacate space which then must be refurbished and released, and not all rent will be paid in a timely fashion. Furthermore, owners often choose to hold a small inventory of space off the market to have available to show prospective tenants. The **natural vacancy rate** is the proportion of potential gross income not collected—even when the use (rental) market is in equilibrium.[3] Of course, if there is an excess supply of leasable space, the actual amount of vacancy and collection losses will exceed the natural rate. Therefore, the second step in projecting *NOI* is to estimate the expected vacancy and collection (*VC*) losses for the property, consistent with market expectations. Again, appraisers should estimate these losses on the basis of (1) the historical experience of the subject property and (2) the experiences of competing properties. The normal range for vacancy and collection losses for apartment, office, and retail properties is 5 to 15 percent of *PGI*, although vacancies well in excess of 15 percent have occurred in overbuilt markets.[4] The expected vacancy and collection loss is subtracted from *PGI*.

---

3. The natural vacancy rate is sometimes referred to as *frictional vacancy,* implying that normal market frictions will cause a portion of *PGI* not to be collected even in stable markets.

4. It is important to note that vacancy and collection loss rates reflect the income lost as a percentage of the *PGI*. This is referred to as the *economic vacancy rate* and, although similar, it may differ from the percentage of space vacant.

In addition to basic rental income, there may be miscellaneous revenue from sources such as garage rentals, parking fees, laundry machines, and vending machines. The miscellaneous income would be added to the potential gross income. The net effect of subtracting the vacancy allowance and adding miscellaneous income is **effective gross income (EGI)**.[5]

Example 9-2   Centre Point

Assuming contract rents, vacancy and collection losses of 10 percent, and no miscellaneous income, the projected *EGI* for the Centre Point Office Building is:

	Potential gross income (*PGI*)	$180,000	
−	Vacancy & collection loss (*VC*)	18,000	(0.10 × 180,000)
=	Effective gross income (*EGI*)	$162,000	

Operating Expenses

The typical expenses owners incur in maintaining and operating rental properties are termed **operating expenses (OE)**. Operating expenses include the ordinary and necessary expenditures incurred during the year (including incidental repairs) that do not materially add value, but keep the property operating and competitive in its market. They are generally divided into two categories: fixed and variable expenses. Fixed expenses do not vary directly with the level of operation (i.e., occupancy) of the property. The most common fixed expenses are property taxes and hazard and fire insurance; owners must pay them whether the property is vacant or fully occupied. Variable expenses, as the name implies, change with the level of operation of the property; they increase as the level of occupancy rises and decrease when occupancy is reduced. Variable expenses include items such as utilities, garbage and trash removal, maintenance, repairs, supplies, and management.

Capital Expenditures

Appraisal analysts commonly include in the reconstructed operating statement an annual "allowance" to recognize the capital expenditures typically required to replace building components as they age and deteriorate. In contrast to operating expenses, **capital expenditures (CAPX)** are replacements and alterations to a building (or improvement) that materially prolong its life and increase its value—they represent additions to the investment. Other publications may refer to this item as a reserve for replacement, replacement allowance, capital and leasing costs, or another similar term. Examples of such expenditures may include roof replacements, additions, floor coverings, kitchen equipment, heating and air-conditioning equipment, electrical and plumbing fixtures, and parking surfaces. In addition, the costs owners incur to make the space suitable for the needs of a particular tenant (i.e., "tenant improvements") are generally included as part of *CAPX,* or as an additional line item.[6]

---

5. Many commercial leases require tenants to reimburse the owner for some, or all, of a property's operating expenses. For example, "expense stops" place an upper limit on the amount of operating expenses that owners must pay. Operating expenses in excess of the "stop" amount are paid by the tenant. Shopping center leases typically require tenants to reimburse the owner for their fair share of all common area maintenance, property taxes, insurance, and other operating expenses—not just those in excess of a stop amount. All of these payments from the tenant are typically displayed as "expense reimbursement revenue" and are added in, along with miscellaneous income, in the calculation of effective gross income. For simplicity, we ignore expense reimbursement income in our cash flow estimates. These issues are further discussed in Chapters 16 and 21.

6. Leasing commissions paid by property owners to brokers who are responsible for finding tenants are not technically capital expenditure, and should be reserved for separately when appropriate.

9.5 How is an operating expense distinguishable from a capital expenditure?

In practice, *CAPX* is often estimated as the expected cost to replace each item, or all items, prorated as a constant annual "expenditure" over the item's expected life. For example, if the cost of replacing a roof is expected to be $47,000 in 15 years (its expected life), the required annual set-aside—often called a reserve—is $1,731, assuming a discount rate of 8.0 percent.[7] In other words, if an owner puts $1,731 into an account or investment that each year yields 8.0 percent, he or she would have a $47,000 reserve balance for roof replacement at the end of 15 years. For simplicity, the *CAPX* shown in Exhibit 9-4 for the Centre Point example is assumed to total 5 percent of the *EGI*.

The recognition of capital expenditures in the estimation of annual net income varies in practice. Most appraisers set aside a reserve for expected capital expenditures annually, as demonstrated above. Others though, may attempt to estimate the actual capital expenditure in the period it is anticipated to occur. As noted later, the treatment of *CAPX* generally reflects the valuation method applied. The use of direct capitalization requires an annualized estimate (reserve) for capital expenditures—given that cash flows beyond the next year are not explicity modeled. In contrast, multiyear DCF models permit the appraiser to be specific about the expected timing of future capital expenditures. Where the estimated *CAPX* appears on the reconstructed operating statement is not consistent in the commercial real estate industry. Most appraisers subtract *CAPX* in the calculation of *NOI*. This is referred to as an "above-line" treatment where the "line" is *NOI*. Other market participants,

Exhibit 9-4 Centre Point Office Building: Reconstructed Operating Statement

		Stabilized Annual Income
Potential gross income (*PGI*)			$180,000
Less: Vacancy and collection losses (*VC*)			18,000
Effective gross income (*EGI*)			162,000
Less: Operating expenses (*OE*)			
Fixed expenses			
Real estate taxes	$15,900		
Insurance	9,200	$25,100	
Variable expenses			
Utilities	$12,800		
Garbage collection	1,000		
Supplies	3,000		
Repairs	5,200		
Maintenance	10,500		
Management	7,200	$39,700	
Total operating expenses			$ 64,800
Less: Reserves for leasing and capital expenditures			
Roof and other exterior expenditures	$ 2,800		
Tenant improvements	3,200		
Leasing commissions	2,100	8,100	
Total reserves for capital expenditures			8,100
Net operating income (*NOI*)			$ 89,100

7. The calculator kystrokes are $N = 15$, $I = 8\%$, $PV = 0$, $PMT = ?$, and $FV = 47,000$.

more typically investment analysts, may treat *CAPX* as a "below-the-line" expenditure—subtracting it from *NOI* to obtain what may be defined as "net cash flow." To add to the confusion, many capitalization rate surveys (e.g., Real Estate Research Corporation's *Real Estate Report*) average together CAP rates based on below-line treatments with CAP rates based on above-line treatments of CAPX. We will subtract capital expenditures above the line in this chapter. However, it is important for analysts to (1) determine how the *CAPX* is estimated and reported in the property and survey data they review, (2) to consistently apply the *CAPX* to the subject property and all comparable properties, and (3) to value the appropriate measure of income.

Concept Check

9.6   If capital expenditures are subtracted from revenues in the calculation of NOI, is this an above-line or a below-line treatment?

In addition to comparing owner-reported expenses for the subject property to similar properties in the market, comparisons to industry averages are also available. Published expense reports that show typical expense levels are available from the Institute of Real Estate Management (IREM: www.irem.org), the Building Owners and Managers Association (BOMA: www.boma.org), the International Council of Shopping Centers (ICSC: www.icsc.org), and the Urban Land Institute (ULI: www.uli.org).

Net Operating Income

www.appraise.com

Site has appraisal chat room, which can be helpful for answering questions.

Investors obtain the final estimate of *NOI* for the first year of operations by subtracting all operating expenses and capital expenditures from *EGI*. With the assumed operating expenses and capital expenditures for the Centre Point Office Building, Exhibit 9-4 shows the stabilized *NOI* in a reconstructed operating statement. In the example, total operating expenses are estimated at $64,800, (40 percent of *EGI*) and total capital expenditures are $8,100 (5 percent of *EGI*). Thus, estimated net operating income is $89,100.

Using Direct Capitalization for Valuation

Direct capitalization, as typically practiced, is the process of estimating a property's market value by dividing a single-year stabilized *NOI* by a "capitalization" rate. The general relationship between market value and income is expressed in the basic income capitalization equation:

$$V = \frac{NOI_1}{R_o} \tag{9-1}$$

where *V* is value, NOI_1 is the projected stabilized income in the next calendar year, and R_o is the capitalization rate. We begin the discussion of direct capitalization by first explaining how capitalization rates can be obtained from the market and how the basic capitalization equation (9-1) can be applied to produce estimates of market value. We then develop some intuition about what a cap rate is, and is not, and discuss the important linkage between cap rates and required internal rates of return (i.e., the discount rate). We then consider two other approaches for estimating the appropriate cap rate.

Abstracting Cap Rates from the Market

Appraisers often rely on recently completed transactions of similar properties to provide a guide for the appropriate cap rate to be used to value the subject property. Rearranging the basic capitalization formula so that:

$$R_o = \frac{NOI_1}{V_o}, \text{ or as applied } R_o = \frac{NOI_1}{\text{Sale price}} \tag{9-2}$$

This allows R_o to be estimated from comparable property sales if the sale price and first-year *NOIs* for the comparables are known. This method of estimating the appropriate cap rate is called **direct market extraction.**[8] The estimated R_o can then be applied, using equation (9-1), to capitalize the estimated first-year *NOI* of the subject property into an estimate of market value.

For example, in evaluating the Centre Point Office Building, assume the appraiser found five comparable properties that sold recently. Comparability is as important here as in the sales comparison approach discussed in Chapter 8. Location, size, age and condition, and intensity of land use should be similar to the subject property. The selected comparables should then be screened to ensure that only recent open market sales are used. Unusual financing terms must be analyzed. If the appropriate adjustment can be quantified, the comparable may be used; if not, it must be excluded. For each comparable property, the appraiser estimates expected *NOI,* making sure that it is based on current market rents and that all appropriate expenses have been deducted. The *NOI* of each comparable is then divided by the sale price of the property. This calculation provides an indicated capitalization rate (*NOI* ÷ Sale price) for each comparable sale, as displayed in Exhibit 9-5. The average of the five comparable capitalization rates (R_o) is 9.9 percent. Dividing the subject property's expected *NOI* of $89,100 by 9.9 percent [as shown in equation (9-1)] produces an indicated value for the subject property of $900,000 ($89,100 ÷ 0.099 = $900,000).

www.blacksguide.com

Provides comprehensive commercial real estate information in 19 U.S. markets.

Concept Check

9.7 Assume the estimated, stabilized, first-year *NOI* of the subject property is $400,000. Also assume that data from the sale of comparable properties indicates the appropriate cap rate is 9 percent. What is the indicated value of the subject property?

In addition to abstracting cap rates directly from comparable sales transactions, appraisers and other market participants may also look to published survey results for evidence on required going-in cap rates. The Real Estate Research Corporation (RERC) regularly surveys the cap rate expectations of institutional investors. These survey results are published quarterly in the *Real Estate Report* (www.rerc.com). RealtyRates.com (www.realtyrates.com), Grubb & Ellis (www.grubb-ellis.com), Legg-Mason Real Estate Services (www.lmres.com), and numerous other firms provide similar information—generally for the price of a subscription.

Three points are worth emphasizing at this stage. First, the sale prices of the comparable properties are publicly recorded and therefore easily obtainable. The comparable *NOIs* are not publicly available; thus, the appraiser must contact the buyer and/or seller of each

Exhibit 9-5 Direct Market Extraction of the Overall Capitalization Rate, R_o

Comparable	First-year *NOI*		Sale Price		R_o	Price ÷ *NOI*
A	$80,000	÷	$ 825,000	=	0.097	10.3
B	114,000	÷	1,200,000	=	0.095	10.5
C	100,000	÷	971,000	=	0.103	9.71
D	72,000	÷	713,000	=	0.101	9.9
E	90,000	÷	910,000	=	0.099	10.1
			Average	=	0.099	10.1

8. This technique is also referred to as the direct comparison method and the comparable sales method.

Industry Issues

A ppraisers are responsible for much more than number crunching these days. The increasing accessibility of information is revolutionizing the appraisal industry. "When I started in the business 40 years ago, we used to spend most of our time gathering information," says Eugene Stunard, president of Appraisal Research Counselors Ltd. in Chicago. The analysis and presentation of the data was typically crammed into the last few hours of the fee, Stunard says. "Now we're spending more time analyzing and understanding data because it is easier to access information," he says.

The booming information age has resulted in an abundant supply of readily available data. A variety of companies, industry associations, and government entities offer economic research, real estate market reports, and databases full of property information. According to Stunard, the rise of publicly traded property owners, and subsequent financial reporting

Booming Information Age Continues to Revolutionize How Appraisers Operate

requirements, makes it easier to access information that used to be closely held among private investors. "Today, all of these transactions are very transparent," he says.

The rise of the Internet is one of the reasons behind the tremendous thirst for information. Data are becoming more readily available through websites that range from fee-based multiple listing services to government offices that offer easy access to both economic and demographic information. State trade and economic development departments offer a wealth of information on economic indicators such as employment and income growth, as well as real estate trends that affect real estate. "Data are becoming ubiquitous," says an appraiser. "The challenge is not finding quality data, but evaluating the data that are available and interpreting what that data mean."

The greater availability of data today has led to the increased use of statistical analysis and geographic information systems. The appraisal reports themselves are becoming more dynamic. Digital cameras are being used to incorporate photos directly into the reports. Appraisers also are able to download or import graphics such as topographic maps and detailed land use maps.

Source: Adapted from Beth Mattson-Teig, "Property Owners Look for Appraisers to Analyze This," *National Real Estate Investor,* January 1, 2000.

---

comparable property for revenue and expense information. These data must generally be adjusted and supplemented by the appraiser. Second, R_o is a "rate" that is used to convert the first-year NOI (the property's overall cash flow) into an estimate of current market value. Thus, R_o is referred to as the **overall capitalization rate,** or the **going-in cap rate.** Third, R_o is *not* a discount rate that can be applied to future cash flows. It is simply the ratio of the first year's annual income to the overall value of the property. Finally, note that the reciprocal of R_o is $1 \div 0.099$, or 10.10. Thus, another way of looking at the relationship between income and value is to say that office buildings similar to the subject property sell for about 10.10 times their estimated first-year NOIs. Thus, the $900,000 market value estimate may also be obtained by multiplying the expected NOI times the abstracted price/income multiple (i.e., $900,000 = $89,100 \times 10.1$)

The direct capitalization approach to estimating value does not require an appraiser to estimate cash flows beyond a stabilized first year. The investors who purchased the comparable properties had *already done so*—their future cash flow estimates are embedded in the sale price of each comparable property and therefore embedded in the abstracted capitalization rates. In contrast to the discounted cash flow approach to valuation, the market value estimate produced by this short-cut method, which relies on prices paid by similar investors for similar properties, may be *more* reliable for the purpose of estimating a property's market value. Why? Because the short-cut requires fewer *explicit* forecasts and judgments than are necessary if the appraiser is constructing a 5- or 10-year discounted cash flow analysis. In effect, the appraiser relies on decisions already made by other market participants to help "read" the market.

Understanding Capitalization Rates

We have just seen that cap rates can be used to convert a stabilized one-year forecast of *NOI* into an estimate of market value. What else can be said about the cap rates we observe in the market? First, the cap rate is a measure of the relationship between a property's current income stream and its price or value. It is not an overall measure of return (i.e., an internal rate of return) because it ignores future cash flows from operations and expected appreciation (or depreciation) in the market value of the property. In this sense, the cap rate is analogous to the dividend yield on a common stock, defined as the projected annual dividend, divided by the current stock price. All else being the same, investors prefer stocks (and commercial properties) with the highest dividend yield (cap rate).

But all else is usually not the same when comparing the investment desirability of stocks and real estate. Cash flows beyond year 1 and changes in the value of the asset can significantly affect internal (total) rates of return. Consider again the Centre Point Office Building. If the property is purchased by an investor for $900,000, and the estimated first-year *NOI* is $89,100, the investor's capitalization rate (dividend yield) is 9.90 percent. If the property is expected to increase in value to $916,650 by the end of year 1, the going-in internal rate of return (IRR), assuming a one-year holding period and no transaction costs, is 11.75 percent and is calculated as follows:

$$y_o = R_o + g = \frac{\$89,100}{\$900,000} + \frac{\$916,650 - \$900,000}{\$900,000}$$

$$= 0.099 + 0.0185 = 0.1175, \text{ or } 11.75\%$$

where

$$R_o = \frac{NOI_1}{\text{Price}} \quad and$$

$$g = \frac{P_1 - P_0}{\text{Price}}$$

The expected internal rate of return is comprised of two parts: the 9.90 percent overall cap rate, sometimes called the "current" yield, and the 1.85 percent rate of appreciation.

This formulation clearly shows that the investor's internal rate of return is obtained from two sources:

1. The property's dividend (i.e., *NOI*).
2. Appreciation (or depreciation) in the value of the property.

If a larger portion of y_o—the required *IRR*—is expected to be obtained from price appreciation (g), then a smaller portion of y_o must be provided in the form of current yield (i.e., cap rates can be lower). This helps explain why cap rates often vary significantly across property types and across the markets; expected appreciation rates can be very different.

Although the relation between required *IRR*s, capitalization rates, and expected price appreciation can be written as $y_o = R_o + g$, it is important to recognize which way causality runs. In the competitive capital markets in the United States, y_o is a function of internal rates of return available on competing investments of similar risk, including stocks, bonds, and other financial assets. Thus, capitalization rates are a function of available returns on other assets and the expected appreciation of the subject property; that is, $R_o = y_o - g$. Thus, multiperiod discount rates, along with expected growth rates, determine market values and, therefore, cap rates.

The point is that y_o, in conjunction with expected appreciation and current rental income, determines the maximum amount investors are willing to bid for a property, which in turn determines actual transaction prices, and thus R_o. Therefore, cap rates do not determine value; cap rates react to changes in cash flow projections and/or changes in the required *IRR*s on competing investment alternatives. Note that this integration of real estate markets with general capital markets can cause a variation in local real estate values and therefore in observed cap rates if, for example, yields on risky corporate bonds were to change.

Concept Check

9.8   If new information suggests that rents in a market are going to increase at a faster rate than what has been projected, what will happen to the cap rates that appraisers abstract from this market after this new information becomes known to market participants?

Other Methods of Estimating Cap Rates

When adequate reliable market data are available, appraisers often prefer to estimate overall cap rates directly from recent transactions of similar income properties using direct market extraction. Often, however, estimates of *NOI* for the comparable properties may not be available or reliable, and the sale prices may reflect special considerations such as favorable financing or an unusual income tax situation. Thus, appraisers often must rely on alternative methods for estimating the R_o to be applied to a subject property. The Centre Point Office Building example is used to illustrate two of these alternative methods: (1) mortgage-equity rate analysis and (2) application of the general constant-growth model formula.

Mortgage-Equity Rate Analysis. Mortgage-equity rate analysis recognizes that the *NOI* produced by a property represents the initial return on the total acquisition price of the property. However, the acquisition is usually financed with a combination of equity (cash) and mortgage debt. Mortgage-equity rate analysis assumes the investor's minimum required cap rate is a weighted average of the required cap rate on debt financing and the required cap rate on equity financing. Thus, appraisers must determine the one-year cap rate on both debt and equity. Appraisers then weight these capital costs by the proportion of each part to the total property value. They then add the two weighted rates to obtain R_o.

The cap rate on mortgage financing, R_m, is easily obtained by observing current lending terms for the type and amount of mortgage financing the typical investor would use if acquiring the subject property. The cap rate on equity financing should reflect the dividend rate investors could earn on alternative investments of equal risk. The **equity dividend rate (R_e)** is estimated by dividing the before-tax cash flow (*BTCF*) available on alternative investments by the typical amount of equity (V_e) investors use to finance similar investments. *BTCF* is equal to the *NOI* minus the expected mortgage payment; **equity** is the difference between the value (sale price) of the property and the value of the mortgage (the mortgage amount). The equity dividend rate (*EDR*) is thus defined as

$$R_e = \frac{BTCF_1}{V_e} \qquad (9\text{-}3)$$

Investors view the equity dividend rate as the one-year income return (i.e., dividend) they could earn on their equity investments in properties similar to the subject property.

The appropriate going-in cap rate, R_o, is a weighted average of R_m and R_e, or

$$R_o = mR_m + (1 - m)R_e \qquad (9\text{-}4)$$

where R_o denotes the overall capitalization rate; m, the loan-to-value ratio; R_m, the mortgage capitalization rate; $(1 - m)$, the equity-to-value ratio; and R_e, the equity capitalization rate (equity dividend rate). Mortgage-equity rate analysis is sometimes also referred to as **band-of-investment analysis.**

Example 9-3 Centre Point

The appraiser has determined that the typical investor can obtain mortgage financing at 70 percent of value for the Centre Point Office Building. The typical cap rate on this debt financing, R_m, is 8.89 percent. The equity dividend rate available on comparable properties is estimated to be 11.5 percent, which was obtained from reviewing market investor surveys and the estimated *BTCF*s of similar recently sold properties. The indicated R_o is calculated as follows:

$$R_o = (0.70)(0.0889) + (0.30)(0.1150) = 0.0967$$

The overall capitalization rate of 0.0967 is a weighted average of the cost of debt and the equity dividend rate (the opportunity cost of equity).

Concept Check

9.9 If the equity dividend rates that investors can earn on comparable properties decrease in a market, what happens to cap rates estimated with a mortgage-equity rate analysis, all else being equal.

Applying the General Constant-Growth Formula. A third approach to determining the appropriate capitalization rate is to apply the constant-growth formula. Recall that the capitalization rate is composed of a required *IRR* on equity and a growth rate: $R_o = y_o - g$. In the Centre Point Office example, the appraiser has determined the overall market discount rate is 11.75 percent. If the appraiser expects the property's *NOI*s and market value to grow, on average, by 2.0 percent per year into perpetuity, then $R_o = (0.1175 - 0.0200) = 0.0975$.

Reconciling Cap Rates and Estimating an Indicated Value

The preceding sections discuss three methods for estimating the going-in cap rate, R_o, for a particular property in a given market: market extraction, mortgage-equity rate analysis, and the general constant-growth formula. The questions that naturally arise are: Which one is correct? or which should I use? All are correct, of course; they are simply different methods of analyzing market data to estimate the value of a property. Even so, the methods will not produce the same numerical results. Real estate markets are not totally efficient, and different methods of analysis will not yield the same conclusions. Nevertheless, if accurate, reliable data are available for the various methods, the resulting going-in cap rates should be quite close because there is only one true "market value."

The appraiser's choice of method(s) depends on data availability and reliability. The preferred method—if reliable price, income, and expense data are available for at least three (and preferably more) comparable properties—is the direct market extraction of R_o. Remember, however, that observed transaction prices should not reflect any nonmarket considerations such as unusual financing or other concessions. Also, income, operating expense, and capital expenditure data must be consistently placed in a reconstructed operating statement format. In other words, direct market extraction requires the same availability, reliability, and consistency of data and analysis for the comparable properties as for the subject property.

Mortgage-equity rate analysis and the general constant-growth formula are substitute methods for deriving R_o. They are often used because appraisers cannot obtain accurate, reliable data for direct market extraction. At times, however, appraisers are able to obtain typical mortgage financing data and equity dividend rates on comparable properties. In these situations, the mortgage equity method may be preferred to direct market extraction.

Exhibit 9-6   Reconciliation of the Indicated R_os

Source	Indicated R_o		Weight (%)		Weighted R_o
Direct market extraction	0.0990	×	50%	=	0.04950
Mortgage-equity rate analysis	0.0967	×	25	=	0.02418
General constant growth formula	0.0975	×	25	=	0.02438
Final R_o: (calculated by summing the weighted R_os)				=	0.09806
				Rounded to:	0.098

Exhibit 9-6 shows how the three indicated cap rates for our example property are reconciled. **Reconciliation** is accomplished by using weights to reflect the degree of confidence the appraiser has in each R_o. This confidence is usually based on the quantity and reliability of the data used to produce the alternative estimates. In this case the appraiser would weight the R_o obtained by direct market extraction twice as heavily as each of the other estimates because he or she has high-quality data for five very comparable properties. The data for the other two methods were acceptable, but the methods are not as directly applicable as direct market extraction. Using this final R_o to capitalize the *NOI* of the subject property produces the following **indicated value** from the direct income capitalization approach:

$$V_O = \frac{\$89,100}{0.098} = \$909,184, \text{ rounded to } \$910,000$$

Appraisers often favor applying the direct capitalization equation to estimate market value because it enables them to rely on summary market evidence without having to estimate incomes and expenses for several years into the future—a task that may be subject to significant error.

Gross Income Multiplier

For some smaller income-producing properties, appraisers may use a variant of the direct income capitalization method known as the **gross income multiplier (*GIM*)** as an additional indicator of value. The *GIM* of a comparable property is defined as the ratio of the property's selling price to its effective gross income.[9]

$$GIM = \frac{\text{Sale Price}}{EGI} \qquad\qquad \textbf{(9-5)}$$

While income capitalization methods generally use income after expenses (i.e., *NOI*), the *GIM* analysis uses the effective gross income of the subject and comparable properties. Hence, it is easily estimated by acquiring recent sale price, rent, and vacancy information. The resulting *GIM*s of the comparable properties are reconciled and subsequently applied to the income of the subject property to estimate an indicated value ($V_o = EGI \times GIM$), where *GIM* is the reconciled multiple from comparable sales data.

9. Estimation of gross income multipliers (GIM) in practice varies. Some appraisers and analysts may estimate the GIM using potential gross income, rather than effective gross income. Analysts and appraisers should take care to note this distinction in interpreting or applying GIMs.

Exhibit 9-7 GIM Analysis for Centre Point Office Building

	Comparable		
	A	**B**	**C**
Recent sale price	$876,400	$986,900	$776,300
Effective gross income (*EGI*)	$158,200	$175,300	$143,500
GIM (sale price ÷ *EGI*)	5.54	5.63	5.41
		Average GIM =	5.53

As shown in Exhibit 9-7, the appropriate *GIM* for the Centre Point Office Building is about 5.53. Multiplying the effective gross income of Centre Point, $162,000, by the abstracted *GIM* results in an indicated value of $895,860 ($162,000 × 5.53), rounded to $896,000.

Several crucial assumptions are implicit in the use of income multipliers to value the subject property. First, it is assumed that the operating expense percentage of the subject and comparable properties are approximately equal. Thus, at times, adjustments may be required to account for operating differences between the comparable properties and the subject properties. For example, if a comparable property's effective gross income includes operating expense payments (e.g., utility fees), but the subject property does not, the expenses would be subtracted from the comparable property's income.

Gross income multiplier analysis also assumes that the subject and comparable properties are collecting market rents. In particular, the application of *GIM* analysis is especially tenuous when the subject and/or comparable properties are subject to long-term leases at rates above or below current market rents. For example, assume the rents of the comparable office properties are at market. In contrast, however, the subject office property is 50 percent leased at rates 25 percent below market. Moreover, the tenant's original 10-year lease has a remaining term of 5 years; thus, it will be 5 years before the entire property can be leased at market rates. Intuitively, the subject property should sell at a lower multiple of current rents than the comparable office properties because the subject's rental income will grow more slowly. Therefore, using, say, the average *GIM* of the comparables would place too high a value on the subject property.

For this reason, it is frequently argued that a *GIM* approach to valuation is more appropriate for apartment buildings than for most office, industrial, and retail properties. Why? Because apartment leases seldom exceed one-year terms. This allows contract rents to closely track movements in market rents. In addition, there is generally less variation in the operating expenses of comparable apartment properties than the variation often observed in other types of commercial property. Moreover, there is generally little variation across apartment properties in the proportion of operating expenses paid by tenants. In contrast, tenants in office and retail properties often reimburse the owner for a significant portion of the property's operating expenses. These reimbursements, however, can vary significantly across properties and even across tenants in a single property. In short, the typical lease structure of apartment properties permits the use of *GIM* analysis more readily than the lease structures of other commercial property types.

Concept Check

9.10 If an appraiser concludes that the rents of a subject property will grow faster than the rents of comparable properties, how would the appraiser adjust for this when reconciling the GIMs abstracted from the comparable sales? How would this adjustment affect the estimate of value for the subject?

Career Focus

A lthough many commercial appraisals are performed for mortgage lending purposes, there are many other reasons to hire a commercial appraiser, including determining an estimate of market rent, property tax appeal, estimation of just compensation for an eminent domain taking, need of an expert witness, or litigation support.

Sources: Information on Career Paths in Commercial Real Estate, University of Cincinnati, www.cba.uc.edu/getreal; and Career Opportunities, Washington State University, www.cbe.wsu.edu/~fire/real_estate

Although the fees for standard commercial appraisals have been flat or declining over the last 10 to 15 years, the outlook for appraisers involved in specialized commercial appraisal and consulting, such as site analysis, buy or lease decisions, property tax appeals, portfolio revaluation, and investment analysis, is quite promising. Many commercial and consulting appraisers work within larger consulting firms, including accounting and market research firms. Computer technology and the availability of electronic databases are having a major impact on the commercial appraisal business.

Using Discounted Cash Flow Analysis for Valuation

The previous sections of this chapter have been devoted to direct capitalization—a valuation process that involves the use of rates or ratios to convert a single-year cash flow forecast into an estimate of market value. Because direct capitalization relies heavily on data from comparable sales, its effective use requires a high degree of comparability between the subject property and the comparable sale transactions. However, such comparability is often difficult for an appraiser to obtain. Recall that, with the possible exception of apartments, commercial properties are often subject to long-term leases. These leases may carry rental rates above or below the current market rate. In fact, multitenant properties can be subject to numerous leases, all with different rental rates, remaining terms, and rent escalation clauses. There also can be a significant variation between the owner and the tenant in the percentage of operating expenses that each pays.

In addition to the heterogeneous nature of commercial leases, the increasing complexity of many transactions also requires adjustments to comparable sale prices that are difficult to quantify. Recent years also have witnessed significant differences in the prices institutional investors (e.g., pension funds and REITs) are willing to pay and the prices noninstitutional investors (e.g., private partnerships, wealthy families) are willing to pay. For these many reasons, the use of DCF models is often a necessity. Moreover, DCF analysis has become the main financial tool used by investors to evaluate the merits of commercial real estate investments. Because appraisers typically are paid to estimate the most probable selling price of a subject property, it may be beneficial for them to use the same valuation framework as investors.

The term *discounted cash flow (DCF) analysis* refers to the process and procedures for estimating (1) future cash flows from property operations, (2) the net cash flow from disposition of the property at the end of the investment holding period, and (3) the appropriate required internal rates of return, and then using these inputs to generate an indicated value for the subject property. To demonstrate the DCF process, we turn again to our Centre Point example. The assumptions in Exhibit 9-2 were used to generate a reconstructed operating statement and an estimate of *NOI* for the first year of operations after acquisition (see Exhibit 9-4). However, the typical expected holding period for investors in properties comparable to Centre Point is assumed to be five years.[10] Thus, the appraiser must prepare a five-year cash flow forecast, often referred to as a **pro forma.**

www. tortowheatonresearch. com

Torto-Wheaton Research (TWR) provides office and industrial real estate forecasts.

www. cushmanwakefield.com

Provides both free and fee-based data on real estate trends.

www.grubb-ellis.com

Provides free statistical reports on local and national real estate trends.

---

10. The most typical holding period assumed in DCF analyses of commercial real estate assets is ten years, although, to our knowledge, an adequate explanation of this assumption has never been offered. We have chosen a 5-year holding period to simplify and reduce the number of required assumptions and calculations.

Exhibit 9-8 Centre Point Office Building: Five Year Pro Forma *NOI*

Year	1	2	3	4	5
Potential gross income (*PGI*)	$180,000	$185,400	$190,962	$196,691	$202,592
− Vacancy & collection loss (*VC*)	18,000	18,540	19,096	19,669	20,259
= Effective gross income (*EGI*)	162,000	166,860	171,866	177,022	182,332*
− Operating expenses (*OE*)	64,800	66,744	68,746	70,809	72,933
− Capital expenditures (*CAPX*)	8,100	8,343	8,593	8,851	9,117*
= Net operating income (*NOI*)	$89,100	$91,773	$94,526*	$97,362	$100,283*

*Subtraction discrepancy due to rounding.

Exhibit 9-8 contains these estimates. Given the assumptions in Exhibit 9-4—*PGI* increasing 3 percent per year, 10 percent vacancy and collection losses, operating expenses at 40 percent of *EGI,* and capital expenditures at 5 percent of *EGI*—*NOI* is expected to increase from $89,100 in year 1 to $100,283 in year 5.

A Word of Caution

As Chapters 4 through 7 clearly demonstrate, many qualitative and difficult to predict economic, social, and legal factors influence real estate cash flows and values. Thus, the usefulness of quantitative valuation tools and techniques, such as discounted cash flow analysis, depends on the quality of the cash flow assumptions employed. How does one learn to develop relevant and realistic cash flow projections? Certainly, familiarity with the material in prior chapters will provide a solid foundation. However, directly related work experience and in-depth knowledge of the local market in which the subject property is located are required for a successful implementation of DCF analysis. Although recent college graduates often hold analytical (i.e. "number crunching") positions within real estate firms, the input assumptions they employ in their analyses are guided by seasoned professionals.

Estimating Future Sale Proceeds

The second major source of property cash flows comes from the disposition (typically, the sale) of the ownership interest in a property. In a sale the invested capital "reverts" back to the owner; hence, the proceeds from the sale are frequently referred to as the **reversion.** Because income properties are usually held for a limited time period, the net cash flow from the eventual sale of the property must be estimated in addition to the cash flows from annual operations.

There are numerous methods available for estimating the sale price at the end of the expected holding period—commonly termed the **terminal value (V_t).** For example, an appraiser may simply assume a resale price or that the value of the subject property will grow at some compound annual rate. However, direct capitalization is the most common method used to estimate terminal value. This is because estimating the sale price at the end of an expected five-year holding period is analogous to estimating the current value at the beginning of year 6. If a **terminal capitalization rate (R_t),** or **going-out cap rate,** of 10 percent (0.10) is deemed appropriate for determining the future sale price (terminal value) of Centre Point, then the estimated sale price at the end of year 5 is:

$$V_5 = \frac{NOI_6}{R_t} = \frac{\$103,291}{0.1000} = \$1,032,910, \text{ or approximately, } \$1,033,000$$

In theory, the sale price at the end of the holding period can be viewed as the present value of the cash flows remaining from that point forward. However, the effort and cost required for the estimation of net operating incomes beyond the end of the holding period may exceed the benefit because the accuracy of estimated cash flows generally declines over time. Note that DCF analysis, as commonly employed, is really a combination of DCF and direct capitalization.

For fully leased, stabilized properties in normal markets, the going-out cap rate is usually assumed to be 1/4 to 3/4 of a percentage point higher than the going-in cap rate—and higher cap rates produce lower value estimates. The higher going-out cap rate at termination usually reflects the assumption that the income-producing ability of properties (i.e., their productivity) will decline over time.

The **net sale proceeds (NSP)** are obtained by subtracting **selling expenses (SE)** from the expected selling price. Selling expenses include brokerage fees, lawyer's fees, and other costs associated with the sale of the property that represent cash outflows. Selling expenses in our example are forecasted to be $58,300, or a little less than 6 percent of the expected sale price. When deducted from the estimated selling price, this leaves an expected NSP of $974,700.

	Sale price (*SP*)	$1,033,000
−	Selling expenses (*SE*)	58,300
=	Net sale proceeds (*NSP*)	$ 974,700

Concept Check

9.11   Explain why DCF analysis, as commonly used in market valuation, is really a combination of DCF and direct capitalization.

Levered versus Unlevered Cash Flows

To this point, we have estimated annual cash flows net of vacancy and collection losses, operating expenses, and capital expenditures. But are the pro forma *NOI*s, if realized, the actual amounts the owner of Centre Point will have available each year to spend, save, or invest elsewhere? The answer is no. Why? Because in many cases, property owners use a combination of equity and mortgage debt to finance an acquisition such as Centre Point. Therefore, the investor's cash flows from operations will be reduced by any payments that are required to stay current (i.e., "service") the mortgage. The use of mortgage debt to help finance capital investment is commonly referred to as **leverage.** Thus, the expected stream of *NOI*s and the expected *NSP* are **unlevered cash flows** because they represent the income-producing ability of the property *before* subtracting the portion of the annual cash flows that must be paid to the lender to service or retire the debt. **Levered cash flows** measure the property's income *after* subtracting any payments due the lender. In addition to ignoring the effects of mortgage debt, unlevered cash flows also do not capture the effects of state and federal income taxes on investor cash flows.

Concept Check

9.12   Are levered cash flows greater in magnitude than unlevered cash flows, all else equal?

Valuing Unlevered Cash Flows

In addition to well-researched and reasonable estimates of cash flows, selection of the appropriate discount rate is also of critical importance. In the appraisal process, where the purpose is to estimate the property's current market value (V_O), the rate used to discount the expected unlevered cash flows (*NOI*s and *NSP*) is the typical investor's required internal

rate of return on comparable properties. We refer to this unlevered discount rate as (y_o). As discussed in Chapter 3, discount rates typically are determined by examining data on comparable property sales, evaluating the required returns on alternative investments of similar risk, talking to market participants, and reviewing investor survey information.

Example 9-4   Centre Point

Assume an appraiser has evaluated the estimates of *NOI* and net sale proceeds previously constructed for Centre Point and now listed in Exhibit 9-9, and has determined they reasonably represent the market's expectations. In addition, assume the appraiser concludes that the overall *market* discount rate (y_o) for the property is 11.75 percent. The *NOIs* and net sale proceeds can then be discounted as shown, producing an estimate of market value of $900,181, or $900,000 when rounded to the nearest $1,000.

Exhibit 9-9   Centre Point Office Building: Present Value of Unlevered Cash Flows

Year	NOI	Net Sale Proceeds	Total Cash Flow	PV Factor @ 11.75%	Present Value
1	$ 89,100		$ 89,100	0.894855	$ 79,732
2	91,773		91,733	0.800765	73,489
3	94,526		94,526	0.716568	67,734
4	97,362		97,362	0.641224	62,431
5	100,283	$974,700	1,074,983	0.573802	$616,827
				Present value =	$900,181

It is clear from this example and our discussion in Chapter 3 that the accuracy of the value estimate depends heavily on the accuracy of the discount rate. We will see in subsequent chapters that the use of debt financing and the existence of state and federal income taxes can have a significant effect on the magnitude and riskiness of investment cash flows. However, our valuation of Centre Point using *NOIs* and the *NSP* appears to ignore financing and income taxes. How can this be explained? The answer lies in the discount rate. Investors in higher income tax brackets require higher going-in *IRRs* to offset their higher tax payments, all else being equal. The amount of leverage also affects the riskiness of the equity investment, which we will discuss further in Chapter 14. For now, it is sufficient to understand that debt financing and taxes are not ignored if the valuation estimate is based on the *NOIs* and *NSP*—these effects are captured in the discount rate.

Valuing Levered Cash Flows

When estimating market value, appraisers are attempting to estimate the most probable selling price; that is, the transaction price most likely to be observed for the subject property. It is therefore important that the appraisal method reflects the valuation techniques used by typical investors when making acquisition decisions. To do so, appraisers sometimes estimate market values by separately valuing the equity and debt. An appealing feature of this approach is that it simulates the thinking of many investors, who are concerned with not only the property's overall productivity, as measured by *NOI*, but also with the cash flows that will flow to them after servicing the debt. Valuation of the equity piece of the productivity pie is accomplished by discounting the expected **before-tax cash flows** (**BTCF**s), rather than the *NOI*s, to determine the value of the equity (V_e). The *BTCF* is calculated by subtracting the estimated annual mortgage payment from the *NOI*. Note that the equity investor has a residual claim on the property's cash flow stream because the lender has the first claim on the cash flows generated by the property.

Concept Check

9.13   Why is the owner's claim on the property's cash flows referred to as a residual claim?

In the Centre Point example, assume the appraiser determines that a *typical* buyer of a similar property could obtain a mortgage loan of $625,000 (approximately 70 percent of the property's value as estimated above), at an annual interest rate of 8.21 percent, amortized monthly over 30 years. The monthly mortgage payment on the loan is $4,677.85; thus, the annual debt service rounds to $56,134 ($4,677.85 × 12).[11] Calculation of the annual *BTCF*s are presented in Exhibit 9-10.

In this method, the estimated proceeds from the sale of the property at the end of the expected holding period will also change. The equity investor will receive $379,386, the difference between the net sale proceeds and the outstanding balance on the mortgage loan in five years. This is termed the **before-tax equity reversion (BTER)**, and its calculation is shown below.

	Sale price	$1,033,000
−	Selling expenses	58,300
=	Net sale proceeds	$ 974,700
−	Remaining mortgage balance	595,314
=	Before-tax equity reversion	$ 379,386

Finally, assume the appraiser determines the appropriate rate used to discount the cash flows to the equity investor, *BTCF* and *BTER,* is 20.0 percent. This is the internal rate of

---

Exhibit 9-10   Centre Point Office Building: Estimated Before-Tax Cash Flows

	1	2	3	4	5
= Net operating income (*NOI*)	$89,100	$91,773	$94,526	$97,362	$100,283
− Debt service (*DS*)	56,134	56,134	56,134	56,134	56,134
= Before-tax cash flow (*BTCF*)	$32,966	$35,639	$38,392	$41,228	$44,149

---

11. The calculation of mortgage payments is explained in Chapter 11. In this example, the calculator keystrokes are $N = 360$, $I = 8.21\% \div 12$, $PV = 625,000$, $PMT = ?$, $FV = 0$.

Exhibit 9-11 Centre Point Office Building: Present Value of Levered Cash Flows

Year	BTCF	BTER	Total Cash Flow	PV Factor @ 20%	Present Value
1	$32,966		$ 32,966	0.833333	$ 27,472
2	35,639		35,639	0.694444	24,749
3	38,392		38,392	0.578704	22,218
4	41,228		41,228	0.482253	19,882
5	44,149	$379,386	$423,535	0.401878	$170,209

Present value = $264,530

return on equity (y_e) required by typical investors for similar properties, assuming typical market financing. Note that the investor's equity discount rate is higher than the overall discount rate (y_e = 20.0 percent, y_o = 11.75) used in the previous DCF method. This reflects the risky nature of the equity investor's residual position.[12] The *BTCF*s and *BTER* can be discounted as shown in Exhibit 9-11, producing an estimate of the value of the equity investment (V_e) of $264,530.

To this value (the market value of the equity) must be added the current market value of the debt (V_m, the original loan amount) to obtain an estimate of the total market value of the property (V_o). That is,

$$V_o = V_e + V_m$$
$$= \$264{,}530 + \$625{,}000$$
$$= \$889{,}530, \text{ or rounded, } \$890{,}000$$

Thus, we have two indicators of market value, $900,000 and $890,000, from the two DCF procedures presented. The first was estimated as the present value of the overall cash flows (*NOI* and *NSP*), while the second was estimated as the sum of the value of the equity (present value of the cash flows to the equity investor) and the value of the mortgage.

Concept Check

9.14 With what piece of the subject property's productivity pie are equity investors most concerned?

Other Approaches

Other approaches and methods may be also used in determining the market value of an income property. In applying the income approach, alternative methods may be used to determine the overall capitalization rates for application in the direct capitalization approach. In addition, an indicated value using the cost approach generally is reported. However, appraisers usually rely less on the cost approach for income properties because of the difficulties in measuring costs and accrued depreciation, as discussed in Chapter 8. Also, variations of the sales comparison approach may be applied; again, less reliance typically is placed on those methods. Income is the most important characteristic for which these properties are purchased, and the greatest reliance thus is placed on the approach that converts income to present value.

---

12. It should be noted that $y_o = y_e$ on projects purchased without the use of mortgage financing. As the use of mortgage financing increases, y_e increases due to the added riskiness of the cash flows expected by the equity investor (see Chapter 14).

Exhibit 9-12 Centre Point Office Building: Reconciliation of Value Indicators

Approach	Indicated V_O	Weight (%)	Weighted V_O
Indicated values from income approach			
DCF analysis (*NOIs*)	$900,000	30%	$270,000
DCF analysis (*BTCFs*)	890,000	30	267,000
Direct capitalization	910,000	30	273,000
GIM analysis	896,000	5	44,800
Indicated value from cost approach	915,000	5	45,750
Indicated value from sales comparison approach	Not applied	0	0
	Weighted V_O added to yield final estimate of value:		$900,550
		Rounded to:	$900,000

Final Reconciliation

Proper application by the appraiser of each of the several income approaches to valuation discussed in this chapter would, in theory, produce identical estimates of market value for Centre Point. Market value is determined by demand and supply conditions, not the methodology chosen by the appraiser to measure it. In practice, of course, we would be surprised if the answers obtained by use of two or more methods were identical. The realities of the imperfect markets that provide valuation inputs, such as market rents, typical expenses, sale prices, and loan terms, will result in discrepancies among market value estimates. Thus, the reconciliation process requires informed judgment and expert opinion; it is not a simple averaging of divergent data.

Exhibit 9-12 summarizes the various indications of market value for the Centre Point Office Building obtained so far. Appraisers obtain a final estimate of value by reconciliation of these indications into a final estimate of value. Relevance and reliability serve as the criteria for determining the weight assigned to the *values* indicated by each approach.

For income-producing properties, the most reliable methods are usually DCF analysis and direct capitalization. Recall that DCF analysis employed market inputs—that is, market-derived rents, expenses, and discount rate. The DCF analysis and direct capitalization should produce similar results, with no more than a 10 percent difference. The difference in this case is about 2.0 percent (ranging from $890,000 to $910,000). In this example, the two DCF methods and the direct capitalization method are each weighted 30 percent, indicating the high level of appropriateness and confidence accorded them by the appraiser. The GIM analysis and the cost approach (not demonstrated here, but assumed to result in an indicated value of $915,000) are each weighted only 5 percent, indicating the lower level of confidence placed on these methods for this particular type of property.

The final estimate of market value, $900,000, is the weighted average of all of the value indications shown in Exhibit 9-12. It reflects the appraiser's best estimate of the current market value of the property, using the valuation methods believed relevant and reliable.

It should be noted that, in practice, appraisers seldom explicitly identify the weights given each method. Alternatively, they apply the weights implicitly in rendering their professional opinion of value. In this example, the weights are identified to describe the process.

Valuing Partial and Other Interests

Alternative capitalization rates and discount rates are often applied in valuing partial interests (and future interests) of the entire property. For example, the "property" valued may be any legal interest in real estate such as a **fee simple estate** (complete ownership of a prop-

Exhibit 9-13 Capitalization Rates, Income, and Value Components

Overall cap rate (R_o)	=	NOI_1	÷	Current property value (V_o)
Terminal cap rate (R_t)	=	NOI_{n+1}	÷	Terminal property value (V_n)
Equity dividend rate (R_e)	=	BTCF	÷	Value of the equity (V_e)
Mortgage constant (R_m)	=	DS	÷	Value of the debt (V_m)
Building cap rate (R_b)	=	Building income	÷	Value of the building (V_b)
Land cap rate (R_L)	=	Land income	÷	Value of the land (V_L)

erty without regard to any leases) or a **leased fee estate** (ownership subject to leases on the property). The value of other estates, such as those in the land only, the building only, lease-hold estates, and other partial interests, may also be estimated.

Whenever a specific property, or a component of or interest in the property, is appraised, the income associated with that particular component or interest must be estimated, and the appropriate rate applied using direct capitalization or DCF procedures similar to those outlined in valuing the overall market value. A detailed description of the valuation of partial interests is beyond the scope of this book; however, examples of some of the capitalization rates (and their symbols) are listed in Exhibit 9-13.

Summary

This chapter focuses on the third approach to market valuation—the income approach. The income approach includes the valuation of income-producing properties by both DCF analysis and direct capitalization. The mechanics of DCF analysis are the same whether the analysis is used for the purpose of making investment decisions or for valuation. For valuation purposes, however, the viewpoint is different; consequently, the data employed may differ from those used in investment analysis for the same property. To estimate the market value of a property using DCF analysis, an appraiser must use market-derived data while investors can enter their own requirements and data. Thus, for appraisal purposes, market data are the inputs, and an estimate of market value is the output.

Direct capitalization involves dividing one year's income by a capitalization rate to estimate market value. The income and cap rate could be for any interest in real estate: the fee simple interest, leased fee interest, leasehold interest, land only, or building only. The only requirement is that the cap rate is obtained for whatever interest produces the income. In most situations, the value of the fee simple interest in a property is estimated, so the relevant income is *NOI*, and the relevant cap rate is an overall cap rate (R_o). Three methods for estimating the appropriate overall cap rate were presented. Once an R_o is selected, it is used to convert a stabilized income estimate into an estimate of market value. In straightforward appraisal situations, direct capitalization can be more accurate and reliable than DCF analysis because the appraiser can rely on the decisions of other investors represented in the sale prices and incomes of comparable properties. It is not necessary to estimate cash flows over a holding period.

The sales comparison and cost approach to market valuation should also be applied when reliable data are available. However, these approaches to commercial propery valuation are usually not considered as relevant or reliable as the income approach and are usually weighted less in the final estimate of market value of income-producing properties.

Key Terms

Band-of-investment analysis 228
Before-tax cash flows 236
Before-tax equity reversion 236
Capital expenditures (*CAPX*) 222
Contract rent 220
Direct capitalization 224
Direct market extraction 225
Effective gross income (*EGI*) 222
Equity 228
Equity dividend rate (R_e) 228
Fee simple estate 238
Going-in cap rate (R_o) 226

Going-out cap rate (R_t) 233
Gross income multiplier (GIM) 230
Income capitalization 217
Indicated value 230
Leased fee estate 239
Leverage 234
Levered cash flows 234
Market rent 220
Mortgage-equity rate analysis 228
Natural vacancy rate 221
Net operating income (*NOI*) 217
Net sale proceeds (*NSP*) 234

Operating expenses (*OE*) 222
Overall capitalization rate (R_o) 226
Potential gross income (*PGI*) 220
Pro forma 232
Reconciliation 230
Reconstructed operating
  statement 218
Reversion 233
Selling expenses (*SE*) 234
Terminal capitalization rate (R_t) 233
Terminal value (V_t) 233
Unlevered cash flows 234

Test Problems

Answer the following multiple choice problems.

1. Which of the following expenses is not an operating expense?
   a. Utilities.
   b. Reserve for replacements and other nonrecurring expenses.
   c. Management.
   d. Mortgage payment.
   e. Advertising.

2. To estimate the value of the equity portion of a real estate investment, an appraiser divides the equity income (BTCF) by which of the following?
   a. Equity yield rate (y_e).
   b. Equity dividend rate (R_e).
   c. Overall capitalization rate (R_o).
   d. Mortgage constant (R_m).
   e. Discount rate (y_o).

3. An overall capitalization rate (R_O) is divided into which type of income or cash flow to obtain an indicated value?
   a. Net operating income (NOI).
   b. Effective gross income (EGI).
   c. Before-tax cash flow (BTCF).
   d. After-tax cash flow (ATCF).
   e. Potential gross income (PGI).

4. Which of the following types of properties probably would not be appropriate for income capitalization?
   a. Apartment building.
   b. Shopping center.
   c. Farm.
   d. Warehouse.
   e. Public school.

5. Reserves for replacement and other nonrecurring expenses are allowances that reflect
   a. The annual depreciation of the building.
   b. The annual depreciation of the long-lived components of the building.

   c. The annual depreciation or appreciation of the entire property.
   d. The annual depreciation of the short-lived components of the building and expenses that occur only occasionally.
   e. The depreciation or appreciation of the land.

6. What overall capitalization rate is indicated by the following characteristics of equity and debt in a transaction?
   $m = 0.80$ a. 14.00 percent.
   $R_M = 0.123432$ b. 12.00 percent.
   $R_E = 0.1400$ c. 12.67 percent.
                        d. 13.25 percent.
                        e. 12.50 percent.

7. An appraiser estimates that a property will produce NOI of $25,000, the y_O is 11 percent, and the growth rate is 2.0 percent. What is the total property value (unrounded)?
   a. $277,778.   d. $243,762.
   b. $227,273.   e. $231,580.
   c. $323,762.

8. If a comparable property sells for $1,200,000 and the effective gross income of the property is 12,000 per month, the gross income multiplier is
   a. 0.12   d. 0.01
   b. 8.33   e. 10
   c. 100

9. The final value estimate produced by one approach is called
   a. Final estimate of value.
   b. Reconciled estimate of value.
   c. Probable sale price.
   d. Indicated value.
   e. Adjusted final sale price.

10. The methodology of appraisal differs from that of investment analysis primarily regarding
    a. Use of DCF analysis.
    b. Use of direct capitalization.
    c. Length of holding period analyzed.
    d. Type of debt assumed in the analysis.
    e. Point of view and types of data used.

Study Questions

1. Data for five comparable income properties that sold recently are shown in the accompanying table.

Property	NOI	Sale Price	Overall Rate
A	$57,800	$566,600	0.1020
B	49,200	496,900	0.0990
C	63,000	630,000	0.1000
D	56,000	538,500	0.1040
E	58,500	600,000	0.0975

   What is the indicated overall cap rate (R_o)?

2. Why is the market value of real estate determined partly by the lender's requirements and partly by the requirements of equity investors?

3. The cap rate on mortgage financing is 7.5 percent for properties similar to the subject. The typical loan-to-value ratio is 75 percent of value. What would be the indicated R_O by simple mortgage equity rate analysis, if equity dividend rates ($R_e s$) are running about 11.0 percent?

4. You are asked to appraise a vacant parcel of land. Your analysis shows that if apartments were constructed, the portion of the NOI attributable to the land would be $30,000 per year. If offices were constructed, the portion attributable to land would be $25,000, and the portion contributed by a small neighborhood shopping center would be $27,500. All of these uses would be legal. If the appropriate R_L is 0.105 (10.5 percent), what is the value of the site?

5. Given the following owner's income and expense estimates for an apartment property, formulate a reconstructed operating statement. The building consists of 10 units that could rent for $550 per month each.

Owner's Income Statement

Rental income (last year)		$60,600
Less: Expenses		
Power	$2,200	
Heat	1,700	
Janitor	4,600	
Water	3,700	
Maintenance	4,800	
Reserves	2,800	
Management	3,000	
Depreciation (tax)	5,000	
Mortgage payments	6,300	34,100
Net income		$26,500

   Estimating vacancy and collection losses at 5 percent of potential gross income, reconstruct the operating statement to obtain an estimate of NOI. Remember, there may be items in the owner's statement that should not be included in the reconstructed operating statement. Using the NOI and an R_o of 11.0 percent, calculate the property's indicated market value. Round your final answer to the nearest $500.

6. You have been asked to estimate the market value of an apartment complex that is producing annual net operating income of $44,500. Four highly similar and competitive apartment properties within two blocks of the subject property have sold in the past three months. All four offer essentially the same amenities and services as the subject. All were open-market transactions with similar terms of sale. All were financed with 30-year fixed-rate mortgages using 70 percent debt and 30 percent equity. The sale prices and estimated first year net operating incomes were as follows:
   Comparable 1: Sales price $500,000; NOI $55,000
   Comparable 2: Sales price $420,000; NOI $50,400
   Comparable 3: Sales price $475,000; NOI $53,400
   Comparable 4: Sales price $600,000; NOI $69,000
   What is the indicated value of the property using direct capitalization?

7. You are estimating the market value of a small office building. Suppose the estimated NOI for the first year of operations is $100,000.
   a. If you expect that NOI will remain constant at $100,000 over the next 50 years and that the office building will have no value at the end of 50 years, what is the present value of the building assuming a 12.2% discount rate? If you pay this amount, what is the indicated initial cap rate?
   b. If you expect that NOI will remain constant at $100,000 forever, what is the value of the building assuming a 12.2% discount rate? If you pay this amount, what is the indicated initial cap rate?
   c. If you expect that the initial $100,000 NOI will grow forever at a 3% annual rate, what is the value of the building assuming a 12.2% discount rate? If you pay this amount, what is the indicated initial cap rate?

8. Describe the conditions under which the use of gross income multipliers to value the subject property is appropriate.

9. In what situations or for which types of properties might discounted cash flow analysis be preferred to direct capitalization?

10. Distinguish between levered and unlevered cash flows. In what sense does the equity investor have a residual claim on the property's cash flow stream if mortgage financing is employed?

11. What is the difference between a fee simple estate and a leased fee estate?

12. What is the difference between contract rent and market rent? Why is the distinction more important for investors purchasing existing office buildings than for investors purchasing existing apartment complexes?

13. Estimate the market value of the following small office building. The property has 10,500 sq. ft. of leasable space that was leased to a single tenant on January 1, four years ago. Terms of the lease call for rent payments of $9,525 per month for the first five years, and rent payments of $11,325 per month for the next five years. The tenant must pay all operating expenses.

During the remaining term of the lease there will be no vacancy and collection losses; however, upon termination of the lease it is expected that the property will be vacant for three months. When the property is released under short-term leases, with tenants paying all expenses, a vacancy and collection loss allowance of 8 percent per year is anticipated.

The current market rental for properties of this type under triple net leases is $11 per sq. ft., and this rate has been increasing at a rate of 3 percent per year. The market discount rate for similar properties is about 11 percent, the "going-in" cap rate is about 9 percent, and terminal cap rates are typically 1 percentage point above going-in cap rates.

Prepare a spreadsheet showing the rental income, expense reimbursements, NOIs, and net proceeds from sale of the property at the end of an 8-year holding period. Then use the information provided to estimate the market value of the property.

Explore The Web

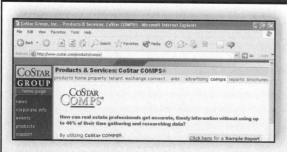

The explosion of online resources is having a profound effect on how appraisers operate. The CoStar Group offers an online data service called CoStar COMPS. With over 689,000 confirmed real estate sale transactions, users have access to a comprehensive commercial real estate database. Because of CoStar COMPS and other competing data providers, due diligence no longer requires hours of digging through records, microfiche and news sources for information and the dozens of subsequent verification calls. CoStar COMPS® employs hundreds of researchers who follow a standarized process to compile and confirm 200+ data fields on a single property. Thousands of transactions are added every month and data are updated daily, making CoStar COMPS® a real-time sales transaction database.

Go to www.costar.com. After browsing the home page, click on "search comparables" under the Comps section. Click on the link to find out how to become a member. Browse the page that describes their comparable database, then download a sample report.

Solutions to Concept Checks

1. When a commercial asset is performing well, there is sufficient cash being generated to both service the debt (i.e., make the mortgage payment) and pay all state and federal income taxes. So, both the lender and the income tax collector(s) benefit from good property performance.

2. Direct capitalization models require an estimate of stabilized income for one year. DCF models require estimates of net cash flows over the entire expected holding period. In addition, the cash flow forecast must include the net income expected to be produced by the sale of the property at the end of the expected holding period. Finally, the appraiser must select the appropriate investment yield (required IRR) at which to discount all future cash flows.

3. Stabilized income means under current market conditions, but adjusted to reflect market rents (not contract rents), "normal" vacancy and collection losses (not current if they are higher than normal), and normal operating expenses and capital expenditures. For example, sometimes an investor feels the current owner is not managing the property well in that rents are lower than the market will bear and expenses are higher than they need be. In putting together the reconstructed operating statement, the potential investor values the property under the assumption that he will quickly stabilize the property (i.e., bring revenues and expenses to market levels).

4. Contract rent is the actual rent being paid under the terms of the lease(s). A listing of these contract rental rates is sometimes called the property's "rent roll." Market rent is the income the property is capable of producing if leased at market rates.

5. Operating expenses include the ordinary and necessary expenditures associated with operating an income producing property. They keep the property competitive in its market, but they do not prolong the useful life of the asset or increase its market value. In contrast, capital expenditures are replacements, alterations, or additions, that do prolong life and/or increase value.

6. When capital expenditures are subtracted (i.e., taken out) in the calculation of NOI, this is referred to as an "above-line" treatment.

7. The indicated value is $4,444,444 ($400,000 / 0.09).

8. If new information suggests that rents are going to increase at a faster rate, but y_O (the required going in IRR) has not changed, then capitalization rates will fall because $R_o = y_o - g$. Said differently, if a larger portion of the required total return is going to come in the form of future rent growth and appreciation, then a small portion needs to be obtained from the current cash flow.

9. The equity dividend rates available on comparable properties can be thought of as equity cap rates (in contrast to overall cap rates). If equity cap rates fall, overall cap rates will fall because they are a weighted average of the equity and debt cap rates.

10. If the appraiser believes that the subject's rents will grow faster than the rents of the comparable properties, then an investor can justify paying a higher price per dollar of current rental income. Thus, the appraiser should adjust upward the GIM abstracted from the market, which would imply a higher value for the subject property.

11. DCF analysis requires an estimate of the value of the property at the end of the assumed holding period. The most common method used to estimate the market value of the property at the end of, say, 10 years, is to capitalize the NOI estimate in year 11 into an end-of-year 10 value. Thus, DCF is a combination of DCF analysis and direct capitalization.

12. In calculating levered cash flows, the mortgage payment is subtracted from the unlevered cash flows. Thus, levered cash flows are smaller in magnitude than unlevered cash flows.

13. The owner's claim is a residual claim, because he or she only gets "paid" if the property produces enough income to cover all operating and capital expenditures, cover the mortgage payment, and cover all state and federal income taxes. The owner then gets what is "left over."

14. Equity investors are most concerned with the equity portion of the "productivity pie." The debt portion of the pie is paid to the mortgage lender.

Additional Readings

The following books contain expanded examples and discussions of real estate valuation and appraisal:

Appraisal Institute. *The Appraisal of Real Estate,* 13th ed., Chicago, Il., American Institute of Real Estate Appraisers, 2001.

Collier, N. S.; C. A. Collier; and D. A. Halperin. *Construction Funding: The Process of Real Estate Development, Appraisal, and Finance.* 3rd ed. New York, NY: John Wiley & Sons, December 2001.

Betts, Richard M., and Silas J. Ely. *Basic Real Estate Appraisal,* 5th ed., Upper Saddle River, NJ, Prentice Hall, 2001.

Fisher, J. D.; and R. S. Martin. *Income Property Appraisal.* Chicago, Il.: Real Estate Education Company, a division of Dearborn Financial, October 1991.

Fisher, J. D.; R. S. Martin; P. Mosbaugh. *Language of Real Estate Appraisal.* Chicago, Il.: Real Estate Education Company, a division of Dearborn Financial, January 1991.

Lusht, Kenneth L., *Real Estate Valuation: Principles and Applications,* Burr Ridge, Il., McGraw-Hill Irwin, 1997.

Smith, Halbert C., Linda Crawford Root, and Jerry D. Belloit, *Real Estate Appraisal* 3rd edition, Upper Saddle River, NJ: Gorsuch Scare Brock Publishers, 1995

The following journals contain numerous articles on real estate valuation and appraisal:

The Appraisal Journal, published quarterly by the Appraisal Institute, Chicago, Il.

Real Estate Review, published quarterly by Warren, Gorham and Lamont, Boston, MA.

Real Estate Issues, published quarterly by the American Society of Real Estate Counselors, Chicago, Il.

The Real Estate Appraiser, published monthly by the Society of Real Estate Appraisers, Chicago, Il.

Financing Real Estate Ownership

Real Estate Finance: *The* **Laws** *and* Contracts

Learning Objectives

After reading this chapter you will be able to:

1. Correctly use these terms concerning an adjustable interest rate: *index, margin, periodic cap, overall cap, payment cap, adjustment period,* and *teaser rate.*

2. With respect to a note, state the meaning of *personal liability, exculpatory clause, demand clause,* and *default.*

3. State the effect of these clauses in a mortgage: insurance clause, escrow clause, acceleration clause, and due-on-sale clause.

4. Contrast a mortgage, a deed of trust, and a contract for deed.

5. List four alternative actions to foreclosure that a lender can take as a remedy for default.

6. State the function of foreclosure, and the role of the following: equity of redemption, statutory redemption, deficiency judgment, and judicial versus power-of-sale foreclosure.

7. Distinguish three types of bankruptcy and what effect each has upon foreclosure.

8. Distinguish acquiring a property "subject to" a mortgage from assuming the mortgage.

Introduction

Most real estate transactions involve debt financing. Most homebuyers lack the cash to purchase their residence outright, most businesses want their cash available in their core business rather than to tie it up in real estate, and many investors want to "leverage" their investment through debt in order to increase equity returns or to be able to acquire more assets with their available cash. In addition, many homeowners find that their best source of financing for household needs is a credit line loan secured by their house. As a result, mortgage debt financing is a major aspect of real estate decisions, and mortgage lending is a major industry in the United States and many other countries.

Mortgage financing is complicated. Because the debt normally is large, long lasting, and secured by a complex asset, it must be crafted to anticipate a multitude of legal events. As a result, it requires some knowledge of law, which is presented in this chapter. In effect, this chapter provides the "rules of the game" for mortgage finance.

In a mortgage loan the borrower always conveys two documents to the lender: a note and a mortgage. The note details the financial rights and obligations between borrower and lender. The mortgage pledges the property as security for the debt.

Several aspects of a mortgage note are important for a borrower to understand. These include computation of the interest rate (if adjustable), whether a loan can be paid off early (and at what cost), whether there is personal liability for a mortgage, what fees can be charged for late payments, and whether the loan must be repaid upon sale of the property. Finally, a borrower should know whether the lender has the right to terminate the loan, calling it due.

In case of default on a mortgage, a lender's ultimate recourse is foreclosure. But foreclosure is costly to implement. The lender needs to know what the alternatives to foreclosure are, and their risks. Bankruptcy frequently accompanies default and can have serious adverse consequences that a lender must understand.

When property is purchased, new mortgage debt is not the only means of financing the purchase. Existing debt may be preserved, in which case the seller and buyer must understand his or her liability. Further, a contract for deed may substitute for mortgage financing. Finally, whenever residential mortgage debt is created both borrower and lender need to understand several Federal laws governing the process.

Concept Check

10.1   What two contracts are always involved in a mortgage loan?

The Note

The **note** defines the exact terms and conditions of the loan. Both the large size of a real estate loan and the long maturity compel the note to be very explicit to prevent misunderstandings between the borrower and lender. The complexity of loan terms can vary with its size and the risks involved. In this section we discuss the major elements common to most mortgage notes.

Interest Rate and Interest Charges

Interest rates can be fixed or variable. Either way, virtually all small- to medium-size real estate loans from standard lenders follow the same conventions for interest rate computation and interest charges.[1] The actual interest charged per month is the annual stated contract interest rate divided by 12, multiplied by the beginning-of-month balance. The payment is due on the first day of the following month. For example, if the contract interest rate on a home loan is 6.00 percent, and the balance on the first day of the month is $100,000, then interest for the month is 0.5 percent ($0.06 \div 12$) $\times$ 100,000, or $500, payable on the first day of the next month.

Concept Check

10.2   What is the monthly interest rate for a mortgage loan with a 12 percent annual rate?

---

1. Standard lenders are banks, savings and loan associations, savings banks, credit unions, mortgage bankers, and mortgage brokers. These are discussed in Chapter 13.

Adjustable Rates

A significant number of mortgage loans use adjustable interest rates. They are common in commercial real estate loans and are the choice of many home borrowers where this loan type is known as an **adjustable rate mortgage (ARM).** Finally, adjustable interest rates are used in virtually all home equity credit line mortgage loans (discussed in Chapter 12). The computation of an adjustable interest rate opens several questions not present when the interest rate is fixed. A number of components must be defined in the note, including the index, margin, method of computing the index, adjustment period, date of change in the interest rate, and determination of any "caps" or limits on interest rate changes. These components are explained below.

www.fhfb.gov/MIRS/
MIRS_rates.htm

Contract mortgage loan index rate.

Index. The **index rate** is a market determined interest rate that is the "moving part" in the adjustable interest rate. In principle, it could be any regularly reported market interest rate that cannot be influenced by either borrower or lender. In practice, a relatively small number of choices are used. With ARM home loans, for example, the most common index rates include U.S. Treasury **constant maturity rates** (most commonly one year in maturity, although longer maturities are used as well), and a **cost-of-funds index** for thrift institutions.[2] Occasionally, a home mortgage index rate may be used as well, such as the national average rate for new loans on existing homes. Home equity credit line loans, commonly offered by banks, rely on the commercial bank "prime rate" as published regularly in *The Wall Street Journal.* Finally, a common index is a **LIBOR** rate, especially for loans on income-producing property.[3] Generally, home mortgage lenders must give notice of interest rate changes to borrowers at least 30 days in advance.

http://research.
stlouisfed.org/fred2/
series/DGS1/22

One-year Constant Maturity Treasury (CMT) index rate.

Not only must an adjustable rate note specify the index, but it must state how it is used at each adjustment period. For example, when the rate is recomputed at the **change date,** the new index value may be the latest published value, a value from a certain number of days earlier, or an average of a recent period.[4]

The one-year constant maturity Treasury rate is displayed in Exhibit 10-1 for the earliest available day in July from 1981 through 2002. Its behavior is representative of other index rates. First, the enormous range in the value of the rate is apparent. Also evident is the downward trend over the last two decades, which is interlaced with numerous significant upward reversals. The year-to-year effect is most evident in the second panel, showing changes in the Constant Maturity Treasury (CMT) rate from one year earlier. It reveals that borrowers have experienced more years of declining rates than rising rates. If one regards any increase of less than 1/2 of 1 percent as a win, the borrower has won 16 of 22 years from 1981 through 2002. Still, many borrowers may not be comfortable with the very apparent possibility of occasional large rate increases. For this reason, most home borrowers prefer caps on changes in the ARM rate, as discussed below.

www.federal reserve.
gov/releases/h15/
update

Reports latest Constant Maturity Treasury rates.

Margin. Added to the index of the adjustable rate is a **margin,** which is the lender's "markup." The margin is determined by the individual lender and can vary with competitive conditions and with the risk of the loan. It normally is constant throughout the life of

---

2. Treasury constant maturity interest rates are computed by the Federal Reserve Board as follows: The one year constant maturity rate, for example, is the average of the market yield, found by survey, on any outstanding U.S. Treasury debt having exactly one year remaining to final repayment, regardless of what the original maturity of the debt was. The Federal Reserve regularly reports several constant maturity rates.

A cost of funds index for thrifts is a weighted average of all the rates of interest on all types of funds deposited with thrift institutions (savings and loan associations and savings banks). The most common cost of funds index used is based on West Coast thrifts (District 12 of the Federal Home Loan Bank system).

3. LIBOR (London Interbank Offering Rate) is a short-term interest rate for U.S. dollar denominated loans among foreign banks based in London.

4. A common choice is to use the latest weekly average available a certain number of days (e.g., 45) before the change date.

Exhibit 10-1 The Most Common ARM Index Rate: One-Year Constant Maturity Treasury Rate

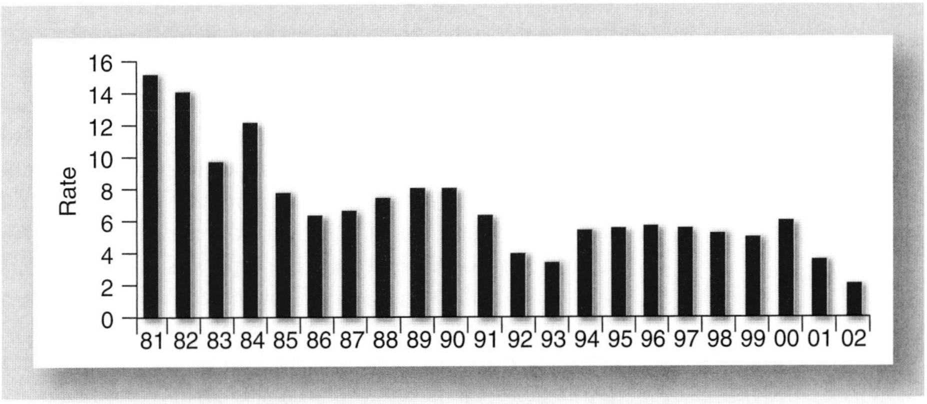

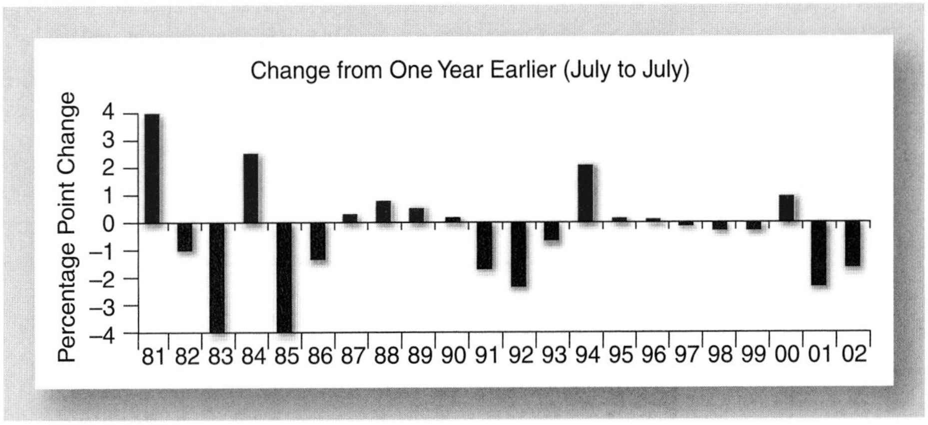

www.freddiemac.com/pmms/pmmsarm.htm

One-year ARM rates and margins

the loan. For standard ARM home loans, the average industry margin has been very stable around 275 basis points (2.75 percentage points). Margins frequently are lower for home equity loans by banks.

Concept Check

10.3 **What are four sources of index interest rates for use in adjustable interest rates?**

Rate Caps. Two kinds of limits, known as caps, commonly restrict the change in ARM adjustable rates: periodic caps and overall caps. **Periodic caps** limit change in the interest rate from one change date to the next. **Overall caps** limit change over the life of the loan. Typically, the caps are binding for both increases and decreases in the index.

Teaser Rates. Most ARM home loans have been marketed with a temporarily reduced interest rate known as a **teaser rate.** This reduction, which may be a percentage point or two below the sum of index plus margin, usually applies for a short time, perhaps one year. The presence of a teaser rate creates a question about how the periodic cap works: Does the cap apply to the teaser rate, or does it apply only to the index plus margin? For example, suppose the periodic cap is 1 percent (100 basis points), the initial index plus margin implies a starting rate of 5.0 percent, but a teaser rate of 3.5 percent applies in the first year.

At the start of year 2, is the new interest rate limited to 4.5 percent (3.5 + 1.0) or to 6.0 percent (5.0 + 1.0)? The answer depends on how the note is written, and the borrower must examine the wording of the note to find the answer. A detailed computation of ARM interest rates and payments, demonstrating the interaction of the teaser rate and caps, is shown in Chapter 11.

Payment Caps. Occasionally lenders offer ARM home loans with caps on payments rather than on the interest rate. For example, while the actual interest rate may be allowed to adjust without limit, the payment may be capped at increases of no more than 5 percent in a single year. Thus, if the payment in the initial year of a loan with annual payment adjustments is $1,000 and there is a 5 percent payment cap, then the maximum payment in year 2 is $1,050 regardless of how much the interest rate (index plus margin) increases. The **payment cap** enables the lender to enjoy the advantage of unconstrained interest rate adjustments while protecting the borrower against the shock of large payment changes. However, it can become very complicated. In particular, it is possible for the interest rate to increase enough that the resulting payment increase still cannot cover the additional interest cost. The unpaid interest must be added to the original balance, causing the loan amount to increase, a result that is known as **negative amortization.** Due to their complexity, payment-capped mortgages have been used infrequently.

www.federalreserve. gov/pubs/brochures/ arms/arms.pdf

Handbook for adjustable rate mortgages (ARMs).

Concept Check

10.4   The two most common types of caps in an adjustable rate mortgage are:

Payments

Payments on standard mortgage loans are almost always monthly. Further, almost all standard, fixed term real estate loans are level payment and fully amortizing.[5] That is, they have the same monthly payment throughout, and the payment is just sufficient to cover interest due plus enough principal reduction to bring about full repayment of the outstanding balance at exactly the end of the term. Exhibit 10-2 shows the pattern of interest and principal payments on a fixed rate, 30-year, level payment, fully amortizing loan. Notice that the payment is largely interest for about the first half of the loan life before it begins to decline. This pattern is very similar for all level payment, long-term loans, although the actual interest share of the payment depends on the interest rate and term.

Not every loan is fully amortizing. A loan may be **partially amortizing,** as noted in the next paragraph; that is, it may pay down partially over a certain number of years, but may require an additional (large) payment of principal with the last scheduled payment. Loans also may be **nonamortizing,** that is, they require interest but no regularly scheduled principal payment prior to the last payment. Finally, some loans may contain negative amortization. As noted before, this means that their scheduled payment is insufficient to pay all of the accumulating interest, causing some interest to be added to the outstanding balance after each payment shortfall, increasing the loan amount.

Concept Check

10.5   What happens to the balance of a loan with negative amortization?

---

5. Amortizing refers to repayment through a series of balance reductions.

Exhibit 10-2 Interest and Principal on a Level-Payment Loan

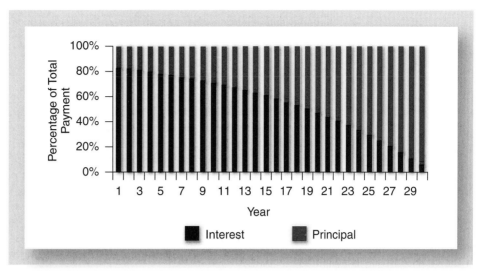

Term

Most real estate loans have a definite term to maturity, usually stated in years. For example, home loans typically have a term to maturity between 15 and 30 years. If a loan is not fully amortizing, it will have two terms. The first is a **term for amortization** that determines the payment, and the schedule of interest and principal payments, just like a fully amortized loan. The second is a **term to maturity** that is shorter. This determines when the entire remaining balance on the loan must be paid in full. This type of loan often is called a **balloon loan.** While it is used infrequently for a primary home loan, it is the dominant form of mortgage loan for income-producing property.

Concept Check

10.6 What is a balloon loan?

Right of Prepayment

There is important variation in the **right of prepayment** on a mortgage loan, and several situations are possible. First, the note may be silent on the matter. In this case, the right of prepayment will depend on the law of the state where the property is located. Under the traditional law of mortgages, which derives from English common law, there is no right to prepay a mortgage before its term, unless explicitly stated. However, some states have enacted statutes to reverse this common law tradition; that is, by statute the borrower automatically has the right to prepay a mortgage loan unless it is explicitly prohibited. Florida, for example, has enacted such a reversal.

A simpler case is where the note is explicit on the right of prepayment. In this case the provisions of the note will prevail. Most standard home loans give the borrower the right to prepay any time, without penalty.[6] However, in recent years prepayment penalties have become more common in larger home loans. In addition, they frequently occur in subprime

---

6. The right of prepayment without penalty is required in the note for standard home loans purchased by Freddie Mac or by Fannie Mae, and for Federal Housing Administration (FHA) and Veterans Affairs (VA) home loans. However loans not eligible for FHA or VA, and loans too large to be eligible for purchase by Freddie Mac or Fannie Mae (over $322,700 for 2003) frequently have prepayment penalties.

home mortgage loans. (Subprime loans are discussed further at the end of this chapter and in Chapter 13.) **Subprime loans,** made to homeowners who do not qualify for standard home loans, can have very costly prepayment penalties that "lock in" the borrower to a very high interest rate.

Prepayment Penalties

For most mortgage loans on commercial real estate, the right of prepayment is constrained through a **prepayment penalty.** This penalty usually is very severe for the first few years of the loan, but declines in the latter half of the loan term. Three types of prepayment penalties have been used. Earlier generation income property loans often specified a prepayment penalty as a percentage of the remaining balance at the time of prepayment. More recent practice has been to specify a **yield maintenance prepayment penalty.** In this approach, a borrower wishing to prepay must pay the balance, plus the present value (as defined in the note) of the interest income that will be lost by the lender due to prepayment. Still more recently, an even more demanding prepayment penalty has been used. This is a **defeasance prepayment penalty,** where a borrower wishing to prepay must usually offer the lender some combination of U.S. Treasury securities that replaces the cash flows of the loan being paid off.

Concept Check

10.7   Of these types of loans, which typically have prepayment restrictions or penalties?
a. Standard home loan. b. Large home loan. c. Subprime loan. d. Commercial property mortgage loan.

Late Fees

Late fees are a significant issue on debt contracts. Many credit card users discover the hard way that late fees are a major source of revenue for credit card lenders. Late fees on standard home loans typically are around 4 to 5 percent of the late monthly payment. Almost universally, they are assessed for standard home loans on payments received after the 15th of the month the payment is due. On subprime loans, and on nonstandard loans in general, late fees can be larger.

Personal Liability

When borrowers sign a note, they assume **personal liability,** in general, for fulfillment of the contract; that is, if the borrowers fail to meet the terms of the note, they are in a condition of **default,** and can be sued. This liability exists for virtually every home loan. Because the lender has this legal recourse against the mortgagor in case of default, these loans often are called **recourse loans.** Recourse is less commonly available with loans on commercial real estate. For commercial loans, the note is often written so as to avoid personal liability on the part of the mortgagor, or borrower. Equivalently, an **exculpatory clause** is negotiated in the note that releases the borrower from liability for fulfillment of the contract. These loans are referred to as **nonrecourse loans.** While they relieve the borrower of personal liability, they do not release the property as collateral for the loan. Thus, the lender still has an interest in the property as security for the loan.

Demand Clause

A **demand clause** permits a lender, from time to time, to demand prepayment of the loan. This clause is common with loans from commercial banks. If the bank determines after periodic review that the borrower's creditworthiness has deteriorated, the bank may exercise a demand clause. While a demand clause is rare in fixed-term, standard home loans (it is prohibited in many), it is quite common in "home equity" credit line loans from commercial banks.

Home Loan Originator

A home loan originator (loan officer or broker) is the sales arm of the home financing industry. An effective loan originator is one who can help to make a home purchase happen. He or she assists brokers and buyers in overcoming the single largest obstacle to completing a successful home purchase: obtaining financing. "Loan officers" work directly for a lending institution. "Brokers" are agents for various lending institutions. Loan originators spend most of their day calling on industry salespersons or meeting with them and their clients. They are active in a variety of industry and community affairs both because they are "people oriented" and because the resulting interactions are the seedbed of their business opportunities. Much of their work occurs in the hours when households are buying homes, which often includes evenings and weekends. Originators have a wide range of educational and experience backgrounds. Most have an undergraduate college degree, frequently in business. Compensation for originators can be good. For brokers it is achieved primarily through transaction-based commissions, though some firms may provide a "draw" against future earnings or a modest salary at the outset. Loan officers, in contrast, are primarily salaried, with more modest upside potential. Residential lending is a blend of sales work and technical expertise. While the broker and loan officer must have a solid knowledge of their products and of complex loan application and closing processes, their core business remains understanding, assisting, and influencing clients.

Concept Check

10.8 What does a demand clause permit a lender to do?

Inclusion of Mortgage Covenants by Reference

The note usually will, by reference, add to its clauses all of the covenants (i.e., legally binding provisions) of the mortgage. In addition, it commonly reiterates some of the important mortgage covenants. Among these is likely to be a so-called due-on-sale clause, and an acceleration clause, which are discussed below.

The Mortgage

The **mortgage** is a special contract by which the borrower conveys to the lender a security interest in the mortgaged property. Because the property is being pledged by the action of the borrower, the borrower is referred to as the **mortgagor,** or grantor of the mortgage claim. The lender, who receives the mortgage claim, is known as the **mortgagee.** Under traditional English common law, a mortgage temporarily conveyed title of the property to the mortgagee/lender. This **title theory** tradition has been largely replaced by the more modern **lien theory.**[7] Under the lien theory, the mortgage gives the lender the right to rely on the property as security for the debt obligation defined in the note, but this right only can be exercised in the event of default on the note.[8]

---

7. The pure lien theory is found, generally, in states west of the Mississippi, while title theory states include Alabama, Maryland, and Tennessee. Many states have a mixture of the traditions.

8. The difference between lien theory and title theory, now largely erased through state laws, is in the time that a mortgagee (lender) has claim to possession and rents of a property. Upon default, according to the pure title theory, a lender has claims extending back to the date the mortgage was created. But by the most extreme interpretation of lien theory, a lender has claim to no income or possession until a statutory redemption period (discussed later) has expired. While state laws have largely limited a lender's claims to those of a lien, state variations remain. The practical implication is that only a knowledgeable attorney should ever attempt to write or interpret a mortgage.

Because the mortgage conveys a complex claim for a long period of time, it must anticipate numerous possible future complications. Most of the clauses in a mortgage are for this purpose. Below is a sample of major clauses in a standard home loan mortgage.

Description of the Property

The mortgaged property must be described unambiguously. Three methods of property description generally are considered acceptable for this purpose (see Chapter 18). These are description by metes and bounds, by government rectangular survey, or by recorded subdivision plat lot and block number. Tax parcel number or street address are insufficient if used alone, since they can be erroneous or ambiguous.

Insurance Clause

An **insurance clause** requires a borrower/mortgagor to maintain property casualty insurance (e.g., fire, windstorm) acceptable to the lender, giving the lender joint control in the use of the proceeds in case of major damage to the property.

Escrow Clause

The **escrow clause,** or impound clause, requires a borrower to make monthly deposits into an **escrow account** of money to pay such obligations as property taxes, casualty insurance premiums, or community association fees. The lender can use these escrowed funds only for the purpose of paying the expected obligations on behalf of the borrower. Note that the obligations involved in some manner affect the ability of the lender to rely on the mortgaged property as security for the debt. The insurance must be paid to protect the value of the property against loss due to physical damage. The property tax and association dues must be paid because both are secured by superior claims to the property, as explained below.

Concept Check

10.9 Why does a mortgage lender want to be able to pay the property taxes on behalf of a mortgage borrower?

Acceleration Clause

In the event a borrower defaults on the loan obligation, an **acceleration clause** enables the lender to declare the entire loan balance due and payable. If this were not so, the default would apply only to the amount overdue. As a result, the cost of legal action against the borrower would almost always exceed what could be recovered. It would never pay to sue in case of default, and the mortgage would be meaningless.

Due-on-Sale Clause

If a property is sold, either in fact or in substance (e.g., through a lease with an option to buy), a **due-on-sale clause** gives the lender the right to "accelerate" the loan, requiring the borrower to pay it off. This right can be waived at the lender's option, of course. It enables the lender to prevent degradation in the quality or reliability of the person(s) paying the loan. This clause became extremely important in the early 1980s when interest rates were very high relative to rates on existing loans. Mortgagors selling their homes had a powerful incentive to preserve old, low interest rate loans that would be attractive to buyers, whereas the lender had an equally powerful incentive to terminate the old loans as soon as possible. The due-on-sale clause became a weapon in the struggle between lenders attempting to terminate low-yield loans and sellers attempting to preserve them.

The presence or absence of a due-on-sale clause is a major distinguishing feature between basic classes of home mortgage loans. So-called conventional home loans (see Chapter 12) almost always contain a due-on-sale clause, giving the lender the right to terminate the loan at sale of the property. By contrast, Federal Housing Administration (FHA) and Veterans Affairs (VA) loans are assumable, as long as the buyer can qualify for the loan. An **assumable loan** means that the buyer can preserve the existing loan.

Hazardous Substances Clause and Preservation and Maintenance Clause

A lender wants to protect the loan security from damage due to negligence or excessive risk taking by the borrower. Therefore, the borrower is prohibited from using or storing any kind of toxic, explosive, or other "hazardous substance" on the property beyond ordinary, normal use of such substances. In addition, the borrower is required to maintain the property in essentially its original condition. Failure to meet either of these provisions constitutes default.

Concept Check

10.10   What types of standard home loans are assumable?

Deed of Trust

In some states, a **deed of trust** is used in place of a mortgage. This arrangement works as follows: As shown in Exhibit 10-3, the borrower conveys a deed of trust to a **trustee,** who holds the deed on behalf of both borrower and lender. If the loan obligation is paid off in accordance with the note, the trustee returns the deed to the borrower. But if the borrower defaults, the trustee exercises the power of sale (discussed later in "Judicial Forclosure versus Power of Sale") to dispose of the property on behalf of the lender. Compared to a mortgage, the power of sale process offers significant advantages to a lender, as we will explain later in the next section.

Exhibit 10-3   Mortgage versus Deed of Trust

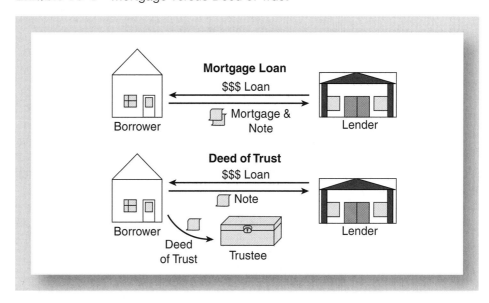

Explore The Web

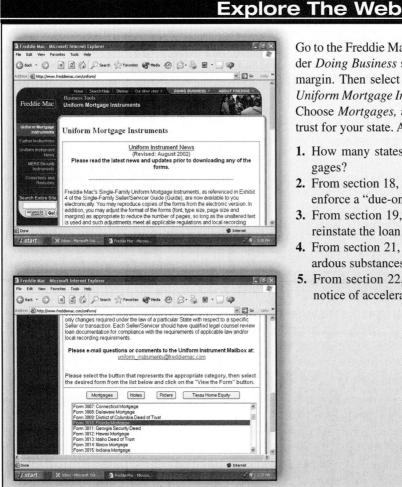

Go to the Freddie Mac website (www.freddiemac.com). Under *Doing Business* select *Single Family* from the left-hand margin. Then select *Forms and Electronic Documents* and *Uniform Mortgage Instruments*. Go to the selection window. Choose *Mortgages,* and download the mortgage or deed of trust for your state. Answer these questions:

1. How many states have deeds of trust rather than mortgages?
2. From section 18, in what circumstances will a lender not enforce a "due-on-sale" clause?
3. From section 19, what actions must a borrower take to reinstate the loan in good standing after acceleration?
4. From section 21, can a borrower store *any* toxic or hazardous substances on the mortgaged property?
5. From section 22, what points must a lender cover in a notice of acceleration?

When Things Go Wrong

Only when something goes wrong does the meaning of the note and mortgage become clear. Below we review the main possibilities when this happens.

Default

Failure to meet the requirements of the note (and, by reference, the mortgage) constitutes *default.* Clearly, however, defaults can range in degree of seriousness. Violations of the note that do not disrupt the payments on the loan tend to be viewed as "technical" defaults. While these violations may require some administrative response, they do not compel legal action. For example, if for some reason hazard insurance were to lapse, the borrower must restore it, but that problem alone would not warrant legal action. When payments are missed (typically for 90 days), however, the lender normally treats the default as serious. In this case, the ultimate response is the process of *foreclosure.* However, foreclosure is a costly and time-consuming action that may damage the borrower's financial and reputational standing. Used unwisely, it could tax the lender's goodwill in the community. Therefore the lender must carefully weigh the use of foreclosure against a range of less drastic remedies that can be pursued. After a brief tour of these less drastic remedies, we will examine foreclosure in depth.

Nonforeclosure Responses to Default

Sometimes when a homeowner misses a mortgage payment, the problem can be mitigated by improved household financial management. In this case, credit counseling, together with possible reorganization of consumer credit obligations, may be a far more constructive and less costly solution than legal action for both borrower and lender.

A more definite response to missed payments may be to allow a temporary reduction of payments. As long as some regular payment is being made, the lender might also allow a missed payment to be deferred. However, there are practical and legal risks in this response. If it is clear that the household will not be able to rectify its financial problem, the solution will only allow losses to compound. Further, any agreement to change the payment schedule on the loan may be interpreted by a court as a "recasting" of the loan. Theoretically, this can then be interpreted by a court as the creation of a new, replacement mortgage. Since the determination of priority among liens (i.e., security claims) generally is by date of creation, this could have disastrous consequences to the lender, as explained below.

Concept Check

10.11 In practice, lenders commonly define default as occurring when a loan is _____ days overdue.

A still more definite response by the lender may be to encourage and facilitate the sale of the property. The lender can agree to cooperate with a prospective buyer by allowing a reasonable plan for the buyer to cure the default. However, this can be risky for the buyer since existing liens will travel with the title.

As a final action short of foreclosure, the lender may accept a **deed in lieu of foreclosure;** that is, the lender may allow the borrower simply to convey the property to the lender. This solution has several attractions. It is faster than foreclosure, less costly, and creates less public attention to the event. The deed in lieu of foreclosure can be beneficial to the lender's public image and to the public perception of the property. Public perception of the property may be especially important for retail and hospitality properties, for which adverse publicity may taint the tenants and damage their business.

But, once again, accepting a deed in lieu of foreclosure has significant risks since financial problems tend to travel in packs. The mortgagor is likely to have other financial problems apart from the property, but which can generate additional liens. Whatever liens have been imposed on the property subsequent to the creation of the mortgage will remain with the property. The lender has no choice but to accept the property subject to these liens.

The worst risk in accepting a deed in lieu of foreclosure is likely to be bankruptcy. The same conditions of distress that caused default on the mortgage may well lead the borrower finally to declare bankruptcy. If this occurs within a year after conveyance of the deed in lieu of foreclosure, the courts can treat the conveyance as an improper disposition of assets, deeming it unfair to other creditors. But the deed in lieu of foreclosure will erase the lender's priority claim to the property as security for the debt. So, when the bankruptcy court reclaims the property, the lender ends up as simply one more in the line of creditors seeking relief through the court.

Concept Check

10.12 Give two reasons a lender might be ill advised to accept a deed in lieu of foreclosure for a distressed property.

Foreclosure

Foreclosure is the ultimate recourse of the lender. It is a legal process of terminating all claims of ownership by the borrower, and all liens inferior to the foreclosing lien. This can enable the lender to bring about free and clear sale of the property to recover the outstanding indebtedness. It is a delicate process because only those claimants who are properly notified and engaged in the foreclosure suit can lose their claims to the property. Thus, there is risk that persons with a claim on the property will remain undiscovered or will be improperly treated in the process. This would result in a defect in the title at a foreclosure sale.

Another concern in foreclosure is the presence of superior liens. In general, liens have priority according to their date of creation, with earlier liens being superior. In addition, local government always has a lien on real estate for property tax obligations that is automatically superior to any private lien. Foreclosure cannot extinguish a superior lien. Therefore, the foreclosing lender must be sure that obligations secured by superior liens—property taxes, assessments, earlier mortgages—are met. Otherwise, the lender is likely to become subject to a subsequent foreclosure initiated by the holder of the superior lien.

Concept Check

10.13   What liens would have priority over the mortgage of a lender?

Lien priority is a major concern to a lender because the highest priority lien receives all net proceeds from the foreclosure sale until that obligation is fully satisfied. Only then does the second lien claimant receive any satisfaction. For example, if a property with a first mortgage loan of $100,000 and a second mortgage loan of $30,000 brings net proceeds of $110,000 from a foreclosure sale, the first mortgagee would receive full satisfaction of $100,000 while the second mortgagee would receive only $10,000. More commonly, net proceeds from foreclosure are less than the amount of the first mortgage, and the second mortgagee receives nothing. Thus, a second mortgage is significantly less secure than the superior mortgage. Subsequent liens are progressively even less secure.

The start of a foreclosure suit does not necessarily spell the end of ownership for the mortgagor. By a legal tradition long part of the English law of equity, the mortgagor has a right, known as the **equity of redemption,** to stop the foreclosure process by producing the amount of the loan balance and paying the costs of the foreclosure process. This right traditionally extends up to the time of actual sale of the property. In many states the right of redemption has been extended further, to some time beyond the sale of the foreclosed property. This period of **statutory right of redemption** varies among states, typically between six months and a year. However, it can range from a few days to as much as two years.

Foreclosure is a costly process to all involved. First, the legal search and notification process can be costly, time consuming, and risky in that it may be difficult to identify all claimants to the property. Second, the sale of the property typically is a distressed sale for a number of reasons: The property tends to be tainted and less marketable, normal market exposure of the property is not feasible, the title is sufficiently questionable so that debt financing for the purchase usually is not available, and, in many cases, the mortgagor may still be able to exercise the statutory right of redemption. Consequently, the price received at a foreclosure sale tends to be low. Finally, the negative public exposure and the time involved must be counted as a cost for all parties involved. Thus, while foreclosure can be regarded by the lender as a potential recourse, it is one that should be used only as a costly last resort. The net recovery by a lender from a foreclosed loan seldom is higher than 80 percent of the outstanding loan balance. As a result, mortgage lenders traditionally have had a strong incentive to avoid loans with high foreclosure risk. It is not surprising that their lending practices tend to err on the side of safety.

Exhibit 10-4   States Having Power of Sale for Residential Mortgages

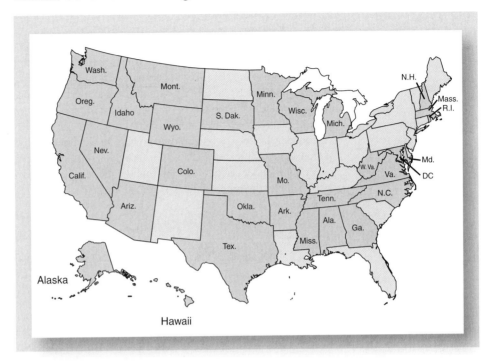

Deficiency Judgment

Because a mortgage loan involves both a note and a mortgage, the lender may have the option, in addition to foreclosure, of simply suing the defaulting borrower on the note.[9] In principle, funds not recovered through foreclosure can be recovered through a **deficiency judgment.** In practice, however, this seldom happens. Many loans on income-producing properties are nonrecourse, as discussed earlier in the chapter, placing the borrower beyond legal reach. Further, lenders recognize that a defaulted borrower usually has extensive financial problems and does not possess the net worth to compensate the lender beyond what is recoverable from sale of the property.

Judicial Foreclosure versus Power of Sale

There are two leading procedures among states of the United States in the treatment of defaulted mortgages, and the difference is significant. In states requiring **judicial foreclosure,** the sale of the foreclosed property must be through a court-administered public auction. In contrast to this are states having the **power of sale,** sometimes referred to as **nonjudicial foreclosure,** which are shown in Exhibit 10-4. In these states either the mortgagee (lender) or the trustee (for a deed of trust) conducts sale of the property. In using this power, the mortgagee or trustee must abide by statutory guidelines that protect the borrower: Typically, they must give proper legal notice to the borrower, advertise the sale properly, and allow a required passage of time before the sale.

The power of sale is advantageous to the lender for several reasons. In almost all cases it is faster and cheaper than a court-supervised auction. Further, with a deed of trust the borrower has no statutory right of redemption. This further shortens the process, ending it with

---

9. In some "power of sale" states the lender is prohibited from both exercising the power of sale and seeking a deficiency judgment. Because of the typical circumstances of financial distress when a borrower defaults, the lender will virtually always elect the power of sale.

finality at sale of the property.[10] The difference between judicial foreclosure and power of sale is so significant that lenders may favor power of sale states in making some types of more risky loans.

The difference between judicial foreclosure and power of sale only partially captures the diversity in foreclosure law among states. There is significant variation within both groups, with many states having completely unique provisions. (See the websites shown for foreclosure law by state.) Texas and Iowa suggest the extremes in variation. In Texas, a power of sale state, there is only a 20-day period for a homeowner to cure a default, and notice of sale requires only another 21 days, making the process unusually quick and easy for the lender. In Iowa, which allows power of sale, but only by voluntary agreement, judicial foreclosure dominates. Further, for farms, there is a redemption period of five years during which the lender can be forced to rent the property to the owner. After five years, the owner still can buy the property back from the lender.

www.foreclosures.com/
pages/statelaws.asp

www.
foreclosureassistance.
com/states.html

Two websites that provide comparative information on mortgage law and foreclosure law, by state.

Concept Check

10.14   Depending on the state, the process of foreclosure sale is either by _____ or_____ . The method most favorable to a lender is_____ .

Bankruptcy and Foreclosure

The risk of **bankruptcy** tends to travel with the risk of foreclosure since both can result from financial distress. When the financial condition of a firm or individual is such that total assets sum to less value than total liabilities, bankruptcy is a possibility. While traditional bankruptcy has little effect on foreclosure, more modern forms can interfere significantly. Three types of bankruptcy must be distinguished, known by their section in the Federal Bankruptcy Code: Chapter 7, liquidation; Chapter 11, court supervised "workout"; Chapter 13, "wage earner's proceedings."

Chapter 7 Bankruptcy.   **Chapter 7 bankruptcy** is the traditional form of bankruptcy wherein the court simply liquidates the assets of the debtor and distributes the proceeds to creditors in proportion to their share of the total claims. So, if total assets sum to 50 percent of total claims, each creditor receives one-half of his or her claim. Because Chapter 7 involves a quick liquidation of assets, it does not disturb liens, and the power to foreclose remains. In short, a Chapter 7 proceeding typically will not seriously threaten the security interest of a mortgagee.

Chapter 11 Bankruptcy.   **Chapter 11 bankruptcy** is a court supervised workout for a troubled business.[11] Once a court accepts the petition of a debtor firm, creditors are suspended from pursuing legal action against the assets of the firm. This follows the view that competition among creditors likely will dismantle an otherwise viable business, which would benefit all the creditors if left intact. Under supervision of the court, the debtor will propose a workout plan, which is presented to creditors for acceptance. If the creditors cannot agree on the plan, a major concern is that the court will then impose a plan on the creditors that is even less acceptable. As part of the workout plan, the court is likely to forestall the possibility of foreclosure on defaulted real estate. The resulting delay can affect the defaulted lender in numerous adverse ways, the principal one being a delay in any possible recovery of funds. Also, the period in which payments are lost is extended, and the value of the property may deteriorate due to neglect.

---

10. In one respect, a deed of trust can favor a mortgagor (borrower). Both standard foreclosure and power of sale afford a mortgagor the right of redemption up to the time of sale. But under the mortgage tradition, the mortgagor must pay off the debt in full (plus litigation expenses) to redeem the property, whereas with the deed of trust the borrower sometimes needs only to pay the amount in default (plus litigation expenses) to redeem the property.

11. The business can be of any legal form: corporation, partnership, proprietorship, or other.

Chapter 13 Bankruptcy. **Chapter 13 bankruptcy** is similar to Chapter 11, but applies to a household. It allows the petitioner to propose a repayment plan to the court. In principle, the plan may not interfere with the claims of a mortgagee upon the debtor's principal residence, but it is likely to forestall any foreclosure proceeding and to allow any arrearages on the loan at the time of the bankruptcy filing to be paid back as part of the debtor's rehabilitation plan. Thus, the lender suffers delay in recovery, if not worse. For the effect of bankruptcy reform legislation on home mortgage lenders, see Industry Issues 10-1.

Concept Check

10.15   Which form of bankruptcy is least harmful to a lender's mortgage interest?

Acquiring a Property with an Existing Debt

When a buyer acquires a property having an existing mortgage loan, the question of personal liability arises. As long as the buyer does not add his or her signature to the note, the buyer takes on no personal liability, although the property still serves as security for the loan and can be foreclosed in the event of default. In this case the buyer is said to purchase the property **"subject to"** the existing loan. The seller remains personally liable for the debt and is said to "stand in surety" for the obligation. This means that in case of default, a lender who fails to obtain satisfaction from the current owner or from the property can go "up the line" to the original borrower. The seller or original borrower may not be comfortable with this contingent liability from the loan. A solution is to have the buyer add his or her signature to the original note, and obtain from the lender a **release of liability** from the note. In this case the buyer is said to *assume* the old loan, that is, to **assume liability** for the note.

An important characteristic of a loan is whether or not a subsequent owner of the property can preserve it. This feature is commonly referred to as **assumability.** As we noted in the discussion of the due-on-sale clause, it is a major distinguishing feature between the broad types of home loans.

Industry Issues

Concept Check

10.16 When a purchaser of mortgaged real estate accepts personal liability for an existing mortgage loan on the property, the borrower is said to _____ .

Real Estate Debt without a Mortgage

It is possible to have a secured real estate loan without a mortgage through the use of a **contract for deed,** or land contract. As the name suggests, this is a contract for sale of a property with the special provision that the actual delivery of a deed conveying ownership will occur well after the buyer takes possession of the property. The idea of the contract for deed is that a seller can finance the sale through installment payments and, by retaining title, have recourse in case of default. As shown in Exhibit 10-5, this arrangement contrasts with the standard real estate sale where both conveyance of possession and conveyance of title occur at the closing. With the contract for deed, the deed is conveyed only after the bulk of the installment payments have been made.

Exhibit 10-5   Standard Sale Timeline versus Contract for Deed Timeline

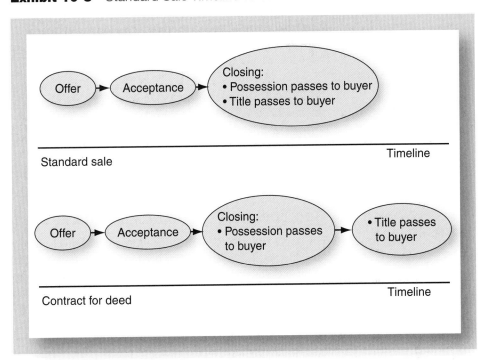

With a contract for deed, the effect of default varies. In the most favorable case for a seller, they can simply evict the would-be buyer and have full recovery of the property. However, this is by no means the typical case. Many courts have given greater recognition to the claims of buyers under contracts for deeds, especially when a personal residence is involved. Then the court may require that a defaulted contract for deed be treated as a mortgage, requiring a foreclosure proceeding. In general, the rights, obligations, and recourses of the parties in a contract for deed depend significantly on the jurisdiction and the nature of the property involved.

The contract for deed has served a number of purposes in real estate, some controversial. On the positive side, it can facilitate financing in situations deemed too risky for standard mortgage financing. For example, it can secure payments by a "speculator" interested in holding land for potential conversion from agricultural use to urban development. A farmer can sell the land on a contract for deed. In case of default, the farmer still has title to the land, and may be able to easily reclaim it outright. Another significant use of the contract for deed is in financing marginal housing, that is, there is some evidence that the land contract is a major means of financing for home purchases in which neither the dwelling nor the borrower can qualify for normal mortgage financing.

There can be a negative side to the contract for deed as well. Because it can be created hastily, there are often few, if any, protections or standards built into the arrangement. It frequently involves unsophisticated buyers who tend to overlook the need for legal and financial advice. Too often the transaction will go forward without a title search (see Chapter 18), and without sufficient legal guidance, leading to serious misunderstandings and grief later. Without a title search, the buyer has no way to know whether the seller can actually deliver clear title. Further, unless the contract is recorded in public records, there is little to prevent the seller from subsequently mortgaging the property to someone else, placing the buyer at risk.

In this situation an unprincipled seller can easily exploit a naïve and uninformed buyer. One example of this is shown in the history of interstate land sales, which affected large areas of the rural South and southwestern United States prior to about 1980. In this activity, it was common to sell land to distant buyers for future retirement homes, at unreasonable prices, expecting the buyer eventually to abandon the purchase. Sales commonly were made through contracts for deed, allowing the seller to easily reclaim the abandoned property for eventual resale to another victim. In the current use of the contract for deed in the sale of marginal homes, there again is little to prevent sellers from exploiting the lack of knowledge and experience of marginal homebuyers.

Concept Check

10.17 How does a sale by contract for deed differ from a normal real estate sale? What does the contract for deed accomplish?

Regulation of Home Mortgage Lending

Few types of business are regulated more extensively than home mortgage lending. Four laws are particularly important because they determine criteria for evaluating home loan applicants and stipulate extensive disclosures in the origination of home loans: the Equal Credit Opportunity Act of 1974, the Consumer Credit Protection Act of 1968 (Truth-in-Lending Act), the Real Estate Settlement Procedures Act of 1974, and the Home Ownership and Equity Protection Act of 1994. In addition, two laws require monitoring of home mortgage lending to reveal discrimination: The Home Mortgage Disclosure Act of 1975 and the Community Reinvestment Act of 1977.

Equal Credit Opportunity Act

Because of what Congress perceived to be a long history of both deliberate and unconscious discriminatory practices in home mortgage lending, in 1974 it enacted the **Equal Credit Opportunity Act (ECOA)**.[12] This act prohibits discrimination in lending practices on the basis of race, color, religion, national origin, sex, marital status, age, or because all or part of an applicant's income derives from a public assistance program. The details of the implementation of this law are extensive, and lenders normally invest extensive time in training employees to assure that the law is observed. Numerous kinds of information are restricted from consideration in evaluating a loan application, including the childbearing plans of a female applicant, whether income is from part-time or full-time employment, and whether there is a telephone listing in the name of the applicant. Fourth, the lender cannot ask for information about a spouse who is not part of the loan application.

Concept Check

10.18 What law prohibits discrimination in lending by race, sex, religion, and national origin? What types of income discrimination does it prohibit?

Truth-in-Lending Act

The **Truth-in-Lending Act (TILA)** is Title 1 of the Consumer Credit Protection Act of 1968. It requires important disclosures concerning the cost of consumer credit. Perhaps the best known of its provisions is the required computation of the annual percentage rate (APR) for most consumer loans, including home mortgage loans. (APR is examined closely

---

12. The detailed implementation of ECOA is through Federal Reserve Regulation B, often referred to in real estate finance circles.

in Chapter 11.) In addition, the law requires disclosure of numerous other aspects of the terms of a home mortgage loan, including the following:

- Whether the loan contains a "demand feature."
- Whether the loan can be assumed.
- Whether the loan has a variable rate.
- Whether property hazard insurance is a required condition of the loan.
- Whether there are late charge provisions.
- Whether the loan has a prepayment charge (penalty).

Finally, under TILA the borrower has the right to **rescind** any loan secured by his or her principal residence for three days following consummation of the loan. That is, the borrower can cancel the loan contract completely. This right must be disclosed to the borrower in a very specific, detailed manner.

Concept Check

10.19   Under the Truth-in-Lending Act, for how many days after closing does a borrower have the right to rescind a mortgage loan agreement?

Real Estate Settlement Procedures Act

The **Real Estate Settlement Procedures Act (RESPA),** enacted initially in 1974, was a response to the confusion and potential for exploitation of homebuyers applying for home financing. The experience of obtaining a home mortgage loan is the most complex business process most households ever experience and many are relatively unprepared for the numerous forms and fees involved. As a consequence, would-be homebuyers are vulnerable to exploitation. Further, it is not difficult for careless or unscrupulous lenders to create forms and procedures that few persons, if any, can understand. Through RESPA, Congress sought to "level the playing field" in home mortgage lending. The law applies if a buyer obtains a new first mortgage home loan from a lender having deposit insurance from the U.S government (e.g., virtually all banks, savings and loan associations, and credit unions), if the loan is insured by the FHA or guaranteed by the VA, or if the loan will be sold in the secondary market to Fannie Mae or Freddie Mac. Its requirements include:

- A standard format closing statement for most home mortgage loan closings (the HUD-1 Settlement Statement, demonstrated in Chapter 20).
- Presentation of a booklet explaining closing fees and the HUD-1 Settlement Statement.
- A good-faith estimate of closing costs, to be provided within three business days of the loan application.
- The opportunity to examine the closing statement at least 24 hours in advance of the loan closing.
- Prohibition of "kickbacks" and referral fees between the lender and providers of services in connection with the loan closing.

Among the services subject to the prohibition against kickbacks are appraisals, property inspections, document preparation, surveys, hazard insurance, mortgage insurance, and title insurance. (Title insurance is explained in Chapter 18; mortgage insurance is explained in Chapter 12.) In addition, RESPA prohibits a lender from specifying the source of title insurance to be used for the loan.

Finally, RESPA limits escrow deposits for interest, property taxes, hazard insurance, community association dues or other items. First, it limits the deposits at closing. Second, it limits the regular monthly deposit that follows. Property taxes serve as an example of how these limits work: The maximum deposit that can be required at closing for property taxes has two parts. First, the initial deposit is limited to the amount that would have been in the account at the time of closing if monthly deposits had been made since the previous payment of property taxes.

Second, any additional "cushion" is limited to one-sixth of the estimated annual obligation (two additional monthly deposits). Thus, if a loan will be closed on January 1 and property taxes are paid on March 1, there would have been ten monthly deposits from the last property tax payment up to the time of closing. So if estimated property taxes are $2,400, the lender would be allowed to require a deposit at closing in the amount of $2,000 (10 × $200) plus a $400 "cushion," for a total of $2,400. The monthly escrow deposit is limited to one-twelfth of the estimated annual obligation. So the maximum monthly deposit for property taxes would be $200. While RESPA does not require payment of interest on these escrow deposits, roughly one-third of states have laws that do require interest payment.

Concept Check

10.20 List five requirements of RESPA for a standard first mortgage home loan.

Home Ownership and Equity Protection Act

In 1994 Congress enacted the **Home Ownership and Equity Protection Act (HOEPA).** This law was passed out of concern for abusive, predatory practices in subprime lending— that is, in lending to homebuyers with limited financial knowledge and inability to qualify for standard mortgage financing. The abusive practices included extremely high interest rates, extremely high fees (commonly rolled into the loan), aggressive selling of optional insurance and "debt protection," severe prepayment penalties to prevent prepayment of loans, short-term balloon payments to force subsequent refinancing, use of undisclosed negative amortization to disguise costs, a general lack of disclosures, and a pattern of encouraging distressed borrowers to refinance into still another abusive loan. Frequently these loans are based only on the amount of home equity of the borrower, without consideration of the borrower's income and ability to make payments. For example, unscrupulous lenders may entice an elderly homeowner with a debt-free residence but little income, to commit to a loan that rapidly consumes the equity in the home.

HOEPA seeks to address most of these abuses. As revised in 2001, it sets trigger APR and fee levels (inclusive of insurance and debt protection charges at closing) for loans to become subject to the law's restrictions.[13] A loan tripping one of these triggers becomes subject to several restrictions: Detailed disclosure of fees is required, prepayment fees can be imposed only within the first five years, balloon payments are prohibited during the first five years, negative amortization is prohibited, and the lender is prohibited from engaging in a pattern of making loans that are not affordable relative to the income of the borrowers. For more about predatory lending, see Industry Issues 10-2.

Concept Check

10.21 When it applies, what disclosures does HOEPA require of a lender? What prohibitions or restrictions does it impose on the loan?

Other Laws Regulating Discrimination in Home Mortgage Lending

Additional laws have been created that affect the practice of home mortgage lending at a community or neighborhood level. Through the **Home Mortgage Disclosure Act (HMDA)** of 1975 and the **Community Reinvestment Act (CRA)** of 1977 Congress has required

---

13. The trigger is either an APR 8 percentage points above the relevant Treasury rate for first mortgage loans (10 percentage points for others), or a combination of points, fees, and insurance amounting to 8 percent of the loan.

Industry Issues

10-2

Predatory Lending

Possibly the most threatening development in home mortgage lending in recent years is predatory lending. It prompted the Congress to enact HOEPA, has gained the attention of many state legislatures, and has catalyzed aggressive campaigns of exposure and education by the U.S. Conference of Mayors, Freddie Mac, Fannie Mae, HUD, and a large number of consumer action groups. A very informative consumer advocate website is www.ACORN.org (Association for Community Organizations for Reform Now). The points below summarize their description of most practices of predatory lending. ACORN also provides rich examples of each of these practices.

- *Financing excess fees into loans.* Borrowers are routinely charged fees of just under 8 percent of the loan amount, compared to the average 1 percent–2 percent assessed by banks to originate loans.

- *Charging higher interest rates than a borrower's credit warrants.* Borrowers with perfect credit are often charged interest rates 3 to 6 points higher than the market rates.

- *Making loans without regard to the borrower's ability to pay.* Some predatory lenders make loans on a homeowner's equity, even when homeowners clearly will not be able to afford their payments. . . . For some lenders, the motivation is the ultimate foreclosure on the house which can then be resold for a profit.

- *Prepayment penalties.* Over two-thirds of subprime loans have prepayment penalties, compared to less than 2 percent of normal prime loans, often as much as six months' interest.

- *Loans in excess of 100 percent of value.* Some lenders regularly make loans for more than a borrower's home is worth with the intent of trapping them as customers for an ex-

tended period. Borrowers frequently are unaware that they owe much more than their homes are worth, and even more frequently unaware of the consequences.

- *Home improvement scams.* Some home improvement contractors target lower-income neighborhoods where owners are unable to pay for needed repairs. The contractor, in collusion with a predatory lender, pressures the owner into financing the work.

- *Single premium credit insurance.* Credit insurance pays off a particular debt if the borrower cannot pay because of sickness, death, or loss of job. Rarely promoted in the "A" lending world, it has been aggressively and deceptively sold in "single premium" form in connection with higher cost loans, and then financed into the home loans.

- *Negative amortization.* Many borrowers are not aware that they have a negative amortization loan and don't find out until they call the lender to inquire why their loan balance keeps going up. Predatory lenders use negative amortization to sell the borrower on the low payment, without revealing that the principal will rise rather than fall.

- *Loan flipping.* Flipping is a practice in which a lender, often through high-pressure or deceptive sales tactics, encourages repeated, costly refinancing. Some lenders will intentionally start borrowers with a loan at a higher interest rate, so that the lender can then refinance the loan to a slightly lower rate and charge additional fees to the borrower.

- *Aggressive and deceptive marketing—the use of live checks in the mail.* One of the methods used routinely and successfully by predatory lenders is the practice of sending "live checks" in the mail to target homeowners. The checks are usually for several thousand dollars and the cashing or depositing of the check means the borrower is entering into a loan agreement with the lender.

Source: http://www.hud.gov/offices/hsg/pred/predInd1.cfm
HUD-Treasury report on predatory lending.

---

www.ffiec.gov/hmda/ default.htm

An official source of information on HMDA.

www.ffiec.gov/cra/ default.htm

An official source of information on CRA.

home mortgage lenders to maintain a record of home loans granted and home loans denied by applicant income level, neighborhood income level, loan purpose (e.g., investment, home improvement, refinancings), applicant gender, and neighborhood area (e.g., census tract). The latter is to address the issue of **redlining** where lenders may tend to avoid certain neighborhoods without regard to the merits of the individual loan applications. This record is publicly available and frequently has been used to exert public pressure on banks, credit unions, and savings associations for more equitable community lending. It has been particularly prominent as a consideration in the evaluation of merger applications by banks and other financial institutions.

Summary

A mortgage loan involves two contracts: a note and a mortgage. The note specifies details of the financial obligation while the mortgage conveys to the lender an interest in the property as security for the debt. The borrower is the mortgagor, who conveys the security interest to the recipient lender, the mortgagee.

Rights of prepayment for a mortgage loan differ by state and type of property. Under the common law tradition, a mortgagor had no right of prepayment unless it was explicitly granted in the mortgage. It is common today, however, for state statutes to give the right to prepay unless it is explicitly prohibited in the loan. Few standard home loans prohibit prepayment, but most commercial mortgage loans impose severe penalties for prepayment.

When a borrower defaults on a loan, the lender may pursue foreclosure, but first may try less drastic strategies ranging from credit counseling to accepting a deed in lieu of foreclosure. Foreclosure, the lender's ultimate response to default, terminates other interests and claims to the security property in order to sell it to repay the debt. The lender is very sensitive to lien priorities because they affect the value of the lender's *security position*. Numerous aspects of state law affect the cost and effectiveness of foreclosure, including the equity of redemption, the statutory right of redemption, and whether the state provides for judicial foreclosure or power of sale. Bankruptcy can jeopardize a lender's ability to foreclose on a loan, particularly if it leads to a court-supervised workout.

The buyers of real property can secure financing through a contract for deed instead of a mortgage. The contract for deed provides for transfer of possession to a buyer, but delays transfer of title until a schedule of installment payments is largely completed.

The home mortgage lending process is heavily regulated by four federal laws. The Truth-in-Lending Act requires disclosure of the annual percentage rate (APR); requires numerous disclosures about late fees, prepayment penalties, and other matters; and requires a three-day rescission period for the borrower. The Equal Credit Opportunity Act (ECOA) prohibits unequal treatment in mortgage lending on the basis of race, color, religion, national origin, sex, marital status, age, or because all or part of an applicant's income derives from a public assistance program. The Real Estate Settlement Procedures Act (RESPA) requires numerous disclosures for most standard home mortgage originations, and requires the use of a standard closing statement, the HUD-1 form. It also prohibits kickbacks from vendors of services provided in connection with the loan and sale.

The Home Ownership and Equity Protection Act (HOEPA) seeks to curtail abusive practices in the origination of subprime loans. It requires disclosures of loan costs, and restricts prepayment penalties, negative amortization, balloon payments, and other aspects of the loan terms. Finally, the Home Mortgage Disclosure Act (HMDA) and the Community Reinvestment Act (CRA) establish public monitoring of potential discriminatory lending by applicant income level, applicant gender, loan purpose, location and neighborhood characteristics.

Key Terms

Adjustable rate mortgage (ARM) 248
Acceleration clause 254
Assumability 261
Assumable loan 254
Assume liability 261
Balloon loan 251
Bankruptcy 260
Change date 248
Chapter 7 bankruptcy 260
Chapter 11 bankruptcy 260
Chapter 13 bankruptcy 261
Community Reinvestment Act (CRA) 266

Constant maturity rates 248
Contract for deed 262
Cost-of-funds index 248
Deed in lieu of foreclosure 257
Deed of trust 254
Default 252
Defeasance prepayment penalty 252
Deficiency judgment 259
Demand clause 252
Due-on-sale clause 254
Equal Credit Opportunity Act (ECOA) 264
Equity of redemption 258

Escrow account 254
Escrow clause 254
Exculpatory clause 252
Foreclosure 258
Home Mortgage Disclosure Act (HMDA) 266
Home Ownership and Equity Protection Act (HOEPA) 266
Index rate 248
Insurance clause 254
Judicial foreclosure 259
Late fees 252
LIBOR 248

Test Problems

1. The element of an adjustable interest rate that is the "moving part" is the:
   a. Teaser rate.
   b. Index.
   c. Margin.
   d. Adjustment period.
   e. None of these.

2. Which of these aspects of a mortgage loan will be addressed in the note rather than in the mortgage?
   a. Prepayment penalty.
   b. Escrow requirement.
   c. Takings.
   d. Acceleration.
   e. Maintenance of property.

3. A lender may reserve the right to require prepayment of a loan at any time they see fit through a(n):
   a. Taking clause.
   b. Acceleration clause.
   c. Demand clause.
   d. Due-on-sale clause.
   e. Escrow clause.

4. When a buyer of a property with an existing mortgage loan acquires the property without signing the note for the existing loan, the buyer is acquiring the property:
   a. By assumption.
   b. By contract for deed.
   c. By deed of trust.
   d. By default.
   e. Subject to the mortgage.

5. Which of these points in a mortgage loan would be addressed in the mortgage (possibly in the note as well)?
   a. Loan amount.
   b. Interest rate.
   c. Late fees.
   d. Escrows.
   e. Loan term.

6. To finance property where either the borrower, the property, or both fail to qualify for standard mortgage financing, a common, *nonmortgage* solution is through the:
   a. Subprime loan.
   b. Deed of trust.
   c. Unsecured loan.
   d. Contract for deed.
   e. Balloon loan.

7. Ways that a lender may respond to a defaulted loan without resorting to foreclosure include all of the following *except*:
   a. Offer credit counseling.
   b. Arrange sale to a third party.
   c. Defer or forgive some of the past-due payments.
   d. Accelerate the debt.
   e. Accept a deed in lieu of foreclosure.

8. If the lender in a standard first mortgage wishes to foreclose cost effectively, it is crucial to have which clause in the mortgage?
   a. Acceleration clause.
   b. Exculpatory clause.
   c. Demand clause.
   d. Defeasance clause.
   e. Taking clause.

9. A common risk that frequently interferes with a lender's efforts to work out a defaulted loan through either nonforeclosure means or foreclosure is:
   a. Equity of redemption.
   b. Statutory right of redemption.
   c. Exculpatory clauses.
   d. Bankruptcy.
   e. Deficiency judgment.

10. The characteristics of a borrower that can be considered by a lender in a mortgage loan application are limited by the:
   a. Truth-in-Lending Act.
   b. Real Estate Settlement Procedures Act.
   c. Equal Credit Opportunity Act.
   d. Home Ownership and Equity Protection Act.
   e. Community Reinvestment Act.

11. The Real Estate Settlement Procedures Act does which of these:
    a. Requires the use of a standard settlement statement for a mortgage loan closing.
    b. Prohibits kickbacks between vendors of closing related services and lenders.
    c. Requires that a borrower receive a good faith estimate of closing costs shortly after a loan application.
    d. Requires that the borrower be able to inspect the closing statement a day before the actual closing.
    e. All of the above.

12. Foreclosure tends to be quickest in states that:
    a. Are title theory states.
    b. Are lien theory states.
    c. Have judicial foreclosure.
    d. Have power of sale.
    e. Have statutory redemption.

13. From a home mortgage lender's perspective which statement is true about the effect of bankruptcy upon foreclosure?
    a. Chapter 7 bankruptcy is the most "lender friendly" form.
    b. Chapter 11 bankruptcy is the most "lender friendly" form.
    c. Chapter 13 bankruptcy is the most "lender friendly" form.
    d. All forms of bankruptcy are equally devastating to a lender's efforts to foreclose.
    e. No form of bankruptcy causes serious problems for a lender seeking to foreclose a mortgage.

14. The most internationally oriented index rate for adjustable rate mortgages is:
    a. Federal Home Loan Bank cost of funds index.
    b. Treasury constant maturity rate.
    c. A LIBOR rate.
    d. A home mortgage loan interest rate index.
    e. The Wall Street Journal prime rate.

15. A type of loan that has grown in volume in recent years, which has raised concerns about predatory lending practices is the:
    a. Adjustable rate mortgage.
    b. Contract for deed.
    c. Purchase money mortgage.
    d. Sub-prime mortgage.
    e. Power of sale mortgage.

16. A partially amortizing loan always will have:
    a. Caps.
    b. Only one stated term.
    c. A balloon payment.
    d. A prepayment penalty.
    e. Recourse.

17. Which of these statements is true about mortgage loans for income producing real estate?
    a. They usually are partially amortizing loans.
    b. They often have a prepayment penalty.
    c. They often are nonrecourse loans.
    d. They can be interest only loans.
    e. All of the above.

18. With what type of loan security arrangement is the deed held by a neutral third party and returned upon payment of the mortgage in full?
    a. Contract for deed.
    b. Mortgage.
    c. Deed of trust.
    d. Non-recourse loan.
    e. Recourse loan.

19. The Truth in Lending Act gives a home mortgage borrower how long to rescind a mortgage loan?
    a. 24 hours.
    b. Two days.
    c. Three days.
    d. A week.
    e. A month.

20. Which statement is correct about the right of prepayment of a home mortgage loan?
    a. All home mortgage loans have the right of prepayment without charge.
    b. Most home mortgage loans have the right of prepayment without charge, but not all, and the borrower should check the loan carefully.
    c. Home mortgage loans give the right of prepayment without charge only in some states.
    d. Home mortgage loans never have the right of prepayment without charge unless it is explicitly stated.
    e. Home mortgage loans never have the right of prepayment without charge.

Study Questions

1. Mortgage law is as clear, consistent, and enforceable in the United States as in any place in the world, and far more so than in many countries. Why is this a vital element of an efficient real estate finance system?

2. The Congress is adopting changes in bankruptcy law that would make Chapter 7 bankruptcy more difficult for households, requiring greater use of Chapter 13, thus providing greater protection to unsecured credit card companies. As a mortgage lender, would you care about this? If so, what would be your position?

3. Residential mortgage terms (mortgage notes) have become increasingly uniform as the mortgage market has become more national and efficient. Is there any downside to this for the homeowner?

4. Most lenders making adjustable rate mortgage (ARM) loans offer a "teaser rate." Is this a good policy or is it misrepresentation?

5. Home mortgage lending is heavily regulated by federal laws. Is this a result of Congressional pandering to consumer groups, or are there good reasons why home mortgage lending should be regulated more than, say, automobile financing?

6. For your own state, determine whether:
   a. It is a judicial or nonjudicial foreclosure state.
   b. The standard home loan is based on a deed of trust or a mortgage.
   c. There is a statutory right of redemption and, if so, how long.
   d. Deficiency judgments are allowed against defaulted homeowners.

Based on this information can you judge whether your state is relatively lender friendly or borrower friendly? For this exercise use the websites noted in the text: foreclosureassistance.com and foreclosures.com.

7. Download one mortgage and one deed of trust from the Freddie Mac website (See Explore the Web). Compare them to see what differences you can find in their clauses.

Explore The Web

Find and download a standard adjustable rate residential mortgage note form appropriate to your state. See http://www.freddiemac.com/uniform/ What is the index rate? How is the adjustment computed? What is the periodic cap? Does it apply to both increases and decreases? Does the cap apply to the first interest rate change? What must a buyer of the property do to have the loan continue after purchase?

Solutions to Concept Checks

1. A borrower always conveys a mortgage and a note to the lender in a mortgage loan.

2. The monthly interest rate for an annual interest rate of 12 percent is 1 percent.

3. The U.S. Treasury constant maturity rate, the cost of funds index rate, the commercial bank "prime rate," the mortgage loan index rate, and the LIBOR rate are all sources for index interest rates for adjustable interest rates.

4. The two most common types of caps in an adjustable rate mortgage are periodic caps and overall caps.

5. A loan balance with negative amortization will increase because the scheduled payment is insufficient to cover the accumulated interest.

6. A balloon loan has an amortization term that determines interest and principal payments as if it were a fully amortized loan and a shorter term for maturity at which the remaining loan balance must be paid in full.

7. Prepayment penalties occur in large home loans, subprime loans, and commercial mortgage loans.

8. A demand clause permits a lender, from time to time, to demand prepayment of the loan.

9. The mortgage lender wants to be able to pay the property taxes on behalf of the borrower because the property tax lien is superior to the mortgage and can preempt it in default.

10. FHA and VA loans are assumable, subject to the buyer's ability to qualify for the loan.

11. In practice, lenders commonly define default as occurring when a loan is 90 days overdue.

12. Lenders may be ill advised to accept a deed in lieu of foreclosure because general liens may remain with the property even after it is conveyed back to the lender. Also, if the borrower claims bankruptcy, the lender may ultimately lose its priority claim to the property.

13. Property taxes, property assessments, and previous mortgages have priority over the mortgage of a lender.

14. Depending on the state, the process of foreclosure sale is either by judicial foreclosure or power of sale. The method most favorable to a lender is power of sale.

15. Chapter 7 bankruptcy is the least harmful type of bankruptcy to a lender's mortgage interest.

16. When a purchaser of mortgaged real estate accepts personal liability for an existing mortgage loan on a property, the borrower is said to assume the loan.

17. A sale by contract for deed differs from a normal real estate sale in that the actual delivery of the deed conveying ownership will not occur until well after the buyer takes possession of the property. This allows the seller to finance the sale through installment payments and to have recourse in case of default.

18. The Equal Credit Opportunity Act prohibits discrimination in lending by race, sex, religion, and national origin. It also prohibits discrimination because an applicant receives income from a public assistance program.

19. Under the Truth-in-Lending Act, a borrower has three days to rescind a mortgage loan agreement.

20. Five requirements of the Real Estate Settlement Procedures Act (RESPA) for a standard home mortgage loan are (1) a standard format closing statement (HUD-1), (2) presentation of a booklet explaining closing fees and the HUD-1 Settlement Statement, (3) good-faith estimate of closing

costs, to be provided within three business days of the loan application, (4) opportunity to examine the closing statement at least 24 hours in advance of the loan closing, and (5) prohibition of kickbacks and referral fees between the lender and providers of services in connection with the loan closing.

21. The Home Ownership and Equity Protection Act (HOEPA) sets trigger annual percentage rate (APR) and fee levels at which loans become subject to the law's restrictions. The trigger is an APR that is 8 points higher than the relevant Treasury rate or a combination of points, fees, and insurance amounting to 8 percent of the loan. After a trigger is set, a detailed disclosure of fees is required, prepayment fees can only be imposed within the first five years, balloon payments are prohibited during the first five years, negative amortization is prohibited, and the lender is prohibited from engaging in a pattern of making loans that are not affordable relative to the income of the borrowers.

Additional Readings

Brueggeman, William B., and Jeffrey B. Fisher. *Real Estate Finance and Investments,* 11th ed. New York: McGraw-Hill Irwin, 2002.

Geltner, David M., and Norman G. Miller. *Commercial Real Estate Analysis and Investments.* Cincinnoti, OH: South-Western Publishing, 2001.

Jennings, Marianne. *Real Estate Law,* 6th ed. Cincinnati, OH: West Legal Studies in Business, a division of Thomson Learning, 2002.

Siedel, George J., III; Robert J. Aalberts; and Janis K. Cheezem. *Real Estate Law,* 5th ed. Cincinnati, OH: West Legal Studies in Business, a division of Thomson Learning, 2003.

Werner, Raymond J. *Real Estate Law,* 11th ed. Cincinnati, OH: South-Western Publishing, 2002.

The Mortgage Bankers Association of America seeks to be a gateway to information about mortgage finance. For information about current regulatory issues, their site is a first choice: http://www.mbaa.org.

chapter eleven

Mortgage Mechanics *and* Calculations

Learning Objectives

After reading this chapter you will be able to:

1. Compute the payment on a loan, and the balance with any number of remaining payments, given the original loan terms: maturity, interest rate, and amount.

2. Compare loan choices using either the lender's yield or the borrower's effective borrowing cost, accounting for the effect of prepayment and the amount of any initial loan fees or loan expenses.

3. State the distinguishing characteristics of an interest-only loan, a partially amortized loan, and an early payment loan.

4. Determine whether a 15-year loan or a 30-year loan is a better financial choice for a borrower, given the borrower's discount rate.

5. Define index, margin, caps and adjustment periods on an adjustable rate mortgage, or ARM, state how the latter two features affect the distribution of interest rate risk between borrower and lender.

6. Compute the required deposit for a buydown mortgage loan.

Introduction

In the previous chapter, we introduced the laws and contracts of mortgages. These are the framework for mortgage creation, or the rules that govern the "game" of mortgage finance. In this chapter we introduce basic analytics of mortgages. We focus on level-payment mortgages since the vast majority of mortgage loans either are, or descend from, a level-payment pattern. It is valuable to know how to find the payment on this type of loan as well as the balance at any time in the life of the loan. Further, it is important to be able to compute the true yield to a lender, the true cost to the borrower, and the value of the debt.

For choices involving mortgage loans, present value is the core criterion. In this chapter we show its application in choosing between different loan maturities. Since adjustable rate mortgages are an important option for borrowers, we also examine the computation of payments and balances for adjustable rate loans. Finally, we consider a sample of more specialized applications of time-value to mortgage computations, including a buydown and a wraparound mortgage loan.

Basic Computations

Five quantitative characteristics of a mortgage are vital to making informed decisions. First, we must know the amount and frequency of the payments involved and, since the vast majority of mortgage loans are paid off early, we must know the *loan balance* at any time as well. Knowing these two benchmark mortgage cash flows enables us to compute three results: the *lender's yield,* the borrower's *effective borrowing cost,* and the present value of the debt. The analytics of a level-payment loan are a straightforward application of the time-value tools presented in Chapter 3. Below, we use the time-value tools to compute these five vital characteristics of a loan.

Payments

Suppose you are a lender being asked for a loan with monthly payments of $1,000 for 30 years, or 360 months. Suppose also that you currently receive interest on similar risk loans of 6 percent, or 0.5 percent per month. As a lender who understands time-value concepts, you know that the amount you will be willing to loan is the present value of the future payments that you expect to receive. Discounting the proposed payments at your opportunity cost of 0.5 percent per month, you calculate the present value, and therefore the maximum loan amount, to be $166,791.61. You can find this result on your calculator as follows:

$166,791.61

Now suppose that another borrower wishes to obtain a similar risk, level-payment loan with a term of 30 years, and in the amount of $166,791.61. (Granted, the borrower is overly precise!) Again, you want an annual interest return of 6 percent on this type of loan. The question is: What payment would you require on this loan? If your answer is $1,000, you are on the way to being a successful lender. You have recognized that this prospective loan is the reverse of our starting example, so the payment you are solving for is the payment we started with in the first place.

This payment-loan relationship generalizes to all fixed-payment loans. The amount of any such loan always is the present value of its future payments, discounted at the loan's interest rate.[1] But since this is so, we always can reverse the logic to find the payment for that loan amount. That is, we simply need to find the regular payment that has a present value equal to the prospective loan amount.

If we did not have calculators and computers "smart enough" to do it for us, we could go about finding the payment as follows: Suppose, for example, we want to find the required monthly payment on a level payment loan of $100,000 for 15 years at an interest rate of 6 percent. First, we can arbitrarily define a convenient payment amount of, say, $100 per month. Then we can find the present value of that payment, repeated for 180 months. Discounting at 6 percent per year (0.5 percent per month), we get a present value of $11,850.35.

---

1. Note that this relationship actually applies to any fixed rate loan, regardless of the payment pattern. That is, the amount of a fixed rate loan always must be the present value of its future payment stream, discounted at the loan's required interest rate. This relationship is the "gate to the kingdom" in analyzing fixed rate loans.

From this, we can construct a "payment factor" per dollar of loan; we simply divide the $100 payment by the resulting loan amount as follows:

Monthly payment factor for 15 years, 6 percent $= \$100 \div \$11,850.35$
$= \$0.084386$

Since this is a somewhat awkward decimal fraction, we can conveniently convert it to payment per thousand dollars of loan by multiplying by 1,000, or:

$1000 \times 0.084383 = \$8.4386$ per $1,000

Simply multiplying this factor by the amount (in thousands of dollars) of a loan with the specified terms gives us the payment for that loan. So, for our example loan, the payment is as follows:

Payment $=$ loan amount in thousands $\times$ monthly payment factor per $1000
$= 100 \times \$8.4386$
$= \$843.86$

With financial calculators we simply key in the four known elements, and it performs the equivalent of these computations instantly:

180	6 ÷ 12	$100,000		0
n	i	PV	PMT	FV
			$843.86	

In general, the calculator solution is a bit more precise because it avoids rounding.

Before computers and calculators were widely available, the loan payment factor was almost universally used to determine payments on a level payment, fixed rate loan. It commonly was known as a **monthly loan constant,** and tables for it abounded in virtually every finance text, and in every mortgage lending office. With modern financial calculators the tables no longer are necessary.

Concept Check

11.2 Find the monthly payment on this loan: $125,000, 15 years, 6.25 percent.

Loan Balance

Finding the **loan balance** also is quite simple, once the logic is clear. Consider the following: We have just used the idea that a loan is the present value of its future payments, discounted at the contract interest rate. This is true at the outset of the loan, but what about after payments have been made? With a bit of thought, you may conclude that it still must be true, and you would be correct!

Here is one way to confirm the point. Consider the 15-year loan in the example above, with a payment of $843.86. The interest charged for the first month is the monthly interest rate times the original balance ($0.005 \times 100,000$), or $500. The remainder of the payment, $343.86, is balance reduction. When this payment is made on the last day of month 1, it also reduces the remaining number of scheduled payments by one, to 179. Discounting 179 monthly payments of $843.86 at their contract interest rate of 6 percent results in a present value of $99,656.14, a reduction of exactly $343.86 from the original loan amount of $100,000. Thus, the present value of the remaining payments is reduced by exactly the amount of the first month's principal payment, making it again equal to the remaining principal balance. Our plot thickens! When each principal payment is made, the present value of the remaining payments decreases by exactly the amount of that principal payment. We leave it to the reader to repeat this experiment for the remaining 179 periods, or until you feel assured that it is true.

We have demonstrated that the balance on a fixed-payment loan always is the present value of the remaining payments, discounted at the loan interest rate. This result makes it easy to find the balance on any fixed-rate loan, at any point in its schedule. Suppose, for example, we want to know the balance at the end of five years (60 months) on the 15-year loan discussed above. All that we need to do is find the present value of the payments remaining at that time. Thus, with 120 months remaining (180 – 60), we can solve as follows:

The present value of $76,009.38 is the balance at the end of the year 5.

Concept Check

11.3 Find the balance on this loan at the end of six years: $125,000, 15 years, 6.25 percent.

Lender's Yield

We have used the idea that the amount of a loan is the present value of its payments, discounted at its contract interest rate. As a working example, suppose we have a loan with payments of $1,000 per month, a term of 360 months, and a contract interest rate of 7 percent. We can determine the loan balance as before:

Thus, we obtain a balance of $150,307.57.

Now we extend this present value relationship. Suppose that we are making this loan, but we charge advance interest, called **discount points,** in an amount ($5,307.57) such that we really only pay out $145,000, net to the borrower. We could then ask, what loan interest rate is this deal equivalent to? That is, if we were to make a new loan, what interest rate would result in $1,000 payments, given an initial balance of $145,000? Notice that we are simply asking what discount rate causes our 360 payments of $1,000 to have a present value of $145,000? Our computation is straightforward.

Recall from Chapter 3 that most calculators and spreadsheets will require either *PV* or *PMT* to be negative. The signs should be consistent with the direction of the cash flow; that is, expenditures negative and incomes positive.[2] The resulting equivalent interest rate is 0.6133 percent per month, although your calculator may show it as an annual rate of 7.36 percent, which is the monthly rate multiplied by 12.

This notion of "equivalent interest rate" usually is referred to as the **lender's yield.** It is the implied discount rate, given all of the cash flows for the loan. Note that lender's yield is an application of the internal rate of return (*IRR*) discussed in Chapter 3.

Concept Check

11.4   Find the lender's yield for this loan: $125,000, 15 years, 6.25 percent, lender "points" and origination fee: $2,500. Assume no prepayment.

Effective Borrowing Cost (EBC)

Closely related to lender's yield is the **effective borrowing cost (EBC).** Mathematically, EBC does not differ from the lender's yield, and is computed exactly the same way (it also is an *IRR*). The difference is in the cash flows used. Normally, when a mortgage loan is created, the borrower must pay certain expenses, but these are not income to the lender. These include **closing costs,** discussed below, such as title insurance, mortgage insurance, recording fees and taxes, an appraisal, and a survey. Since the borrower pays these costs but the lender does not receive all of them as income, the lender's cash flows from the loan are not the same as what the borrower pays out. EBC is simply the implied discount rate (yield) from the borrower's perspective. For example, suppose our original 7 percent loan has closing expenses of $8,000 ($5,307.57 in points, plus $2,692.43 in other closing expenses), then the borrower will receive $150,307.57 *less* $8,000, for net loan proceeds of $142,307.57, after paying the expenses. We can find the implied discount rate for these cash flows as follows:

7.55%

The solution is 7.55 percent, which is greater than the lender's yield.

APR: A Special Application of EBC. An important special application of EBC is the **annual percentage rate (APR)** which is required by the *Truth-in-Lending Act (TILA)* to be reported on virtually all home mortgage loans. The APR is computed under the assumption of no prepayment; that is, it is a yield to maturity. The items that must be accounted for as up-front expenses are governed by Federal Reserve Regulation Z, and are rather detailed. In brief, they include the following:

- All finance charges in connection with the loan, including discount points and origination fees, underwriting fee, loan processing fee or document preparation fee, and required mortgage insurance.
- All compensation to originating brokers.

---

2. A more analytically precise reason for the sign requirement is that you are solving the following equation for i:

$$0 = PV + Pmt \sum_{j=1}^{n} \frac{1}{(1+i)^j} + \frac{FV}{(1+i)^n}$$

Note that the equation requires at least one of the cash flows to be negative, and at least one to be positive.

Industry Issues

11-1

What Does APR Really Tell You?

n 1968, when Congress enacted the Consumer Credit Protection Act, it took a big step toward rescuing consumer credit contracts from the jungles of confusion and deception. Better known as the Truth-in-Lending Act, this law created, among other things, the annual percentage rate (APR) which was to enable consumers to compare interest charge apples to interest charge apples. APR has become part of the consumer language. But how far out of the jungle has APR really brought us? Well, most of the way. It turns out that there are more aspects to credit costs than APR accounts for. And this problem is by far the most significant in the biggest of all consumer purchases, a home. First, APR requires a lender to account for all finance charges . . . or does it? The way the implementing regulation, Federal Reserve Regulation Z, is written, some significant charges typically don't count. These can include appraisal fees, lender's title insurance, a survey, and state taxes on the mortgage. As long as these charges are from a source that is neither related to the lender nor stipulated as the source by the lender, they are left in the jungle. So, the APR computation never accounts for them. Worse, if they vary between loans, any chance to account for them in the comparison is lost. Finally, even if APR is computed correctly, it still has a built-in bias. APR is a yield to maturity, whereas virtually no home loan is outstanding until maturity. And as the loan is paid off earlier in its life, the effect of front-end finance charges upon the true cost of financing is much greater. So APR systematically understates the importance of front-end finance fees in the true cost of home mortgage debt. Homebuyers beware, at least a little bit!

www.federalreserve. gov/regulations/regref. htm#z

A peek at Federal Reserve Regulation Z, itself. Click on the top arrow. Then browse, for example, in the pdf/text files on finance charges, right of rescission, and determination of the APR.

- Other charges if the lender receives direct or indirect compensation in connection with the charge, if the charge is paid to an affiliate of the lender, or if the lender stipulates who is to provide the service. (Typically, this *excludes* items such as the appraisal fee, survey fee, state tax on the mortgage, possibly a lender's title insurance, and borrower's legal fees.)
- Premiums for required credit life, accident, health, or loss-of-income insurance or for debt cancellation coverage.

While the annual percentage rate can be thought of as approximating the true effective borrowing cost, there are two potentially important differences. (See Industry Issues 11-1.) First, the expense items required to be included, though extensive, may still omit a few significant ones for a particular case. Second, APR always is based on the assumption of no prepayment.

Concept Check

11.5   Find the EBC for this loan: $125,000, 15 years, 6.25 percent, lender "points" and origination fee: $2,500, plus other up-front costs of $3,500. Assume no prepayment.

Prepayment, Lender's Yield, and Effective Borrowing Cost.   We will consider one more example of both lender's yield and effective borrowing cost (EBC), incorporating prepayment. A home mortgage loan rarely survives to maturity. Homeowners move, or they wish to draw accumulated equity from their homes from time to time for other uses, or they simply wish to take advantage of better interest rates; for all these reasons they replace their current mortgage loan. Therefore we want to be able to determine the effective borrowing cost with the loan prepaid at some point in the future. Suppose that our example loan is expected to be paid off early, at the end of seven years. What does this do to the lender's yield and the EBC? The balance at the end of seven years, the present value of the remaining 276 payments, is $137,001.46. So, if a lender acquires this loan for a net disbursement of $145,000, the computation of lender's yield would be:

7.68%

with a resulting yield of 7.68 percent. By contrast, if the borrower received net loan proceeds of $142,307.57, the EBC would be as follows:

8.03%

with a resulting EBC of 8.03. In general, whenever a lender charges "up-front" points on a loan, the earlier the loan is paid off, the higher is the lender's yield. For the same reason, since a borrower virtually always encounters up-front expenses in obtaining a mortgage loan, the earlier the borrower pays off the loan, the higher is the EBC.

Concept Check

11.6 What assumption about prepayment is made in computing the annual percentage rate (APR)?

Up-front Costs, Holding Period, and Effective Borrowing Cost

Since almost every mortgage loan is paid off before it is fully amortized, the computation of EBC with prepayment deserves more attention. Clearly the EBC depends on two aspects of the prepayment scenario: how large the up-front financing costs are and how long until the loan is prepaid (holding period). Before exploring the effect on EBC, as these two factors vary, we focus on the several elements of up-front financing costs.

Up-front Financing Costs. Lenders charge discount points to increase the yield on a loan. But there are other up-front fees as well. In addition to discount points, home borrowers often pay a loan origination fee equal to 1 percent of the loan amount. Other borrower costs usually include loan application and document preparation fees ($200–$700), the cost of having the property appraised ($250–$400), credit check fee ($35–$75), title insurance (0.5 percent–1.0 percent of the loan amount), mortgage insurance (over 2 percent of the loan amount if purchased with a single advanced premium), charges to transfer the deed and record the mortgage ($40–$200), survey costs ($200–$300), pest inspection ($25–$75), and attorneys' fees. (Mortgage insurance is discussed in Chapter 12.) Though many of these fees will occur with any mortgage loan, discount points and other terms can vary. Therefore, borrowers should shop around and compare more than just contract interest rates.

Multiple EBC Scenarios. To consider the effect of up-front financing costs on the effective (or true) cost of borrowing, consider an 8.50 percent, 30-year, $100,000 level-payment mortgage with a monthly payment of $768.91. Assume up-front financing costs, including all costs except discount points, equal $2,000. Exhibit 11-1 displays the effective borrowing cost for different combinations of discount points and number of years the loan remains outstanding. If there are no discount points and the borrower

Exhibit 11-1 Effective Borrowing Cost with Different Numbers of Discount Points and Years Outstanding*

Discount Points	Number of Years Loan Is Outstanding					
	2 Yrs.	4 Yrs.	6 Yrs.	8 Yrs.	10 Yrs.	30 Yrs.
0.00	9.61%	9.11%	8.94%	8.86%	8.81%	8.72%
0.50	9.89	9.26	9.05	8.95	8.89	8.78
1.00	10.18	9.42	9.17	9.05	8.97	8.83
1.50	10.46	9.57	9.28	9.14	9.06	8.89
2.00	10.75	9.73	9.40	9.23	9.14	8.95
2.50	11.04	9.89	9.51	9.33	9.22	9.01

*30-year fixed payment mortgage with contract rate of 8.5 percent and other up-front financing costs of $2,000.

repays the loan after two years, the effective borrowing cost is 9.61 percent. The calculator keystrokes are:

24		$98,000	−$768.91	−$98,421
n	**i**	**PV**	**PMT**	**FV**

9.61%

The EBC of 9.61 percent is greater than the 8.50 percent contract rate because of the $2,000 in total up-front financing costs.

Adding discount points to the $2,000 in other up-front costs increases the EBC because it decreases the net loan proceeds *without* altering the scheduled monthly payment or remaining loan balances. One discount point (equal to $1,000 on a $100,000 loan) decreases the net loan proceeds to $97,000 and increases the EBC to 10.18 percent with a two-year holding period. The payment of 2 1/2 discount points would increase the EBC to 11.04 percent. The effect of up-front financing costs on the EBC decreases as the holding period increases. For example, with 2 1/2 discount points the EBC decreases from 11.04 percent with a two-year holding period to 9.22 percent if the loan remains outstanding for 10 years. As the holding period increases toward 30 years, the EBC will approach, but not equal, the contract interest rate of 8.5 percent.

Concept Check

11.7 Find the lender's yield for this loan: $125,000, 15 years, 6.25 percent, lender "points" and origination fee: $2,500. (Assume prepayment after four years.)

Implications for Borrowers. Borrowers who *expect* they may have to move relatively soon should choose to pay few or no discount points and a slightly higher contract interest rate. Conversely, borrowers who expect to keep the loan outstanding for a long period of time should consider paying discount points to *buy down* the interest rate. Why? The monthly savings from paying the discount points to reduce the contract rate will be greater the longer the loan remains outstanding. Note that because the length of time the loan will be outstanding is uncertain, the effective or true cost of each mortgage option can only be estimated at the time of origination.

The last column in Exhibit 11-1 is the EBC with no prepayment (i.e., to maturity). Note that this, approximately, is APR. Thus, the table reveals how much error can result through comparing APRs between loans when the borrower expects to have the loan for just a few years. EBC is much more sensitive to up-front costs for short holding periods, so "buying down" the contract interest rate through points is much more costly to the borrower for short holding periods.

Concept Check

11.8 Find the EBC for this loan: $125,000, 15 years, 6.25 percent, lender points and origination fee: $2,500, plus other up-front costs of $3,500. Assume prepayment at the end of four years.

Some Final Notes on Estimating Closing Costs. Under the Real Estate Settlement and Procedures Act (RESPA), discussed in Chapter 10, an estimate of closing costs is required to be furnished by the lender for virtually every standard home loan application.[3] However, as discussed in more detail in Chapter 20, the estimated closing expenses include both the cost of acquiring legal ownership of the property and the costs of obtaining the mortgage financing, if applicable. For the purposes of estimating EBC, only those up-front expenses associated with obtaining the mortgage funds should be included (e.g., discount points, loan origination fees, credit report, appraisal fee). In particular, those settlement costs associated with obtaining ownership of the property (e.g., buyer's title insurance, if required, and attorney fees) should not be included in the EBC calculation. A simple test should be applied to estimated closing expenses: If the expense would be incurred even if no mortgage financing were obtained, it is an expense associated with obtaining ownership and should not be included in the EBC calculation.

www.hud.gov/offices/ hsg/sfh/res/respa_hm. cfm

All about RESPA from HUD's mouth.

Concept Check

11.9 Name an up-front expense in purchasing a home that would *not* be used in computing EBC for the loan involved.

Fixed-Rate Mortgages

When a loan's interest rate is fixed, time-value tools can illuminate numerous loan decisions through the application of present value. Below we demonstrate this by applying present value to the choice of loan term. In Chapter 12, we will show the application of present value to other mortgage loan decisions.

Level-Payment, Fully Amortized Mortgages

Single-family mortgages can take any form negotiated between a borrower and a lender, as noted in Chapter 10. Historically, however, the most common form has been a fixed-rate, level-payment, fully amortized mortgage. Fully amortizing mortgages are paid off completely by periodic (virtually always monthly) payments. At maturity, the loan balance is zero. The majority of single-family residential loans are of this type. As the loan is amortized, the owner's equity interest grows, so long as the property value does not decline.

---

3. Commercial loans are not covered by RESPA. Residential mortgage loans are defined as those issued to finance the acquisition of one- to four-family homes, condominiums, and cooperatives.

When fully amortizing loans call for equal periodic payments they are known as **level-payment mortgages (LPMs).** (A display of typical level-payment principal and interest payments appears in Exhibit 10-2.) Before adjustable rate mortgages were introduced, the dominance of LPMs in the home loan market was unchallenged. With adjustable rate mortgages (discussed later), monthly payments can change as interest rates vary, although the loans remain fully amortizing.

The Choice of Loan Term: A Question of Present Value

The most common loan term on an LPM is 30 years. However, 15-year mortgages have increased in popularity, 40-year mortgages are available from some lenders, and other maturities are always possible. There is an illusion in shorter home mortgages. With a 15-year loan, the borrower pays substantially less interest over the life of the loan than with a 30-year loan. For example, consider a $90,000 LPM with an annual interest rate of 9 percent. With 30-year amortization, the monthly payment is $724.16; with 15-year amortization, the payment is $912.84. As calculated in Exhibit 11-2, total interest paid over the life of the 30-year and 15-year mortgages would be $170,698 and $74,311, respectively.

At first glance, the 15-year mortgage appears to provide an interest saving equal to $96,387 ($170,698 − $74,311). But does this make the 15-year loan better, as is often asserted? Note that this saving is stretched over a very long time, and therefore cannot be worth its "face" amount (undiscounted value). Instead of comparing the accumulated interest of the loans, our understanding of time-value compels us to compare their *present values.* To reinforce this idea, remember, if we have money in hand now, we can put it to use at some productive return (even if this is simply to eliminate existing debt and interest costs). By this reasoning, money received later is less valuable due to lost use, but payments deferred are better because we retain use of the payment money for a longer time. Since all of these points are captured in the concept of present value, the relevant question between the 15-year and 30-loan is: which has the smaller present value? The answer may not be obvious.

To compare the present values of the two loans, we need a discount rate. Recall that the discount rate represents our opportunity cost, that is, the return that we can get on money available to use now. One use of available money is to lessen the amount of debt we owe, thereby escaping future interest payments. In this case, our opportunity cost equals the interest rate on the payments that we escape. But what result do we get in comparing the present values of the two example loans above, discounted at their interest rate of 9 percent? Do we really need to calculate to get the answer? Recall that both loans were originated at 9 percent. We know that the balance on a loan is the present value of its payments, discounted at the loan interest rate. Thus, discounting both loans at their contract interest rate of 9 percent will simply confirm that each loan is worth its original balance of $90,000. In present value, our true measure of value, the loans are equivalent, regardless of the difference in total interest charges. Because the greater interest charges on the 30-year loan come much later in time, their present value is reduced to the point that it is equal to the present value of the 15-year loan. As a result, we are indifferent between the two loans.

Exhibit 11-2   Total Interest Paid on 9 Percent LPM of $90,000

	30-Year	15-Year
Monthly payment	$ 724.16	$ 912.84
Total payments (loan term × monthly payment)	260,698	164,311
Minus: Principal amortization	90,000	90,000
Equals: Total interest	$170,698	$ 74,311

Concept Check

11.10 Under financially unconstrained circumstances, which of these fixed-rate mortgage loans would a borrower prefer, and why? 15-year, 7 percent. 30-year, 7 percent. Explain your answer.

Two changes can make this comparison more challenging. First, 15-year mortgages typically are offered at a lower interest rate than 30-year mortgages. How does this affect the choice? Note that the logic we use remains the same.[4] That is, whichever loan we consider, an alternative use of available money is to lessen the amount of debt contemplated, thereby "earning" interest cost savings at the rate charged on the loan. Thus, the appropriate discount rate for each loan is its own interest rate. The result will be that each loan again has a present value equal to its principal amount. For example, if we are considering two $90,000 loans, with the 30-year loan at 9.0 percent and the 15-year loan at 8.5 percent, then we would discount the 30-year loan at 9.0 percent and the 15-year loan at 8.5 percent. The result is that each loan still would have a present value of $90,000.[5]

Concept Check

11.11 Under financially unconstrained circumstances, assuming that the difference in interest rates result purely from the difference in loan maturity, which of these fixed-rate mortgage loans would a borrower prefer, and why? 15-year, 7 percent; 30-year, 7.4 percent. Explain your answer.

This comparison begins to differ, however, if borrowers are financially constrained. For example, most young households tend to be financially illiquid and have many potential high-return uses for additional cash. They may need to reduce credit card debt, to acquire a car that works, or to buy clothing for children. If the household cannot borrow all that it needs at the mortgage loan interest rate, then its opportunity cost (i.e., discount rate) is higher than the mortgage interest rate. It is likely to be somewhere between the mortgage rate and the rate that the household is willing to pay for large credit card balances. Suppose, for example, that the household contemplating the two loans above has large credit card balances at an interest rate of 15 percent. Then any cash not going to mortgage loan payments could earn at least 15 percent by reducing the credit card balances, thereby avoiding interest costs. Thus, the household should compare the present value of the two loans with both discounted at 15 percent. The payment on the 30-year, 9.0 percent loan is $724.16 while the payment on the 15-year, 8.5 percent loan is $886.27. The resulting computations for the two loans are as follows:

30-Year Loan

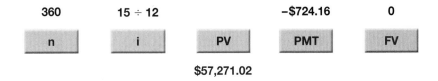

360	15 ÷ 12		−$724.16	0
n	i	PV	PMT	FV

$57,271.02

---

4. We assume that both loans are competitively priced; that is, they have competitive interest rates for their terms and risk.

5. Students of finance will recognize that the difference in interest rates between the 15-year and 30-year loans correspond to different maturities or durations on a yield curve. It follows that the two loans should be valued or discounted at different, appropriate rates from the yield curve.

15-Year Loan

	180	15 ÷ 12		–$886.27	0
	n	i	PV	PMT	FV

$63,323.68

The present value of the 15-year loan is $63,323.68, while the present value of the 30-year loan is $57,271.02, meaning that the longer loan is decidedly more favorable. In general, when the opportunity cost of the household is substantially greater than the mortgage interest rate, the household will be financially better off with longer-term mortgage debt.

Concept Check

11.12 Under financially constrained circumstances whereby the borrower is paying 15 percent on large credit card balances, which of these fixed-rate mortgage loans would the borrower prefer, and why? 15-year, 7 percent; 30-year, 7.40 percent. (Note that the amount of the loan does not matter in this problem, only the terms. Thus, you can pick any convenient amount to examine.) Explain your answer.

How popular are 15-year mortgages? In 2002 about 15 percent of conventional single-family mortgage originations were 15-year mortgages. (Conventional loans are the largest single class of home mortgage loans. They are discussed in Chapter 12.) Inspection of Exhibit 11-3 reveals that, except for 1992, this percentage has remained in the 9 to 12 percent range during the 1990s. Casual evidence indicates that 15-year mortgages are more popular among mature households than among younger and first-time homebuyers that are likely to be financially constrained. Also, the use of 15-year mortgages is decidedly more pronounced among homeowners who are refinancing. According to a 1999 survey conducted by Freddie Mac, 31 percent of refinancing borrowers originally holding 30-year LPMs decided to refinance into 15-year loans. Of borrowers refinancing 15-year LPMs, 67 percent opted to stay with the same product.

Alternative Amortization Schedules

Numerous alternatives to a fully amortizing loan can be available, as noted in Chapter 10. For example, borrowers may arrange to pay only interest over the life of the loan, and to then pay off the loan completely in one repayment of principal at maturity. Alternatively, borrowers may partially amortize the loan and then pay a large lump-sum payment at maturity. In addition, borrowers may select, for example, a 30-year fully amortizing loan, and then make additional payments to reduce principal more quickly than scheduled. These alternative patterns of amortization identify loans as *interest-only mortgages, partially amortized mortgages,* or *early payment mortgages,* respectively.

Exhibit 11-3 Percentage Share of Conventional Single-Family Mortgage Market by Product and Year

Loan Product	1990	1992	1994	1996	1998	1999	2000	2001	2002
30-year fixed-rate	51%	53%	45%	56%	73%	66%	66%	71%	64%
15-year fixed-rate	12	17	10	12	12	9	7	13	15
ARMs	28	20	39	27	12	21	24	12	17
Balloons/other	9	10	6	5	3	4	3	4	4
Total	100%	100%	100%	100%	100%	100%	100%	100%	100%

Source: Federal Housing Finance Board. www.fhfb.com

Industry Issues

Fannie Mae's Argument on the Merits of a 15-Year Mortgage

The following statement is quoted directly from the website of Fannie Mae, June 14, 2003. In what respects do you agree, and in what respects do you disagree, with these arguments for a 15-year mortgage?

Fifteen-Year Fixed-Rate Mortgage

You pay off a 15-year fixed-rate mortgage in half the time it would take you to pay off the traditional 30-year fixed-rate mortgage. This shorter term makes it possible for you to build up equity in your home faster, which can let you move up more quickly to a more expensive home or save more in preparation for retirement or a child's education. This loan is particularly attractive if you're refinancing your mortgage because you can

Source: www.fanniemae.com/homebuyers/findamortgage/mortgages Select "By product type," then "fixed rate," then "15 year."

shorten your loan term plus enjoy a lower interest rate. Fifteen-year mortgages are usually offered at interest rates lower than those available with 30-year mortgages. However, higher monthly payments may make it more difficult to qualify for the 15-year fixed-rate mortgage compared to the 30-year fixed-rate mortgage.

Key Features

- A 15-year mortgage offers a lower interest rate than a 30- or 20-year mortgage. This saves you a significant amount of interest over the life of the loan. For example, with a $100,000 loan at 8.25 percent interest, the 15-year mortgage will save you $95,000 in interest payments over the life of your loan, compared to the same mortgage amount for a 30-year term. However, monthly mortgage payments will be higher.
- The shorter-term allows you to own your home outright sooner.

Interest-Only (Straight-Term) Mortgages. **Interest-only mortgages** are repaid in full with one payment on maturity of the loan. During the life of the loan, however, borrowers make interest payments periodically (e.g., monthly). For example, assume the borrower and lender agree to a $90,000, seven-year, interest-only loan at 6 percent. The monthly payment is $450.00 ($0.06 \div 12 \times \$90,000$). If the loan were to be fully amortized over 30 years, the monthly payment would equal $539.60. The $89.60 difference is principal amortization. Unlike the amortizing mortgage, the loan balance on the interest-only loan would remain constant at $90,000.

Interest-only loans are seldom used to finance single-family homes, but they are often used in commercial real estate financing and in land transactions. Typically, developers purchase land with interest-only loans, expecting to be able to repay the loans after the development and sale of lots.

Partially Amortizing Mortgages. *Partially amortizing mortgage loans* require periodic payments of principal, as well as interest, but they are not paid off completely over the loan's term to maturity. Instead, as noted in Chapter 10, the loan has a separate term for amortization, longer than the term to maturity. The balance at maturity is called a balloon and is satisfied with a *balloon payment*. For example, assume the $90,000, 9 percent loan would be amortized over 30 years, but the term to maturity is 7 years. The monthly payment is, again, $724.16. However, the remaining mortgage balance at the end of year 7 would equal $84,276. The borrower at that time must either (1) negotiate a new $84,276 loan with the original lender at current rates, (2) negotiate a loan with a new lender and use the proceeds to pay off the original lender, or (3) sell the property and use the sale proceeds to pay off the original lender.

Partially amortized loans are not often used to finance home purchases. Still, in recent years, a "borrower friendly" form has been fostered by the influence of Freddie Mac and Fannie Mae.[6] Qualifying loans must be first mortgages, with 5- or 7-year terms, and an option for

---

6. Both Freddie Mac and Fannie Mae established programs to purchase balloon loans that fit their prespecified terms.

the borrower to refinance for the remainder of a 30-year term. A balloon loan also may be used where the seller of the home is providing some or all of the mortgage financing (i.e., in "seller-financed" deals). The partial amortization keeps the borrower's payments at a fully amortized level, but lessens the lender's interest rate risk and default risk associated with the longer term.[7]

Concept Check

11.13 Find the balloon payment on this mortgage loan: $100,000, 6.5 percent, 30-year amortization, but 7-year term to maturity.

Early Payment Mortgages. An **early payment mortgage (EPM)** results if principal payments exceed the schedule of principal payments for an LPM. Lenders have offered numerous EPM plans. One example, sometimes called a "growing equity mortgage," begins with the standard, 30-year level payment, but increases the payment by 4 percent each year. Since all of the increases go to principal reduction, interest charges diminish faster, requiring less of the payment. The result is that the loan pays off in less than 15 years.[8]

Almost any first mortgage home loan can become an EPM if the borrower chooses to make regular supplemental principal payments. As discussed in Chapter 10, most "prime" home loans give the borrower the right to prepay, in whole or in part, with only some "subprime" loans and large prime loans limiting prepayment.

Despite the freedom to pay down a loan early, it may not be financially wise for a borrower to do so. The primary decision criterion in this case is the same one used to evaluate the desirability of a 15-year loan relative to a 30-year loan. If borrowers can invest the prospective prepayment amount in an alternate use at a higher risk adjusted return than the interest rate on the loan (e.g., by paying off expensive credit card debt), they would be ahead financially to elect the alternate use and not pay down the home loan.

Adjustable Rate Mortgages

The most popular alternative to a level-payment mortgage in the home loan market is the *adjustable rate mortgage (ARM).* While the share of home borrowers electing ARM loans over LPMs is quite volatile, in recent years it typically has exceeded 20 percent, as shown in Exhibit 11-3.

The Mechanics of Adjustable Rate Mortgages

The interest rate on ARMs originated in the United States must be tied to a published index of interest rates that is beyond the control of the lender. As discussed extensively in Chapter 10, the most common indexes are averages of U.S. Treasury rates and an average cost of funds for thrift institutions. At a predetermined *change date,* the loan interest rate will fall or rise as the index falls or rises.

When the ARM market first began to develop in the early 1980s in response to high and volatile interest rates, lenders and borrowers experimented with numerous ARM designs. Between 400 and 500 different types of ARM products were being offered in early 1984.[9] Over time, the terms of ARMs have become more uniform. One of the most popular is a one-year ARM based on a 30-year amortization. With a one-year ARM, the initial contract rate remains in effect for one year and adjusts annually thereafter.

---

7. *Interest rate risk* is the risk that a fixed-income asset will decrease in value due to a rise in market interest rates, or, equivalently, that the investor experiences a below-market yield.

8. The exact maturity depends on the contract interest rate.

9. Jack M. Guttentag, "Recent Changes in the Primary Mortgage Market," *Housing Finance Review* (July 1984), pp. 221–55.

Example 11-1 Example without Caps

Consider a $100,000 ARM with a 30-year amortization schedule. The adjustment period is one year, the *index rate* is the one-year Treasury Constant Maturity rate (See Chapter 10), and the *margin* is 2.75 percentage points (275 basis points). Also assume that the current rate on the one-year Treasury securities is 3.25 percent—which would seem to imply a 6.00 percent interest rate (3.25 + 2.75). However, the first-year contract interest rate is a *teaser rate,* discounted to 4.50 percent.

The first three years of the loan are summarized in Exhibit 11-4. The monthly payment in year 1, by our standard method of computation, is $506.69 and the remaining mortgage balance at the end of year 1 is $98,386.77. If the interest rate on one-year Treasury securities is still 3.25 percent at the end of year 1, the contract interest rate in year 2 will equal the one-year Treasury rate plus the margin, or

$$= 3.25\% + 2.75\%$$
$$= 6.00\%$$

Thus, the monthly payment in year 2 will equal $597.21.[10]

Note that even though the Treasury index rate remained unchanged at 3.25 percent, the contract rate increased 1.50 percentage points to 6.00 percent on the first change date. In the third year the index rises from 3.25% to 3.50 percent. Thus the Treasury index plus margin increases accordingly, or

$$= 3.50\% + 2.75\%$$
$$= 6.25\%$$

This results in a new payment of $612.61 for year 3, based on a beginning balance of $97,088.11.

Exhibit 11-4 Adjustable Rate Loan with Teaser but No Caps: Interest Rates and Payments

Loan Assumptions
   Initial amount: $100,000   Caps: None
   Term: 30 years (360 months)
   Margin: 2.75% (275 basis points)

	Year		
	1	**2**	**3**
Index	3.25%	3.25%	3.50%
Teaser rate	4.50%		
Interest rate	4.5%	(3.25 + 2.75) 6.00%*	(3.50 + 2.75) 6.25%*
Beginning balance	$100,000	$98,386.77	$97,088.11
Months remaining	360	348	336
Monthly payment	$506.69	$597.21	$612.61

*Interest rate equals (index + margin) after year 1.

10. The calculator keystrokes are: $N = 348$; $I = 6.00 \div 12$; $PV = \$98,386.77$; $PMT = ?$; and $FV = 0$.

Concept Check

11.14   Given the following information for a 30-year $75,000 uncapped ARM loan, find the balance at the end of year two: Margin, 2.75 percent, index for year 1, 2.50 percent; Index for year 2, 2.75 percent; teaser, 4.00 percent.

Initial Adjustment Periods, Rate Caps, and Other Options

Despite the popularity of the one-year ARM, a growing borrower preference for longer initial **adjustment periods** has led to some additional choices in recent years. According to a recent survey by Freddie Mac, 80 percent of lenders also offered the three-year–one-year ARM in addition to the standard one-year product. With a three-year–one-year ARM, the interest rate is fixed for three years and then adjusts annually thereafter. The survey also revealed that 76 percent of lenders offered a five-year–one-year ARM, 63 percent offered a seven-year–one-year ARM, and 56 percent made available a ten-year–one-year product. The longer-term alternatives allow ARM borrowers to defer the first adjustment for 3, 5, 7, or 10 years, respectively, before the payments start to reflect changes in the index to which the loan interest rate is tied.

Because ARM borrowers and lenders share the interest rate risk, ARM interest rates are typically lower than those on fixed-rate loans. However, the less interest rate risk the borrower assumes, the higher the interest rate charged during the initial adjustment period. Thus, three-year–one-year ARMs have higher initial rates than standard one-year ARMs, five-year–one-year ARMs have higher rates than three-year–one-year ARMs, and so on. Exhibit 11-5 displays the ARM share of conventional originations from 1985 through 2002. Over this time period, the ARM share has varied from 12 to 58 percent, and it has been highly positively correlated with both the *level* of rates on 30-year LPMs and with the

Exhibit 11-5   Mortgage Rates and ARM Share of Conventional Originations

Year	Average Rate 30-Year Mortgages*	Average Rate 1-Year ARMs[†]	30-Year Rate Less 1-Year Rate	ARM Market Share
1985	12.4%	10.0%	2.4%	51%
1986	10.2	8.4	1.8	30
1987	10.2	7.8	2.4	43
1988	10.3	7.9	2.4	58
1989	10.3	8.8	1.5	38
1990	10.1	8.4	1.8	28
1991	9.3	7.1	2.2	23
1992	8.4	5.6	2.8	20
1993	7.3	4.6	2.7	20
1994	8.4	5.3	3.0	39
1995	7.9	6.1	1.9	33
1996	7.8	5.7	2.1	27
1997	7.6	5.6	2.0	22
1998	6.9	5.6	1.3	12
1999	7.4	6.0	1.4	21
2000	8.3	7.0	1.3	24
2001	7.1	5.8	1.3	12
2002	6.8	4.6	2.2	17

*Federal Housing Finance Board, Monthly Interest Rate Survey. www.fhfb.gov
[†]Freddie Mac Primary Mortgage Market Survey. www.freddiemac.com/pmms/

"spread" between 30-year rates and ARM rates. The pattern suggests that home borrowers will pay a substantial price for reduction of interest rate uncertainty, and are more willing to pay this spread as all interest rates are lower.

As noted in Chapter 10, ARM loans often have both an annual *periodic cap* and an *overall cap.* Assume our example one-year ARM has a 1 percent annual adjustment cap and a 5 percent overall cap. Exhibit 11-6 shows interest rates, payments, and beginning balances for the first three years. We assume again that the yield on one-year Treasury securities at the end of year 1 remains unchanged at 3.25 percent. Then the contract rate in year 2 again would be 6 percent in the absence of an annual cap (3.25 + 2.75). But in our example it is constrained by the annual cap to move no more than 1.00 percent (100 basis points). Thus the resulting rate is less:

$$= 4.50\% + 1.00\%$$
$$= 5.50\%$$

This results in a payment of $566.26 for year 2.

It is important to note that not every loan will result in an interest rate of 5.5 percent in this situation. Whether the rate change from the first year to the second is constrained by the periodic cap depends on how the note is written. The question is whether the cap applies to the teaser rate, or whether it applies only to the index plus margin. Notes have been written with both arrangements.

In the third year, the interest rate is determined in the manner that will apply in all subsequent years. The rate change is the lesser of the change in the index or the periodic cap limit. Thus, for our loan, the change is the lesser of 1 percent or the index change. Normally, the cap applies for both positive and negative changes, although this again can depend on how the note is written. For year 3 in our example the index change is 0.25 percent (25 basis points). Since this is less than the periodic cap, the interest rate rises to 6.25 percent on

Exhibit 11-6 Adjustable Rate Loan with Teaser Rate and Caps: Interest Rates and Payments

Loan Assumptions			
Initial amount: $100,000		Caps: None	
Term: 30 years (360 months)		Periodic (annual): 1.00%	
Margin: 2.75% (275 basis points)		Overall: 5.00%	

		Year		
		1	**2**	**3**
Index		3.25%	3.25%	3.50%
Teaser rate		4.50%		
Interest rate		4.50%	Lesser of: (3.25 + 2.75) or (4.50 + 1.00) 5.50%*	Lesser of: (3.50 + 2.75) or (5.50 + 1.00) 6.25%*
Beginning balance		$100,000	$98,386.77	$97,976.54
Months remaining		360	348	336
Monthly payment		$506.69	$566.26	$611.85

Overall maximum interest rate: 9.50% (4.50 + 5.00)

*Assumes that periodic cap applies to any initial interest rate, including "teaser" rate.

the change date for year 3. This results in a new payment of $611.85, based on a beginning-of-the-year balance of $96,967.54.

The use of rate caps in an ARM loan shifts the risk between borrower and lender. If interest rates rise in an LPM, the borrower's payments are unaffected, while the value of the lender's asset (the loan) falls.[11] If interest rates rise in an unconstrained ARM, so does the borrower's payment, leaving the value of the lender's asset unaffected. Thus, the LPM places all the interest rate risk of the loan on the lender and none on the borrower, while an unconstrained ARM does just the opposite. Caps, on the other hand, reallocate interest rate risk someplace between these extremes.

This shift of interest rate risk back to the lender is a cost to the lender. How do lenders balance the pricing of ARMs with rate caps relative to ARMs without such caps? They must in some fashion increase the *expected* return on the ARM with caps. Thus, borrowers who choose ARMs with rate caps can expect a higher initial contract interest rate, a higher margin, more up-front financing costs, or some combination of the three.

Many have observed that in this interest rate risk tug-of-war between borrower and lender, the lender has more knowledge and alternatives in managing interest rate risk than most households have. This suggests that an efficient market solution in designing home loans would place more of the interest rate risk with the lender. From this view, it is not surprising that most households still strongly prefer LPMs and, if they have an ARM, they want it with caps.

The recent ARM innovations discussed earlier, such as the three year-one year ARM, five year-one year ARM and so forth, are a creative truce in the interest rate risk tug-of-war. They allow a borrower to select an ARM where the payment is fixed for approximately the amount of time that the borrower will have the loan. For example, a borrower who expects to move or refinance within five years can select a five year-one year ARM, and their payment may never change before paying off the loan. Thus, the borrower is paying for only the protection against interest rate risk that is valuable to them, while the lender's interest rate risk is much less than with a standard LPM.

It should be apparent that ARMs contain a wide variety of features and provisions. When comparing a particular ARM to a fixed-payment mortgage or to other ARMs, a borrower should calculate the payments and effective borrowing cost (EBC) of the ARM under several different assumptions about changes in the index interest rate. Lenders disclose the payments that would occur if the interest rate increases to the limit of the caps. The borrower must then determine whether the resulting payment is tolerable and whether it is ever likely to occur. This suggests that "ARM wrestling" requires the consideration and comparison of all of the following:

- Initial interest rates.
- Initial adjustment period.
- Margins.
- Adjustment rate caps.
- Overall caps.
- Discount points.
- Other up-front financing costs.

Concept Check

11.15   Given the following information for a 30-year, $75,000 capped ARM loan, find the interest rate and ending balance for year 2: Margin, 2.75 percent, index for year 1, 2.50 percent; Index for year 2, 2.75 percent; teaser, 4.00 percent; periodic cap, 1.00 percent, overall cap, 5.00 percent. Assume that the cap applies to the teaser rate.

---

11. The market now discounts the loan's payment stream at a higher discount rate.

Exhibit 11-7   Interest Rate Buydown

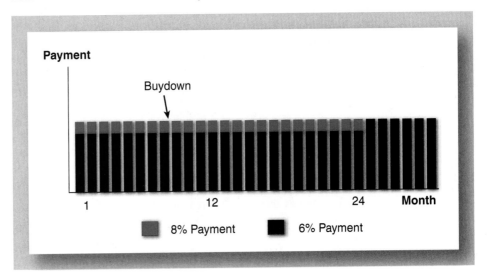

Other Mortgage Types and Uses

The variety of ways that time-value tools apply to mortgages is virtually limitless. As two further important examples we examine buydowns, and wraparound loans.

Interest Rate Buydown

A **buydown mortgage** is a normal LPM in which the early payments are partially paid out of a lump sum deposit made at the time of origination. A common use of this arrangement is by a builder who prefers to make a concession to a buyer through the mortgage financing of a house, rather than by lowering its price. For example, if the market mortgage rate is 8 percent, a builder might want to "buy down" the first 24 payments to be equivalent to payments on a 6 percent loan. The arrangement to be worked out with a cooperating lender is suggested in Exhibit 11-7. The builder can make a deposit with the lender equal to the present value of the 24 payment reductions. Then, at each payment date the "shortfall" between the 8 percent actual payment amount and the 6 percent artificial payment amount is covered with funds from the deposit.

Suppose the loan in question is for $100,000 with a term of 30 years. Then the normal monthly payment would be as follows:

However, the builder wishes to offer a payment equivalent to a 6.00% loan, which we would find as follows:

This means that the builder must provide the lender with the difference between the required payment and the desired payment ($733.77 − 599.55 = $134.22) for the first 24 months. The builder will give the lender a deposit that is the present value of this series of "shortfall" payments. Assuming that the deposit will yield the current mortgage interest rate of 8 percent, the amount of the deposit may be found as follows:

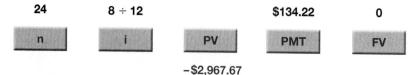

−$2,967.67

That is, $2,967.67 invested at a return of 8 percent can exactly provide the needed series of supplemental future payments. Chances are, however, the lender will place the deposit in a savings account yielding a rate lower than the current mortgage interest rate. If, for example, that savings rate is 5 percent, then the required deposit is as follows:

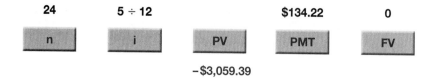

−$3,059.39

And the builder must make the larger deposit; that is, a larger initial amount is required to generate the needed series of supplemental payments.

Concept Check

11.16   What deposit would a builder need to make to buy down a $125,000, 6.5 percent, 30-year mortgage to look like a 4 percent mortgage for the first two years? Assume that the related deposit yields 4 percent.

Wraparound Mortgages

Sometimes a buyer and seller of a property wish to preserve an existing loan, but the buyer needs additional financing as well. This may arise in the financing of income-producing property because the seller's current loan is "locked" against prepayment. In home loans it may result because a buyer wants to avoid the transaction costs of a new first mortgage, or because the existing loan has a below-market interest rate. (With the home loan case, preserving the existing loan will depend on either the loan being assumable, as discussed in Chapter 10, or on the cooperation of the original lender.)

As an example, suppose a homebuyer wants to purchase a house with a price of $150,000 that has the following existing first mortgage loan:

Current balance:	$100,000
Remaining term:	25 years
Interest rate:	5.5 percent
Payment:	$614.09[12]

Suppose, further, that the current market mortgage interest rate is 5.75 percent. The buyer has $30,000 in cash, and thus needs additional financing in the amount of $20,000 for a total of $120,000. However, refinancing will cost 6 percent of the loan amount and result in a higher effective borrowing cost (EBC). One option for the borrower might be to arrange

---

12. It is not necessary to know the original balance on this loan to find its payment. The information given about its current status is entirely sufficient to find the payment.

second mortgage financing in the amount of $20,000, perhaps through a purchase-money mortgage (discussed in Chapter 12) with the seller. However, since the purchase-money mortgage would be a second mortgage, its risk will compel the seller to ask for an interest rate significantly above the current rate on first mortgages, and to require a relatively short term of, say, 10 years. This could result in a very difficult payment schedule for the buyer.

Another solution is a **wraparound mortgage** between the buyer and seller. For example, the seller could "take back" from the buyer the following mortgage loan:

Face loan amount:	$120,000
Term:	25 years
Interest rate:	5.90 percent
Payment:	$765.84

The loan will be secured by a second mortgage on the property. However, it differs from the usual second mortgage: Rather than having the buyer make two loan payments (for the new loan and the existing loan) the buyer will make the single payment of $765.84 to the seller. The seller in turn will continue to make the payment of $614.09 on the old first mortgage loan. Arguably this is safer for the seller because the seller controls the payment on the senior debt and always knows its status. It is advantageous to the buyer because the buyer has a much more manageable single payment instead of making payments on the old first mortgage and, in addition, paying on a purchase-money second mortgage. Thus, the wraparound loan arrangement could be attractive to both parties.

The wraparound arrangement becomes more interesting when one examines the return to the seller/lender. The characteristics of this wraparound arrangement are displayed in Exhibit 11-8. First consider how much the seller actually is receiving on the wraparound loan, suggested in the right-hand panel. The answer is the difference between what the buyer pays and what the seller must pay to the old lender, that is:

$$\text{Net wraparound payment to seller} = \text{Wraparound payment} - \text{Old loan payment}$$
$$= \$765.84 - \$614.09$$
$$= \$151.75$$

But we also must ask how much the seller has actually loaned to the buyer. The price of the house was $150,000, and the equity of the seller was the price less the existing debt ($150,000 − $100,000 = $50,000). The seller was paid $30,000 of this equity as a down payment. Thus, the amount that the seller has deferred, or loaned, is only $20,000. (See the left-hand panel of Exhibit 11-8.) In summary, the seller has effectively loaned $20,000 in

Exhibit 11-8 Wraparound Mortgage Loan

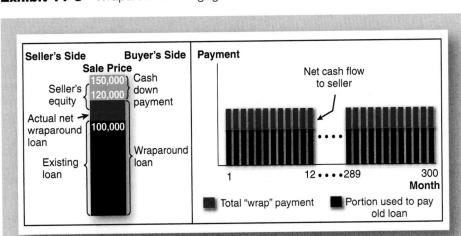

return for 25 years of payments amounting to $151.75 per month. What is the resulting yield on this wraparound loan? We can find it as follows:

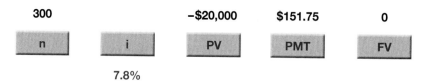

7.8%

Thus, in a market where lenders are receiving 5.75 percent for first mortgage loans, the seller has made a loan yielding 7.80 percent. Even so, the effective cost of this financing to the borrower is better than that available from the market on a first mortgage loan. Since a new loan of $120,000 would cost the borrower 6 percent in origination costs, the borrower effectively would need to borrow a larger amount, $127,700 to actually receive $120,000. The payment on this loan, based on the full $127,700, is $803.37. Thus the borrower's effective borrowing cost, adjusted for expenses, may be computed as follows:

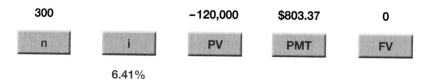

6.41%

So, in a market where the EBC is 6.41 percent, our wraparound borrower achieves an EBC of 5.90 percent.

Summary

To work with mortgage loan computations, one must be able to find the loan payment and the balance at any time in the life of the loan. These cash flows enable one to compute the lender's yield as well as the borrower's effective borrowing cost. Further, these cash flows are the requisite inputs to present value analysis, the central criterion for making mortgage-related decisions.

For fixed-rate loans an important example of decision analysis is the choice of loan maturity (often a choice between a 15-year loan and a 30-year loan). Analysis with present value reveals that the most beneficial choice is not always the loan that has the lowest payment, nor is it always the loan with the least accumulated interest or the loan that pays off the fastest. Opportunity cost (discount rate) of the borrower, frequently measured by the cost of high-interest debt, is a central determinant of the best loan choice.

Adjustable rate loans involve recomputation of the loan payment each time the interest rate changes. Careful attention is warranted in how to compute the new interest rate, particularly in the first few years where a teaser may interact with caps in different manners, depending on the provisions of the note.

There are many additional applications of time-value concepts in mortgage lending. One example is an interest rate buydown where, typically, a builder will seek to reduce the cost of a new home by depositing an amount with the lender sufficient to offset payment reductions to the homebuyer for a year or more. A second application of time-value concepts is a wraparound mortgage, which is a special form of purchase-money mortgage where old financing is preserved and continues to be paid by the seller.

Explore The Web

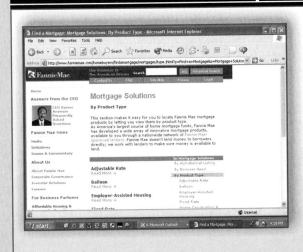

Fannie Mae's Mortgage Menu

On the Fannie Mae website (www.fanniemae.com) from the left-hand margin, under "For Home Buyers & Homeowners," select "Find a Mortgage." Then, in the last paragraph, select "Mortgage Solutions." Finally, under Mortgage Solutions, select "By Product Type." This should get you to the page displayed. From there, explore the mortgage products that Fannie Mae supports. How many different ARM programs can you identify? How many different fixed-rate programs? Who might be interested in the fixed-rate pledged asset mortgage? Who would be interested in a biweekly mortgage? What is Fannie Mae's "InterestFirst mortgage? How does its "Simultaneous Seconds Program" compare to the wraparound mortgage discussed in this chapter?

Key Terms

Adjustment period 288
Annual percentage rate (APR) 277
Buydown mortgage 291
Closing costs 277
Discount points 276

Early payment mortgages (EPM) 286
Effective borrowing cost (EBC) 277
Interest-only mortgages 285
Lender's yield 277

Level-payment mortgage (LPM) 282
Loan balance 275
Monthly loan constant 275
Wraparound mortgage 293

Test Problems

Answer the following multiple choice problems.

1. The most typical adjustment interval on an adjustable rate mortgage (ARM) is:
   a. Six months.
   b. One year.
   c. Three years.
   d. Ten years.
   e. None of the above.

2. A characteristic of a partially amortized loan is:
   a. No loan balance exists at the end of the loan term.
   b. A balloon payment is required at the end of the loan term.
   c. All have adjustable interest rates.
   d. All have a loan term of 15 years.
   e. None of the above.

3. If a mortgage is to mature (i.e., become due) at a certain future time without any reduction in principal, this is called:
   a. A second mortgage.
   b. An amortized mortgage.
   c. A limited reduction mortgage.
   d. An interest-only mortgage.
   e. An open-end mortgage.

4. The dominant loan type originated by most financial institutions is the:
   a. Fixed-payment, fully amortized mortgage.
   b. Adjustable rate mortgage.
   c. Purchase-money mortgage.
   d. FHA-insured mortgage.

5. Which of the following statements is true about 15- and 30-year fixed-payment mortgages?
   a. Thirty-year mortgages are more popular than 15-year mortgages among home owners who are refinancing.
   b. Borrowers pay more total interest over the life of a 15-year mortgage than on a 30-year loan.
   c. The remaining balance on a 30-year loan declines more quickly than an otherwise comparable 15-year mortgage.
   d. Assuming they can afford the payments on both mortgages, borrowers usually should choose a 30-year mortgage over an otherwise identical 15-year loan if their discount rate (opportunity cost) exceeds the mortgage rate.

6. Adjustable rate mortgages (ARMs) commonly have all the following *except:*
   a. A teaser rate.
   b. A margin.
   c. An index.
   d. A periodic interest rate cap.
   e. An inflation index.

7. Annual percentage rate was created in:
   a. The Truth-in-Lending Act of 1968.
   b. The Real Estate Settlement Procedures Act of 1974/1977.
   c. The Equal Credit Opportunity Act of 1974.
   d. State real estate licensing laws.
   e. Rules of the Federal Trade Commission.

8. On a level-payment loan with 12 years (144 payments) remaining, at an interest rate of 9 percent, and with a payment of $1,000, the balance is:
   a. $144,000.
   b. $100,000.
   c. $87,871.
   d. $76,137.

9. On the following loan, what is the best estimate of the effective borrowing cost if the loan is prepaid in six years?

Loan amount:	$100,000
Interest rate:	7 percent
Term:	180 months
Up-front costs:	7 percent of the loan amount

   a. 8.2 percent.
   b. 8.4 percent.
   c. 8.5 percent.
   d. 8.7 percent.
   e. 9.0 percent.

10. Lender's yield differs from effective borrowing cost (EBC) because:
   a. Lender's yield is strictly a yield to maturity and EBC is not.
   b. EBC is strictly a yield to maturity and lender's yield is not.
   c. EBC accounts for additional up-front expenses that lender's yield does not.
   d. Lender's yield accounts for additional up-front expenses that lender's yield does not.

Study Questions

1. Calculate the original loan size of a fixed-payment mortgage if the monthly payment is $1,146.78, the annual interest rate is 8.0 percent, and the original loan term is 15 years.

2. For a loan of $100,000, at 7 percent interest for 30 years, find the balance at the end of 4 years and 15 years.

3. On an adjustable rate mortgage, do borrowers always prefer smaller (tighter) rate caps that limit the amount the contract interest rate can increase in any given year or over the life of the loan? Explain why or why not.

4. Consider a $75,000 mortgage loan with an annual interest rate of 8 percent. The loan term is 7 years, but monthly payments will be based on a 30-year amortization schedule. What is the monthly payment? What will be the balloon payment at the end of the loan term?

5. A mortgage banker is originating a level-payment mortgage with the following terms:

Annual interest rate:	9.0 percent
Loan term:	15 years
Payment frequency:	Monthly
Loan amount:	$160,000
Total up-front financing costs (including discount points):	$4,000
Discount points to lender:	$2,000

   a. Calculate the annual percentage rate (APR) for Truth-in-Lending purposes.
   b. Calculate the lender's yield with no prepayment.
   c. Calculate the lender's yield with prepayment in five years.
   d. Calculate the effective borrowing cost with prepayment in five years.

6. Give some examples of up-front financing costs associated with residential mortgages. What rule can one apply to determine if a settlement (closing) cost should be included in the calculation of the effective borrowing cost?

7. A homeowner is attempting to decide between a 15-year mortgage loan at 5.5 percent and a 30-year loan at 5.9 percent. What would you advise? What would you advise if the borrower also has a large amount of credit card debt outstanding at a rate of 15 percent?

8. Consider the following wraparound loan given by a seller to a buyer:

   Existing debt

Current loan balance:	$90,000
Payment:	$579.87
Remaining term:	25 years

   Proposed wraparound loan

Balance:	$130,000
Term:	25 years
Interest rate:	6.5 percent

   a. How much is the seller really lending to the buyer?
   b. What is the true yield for the seller?

9. Suppose an ARM loan has a margin of 2.75 percent, an initial index of 3.00 percent, a teaser rate for the first adjustment period of 4.00 percent, and caps of 1.00 and 5.00 percent. If the index remains unchanged for the second adjustment period, what will be the interest rate on the loan? If there is more than one possible answer, what does the outcome depend on?

10. A builder has available a new home that would normally be financed with an $80,000 loan at 8.5 percent with monthly

payments over a 30-year term. The builder is offering potential buyers an $80,000, 30-year loan that carries a 6.5 percent annual interest rate for 3 years. After 36 monthly payments, the contract rate would increase to 8.5 percent. The builder has worked out an arrangement with First Federal Savings and Loan. First Federal will originate and own the mortgage. If the home is purchased with the interest rate buydown, the builder's selling price is $107,000. If purchased without the buydown, the selling price is $100,000.

a. Assuming that the lender obtains a yield of 3.5 percent on any deposits, how much would you expect the builder to have to pay First Federal up-front to buy down the payments on each loan for 3 years?

b. Would you recommend that the buyer make use of the interest rate buydown? Explain.

11. Assume the following for a one-year adjustable rate mortgage loan that is tied to the one-year Treasury rate:

Loan amount:	$150,000
Annual rate cap:	2%
Life-of-loan cap:	5%
Margin:	2.75%
First-year contract rate:	5.50%
One-year Treasury rate at end of year 1:	5.25%
One-year Treasury rate at end of year 2:	5.50%
Loan term in years:	30

Given these assumptions, calculate the following:

a. Initial monthly payment.
b. Loan balance end of year 1.
c. Year 2 contract rate.
d. Year 2 monthly payment.
e. Loan balance end of year 2.
f. Year 3 contract rate.
g. Year 3 payment.

12. Assume the following:

Loan Amount:	$100,000
Interest rate:	10 percent annually
Term:	15 years, monthly payments

a. What is the monthly payment?

b. What will be the loan balance at the end of nine years?

c. What is the effective borrowing cost on the loan if the lender charges 3 points at origination and the loan goes to maturity?

d. What is the effective borrowing cost on the loan if the lender charges 3 points at origination and the loan is prepaid at the end of year 9?

Explore The Web

Accurate interest rate information for residential mortgage markets is available online from Freddie Mac and Fannie Mae. Go to the Freddie Mac home page: www. freddiemac.com/ and download the latest primary mortgage market survey.

What was the average interest rate charged on 30-year,

fixed-rate residential mortgages last week?

What was the average 15-year fixed rate?

What was the one-year ARM rate?

Do these figures represent an increase or a decrease over the previous week's rates?

Solutions to Concept Checks

1. Five important measures that are important to mortgage loan analytics are (1) loan payment, (2) loan balance (at any time in the life of the loan), (3) lender's yield, (4) effective borrowing cost, and (5) present value.

2. The monthly payment for a loan of $125,000, 15 years, and 6.25 percent is $1,071.78.

3. The balance after six years on the 6.25 percent, 15-year $125,000 loan is $88,359.45.

4. The lender's yield on the 6.25 percent, 15-year $125,000 loan, assuming no prepayment and assuming that the lender receives points and an origination fee of $2,500, is 6.57 percent.

5. The EBC on the 6.25 percent, 15-year $125,000 loan, assuming no prepayment and total up-front costs to the borrower of $2,500 in points and origination fee plus $3,500 in other up-front costs, is 7.03 percent.

6. In computing APR, it is assumed that the loan goes to maturity (no prepayment).

7. If the 6.25 percent, 15-year, $125,000 loan is prepaid at the end of four years, and if points and origination fees sum to $2,500, the lender's yield is 6.87 percent.

8. If the 6.25 percent, 15-year, $125,000 loan is prepaid at the end of four years, and if total up-front costs to the borrower are $6,000, then the EBC is 7.77 percent.

9. An up-front expense in purchasing a house that should not be included in computing EBC is buyer's title insurance.

10. Under financially unconstrained circumstances, a homebuyer should be indifferent between 15-year and 30-year loans at the same interest rate of 7 percent, unless one considers there is a maturity premium in interest rates. If a maturity premium is considered, the 30-year, 7 percent loan is at a lower rate than the 15-year loan, and would be a lower-cost choice.

www.mhhe.com/lingarcher1e

11. If a financially unconstrained borrower considers the interest rate difference between a 15-year loan at 7.0 percent and a 30-year loan at 7.4 percent to be attributable strictly to maturity difference, then the borrower would be indifferent between the loans.

12. Using the example of a $100,000 loan and discounting at 15 percent, the 15-year, 7 percent loan has a present value (cost) of $64,221 while the 30-year 7.4 percent loan has a present value (cost of $54,758. Thus the 30-year loan is the least cost choice.

13. The balance at the end of seven years on a 6.5 percent, 30-year, $100,000 loan would be $90,416.25.

14. For the uncapped ARM the balance at the end of year 2 is $72,616.39. The initial payment, at 4 percent, is $358.06. The payment in year 2, at 5.5 percent, is $424.05.

15. For the capped ARM the balance at the end of year 2 is $72,519.46. The initial payment, at 4 percent, is $358.06. The payment in year 2, at 5 percent, is $401.45.

16. To buy down the loan so that the payments of the borrower are equivalent to payments at 4 percent for 24 months, and assuming that any deposit grows at 4 percent, the appropriate buydown would be $4,451.72.

Additional Readings

Brueggeman, W. B., and J. D. Fisher. *Real Estate Finance and Investments,* 11th ed. New York: McGraw-Hill Irwin, 2001.

Clauretie, T. M., and G. S. Sirmans. *Real Estate Finance: Theory and Practice,* 4th ed. Cincinnati, OH: South-Western Publishing, 2002.

Dennis, M. W. *Residential Mortgage Lending,* 4th ed. Cincinnati, OH: South-Western Publishing, 1994.

Eldred, G. W. 106 *Mortgage Secrets All Borrowers Must Know—But Lenders Won't Tell.* New York: John Wiley, 2003.

Friedman, J. P., and J. C. Harris. *Keys to Mortgage Financing and Refinancing.* 3rd ed. Hauppauge, NY: Barron's Educational Series, 2001.

chapter twelve

Residential Mortgage Types *and* Borrower Decisions

Learning Objectives

After reading this chapter you will be able to:

1. List two secondary mortgage market institutions and four types of primary mortgage market lenders, and state two effects of the secondary mortgage market upon home mortgage lending.

2. State the distinguishing characteristics of conventional loans, conforming and nonconforming conventional loans, and "jumbo" conventional loans.

3. Define private mortgage insurance, state what it accomplishes, and why it is important to borrowers.

4. State the special purposes served by purchase-money mortgages, package mortgages, and reverse mortgages, and name two borrower advantages of a home equity credit line mortgage over unsecured consumer loans.

5. Determine whether refinancing is financially desirable given the terms and amount of an existing loan, the terms of a new loan, the expected life of the existing loan, and the costs of refinancing.

6. State two factors that commonly influence the likelihood that a home borrower will default on a home mortgage loan.

Introduction

A home is the largest single purchase most households ever make, and they usually must borrow the necessary funds. Therefore, a system of mortgage lending has developed in which people with excess funds lend them to people who need money to buy houses. With mortgage credit available, households can purchase homes now and pay for them, with interest, over 10, 20, or 30 years.

Even many households that could pay cash for a home choose to borrow because the interest rates and terms of borrowing on home loans may be favorable relative to rates and terms on credit cards, car loans, and other consumer debt. So these households can use the funds freed by the mortgage borrowing to invest in other assets and, they hope, earn a rate of return that is greater than the cost of the mortgage funds. This strategy, discussed in Chapter 14, is known as *positive financial leverage.* The use of borrowed funds also allows households to better diversify their portfolios of investments. If home purchasers needed to pay all cash, many household portfolios would be even more overweighted in housing than they are currently. For these reasons—lack of funds, the possibility of positive financial leverage, and a better diversified portfolio—most homebuyers borrow at least a portion of the needed funds.[1]

The first part of this chapter introduces the various types of mortgage loans commonly available to homeowners and the types of decisions to be made about them. In addition to selecting a mortgage type, homeowners must evaluate the various costs associated with the loan and their desired loan-to-value (LTV) ratio or leverage. After obtaining the mortgage funds, borrowers usually have the option to prepay the mortgage, as well as the option to default. Good decisions regarding the financing of real estate can improve the value of the property, and add to the owner's wealth. Effective approaches to these numerous borrower decisions are demonstrated. (We discuss the commercial mortgage market in Chapter 14.)

The many types of available residential loans can be thought of as the **mortgage menu.** What determines the items on a lender's mortgage menu? Similar to restaurant food and other consumer products, lenders in the highly competitive residential mortgage market offer only those mortgage products for which there is a profitable market. In recent years residential lenders across the United States have added hundreds of different products to their mortgage menus. The majority of these added mortgage products have been dropped, either because borrowers did not "order" them or because lenders could not profit sufficiently by offering them. For example, U.S. housing economists have long argued that payments on residential mortgages should be tied (i.e., indexed) to inflation. However, despite the sound economic rationale for indexed mortgages and the willingness of numerous lenders to originate them, they have never caught on with borrowers and therefore remain absent from lenders' mortgage menus.

The Primary and Secondary Mortgage Markets

www.freddiemac.com, www.fanniemae.com

The two entities, Freddie Mac and Fannie Mae, that are the foundation of the modern secondary mortgage market.

The market for home mortgage loans can be divided into the primary mortgage market and the secondary mortgage market. The **primary mortgage market** is the loan origination market, in which borrowers and lenders come together. Numerous institutions supply money to borrowers in the primary mortgage market, including savings and loan associations, commercial banks, credit unions, and mortgage banking companies. Increasingly, this lending has been done through a mortgage broker. These direct sources of home mortgage funds are discussed in detail in Chapter 13.

Mortgage originators can either hold the loans in their portfolios or sell them in the **secondary mortgage market.** The largest purchasers of residential mortgages in the secondary mortgage market are **Fannie Mae** and **Freddie Mac.** These **government-sponsored enterprises (GSEs),** also discussed in Chapter 13, were created by acts of Congress to promote an active secondary market for home mortgages by purchasing mortgages from local originators. The existence of a well-functioning secondary market makes the primary mortgage market more efficient. If mortgage originators are able to sell their mortgage investments quickly, they obtain funds to originate more loans in the primary market. In today's world, the secondary market institutions, especially the GSEs, play a leading role in the home mortgage market. The menu of loans that the GSEs are willing to buy heavily influences the menu of loans that lenders are willing to originate.

---

1. One indication of average loan-to-value ratio for home mortgages is the ratio of total non-farm residential debt to total value of non-farm residential structures; it was 54 percent in 2000. However, the extreme variation in use of mortgage debt is suggested by the fact that 36 percent of owner-occupied residences in 2001 were without any mortgage debt. (See Tables 948 and 1159, *Statistical Abstract of the United States 2002,* U.S. Department of Commerce, Bureau of the Census, Washington D.C.)

Concept Check

12.1   The difference between the mortgage primary market and secondary market is:

_____ .

Conventional Mortgage Loans

The most common type of home loan is a **conventional mortgage loan.** This refers to any standard home loan that is not insured or guaranteed by an agency of the U.S. government.[2] Thus, it includes all standard home loans except those known as FHA (Federal Housing Administration) and VA (Veterans Affairs) loans, which we discuss later in this chapter. Conventional home loans preceded FHA and VA loans historically, but, as we will observe later, derived their modern form from the influence of these "government" mortgages. Conventional mortgages can be either fixed rate or adjustable rate (see Chapter 11).

Concept Check

12.2   What is a conventional home mortgage loan?

Fixed-Rate Conventional Mortgages

The predominant form of conventional mortgage remains the (fixed-rate) level-payment mortgage (LPM). As noted in Chapter 11, over 70 percent of home loans in the last decade were fixed-rate, and over 70 percent of loans on new homes were conventional. The fixed-rate conventional home loan has evolved dramatically in its forms twice in modern history. The first time was the 1940s, a decade that saw the birth of the LPM, though on much more limited terms than today. The evolution of the conventional LPM was enormously accelerated following World War II by the birth of private mortgage insurance (PMI), discussed below. Only after the introduction of the PMI did lenders view it feasible to offer conventional LPMs for maturities much longer than 15 years, or for loan-to-value ratios exceeding 80 percent.

A second important period in the evolution of the conventional fixed-rate home loan is the present. The dramatic changes in the structure of home lending, including rapid concentration of the industry and the growing strength and influence of Fannie Mae and Freddie Mac (discussed in Chapter 13), have brought about a dazzling evolution in the variety of conventional home loans being offered, particularly for groups in our society that have historically faced special problems in obtaining home financing. (See Industry Issues 12-1). Hence, while the 80 to 90 percent loan-to-value, 30-year LPM remains the predominant form of conventional loan, there is rapid growth in a rich variety of alternatives.

An important distinction among conventional mortgage loans is the difference between conforming and nonconforming. A **conforming conventional loan** is one that meets the standards required for purchase in the secondary market by Fannie Mae or Freddie Mac. Although both of these government-sponsored agencies (GSEs) are now privately owned, they are subject to government oversight, and Congress sets the maximum size of home mortgages they are allowed to purchase from originating lenders. To conform to the underwriting standards of the GSEs, a loan must use standard GSE documentation, including the application form, mortgage, note and appraisal form. It must not exceed a certain percentage of the property's value, monthly payments on the loan must not exceed a certain percentage of the borrower's income, and the loan must not exceed $322,700 on

---

2. By standard home loan we refer to loans from such "third party" lenders as banks, savings and loans, credit unions, mortgage bankers, or brokers arranging similar mortgages. This excludes purchase money mortgages between seller and buyer, or similar personal loans.

single-family homes.[3] Loans that fail one or more of these underwriting standards are termed **nonconforming conventional loans.** Nonconforming loans that exceed the dollar limit are called **jumbo loans.** Jumbo loans have accounted for about 8 percent of total single-family mortgage originations since 1990. Because conforming loans can be more readily bought and sold in the secondary mortgage market (i.e., they are more liquid), they carry a lower contract interest rate than otherwise comparable nonconforming loans. Over the last several years, this interest rate advantage has averaged approximately 0.25 percentage points. On a $90,000 loan, this translates into monthly payment savings of $16, assuming the contract interest rate on a conforming mortgage is 8 percent. In addition, quoted rates and points on nonconforming loans are much less uniform from lender to lender and region to region.

Adjustable Rate Mortgages

Another milestone in the evolution of conventional loans was the rise of the adjustable rate mortgage (ARM). Fixed-payment mortgages serve lenders and borrowers well when mortgage interest rates are relatively low and stable. Unfortunately, during the late 1970s and early 1980s, interest rates on LPMs increased dramatically, averaging 14.4 percent from 1979 through 1982. Beginning in the mid-1970s, mortgage rates also became more volatile (i.e., less predictable). This increase in the level and volatility of mortgage rates caused two major problems. First, the higher required monthly payments on a LPM made housing less affordable. Second, the increased volatility of mortgage rates made lenders nervous. Why? Savings and loans (S&Ls) and other depository institutions were in the business of making long-term LPMs using short-term deposits and savings. As long as they could issue liabilities (savings accounts) at little more than 5 percent and loan the money through LPMs at 8 percent, they were prosperous and happy. But when the interest rate paid to depositors increased suddenly, they were in trouble. While their average cost of deposits could rise immediately, their yield on LPMs could only rise with replacement of the LPMs through loan "turnover," a far slower process. When interest rates, both short term and long term, accelerated in the late 1970s and early 1980s, the average spread that many LPM lenders were earning on their fixed-rate mortgage investments actually became *negative.* As discussed in Chapter 13, this negative spread contributed to the eventual failure of many S&Ls.

Concept Check

12.3   What were three major events in the evolution of conventional mortgages since the 1930s?

In financial management terms, funding long-term LPMs with short-term deposits and savings creates a severe **maturity imbalance problem** for depository institutions because their assets (e.g., mortgages) are very long term, whereas their liabilities (e.g., savings deposits and certificates of deposit) are short term. To address the maturity imbalance problem and to avoid or reduce their exposure to the interest rate risk associated with making LPMs, many lenders began searching for alternatives to the LPM. For depository lenders, the most compelling alternative home mortgage is the *adjustable rate mortgage (ARM).* Not only has it become a core product for their business, but ARMs have evolved significantly in recent years to make them more attractive to home borrowers. (Again, see Industry Issues 12-1).

---

3. Higher dollar limits apply in Alaska, Hawaii, Guam, and the U.S. Virgin Islands. The limit stated is as of January 2003. It increases each year, keyed to inflation.

12-1

Ice Cream Parlor Mortgages?

First it was mortgage interest rates that changed constantly. Now it seems to be the menu of mortgages itself. The days of plain vanilla home loans are gone. Time was . . . that a home buyer would choose between a couple of fixed-rate, level-payment loans (15-year and 30-year), or a handful of ARMs distinguished by how fast the rate adjusted and how much the rate change was restricted by caps; only a few "wild-eyed" economists carried on about alternative types of home loans.

But now the wild-eyed economists are looking tame. Some of the biggest home lenders in the country, in league with none other than Fannie Mae, have rolled out menus of mortgages to compete with Baskin and Robbins. And some of the flavors are seriously exotic. Want an interest-only home loan? You got it! Your lender will dish it up, because Fannie Mae will buy it from them. It can be interest only for up to 15 years before regular amortization begins. Want 100 percent financing? No problem if you have good credit and you can find a relative who will pledge some of their retirement savings as security for a while. Again, your lender will dish it up because Fannie Mae will buy it. Want a mortgage where you can skip a payment occasionally? If you have good credit, see a lender about Fannie's "PaymentPower" plan. It allows borrowers who are current on payments to "take a month off" up to twice a year for a total of 10 skipped payments. But a loan program of Washington Mutual may be the current sundae supreme of the mortgage parlor. WaMu's "Option ARM" allows you to choose among four payment choices: You can elect an interest-only payment, a 30-year amortization payment, a 15-year amortization payment, or a minimum payment based on an artificially low interest rate. This minimum payment will result in "negative amortization," and a new, larger, minimum payment will be set yearly to amortize the increased balance. The payment will increase each year, but is guaranteed to increase no more than 7.5 percent as long as the outstanding balance is below something like 125 percent of the initial loan amount. Meanwhile the loan collects interest at some short-term, variable interest rate. (A note to other "wild-eyed" economists: You may remember that one of the "craziest" mortgages ever proposed was the "dual rate mortgage" advocated by Nobel Prize winner Franco Modigliani and some of his friends at MIT. Well, here it is from WaMu, slightly disguised, with options added.)

The mortgage parlor has one big difference, of course, from Baskin and Robbins. You don't need to go out of your house to shop. You can examine all of these loans, and at least 31 flavors more, with interest rate quotes for most, on the Internet. Try some of these parlors:

www.wamuhomeloans.com/loanchoices/index.jsp
WaMu's mortgage flavors.

www.countrywide.com/purchase/l_loantypes.asp
Countrywide Home Loan's choices.

www.wellsfargo.com/mortgage/homeloanworkbench/
Wells Fargo's servings.

www.fanniemae.com/homebuyers/findamortgage/mortgages
Fannie Mae's menu.

Private Mortgage Insurance

www.mgic.com

Website of the original mortgage insurance company.

Private mortgage insurance (PMI) protects a lender against losses due to default on the loan. It gives no other protection; that is, it does not protect against legal threat to the lender's mortgage claim, nor does it protect against physical hazards. It indemnifies the lender, but not the borrower. Lenders generally require private mortgage insurance for conventional loans over 80 percent of the value of the security property. Private mortgage insurance companies provide such insurance, which usually covers the top 20 percent of loans. In other words, if a borrower defaults and the property is foreclosed and sold for less than the amount of the loan, the PMI will reimburse the lender for a loss up to 20 percent of the loan amount. Thus, the net effect of PMI from the lender's perspective is to reduce default risk.[4] This reduction of default risk was sufficient to make LPMs a viable risk for lenders where they had never been before.

---

4. Another type of insurance, mortgage life insurance, provides for the continuing payment of the mortgage after the death of the insured borrower. This special form of life insurance enables the survivors of the deceased to continue living in the house. Mortgage life insurance has sometimes been criticized because it is no different, in substance, from other life insurance, but often has been relatively expensive.

12.4   Whom does private mortgage insurance protect? Against what?

Example 12-1   How PMI Works

Assume a borrower purchased a $100,000 home with 5 percent cash and a $95,000 loan. The initial LTV ratio is quite high (95 percent), so mortgage insurance is required in the amount of $19,000—20 percent of the loan. Suppose the borrower defaults after the loan has been paid down to $94,000. Suppose further the market value of the property falls and the property is sold for $90,000. The lender then looks to the mortgage insurer for compensation for the $4,000 loss.

Mortgage insurance companies have generally followed the practice of reimbursing the lender in full should a foreclosure become necessary. In this example, this option provides a zero net loss for the lender and a $4,000 loss for the insurance company. The outcomes of this option are summarized as follows:

Lender's position:

Payment from insurer	$94,000
Loss of mortgage asset	(94,000)
Net loss	$0

Insurance company position:

Takes ownership of property	$90,000
Pays remaining balance to lender	(94,000)
Net loss	$(4,000)[5]

12.5   Lenders usually require mortgage insurance for loans in excess of _____ .

Typical Terms of Private Mortgage Insurance.   Premiums on PMI can be paid by the borrower in a lump sum at the time of loan origination or in monthly installments added to the mortgage interest rate. For example, a one-time premium equal to 2.5 percent of the loan amount may be required at closing. For our example, this would mean a premium payment at closing of $2,375 (0.025 × $95,000). Alternatively, a monthly premium payment equal to, say, 0.0417 percent (0.5 percent annually) of the remaining loan balance may be included in the monthly mortgage payment and passed on by the lender to the insurance company. Thus, the first month's premium in our example would be $39.62 (0.000417 × $95,000). The premium would decline as the balance of the loan is amortized.

Mortgage insurance rates vary with the perceived riskiness of the loan: Higher loan-to-value ratio, longer loan term, and weaker credit record of the borrower all result in a higher mortgage insurance premium. Also premia on loans for second homes or for investment property are higher than owner-occupied residences, while premia on loans due to corporate relocation are lower. Finally, a "cash-out" refinancing loan (i.e., one that is larger than the loan it replaces) requires a higher insurance premium. These effects are readily apparent, for example, in the MGIC (Mortgage Guarantee Insurance Corporation) rate summaries found in the MGIC Web reference.

www.mgic.com/pdf/
71-6704.pdf/

A summary of MGIC mortgage insurance rates for a wide variety of loan types, borrower characteristics, and insurance programs.

---

5. The above discussion ignores the transaction costs that the insurer would incur in the process of taking title to a property and subsequently selling it in the open market. These costs increase the net loss associated with taking title to the property.

Cancellation of PMI coverage may be allowed if the borrower has a record of timely payments and the remaining loan balance is less than 80 percent of the *current* market value of the home. A new appraisal, paid for by the borrower, is typically required as proof of the increase in the value of the property. Under the Homeowners Protection Act of 1998, a borrower with a good payment record has the right to terminate PMI when the loan reaches 80 percent of the original value of the residence. The PMI company is required to terminate insurance when the loan reaches 78 percent of the original value of the residence.

Government-Sponsored Mortgage Programs

Many U.S. housing experts believe that an inadequate level of housing production would occur if government policies and programs were not in place to help middle- and lower-middle-income households obtain mortgages and purchase homes. The quest for fairness in housing and mortgage finance markets is viewed as a legitimate and ongoing concern of governments, and was adopted as national policy of the United States in the National Housing Act of 1949.[6]

With some exceptions, the predominant approach to making better housing available has been through intervention in the private mortgage markets. This approach is thought to capitalize on the efficiencies of private industry in supplying the funds and managing the risks of the housing finance system. Further, by leaving much of housing assistance to private industy, the approach allows the government to identify and concentrate on those areas in which the private market is unable to provide solutions to perceived problems.

Some government programs make loans directly to homebuyers in the primary market. Examples at the federal level include the Farmers Home Administration (FmHA) and the Farm Credit System. In addition, state governments issue tax-exempt debt to support loans with below-market interest rates for first-time homebuyers. Many state and local housing agencies also offer low-interest loan programs to low- and moderate-income households. The most prominent government-sponsored housing finance programs that operate in the primary market at the national level are the **Federal Housing Administration (FHA)** default insurance program and the **Veterans Affairs (VA)** program that provides guarantees on loans made by private lenders to qualified veterans.

Concept Check

12.6   Name two government agencies that provide direct financing assistance to selected eligible households.

FHA-Insured Loans

www.hud.gov/offices/h sg/sfh/insured.cfm

Main website of the Federal Housing Administration (FHA).

The FHA insures loans made by private lenders that meet FHA's property and credit-risk standards. The insurance is paid for by the borrower and protects the FHA-approved lender against loss of capital from borrower default. Unlike conventional mortgage insurance, which protects the lender against some *portion* of the potential loan loss, **FHA mortgage insurance** covers any lender loss after foreclosure and conveyance of title of the property to the U.S. Department of Housing and Urban Development (HUD). Currently, the FHA borrower pays both an up-front premium equal to 1.5 percent of the loan amount and a monthly premium for 5 to 10 years, as explained below.

The up-front insurance premium can be included in the loan amount and thus paid over the life of the loan. On a 30-year, 7 percent loan of $80,000, the up-front **mortgage insurance premium (MIP)** is $1,200 (0.015 × 80,000). Thus, the total amount borrowed would

---

6. Among the national goals expressed in the National Housing Act was "a decent home and a suitable living environment for every American family."

be \$81,200, and the amount added to the monthly payments to amortize the up-front MIP would be \$7.98. The total monthly payment (including the amortization of up-front MIP) would be \$540.23.[7]

    In addition to the up-front MIP, FHA borrowers also must pay an annual premium. If the loan is for longer than 15 years, this MIP is equal to 0.50 percent of the average outstanding loan balance in each year. This annual premium is divided by 12 and added to each monthly payment during the year. If the loan is for 15 years or less, the MIP is equal to 0.25 percent. If the loan is for 15 years or less *and* if the loan-to-value ratio is below 90 percent, there is no MIP. The higher the initial LTV ratio, the longer the monthly premium must be paid. The \$81,200 loan will have an average outstanding balance during the first year of amortization of \$80,826.71. Thus, the annual premium in the first year would be 0.005 × \$80,826.71 = \$404.13. This amount is divided by 12 and the result is added to the monthly payments (\$404.13 ÷ 12 = \$33.68). This premium decreases each year as the outstanding balance decreases.

Concept Check

12.7   What is the up-front fee for FHA insurance? What is the MIP for a 30-year loan?

    The premiums are automatically cancelled when the loan-to-original value reaches 78 percent, provided that MIP payments have been made for at least five years.[8] For loans of 15 years or less, however, this cancelation is irrespective of how long the MIP has been paid. In no case does this automatic cancelation of the MIP cause discontinuation of insurance coverage. FHA is required each year to advise the borrower of these cancelation provisions. The monthly premiums paid by borrowers are deposited by FHA into the Mutual Mortgage Insurance Fund, which reimburses lenders in case of foreclosure. As with private mortgage insurance, FHA insurance increases the effective borrowing cost of the mortgage.

Concept Check

12.8   At a certain loan-to-value ratio, PMI must be canceled by the provider. For FHA insurance, MIP payments must be terminated. What is this "trigger" LTV ratio?

https://
entp.hud.gov/idapp/
html:hicostlook.cfm

Shows FHA current loan limits in general and for any specific county.

    The FHA insures mortgages for various types of properties. Some of the programs, for example, insure loans for low-income housing, nursing homes, cooperative apartments, and condominiums. The most widely used FHA program insures single-family home mortgages and is authorized by Title II, Section 203(b) of the National Housing Act. Thus, the insured loans are often called **Section 203 loans.** The maximum amount on these loans varies from area to area and is increased each year. As of January 1, 2003, the limit for single-family homes in low-cost areas was \$154,896, while in high-cost parts of the country the limit was \$280,749. Within these extremes, other limits are often established on a county-by-county basis. FHA-approved lending institutions, such as banks, mortgage companies, and S&Ls, can make insured Section 203(b) loans.

    The down payment calculation on FHA loans, as of October 1998, is based on the value of the property (i.e., the lesser of the purchase price or appraised value) and, to a very small

---

7. The calculator keystrokes are $N = 360$, $I = 7\% \div 12$, $PV = 81,200$, $PMT = ?$, and $FV = 0$.

8. The 78 percent rule for cancelation is consistent with requirements of the Home Owner's Protection Act of 1998, which Congress enacted to limit excessive terms for PMI.

extent, on average closing costs in the state. For "low closing cost states" the loan amount is a percentage of the value as follows:

Value/Sales Price	Loan Percentage of Value[9]
$50,000 or lower	98.75 percent
Over $50,000 up to $125,000	97.65 percent
Over $125,000	97.15 percent

The appropriate percentage is applied to the value/sale price exclusive of any closing costs, but the loan can exceed this limit by the amount of the MIP. The borrower must make a cash down payment of at least 3 percent of the value/sale price, but cash paid for closing costs counts toward this requirement.

Example 12-2   Determining the Amount of an FHA Loan

Consider a house with a purchase price of $110,000, an appraised value of $113,000, and closing costs of $5,000. Assuming that the house is in a low closing cost state, the maximum loan with MIP included, would be $109,065 ($110,000 \times (.9765 + 0.015)$). Minimum cash down payment would be $3,300 ($0.03 \times $110,000$). Since the total acquisition cost (price plus closing costs) is $115,000, the down payment is $5,935 ($115,000 - 109,065$). Thus, the minimum cash down payment of $3,300 automatically is satisfied.[10]

Because FHA-insured loans are made with higher LTVs and because the FHA assumes the entire risk of default, premiums charged by the FHA are usually higher than otherwise comparable private mortgage insurance premiums.

Importance of the Federal Housing Administration. It would be hard to overstate the importance of the FHA in the history of housing finance. Before the FHA was established in 1934, the typical home loan was relatively short term (5 to 15 years) and required principal repayment in full at the end of the term of the loan—that is, loans were nonamortizing. The FHA was organized to demonstrate the feasibility of home lending with long-term, amortized loans through insurance protection for lenders participating in the program. In short, the FHA program created the single most important financial instrument in modern housing finance, the level-payment, fully amortizing loan. Further, through its power to approve or deny loans, the FHA heavily influenced housing and subdivision design standards throughout the United States during the middle of the 20th century. Today, FHA mortgage insurance is still an important tool through which the federal government expands home ownership opportunities for first-time homebuyers and other borrowers who would not otherwise qualify for conventional loans at affordable terms. In 2001, the FHA insured close to 1.2 million homes, valued at over $131 billion, and it continues to play a potentially important role in housing finance innovation with its nascent home equity conversion mortgage (HECM) program, discussed later in the chapter.

Concept Check

12.9   What was the greatest historic contribution of the FHA?

9. For "high closing cost" states the percentages are 98.75 percent for $50,000 or less, and 97.75 percent for any value greater.

10. The reader familiar with past calculations for an FHA down payment will appreciate that the calculation has been simplified significantly.

Career Focus

Mortgage Broker

A mortgage broker is an independent agent who specializes in the origination of residential and/or commercial mortgages. Mortgage brokers normally defer the actual funding and servicing of loans to capital sources who act as loan "wholesalers." There are approximately 20,000 mortgage brokerage operations across the nation that originate over half of all residential loans in the United States. Their role in home mortgage lending has grown in recent years.

A mortgage broker is also an independent contractor working, on average, with 40 wholesale lenders at any one time. By combining professional expertise with direct access to hundreds of loan products, a broker provides consumers the most efficient and cost-effective method of offering suitable financing options tailored to the consumer's specific financial goals. The wholesale lender underwrites and funds the home loan, may service the loan payments, and ensures the loan's compliance with underwriting guidelines. The broker, on the other hand, originates the loan. A detailed application process, financial and creditworthiness investigation, and extensive disclosure requirements must be completed for a wholesale lender to evaluate a consumer's home loan request. The broker simplifies this process for the borrower and wholesale lender, counseling consumers on their loan package choices, and enabling them to select the right loan for their homebuying needs. An important part of the business of many mortgage brokers is working with marginal borrowers who only qualify for subprime loans.

Mortgage brokers have a national industry association, the National Association of Mortgage Brokers (www.namb.org). An important service of the NAMB is to provide information and training relating to the complex laws and regulations pertinent to home mortgage lending. The association provides two certifications for members: Certified Mortgage Consultant and Certified Residential Mortgage Specialist. Both are attained through a combination of education and experience requirements. Brokers normally are compensated primarily through fees and commissions. They often combine mortgage brokerage with some closely related real estate occupation. Brokers must be licensed in the state where they practice.

Source: Information partially excerpted from the website of the National Association of Mortgage Brokers. www.namb.org

VA-Guaranteed Loans

www.homeloans.va. gov/veteran.htm

Main website for the VA home loan program.

The Department of Veterans Affairs (VA) is a cabinet-level government department whose purpose is to help veterans readjust to civilian life. **VA-guaranteed loans** help veterans obtain home mortgage loans with favorable terms for which they might not otherwise qualify. For a private lender making a loan to a qualified veteran, the VA guarantee protects against default loss up to a maximum percentage of the loan amount. This guarantee begins at 50 percent of the amount of the loan for loans up to $45,000 and declines in steps to 25 percent for loans in excess of $144,000.[11] The maximum guarantee is $60,000. Thus, for a loan of $144,000 the guarantee is $36,000. For a loan of $240,000 the guarantee is the maximum of $60,000, and since most lenders want at least 25 percent protection of their loan, this typically is the largest amount of VA loan available. If a veteran defaults, the VA will reimburse the lender for any loss up to the guaranteed amount after the property has been foreclosed and sold.

Concept Check

12.10 What is the maximum loan-to-value ratio for a VA loan? What is the guarantee fee for a maximum loan?

The VA will guarantee loans to eligible veterans up to 100 percent of a property's value. For this, the VA charges a funding fee that is a percentage of the loan, with the percentage

11. Note that the guarantee is unrelated to the loan-to-value ratio. This maximum loss amount was effective beginning December 27, 2001.

based on the down payment. The percentage is 2.0 percent on loans with no down payment, 1.5 percent on loans with a 5.0 to 9.99 percent down payment, and 1.25 percent on loans with a 10 percent or higher down payment. The funding fee can be added to the loan amount but closing costs cannot be included in the amount of the loan. In 2002 the VA guaranteed loans on more than 328,000 homes. In areas where eligible veterans cannot obtain loans from approved VA lenders, the VA can make direct loans to them.

Other Mortgage Types and Uses

Mortgages on real property can be used in different ways to accomplish different functions in a transaction. Mortgages identified by the function they play in achieving certain objectives include purchase money mortgages, package mortgages, reverse annuity mortgages and home equity loans.

Purchase-Money Mortgage

Whenever a seller lends all or part of the purchase price of a property to a purchaser, and the loan is secured by a mortgage on the property, the mortgage is termed a **purchase-money mortgage (PMM).** The mortgage is given by the buyer simultaneously with receipt of the title to the property. Though it usually is a loan from the seller, it could be from a third party. Such mortgages, briefly discussed in Chapters 10 and 11, are often used in transactions involving single-family homes. Their primary functions are to provide purchasers with higher loan-to-value ratios than they are able or willing to obtain from a traditional mortgage lender, to provide purchasers with a lower cost of financing than is generally available, or to provide both.

Example 12-3 A Purchase-Money Mortgage

Suppose the Browns want to sell their home for $100,000. The Greens want to buy it but can pay only $10,000 in cash. They can borrow $80,000 with a first mortgage from Third Federal Savings and Loan, but they are still short $10,000. The Browns agree to lend them $10,000, with a second mortgage—a PMM. In effect, the Browns are "taking paper" in lieu of $10,000 in cash at closing. The second mortgage will have a position inferior to the first mortgage in the event of default.

Usage. Purchase-money mortgages are used to finance other types of real estate as well. Landowners often partially finance the sale of large tracts for development with a PMM. They take cash for a portion of the sale price but finance the remainder themselves. The PMM is paid off from the proceeds of lots as they are developed and sold. The landowner, in effect, is a partner of the developer.

Concept Check

12.11 What is a purchase-money mortgage?

Package Mortgage

A **package mortgage** provides additional funds for homebuyers. The mortgage includes home-related items of personal property such as a range, dishwasher, refrigerator, and furnishings. When these items are included in the mortgage, the lender can lend a larger amount, and the homebuyer can amortize the purchases over a much longer period, usually at a lower rate, than if the items were financed by a consumer loan.

Home Equity Loan

A form of second mortgage, the **home equity loan,** has become quite popular in recent years. Home equity loans owe their popularity to lower interest rates and longer terms than other consumer debt, tax-favored status, and easy availability, not to mention aggressive marketing by lenders. Although traditionally used to finance home improvements, home equity loans have become all-purpose loans.

Types of Loans. Banks and savings institutions dominate home equity lending, but credit unions, finance companies, brokerage houses, and insurance companies also offer these loans. The loans come in two forms:

1. *Closed-end loan*—a fixed amount is borrowed all at once and repaid in monthly installments over a set period, such as 10 years.
2. *Open-end line of credit*—money is borrowed as it is needed, drawn against a maximum amount that is established when the account is opened. Interest is paid on the balance due, just as with a credit card. This type of credit commonly requires a minimum monthly payment equal to a percentage (e.g., 1.5 percent) of the outstanding balance. This gives the debt a much longer term than consumer debt. Normally, the interest rate is adjustable, most commonly based on the prime rate published in *The Wall Street Journal,* plus a margin ranging from zero to perhaps 1.5 percent. Open-end lenders frequently provide a book of special checks that allows the borrower to tap the line of credit as if it were a checking account.

How much can one borrow? The limit is set by a total mortgage loan-to-value (LTV) ratio such as 75 percent or 80 percent. The maximum home equity loan is the amount that increases total mortgage debt up to that LTV limit. If a house is appraised at $200,000, has a $100,000 mortgage balance, and the lender sets a 75 percent LTV ratio, a homeowner could borrow $150,000, minus the $100,000 existing debt, or an additional $50,000.

Tax Advantages. Interest on consumer debt, such as loans to finance the acquisition of automobiles, college tuition, and household appliances and electronics, is *not* tax deductible. But interest on home equity loans up to $100,000 is generally 100 percent deductible for federal and many state tax returns.

Concept Check

12.12   Give three reasons why homeowners might be interested in a home equity loan rather than a consumer loan.

www.reversemortgage.org/index.html

National Reverse Mortgage Lenders Association, a primary reverse mortgage trade organization.

www.aarp.org/revmort/

AARP's reverse mortgage page, a wealth of links and references.

Reverse Mortgage

Many older, retired households suffer from constrained income and a resulting reduction in their quality of life. Over 80 percent of older households are homeowners, often with little or no mortgage debt on their residence. But even when income is constrained, they remain unwilling to sell their homes for many reasons. In short, a very significant percentage of older households are "house poor," with little income, but substantial illiquid wealth in their home. A **reverse mortgage** is designed to mitigate this problem. It offers additional monthly income to these homeowners through various loan disbursement plans, using the home as security for the accumulating loan. Essentially, a reverse mortgage allows homeowners to liquidate a portion of their housing equity without having to sell the house and move.

12.13 For whom is a reverse mortgage intended? What problem does it address?

Example 12-4   A Simple Reverse Mortgage

In a fixed-term, level-payment reverse mortgage, sometimes called a reverse annuity mortgage, or RAM, a lender agrees to pay the homeowner a monthly payment, or annuity, and to be repaid from the homeowner's equity when he or she sells the home or obtains other financing to pay off the RAM. A fixed-term RAM provides a fixed payment for a certain period of time, say, 10 years. For example, consider a household that owns a $100,000 home free and clear of mortgage debt. The RAM lender agrees to a $70,000 RAM for 10 years at 9 percent. Assume payments are made *annually,* at the beginning of each year, to the homeowner. The annual payment on this RAM would be $4,226.98. The calculator keystrokes are:

10	9	0		−$70,000
n	i	PV	PMT	FV
			$4,226.98	

The annual payment, accrued interest, and accumulated loan balance are displayed in Exhibit 12-1.

Note that the disbursement and loan payment pattern on a RAM are not at all like a typical mortgage from which the borrower receives the entire loan proceeds at closing and then immediately begins to make monthly payments of interest and principal. With our RAM example, the loan proceeds are distributed to the borrower in periodic amounts. Interest on the loan disbursements begins to accumulate immediately. However, no payments of any kind are made on the loan until the borrowers, or their heirs, pay off the loan with proceeds from the sale of the house (or other assets from the borrower's estate).

Exhibit 12-1   Reverse Annuity Mortgage*

Year	Beginning Balance	Payment	Ending Interest	Balance
1	$ 4,227	$4,227	$ 380†	$ 4,607‡
2	8,834	4,227	795	9,629
3	13,856	4,227	1,245	15,104
4	19,331	4,227	1,740	21,070
5	25,297	4,227	2,277	27,574
6	31,801	4,227	2,862	34,663
7	38,890	4,227	3,500	42,390
8	46,617	4,227	4,196	50,813
9	55,040	4,227	4,954	59,993
10	64,220	4,227	5,780	70,000

*$70,000, 9 percent, 10-year loan.

†9 percent of beginning balance.

‡Beginning balance, plus payment, plus interest.

Industry Issues

Charles and Joan H., aged 79 and 77, respectively, have 26 miniature flags in their downstairs living room. Each represents the country of a foreign exchange student they have befriended. Although the couple are no longer a host family, they've kept in close contact with many of their former exchange students. Three of them—Christine from France, Gabrielle from Mexico, and Carlos from Brazil—got married in 2002. Charles and Joan were invited to attend all three weddings, which were held in their friends' native countries.

To raise the money to attend the weddings, they decided to get a reverse mortgage. "We got the reverse mortgage, so that we could go to France and Brazil," explained Joan. "Later we were invited to Gabrielle's wedding in Mexico. Getting the reverse mortgage was a smart move, because we didn't have to dip into our savings."

Their four bedroom ranch-style home, where they've lived for 50 years, was appraised at $100,000. They obtained a $54,847 reverse mortgage, after payment of closing costs. The loan closed on February 25, 2002. The couple took out an initial draw of $8,000 to pay for the first two trips, and left the balance in a line of credit.

In addition to paying for their travel, Charles and Joan also used the funds from their reverse mortgage to buy a computer. The computer, Joan said, "opened up a whole new world for us." The couple now uses e-mail to keep in touch with their children and other friends. "I used the Internet to purchase our plane tickets, reserve hotel rooms, and make other travel arrangements," she noted. "I doubt we could have done any of this without our reverse mortgage, which is why we're advising our friends to get one, too."

Source: Excerpt from website of National Reverse Mortgage Lenders Association. http://www.reversemortgage.org/realborrowers.htm

---

"Mortality" Risk. If the property is sold or the homeowner dies prior to the end of the 10-year term, the accumulated loan balance can be paid off with the sale proceeds. If the owner is still living, the loan balance must still be paid to the lender, which may force a sale of the house—and likely produce a great deal of negative publicity for the lender. To address this "mortality risk," several departures from the fixed-payment, fixed-term RAM have emerged. In one, the payments to the homeowner cease at the end of the loan term, but the owner is allowed to stay in the house as long as he or she chooses or lives. Interest on the unpaid mortgage balance simply continues to accrue at the contract rate. The homeowner's heirs then use the sale proceeds or other estate assets to satisfy the outstanding obligation.

Concept Check

12.14 What is the unique risk of a reverse mortgage? How is it mitigated?

Roles of FHA and Fannie Mae. Two important steps in the development of reverse mortgages were the creation of reverse mortgage insurance and the creation of a secondary market. In 1987 Congress created the FHA Home Equity Conversion Mortgage (HECM) program to provide insurance for reverse mortgages. This program set the framework, in large part, for acceptable forms of the mortgage. It provides guidelines for maximum loans that depend on the age of householders and the value of the residence. It provides for a variety of acceptable disbursement plans, including lump sum, annuity (level payment), and credit line. It provides mortgage insurance for reverse mortgages originated by FHA-approved lenders. More specifically, if the proceeds from the sale of the home are not suf-

www.hud.gov/offices/
hsg/sfh/hecm/
hecmhome.cfm

HUD's reverse mortgage
website.

www.fanniemae.com/
homebuyers/
findamortgage/
mortgages/

Select "by product types," then
"reverse mortgages" for
Fannie's "Home Keeper"
website.

ficient to pay the amount owed, HUD will pay the lender the amount of the shortfall. In 1996 Fannie Mae began offering a reverse mortgage purchase program, called "Home Keeper," to lenders across the country. After the origination of these two programs, there was slow but growing acceptance of the concept among conventional lenders. Between 2000 and 2002, however, the rate of growth in reverse mortgages insured under FHA's HECM program increased dramatically, rising to 8,127 in 2001, to 14,181 in 2002, and continuing at a similar pace into 2003. This is a significant change, since there had been little more than 50,000 reverse mortgages created under the two main programs since 1989. Many analysts predict the demand for these loans will grow as the baby-boom generation continues to age.[12]

The Borrower's Mortgage Loan Decisions

Once a household has selected a home to purchase, it faces a number of financing decisions. First, the buyer must choose a mortgage from the mortgage menu. It must decide the maturity of the loan, which can range from a balloon loan with a maturity of five years to a 30-year LPM. Then it frequently must choose the most suitable combination of interest rate and up-front points. In Chapter 11 we showed how the maturity decision is addressed by comparing present values of mortgages and how the interest rate–points tradeoff is addressed by comparing effective borrowing costs (EBC).

But there are other mortgage choices as well. Increasingly, borrowers can consider alternatives to the level payment loans discussed in Chapter 11, including a mortgage with reduced payments in the early years to increase affordability, or an *early payment mortgage* with scheduled increasing payments. In choosing between fixed rate loans a comparison of present values, as done in Chapter 11, always is a good guide to making the mortgage choice. But households may consider an ARM instead of a fixed rate loan, or a mortgage with the interest rate fixed for only a few years, followed by an adjustable rate. In any case, a borrower must decide whether to seek the maximum loan-to-value ratio or something less, entailing a lower EBC.

After the mortgage has been originated, the household usually has the option to prepay the mortgage (in whole or in part) and the option to default. Borrowers typically do not give serious consideration to default unless the value of the property has fallen well below the remaining mortgage balance. Prepayment may result from a household's decision to move, to refinance for a lower interest rate, or to obtain a larger mortgage, drawing some of the household's equity out of the property.

In this section we extend the use of EBC and present value to some of these additional mortgage decisions. We look to EBC to help with the extremely complex choice between fixed rate and adjustable rate. We also consider EBC as a guide to making the loan-to-value choice. Finally, we use present value to address the question of refinancing.

Mortgage Choice

When prospective buyers of single-family homes seek financing, they must consider several provisions of the mortgage contract that can affect the cost of both the financing and the property, as detailed in Chapter 11. While the contract interest rate is the most obvious component of the cost of debt, we have shown that up-front closing costs are important as well, and become increasingly significant as the loan holding period is shorter. The effect of the holding period is almost always an issue in mortgage loan decisions since virtually every home mortgage gets paid off early due to the borrower moving, or wanting to "cash out" equity from the home, to own debt-free, or to obtain a lower interest rate.

---

12. RAMs have received increased attention in recent years from practitioners and academics, as well as from policy makers. Evidence of this interest is that an entire issue of the *Journal of the American Real Estate and Urban Economics Association* (vol. 22, no. 2, Summer 1994) was devoted to articles on RAMs.

Comparing Mortgage Options. Borrowers selecting among different mortgage types should calculate the effective borrowing costs (EBCs) of the various options. Consider the choice between the 8.50 percent LPM in Exhibit 12-2 with 1 1/2 discount points and a one-year adjustable rate mortgage (ARM) with a 6.00 percent first year interest rate, a margin of 2.75 percent, no interest rate caps, 1 1/2 discount points, and $2,000 in other up-front financing costs. The first row in Exhibit 12-2 displays the EBCs on the LPM for various holding periods. The second row contains the EBCs of the ARM, assuming the yield on one-year Treasury securities (the index rate) is 5 percent at the beginning of years 2 through 10. With a margin of 2.75 percent, this means the contract rate will be 7.75 percent in years 2 through 10. If the index rate remains at 5 percent, the ARM is less expensive than the LPM, regardless of the holding period.

However, if the yield on one-year Treasury securities rises to 6 percent at the beginning of years 2 and 3, 7 percent at the beginning of year 4, and remains at 7 percent in years 5 through 10, the desirability of the ARM relative to the LPM depends on the period of time the loan is outstanding. For relatively short holding periods (i.e., less than six years), the ARM is less expensive than the LPM. For longer periods, however, the LPM is the preferred option. Note that the EBC of the ARM is affected by both the holding period *and* the course of future short-term interest rates—both of which are difficult to predict.

What does this uncertainty in the EBC of ARMs imply for mortgage choice? If the effective borrowing cost of the ARM is not significantly lower than that of a comparable LPM, the ARM is an inferior choice. If the EBC of the ARM *is* significantly lower, then the choice will depend on the risk tolerances of the borrower. The pertinent question becomes: Is the borrower comfortable with the possible future rate increases?

Concept Check

12.15 In comparing alternative mortgage choices, what is the principal tool of comparison?

Loan Size

A borrower must consider several factors in determining how much debt to obtain. First, the use of mortgage debt depends on the relative costs of debt and equity financing. Consider a household that has agreed to purchase a home for $100,000. Assume that the household currently owns several other assets, including $100,000 in corporate bonds. This household has two basic financing options: (1) sell the $100,000 in bonds and put its own money into the house or (2) debt finance a portion of the purchase price. If the household chooses the first option, it is, in effect, lending the money to itself. What is the cost of this

Exhibit 12-2 Effective Borrowing Cost of LPM versus ARM*

| Mortgage Choice/Interest Rate Scenario | Number of Years Loan Is Outstanding | | | | |
	2 Yrs.	4 Yrs.	6 Yrs.	8 Yrs.	10 Yrs.
8.5 percent LPM/any interest rate scenario	10.46%	9.57%	9.28%	9.14%	9.06%
1-year ARM, 6.0% initial contract rate, index rate 5% at the beginning of all 10 years	8.77	8.30	8.15	8.07	8.03
1-year ARM, 6.0% initial contract rate, index rate 5% at the beginning of year 1; 6% at the beginning of years 2 and 3; 7% at the beginning of years 4–10	9.25	9.24	9.38	9.44	9.48

*Calculations assume 1.5 discount points, other up-front financing costs of $2,000, and a 30-year loan term. The ARMs have a margin of 2.75 percent and no rate caps.

self-financing? It is the rate of return that the household could have earned from keeping the bonds. This forgone rate of return is the household's cost of equity (or self-financing). If the risk-adjusted cost of self-financing is *equal* to the effective borrowing cost (EBC) of the debt financing, the borrower is indifferent between the two options from a financial perspective. However, if the cost of self-financing exceeds the EBC, the household has an incentive to finance some, if not all, of the purchase with debt. A second consideration is the interaction of loan-to-value ratio and EBC. Due mainly to the cost of mortgage insurance, a higher LTV ratio results in a higher EBC.

The Refinancing Decision

Because of frequent declines in mortgage interest rates, a large percentage of home mortgage originations in the last 15 years have been refinancings. The powerful relationship between interest rate declines and refinancing activity is shown in Exhibit 12-3. From 1990 to 2001, 39 percent of conventional single-family originations were refinancings, including cumulative annual percentages of 52, 58, 52, and 57 in 1992, 1993, 1998, and 2001, respectively. Because of the size of the costs and benefits involved, refinancing is a decision that mortgage borrowers should consider carefully.

Refinancing is an investment problem. So the core question is whether the present value of the future loan payment reductions (the benefit), exceeds the immediate refinancing cost. That is, we need to determine whether the *NPV* of refinancing is positive, where *NPV* is:

$$NPV = PV \text{ of Loan payment reductions} - \text{Cost of refinancing}$$

The costs of refinancing were explored above. They may range from 4 percent to 9 percent of the cost of a new loan, with the cost of mortgage insurance usually the greatest variable factor.

Finding the present value of payment reductions from refinancing is greatly simplified if the payment reductions are "dismantled." Note, as shown in Exhibit 12-4, that the payment reductions really are the differences, month by month, in the payment on the old loan and the payment on the new loan. As a result, the present value of the payment reductions is simply the difference in the present values of the two loans, that is:

$$PV \text{ of Loan payment reductions} = PV \text{ of old loan} - PV \text{ of new loan}$$

Exhibit 12-3 Drops in Interest Rates Cause Mortgage Refinancing

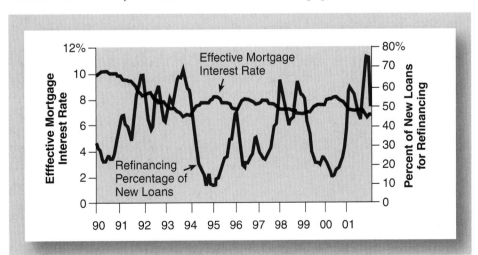

Source: Federal Housing Finance Board, www.fhfb.gov; Freddie Mac, www.freddiemac.com

Exhibit 12-4 The Benefit of Refinancing Is the Difference Between Two
Present Values

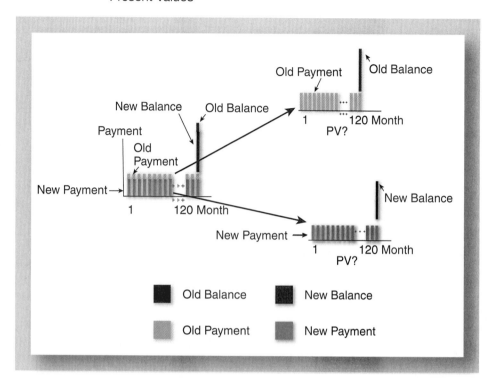

To determine the present value of the payment reductions, we must specify the opportunity cost of the borrower. Since borrowers rely on the current mortgage loan interest rate to make decisions about additional mortgage debt, that rate commonly is used as the opportunity cost of mortgage borrowing.[13] Accepting this as the discount rate leads to a very simple means of computing the present value of payment reductions. First, recall that when we discount any fixed rate mortgage loan by its own interest rate, the resulting present value is simply the balance of the loan. So the present value of the new loan always equals its balance. This will be true regardless of whether the loan is expected to be prepaid at some point in the future, or not. In this analysis, we need to find the difference between the present value of the existing loan and the present value of the new loan. We have the latter, so we are halfway there.

The present value of the existing loan is more complex. Unlike the new loan, the time to payoff (the holding period) matters. In general, the present value of the existing loan is the sum of the present value of the payments up to the time the loan is prepaid, if ever, and the present value of the payoff balance. Suppose the existing loan is $90,000, has 15 years remaining, and has an interest rate of 8 percent. This is sufficient information to determine the payment as follows:[14]

180	8 ÷ 12	$90,000		0
n	i	PV	PMT	FV

−$860.09

13. This makes sense if we believe that the borrower can reasonably borrow as much or as little as he or she prefers at that rate.

14. We do not need to know how old the loan is or what its original balance was. Remaining term, the interest rate, and the current balance are sufficient information to determine every aspect of the future cash flows of a level-payment loan.

Exhibit 12-5 Net Benefits of Refinancing for Various Times to Loan Prepayment

	Number of Years to Prepayment of New Loan					
	2	4	6	8	10	15
Present value of old loan	$93,268.77	$95,926.01	$98,030.87	$99,635.40	$100,785.39	$101,923.32
Present value of new loan	90,000.00	90,000.00	90,000.00	90,000.00	90,000.00	90,000.00
PV of payment reductions	3,268.77	5,926.01	8,030.87	9,635.40	10,785.39	11,923.32
Cost of refinancing	6,300.00	6,300.00	6,300.00	6,300.00	6,300.00	6,300.00
Net refinancing benefit (*NPV*)	(3,031.23)	(373.99)	1,730.87	3,335.40	4,485.39	5,623.32

Existing loan is $90,000, 15 years remaining, 8 percent interest rate. Current market interest rate is 6 percent.

Assume you expect to pay off the loan at the end of six more years (72 months), leaving 108 months at payoff. Following our earlier method, we compute the balance at payoff as the present value of the 108 remaining payments. This gives a balance of $66,065.42.[15] Now we have the necessary information to compute the present value of the loan, prepaid. Discounting at the current loan interest rate of 6 percent, our computation is:

Thus, the present value of the existing loan, prepaid at the end of six years, is $98,030.87.

Concept Check

12.16 In the refinance decision, it is beneficial to refinance only if the present value of _____ less the present value of _____ exceeds _____ .

We have said that this present value is sensitive to the number of years the loan is outstanding (i.e., the holding period of the borrower). We explore the effect of this in Exhibit 12-5, using the loan terms above and assuming that refinancing costs are 7 percent of the new loan, or $6,300. The present value of payment reductions ranges from $3,268.77 for a two-year holding period to $11,923.32 with no prepayment in a 15-year holding period. Subtracting from this the cost of refinancing results in a net benefit of refinancing (*NPV*) ranging from negative $3,031.23 for a two-year holding period to positive $5,623.32 for a 15-year holding period.

It is clear from Exhibit 12-5 that the benefit of refinancing depends heavily on the expected holding period of the borrower. Under the assumptions of the example, refinancing is not beneficial unless the holding period for the new loan extends further than four years.

The benefit of refinancing depends on other factors as well. One of the principal ones is the spread between the interest rate on the existing loan and the new loan. Exhibit 12-6 shows the benefit of refinancing for a range of interest rate reductions (spreads) and holding periods, assuming, again, a $90,000, 15-year existing loan, a current loan rate of 6 percent, and refinancing costs of $6,300. Under these conditions, refinancing to gain a 1.0 percent interest rate reduction never makes financial sense. At a 2.5 percent reduction, in

15. This computation is as follows: $N = 108$, $I = .667$/month, $PV = ?$, $PMT = 860.09$, and $FV = 0$.

Exhibit 12-6 Refinancing Benefit (NPV) for Various Loan Interest Rate Spreads and Holding Periods

Interest Rate Spread	Monthly Payment Reduction	Holding Period (Years)					
		2	**4**	**6**	**8**	**10**	**15**
1.0	$ 49.47	$(4,671)	$(3,355)	$(2,320)	$(1,538)	$ (981)	$ (437)
1.5	74.84	(3,852)	(1,869)	(303)	886	1,734	2,569
2.0	100.62	(3,031)	(374)	1,731	3,335	4,485	5,623
2.5	126.79	(2,208)	1,129	3,782	5,811	7,272	8,726

Existing loan is $90,000, 15 years remaining. Current market interest rate is 6 percent. Cost of refinancing is $6,300 (7 percent of the loan amount).

contrast, refinancing is beneficial even for a four-year holding period. Of course, these results will improve dollar for dollar as the cost of refinancing is less.

Concept Check

12.17 The benefit of refinancing _____ as the expected holding period is longer and _____ as the spread is greater.

Refinancing Rules of Thumb. These results shed light on some "rules of thumb" widely referred to in news media as refinancing guides. Probably the most common rule of thumb has been a rule of interest rate spread; that is, the borrower should refinance when the interest rate spread between the existing loan and a new loan reaches 2 percentage points or some other level. However, it is clear from Exhibit 12-6 that a "spread" rule of thumb cannot cover the important variations in the benefits. In the table, a 2 percent spread rule only is correct for a holding period of six years or more. Moreover, this will change if the costs of refinancing change. In short, any interest rate spread rule of thumb is unable to account for a variation in refinancing benefits due to cost or holding period differences. It offers a one-dimensional solution to address a problem of at least three dimensions.

A second refinancing rule of thumb concerns a form of payback period. This approach divides the total cost of refinancing by the monthly payment reduction. For our example, the monthly payment reduction resulting from a new loan is shown in column 2 of Exhibit 12-6. Dividing each of these payment reductions into the assumed cost of refinancing ($6,300) shows that the payback period varies considerably with the interest rate spread. The interest rate spreads and resulting payback periods are as follows:

1.0 percent spread	127 months
1.5 percent spread	84 months
2.0 percent spread	63 months
2.5 percent spread	50 months

These results are remarkably consistent with the *NPV* results in Exhibit 12-5 in that the payback periods correspond closely to the minimum holding period for the NPV of refinancing to become positive. The exception is the 1 percentage point spread case. There, the undiscounted "payback period" results overstate the possibility of a beneficial refinancing due to the long payback period required. The higher the current mortgage interest rate, the greater will be this overstatement due to the absence of discounting in the payback rule.

In general, for shorter holding periods and larger interest rate spreads, the so-called payback period rule can give roughly the same decision signal as net present value. *NPV,* however, is more robust and informative, and not that much more difficult to compute with modern equipment.

Explore The Web

Mortgage Select's Mortgage Refi Calculator

Go to this website: www.mortgageselect.com/Calcs/Refinance.asp?referrer=162

Assume that you have the following existing mortgage: $100,000, 6 percent, 30 years, with 25 years remaining. Assume that you can replace it with this mortgage: $100,000, 5 percent, 30 years. Assume that savings will yield 2.5 percent. See if the result that you get from this calculation corresponds to your results using present value. Does a present value analysis break even at about the same time as what is indicated from the Web calculator?

Because home mortgage refinancing is a major financial decision that affects virtually all homeowners, many refinancing guides have appeared on the Internet. Regrettably, most are less sophisticated, and less adequate than the analysis presented here. One of the better examples, a graphical approach, appears in Explore the Web.

Concept Check

12.18 Which rule of thumb has a better chance of giving a valid result: interest rate spread rule or payback period?

Refinancing and Income Taxes. The refinancing decision is complicated by income tax effects. Since home mortgage interest is deductible from income being taxed, mortgage interest cost can be lower than the EBC. As a result, the interest payment reduction from refinancing is less valuable after tax. This works as follows: Suppose, for example, you are paying 30 cents in income taxes for every additional dollar of income. Then a mortgage interest tax deduction offsets your mortgage interest cost at the same rate, and 10 percent interest would cost 7 percent after taxes. But by the same logic, a new 9 percent loan will cost, after the tax deduction, 6.3 percent. Thus, the before-tax interest rate reduction of 1.0 percent is diminished, after tax, to:

$$7.0\% - 6.3\% = 0.7\%^{16}$$

In this example, suppose the present value of interest savings is about 30 percent greater than the refinancing cost. Then, after tax, it is about equal to cost, and NPV is close to zero.

Implicit Opportunity Cost of Refinancing. Refinancing involves an additional implicit cost. Suppose you refinance, and then loan interest rates decline. You have incurred the opportunity cost of missing the better deal. This cost is limited by the fact that if rates fall

---

16. Unfortunately, the tax effect is not, in reality, this straightforward. Borrowers only benefit from interest deductions to the extent that their total deductions exceed the standard deduction. For an increasing portion of households in the United States, mortgage interest deductions have little or no tax benefit, and the before-tax analysis above is the correct one.

sufficiently, you always can simply incur the cost of refinancing again and obtain the new rate.[17] We offer two observations on this risk of "jumping too early." Most financial economists argue that we never know whether interest rates will go up or down from where they currently are. Thus, the chance of rates falling further is 50 percent. This means that the expected value of the risk of jumping too early can never be greater than half the cost of refinancing again. We suspect it is a good bit less.

Accepting this reasoning, the borrower would require a greater decline in interest rates before refinancing is beneficial. Specifically, the borrower could increase the estimated cost of refinancing by 25 to 35 percent to account for this potential lost opportunity. Then the borrower would repeat the analysis just as we did in Exhibit 12-5 earlier.

The Effect of Income Taxes, Implicit Opportunity Cost and Borrower's Effort on the Refinancing Decision. We have noted two reasons why a borrower may regard our quantitative analysis of the refinancing decision as overstating the benefits. A third is that the experience of refinancing may be time-consuming and stressful for many homeowners. It is not possible to fully quantify all of these factors influencing the refinance decision. A plausible rule of thumb may be that these factors justify increasing the estimated cost of refinancing by 50 percent or more. Thus, the basic computations above are "upper bounds" on the benefit of refinancing. Since the *NPV* of refinancing decreases dollar for dollar with increased costs of refinancing, an easy decision test might be the following: Double the estimated cash cost of refinancing and see whether the net present value remains positive.

Refinancing Decisions with a Debt Increase. Many times a homeowner is interested in replacing an old mortgage loan with a larger loan, thus drawing out some of his or her equity from the home. These "cash-out" refinancings often are to replace high-cost consumer debt such as credit card debt, a car loan or a personal credit line loan. The analysis of a "cash-out" decision is analytically no different than our analysis above. The only changes are in the amounts to be used for the old loan balance and payments. The old loan amount becomes the total of all the existing debt to be replaced. Similarly, the payments on the old loan include the payments on all of the old debt. Thus, instead of finding the present value of one old loan, you find the present value of all the existing loans to be replaced, and sum the results. As above, you would discount each old loan at your appropriate discount rate, commonly the interest rate on the new, replacement loan. The equation for NPV becomes the following:

$$NPV = (\text{PV of All Existing Loans} - \text{PV of New Loan}) - \text{Cost of Refinancing}$$

The Default Decision

Default occurs when the mortgage borrower ceases to make timely payments of principal and interest. When this occurs, the lender must either renegotiate the terms of the mortgage with the borrower or take action to obtain title to the property. From the lender's perspective, the degree of default risk is related (1) to the probability that the market value of the home will fall below the remaining loan balance (plus the costs of foreclosure) and (2) to the risk that the lender will not be able to take possession of the home from the borrower in a timely fashion.

How prevalent is mortgage default? According to the Mortgage Bankers Association, payments on 4.7 percent of all outstanding single-family mortgages (conventional and FHA and VA) were past due, on average, during the first quarter of 2002. The past due delinquency rate averaged 4.3 percent a year from 1990 to 1999. However, only a small portion of these past-due mortgages end up in foreclosure. For example, lenders initiated foreclosure proceedings on only 0.35 percent of outstanding single-family loans, on average, during the fourth quarter of 2002.

---

17. Note that if refinancing were costless, this problem would not exist.

Why do borrowers become delinquent and sometimes default? There are two primary explanations. The first has to do with the borrower's ability to pay. The loss of employment, divorce, and other shocks to the household may hamper the borrower's ability—or willingness—to continue to service the debt. The second explanation centers on the amount of equity in the property. Borrowers with positive equity may not default even if a household shock renders them unable to make payments. To avoid the monetary and psychic costs of default, borrowers with positive equity can sell the property and use the proceeds to satisfy the outstanding loan balance. However, if the value of the home falls below the value of the outstanding mortgage (negative equity), the borrower has an incentive to default.

Concept Check

12.19   What two conditions typically must be present to result in home mortgage default?

Do borrowers immediately default if the value of their home falls below the value of the mortgage? Many homeowners with negative equity continue to make their monthly payments, perhaps because of fear of a bad credit rating, the financial and nonfinancial costs of forced relocation (they must live somewhere!), the house has more value to them than it would if sold in the open market, or they expect property values to recover. It appears that when a household encounters both negative equity and a household shock (e.g., divorce, loss of employment, or other catastrophe), default becomes more likely. However, if house prices decline precipitously, as they did in many parts of Texas, Oklahoma, and Colorado during the mid- to late-1980s, there is a widespread convergence of negative equity and unemployment, and households are increasingly likely to give the house back to the lender.

Summary

Prospective homebuyers are confronted with a number of choices and options when deciding what type of mortgage financing to obtain. Conventional loans (i.e., those that do not enjoy some form of government support) are clearly the dominant choice, accounting for roughly 85 percent of all single-family home loans. If these loans conform to standards set by Freddie Mac and Fannie Mae, they are frequently sold in the secondary mortgage market. With the development of elaborate secondary markets for residential mortgages, lenders have become dependent on and responsive to the requirements of the secondary market. They sell a majority of their fixed-rate loans into the secondary market as soon as, if not before, they actually create the loans. Because of these intricate linkages between primary and secondary mortgage market activities, it is impossible to gain an in-depth understanding of one market without first having a working knowledge of the other.

Conventional versus government-guaranteed financing is not the only mortgage choice potential borrowers face. They must also select a payment schedule that matches their risk tolerance and affordability concerns. Thirty-year, fixed-rate mortgages are currently the most popular alternative, while adjustable rate mortgages are gaining ground. Fifteen-year, fixed-rate mortgages still account for a sizable fraction of the market, while other options such as interest-only loans, partially amortized mortgages, and early payment mortgages are also available.

Homebuyers who borrow more than 80 percent of the purchase price are required to purchase private mortgage insurance (PMI). PMI typically insures the lender against default loss of up to 20 percent of the loan amount. If the lender must foreclose, the insurer will generally reimburse the lender for the remaining loan balance, take title to the property, and sell the asset for its current market value. PMI can be paid either as a lump sum or in monthly installments. After the loan has been paid down sufficiently, borrowers are permitted to cancel their mortgage insurance.

www.mhhe.com/lingarcher1e

Potential buyers should be aware of many alternative mortgage instruments that can alter the required payment schedule. For example, sellers may issue purchase-money mortgages to alleviate buyer affordability problems, or buyers may "buy down" the interest rate to alter the payment schedule. Reverse mortgages allow older homeowners to draw equity out of their residence. Package mortgages, which include home-related items such as appliances and furnishings, are particularly valuable to first-time homebuyers. Finally, a form of second mortgage, the home equity loan, is also very popular.

Borrowers, who should select the appropriate mortgage type based on effective borrowing cost, also face default and refinancing decisions. Basic financial theory indicates that the borrower should refinance when the present value of the payment savings exceeds the costs associated with the refinancing. In actuality, an additional potential cost to refinancing today is the inability to refinance at even lower rates tomorrow. Further, the benefits of refinancing depend on whether the borrower expects to treat mortgage interest as an itemized (i.e., explicit) deduction for taxes. As for default, basic financial theory again indicates that the borrower should default if and when the current market value of the property falls below the value of the outstanding mortgage. In reality, many homeowners with negative equity continue to make their monthly payments, perhaps because of fear of a bad credit rating or because the house has more value to them than it would if sold in the open market. In addition, there is the possibility that changed market conditions could bring improved value to the residence.

Key Terms

Conforming conventional loan 301
Conventional mortgage loan 301
Fannie Mae 300
Federal Housing Administration
   (FHA) 305
FHA mortgage insurance 305
Freddie Mac 300
Government-sponsored enterprise
   (GSE) 300

Home equity loans 310
Jumbo loans 302
Maturity imbalance problem 302
Mortgage insurance premium
   (MIP) 305
Mortgage menu 300
Nonconforming conventional loan 302
Package mortgage 309
Primary mortgage market 300

Private mortgage insurance
   (PMI) 303
Purchase-money mortgage
   (PMM) 309
Reverse mortgage 310
Secondary mortgage market 300
Section 203 loan 306
Veterans Affairs (VA) 305
VA-guaranteed loan 308

Test Problems

Answer the following multiple choice problems:

1. Private mortgage insurance (PMI) is usually required on _____ loans with loan-to-value ratios greater than _____ percent.
   a. Home, 75 percent.
   b. Home, 60 percent.
   c. Income property, 75 percent.
   d. Income property, 80 percent.
   e. None of the above.

2. The dominant loan type originated and kept by most depository institutions is the:
   a. Fixed-payment, fully amortized mortgage.
   b. Adjustable rate mortgage.
   c. Purchase-money mortgage.
   d. FHA-insured mortgage.

3. Which of the following mortgage types has the most default risk, assuming the initial loan-to-value ratio, contract interest rate, and all other loan terms are identical?
   a. Interest-only loans.
   b. Early payment loans.
   c. Partially amortized loans.
   d. There is no difference in the default risk of these loans.

4. A mortgage that is intended to enable older households to "liquify" the equity in their home is the:
   a. Graduated payment mortgage (GPM).
   b. Adjustable rate mortgage (ARM).
   c. Purchase-money mortgage (PMM).
   d. Reverse annuity mortgage (RAM).

5. A jumbo loan is:
   a. A conventional loan that is large enough to be purchased by Fannie Mae or Freddie Mac.

b. A conventional loan that is too large to be purchased by Fannie Mae or Freddie Mac.

c. A multiproperty loan.

d. A VA loan that exceeds the normal limits.

6. The maximum loan-to-value ratio for an FHA loan over $50,000 is approximately:

a. 90 percent.

b. 98 percent.

c. 99 percent.

d. 100 percent.

7. The maximum loan-to-value ratio on a VA-guaranteed loan is:

a. 90 percent.

b. 98 percent.

c. 99 percent.

d. 100 percent.

8. Conforming conventional loans are loans that:

a. Are eligible for FHA insurance.

b. Are eligible for VA guarantee.

c. Are eligible for purchase by Fannie Mae and Freddie Mac.

d. Meet federal Truth-in-Lending standards.

9. Home equity loans typically:

a. Are fixed-rate, fixed-term loans.

b. Are first mortgage loans.

c. Are originated by mortgage bankers.

d. Have tax-deductible interest charges.

10. The best method of determining whether to refinance is to use:

a. Present value analysis.

b. Effective cost of borrowing.

c. An interest rate spread rule.

d. A payback rule.

11. Probably the greatest contribution of FHA to home mortgage lending was to:

a. Establish the use of the level-payment home mortgage.

b. Create mortgage insurance for conventional loans.

c. Create the adjustable rate mortgage.

d. Create the home equity loan.

Study Questions

1. On an adjustable rate mortgage, do borrowers always prefer smaller (i.e., tighter) rate caps that limit the amount the contract interest rate can increase in any given year or over the life of the loan? Explain why or why not.

2. Explain the potential tax advantage associated with home equity loans.

3. Distinguish between conforming and nonconforming residential mortgage loans and explain the importance of the difference.

4. Discuss the role and importance of private mortgage insurance in the residential mortgage market.

5. Explain the maturity imbalance problem faced by savings and loan associations that hold fixed-payment home mortgages as assets.

6. Suppose a homeowner has an existing mortgage loan with these terms: Remaining balance of $50,000, interest rate of 8 percent, and remaining term of 10 years (monthly payments). This loan can be replaced by a loan at an interest rate of 6 percent, at a cost of 8 percent of the outstanding loan amount. Should the homeowner refinance? What difference would it make if the homeowner expects to be in the home for only five more years?

7. Assume an elderly couple owns a $140,000 home that is free and clear of mortgage debt. A reverse annuity mortgage (RAM) lender has agreed to a $100,000 RAM. The loan term is 12 years, the contract interest rate is 9.25 percent, and payments will be made at the end of each month.

a. What is the monthly payment on this RAM?

b. Fill in the following partial loan amortization table:

Month	Beginning Balance	Monthly Payment	Interest	Ending Balance
1	_____	_____	_____	_____
2	_____	_____	_____	_____
3	_____	_____	_____	_____
4	_____	_____	_____	_____
5	_____	_____	_____	_____

c. What will be the loan balance at the end of the 12-year term?

d. What portion of the loan balance at the end of year 12 represents principal? What portion represents interest?

8. Five years ago you borrowed $100,000 to finance the purchase of a $120,000 home. The interest rate on the old mortgage loan is 10 percent. Payments are being made *monthly* to amortize the loan over 30 years. You have found another lender who will refinance the current outstanding loan balance at 8 percent with monthly payments for 30 years. The new lender will charge two discount points on the loan. Other refinancing costs will equal $3,000. There are no prepayment penalties associated with either loan. You feel the appropriate opportunity cost to apply to this refinancing decision is 8 percent.

a. What is the payment on the old loan?

b. What is the current loan balance on the old loan (five years after origination)?

c. What would be the monthly payment on the new loan?

d. Should you refinance today if the new loan is expected to be outstanding for five years?

Explore The Web

1. Go to the Freddie Mac home page http://www. freddiemac.com/ and download information regarding Freddie Mac's role in the mortgage market. Briefly discuss the role secondary market institutions play and how they increase the efficiency of real estate markets.

2. Repeat question 2 using data from Fannie Mae: http://www.fanniemae.com/

Solutions to Concept Checks

1. The difference between the mortgage primary market and secondary market is that in the primary market, new loans are created by borrowers and lenders; in the secondary market, existing loans are sold by one investor to another.

2. A conventional home mortgage loan is simply any standard home mortgage loan not insured or guaranteed by the U.S. government.

3. Three major developments in the history of conventional mortgage loans since the 1930s were (1) introduction of the LPM, assisted by private mortgage insurance; (2) introduction of adjustable mortgage loans; (3) introduction of numerous alternatives to the standard 80–90 percent LPM beginning in the late 1990s.

4. Private mortgage insurance protects the lender from losses due to default. It indirectly aids the borrower by making the LPM a viable investment for lenders.

5. Lenders usually require mortgage insurance for loans in excess of 80 percent of value.

6. Two government agencies that provide direct housing assistance are the Farmers Home Administration and the Farm Credit System.

7. The up-front MIP for FHA mortgage insurance is 1.5 percent of the loan. It can be added to the loan amount. The monthly MIP for an FHA loan of 30 years is 0.5 percent of the average outstanding balance.

8. When the loan balance is below 78 percent of original value, both PMI and MIP must be discontinued.

9. The greatest historic contribution of the FHA was to introduce the level-payment mortgage and to demonstrate its viability.

10. The maximum loan-to-value for a VA loan is 100 percent. This requires a guarantee fee of 2 percent.

11. A purchase-money mortgage is a mortgage loan created simultaneously with the transfer of a property between buyer and seller. It typically is given by the buyer to the seller, but can be from a third party as well. It generally is a second mortgage loan.

12. Three attractions of a home equity mortgage loan include (1) a better interest rate than found with consumer loans, (2) longer term, and (3) tax deductibility of the interest.

13. Reverse mortgages are for older households who need more cash flow and who have substantial wealth accumulated in their residence.

14. The unique risk of a reverse mortgage is that the mortgage will "outgrow" the value of the securing residence. Special mortgage insurance has been created by the FHA to indemnify the lender in case this occurs, without causing the borrower to lose the home.

15. In comparing alternative mortgage choices, the principal tool is effective borrowing cost.

16. In the refinance decision, it is beneficial to refinance only if the present value of the old loan less the present value of the new loan exceeds the cost of refinancing.

17. The benefit of refinancing increases as the expected holding period is longer and increases as the spread is greater.

18. The payback period rule of thumb comes closer to the present value computation for refinancing than a spread rule can. Therefore, it is superior to the spread rule.

19. Typically, a homeowner does not default unless the loan exceeds the value of the residence, and the household has experienced some traumatic economic event such as death, unemployment, or divorce.

Additional Readings

Brueggeman, William B., and Jeffrey D. Fisher. *Real Estate Finance and Investments,* 11th ed., New York: McGraw-Hill Irwin, 2002.

Clauretie, T. M., and G. S. Sirmans. *Real Estate Finance: Theory and Practice,* 4th ed., Cincinnati, OH: South-Western Publishing, 2002.

Eldred, G. W. *106 Mortgage Secrets All Borrowers Must Know—But Lenders Won't Tell.* New York: John Wiley, 2003.

Fabozzi, Frank J., and Franco Modigliano. *Mortgage and Mortgage-Backed Securities Markets.* Cambridge: Harvard Business School Press, 1992.

Friedman, J. P., and J. C. Harris. *Keys to Mortgage Financing and Refinancing,* 3rd ed., Hauppauge, NY: Barron's Educational Series, 2001.

Garton-Good, J., and J. Good-Garton. *All About Mortgages: Insider Tips for Financing and Refinancing Your Home,* 2nd ed. Chicago: Dearborn Publishing, 1999.

Dennis, M. W. *Residential Mortgage Lending.* 4th ed., Cincinnati, OH: South-Western Publishing, November 1, 1994.

Wiedemer, John P. *Real Estate Finance,* 9th ed., Cincinnati, OH: South-Western Publishing, 2001.

chapter thirteen

Sources *of* Funds *for* Residential Mortgages

Learning Objectives

After reading this chapter you will be able to:

1. Contrast the traditional system of home mortgage lending with the modern, post-1980 system in terms of lenders and methods of doing business.

2. List four depository home mortgage lenders by size of market share, list two nondepository lenders, and identify the core difference between the latter two.

3. List the three major functions of mortgage banking, identify a major risk to be managed in each function, and how it is managed.

4. Distinguish the roles of Fannie Mae, Freddie Mac and Ginnie Mae in secondary mortgage markets by types of loans affected and by function.

5. List critical aspects of mortgage lending for which Fannie Mae and Freddie Mac have created uniformity, and state how this has improved mortgage markets.

6. State what home mortgage underwriting is, list the "three Cs" of traditional underwriting, and list what has changed or is changing with each "C" in the evolution of "automated underwriting."

7. List three reasons that automated underwriting is replacing traditional methods.

8. Identify three "deficiencies" of home loan applicants that can make them candidates for a "subprime" home mortgage loan.

Introduction

This chapter continues our examination of the residential mortgage market. In the preceding chapter, we discussed the most common types of mortgage instruments available to homeowners, including level-payment mortgages (LPMs) and adjustable rate mortgages (ARMs). We also contrasted conventional mortgages with government insured or guaranteed mortgage loans, and examined how the lender is protected through private mortgage insurance, FHA insurance, or the VA guarantee. We then considered several financing decisions a household faces after deciding to purchase a home, including the amount of mortgage debt to use, the type of loan to select from the mortgage menu, and the trade-off between the contract interest rate and the number of up-front discount points. We also considered two decisions that many borrowers face after obtaining mortgage funds: refinancing and default. We did not discuss where and how households obtain home loans.

This chapter first discusses the various sources of these home mortgage funds in the primary market—savings institutions, mortgage bankers, and commercial banks—as well as the most prominent government-sponsored programs that operate in the primary market. We then discuss the major purchasers of home loans in the secondary mortgage market, and the important role that secondary market securities play in real estate finance. Next, we outline the typical process residential lenders use when deciding whether to provide mortgage funds to a household. Finally, we examine the alternatives to the traditional home loan that have emerged in recent years for marginal home borrowers.

The effectiveness of our mortgage finance system has profound effects on the value of real estate. For example, few would question that increased availability and lower cost of mortgage funds have buoyed the housing market of the United States in recent years, increasing home ownership rates and sustaining strong housing appreciation. Our mortgage finance system is complex, and has gone through profound shock and change, as we will show. Still, it remains the most successful in the world. Whether it will continue to successfully adapt to changes in our society and in the world economy will have significant implications for the value of real estate in the future.

The Market for Residential Finance

Mortgage borrowers must compete to borrow funds in the credit markets. They must bid against other individuals, partnerships, corporations, financial institutions, state and local governments, and the federal government. Total mortgage debt outstanding at the end of first quarter 2003 exceeded $8.7 trillion. Exhibit 13-1 identifies the four major types of mortgage debt. Residential (home) mortgage debt exceeded $6.6 trillion and accounted for 76 percent of total outstanding mortgage debt. Loans for acquisition of apartment (multifamily) buildings represented 6 percent of the total, and loans to fund commercial real estate investments (e.g., office buildings, shopping centers, and warehouses) accounted for 16 percent of the total.

Exhibit 13-1 Mortgage Debt Outstanding by Type of Loan
(First Quarter, 2003, in Billions of Dollars)

Loan Type	Amount	Percent of Total
Residential (1–4 family)	$6,644	76%
Apartment (multifamily)	507	6
Commercial	1,425	16
Farm	127	2
Total	$8,703	100%

Source: *Federal Reserve Bulletin,* June 2003, Table 1.54, "Mortgage Debt Outstanding."

How large is the $6.6 trillion in outstanding residential debt? By way of comparison, the gross debt of the U.S. government was approximately $3.7 trillion at the end of 2002. The $6.6 trillion also is approximately twice as large as the value of all outstanding corporate bonds and more than three times as large as the amount of outstanding consumer debt.[1]

The institutions of residential real estate finance involve two stories: a traditional one and a modern one. The traditional story is about the role of depository lenders while the modern one is about the process known as mortgage banking, about securitization, and about the secondary market. In today's world the two stories intertwine in elaborate ways that we will explore.

Depository Lenders in the Primary Market

Depository institutions, such as savings and loan associations, savings banks, credit unions, and commercial banks, are major sources of home financing. These institutions also are called **financial intermediaries** because they bring together depositors and mortgage borrowers. They collect the savings (often small) of many individuals, households, and organizations, and then lend larger sums to individuals, households, and organizations that need them.

Savings Institutions (Thrifts) and Their Decline

Savings institutions, or thrifts, include **savings and loan associations (S&Ls), savings banks,** and credit unions. Together, the savings and loan associations and savings banks are a form of real estate financing system specialized for real estate finance, and one that is fading from view. Prior to the late 1970s, the financial system in the United States was localized to a degree difficult to imagine today. This contrast is suggested in Exhibit 13-2. In this old regime (left-hand portion), households deposited their short-term savings in local thrift

Exhibit 13-2   Traditional and Modern Housing Finance

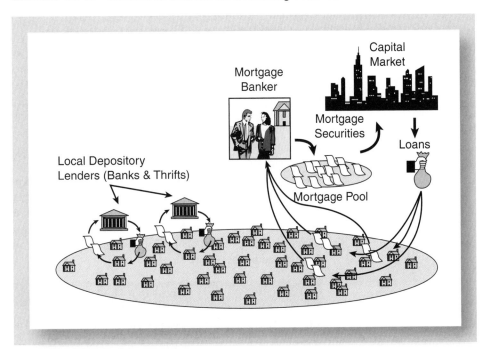

1. The source for these comparisons is the *Federal Reserve Bulletin,* July 2003, Tables 1.54, 1.41, 1.59, and 1.55.

institutions, which in turn used the savings to make mortgage loans to local borrowers. S&Ls and savings banks served as the backbone of mortgage finance, especially for home lending. Even the commercial real estate loans originated by S&Ls were typically for commercial facilities to support neighborhood development and housing. Savings banks, which were largely in the northeastern and Middle Atlantic states, were slightly more diversified in their investments. Still, they were far more like S&Ls than like banks. (There were, of course, exceptions among the thousands of thrifts. A few engaged heavily in nonresidential real estate finance, especially on the West Coast.)

This system worked exceedingly well in the post–World War II years. Despite a fatal vulnerability, the asset-liability maturity mismatch, the world of thrifts was rosy because interest rates remained low and stable.

But the thrifts became victims of their own system. When Congress created deposit insurance in 1933 and 1934 to save depository institutions from the financial panic of the Great Depression, in return for this salvation it also cocooned them in a vast array of regulations to assure their "safety and soundness." These regulations, which fiercely protected the local, narrowly scoped depository institutions, resulted in a localized system of real estate finance through thrifts, which thrived into the late 1970s.

However, the economic world changed dramatically during the 1970s. Names like Sony, Toshiba, Honda, Toyota, and others largely unrecognized in the United States became household words. Suddenly the U.S. economy and financial system were far more international than Congress, financial regulators, or even depository managers had ever conceived. This brought tides in the flows of capital funds never before seen, and interest rate volatility previously unknown. This change converged with an overheated economy in the late 1970s that began to fuel the fires of inflation. Meanwhile, as housing demand boomed— What better way to hedge inflation than to buy a bigger house?—thrifts were creating record levels of 30-year, fixed-rate home loans, funded by short-term local deposits. Throughout the thrift industry the "good times rolled" as never before. The only problem was to find attractive-enough toasters, golf bags, and other premiums to attract savings deposits that were earning less than the rate of inflation. (Thrifts had added to their cocoon in 1966 by agreeing to join with banks under "Regulation Q," which capped interest rates payable for savings deposits.)

But the party music turned to an ominous tone in the late 1970s when money market funds were born and savers suddenly could get a decent return on their short-term savings from Wall Street. **Disintermediation** raged as huge blocks of savings were diverted from thrifts to Wall Street.[2] Out of desperation, thrifts were forced to subvert "Reg Q," creating competitive market-yield savings deposits, and to organize unregulated "service corporation" subsidiaries to engage in hopefully high-yield, but risky, ventures. Then, in 1979 the good times collapsed. The Federal Reserve saw fit to "declare war" on inflation by restricting the growth of the money supply, and the result was catastrophic to the old housing finance system in the United States. Suddenly thrifts, gorged with new 30-year, fixed-rate home loans saw the cost of their deposits rise to, and even go above, the yield on their loan portfolios. In substance, a large percentage of thrifts were permanently crippled or dead at that point. Their net worth would be ravaged before rates began to fall in the middle 1980s, and most were left weak and vulnerable, if not desperate, thereafter. But savings associations were "money machines" that, thanks to deposit insurance, could continue to attract savings and pay interest out of their mortgage loan cash flows even as they "bled to death" through capital losses.

Concept Check

13.1   The basic financial vulnerability of savings and loan associations was:_____

---

2. *Disintermediation,* a horror word to depository institutions, refers to conditions when the growth of deposits becomes negative, due to other, more attractive, direct investment opportunities.

For the next decade, thrifts went through an inexorable and turbulent demise. As they fell, they created widespread "collateral damage" to overwhelmed regulators, to pressured members of Congress, and to taxpayers. Congress had raised deposit insurance from $40,000 to $100,000 per account for all depositories, and stripped off the cocoon of regulation beginning with the watershed Depository Institutions Deregulation and Monetary Control Act of 1980 (DIDMCA). The new laws enabled thrifts to invest in a wide variety of assets and may have saved some thrifts on the margin, or at least prolonged their demise. But because Congress failed to create adequate accountability, stripping off the regulations while increasing deposit insurance also served to give desperate thrifts more ways to exploit their "default option" by taking flagrant risks and to fall sensationally. A handful of thrifts created financial scandals and Congressional influence scandals of an order not seen again until the era of Enron. By 1989 the Federal Savings and Loan Insurance Corporation (FSLIC) had a mammoth deficit from covering savings deposits of failed thrifts, and it was estimated that taxpayers would need to cover its losses to the extent of at least $50 billion. Ultimately, some 1,300 thrifts failed.

In 1989 Congress enacted the Financial Institutions Reform, Recovery and Enforcement Act (FIRREA), which took major steps to establish depository institution accountability. The act finally created long-called-for risk-based capital standards for depository institutions. This was an effort, explained below, to "charge" financial institutions for risky behavior through higher net worth requirements. Its goal was to supplant the conventional regulatory approach of attempting to suppress risky behavior through restrictions—an approach that was always one step behind the actions of bank or thrift managers, and which ignored the incentives to engage in the risky behavior. FIRREA has affected many aspects of the mortgage lending business, including the portfolio (asset) requirements of regulated lenders, the licensing of real estate appraisers, and the minimum capital requirements of depository institutions.

To become a "Qualified Thrift Lender" under FIRREA, a S&L was required to hold at least 70 percent of its investments in residential mortgage loans or mortgage-backed securities. Core capital (net worth) requirements mandated that S&Ls have equity capital (i.e., common stock, retained earnings, and other liquid assets) equal to at least 3 percent of the value of the S&L's assets. In addition, S&Ls had to retain as equity capital an amount equal to at least 8 percent of the value of its **risk-weighted assets.** Assets are assigned a risk measure (or weight) by federal regulators of 0 to 200 percent. For example, a home mortgage loan carries a 50 percent weight. If the S&L makes an $80,000 loan, $3,200 in capital is required to support the loan ($0.50 \times 0.08 \times \$80,000$). If the risk weighting (level) is 0 (e.g., government bonds), no additional risk-based capital is required beyond the 3 percent core capital. Thus, the risk-based capital requirements compel the owners of financial institutions to have more equity capital at risk if they choose more risky investments. The resulting high capital requirements for real estate lending other than the simplest of home loans appears to have encouraged large numbers of thrifts to withdraw from development and construction financing, although one of their traditional spheres of activity was financing residential subdivison development.

Concept Check

13.2   A major new regulatory approach for thrifts introduced by the FIRREA was to impose _____ capital standards.

As a result of the closing of weak S&Ls and the strengthening of capital requirements, the thrift industry of the late 1970s shrank drastically in numbers, asset size, and its share of mortgage lending. While S&Ls were 4,000 strong in 1980, they numbered about 1,200 at the end of 2001, a decline of about 70 percent. While all thrifts had total assets in 1980 equal to 51 percent of commercial bank assets, their total assets at the beginning of 2000 was only 20 percent of bank assets. While S&Ls originated over one-half of all home

Industry Issues

13-1

Hubby, Wife are Golden Duo at Golden West Financial (World Savings)

In an era of debt downgrades and profit disasters, Herb and Marion Sandler (at Golden West's World Savings) are models of prudent management. They are risk averse: Golden West focuses on plain-Jane home loans—"the safest type of lending," Herb says. "No commercial loans, subprime, or loans for high-end homes in Silicon Valley." They are rational: While Herb, 70, and his wife and co-CEO, Marion, 71, have done 30 deals in four decades (Golden West's assets top $58 billion), they avoid acquisitions that dilute earnings. In his wallet Herb carries the words of his hero, Warren Buffett: "If a CEO is enthused about a particularly foolish acquisition, both his internal staff and his outside advisors will come up with whatever projections are needed to justify his stance. Only in fairy tales are emperors told that they are naked."

Equally impressive, the Sandlers have survived as a couple. Herb met Marion 42 years ago. A Wall Street analyst following financial services companies, she convinced Herb, a lawyer, that S&L bosses were weak managers; they could do better. They quit their jobs, drove west in a Chevy convertible, borrowed $3 million, and bought a tiny S&L. "She gave me the courage to do this," says Herb.

In many ways Herb and Marion are throwbacks to a simpler time. They do their advertising in-house. ("How may we help you?" is the pitch for Golden West's World Savings banks.) In investor meetings they shun slides—they view them as unimaginative.

It's corny, but it works. Over the past decade Golden West stock has delivered on average a 20.5 percent total return to investors versus 11.5 percent for the S&P. Herb and Marion recently unearthed a list from 1989 of the then-largest S&Ls. Of the 20 on that list, 19 have died or been acquired; Golden West is the only independent survivor.

As of 2003, Golden West is the second largest thrift, behind Washington Mutual. It was the first thrift ever to receive a Moody's AA credit rating, and has enjoyed 35 years of 20 percent growth in earnings per share. In 2003 the Sandlers were named to *USBanker's* All Star Banking Team of 2002, and Marion Sandler has been recognized as among the 100 most influential women in business.

Source: Excerpts from "Hubby, Wife are Golden Duo" Patricia Sellers, an article *Fortune*, March 4, 2002.

---

www.fdic.gov/bank/historical/index.html

A Federal Deposit Insurance Corporation (FDIC) site with extremely rich documentation and discussion of the story of thrift and bank struggles since 1980.

mortgage loans from 1975 to 1979, by the end of 1997 their share of home loan originations was barely 15 percent.

Today thrifts are little more than a shadow of their original role in home mortgage finance. The survivors, however, are a profitable and stable, if more modest, industry. But, while the CEOs of thrifts often were among the leading financial figures in cities of the Sun Belt, there are no thrifts in many of these cities today. Surviving thrifts have reshaped into a variety of forms. Many have sought to assume the role of a community bank. Others have become, in substance, mortgage bankers. Still others have evolved "boutique" roles with an emphasis on specialty areas of real estate finance. For example, a few have concentrated on marginal, or subprime home lending, with mixed success. Others have concentrated on commercial or multifamily mortgage lending.

One notable exception to disappearing thrifts is Washington Mutual ("WaMu"), based in Seattle, Washington. After buying up numerous other thrifts and amassing the largest portfolio of home mortgage servicing in the United States, and achieving the largest volume of home loan originations in the industry by 2001, WaMu has expanded to nonresidential lending. Thus, while still serving the classic markets of the thrift, it has grown to become one of the 10 largest financial institutions in the country. Most other large thrifts continue to disappear, however, through acquisition by other large thrifts or by bank holding companies. Of the 20 largest thrifts in 1989, only one, Golden West Financial Corporation of Oakland, California, has retained continuity of ownership. (See Industry Issues 13-1.) One common theme among thrifts that remain in home mortgage lending is the origination of adjustable rate mortgages. In recent times ARMs have represented 40 percent of thrift home loan originations.

Credit Unions

Credit unions also are a form of thrift, with over 11,000 operating in the United States. Their charters restrict them to serving a group of people who can show a common bond such as employees of a corporation, government unit, labor union, or trade association. In years past, credit unions played only a marginal role in home mortgage lending. However, they have been able to expand the definition of their "common bond" of membership in recent years, enabling many to grow considerably in size and diversity of services. This has brought them to greater activity in home mortgage lending. Most credit unions today can offer home mortgage loans and home equity credit lines. However, their role is likely to be as a mortgage broker (discussed below) rather than as a traditional depository lender. Altogether, their share of total home mortgage lending appears to remain around 3 percent.

Commercial Banks

Banks historically have served several roles in real estate finance. The core business of **commercial banks** traditionally has been to make short-term loans to businesses for inventory financing and other working capital needs. But a very important adjunct of this business always has been to meet the real estate finance needs of business customers. This included financing of business-related real estate, mortgage loans for personal residences, and sometimes financing of investment real estate. In addition, with the demise of thrifts as the primary source of financing for residential subdivision development and for home construction, banks have captured much of these real estate roles as well. Finally, of course, virtually all banks offer home loans as a service to nonbusiness customers. Similar to S&Ls, banks are increasingly likely to immediately sell their fixed-rate residential originations in the secondary mortgage market.

Larger commercial banks have traditionally provided funds for real estate finance in two other ways. First, they make short-term construction loans that provide funds for the construction of multifamily, commercial, and industrial buildings. The timing and risks of construction lending are not unlike business inventory lending, and therefore tend to be "natural" for banks. Thus, they have traditionally dominated the commercial construction lending business. Second, some large commercial banks also have specialized in providing short-term funds to mortgage banking companies (which will be discussed below) to enable them to originate mortgage loans and hold the loans until the mortgage banking company can sell them in the secondary mortgage market. This type of financing is termed **warehousing** because the mortgage bankers put up the originated loans as security for the bank financing and the loans are "stored" (at the bank or with a trustee) for a relatively short time.

Banks have gone through much stress and change since 1980. The same initial legislation that deregulated thrifts, DIDMCA, began a series of empowerments to commercial banks that ultimately has led the industry to a profound transformation. Powers that banks had lost by the reforms of the early 1930s slowly were regained through a complex sequence of state legislative actions, Congressional actions, and regulatory changes. This transformation in their governing framework was essentially completed in 1994.[3] In the process, banks regained powers to engage in insurance and securities businesses, in real estate investment and development, and gained the ability to engage in interstate branching, acquisitions, and mergers.

Parallel to the broadening of bank powers came significant changes in the workings of bank regulation. Historically, the regulatory framework of banking was labyrinthine. State-chartered banks generally were regulated by their state, the FDIC, and the Federal Reserve

---

3. Congress enacted the Riegle Community Development and Regulatory Improvement Act of 1994 which addressed, among other issues, simplification and efficiency of regulation; and the Riegle-Neal Interstate Banking and Branching Efficiency Act of 1994 which provided for the possibility of full interstate branching, acquisitions and mergers by 1997. The latter law effectively finished a process that already had become far advanced. State legislation enabling reciprocal interstate banking through bank holding companies was well advanced by the early 1990s.

System (Fed). Federally chartered banks were regulated by the Office of the Controller of the Currency, by the FDIC, and by the Fed. This system was replete with duplication of requirements and conflicting rules. Thus, a crucial part of the transformation was elimination of much of the duplication and inefficiency in regulation, permitting larger, more complex, multistate operations. Out of this transformation in bank powers and bank regulation, completed in the mid-1990s, has come the megabanks of today.

Concept Check

13.3 Name three ways that banks traditionally have served mortgage lending.

The new world of deregulated banking has brought still another relationship of banking to residential real estate finance. Several megabanks have identified megascale residential mortgage banking as a business opportunity. Wells Fargo, Bank of America, Chase Manhattan, National City Bank, Citigroup, and other banking groups hold mortgage banking subsidiaries that not only are among the largest mortgage bankers in the country, but also have reached unprecedented levels of market share. This phenomenon is discussed further below.

Concept Check

13.4 Today the largest market share in home mortgage lending among depository lenders is held by:

Nondepository Lenders in the Primary Market

The depository lenders discussed in the previous section historically dominated the home mortgage origination business before the 1980s. Using savings deposits, these institutions funded long-term home mortgage loans and then held the whole loans as investments. That is, they were **portfolio lenders.** However, as financial institutions in the United States suffered through the 1980s and early 1990s, mortgage companies emerged as the central element for a new system of home mortgage originations. Mortgage companies have accounted for over 50 percent of all conventional home mortgage originations since 1993. Their share of the FHA/VA originations market (discussed below) is even larger—exceeding 80 percent.[4]

Mortgage companies vary widely in the scope of their activities. **Mortgage bankers** are full-service mortgage companies: They process, close, provide funding, and sell the loans they originate in the secondary mortgage market. They also typically service the loans they have sold (e.g., collect monthly payments). However, some mortgage companies specialize in the details of loan origination. These firms are referred to as **mortgage brokers.** Brokers do not provide the funding (or capital) for the loan, nor do they typically service the loans after selling them. Instead, they serve strictly as an intermediary between those who demand mortgage funds (borrowers) and those who supply the funds (lenders or secondary market investors).

Concept Check

13.5 Name two ways that mortgage brokers differ from a typical mortgage banker.

---

4. Based on the top 15 FHA/VA originators which accounted for approximately 92.5 percent of all FHA/VA originations in 2001. Source: *The 2002 Mortgage Market Statistical Annual,* vol. 1. Inside Mortgage Finance Publications, Inc. Bethesda, Md, 2002.

Mortgage Bankers

Mortgage bankers lend funds for home financing. They are not financial intermediaries, however, because they do not accept deposits. They combine a small portion of equity with vast amounts of borrowed capital to originate loans. They then sell the loans as rapidly as possible to institutional investors and secondary mortgage market participants. Thus, they are not portfolio lenders. The home loans originated by mortgage bankers are usually either FHA or VA loans or are conforming loans that meet the purchase requirements of Fannie Mae and Freddie Mac. The guarantee or insurance and underwriting standards for these loans mitigate much of the default risk of home mortgage loans for lenders, allowing the loans to be more easily sold to investors in the secondary market.

The mortgage banking process creates two valuable financial assets: the loan and the rights to service the loan. As depicted in Exhibit 13-3, the process begins with the loan application of a borrower. The loan always is sold, but through a variety of ways. Since the servicing rights are the profit center of mortgage banking, they may be retained or sold, depending partly on the size of the firm. This mortgage banking process is explored in more detail in the following sections.

www.mortgagebankers. org/resident/

The home mortgage lending page of the Mortgage Bankers Association of America, the primary organization, in the mortgage banking industry. This website is a reference point for the entire industry.

Loan Commitments and Funding. If the borrower is applying for a level-payment mortgage, the lender usually offers the applicant several choices on when to "lock in" the contract interest rate. These choices may include the time the loan application is taken, when the lender commits to fund the loan, or when the mortgage loan is acquired (at closing).

The major traditional source of funding for mortgage companies, discussed above, is bank "warehouse" lines of credit. These enable the mortgage companies to originate far more home loans than their equity capital alone would support. When the loans are sold in the secondary mortgage market, the bank line of credit is paid down and the process starts again.

Pipeline Risk. The period between loan commitment and loan sale exposes mortgage bankers to considerable risk called **pipeline risk.** For example, assume during a given week that a lender commits to originate and fund a number of 30-year, fixed-payment mortgages.

Exhibit 13-3 The Mortgage Banking Process Creates Two Financial Assets:
A Loan and Servicing

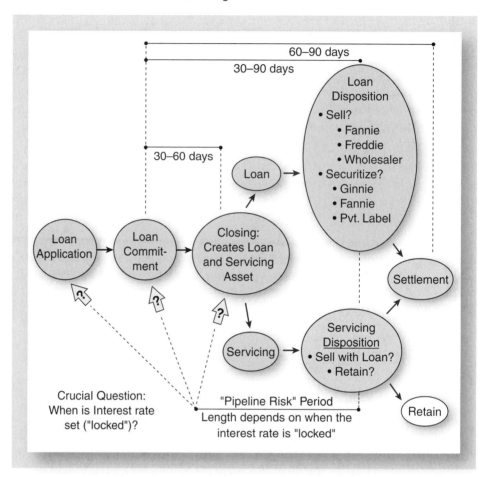

These commitments are added to the originator's **mortgage pipeline**—a term used to describe loans from the time a lender has made a commitment to lend through the time loans are sold to an investor. Also, assume borrowers choose to lock in an 8 percent contract rate when they receive the commitment. The approved borrowers often have 45 to 60 days to close ("take down") the loans. If mortgage interest rates decline, some of the borrowers may choose not to close the loan at the end of the 45 or 60 days because, in the meantime, they have obtained a lower rate from another lender. This potential loss of borrowers is called pipeline **fallout risk.** If interest rates rise after the lender makes the commitment at 8 percent, a larger percentage of loans in the pipeline will close because borrowers will be unable to find a better deal.

Concept Check

13.6 Pipeline risk refers to the period in mortgage banking between making a
_____ for a loan and _____ the loan.

However, if rates rise over the commitment period, the contract rate at closing will be less than the current market rate and the mortgage banker will have to sell the newly originated loan at a discount (for *less* than the amount originated). This threat is called **interest rate risk.**

Interest rate risk and resulting price declines over the loan pipeline cycle can be disastrous to a mortgage banking firm. Many firms have disappeared overnight by not being prepared for it. Thus, mortgage bankers seek to hedge the risk. One hedging technique is to purchase a **forward commitment** from a secondary market investor with a prespecified future selling price. This commitment obligates the secondary market investor to purchase, and the mortgage banker to sell, a prespecified dollar amount of a certain type of loan. The commitment is for a limited period of time, usually 30 days to six months. The forward commitment also will specify the price (and therefore the yield) at which the mortgages will be purchased. For example, the secondary market investor may commit to purchase $20 million of 9 percent fixed-rate loans at a price of "99." This means that the investor will pay the mortgage banker $99 per $100 of outstanding mortgage principal for any 9 percent mortgage delivered to the investor during the commitment period.

Mortgage bankers know from experience that only part of the loan commitments they issue will be taken down by the borrowers. For this reason, they often purchase **standby forward commitments** from secondary market investors that give them the right, but not the obligation, to sell a certain dollar amount of a certain loan type to the issuer of the standby commitment. If a larger than expected portion of the loans in the mortgage banker's pipeline are taken down by borrowers, perhaps because interest rates have risen, the option to sell the mortgages is exercised by the mortgage banker. However, if mortgage rates have fallen over the commitment period and an unexpectedly large amount of pipeline fallout occurs, the mortgage banker is not obligated by the standby commitment to deliver mortgages that are not in hand.

Concept Check

13.7   Forward sales and standby forward sales are ways that a mortgage banker can _____ pipeline risk.

Exhibit 13-4 depicts a strategy some mortgage bankers use to protect against changes in interest rates over the commitment period. The rectangle represents the total number of mortgages, or pipeline, of a specific type (e.g., 30-year LPMs with 8.5 percent contract rates) on which the mortgage banker has issued commitments to borrowers. The top part represents the portion of the pipeline the lender is confident will be taken down by borrowers, regardless of changes in interest rates. This portion of the pipeline exposes the lender to interest rate risk. But since it is predictable in amount, it can be hedged by obtaining forward commitments, which effectively presell the loans. The bottom portion of

Exhibit 13-4   The Three Mortgage Banking "Pipeline" Risk Situations

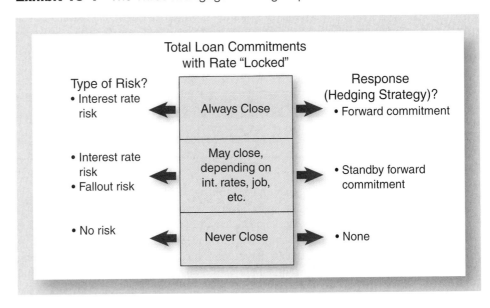

the pipeline represents the loans the lender strongly expects not to be taken down. This portion does not need to be hedged at all. The middle portion of the pipeline is the most complex. It exposes the lender to interest rate risk if interest rates rise, but to fallout risk if rates fall. Thus, the lender cannot simply "sell forward" this portion of the loans as with the first portion. The mortgage banker is willing to buy a costly standby forward commitment to be protected against interest rate increases, and not have to deliver if this portion of the pipeline is not taken down by borrowers. Experience and an understanding of current interest rate expectations dictate the relative size of the three rectangles. Management of the pipeline risk is uniquely critical to the safety of a mortgage banking firm. Therefore, the person responsible for it is a crucial individual in the company, and typically very well rewarded for bearing the responsibility.

Servicing. The primary source of revenue in mortgage banking is the right to service the loans created. **Loan servicing** includes collecting the monthly payment from the borrower and remitting principal and interest payments to the investor(s). It also includes ensuring that the borrower's monthly escrow payments for hazard insurance and property taxes are sufficient to allow the servicer to pay in full the annual insurance premium and property taxes on behalf of the borrower when they are due. Servicers also are responsible for sending out notifications if borrowers are delinquent with their payments, and managing default, even foreclosure, should it arise. Mortgage bankers and other servicers receive a monthly fee for servicing the loans, which amounts to 0.25 to 0.44 percent (annually) of the outstanding loan balances. For example, if the outstanding balance of a loan at the beginning of a month is $100,000, and the annual servicing fee is 0.375 percent, then the servicer's fee for that month would be $31.25 ($0.00375 \div 12 \times \$100,000$). If the borrower's monthly mortgage payment is $750, the servicer would keep $31.25 and pass $718.75 on to the secondary market investor that owns the mortgage. Servicing rights may be retained by the loan originator or sold. Commonly, servicing has had a market value of 1 to 2 percent of the amount of the loan.

Other Sources of Revenue. Mortgage bankers may earn revenues from several other sources in addition to servicing. Like all home loan originators, mortgage bankers normally charge borrowers a nonrefundable application fee of between $50 and $200 at the time of the loan application. Mortgage bankers also charge an origination fee that is payable if and when the loan closes. The origination fee is typically 1 percent of the loan amount and is separate from any discount points the mortgage banker may require the borrower to pay at closing. Normally, the origination fee does not cover the total cost of origination, which includes direct expenses plus the commission of the loan representative who takes the loan application and works with the borrower in documenting and processing the required paperwork. The shortfall is viewed as a cost for creating the servicing rights to the loan. Mortgage bankers also stand to make (or lose) money when they sell loans into the secondary market without forward commitments or other hedges, but this is widely regarded as a very risky source of revenue, at best.

Concept Check

13.8   The primary source of mortgage banking profit is from _____ .

Megamortgage Banking. The birth of megabanking and the explosion of cybercommunication have converged to drastically affect home mortgage lending, especially mortgage banking. Unprecedented economies of scale now appear possible in mortgage banking, given enough capital and potential volume of business. As mentioned above, the new megabanks have committed to this possibility, have acquired mortgage banking subsidiaries, and are well along in wedding the mortgage banking process with cyberspace.

Exhibit 13-5 Consolidation in the Top 20 Home Mortgage Lenders

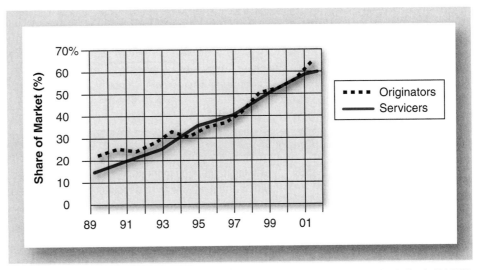

Source: The *2002 Mortgage Market Statistical Annual*, vol 1. Inside Mortgage Finance Publications Inc. Bethesda, Md. 2002.

The result has been a transformation in borrower interface and scale of operation. The megamortgage bankers operate in four modes: traditional "face-to-face" (retail) lending, purchases of loans from smaller mortgage bankers (wholesale lending), Internet lending, and lending through mortgage brokers. In all of this, they exploit the most advanced electronic communications systems. Perhaps the most significant impact of the megamortgage banking approach up to the year 2002 has been the increased reliance on the Internet and on mortgage brokers (discussed below). Some large traditional mortgage banking firms have simply eliminated their retail operations, turning primarily to wholesale, broker operations, and the Internet for their business.

Another effect of megamortgage banking has been the unprecedented rise in industry concentration, shown in Exhibit 13-5. In 1989 the top 20 originators of home mortgages accounted for 23 percent of all first-lien home mortgage originations. (The top 10 originators accounted for 15 percent.) But in 2001 the top 20 originators accounted for nearly 65 percent of these originations (and the top 10 accounted for over 51 percent). As can be seen from Exhibit 13-5, the concentration of home mortgage servicing has been just as dramatic. An important consequence of this new concentration is that megamortgage banking has reached a scale where the lenders can afford the "front-end" cost to innovate with new loan products to an unprecedented extent. (See Industry Issues 12-1.)

Mortgage Brokers

Mortgage lending has become increasingly complex. As a result, the demand for knowledgeable mortgage brokers has increased significantly. As mentioned previously, a mortgage broker operates differently from a mortgage banker in that a broker does not actually make loans. Instead, a mortgage broker specializes in serving as an intermediary between the borrower (the customer) and the lender (the client). Many mortgage brokers serve as correspondents for large mortgage bankers who desire to do business in an area but do not feel the volume of business justifies the expense of staffing a local office. As compensation, the broker receives a fee for taking the loan application and a portion of the origination fee if and when the loan closes. Many industry analysts expect the role of mortgage brokers to continue to grow in conjunction with the explosion in information technology. As brokers gain access to instantaneous interest rate quotes from multitudes of mortgage originators, their ability to find the lowest-cost option for borrowers should increase the value of their services.

www.namb.org

Website of the National Association of Mortgage Brokers.

In this growth of mortgage brokers also lies some concern. It has been argued that mortgage brokerage frequently can be a part-time activity wherein the broker generates a fee through a one-time involvement with the borrower. Under these conditions, problems could arise. First, the broker could be only marginally knowledgeable. Second, and more importantly, there is the risk of moral hazard. The broker is offering a complex service on a one-time basis to borrowers, many of who may be poorly informed. Since the broker often has no continuing involvement with the loan or borrower, this creates an incentive for exploitation.

Concept Check

13.9 Why might there be more concern about moral hazard in mortgage brokerage than with mortgage banking or depository mortgage lenders?

Other Nongovernment-Sponsored Lenders in the Primary Market

With the ascendancy of mortgage banking in real estate lending has come dramatic growth in the secondary mortgage market. This has encouraged large finance companies to enter the home mortgage origination business. For example, companies with experience in other types of consumer lending, such as GE Financial Network, General Motors Acceptance Corporation, and AT&T Capital, are now underwriting home loans. Several finance companies (e.g., Household Finance) also are originating home loans. Nevertheless, these other sources still account for less than 1 percent of the residential originations market.

The Secondary Market for Residential Mortgages

The ultimate source of funds for mortgage lending depends on whether the loans are sold in the secondary market, and to whom. Well-developed private secondary markets exist for many stocks and bonds, and for some physical assets. But the secondary market for residential mortgages before government involvement in the early 1970s was, to state it kindly, informal. About the only secondary market for mortgages involved lenders, usually mortgage bankers, loading bundles of FHA loans in a suitcase and carrying them up to northeastern states to "peddle" them to insurance companies or savings banks who had a shortage of local loan investment opportunities.[5]

The reasons for a weak private secondary mortgage market included the variation in mortgage instruments among states, the differences among properties that serve as collateral for the mortgage, differing appraisal practices, and varying loan standards and underwriting practices of lending institutions (i.e., the process and policies for evaluating the risks of mortgage loan default). This lack of standardization made it extremely difficult for purchasers in the secondary mortgage market to analyze the risk and return characteristics of mortgage investments, which in turn increased the return (or yield) they required on mortgage investments—if they were willing to invest at all. The originating lenders then passed on these higher required yields to mortgage borrowers in the form of higher mortgage rates.

The absence of an effective secondary market created liquidity problems for mortgage originators because loans could not be quickly and easily sold. It also resulted in fewer loans and higher mortgage interest rates for homebuyers, and created sizable home mortgage interest rate differentials among growth areas of the United States, such as California and Florida, and the more mature areas of the Northeast and Midwest. Finally, in periods of increased interest rates, disintermediation would restrict flows of savings into thrifts,

---

5. As described by a veteran mortgage banker, Mr. David Ginn.

leaving local mortgage lenders without funds to lend and unable to sell the loans they already had originated. As a result, horror stories were not uncommon in the late 1960s and early 1970s of lenders simply "shutting the credit window" and bringing otherwise active local housing markets to a standstill.

The lack of a well-functioning secondary market for residential mortgages was addressed in 1968 by Congress. It spun *Fannie Mae* (then, the Federal National Mortgage Association, or FNMA) out of the Department of Housing and Urban Development to establish it as a separate, quasi-private corporation to act as a buyer of FHA and VA loans. In the same act Congress created the Government National Mortgage Association **(GNMA),** popularly known as Ginnie Mae, as a unit within HUD. Among its intended roles was to guarantee mortgage-backed securities based on pools of FHA, VA, and Farmers Home Administration (FmHA) loans. (See below.) Two years later, recognizing the need for a secondary market for conventional loans, Congress also created *Freddie Mac* (then known as the Federal Home Loan Mortgage Corporation). These steps laid the groundwork for a revolutionary system of housing finance which, out of the wreckage of the thrift-based system, would burst forth 10 years later.

Mortgage-Backed Securities

Perhaps the most important innovation that occurred in residential mortgage markets since World War II was the development of the market for mortgage-backed securities (MBSs). This process for the GNMA MBS is depicted in Exhibit 13-6. Passthrough MBSs are created by pooling a group of similar mortgages. The owner then uses the mortgage pool as collateral for the issuance of a new security—the MBS. For example, a mortgage banker assembles a $100 million pool of 7.5 percent, 30-year, level-payment mortgages. The mortgage banker then sells an undivided interest, or participation, in the mortgage pool to many investors who are promised an 7 percent rate of interest on their invested capital. The issuer continues to service the underlying mortgages, collecting payments from borrowers and "passing through" to each security holder (1) its pro rata (proportionate) share of any principal repayments on the underlying mortgages and (2) 7 percent interest on its share of any outstanding principal that the issuer of the MBS has not returned to the investors. The difference between the 7.5 percent rate on the underlying mortgages and the 7 percent rate paid to investors is kept by the MBS issuer. This "spread" must cover the issuer's issuance and servicing costs, and the cost of absorbing the default risk in the pool of mortgages. When a

Exhibit 13-6 The GNMA Mortgage-Backed Security Process

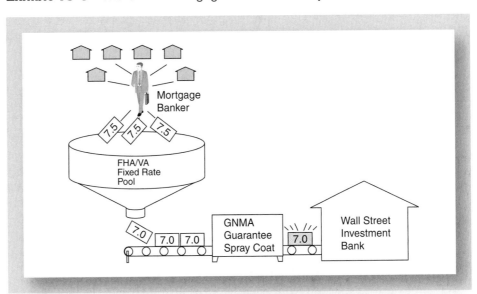

Exhibit 13-7   Securitization of Home Mortgages

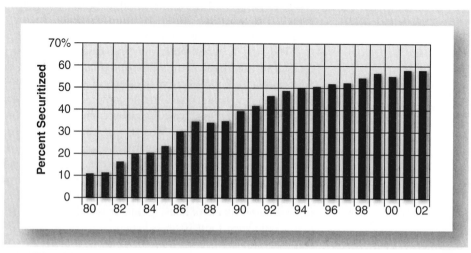

Source: *Federal Reserve Bulletin,* June 2003, Table 1.54.

mortgage is used as collateral for the issuance of a MBS, the underlying mortgage is said to be "securitized." Agencies and private companies that pool mortgages and sell MBSs are sometimes called **conduits.**

Between one-half and two-thirds of all residential mortgage loans originated in the United States are now sold into the secondary mortgage market and used as collateral for the issuance of mortgage-backed securities. This securitization of pools of standardized residential mortgages has greatly increased the liquidity and efficiency of the mortgage market. By attracting nontraditional investors, such as pension funds, life insurance companies, and mutual funds, MBSs have brought many new sources of investment capital into the residential mortgage market. The dramatic change that securitization represents in home mortgage lending is indicated in Exhibit 13-7. In 1980 just over 10 percent of all home mortgages were securitized. At the beginning of 2002 almost 60 percent had been securitized and sold in the secondary market.

Concept Check

13.10   The three main government-related entities involved in creation or support of residential mortgage backed securities are: _____

Purchasers of Residential Mortgages in the Secondary Market

Through the three formative decades of the home mortgage secondary market, up to 2002, the story of the market was the story of Ginnie Mae, Fannie Mae, and Freddie Mac. To be sure, other entities played significant and productive roles, including private conduits and state government housing agencies. But it was in the game defined by "Ginnie," "Fannie," and "Freddie" that the others played. Below is an "up close and personal" of these players.

Ginnie Mae (GNMA)

Ginnie Mae is the popular name for the Government National Mortgage Association (GNMA), a government-owned and financed corporation, which originally was charged with three functions. The first was to liquidate certain assets left behind by Fannie Mae as it was removed from HUD. Second was to subsidize the cost of housing for low-income families. This was to be accomplished by what was called the "tandem" program. The National Housing Act of 1968 which established the modern Ginnie Mae, also created the largest subsidized housing finance programs in history, launching massive below-market interest rate FHA loan programs for home ownership and for construction of rental housing. Ginnie Mae would purchase these below-market interest rate mortgages at face value (or par)—instead of at their true, discounted value—from the private lenders originating them. It then would sell them to Fannie Mae at market value. Thus, the difference between the loan's par value and discounted value would be absorbed by Ginnie Mae, providing a subsidy that made the loans viable for lenders.

Concept Check

13.11 GNMA's role in residential mortgage-backed securities is to guarantee _____ to the investors in the securities.

But Ginnie Mae's most enduring activity came to be as the guarantor of mortgage-backed securities. The Ginnie Mae MBS became the definitive mortgage "pass-through" security. Through its first 20 or more years, it remained the most liquid and widely held single type of MBS. Further, it was the security that introduced much of the investment community to MBSs. In this program Ginnie Mae does not issue, buy, or sell mortgages or MBSs. Rather, as suggested in Exhibit 13-6, its role is to guarantee the timely payment of principal and interest on MBSs issued by private lenders. Ginnie Mae primarily guarantees MBSs backed by pools of FHA-insured or VA-guaranteed fixed-rate mortgages. These securities carry the full faith and credit of the U.S. government. Ginnie Mae mortgage-backed securities are thus free of default risk—just like Treasury securities—and therefore trade at relatively low yields. By linking housing and mortgage markets to the capital markets, this tremendously successful program has channeled vast sums of investment capital into the residential mortgage market. In the first quarter of 2003, $512 billion in MBSs guaranteed by Ginnie Mae were outstanding, or about 8.0 percent of the residential mortgage market. While the market share of the Ginnie Mae MBS has yielded to the growth in recent years of MBSs based on conventional loan pools, it remains among the largest and most liquid of MBSs.

www.ginniemae.gov/

Website of Ginnie Mae. Information for homebuyers, issuers, and investors.

Fannie Mae

Fannie Mae was created as the the Federal National Mortgage Association in 1938 to provide a secondary market for FHA-insured mortgages and, later, VA-guaranteed loans. Congress expected it to set an example for private lenders and investors of how to operate in the secondary mortgage market. In 1968 Fannie Mae became a private, self-supporting company. However, it could continue to borrow with government assistance (the importance of which is discussed below). Under a congressional charter, Fannie Mae continues to be obligated to help attain the national goal of safe and decent housing for low- and moderate-income families. In 1970 Fannie Mae was authorized to purchase conventional mortgages in addition to FHA-insured and VA-guaranteed loans, but it remained focused on FHA and VA loans throughout the 1970s. Although Fannie Mae does not lend money directly to homebuyers, it helps ensure that mortgage funds are consistently available and affordable by buying mortgages from qualified lenders who are making home loans.

Fannie Mae now has well-developed programs for the purchase of both conventional and government-underwritten residential mortgages from mortgage companies, commercial banks, savings and loan associations, and other approved lenders. The majority of these acquired mortgages are combined into packages or mortgage pools, mortgage-backed securities are written against the pools, and the MBSs are then sold to investors. The agency obtains its funds for the acquisition of mortgage pools by selling stock in the public capital market (its stock is traded on the New York Stock Exchange), selling MBSs, obtaining (forward) commitment fees from originating lenders for loan purchases, earning interest on its mortgage portfolio and other investments, and selling notes and bonds to fixed-income investors.

Concept Check

13.12   Whereas Fannie Mae was created to purchase _____ and _____ mortgages, it now also buys _____ mortgages.

www.fanniemae.com/ index.jhtml

Fannie Mae. Under "For Business Partners," select "Single-Family" and explore loan purchase programs. Under "Mortgage-Backed Securities," explore MBS programs.

In early 2003 Fannie Mae held $181 billion in mortgages in its portfolio, or about 3 percent of the $6.6 trillion in outstanding residential mortgages (see Exhibit 13-8). In addition, approximately $1.58 trillion in MBSs issued by Fannie Mae and owned by a wide variety of investors were outstanding. Because the MBS investors are the actual owners of the mortgage pools used as collateral for the MBSs, these mortgages are not listed as Fannie Mae assets. The MBSs issued and insured by Fannie Mae, along with their outright ownership of $181 billion in mortgages, accounted for 26 percent of the outstanding residential mortgage market.

Freddie Mac

Freddie Mac's purpose, like that of Fannie Mae, is to develop the private secondary mortgage market. It was originally designed to create an active secondary market for mortgages originated by savings and loan associations. The S&Ls had not found Fannie Mae particularly helpful because S&Ls primarily originated conventional loans and Fannie Mae was not authorized to purchase conventional loans until 1970. Freddie Mac currently buys almost exclusively conventional loans from all types of lenders. The majority of these loans

Exhibit 13-8   Holders of Outstanding One- to Four-Family Residential Mortgage Debt

(1st Qtr. 2003, in billions of dollars)

Commercial banks	$1,245	(19)%		
Savings institutions	663	(10)%		
Life insurance companies	5	(−0)%		
Financial Institutions			$1,913	(29)%
Fannie Mae	$181	(3)%		
Freddie Mac	36	(1)%		
Other federal agencies	19	(<1)%		
Total federal agencies			$236	(4)%
MBSs guaranteed by Fannie Mae	$1,576	(24)%		
MBSs guaranteed by Freddie Mac	1,064	(15)%		
MBSs guaranteed by Ginnie Mae	489	(8)%		
Private MBS pools	727	(11)%		
Total MBS pools*			$3,856	(58)%
Individuals and others†			$ 564	(9)%
All holders			$6,644**	(100)%

*Outstanding balances of MBSs insured or guaranteed.

†Others include mortgage companies, REITs, noninsured pension funds, credit unions, finance companies, and state and local credit unions.

**Total differs from subtotals by $75 billion in original data.

Source: *Federal Reserve Bulletin,* June 2003, Table 1.54.

**www.freddiemac.com/
singlefamily/**

Freddie Mac, single-family loan
business page. Explore various
aspects of their loan purchase
programs.

**www.freddiemac.com/
mbs/**

The entry page to Freddie Mac's
mortgage security programs.

are pooled and used as collateral for the issuance of MBSs. Thus, Freddie Mac and Fannie Mae are operationally quite similar. Freddie Mac, however, has put greater emphasis on issuing MBSs; in 2003, Freddie Mac held only $36 billion in mortgages while it had $1.06 trillion in outstanding MBSs. In total, 17 percent of all residential mortgages outstanding, are either held or securitized by Freddie Mac.

Concept Check

13.13   In 2002 the share of all residential mortgage loans either owned or securitized by Fannie Mae and Freddie Mac, together, is _____ percent.

The Importance of Fannie Mae and Freddie Mac

Fannie Mae and Freddie Mac have set the rules for the secondary market in conventional mortgage loans. It is through their common efforts that the uniformity of documents, procedures, and underwriting standards so badly missing up to 1970 has been established. Today, conventional home mortgage loans rarely are originated without using the application form, the mortgages, the mortgage notes, and an appraisal report form evolved by Freddie Mac and Fannie Mae. Similarly, conventional loan underwriting standards are heavily influenced, if not defined, by what is marketable to these two institutions. The markets and opportunities of other secondary market participants appear to consist largely of what Freddie and Fannie classify as "nonconforming" and ineligible for purchase. Many other secondary market investors will only purchase mortgages that meet the underwriting standards of government-sponsored enterprises (GSEs). Because of this GSE-induced standardization, investors today are better able to buy and sell mortgages and MBSs because the risk/return characteristics of these securities are more easily analyzed. Moreover, the GSEs have provided liquidity to mortgage originators at critical times. The GSEs also have helped increase the flow of investment dollars into the mortgage market as their activities have helped to attract investors who ignored mortgage investments prior to the development of the secondary mortgage market and MBSs.

Concept Check

13.14   Fannie Mae and Freddie Mac jointly brought about uniform _____ , _____ , _____ , and _____ documents for home mortgage loans, and the use among lenders of uniform _____ standards.

Today, Fannie Mae and Freddie Mac have become two of the largest corporations in the United States.[6] Together, they are estimated in early 2003 to hold or to have securitized 43 percent of all home mortgages, and 80 percent of all "conforming" conventional mortgages. When these government-sponsored enterprises purchase loans in the secondary market, the originating lenders, or a firm that has purchased the servicing rights, continue to service the loans, remitting in bulk to the GSEs the payments they receive from borrowers.

One of the key functions of the GSEs is to issue forward commitments to purchase loans from qualified originators. As discussed above, by issuing (selling) a commitment, the GSE pledges to purchase "qualified" loans from originators over a specified period of time. With a fixed-price commitment, the GSE bears the interest rate and price risk. Many argue that it is efficient for the GSEs to assume from originators the interest rate risk

6. In early 2003 Fannie Mae is second largest and Freddie Mac is fifth largest by assets. As reported in *Fortune 500's Largest U.S. Corporations,* April 14, 2003.

Industry Issues

Competitors Want Fannie, Freddie Out of Their Business

The self-styled FM Policy Focus, formerly called FM Watch, has been lobbying Congress for the past few years to rein in the so-called mission creep of Freddie Mac and Fannie Mae beyond their original purpose of facilitating a secondary market for home loans.

The FM Policy Focus sees initiatives by one or both of the two secondary mortgage market giants to get into private mortgage insurance, consumer lending through the purchase of home equity loans, and the origination market through the setting of underwriting standards, beyond the mission the two companies were chartered for, according to a Washington lobbyist representing the group. "At some point, they get into everybody's else's business because there's no place else to go," he said. "The power of the GSEs is so strong that whatever market they enter into they can dominate."

Source: Ed Roberts, Washington Bureau Chief, *Credit Union Journal*, 7, no. 24, June 16, 2003. Copyright © 2003 Thomson Media Inc. All Rights Reserved.

The group was started by Bank of America, JP Morgan Chase, GE Capital, Household Finance, Wells Fargo, and American International Group, all powerhouses themselves in the mortgage and other financial services markets.

But sources familiar with the group say the competing financial giants would also like to increase their own ability to compete in the giant secondary mortgage market, which is currently monopolized by Fannie Mae and Freddie Mac. Some of these companies already buy mortgages from credit unions and banks but are at a disadvantage to Fannie and Freddie.

However, an oft-mentioned goal of eliminating the borrowing advantage of the GSEs through the guaranteed line of credit with the U.S. Treasury, the so-called implied federal guarantee, is not a current aim of the group, said the lobbyist.

"Our goal from day one has been for a strong single regulator that has the means and ability to regulate the GSEs, both their debt and their mission," said the lobbyist, who called OFHEO (the current regulator of the GSEs) a "joke." The next aim is to work for passage of greater disclosure requirements for the GSEs, currently pending in Congress.

---

associated with fixed-rate mortgages because their size and market knowledge allow them more easily to hedge their interest rate exposure over the commitment period.

Concept Check

13.15   A central function of Fannie Mae and Freddie Mac is to issue _____ .

Finally, it should be noted that the federal government has no direct responsibility for the obligations of the GSEs, and these obligations are not included in the federal budget. However, capital market investors assume the GSEs are supervised closely enough to ensure that they will not default on the debt they issue to help fund their mortgage purchases. Moreover, investors clearly believe the government (i.e., the taxpayers) will step in and pay off the debts of the GSEs, if necessary. Evidence of the close relationship GSEs enjoy with the federal government is that they are able to borrow money in the capital markets at rates only slightly above those paid by the U.S. Treasury.[7] Many private participants in the secondary market have argued that the government's implicit guarantee of the liabilities of

---

7. The GSEs are monitored by the Office of Federal Housing Enterprise Oversight (OFHEO), whose authority comes from the Federal Housing Enterprise Financial Safety and Soundness Act passed by Congress in 1992. OFHEO seeks to ensure that GSEs have sufficient capital to withstand significant increases in defaults on the mortgages used as collateral for the MBSs they issue. In June 2003, their capacity to fulfill this mission was being vigorously challenged by many of the largest private financial organizations in the country. (See Industry Issues 13-2.)

GSEs should be eliminated because it gives the GSEs an unfair competitive advantage—the implicit guarantee lowers their cost of obtaining funds. Furthermore, some observers argue that the primary beneficiaries of this guarantee are the private investors who own the publicly traded stock of the GSEs. The proper relationship between the GSEs and the federal government is the topic of an ongoing public policy debate.

Federal Home Loan Banks

The most recent entrant into the secondary mortgage market is an institution that dates back to the 1930s. Originally, the system of 12 Federal Home Loan Banks (FHLBs) was created to provide liquidity to savings and loan associations. They are privately owned by their members (originally, thrift institutions) and, like the GSEs, borrow as if they were backed by the U.S. government. Thus, they enjoy a low cost of funds. Moreover, since their stock is not publicly traded, they do not need the same level of earnings as the GSEs. As the savings and loan industry receded, the FHLB system was reconstituted to serve as the "wholesale" lender (i.e., provider of liquidity) to all thrifts, banks who elect to become members, insurance companies, and credit unions. In the late 1990s, the FHLBs developed a secondary mortgage market operation. While still small in 2003, this program has the possibility of growing into a competitor of the two GSEs, for the business of its members.

Life Insurance Companies

Historically, one of the largest sources of funds for *commercial* mortgages has been the approximately 1,900 life insurance companies. These companies obtain large amounts of investable funds from policyholders. Policy premiums must be held and invested during the time between the policy origination and payout at the time of death. Although life insurance companies (LICs) are not depository institutions, they are heavily regulated by the various states that charter them as well as those states in which they do business.

Although LICs invest mostly in corporate stocks and bonds and government securities, they also invest in residential mortgages. However, they make relatively few loans *directly* to finance single-family homes. In fact, LICs hold less than 1 percent of the value of all home loans originated in the primary market. However, many LICs provide funds for home mortgage finance by purchasing the MBSs issued by Fannie Mae and Freddie Mac, or guaranteed by Ginnie Mae. Life insurance companies also purchase private MBSs that are issued by mortgage companies, commercial banks, Wall Street investment banks, and other nongovernment entities. By purchasing these MBSs in the secondary market, LICs, pension funds, and other investors pump funds *indirectly* into the primary mortgage market.

Other Secondary Market Purchasers

In addition to the GSEs, there are a number of federal credit agencies that support the primary and secondary mortgage market. The list includes the Farm Credit System, the Federal Agricultural Mortgage Corporation (Farmer Mac), the Farmers Home Administration (FmHA), the Financing Corporation (FICO), and the Federal Financing Bank (FFB).

State and local housing finance agencies also are a significant source of mortgage financing for first-time homebuyers and for those engaged in developing low- and moderate-income housing. The key to the success of these state and local programs has been the ability to finance their activities by issuing bonds exempt from federal taxation. Because investors in these bonds do not pay federal taxes on the interest they receive, the bonds can be issued with interest rates that are only 70 to 80 percent of the rates on typical bonds, which pay interest that is taxable to the investor. During recent years, Wall Street investment banks and other private companies also have taken on a greater role in the secondary mortgage market. Many of these firms have established mortgage conduits. These conduits acquire mortgages from a variety of primary mortgage market sources and then use the mortgages to create and sell MBSs.

The Lender's Mortgage Loan Decisions

The lender's process of determining whether to make a mortgage loan is called **loan underwriting.** It is a matter of determining whether the risks of the loan are acceptable. The process has undergone dramatic change since the mid-1990s, with traditional manual methods giving way to automated methods.

Traditional Home Mortgage Underwriting

Traditional home mortgage underwriting is said to rest on three elements, like a three-legged stool. The legs are collateral (the house), creditworthiness (willingness to pay), and capacity (income). These are often referred to as the "three Cs" of mortgage underwriting.

Collateral. To evaluate the loan **collateral,** an appraisal of the residence is required. The Uniform Residential Appraisal Report, created jointly by Fannie Mae and Freddie Mac, became virtually the universal document format for this purpose (see Exhibit 8-12).

The appraisal is important because the loan-to-value ratio always has been recognized as an important factor in mortgage loan risk. For example, studies of loans bought by Freddie Mac from the 1975–1983 period revealed a decade later that loans with a loan-to-value ratio above 90 percent were 25 times more likely to default than loans originated with a loan-to-value ratio below 70 percent, and the severity of loss from default was over twice as great.[8]

Despite the importance of the loan-to-value relationship in underwriting, the role of an appraisal has been reduced. Because appraisal is a costly and time-consuming part of underwriting, the search for substitutes has been active. For example, to simply refinance an existing loan—already paid down for some years—it is arguable that an appraisal is not needed. More generally, substantial progress has occurred in developing long-distance, electronic appraisal substitutes, called *automated valuation models* (see Chapter 8).

Creditworthiness. Until the 1990s, evaluation of borrower creditworthiness was perhaps the most complex and uncertain element in underwriting. It involved obtaining a credit report for the applicant, and then examining the pattern of balances and payment punctuality. Consistent and reliable rules of interpretation were difficult to define, so considerable judgment could be necessary to evaluate a report. This process began to be replaced by the use of statistical **credit scoring** during the mid-1990s, as explained below. This set the stage for a virtual revolution in loan underwriting.

Capacity (Ability to Pay). From the beginning of the FHA and conventional lending, two payment burden ratios were important elements of underwriting.[9] The first, commonly known as the **housing expense ratio,** or "front-end" ratio, is defined as:

$$\text{Housing expense ratio} = \text{PITI} \div \text{GMI}$$

PITI is the monthly payment of principal and interest on the loan plus monthly payments into an escrow account toward property taxes and hazard insurance. GMI is the borrower's gross monthly income. For conventional loans, a standard threshold for this ratio was 28 percent by the mid-1990s. For FHA loans it was 29 percent, reflective of slightly more tolerant standards.

The second underwriting ratio, commonly called the **total debt ratio,** or "back-end" ratio, is defined as:

$$\text{Total debt ratio} = (\text{PITI} + \text{LTO}) \div \text{GMI}$$

---

8. Robert B. Avery, Raphael W. Bostic, Paul S. Calem and Glenn B. Canner, "Credit Risk, Credit Scoring, and the Performance of Home Mortgages," *Federal Reserve Bulletin,* July 1996.

9. VA underwriting originally used a different approach, which computed the amount of income available for a housing payment. FHA adopted the versions of the ratios presented here in the early 1990s.

LTO (long-term obligations) is the sum of payments for other repeating obligations that extended for more than, say, 10 months, including such obligations as car lease payments and child support. For conventional loans, a standard threshold for the total debt ratio came to be 36 percent by the mid-1990s. The threshold for FHA was 41 percent, again reflecting more tolerant standards. A profound change, discussed below, is that these two ratios no longer serve as cutoffs for mortgage underwriting to the extent that they did until the mid-1990s.

Concept Check

13.16 The housing expense ratio is computed as: _____

Since gross monthly income is the denominator in all of the expense ratios, how it is determined is important. Often computing the "quantity and quality" of GMI involves much more than taking a single number from a paycheck stub. Rather, there may be multiple jobs, multiple borrowers, and uncertain employment situations to consider. Because of the many judgments involved, biases and abuses can result. As a result, this step has become the most carefully regulated part of the underwriting process. As explained in Chapter 10, the Equal Credit Opportunity Act (ECOA) regulates extensively what information can be used and what income can be excluded from the process. Underwriters typically receive many hours of training related to the requirements of ECOA.

Concept Check

13.17 The "three Cs" of home loan underwriting are: _____

Modern Home Mortgage Underwriting

In the middle 1990s radical change began to occur in the process of home loan underwriting with the introduction of credit scoring. The use of individual credit reports in loan applications was largely replaced in a very short time by the FICO score, a product by the Fair Isaac Corporation. So, on the FICO scale that ranges from 300 to 850, it became the prevailing practice to regard applicants with a FICO score above 660 as "high quality" whereas an applicant whose FICO score was below 620 was "risky."[10] The credit scoring methodology rapidly evolved to **automated underwriting,** and has virtually replaced the traditional approach. The modern approach relies on a statistically derived equation to determine the level of default risk with a loan application. This approach exploits the combination of cybertechnology and the vast lending experience embedded in the giant loan portfolios of Freddie Mac, Fannie Mae, and of the new megamortgage lenders. Applying multivariate statistics to past loans, researchers build an equation (index) to predict default from the data of the loan application "package." The equation can then be used to evaluate almost instantly a new application submitted electronically by a lender for a prospective borrower. The system classifies the loan application according to its computed risk index. If the index is favorable, the loan application is classified as accepted, and the loan, if originated, will be accepted for purchase without further question. At some lower index value, the loan must be underwritten manually and then considered for purchase. At some still poorer index value, the loan application is likely not to be acceptable for purchase unless underlying problems in the application are solved.

10. *Automated Underwriting: Making Mortgage Lending Simpler and Fairer for America's Families,* Freddie Mac, 1996.

Automated underwriting now is used in virtually all home mortgage lending. Lenders not selling to "Freddie" or "Fannie" still can "rent" the use of their systems.[11] Further, these systems have been adapted for use with FHA and VA loan applications. Finally, several of the giant mortgage lenders of today have evolved their own proprietary automated underwriting systems.

Concept Check

13.18   In modern automated underwriting, a critical difference from the traditional approach is that credit evaluation is accomplished through a _____ .

This technology has proved to dominate manual traditional underwriting in many important ways. First, it is capable of being virtually instantaneous whereas traditional underwriting could require days, or more. Second, its use is totally electronic and thus has much lower marginal cost per loan than manual underwriting. Most importantly, it has proved to be much "smarter," on average, than manual methods. Its success in identifying risky loans has made it a critical enabling factor for Fannie Mae, Freddie Mac, and the giant lenders to safely undertake "affordable housing" loan programs that would be prohibitively risky otherwise. Thus, through underwriting cost reductions and improved risk discrimination, automated underwriting has made home ownership available to large numbers of households for whom it previously was inaccessible.[12]

Cash Down Payment Requirement

In both traditional and modern home loan underwriting, a standard practice has been to require some portion of the down payment to be in cash. As noted in Chapter 12, this was a minimum of 3 percent of the house value for FHA loans. For conventional loans it usually was greater. Some economists have argued that this requirement is questionable since true equity is not what one puts into a house, but what one can recover from it. Others explain the requirement as a signal. Putting cash into the purchase indicates that the borrower believes in the purchase and intends to stay with it.

http://www.freddiemac.com/lp/

Website for Freddie's Loan Prospector automated underwriting.

Concept Check

13.19   Two important advantages of automated underwriting are that it is _____ and it enables lenders to more safely make _____ loans.

Home Financing for Marginal Borrowers

The creation of the long-term, level-payment loan, the creation of mortgage insurance, and the evolution of modern residential lending institutions since World War II went far to make home ownership available to mainstream American households. But some groups in the

11. Freddie Mac's automated underwriting system is called Loan Prospector, while Fannie Mae's is called Desktop Underwriting.

12. Some critics have questioned whether automated underwriting is merely a vehicle by which the GSEs are moving home mortgage lending into excessive risk-taking. However, in contrast to extensive tests of the validity of the analysis underlying automated underwriting (AU), the critics have not yet offered any substantial research that challenges its use. Examples of research supporting AU include: *Automated Underwriting: Making Mortgage Lending Simpler and Fairer for America's Families,* Freddie Mac, 1996, and references therein. Particularly important is: Robert B. Avery, Raphael W. Bostic, Paul S. Calem and Glenn B. Canner, "Credit Risk, Credit Scoring, and the Performance of Home Mortgages," *Federal Reserve Bulletin,* July 1996.

society still have found this dream chronically difficult to achieve. Among these are minority households, lower-income households, and even some moderate-income households lacking accumulated wealth. The barrier to home ownership has two aspects: qualifying for a loan and making a down payment. Three developments have brought important relief to this problem. The first was automated underwriting, discussed in the previous section. The other two are new kinds of lending programs: affordable housing loans and subprime loans.

Affordable Housing Loans

In the mid-1990s a powerful convergence of GSE capability and public interest led to a harvest of **affordable housing loan** programs. By the beginning of the 1990s, Fannie Mae and Freddie Mac had achieved unprecedented scale and experience in operating a secondary mortgage market. Their new strengths enabled them to make a commitment to weed out inefficiencies of the past lending tradition, and to begin a search for better underwriting methods that finally led to automated underwriting. At the same time Congress showed renewed interest in the problem of affordable housing. Today both GSEs offer to lenders a rich menu of loan purchase programs exclusively for low- and moderate-income households. These include loan programs with new lows in the required down payment and new degrees of flexibility in underwriting standards. Some of these loans require less than 3 percent of the loan amount in cash down payment.

A core element of affordable housing loans is a relatively low down payment (5 percent or less). A second element often is to allow unusual flexibility in one of the "three Cs" of underwriting while maintaining the other two at more normal standards. For example, a loan program may allow the down payment to go below 3 percent while maintaining fairly restrictive payment burden ratios and minimum credit score. This strategy results in loans designed to address a range of particular borrower limitations without "layering" and compounding the risks involved. For example, this superlow down payment loan can make homeownership accessible to a moderate income, good credit household that lacks accumulated wealth.

Concept Check

13.20 In recent years the combination of GSE underwriting and risk management capability, together with increased Congressional interest, has brought about an unprecedented variety in the types of _____ loans.

Explore The Web

Affordable Housing Loan Programs of Freddie Mac

Go to www.freddiemac.com/sell/expmkts/affprod.html. From the home page, select "Doing Business," then "Single-family," then "Affordable Products." Note that there are loan programs to address several special problems that tend to disqualify persons from standard home loans. Explore the variation in the programs within one or more groups. Can you determine among the "affordable" products why there are several choices?

Subprime Lending

Most "affordable" housing loans still permit only slightly deficient credit quality. This leaves a significant population of households that cannot qualify, even for affordable home loans. In addition, some creditworthy borrowers have sought refinancing at extremely high loan-to-value levels (in excess of 100 percent). Often they have done this in the hope of replacing high-interest, high-payment consumer debt with more favorable mortgage debt. Still others may be creditworthy and may want a conventional loan-to-value ratio, but lack adequate income documentation to qualify for prime financing. These three types of borrowers—those with weak credit, those who seek 100 percent financing and more, and those who cannot document their income—have been the clientele for *subprime loans*. Subprime loans are at a substantially higher interest rate than prime loans (200 to 600 basis points), carry greater fees, and often include prepayment penalties. Despite the more difficult terms, these types of loans have grown exponentially since the early 1990s to a $160 billion industry in 1999.

Concept Check

13.21 The three clienteles for subprime loans include households that _____, _____, or _____ _____ .

Subprime lending has been the subject of major controversy. Defenders of the industry argue that these costly loans still benefit the borrowers. The target households cannot qualify for higher-quality home financing, and the terms of the subprime loan typically are better than credit card and personal loans that the household would be forced to depend on otherwise. But others point to horror stories of "predatory" lending practices in this largely unregulated industry.[13] (See Industry Issues 10-2.) Further, they note that the lack of uniform contracts and practices makes it particularly difficult for the ill-informed and vulnerable borrower to understand their alternatives.

Controversy also surrounds the proper role of Fannie Mae and Freddie Mac in subprime lending. Consumer advocates urge the two government-sponsored enterprises to become involved in order to bring uniform practices and contracts to the industry. Further, they argue that Freddie Mac and Fannie Mae would bring competition, liquidity, and lower interest rates to the industry. Most existing subprime lenders, on the other hand, strongly oppose the entry of the two GSEs. They argue that Freddie Mac and Fannie Mae would skim all the nearly qualified borrowers who currently subsidize still weaker borrowers. This would leave only the poorest risk borrowers for the rest of the industry. Finally, many of the private megalenders have lobbied Congress to keep the GSEs out of subprime lending, arguing that they constitute unfair, subsidized competition.

Despite the controversy, the GSEs have been cautiously testing subprime loan programs. For example, both offer to purchase loans at a higher interest rate than their standard loans when the borrower has only a slightly deficient credit record. However, with 24 months of "on-time" payments, borrowers can have their loans reclassified as standard loans and receive a reduction in the interest rate charged. Some expect the GSEs to eventually purchase 50 percent of all subprime loans.

www.hud.gov/offices/
hsg/pred/predlnd1.cfm

HUD-Treasury reports on predatory lending.

www.mbaa.org/
resources/predlend/

Mortgage Bankers resource site on predatory lending.

---

13. Congress addressed the predatory lending problem by enacting the Home Owners Equity Protection Act of 1999. It is discussed in Chapter 10.

Summary

Homebuyers have a number of choices when deciding where to obtain mortgage financing. Altogether, depository institutions such as thrifts, credit unions, and commercial banks have diminished as a source of home loans, largely due to the drastic decline of thrifts. Still, thrifts account for perhaps 15 percent of home mortgage loans (specializing in ARMS), and depositories account for over 40 percent of all conventional one- to four-family residential mortgage originations being made. Mortgage banking companies account for almost all of the remaining originations. Their increasing role is evidence of a larger shift from "portfolio" lending to reliance on the secondary market and securitization.

More than half of all residential mortgage loans originated in the United States are now sold into the secondary mortgage market. The largest purchasers of residential mortgages in this market are Fannie Mae and Freddie Mac. These government-sponsored enterprises (GSEs) also are the largest issuers of residential mortgage-backed securities (MBSs), which are written against pools of mortgages purchased from primary market originators.

In developing and facilitating the secondary market in residential mortgages, Fannie Mae and Freddie Mac have developed standardized documents and procedures for loans submitted to them for purchase. This has brought wide conformity to the primary, as well as the secondary, mortgage market. Because of this standardization, investors today are much better able to buy and sell mortgages and MBSs because the risk return characteristics of these securities are more easily analyzed. The increased standardization and liquidity provided by the GSEs has greatly improved mortgage market efficiency.

When underwriting home loans—that is, when deciding whether to extend credit—lenders traditionally have examined the "three Cs" of a borrower: creditworthiness, collateral (appraised value) and capacity (income). Though the same issues are examined today, the approach has changed radically through the use of credit scores, appraisal substitutes, and automated underwriting. Because of the advances in lending operations and in underwriting, and because of increased awareness and enforcement of civil rights legislation, many lenders have created new programs designed to extend credit to low- and moderate-income borrowers, particularly ethnic minorities, who do not meet traditional standards. This venture into "marginal" lending continues with the emergence of subprime lending. Amidst some controversy about abusive lending practices and what role GSEs should have in such lending, subprime loans have become a fast growth industry, serving three main clienteles: creditworthy borrowers seeking very high loan-to-value ratios, borrowers with a weak credit record, and borrowers unable to document their income capacity.

Key Terms

Affordable housing loan 349
Automated underwriting 347
Collateral 346
Commercial banks 331
Conduits 340
Credit scoring 346
Credit unions 331
Disintermediation 328
Fallout risk 334
Financial intermediaries 327

Forward commitment 335
Government National Mortgage
    Association (GNMA) 339
Housing expense ratio 346
Interest rate risk 334
Loan servicing 336
Loan underwriting 346
Mortgage bankers 332
Mortgage brokers 332
Mortgage pipeline 334

Pipeline risk 333
PITI 346
Portfolio lenders 332
Risk-weighted assets 329
Savings and loan associations
    (S&Ls) 327
Savings banks 327
Standby forward commitment 335
Total debt ratio 346
Warehousing 331

Test Problems

Answer the following multiple choice problems:

1. Mortgage banking companies:
   a. Collect monthly payments and forward them to the mortgage investor.
   b. Arrange home loan originations, but do not make the actual loans.
   c. Make home loans and fund them permanently.
   d. None of the above.

2. In recent years, the mortgage banking industry has experienced:
   a. Decline.
   b. Decentralization.
   c. Limited consolidation.
   d. Rapid consolidation.

3. Currently, which type of financial institution in the primary mortgage market provides the most funds for the residential (owner-occupied) housing market?
   a. Life insurance companies.
   b. Savings and loan associations.
   c. Credit unions.
   d. Commercial banks

4. For all except very high loan-to-value conventional home loans, the standard payment ratios for underwriting are:
   a. 28 percent and 36 percent.
   b. 25 percent and 33 percent.
   c. 29 percent and 41 percent.
   d. 33 percent and 56 percent.

5. The numerator of the standard housing expense (front-end) ratio in home loan underwriting includes:
   a. Monthly principal and interest.
   b. Monthly principal, interest, and property taxes.
   c. Monthly principal, interest, property taxes, and hazard insurance.
   d. All of these plus monthly obligations extending 10 months or more.

6. The most profitable activity of residential mortgage bankers is typically:
   a. Loan origination.
   b. Loan servicing.
   c. Loan sales in the secondary market.
   d. Loan brokerage activities.

7. Potential subprime borrowers include persons who:
   a. Are creditworthy but want a 100 percent or higher LTV loan.
   b. Are credit-impaired.
   c. Persons with no documentation of their income.
   d. All of these.

8. Savings banks are now virtually indistinguishable from:
   a. Credit unions.
   b. Savings and loan associations.
   c. Commercial banks.
   d. Mortgage bankers.

9. The reduced importance of certain institutions in the primary mortgage market has been largely offset by an expanded role for others. Which two are these?
   a. Commercial bankers; savings and loan associations.
   b. Mortgage bankers; commercial banks.
   c. Commercial banks; mortgage bankers.
   d. Savings and loans associations; mortgage bankers.

10. *Warehousing* refers to:
    a. Short-term loans made by mortgage bankers to commercial banks.
    b. Short-term loans made by commercial banks to mortgage bankers.
    c. Long-term loans made by commercial banks to mortgage bankers.
    d. Short-term loans to finance the construction of industrial warehouses.

Study Questions

1. What is the primary purpose of the risk-based capital requirements that Congress enacted as part of the Financial Institutions Reform, Recovery, and Enforcement Act (FIRREA)?

2. Explain what is meant by *forward commitments* and *standby forward commitments*. Which part of the mortgage banker's pipeline is often hedged with forward commitments? With standby forward commitments? Why?

3. Describe the basic activities of Fannie Mae in the secondary mortgage market. How are these activities financed?

4. Explain the importance of Fannie Mae and Freddie Mac to the housing finance system in the United States.

5. Describe the activities mortgage bankers often engage in to generate income.

6. Describe the mechanics of warehouse financing, in mortgage banking.

7. Explain how affordable housing loans differ from standard home loans.

8. List three "clients" for subprime home mortgage loans.

9. You have just signed a contract to purchase your dream house. The price is $120,000 and you have applied for a $100,000, 30-year, 5.5 percent loan. Annual property taxes are expected to be $2,000. Hazard insurance will cost $400 per year. Your car payment is $400, with 36 months left. Your monthly gross income is $5,000. Calculate:
   a. The monthly payment of principal and interest (PI).
   b. One-twelfth of annual property tax payments and hazard insurance payments.
   c. Monthly PITI (principal, interest, taxes, and insurance).
   d. The housing expense (front-end) ratio.
   e. The total obligations (back-end) ratio.

10. Contrast automated underwriting with the traditional "three Cs" approach.

Explore The Web

1. In home mortgage lending today, automated underwriting based on a single statistical risk equation, has largely replaced the traditional method of risk evaluation through separate examinations of the "three Cs": collateral, creditworthiness, and income capacity. Central to the automated risk equation is the borrower's credit score (FICO score). Go to the FICO score website: http://www.myfico.com and read about the use of FICO scores. You may want to pay the modest fee required to obtain your FICO score, plus an analysis of factors that could improve it.

2. Go to Fannie Mae's website and find their "affordable housing" loan programs. Compare them to Freddie Mac's.

Solutions to Concept Checks

1. The vulnerability of savings and loan associations was asset-liability maturity mismatch.

2. A major new regulatory approach for thrifts introduced by FIRREA was to impose risk-based capital standards.

3. Three ways that commercial banks have served mortgage lending is by making mortgage loans to its regular customers, by providing "warehouse" lines of credit to mortgage bankers, and through construction lending.

4. Today the largest market share in home mortgage lending among depository lenders is held by commercial banks.

5. Mortgage brokers differ from mortgage bankers in that they neither fund mortgage loans nor service them.

6. *Pipeline risk* refers to the period in mortgage banking between making a commitment for a loan and selling the loan.

7. Forward sales and standby forward sales can hedge a mortgage banker's pipeline risk.

8. The primary source of mortgage banking profit is from loan servicing.

9. There might be more concern about moral hazard among mortgage brokers than among mortgage bankers or depository mortgage lenders because brokers have no continuing involvement with the loan or borrower after the loan is made.

10. The three main government-related entities involved in creation or suppport of residential mortgage backed securities are Ginnie Mae, Fannie Mae, and Freddie Mac.

11. Ginnie Mae's role in residential mortgage-backed securities is to guarantee timely payment of interest and principal to the investors in the securities.

12. Whereas Fannie Mae was created to purchase FHA and VA mortgages, it now also buys conventional mortgages.

13. In 2002 the share of all residential mortgage loans either owned or securitized by Fannie Mae and Freddie Mac together was about 43 percent.

14. Fannie Mae and Freddie Mac jointly brought about uniform application, mortgage, note, and appraisal documents for home mortgage loans, and the use among lenders of uniform underwriting standards.

15. A central function of Fannie Mae and Freddie Mac is to issue forward commitments to buy loans.

16. The housing expense ratio is computed as PITI/GMO, or principal, interest, taxes, and insurance divided by gross monthly income.

17. "Three Cs" of home loan underwriting are collateral, creditworthiness, and capacity.

18. A critical difference in modern automated underwriting from the traditional approach is that credit evaluation is accomplished through a credit score.

19. Two important advantages of automated underwriting are that it is faster and it enables lenders to more safely make affordable housing loans.

20. In recent years the combination of GSE underwriting and risk management capability, together with renewed Congressional interest, has brought about an unprecedented variety in the types of affordable housing loans.

21. The three clients for subprime loans include households that have weak credit, want 100 percent financing, or cannot document their income.

Additional Reading

Substantial portions of the following books are devoted to residential mortgage financing:

Brueggeman, William B., and Jeffrey D. Fisher. *Real Estate Finance and Investments,* 11th ed. New York: McGraw-Hill Irwin, 2002.

Clauretie, T. M., and G. S. Sirmans. *Real Estate Finance: Theory and Practice,* 4th ed. Cincinnati, OH: South-Western Publishing, 2002.

Fabozzi, Frank J., and Franco Modigliano. *Mortgage and Mortgage-Backed Securities Markets.* Cambridge: Harvard Business School Press, 1992.

Lederman, J. *The Handbook of Mortgage-Banking: Trends, Opportunities, and Strategies,* 2nd ed. New York: McGraw-Hill, 1993.

Weicher, J. C. *The Home Equity Lending Industry: Refinancing Mortgage Borrowers with Impaired Credit.* Indianapolis: Hudson Institute, 1997.

Wiedemer, John P. *Real Estate Finance,* 9th ed. Cincinnati, OH: South-Western Publishing, 2001.

chapter fourteen

Commercial Mortgage Types *and* Decisions

Learning Objectives

After reading this chapter you will be able to:

1. Identify the most common types of long-term commercial mortgages and the most common provisions contained in these mortgages.

2. Identify and explain four alternative financing structures and explain their advantages and disadvantages from the borrower's perspective.

3. Define and explain positive and negative financial leverage and the risks to the borrower associated with the use of borrowed funds.

4. Identify and explain the items commonly included in a loan submission package.

5. Identify the characteristics of the loan application on which lenders focus when making their funding decisions.

Introduction

In this chapter we discuss the permanent financing of commercial real estate properties. Permanent financing refers to the long-term debt financing of existing properties that are operating and producing income. Permanent financing for commercial real estate is provided by a wide variety of lenders, including mortgage bankers, savings institutions, commercial banks, the government-sponsored enterprises (GSEs), the Department of Housing and Urban Development (HUD), life insurance companies, and pension funds.[1] A detailed discussion of the role and importance of these lenders as sources of commercial mortgage credit is contained in Chapter 15.

We first discuss commercial loan documents and contract provisions. We then consider the most common types of long-term commercial mortgages. Unlike residential mortgage

1. GSEs, or government sponored enterprises, include Freddie Mac and Fannie Mae, discussed in Chapter 13.

markets, 25- or 30-year mortgages are found infrequently, as mortgages with 5- to 10-year terms are the most common. Alternative financing arrangements, such as floating-rate loans and sale-leasebacks, are then considered. In addition to choosing a financing structure, commercial property investors also must determine, subject to lender restrictions, the size of the mortgage that is most advantageous to them. Here investors must carefully consider the cost of available mortgage financing, the cost of equity (or self) financing, and the effect of debt (i.e., financial leverage) on investment risk and return.

We next discuss the loan application process. Prospective borrowers must submit a loan application package to the commercial lender. The size and details of the package vary with the size of the loan request, with the type of property used as collateral (e.g., office, apartment), and on whether the loan proceeds will be used to finance an existing property or a proposed development. Once the loan application and related material are submitted for funding consideration, the lender decides to approve, reject, or renegotiate the loan terms and conditions.

The chapter concludes with a brief overview of the various types of short-term (i.e. nonpermanent) mortgage debt often used to finance the development and construction of new properties, including land acquisition loans, land development loans, and construction loans.

Loan Documents and Provisions

As discussed in Chapters 12 and 13, the underwriting requirements of Fannie Mae and Freddie Mac have precipitated a great deal of product standardization in the residential mortgage market. In contrast, most commercial mortgages are not made in conformity with any specific standards or regulations. Indeed, one of the most confusing aspects of commercial real estate lending is the number of mortgage products available to potential borrowers. Nevertheless, all is not chaos. Commercial and residential lenders use the same basic types of documents, and many of the same standard clauses apply. These documents and provisions are briefly described in the remainder of this section. (Chapter 10 provides more detailed explanations of mortgage loan documents.)

The Note

As in residential mortgage financing, the *note* is the document used to create a legal debt. In residential property financing, the note is usually a relatively simple document. In commercial property financing, however, the note is usually quite lengthy. It contains the terms of the loan and the provisions agreed to by each party. It presents in detail the borrower's obligations in various situations. The provisions typically deal with such matters as these:

- Amounts and timing of periodic payments.
- Penalties for late payments.
- Record keeping.
- Hazard insurance requirements.
- Property maintenance.
- Default.

Normally the note creates personal liability for borrowers, but this is unacceptable in the case of many commercial property loans. Therefore, a special legal entity is usually created as the borrower, and it is this entity that actually is named on the note. This special entity has one asset: the mortgaged property. Thus, in the event of default, the only recourse the lender has is still the mortgaged property. This arrangement shields the actual borrower(s) from personal liability and makes the loan nonrecourse.[2]

---

2. In recent years lenders have been unwilling to relieve borrowers from personal liability in the event of fraud, environmental problems, or unpaid property tax obligations. Therefore a "bad boy carve-out" clause is included in the note. This clause pierces the single-purpose borrowing entity to hold the actual borrower liable for such problems.

From the perspective of the equity investor, nonrecourse financing can significantly reduce the downside risk associated with investing in commercial real estate. If rents and property values should fall, equity investors have the option to walk away from the property and mortgage, bearing no personal responsibility to repay the debt. Although legal, creditworthy borrowers are loath to exercise this option because they understand that nonrecourse does not mean "not responsible." Nevertheless, when nonrecourse financing is coupled with high loan-to-value ratios (LTVs), equity investors can limit their downside risk without constraining their upside potential.

Concept Check

14.1 Distinguish between recourse and nonrecourse loans. Which is the industry standard?

Two final points about nonrecourse financing are worth highlighting. First, the benefits of nonrecourse financing are not free. Rather, borrowers pay for the nonrecourse option in the form of higher contract interest rates or higher up-front financing costs, or both. Second, although nonrecourse loans dominate the mortgage lending practices of pension funds, life insurance companies, and commercial mortgage-backed security (CMBS) originators, banks and savings and loans are likely to require some form of credit "enhancement," which the borrower may provide directly by agreeing to a recourse loan. Alternatively, the borrower may arrange for a third party (perhaps another bank or wealthy individual) to guarantee the loan payments or, perhaps, to insure the lender against losses in excess of some prespecified amount. Of course, the borrower must pay a risk-appropriate fee to the third party for this service.

The Mortgage

The commercial mortgage creates security for lenders. As in a residential mortgage, it states that lenders can have the property sold to satisfy the debt if borrowers default on any of their obligations. Lenders must follow foreclosure proceedings, determined by state law, just as in residential foreclosures. To protect the lender's security interest in the mortgaged property, many commercial mortgages contain a due-on-sale clause. As in residential lending, this clause precludes the mortgage from being assumed by a subsequent purchaser of the

www.mbaa.org

Mortgage Bankers Association.

www.namb.org

National Association of
Mortgage Brokers.

collateralized property without permission of the lender. This protects the lender from a degradation of credit risk that may occur if a less creditworthy borrower was allowed to assume the loan. It is worth noting that default and foreclosure are much more common in commercial loans than in residential loans.

Common Types of Permanent Mortgages

Three main repayment mechanisms are used for long-term commercial mortgages: fully amortizing loans, partially amortizing loans, and interest-only loans. Recall from Chapter 11 that on a fully amortized loan, the principal repayment portion of the periodic payment is large enough to reduce (i.e., amortize) the outstanding balance to zero over the term of the loan. On a partially amortized loan, the payments are based on an amortization schedule that is longer than the actual term of the loan. Thus, the outstanding balance is reduced, but not to zero, at loan maturity. This requires the borrower to satisfy the remaining mortgage balance with a balloon payment.

Concept Check

14.2 All else being the same, are fully amortizing or partially amortizing loans more risky for the lender?

Balloon Mortgages

The **balloon mortgage** is the most common instrument used to finance commercial property. Payments are typically based on a 25-year or 30-year amortization schedule, but the loan matures in 5, 7, or 10 years.[3] Exhibit 14-1 contains selected results from surveys of commercial mortgage lenders completed in September 1999 and 2002. The average rate on 5-year balloon mortgages of $5 million and up with 25- to 30-year amortization was 4.89 percent in September of 2002. Assuming, for example, a 30-year amortization schedule and a $5 million mortgage, this implies a monthly payment of $26,506 and a remaining mortgage balance at maturity (RMB_5) of $4,584,226. The borrower must satisfy the $4,584,226 obligation by either selling the property at the end of the five-year term or by refinancing (perhaps with the original lender) at the then-current interest rate.

The relatively short loan term on a balloon mortgage reduces the lender's interest rate risk. If interest rates increase after the origination of a balloon mortgage, the value of the remaining payments, and therefore the value of the mortgage, falls less than if the loan were outstanding the full 25 or 30 years. For example, if interest rates were to rise from 4.89 percent to 5.20 percent immediately after origination of the five-year, 4.89 percent balloon

Exhibit 14-1 Average Interest Rates on Fixed-Rate Commercial Mortgages

	September	
Loan Term (Years)	**2002**	**1999**
5	4.89%	7.85%
7	5.26	8.07
10	5.75	8.07

Source: *Barron's/John B. Levy & Co. National Mortgage Survey,* September 1999 and 2002. For loans of $5 million and up that can be funded in 60–120 days with 0–1 discount points and 25–30 year amortization schedules.

3. A bullet loan is an interest-only balloon loan.

Exhibit 14-2   10-Year Prime Mortgage Rate versus 10-Year Treasury Yield
(January 1990 to September 2002)

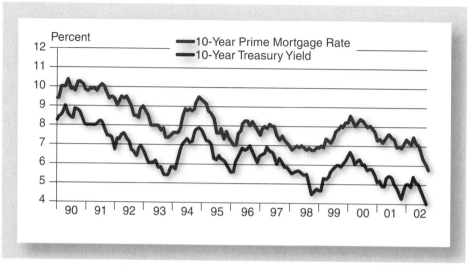

Source: *Barron's/Levy National Mortgage Survey* published by John B. Levy & Company (www.jblevy.com), which provides commercial real estate financing services and interest rate tracking.

mortgage, its market value would decline from $5,000,000 to $4,934,435, assuming the loan is held to maturity.[4] However, if both the term of the loan and the amortization period were 30 years, the present value of the remaining payments, and therefore the value of the loan, would decline to $4,827,076.[5]

Although reducing the term of the mortgage to 5 years reduces the lender's exposure to interest rate risk, the 25- or 30-year amortization schedule keeps the payment low and therefore does not reduce the *affordability* of the mortgage relative to a 25- or 30-year mortgage. Exhibit 14-1 also reveals that commercial mortgage rates in 2002 were significantly lower than in 1999. In fact, mortgage rates in early 2002 were at their lowest levels since the early 1960s.

The contract rates on commercial mortgages reported in Exhibit 14-1 are determined by the perceived riskiness of mortgage investments relative to a riskless alternative. The widely used riskless benchmark is the investment yield (going-in *IRR*) available on a U.S. Treasury security. The expected yields on both 10-year commercial mortgages and 10-year Treasury securities are plotted in Exhibit 14-2. The exhibit clearly demonstrates that commercial mortgages are priced in relation to comparable maturity Treasury securities; that is, movements in mortgage rates are highly correlated with changes in available returns on riskless Treasury securities.[6] While the yield spread (mortgage rate minus Treasury rate) required by mortgage lenders has ranged since 1990 between 100 basis points (one percentage point) and 275 basis points, the directions of change have followed "Treasuries" very closely. Mortgage yield spreads increase with mortgage term; thus, borrowers using

---

4. The calculator keystrokes are $N = 60$, $I = 5.20 \div 12$, $PV = ?$, $PMT = 26,506$, and $FV = 4,584,226$.

5. The calculator keystrokes are $N = 360$, $I = 5.20 \div 12$, $PV = ?$, $PMT = 26,506$, and $FV = 0$. If the lender did not expect the below-market rate loan to be outstanding the full 30 years, the decline in value would be less.

6. U.S. Treasury securities that pay periodic interest are not, technically, risk free because investors are subject to reinvestment risk, which is the risk that interest rates will fall and the periodic payments will have to be reinvested at lower rates. Also, available yields on Treasury securities are stated in *nominal* terms. However, the *real* return earned by investors is risky because it depends on the rate of general inflation in the U.S. economy over the investment holding period. Despite these limitations, the nominal returns on interest-paying Treasury securities are the most common benchmarks used to measure the "riskless" rate of return available to real estate investors.

Explore The Web

What has happened to commercial mortgage spreads since late 2002? To update the information in Exhibit 14-2, go to the website of the Mortgage Bankers Association (www.mbaa.org). Once there, click on the "Commercial Finance" tab near the top of the home page. After browsing the latest commercial real estate finance news, click on "industry data" in the left margin. Find the link to commitment rates at life insurance companies. What has happened since late 2002 to commercial mortgage spreads on fixed-rate loan commitments by life insurance companies?

5- and 7-year mortgages face smaller risk premiums than 10-year borrowers. Yield spreads increase with the mortgage term, primarily because the lender's interest rate risk exposure increases with the loan term, as demonstrated earlier.

Concept Check

14.3   When calculating present values, expected future cash flows must be adjusted for their magnitudes, timing, and risk. Which of these three is adjusted for when discounting at the riskless Treasury rate?

Restrictions on Prepayments

As discussed in Chapter 10, homeowners typically have the right to prepay costlessly the remaining loan balance on residential mortgages, which is often referred to as the **par value** of the mortgage. In sharp contrast, most fixed-rate commercial mortgages do not allow borrowers to freely prepay at par, as they contain either a lock-out provision, a prepayment penalty, or occasionally, both. A **lockout provision** prohibits prepayment of the mortgage for a period of time after its origination. For example, a commercial mortgage can have a 10-year loan term, a 25-year amortization schedule, and a 5-year lockout period. Lockout periods reduce the risk that lenders will have to reinvest the remaining loan balance at a lower rate when borrowers prepay mortgages with above-market rates. Thus, lockout provisions reduce lenders' **reinvestment risk,** all else being equal.

Concept Check

14.4   Assume a 10-year, 7 percent, commercial mortgage loan with a $1,400,000 remaining balance is paid off by the borrower after 3 years. Assume interest rates have declined to 5 percent since origination. If the $1,400,000 is invested for the remaining 7 years at 5 percent, to what amount will the principal balance increase if interest is compounded monthly? What if the lump sum is invested at a 7 percent annual rate with monthly compounding?

Some commercial mortgages contain **prepayment penalties** instead of, or in addition to, lockout provisions. These penalties may be expressed as a percentage of the remaining loan balance, say, 2 to 4 percent. Prepayment penalties can significantly increase the cost of refinancing and, therefore, reduce the benefits. An alternative form of prepayment penalty is a **yield-maintenance agreement.** With such an agreement, the penalty that borrowers pay depends on how far interest rates have declined since origination. Why tie the penalty to interest rate movements? When interest rates decline and borrowers prepay at par, lenders must reinvest the remaining loan balance at current (i.e., lower) rates. Effectively, lenders lose the present value of the difference between the payments on the old mortgage and the payments on a new mortgage at current rates. With a yield-maintenance agreement, the prepayment penalty can be set to approximate this lost present value, or some portion of it.

Finally, a process called defeasance is also used by some commercial lenders to protect themselves from prepayments that arise from declining mortgage rates. With defeasance, a borrower who prepays must purchase for the lender a set of U.S. Treasury securities whose coupon payments replicate the cash flows the lender will lose as a result of the early retirement of the mortgage. Thus, similar to yield maintenance agreements, defeasance clauses provide borrowers with the flexibility to prepay (i.e., they are not locked out). However, the clauses are designed in a way that the borrower's cost of purchasing the Treasury securities for the lender effectively eliminates any interest savings associated with the mortgage prepayment.

Alternative Financing Arrangements

Although the use of fixed-rate balloon mortgages from a third-party lender is common, alternative mortgage products and financing structures do exist. These alternatives are discussed in the following section.

Floating Rate Loans

Some commercial mortgages have adjustable, or floating, interest rates. The index on a **floating-rate mortgage** is typically the prime rate—the rate banks charge their best customers—or, increasingly, the London Interbank Offer Rate—commonly referred to as LIBOR. Floating-rate loans decrease the lender's interest rate risk, which tends to reduce the rates on floating-rate loans relative to fixed-payment mortgages, all else being the same. However, floating-rate mortgages can increase the default risk of a mortgage because the borrower may not be able to continue to service the debt if payments on the loan increase significantly. Chapter 11 provides examples of how to calculate the revised payments on mortgages that have interest rates tied to a market index.

Installment Sale Financing

A popular method of deferring the taxes due on the sale of a commercial property is the **installment sale.** Under this method, the seller allows the buyer to pay the purchase price over a number of years. In effect, the seller collects a down payment and then loans the buyer the remainder of the purchase price. Subsequent to the sale, the buyer makes periodic payments to the seller (lender) that consist of both interest and principal amortization. Because the seller receives the sale proceeds (i.e., the principal on the installment loan) over a number of years, the Internal Revenue Service (IRS) allows the seller to recognize the taxable gain from sale as the sale proceeds are collected from the buyer. Spreading the recognition of the taxable gain over several years reduces the present value of the tax payments.

There is a potential cost, however, associated with this strategy: The seller does not immediately receive the full amount of the sale proceeds from the buyer. If the interest rate the seller charges the buyer is less than the seller's risk-adjusted opportunity cost, the seller's wealth is decreased by the installment sale loan. This loss would need to be balanced against the benefits of tax deferral. Nevertheless, the availability of installment sale tax treatment allows investors to pursue market timing and portfolio reallocation strategies without triggering large capital gains.

Because the installment sale may provide the seller with significant tax benefits, the seller may be willing to offer the buyer-investor a below-market rate of interest. Installment sales are also popular with buyers because the seller often uses underwriting standards that are less strict than those used by traditional third-party lenders (e.g., banks, insurance companies). This underwriting flexibility may allow the investor to increase the ratio of total debt to total property value, thereby minimizing the investor's required down payment.[7]

Concept Check

14.5   If the interest rate on the installment sale loan is equal to the seller's risk-adjusted opportunity cost, the use of the installment sale is unambiguously advantageous to the seller. Explain why.

Joint Ventures

A **joint venture** (JV) produces a borrower-lender relationship in which a lender receives a portion of the cash flows from operation or sale of the property, or both, as well as scheduled mortgage payments. The lender accomplishes this by acquiring an ownership (equity) interest in the property. Thus, the lender supplies a portion of the required equity capital in addition to providing the permanent debt financing. The joint venture lender's total return therefore comes from two sources: a return on the mortgage investment (i.e., the debt service) and a return on the equity investment (i.e., the lender's share of the property's cash flow).

Many real estate JVs involve the construction of new properties, with the lender (often a large life insurance company) providing the majority of the debt and equity capital. For example, the JV lender will typically finance 75 to 80 percent of the total development costs, and additionally provide a significant portion of the required equity. The developer primarily provides the expertise in project selection, development, construction, and management. The developer and JV lender/investor will split the cash flow from operations and sale equally, or in any other manner agreed upon. Obviously, such arrangements require a complex partnership agreement to cover the rights and obligations of each party. (Partnerships are discussed in more detail in Chapter 15.) In recent years, many publicly traded real estate investment trusts (REITs) have also pursued JVs with established local builders. These development JVs provide the REIT with higher expected returns than what is generally available on acquisitions of existing properties. However, these higher expected returns come at a cost of higher risk.

Developers and investors in need of capital may find a joint venture structure attractive because it reduces the amount of equity capital the investor must contribute to the deal. The reduction in equity capital occurs because the total financing provided by the lender (debt *and* equity) generally exceeds the maximum amount of straight debt financing usually available from traditional lenders. However, the lender's participation in the cash flow stream reduces the upside potential of the borrower's return, because the lender will share in any larger-than-expected increases in rents, resale values, or both.

Concept Check

14.6   If joint ventures reduce the property owner's upside potential, why do owners sometimes seek a JV partner?

Sale-Leasebacks

Sale-leasebacks are an alternative vehicle for financing commercial property. With a *land* sale-leaseback, the borrower either currently owns or purchases the building(s) and other improvements. The other party to the transaction, often an institutional investor such as an

---

7. Installment sales of commercial property are similar in structure to a "contract for deed" financing arrangement between the buyer and seller of a home (see Chapter 10).

insurance company, purchases the land and leases it back to the borrower. Usually, the institutional investor also provides the long-term mortgage for the building if the land and structure are to be acquired. The institutional investor's cash flow comes from (1) debt service on the mortgage note that has financed the building acquisition and (2) lease payments on the land. Because the investing institution has a long-term economic interest in the land, it benefits from any price appreciation. Although the borrower relinquishes his or her economic interest in the land, depreciation deductions on the building improvements are retained which, along with the lease payments on the land and the interest payments on the building mortgage, are generally fully deductible. (Income taxes are discussed in detail in Chapter 22.)

Institutions sometimes negotiate the purchase of both the land and building of an existing property or underwrite the development and construction costs for a proposed new property. The property is then leased back to the user of the property, who becomes a rent-paying tenant (lessee). With such a complete sale-leaseback, the tenant obtains the use of a structure that is presumably well suited to its needs. The arrangement also allows funds that are not invested in the land and building to be invested in other assets or in other facets of the tenant's business. In many cases, the tenant's primary business is not real estate. Thus, it may make more sense to *sell* the property to an investor who specializes in real estate and then lease the property back on a long-term basis. Proceeds from the sale can then be invested in the tenant's core business. This strategy is especially useful for a company that is looking at the rapid expansion of its locations, yet suitable facilities do not exist. Walgreens and Eckerds drugstores are prime examples. From the tenant's viewpoint, a complete sale-leaseback also carries the advantages of 100 percent financing and the deductibility of lease payments for tax purposes. However, appreciation in the value of the property accrues to the purchaser of the land and buildings, as do the depreciation deductions for tax purposes.

Concept Check

14.7   For a company whose primary business is not the development, ownership, or management of commercial real estate, what is the primary reason it may be better off leasing rather than owning its real estate?

Other Products and Structures

In addition to the financing options discussed above, numerous others are available. For example, borrowers may choose to obtain more than one mortgage on a property. So-called "second mortgages" usually carry higher interest rates than first mortgages, but the rates may still be below the borrower's perceived cost of equity financing. Another method of obtaining additional leverage is to employ **mezzanine financing** on top of a traditional first mortgage. Such debt is generally secured by the borrower's pledge to the lender of an equity interest in the borrower's partnership or business; it is not secured by a lien on the property. With a **participation loan,** the lender receives a specified portion of a property's net operating income (*NOI*) or sale proceeds, in addition to interest and principle on the note.

Government-Sponsored Programs

Similar to the owner-occupied housing market, the U.S. government provides multiple incentives to encourage the construction and ownership of affordable multifamily housing. Sponsoring and encouraging the construction of affordable rental housing meets the government's public policy goal of providing adequate housing for all U.S. citizens. The Department of Housing and Urban Development (HUD) administers most of the federal government's multifamily initiatives, although certain tax credit programs are the responsibility of the Internal Revenue Service. As with the home loan mortgage market, HUD

Industry Issues

Source: Adapted from Mike Fickes, "The Move to Sale-Leasebacks," *National Real Estate Investor,* July 1, 2002.

14-1

The Net Lease and Sale-Leaseback Industry Continues to Grow

Often referred to interchangeably, the terms *net lease* and *sale-leaseback* describe transactions that produce a similar result. In a sale-leaseback, a company that owns real estate, sells it to another company, and then leases it back on a long-term basis—usually agreeing to pay all required operating expenses of the property. The sale generates cash, which replaces the asset on the company's balance sheet. With a net-lease transaction, a company in need of an asset leases the property from a net-lease provider, which finances the purchase. In both cases, the company receives effective control over an asset it doesn't own under a long-term lease. Once viewed as a last resort for corporations in need of cash, these vehicles have emerged as financial management tools available to healthy as well as struggling companies.

Take Walgreens, for example. In the early 2000s, the Deerfield, Illinois, company sold 42 newly built, stand-alone stores in 16 states for $150 million. The company now operates those stores under 25-year leases held by Cornerstone Capital Corp. of Dublin, Ohio.

Proceeds from the deal helped pay down some $650 million in commercial paper debt, a portion of which had resulted from store acquisitions. Although Walgreens used sale-leaseback cash to pay off short-term debt that had accumulated against long-term real estate assets, the company says the most important reason for the transaction was to rearrange the company's capital structure. "For us, returns on investments in real estate are not nearly as good as the returns we get from operating drugstores," says a company spokesperson. While real estate returns typically range between 5 percent and 8 percent, Walgreens' shareholders expect returns of about 18 percent after taxes. According to Walgreens, "Real estate ownership would dilute those returns."

---

www.cmalert.com

Commercial Mortgage Alert site delivers news, analysis, and statistics on all aspects of the commercial real estate finance business.

www.property.com

An established portal to news and information on the commercial mortgage market.

www.GlobeSt.com

Another portal to commercial real estate news and information.

provides loan guarantees for multifamily mortgages through the Federal Housing Administration (FHA). HUD's initiatives include a program for the purchase and refinancing of existing, qualified, low-income properties that allows higher loan-to-value ratios (*LTVs*), a low-income program that targets new construction and substantial rehabilitation, as well as programs that finance rental housing for the elderly and subsidize the interest rates on multifamily properties targeted to low-income families. HUD also uses the "Section 8" program to allow local housing authorities to subsidize the rent payments of low-income households.[8]

Freddie Mac offers a variety of multifamily loan types including affordable housing, housing for the elderly, construction and permanent loans, and refinancings. Fannie Mae is also an active participant in the multifamily mortgage business supplying a wide variety of loans targeted at the elderly and low- and moderate-income households.[9]

The Borrower's Decision-Making Process

Once investors have decided to purchase a commercial property, they are faced with a number of decisions. First, as discussed above, they must choose a financing structure. Do they use a standard balloon mortgage or a floating-rate loan, or do they pursue a more complicated structure such as a joint venture or sale-leaseback. Owners must also choose their desired amount of debt, although maximum loan size is typically limited by the income-producing ability and market value of the property.

---

8. For more information on HUD programs see Gary W. Hutto, *Commercial Real Estate Finance Basics* (Washington, DC: Mortgage Bankers Association of America, 2000) or visit the HUD website www.hud.gov

9. For more information on Fannie Mae and Freddie Mac multifamily mortgage programs, see Hutto, *Commercial Real Estate Finance Basics* (2000) or visit the Fannie (www.fanniemae.com) or Freddie (www.freddiemac) websites.

Typical Loan Terms

Exhibit 14-3 contains typical loan terms on standard fixed-rate commercial mortgages as of the third quarter of 2002. This information was obtained from RealtyRates.com.[10] The average interest rate spread over 10-year Treasuries reported by survey respondents ranged from 2.22 percentage points (222 basis points) for apartment loans to 2.61 percent for loans on office buildings, with the spreads for industrial and retail loans nearly identical to office spreads.

Additional evidence that apartment loans are, on average, viewed by lenders to be less risky than other property types can be found in the lower average debt coverage ratio (1.37). The **debt coverage ratio (*DCR*)** is defined as:

$$DCR = \frac{NOI}{DS}$$

where *NOI* is generally the net operating income estimated for the first year of operations and *DS* is the annual debt service. The *DCR* shows the extent to which *NOI* can decline from expectations before it is insufficient to service the debt. It therefore provides an indication of the safety associated with the use of borrowed funds. Lenders usually seek a 1.2 to 1.3 *DCR,* but vary their requirements depending on the risk characteristics of the loan and competitive market pressures.

Exhibit 14-3 also reveals that apartment loans have higher average loan-to-value ratios (*LTV*s). This ratio measures the percentage of the price (or value) encumbered by debt. The higher the ratio, the less protection the lender has from loss of capital in the event of default and foreclosure (the *LTV* and *DCR* are discussed further in a later section). In no case did lenders or investors report *LTV*s that exceeded 90 percent and, for nonapartment properties, the maximum *LTV* was 80 percent. Although not reported in Exhibit 14-3, interest rate spreads are lower for floating-rate loans largely because borrowers, not lenders, are absorbing the interest rate risk. Thus, lenders can (and must) offer lower rates on floating-rate loans.

Concept Check

14.8 What is the relation between the probability of default and (1) the *LTV* and the (2) *DCR*?

There was significant variation across property types in the average loan term reported by survey respondents. Apartment loans had a 21-year average term. The average loan term for industrial properties was 12 years, whereas the averages for office and retail loans were just 8 and 6 years, respectively. Clearly, lenders are more willing to commit to longer-term loans when the property pledged as collateral for the loan is apartments. Despite significant variation in average loan terms across property types, amortization periods were quite similar, with averages ranging from 25 to 28 years.

Finally, apartment borrowers were typically required to set aside $250 a year for each apartment unit. The accumulated balances in these reserve accounts are used to fund nonrecurring capital costs, such as replacing carpeting, appliances, roofs, and heating and air-

---

10. The RealtyRates.com Investor Survey represents one of the most comprehensive data sets of investment activity compiled for the commercial real estate industry. The information and data maintained encompass all markets nationally, but includes only class A and B properties. Class "A" properties usually command the highest rents because they are most prestigious in their tenancy, location, and overall desirability. Class "B" properties command lower rents than class A properties for one or more reasons; for example, less desirable location or tenant mix, fewer amenities, or more advanced age. The 2002 third quarter survey is based on information provided by 312 commercial real estate appraisers, brokers, developers, investors, and lenders. More complete information on survey methodologies is available at www.RealtyRates.com.

Exhibit 14-3 RealtyRates.com Investor Survey of Permanent, Fixed-Rate Financing
(3rd Quarter 2002)

	Apartment	Industrial	Office	Retail
Spread over 10-Year Treasury				
Average	2.22%	2.57%	2.61%	2.60%
Min.	1.31	1.49	1.49	1.49
Max.	3.75	4.20	3.92	4.40
Debt Coverage Ratio				
Average	1.37	1.39	1.50	1.43
Min.	1.11	1.20	1.20	1.20
Max.	1.80	1.60	1.80	1.80
Loan-to-Value Ratio				
Average	75%	72%	73%	73%
Min.	60	60	60	60
Max.	90	80	80	80
Amortization (Yrs.)				
Average	26	25	28	26
Min.	15	20	20	20
Max.	35	30	30	30
Term (Yrs.)				
Average	21	12	8	6
Min.	3	3	3	2
Max.	40	30	30	10
Lender Reserve Requirements				
Typical	$250/yr.	$0.15/sq.ft.	$0.20/sq.ft.	$0.15/sq.ft.
Min.	$150/yr.	$0.10/sq.ft.	$0.15/sq.ft.	$0.15/sq.ft.
Max.	$250/yr.	$0.15/sq.ft.	$0.20/sq.ft.	$0.25/sq.ft.

Source: www.RealtyRates.com

conditioning units. Industrial and retail owners were typically required to set aside $0.15 per square foot per year for nonrecurring capital costs. On average, office properties require slightly higher reserves ($0.20 per sq.ft.).

Concept Check

14.9 If $100,000 must be accumulated for a major roof repair that will be required at the end of four years, how much must be set aside each year if the annual deposits will earn 3 percent compounded annually?

We next discuss the borrower's choice of loan size, carefully considering the advantages and disadvantages of using financial leverage. We then discuss the trade-offs between the various financing structures that borrowers must be aware of when searching for and negotiating a commercial mortgage. The ongoing prepayment and default decisions borrowers face after origination are then considered.

Loan Size

There are two basic reasons why real estate investors and homeowners borrow funds—use financial leverage—for real estate investments. The first reason is limited financial resources. If an investor desires to purchase real estate but has insufficient wealth to pay cash for the property, then borrowing is not an option. The second reason for the use of mortgage financing is that it alters the expected risk and return of real estate investments. In particular, the use of leverage amplifies the rate of return that investors earn on their invested equity. This *magnification* of equity returns is known as positive (or negative) financial leverage, and may induce investors to at least partially debt-finance (use "other people's money") even if they have sufficient wealth to avoid borrowing.

When is the use of leverage favorable? The use of financial leverage will increase the going-in *IRR* on equity when the cost of borrowing is less than the unlevered going-in *IRR;* that is, the *IRR* calculated assuming the property is purchased with 100 percent equity financing. In other words, as long as each borrowed dollar is earning a greater return than it costs, the net difference goes to the owner, enhancing the equity yield. Although the use of leverage may increase the investor's going-in *IRR* on equity, it should be stressed that financial leverage also increases the riskiness of the equity investment by increasing the risk of default *and* by making the *realized* return on equity more sensitive to changes in rental rates and resale values. Thus, the increase in *expected* return from the use of debt may not be large enough to offset the corresponding increase in risk.

Financial Risk

Recall that mortgage lenders have a claim on operating cash flows that is superior to the claims of the equity investor. However, so long as the net operating income (*NOI*) from monthly operations exceeds the promised mortgage payment (i.e., the property is "cash flowing"), satisfying the lender's claim is not a problem. Increasing the amount of borrowed funds—and thus the promised mortgage payment—increases the probability that *NOI* will be insufficient to cover (service) the mortgage payment obligation. The risk that *NOI* will be less than debt service is often referred to as **financial risk.** Default risk is the risk that borrowers will cease to make timely payments of principal and interest, as required by the mortgage agreement. Such behavior could lead to lender foreclosure on the property if not cured by the borrower. As the amount of leverage increases beyond a critical level, it becomes increasingly likely that debt service will exceed the *NOI.* If the property is not cash flowing, the borrower will have to draw on money from other sources to avoid default.

Concept Check

14.10 Define *financial risk.* From the lender's perspective, is it more closely linked to the risk of default or prepayment?

Increased Variability of Equity Returns from Leverage

The use of debt financing affects the amount and the variation (from expectations) of before-tax cash flows available for distribution to the equity investor. More specifically, the variability of the equity investor's *IRR* increases with the amount of financial leverage. This is because a given amount of variation in *NOI* will have increasingly larger effects on the equity return as the use of debt increases.

To demonstrate the acute sensitivity of equity returns to the use of debt financing, consider the example summarized in Exhibit 14-4. A lender is offering a $10 million fixed-payment mortgage with a 7.625 percent interest rate and, for simplicity, *annual* payments. With a loan term of 10 years and a 30-year amortization schedule, the annual payment is

Exhibit 14-4 Assumptions for a Loan on Gatorwood Apartment Complex

Input	Assumption
Number of units	296 units with average monthly rent of $534.91
Purchase price	$13,375,000
Projected increase in gross rents	3% per year
Vacancy and collection losses	10% per year
Operating expenses	$400,000 in year 1, increasing 3.5 percent thereafter
Capital expenditures	$37,500 in year 1, increasing 3.5 percent thereafter. Expenditures are reserved for in calculation of *NOI* (i.e., an above-line treatment)
Holding period	5 years
Estimated selling price in year 5	Year 6 net operating income capitalized at 10%
Selling expenses	5% of sale price
Financing:	
Loan amount	$10,000,000 (equals 74.7664% of price)
Interest rate	7.625%
Amortization schedule	30 years, *annual* payments
Loan term	10 years

Exhibit 14-5 Gatorwood Apartment Complex Before-Tax Cash Flows from Annual Operations

	1 yr.	2 yr.	3 yr.	4 yr.	5 yr.
Potential gross income (*PGI*)	$1,900,000	$1,957,000	$2,015,710	$2,067,181	$2,138,467
− Vacancy and collection loss (*VC*)	190,000	195,700	201,571	207,618	213,847
= Effective gross income (*EGI*)	1,710,000	1,761,300	1,814,139	1,868,563	1,924,620
− Operating expenses (*OE*)	400,000	414,000	428,490	443,487	459,009
− Capital expenditures (*CAPX*)	37,500	38,812	40,171	41,577	43,032
= Net operating income (*NOI*)	1,272,500	1,308,488	1,345,478	1,383,499	1,422,579
− Debt service (*DS*)	857,038	857,038	857,038	857,038	857,038
= Before-tax cash flow (*BTCF*)	$ 415,462	$ 451,450	$ 488,440	$ 526,461	$ 565,541

www.lmres.com/ ourBusinesses/ financing/ mortgagecalculator.asp

Use this free online calculator offered by Legg Mason to figure the mortgage payment for Gatorwood.

$857,038.[11] Assume the borrower expects to sell the property at the end of five years, at which time the remaining mortgage balance will equal $9,449,517. The holding period cash flows from annual operations implied by the assumptions in Exhibit 14-4 are contained in Exhibit 14-5. The before-tax equity reversion (*BTER*), calculated in Exhibit 14-6, is equal to $4,446,569. This *BTER,* along with the *BTCF*s in Exhibit 14-5 and the initial equity investment of $3,375,000, produce an estimated before-tax *IRR* on equity of 18.52 percent.[12]

Concept Check

14.12 What is the monthly loan payment on a fixed-rate mortgage with a 7.625 annual contract rate and 30-year amortization? What will be the total annual payments on this loan?

11. The calculator keystrokes are $N = 30$, $I = 7.625$, $PV = -10,000,000$, $PMT = ?$, and $FV = 0$.

12. The calculator keystrokes are $N = 5$, $I = ?$, $CF_0 = -3,375,000$, $CF_1 = 415,462$, $CF_2 = 451,450$, $CF_3 = 488,440$, $CF_4 = 526,461$, and $CF_5 = 5,012,110$. The cash flow in year 5 is equal to the *BTCF* in year 5, $565,541, plus the *BTER* of $4,446,569.

Exhibit 14-6 Proceeds from Sale of Gatorwood Apartments*

	Selling price (*SP*)	$14,627,459†
−	Selling expenses (*SE*)	731,373
=	Net selling price (*NSP*)	13,896,086
−	Remaining mtg. balance (*RMB*)	9,449,517
=	Before-tax equity reversion (*BTER*)	$ 4,446,569

*See Exhibit 14-4 for required assumptions.

†Equal to *NOI* in year 6 ($1,462,746) capitalized at 10 percent.

We now investigate the sensitivity of before-tax cash flows (*BTCF*s) and equity *IRR*s to variations in the initial *LTV* and in the assumed annual rate of growth in rental income. These sensitivities are displayed in Exhibit 14-7. The results in the first column were calculated with a spreadsheet assuming a zero percent *LTV*. Columns 2 through 4 assume initial loans of $5,350,000, $8,025,000, and $10,000,000, respectively. First, note that estimated *NOI* is assumed to be unaffected by the *LTV*.[13] In the absence of financial leverage (column 1), the estimated *BTCF* equals the *NOI* of $1,272,500, and the required initial equity investment is equal to $13,375,000—the purchase price of the property. The equity dividend rate (*BTCF* ÷ equity) is 9.51 percent. Annual debt service with a $5,350,000 loan is $458,515. This results in a *BTCF* of $813,985 and an equity investment of $8,025,000. The estimated *BTCF* continues to decrease as the *LTV* increases, but so does the required equity investment. Note that the equity dividend rate increases as the amount of leverage increases. This positive relation between the equity dividend rate and the *LTV* will be observed whenever the annual mortgage constant is *less* than the overall capitalization rate. The annual mortgage constant (annual payment ÷ loan amount) in this example is equal to 8.57 percent, and the going-in cap rate (*NOI* ÷ price) is 9.79 percent.[14] Thus, increasing leverage increases the estimated equity dividend rate in this example.

Concept Check

14.13 When will the use of leverage increase the going-in *IRR* on equity?

The middle section of Exhibit 14-7 displays the going-in *IRR* for annual growth rates in gross rents ranging from −1 to +8 percent. The assumed probability of each growth rate scenario is listed in parentheses. With no leverage and a 1 percent annual decline in rents, the internal rate of return (*IRR*) on equity is 5.2 percent. The use of financial leverage will increase the going-in *IRR* on equity if the unlevered *IRR* exceeds the borrower's cost of debt. Because there are no up-front financing costs in our example, the cost of debt (i.e., the effective borrowing cost) is equal to the contract rate of 7.625 percent. Thus, increasing the *LTV* will *decrease* the calculated *IRR* on equity if gross rents decrease 1 percent per year because 5.2 percent (the unlevered *IRR*) is less than the 7.625 percent cost of debt. With rental growth rates of approximately 1 percent or higher, increasing the use of leverage in-

---

13. In a simple world, the amount of debt financing (leverage) will not affect the income-producing ability of the property. However, if the incentives of the borrower and lender are not aligned, leverage may impact the operating decisions of the borrower, and thus *NOI*.

14. The annual mortgage constant can also be determined with the following keystroke sequence: $N = 30$, $I = 7.625$, $PV = -1$, $PMT = ?$, and $FV = 0$.

Exhibit 14-7 The Effects of Debt Financing on Cash Flows, IRRs, and Risk

Initial loan amount	$0	$5,350,000	$8,025,000	$10,000,000
Initial loan-to-value ratio	0%	40%	60%	75%
NOI in year 1	$ 1,272,500	$1,272,500	$1,272,500	$ 1,272,500
− Debt service	—	458,515	687,773	857,038
= *BTCF*	$ 1,272,500	$ 813,985	$ 584,727	$ 415,462
Initial equity*	$13,375,000	$8,025,000	$5,350,000	$ 3,375,000
BTCF/initial equity	9.51%	10.14%	10.93%	12.31%
Growth rate in rents:	*IRR*	*IRR*	*IRR*	*IRR*
−1% (5% probability)	5.2%	3.4%	0.8%	−5.0%
+1% (20% probability)	8.0	8.2	8.5	9.0
+3% (50% probability)	10.6	12.5	14.8	18.5
+5% (20% probability)	13.3	16.6	20.3	26.2
+8% (5% probability)	17.1	22.2	27.6	35.7
Mean *IRR*	10.7%	12.5%	14.6%	17.8%
Standard deviation of *IRR*	2.5	4.0	5.7	8.5
Mean return/standard deviation	4.2	3.1	2.6	2.1

*The initial equity is equal to the total purchase price minus the loan amount.

creases the going-in *IRR* because the unlevered *IRR* for these growth rates is greater than the 7.625 percent cost of debt.

Although increased financial leverage increases, in some cases substantially, the going-in *IRR* when rental growth rates exceed approximately 1 percent per year, this benefit of financial leverage must be weighed against the cost of increased risk. Given the assumed distribution of rental growth rates, the mean and standard deviation of the internal rate of return, assuming no leverage, are 10.7 percent and 2.5 percent, respectively. With a 40 percent *LTV*, the going-in *IRR* on equity increases to 12.5 percent. However, the standard deviation of the *IRR* increases to 4.0 percent. Thus, higher expected returns on equity can be "purchased" with additional leverage—but at the "price" of significantly increased risk (standard deviation). In fact, the mean return per unit of risk decreases steadily as leverage increases.

The use of mortgage debt to help finance the acquisition of real estate is pervasive. Therefore, its effect on risk and return should be clearly understood. Many market participants recommend extensive use of debt. One of the basic tenets of the numerous "get rich by investing in real estate schemes" is to make maximum use of "other peoples' money." The discussion and example above, however, demonstrate that leverage is a double-edged sword. Its use will enhance equity returns when the property is performing well. However, if the property performs poorly, the use of debt can make a bad situation worse, although the right to default can limit the amount of downside risk when nonrecourse financing is used.

Concept Check

14.14 After watching a late night "get rich by investing in real estate" cable TV show, your roommate reports that the key ingredient to successful real estate investing is using "lots" of mortgage debt. What response would be appropriate and also allow you to contradict your roommate?

Exhibit 14-8 Financing Commercial Property: A Borrower's Perspective

	Straight Debt	Joint Venture	Land Sale-Leaseback	Complete Sale-Leaseback
Property price risk	High	Moderate	Moderate	None
Influence on property management	Strong		→	None
Depreciation deductions	Full	Shares	Full	None
Priority of claim to cash flow	Send to lenders'	Partners with lender	Claim second to lenders' and land owners'	No ownership interest
Maximum amount of leverage	80% of value		→	100% of value

Choosing among Alternative Financing Structures

In previous sections we discussed a number of debt financing options available on commercial properties. When comparing commercial mortgage structures, it is important to be aware of how borrowers and lenders evaluate the trade-offs between the various financing structures and contract provisions. When the borrower must give up something in order to benefit along another dimension of the financing structure, decision making becomes more difficult.

Exhibit 14-8 summarizes the spectrum of financing alternatives along several dimensions. With respect to bearing the risk of future property price fluctuations, straight debt is the most risky from the borrower's perspective because the lender does not share in future sale proceeds. A joint venture agreement reduces the effects of price fluctuations on the borrower's return because the lender shares in the risk of property price changes. Borrowers, effectively, sell off a portion of the benefits of equity ownership to the joint venture lender. With a land sale-leaseback, borrowers bear the price risk associated with the building or buildings, while sale/leaseback investors absorb the price risk associated with the land. Investors bear all of the property price risk in a "complete" sale-leaseback.

Straight debt places full responsibility for the management of the property on the borrower, while joint venture agreements can give lenders an increased say in management decisions. Complete sale-leasebacks, the other extreme, eliminate the borrower's control of the property. With straight debt, the borrower claims the full amount of the available tax depreciation deductions. These tax deductions are typically shared with an institutional partner in a joint venture agreement and lost completely in a sale-leaseback that involves both the land and improvements.

With straight debt, the borrower's claim on property cash flows is second, or residual, to the lender's, whereas in joint ventures, borrowers become partners with the lender. With land sale-leasebacks, the borrower's cash flow claims are subordinate to both the mortgage and lease payments. With complete sale-leasebacks, the borrower has no claim on the property's cash flows. If straight debt is used, total mortgage financing is generally limited to 80 percent of the property's market value (apartment borrowers may have higher limits). Joint ventures and land sale-leasebacks may require less borrower equity, whereas complete sale-leasebacks effectively provide the borrower with 100 percent financing. As this discussion suggests, the relative costs and benefits of the various options are difficult to assess and highly dependent on the specific terms of the agreements.

In general, it appears that most commercial owners are inclined to use some mix of straight debt and equity to finance properties, bearing the full price risk, but retaining the full "upside potential" and full control. However, the scarcity or opportunity cost of their equity capital can compel them to consider alternatives. Then, by giving up more aspects of ownership (moving to the right in Exhibit 14-8) they can reduce their equity commitment while still mitigating the risks of high leverage.

Concept Check

14.15   With straight debt, the borrower absorbs all the risk associated with changes in the value of the property. This sounds bad! Can you put a more positive spin on it?

The Prepayment and Default Decisions

As with residential mortgages, the most accurate guide to a commercial mortgage refinancing decision is net present value. This decision rule compares the present value of future payment reductions to the immediate costs of obtaining a new loan. The costs of refinancing an existing commercial mortgage are large and can vary depending upon the number of points and fees charged by the new lender. In addition, the up-front costs of commercial refinancing typically include a prepayment penalty on the existing mortgage. Moreover, lockout provisions may preclude the borrower from refinancing. For these reasons, the risk to the lender of a prepayment due to a decline in interest rates or a borrower move is often small relative to residential mortgages.

What is the most significant risk faced by commercial mortgage lenders? The signature risk of commercial mortgage lending is default risk. Putting aside transaction costs and other considerations (including the borrower's credit rating), commercial borrowers would tend to default on their loans if the value of the property were to fall below the value of the remaining mortgage balance. This is especially true if the mortgage is nonrecourse. However, the evidence indicates that commercial borrowers do not default the minute the mortgage balance exceeds the value of the property. Many borrowers with negative equity continue to make payments because they expect the value of the property to increase.

The propensity of commercial borrowers to default also is impeded by the costs of default. These costs include direct costs such as penalty fees or any recourse the lender holds to other assets of the borrower, and indirect costs such as greater difficulty or higher cost of obtaining mortgage financing subsequent to the default. Nevertheless, commercial mortgage defaults regularly occur (see Industry Issues 14-2). According to the American Council of Life Insurance Companies, over 7 percent of outstanding commercial mortgage loans issued by U.S. life insurance companies were delinquent in late 1992. By the second quarter of 1996, the delinquency rate had fallen to 2.6 percent and in the second quarter of 2002 the rate was just 0.22 percent. However, by late 2002 the delinquency rate had increased to 2.1 percent. In contrast, home loan foreclosure rates have rarely risen above one third of one percent since World War II.

Concept Check

14.16   Yield spreads on commercial mortgages since 1990 are displayed in Exhibit 14-2. What accounts for the majority of this spread over Treasury securities?

Requesting a Permanent Loan

There are three basic steps involved in obtaining debt financing for a commercial property investment. First, the prospective borrower submits a loan application. Second, the lender analyzes the information contained in the loan application, as well as other information, and decides whether or not to fund the loan. This process is referred to as the **loan underwriting process.** If the decision is made to fund the loan, a formal commitment is made to the borrower. After both the borrower and lender have satisfied the terms of the agreement, the loan is "closed." This section discusses step 1: the loan application process. The lender's decision-making process is discussed in the next section, while the loan closing process is

Industry Issues

Source: Adapted from Richard D. Hylton, "The Building That Ate Chicago," *Fortune*, October 4, 1993. Copyright Time Inc.

14-2

The Building That Ate Chicago

A t 110 stories, the Sears Tower dominates Chicago's urban skyline. At 3.6 million square feet, it also carries considerable sway in the Windy City's real estate market. But this prominent structure, America's tallest, is no longer a source of profits for Sears. In 1994 the Sears Tower fell into foreclosure, heaping hundreds of millions of dollars in losses on some of the country's biggest investors.

What prompted the country's biggest retailer to join the rolls of corporate deadbeats? Money—lots of it. The loans were nonrecourse, meaning that in the event of default, the lenders could lay claim only to the building, not to any of Sears's other assets.

In the late 1980s, Sears struck an arrangement with a consortium of lenders to mortgage the building for $850 million, even as real estate markets were collapsing. The lending consortium included Metropolitan Life and New York Life, as well as the pension funds of Ameritech and AT&T. In some ways the mortgage offered more advantages to Sears than an outright sale: It allowed the retailer to pull cash out of the building without paying some $150 million in capital gains tax that a sale would trigger.

However, the real estate recession pushed vacancies up and rents down. By late 1993 the value of the Sears Tower had fallen to about $400 million, less than half the loan amount. Many observers were certain Sears would avoid the embarrassment of foreclosure. They were wrong.

---

discussed in detail in Chapter 20. It should be pointed out that the following discussion applies most directly to situations in which the borrower does not have an ongoing relationship with the lender. If the borrower and lender have a larger business relationship, the loan application process may be decidedly less formal.

Loan Application Package

A loan application is a nonbinding document that indicates to a lender that the borrower is agreeable to its loan terms. When seeking a long-term mortgage loan, investors must provide prospective lenders with the information they need to assess the profitability and risk of the proposed loan. The required information is usually filled in on a number of prepared forms which are bound together with other information as a loan application package. Unlike residential loans, a commercial loan application is not a standardized form because it is designed by lenders to suit their specific requirements. However, pressure to standardize commercial loan documents continues to mount as the secondary market for commercial mortgages continues to expand.

Relative to residential loans, the underwriting process for commercial loans is more complicated and focuses more on the property used as collateral for the loan. The primary reason for this difference in emphasis is the anticipated source of funds for loan repayment. Lenders expect that payments on residential loans will come from the personal income of the borrower. Payments on commercial loans are expected to come from income generated by the property. As a result, the commercial loan underwriting process focuses first on the property being pledged as collateral for the loan.

The size and details of the application package vary with the size of the loan request, the type of property being used as collateral (e.g., office, apartment), and whether the loan proceeds will be used to fund an existing property or a proposed development. However, loan application packages usually include the following items.

1. *Loan application.* The loan application is the specific document in the package that requests funds. It specifies the amount (or percentage of value) requested, the maturity of the loan, the interest rate, commitment terms, and identity of the borrower(s). It also usually includes the borrower's financial statements, a credit report, a projection of how the loan is to be repaid, and the borrower's experience with similar projects.

2. *Property description.* The property that will secure the loan and its location must be described in considerable detail. Maps and photos of the area are usually included, as are surveys, plot plans, and topographical maps.

3. *Legal aspects.* Lenders require a precise description of the property and identification of any easements or encroachments. Information about property taxes, special assessments, and deed restrictions must also be included. Environmental impact statements or other reports must be included, as required. The environmental site assessment has become increasingly important in the lender's decision-making process because of recent regulatory changes and because several recent court rulings have held lenders liable for cleanup costs on contaminated properties when they foreclose and take title. (See Chapter 6 for more detail on environmental reports.) Loan applicants also must provide a favorable title opinion or a commitment for title insurance. Lenders want to make certain a long-term mortgage loan will constitute a first lien on the property.

4. *Cash flow estimates.* Because the main source of repayment for commercial loans is cash flow from rental operations, the lender will usually require a copy of the property's financial statements (if it is an existing property) and a copy of the rental rates paid by each tenant (sometimes called the rent roll). In many cases, lenders also require the borrower to provide a cash flow pro forma, that is, a discounted cash flow analysis. How much weight is placed on the applicant's estimate of the property's future income-producing ability depends on the skills and knowledge of the lender's underwriting staff and the reputation of the loan applicant.

5. *Appraisal report.* Lenders typically require a third-party fee appraisal of the property's market value. Maximum loan amounts are often a percentage of the agreed upon sale price or the estimated market value of the property, whichever is less. Federally regulated lenders must order appraisal reports from state certified appraisal firms; borrowers cannot shop appraisers to find the highest value estimate. Lenders often place considerable weight on the estimate of market value contained in the appraisal report. However, estimates of the property's future net cash flows, from which the loan payments will be made, dominate the underwriting practices of most commercial mortgage lenders. As in many business situations "cash is king."

www.LoopLender.com

Affiliated with LoopNet.com, this site provides information on current rates and permits an online mortgage search.

Channels of Submission

Prospective borrowers often submit loan requests directly to commercial banks, savings and loans, mutual savings banks, life insurance companies, or pension funds. These institutions have commercial property lending units that consider such requests. Informal discussions with loan officers in these firms inform would-be borrowers of the expected items in a loan application package.

Another channel for loan requests is through mortgage bankers and brokers. Many of these firms enjoy close business relationships with several lenders. A business relationship in which a large lender agrees to purchase loans or to consider loan requests from a mortgage banker or broker is frequently termed a **correspondent relationship.** Many mortgage brokers specialize in seeking loan opportunities and in putting together loan application packages that meet the requirements of both institutional and noninstitutional lenders. In short, mortgage brokers help borrowers and lenders find each other. They may also assist borrowers in assembling loan application packages. For these services, brokers receive a fee from the lender at closing that typically ranges from 1/2 to 1 percent of the loan amount.

The Lender's Decision-Making Process

The borrower submits—either directly or through a mortgage broker—the loan application package to the lender for funding consideration. Usually one of the lender's loan underwriters is assigned primary responsibility for analyzing the loan, summarizing the application information on internal forms, and making a recommendation to a loan committee to

Explore The Web

Looking for up-to-date information on commercial real estate loan terms? Go to the home page of the International Real Estate Digest (www.ired.com) and click on "Mortgage Finance" in the left margin. To examine an extensive list of mortgage companies in your state, click on the U.S. map, then click on "RealWebFunds Commercial Mortgage Financing."Once there, click on "Common Index Rates" in the left margin.

What is the current yield on 1, 5, and 10-year Treasury securities and what have been the trends in these yields over the last year? Now click on "Mortgage Rates" in the left margin. How do current rates on a prototypical fixed-rate loan vary across property types? How sensitive are rates to the original loan-to-value ratio? Now go back to the RealWebFunds home page and prequalify a hypothetical loan of your choosing.

approve, reject, or renegotiate the loan terms and conditions. We first discuss some qualitative issues and standards mortgage lenders consider in evaluating the property and the borrower. We subsequently review the ratios and return measures commonly used in the quantitative analysis of the loan application.

The Property and the Borrower

When evaluating the loan application, lenders concentrate on the characteristics of the application that will have the most influence on the performance of the property used as collateral. In particular, lenders generally consider the following characteristics:

- **Property type.** Each commercial property type represents an investment in a diverse business with different operating margins, regulatory constraints, and supply and demand fundamentals.
- **Location.** Local markets have a significant effect on how properties perform. For this reason, lenders often perform the same kinds of market and feasibility analyses undertaken by investors and appraisers.
- **Tenant quality.** Tenants typically fulfill their lease obligations as long as their business is profitable. Lenders are therefore concerned about the number of tenants in each property and their creditworthiness.
- **Lease terms.** Cash flow from operations is derived from leases. Therefore, lenders must evaluate important lease terms such as base rental rates, escalation clauses, expense payment provisions, and renewal and cancelation options. (Commercial leases are discussed in detail in Chapter 21.)
- **Property management.** Property management can significantly affect the operating performance of a property. Thus, lenders must evaluate the manager's experience and knowledge of the local market. (Property management is discussed in detail in Chapter 17.)
- **Building quality.** The age, design, and physical appearance of the building can dramatically affect its income-producing ability. In particular, lenders should be concerned about any deferred maintenance or required capital expenditures that may affect the ability of the borrower to service the debt.
- **Environmental concerns.** As previously mentioned, environmental issues and concerns have become increasingly important.
- **Borrower quality.** Although the nonrecourse nature of most commercial loans causes the lender to focus on the property, borrower quality is still an important consideration.

Concept Check

14.17 What characteristics of the commercial loan application should the lender carefully evaluate?

Maximum Loan Amount

Several factors may determine whether the borrower's requested loan amount is too high. First, lenders usually set limits on loan-to-value ratios that vary by property type and often by the market in which the property is located. Second, the lender underwrites the property's first year *NOI;* that is, they estimate what they believe will be the net operating income of the property. From this, the lender backs out a maximum loan amount—given an interest rate, amortization period, and minimum required debt coverage ratio.

The debt coverage ratio (*DCR*) for our Gatorwood Apartment example, assuming a $10 million loan, is:

$$DCR = \frac{Net\ operating\ income}{Debt\ service} = \frac{\$1,272,500}{\$857,038} = 1.5$$

Because *NOI* in the first year of operations is expected to be half again as large as the prospective mortgage payment, there appears to be sufficient protection against a decline in rental rates and net operating income.[15]

If the lender feels that $1,272,500 is a reasonable estimate of first year *NOI,* the *DCR* can be used to calculate the maximum allowable loan given the lender's minimum acceptable *DCR.* For example, if the lender requires the *DCR* to be 1.25 or greater, we can obtain the maximum debt service payment by rearranging the *DCR* formula as follows:

$$Maximum\ debt\ service = \frac{NOI}{Minimum\ DCR} = \frac{\$1,272,500}{1.25} = \$1,018,800$$

This maximum annual debt service, together with a 7.625 percent interest rate, annual payments, and a 30-year term, implies a maximum loan of $11,878,124 (an 88.8 percent *LTV*).[16] Although it appears the property can support a $11,878,124 loan, the loan limit will be determined by the lender's maximum allowable *LTV* if it is less than 88.8 percent, which is very likely.

An additional financial ratio often employed by lenders when underwriting a commercial loan is the **break-even ratio** (*BER*), defined as:

$$BER = \frac{Operating\ expenses\ +\ Capital\ expenditures\ +\ Debt\ service}{Potential\ gross\ income}$$

The *BER* measures the ability of an income property to cover its obligations; the lower the *BER,* the greater the decline in gross revenue—or the increase in expenses—can be before investors experience a negative cash flow from property operation.

The year 1 *BER* for Gatorwood is:

$$BER = \frac{\$400,000\ +\ \$37,500\ +\ \$857,038}{\$1,900,000} = 0.681,\ or\ 68\%$$

The margin of safety between cash inflows and cash outflows is the difference between 100 percent and the break-even ratio. For apartment properties, the *BER* typically varies between 60 and 80 percent; thus, Gatorwood provides the lender with a fairly high tolerance for increases in vacancies and expenses.

---

15. Commercial lenders are more likely to employ an above-line, rather than a below-line, treatment when underwriting commercial loan applications. Thus, we employ an above-line treatment of *CAPX*s in our Gatorwood example.

16. The calculator keystrokes to find the maximum loan amount are: $N = 30$, $I = 7.625$, $PV = ?$, $PMT = 1,018,000$, and $FV = 0$. To calculate the maximum *LTV,* simply divide the maximum loan amount of $11,878,124 by the purchase price (value), given in Exhibit 14-4, of $13,375,000.

Career Focus

Construction lending is the most complicated end of the financing spectrum. Thus, construction lenders are often hired from among the ranks of experienced mortgage lenders. The job requires a solid knowledge of lending regulations, loan documentation, loan underwriting, construction,

Construction Lenders

development, accounting for draws against the loan during construction, and permanent loan commitments. In addition, construction loan officers need to assess project feasibility and the probability of the builder/developer being able to complete a project on time and within the budget. These skills require significant experience.

Concept Check

14.18 You are analyzing the potential acquisition of a small apartment property. Some of the estimates from the first year pro forma are as follows: potential gross income, $185,000; vacancy and collection losses, $18,500; annual debt service, $72,643; operating expenses, $58,275; capital expenditures, $0. Calculate the *DCR* and the *BER*.

The Economic Justification

If the requested loan amount does meet the lender's underwriting guidelines, a decision must be made about whether the entire loan proposal makes sense on economic grounds. This decision requires that the lender check the cash flow and resale projections contained in the appraisal report and in the borrower's application package—that is, the lender must perform a **due diligence** analysis to determine, essentially, that the potential borrower has not misrepresented the property in any way. The lender is also aware that if the property produces an adequate return for the borrower, there is little chance the borrower will default on the mortgage. Thus, the lender may estimate the going-in capitalization rate and the equity dividend rate, as well as the borrower's going-in *IRR* on equity.

From Application to Commitment

Usually, a commercial real estate loan will take 90 days from the signing of the sale contact until closing, but some loans can be processed in as little as 45 days. Processing time depends on numerous factors such as the type and size of loan, the number and complexity of the existing leases, and whether the borrower and lender are familiar with each other's requirements. While the application is nonbinding, a **loan commitment** is a written agreement that commits the lender to make a loan to the borrower provided the borrower satisfies the terms and conditions of the commitment. As part of the commitment process, the lender will usually offer the borrower the opportunity to "lock in" the interest rate on the loan. If the rate is not locked, the borrower and lender agree to a spread. For example, the lender may commit to close a 10-year loan at a rate 175 basis points (1.75 percentage points) above the yield on 10-year Treasury securities. If the yield on 10-year Treasury securities increases after the loan commitment but before closing, the contract interest rate will increase. To protect against such increases, the borrower is often willing to pay a nonrefundable fee to obtain a **rate lock agreement.**

Land Acquisition, Development, and Construction Financing

The development, construction, and operation of large income properties take time and different types of effort. The developer may acquire land that must then be made ready (i.e., improved) for construction. The improved land may be sold as individual lots, which is typical with new home development, or it may be used as an industrial or office park, or as a site for some other form of income-producing property. Different financing requirements usually are involved in the various phases of a property's life, and lending arrangements have evolved to serve these needs. **Land acquisition loans** finance the purchase of the raw land: **Land development loans** finance the installation of the on-site and off-site improvements to the land (e.g., sewers, streets, and utilities) that are necessary to ready the land for construction. **Construction loans** are used to finance the costs associated with erecting the building or buildings (i.e., "going vertical").

Some lenders may be willing to make acquisition, development, and construction (ADC) loans. In these loans, the same lender advances enough money for the developer to purchase the land and develop it to the point that it is ready for a building to be constructed on it. Then the lender advances additional funds for construction, with the developed land and partial construction serving as security for the loan. The existence of one lender and one set of loan documents simplifies the financing process and eliminates potential conflicts of interest between the various lenders. In some cases, the developer may obtain a single, short-term permanent mortgage—or **miniperm loan**—from a lender that provides financing for the construction period, the lease-up period, and for several years beyond the lease-up stage. Developers may be attracted to miniperms, which enable them to proceed with construction without long-term financing, if they expect to sell the project or refinance into a permanent loan before the term of the miniperm loan expires. (Land acquisition, land development, and construction loans are discussed in more detail in Chapter 24.)

Ultimately, the success of land development and construction loans depends on the developer's ability to complete projects with market values in excess of development and construction costs. The developer's failure to create adequate value at any stage of the development process may result in default and foreclosure. As discussed in Chapter 2, development and construction loans lie on the high end of the real estate risk spectrum.

Summary

Most commercial properties require debt financing tailored to meet the unique aspects of the situation. While many of the same institutions (e.g., commercial banks, life insurers, savings institutions) that originate home loans also provide commercial property financing, the loan terms are considerably different. For example, commercial mortgages are typically shorter in term and limit or penalize prepayment. Also, unlike residential mortgage financing, commercial property financing has historically been nonrecourse.

The three main repayment mechanisms used in the market for long-term (permanent) commercial mortgages are fully amortizing loans, partially amortizing loans, and interest-only loans. Fixed-rate, partially amortizing mortgages with balloon payments are the most commonly used structure, although it is not uncommon for commercial mortgages to have adjustable, or floating, interest rates. Fixed-rate commercial mortgages do not typically allow borrowers to freely prepay at par because they contain either a lockout provision, a prepayment penalty such as a yield-maintenance agreement or defeasance, or both. Floating-rate loans generally are prepayable at par without penalty. The availability of installment sale financing, joint ventures, and sale-leaseback financing provides alternative financing structures for investors and property owners to consider.

After selecting the appropriate financing structure, investors must next choose their desired loan amount. Borrowed funds magnify the equity returns to a given project, both positively and negatively. By employing higher loan-to-value ratios—using more financial leverage—investors can generally increase their expected returns. By doing so, however, they also increase the variability of equity returns and the probability that net operating income will not be sufficient to cover the mortgage payment obligation. This latter concern is often referred to as *financial risk*. Other decisions facing commercial borrowers subsequent to loan origination include the decision to prepay and the decision to default. In both situations, net present value calculations should guide decision making, remembering of course that it is important to include all potential costs, such as a diminished credit rating, when selecting the default option.

To obtain debt financing for a commercial property investment, the prospective borrower must usually submit a formal loan application package. This package typically includes items such as the loan application, property description, legal aspects, cash flow estimates, and appraisal report. Prospective lenders must then evaluate both the property and the borrower to determine if they wish to fund the mortgage. When evaluating the loan application, lenders pay particular attention to the property type, location, tenant quality, lease terms, property management, building quality, environmental concerns, and borrower quality. When determining the maximum loan amount, lenders often employ the debt coverage ratio.

Key Terms

Balloon mortgage 357
Construction loans 377
Correspondent relationship 373
Debt coverage ratio (*DCR*) 364
Due diligence 376
Financial risk 366
Floating-rate mortgage 360
Installment sale 360

Joint venture 361
Land acquisition loans 377
Land development loans 377
Loan commitment 376
Loan underwriting process 371
Lockout provision 359
Mezzanine financing 362
Miniperm loan 377

Participation loan 362
Par value 359
Prepayment penalties 359
Rate lock agreement 376
Reinvestment risk 359
Sale-leasebacks 361
Yield-maintenance agreements 359

Test Problems

Answer the following multiple choice problems:

1. Due-on-sale clauses are included in commercial mortgages primarily to protect lenders from:
   a. Interest rate risk.   c. Reinvestment risk.
   b. Default risk.   d. Prepayment risk.

2. Consider a 30-year, 7 percent, fixed-rate, fully amortizing mortgage with a yield maintenance provision. Relative to this mortgage, a 10-year balloon mortgage with the same contract interest rate and yield maintenance provisions will primarily reduce the lender's:
   a. Interest rate risk.   c. Reinvestment risk.
   b. Default risk.   d. Prepayment risk.

3. Lockout provisions are primarily intended to reduce the lender's:
   a. Interest rate risk.   c. Reinvestment risk.
   b. Default risk.   d. Par value risk.

4. The tax benefits associated with installment sales are:
   a. Captured exclusively by the buyer.
   b. Captured exclusively by the seller.
   c. Often shared by the buyer and seller.
   d. Often shared by the seller and a third-party lender.

5. Which of the following statements is most accurate?
   a. Joint ventures increase the amount of equity capital the developer/borrower must invest in the project.
   b. Joint ventures decrease the amount of equity capital the developer/borrower must invest in the project.

   c. Joint ventures give the developer/borrower a priority claim on the property's cash flows.
   d. Joint ventures increase the developer/borrower's exposure to the risk of property price fluctuations.

6. Which of the following financing structures provides for 100 percent financing?
   a. Straight debt.
   b. Joint venture.
   c. Land sale-leaseback.
   d. Complete (land and building) sale-leaseback.

7. Using financial leverage on a real estate investment can be for the purpose of all of the following except:
   a. Greater diversification.
   b. Greater expected return on the leveraged investment.
   c. Being able to acquire the property.
   d. Reduction of financial risk for the leveraged investment.

8. Increasing the amount of mortgage debt on a property will increase the equity investor's expected *IRR* if:
   a. The going-in cap rate exceeds the loan constant.
   b. The unlevered *IRR* exceeds the borrower's before tax cost of debt.
   c. The unlevered *IRR* exceeds the borrower's after tax cost of debt.
   d. NOI is greater than the mortgage payment.
   e. None of the above.

9. Which of these ratios is an indicator of the financial risk for an income property?
   a. Debt coverage ratio.
   b. Loan-to-value ratio.
   c. Equity dividend rate.
   d. Both **a** and **b**, but not **c**.
   e. All three, **a**, **b**, and **c**.

10. If the property's *NOI* is expected to be $22,560, operating expenses $12,250, and the debt service $19,987, the debt coverage ratio (*DCR*) is approximately equal to:
    a. 0.89.
    b. 1.13.
    c. 1.84.
    d. 1.74.
    e. None of the above.

Study Questions

1. Discuss several differences between long-term commercial mortgages and their residential counterparts.
2. Answer the following questions on financial leverage, value, and return:
   a. Define financial risk.
   b. When will increasing the loan-to-value ratio at origination increase the going-in *IRR* on a proposed commercial property investment?
   c. Should the investor select the origination *LTV* that maximizes the calculated *IRR* on equity? Explain why or why not.
3. Distinguish between recourse and nonrecourse financing.
4. Explain lockout provisions and yield-maintenance agreements. Does the inclusion of one or both of these provisions affect the borrower's cost of debt financing? Explain.
5. Assume the annual interest rate on a $500,000 7-year balloon mortgage is 6 percent. Payments will be made monthly based on a 30-year amortization schedule.
   a. What will be the monthly payment?
   b. What will be the balance of the loan at the end of year 7?
   c. What will be the balance of the loan at the end of year 3?
   d. Assume that interest rates have fallen to 4.5 percent at the end of year 3. If the remaining mortgage balance at the end of year 3 is refinanced at the 4.5 percent annual rate, what would be the new monthly payment assuming a 27-year amortization schedule?
   e. What is the difference in the old 6 percent monthly payment and the new 4.5 percent payment?
   f. What will be the remaining mortgage balance on the new 4.5 percent loan at the end of year 7 (four years after refinancing)?
   g. What will be the difference in the remaining mortgage balances at the end of year 7 (four years after refinancing)?
   h. At the end of year 3 (beginning of year 4), what will be the present value of the difference in monthly payments in years 4–7, discounting at an annual rate of 4.5 percent?
   i. At the end of year 3 (beginning of year 4), what will be the present value of the difference in loan balances at the end of year 7, discounting at an annual rate of 4.5 percent?
   j. At the end of year 3 (beginning of year 4), what will be the total present value of lost payments in years 4–7 from the lender's perspective?

   k. If the mortgage contains a yield maintenance agreement that requires the borrower to pay a lump sum prepayment penalty at the end of year 3 equal to the present value of the borrower's lost payments in years 4–7, what should that lump sum penalty be?

6. Consider the stand-alone corner locations favored by both Walgreens and Eckerds for locating their drugstores. In most cases, Walgreens and Eckerds do not own these properties. Instead, they lease the properties on a long-term basis from institutional owners. What do these companies gain by leasing instead of owning? What do they lose?

7. Consider the following table of annual mortgage rates and yields on 10-year Treasury securities:

Year	Mortgage Rate	10-Year Treasury Yield
1985	12.42%	10.82%
1986	10.18	7.68
1987	10.20	8.38
1988	10.33	8.85
1989	10.32	8.50
1990	10.13	8.55
1991	9.25	7.86
1992	8.40	7.01
1993	7.33	5.87
1994	8.36	7.08
1995	7.95	6.58
1996	7.81	6.44
1997	7.67	6.35
1998	6.95	5.26
1999	7.43	5.64
2000	8.06	6.03
2001	6.97	5.02
2002	6.54	4.61

   a. What is the average annual spread on mortgage rates relative to 10-year Treasury securities?
   b. What is the correlation between annual mortgage rates and Treasury yields over the 1985–2002 period? (Use your financial calculator or the statistical functions in Excel.)

8. List and briefly describe the typical items included in a commercial mortgage loan application package.

9. List at least six characteristics of a commercial mortgage loan application that the lender should carefully evaluate.

10. You have decided to purchase an industrial warehouse. The purchase price is $1 million and you expect to hold the property for five years. You have narrowed your choice of debt financing packages to the following two alternatives:
    - $700,000 loan, 6 percent interest rate, 30-year term, annual, interest-only payments (the annual payment will not include any amortization of principal), and $50,000 in up-front financing costs.
    - $750,000 loan, 6 percent interest rate, 30-year term, annual, interest-only payments. No up-front financing costs.

    What is the difference in the present value of these two loan alternatives? Assume the appropriate discount rate is 6 percent.

11. You are considering the purchase of an industrial warehouse. The purchase price is $1 million. You expect to hold the property for five years. You have decided to finance the acquisition with a $700,000 loan, 6 percent interest rate, 30-year term, and annual interest-only payments (that is, the annual payment will not include any amortization of principal). There are $50,000 in up-front financing costs. You estimate the following cash flows for the first year of operations:

$135,000	Effective gross income
27,000	Operating expenses
$108,000	*NOI*

    a. Calculate the overall rate of return (or "cap rate").
    b. Calculate the debt coverage ratio.
    c. What is the largest loan that you can obtain (holding the other terms constant) if the lender requires a debt service coverage ratio of *at least* 1.2?

12. Distinguish among land acquisition loans, land development loans, and construction loans. How would you rank these three with respect to lender risk?

13. Discuss the potential advantages of a miniperm loan from the perspective of the developer/investor, relative to the separate financing of each stage of the development.

14. You are considering purchasing an office building for $2,500,000. You expect the potential gross income (*PGI*) in the first year to be $450,000; vacancy and collection losses to be 9 percent of *PGI;* and operating expenses and capital expenditures to be 42 percent of effective gross income (*EGI*). You will finance the acquisition with 25 percent equity and 75 percent debt. The annual interest rate on the debt financing will be 5.5 percent. Payment will be made monthly based on a 25-year amortization schedule.
    a. What is the implied first year overall capitalization rate?
    b. What is the expected debt coverage ratio in year 1 of operations?
    c. If the lender requires the *DCR* to be 1.25 or greater, what is the maximum loan amount?
    d. What is the break-even ratio?

Explore The Web

Through their Program Plus lender network, Freddie Mac works to finance rental properties that are affordable to families with low and very low incomes and rental properties that are located in underserved areas. Freddie Mac and Fannie Mae have long histories of increasing the availability of affordable rental units in the United States. More than 90 percent of the more than one million rental units Freddie Mac has financed are affordable to people whose incomes are at or below the area median income.

Freddie Mac and Fannie Mae provide a full range of competitively priced mortgage products for the acqui-

sition, refinance, or rehabilitation of multifamily properties. Go to the Freddie Mac website (www. freddiemac.com) and browse the home page. Then search for information on their multifamily loan products. This search will eventually lead you to www.freddiemac.com/multifamily/product.htm, where you will see links to a variety of multifamily mortgage products. Examine the descriptions of the following loan types: fixed-rate amortizing, interest-only mortgages, rate-reset mortgages, and fixed-to-float mortgages. Explain how rate-reset and fixed-to-float mortgages compare to the standard financing options discussed in this chapter.

Solutions to Concept Checks

1. With recourse loans, the borrower has personal liability for the amount borrowed. This means that if default and foreclosure occurs and the foreclosure sale proceeds are less than the amount due the lender, the lender may come after other borrower assets to satisfy the lender's claim. With nonrecourse loans, the borrower is not personally liable for the loan. Thus, the lender can look only to the property pledged as collateral for the loan to satisfy any shortfalls that occur

from the foreclosure sale. The industry standard is a nonrecourse loan.

2. With a partially amortizing loan, the loan balance is not zero at the end of the loan term. This means that the remaining loan balance must be paid off or refinanced. If the value of the property has fallen below the remaining loan balance, the borrower may simply choose to default. With a fully amortizing loan, the balance of the mortgage is zero at the end of

the loan term. This reduces the probability of default throughout the life of the loan. Thus, partially amortizing loans are more risky for the lender.

3. When discounting at the riskless Treasury rate, investors are adjusting for the *timing* of the cash flows because the Treasury rate represents their opportunity cost of waiting for the future cash flows. To adjust for risk, the appropriate risk premium must be added to the riskless Treasury rate.

4. If the $1,400,000 principal balance is reinvested at 5 percent, compounded monthly, for the remaining seven years, the balance will increase to $1,985,804. If invested at 7 percent, compounded monthly, for the remaining seven years, the principal balance will increase to $2,281,992. This illustrates why lenders do not want borrowers to prepay 7 percent mortgages in a 5 percent interest rate environment; lenders do not want to reinvest the loan balance at 5 percent when they are earning 7 percent on the mortgage.

5. If the interest rate on the installment sale loan is equal to the seller's risk adjusted opportunity cost, then the installment loan (ignoring the tax deferral) will be a zero net present value "project" for the seller lender. Because we know that the present value of the tax deferral is positive, then the use of the installment sale is unambiguously advantageous. However, if the interest rate on the installment note is less than the seller's opportunity cost, then the seller will be losing money on the loan portion of the deal. And this loss may be enough to offset the positive value of the tax deferral.

6. Developers will often seek a joint venture (JV) partner because they are in need of capital. Joint ventures allow the developer to attain more capital than would otherwise be available under traditional debt financing. With a JV partner, the developer is also sharing the downside risk of the development project. For these two reasons, the developer may be willing to share the upside potential with a JV partner.

7. Leasing allows funds that are not invested in the land and building to be invested in other assets or in other facets of the tenant's business. If they expect returns on capital invested in their primary business to exceed the returns on their real estate holdings, they are better off leasing. In addi-

tion, leasing effectively provides 100 percent financing of the real estate and the entire lease payment is deductible for tax purposes.

8. Loans with higher *DCR*s and lower *LTV*s have lower probabilities of default.

9. To accumulate $100,000 by the end of four years, $23,903 must be deposited annually at a 3 percent interest rate compounded annually.

10. Financial risk is the risk that *NOI* will be less than debt service. From the lender's perspective, financial risk is more closely linked to default risk.

11. The monthly loan payment is $70,779, and the total annual payments equal $849,352.

12. The use of financial leverage will increase the going-in *IRR* on equity if the unlevered *IRR* exceeds the borrower's cost of debt.

13. Leverage will increase equity returns when a property is performing well; however, leverage in a poorly performing property will reduce returns even further.

14. With straight debt, the borrower absorbs all of the risk associated with changes in property value. However, if the property increases in value, the borrower captures all of this appreciation. In a joint venture, the borrower would have to share this appreciation (upside) with the JV partner. In a land sale-leaseback, the borrower benefits only from the appreciation in the value of the building improvements—the land is owned by the investor. In a complete sale-leaseback, the borrower cannot benefit in any way from property appreciation—the borrower is simply a tenant.

15. The majority of the spread of commercial mortgages over Treasuries is default risk.

16. The characteristics of the commercial loan application that the lender should carefully evaluate are property type, property location, tenant quality, terms of the existing lease, quality of the property management, building quality, environmental issues, and borrower quality.

17. The *DCR* is equal to *NOI* ÷ debt service = $108,225 ÷ $72,643 = 1.49. The *BER* is equal to (*OE* + *CAPX* + *DS*) ÷ *PGI* = ($58,275 + $0 + $72,643) ÷ $185,000 = 0.71.

Additional Readings

Brueggeman, William B., and Jeffrey D. Fisher. *Real Estate Finance and Investment,* 11th ed. New York: McGraw-Hill Irwin, 2001.

Clauretie, T. M., and G. S. Sirmans. *Real Estate Finance: Theory and Practice,* 4th ed. Cincinnati, OH: South-Western Publishing, 2002.

Collier, N. S., C. A. Collier, and D. A. Halperin. *Construction Funding: The Process of Real Estate Development, Appraisal, and Finance,* 3rd ed. New York: John Wiley, 2001.

Friedman, J. P., and J. C. Harris. *Keys to Mortgage Financing and Refinancing,* 3rd ed. Hauppauge, NY: Barron's Educational Series, January 1, 2001.

Gelter, D. M., and N. G. Miller. *Commercial Real Estate Analysis and Investments.* Cincinnati, OH: South-Western Publishing, 2000.

Gray, K. D., and J. R. White. *Shopping Centers and Other Retail Properties: Investment, Development, Financing, and Management.* New York, John Wiley, 1996.

Lederman, J. *The Handbook of Mortgage-Banking: Trends, Opportunities, and Strategies,* 2nd ed. New York: McGraw-Hill, 1993.

Madison, Michael. *Modern Real Estate Finance and Land Transfer: A Transactional Approach.* Gaithersburg, MD: Aspen Law & Business, 1999.

Wiedemer, John P. *Real Estate Finance.* Upper Saddle River, NJ: Prentice Hall, 2001.

www.mhhe.com/lingarcher1e

chapter fifteen

Sources of Commercial Debt *and* Equity Capital

Learning Objectives

After reading this chapter you will be able to:

1. Describe the size of the U.S. commercial real estate market relative to alternative asset classes such as stocks and bonds.

2. Identify the primary sources of public and private equity capital and discuss their relative importance.

3. Identify five ownership structures for pooling private equity capital and explain the advantages and disadvantages of each.

4. Identify the primary sources of public and private mortgage debt and discuss their relative importance.

5. Discuss the role private syndications play in commercial real estate markets.

6. Comment on the size and importance of the real estate investment trust (REIT) market.

7. Explain how REIT income is measured and how REITs are valued.

Introduction

Several of the preceding chapters focus on building a framework for understanding how commercial real estate assets are valued. But little attention has been paid to the types of investors that actually acquire commercial real estate or to the forms of ownership (e.g., partnership, corporation) these investors employ when purchasing real estate. Similarly, Chapter 14 discussed the most common mortgage products used by equity investors to finance commercial real estate investments. Again, the emphasis in Chapter 14 was on the description of common commercial mortgage products and the decision-making processes of borrowers and lenders, not on the role and importance of each of the various lenders who provide mortgage credit.

In this chapter we discuss the most common public and private equity investors and the ownership structures these investors use when purchasing commercial real estate. We then dis-

Exhibit 15-1   Relative Size of Investable Asset Categories

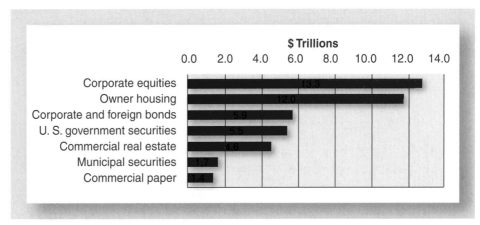

Source: Flow of Funds Accounts of the United States, Federal Reserve, September 2002, various tables, www.federalreserve.gov.

cuss the sources (i.e., holders) of commercial mortgage debt. In short, it is time to answer the following question: Who owns and finances the stock of U.S. commercial real estate assets?

How Large Is the U.S. Commercial Real Estate Market?

Before discussing the roles and importance of the various real estate owners and lenders, it is important to emphasize that commercial real estate plays a significant role in the U.S. (and other) economies. The estimated market value of investable commercial real estate (as of September 2002) is $4.6 trillion.[1] To put this into perspective, this $4.6 trillion estimate is displayed in Exhibit 15-1 along with the market values of other asset classes in U.S. capital markets. Exchange-traded corporate equities (stock) is the dominant asset class with a total stock market capitalization of $13.3 trillion. With an estimated market value of approximately $12.0 trillion, owner-occupied housing rivals the corporate equity market in size. Corporate and foreign bonds and U.S. government securities provide investors with an additional $5.9 trillion and $5.5 trillion, respectively, in investable assets. At $4.6 trillion in market value, commercial real estate compares favorably in size to the corporate bond and government securities markets; moreover, it is approximately three times the size of both the municipal securities and commercial paper market. Clearly, the commercial real estate market is a significant component of investable wealth in the United States.

As displayed in Exhibit 15-2, the $4.6 trillion total market value of commercial real estate can be broken into four quadrants: publicly traded equity capital, $168 billion; privately held equity, $2,397 billion; publicly traded mortgage debt, $403 billion; and privately held mortgage debt, $1,662 billion. We first turn our attention to the sources of equity capital.

Concept Check

15.1   According to Exhibit 15-1, what is the total estimated value of owner-occupied housing and commercial real estate? How much bigger than corporate stocks is the total value of U.S. real estate in percentage terms? Than corporate and foreign bonds? Than U.S. government securities?

---

1. This estimate comes from *Emerging Trends in Real Estate 2003,* (New York: Lend Lease Real Estate Investments and PricewaterhouseCoopers LLP, 2003), chap. 2; or emergingtrends@lendleaserei.com

Exhibit 15-2 Value of U.S. Commercial Real Estate

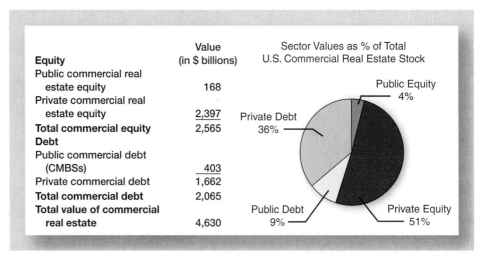

Equity	Value (in $ billions)	
Public commercial real estate equity	168	
Private commercial real estate equity	2,397	
Total commercial equity	2,565	
Debt		
Public commercial debt (CMBSs)	403	
Private commercial debt	1,662	
Total commercial debt	2,065	
Total value of commercial real estate	4,630	

Sector Values as % of Total U.S. Commercial Real Estate Stock

Public Equity 4%
Private Debt 36%
Public Debt 9%
Private Equity 51%

Source: *Emerging Trends in Real Estate 2003,* published jointly by Lend Lease Real Estate Investments and Pricewater-houseCoopers LLP, 909 Third Avenue, New York, NY 10022; and the *Federal Reserve Bulletin,* March 2003, table 1.54.

Sources of Commercial Real Estate Equity Capital

Investors can hold ownership (equity) positions in commercial real estate through either direct private investment or real estate securities. With direct private investment, individual and institutional investors purchase and hold title to the properties. Purchasing individual properties directly in the private market gives investors complete control of the asset: Who leases it, who manages it, how much debt financing is used, and when it is sold. With securities, in contrast, individuals and institutions invest funds in a separate ownership entity which, in turn, purchases and holds title to the real estate. **Securitized investments** therefore pool money from multiple investors. Securitized investments are purchased and resold in either "public" or "private" markets. We define public markets as those in which securities are bought and sold on a centralized public exchange, such as the New York Stock Exchange. Private markets are characterized by individually negotiated transactions that take place without the aid of a centralized market. Exchange-traded assets provide investors with a relatively high degree of liquidity and relatively low transaction costs. In contrast, private markets are generally characterized by high transaction costs and low liquidity.[2]

Concept Check

15.2   What are the advantages of private ownership of commercial real estate? What are the disadvantages?

Publicly Owned Commercial Real Estate

Approximately $168 billion of commercial real estate equity is held in the form of publicly traded **real estate investment trusts (REITs).** There are three major types of REITs. **Equity REITs** invest in and operate commercial properties, whereas **mortgage REITs** purchase mortgage obligations (typically commercial) and thus become, effectively, real

2. A liquid market is one in which assets can be sold quickly for fair market value. Although most REITs trade on an established public market, there is no requirement that REITs be publicly traded companies. REIT securities that are not listed on an exchange or traded over-the-counter are called "private" REITs.

Explore The Web

To examine the recent stock market performance of Equity Residential Properties (EQR), go to the NAREIT website (www.nareit.com). Click on "Investing in REITs," then on "REIT Performance Information." Retrieve information on EQR. What was EQR's total return in the last month? The last year? The last five years? How do these returns compare to other publicly traded apartment REITs?

estate lenders. An example of a mortgage REIT is Annaly Mortgage Management, Inc. (www.annaly.com; ticker symbol NLY). Annaly owns and manages a portfolio of mortgage-backed securities. Its principal business objective is to generate net income for the distribution to shareholders from the spread between the interest income on the mortgage-backed securities owned by the REIT and the costs of borrowing to finance their acquisitions. **Hybrid REITs** invest a significant percentage of their assets in both properties and mortgages. An example of a hybrid REIT is iStar Financial Inc. (www.istarfinancial.com; ticker symbol SFI). This REIT provides structured financing nationwide to private and corporate owners of real estate, including senior and junior mortgage debt, mezzanine financing, and corporate net lease financing (all discussed in Chapter 14).

REITs have been described as mutual funds for real estate in that they afford the same advantages to investors: portfolio diversification and liquidity. Diversification comes from the large portfolios that a REIT can own on behalf of shareholders. For example, Equity Residential Properties (www.eqr.com; ticker symbol EQR), the largest U.S. REIT that specializes in apartment investments, owns more than 1,000 properties in 35 states. Each EQR shareholder owns an interest in these 1,000 plus properties. Liquidity for REITs is achieved because shares of stock traded on a major stock exchange are more easily disposed of than the underlying properties which are traded in private markets.

REITs are corporations and therefore shareholders receive the same limited liability protection as shareholders in regular C corporations. (C corporations are discussed more fully later in this chapter.) Unlike a C Corporation, however, REITs are not taxed at the entity level if they satisfy a set of restrictive conditions on an ongoing basis. The most important of these conditions are as follows.[3]

First, at least 100 investors must own a REIT's shares; to ensure diversified ownership, no five investors can own more than 50 percent of a REIT's shares. A REIT must distribute at least 90 percent of its taxable income to shareholders in the form of dividends, which limits the ability of a REIT to retain earnings for future investments.[4] Fully 75 percent of the value of a REIT's assets must consist of real estate assets, cash, and government securities. Real estate mortgages and mortgage-backed securities are considered real estate for the purposes of this test. At least 75 percent of the REIT's gross income must be derived

---

3. On May 28, 2003, President Bush signed the "Jobs and Growth" Tax relief package. This bill cuts income tax rates on most dividends and capital gains received by individuals to a 15 percent maximum. Because REITs generally do not pay taxes at the corporate level, the majority of REIT dividends will continue to be taxed at the shareholder's ordinary income tax rate. For more information, visit the NAREIT website (www.nareit.com).

4. Prior to 2001, this percentage was 95 percent.

Industry Issues

At the close of trading on October 9, 2001, Standard & Poor's added Equity Office Properties (EOP) to its S&P 500 Index—one of the most widely used benchmarks of U.S. stock performance. EOP replaced Texaco Inc. Since then, four additional REITs have been added to the S&P 500: Apartment Investment & Management (AIV), Equity Residential Properties (EQR), Plum Creek Timber (PCL), and Simon Property Group (SPG). According to industry analysts, the inclusion of REITs in the S&P 500 is a significant step that underlines the notable growth of real estate stocks over the past decade and their increasing role in the overall stock market.

Standard & Poor's uses the following guidelines for the addition and deletion of stocks: investability (are there sufficient shares available for purchase?), liquidity, financial viability, and stock market capitalization.

from real estate assets. The last two requirements ensure that REITs invest primarily in real estate. In exchange for meeting these and several other requirements, REITs, effectively, do not pay federal income taxes. This leaves more cash flow available to pay dividends to investors (who do pay taxes on the dividends).[5]

Concept Check

15.3 What are some major advantages of investing in REITs?

The REIT market has grown significantly over the last 10 years and REITs are now more broadly accepted by mutual funds and other institutional investors, especially pension funds. Further evidence of the rise in the size and stature of the REIT market is that in 2001 the first REIT, Equity Office Properties (www.equityoffice.com; ticker symbol EOP), was added to the S&P 500, a bellwether stock return index published by Standard & Poor's that includes 500 of the largest and most important U.S. corporations. With more than 700 properties, EOP is the nation's largest office building owner and manager as well as the largest U.S. REIT. As of June 2003, four additional REITs had been added (see Industry Issues 15-1). Despite the growing importance of REITs, the $168 billion in total market value represents only 4 percent of the total value of domestic commercial real estate. The REIT market is discussed in more detail in a later section of the chapter.[6]

It is worth noting that a significant amount of commercial real estate is owned by corporations and other business entities that are not primarily in the commercial real estate business—for example, telephone and communications companies, publicly owned auto manufacturers, banks, and restaurant chains. This real estate cannot be invested in directly or in a securitized form and is therefore generally excluded from discussions of the U.S. commercial real estate market. To illustrate, Bank of America (BOA), a large commercial bank, owns its office tower headquarters in Charlotte, North Carolina. However, should BOA decide to divest, this office tower would become part of the investable commercial real estate universe. The market value of U.S. real estate held by non-real estate corporations, including the BOA office tower, probably approaches $2 trillion.

---

5. For a complete list of what a company must do to qualify as a REIT, go to www.nareit.com, click on "About REITs," then "Frequently Asked Questions."

6. Real estate operating companies (REOCs) are publicly traded real estate companies that have chosen not to be taxed as REITs. A number of large hospitality companies, as well as several large homebuilders, function as REOCs. Because the total market capitalization of REOCs is quite small (approximately $15 billion) and because the primary business of most REOCs is not long-term real estate investment, REOCs are not discussed further. Publicly traded real estate limited partnerships, once an important component of U.S. real estate markets, now represent less than $500 million in assets and are also not discussed here.

Concept Check

15.4 Provide some additional examples of noninvestable commercial real estate held by non-real estate entities.

Privately Owned Commercial Real Estate

Lend Lease estimated that the value of privately owned, but investable, commercial equity capital as of September 2002 was $2,397 billion, or 51 percent of the total value of U.S. commercial real estate. As can be seen in Exhibit 15-3, this $2,397 billion in market value represents direct investments by institutional investors such as pension funds, foreign investors, life insurance companies, commercial banks and savings associations, as well as securitized ("pooled") investments by private, noninstitutional, investors. We next discuss these sources of private equity capital.

Pension Funds. Pension funds have long been recognized as a major potential source of real estate equity capital. However, pension funds have often viewed real estate as too risky, too difficult to manage, and too illiquid. Moreover, real estate markets are often characterized by a lack of information necessary for performing the quantitative investment analysis that pension funds or their advisors generally undertake.

www.prea.org

Pension Real Estate Association.

Despite this history, pension funds have become an important participant in commercial real estate equity markets, especially in recent years. The value of real estate owned by pension funds is estimated to be $149 billion. Thus, pension funds control approximately 3 percent of the total commercial real estate market, although this percentage seems likely to grow in the coming years. Certainly, the early years of the 21st century witnessed an increased interest in real estate by pension funds that resulted from the significant losses most funds realized on their stock market portfolios (see Industry Issues 15-2). Finally, it is important to note that pension funds and their advisors and consultants have been pushing the industry to increase the sophistication of real estate investment decision making. Their influence on commercial markets is disproportionate to the relatively small percentage of assets they own and is helping to increase the supply of market-level and property-level information available to all investors.

Exhibit 15-3 The Value of U.S. Commercial Real Estate Equity

	Value (in $ billions)		Value (in $ billions)
Public commercial real estate equity (REITs)	168	**Private Commercial Real**	
Private commercial real estate equity	2,397	**Estate Equity**	
		Pension funds	149
Total Commercial Equity	2,565	Foreign investors	47
		Life insurance companies	32
Public commercial debt (CMBSs)	403	Commercial banks	3
Private commercial debt	1,662	Savings associations	1
Total Commercial Debt	**2,065**	Noninstitutional investors	2,166
Total value of commercial real estate	4,630	**Total privately held equity**	**2,397**

Source: *Emerging Trends in Real Estate 2003,* published jointly by Lend Lease Real Estate Investments and PricewaterhouseCoopers LLP, 909 Third Avenue, New York, NY 10022; and the *Federal Reserve Bulletin,* March 2003, table 1.54.

Industry Issues

Rising Allocations: Pension Plans Reassess Property Plays

The real estate industry has never seen this much cash. Pension funds, along with foreign buyers and individuals burned by the stock market, are pouring money into commercial real estate. But it is pension funds, which have strict limitations on how much money they can allocate to an asset class, that are leading the charge. Many are increasing the percentage of cash they allocate to real estate, which is now seen as one of the most stable investments available. Other funds are meeting with consultants to consider increased real estate allocations.

Despite the new money pension funds are shoveling into real estate, they may not be able to invest as much as they would like. Pension funds are constrained by how much risk they can expose themselves to. Many have implemented maximum real estate

allocations of 3 to 5 percent. And unlike other major investors, pension funds cannot make swings in their investment approach overnight. Many are in two- to three-year cycles in terms of reviewing allocations.

Despite these limitations, some pension funds are angling to maximize their real estate exposure and, according to some observers, they are setting off an all-out bidding war for available properties. However, pension funds themselves are facing more competition for real estate assets from a nontraditional source. As the stock and bond markets falter and mortgage rates remain low, wealthy individuals, generally in the form of limited partnerships, are chasing real estate assets that were previously too expensive.

But investment climates are never stable. When mortgage rates, currently at historical lows, go up, when the stock market looks more compelling, or when the real estate market weakens, some of this new money will exit the commercial real estate market.

Source: Adapted from Neil Weilheimer, "Rising Allocations: Pension Funds Reassess Property Plays," *Commercial Property News*, November 16, 2002, www.cpnonline.com

---

Pension funds must decide whether to make their real estate investments directly or to pursue their investment strategy by investing in REITs or commingled real estate funds. If the pension fund chooses to make direct investments, it must then decide whether to set up an in-house staff to make and oversee investments or to employ a pension fund advisory firm to handle its real estate investments.

Commingled Real Estate Funds. Commingled real estate funds are offered by major banks, life insurance companies, investment banks, and real estate advisory firms to pension funds for investment in real estate. Because many pension funds do not have the in-house expertise required for real estate investment, fund managers collect contributions from multiple pension funds and "commingle" them to purchase properties. About one-half of pension fund investments in real estate are placed with managers of commingled funds. The remainder is invested directly in real estate, usually through local real estate companies. Liquidity has been a problem in market downturns. Some pension fund investors who intended to move money out of certain commingled real estate funds have had to wait long periods for their redemption request to be satisfied. This at least partially explains the increase in the ownership of publicly traded REITs by pension funds.

Life Insurance Companies. Life insurance policies involve the payment of premiums by the insured in exchange for benefits to be paid upon the death of the insured. Using mortality tables, life insurers are able to predict the mortality rates of policyholder groups with a high degree of accuracy. As a result, the liabilities of life insurers can be characterized as both long term and predictable. In order to match the maturity of their assets to the maturity of their liabilities, it makes sense for life insurance companies to invest on a long-term basis. Moreover, because their liabilities are fairly predictable, it is not necessary that their assets be highly liquid; large unexpected payments to policyholders are unlikely. These characteristics make life insurance companies well suited for investment in commercial real

ost of today's large-scale real estate transactions ($10 million and up) involve institutional investors, such as real estate investment trusts (REITs), the larger life insurance companies, international investors, and pension funds. These institutional investors generally utilize commercial brokers in the local markets, but they rely on internal staff to review and analyze proposed

Institutional Real Estate Investors

investments. When hiring, these institutions frequently look for a real estate background, strong analytical skills, the ability to manage portfolios, and excellent communication skills. Increasingly, they are also looking for an MBA degree or a specialized graduate degree such as an MS in real estate when staffing positions. Industry experience and advanced degrees are important because institutional investors must be knowledgeable about industry market trends, tax law trends, regulatory trends, geographically-based economic trends, demographic trends, and global economic trends, in addition to property specific issues.

Source: *Information on Career Paths in Commercial Real Estate,* University of Cincinnati, www.cba.uc.edu/getreal

---

estate markets, which are characterized by low liquidity and high transaction costs. And, indeed, life insurers have traditionally been a major source of commercial real estate capital. In 2002 life insurers owned $32 billion of commercial real estate assets. As we shall see, however, they are much more active as suppliers of commercial mortgage capital.

Concept Check

15.5 What characteristics make life insurance companies well suited for commercial real estate investments?

Other Institutional Investors. At times foreign investors have grabbed headlines for their active participation in United States real estate markets. After pouring more than $70 billion into U.S. real estate during the 1980s, Japanese investors became active sellers in the 1990s. In 2002 foreign investors controlled approximately $47 billion in U.S. real estate. Exhibit 15-3 shows that commercial banks and savings associations own just $3 billion and $1 billion, respectively, in commercial real estate equity. Moreover, the vast majority of these limited holdings are not the result of direct equity investments. Rather, these holdings represent "real estate owned" (REO); that is, real estate obtained by the institution as a result of default and foreclosure.

Pooled Investments. A striking feature of Exhibit 15-3 is that institutional investors (e.g., pension funds, life insurers) control just 10 percent of private commercial equity capital. The remaining 90 percent of private equity ($2,166 billion) is owned by "noninstitutional" investors. Who are these noninstitutional investors? Certainly, individual investors, or investors who own property jointly with other family members, account for a portion of this noninstitutional equity ownership. But in terms of market value, individual investors, sometimes referred to as sole proprietors, account for very little of the noninstitutional total of commercial real estate assets because these are relatively expensive to build or acquire. Even modest office buildings, strip shopping centers, and apartment buildings often require more equity capital than individual investors are able or willing to contribute.

More commonly, groups of private investors pool their equity capital when purchasing commercial real estate. The pooling of equity capital by investors to purchase real estate in the private market is often referred to as syndication. A **syndicate** is a group of persons or legal entities who come together to carry out a particular activity. A real estate syndicate, therefore, is a group organized to develop a parcel of land, buy an office building, purchase an entire portfolio of properties, make mortgage loans, or perform other real estate activities.

With pooled ownership structures, investors can receive the income, appreciation, and tax benefits produced by direct investments. In addition, if the syndicate purchases multiple properties, investors receive the benefits associated with investing in portfolios of properties including:

- Diversification.
- Economies of scale in the acquisition, management, and disposition of properties.
- The ability to obtain debt financing at the portfolio level.
- The expertise of the management team assembled by the organizer of the ownership structure.

In exchange for these benefits, investors generally relinquish management control to the active manager(s) and must compensate the syndicator-manager with fees, salary income, a disproportionate share of the equity ownership, or some combination of the three. Certainly it is important that the interests and incentives of the manager are closely aligned with those of the investors. Private real estate syndications are discussed in more detail later in the chapter.

Concept Check

15.6   What are real estate syndications and what do they do?

Forms of Ownership for Pooled Equity Investments

The choice of ownership form for a property or portfolio of properties to be owned by an entity is driven largely by management control issues, federal income tax issues, and the ability of some or all of the investors to avoid personal liability for the debts and obligations of the entity. Other objectives such as the ability to access debt and additional equity capital and the ability of investors to dispose of their interests in the organization also affect the decision.

We first discuss and compare alternative ownership structures for pooled equity investments. Subsequent sections provide a more detailed look at real estate limited partnerships and real estate investment trusts.

Concept Check

15.7   For the purposes of investing in commercial real estate, what characteristics are desirable in an ownership form?

C Corporation

A **C corporation** constitutes a legal and taxable entity that is separate from the owners who are the shareholders in the corporation. Thus, the C corporation earns income and incurs tax liabilities. C corporations pay income taxes on net corporate income and have their own tax rate structure and rules. Dividends paid to shareholders are not deductible by the corporation and are taxable to the shareholders. Thus, one of the major disadvantages of using a C corporation to invest in commercial real estate is that the income from the underlying property or properties may be taxed twice. C corporation income is currently subject to federal tax rates as high as 39 percent and, in 2003, individuals could be taxed at federal rates as

More Companies Create Value through Strategic Real Estate Plans

n recent years, hundreds of companies including Chevron Corp., Dole Food Co., Exxon, Pacific Gas & Electric Co., Pacific Telesis Group, Prudential Insurance, Sears Roebuck, Sun Oil, and Westinghouse Electric Corp. have decided to sell off billions of dollars of corporate real estate assets. Such sales are expected to accelerate in coming years. In some cases, companies are selling assets that no longer are needed for their operations. In many situations, however, possession and control of the real estate assets is critically important even if ownership of the assets is not. Thus, selling companies frequently lease back the assets on a long-term basis by signing a triple net lease. These sale-leaseback transactions, also discussed in Chapter 14, provide many potential benefits to the selling firm.

Although the value of corporate real estate can be significant, it historically has been an overlooked and underutilized asset on corporate balance sheets. But as companies have gradually realized its importance as a strategic asset, they are beginning to take a proactive approach to its management. Many corporations are developing strategic real estate plans.

While such plans may differ in their particulars, companies generally have common goals. Among them are to increase shareholder value, optimize returns on existing real estate assets and any assets acquired in the future, move highly leveraged real estate off the balance sheet, realize tax-deductible losses, increase liquidity, raise capital for various corporate purposes (including growth and expansion), and redeploy corporate resources from real estate to core businesses.

Source: Adapted from Barry Barovick and Stephen Duffy, *Real Estate News Line*, 13, No. 2 (February/March, 1996), Ernst and Young Kenneth Leventhal real estate group.

high as 35 percent. Thus, the effective tax rate on income from properties can be as high as 60 percent.[7] For shareholders a C corporation provides limited liability for obligations of the corporation. This limited liability includes liability from contractual obligations as well as obligations arising from tort actions brought against the corporation.

C corporations are not a desirable structure for entities whose primary purpose is to acquire and own commercial real estate because there are alternative ownership structures that provide limited liability but avoid double taxation. Although C corporations are not typically used if the primary business of an ownership entity is to invest in commercial real estate, many regular C corporations do own a significant amount of real estate (e.g., General Motors, Microsoft, McDonalds). Moreover, these corporations are gradually recognizing the importance of real estate as a strategic asset and are beginning to be more involved in its management (see Industry Issues 15-3).

Concept Check

15.8 Why are C corporations seldom used by investors to purchase commercial real estate?

S Corporation

A **Subchapter S corporation** possesses the same limited liability benefits for its shareholders as C corporations. However, although an S corporation is a separate *legal* entity, it is not a separate *taxable* entity; that is, S corporations pay no income taxes, and taxable

---

7. This is calculated as $[1 - (1 - 0.39) \times (1 - 0.35)] = 0.60$. The maximum tax rate on corporate capital gains is also 35 percent. Note that the existence of a state income tax would push this effective tax rate even higher.

income is passed through to its stockholders who become liable for the tax.[8] A major draw-back of S corporations for some investor groups is that they must not have more than 75 shareholders. Also, an S corporation's cash flow and taxable income must be allocated to each shareholder in proportion to his or her ownership of the corporation. Allocation of these items based on some other criteria—that is, "special" allocations—is not allowed. This may limit the attractiveness of S corporations as pooled investment structures because real estate owners often seek to structure an ownership entity in a manner that allows the owners to share cash flow and taxable gains or losses in a disproportionate manner. S Corporations, however, are popular with individual investors who are the sole equity investors in a property or properties. Such investors are seeking to avoid unlimited liability and double taxation and are, of course, unconcerned that special allocations are not allowed.

General Partnership

A **general partnership** is treated as a conduit for tax purposes; taxable income and losses flow through to the individual partners who pay the tax. Thus, double taxation does not exist. A partner's share of income, losses, and cash flow is determined by the partnership agreement and may vary from item to item. In particular, if certain conditions are met, a partnership can allocate cash flow and tax liabilities in a manner different from each partner's interest in the partnership.

A major disadvantage of a general partnership is that all partners have unlimited liability. General partners are liable for *all* debts of the partnership, including contractual debts and debts arising from legal actions against the partnership. General partners are also liable for wrongful acts committed by other partners in the course of the partnership's business. Therefore, the personal assets of the general partners are subject to the claims of the partnership's creditors. For this reason, real estate general partnerships are fairly uncommon and those that do exist tend to have only a few partners.

Limited Partnership

A **limited partnership** is created and taxed in the same way as a general partnership. However, a limited partnership allows some of the investing partners to limit their personal liability to an amount equal to their total investment in the partnership. A limited partnership must have at least one "general" partner and one "limited" partner. The former assumes unlimited liability for the debts of the partnership; the latter places at risk of loss only the amount of his or her equity investment. Moreover, the responsibility for the management of the partnership rests with the general partner(s) who is frequently a knowledgeable real estate builder, broker, or investor. Note that the general partner can be a corporation, which creates limited liability for the owner(s) of the corporation acting as the general partner. With regard to cash distributions and double taxation, limited partnerships are similar to general partnerships—double taxation does not exist.[9]

The flow-through feature of a limited partnership coupled with limited liability for the limited partners largely explains why the limited partnership form of ownership has been a preferred ownership form of commercial property investors. However, the Internal Revenue Service does not allow an organization of individuals to call themselves a partnership—and

---

8. Although losses of an S corporation flow through to its shareholders, the ability of the shareholders to utilize these losses is subject to several limitations. First, shareholders cannot utilize tax losses in excess of the amount they have invested, their at-risk basis. The at-risk basis is generally equal to the amount paid for the stock, minus allocated tax losses, minus cash distributions received. The debts and liabilities of the S corporation do *not* increase the shareholder's at-risk basis in the stock. Thus, if the S corporation takes out a mortgage on property it owns, no part of the mortgage is included in the amount the individual shareholders have at risk. This could significantly limit the amount of tax deductions that can be used by shareholders. Shareholder loans to the S corporation do increase the shareholder's basis.

9. The ability of limited and general partners in a limited partnership to utilize losses is identical to the treatment afforded participants in a general partnership. However, all tax losses may be subject to a separate set of restrictions referred to as *passive activity loss restrictions*. This topic is discussed in Chapter 22.

The remaining privately held mortgage debt is owned by savings institutions (7 percent), pension funds (2 percent), and "other" investors, primarily federal, state, and local credit agencies that supply mortgage funds for the acquisition of low- and moderate-income rental housing. Savings institutions, after the debacle of the late 1980s and early 1990s (see Chapter 13), have become relatively less important as commercial property lenders. As previously discussed, pension funds invest vast sums for their participants' future retirement benefits, and some are gradually increasing the portion of their portfolios invested in high-grade commercial real estate, either directly through equity investments or indirectly through long-term mortgages and commercial mortgage-backed securities (CMBSs).

The fastest-growing source of long-term commercial mortgage funds are investors in publicly traded CMBSs. Whereas residential MBSs are issued against a pool of residential mortgages, CMBSs are backed by a pool of commercial mortgages or, perhaps, a single large commercial loan. The outstanding principal balances of CMBSs backed by the government-sponsored enterprises (GSEs) totaled $87 billion in September of 2002 (see Exhibit 15-5). The outstanding principal balances of "private label" CMBS securities (i.e., those not issued or backed by a government agency) totaled $307 billion. Thus, the total outstanding value of CMBSs was $394 billion, which represents 19 percent of total commercial mortgage debt outstanding. The remaining $9 billion in publicly traded commercial debt represents the unsecured debt issued by publicly traded REITs.

Concept Check

15.10   What is the fastest-growing source of commercial mortgage funds?

Mortgage Originators Versus Long-Term Holders

The mortgage data displayed in Exhibit 15-5 depicts the holdings of long-term investors in the "permanent" commercial mortgage market. In many cases, these long-term holders purchase their mortgage assets in the secondary mortgage market. For example, although foreign investors own $214 billion in commercial mortgages, they generally do not originate loans in the primary market. Instead, they are active purchasers in the secondary market, as are life insurance companies; federal, state, and local credit agencies, and pension funds. In addition, the commercial mortgages packaged and resold to investors as CMBSs are largely originated by entities that do not appear in Exhibit 15-5.

Who, then, originates the mortgages purchased by life insurers, foreign investors, pension funds, and CMBSs issuers? Some are originated by other long-term mortgage holders. For, example, although timely and accurate data on commercial originations are not available, commercial banks are responsible for approximately three-fourths of all long-term commercial originations. However, they hold just 37 percent of the outstanding stock. Thus, they are net sellers in the secondary market along with savings institutions.

Another important source of commercial originations is mortgage banking companies. Recall from Chapter 13 that residential mortgage banking firms process, close, provide the loan funds, and then sell the loans they originate in the secondary market. In contrast to mortgage bankers, mortgage brokers (often referred to as "correspondents,") do not provide the funding (capital) for the loans; instead they serve as an intermediary between those who demand funds (i.e., the borrowers) and those who are willing to supply the funds (i.e., the long-term investors). Commercial mortgage bankers and brokers feed the appetites of many of the holders displayed in Exhibit 15-5 for long-term commercial mortgage investments. Thus, although mortgage banking and brokerage firms do not appear in Exhibit 15-5, their roles "as intermediaries" in the commercial mortgage market are significant.

Concept Check

15.11   Why aren't mortgage bankers listed as a source of funds in Exhibit 15-5?

Explore The Web

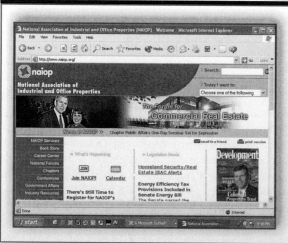

The National Association of Industrial and Office Properties (NAIOP) maintains a comprehensive database of articles and data meant to support commercial real estate development, investment, and financing. To see who is financing the latest commercial deals, go to www.naiop.org. On the home page, look for the "dealmakers" link. Click on that for a summary of the latest deals.

Development and Construction Lending

To this point we have concerned ourselves entirely with the originators and holders of long-term commercial mortgages. However, as discussed in Chapter 14, the development and construction of commercial properties generally is financed with separate land acquisition, land development, and construction loans.

Development and construction lending can be extremely risky. The primary risk of a construction loan is that the developer will fail to complete the project in a timely manner or fail to complete it at all. Builders may experience cost overruns, poor weather, strikes, structural or design problems, or difficulties with subcontractors. The builder may simply be a bad manager. In addition, failure to pass various building code inspections may delay the ability of tenants to occupy the building (and pay rent). All of these risks are assumed by the construction lender. Thus, construction lenders must have specialized skills in monitoring and controlling the construction process.

Concept Check

15.12   Why are so many long-term mortgage lenders not involved in construction lending?

Because the risks of development and construction financing are significant and much different in nature than the risks of long-term lending, the capital sources for short-term development and construction loans differ significantly from the providers of permanent financing displayed in Exhibit 15-5. The construction loan market is dominated by commercial banks, who hold approximately four-fifths of outstanding construction loans on commercial properties. The remainder of the construction market is served primarily by savings institutions and federal, state, and local credit agencies.

How Information Standards Help Attract More Capital

As an asset class, real estate is beginning to attract more investment by pension funds and other institutional investors, but it has yet to achieve comparable stature with the larger and more established stock and bond markets. Accurate, unbiased information is very important to potential investors. In the perception of investors, however, the real estate market has lacked consistent standards for compiling, measuring, and disclosing information comparable to those that govern public trading in stocks and bonds.

Real estate has traditionally been an entrepreneurial business, with properties bought and sold in private markets. Information has not been consistently reported and property valuations have been based on appraisals that may lag current market conditions. Because of such ambiguities, investors have been uncertain as to the true value of their prospective investments, and the overall liquidity of these investments has been impaired. Moreover, unlike public stock and bond markets, it is difficult to even calculate the historical total return performance of commercial properties.

With definitive information standards and more accurate and timely data to guide them, institutional investors can better analyze individual properties and portfolios, as well as REITs and mortgage-backed securities. Moreover, they can compare the performance of real estate with other asset classes. This gives investors a higher comfort level and helps to attract investment capital to real estate.

Recognizing the need for guidelines, the National Council of Real Estate Investment Fiduciaries (NCREIF; www.ncreif.org), the Pension Real Estate Association (PREA; www.prea.org), and the National Association of Real Estate Investment Managers (NAREIM; www.nareim.org) created a task force in 1994 and compiled a recommended set of information standards. The creation of consistent information guidelines for the real estate industry and the ongoing development of benchmark return indexes is bringing more liquidity and capital into the commercial real estate market.[11]

A Closer Look at Real Estate Syndications

As previously defined, a syndicate is a group of persons or legal entities who come together to carry out a particular activity. Private real estate syndicates have been most frequently organized as limited partnerships, but also may be organized as S corporations and limited liability companies.

The syndicator organizes the investors and manages the activities of the entity. Much of the syndicator's work is raising money. The other members of the real estate syndicate are usually money partners or investors. Syndicators generally enhance the productivity of real estate because without their efforts and organizational skills, fewer new development projects would be initiated, fewer existing property transactions would occur, and fewer mortgage loans would be made.

From the perspective of the investors, substantial costs may offset the benefits of investing in real estate through syndications. The sponsor of the syndication and the professionals hired by the syndicator—lawyers, accountants, and real estate acquisition personnel—must charge fees for creating and managing the organization. Because of these fees, not every dollar contributed by investors is actually invested in properties. Nevertheless, private syndications in the form of limited partnerships, S corporations, and LLCs are still the most important source of equity capital for small- and medium-sized real estate investments. Moreover, private limited partnerships, sponsored by a diverse mix of local syndicators, are making inroads in markets that once were the domain of institutional investors. Some estimates suggest local syndications in recent years have accounted for more than one-fourth of all commercial real estate acquisitions over $5 million in size.[12]

The Role of the Syndicator/Organizer

In private real estate deals (offerings), syndicators typically act as their own brokers and attempt to market the investment opportunity to a select group of investors. Because the risks and returns from real estate syndications are difficult for potential investors to evaluate, the

---

11. This section draws on Jack Haly and David Duncan, "Development and Information Standards Could Help Attract More Capital to Real Estate Markets," *Real Estate Newsline* (E&Y Kenneth Leventhal Real Estate Group) 13, no. 1 (January 1996).

12. See *Emerging Trends in Real Estate 2003,* (New York: Lend Lease Real Estate Investments and PricewaterhouseCoopers LLP, 2003), p. 2.

Exhibit 15-6 Syndication Process: The Role of the Syndicator

Origination Phase ⟶	Operation Phase ⟶	Completion Phase
The syndicator:	The syndicator:	The syndicator:
• Develops the concept for the syndication	• Manages the syndication	• Prepares the properties for sale
• Organizes the legal entity (e.g., limited partnership or S corporation)	• Manages the property (frequently)	• Sells the property (frequently)
• Has offering memorandums drafted	• Raises additional investment capital if required	• Dissolves the organization or resyndicates
• Markets ownership interests to investors		• Organizes the final cash payments and allocations of the capital gain tax liability
• Acquires the real estate		

success of an offering often depends on the reputation and track record of the syndicator. Today's private syndicator is a businessperson who usually is well known in the local real estate community. Typically, the private syndicator has a background in real estate, most often in brokerage or development.

Syndicators organize, manage, and control the investment vehicle from origination through dissolution. As shown in Exhibit 15-6, the syndicator's role in the syndication process is most important during origination. Much of the syndicator's work in this phase involves coordination with lawyers on the preparation of the offering documents, with accountants to set up the syndicate's accounting system, and with real estate brokers to acquire the property or properties. These activities may be done in-house or with the aid of outside professionals. Real estate brokerage, for example, is typically handled in-house whereas legal counsel typically comes from outside law firms.

Concept Check

15.13 As an investor in a real estate syndication, you obtain the real estate skills of the syndicator/organizer. What's the bad news?

During the operations phase, the syndicator manages the syndicate and, frequently, the property. Managing the syndicate involves making sure investors receive their cash or dividend distributions, typically on a quarterly basis, as well as their share of the annual tax liability produced by the syndicate. Many syndicators, especially larger ones, have an in-house property management division. For syndications with continual lives, such as S corporations and LLCs, the syndicator/manager may be required to raise additional equity capital or refinance existing mortgage debt. Finally, the completion or dissolution phase may involve the sale of the property or properties and dissolution of the syndicate/corporation.[13]

www.crewnetwork.org

Association of Commercial Real Estate Woman (CREW) for women in commercial real estate.

Regulation

Depending on the number of investors, the wording of the syndication or partnership agreement, and the manner in which the investment opportunity is marketed to potential investors, the sale of a participating interest in commercial real estate can be considered a sale of securities. Both federal and state laws control the sale of securities to the general public. Government regulation is usually rationalized by the argument that markets will fail and innocent consumers will be hurt without the intervention of a disinterested third

---

13. For a detailed example of a private real estate syndication, including cash flow projections and return calculations, see William B. Brueggeman and Jeffrey D. Fisher, *Real Estate Finance and Investment,* 11th ed. (New York: Mc Graw-Hill, 2001), Chap. 12.

party. The general argument for regulating real estate syndications is that investors require information to make rational investment decisions; therefore, without government regulation requiring syndicators to *disclose* and *disseminate information,* the market would not operate efficiently.

State regulation of real estate securities varies considerably. However, most states require the registration of syndicated offerings. If the offering is made to potential buyers in multiple states, or to more than 35 individuals within a state, registration is also required with the federal regulator, the Securities and Exchange Commission.[14]

Evaluating a Syndication Opportunity

A word of caution is in order regarding the advisability of investing in commercial real estate through local syndications. The syndication agreement generally creates a principal/agent relationship in which the syndicator (the agent) is empowered to act on behalf of the investors (the principals). As is true of all principal/agent relationships, the principals must be concerned that the agent will act in the agent's best interest, *not* in the best interests of the principals. These "moral hazard" concerns are generally more pronounced in situations in which the agent has a significant information advantage over the principals—and this is precisely the situation in most local real syndications. This creates an environment in which the syndicator can use his or her information advantage to take unfair advantage of the investors. For example, the syndicator may "carve out" large upfront fees that reduce the amount of capital invested in the enterprise. Moreover, if the syndicator's return is "front-loaded," this may reduce his or her incentive to maximize the value of the syndicated assets through aggressive property management. Another example of possible moral hazard is that the agent may choose to sell the syndicated assets at a time that is most advantageous to her, not at a time that maximizes investor returns. Finally, investors must be aware that agents have a strong incentive to downplay the risks associated with the venture.

In short, investors should carefully analyze the legal and economic ramifications of the offering before investing in a real estate syndication, preferably in consultation with a knowledgeable but disinterested third party and a real estate attorney. In the end, however, investment in a real estate syndication requires, at least to some degree, a "leap of faith" that is not warranted unless the investor has complete confidence in the reputation and ability of the syndicator. To close this section, we offer a simple rule of thumb: "Just say no" to unsolicited syndication offers from individuals with whom you are not *completely* comfortable. We wish we had followed this simple rule a time or two in the past.

A Closer Look at Real Estate Investment Trusts

This section traces the rapid development of the U.S. REIT industry in recent years. The management and investment strategies of REITs are then discussed. We then turn our attention to REIT valuation and the performance of REITs as an asset class.

The Growing Importance of Public Real Estate Markets

One measure of the importance of a publicly traded asset class in the U.S. economy is its stock market capitalization. The market capitalization of an individual stock is equal to the number of publicly traded shares times the current market price of the stock. At year-end 1991, the total market capitalization of all exchange-traded REITS was only $13 billion (see Exhibit 15-7).[15] During the entire 10-year period from 1982 to 1991, there were 116 initial

---

14. For more on the regulation of commercial real estate securities, see, for example, William B. Brueggeman and Jeffrey D. Fisher, *Real Estate Finance and Investment,* 11th ed. (New York: McGraw-Hill, 2001), chap. 12

15. *Exchange-traded* means the shares are traded on the New York Stock Exchange, the American Stock Exchange, or over the counter on the National Association of Securities Dealers Automated Quotation (NASDAQ) system.

Exhibit 15-7 Historical Stock Offerings and Total Market Capitalization of REITs

	Initial Equity Offerings		Secondary Equity Offerings		Secondary Debt Offerings		Year-End Market Capitalization
	No.	($ Mil.)	No.	($ Mil.)	No.	($ Mil.)	($ Mil.)
1982–91	116	$9,384	133	$5,178	103	$9,495	$12,968*
1992	8	919	24	1,054	26	4,642	15,912
1993	50	9,335	50	3,856	41	5,135	32,159
1994	45	7,176	52	3,944	49	3,651	44,306
1995	8	939	93	7,321	95	4,245	57,541
1996	6	1,107	139	11,201	76	4,754	88,776
1997	26	6,296	292	26,378	145	12,597	140,534
1998	17	2,129	297	19,379	160	16,874	138,301
1999	2	292	100	6,444	103	10,477	145,387
2000	0	0	42	2,834	72	7,542	138,714
2001	0	0	79	6,082	48	12,670	154,899
2002	3	608	110	7,776	74	11,383	161,937

*As of year-end 1991.

public offerings (IPOs) of REIT stocks. These 116 IPOs raised $9.4 billion in equity capital. Another 133 secondary equity offerings raised an additional $5.2 billion in capital for publicly traded REITs during this 10-year period, while 103 secondary debt offerings raised $9.5 billion.

After 1991 the real estate investment trust market exploded with 95 initial public offerings in 1993–94. Secondary equity offerings by REITs also increased significantly during the early- to mid-1990s. Since 1994 the REIT IPO market has cooled with just 62 issues coming to market over the 1995–2002 period. However, existing REITs have been tapping the secondary market for equity and debt. The total dollar value of debt and equity security offerings by publicly traded REITs is displayed graphically in Exhibit 15-8. Clearly, the largest surge in capital raising occurred during the 1997–1998 period, although significant activity also occurred in 1993–1994 and in late 2001, early 2002.

Not surprisingly, capital raised through debt and equity security offerings is primarily used by equity REITs to acquire properties. By year-end 2002 the value of properties owned by REITs exceeded $375 billion. Over the 1991–2002 period, the total market capitalization of the REIT market, including mortgage and hybrid REITs, increased from $13 billion to $162 billion. As can be seen in Exhibit 15-9, approximately 25 percent of this $162 billion represents the market value of the 35 REITs that specialize in retail property investments. The representation of other property types includes office properties, 17 percent; apartments, 16 percent; and diversified properties, 8 percent.

www.nmhc.org

National Multifamily Housing Council, a national association representing the interests of the nation's larger and most prominent apartment firms.

www.icsc.org

International Council of Shopping Centers (ICSC), a global trade association that represents shopping center owners, developers, managers, investors, and lenders.

REIT Management

Most REITs are actively managed operating companies. Property management is either carried out internally or by management that works solely for the benefit of the REIT shareholders. Property investments are generally focused by property type and/or geographic market because this specialization allows shareholders to benefit more fully from the specific expertise of the REIT management team.

Over the last decade, REITs have attracted significantly more institutional investors, which has been attributed to the growing acceptance of REITs among pension fund investors as viable alternatives to direct investments in real estate and to the prospects of greater liquidity in the REIT market. Further evidence that the REIT market is attracting a wider range of investors can be found in the number of mutual funds that invest in REIT

Exhibit 15-8 Securities Offerings by REITs
(First Quarter 1992 to Second Quarter 2003)

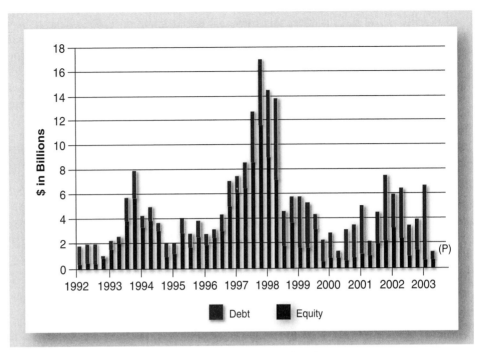

Source: National Association of Real Estate Investment Trusts, (www.nareit.com)

Exhibit 15-9 REITs by Property Type and Percent of Market Capitalization
(as of May 30, 2003)

Type of REIT	No. of Companies	Total Market Capitalization (%)
Retail	35	25%
Office	20	17
Apartments	20	16
Diversified	18	8
Industrial	8	6
Mixed office/industrial	7	5
Health Care	13	5
Mortgage REITS	20	5
Lodging/resorts	16	4
Specialty	6	4
Self-storage	3	3
Manufactured homes	5	2
Totals	171	100%

Source: National Association of Real Estate Investment Trusts, www.nareit.com.

securities. By May 2003 over 70 REIT mutual funds owned $15.9 billion in REIT stocks; there had been only a handful of such dedicated REIT mutual funds in the early 1990s.

A final development has been the evolution of the **umbrella partnership REIT (UPREIT).** As an UPREIT, the REIT is a managing partner and typically majority owner in a single large umbrella partnership which in turn owns all or part of individual property partnerships. Owners transferring their individual partnership interests into the umbrella partnership can receive umbrella partnership units or REIT shares in return for their original partnership interests. Although the properties that made up the original partnership have effectively been sold to the acquiring UPREIT, the exchange of partnership units is *not* treated as a sale for federal income tax purposes. This is extremely important. Why? Because many of these property owners would face significant tax liabilities if they engaged in a "regular" taxable sale. As a result, the owner would be much less likely to transfer the property or properties to the REIT. As a result of this nontaxation, the UPREIT structure has played a critical role in the conversion of private ownership of real estate to public REIT ownership.[16]

Concept Check

15.14 You are the general partner in a limited partnership that owns a portfolio of five large apartment complexes. For various reasons, the partnership is to be dissolved and the properties disposed of. Both a large pension fund and an UPREIT have offered to buy the portfolio at similar prices/values. What is the primary advantage of finalizing negotiations with the UPREIT?

REIT Valuation

REITs typically use income capitalization and discounted cash flow techniques (see Chapter 9) to make individual property acquisition and disposition decisions. That is, REITs seek to purchase properties that have positive net present values (*NPV*s) and going-in internal rates of return (*IRR*s) in excess of the REIT's opportunity cost of capital. But how are the REITs themselves valued? Said differently, how do capital market investors determine the appropriate price to pay for a share of stock in a REIT which in turn holds a portfolio of commercial properties or mortgages?

In general, REIT stocks are valued similarly to the stocks of other public companies; that is, investors attempt to forecast the stream of dividends the REIT will pay out over time. This projected dividend stream is then converted into a present value using a discounted cash flow model. In practice, however, long-term dividend projections are difficult to develop. Thus, investors also use other indicators of relative value in their REIT acquisition and disposition decisions.

One commonly employed approach to assessing the attractiveness of a REIT centers on the concept of **net asset value (*NAV*)**. *NAV* is equal to the estimated total market value of a REIT's underlying assets, less all liabilities having a prior claim to cash flow—including mortgages. To estimate the market value of the REIT's property holdings, individual property appraisals—formal or otherwise—are not performed. Rather, analysts estimate the aggregate net operating income (*NOI*) of the REIT's property holdings. This aggregate *NOI* is then converted into an estimate of market value by capitalizing it at the appropriate (weighted average) cap rate for the portfolio. (Capitalization rates are discussed in detail in Chapter 9.) The capitalization process uses information from the private real estate market to perform something resembling a mass appraisal of the REIT's properties. The ability to use information from the well-functioning private real estate market to value shares of publicly traded REITs is unique and distinguishes the REIT market from other industries where the assets are not separately traded in a private market.

---

16. It should be pointed out that the capital gain that is not taxable at the time that the partnership units are exchanged is not excluded from taxation. If the investor subsequently disposes of the partnership units or shares acquired from the UPREIT in the exchange, the capital gain that previously went untaxed will be added to the taxable gain reported on the sale of the UPREIT stock. Thus, the UPREIT structure does not eliminate accrued tax liabilities; rather, it allows them to be deferred, perhaps indefinitely.

How is the estimate of net asset value used to make acquisition decisions? If the total stock market capitalization of a REIT is greater than its *NAV,* the REIT is said to be selling at a premium to *NAV.* Although some of this premium may reflect the market's assessment of the ability of the REIT's management team to create value, a stock price in excess of per share *NAV* may indicate that the REIT is overpriced relative to the value of the real estate assets currently in the portfolio. Conversely, REITs selling at discounts to net asset value may signal buying opportunities for investors or, perhaps, takeover opportunities for other management teams.

Concept Check

15.15 In the *NAV* calculation, how is the value of the portfolio of properties estimated?

---

www.reits.com

REITNet provides access to information and decision-making tools needed to evaluate REIT investments.

Analysts and potential REIT investors may also track and compare the ratio of a REIT's current stock price to estimated income per share. For example, if the stock of an office REIT is currently selling for $20 per share and analysts forecast that current year net REIT income per share will be $1, the current price-income multiple is $20. This multiple could then be compared to that of other similar office REITs. If the average office REIT has a current price-income multiple of, say, $22 per share, it *may* indicate that the stock of the office REIT in question is undervalued, although numerous other explanations are likely to exist. Investors also consider the amount of financial leverage used by REITs when valuing individual companies. The ratio of debt to total market capitalization for the REIT industry is approximately 45 percent. Investors tend to punish the stock prices of REITs that use more leverage than is typical.

Measuring REIT Income

According to generally accepted accounting principles (GAAP), a corporation's net income includes a tax deduction for the depreciation and amortization of certain financial and fixed assets. Tax depreciation, discussed in detail in Chapter 22, is the process whereby the cost of depreciable improvements is allocated (i.e., expensed) over the cost recovery period of the asset. Mechanically, depreciation and amortization expenses therefore reduce reported net accounting income. However, these expenses do not represent actual cash outflows. Thus, if a corporation's assets are primarily depreciable, as are most of the assets of an equity REIT, net income may not accurately measure the net cash flow available to distribute to investors as dividends.

The REIT industry's response to this issue was to create a supplemental earnings measure that adds back depreciation and amortization expenses to GAAP net income. This calculation is termed **funds from operations (FFO)** and is defined as:

$$
\begin{aligned}
\text{FFO} \;=\; &\text{Net income (GAAP)} \\
&+\; \text{Depreciation (real property)} \\
&+\; \text{Amortization of leasing expenses} \\
&+\; \text{Amortization of tenant improvements} \\
&-\; \text{Gains (losses) from infrequent and unusual events}
\end{aligned}
$$

If a REIT has a higher FFO multiple (i.e., share price ÷ FFO per share) than the average REIT with which it competes, it may indicate the REIT is overpriced or that the market perceives the REIT to have higher-quality management and/or more income growth potential than similar REITs.

Many industry analysts and observers have argued that FFO is too easily manipulated by REITs, thus reducing its usefulness as an income measure. For example, what is an "infrequent" or "unusual" event? Recently, some industry analysts and other market participants began advocating the use of GAAP net income, despite its limitations, because they believe the calculation of GAAP net income is much less susceptible to interpretation

Exhibit 15-10 Comparison of Historical Total Returns

(Annualized returns, as of April 30, 2003)

Holding Period (in years)	Equity NAREIT Index	S&P 500	Russell 2000
1	−0.1	−13.5	−20.8
3	12.9	−13.0	−6.4
5	5.1	−2.4	−2.5
10	9.4	9.7	7.5
15	10.0	11.3	8.6
20	11.2	12.0	8.5

Source: National Association of Real Estate Investment Trusts, www.nareit.com

and firm manipulation. The National Association of Real Estate Investment Trusts (NAREIT) has recognized that GAAP income is the primary earnings measure for real estate companies. However, NAREIT believes that FFO remains a useful measure of a REIT's cash flow.[17]

Concept Check

15.16 Why is GAAP net income not an appropriate metric of a REIT's ability to generate cash flow for investors?

REIT Investment Performance

To obtain evidence on the return performance of publicly traded REITs, we analyze data obtained from the National Association of Real Estate Investment Trusts. The NAREIT Index tracks the total return (income plus capital appreciation) pattern of all exchange-traded REITs. For comparison purposes, we also report total returns on the S&P 500 and the Russell 2000. The Russell 2000 is a "small cap" index that tracks the performance of 2,000 publicly traded companies that rank 1,001 to 3,000 in U.S. stock market capitalization. Exhibit 15-10 presents annualized total returns for each index over selected holding periods.

Over recent time periods, REITS as a group have significantly outperformed both large cap and small cap stocks. Over the prior one-year period, REITs produced a negative total return of 0.1 percent, while the S&P 500 and the Russell 2000 generated negative total returns of 13.5 and 20.8, respectively. Returns on the stock indexes have been negative for at least the prior three years. In contrast, REITs produced a 12.9 percent annualized return over the prior three-year period. Even when looking back 10 years, REITs have generated a 9.4 percent annualized return, just slightly less than the return earned by those who invested in the S&P 500 and significantly greater than the 8.5 percent return earned on the Russell 2000. When evaluating the historical performance of the three asset classes, it is important to recognize that Exhibit 15-10 contains only mean returns, unadjusted for risk. Rational investors should also consider the volatility of returns and their comovement with the returns on other asset classes when making investment decisions. Measuring and evaluating risk is discussed in detail in Chapter 23.

17. See "White Paper on Funds from Operations," National Association of Real Estate Investment Trusts, April 2002. This article is available on the NAREIT website (www.nareit.com). Adjusted funds from operations (AFFO) also is widely reported and used by REIT industry participants. AFFO is equal to FFO minus certain recurring capital expenses.

Summary

The market value of investable commercial real estate assets in the United States is approximately $5 trillion. In this chapter we answer the following question: Who owns these commercial real estate assets and who provides the debt financing that is so often used in conjunction with investors' equity to acquire and hold these assets?

Investors can own commercial real estate either through direct investment or through real estate securities. With direct equity investment, individual and institutional investors purchase and hold title to the properties, thereby gaining complete control of the assets. With commercial real estate securities, funds are invested in a separate ownership entity which in turn purchases and holds title to the real estate.

Securitized equity investments can be purchased and resold in public markets or they can be privately owned. Publicly traded securities, including many real estate investment trusts (REITs), are bought and sold on public stock exchanges, such as the New York Stock Exchange. These exchange-traded assets provide investors with a high degree of investment liquidity and relatively low transaction costs. However, only a very small percentage (approximately 6 percent) of commercial real estate equity is traded in public markets. The remaining 94 percent (about $2.4 trillion) is privately owned. Approximately $232 billion of this remaining 94 percent is owned by pension funds, foreign investors, life insurance companies, commercial banks, and savings associations. The remaining $2.2 trillion is held by private, noninstitutional investors.

Who are these noninstitutional investors that own and control the vast majority of the commercial real estate stock? Individual investors account for only a small portion. More commonly, groups of private investors pool their equity capital when purchasing commercial real estate. A real estate syndicate is a group organized to develop a parcel of land, buy an office building, purchase an entire portfolio of properties, make mortgage loans, or perform other real estate activities. Examples of pooled ownership structures that purchase real estate directly in the private market include general and limited partnerships, S corporations, and limited liability companies. The relative advantages and disadvantages of each ownership structure are discussed with special attention given to the prominent role played by limited partnerships and, more recently, limited liability companies.

The chapter then covers the sources of commercial mortgage debt. Unlike the equity market, where just 6 percent of assets are publicly traded, approximately 20 percent of outstanding commercial mortgage debt is publicly traded, primarily in the form of commercial mortgage-backed securities (CMBSs). Investors in CMBSs represent the fastest-growing source of long-term commercial mortgage funds. The remaining 80 percent of outstanding commercial mortgage debt is privately held by institutional and individual investors. Commercial banks are the largest single source of private mortgage funds. Life insurance companies and foreign investors are also major participants in the long-term commercial mortgage market. The remaining privately held mortgage debt is primarily owned by savings institutions, pension funds, and federal, state, and local credit agencies that supply mortgage funds for the acquisition of low- and moderate-income rental housing.

Finally, the chapter takes a closer look at REITs. In particular, we discuss the growing size and importance of the REIT market, how REIT income is measured, how REITs are valued, and how REITs as an asset class have performed relative to the investment returns of alternative stock investments.

Key Terms

C Corporation 390

Commingled real estate funds 388

Equity REITs 384

Funds from operations (FFO) 403

General partnership 392

Hybrid REITs 385

Limited liability company (LLC) 393

Limited partnership 392

Mortgage REITs 384

Net asset value (NAV) 402

Pension funds 387

Real estate investment trusts (REITs) 384

Securitized investments 384

Subchapter S corporation 391

Syndicate 389

Umbrella partnership REIT (UPREIT) 401

Test Problems

Answer the following multiple choice problems:

1. Double taxation is most likely to occur if the commercial properties are held in the form of a(n):
   a. S corporation.
   b. Limited partnership.
   c. C corporation.
   d. Real estate investment trust.
   e. Limited liability company.

2. With regard to double taxation, distributions, and the treatment of the losses, general partnerships are *most* like:
   a. S corporations.
   b. C corporations.
   c. Limited partnerships.
   d. Real estate investment trusts.

3. Special allocations of income or loss are available if the form of ownership is a(n):
   a. S corporation.
   b. Real estate investment trust.
   c. Limited partnership.
   d. C corporation.

4. Real estate syndicates traditionally have been legally organized most frequently as:
   a. S corporations.
   b. C corporations.
   c. Limited partnerships.
   d. Real estate investment trusts.

5. A real estate investment trust generally:
   a. Must have fewer than 100 shareholders.
   b. Can only invest directly in income-producing properties.
   c. Can pass tax losses through to shareholders.
   d. None of the above.

6. Which of the following forms of ownership involve both limited *and* unlimited liability?
   a. Limited partnerships.
   b. Corporation.
   c. General partnership.
   d. Sole partnership.
   e. None of the above.

7. Which statement is *false* concerning the limited partnership form of ownership?
   a. The general partner has nearly complete control and is liable for debts and actions of the partnership.
   b. The limited partners have little management control and are not liable except to the amount of their investment.
   c. The limited partners cannot enjoy tax deduction benefits, but the general partners can.
   d. The partnership is not a taxable entity.
   e. None of the above.

8. Which of these lenders is most likely to provide a construction loan?
   a. Savings and loan association.
   b. Credit union.
   c. Commercial bank.
   d. Life insurance company.
   e. Real estate investment trust.

9. Which of these loans is a life insurance company most likely to invest in?
   a. Single-family home loan.
   b. Small commercial property loan (nonconstruction).
   c. Large office building loan (nonconstruction).
   d. Large construction loan.
   e. Small construction loan.

10. Which of these financial firms is most likely to invest in a large, long-term mortgage loan on a shopping center?
   a. Credit union.
   b. Commercial bank.
   c. Savings and loan association.
   d. Life insurance company.
   e. Mortgage banker.

Study Questions

1. For what debt in a general partnership is each of the general partners liable?

2. Why are many pension funds reluctant to invest in commercial real estate?

3. Discuss the role life insurance companies play in financing commercial real estate.

4. Approximately 90 percent of investable commercial real estate (on a value-weighted basis) is owned by "noninstitutional" investors. Who are these investors?

5. Briefly describe a commingled fund. Who are the investors in these funds and why do these investors use commingled funds for their purchases?

6. There are three primary considerations that affect the form in which investors choose to hold commercial real estate. List each and explain how they affect the choice of ownership form.

7. Explain what is meant by the double taxation of income.

8. What are the major restrictions that a REIT must meet on an ongoing basis in order to avoid taxation at the entity level?

9. Compare the tax advantages and disadvantages of holding income-producing property in the form of a REIT to the tax advantages and disadvantages of holding property in the form of a real estate limited partnership. Does either form of ownership dominate *from a tax perspective?*

10. Of the more than $2 trillion in outstanding U.S. commercial real estate debt, what percent is traded in public markets? What percent is traded in private markets? What institutions or entities are the long-term holders of private commercial real estate debt? What is the fastest growing source of long-term commercial mortgage funds?

11. Distinguish among equity REITs, mortgage REITs, and hybrid REITs.

12. Define funds from operations (FFO) and explain why this measure is often used instead of GAAP net income to quantify the income-producing ability of a real estate investment trust.

13. How have equity REITs, measured in terms of total returns, performed in recent years relative to alternative stock investments?

Explore The Web

Real estate investment trusts have become a popular vehicle for real estate investment. Investors can monitor the performance of REITs, as well as non-REIT stocks and bonds, using the Web page of the National Association of Real Estate Investment Trusts (NAREIT). Go to the NAREIT home page: http://www. nareit.com/ and download the latest REIT performance report. In 500 words or less, analyze the recent performance of REITs and compare their returns to those realized on portfolios of stocks and bonds. Have REITs outperformed stocks and bonds over the last 12 months? Have equity, mortgage, or hybrid REITs exhibited the strongest recent performance?

Solutions to Concept Checks

1. The estimated value of U.S. real estate is $16.6 trillion ($12.0 housing + $4.6 commercial). This is 25 percent greater than the stock market ($16.6/$13.3), 2.8 times the value of corporate and foreign bonds, and 3.0 times the value of outstanding U.S. government securities.

2. With private ownership, the investor has complete control of the asset, including how it is managed, how it is financed, and when it is sold. The disadvantages include high transaction costs when buying and selling and low liquidity.

3. REIT investors obtain more diversification by investing in REITs than they could obtain on their own. Also, shares of publicly traded REITs are much more liquid (easier to sell) than the individual properties.

4. Restaurant properties owned by the restaurant companies, branch offices of banks owned by the banks, government-owned office buildings, plant and equipment owned by steel corporations, drugstores owned by the companies, hospitals and medical office buildings owned by the hospitals or doctors. Note that these properties could be sold to investors and then leased back. Doing so would move these properties into the investable category.

5. Life insurance companies have liabilities that are both long term and, due to the law of large numbers, fairly predictable. Thus, the life insurance companies do not need to be (and probably should not be) active traders of their assets. Thus, they can effectively amortize the relatively high acquisition costs of real estate over longer holding periods. It is unlikely that they will need to sell to cover an unexpected need for cash.

6. A real estate syndication is a group of investors or legal entities that is organized to develop or purchase real estate, usually with the intention of holding the assets as long-term investments. The syndicate must choose a form of ownership to conduct its business, such as a limited partnership or a limited liability company.

7. It is desirable to avoid double taxation of the income produced by the underlying assets (properties), to put the management of the enterprise in the hands of those with experience and expertise, and to allow the investors (or at least the passive investors) to avoid unlimited liability for the debts and obligations of the partnership.

8. C corporations are seldom used by investors to purchase and hold commercial real estate, primarily because the structure does not permit the enterprise to avoid double taxation. Thus, for the purposes of making long-term investments in commercial real estate, this structure is dominated by limited liability companies and limited partnerships.

9. The primary advantage of a limited partnership relative to a general partnership is that the passive limited partners can avoid unlimited liability for the debts and obligations of the partnership. In a general partnership, all partners must assume unlimited liability.

10. The fastest-growing source of commercial mortgage funds is commercial mortgage-backed securities.

11. Mortgage bankers originate commercial mortgage loans, but do not hold them as long-term investments. Exhibit 15-5 provides information on the holders of commercial mortgages, not the originators.

12. Construction lending is a much different business than long-term lending and has significantly more risk for the lender. It is primarily short-term lending that requires significant knowledge of the development and construction business.

13. The bad news to the investor in a real estate syndication is that you must pay for the knowledge and experience supplied by the syndicator/organizer. The syndicator will usually charge an up-front fee equal to a flat amount or some percentage of the equity capital raised. Either way, less than 100 percent of the money contributed by investors is actually used to purchase properties. In addition, the syndicator will often get a percentage of the net annual cash flows or the net

selling price in excess of the percentage of the original equity capital he or she contributes. This also reduces the cash flows and returns of the limited (passive) investors.

14. By "selling" the property to the UPREIT you can avoid the immediate recognition of the accrued capital gain. There can be significant value associated with tax deferral.

15. To calculate the value of the portfolio of properties owned by the REIT, the net operating income (*NOI*) to be produced by all of the underlying properties is estimated and then aggregated. This total *NOI* is then converted into an estimate of the market value of the portfolio by capitalizing the aggregate *NOI* at the appropriate cap rate. This is akin to applying direct capitalization on an aggregate basis.

16. GAAP net income understates the true ability of a REIT to generate cash flow because it includes deductions for noncash expenses, such as tax depreciation. These noncash deductions should be added back to get a true picture of the income-producing ability of the REIT.

Additional Readings

Block, R. L. *Investing in REITS: Real Estate Investment Trusts,* rev. and updated ed. Burlington VT. Bloomberg Press, 2002.

Brueggeman, William B., and Jeffrey D. Fisher. *Real Estate Finance and Investment,* 11th ed. New York: McGraw-Hill Irwin, 2001.

Chan, S. H., J. Erickson, and K. Wang. *Real Estate Investment Trusts: Structure, Performance, and Investment Opportunities.* New York: Oxford University Press, 2003.

Garrigan, R. T., and Parsons, J. F. C. *Real Estate Investment Trusts: Structure, Analysis and Strategy.* New York: McGraw-Hill, 1997.

Gelter, D. M., and N. G. Miller. *Commercial Real Estate Analysis and Investments.* Cincinnati, OH: South-Western Publishing, 2000.

Imperiale, R. J. K. *Lasser Pro Real Estate Investment Trusts.* New York: John Wiley, 2002.

Mullaney, J. A. *REITs: Building Profits with Real Estate Investment Trusts.* New York: John Wiley, 1997.

Wiedemer, John P. *Real Estate Finance.* Upper Saddle River, NJ: Prentice Hall, 2001.

Investment Valuation

5

Valuing Investment Opportunities

Learning Objectives

After reading this chapter you will be able to:

1. List the primary difference between market value and investment value.

2. List and discuss the three steps required in a discounted cash flow analysis of a potential commercial real estate investment.

3. Calculate the effects of mortgage debt on cash flows, values, and returns.

4. Demonstrate how risk is incorporated into investment valuation and decision making.

5. Calculate the net present value and internal rate of return on a proposed investment, given assumptions about cash flows and required rates of return.

6. Calculate and interpret the basic cash flow multipliers, profitability ratios, and financial ratios that apply to real estate investment decisions.

7. Explain why real estate investors borrow money and calculate what effect financial leverage has on investment decisions, given assumptions about the mortgage and future cash flows.

8. Explain how income taxes affect property cash flows and values.

Introduction

We examined the concept of market value and its measurement in Chapters 8 and 9. Professional real estate appraisers are often called upon to estimate the market value of parcels of real estate because market value is the basis for economic transactions. A buyer does not usually wish to pay more, nor the seller take less, than the market value of the property.

Nevertheless, for many purposes the market value estimate is not the whole story. Since most decisions that determine the role of real estate assets in shaping the future of neighborhoods and cities are made with an investment motive, it is our contention that the professional approach to the study of real estate must employ investment valuation as its base. Investment calculations, whether implicit or explicit, are made whenever a property transaction is contemplated; when a maintenance or repair decision is made; when a structure is modernized, renovated, converted, abandoned, or demolished; and when a site is developed with a new set of improvements. This chapter presents the framework for making single-asset real estate investment decisions.[1]

First, however, a word of caution. The future cash flows at the heart of investment valuation are, in the "real world," estimated with significant uncertainty. In prior chapters, especially Chapters 4 to 7, we sought to explain and demonstrate the importance of the complex economic, social, and legal processes that affect real estate markets and, hence, the income-producing ability of commercial real estate. For example, in Chapter 6 we discussed growth management and local land use regulations. Why? Because these rules and regulations may affect the future income-producing ability, and therefore the value, of a property. Similarly, the numerous "imperfections" in real estate markets, such as a lack of adequate data, the large economic size of parcels, and the immobility of land and structures, are all discussed in Chapter 5 because of their potential effect on rents and property values.

As these prior chapters clearly demonstrated, many qualitative and difficult-to-predict factors influence real estate cash flows. In this chapter, however, we largely assume that the influences of these myriad factors have already been converted into assumptions and projections of future rents, vacancies, operating expenses, and resale values. This allows us to focus on how these often tenuous assumptions are used by the industry to quantify the investment value of commercial real estate. Despite the emphasis in this chapter on quantitative decision tools, students should not conclude that investment valuation is simply a matter of "getting the numbers to add up." Although quantitative valuation tools and techniques, such as discounted cash flow analysis, are widely used in commercial real estate markets, the usefulness of investment valuation is limited by the quality of the cash flow assumptions employed. Thus, most all of the concepts discussed in prior chapters should help form the investor's projections of future rents, vacancies, operating expenses, and future sale prices. In short, the "garbage in, garbage out" maxim applies directly to real estate decision making.

Investment Valuation versus Market Valuation

Investment value was defined in Chapter 8 as the maximum the buyer would be willing to pay and the minimum the seller would be willing to accept. How is investment value calculated? The investment calculation begins where the market value calculation ends. The calculation of market value will have already taken into account the general, or average, investment conditions in the market. To the extent that a particular investor's situation is different, the price the investor is willing to pay will differ from market value. For example, investors may vary with respect to their expectations of future rents and vacancies. The amount and cost of equity and debt financing also will generally vary across investors and this may affect how much a particular investor is willing to pay for a particular property. Thus, explicit assumptions about how the acquisition is to be financed should be included in an investment valuation. Finally, expected income tax consequences usually are significant; thus, many investors choose to incorporate future income tax consequences into their analysis of a proposed investment.

Concept Check

16.1　How does investment value differ from market value?

---

1. When assets are acquired, their value is affected by the composition of the investor's current portfolio, including stocks, bonds, and other real estate assets. These portfolio considerations, and the effect they have on risk and return, are considered in more detail in Chapter 23.

Exhibit 16-1 Property Assumptions for Centre Point Office Building

- Total acquisition price: $885,000.
- Property consists of nine office suites, four on the first floor and five on the second.
- Contract rents: six suites at $1,800 per month and three at $1,400 per month.
- Annual market rent increases: 3% per year.
- Vacancy and collection losses: 10% per year.
- Operating expenses: 40% of effective gross income each year.
- Capital expenditures: 5% of effective gross income each year.
- Expected holding period: 5 years.
- Expected selling price in year 5: Year 6 *NOI* capitalized at 10%.
- Selling expenses in year 5: $58,300.

In Chapter 9 we discussed the mechanics of constructing cash flow projections for appraisal. In the next section we show the mechanics of constructing cash flow projections for a particular investor.

Investment Value Calculation

Similar to the discounted cash flow (DCF) method used for market valuation in Chapter 9, the calculation of investment value has three basic components: estimating net cash flows from annual rental operations, estimating cash proceeds from the eventual sale of the property, and converting these uncertain cash flow projections into present value.

Centre Point Office Building Example

To demonstrate how commercial real estate appraisers estimate the cash flows from an existing commercial property, Chapter 9 provided a detailed case example: the Centre Point Office Building. We now return to this case example to demonstrate investment valuation and decision making. For convenience, the basic assumptions for this potential investment are reproduced in Exhibit 16-1.

Potential gross income (*PGI*) in the first year of operations is estimated to be $180,000 and vacancy and collection loses are estimated at $18,000, resulting in an effective gross income (*EGI*) of $162,000.[2] Total operating expenses in the first year are estimated at $64,800 (40 percent of *EGI*) and capital expenditures are projected to be $8,100 (5 percent of *EGI*). These assumptions produce an estimated *NOI* of $89,100 in year 1. (Please see Chapter 9 for more discussion of these calculations.)

Although the expected cash flow in the first year of operation is a significant determinant of the property's investment value, pro forma cash flow projections over the expected investment horizon are required. This is because real property assets have long economic lives (50–100 years) and because investors tend to hold properties for long periods in order to recover the significant transaction costs associated with buying and selling commercial real estate. However, even if a particular investor expects to hold a property for only, say, three years, the market/resale value of the property after three years is a function of the expected ability of the property to generate cash flows *after* year 3. Therefore, an expected three-year holding period in no way relieves the investor of the burden of forecasting the income-producing ability of the property in year 4 and beyond.

Another advantage of longer projection periods is that it forces the investor to consider all of the economic, social, and legal changes that could affect the long-term, income-

2. The *PGI* of $180,000 is equal to $12 \times [(6 \times \$1,800) + (3 \times \$1,400)]$.

Exhibit 16-2 Centre Point Office Building: Five-Year Operating Pro Forma

	1	2	3	4	5
Potential gross income (*PGI*)	$180,000	$ 185,400	$ 190,962	$ 196,691	$ 202,592
− Vacancy and collection loss (*VC*)	18,000	18,540	19,096	19,669	20,259
= Effective gross income (*EGI*)	162,000	166,860	171,866	177,022	182,332
− Operating expenses (*OE*)	64,800	66,744	68,746	70,809	72,933
− Capital expenditures (*CAPX*)	8,100	8,343	8,593	8,851	9,117
= Net operating income (*NOI*)	$89,100	$91,773	$ 94,526*	$ 97,362	$100,283*

*Subtraction discrepancy due to rounding.

Exhibit 16-3 Reversion Cash Flow

Sale price (*SP*)	$1,033,000
− Selling expenses (*SE*)	58,300
= Net sale proceeds (*NSP*)	$974,700

www.realestateindex.com

National Real Estate Index provides information on recent trends in rent and property price appreciation.

producing ability of the property. Such an exercise does not guarantee accurate projections, but it does reduce the likelihood that key issues and variables will be overlooked.

Concept Check

16.2 Ten years is the most commonly assumed holding period in commercial real estate appraisal and investment analysis? Any ideas why?

Despite the prevalence of 10-year investment horizons, we assume for simplicity that the Centre Point Office Building will be sold five years after its acquisition. Exhibit 16-2 contains the projected cash flow for each year of the expected five-year holding period. Based on the assumptions in Exhibit 16-1, *NOI* is expected to increase from $89,100 in year 1 to $100,283 in year 5.

As discussed in Chapter 9, there are numerous methods available for estimating the sale price, or terminal value, at the end of the expected holding period. However, direct capitalization is the most common. If a going-out (terminal) cap rate, R_t, of 10 percent (0.10) is deemed appropriate for determining the future sale price of Centre Point, then the estimated sale price at the end of year 5 is:

$$V_5 = \frac{NOI_6}{R_t} = \frac{\$103,291}{0.1000} = \$1,032,910 \text{ or approximately, } \$1,033.000$$

Selling expenses in our example are projected to be $58,300, or a little less than 6 percent of the expected sale price. When deducted from the estimated selling price, this leaves an expected net sale proceeds (*NSP*) of $974,700 (see Exhibit 16-3).

Concept Check

16.3 Summarize the calculation of net operating income (*NOI*).

The projected stream of *NOI* is the fundamental determinant of Centre Point's value. In an analogy to the stock market, *NOI* is the annual "dividend" expected to be produced by the property. It must be sufficient, along with future sale proceeds, to provide the investor with an acceptable going-in internal rate of return.

Treatment of Capital Expenditures

As indicated previously, many components of commercial properties wear out faster than the building itself; thus, owners can expect to replace them several times during the building's economic life. In addition, investors typically expect to incur "retenanting" expenses when leases expire and the vacant space must again be made ready for occupancy. These tenant improvements may be relatively minor. To re-lease an apartment, for example, owners may simply apply a fresh coat of paint and clean the carpet. However, in some situations these expenditures can be quite large. For example, the re-leasing of office space often requires that substantial changes be made to the space, such as removing or adding walls, raising ceilings, and altering electrical capacity. Most office leases provide a new tenant with a tenant improvement allowance, or "TI." This lease provision obligates the landlord to incur a prespecified dollar amount of expenditures, perhaps $5 to $10 per square foot, to improve the space to the tenant's specifications.[3]

Various terms are applied to nonrecurring capital expenses and tenant improvements in pro forma cash flow projections. Examples include "capital costs," "capital expenditures," and "reserve for capital expenditures." The tradition in real estate appraisal is to refer to the projected expenses as reserves. The investment community increasingly refers to these items as capital expenditures. We adopt the latter convention here (and, for consistency, did so in Chapter 9).

In addition to inconsistent terminology, the placement of these nonrecurring capital expenditures in pro forma cash flow projections has not been standardized. In appraisal, capital expenditures (*CAPX*) have traditionally been treated as "above-line" expenses, meaning they are included in the calculation of *NOI*. Alternatively, however, nonrecurring capital expenditures may be treated as "below-line" expenses; that is, they are subtracted *from NOI*.

Concept Check

16.4   What is the more traditional treatment of *CAPX*?

Although many investors and analysts treat capital expenditures as below-line costs, we continue to use the above-line treatment depicted in Exhibit 16-2 to be consistent with our treatment of such costs in Chapter 9.

How does the investor distinguish between operating expenses and capital expenditures in historical data or in future projections? The key characteristic of an operating expense is that the expenditure is necessary to keep the property operating and competitive in its local market. By definition, however, an operating expense does not add to the market value of the property. For example, minor roof repairs are occasionally required on commercial properties, but they do not affect the market value of the property, nor do they extend it useful life. In contrast, major roof replacements do affect the market value of the property and, as a result, are considered capital expenditures, not operating expenses.[4]

---

3. When new leases are signed on some types of commercial properties, the leasing agents are usually entitled to leasing commissions that typically range from 2 to 4 percent of the face value of the lease (monthly rent times number of months). Although leasing commissions are not technically capital expenditures, we will not differentiate such expenses in the examples and discussion that follows.

4. As we shall see in Chapter 22, the distinction between operating expenses and capital expenditures also has significant income tax ramifications because operating expenses are deductible for tax purposes in the year in which they are paid. Although capital expenditures generally require an immediate cash outflow, they are not immediately deductible. Instead, they must be added to the property's tax basis and then expensed (i.e., recovered) over a period of time that is meant to approximate the economic life of the improvements.

Commercial Real Estate Investors Continue to Overpay

Are investors overpaying for office and apartment properties? It appears so, based on 2002 data compiled by Reis Inc. (www.reis.com), a New York–based real estate research firm, and by Real Capital Analytics Inc. (www.rcanalytics.com), a New York company that tracks real estate investment sales.

Office landlords continued to receive diminishing net rents in the second quarter of 2002, thereby bringing down property values. According to Reis, the intrinsic value of office properties in the top 50 U.S. markets dropped to an average of $141.67 per square foot, a decline of 1.9 percent from the previous quarter. In contrast, based on actual sales that closed during the 12 months ended June 30, 2002, office properties traded for $152 per square foot, on average, according to Real Capital Analytics. The average intrinsic value of rental-apartment properties rose 1.5 percent from the previous quarter to an average of $65,769 per unit. But apartment properties still sold, on average, for greater than the intrinsic value: about $66,115 per unit, according to Real Capital Analytics.

"I think there's a disconnect between intrinsic value and the prices being paid," says Lloyd Lynford, chief executive of Reis. But Robert White, Jr., president of Real Capital Analytics, doesn't see any disconnect. He says that in many markets, investors are buying newer, higher-quality properties, which may skew the average sales numbers. Given that, he says, investors aren't paying more than they should. Sale prices have held up well considering all the discounts and concessions that landlords are offering tenants, particularly in the apartment sector, says Craig Leupold, a senior analyst at Green Street Advisors Inc. (www.greenstreetadvisors.com), a real estate–stock research firm in Newport Beach, California.

Source: Adapted from Ray. A. Smith, "Real Estate Investors Continue to Overpay," *The Wall Street Journal Online,* August 27, 2002.

Evaluating the Cash Flow Estimates

The key to meaningful cash flow analysis, of course, is to use meaningful cash flow estimates. Therefore, investors should consider some important questions when projecting the future level of rents, vacancies, operating expenses, and capital expenditures. The answers to these questions will assist in the evaluation of the completeness and accuracy of the pro forma cash flow projections.

www.boma.org

Building Owners and Managers website provides detailed operating income and expense information for 29 U.S. cities.

www.icsc.org

International Council of Shopping Centers website provides operating income and expense information for U.S. shopping centers.

1. Are the sources of income and expenses appropriate? Investors should include only those sources of income and expenses that relate directly and entirely to the income-producing ability of the property. Operating expense estimates should not include financing costs and federal income taxes because these expenses are specific to the investor. Estimates of operating expenses also should exclude capital expenditures and business-related expenses not directly attributable to the operation of the property (e.g., unnecessary "business" lunches and club memberships).

2. Have the trends for each revenue and expense item been considered? Investors should avoid considering only short-term or current events to the detriment of long-term trends. For example, current vacancy rates may be high relative to historic averages. Thus, current market conditions could easily bias upwards a forecast of future vacancy rates. No assumptions are more critical to investment valuation than rental growth rate and vacancy assumptions.

3. What about comparable properties? Considering only the experience of the subject property, regardless of its current status, is often too narrow a perspective. Similar to appraisers, investors should obtain information about revenue and expense items for comparable properties whenever possible. As an example, property tax trends for frequently reassessed comparable properties may be better for forecasting the future property taxes of the subject property than its own past property tax trends. Obtaining this information on comparable properties requires that investors develop and maintain relationships with various market participants such as appraisers, brokers, lenders, and other investors.[5] Also, as discussed in detail in Chapters 8 and 9, numerous other sources of comparable data and information are available on the Internet and elsewhere.

4. What are the prevailing social and legal environments? Local zoning, land use, and environmental controls evolve continuously at both the state and local level. Changes in these rules and regulations can have a dramatic effect on property values and returns. Accurately predicting such changes is an impossible task, especially given that many changes are based on political, not economic, considerations. An understanding, however, of current local controls and regulations is a prerequisite for successful real estate investing, even if changes are difficult to predict.

Effects of Debt Financing on Pro Forma Cash Flows

Many investors make at least some use of debt financing—also called financial leverage—when acquiring real estate. The use of financial leverage affects the amount of cash (equity) required at acquisition, the net cash flows from rental operations, the net cash flow from the eventual sale of the property, and the risk and return of the required equity investment.

Why Do Investors Borrow?

Two basic reasons explain why real estate investors use financial leverage. The first reason is limited financial resources. If an investor desires to purchase real estate but does not have sufficient assets to pay cash for the property, then borrowing is the only alternative. The price the investor/borrower must pay is the interest rate on the borrowed funds.

Explore The Web

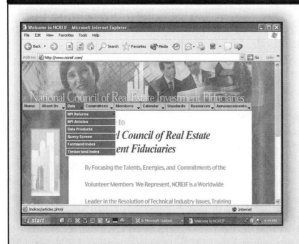

The National Council of Real Estate Investment Fiduciaries (NCREIF) is an association of real estate investment professionals who share a common interest in their industry. They are investment managers, pension plan sponsors, academicians, consultants, appraisers, CPAs, and other service providers who have a significant involvement in pension fund real estate investments. They come together to address vital industry issues and to promote research. Produced quarterly, the NCREIF Property Index (NPI), shows real estate performance returns using data submitted to NCREIF by its Data Contributing Members. The NPI is used as an industry benchmark to compare an investor's own returns against the industry average and against returns on stocks and bonds.

Go to the NCREIF home page (www.ncreif.com). Under "Data" choose "NPI Articles" and read NCREIF's latest *Performance Report Highlight*. Then click on "Data" once again and select apartment returns under "NPI Returns." Using your calculator or, preferably, a spreadsheet, calculate the average quarterly total return on U.S. apartment investments since the first quarter of 1990. How does this return compare to the performance of other property types?

---

5. A significant amount of historical information on typical operating expense levels is available, by property type, for the United States and major submarkets. See, for example, the following annual publications of the Institute of Real Estate Management (IREM): *Income/Expense Analysis: Office Buildings; Income/Expense Analysis: Shopping Centers;* and *Income/Expense Analysis: Conventional Apartments.* IREM's website is www.irem.org

The second reason for the use of mortgage financing is that it alters the expected risk *and* return of real estate investments. In particular, the use of financial leverage amplifies the rate of return investors earn on their invested equity. Positive *magnification* of equity returns is known as positive financial leverage, and it may induce investors to partially debt-finance (i.e., use "other people's money") even if they have sufficient capital resources to avoid borrowing.[6] As discussed in Chapter 14, however, financial leverage may magnify returns in a negative direction if the property underperforms.

Concept Check

16.5 Why might a real estate investor borrow to help finance an investment even if she could afford to pay 100 percent cash?

Effect on Initial Investment

When a mortgage loan is obtained, the cash down payment (i.e., equity) required at property acquisition, $E,$ is equal to:

$$E = \text{Acquisition price} - \text{Net Loan Proceeds}$$

where the net loan proceeds equal the face (or stated) amount of the loan, minus up-front financing costs paid to the lender. Recall that up-front financing costs include any charges or fees the borrower pays to obtain the mortgage financing. Examples include discount points, loan origination fees, and costs associated with having the property surveyed or appraised.

Assume the $885,000 Centre Point acquisition price is to be financed with a 30-year, 8% mortgage loan. The loan amount will equal 75 percent of the purchase price, or $663,750. Total up-front financing costs will equal 3 percent of the $663,750 loan amount, or $19,913. Thus, the required equity down payment is:

$$E = \$885,000 - (\$663,750 - \$19,913) = \$241,163$$

---

6. For a detailed discussion of this question, please see David G. Gelter and Norman M. Miller, *Commercial Real Estate Analysis and Investments* (Cincinnati, OH: South-Western Publishing, 2000), Chaps. 13 and 15.

16.6   Define net loan proceeds.

Effect on Cash Flows from Operations

Before-tax cash flow from operations (*BTCF*) is defined as net operating income (*NOI*) minus the mortgage payment (debt service). The general form for estimating *BTCF* is shown in Exhibit 16-4.

    BTCF is the amount of money left over from rental operations each year after paying all operating expenses, capital costs, and servicing the mortgage debt.

16.7   Why is *BTCF* a better measure of investor cash flow than *NOI*?

    Consider again the Centre Point Office Building example. The monthly payment on the $663,750 mortgage loan is $4,870.36; annual payments total $58,444.[7] Estimates of the *BTCF*s for the expected five-year holding period are displayed in Exhibit 16-5. The *BTCF* is $30,656 in year 1 and is expected to increase to $41,838 in year 5. As discussed in Chapter 9, the *BTCF*s are considered levered cash flows because they represent cash flows to the equity investor *after* the effects of financial leverage (i.e., debt service) have been subtracted. In contrast, the *NOI*s are unlevered cash flows because they represent returns on the entire investment (in this case $885,000), not just the portion of the investment financed with equity capital.

Exhibit 16-4   General Form for Estimating Before-Tax Cash Flows from Operations

$$
\begin{array}{rl}
 & \text{Net Operating Income } (NOI) \\
- & \text{Debt service } (DS) \\
\hline
= & \text{Before-tax cash flow } (BTCF)
\end{array}
$$

Exhibit 16-5   Centre Point Office Building: Estimated Before-Tax Cash Flows

	1	2	3	4	5
= Net Operating Income (*NOI*)	$89,100	$91,773	$94,526	$97,362	$100,283
− Debt Service (*DS*)	58,444	58,444	58,444	58,444	58,444
= Before-Tax Cash Flow (*BTCF*)	$30,656	$33,329	$36,082	$38,918	$41,838*

*Subtraction discrepancy due to rounding.

7. The keystrokes for this calculation are $N = 360$; $PV = -663,750$; $PMT = ?$; $FV = 0$; and $I = 8 \div 12$. This series of keystrokes produces a monthly payment of $4,870.36. The calculation of mortgage payments is discussed in detail in Chapter 11.

Computer-Aided Discounted Cash Flow Analysis

he widespread adoption and use of spreadsheet programs such as Microsoft's Excel has greatly facilitated the quantitative analysis of real estate development and acquisition decisions. However, creating a spreadsheet capable of analyzing, say, a large office property with 50 tenants and leases is a task too time consuming even for the most accomplished spreadsheet users. Fortunately, there are numerous ready-to-use software programs

available to commercial real estate investors that are capable of handling even the most sophisticated analytical requirements encountered in today's commercial leases and transactions. ARGUS, developed by Realm Business Solutions (www.realm.com), is one widely used valuation tool. Competitors to ARGUS include RealData (www.realdata.com), Real CashFlow (www.realcashflow.com), and planEASe (www.planease.com).

Exhibit 16-6   General Form of the Calculation of Before-Tax Equity Reversion

Net sale proceeds (*NSP*)		$974,700
− Remaining mortgage balance (*RMB*)		631,026
= Before-tax equity reversion (*BTER*)		343,674

Effect on Cash Flow from Sale

The before-tax equity reversion (*BTER*) is defined as the net selling price minus the remaining mortgage balance (*RMB*) at the time of sale. The loan balance in year 5 on the Centre Point mortgage will be $631,026.[8] Thus, the estimated *BTER* in year 5 is $343,674. A summary of this calculation is provided in Exhibit 16-6.

More Detailed Cash Flow Projections

Exhibits 16-2 through 16-6 present the general form of commercial real estate pro formas. These exhibits show the major categories of revenues and expenses. However, it would be misleading to leave readers with the impression that investors regularly make investment decisions based on pro formas that contain only these major categories of revenues and expenses. Exhibit 16-7 contains an example pro froma used for the analysis of Exodus Center, a 50,000-square-foot office building. This pro forma was calculated using ARGUS, a widely used software program for performing discounted cash flow analyses (see Industry Issues 16-2 for more information on available software programs). Currently, four tenants occupy space in the Exodus Center subject to long-term leases with different maturities, lease rates, and other terms. A total of 12,000 square feet is currently vacant.

The cash flow projections in Exhibit 16-7 differ from our Centre Point pro forma in the amount of detail provided. For example, in addition to contract rent, the owner of Exodus Center is reimbursed by the tenants for a portion of the property's operating expenses. This reimbursement revenue, along with revenue from leasing roof space for a communications antennae, increases the gross income of the office building. Typical pro formas will also provide more detail on projected operating expenses, as seen in Exhibit

www.ncreif.org

National Council of Real Estate Investment Fiduciaries. Tap into the real estate investment community through this organization.

---

8. The calculator keystrokes are: $N = 300$, $I = 8 \div 12$, $PV = ?$, and $PMT = 4,870.36$. The calculation of remaining mortgage balances is explained in more detail in Chapter 11.

Exhibit 16-7   ARGUS Pro Forma for Exodus Office Building

For the Years Ending	Year 1 Dec-2002	Year 2 Dec-2003	Year 3 Dec-2004	Year 4 Dec-2005	Year 5 Dec-2006	Dec-2007
Potential Gross Revenue						
Base Rental Revenue	$ 659,088	$696,338	$731,988	$761,820	$783,633	$949,407
Absorption & Turnover Vacancy	(156,625)		(20,286)		(34,271)	(94,028)
Scheduled Base Rental Revenue	502,463	696,338	711,702	761,820	749,362	855,379
Expense Reimbursement Revenue						
Real Estate Tax	4,071	11,083	11,593	13,096	13,546	3,497
Insurance	345	949	1,002	1,142	1,195	311
Utilities	3,952	12,551	13,046	15,121	15,337	3,832
Repairs and Maintenance	2,136	6,650	6,929	8,010	8,158	2,049
Grounds & Security	2,047	5,632	5,945	6,785	7,087	1,845
Total Reimbursement Revenue	12,551	36,865	38,515	44,154	45,323	11,535
Antennae	15,000	15,450	15,914	16,391	16,883	17,389
Total Potential Gross Revenue	530,014	748,653	766,131	822,365	811,568	884,303
Effective Gross Revenue	530,014	748,653	766,131	822,365	811,568	884,303
Operating Expenses						
Real Estate Tax	82,500	84,150	85,833	87,550	89,301	91,087
Insurance	7,000	7,210	7,426	7,649	7,879	8,115
Utilities	80,082	95,275	96,615	101,077	101,116	99,753
Repairs and Maintenance	43,299	50,470	51,287	53,544	53,776	53,371
Grounds & Security	41,500	42,745	44,027	45,348	46,709	48,110
Total Operating Expenses	254,381	279,850	285,188	295,168	298,781	300,436
Net Operating Income	275,633	468,803	480,943	527,197	512,787	583,867
Debt Service						
Interest Payments	239,034	237,014	234,762	232,322	229,680	
Principal Payments	25,061	27,141	29,384	31,833	34,475	
Obligation Points & Fees	30,000					
Total Debt Service	294,155	264,155	264,156	264,155	264,155	
Leasing and Capital Costs						
Tenant Improvements	261,000	17,562	65,670			388,545
Leasing Commissions	78,300	9,217	24,343			205,840
Roof Repair			55,000			
Total Leasing & Capital Costs	339,300	26,779	145,013			594,485
Cash Flow after Debt Service but Before Taxes	($357,822)	$177,869	$ 71,774	$263,042	$248,632	($10,618)

16-7. In addition, the components of the mortgage payment are disaggregated. Finally, ARGUS refers to capital expenditures (*CAPX*) as leasing and capital costs, and allows tenant improvements, expected leasing commissions, and other items (e.g., roof repairs) to be separately forecasted. Despite the simplifying assumptions made in our Centre Point example problem, Exhibits 16-2 through 16-6 do contain all the major categories of operating revenues and expenses.

Investment Valuation Using Discounted Cash Flow Models

Discounted cash flow analysis has become the main financial analysis tool used to evaluate the investment desirability of commercial real estate. Although much of the effort in DCF analysis goes toward the estimation of future cash flows, net present value and the going-in internal rate of return on equity are the bottom-line concerns of investors. In this section we demonstrate the use of these two investment criteria.

Net Present Value

We explained in Chapters 2 and 3 that real estate decision making fundamentally involves comparing the costs of various decisions, including the decision to purchase a property, to the benefits. The net present value (*NPV*) of an investment decision was defined as the difference between the present value of the cash inflows (PV_{in}) and the present value of the cash outflows (PV_{out}) or:

$$NPV = PV_{in} - PV_{out}$$

Net present value is interpreted using the following very simple, but very important, decision rule: If the *NPV* is greater than zero, the property should be purchased, assuming the investor has adequate resources, because it will increase the investor's wealth. If the calculated *NPV* is negative, the investment should be rejected because the investor expects to earn a return less than his or her required rate of return for such an investment. If the *NPV* equals zero, the investor is indifferent.

To illustrate the calculation of *NPV* in an investment setting, consider again our Centre Point example with a required equity investment of $241,163. In exchange for this down payment, the investor will acquire a set of property rights. These rights are expected to produce the *BTCFs* and *BTER* shown previously in Exhibits 16-5 and 16-6. Assume 16 percent is the levered discount rate currently being used by investors to value investments of similar risk and leverage to Centre Point. The projected cash flows and their present values are displayed in Exhibit 16-8.

The present value factor (*PVF*) for each year equals the present value of the right to receive a lump sum payment of $1 at the end of that year, given a 16 percent discount rate.[9] Multiplying the expected cash inflows by the *PVFs* results in present value. The total present value of the levered cash flows is $279,354. Thus,

$$NPV = PV_{in} - PV_{out}$$
$$= \$279,354 - \$241,163$$
$$= \$38,191$$

Exhibit 16-8   Levered Cash Flows from Centre Point Office Building

Year	Annual *BTCF*	*BTER*	Total *CF*	*PVF* @ 16%	Present Value
1	$30,656		$ 30,656	0.862069	$ 26,428
2	33,329		33,329	0.743163	24,769
3	36,082		36,082	0.640658	23,116
4	38,918		38,918	0.552291	21,494
5	$41,838	$343,674	$385,512	0.476113	183,547
			Total present value of levered inflows	=	$279,354

9. For example, the present value factor of 0.743163 for year 2 can be calculated with the following keystrokes: $N = 2$, $I = 16\%$, $PV = ?$, $PMT = 0$, and $FV = 1$.

Exhibit 16-9 Net Present Values at Different Discount Rates

Required Internal Rate of Return (y_e)	Net Present Value
12.00%	$ 81,943
14.00	58,993
16.00	38,191
18.00	19,298
20.00	2,106
20.2584	0
22.00	(13,565)
24.00	(27,878)

Using our net present value decision rule, the levered Centre Point investment should be accepted because the investor's current wealth would be increased by $38,191 as a result of undertaking the investment.[10]

To further analyze the *NPV* method, the *NPV*s at different discount rates can be calculated using either the format demonstrated in Exhibit 16-8, a handheld calculator, or a spreadsheet program. Spreadsheet programs are ideally suited to solving such problems. The *NPV* calculations are presented in Exhibit 16-9.

Note that as the required going-in *IRR* increases, *NPV* declines. Also note that *NPV* equals zero only when the cash flows are discounted at *exactly* 20.2584 percent. At lower discount rates, *NPV* is positive, indicating an accept decision. When the discount rate exceeds 20.2584 percent, *NPV* is negative, indicating a reject decision.

Internal Rate of Return

It is often not very meaningful to express investment performance in terms of dollars. For example, if the investor were to determine that the Centre Point Office Building before-tax *NPV* is $38,191, it may be difficult for the investor to evaluate how this investment compares to other investment opportunities such as stocks, bonds, and other real estate investments. If, however, the investor expects the Centre Point investment to provide, say, a 20 percent *IRR,* this facilitates more direct comparisons to available returns on other investment opportunities. Although certain technical problems are associated with its use, the internal rate of return (*IRR*) continues to be the standard, comprehensive measure of investment returns in real estate and other business fields, such as corporate finance.

How is the *IRR* defined? The *IRR* on a proposed investment is the discount rate that makes the net present value of the investment equal to zero. The only method for calculating the *IRR* in the absence of a calculator or spreadsheet program is trial and error. Let's return to our Centre Point example. Suppose we select 16 percent as the equity discount rate. At this rate the net present value of the levered before-tax cash inflows is $38,191. Thus, the *IRR* is not equal to 16 percent.

Concept Check

16.8   Define the internal rate of return.

But is the *IRR* higher or lower than 16 percent? To answer this question, note that the present value (*PV*) at 16 percent is $38,191 greater than the required cash outflow. To lower

---

10. The calculator keystrokes are $CF_0 = -241,163$, $CF_1 = 30,656$, $CF_2 = 33,329$, $CF_3 = 36,082$, $CF_4 = 38,918$, and $CF_5 = 385,512$.

Exhibit 16-10 Computation of Internal Rate of Return for Centre Point Office Building

Year	Cash Flows	Present Values			
		16%	**18%**	**20.2584%**	**22%**
0	$(241,163)	$(241,163)	$(241,163)	$(241,163)	$(241,163)
1	30,656	26,427	25,979	25,491	25,128
2	33,329	24,769	23,936	23,046	22,392
3	36,082	23,116	21,961	20,746	19,871
4	38,918	21,494	20,073	18,607	17,567
5	385,512*	183,547	168,511	153,271	142,639
Net present value		$ 38,191	$ 19,298	$ 0	$ (13,565)

*The cash flow in year 5 is the sum of the *BTCF* in year 5 and the estimated *BTER*.

the net present value in the direction of zero, we must increase the discount rate. With an 18 percent discount rate, the *NPV* of the cash inflows is $19,298, still in excess of zero. However, at 22 percent, the NPV of the levered cash flows is −$13,565. Thus, a 22 percent discount rate is too high. This indicates that the discount rate that makes the *NPV* equal to zero, the *IRR*, is somewhere between 18 and 22 percent. As shown in Exhibit 16-10, the discount rate that makes *NPV* equal to zero and, therefore, exactly solves the *IRR* equation, is 20.2584 percent.[11]

Should the project be accepted or rejected? Because investors require a 16 percent return on levered equity invested in projects of similar risk and the going-in *IRR* is approximately 20 percent, the project should be accepted. The decision rule for the internal rate of return method is, therefore,

If $r \geq y_e$, accept

If $r < y_e$, reject

where r is the estimated *IRR* and y_e is the required going-in *IRR* on equity.

Comparing Net Present Value and the Internal Rate of Return

When calculating Centre Point's *NPV,* we selected a discount rate (16 percent) and solved for present value. With *IRR,* we are *solving* for the discount rate that makes *NPV* = 0. Net present value and the internal rate of return use the same cash inflows and outflows in their calculations. Therefore, we would expect that decisions using the two DCF methods would be fairly consistent and, to a large extent, this is true. Both *NPV* and *IRR* produce the same accept/reject signal with respect to a particular investment opportunity—if a project's *NPV* is greater than zero, the *IRR* will exceed the required going-in *IRR* (y_e).

However, the *IRR* has some inherent assumptions that make its use as an investment criterion problematic in some situations. For example, the *IRR* method does not discount cash flows at the investor's required rate of return (y_e). This is significant because both *NPV* and *IRR* (implicitly) assume that the cash flows from an investment will be reinvested. With the net present value method, cash flows are assumed to be reinvested at the investor's required rate of return. However, with the internal rate of return method, it is implicitly assumed that cash flows are reinvested at the *IRR,* not the actual rate investors expect to earn on reinvested cash flows.

11. Financial calculators also allow the user to solve for the *IRR* of a stream of uneven cash flows by using the cash flow (*CF*) key. In this example, −241,163 would be entered as CF_0, 30,656 as CF_1, 33,329 as CF_2, and 36,082, 38,918, and 385,512 (41,838 + 343,674) as CF_3, CF_4, and CF_5, respectively. Then solve for *I*. The calculations that appear in Exhibit 16-10 were actually performed with Microsoft EXCEL.

A related problem with the use of the *IRR* as a decision criterion is that it will not necessarily result in wealth maximization for the investor. In particular, the *IRR* may produce
a different ranking than NPV of alternative investment opportunities. If all positive *NPV*
investments cannot be purchased by the investor—perhaps because of limited financial resources—the use of *IRR* instead of *NPV* may lead to the selection of a project with a lower
NPV than one of the rejected projects.

An additional difficulty with the *IRR* decision criterion is that multiple solutions are possible for investments where the sign (+ or −) of the cash flows changes more than once over
the expected holding period. That is, more than one discount rate may equate the present
value of future cash flows with the initial investment. In most commercial real estate investments, an initial cash outflow (−) is followed by a series of cash inflows (+) from operations
and sale of the property. It is possible, however, that the net cash flow from operations could
be negative in some future year(s)—perhaps due to large capital expenditures. This additional
"sign flip" could result in multiple *IRR*s. This is problematic because investors may not be
aware that multiple *IRR* solutions to their investment problems exist, and it is not clear which
IRR investors would choose even if they were aware of multiple solutions.

Concept Check

16.9   List three technical problems potentially associated with the use of the internal rate
of return as your final investment criterion.

For all these reasons, the use of net present value (*NPV*) is preferable to the *IRR* for
making decisions regarding single property investments. However, the *IRR* is widely used
for making comparisons across different investment opportunities.

Effects of Debt on Return and Risk

When will the increased use of financial leverage increase *NPV* and *IRR*? To explore this
question, consider Exhibit 16-11. If 75 percent of the acquisition price is borrowed, and
up-front financing costs equal 3 percent of the loan amount, then increasing the leverage
rate to 80 percent from 75 percent increases the *NPV* (assuming $y_e = 16$ percent) to
$48,362 from $38,191. The going-in *IRR* increases to 22.4 percent from 20.3 percent.

Exhibit 16-11 The Effects of Leverage

Mortgage as a % of Acquisition Price	$NPV\ y_e = 16\%$	IRR
0%	$(113,843)	12.2%
60	7,784	16.6
70	28,035	18.7
75	38,191	20.3
80	$48,362	22.4

Conversely, decreases in the leverage rates reduce *NPV*s and *IRR*s. Thus, based on the given set of input assumptions, the Centre Point investment opportunity displays positive financial leverage.

How can these patterns be explained? Note that the effective borrowing cost for the Centre Point Office Building is 8.76 percent, including the effect of up-front financing costs.[12] However, if the investor's required equity yield remains 16 percent, he has an incentive to substitute debt for the more expensive equity financing. Put differently, if the investor can borrow an additional dollar at an effective rate of 8.76 percent, then an additional dollar can be left invested in other assets (presumably of similar risk) that are expected to earn 16 percent.

Concept Check

16.10 When will the use of leverage increase the calculated *IRR*? The calculated *NPV*?

Despite the potential return-enhancing effects of leverage, it was determined in Chapter 14 that financial leverage increases the riskiness of the equity investment by increasing the risk of default and by making the return on equity more sensitive to changes in rental rates and expense levels (see, in particular, Exhibit 14-7). Thus, going-in *IRR*s on equity *should* increase as the amount of leverage increases. As a result, the decision to substitute more debt financing for equity financing is complicated because the increase in *expected* return from the increased use of debt may not be large enough to offset the corresponding increase in risk and required return.

Partnerships and Other Direct Forms Of Ownership

The before-tax cash flows (*BTCF*s) and before-tax equity reversion (*BTER*) displayed in Exhibits 16-5 and 16-6 represent the *total* cash flow available for distribution to equity investors—after the payment of operating expenses, capital expenditures, and debt service. To this point we have implicitly assumed there is but one equity investor who is entitled to receive these cash flows. As emphasized in Chapter 15, however, the majority of commercial properties in the United States, both large and small, are held not by individuals but by multiple investors in the form of partnerships, limited liability companies, and other ownership entities. Investment through partnerships and limited liability companies is considered "direct" investment because all cash flow and income tax consequences of real estate ownership "flow through" directly to the individual investors. There is no separate

---

12. The keystrokes for this calculation are $N = 60$; $PV = 643,837$; $PMT = -4,870.36$; $FV = -631,026$; and $I = ?$, where $643,837 equals the net loan proceeds ($663,750 - $19,913). $FV = -631,026$ is the remaining mortgage balance at the end of year 5. Effective borrowing costs are explained in Chapter 11.

corporate entity that collects the cash flows, pays corporate income taxes, and distributes all or part of the net corporate cash flow to investors in the form of dividends.

How does investment through a partnership or limited liability company affect investment valuation? Investment in real estate partnerships, for example, is governed by a partnership agreement, which prescribes the percentage of the required equity capital that must be contributed by each investor, as well as the portion of the *BTCF*s and *BTER* that are distributed to the various investors. In some cases the partnership agreement requires all investors to contribute their **pro rata share** of the total required equity investment in exchange for a prorated share of the *BTCF*s and the *BTER*. For example, if there are 10 investors, each would be required to contribute 1/10 of the required equity investment in exchange for 1/10 of all future cash flows. In such a case, the cash flows and returns for all 10 investors will be identical.

However, in many cases the partnership agreement calls for certain investors to receive a higher percentage of some future cash flows than their initial equity contribution would warrant. This is almost always the case for the syndicator (i.e., promoter) of the investment opportunity, who usually contributes significant time and resources to create the partnership entity. Moreover, the general partner in a limited partnership is exposed to unlimited liability. Thus, the general partner needs to earn a higher *expected* return than the limited partners in order to be induced to undertake the venture. In short, it is important to understand that the estimate of property level cash flows may be just the first step in determining the cash flows and returns expected by various investors in the ownership entity.

Concept Check

16.11 Why is the estimation of property level cash inflows and outflows often just the first step in determining the cash flows and returns expected by various investors in the ownership entity?

Effects of Income Taxes

The direct ownership of commercial real estate is expected to produce cash flows from rental operations and cash flow from the eventual sale of the property. Recall, however, that mortgage lenders have a claim on cash flows that is superior to the claim of the equity investor. Moreover, property cash flows are subject to federal income taxation. Investors receive only that which is left after the lender(s) and the state and federal government collect their share of the cash flows. The claims of the state and federal government on property level cash flows are substantial. Maximum federal income tax rates on individuals are 35 percent. Although some states do not have an income tax, many do and the maximum tax rate in some states approaches 10 percent. Thus, many real estate investors face a combined state and federal tax rate that exceeds 45 percent! Consequently, the measure of investment value most relevant to investors is the present value of the **after-tax cash flow (ATCF)** from operations and sale. Although investors are not expected to be income tax experts—tax accountants and attorneys are readily available—wise investors should not make a commitment to purchase commercial real estate without a clear understanding of the income tax implications.

Unfortunately, the portion of the federal tax code that affects commercial real estate is extensive and complex. In particular, the income subject to taxation generally differs, often significantly, from the actual cash flow generated by the property because some expenditures that reduce net investor cash flows (e.g., capital expenditures and the principle portion of mortgage payments) are *not* tax deductible. Conversely, federal income tax law allows investors to claim deductions for several items that are not associated with a concurrent cash expenses. In particular, capital expenditures are not immediately deductible for income tax purposes when paid. Rather, they are required to be expensed (i.e., depreciated) over time.

Exhibit 16-12 Centre Point Office Building: After-Tax Cash Flows from Annual Operations

	1	2	3	4	5
Net operating income (*NOI*)	$89,100	$91,773	$94,526	$97,362	$100,283
− Debt service (*DS*)	58,444	58,444	58,444	58,444	58,444
= Before-tax cash flow (*BTCF*)	$30,656	$33,329	$36,082	$38,918	$ 41,839
− Tax liability (*TAX*)	7,645	8,658	9,708	10,798	6,951
= After-tax cash flow (*ATCF*)	23,011	24,671	26,374	28,119	34,887*

*Subtraction discrepency due to rounding.

Exhibit 16-13 Centre Point Office Building: Estimated After-Tax Cash Flow
from Sale

Before-tax equity reversion (*BTER*)	$343,674
− Taxes due on sale (*TDS*)	32,032
= After-tax equity reversion (*ATER*)	$311,642

For example, if the Centre Point Office Building is purchased at a price equal to $885,000, this capital expenditure is *not* fully deductible in the year in which the investment is undertaken, as most investors would prefer. Rather, the $885,000 expenditure must be expensed—under current federal tax law—over 39 years. As we shall see in Chapter 22, the allowable annual deduction for our Centre Point property is $18,154. This deduction, referred to as depreciation, reduces the investor's taxable income by $18,154. However, it is extremely important to recognize that the investor does expend $18,154 in depreciation each year—the "check" for the purchase price was actually written when the property was purchased. Hence, the complication in income tax calculations: Allowable tax deductions in any year do not equal cash expenditures. Therefore, we cannot simply apply an assumed rate of tax to our *BTCF* and *BTER* estimates.

Concept Check

16.12 To calculate the expected income tax liability in a given year, why can't the analyst simply apply the investor's tax rate to the estimated *BTCF*?

So, what do we do? Because even an introductory treatment of real estate tax calculations requires considerable time and effort to work through, we simply report five-year projections of annual tax liabilities and after-tax cash flows from operations for our Centre Point example (see Exhibit 16-12). These calculations assume the investor faces a 30 percent tax rate on additional taxable income. Exhibit 16-13 displays the taxes due on the sale of Centre Point and the resulting **after-tax equity reversion (ATER)** at the end of the expected five-year holding period. The estimated tax liability in year 1 is $7,645, or 25 percent of *BTCF*. Estimated taxes due on sale are $32,032, or 9 percent of the before-tax equity reversion. Interested readers are referred to Chapter 22 for detailed explanations of these calculations.

Two points are worth emphasizing. First, the estimated tax liability in each year is a significant percentage of the before-tax cash flow. Thus, *BTCF* estimates significantly overstate the amount of cash that investors will actually net from the investment. Second, estimated tax liabilities are *not* calculated by applying the assumed tax rate to the before-tax cash flows. As we have stressed above, *cash flow is not the same as taxable income!*

Exhibit 16-14   After-Tax Cash Flows from Centre Point Office Building

Year	ATCFs	ATER	Total CF	PFV @ 11.2%	Present Value
0	$(241,163)		$(241,163)	0.000000%	$(241,163)
1	23,011		23,011	0.899281	20,693
2	24,671		24,671	0.808706	19,952
3	26,374		26,374	0.727253	19,181
4	28,119		28,119	0.654005	18,390
5	34,887	$311,642	346,529	0.588134	203,805
				Net present value =	$40,858
				Internal rate of return =	15.4%

Effects on Discount Rates

Given the required equity investment of $241,163, the $ATCFs$ from annual operations (Exhibit 16-12) and the $ATER$ (Exhibit 16-13), we are now in a position to calculate the levered, after-tax, NPV and IRR for Centre Point. However, one additional decision is required: What is the appropriate discount rate to apply to the *after-tax* cash flows? Recall that we discounted the levered, *before-tax* cash flows from Centre Point at a 16 percent rate; we assumed that if the investor did not purchase Centre Point, he or she could invest in an alternative project, of similar risk, and earn a 16 percent pretax return. That is, we assumed y_e was equal to 16 percent. However, the investor is not giving up a 16 percent *after-tax* return by acquiring Centre Point. Rather, by not investing in the alternative asset, the investor would be forgoing the 16 percent before-tax return minus the taxes that would be paid on that return. If the income tax on the income from comparable risk investments is 30 percent, the investor is giving up an 11.2 percent after-tax return—16 percent × (1 − 0.30)—by acquiring Centre Point. Thus, 11.2 percent is an appropriate going-in, after-tax, internal rate of return, assuming, of course, that 16 percent is an accurate measure of the investor's before-tax opportunity cost.

Effects on Net Present Value and the Internal Rate of Return

Assuming an 11.2 percent required after-tax return on equity, the total present value of the $ATCFs$ and the $ATER$ is $282,021, yielding an NPV of $40,858 and an IRR of 15.4 percent. The project should therefore be accepted. These calculations are summarized in Exhibit 16-14.[13]

Exhibit 16-15 summarizes the effects of debt financing and income taxes on the Centre Point internal rate of return. Note that financial leverage increases the before-tax IRR to 20.3 percent from 12.2 percent. This result suggests that the benefits of debt financing are substantial. However, the use of debt financing increases the riskiness of the investor's return on equity. Thus, it is inappropriate to apply the 11.75 percent unlevered discount rate to the levered cash flows. Assume a 4.25 percentage point risk premium is deemed appropriate for the 75 percent leverage that is employed. The levered discount rate is therefore 16 percent (11.75 + 4.25) and the levered NPV declines to $38,191.

What about the effect of taxes? Income taxes reduce the levered going-in IRR from 20.3 percent to 15.4 percent. However, if 11.2 percent is the appropriate after-tax levered discount rate, the levered NPV is only marginally affected by income taxes. Finally, note that although the investor's tax rate on ordinary income is 30 percent, the after-tax IRR is not 30 percent lower than the before-tax IRR; rather the effective tax rate is 24 percent [1 − (15.4% ÷ 20.3%)].

---

13. The NPV and IRR also can be solved for using a spreadsheet program or the cash flow (CF) keys of a financial calculator.

Exhibit 16-15 Effect of Debt and Taxes on IRRs and NPVs: Centre Point Office Building

	IRR	*NPV*
Unlevered, before-tax (*NOI*s)	12.2%	$15,181 (with 11.75% discount rate)
Levered, before-tax (*BTCF*s)	20.3	38,191 (with 16.0% discount rate)
Levered, after-tax (*ATCF*s)	15.4	40,858 (with 11.2 % discount rate)

Concept Check

16.13 Why is it inappropriate to discount after-tax cash flows at the investor's before-tax opportunity cost?

Why is the *effective* tax rate lower than the actual tax rate faced by the investor? First, as we shall see in Chapter 22, depreciation allows investors to defer the recognition of a portion of each annual cash flow until the property is sold. This deferral is valuable. Second, the rate of tax paid by the investor if and when the property is sold is generally less than his or her ordinary tax rate. The ability to defer taxes with depreciation and to convert some of the deferred ordinary income to income taxed at a lower rate both contribute to the result that the effective tax rate on commercial property investments is less than the tax rate on the investor's ordinary income. For most investors, their effective tax rate on commercial real estate investments is less than the effective rate of tax they pay on alternative investments such as stocks and bonds. This is an important advantage to investors in many real estate investment opportunities.

Finally, note that the levered, after-tax *IRR* of 15.4 percent is still greater than the unlevered, before-debt *IRR* of 12.2 percent. This suggests that the expected benefits of debt financing more than offset the negative effect of taxes.

Other Investment Criteria

In addition to calculating the net present value and the going-in internal rate of return of a potential acquisition, an investor may find it desirable to analyze a number of key ratios. Indeed, before the introduction of discounted cash flow analysis, real estate investment decisions were based on ratio analysis, and it is still frequently used to guide real estate investment decisions. These ratios—or *rules of thumb*—can be grouped into three categories: profitability ratios, multipliers, and financial ratios.

Profitability Ratios

The ultimate determination of an investment's desirability is its capacity to produce income in relation to the capital required to obtain that income. Two frequently used profitability ratios are discussed in this section: the capitalization rate and the equity dividend rate.

Capitalization Rate. The going-in capitalization rate on an acquired property—known as the overall cap rate—is defined as:

$$R_o = \frac{NOI_1}{Acquisition\ price}$$

R_o indicates the (first year) cash flow return on the total investment—that is, the return on funds supplied by both equity investors and lenders. As such, it measures the *overall*

Exhibit 16-16 Range and Average Going-in Cap Rates by Property Type and Class of Property: South Region of the United States
(First Quarter 2003)

	Warehouse	Regional Mall	Neighborhood Shopping Center	CBD Office	Apartment
Class A properties	8.0 – 9.5%	7.0 – 10.0%	8.0 – 10.0%	7.0 – 10.5%	7.0 – 9.5%
Average	9.0%	8.8%	9.1%	9.0%	8.2%
Class B properties	9.0 – 10.0%	8.0 – 12%	8.5 – 10.5%	8.5 – 11.0%	8.0 – 9.5%
Average	9.5%	9.7%	9.5%	9.9%	8.8%
Class C properties	10.0 – 10.7%	9.5 – 12.0%	9.5 – 11.0%	9.0 – 12.0%	9.0 – 10.0%
Average	10.2%	10.6%	10.3%	10.8%	9.8%

Source: Real Estate Research Corporation, *Real Estate Report,* first quarter 2003.

income-producing ability of the property.[14] To illustrate, consider again the Centre Point Office Building, which has an acquisition price of $885,000 and an estimated first-year net operating income of $89,100. The going-in capitalization rate therefore is:

$$R_o = \frac{\$89,100}{\$885,000} = 0.1007, \text{ or } 10.1\%$$

Is 10.1 percent an acceptable overall cap rate? This question can only be addressed by comparisons with cap rates on similar properties in the market. The Real Estate Research Corporation (RERC) regularly surveys the going-in cap rate expectations of a sample of institutional investors. Published quarterly in the *Real Estate Report,* this survey provides useful information on cap rate trends in the United States. Portions of several tables from the first quarter 2003 report are reproduced in Exhibit 16-16. All figures are for the South, one of four regions in the United States for which RERC reports separate results. Class A properties are defined by RERC as new or newer quality construction in prime to good locations. Class B properties are defined as aging, formerly class A properties in good to average locations. Finally, class C properties are defined as older properties with functional inadequacies and/or marginal locations.

Exhibit 16-16 reveals several notable patterns. First, required going-in cap rates vary significantly by property quality. For example, cap rates for class A regional malls ranged from 7.0 to 10.0 percent with an 8.8 percent average, whereas class C cap rates for malls ranged from 9.5 to 12.0 percent with a mean of 10.6 percent. Class C properties have less predictable cash flows or are likely to produce less rent growth than class A and B properties. Class C properties must therefore sell for a lower price *per dollar of current income,* which implies higher cap rates.

Exhibit 16-16 also reveals a significant amount of variation in cap rates by property type in terms of both averages and ranges. Apartment cap rates are generally lower than other property types, although there is considerable variation even within the class A properties. In contrast, investors in warehouse properties require higher going-in cap rates than apartment investors, but the variation among warehouse investors responding to the survey is much smaller. Centre Point's going-in rate of 10.1 percent is approximately equal to the 9.9 percent average cap rate for class B office properties located in central business districts.

It is extremely important when comparing cap rates across properties to be consistent in the treatment of capital expenditures. If the estimated net operating income for the subject property does not include a deduction for estimated capital expenditures, the investor

14. The role of the capitalization rate in commercial property appraisal is discussed in Chapter 9.

must take significant care to ensure that cap rates obtained from comparable properties do not include estimated capital costs in the *NOI*, which would lower the cash flow estimate and, therefore, the calculated capitalization rate.

Concept Check

16.14 Why do class B properties sell at higher going-in cap rates than class A properties?

Equity Dividend Rate. Because many commercial property investments involve the use of mortgage funds and because the cost of mortgage debt may differ across investment opportunities, the use of the capitalization rate as a measure of profitability has limitations. Another profitability measure—the **equity dividend rate (EDR)**—is defined as

$$EDR = \frac{Before - Tax\ cash\ flow}{Equity\ investment}$$

The equity dividend rate shows investors what percentage of their equity investment is expected to be returned to them in cash (before income taxes). Note that the difference between the *EDR* and R_o is that the effects of debt financing have been subtracted from both the numerator and the denominator of the *EDR*. Thus, the cash flow in the numerator measures the amount received by the equity investor after paying all operating and capital expenses *and* after servicing the debt. This "residual" cash flow is then compared to the equity investors' cash investment. For this reason, the equity dividend rate is also referred to as the "cash-on-cash" return.

The *EDR* for the Centre Point Office Building is:

$$EDR = \frac{\$30,656}{\$241,163} = 0.1271,\ or\ 12.7\%$$

The estimated *EDR* of 12.7 percent can be compared to similar properties to determine its relative magnitude. Note that the *EDR* for Centre Point exceeds R_O; thus, positive financial leverage is expected.

Multipliers

Two cash flow multipliers may be calculated by potential investors: the net income multiplier and the (effective) gross income multiplier. The **net income multiplier, (*NIM*,)** is defined as:

$$NIM = \frac{Acquisition\ price}{NOI_1}$$

Recall that the overall cap rate is equal to year 1 net operating income divided by the acquisition price. The *NIM* is, therefore, simply the reciprocal of the cap rate—properties with a relatively high cap rate (overall return) sell for a lower multiple of *NOI*.

The gross income multiplier, (*GIM*) is defined as:

$$GIM = \frac{Acquisition\ price}{Effective\ gross\ income}$$

The gross income multiplier, also discussed in Chapter 9, is employed more frequently than the net income multiplier; however, it must be used with great care. To compare gross income multipliers, the properties should be traded in the same market and should be equivalent in expense patterns, risk, location, physical attributes, time, and terms of sale.[15]

---

15. The *GIM* is sometimes calculated using potential, instead of effective, gross income.

For Centre Point, the *NIM* and *GIM* are:

$$NIM = \frac{\$885,000}{\$89,100} = 9.9$$

$$GIM = \frac{\$885,000}{\$162,000} = 5.5$$

www.nationalreia.com

National Real Estate Investors Association. Data and information for real estate investors

Income multipliers can be used to provide a quick assessment on whether a property is priced reasonably in relation to its gross or net income. While multipliers vary greatly, the range for annual gross income multipliers is normally between 4 and 8. Net income multipliers for office properties usually range between 5 and 12. The multipliers for Centre Point are within the realm of reasonable expectations for an office property.

Financial Risk Ratios

Financial risk ratios measure the income-producing ability of the property to meet operating and financial obligations. As we saw in Chapter 14, these ratios are helpful to lenders in assessing the risk of lending to investors on particular projects. Commercial lenders typically require that borrowers include estimates of these ratios in the loan application package submitted to lenders. Lenders are concerned whether properties will generate sufficient income to service the debt and, eventually, ensure that the loan principal will be repaid. Several ratios that are widely used for this purpose are discussed below.

Operating Expense Ratio. This ratio expresses operating expenses as a percentage of effective gross income (*EGI*); thus the **operating expense ratio (OER)** is:

$$OER = \frac{Operating\ expenses}{Effective\ gross\ income}$$

The *OER* in year 1 for Centre Point is calculated as:

$$OER = \frac{\$72,900}{\$162,000} = 0.45\ or\ 45\%$$

The greater the *OER*, the larger the portion of effective rental income consumed by operating expenses. Knowledgeable market participants are aware of typical operating expense ratios; thus, this ratio may provide information to investors and lenders. For example, if the *OER* of a property is higher than average, it may signal that expenses are out of control or, perhaps, that rents are too low. This may indicate a "turnaround" opportunity for a buyer. However, investors should not simply seek properties with low *OER*s; as discussed earlier, ratios are most useful as preliminary screening devices.

Loan-to-Value Ratio. This ratio measures the percentage of the acquisition price (or current market value) encumbered by debt. If property values decline after the origination of the mortgage, the *loan-to-value ratio (LTV)* may increase even though scheduled principal amortization is reducing the remaining mortgage balance. To protect their invested capital in the event that property values do fall, commercial mortgage lenders generally require that the initial *LTV* not exceed 75 to 80 percent. In equation form:

$$LTV = \frac{Mortage\ balance}{Acquisition\ price}$$

For our Centre Point example, the initial *LTV* is:

$$LTV = \frac{\$663,750}{\$885,000} = 0.75\%,\ or\ 75\%$$

Debt Coverage Ratio. As discussed in Chapter 9, the debt coverage ratio (*DCR*) shows the extent to which net operating income (*NOI*) can decline before it is insufficient to service the debt. It therefore provides an indication of the safety associated with the use of borrowed funds and is defined as:

$$DCR = \frac{Net\ operating\ income}{Debt\ service}$$

For the example property:

$$DCR = \frac{\$89,100}{\$58,444} = 1.52$$

The debt coverage ratio provides an indication of safety from legal default in the event rental revenues fall and the mortgage payment is in jeopardy. According to the data presented in Exhibit 14-3, office property lenders require this ratio to be *at least* 1.2, with 1.50 as the average *DCR* for office properties in late 2002. Thus, Centre Point's 1.52 coverage ratio would seem to provide the investor (and lender) with a satisfactory safety margin. Required *DCR*s, however, can vary significantly across property types. For example, required *DCR*s for hotel properties often exceed 1.6. The common ratios used in the analysis of commercial real estate investments are summarized in Exhibit 16-17.

Exhibit 16-17 Common Ratios Used in Real Estate Investment Analysis

Ratio	Form	Use	Comment
Capitalization rate	$\frac{NOI}{Acquisition\ price}$	To indicate one-year return on total investment (both lender and equity position)	Also called overall cap rate—is more commonly applied in appraisals
Equity dividend rate	$\frac{BTCF}{Equity\ investment}$	To indicate the investor's one-period rate of return on equity	Ignores tax consequences, future year cash flows, and changes in property values
Net income multiplier	$\frac{Acquisition\ price}{NOI}$	To indicate relationship between total price and first-year *NOI*—measures price per current dollar of *NOI*	A quick method of comparing the price per dollar of net income of one property to others sold in the market
Gross income multiplier	$\frac{Acquisition\ price}{EGI}$	To indicate the relationship between total price and *EGI*—measures price per current dollar of *EGI*	A quick method of comparing the price per dollar of gross income of one property to others sold in the market
Operating expense ratio	$\frac{OE}{EGI}$	To indicate the portion of rental income consumed by operating expenses	Range is 25–50 percent of *EGI*, but varies significantly by property type
Loan-to-value ratio	$\frac{Mortgage\ balance}{Property\ value}$	To measure the degree of financial leverage	Maximum allowable on commercial property usually 75–80 percent, borrowers often seek maximum
Debt coverage ratio	$\frac{NOI}{Debt\ Service}$	To see how much *NOI* can decline before it will not cover debt service	Lenders usually seek a minimum *DCR* of 1.20 to 1.30, but may vary their requirements

Limitations of Ratio Analysis

There are two basic arguments for using ratios instead of discounted cash flow valuation methods. First, ratios are much easier to calculate and more widely understood than *NPV* and *IRR* (internal rate of return). Second, because DCF analysis requires estimation of *NOI*s (net operating incomes), *BTCF*s (before-tax cash flows), *NSP*s (net sale proceeds), and *BTER*s (before-tax equity reversions), often many years into the future, some believe the numbers can be easily manipulated to achieve any result the analyst desires (again, the "garbage in, garbage out" problem).

In contrast, the basic shortcoming of multipliers and single period rate of return measures is that they do not consider future cash flows. For example, the estimated net income multiplier (*NIM*) of 9.9 for Centre Point may be low relative to similar properties. But does this necessarily imply that the current asking price is too low and that the property should be purchased? Perhaps, but the investor should consider alternative explanations for the apparently low multiplier. For example, it is possible that the current owner has not maintained the property well. This deferred maintenance would have to be taken care of shortly after purchase if the property is going to be competitive in the local office rental market. Given that potential investors anticipate substantial capital expenditures subsequent to the purchase, they are willing to pay less today for each dollar of current *NOI*. This pricing behavior implies a lower net income multiplier.

Another possible explanation for a relatively low *NIM* (high cap rate) is that the property may be located in an office market that is declining relative to most office markets in the area. As a result, potential investors are forecasting less growth in rental rates than in other markets. Given lower growth rates in rents, investors again are going to bid less today for each dollar of current *NOI*—thereby lowering the *NIM*. Note that lower multipliers imply higher current yields—that is, capitalization rates. If investors expect less growth in rental income and, therefore, appreciation in a particular market, they must be compensated in the form of a higher income return. However, differences in rental growth rates are ignored if investment decisions are based solely on comparisons of *NIM* or capitalization rates.

Although ratios have their place in real estate investment analysis, there are serious problems associated with their use. Ratios are single-period, before-tax measures and are void of formal decision rules. Their strength comes in isolating specific aspects of a property or investment and facilitating *comparisons* with similar investment opportunities. For example, an operating expense ratio of 60 percent says nothing about the acceptability of the investment, but when compared with similar properties having 40 percent operating ratios, it illuminates an undesirable feature and perhaps an opportunity associated with the investment.

In conclusion, both ratio analysis and discounted cash flow analysis seem to have their place in real estate investment decisions. Ratios may provide quick signals to alert the investor to deviations between the subject property and "typical" properties. On the other hand, net present value and the internal rate of return provide a comprehensive evaluation of the property. These methods, however, require considerable data, many assumptions, and much judgment.

Concept Check

16.15 What is the major shortcoming of most ratios when they are used to make investment decisions?

Varying the Assumptions

As emphasized earlier, cash flow projections should be based on well-researched, realistic input assumptions. However, it is clear that the investor's point estimates of rental income growth, future vacancies, operating expenses, and future resale prices will prove to be wrong, either by a little or perhaps a lot. When considering a proposed acquisition, investors should recalculate *NPV*s and *IRR*s using both optimistic and pessimistic input assumptions in order to draw contrasts to the base case (i.e., most likely) scenario. Such an exercise allows investors to determine how sensitive their point estimates of *NPV* and *IRR* are to variations in important input assumptions.

Although values and rates of return can be determined by hand calculation, the computations are greatly facilitated by the use of personal computers, especially when a variety of input assumptions are considered. The use of spreadsheet programs such as Excel allows investors to quickly calculate the effect of a changed variable assumption on cash flows, values, and rates of return. Numerous spreadsheet programs that facilitate the valuation and investment decision-making process are available for investors to purchase, or the analyst may custom-design a spreadsheet. For complex analyses involving numerous leases, properties, or both, sophisticated PC-based programs such as ARGUS, RealData, and planEASe can be purchased, although the cost of these programs far exceeds the modest price of most spreadsheet software.

Summary

Investment is one of the most interesting and important areas of study in the field of real estate. Whether the student is considering a career in a corporation or institution that invests in real estate, or is seeking knowledge for personal investment reasons, several questions must be answered to make better-informed investment decisions.

This chapter presents the conceptual and analytical framework for making single-property real estate investment decisions. The framework has three basic components: forecasting net cash flows from the operation of the property, forecasting cash proceeds from the eventual sale of the property, and converting these future cash flow streams into present values.

Our perspective is that of the investor in commercial real estate who has a unique set of holding period and financing requirements, and expectations about the future that may differ from those of other investors. The objective of analyzing real estate investments, therefore, is to compare the values of all property rights in real estate investment opportunities against required equity investments. The total present value of the set of property rights to be acquired is the investment value of the equity; if this value is greater than the required cash investment, equity investors are on solid financial ground to proceed with the investment. Other important factors that are difficult to quantify may steer investors away from real estate investments.

We would be less than forthcoming if we were to leave you with the impression that the production of pro forma cash flow estimates and the calculation of net present values and internal rates of return is all that is required for successful real estate investment. Many market participants are not well versed in discounted cash flow valuation models and some may produce them more for the sake of appearance than as a serious step in the analysis of the property. But discounted cash flow analysis should be treated seriously. Although no one possesses a crystal ball, lenders, potential investment partners, and other market participants are increasingly likely to consider DCF analysis as fundamental to sound decision making. Put another way, individuals who are not comfortable with DCF tools and techniques are finding their job prospects in commercial real estate to be increasingly limited.

Key Terms

After-tax equity reversion (*ATER*) 427	Equity dividend rate (*EDR*) 431	Operating expense ratio (*OER*) 432
After-tax cash flow (*ATCF*) 426	Net income multiplier (*NIM*) 431	Pro rata share 426

Test Questions

Answer the following multiple choice questions:

1. Income multipliers:
   a. Are useful as a preliminary analysis tool to weed out obviously unacceptable investment opportunities.
   b. Are adequate as the sole indication of a property's investment worth.
   c. Relate the property's price or value to after-tax cash flow.
   d. None of the above.

2. The overall capitalization rate:
   a. Is the reciprocal of the net income multiplier.
   b. Incorporates the effects of expected future rent growth.
   c. Considers the risk associated with an investment opportunity.
   d. All of the above are true.

3. The operating expense ratio:
   a. Highlights the relationship between net operating income and operating expenses.
   b. Shows the percentage of potential gross income consumed by operating expenses.
   c. Expresses operating expenses as a percent of effective gross income.
   d. Is the reciprocal of the break-even ratio.

4. The equity dividend rate:
   a. Incorporates income tax considerations.
   b. Expresses before-tax cash flow as a percent of the required equity cash outlay.
   c. Expresses before-tax cash flow as a percent of the property's acquisition price.
   d. Expresses net operating income as a percent of the required equity cash outlay.

5. A real estate investment is available at an initial cash outlay of $10,000 and is expected to yield cash flows of $3,343.81 per year for five years. The internal rate of return is approximately:
   a. 2 percent.
   b. 20 percent.
   c. 23 percent.
   d. 17 percent.

6. The net present value of an acquisition is equal to:
   a. The present value of expected future cash flows, plus the initial cash outlay.
   b. The present value of expected future cash flows, less the initial cash outlay.
   c. The sum of expected future cash flows, less initial cash outlay.
   d. None of the above.

7. Present value:
   a. In excess of zero means a project is expected to yield a rate of return in excess of the discount rate employed.
   b. Is the value now of all net benefits that are expected to be received in the future.
   c. Will always equal zero when the discount rate is the internal rate of return.
   d. Will always equal a project's purchase price when the discount rate is the internal rate of return.

8. The internal rate of return equation incorporates:
   a. Future cash outflows and inflows, but not initial cash flows.
   b. Future cash outflows and inflows, and initial cash outflow, but not initial cash inflow.
   c. Initial cash outflow and inflow, and future cash inflows, but not future cash outflows.
   d. Initial cash outflow and inflow, and future cash outflow and inflow.

9. The purchase price that will yield an investor the lowest acceptable rate of return is:
   a. The property's investment value to that investor.
   b. The property's net present value.
   c. The present value of anticipated future cash flows.
   d. Computed using the risk-free discount rate.

Study Questions

Use the following information to answer questions 1–4.

You are considering the purchase of an office building for $1.5 million today. Your expectations include the followings: first-year gross potential income of $340,000; vacancy and collection losses equal to 15 percent of gross potential income; operating expenses equal to 40 percent of effective gross income. Capital expenditures equal 5 percent of *EGI*. You expect to sell the property five years after it is purchased. You estimate that the market value of the property will increase 4 percent a year after it is purchased and you expect to incur selling expenses equal to 6 percent of the estimated future selling price.

1. What is estimated effective gross income (*EGI*) for the *first* year of operations?

2. What is estimated net operating income (*NOI*) for the *first* year of operations?

3. What is the estimated overall cap rate (R_O) using *NOI* for the *first* year of operations?

4. What will be the net sale proceeds from the sale of the property at the end of year 5?

5. A retail shopping center is purchased for $2.1 million in 2000. During the next four years, the property appreciates at 4 percent a year. At the time of purchase, the property is financed at a 75 percent loan-to-value ratio for 30 years at 8 percent with monthly amortization. At the end of year 4, the property is sold with 8 percent selling expenses. What is the before-tax equity reversion?

6. An office building is purchased with the following projected cash flows:
   - *NOI* is expected to be $130,000 in year 1 with 5 percent annual increases.
   - The purchase price of the property is $720,000.
   - 100 percent equity financing is used to purchase the property.
   - The property is sold at the end of year 4 for $860,000 with selling costs of 4 percent.
   - The required levered rate of return is 14 percent.
   a. Calculate the levered internal rate of return (*IRR*).
   b. Calculate the levered net present value (*NPV*).

7. With a purchase price of $350,000, a warehouse provides for an initial before-tax cash flow of $30,000, which grows by 6 percent a year. If the before-tax equity reversion after four years equals $90,000, and an initial equity investment of $175,000 is required, what is the *IRR* on the project? If the going-in levered rate of return on the project is 10 percent, should the project be undertaken?

8. You are considering the acquisition of an office building. The purchase price is $775,000. Seventy-five percent of the purchase price can be borrowed with a 30-year, 7.5 percent mortgage. Payments will be made *annually*. Up-front financing costs will total 3 percent of the loan amount. The expected before-tax cash flows from operations, assuming a five-year holding period, are as follows:

Year	BTCF
1	$48,492
2	53,768
3	59,282
4	65,043
5	71,058

The before-tax cash flow from the sale of the property is expected to be $295,050. What is the net present value of this investment, assuming a 12 percent required rate of return on levered cash flows? What is the levered internal rate of return?

9. An investment opportunity having a market price of $100,000 is available. You could obtain a $75,000, 25-year mortgage loan requiring equal monthly payments with interest at 9.5 percent. The following operating results are expected during the first year:

Effective gross income	$25,000
Less operating expenses	$13,000
Net operating income	$12,000

For the first year only, determine the:
   a. Gross income multiplier
   b. Operating expense ratio
   c. Debt coverage ratio
   d. Overall rate
   e. Equity dividend rate

10. You are considering the purchase of a quadruplex apartment. Effective gross income during the first year of operations is expected to be $33,600 ($700 per month per unit). First-year operating expenses are expected to be $13,440 (at 40 percent of *EGI*). Ignore capital expenditures. The purchase price of the quadruplex is $200,000. The acquisition will be financed with $60,000 in equity and a $140,000 standard fixed-rate mortgage. The interest rate on the debt financing is 8 percent and the loan term is 30 years. Assume, for simplicity, that payments will be made *annually* and that there are no up-front financing costs.
   a. What is the overall capitalization rate?
   b. What is the effective gross income multiplier?
   c. What is the equity dividend rate (the before-tax return on equity)?
   d. What is the debt service coverage ratio?
   e. Assume the lender requires a minimum debt coverage ratio of 1.2. What is the largest loan that you could obtain if you decide that you want to borrow more than $140,000?

11. You are considering the purchase of an apartment complex. The following assumptions are made:
   - The purchase price is $1 million.
   - Potential gross income (*PGI*) for the first year of operations is projected to be $171,000.
   - PGI is expected to increase 4 percent per year.
   - No vacancies are expected.
   - Operating expenses are estimated at 35 percent of effective gross income. Ignore capital expenditures.
   - The market value of the investment is expected to increase 4 percent per year.
   - Selling expenses will be 4 percent.
   - The holding period is four years.
   - The appropriate unlevered rate of return to discount projected *NOIs* and the projected *NSP* is 12 percent.
   - The required levered rate of return is 14 percent.
   - 70 percent of the acquisition price can be borrowed with a 30-year, monthly payment mortgage.
   - The annual interest rate on the mortgage will be 8 percent.
   - Financing costs will equal 2 percent of the loan amount.
   - There are no prepayment penalties.
   a. Calculate net operating income (*NOI*) for each of the four years.
   b. Calculate the net sale proceeds from the sale of the property.
   c. Calculate the net present value of this investment, assuming no mortgage debt. Should you purchase? Why?
   d. Calculate the internal rate of return of this investment, assuming no debt. Should you purchase? Why?
   e. Calculate the monthly mortgage payment. What is the total per year?
   f. Calculate the loan balance at the end of years 1, 2, 3, and 4. (*Note:* The unpaid mortgage balance at any time is equal to the present value of the remaining payments, discounted at the contract rate of interest).
   g. Calculate the amount of principal reduction achieved during each of the four years.

h. Calculate the total interest paid during each of the four years. (Remember: Debt service = Principal + Interest.)

i. Calculate the (levered) required initial equity investment.

j. Calculate the before-tax cash flow (*BTCF*) for each of the four years.

k. Calculate the before-tax equity reversion (*BTER*) from the sale of the property.

l. Calculate the (levered) net present value of this investment. Should you purchase? Why?

m. Calculate the (levered) internal rate of return of this investment. Should you purchase? Why?

n. Calculate, for the first year of operations, the
   (1) Overall (cap) rate of return.
   (2) Equity dividend rate.
   (3) Gross income multiplier.
   (4) Debt coverage ratio.

12. The expected before-tax *IRR* on a potential real estate investment is 14 percent. The expected after-tax *IRR* is 10.5 percent. What is the effective tax rate on this investment?

Explore The Web

Go to the CCIM Institute home page, www.ccim.com. Click on the "education" link at the top of the page. Follow the links to designation requirements, course descriptions and schedules, frequently asked questions, and other valuable information. What must you do to attain your CCIM designation?

Solutions to Concepts Checks

1. Investment value is very similar to market value in that it is a function of three things: (1) estimated cash flows from annual operations, (2) estimated cash proceeds from the eventual sale of the property, and (3) the discount rate applied to these future cash flows. When estimating market value, the cash flow forecasts and discount rate are based on the expectations of the *typical*, or average, investor. The calculation of investment value is based on the expectations and return requirements of a *specific* investor.

2. There is no clear answer to this. One is tempted to answer that a 10-year holding period is typically assumed because 10 years of annual cash flows is all one can comfortably fit on an 81/2-by-11-inch piece of paper set on landscape. A better, less cynical, answer is that 10 years is the maximum period over which investors can foresee with any accuracy changes in the economic environment, including changes in local supply and demand conditions for commercial real estate. Moreover, except for apartment properties, many commercial properties are subject to long-term leases that make the prediction of rental income, in the absence of lease default, possible over periods as short as 10 years. Beyond 10 years, however, the cost associated with developing a detailed cash flow forecast probably exceeds the value.

3. Effective gross income (*EGI*) is equal to potential gross income minus vacancy and collection losses, plus miscellaneous income. Net operating income (*NOI*) is equal to *EGI* minus operating expenses (*OE*s) and capital expenditures (*CAPX*), although in a below-line treatment of *CAPX*, they would be subtracted from *NOI*.

4. The more traditional treatment of nonrecurring capital expenditures is to treat them above line with an estimated reserve for replacement. Recall that before the advent of computers and spreadsheets, direct capitalization was the only feasible income approach to valuation. When capitalizing a single-year estimate of stabilized *NOI* into a value estimate, it is necessary for the analyst to deduct from rental income the expected annualized cost of nonrecurring capital expenditures. However, with the advent of spreadsheet programs and prepackaged software, the construction and estimation of multiperiod discounted cash flow models is feasible. Thus, instead of estimating an annual reserve, analysts may choose to make explicit forecasts of future capital expenditures.

5. Borrowing—that is, the use of "other people's money"—is also referred to as the use of financial leverage. If the overall return on the property exceeds the cost of debt, the use of leverage can significantly increase the rate of return investors earn on their invested equity. This expected magnification of return often induces investors to partially debt-finance even if they have the accumulated wealth to pay all cash for the property.

6. Net loan proceeds equal the face amount of the loan minus all costs associated with obtaining the mortgage. It can be thought of as the actual cash that the borrower nets from the lender at closing. Recall, however, that mortgage payments are based on the face value of the loan, not the net loan proceeds.

7. The investor does not get to pocket the net operating income of the property if the acquisition has been partially debt financed. Rather, the investor/borrower must pay the promised mortgage payment out of the property's *NOI*. Thus, BTCF better reflects the amount of cash the investor will net from the investment after servicing the debt, but before income taxes.

8. The internal rate of return (*IRR*) is the discount rate that equates the present value of the expected future benefits of an investment to the cost of the investment. Note that this implies another definition of the *IRR*—the discount rate that makes *NPV* equal to zero.

9. Three technical problems potentially associated with the use of the *IRR* as a final investment criterion are (1) the *IRR* implicitly assumes that cash flows are reinvested at the *IRR;* (2) ranking projects based on their going-in *IRR*s may produce a different ranking than the *NPV* criterion—and the *NPV* ranking is always correct; and (3) multiple *IRR* solutions are possible.

10. Increasing the amount of leverage will increase the calculated *IRR* if the unlevered (i.e. the zero percent *LTV*) *IRR* exceeds the effective borrowing cost. Leverage will increase the calculated *NPV* so long as the going-in *IRR* on equity exceeds the effective borrowing cost.

11. The majority of commercial properties in the United States are not purchased by individuals, but by multiple investors in the form of partnerships, limited liability companies, and other ownership entities. Thus, the property level cash inflows and outflows must be allocated to the various investors in order to calculate a particular investor's going-in *IRR* and *NPV.*

12. The analyst cannot simply apply an investor's tax rate to the estimated before-tax cash flows to calculate income tax liability in a given year because some cash expenditures that reduce *BTCF,* such as capital expenditures and the principal portion of mortgage payments, are not deductible in the cal-culation of taxable income from property operations. On the other hand, tax law allows investors to take deductions for several items that are not associated with actual cash expenses. In short, taxable income can vary significantly from *BTCF,* so the analyst cannot simply multiply the estimated *BTCF* by the investor's tax rate.

13. The appropriate after-tax discount rate should reflect the after-tax return the investor can earn on alternative taxable investments of similar risk. For example, if the investor views his or her opportunity cost of investing in a real estate project to be the 12 percent before-tax return expected on his or her current stock portfolio, what return is the investor giving up on an after-tax basis? If the cash flows produced by the stock investments would be taxed at a rate of 30 percent, then the investor is really giving up an 8.4 percent after-tax return [$8.4 = 12 \times (1 - 0.30)$] by investing in real estate instead of stocks.

14. Relative to class A properties, class B properties are more risky and/or are expected to produce smaller rental increases over time. Both effects reduce the amount a rational investor is willing to pay today per dollar of current net operating income. When values/prices fall relative to current net operating income, cap rates increase.

15. A major shortcoming of using ratios to make investment decisions is that they generally ignore cash flows beyond the first year of operations. Thus, unlike *NPV* and *IRR*, ratios are not able to capture the magnitude and timing of all expected future cash flows.

Additional Readings

Blair, Gwenda. *The Trumps: Three Generations That Built an Empire.* New York: Simon & Schuster, 2000.

Brueggeman, William B., and Jeffrey D. Fisher. *Real Estate Finance and Investments,* 11th ed. New York: McGraw-Hill, 2001.

Cook, W. B. *How to Pick Up Foreclosures: A Step-By-Step Guide for Getting Super Discounted Property before the Auction,* 2nd ed. Bridgewater, Nova Scotia; Lighthouse Publishing, 1997.

Cruikshank, J. L., and W. J. Poorvu. *The Real Estate Game: The Intelligent Guide to Decision-Making and Investment.* New York: Free Press, 1999.

Friedman, Jack P. *Keys to Investing in Real Estate.* Hauppauge, NY: Barron's Educational Series, 2000.

Gelter, D. M., and N. G. Miller. *Commercial Real Estate Analysis and Investments.* Cincinnati, OH: South-Western Publishing, 2000.

Greer, G. E., P. T. Kolbe, and M. T. Lush. *Investment Analysis for Real Estate Decisions,* 5th ed. Chicago: Dearborn Trade Publishing, March 2003.

Jaffe, Austin J., and C. F. Sirmans. *Fundamentals of Real Estate Investment,* 3rd ed. Upper Saddle River, NJ: Prentice Hall, 1995.

Kennedy, D., R. T. Kiyosaki, and G. Sutton. *Real Estate Loopholes: Secrets of Successful Real Estate Investing.* New York: Warner Books, 2003.

Shemin, R. *Secrets of a Millionaire Real Estate Investor.* Chicago: Dearborn Publishing, 2000.

Tanzer, M. *Real Estate Investments and How to Make Them,* 3rd ed. Old Tappan, NJ: Prentice Hall, 1997.

Tompos, A. W. *Analyzing Investment Properties,* 2nd ed. Cincinnati, OH: South-Western Publishing, 2001.

Enhancing Value *through* Ongoing Management

Learning Objectives

After reading this chapter you will be able to:

1. List five differences between the typical functions of property managers and asset managers.

2. Calculate the leasing commission to a broker, given the terms of the lease and the commission percentage.

3. Identify the optimal tenant mix in apartment properties and shopping centers.

4. List at least five elements of a typical commercial lease.

5. Perform a discounted cash flow analysis of a maintenance or repair decision, given the cost of the repair and the loss of income averted by the repair.

6. Describe specific steps managers must take to fulfill their fiduciary responsibility to their owners.

7. List three of the most prominent professional property manager designations.

8. Describe two functions of real estate asset managers that clearly distinguish their duties from stock and bond asset managers.

9. Explain why benchmarks are important in the evaluation of asset managers.

10. Describe the most recent trend in corporate real estate management.

Introduction

The previous chapter and, indeed, much of this book deals with investment valuation; that is, how do investors evaluate the desirability of potential investment opportunities? Every investment decision involves the same two elements: the initial costs and the value of the future benefits. Making good acquisition decisions is important because, by their nature, they cannot be undone easily or costlessly.

But what about after the property is acquired? The long-term ownership of real estate puts investors in the business of providing services to users of the space; the provision of these services is extremely management intensive. Owners or their agents must repeatedly make management decisions that affect the value of the property and the investors' return on equity. Ongoing asset management is particularly important to the success of commercial real estate investments. Unlike many publicly traded stock and bond investments, which can be bought and sold inexpensively in liquid markets, the going-in and going-out transaction costs of commercial real estate investments are high (as a proportion of asset value). As a result, internal rates of return are generally maximized by holding the assets for longer periods of time, often in excess of 10 years. In addition, the majority of the holding period return produced by investments in existing commercial properties comes from periodic net rental income, not from appreciation in the value of the property. Because of both factors—long holding periods and total returns generated primarily by the property's net operating income—commercial real estate returns are determined in no small part by how well the ongoing asset management function is performed.

Concept Check

17.1   Why is ongoing asset management so important in commercial real estate markets?

We classify ongoing, or continuing, management decisions into two categories: (1) those that have to do with the day-to-day operations of the property and (2) those that affect the physical, financial, or ownership structure of the property. **Property managers** are in charge of the day-to-day operations of the property. Typical functions include marketing the property to prospective tenants, selecting tenants, signing leases, collecting rent, maintaining the property, complying with all applicable landlord-tenant laws, maintaining tenant relations, and communicating with the property owner. Property management is the core function of real estate management. As we have stressed numerous times throughout the text, net operating income (*NOI*) is the fundamental determinant of property value and the activities of property managers have a significant impact on *NOI*.

The real estate industry applies the label **asset manager** to managers who are responsible for the decisions that affect the physical, financial, or ownership structure of the property. For example, an asset manager may recommend or be responsible for decisions involving rent adjustments, the timing and magnitude of required capital expenditures, refinancing, rehabilitation, modernization, expansion, conversion of the property to an alternative use, divestiture, or even abandonment. Asset managers typically work for institutional investors such as pension funds and life insurance companies, or for the managers of real estate syndications and real estate investment trusts (REITs). Asset managers work as liaisons between investors and their real estate investments and are involved in strategic decision making regarding the design of the investor's real estate portfolio, individual property purchases, and property dispositions. They may contract with property management firms on behalf of their investors, and make periodic reports to investors regarding the performance of their property portfolios.

Although the responsibilities of an asset manager may differ from one professional setting to the next, the asset manager occupies a higher position in the decision-making hierarchy than property managers. Asset managers typically have an MBA with a concentration in finance or real estate, a specialized MS or MA degree in real estate, or are well-trained undergraduates.

Owners as Managers

Sometimes property owners choose to perform both the property and asset manager functions themselves. This is frequently the case with smaller properties, especially those in which the owner occupies a portion of the space. Many successful real estate entrepreneurs began their careers by purchasing, renting, and managing small residential properties, such as single-family homes and duplexes. Most "get rich quick in real estate" formulas marketed on late night cable television and in hundreds of "how-to" books center around the acquisition of small residential properties which are currently being poorly managed. The get rich formulas then call for intensive management of the property, perhaps including rehabilitation or modernization of the structure. Once the owner/manager has "turned around" these underutilized (and presumably undervalued) properties, they are then held as investments or sold in the market for large profits—or at least that is the theory. In any case, however, successful implementation of the strategy requires intensive management of the property.

Although many small rental properties are owner managed, most apartment, office, and retail properties employ professional property managers. In some cases, a single third-party manager performs both the property and asset management functions listed above. This is most likely to occur when the manager has been hired to oversee a single property. However, as the size of the owner's portfolio increases, it is increasingly likely that he or she will employ an asset manager, who will in turn hire one or more property managers.

We begin by discussing the management functions typically performed by property managers. We then explore the importance and contents of property management agreements and briefly tour the professional associations that support the property management industry. We then turn our attention to asset management, including the decisions to improve, alter, demolish, and reuse property. We conclude with a brief introduction to the world of corporate real estate asset management.

Functions of a Property Manager

As we argued above, the successful ownership of commercial real estate requires that space be leased to tenants at competitive rental rates. Once leased, the property and tenants must be managed—the ownership of commercial real estate is management intensive. Even if the primary goal of the investor is to maximize his or her return on investment, the ownership of commercial real estate is not a passive activity; operating a rental property is a form of business that requires ongoing management. These management responsibilities include marketing the property, finding and selecting tenants, signing leases, collecting rents, complying with applicable landlord-tenant laws, maintaining tenant relations, communicating with the owner, and maintaining the premises. Each of these management functions is discussed below.

Marketing the Property

Leases are the engines that drive property values, but they are perishable assets. Most commercial space must therefore be marketed on a continual basis so that desirable replacement tenants can be found in a timely fashion as leases expire. The objective of the marketing plan should be to attract as many prospects as possible from the pool of possible tenants. There are many promotional tools available to managers to attract tenants, including newspaper advertising, other print media, signs, brochures, direct mail, cold calling, press releases, broadcast advertising, and the Internet. With a limited budget for marketing, choosing an effective combination of promotional tools is critically important to the success of any rental property. It requires a thorough knowledge of the property for lease and a clear understanding of the market for that type of space. This is where the experience and ability of the property manager can produce significant benefits for the owner.

Who Should Lease the Property? A critical question, directly related to the marketing of the property, is who should be primarily responsible for finding tenants and negotiating leases? In the case of apartment properties, the on-site manager or staff usually shows vacant apartments. Because standard form leases are used and relatively little negotiation occurs, the manager may handle the entire leasing process. Leasing is more complex, however, in the case of office buildings, shopping centers, industrial buildings, and other commercial space. The owner has three basic leasing options: use (1) an independent leasing broker, (2) an in-house leasing agent, or (3) the property manager. Each of these alternatives has advantages and disadvantages depending on the leasing situation.

Concept Check

17.2   For nonresidential property, the owner has three primary choices when selecting the person or entity to be responsible for leasing the property. What are these choices?

The use of a leasing broker working for a local or national brokerage firm can offer the services of an organization geared solely to leasing or, as is more frequently the case, to leasing and selling commercial property. Similar to the sale of real estate, owners enter into an agreement with a brokerage firm to lease the property. As an agent, the brokerage firm has a fiduciary responsibility (discussed at length in Chapter 19) to the owner. Leasing agents working for the broker function as subagents of the listing broker. Brokers or agents that specialize in helping tenants find suitable space are often referred to as tenant representatives, or **tenant reps.**

Concept Check

17.3   "Tenant reps" are licensed real estate brokers who specialize in what?

Brokers are usually paid on a commission basis at the time the lease is consummated. Generally, the commission is equal to a predetermined percentage of the face amount of the lease. The face amount of the lease, in turn, is equal to the total scheduled payments over the entire lease term. The percentage applied to the face value of the lease usually ranges from 3 to 5 percent. For example, if an office tenant signs a five-year lease with monthly payments of $10,000, and if the percentage commission rate is 4 percent, the leasing agent will be owed a $24,000 commission [$0.04 \times (\$10,000 \times 12 \times 5)$] when the lease is signed.

Concept Check

17.4   A tenant and owner just signed a three-year office property lease that calls for monthly payments of $6,500. The tenant was procured by a leasing agent. What commission is due the agent if the commission is specified to be 5 percent of the face value of the lease?

Leasing agents generally have but one responsibility: leasing space. Therefore, they are totally focused on that goal. Good leasing brokers are always in the market and aware of new tenants in the area, as well as the potential space needs of tenants currently signed to leases. A disadvantage is that the services of leasing agents are expensive. However, they operate in a very competitive market; therefore, what they are paid is some indication of the complexity and volatility of their job.

In contrast to leasing brokers, an in-house leasing agent is an employee of the property owner and is usually paid a salary plus a performance bonus. This person devotes 100 percent of his or her time to the owner's property and is thus able to become intimately familiar with it. The use of in-house leasing agents is common in the marketing of newly constructed shopping centers and, to some extent, multitenant office properties. The use of in-house agents is less likely to be observed in the marketing of existing buildings that are fully occupied.

Finally, the owner may simply use the property manager as the leasing agent. This is frequently the case with apartment properties. The obvious advantage of this strategy is that the property manager is already familiar with the property, the tenants, and the goals of the owners. A disadvantage is that the property manager may not have sufficient expertise to negotiate complex office, industrial, and shopping center leases.

Selecting Tenants

In leasing commercial property, care must be taken to assure that the prospect is willing and able to pay the rent. Tenant quality is a significant determinant of the income-producing ability of the property. Ideally, the property is of sufficient quality and desirability to allow some choice of tenants, thereby minimizing rental collection problems and other problems.

Creditworthiness. When leasing nonresidential properties, owners would prefer to rent exclusively to credit tenants. **Credit tenants** are companies whose general debt obligations are rated "investment grade" by one or more of the U.S. rating agencies, such as Standard and Poor's and Moody's. The rationale for preferring such companies as tenants is that, if these companies have been judged to be creditworthy enough to borrow at preferential rates in the U.S. bond market, they are very unlikely to default on a lease obligation. Certainly, credit tenants such as General Motors, Microsoft, Walgreens, and Bank of America are extremely desirable tenants, and such companies do occupy a significant amount of space in commercial properties. However, as we document in Chapter 15, the vast majority of commercial properties in the United States are small projects leased to small- and medium-size businesses that do not bring an investment-grade rating with them to the negotiating table.

Think for a moment about your favorite neighborhood shopping center. Although the center may be "anchored" by a prominent grocery store, such as a Publix or a Kroger, the majority of the stores are likely to be local service businesses such as restaurants, dry cleaners, and barbershops. To make risk even more difficult to assess, some of these businesses may be new, or at least new to the area. Nevertheless, the previous operations and credit quality of these lease applicants must be thoroughly investigated. The information to be verified and analyzed is usually supplied by the prospective tenant on the lease application. Financial records such as existing bank accounts and sources of income can be verified through a credit bureau. Evicting an undesirable tenant can be expensive but often can be avoided by careful screening of lease applications.

Concept Check

17.5   What is a credit tenant?

Residential Properties. Residential prospects may be asked to pay the fee for a credit check and they usually are required to leave a refundable deposit to reserve the unit until the credit check has been completed. When qualifying residential applicants, an applicant's past payment record, sources and amount of income, and level of indebtedness are the main concerns when evaluating rent-paying ability. Generally, the manager will contact the applicant's current landlord as well as past landlords, if possible, to collect additional information on the applicant's willingness and ability to pay. The ratio of prospective rent to gross monthly income is also a valuable screening tool; generally, this ratio should not exceed 30 percent. Overtime pay and earnings from a second job should not be used when calculating a prospect's income-to-rent ratio. The amount of prospective rent as a percentage of the applicant's current income, however, is not a definitive measure of his or her ability to pay rent. Household size and the number of family members employed are also important factors.

All else being equal, managers prefer to lease residential units to households whose prior history indicates a probability of a long-term occupancy. This is sometimes referred to in the industry as **permanence potential.** Reducing tenant turnover decreases vacancies as well as costs for repair, cleaning, and re-leasing.

Tenant Mix. In addition to creditworthy tenants, managers of multitenanted properties must also be concerned with tenant mix. **Tenant mix** "is the synergism created by the right grouping of tenants."[1] Synergism, simply stated, means that with the right mix of tenants "the whole is greater than the sum of its parts." In residential properties, this concept implies that managers should seek tenants with similar characteristics. This is why we frequently observe apartment complexes that cater to clienteles such as college students, young working professionals, or retirees. Mixing these groups is generally not a preferred strategy.

Concept Check

17.6   Provide an example of a suboptimal tenant mix in an apartment complex.

The appropriate mix of tenants is often even more important in commercial properties, especially shopping centers and, to some extent, office buildings. According to Alexander and Muhlebach, "the strength of the synergism created by several merchants in close proximity is dependent upon which merchants are grouped together." The correct mix in a shopping center "will maximize each tenant's sales potential and the center's rent potential."[2] A tenant unsuited to a location in a shopping center (e.g., a law firm) is not likely to attract customers for an adjoining men's clothing store. This explains why regional malls, for example, are tenanted primarily by fashion stores and gift shops. Someone shopping for a new suit at a department store is much more likely to stop at a nearby shoe store than a nearby bakery or drugstore. In contrast, neighborhood shopping centers anchored by a grocery store, which provides necessary food goods, will be occupied primarily by tenants who service the daily needs of those frequenting the grocer; for example, dry cleaners, beauty salons, liquor stores, and, of course, take-out Chinese restaurants!

Signing Leases

The last steps in a successful marketing and leasing program are negotiating and executing the lease. The lease is a contract between the owner (lessor) and the tenant (lessee) that transfers exclusive use and possession of the space to the tenant under the terms of the lease in return for rent or other consideration. Since the lease is the document that describes the rights and obligations of the owner and tenant, it is the primary determinant of a property's net rental income. In short, leases are the engines that drive property values.

---

1. Alan A. Alexander and Richard F. Muhlebach, *Managing and Leasing Commercial Properties,* Chicago: Institute of Real Estate Management of the National Association of Realtors, 1990), p. 292.

2. Ibid.

Property Management

The career of property manager requires good interpersonal and analytical skills and a fair amount of negotiating prowess. This career path usually starts as an on-site, assistant manager. Subsequent positions include becoming a property manager, a supervisor of several property managers, a regional manager for a large property management firm, or the owner of your own property management company. An additional attraction of a property management career is that it is a very good way to learn about many aspects of the commercial real estate industry; thus, property management can be a very good stepping-stone to jobs in development, investments and syndication, and investment management.

Source: Authors' research and Mariwyn Evans, *Opportunities in Real Estate Careers* (Chicago: VGM Career Books, 2002).

A 1997 survey by the Institute of Real Estate Management (IREM) found that 41 percent of its members worked for a property management company and 35 percent worked for a full-service real estate firm (meaning the firm probably offered a full set of brokerage services—sales and leasing—as well as property management services). Over 30 percent of those surveyed worked for a firm with 10 or fewer employees, although the typical management company had 11–20 employees. The survey found that members received an average total compensation of $86,366. Exhibit 17–1 lists the top national property managers.

Property management is a field that offers considerable opportunities for women. The IREM survey found that 34 percent of its members and 49 percent of its professional designation candidates were women.

An enforceable lease, at a minimum, must meet the usual requirements of a valid contract: competent parties, mutual agreement, lawful objective, and sufficient consideration. The additional elements of a typical commercial lease are:

1. A beginning and ending date, and any provisions relating to renewal and cancellation.
2. Identification of the property owner and tenant.
3. A legal description of the leased premises.
4. The rental terms, including the amount of rent to be paid each period, the date it is due, and the place of payment.
5. Signatures of the parties to the lease.

Rent is usually paid monthly and due on the first day of the month. Commercial leases with durations longer than one year often include clauses that specify the method of adjusting rental payments over time.

The *net* rental income generated by a lease is a function of the proportion of operating expenses paid by the tenant. In a **gross lease,** the tenant makes a single rental payment and the owner pays all of the property's operating expenses. In a **net lease,** the tenant is responsible for a clearly defined portion of operating expenses. Net leases are sometimes referred to as single net, double net, or triple net. In a single net lease, the tenant is responsible only for the payment of property taxes; in a double net (or net-net) lease, the tenant must pay (or reimburse the owner for) property taxes and fire and hazard insurance. In a triple net lease, the tenant is responsible for all of the property's operating expenses. However, be aware that these definitions of "netness" are often inadequate to describe the responsibilities of the owner and tenant in many situations, and extreme care must be taken by both sides to carefully read and negotiate the operating expense provisions of the lease.

Concept Check

17.7 Distinguish among gross, net, net-net, and triple net commercial leases.

If a lease does not state a specific purpose for which the property may be used, and if certain uses are not specifically disallowed by the lease, the tenant may use the property for

Exhibit 17-1 Some Top National Property Managers
(As of June 2003)

Trammell Crow Co. www.trammellcrow.com
  Manages 75,000 apartment units and 250 million sq. ft. of commercial space.

CB Richard Ellis Inc. www.cbrichardellis.com
  Full service firm that manages 850 million sq. ft. of commercial property.

Cushman & Wakefield Inc. www.cushmanwakefield.com
  Full service firm that manages 325 million sq. ft. of commercial property.

Pinnacle Realty Management Co. www.aof-ahc.com
  Apartment management firm with 115,000 units under management.

Jones Lang LaSalle Inc. www.joneslanglasalle.com
  Full service management firm with 725 million sq. ft. of commercial space under management.

any legal purpose. Generally, however, a particular use is specified by the lease and a contrary use may be cause for termination of the lease.

It is not uncommon to encounter a commercial lease of 100 pages or more containing lengthy clauses that detail the duties and responsibilities of the owner and the tenant. Each clause has a specific purpose and negotiated revisions must be analyzed to determine their effect on property operations, income, and value. Of particular importance are the responsibilities of both parties to pay specific operating expenses. Clearly, the property manager must understand the purpose of each clause. Because of their importance and complexity, and because their terms vary significantly across property types, we devote an entire chapter (21) to commercial leases and leasing strategy.

Collecting Rent

Most tenants pay their rent on time, but some will not. The property manager is responsible for the *prompt* collection of rent. Maintenance and repair expenditures, property taxes, utility bills, and other expenses of the property are paid out of rental income, and these expenses accumulate day to day. Thus, the timely collection of rental income is imperative. This undoubtedly explains why property management contracts tie the manager's compensation directly to rent collections.

Concept Check

17.8 What is the owner's motivation for tying the property manager's compensation to the amount of rental income collected?

Inevitably, some tenants will be delinquent with their rent payments. Managers should follow a strict and well-specified procedure for collecting overdue rent payments, as well as any applicable late fees. In the event the tenant does not become current on his or her lease payments, the manager may be forced to initiate eviction proceedings. Delinquency, collection, and eviction rights and procedures are always controlled by statute and the property manager must clearly understand both the laws and the common practices that govern these matters.[3]

3. For an expanded discussion of these issues, see Institute of Real Estate Management, *Principles of Real Estate Management,* 14th ed. (Chicago; IREM, 2001) chap. 8.

Complying with Landlord-Tenant Laws

State laws govern the landlord-tenant relationship and state courts are strict interpreters of commercial real estate lease agreements. So long as the lease document satisfies the requirements for a valid lease, federal and state law and the courts system are largely neutral with respect to the rights and obligations of commercial owners and tenants. This reflects the assumption that tenants occupying office buildings, shopping centers, and industrial buildings are competent businesspersons fully capable of representing their position in lease negotiations.

In sharp contrast, however, state legislators have been extremely proactive in recent years in passing legislation aimed at protecting the rights and interests of households in residential rental properties. Presumably, this reflects the concern that property owners have a significant information advantage relative to potential tenants and that, left unchecked, owners would use this advantage to negotiate one-sided lease agreements.

The apparent intent of state-based landlord-tenant laws is to "level the playing field" on which owners and households negotiate lease terms. This is accomplished by clearly spelling out the rights and obligations of both owners and tenants. For example, these laws typically:

- Limit the size of the security deposit an owner can require.
- Require an owner to maintain the premises in a suitable condition for living.
- Limit the ability of an owner to enter the premises except in cases of emergency.
- Specify how many days' notice must be given before a landlord can terminate the lease.
- Permit a tenant to recover any prepaid rent and security deposit whenever a lease is terminated because of the landlord's noncompliance.

Tenants also have certain rights and obligations under these state laws. For example, a tenant must not willfully damage the premises, must use the facilities in a reasonable manner, and must comply with local housing and building codes concerning trash disposal and keeping the premises clean and safe.[4]

Concept Check

17.9   Why do state lawmakers and courts seem more concerned with the welfare of apartment tenants than nonresidential tenants?

Maintaining Tenant Relations

Most owners of commercial real estate invested because of a profit motive—they had no burning desire to enter a service business. Nevertheless, owning and operating real estate *is* a service business and, similar to every other business, the customer must be kept satisfied. The existence of long-term leases does prevent tenants from immediately walking away if they become dissatisfied. However, leases expire and a high rate of turnover adds significantly to operating costs; tenant dissatisfaction can be very damaging to both current and future occupancy. Every communication with a tenant is an opportunity to build—or destroy—goodwill; thus successful property managers are invariably skilled communicators who deal with tenant requests respectfully, conscientiously, and promptly.

Communicating with Owners

In addition to performing the tasks specified by the management agreement, successful property managers are skilled at communicating with the owner, or with the owner's asset manager if the property manager does not report directly to the owner. Owners, or asset

---

4. Although state landlord-tenant laws vary, some uniformity is provided by the Uniform Residential Landlord and Tenant Act (URLTA), which has been adopted by 14 states. The lease provisions required by URLTA can be found at www.law.cornell.edu/topics/landlord_tenant.html.

managers acting on their behalf, are interested in the performance of the property, but some judgment on the part of the property manager may be involved in deciding the frequency of communications and the level of informational detail supplied to the owner. In addition to the standard reports on property performance (e.g., vacancies, turnover rates, collection losses), a good property manager will also offer his or her perspective and advice on decisions that ultimately rest with the asset manager or owner. For example, the property manager may feel strongly that a substantial rehabilitation of all or part of the premises is required to maximize the value of the property. If so, it is important that this recommendation be effectively communicated.

Repairing and Maintaining the Premises

Although tenants may be responsible through their lease agreements for maintaining interior walls and some of the heating and air-conditioning equipment, commercial properties are usually maintained, in large part, by the owner. Various levels of maintenance are required, depending on the type of property and the terms of the lease. The objective of maintenance and repair work, like every other aspect of property management, should be to meet the goals of the property owners, which usually center on maximization of the property's market value.

The property manager should develop a comprehensive maintenance program approved by the owner or the asset manager. This program should include a plan for replacing short-lived items, as well as anticipating nonrecurring capital expenditures, such as roof replacements and the repair and the resurfacing of parking lots. A comprehensive maintenance program that includes annual and seasonal inspections forces a manager to be proactive rather than reactive in dealing with potential problems. The ability to react promptly and effectively will produce long-term savings in operating costs.

A comprehensive maintenance program also aids with tenant retention. If tenants are satisfied with their environment, they will be less likely to vacate their space when their lease terms expire. This will reduce vacancies and lease turnover costs. Tenant safety is also an issue. Owners are responsible for fire prevention, sanitation, and security. If someone is injured as a result of neglected maintenance, the economic consequences can be severe— even if liability insurance is in place. Regular maintenance reduces potential hazards and provides a safer environment for everyone on the property.

Concept Check

17.10 List two benefits of a comprehensive maintenance program.

Maintenance and repair of the property is an ongoing process that can be separated into four principal categories.[5]

1. **Custodial maintenance** is the day-to-day cleaning and upkeep required to maintain value—and tenants.
2. **Corrective maintenance** is the ordinary repairs to a building and its equipment on a day-to-day basis. Examples include fixing a leaking roof, repairing a broken window, painting, stripping and refinishing a floor, and other routine tasks.
3. **Preventive maintenance** is a program of regular inspections and care to avert potential problems.
4. **Deferred maintenance** is ordinary maintenance not performed at the time a problem is detected.

By deferring maintenance and repairs, managers can boost the short-run *NOI* of the property. However, a deteriorated building is the end result of successive decisions over a longer period of time to forgo adequate maintenance and repairs. Thus, deferred maintenance will eventually diminish the use, occupancy, and value of the property.

5. See Institute of Real Estate Management, *Principles of Real Estate Management,* 14th ed. (Chicago: IREM, 2001), p. 140.

Maintenance as an Investment Decision. The decision to spend on maintenance and repairs is the most frequent ongoing investment decision property owners face. Ideally, maintenance and repairs should be performed over the investment holding period to the point where the present value of the outlays for maintenance and repair equals the present value of the loss of net income and reversion value averted over the holding period. Stated differently, expenditures for maintenance and repairs should be made at a level that maximizes the internal rate of return on equity over the investment holding period.

Example 17-1   Ongoing Maintenance Decisions

Consider the following simple example. If a property owner spends on average, $10,000 a year for 10 years on maintenance and repairs, her cash flow will be reduced annually by this amount. However, if she does not spend this amount, she will not be able to keep rents at market levels, vacancies will increase, the resale value of the property in 10 years will be lower, or all will occur. Assume that she would lose about $8,000 a year in net income and would realize a loss of $75,000 in lower property value at the time of sale. The maintenance and repair outlays represent a cost to the investor; the loss of net income and reversion value averted are the investor's gains. If 10 percent is the appropriate rate of discount, the investor concludes that the present value of the $10,000 annual maintenance and repair outlays, or $61,446, is less than the present value of the averted loss, or $78,073.[6]

In this example, the property is kept in a state of "normal" maintenance and repair over the investor's holding period. There would be a limit, however, to the amount that would be spent on maintenance and repair over the holding period. This limit would be reached when the present value of the cash outlays for maintenance and repair equals the present value of the loss averted.

Concept Check

17.11   Investment in maintenance can be thought of as positive or negative net present value "projects." What are the inflows associated with a maintenance expenditure? What are the outflows?

Although the above property example depicts the economics of the maintenance and repair decision, it is obvious that market imperfections and other characteristics of real estate as an investment prevent such precision in the maintenance and repair calculations and decision. Investors generally cannot accurately project the loss in net income or reversion value over the entire investment holding period. Moreover, the length of the investment holding period is itself an uncertain variable. The time horizon involved in the maintenance and repair decision is, as a practical matter, the foreseeable short run. An investor can recognize how the property compares with other properties in the market and can judge the level of maintenance and repair necessary to keep the property competitive in the short run.

The simple example also overlooks the requirement of larger expenditures on maintenance and repair as the building ages, to prevent a given loss in net income and reversion value. The onset of physical deterioration cannot be postponed indefinitely by maintenance and repairs, and both functional and locational obsolescence can render additional mainte-

---

6. The keystrokes for calculating the $61,446 present value of the $10,000 annual expenditure are: $N = 10$, $I = 10$, $PV = ?$, $PMT = 10,000$, and $FV = 0$. The present value of the reduction in annual income that is averted by the maintenance program is $49,157 and the calculator keystrokes are $N = 10$, $I = 10$, $PV = ?$, $PMT = 8,000$, and $FV = 0$. The present value of the reduction in reversion value that is averted is $28,916 and the calculator keystrokes are $N = 10$, $I = 10$, $PV = ?$, $PMT = 0$, and $FV = 75,000$. Thus, the total present value of the averted loss is $78,073 ($49,157 + $28,916).

17-1

Mold Worries Creep into Commercial Property Deals

Mold has become a huge legal and financial problem for homeowners and insurers, not to mention a significant health concern. Now it is turning into a big headache for commercial properties—from apartments to hotels to shopping centers.

Archstone-Smith, a major owner of apartments in 22 states, recently said it will have to spend close to $20 million to contend with a mold outbreak at one of its high-rise properties in southeast Florida. Hilton Hotels Corp. recently shut one of six towers that comprise the Hilton Hawaiian Village in Waikiki after investigators discovered mold. Hilton so far has written off $20 million for the cleanup. Mold is even affecting big real-estate transactions. In 2002 a buyer abandoned at the last minute a $30 million deal to purchase a 250-unit apartment complex in the Southwest because it had mold, according to Jones Lang LaSalle Inc., a Chicago real estate services firm that represented the apartments' owner. Real estate attorneys say mold inspections are increasingly becoming part of the industry's due diligence process before taking on a transaction.

The fungal growth, found in damp or wet conditions, has been blamed for a number of health problems, including breathing difficulties, headaches, nausea, gastrointestinal ailments, skin rashes, severe allergic reactions, and neurological damage. Mold-related expenses cost companies that underwrite homeowners' insurance $1.3 billion in 2001, a number that is expected to grow this year, says the Insurance Information Institute, a New York–based trade group.

Insurers and real estate professionals contend the recent attention about mold has been stoked in part by trial lawyers. Jones Lang LaSalle estimates that more than 9,000 claims of personal injury, property damage, or other loss caused by mold are pending in the nation's courts, and awards for property damage alone typically range from $200,000 to $400,000. Legislators across the country are calling for more research into mold. To complicate life even further for owners and managers, insurers have begun excluding mold coverage in some of their liability policies when customers renew. Some insurers have even started excluding mold from their property damage policies as well.

Source: Adapted from Ray A. Smith, "Mold Worries Creep into Property Deals," *The Wall Street Journal Online,* December 10, 2002.

Recenter.tamu.edu

Texas A&M University Real Estate Center website contains extensive information on mold with links to other sites.

www.naiop.org

National Association of Industrial and Office Properties website contains numerous mold resources for real estate professionals.

nance and repair expenditures infeasible. Decisions made early in the investment holding period to keep the property in good repair may not be made later when no amount of expenditure on maintenance and repair will overcome the debilitating effects of a neighborhood in transition to another land use or of a functionally obsolete heating system. However, a property manager can recognize when market conditions have changed to the extent that maintenance and repair can no longer prevent loss of net operating income.

An owner whose property is in a strong market position, where fewer services can be offered to tenants for the same dollar of rental income, and where the owner will not lose tenants if the property is undermaintained, can reduce maintenance and repairs without affecting the rental income or the value of the property. Such an owner faces a relatively inelastic demand, where the quantity of rental services demanded is not as responsive to price as it is in less desirable markets.[7]

Property Management Agreements

The above discussion of the functions of a property manager clearly indicates that the manager assumes the role of the owner in conducting the day-to-day operations of the property. Tenants often do not know who actually owns the property; thus, they often view the manager as the "landlord." This view is justified because the property manager can have the legal authority to advertise the property for lease, set rents, negotiate and sign leases, hire

---

7. Another take on the value of maintenance and repairs is that the payoff from these expenditures tends, in our opinion, to vary positively with the expected growth rate in market rents.

Exhibit 17-2 Contents of a Management Agreement

- Parties to the agreement
- Description of the property
- Term of the agreement
- Responsibilities of the manager
  - Financial management
  - Reports to ownership
  - General property management
- Obligations and responsibilities of the owner
  - Insurance
  - Operating and reserve fund
  - Liability
  - Legal and regulatory compliance
- Compensation for management services
- Provision for termination of agreement

Source: Institute of Real Estate Management, *Principles of Real Estate Management,* 14th ed. (Chicago: IREM 2001), p. 84.

and pay employees to operate and maintain the property, collect rents, and file all necessary reports to federal, state, and local agencies. Like the broker who operates on behalf of the seller under a listing agreement, the property manager works under a **management agreement** between the property owner and the property management firm. This agreement must be carefully prepared and negotiated and must clearly establish the manager's duties, authority, and compensation.

The typical contents of a management agreement are listed in Exhibit 17-2. With respect to financial management, the agreement should carefully specify any requirements on the part of the manager to maintain separate accounts for monies collected from tenants. The manager's authority to negotiate and execute lease contracts must be clarified, as should his or her authority to hire and fire employees and to enter into service contracts with vendors. Although the management agreement may be arranged for virtually any time period, many property managers prefer a three-year contract to provide adequate time to implement the agreed upon management plan.

Owners also have responsibilities which must be detailed in the management agreement. For example, the owner is usually required to provide the manager with all essential documents such as existing leases, insurance policies, and employment and service contracts. Of course, owners must provide the manager with adequate resources to fund operating and capital expenditures as they occur.

An important characteristic of the management contract is that it creates an **agency relationship** between the manager and owner. This agency relationship empowers the manager/agent to serve as the owner's fiduciary; thus the manager's words and actions are binding on the owner. The implications of this agency relationship are explored in more detail in the following Career Focus.

Concept Check

17.12 What type of relationship is created between the owner and the manager by the property management contract?

The typical management agreement requires the manager to obtain permission from the owner or, perhaps, from the asset manager before making any structural changes to the property. In short, the authority of the management agent is limited to the normal operating tasks of managing real estate. Rehabilitation, modernization, and conversion of the property to another use are covered by other express grants of authority by the owner. Generally, the management agreement can be terminated when the term of the agreement expires, by notice from either the owner or the managing agent according to contract provisions, or by mutual agreement.

Concept Check

17.13 The property management agreement usually conveys authority to the manager to perform what kinds of tasks?

Management Fees

The management agreement provides for a management fee, which is usually a percentage of effective gross income. Typically, the percentage is lower for larger properties because of the economies of scale associated with providing property management services. The fee usually ranges from 3 to 6 percent, although higher fees are not uncommon for smaller, more-management intensive, properties. It is usually appropriate for the manager to negotiate separate fees for leasing a new building, overseeing rehabilitation or remodeling projects, or any services provided by the manager that are not part of regular management duties.

As with any fiduciary relationship, property management contracts should be written to align as closely as possible the interests of the agent (manager) with those of the principal (owner). Generally, the owner's interests are best served by management decisions that maximize net operating income and the long-term value of the property. However, the typical property management fee is a percentage of *gross* rental income. This would seem to create an obvious agency problem in that the agreement does not give managers the incentives to control operating expenses while they attempt to increase rental income. For example, the manager may be tempted to overmaintain the property or to engage in costly and inefficient marketing and promotion strategies in an attempt to boost occupancy and gross rental income.

Concept Check

17.14 A direct result of "agency theory" is that owners would be better off if property management fees were based on net operating income. Why?

Basing the property management fee on net rental income i.e., (*NOI*) rather than effective gross income (*EGI*) would, in theory, better align the interests of the owner and manager. However, this arrangement is seldom observed. One explanation for basing the management fee on *EGI* is that the amount of collected rental income is easy to verify, whereas the calculation of "net" income is complicated by the requirement to fully account for all operating and capital expenses. Moreover, the use of net income presents other problems. For example, if management compensation is based on monthly *NOI*, the manager may have an incentive to delay discretionary spending for maintenance and repairs. Such a strategy may boost *NOI* in the short run, but could be harmful to the owner's interests in the longer run. In short, although there appears to be an incentive compatibility issue associated with the use of gross rental income as the basis for the management fee, the simplicity of its calculation is a clear advantage. In addition, professional property managers are keenly aware they will not be retained by the owner when the contract expires if they have not worked hard to maximize the net income of the property. The incentive to keep the owner's business is clearly a strong one.[8]

Professional Associations and Designations

College courses in property management are not widely available. Instead, most property managers learn the profession primarily by working in the industry. However, a number of professional and trade organizations exist in the field of property management. Of these, the Institute of Real Estate Management (IREM) and the Building Owners and Managers Association International (BOMA) are probably the best known. These and other groups provide both entry-level and continuing professional education for their members and work to enhance the status of professional property managers. To this end, IREM and BOMA promote standards of conduct and performance to which their members are required to adhere. Both of these groups offer professional designations which identify holders as having attained specific levels of competence or experience in property management.

IREM awards the certified property manager (CPM) designation to members who successfully complete a set of required courses in property management. IREM also offers the Accredited Resident Manager (ARM) designation for those individuals specializing in the management of apartment buildings. The Accredited Management Organization (AMO) designation is awarded to management companies that meet the necessary requirements for certification. IREM also publishes the *Journal of Property Management*, which contains a career opportunities (i.e., positions available) section.

BOMA provides educational programs aimed primarily at owners and managers of office buildings. Courses include design, operation and management, accounting, insurance, and law. BOMA confers the Real Property Administrator (RPA) designation to those who successfully complete the required course work and pass the accompanying comprehensive exam.

---

8. Readers familiar with principal-agent theory are aware that many agency problems can be solved, or at least mitigated, by repeated "games" between the principal and the agent. Each time a game is played—that is, each time a contract is signed and the parties perform—both sides reveal information about their intentions and abilities. This information can then be used by both sides to negotiate a "better" replacement contract. The problem with property management contracts is that, given their long-term nature, renegotiation does not frequently occur and therefore the contractual relationship cannot be refined. Note that agency problems are especially severe in real estate brokerage; property owners often have a severe information disadvantage *and* the game with the agent is usually "played" just once.

ccording to the Institute of Real Estate Management (IREM), typical employers of property managers include the following:

Who Hires Property Managers?

- *Development companies,* where staff manage company-owned properties and may take care of tasks from marketing to renovating properties.
- *Full-service real estate companies,* where property management may be one of several functions handled by the firm.
- *Property management firms,* which specialize in fee-based management services.

Source: Adapted from Mark Rowh, *Careers in Real Estate,* (Chicago: VGM Career Books, 2002), pp. 63–64.

- *Real estate investment trusts (REITs),* which have property management subsidiaries or employ property management firms.
- *Commercial banks,* who must manage properties obtained in foreclosure.
- *Corporations,* which often employ in-house staff of outside managers to oversee properties owned for conducting business.
- *Government agencies,* which employ managers for government housing programs as well as maintenance of the vast stock of government-owned real estate.
- *Insurance companies,* which often own real estate as part of their investment programs.
- *Other property owners and users,* including colleges and universities, the military, and nonprofit organizations.

Exhibit 17-3 Property Management—Just One Aspect of Asset Management

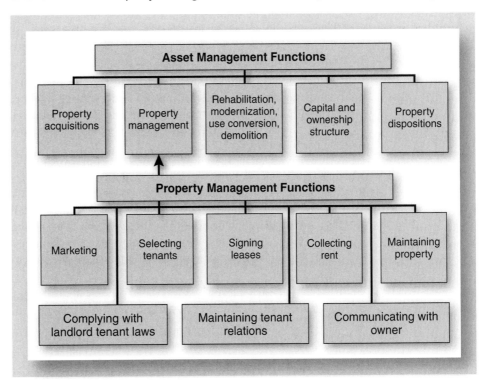

Asset Management

The typical functions of a property manager we have described are summarized in the bottom portion of Exhibit 17-3. These functions encompass the decisions associated with managing the property on a day-to-day basis. Although important, property management is but one of many asset management functions that must typically be performed during the investment holding period, as is depicted in the top portion of Exhibit 17-3. We first summarize the development of the real estate asset management profession, then briefly describe the major functions of an asset manager.

The Development of a Profession

Unlike the core function of property management, asset management, broadly defined, is a relatively new profession in the United States. Prior to the 1970s, institutional investors such as pension funds, life insurance companies, commercial banks, and savings and loan associations did not actively invest in commercial real estate (although many of these institutions were active mortgage lenders). The vast majority of commercial real estate assets were privately held by individuals, wealthy families, and private partnerships. These entities included a knowledgeable equity investor, usually the syndicator or general partner, who undertook the responsibilities of a "managing equity investor."

For a variety of reasons (see Chapter 15), including the perceived value of real estate as a portfolio risk diversifier, institutional investors began in the 1970s to invest in commercial real estate. Although the progress was slow, real estate was beginning to be viewed by many institutional investors as a legitimate asset class—in addition to stocks, corporate bonds, and U.S. Treasury securities—worthy of inclusion in a mixed-asset portfolio. With new investment funds flowing in from pension funds, commercial banks, life insurance companies, and foreign investors, the commercial real estate market, and the capital and financing vehicles used to feed the market, were transformed beyond recognition. For institutions to invest prudently in this transformed, but still highly regulated world, a new breed of third-party asset managers was required to take on, in a fiduciary capacity, the role of managing equity investor.

In summary, it is helpful to refer back to Exhibit 15-3 and the accompanying discussion. There we learned that approximately 90 percent of the total value of U.S. commercial real estate equity is held by noninstitutional investors, including sole proprietors, wealthy families, limited partnerships, and limited liability companies. The required asset management functions in these entities are typically carried out by the managing equity investor—that is, the general partner in a limited partnership or the managing partner in an LLC. Managing equity investors may, in turn, perform the property management duties themselves (if the entity's assets are relatively small and local), use a property management subsidiary of their firm (with approval from the investors), or hire an independent third-party property management firm.

What about the 10 percent of U.S. commercial real estate held by institutional investors? For the most part, these institutional investors are generally passive, preferring instead to hire nationally recognized asset managers—also called investment advisers—to invest in and manage commercial real estate on their behalf. Thus, the counterparts to the "managing equity investors" operating in the private entrepreneurial investment arena are "asset managers" and "investment advisers" operating in the institutional and securitized arena.[9] Some of the largest U.S. asset managers/advisers are listed in Exhibit 17-4.

Concept Check

17.15 What kinds of functions do asset managers operating in the institutional and securitized arena perform that are similar to those operating in the private entrepreneurial investment market?

Asset Management Functions

An important function performed by many asset managers is to find specific assets in which the owner/client can invest. Once assets have been identified for purchase, the manager must line up the financing, negotiate the acquisition price, and then oversee the due diligence and closing processes. These activities are required because whole assets are typi-

---

9. We attribute the term *managing equity investor* to S. S. Pyhrr, J. R. Cooper, L. E. Wofford, S. D. Kapplin, and P. D. Lapides, *Real Estate Investment: Strategy, Analysis, and Decisions,* 2nd ed. (New York: John Wiley, 1989).

Exhibit 17-4 Some Top Asset Managers/Investment Advisers
(as of July 2003)

	Assets Under Management 2003 (in $ billions)
Jones Lange LaSalle Inc. www.joneslanglasalle.com	$21
Lend Lease RE Investments Inc. www.lendleaserei.com	49
JP Morgan Fleming www.jpmorgan.com	22
Prudential RE Investors www.prudential.com	15
AEW Capital Management L.P. www.aew.com	7
RREEF www.rreef.com	19

Note: A detailed list of firms providing real estate advisory services to institutional clients can be found in the *Commercial Property Goldbook* published by *Commercial Property News* magazine.

cally traded in the private real estate market, so investors generally end up with a controlling ownership interest in the property. As Geltner and Miller pointed out, these functions distinguish real estate asset managers from those who manage stock and bond portfolios for investors.[10] Managers of stock portfolios, for example, do not have to go out and *find* assets in which to invest—thousand of stocks (and other securities) are traded on public exchanges. Nor do they have to negotiate purchase prices—securities are purchased at market value in the public exchanges.

Once commercial properties are acquired, the asset manager must monitor and control operating performance. Usually this will entail making periodic site visits, preparing long-term budgets for capital expenditures, and analyzing and, when necessary, appealing—property tax assessments. Although decisions on whether to improve the property are required less frequently than ongoing maintenance and repair decisions, asset managers must recognize and report to owners value-enhancing opportunities for rehabilitation, historic preservation, remodeling, modernization, or conversion to a more profitable use. If an improvement decision is implemented, the asset manager is usually responsible for overseeing the completion of the improvement.

Although most commercial mortgages cannot be costlessly prepaid if mortgage interest rates decline (see Chapter 14), the asset manager should periodically consider whether the owner's cost of capital could be reduced by changing the loan-to-value ratio or by otherwise altering the financing package. Asset managers also must be aware of opportunities to restructure the equity ownership of the project, perhaps through joint venture partnerships, joint venture buyout options, land sale-leasebacks, or complete sale-leasebacks. (These alternative financing structures are discussed in Chapter 14.) Finally, the asset manager must continually monitor local market conditions and assess whether or not to recommend the sale of the property.

Performance Evaluation and Compensation

During the early years of the real estate investment management industry, the 1970s and 1980s, managers were generally compensated based on the market value of assets under management. Typical asset management fees ranged from 0.5 to 1.5 percent of the value of managed assets.

Similar to the problems with basing a property manager's compensation on gross rental income, the policy of compensating asset managers based strictly on the value of the assets under management produces a clear agency problem. Generally, an owner's interests are

10. See David Geltner and Norman G. Miller, *Commercial Real Estate Analysis and Investments* (Cincinnati, OH: South-Western Publishing, 2001), p. 706.

best served by asset management decisions that maximize the investor's internal rate of return on the capital. However, if managers are compensated based on the value of the assets under management, they clearly have a primary incentive to find, acquire, and *hold* assets on behalf of the investor. The compensation scheme clearly offers no incentive for managers to *sell* properties, even if current conditions suggest they should, nor are they motivated to select for acquisition only those properties with the highest going-in internal rates of return.

To better align the interests of owners and managers, the industry has moved rapidly in the last decade to performance-based compensation for asset managers. With a performance-based management contract, a manager's fees are tied directly to the rate of return earned by investors on the portfolio of properties managed by the advisor.

If some or all of the manager's compensation is to be based on the return performance of the assets under management, the owner and manager must agree at the outset on the appropriate benchmark for evaluation. A **benchmark** is a reference point that can be used as a standard to quantify the relative performance of an asset manager (an agent) on behalf of an investor (a principal). There are three major functions of evaluation benchmarking in the private real estate investment industry:

1. To aid the communication between the principal and agent regarding investment objectives, strategy, and tactics.
2. To help align the interests of the principal and agent.
3. To evaluate the actual performance of the agent over the period of the management contract (typically 3 to 5 years).

Although the last of these three—performance evaluation—is typically thought of as *the* purpose of benchmarking, the first two are equally important.

Concept Check

17.16 Describe the traditional compensation scheme for asset managers and the incentive problem it creates.

---

www.ncreif.com

National Council of Real Estate Investment Fiduciaries.

www.nareit.com

National Association of Real Estate Investment Trusts.

www.wilshire.com/ Indexes/RealEstate

Wilshire Associates.

What return indexes can be used to evaluate the performance of the manager/adviser? If the manager has been hired by the owner to acquire and manage a portfolio of publicly traded real estate investment trusts (REITs), there are a number of potential benchmark REIT indexes from which to chose, including the various indexes and subindexes produced by the National Association of Real Estate Investment Trust (NAREIT) and Wilshire Associates (see Chapter 15). However, the majority of real estate investment advisers are employed by U.S. investors to acquire and manage portfolios of *privately* held and traded commercial real estate assets. In the private arena, the choice of benchmarks is limited in large part to the return indexes produced by the National Council of Real Estate Investment Fiduciaries (NCREIF), although the use of NCREIF indexes for benchmarking purposes has some significant limitations.[11]

A Closer Look at the Decision to Improve or Alter a Property

During the investment holding period, decisions to improve the structure are less frequent than the decision to maintain and repair it. In contrast to maintenance and repair expenditures, which are operating expenses, the improvement (alternation) decision involves a capital expenditure meant to increase the value of the structure. This increase in value can result from a larger net operating income, extending the building's remaining economic life, or changing the discount rate used to convert future income into present value.

---

11. For a detailed discussion of commercial real estate benchmarking, see David Geltner and David C. Ling, *Benchmarks & Index Needs in the U.S. Private Real Estate Investment Industry: Trying to Close the Gap* (Real Estate Research Institute Study for the Pension Real Estate Association, 2000).

An improvement to the structure can involve rehabilitation, historic preservation, re-modeling, modernization, conversion, or adaptive reuse. **Rehabilitation** is the restoration of a property to satisfactory condition without changing the floor plan, form, or style of the structure. Rehabilitation removes the effects of prolonged undermaintenance, and may in-volve painting, replacement of a roof, replastering, or replacement of deteriorated portions of the building.

Remodeling changes the floor plan, form, or style of a structure to correct functional or economic deficiencies. Remodeling may rearrange partitions to alter a floor plan, or it may replace obsolete electrical, plumbing, and heating systems. Remodeling may result in a conversion of the property from a use no longer suitable for the site to one that is com-petitive in the market. An **adaptive reuse** is a conversion in which the remodeling produces a creative reuse of the structure that is different from its original purpose. From an eco-nomic point of view, remodeling and substantive rehabilitation are positive actions that add value to the property. Maintenance and repair, on the other hand, are preventive measures undertaken to prevent a loss of value.

Capital improvements can affect rents, vacancy and collection losses, operating ex-penses, financing expenses, and the reversion value of the property at the end of the in-vestment holding period. Many improvement decisions will affect rents, in some cases be-cause after alteration the building will have more rentable area or because the quality of the services the building provides will have increased. Vacancy and collection losses also may be reduced if the improved property is more competitive in its market. Property tax pay-ments and insurance premiums may increase if the improvements increase the value of the property. Other expenses (e.g., utilities), can perhaps increase because the building is now larger, or decrease because of the greater efficiency of the improvement.

Capital improvements must be financed with additional debt, new equity, or both. In all likelihood, the equity *IRR* will be different following the improvement, perhaps because the new debt has different terms or because the loan-to-value ratio has been changed.

Example 17-2 MedFirst Office Building

An improvement should be undertaken only if the value added to the property at least equals the cost of the improvement. Consider, as an example, the MedFirst office building. MedFirst is a 10-year-old medical office building on a major traffic artery near downtown. Other small office buildings of fairly high quality occupy the area, and this usage is ex-pected to continue. The building contains 9,000 gross square feet and 7,650 square feet of net rentable area. Rental rates are currently $14 per square foot.

Exhibit 17-5 provides a "before and after" valuation analysis of a $130,000 rehabili-tation of the MedFirst building. Net operating income is expected to increase from $66,134 before rehabilitation to $79,726 after; this increase is the net result of higher rents, lower vacancy, a lower operating expense ratio, and lower capital expenditures. The market value of the MedFirst property is expected to be $995,844 after rehabilitation, a gain of $151,019. The gain in property value is compared with the cost of the improvements, which include material, labor, the contractor's profit, architect's fees, and an allowance for contingencies. Further, if undertaking the improvements prevented renting part or all of the structure for a period of time, the present value of the lost rental income should be included as a cost. The estimated total cost of the improvements to the Medfirst building is $130,000.

The value added ($151,019) exceeds the estimated cost of improvements ($130,000) by $21,019, which is about 16 percent of the cost of improvements. The uncertainty sur-rounding estimated rents, vacancy level, operating and capital expenditures, and the ex-pected costs of the improvements results in a need for this margin of safety of value added over cost. The investor contemplating this rehabilitation project would undertake it only if sufficient confidence existed in the factors influencing the postrehabilitation value and the total improvement cost.

Exhibit 17-5   Valuation of the Rehabilitation of MedFirst Office Building

	Before	**After**
Rent per sq. ft.	$14.00	$15.80
Net rentable area (sq. ft.)	7,650	7,650
Vacancy and collection losses	5%	3%
Operating expense ratio	30%	28%
Annual capital expenditures as a percent of effective gross income	5%	4%
Net operating income	$66,134	$79,726
Cap rate for building income	0.09	0.09
Market value of building	$734,825	$885,844
Site value (from market)	$110,000	$110,000
Total market value	$844,825	$995,844
Gain in value		$151,019
Cost of improvements		$130,000
Excess over cost		$ 21,019 (or 16%)

Tax Consequences. The basis for tax depreciation and the annual tax depreciation expense will be changed by rehabilitation, depending on the type of property and its use. In addition to a larger depreciation deduction, certain types of commercial real estate enjoy tax benefits intended to promote the continued use of existing structures. As will be discussed in Chapter 22, these additional tax benefits are available for renovation of commercial building (but not apartments) which have been in use for 50 or more years and for the preservation and rehabilitation of historic structures. Potential tax consequences are ignored in the above analysis, but should be included in the final analysis.

Demolition and Reuse

Casual inspection of any urban area will reveal demolitions of existing buildings. Sometimes the site is to be left vacant or perhaps put to an interim "taxpayer" use, such as a parking lot; at other times, another building is immediately constructed on the site. Demolition will occur only after the existing building has accumulated substantial physical deterioration and functional and locational obsolescence. In some instances, the building may have been abandoned at the time of demolition and removed only after the court found it to be a hazard to public health and safety. However, the removal of relatively new buildings for a replacement use can also sometimes be observed. Such demolitions may be the result of a "taking" for a public purpose (see Chapter 6), or they may reflect profit-motivated decisions in the private sector.

   The speed of reuse will depend upon the factors that affect the demand for land uses feasible at the given location and upon competition of alternative sites. At the time of reuse, the value of the site is determined by the new building, which is judged to be the highest and best use of the site. As discussed in Chapter 8, if an existing improvement already occupied the site, it no longer represented the highest and best use of the site.

   Reuse of an urban site occurs when the site value under the new structure is sufficient to permit acquisition of the site and existing building at market value and to pay the cost of demolition and preparation of the site for the new structure. The reuse must yield a competitive return on the required investment.

Managing Corporate Real Estate Assets

In Chapter 15 we estimated that non-real estate corporations own approximately $2 trillion in real estate. These real estate assets account for 25 to 40 percent of the total assets of

Industry Issues

17-2

Finding New Uses for Outdated Malls

Where do old malls go when they die? Nowhere, of course, and that's the problem. The nation's stock of regional malls was built mostly in the 1960s and 1970s, and an increasing number are becoming obsolete in terms of their size and location. Many are now too small and suburban growth has passed them by, leaving landlords and communities with bulky eyesores that have few apparent alternative uses and presenting a redevelopment problem that will dog suburban landscapes for years. In the summer of 2001, the International Council of Shopping Centers published a comprehensive inventory that put the number of fully functioning, two-anchor regional malls encompassing more than 400,000 square feet in the United States at about 1,100.

The redevelopment of the former Eastlake Square Mall in Tampa, Florida, might offer some lessons. Developed by the DeBartolo family in 1975, the one-million-square-foot property seemed like a reasonable bet, but before long it was eclipsed by competing developments that offered more attractive anchors than Eastlake's dowdy collection, which included now-defunct discount retailers Service Merchandise Co. and Montgomery Ward & Co. By 1994 the DeBartolos returned the property to its lender, a unit of John Hancock Financial Services Inc. The mall closed for good in 1996.

After much study and discussion, Divaris Real Estate, Tampa, a local developer, and HOK, a St. Louis-based design firm, proposed to convert the mall into a multitenant office campus. It took a lot of effort. Surprisingly, such a conversion hadn't been done before, and the Tampa-area brokerage community was far from convinced that major tenants would accept moving into an old mall, especially given its appearance at the time.

After much hand-wringing, Hancock committed $55 million to what was essentially a speculative office development—never a sure bet. The project, known as Netp@rk Tampa Bay, is still a work in progress but is now 70 percent leased and home to 3,000 employees. The HOK design has won praise for its open, airy look and interior "main street" that allows tenants of different companies to interact in common areas. The building also provides separate exterior entrances for convenience. The Eastlake conversion demonstrates that the nation's rapidly aging fleet of regional malls can find another useful life after economic death.

Source: Adapted from Dean Starkman, "Finding New Uses for Outdated Malls," *The Wall Street Journal Online,* March 12, 2003. www.realestatejournal.com.

---

large industrial firms.[12] Corporate real estate includes not only specialized production and storage facilities, but also retail outlets, industrial warehouses, and office buildings that contain space suitable and attractive to a broad range of potential users.

Despite the magnitude of their real estate holdings, non-real estate corporations have historically expended little effort to manage these assets effectively. A study in the early 1980s revealed that only 40 percent of U.S. corporations clearly and consistently evaluated the performance of their real estate assets and that only 20 percent compared the returns on their real estate assets to returns available on alternative assets. Instead, corporations have largely viewed real estate as a necessary evil, which requires the significant commitment of corporate capital for relatively long periods of time. Companies typically build up a real estate portfolio to meet the needs of their principal business activities. And, although firms may carefully examine the initial acquisitions of real estate assets, most spend little time thinking strategically about these assets once they have been added to the corporate balance sheet.

In recent years, many corporations have begun to pay increased attention to their real estate assets. Some now employ in-house corporate real estate and facilities management personal, while others rely primarily on asset management consultants to help them rethink and restructure their real estate holdings. Many of the same firms that supply asset and investment advisory services to institutional real estate investors also supply consulting and

---

12. This estimate come from M. J. Seiler, A. Chantrath, and J. R. Webb, "Real Estate Ownership and the Risk and Return to Stockholders," *Journal of Real Estate Research* 22, no. 1 (2001), pp. 199–212; and Y. Deng and J. Gyourko, "Real Estate Ownership by Non-Real Estate Firms: An Estimate of the Impact on Firm Returns," working paper, University of Pennsylvania, Wharton School of Business, 1999.

Many real estate professionals are employed by firms to provide in-house, site-selection, and development expertise. For example, firms like fast-food restaurants, convenience store franchisers, supermarkets, and retailers are prospective employers for corporate real estate specialists. Site selection and development work require knowledge of a firm's product, the demographics it serves, and the linkages the firm requires to its customers and suppliers. Site selection experts must understand urban growth patterns, transportation linkages, and market analysis. They must also be able to interpret the impact of zoning requirements, building codes, site frontage and visibility, topography, easements, drainage, utility services, and soils on a firm's site-choice decision. In addition, they need to be able to assess market values in order to negotiate reasonable purchase prices on behalf of their employer. Courses in appraisal, investment analysis, development, and urban planning will be beneficial to those who expect to pursue a career in corporate real estate.

Source: *Career Opportunities,* Washington State University, www.cbe.wsu.edu/~fire/real_estate

www.corenetglobal.com

Global Corporate Real Estate Network (CoreNet)—world's largest association for corporate real estate professionals.

management services to non-real estate companies. In addition, corporate real estate heads or consulting asset managers often deal with site analysis, buy versus lease decisions, acquisition and disposition, portfolio refinancing and sale leaseback arrangements, property tax appeals, and a host of facility management decisions.

Perhaps the most significant recent development in corporate real estate management has been the increased activity in the sale-leaseback and net-lease markets. Increasingly, corporations are recognizing that it is not always necessary to own a real estate asset to have control over its use. With leasing, corporate users can control and use properties without having to commit the resources necessary to own them. As a result, many corporate property owners are executing sale-leaseback transactions and then entering into (triple) net lease arrangements with the buyers of the property. With a sale-leaseback, corporate sellers can convert illiquid real estate assets into cash and the sale proceeds can then be plowed back into the main business and core assets of the company.

A few examples help to illustrate the trend. In 2001 Discount Auto Parts sold 101 of its stores for $62 million in an effort to free up capital for its core business operations. In 1999 Reader's Digest Association sold its Canary Wharf headquarters in London for $100 million and leased back space in the building. Blue Cross/Blue Shield of Illinois recently sold two of its office buildings, totaling 120,000 square feet, to a net lease investor while simultaneously signing a 10-year lease to occupy them. A spokesperson for the insurance company said that the motivation for the sale was that real estate wasn't a core asset. The increasing propensity of non-real estate companies to lease their real estate assets was further fueled by the economic downturn of the early 2000s. In a slowing economy, many companies needing to improve their balance sheets and free up capital for their core businesses executed sale-leaseback transactions.

If corporate America is discovering the benefits of sale-leaseback and net leases, who is taking the opposite side in these transactions? Interestingly, a broad range of investors, including pension funds, limited partnerships, and other investment opportunity funds, have come to regard net lease investments as one of the most stable and valuable property segments (see Explore the Web for a brief description of several net lease firms). Conferences have focused on "net lease" properties, players are suddenly commonplace, and other information on this segment of the commercial real estate industry is now readily available.[13]

13. See, for example, the *2003 Guide to Net Lease Players,* a supplement to *Commercial Property News,* VNU Business Publications, April 16, 2003.

Industry Issues

Corporate Tenants Paying Closer Attention to Their Real Estate

Corporate clients, faced with a volatile business climate, are paying much stricter attention to their real estate portfolio and demanding greater flexibility on everything from the length of leases to expansion rights to the number and location of the buildings they occupy. "There is reservation in corporate confidence as to what the long-term business viability is going to be or when growth will really happen," said Garry Weiss, senior VP and national director of integrated industrial solutions at First Industrial Realty Trust Inc., "so the greatest attribute that we can provide a corporate real estate director is to try to be a partner in their business and understand what they need." "We try to go in as a business partner and treat their portfolio as we would our own," said Pamela Zoellner, senior managing director at Cushman & Wakefield. For developers, closer partnership with their corporate clients means being flexible enough to respond to the distinct—and sometimes diametrically opposed—needs of each tenant.

"In the past few years, there has been an ever-increasing move by corporate America to finally take a really close look at their real estate portfolio," said J. Leonard Caldeira, managing principal at Staubach Midwest LLC. "One area that has definitely caught their attention is lease terms. Companies want to be able to react to changing demand, changing locations and the changing nature of their product very, very quickly. As a result, corporate tenants continue to push for shorter and shorter terms. Nobody wants a 10-year lease." Many tenants are reluctant to sign even five-year leases. And, as a result of their strong bargaining position, corporate users who might have formerly given developers business are hedging their futures with leases rather than investing scarce capital in a building. More and more now, they want to deploy their capital into their core businesses rather than owning the real estate.

Source: Adapted from Amy S. Choi, "Industry Stretches Amid Changing Tenant Needs," *The Wall Street Journal Online,* July 26, 2002.

Explore The Web

The following firms (as of July 2003) are significant players in the corporate sale-leaseback and net lease industry. After visiting their websites, answer the following questions for each firm:

1. Do they operate as a public corporation or as a private limited partnership or LLC?
2. Could you invest in the company?
3. What is their most significant recent transaction?
4. What is the composition of their portfolio by property type and by geographical location?

Capital Lease Funding (www.caplease.com)
An investment company whose primary focus is on the net lease marketplace. It has financed more than $2.5 billion worth of credit tenant loans covering more than 400 properties net-leased to more than 60 credit tenants.

W. P. Carey & Company (www.wpcarey.com)
An investment firm that provides capital to companies through corporate net lease or sale-leaseback structures. It owns or manages 500 properties throughout the United States and Europe.

Commercial Net Lease Realty (www.cnlreit.com)
CNL is a publicly traded REIT that owns, builds, and manages single-tenant, net leased properties nationwide.

U.S. Realty Advisors L.L.C. (www.usrealtyadvisors.com)
A private investment company that specializes in the acquisition of real estate properties net-leased to corporate and other credit tenants.

Concept Check

17.17 What is the most significant recent development in corporate real estate management?

Summary

Owners of income-producing real estate often seek the services of professional property managers. Unlike asset managers, property managers work at or near the site or sites they are managing. Property managers are responsible for negotiating leases, ensuring that tenants are satisfied, that rent is paid, and that rents reflect market conditions. Property managers work to maintain property values by skillfully selecting tenants, negotiating leases, dealing with tenant needs, accounting for income, managing operating expenses, and physically maintaining the property. Effective property managers must know their market—that is, know the competitive rental rate for their property and what concessions, if any, are being offered to tenants by direct competitors. They must be skilled at marketing their properties, understand laws regarding contractual relationships between landlords and tenants, be able to control operating expenses, and have a good understanding of property maintenance and repair issues. They are responsible to the owners, either directly or indirectly through an asset manager.

Although important, property management is one of many asset management functions that must typically be performed during the investment holding period. For example, asset managers are often charged with finding and acquiring properties on behalf of the owner/investor. Once the property is acquired, asset managers must hire and then oversee the property manager, unless the firm provides property management services. Asset managers must recognize and report to owners value-enhancing opportunities for rehabilitation, remodeling, modernization, or conversion of the property to a more profitable use. If such expenditures are undertaken, the asset manager is usually responsible for overseeing the completion of the improvements. Asset managers also may recommend changes in the capital or ownership structure, as well as recommend advantageous times to sell the property.

Key Terms

Adaptive reuse 459
Agency relationship 452
Asset manager 441
Benchmark 458
Corrective maintenance 449
Credit tenants 444

Custodial maintenance 449
Deferred maintenance 449
Gross lease 446
Management agreement 452
Net lease 446
Permanence potential 445

Preventive maintenance 449
Property managers 441
Rehabilitation 459
Remodeling 459
Tenant mix 445
Tenant reps 443

Test Questions

1. The Institute of Real Estate Management awards which of the following designations?
   a. REM.
   b. CPM.
   c. MAI.
   d. RPA.

2. A contractual relationship where an individual must act in the best interests of a principal when dealing with a third party is termed:
   a. An agency relationship.
   b. A lease arrangement.
   c. A tenant-landlord relationship.
   d. A joint venture contractual arrangement.

3. The requirement of a real estate manager to act in the best interests of the landlord when dealing with a tenant is termed:
   a. An associate responsibility
   b. Due process

   c. A fiduciary responsibility
   d. An implied responsibility of the employment contract.

4. Which of these is *not* typically a responsibility of a property manager?
   a. Marketing and leasing.
   b. Tenant relations.
   c. Maintenance programs.
   d. Income tax analysis.

5. Remodeling and rehabilitation:
   a. Are preventive measures undertaken to prevent a loss in value.
   b. Are most likely categorized as operating expenses.
   c. Are expected to add value to the property.
   d. Can usually be undertaken by the property manager without consulting the owner or asset manager.

www.mhhe.com/lingarcher1e

6. Both the owner and the manager may be better off if property management compensation were based on a percentage of the property's:
   a. Potential gross income.
   b. Effective gross income.
   c. Net operating income.
   d. Market value.

7. The following are necessary for a lease to be valid, except:
   a. Consideration.
   b. Written leases, if longer than one year, in most states.
   c. Tenant's contact phone number, or address, in the event of an emergency.
   d. Statements to the effect that the tenant agrees to lease the property for a specified period and that the owner and the tenant agree to the terms of the rent.

8. The lease in which the tenant pays real estate property taxes, insurance, and all utility and maintenance expenses is termed a(an):
   a. Net-net lease.
   b. Pass-through lease.
   c. Expenses lease.
   d. Triple-net lease.

9. Demolition of an existing property on an urban site will likely occur:
   a. After the building has been abandoned for a reasonable period of time.
   b. When the highest and best use of the property is a tax-payer use, such as a parking lot or recreational park.
   c. When the site value, assuming a new use, exceeds the value of the site under its existing use, plus the cost of demolition.
   d. When the site value, under its existing use, exceeds the cost of demolition.

10. For non-real estate corporations, which of the following is not a potential advantage of a real estate sale-leaseback?
    a. The firm can convert an illiquid asset into cash.
    b. More of the firm's capital can be invested in its core business.
    c. The firm benefits from property appreciation that occurs after the sale-leaseback.
    d. The firm may reduce its overall cost of capital.

Study Questions

1. An investor purchased a property with an equity investment of $100,000 and an $800,000 mortgage. She has held the property for five years, and the mortgage now has a balance of $750,000. The market value of her property is estimated to be $950,000. What is her present equity investment?

2. What should be included as costs to be matched by value added after rehabilitation?

3. In what ways are the maintenance and repair decision and the rehabilitation decision similar? How do they differ?

4. What factors can change after rehabilitation of a property to produce a higher "after" value than "before" value?

5. What does the property management agreement accomplish?

6. How does routine maintenance and repair affect a property's performance?

7. Define *deferred maintenance* and list some examples.

8. How is the financial compensation for property managers usually determined? What "agency" problem does this seem to create?

9. Why is the tenant mix critically important to the performance of shopping center investments?

10. In the real estate asset management/investment advisory business, why has performance-based management replaced, or at least supplemented, the "traditional" scheme for compensating managers?

11. In the context of asset management agreements in the private commercial real estate industry, what is a benchmark index? What is the most typical benchmark index?

12. With respect to complying with applicable landlord-tenant laws, would you rather be managing an apartment complex or an office building? Explain.

Explore The Web

Landlord-tenant law governs the rental of commercial and residential property. It is composed primarily of state statutory and common law. A number of states have based their statutory law on the Uniform Residential Landlord and Tenant Act (URLTA). Cornell University Law School maintains a website (www.law.cornell.edu/topics/landlord_tenant.html) that contains useful information on landlord-tenant laws along with links to federal and state legislative reference materials. Visit the website and read the responsibilities of both landlord and tenants under URLTA.

www.mhhe.com/lingarcher1e

Solutions to Concept Checks

1. Ongoing asset management is so important in commercial real estate markets because the ownership of commercial real estate is characterized by long holding periods, which requires a prolonged period of ongoing management. Also, a significant portion of the total return on real estate investment usually comes in the form of periodic net rental income, not appreciation in property value. The maximization of periodic income requires significant management effort.

2. The owner has three basic choices for leasing nonresidential property: use an independent leasing agent/broker, use an employee, or use the property manager. Each has advantages and disadvantages.

3. Tenant reps are licensed real estate brokers who specialize in helping tenants find suitable rental space.

4. The leasing commission is $11,700 ($6,500 \times 12 \times 3) \times 0.05$.

5. Credit tenants are large companies whose publicly traded debt has been rated "investment grade" by one or more of the independent rating agencies.

6. An example of a suboptimal tenant mix in an apartment complex is a mixture of young families with children and retired couples without children.

7. In a gross commercial lease, the landlord is responsible for all operating expenses. In a net lease, the tenant picks up responsibility for property taxes, and in a net-net lease the tenant pays both property taxes and insurance. In a triple net lease, the tenant pays all operating expenses.

8. All operating expenses for which the owner is responsible are paid out of the property's rental income. Thus, owners have an incentive to make sure the property's rental income is maximized. Tying the property manager's compensation to rent collections helps ensure that rental income is maximized.

9. State lawmakers and courts seem more concerned over the welfare of apartment tenants than commercial tenants because apartment seekers are assumed to be in the market infrequently; thus, it is assumed that knowledgeable apartment owners and managers have a significant informational advantage over prospective tenants. In contrast, commercial tenants are assumed to be fully capable of negotiating with commercial owners.

10. A written comprehensive maintenance program forces a manager to be proactive in planning for and dealing with required maintenance expenditures. This preparedness increases the ability of the manager to react quickly and effectively which, in turn, produces cost savings and satisfied tenants.

11. The inflows associated with an investment in maintenance are some combination of: increased rents, decreased vacancies, and higher future sale prices. The outflow is the up-front cost of the maintenance expenditure.

12. A property management contract creates an agency relationship, which establishes a fiduciary responsibility on the part of the manager to act in the best interests of the owner.

13. The authority of property managers is usually limited to the normal day-to-day task of operating the property. Permission of the owner or the asset manager, if the latter is a different entity than the property manager, is typically required for capital expenditures, especially those that entail significant rehabilitation, modernization, or expansion of the property.

14. Owners would seem better off if property management fees are based on net operating income because when such fees are based on gross rental income, the manager has an incentive to maximize occupancy and rental income, perhaps with insufficient regard for limiting operating expenses. In contrast, net operating income is the property's fundamental determinant of value; thus, if the manager is given an incentive to maximize it, the incentives of the owner and the manager would seem to be aligned.

15. Asset managers perform tasks in the institutional and securitized arena that are similar to those of managing equity investors.

16. Traditionally, asset management fees were based strictly on the market value of assets under management. This provided an incentive for managers to acquire and hold properties with insufficient regard for the purchase price and to continue to hold properties even if the interests of the owner would be best served by disposing of the asset.

17. The most significant development in corporate real estate management is the increased propensity of non-real estate firms to sell their real estate assets, redeploy the capital back into the main business of the company, and then lease the property back on a long-term basis to assure the company of its use and control.

Additional Readings

Baird, F. M.; R. C. Kyle, and M. S. Spodek. *Property Management,* 6th ed. Chicago: Real Estate Education Company, 1999.

Evans, M., and M. B. Simmons. *Opportunities in Property Management Careers.* New York: McGraw-Hill/Contemporary Books, 2000.

Income Expense Analysis: Conventional Apartments 2002. Chicago: Institute of Real Estate Management, 2002.

Income Expense Analysis: Office Buildings 2002. Chicago: Institute of Real Estate Management, 2002.

McLean, A. J. *Buying and Managing Residential Real Estate.* New York: McGraw-Hill, 1989.

Portman, J., and M. Stewart. *Every Tenant's Legal Guide,* 3rd ed. Berkeley, CA: Nolo Press, December 2002.

Robinson, L. *Landlording: A Handy Manual for Scrupulous Landlords and Landladies Who Do It Themselves,* 9th ed. Southbend, IN: Express, 2001.

part six

Acquiring *and* Disposing *of* Ownership Interests

OUTLINE

Conveying Real Property Interests

Learning Objectives

After reading this chapter you will be able to:

1. State three ways that a deed differs from normal business contracts.

2. Distinguish these clauses of a deed: words of conveyance, habendum clause, and exceptions and reservations; and state the importance of "delivery."

3. Distinguish between these deeds by the covenants they contain and when each deed is used: general warranty, special warranty, bargain and sale, quitclaim.

4. List four examples of involuntary conveyance of property with a deed.

5. List two voluntary and two involuntary transfers of property without a deed.

6. State the effect of the Statute of Frauds, of recording statutes, of constructive notice, and actual notice on conveyance of real estate.

7. State two reasons why determining title in real estate requires a title search.

8. Identify and distinguish two forms of evidence of title.

9. List and distinguish three "legal" descriptions of land, and be able to identify and interpret each.

Introduction

The conveyance of real estate interests is uniquely complicated for three reasons:

1. Real property is a complex bundle of rights, as we have observed in Chapter 4, and the interests must be described with care.
2. Since land and rights to land are enduring, transactions long ago affect the bundle of rights conveyable to a buyer today.
3. Since all land parcels adjoin other parcels, any error in the description of land represents a loss to some owner. Therefore methods of describing land must be very accurate.

Much is at stake in real property conveyance. If the transfer is flawed by being unclear or uncertain, the property can lose much of its value because buyers cannot be sure what they would get. This risk of defective transfer has compelled our legal system to create unique arrangements for the conveyance of real property. It has evolved special concepts, special documents, special legal procedures, and even special government institutions to address the unique challenges involved. In this chapter we tour the distinctive aspects of real property conveyance.

Concept Check

18.1   List the three features of real property that introduce special challenges for the orderly transfer of ownership.

Deeds are the primary means of conveying interests in real property. They are a special form of contract, distinguished by a group of clauses that determine the exact property interest being conveyed. Deeds vary in "quality" by the strength of covenants (i.e., promises) they contain. Under some circumstances, however, property can transfer to a new owner without a deed and even with no explicit document at all.

No deed or other document can convey rights that a person does not have. Thus, recording statutes create a system of publicly recorded documents that provide "constructive notice" of real property transfers. From these documents, and from inspection of the property, "evidence of title" can be derived. An important element of all property records is an accurate description of the land. Only three methods of description are acceptable in modern practice for this purpose.

Deeds

A **deed** is a special form of written contract used to convey a permanent interest in real property. It had its origin in England in 1677, when Parliament passed the "Statute for the Prevention of Frauds and Perjuries" which required, for the first time, that conveyances of title to real property be in writing.

A deed can convey a wide variety of permanent real property interests. Depending on its wording, it can convey the full fee simple absolute or a lesser interest such as a life estate, a conditional fee, or an easement (see Chapter 4). Through restrictive clauses called deed restrictions, the deed also may "carve out" reductions in the rights conveyed. Similarly, the deed also can carve out easements. For example, the deed can withhold mineral rights, timber rights, or water rights, implying an easement of access to pursue these claims. Other easements that may be retained could be for access to adjacent property of the seller, or an easement in gross for a variety of commercial uses.

Concept Check

18.2   What is a deed a special form of? What is its purpose?

Requirements of a Deed

While deeds are not restricted to a particular physical form, all deeds contain a number of elements:

1. Grantor (with signature) and grantee
2. Recital of consideration
3. Words of conveyance
4. Covenants

5. Habendum clause
6. Exceptions and reservations clause
7. Description of land
8. Acknowledgment
9. Delivery

Grantor and Grantee. The person or entity conveying the real property interest is the **grantor,** while the recipient is the **grantee.** Unlike most contracts in which both parties must be legally competent and of legal majority age, only the grantor must meet these conditions for a deed. In principle, the grantee would not even need to exist at the time of conveyance. For example, a grantor technically could convey property to a firstborn grandchild. As long as there is no ambiguity about the arrival of the child, the deed should be effective (if inadvisable).

Concept Check

18.3   In a normal contract _____ must be legally competent, whereas in a deed _____ must be legally competent.

Recital of Consideration. Unlike normal "in-progress" (i.e., executory) contracts that require mutual obligations between parties and future performance, consideration is not important to a valid deed. When a grantor conveys property, the event is done, and details of the grantee's financial obligation to the grantor are spelled out elsewhere. Still, it is traditional to have a statement of consideration in deeds, and some states actually require it. However, it is not necessary to state the true consideration. A statement such as "for ten dollars and other good and valuable consideration" is often used.

Words of Conveyance. Early in the deed will be words such as "does hereby grant, bargain, sell, and convey unto. . ." These **words of conveyance** serve two main purposes. First, they assure that the grantor clearly intends to convey an interest in real property. Second, they indicate the type of deed offered by the grantor. For example, either the words above or the words "convey and warrant" generally are taken to indicate a general warranty deed, while the words "convey and quitclaim" indicate a quitclaim deed. (See the discussion of types of deeds in the next section.) The practical message from these subtleties is that a competent legal professional always should prepare words of conveyance.

Covenants. The covenants in a deed are the most important differences among types of deeds, as discussed below. **Covenants** are legally binding promises for which the grantor becomes liable; that is, if the promises prove to be false, the grantee can sue for damages. The three normal covenants are:[1]

1. **Covenant of seizin**—a promise that the grantor truly has good title, and that they have the right to convey it.
2. **Covenant against encumbrances**—a promise that the property is not encumbered with liens, easements, or other such limitations except as noted in the deed.
3. **Covenant of quiet enjoyment**—a promise that the property will not be claimed by someone with a better claim to title.

Concept Check

18.4   What are the three covenants that distinguish the "quality" of deeds? What does each promise?

---

1. The common law tradition provided for six covenants. In modern practice, they have been reduced to the three discussed.

Habendum Clause. The **habendum clause** defines or limits the type of interest being conveyed. The legal tradition recognizes certain words and phrases as signals of various real property interests. For example, in the wording "to John Smith and to his heirs and assigns forever," the words "to his heirs and assigns forever" are regarded as distinguishing a fee simple interest from a life estate. Similarly, the words "to John Smith for use in growing timber" may be interpreted as conveyance of a timber easement rather than a fee simple absolute interest. Adding the words "so long as" is likely to be interpreted in a court as a reverter clause, and the estate conveyed as a conditional fee (see Chapter 4 for conditional fee and reverter). Since the court must interpret what is written rather than what the grantor later claims he or she intended, it is again critical that this wording be drafted under supervision of a competent legal professional.

Concept Check

18.5   The type of deed is determined in the _Words of Conveyance_ by certain traditional phrases. The nature of the property interest being conveyed is determined by wording of the _Habendum_ clause.

Exceptions and Reservations Clause. An **exceptions and reservations clause** can contain a wide variety of limits on the property interest conveyed. This clause may contain any "deed restriction" the grantor wishes to impose on the use of the property. Here the grantor may carve out mineral rights, timber rights, water rights, or a variety of easements.

Description of Land. The important requirement for the land description is that it be unambiguous. Some traditional methods of property description are ill advised at best, even though they may work in most cases. Street addresses, for example, can be ambiguous in older, transitional, or nonresidential urban neighborhoods where use of an address may have subtly changed over time. A tax parcel number is convenient, but can be erroneous. A very old method of land description is by monuments, or prominent features of the land, such as reference to bends in rivers, large rocks, ridges, and forks in roads. But over a long period of time even prominent features of the land can change. In modern practice, three methods have been deemed sufficiently accurate and durable to be accorded special favor for use in legal documents. These "legal descriptions" are metes and bounds, subdivision plat lot and block number, and government rectangular survey. They are explained later in the chapter.

Concept Check

18.6   Any property interest not being conveyed to the grantee is stated in what clause?

Concept Check

18.7   Name three acceptable methods of land description for deeds and other public records.

Acknowledgment. The purpose of **acknowledgment** is to confirm that the deed is, in fact, the intention and action of the grantor. It is accomplished by having the grantor's signature notarized, or the equivalent. In some states, witnesses also must sign the deed, attesting to the grantor's signature. While acknowledgment is not always required to make a deed valid (i.e., enforceable), it is required for a deed to be placed in public records.

Explore The Web

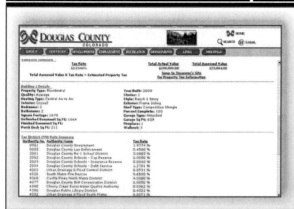

Most local property tax assessment authorities have made their records available on the Web. If you know the address or owner's name, you probably can locate the property in the local (county) property records over the Internet. Select a property of interest to you, anywhere in the United States. Locate the local tax assessor's website and see what information you can find for the property. On the left is a typical example of the information about a residence that is available from a county property tax assessor website.

Delivery.   A deed must be "delivered" to be valid. **Delivery** refers to an observable, verifiable intent that the deed is to be given to the grantee. Normally, this is accomplished when the grantor hands the deed to the grantee at closing. However, it also may occur through third parties, such as the attorney of either party. Delivery may fail to occur even if a deed is handed to the person named as grantee. For example, suppose the owner of real property prepares a deed and places it in a safe-deposit box (or desk drawer). Then someone, perhaps a relative, finds the deed and hands it to the person named as grantee. Or suppose an owner prepares a deed and gives it to his or her attorney, without instructions to deliver it, but the attorney gives it to the named grantee. In neither of these cases did legal delivery take place, and neither deed is valid.

Concept Check

18.8   What does delivery of a deed refer to with regard to the grantee?

Types of Deeds

No deed can convey what a grantor does not possess. There are several ways that a deed can be "empty." Property identified in a current deed might have been conveyed by the grantor at an earlier time by intention, making the current deed fraudulent. Also, the property may have been conveyed by mistake, or by one of several involuntary conveyances that we discuss below. Further, the grantor may unwittingly have failed to receive the rights to begin with, perhaps through a deed that was never successfully delivered. In all of these cases, it is beyond the power of the would-be grantor to convey the property anew. Someone else now holds the rights who is not bound to give them up.

Although deeds can only deliver what a grantor actually owns, they still can vary in "quality." Below are five types of deeds that appear in common practice. The main difference between them is the number of covenants for which the grantor is liable if the title turns out to be defective. Additional differences are in the prevailing usage of each type, and how that affects presumptions about title.

General Warranty Deed.   The **general warranty deed** includes the covenant of seizin, the covenant of no encumbrances, and the covenant of quiet enjoyment. In short, it contains the full set of legal promises the grantor can make. Thus, it is considered the "highest-quality" deed and affords the maximum basis for suit by the grantee in case the title is defective.

Special Warranty Deed. The **special warranty deed** is identical to the general warranty deed, except that it limits the time of the covenant of encumbrances to the grantor's ownership. That is, the grantor asserts only that he or she has created no undisclosed encumbrances during ownership, but asserts nothing about encumbrances from previous owners. Conveying title using a special warranty deed does not imply questions about the validity of the deed. In that sense, the special warranty deed is a "quality" deed.

Deed of Bargain and Sale. The **deed of bargain and sale** has none of the covenants of a warranty deed. Nevertheless, it purports to convey the real property, and appears to imply claim to ownership. It commonly is used by businesses to convey property because, while implying ownership, it commits the business to no additional covenants which are sources of liability.

Quitclaim Deed. The **quitclaim deed** has none of the covenants of the warranty deed. Also, its words of conveyance read something like "I . . . hereby quitclaim . . ." as opposed to "I . . . hereby grant or convey . . ." Thus, a quitclaim deed is worded to imply no claim to title, only to convey what interest the grantor actually has. Courts therefore regard a quitclaim deed as a questionable conveyance of title. Its very use may create a "cloud" on the title that must be cleared in order to obtain a fully **marketable title**—one that is free of reasonable doubt.[2]

A primary use of the quitclaim deed is to extinguish ambiguous interests in a property as a means of removing clouds or threats to a marketable title. The title to a property may be clouded, for example, by a defective release of dower or elective share rights, or it may be clouded by disputes stemming from divorce proceedings. In such cases, restoring a marketable or clear title may require negotiating with the person with the questionable claim to release it through a quitclaim deed. The quitclaim deed also may be used by a landowner, perhaps a developer to **dedicate** (i.e., to convey) certain lands of a subdivision to the local government.

Judicial Deeds and Trustee's Deeds. The **judicial deed,** sometimes called an officer's deed or sheriff's deed, is one issued as a result of court-ordered proceedings. It may include deeds issued by administrators of condemnation proceedings or administrators of foreclosure sales. A **trustee's deed** is issued by the trustee in a court-supervised disposition of property—for example, by an executor and administrator of an estate, a guardian of a minor, a bankruptcy trustee, or an attorney in divorce proceedings. The quality of all these deeds may depend on the proceeding involved. In foreclosure sales, particularly, there are complex and demanding notification requirements to assure that all parties with a legal interest in the property are given the opportunity to defend their interest. It is not infrequent that the notification process is flawed, leaving some latent claim to title "alive" following the sale and issuance of a deed.

The array of deeds has implications for real estate investment and transactions. When a property can be acquired only through a relatively weak deed such as a quitclaim deed or judicial deed from foreclosure, the grantee may need to gain additional assurance that the property title is safe. In many conveyances with a trustee's deed, the circumstances probably imply an especially strong need for title insurance (discussed in a later section) as both buyer protection and assurance of good title.[3] Title insurance will defend and indemnify the grantee against attack on the title. In addition, if a question arises concerning marketable title at subsequent sale of the property, the insurance normally will compensate for any legal costs in curing the problem.

2. More specifically, marketable title is a claim to title that "reasonable persons," knowing the evidence of ownership, would regard as free from reasonable doubt.

3. A commitment from a title insurer has two benefits. It implies that the insurer regards the title as having low risk, and it provides indemnification should a threat to title actually occur.

Concept Check

18.9   What is the highest-quality deed?
       What deed do businesses often use to convey real estate?
       What deed is used mainly to relinquish ambiguous or conflicting claims?

Modes of Conveyance of Real Property

While the vast majority of conveyances of real property are private grants through a deed, there are other modes of transfer. Some of these, as suggested before, may result in a less than marketable title. Some conveyances occur in the absence of any kind of document. We next survey the variety of these modes.

Voluntary Conveyance by a Deed

The great majority of real property conveyances are voluntary. Among these, most are private transfers from one owner to another. The transfer may result from a sale and purchase, a gift, or an exchange. In these cases the transfer usually is by a warranty, special warranty, or bargain and sale deed. One exception is voluntary conveyance of public property by a government to a private citizen. This kind of conveyance is accomplished by a document known as a **patent,** and the interest conveyed also is referred to as a patent. An important point about all of these voluntary conveyances is that, typically, they are legally simple, especially when the deed is a "quality deed," and there is little risk of the title becoming clouded (i.e., unmarketable) by the transfer.

Involuntary Conveyance by a Deed

Several kinds of conveyances result from events beyond control of the grantor. These include probate proceedings to settle the grantor's estate, sale of property in bankruptcy proceedings, divorce settlement, condemnation proceedings, and foreclosure. We review each of these below:

Probate. At the death of a property owner, the property will convey in one of two modes: **testate**—in accordance with a will, or **intestate**—without a will. Either way, state laws of **probate** where the property is located will govern the disposition procedure. The final conveyance of property in the probate process is by either a judicial deed or a trustee's deed. An increasing number of states have adopted some version of the Uniform Probate Code (UPC), thus providing increasingly uniform terminology and standards for probate. Under the UPC, the decedent will have a "personal representative" who is responsible for administration of the procedure. If a will dictates the distribution of the decedent's real property, the property is said to be **devised,** or conveyed by devise. If there is no will, the property is conveyed by the **law of descent.** The law of descent for the state containing the property determines its distribution among the heirs, and these laws vary significantly among the states. An important implication is that any real property owner should draw up an explicit will rather than leave the distribution of the estate to intestate surprise.

**www.nccusl.org/
nccusl/uniformacts-
alphabetically.asp**

Source of the Uniform Probate Code (and other model laws); a "google" search of numerous websites can give a sense of what the UPC is about. It is a major streamlining of very old statutes.

Concept Check

18.10   When property is conveyed to heirs in accordance with a will, it is said to be conveyed _____ or conveyed by _____ , whereas when property is conveyed to heirs without a will it is said to be conveyed _____ or conveyed by _____ .

Bankruptcy. In a bankruptcy proceeding, real property of the debtor, unless preempted by a defaulted mortgage, may be included in other assets to be liquidated on behalf of the creditors. The court will appoint a trustee to conduct the liquidation, and the property will be conveyed by a trustee's deed. If the trustee follows requisite procedures, including obtaining permission of the court, sale of the property can be straightforward. However, since more things can go wrong than in a voluntary conveyance, the buyer has at least some additional risk, which is best alleviated through title insurance (discussed below).

Divorce Settlement. In a divorce settlement, real property may transfer by a "final judgment of dissolution," instead of a deed. Often the disposition will be directed by a "property settlement agreement." It may award the property directly through the final judgment, or it may call for a trustee's deed. If the settlement agreement awards the property to one spouse, but awards the other spouse some compensation from the property, then the latter spouse retains what amounts to a lien on the property until the compensation requirement is fulfilled.

Condemnation. By the power of *eminent domain,* government can take private property for public purpose through due process, and with just compensation. The process of exercising this power is known as *condemnation.* (Eminent domain and condemnation are discussed in Chapter 6.)

Foreclosure. As discussed in Chapter 10, foreclosure can be either judicial or power of sale (nonjudicial). In both cases the foreclosed property, with few exceptions, is disposed of by public sale.[4] In judicial foreclosure, however, the process is administered by a court. Under power of sale, the process is administered by a trustee, subject to state law that specifies the procedure, particularly for advertising and notification requirements. Title will convey by either a deed from the court or from a trustee. Foreclosure is a complicated procedure, typically arising from legally messy circumstances. Therefore, the title obtained at foreclosure sale usually has significantly more risks than normal.

Concept Check

18.11 Name four events that can result in the conveyance of real property involuntarily through some type of deed.

Voluntary Conveyance without a Deed

There are multiple ways an easement can arise incidental to a voluntary conveyance of property. These include variations of implied easements and easement by estoppel.

Implied Easements. An **implied easement** is not created by an explicit deed or an explicit clause in a deed. It often is created when a subdivision map is placed in the public records. On the map will be utility easements and possibly easements of access such as bike paths or footpaths that do not appear in any specific deed. While they are in the public records for all to see, the prospective grantee must realize that they may only be detectable by examination of the map or by careful inspection of the property.

An easement by prior use and an easement of necessity both arise when a landowner subdivides land, conveying part of it in a way that causes a parcel to be landlocked. By common law tradition, land is to be useful, and therefore must be accessible. An owner cannot convey land in a manner that makes it inaccessible. When a path of access across part

---

4. The exceptions are in Connecticut and Vermont, where a lender may be able to take title of the foreclosed property directly through a court supervised process known as strict foreclosure.

of the property to a now landlocked parcel preexists, and if the sale leaves that path as the only access and egress, then the path becomes an implied **easement by prior use.** If the landlocked parcel has no prior path of access and egress, then an implied **easement of necessity** is automatically created.

Trouble can arise with these implied easements when the servient parcel bearing the easement subsequently passes to a new owner. There will be no indication of the easement in public records, even though it must exist.

Easement by Estoppel. **Easement by estoppel** can occur if a landowner gives an adjacent landowner permission to depend on her land. For example, suppose a landowner gives a neighbor permission to rely on sewer access or drainage across his or her land. Courts may subsequently enforce that claim against the landowner (estop any attempt to deny access), or against subsequent purchasers of the land, acting on behalf of the benefiting (dominant) parcel.

Concept Check

18.12 What are two types of easements that are created without a deed, but with the knowledge of the grantor?

Involuntary Conveyance without a Deed

An owner of land may involuntarily and unknowingly give up rights to land. The interest sacrificed can be either an easement, called an **easement by prescription,** or title to the land, or title by **adverse possession.** This can occur if others use the property and their use meets five conditions, which must be:

1. *Hostile to the owner's interests,* and under claim of right (i.e., without the owner's permission and acting like an owner).
2. *Actual*—the land must be employed in some natural or normal use.
3. *Open and notorious*—there can be no effort to disguise or hide the use from the owner or neighbors.
4. *Continuous*—possession must be uninterrupted by a period specified by state law; this period can be as short as 5 years or as long as 20 years.
5. *Exclusive*—the claimant cannot share possession with the owner, neighbors, or others.

These requirements generally apply both to title by adverse possession and to easement by prescription, although the requirement of exclusive possession may be interpreted less strictly for an easement by prescription. In addition to these requirements, some states require under adverse possession that the claimant has paid property taxes on the property for a period of time before acquiring title.

Concept Check

18.13 Real property can convey to a new owner without a deed, and without the consent or knowledge of the original owner. A fee simple interest being conveyed in this manner is said to convey by _____ , while an easement is said to convey by _____ .

An owner also can involuntarily gain rights to land through the action of water bordering the property. By means of **accretion,** water may deposit soil, which can become the property of the owner. By **reliction,** subsiding water may leave additional land as property of the owner.

Real Property Complexity and Public Records

In Chapter 4 we explored the complex variety of the "bundles of rights" in real property. In this chapter we have reviewed the multitude of ways that these rights can be conveyed from one owner to the next over many generations. Clearly, therefore, within the property rights system that we have described, the only way to be certain what rights are obtainable for a parcel of land, and from whom, is to be able to account for the complete legal history of the property.[5] Thus our society has established a framework of laws, public record systems, and procedures to preserve this real property history. We describe this system in the sections below.

The Doctrine of Constructive Notice

The common law tradition holds that a person cannot be bound by claims or rules he or she has no means of knowing. The corollary is that once a person is capable of knowing about a claim or rule, he or she can be bound by it. This is the **doctrine of constructive notice.**

Statute of Frauds

Every state has adopted some form of the original **Statute of Frauds** (1677) by enacting a law requiring any contract conveying a real property interest to be in writing. Thus, deeds, long-term leases, and mortgages must be in writing to be enforceable.

Recording Statutes

Every state also has implemented the doctrine of constructive notice through the enactment of **recording statutes.** These laws require that a document conveying an interest in real property must be placed in the public records to be binding on the public. Once in the public records, the document is binding on everyone, whether or not they make an effort to learn of it. Thus, deeds, mortgages, mechanics' liens, attachments from court judgments, and other instruments that convey real property interests must be placed in local public records to be enforceable.[6] This recording process is maintained at the county level (parish or township where counties do not exist) and is an important function of the traditional county courthouse. A registrar of deeds, clerk of the court, or similar officer is charged with the responsibility of maintaining the property recording system.

Concept Check

18.14 All persons are presumed to be informed of legal documents placed in public records according to the doctrine of _recording statutes_ .

Concept Check

18.15 Agreements to convey an interest in real property must be in writing to be enforceable by requirement of the _statute of Frauds._

When a grantee receives a deed, or when a mortgagee receives a mortgage, it is important to record it as soon as possible since priority of real property claims is by chronology of recording (see Chapter 10). If a mortgage, for example, is not recorded, an unscrupulous mortgagor could immediately issue a second, competing mortgage. If the

---

5. The property system we have described is common to countries with an English tradition. In other traditions, much less emphasis is placed on property history and more on a system of registration.

6. Long-term leases generally are enforceable on the basis of actual notice, discussed on page 478.

second one issued is recorded first, it gains first priority, regardless of the original understanding with the mortgagor, and the aggrieved mortgagee is powerless to correct the problem. Similarly, if an unscrupulous owner sells a parcel of land twice, the grantees recording their deed first become the true owners of the property.

Actual Notice

Unfortunately, recording statutes cannot assure complete knowledge of real property interests. Earlier in this chapter we noted that real property could be conveyed through adverse possession, prescription, implied easements, and estoppel easements. In addition, the property may be subject to a lease. None of these conveyances appears in recorded documents, but each is enforceable on the basis of actual notice. If the asserted claim is open, continuous, and apparent to all who examine the property, it meets the requirements for **actual notice** and is considered to have the same force as constructive notice. The obvious implication of actual notice is that property should never be acquired until it has been inspected. By the same token, when the validity of title is being examined, as discussed below, part of the process must be to inspect the property.

Concept Check °

18.16   Name two types of legal notice that can provide evidence of a real property interest.

Title

It is clear from the complexity and length of ownership history that no single document can prove ownership of land; that is, there is no single form that we can meaningfully refer to as the "title." Rather, title must be a *collection* of evidence. This evidence must point to some person (or entity) as the holder of the fee (titled) interest. From the discussion above, two kinds of evidence are pertinent: constructive notice and actual notice. In short, the problem of establishing title is one of searching the public records for pertinent evidence, and then examining the property for any undetected evidence from current occupancy and use.

Title Search, Title Abstract, and Chain of Title

The task of examining the evidence in the public records is called a **title search.** The object is to construct a **chain of title**—a set of deeds and other documents that traces the conveyance of the fee, and any interests that could limit it—from the earliest recorded time for the particular property to the current owner. If no breaks in this chain are discovered (i.e., no paths lead away from the current owner) then a complete chain is established. Events that must be accounted for in this process may include sales, gifts, marriages, estate settlements, divorces, mortgages, foreclosures, condemnations, and others.

Traditionally, each relevant document was summarized, and the document summaries were compiled into a chronological volume called a **title abstract.** Since the relevant public records might be housed in multiple offices and since each county historically has created its own system of public records, the title search process must be carried out by a knowledgeable person with local expertise. Further, since many of the documents can be subject to interpretation, only a competent legal expert can draw final conclusions about the chain of title. Thus, the title abstract was constructed and then given to an attorney for final interpretation. With electronic document storage and retrieval, the customary title abstract has largely been replaced by electronic equivalents.

Concept Check

18.17   What is the object of a title search?

18-1

Title Insurance: Robber Barons?

Are title insurers the last of the robber barons? Like the feudal lords along the Rhine River who held up shippers for ransom in an earlier era, title insurers have become the gatekeepers for home purchases. Since title insurance is required for most home mortgage loans, it has grown as the choice for evidence of title as well. But not without controversy. In Colorado, California, Florida, New York, and other states, regulators and class action suits have accused the industry of providing the buyers less than they pay for. While evidence seems sketchy, it has been reported that less than 10 cents of the typical title insurance dollar is paid out in claims, in contrast to automobile insurance, for example, where something like 90 percent is paid out. Much of the rest of the premium, some critics report, goes to lavish marketing efforts to the real estate industry. Moreover, some studies have indicated that about half of the claims paid out result from errors or oversights in conducting the title examination that is being insured.

Title insurance defenders counter that the premium covers not just insurance but the cost of maintaining the "title plant" or record base and for closing-related services, which the home-buyer would need to pay for anyway. The pricing of closing services remains murky, and thus the merit of this argument is not clear. However, perhaps some indication of the pricing of title insurance is found from the state of Iowa. There, a division of the Iowa Finance Authority, a state agency, provides all title insurance. Insurance (called a Title Guaranty Certificate) is $1 per $1,000 of value, plus $150 to $300 for preparation of a title abstract. Thus, the cost of title insurance on a $150,000 house would be between $300 and $450, compared to 1/2 to 1 percent of value from private companies, or $750 to $1,500.

What are homebuyers to do, besides support their local investigator and class action lawyer? Shop! It turns out that you can compare prices of providers, and should do so as soon as title insurance is on your horizon. Further, if the property was previously insured in the last three years or so, you may be able to go back to the most recent insurer and negotiate a lower "update" premium. Start by checking industry websites for pricing and provider information. Try these, for example:

http://titlefees.firstam.com/Titlefees.asp

http://ldi.stewart.com/titleagentsearch/search.asp

Evidence of Title

Demonstrating a good title is a central part of any real estate transaction. A contract for sale of real estate usually calls for the seller/grantor to provide **evidence of title** as a requisite to completing the sale. The seller traditionally can meet this requirement in one of two ways:

1. Title abstract, together with an attorney's opinion of title. (Note that the abstract alone is not sufficient.)
2. Title insurance commitment.

Title Abstract and Attorney's Opinion. The **title abstract with attorney's opinion** is the traditional evidence of title. Its logic follows closely from the nature of the title search described above.

Title Insurance Commitment. A **title insurance commitment** is deemed equivalent to the traditional abstract and opinion of title. The logic of relying on a title insurance commitment as evidence of title is that the insurer would not make a commitment before conducting a title search and assuring a good title beyond reasonable doubt. **Title insurance** protects a grantor (or mortgagor) against the legal costs of defending the title and against loss of the property in case of an unsuccessful defense. Therefore, the insurer will refuse to commit if good title is in doubt.

Title insurance has become the predominant type of evidence of title because the tradition of abstract with attorney's opinion, even if executed perfectly, cannot guard against certain risks. Among these are defective deeds (e.g., those improperly delivered), forgeries, flaws due to incorrect marital status (e.g., failure to reveal a marriage), and incapacity of a grantor due to insanity or minority age. Title insurance provides indemnification against these risks, among others. Litigation may be necessary to defend even a good title, and title insurance covers this cost.

T itle researchers examine and analyze past deeds and other records that are on file with state and county registry offices. Many title insurance companies also maintain their own files for title research. Examiners check deeds, mortgages, court documents, and other records affecting property conveyance, and examine surveys of the property to assure that there is no dispute over the boundary lines. They also may check the property in person to be certain that there are no buildings, power lines, or other constructions encroaching on the property. In addition, they will check tax records to be sure all payments have been made. Basic skills and knowledge involved include:

- Considerable knowledge of forms and terminology as applied to real estate.
- Considerable knowledge of sources and procedures pertaining to title abstracts.
- Ability to search title records and to provide concise, accurate reports of findings.

Title Researcher and Examiner

- Ability to make routine decisions in accordance with regulations and procedures.
- Ability to establish and maintain effective working relationships with associates, property owners, appraisers, and the public.

If the examiner finds defects in the title, he or she will contact the necessary parties to determine the best means of correction, and assist in resolving the problem. Finally, the examiner will prepare a report.

Some companies hire high school graduates (normally with experience) and train them. Other companies prefer college graduates with courses in accounting, business, prelaw, and real estate. Title examiners may work for state, county, or local governments and may focus on condemnation cases. Also, they may work for utility companies or private title companies. They commonly are salaried employees with full fringe benefits. Entry positions start at under $20,000, whereas, senior, supervisory positions as examiners can pay over $50,000.

www.alta.org/ cnsrinfo/eduabtti/

American Land Title Association is the umbrella organization of the title insurance industry—a very rich site for information about title insurance and the industry.

There are important limits or exceptions to title insurance. First, it is not hazard insurance; that is, it does not protect the owner from the threat of physical damage to the property. It only protects against legal attack on the owner's title. Second, title insurance typically excepts any facts that an inspection and survey of the property would reveal. For example, title insurance will not protect against claims of title brought by a current occupant of the property, and it will not protect against the risk of **encroachments,** the intrusions on the property by structures of adjacent land parcels. In addition, title insurance normally does not insure against limitations on the property placed by government through the exercise of police power—that is, zoning, building codes, environmental laws, and others.

Torrens Certificate. A third, rarely used means of providing evidence of title is through a Torrens Certificate introduced by Sir Robert Torrens in Australia in 1858. A property is first converted to the Torrens system by going through a careful title search and examination. Then a **Torrens certificate** is issued that is accepted as evidence of good title. From that point on, no mortgage, deed, or other conveyance is binding until presented to the Torrens office where it is noted in an updated Torrens Certificate. The intent is to simplify title conveyance. However, time has not been favorable to the system. Though it has been used in a handful of U.S. cities, including Boston, New York, Minneapolis–St. Paul, and Chicago, it seldom appears today.

Concept Check

18.18 List the two main forms of evidence of title.

Marketable Title Laws. The past history of a property, once constructed, remains the same, and only recent conveyances alter the status of title. Recognizing this, an increasing number of states have sought to simplify title search and title risk through **marketable**

title laws. By these laws, certain types of claims, including restrictive covenants and even easements in some cases, may cease to be binding if they do not *reappear* in recorded documents that postdate a so-called root of title. (Presumably, actual notice of easements is not affected.) The "root of title" conveyance is the last conveyance of the property that is at least a certain number of years old (typically 30 to 40 years). With some exceptions, a title that is good back to the root of title may be regarded as fully marketable. Thus, the marketable title act provides, with some exceptions, a statute of limitations on title search.

Land Descriptions

At the outset of the chapter, we noted three aspects of real property transactions that make them uniquely complicated, the first two were the complexity of real property "bundles of rights," and the long history of property ownership. The third complicating aspect is the need for precise descriptions. Since land parcels are defined on a continuous surface, adjacent everywhere to other land parcels, description is challenging. It cannot be accomplished, for example, by a machine-readable code number. Errors in a land description must imply a loss to some landowner that could be substantial.

While the basic requirement of a land description is to be unambiguous, only the three methods presented below are recognized as reliably clear for use in legal documents.[7]

Metes and Bounds

The method of **metes and bounds** is the oldest of the three forms of land description. In ancient practice, *metes* referred to measures, and *bounds* referred to the identifiable boundaries of surrounding parcels of land. Without systematic reference points such as the longitude and latitude we use today, there was no simple place to begin a survey. The point of beginning, always critical, had to be defined in terms of any existing reference points available. Thus, the best the surveyor could do was to make good use of trees, large rocks, and identifiable boundaries of neighboring properties. (See Industry Issues 18-2)

In its modern version, metes and bounds is a very precise, compass-directed walk around the boundary of a parcel. The boundary is defined by a point of beginning and a sequence of directed distances (metes, in Old English) that eventually lead back to the point of beginning. The point of beginning is a marker or monument that is presumed to be permanent. In early times the point of beginning might be a notable feature of the land, such as a large oak tree or a boulder. However, because such "permanent" features of land have a way of changing through time, modern practice is to install a steel or concrete marker as the point of beginning.

A metes and bounds description is the most flexible of descriptions, and is capable of describing even the most irregular of parcels. However, it should neither be created nor interpreted except by a trained surveyor. An example of a very simple metes and bounds description is shown in Exhibit 18-1. Notice that the four sides of the Glowing Hills Subdivision are defined in a clockwise sequence by pairs of precise compass headings and distances. Each compass heading has three elements. First is a reference direction (N, E, S or W). Next is the degrees, minutes, and seconds of rotation from that direction. Third is the direction of rotation. Thus, the first compass heading gives a rotation of 89 degrees, 36 minutes and 01 seconds away from north, rotating to the west. The distance in that direction is 1,274.03 feet.

Concept Check

18.19 Metes and bounds land description can be summarized or described as a
_____ and a series of _____ .

---

7. Historically, street addresses, tax parcel numbers, and prominent features of the land (monuments) have been used to identify parcels. These methods, however, produce too many failures to be acceptable in modern practice.

18-2

Metes and Bounds: The Surveyor's Bread and Butter

n about 20 states the basic property description system is by metes and bounds. These include the original 13 colonies, along with Vermont, Maine, West Virginia, Texas, and parts of Ohio, Kentucky, and Tennessee. Some of these systems have more meat than others! In Kentucky and Tennessee, for example the system has been referred to as "indiscriminant metes and bounds," and had to describe land without the assistance of a compass, and with few systematic points of beginning. For example, read the description of a property in Mercer County, Kentucky:

Beginning at the mouth of a branch at an ash stump thence up the creek south 20 poles to 2 beech, thence east 41 poles to a small walnut in Arnett's line, thence north 50 east 80 poles to a linn hickory dogwood in said line, thence north 38 poles to an

ash, thence west 296 poles with Potts's line till it intersects with Tolly's line, thence south 30 west 80 poles to a whiteoak and sugar, thence east 223 poles to beginning.*

Often, descriptions followed creeks or rivers, and used the term "meander" to describe a boundary that simply followed the streambed. In this system distance is measured in 16 1/2 foot lengths, which are interchangeably known as poles, rods, or perches. A common device in measuring for these early descriptions was the "chain" (shown below[†]) which was 66 feet in length, or 4 perches.

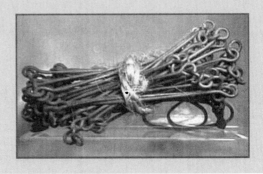

Information obtained from a helpful, but unsigned Web source: www.outfitters.com/genealogy/land/metesbounds.html

[†]Another enjoyable site on early surveying in Tennessee is www.tngenweb.org/tnland/terms.htm. The chain illustration is from that website.

Exhibit 18-1   Metes and Bounds Description: Glowing Hills Subdivision

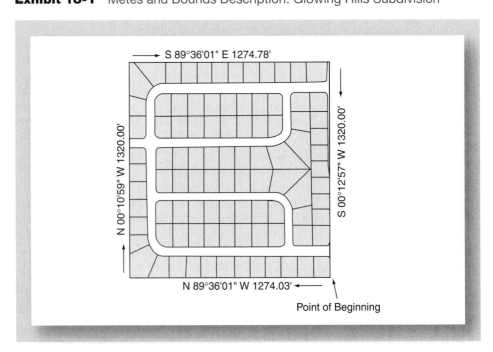

From the point of beginning, north 89° 36 minutes and 01 seconds west 1,274.03 feet, thence north 00° 10 minutes and 59 seconds west 1,320.00 feet, thence south 89° 36 minutes and 01 seconds east 1,274.78 feet, thence south 00° 12 minutes and 57 seconds 1,320.00 feet to the point of beginning.

Subdivision Plat Lot and Block Number

Most urban property is part of a platted subdivision. When a platted residential or other subdivision is created, a surveyed map of the subdivision is placed in the public records with each parcel identified by **plat lot and block number.** Since the original survey is contained in the recorded plat map, the lot and block number on that map provide an unambiguous description of the property.

The recorded plat map contains other important information as well. It usually shows the location of various easements such as utilities, drainage, storm water retention, and bicycle paths. In addition, it may contain a list of restrictive covenants, although it is more common in current practice to record the restrictions in an associated declaration.

Exhibit 18-2 shows a simple subdivision plat map based on an actual subdivision. It contains four blocks, each with lots numbered beginning with 1. Note that Block 1 extends around three sides of the subdivision, with lots running from 1 to 32. Though the subdivision is quite simple, it nevertheless contains numerous easements. A utility easement borders every lot. In addition, drainage easements for storm sewers affect six lots. Finally, a common path cuts through all four blocks leading to an adjacent elementary school and park. Often such a path is an easement across some of the lots. In this case, however, the path is the common property of all owners in the subdivision.

Government Rectangular Survey

A large portion of the United States, after the 13 colonies and the earliest post-Revolutionary new states, was originally described by government rectangular survey. This process of survey began with the Old Northwest Territory (Ohio, Indiana, Illinois, and

Exhibit 18-2 Subdivision Plat Map with Lot and Block Number

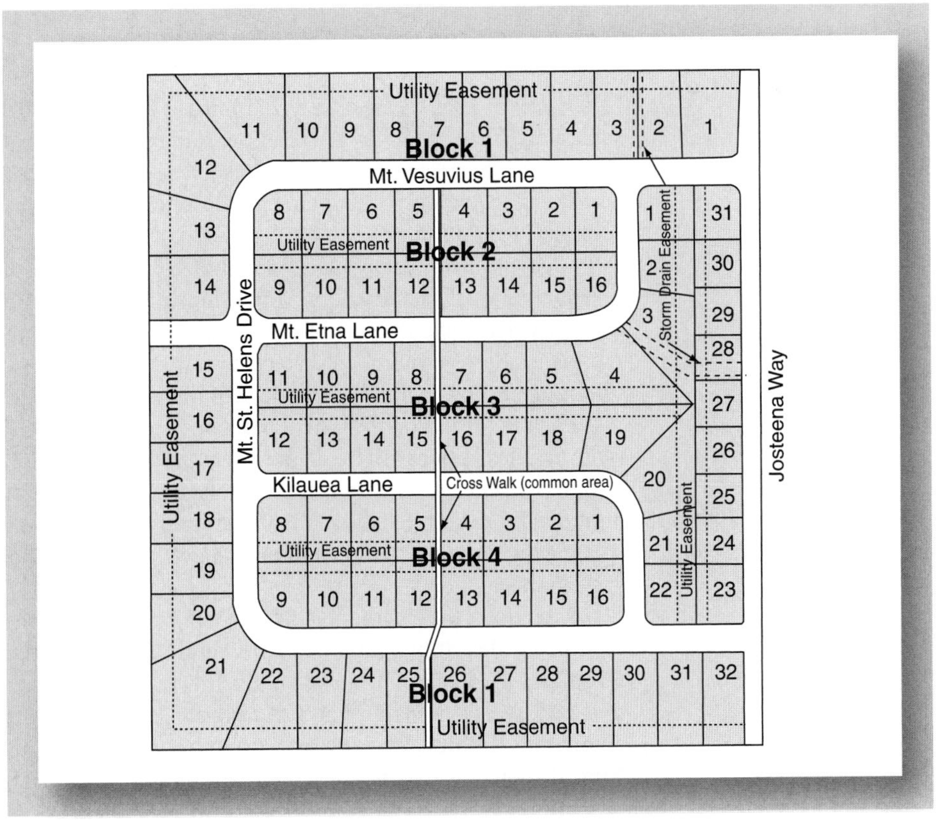

Exhibit 18-3 Principal Meridians and Base Lines of the United States

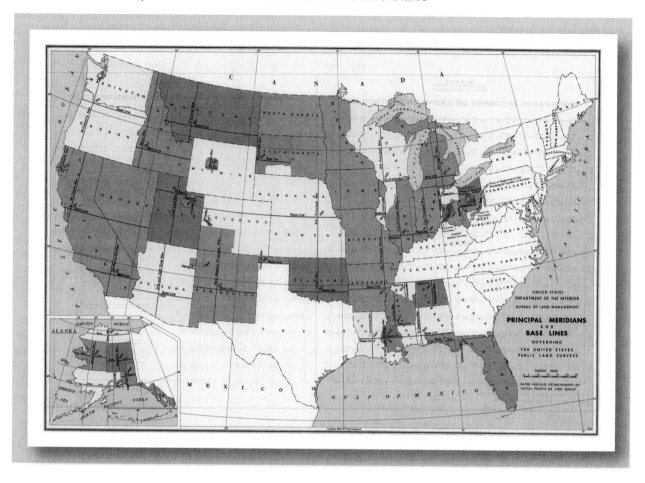

Michigan) in 1789. As shown in Exhibit 18-3, numerous different regions were surveyed separately. For each region a **baseline,** running east and west, and a **principal meridian,** running north and south, were established as reference lines. From these lines a grid system was surveyed involving **checks** (24 miles square), **townships** (6 miles square), and sections (1 mile square).

A government rectangular description relies on townships and section numbers as the essential units of identification. Townships are numbered east or west from the principal meridian. They are separated, east and west, by **range lines,** which parallel the principal meridian. They are numbered south or north from the baseline by **tier lines** (sometimes referred to as township lines), which parallel the baseline.

Each township of six square miles is subdivided into 36 numbered sections, laid out (with rare exceptions) in the pattern shown in Exhibit 18-4. The numbering begins in the northeast corner of the township and ends in the southeast corner, going back and forth horizontally in between. Note that a **section** is not simply any one-square-mile area. It is a specifically surveyed and identified square mile within the framework of the rectangular survey system.

A section (which contains 640 acres) is subdivided, as necessary, according to a set of simple rules. It typically is quartered (160 acres), and each quarter section can again be quartered (40 acres), and so on. Sections can be halved without ambiguity (e.g., north one-half, west one-half), but a description never uses the term "middle" because it is ambiguous. Exhibit 18-5 displays a number of sample subdivisions for a typical section. Note that halves and quarters can be combined to form L-shaped or other blocklike properties.

Exhibit 18-4   One Township, with Numbered Sections: Tier 24 South, Range 27 East

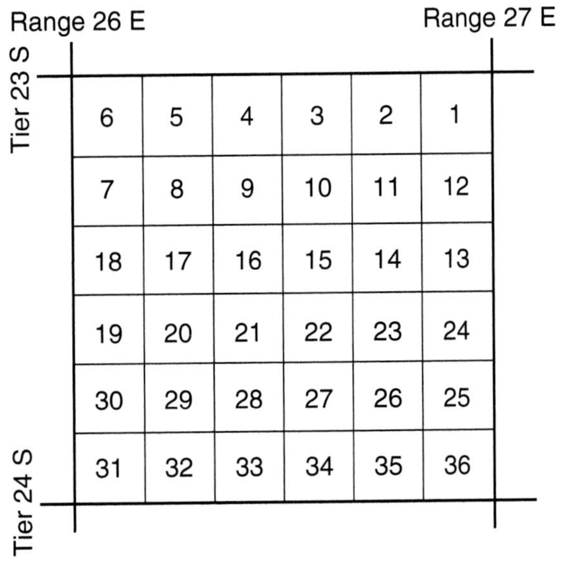

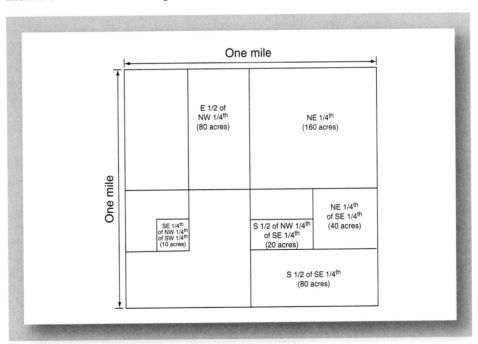

Range 26 E | | | | | | Range 27 E

Tier 23 S

6	5	4	3	2	1
7	8	9	10	11	12
18	17	16	15	14	13
19	20	21	22	23	24
30	29	28	27	26	25
31	32	33	34	35	36

Tier 24 S

Exhibit 18-5   Subdividing a Section

One mile

One mile

E 1/2 of NW 1/4th (80 acres)

NE 1/4th (160 acres)

SE 1/4th of NW 1/4th of SW 1/4th (10 acres)

S 1/2 of NW 1/4th of SE 1/4th (20 acres)

NE 1/4th of SE 1/4th (40 acres)

S 1/2 of SE 1/4th (80 acres)

Clearly, the **acre** is an important measure in rectangular survey descriptions and in land measure generally. It is a measure of land area, with no specific configuration, containing 43,560 square feet. Note that this implies that a square lot of slightly over 200 feet on a side constitutes an acre. Ninety yards of the standard American football field constitutes approximately an acre.

Exhibit 18-6 Government Rectangular Survey Description of a Familiar Florida Site

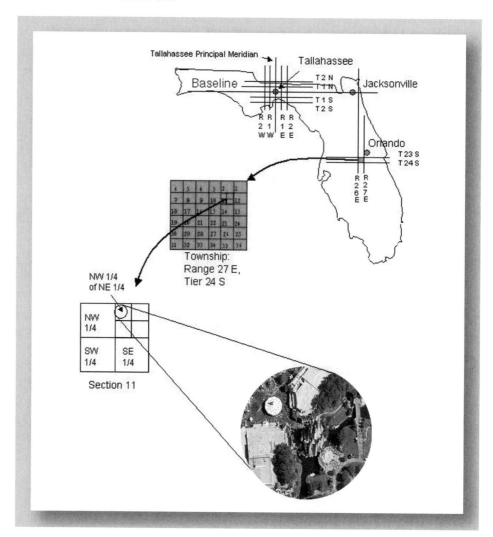

Exhibit 18-6 shows the government rectangular description for a familiar Florida location (shown in the aerial photo). The property is located in the 27th north-south range of townships east of the Tallahassee principal meridian and in the 24th east-west tier of townships south of the baseline. (The principal meridian and baseline intersect near Florida's state capitol building.) The section is number 11, which always is in the second row from the top of the township, one removed from the right-hand boundary. The parcel of interest is in the northeast quarter of section 11, and within that quarter it lies in the northwest quarter. We leave it to the reader to figure out what the property is.

Concept Check

18.20 What is the oldest form of the three main land descriptions?
What is the most common form of urban land description?
What is the most common rural land description in most states?

Summary

Conveyance of real property is complicated by three characteristics. First, real property interests can be complex. Second, because land is enduring, the history of real property ownership is very long. Third, describing land is critical because all land parcels adjoin other parcels; any errors in description inevitably favor one owner and hurt another.

Deeds are the principal means of conveying title or other interests in real property. They are a special form of contract. They differ from a normal business contract by not requiring a legally competent grantee, by not requiring explicit consideration, and by the requirement that they must be in writing. Deeds contain a number of specialized clauses necessary to define the bundle of rights and the precise location being conveyed. Deeds vary in "quality" in accordance with the number of covenants they contain. Finally, a deed is valid only if it has been "delivered" from the grantor to the grantee.

Transfers of property also can occur without a deed or any other explicit document. This can occur through an easement by implication, an easement by estoppel, by adverse possession, or by prescription. In these cases, an easement or the possession of the property, in whole or in part, is not recorded in the public records. However, the existence of the claim is often visibly detectable. Thus, actual inspection of property is always important.

The complexity of real property interests, together with their long history, make it challenging to determine what rights to a parcel are available today. The Statute of Frauds provides an essential first step by requiring every conveyance of real property to be in writing. Recording statutes require that deeds and other conveyances of real property interests must be placed in public records to be enforceable. Finally, the doctrine of constructive notice holds that all persons must honor any valid deed or other conveyance thus recorded and available for examination. However, it does not relieve a grantee from directly inspecting the property for "actual notice" of unrecorded claims to the land.

The resulting real property record systems make it possible to create "evidence of title" for a parcel of land. The first step is to construct a "chain of title" tracing ownership back through the record system for as long as it is deemed necessary. A qualified legal expert examines the conveyances in the chain to assure that they imply an unbroken transfer of the property interest in question down to the grantor. The substance of this search and evaluation can result in two main types of evidence of title. The most traditional form is title abstract with attorney's opinion. A more modern form is a title insurance commitment, which also offers the advantage of financial protection against title challenges.

In the sensitive issue of land description, three methods of legal descriptions are accepted for public records: metes and bounds, subdivision plat lot and block number, and government rectangular survey.

Key Terms

Accretion 476	Dedicate 473	Exceptions and reservations clause 471
Acknowledgment 471	Deed 469	General warranty deed 472
Acre 485	Deed of bargain and sale 473	Grantee 470
Actual notice 478	Delivery 472	Grantor 470
Adverse possession 476	Devised 474	Habendum clause 471
Baseline 484	Doctrine of constructive notice 477	Implied easement 475
Chain of title 478	Easement by estoppel 476	Intestate 474
Checks 484	Easement by prescription 476	Judicial deed 473
Covenants 470	Easement by prior use 476	Law of descent 474
Covenant against encumbrances 470	Easement of necessity 476	Marketable title 473
Covenant of quiet enjoyment 470	Encroachment 480	Marketable title laws 480
Covenant of seizin 470	Evidence of title 479	Metes and bounds 481

Test Problems

1. Which of these is *not* a requirement of a valid deed?
   a. Competent grantor.
   b. Competent grantee.
   c. In writing.
   d. Habendum clause.
   e. Delivery.

2. The interest being conveyed by a deed is specified in the:
   a. Words of conveyance.
   b. Habendum clause.
   c. Property description.
   d. Exceptions and reservations clause.
   e. Covenant of seizin.

3. The "highest-quality" form of deed is the:
   a. General warranty deed.
   b. Special warranty deed.
   c. Deed of bargain and sale.
   d. Quitclaim deed.
   e. Judicial deed.

4. A deed used mainly to clear up possible "clouds" or encumbrances to title (conflicting interests) is the:
   a. General warranty deed.
   b. Special warranty deed.
   c. Deed of bargain and sale.
   d. Quitclaim deed.
   e. Judicial deed.

5. If a landowner sells the front part of a parcel of land, retaining the back portion as a "landlocked" parcel, and if there is an existing informal path across the front parcel to the back one, the seller is likely to retain the path as a (an):
   a. Easement in gross.
   b. Joint driveway easement.
   c. Implied easement by prior use.
   d. Easement by estoppel.
   e. Prescriptive easement.

6. If a neighboring landowner drives across a person's land openly and consistently for a number of years the neighbor may acquire an easement by:
   a. Estoppel.
   b. Implication.
   c. Accretion.
   d. Prescription.
   e. Necessity.

7. If documents conveying interests in real property are properly recorded in the public records, they are binding or enforceable on all persons, regardless of whether those persons are aware of the documents, by the:
   a. Statute of Frauds.
   b. Recording statutes.
   c. Doctrine of constructive notice.
   d. Doctrine of actual notice.
   e. Evidence of title acts.

8. Which of these is a widely used form of "evidence of title"?
   a. Abstract of title.
   b. Title insurance commitment.
   c. Torrens certificate.
   d. Title certificate.
   e. General warranty deed.

9. The most common form of legal description for urban residential property is the:
   a. Street address.
   b. Tax parcel number.
   c. Plat lot and block number.
   d. Metes and bounds description.
   e. Government rectangular survey.

10. Factors that make it uniquely difficult to establish clear title in real estate compared to most personal property items include:
    a. Size of real estate.
    b. Length of the ownership history in real estate.
    c. Value of real estate.
    d. Land use controls.
    e. Serious deficiencies of property law in the United States.

Study Questions

1. Explain how title insurance works. What risks does it cover? Who pays, and when? What common exceptions does it make?

2. If a grantee obtains title insurance, what value, if any, is there in the covenant of seizen in a warranty deed?

3. The use of Torrens certificates, never large in the United States, has diminished in recent years. Explain how marketable title laws, recently adopted in many states, might have made Torrens certificates less interesting and useful.

4. Name at least six adverse (conflicting) claims to property or other title defects that will not be evident from a search of property records but which might be detected by inspection of the property and its occupants.

5. Why might it be advisable to require a survey in purchasing a 20-year-old home in an urban subdivision?

6. Describe the shaded property in the diagram by government rectangular survey.

7. Some people in the real estate industry have suggested that it is good to require a title insurance commitment as evidence of title for rural property, but that it is satisfactory to use the less costly abstract and attorney's opinion as evidence of title for a residence in an urban subdivision. Discuss the merits or risks of this policy.

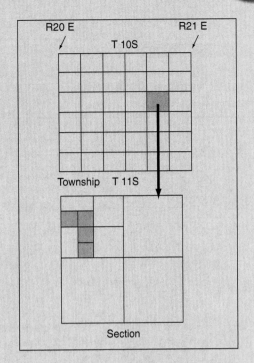

Explore The Web

As noted in the chapter, most local government property appraisers (or assessors) have made their records and maps available today on the Internet. Find the website of your local property appraiser. Then, for property of your choice, find the property description. Does the site give the area of the parcel? Is there a map of the parcel? Does the site also provide aerial photos?

Solutions to Concept Checks

1. Three features of real property that introduce special challenges for orderly transfer of ownership are:
   a. Real property interests can be very complex.
   b. Ownership has a very long history.
   c. All real property is bounded by other properties, so description errors always matter.

2. A deed is a special form of contract for the purpose of conveying a permanent interest in real property.

3. In a normal contract, all parties must be legally competent, whereas in a deed only the grantor must be legally competent.

4. The three covenants that distinguish the "quality" of deeds are:
   a. Seizin, which promises that the grantor actually holds title.
   b. No encumbrances, which promises that there are no undisclosed encumbrances.
   c. Quiet enjoyment, which promises that no superior claim to title will appear.

5. The type of deed is determined in the words of conveyance by certain traditional phrases. The nature of the property interest conveyed is determined by the wording of the habendum clause.

6. Any property interest not being conveyed to the grantee is stated in the exceptions and reservations clause.

7. Three acceptable methods of land description for deeds and other public records are metes and bounds, subdivision plat lot and block number, and government rectangular survey.

8. Delivery of a deed refers to observable and verifiable intent that the deed is to be given to the grantee.

9. The highest-quality deed is the general warranty deed. A deed which businesses often use to convey real estate is the bargain and sale deed. A deed used mainly to relinquish ambiguous or conflicting claims is the quitclaim deed.

10. When property is conveyed to heirs in accordance with a will, it is said to be conveyed testate or by devise, whereas when property is conveyed to heirs without a will it is said to be conveyed intestate or by descent.

11. Four events that can cause an owner to convey real property involuntarily through some type of deed are condemnation, bankruptcy, foreclosure, and divorce.

12. Two types of easements that are created without a deed, but with the knowledge of the grantor, are an implied easement and an easement by estoppel.

13. Real property can convey to a new owner without a deed, and without the consent or knowledge of the original owner. A fee simple interest conveyed in this manner is said to convey by adverse possession, while an easement is said to convey by prescription.

14. All persons are presumed to be informed of legal documents placed in public records by the doctrine of constructive notice.

15. Agreements to convey an interest in real property must be in writing to be enforceable by requirement of the Statute of Frauds.

16. Two types of legal notice that can evidence a real property interest are constructive notice and actual notice.

17. The objective of a title search is to construct a chain of title.

18. The two main forms of evidence of title are abstract with attorney's opinion and a title insurance commitment.

19. A metes and bounds land description can be summarized or described as a point of beginning and a series of directed distances.

20. The oldest form of the three main land descriptions is metes and bounds. The most common form of urban land description is subdivision plat lot and block number. The most common rural land description in most states is the government rectangular.

Additional Readings

The following real estate law texts offer excellent additional material on many of the subjects in this chapter:

Jennings, Marianne. *Real Estate Law,* 6th ed. Cincinnati, OH: West Legal Studies in Business, a division of Thomson Learning, 2002.

Siedel, George J., III, Robert J. Aalberts, and Janis K. Cheezem. *Real Estate Law,* 5th ed. Mason, OH. Thomson, 2003.

Werner, Raymond J. *Real Estate Law,* 11th ed. Cincinnati, OH: South-Western Publishing, 2002.

chapter nineteen

Real Estate Brokerage *and* Listing Contracts

Learning Objectives

After reading this chapter you will be able to:

1. Describe the brokerage function.

2. State three reasons sellers use brokers.

3. Explain the real estate licensing process.

4. Explain the difference between licensing and certification.

5. Explain how commission rates are determined.

6. List and describe three types of listing contracts.

7. Describe three types of agency relationships in real estate brokerage.

8. List at least three protective provisions each for a property owner and broker that should be included in a listing contract.

9. List the ways that a listing contract can be terminated.

Introduction: Brokerage—The Best-Known Type of Real Estate Business

Many people think of real estate brokerage as *the* real estate business. Although we take a much broader view of real estate, we agree that brokerage is one of the largest and most visible parts of the real estate business. Also, most people are more apt to come in contact with real estate brokers or salespeople than other real estate professionals.

Real estate brokerage also tends to be better known than other real estate businesses because it is easier to enter than other types. Educational requirements are not extensive, and capital requirements are not as high as in other businesses; a small office, a telephone, and a car may be the only requirements. Although many people enter the business, many also leave it; turnover is high.

Yet, real estate brokerage is a demanding occupation for those who would succeed. It requires a great deal of knowledge, skill, and effort. It also can be quite rewarding monetarily and personally. As with any other business or profession, however, the price of success is educational preparation, dedication to the welfare of customers, and hard work.

Concent Check

19.1   Name three conditions that represent the "price of success" in real estate brokerage.

Real Estate Brokers as Market Facilitators

www.realtor.org

Home page of the National Association of Realtors (NAR), the umbrella organization for the real estate brokerage industry, and more.

Real estate brokers serve as intermediaries. They are the catalysts of real estate transactions; they help make markets work by bringing buyers and sellers together physically and emotionally to create sales and purchases. For this reason they may be regarded as *facilitators of market value.* Without their services, it would be more difficult and costly to buy and sell properties, and real estate values—at least in some markets—would undoubtedly be lower.

For this service, brokers are paid a fee, usually called a **commission.** Commissions are typically paid by sellers, but they may be paid by buyers or—in some unusual situations—by both sellers and buyers. Exhibit 19-1 shows the nature of the brokerage function.

Concent Check

19.2   Without real estate brokers, real estate values would be lower. Explain this statement.

Commissions usually are determined as a percentage of the gross sale price, though other arrangements are possible. For example, an owner and broker may agree to a **net listing,** whereby the seller is assured a certain fixed net price for the property and the broker is allowed to retain any amount of the actual sales price above that figure.

Exhibit 19-1   The Brokerage Function

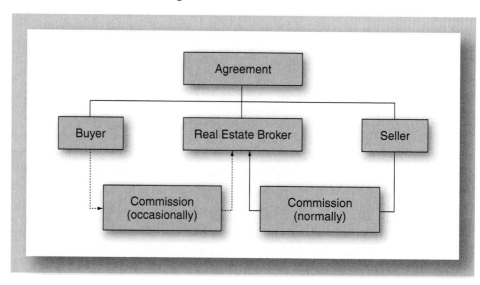

Economic Rationale for Employing a Broker

Brokers are employed to sell properties because they perform a useful service. Brokers have specialized knowledge of the real estate market and have developed expertise in selling properties. Furthermore, they spend time and effort in finding buyers for listed properties. Successful brokers have knowledge and expertise in the following areas:

- Prices and terms of recent market transactions for similar properties.
- Marketing procedures that have been successful in the past.
- Legal obligations of buyers and sellers.
- Similar properties, prices, and terms currently listed for sale.
- Needs of prospective buyers who seek out brokerage firms as sources of properties.
- Procedures that buyers and sellers should follow in consummating a transaction (e.g., how to obtain a title search, financing, insurance, utility services, and the like).

While some property owners attempt to sell their properties themselves to avoid a brokerage commission, they often find they are ill equipped for this task, and they may end up with less cash than if they had employed a broker. Consider the two alternative transactions in Exhibit 19-2 for the same property—one without and the other with a broker. The gain to the owner by using a broker is the result of a number of factors. While some owners may believe otherwise, buyers tend to negotiate prices downward by at least a portion of the commission when they know a broker is not involved. Furthermore, the asking price may be lower to begin with because a seller who does not employ a broker has access to fewer prospective buyers. And sellers may waste time with unqualified buyers. In other words, an owner-seller must usually rely on a "thinner" market than a broker, and the selling time may be longer.

Concept Check

19.3 Name five areas in which an expert real estate broker has special knowledge.

Careful readers of Exhibit 19-2 may agree with these points, but may also realize that by ignoring his or her time in the calculation, the owner would be ahead not to use a broker. But even though the owner's time is not a cash cost, it normally should be counted, since he or she must typically take time off from a job or give up other valuable or pleasurable activities. Owners also subject themselves to greater legal risks, financial risks, and potential frustration because they are less aware of the pitfalls of selling property than brokers who specialize in this activity.

The net result is that sellers who employ brokers often end up better economically than sellers who do not employ brokers. Arguably, brokerage commissions are quite low in relation to the service provided and to the costs borne by brokerage firms (see Industry Issues 19-1). If this were not so, most owners would not use brokers, and the number of brokerage firms would decline dramatically.

Exhibit 19-2 Transactions with and without a Real Estate Broker

		Without Broker	With Broker
Price		$95,000	$100,000
Owner's marketing costs	$1,000	—	—
Time of owner (60 hrs. @ $50 per hr.)	3,000	4,000	—
Commission (6 1/2%)		—	6,500
Proceeds to owner		$91,000	$ 93,500

Industry Issues

19-1

The Effect of Competitive Market Forces on Commission Rates

Brokerage commissions are, by practice, a certain percentage of the sale price of a property. Usually, the salesperson must split with the brokerage firm (e.g., 50 percent each) any commission earned from the sale of a property the salesperson listed or from the sale of a property by the salesperson. This is because the broker provides training, office space, telephones, and secretarial support so the salesperson can produce listings and sales.

By law, brokerage commissions must be established by negotiations between the broker and clients. Many brokers in the same area are members of a multiple listing service and charge similar commission rates, which has led some observers to suspect price fixing. This pattern, however, apparently results from competitive market forces that drive rates to their lowest possible levels, rather than from collusion among brokers. Because entry into real estate brokerage is relatively easy (consider the number of real estate brokers listed in your local Yellow Pages), and because there are many potential brokers in most markets, it is very difficult to argue that long-term price collusion is viable.

Concept Check

19.4 What is a cost of selling a property that tends to be overlooked by prospective "for-sale-by-owners"?

Law of Agency

Real estate brokers and salespersons operate under the **law of agency,** which gives a broker or salesperson the right to act for a **principal** in trying to buy or sell a property. In acting for another person, brokers automatically fall into the category of agents (except when the category of *transaction broker* is created, as explained below), which means the broker must "stand in the shoes" of the principal. Thus, a broker must look out for the best interests of the principal and can do nothing to compromise a principal's interests, position, or bargaining power.

Concept Check

19.5 An agent's relationship to a principal is characterized by what phrase?

Types of Agents

In general, three types of agents can be created by the scope of the relationship between a principal and an agent. The broadest scope of authority is the **universal agent,** to whom a principal delegates the power to act in *all* matters that can be delegated in place of the principal. A **general agent** is delegated by the principal to act within the confines of a business or employment relationship. An insurance agent, for example, may be a general agent of the insurance company if the agent can sign contracts that bind the company, supervise employees of the company, and in other ways carry out the business of the company. Similarly, a property manager is a general agent if he or she can rent apartments, collect rents, handle tenant relations, supervise maintenance, and perform accounting functions, but is not an employee of the property owner. Further, as discussed below, a salesperson in a real estate brokerage firm is a general agent of the firm's owning broker. A **special agent** is authorized by the principal to handle only a specific business transaction or to perform only a specific function. In most cases a real estate broker acts in the capacity of a special agent in representing the buyer or seller to purchase or dispose of a property.

Fiduciary Responsibilities

Agents have a **fiduciary relationship** with their principals. This relationship, by legal tradition, carries several special responsibilities. As fiduciaries, agents must observe the following duties:

Integrity

1. *Disclosure*—Be completely open and honest with their principals.
2. *Confidentiality*—Never betray confidential information about their principals, their financial status, or their motivations.
3. *Accounting*—Keep the principal informed about financial aspects of their assignment.
4. *Obedience*—Follow the instructions of their principal to the limits of what is legal. If agents regard the orders of the principal to be legal but unethical, they should withdraw from the relationship rather than disobey.
5. *Loyalty*—Never subordinate the best interest of their principal to the interests of others.
6. *Skill and Care*—Represent the interests of their principals to the best of their ability— in the same way they would represent themselves, acquiring and applying the necessary skills, knowledge, and information about relevant laws and regulations, the market and subject property.

A principal in a fiduciary relationship also has duties. These are to be open, honest, and fair with the agent. This implies also that the principal will cooperate with the agent in providing information about the property (e.g., repair and expense records and defects) when requested by the agent. When the agent has successfully completed the task assigned (the sale of the property), the agent is entitled to prompt payment for services rendered.

Concept Check

19.6 The broker has what kind of relationship to the principal? What are the six duties owed the principal?

Real Estate Agents

An *agency relationship* is created between a seller and a broker when both parties agree to a **listing contract.** Such a contract may be written or oral, and it establishes the rights and duties of each party. In most listing contracts the sellers agree to make the properties available for purchase at a specified price for a specified period of time (e.g., four months). They also agree to pay the broker a specified fee or a certain percentage of the selling price when the broker finds a buyer who is "ready, willing, and able" to purchase the property, or upon closing of the transaction. Brokers usually agree to use their best efforts to try to sell the property on terms acceptable to the sellers. (A detailed listing contract, Exhibit 19-8, is discussed below.)

**www.realtor.org/
mempolweb.nsf/pages/
code?opendocument**

NAR code of ethics

Concept Check

19.7 What are the three basic types of agency relationships? Which of these refers to a broker's relationship to a principal?

An agency relationship also can exist between a buyer and a broker. In a **buyer agency agreement** a broker agrees to use his or her best efforts to find properties meeting the requirements of the buyer. The buyer agrees to pay the broker a commission or a fee upon consummating a purchase or to permit the broker to share a commission paid to the seller's broker.

Salespersons must be affiliated with a broker, from whom they derive their agency status. As general agents of their broker, they assume all of the special agency obligations that the broker has created, thus becoming special agents to any of the broker's principals.

Subagency. Modern real estate brokerage normally relies on a **multiple listing service (MLS)** through which brokers have access to each other's listings. Brokers who are members of the MLS can make their listings available to be sold by other broker members, and the commission is split between them. In this **subagency** arrangement, the chain of agency becomes rather long, but clear. The listing salesperson represents the listing broker, and both become special agents to the seller-principal. A selling broker and any affiliated salespersons traditionally become subagents of the listing broker, and thus are special agents of the seller as well. So every person in this chain is a special agent to the seller, and owes the same level of loyalty, confidentiality, trust, obedience, disclosure, accounting, care, skill, and due diligence to the seller-principal.

Dual Agency. Another agency relationship that can be created under the laws of many states is dual agency. In these situations the broker is an agent of both a seller and a buyer, and the broker owes equal loyalty to both. A **dual agency** must be disclosed to all parties in the transaction, and both principals must give their informed written consent. While the broker owes equal loyalty to both parties, it cannot be *undivided* loyalty. For example, a dual agency broker cannot inform the seller that the buyer will pay more than the price stated in the written offer or that the seller or buyer will accept financing terms other than those offered. Similarly, the broker cannot reveal to the buyer that the seller will accept a price lower than the listing price, unless instructed in writing to do so.

Concept Check

19.8   What is the name of a very complicated agency relationship that arises when one firm represents both seller and buyer?

Concept Check

19.9   In MLS property listings, the broker selling a listing traditionally was an agent of the seller, in spite of all appearances otherwise, by virtue of what kind of required agency relationship?

Comparison of Traditional Agency Relationships. A variety of agency relationships for real estate brokerage are compared in Exhibit 19-3. The first case, traditional brokerage, involves a seller-principal listing with a broker (through a salesperson). Through MLS and subagency, the resulting special agency relationship runs through the seller-broker all the way to the salesperson in direct contact with the buyer. However, the relationship between that salesperson and the buyer is "arm's length." Thus, the buyer is simply a customer of the seller-broker firm rather than a client.

In the second case, where there is both a seller agency and buyer agency, two special agency relationships confront each other at the interface between the brokers. The two brokerage firms can deal at arm's length in the transaction. Until recently, however, transactions involving both seller-principal and buyer-principal had special difficulties. MLS membership generally required subagency. Therefore, the buyer's broker dealing with an MLS listing was, by contract, also a subagent of the seller and unavoidably a dual agent (the third case in Exhibit 19-3). To avoid this problem the requirement of subagency generally has been dropped from MLS membership.

The fourth case represents the basic example of dual agency. A single broker has both the listing contract with the seller and a buyer agency agreement with the purchaser. As noted below, this is an increasingly common situation, often treated through the use of designated agents, one for the buyer and one for the seller.

Exhibit 19-3 Types of Brokerage Relationships

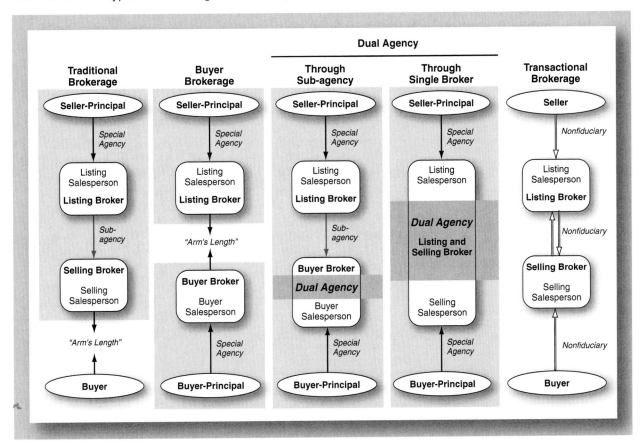

The fifth case, transaction brokerage, is a recent effort to replace the classical agency relationship. Some background on the problems of agency is helpful to understand it.

Concept Check

19.10 Brokerage firms are increasingly faced with an unintended internal dual agency problem because of the increase in what practice?

Problems in Real Estate Agency Relationships and Disclosures

The nature of the real estate brokerage business tends to confuse and stress the traditional agency relationships described above. For example, many thoughtful observers have questioned whether it is possible for a broker serving as a dual agent to simultaneously "stand in the shoes" of both a buyer and a seller. Yet the occurrence of this conflict grows with the increasing practice of buyer brokerage. To mitigate the concern about dual agency, virtually every state has imposed strict requirements of disclosure and written consent for the buyers and sellers involved. Many observers still question whether this is sufficient protection since the nature of the problem is subtle and challenging to understand. One solution that a number of states have resorted to in dual agency is to provide for **designated agents.** When a brokerage firm is serving both a buyer and seller as clients, this arrangement allows the broker to designate a separate salesperson to represent each client. These persons are charged to maintain an "arm's-length" relationship within the firm, though the broker remains privy to the affairs of both clients. There is debate whether any such device is sufficient to solve the dual agent conflict. Meanwhile, numerous legal challenges to dual agency have emerged.

Exhibit 19-4 The Problem of Unintentional Dual Agency

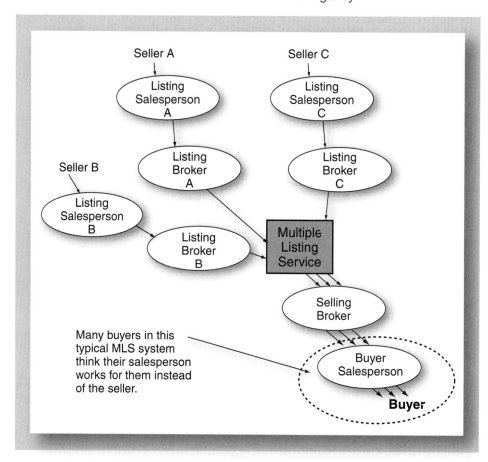

Probably the most common problem in real estate brokerage relationships is *unintended* dual agency. As noted above and depicted in Exhibit 19-4, the normal brokerage practice of today depends on MLS systems, with a salesperson working with the buyer as a subagent of the seller. Yet that salesperson typically "represents" numerous listings, has no direct contact with the seller, and meanwhile is actively engaged in fostering a personal relationship with the buyer. Under these conditions it is no surprise if many buyers believe that the selling agent represents them rather than the seller. Again, while states have adopted extensive disclosure requirements to clarify the loyalty of the salesperson engaged in subagency, legal challenges of this arrangement continue to arise. Some states now have gone so far as to enact laws stipulating that a salesperson showing a house to a prospective buyer automatically becomes the agent of the buyer unless the salesperson declares otherwise in writing at the outset of the dealings.[1]

Concept Check

19.11 What might a broker do to mitigate the dual agency problem occurring within the firm due to the firm's being both a listing broker and a buyer broker?

---

1. See, for example, Illinois, Virginia, Maryland, and the District of Columbia.

Explore The Web

Go the website of the Association of Real Estate License Law Officials (ARELLO) at www.arello.com/site/rulesLaws.jsp#USRules-Laws. Find your state on the list. If your state is not listed on the ARELLO website, find yours using a search engine and such key words as "*yourstate* real estate license." As examples, for New York, this leads you to: http://dos.state.ny.us/lcns/realest.html; for California, http://www.dre.ca.gov/; and for Illinois, http://www.obre.state.il.us/realest/REALEST.HTM. Then go to the online "Rules and Laws." Find out what the law is in your state regarding dual agency. Is it legal? What disclosure is required? If a broker or salesperson fails to disclose his or her agency relationship to a customer (i.e., the prospective buyer) does your state law make them automatically an agent of the customer?

Transaction Brokers

The inherent tendency for real estate brokerage to result in dual agency has prompted about half of all states to create a new type of brokerage relationship known as a **transaction broker** or *facilitating or intermediary broker* (shown as the fifth case in Exhibit 19-3). In this relationship a broker assists with a transaction between a buyer and seller, but the broker does not represent either party. Transaction brokers are required to exercise skill, care, and diligence in dealing with the parties, and they must deal honestly and fairly with both parties. In other words, they owe both parties the standard business characteristics of competence and fair dealing, but they are not bound by the strict fiduciary requirements of agents. A transaction broker's status must also be disclosed in writing to all relevant parties.[2]

Agency problems within real estate brokerage remain difficult to fully solve, and no proposed solution is perfect. Therefore wise practice in use of brokerage services includes two steps: First, be sure that you clearly understand whom a broker represents. Second, in all cases provide information to the broker strictly on a need to know basis. That is, do not impart any more information about your income, motivations for sale, financing alternatives or other financial matters than is clearly pertinent to the transaction.

Concept Check

19.12   What is a broker who represents neither buyer nor seller called?

Licensing of Real Estate Brokers and Salespersons

All 50 states and the District of Columbia have **licensing laws** that regulate persons and companies that engage in the brokerage business. In all of these jurisdictions, a license is required to conduct real estate brokerage activities, which include the purchase, sale, renting, leasing, auctioning, and managing of real estate for others.

---

2. The adoption of designated agency and of transaction or facilitating brokerage by states is detailed in an unpublished survey of the Association of Real Estate License Law Officials (ARELLO) completed in 1999.

State licensing laws generally prescribe two levels of real estate brokerage licensing—the broker license and the salesperson license. The most complete license is the **broker license,** because only a broker is permitted to own and operate a real estate brokerage business. Brokers are responsible for the completion of documents used in sales and leases negotiated by people in their business, for handling money held in trust for clients (e.g., earnest money deposits or rent collected), and for the actions of their employees. Each real estate sales office, therefore, must have at least one licensed broker.

To enter the brokerage business, one must first obtain a **salesperson license.** The salesperson can be either an employee of a broker or an independent contractor of the brokerage firm. The salesperson may perform business activities, such as negotiating listing contracts or contracts for sale, but must perform them in the name of the broker. Also, laws and regulations usually strictly forbid salespersons from holding client moneys in trust; these funds must be delivered to the broker or the broker's trust account shortly after receiving them.

Concept Check

19.13 List five real estate services which require licensing to be performed for others.

Brokerage Licensing Administration

As shown in Exhibit 19-5, the line of authority for real estate brokerage licensing begins with the legislative branch of state government, which originates licensing laws and amendments. Interpretations of state licensing laws take the form of rules and regulations set by the state's **real estate commission.** The commission is usually comprised of prominent brokers and nonbroker (i.e., public interest) members. In some states, the commission is part of the department of state government responsible for licensing many occupations (e.g., appraisers, barbers, contractors, and morticians).

The real estate commission has several functions. First, it specifies educational requirements for applicants and licensees. It may also prescribe courses and determine whether other courses, usually offered outside the state, are equivalent to those prescribed. The second function is to provide examinations. Passing the state license examination is the

Exhibit 19-5 Organizational Structure for Administering Real Estate Licensing Laws

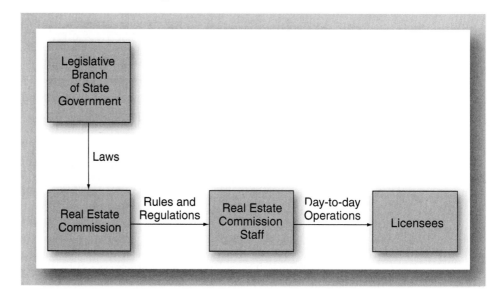

determining factor in obtaining a real estate license. Finally, the commission enforces the license law and regulations implementing the law. The commission must hold hearings for licensees accused of violating state licensing laws and has the right to reprimand licensees and to suspend or revoke their licenses.

The commission staff carries out the day-to-day business of administering the license law. The chief administrative officer is responsible to the commission for developing educational materials, record keeping, collecting license fees, and researching complaints against licensees.

How to Obtain a Real Estate License

Unlike a driver's license, a real estate license obtained in one state does not necessarily qualify one to practice real estate brokerage in another state. Nevertheless, the requirements for obtaining brokerage licenses generally have become more uniform among the states in recent years. A greater degree of reciprocity exists today than in the past, especially with respect to education and examination requirements. To answer the question of how to obtain a broker's license, we examine the various licensing requirements, which include exemptions, general requirements, education, examinations, and experience.

Exemptions. Some persons who buy, sell, rent, or lease real estate for others are exempt from licensing laws. Usually attorneys, because of their extensive legal training, are exempt. Other exempt categories may include resident managers, government employees (e.g., state transportation department employees), trustees, executors, and those with the power of attorney. These exemptions either involve public employees or persons who have a special relationship with the parties for whom they perform brokerage services.

General Requirements. Anyone interested in obtaining a salesperson license must apply to take the salesperson license examination. On the application, individuals must demonstrate that they have satisfied a set of general requirements, such as minimum age (usually 18 years for a salesperson license and 21 years for a broker license), general education (usually a high school diploma), and a good reputation. Some states require references. Finally, they must satisfy any specified prelicensing education requirements of the state. In most states the minimum prelicensing education is at least 45 classroom hours of prescribed material.

Once applicants satisfy these general and educational requirements and pay a fee, they may sit for the state examination. If they earn a passing grade, applicants may receive or apply for a license from the state real estate commission. Another fee may be required then. Applicants for a license usually must specify a broker (i.e., a sponsor) with whom the license will be placed.

Traditionally, applicants for brokerage licenses had to demonstrate their financial capacity to cover damage judgments brought against them by clients. Some states now, however, have established a **recovery fund** with moneys from license fees. Payments from this fund can be used to pay some types of judgments against licensees. Other states require licensees to purchase **errors and omission insurance** to cover damages arising from professional mistakes.

Experience Requirements. Generally, states do not impose a brokerage experience requirement (i.e., an apprenticeship) for obtaining salesperson licenses. For a brokerage license, however, an applicant must have actual experience as a salesperson in addition to taking further course work in real estate. This experience requirement involves at least one year and does not exceed five years.

License Law Infractions

State licensing laws prescribe behavioral requirements with which licensees must comply to keep their licenses. Most laws specify that licensees must not behave in an unethical,

www.arello.com/site/ rulesLaws.jsp

The same ARELLO link to state regulations used in Explore the Web concerning the problem of dual agency can also take you to the licensing requirements for most states.

fraudulent, or dishonest manner toward their clients and prospective buyers. License laws generally seek to prevent the following activities:

- *Mishandling trust money,* including practices such as commingling trust money with personal funds and accepting noncash payments in trust.
- *Improper handling of fees,* including paying commissions to licensees not in the broker's employ and paying commissions to unlicensed persons.
- *Failure to provide required information,* including failure to provide copies of contracts to all relevant parties and failure to inform buyers of closing costs.
- *Misrepresentation and fraud,* including taking kickbacks without the employer's knowledge, false advertising, and intentionally misleading clients or prospective buyers.
- *Improper business practices,* including offering property at terms other than those specified by clients or failure to submit all offers to clients.

Certification of Real Estate Occupations

There are a number of certification or designation programs in real estate brokerage. Practitioners voluntarily seek designations and certificates from trade or professional organizations because they want to differentiate themselves from those with less training, experience, and professionalism. With these credentials they expect to obtain more customers or be able to charge higher fees. Various institutes, societies, and councils affiliated with the **National Association of Realtors** (NAR) offer designations in specialty fields of the real estate brokerage business. In addition, minority brokers may seek designations through the National Association of Real Estate Brokers. Some of these designations are primary signaling devices within a particular segment of the real estate business (e.g., property management, industrial and office properties, and real estate counseling).

Brokerage and salesperson licensees may choose to become affiliated with a local Board of Realtors, which is associated with the NAR as a Realtor (broker) or Realtor-Associate (salesperson).[3] Salespersons working under a broker member of a Board of Realtors are also required to belong to the board. Typically the board charges the broker for all of the firm's members, who in turn usually charge the salespersons for their memberships. Such affiliations are secondary signals to the public that licensees abide by the NAR code of ethics, in addition to the primary signaling device of state licensing.

www.realtor.org

Scroll down and select "Real Estate Specialties" for a very large set of links to NAR specialty affiliates and other sites.

The Marketing Function

Market Segmentation and Specialization and Service

Real estate brokerage firms, like most firms that have a marketing function, practice **market segmentation;** that is, they attempt to identify **submarkets** in which they can specialize and concentrate. Some brokers specialize by property type; they serve sellers and buyers of commercial, industrial, residential, agricultural, office, or recreational properties. Sometimes brokers limit their activities to a particular section of a city, such as the southeast or northwest. Brokers who specialize in large commercial or industrial properties may operate over a wide geographic area, sometimes even nationally or internationally.

In all cases, however, successful brokers are able to relate to the needs of buyers and sellers and help them solve their problems. Obviously, sellers want to sell properties quickly for as high a price as they can obtain. Buyers want to find properties that will best serve their needs quickly for as low a price as possible. Thus, the broker's role is to facilitate the transaction process, and guide the client successfully through the steps of the process. Successful brokers understand that clients must be pleased with their service and

---

3. The term Realtor® is a federally registered collective trademark. Only active brokers who are members of local and state Boards of Realtors affiliated with NAR are permitted to use this trademark.

R eal estate brokers and salespersons are people oriented. They are persons who can understand the instructions, requests, and feelings of others. Moreover, they are comfortable guiding and persuading others to make decisions. Finally, they are positive persons who are basically optimistic, enthusiastic, and self-motivated. At least 75 percent of brokers and salespersons are involved in residential sales. However, within that sphere are a wide variety of products, clients, and firms. Though there are very large brokerage organizations, the typical residential firm is small, with two-thirds of firms having no more than five persons. Few occupations see more diversity in the background of the persons involved. About 80 to 90 percent of brokers and salespersons come to real estate from another career, and their backgrounds virtually span the spectrum of service occupations from accounting to zoo keeping.

Residential Real Estate Brokerage

While the educational level of persons in brokerage and sales is varied, slightly more than two-thirds of salespersons have a college degree.

A strong attraction for many who pursue real estate brokerage is the opportunity to be self-employed. By the same token, it is a field offering little income security. While the potential is good, the income can be uncertain and volatile. While the median income for brokers and salespersons, according to Department of Labor data is around $30,000, a National Association of Realtors survey in 2001 showed 23 percent of its membership had an income in excess of $100,000. Work hours for brokers and salespersons are relatively long. Less that 15 percent of the industry are part-time workers, and the remainder average over 45 hours a week. In addition, the hours regularly involve evenings and weekends.

continue to be satisfied after the transaction is closed. As marketing specialists, real estate brokers know that they have only one thing to sell—their service.

Commercial Brokerage

www.sior.com

Home page of a leading professional organization for commercial property brokers and other professionals.

Although the function of commercial brokerage is the same as that of residential broker-age—facilitating transactions between buyers and sellers—the activities of commercial brokers usually differ considerably from those of residential brokers. Almost all types of properties except one- to four-family residential properties, public properties (e.g., schools, municipal buildings, court houses), and churches can be included in the catch-all commercial category. In reality, it includes almost all income-producing properties.

Relative to residential transactions, commercial transactions are larger and the parties are more knowledgeable. Thus, brokers often seek to match potential buyers with the owners of specific properties and then "get out of the way." Even in these cases, however, potential buyers will want important information about the property and perhaps competing properties. They will want a multiyear record of past income and expenses; detailed information about current leases, together with summary information about the implications of the leases for projected income, expenses, and tenant turnover; and information on major repairs, additions, or renovations. In short, they will want a complete and detailed cash flow analysis as discussed in Chapter 16. In addition, they will want certifications of inspections and compliance with all relevant laws and regulations. Buyers also may want inspections to detect the presence of any hazardous wastes on the property. The broker often must work with the seller in obtaining and providing all requested information. Thus, an important part of the broker's service is to put together a printed marketing information package for a listed property and reports to enable a prospective buyer to complete "due diligence" for the property. This can include a detailed description of the property, adequate market information to evaluate the market context of the property, descriptions of competitive properties, details of current leases and tenants, one or more cash flow "pro formas" or cash flow projection displays and other items. The broker must be capable of collecting this information and assembling it into an effective professional "sales package."

Commercial brokers also must negotiate compromises between buyers and sellers when they reach an impasse over a particular issue. Often a major obstacle is the price;

Commercial property brokerage involves the sale and leasing of income-producing properties. These include all manner of rental properties as well as owner-occupied properties of businesses or other entities. The types of properties span office buildings, hotels, restaurants, apartments, retail stores, shopping centers, industrial plants, and a host of specialty properties. Most commercial brokers and salespersons will specialize in one or a few of these property types, sometimes becoming established as an expert for a type of specialty property at the national or international level.

Commercial real estate brokers, unlike residential brokers, deal with two separate clienteles. On the one hand, they are involved with actual occupants, that is, as a leasing agent or tenant representative. On the other hand, they are dealing with income property investors. They must market the space to the first group and ownership of the properties to the second. Most of the large commercial brokerage companies in the United States provide a great deal of local market data and research so they can service a cadre of sophisticated clients who are making

Commercial Real Estate Brokerage

multimillion dollar investment decisions. Several trade organizations represent the various commercial real estate subspecialties, including the American Industrial Real Estate Association, the Hotel and Motel Brokers of America, the National Association of Industrial and Office Properties, the Real Estate Exchange—a forum for women in commercial real estate, the International Council of Shopping Centers, and the Society of Industrial and Office Realtors. Additionally, the CCIM Institute provides a well-established industry designation, Certified Commercial Investment Member (CCIM), and a supporting education program for the designation.

About 6 percent of real estate brokers are involved with commercial real estate. In general, commercial brokers and salespersons work on a straight commission basis, though newer members in the profession may be given a draw or salary since deals often require many months to consummate. Commissions on commercial sales can range between 2 and 10 percent, while leasing commissions may be 4 to 7 percent. Where the average residential broker earned $47,500 per year in 2001, the average commercial broker earned around $60,000.

brokers often find it in their best interest to suggest a compromise, which might involve creatively placing non-real estate consideration on the negotiating table as well. Not infrequently, the broker is required to lower the commission in order to bring the asking and bid prices into line.

Concept Check

19.14 Two important functions of a commercial real estate broker are to provide the prospective buyer with _____ , and to negotiate _____ .

Residential Brokerage

Almost all brokers in a community have the same inventory (e.g., the list of MLS properties), and buyers could learn about some of these properties by reading classified advertising. Therefore, a broker's property inventory is not the main reason buyers and sellers use brokers or choose one brokerage firm over others. Rather, it is the service the firm is expected to provide.

Potential customers usually choose a brokerage firm on the basis of the firm's reputation in the community, personal acquaintance with the broker or a salesperson, or recommendation by a satisfied customer. Some customers may also rely on the reputation or general image of a brokerage franchise operation such as RE/MAX, ERA, Century 21, Prudential Preferred Properties, or Coldwell Banker.

The service provided by a brokerage firm is to help clients make a decision and then to help them implement that decision. For example, buyers will usually need information about alternative choices of properties in the market, their prices, and how they may meet the buyer's needs. The broker or salesperson can obtain information about such matters as utility expenses, taxes, maintenance, and legal issues regarding alternative properties. The broker or salesperson can also suggest ways of modifying or using the property in particular ways needed by the buyer. Finally, the broker or salesperson can help the buyer find and compare financing alternatives. Overall, the objective of a broker or salesperson should be to help the client (buyer or seller) to analyze the proposed purchase or sale and to guide the client to a decision with which he or she is comfortable.

Concept Check

19.15   Name three factors that might influence a customer's choice of brokerage firm.

Discrimination Prohibited. Federal and state laws prohibit **discrimination in housing** on the bases of race, color, religion, national origin, sex, familial status, and handicap. The main federal law prohibiting discrimination is Title VIII of the Civil Rights Act of 1968, commonly called the Fair Housing Act. This law declares the following acts to be illegal:

1. Refusing to sell, rent, or deal with any person.
2. Offering terms and conditions that differ among buyers or renters, influenced by the prohibited characteristics.
3. Advertising housing as available only to certain buyers.
4. Denying that housing is available for sale or rental when it is actually available.
5. Persuading someone to sell housing by telling him or her that minority groups are moving into the neighborhood, a practice commonly called "blockbusting."
6. Denying home loans or varying home loan terms on the basis of prohibited characteristics.
7. Denying or limiting the use of real estate services to anyone on the basis of prohibited characteristics.
8. Coercing, intimidating, or interfering with any person in the exercise or enjoyment of these federal rights.

An important exemption to the Fair Housing Act is for owner-occupants living in a unit of a residential building serving four or fewer households, including single-family homes. In other words, by the exemption to this law, owners of such units may discriminate on the prohibited bases, provided they do not employ the services of a broker or agent. For *racial* discrimination, however, the one- to four-unit exemption is overridden by another federal law. In June 1968 the U.S. Supreme Court in the case of *Jones v. Mayer Co.* held that the Civil Rights Act of 1866, barring "all racial discrimination, private as well as public, in the sale or rental of property," preempts the 1968 law.[4]

Concept Check

19.16   What are the seven factors on which discrimination is prohibited under the fair housing laws?

Another exemption pertains to discrimination against "familial status." In multifamily residential facilities operated for "elderly" persons, defined to be individuals 62 years and over, the owners or management can refuse to sell or rent to persons under 62, or to families having children.[5] State laws generally mirror the Fair Housing Law.

The federal and state fair housing laws apply equally to property owners and their agents. In other words, discrimination on any of the specified bases by anyone involved in

---

4. See *Fred v. Kokinokos,* D.C. Ill. 1973, 381 F. Supp. 165. In 1868 the substance of the Civil Rights Act of 1866 was incorporated into the 14th Amendment to the Constitution of the United States.

5. The age limit is dropped to 55 when at least 80 percent of the units are occupied by at least one person 55 years or older.

19-2

Actions Are More Important than Words in Deciding Whether Discrimination Occurred

A recent case* alleging housing discrimination decided in June 1999 by a U.S. District Court demonstrates that agents and brokerage firms cannot be held liable when they follow the law and act in good faith, in spite of comments that might suggest otherwise. In *Ileka v. Lyons,* the African-American plaintiffs argued initially that the white defendant, Mary Lyons, refused to sell them a house after they had made an offer in July 1997, and that the listing agent (Mary Small) and her brokerage firm (Erickson Realty and Management Co.) had aided and abetted in the discrimination. The seller claimed health reasons and the

Ileka, Ileka, and Leadership Council for Metropolitan Open Communities, Inc. v. Mary Lyons, Michael Lyons, Kevin Lyons, James P. Heywood, Mary Small, and Vincent R. Innocenti, d/b/a Erickson Realty and Management Co., No. 98 C 986, U.S. District Court for the Northern District of Illinois, Eastern Division.

inability to find suitable alternative housing, and not racial prejudice, had caused her to refuse the offer.

Subsequently, in July 1998, the Ilekas bought the house from the seller, leaving only the agent and brokerage company as defendants in the case alleging violations of the U.S. Fair Housing and Civil Rights Acts.

In spite of a comment by the agent to the seller when she listed the property and agreed to place the listing in the MLS that "the blacks will come," the court found that the company and agent did not refuse to deal with the buyers. Rather, the agent Mary Small had placed the property in an MLS accessible to African-American buyers. Furthermore, she had tried to find suitable alternative housing for the seller, Mary Lyons, which would have facilitated the sale. The court also found no evidence that the agent had attempted to sell the house to white buyers and concluded that there had been no "coercion, intimidation, threat, or interference" by the defendants against either the seller or the buyers.

a housing transaction is prohibited, unless covered by an exemption. (See Industry Issues 19-2 for an example of how the courts determine whether discrimination may have occurred.)

Concept Check

19.17 Name the 1968 case in which the U.S. Supreme Court ruled that discrimination by race is absolutely prohibited in any form or at any level.

Internet Marketing. The Internet is increasingly being used to market properties. From the website of the National Association of Realtors (www.realtor.com) buyers can find residential properties listed by Realtors all across the country. The website, www.homestore.com is closely related to NAR, but includes links to other real estate professionals in addition to Realtors.

Commercial properties are also marketed over the Internet. The CCIM Institute (www.ccim.com), for example, has an Internet listing service called CCIMNet Properties (www.ccimnet.com). Real Estate Mag (www.mortgagemag.com) provides links to hundreds of residential and commercial property listings. Both Co-Star (www.costar.com) and LoopNet (www.loopnet.com) provide online listing, trading, and information for commercial real estate professionals (See Industry Issues 19-3). By all indications, the **Internet marketing** of real properties will continue to grow. Additional examples of sites with Internet marketing of homes and related services are:

www.cre.org

Provides links to the organizations whose websites are shown in the text, and to other real estate websites.

www.century21.com/home.aspx
www.homegain.com/h/index_html
http://list.realestate.yahoo.com/

19-3

Online Commercial Listing Services Are Happening

A weak commercial real estate market and resulting cost consciousness may be bringing profits to one facet of the industry, online listing services. The savings from going to online listings can be substantial for a large commercial brokerage service, perhaps $150,000 a year through reduction of research and marketing expenses, according to one study completed for the Society of Industrial and Office Realtors. Thus, it is not surprising that thousands of commercial brokerage firms of all sizes have logged on to the leading systems, Co-Star www.costar.com and LoopNet www.loopnet.com/qry.asp.

While LoopNet recently announced its first quarter of profitability (fourth quarter of 2002), the dominant Co-Star reported its sixth straight quarter of positive income growth. But the long-term viability of these enterprises appears to depend on their ability to maintain the quality of their data. This is a major challenge because acquiring accurate commercial real estate information is very difficult. Both Co-Star and LoopNet have distinguished their approach to the business from a number of failed online listing competitors by their willingness to put serious capital into data collection. Co-Star has a staff of some 500 who make six million phone calls a year and drive a million miles to collect and verify data. From this, Co-Star provides not only listing information but more complete market data for the 50 major markets in which it operates. LoopNet follows a different model, relying on local broker networks in 340 markets.

The competition between these two ventures, along with some apparent new participants including the CCIM Institute, will likely depend on three factors: volume of users, breadth of market coverage, and quality of data. While Co-Star touts its independent, wide-ranging research approach, LoopNet points to the growing success of its reliance on local brokers, arguing that, with a stake in the transactions, local brokers have the greatest incentive to assure that the information they share is valid.

Source: Based on "Profit and Loss Online: Co-Star LoopNet Begin to Realize Profits as Smaller Rivals Test Viability." Jessica Roe, *Commercial Property News,* March 16, 2003.

International Aspects of Brokerage

World economies have become increasingly intertwined. As part of these economies, real estate markets have also become internationalized. This trend has been labeled the *globalization* of real estate markets. Many U.S. companies and investors have purchased real estate in foreign countries, and many foreign companies and investors have purchased U.S. real estate. In the 1980s Japanese companies purchased a number of prominent buildings in the downtowns of major U.S. cities for relatively high prices, attracting media attention. Since that time, however, Japanese investors have sold some of these properties, and foreign ownership of certain properties (e.g., Rockefeller Center in New York City) has ended in bankruptcy. In addition to Japanese investors, Canadian, Dutch, British, and German investors are, or have been, very active.

A number of large firms in the United States and abroad find foreign investment to be a lucrative part of their business. While some of the largest purchases of U.S. real estate have been made without the aid of brokerage firms, most deals have involved brokers. The commission on a typical transaction can be several million dollars, and the brokerage firms are expected to earn these large commissions by being of real service to buyers and sellers. For example, they normally will need to provide even more supporting information about properties and markets to foreign investors than to domestic customers.

Although most foreign investors speak English or have English-speaking staffs, most U.S. brokers must work through cooperative arrangements with local brokers in non-English-speaking countries. Brokers who deal with foreigners must be sensitive to the cultures, customs, and mores of other countries. Speaking a foreign language can facilitate communication with a client and also increase a broker's sensitivity to other cultures. To deal in international real estate, U.S. brokers must think increasingly in terms of a global market and be prepared to deal with foreign investors on their own terms.

www.ired.com

The International Real Estate Digest provides over 50,000 links to real estate related websites throughout the world.

Listing Contracts

A listing contract is an agreement between the owner of real estate and a real estate broker or brokerage firm that requires the broker to attempt to sell the property. If the broker is successful in finding a buyer, the agreement requires the owner to pay the broker a fee or commission. The broker's fee or commission is usually calculated as a percentage of the selling price (e.g., a commission of 6 percent on a selling price of $100,000 is $6,000). If the broker is unsuccessful in selling the property, the agreement lapses after a specified time period (or reasonable time period if a time period is not specifically stated), and neither party has any further obligation.

As discussed previously in this chapter, the broker, as an agent, has a fiduciary relationship with the principal and therefore cannot do anything that would not be in the best interests of the principal. For example, the broker may not purchase the property for himself or herself secretly through a third party. The broker could, of course, purchase the property openly and directly from the principal, provided the complete identity of the broker and his or her relationship to the principal is known by the principal. Furthermore, the broker-agent cannot withhold information from the principal. The broker must present every offer to purchase the property to the principal, even if the agent considers an offer too low, since it may be in the principal's best interest to sell the property quickly, no matter how low the offer.

Additionally, the broker-agent may not attempt to frighten the principal into accepting a low offer or suggest to a prospective buyer that the seller will accept a price lower than the listed price, unless the principal has specifically instructed him to convey such information to a prospective buyer. (A broker can, of course, state the obvious fact that the seller *might* accept a lower price and that he or she is obligated to present every offer to the seller.)

Critical to any listing contract is the question of when the broker becomes entitled to a commission. Traditionally, the broker is entitled to a commission upon finding a buyer who is ready, willing, and able to purchase the property at the price and terms specified in the listing contract. Of course, if the seller accepts (signs) an offer with different terms and conditions, then the broker also is entitled to the commission. A number of situations can cause a seller to refuse an offer, as shown in Industry Issues 19-4. If the seller refuses to sell upon being presented with an offer meeting the original terms and conditions, or cannot deliver the property for any reason due to his or her fault, the broker is entitled to the full commission, and has grounds for suit. If both buyer and seller sign a contract but then agree to cancel it, the broker still is entitled to a commission. If a contract is contingent upon the buyer obtaining financing, or upon any other condition, then the broker generally is not entitled to a commission until the condition has been fulfilled. Recourse for the broker, seller, and buyer, in the event of failure to perform by one of the parties, is discussed in Chapter 20.

Concept Check

19.18 What must a broker do to be entitled to a commission under a listing contract?

Types of Listing Contracts

There are three basic types of listing contracts, although only two—the *open listing* and the *exclusive right of sale listing*—are used with much frequency. Another term, *multiple listing,* is sometimes confused as a type of listing; however, multiple listing is actually a cooperative arrangement among brokerage firms to share their listings. It is not a basic type of listing contract between a seller and a broker.

Industry Issues

A Ready, Willing, and Able Buyer

Lloyd and Edna Evans desired to sell their property. They employed the services of Fleming Realty and Insurance, Inc., a corporation engaged in providing real estate brokerage services. These parties entered into a listing agreement containing the usual provision that required the Evanses to pay a commission if Fleming obtained a ready, willing, and able purchaser. The broker located Neal Hasselbach, who signed a standard purchase agreement offering to buy the Evans property on the terms specified in the listing agreement. In essence, in this document Mr. Hasselbach offered to pay the asking price to the Evanses. Based on their fears that Mr. Hasselbach was not financially able to purchase their property, Mr. and Mrs. Evans refused to sign a sales contract with this buyer.

Issue: Did Fleming Realty and Insurance procure a ready, willing, and able buyer, and was it therefore entitled to the agreed-upon commission?

Decision: Yes.

Reasons: The evidence at the trial court showed that Hasselbach had a net worth, in cash and property, in excess of $250,000. The proposed contract for the Evanses' land totaled $155,840, to be paid in a down payment of $35,000 and 10 annual installments of $12,184 each. The jury's conclusion that Hasselbach was financially able to perform this sale contract was reasonable. Since the buyer fulfilled the requirements of the listing agreement's procuring clause, the broker was entitled to collect the commission established even though the sale was not closed.

Source: *Fleming Realty and Insurance Inc. v. Evans*, 259 NW 2d 604 (Neb. 1977).

Open Listing

The **open listing** is a contract between a property owner and a broker that gives the broker the right to market the property. The distinguishing characteristic of the open listing is its lack of exclusivity. The property owners are not precluded from listing the property with other brokers. If they do list the property with two or more brokers, only the broker who procures a buyer will be owed a commission. If the owners sell the property themselves, none of the brokers will be owed a commission.

The open listing is sometimes used with large, special-purpose, or otherwise difficult-to-sell properties. The owners may not be willing to tie up the property with one broker. A single brokerage firm may not operate in a wide enough geographic area or have sufficient expertise, so the owners may list with several brokers to obtain a wider market for their property. A broker may be willing to accept such a listing because he or she believes (1) there is a good chance of selling the property, and the owner will not accept an exclusive agency or exclusive right of sale listing, or (2) there is not a good chance of selling the property, but there is little to lose in accepting the listing; in other words, there is *some* chance the property will sell and yield a commission.

Exclusive Agency Listing

This type of listing contract requires the sellers to pay a commission to the broker if the property is sold by anyone other than the owners. The owners, however, retain the right to sell the property without incurring liability for a commission.

This type of listing is used infrequently. Since the owner can sell the property and avoid paying a commission, the **exclusive agency listing** provides far less protection to the broker than the exclusive right of sale listing discussed below. Thus, brokers are usually less willing to spend time and effort to market properties listed under the exclusive agency arrangement.

Exclusive Right of Sale Listing

For the **exclusive right of sale listing** contract, the sellers list their property with one broker and agree to pay that broker a commission if the property is sold within a specified time or, if not specified, within a reasonable time. Thus, the broker will be owed a commission if any other brokers *or even the owner* sell the property during the contract period. A typical exclusive right of sale listing contract form is shown at the end of the chapter in Exhibit 19-7. Note the operative words in provision 1, "SELLER gives BROKER the EXCLUSIVE RIGHT TO SELL the real and personal property . . . described below . . ."

For several reasons, the exclusive right of sale feature is included in the vast majority of brokerage arrangements. Although one might think at first that such a feature would create an unfair burden on sellers, the exclusivity provision has produced faster sales. With the exclusive right of sale, brokers are more willing to commit their firms to engage in thorough marketing programs for properties and to spend whatever time is necessary to sell them. Under this arrangement, brokers usually advertise in public media, prepare photographs and brochures about listed properties, and work long hours to obtain buyers.

Second, brokers have realized that to justify their best efforts, they must have the protection provided by the exclusive right of sale provision. Thus, most brokers require sellers to accept this feature. Owners may, of course, refuse and attempt to find a broker who will accept an open or exclusive agency listing, but most do not.

Finally, a multiple listing service (MLS) accepts only exclusive right of sale listings. Other types of listings would undermine the workings of an MLS. For example, if an MLS property were sold by an owner or a broker who was not a member of the MLS, the MLS broker would probably lose the commission. It would not take many such sales to put the MLS out of business. Thus, to obtain the advantages of having their properties listed by an MLS, owners must agree to an exclusive right of sale listing contract with their broker.

Innovation in Brokerage

Because real estate brokerage firms are small and numerous it is not surprising that there is constant experimentation with new approaches to the business. For example, many firms have explored fixed fee services in the past. Today the emergence of the Internet has enhanced the possibilities for innovation, and some firms are attempting to "unbundle" traditional brokerage services. They are offering various degrees of brokerage service ranging from nothing except administrative and document assistance for perhaps a one percent fee to a nearly complete "package" of services including listing on MLS plus all other services except showing the property, all for a fee of perhaps one percent less than full brokerage service. Only time will reveal which of these experiments thrives.

To the extent that real estate brokerage is an information service it can be heavily affected by the emergence of the Internet. As we have noted, this medium has been embraced by the brokerage industry. Many, however, point out that real estate is an extremely complex good, with many non-financial characteristics. As a result, another important part of brokerage is counseling: educating, guiding, and assisting both buyer and seller through the transaction process. It is not clear that the value of this service is diminished by the presence of the Internet. Therefore, it remains difficult to determine how much fundamental change the Internet will bring to the industry.

Concept Check

19.19   When is a broker entitled to a commission in an open listing? Exclusive agency listing? Exclusive right-of-sale listing?

Listing Contract Provisions

While most brokers use standard, preprinted listing contract forms (see Exhibit 19-7) and most property owners are willing to sign such forms, both parties to such a contract should be certain their interests are protected. For example, when signing a listing contract, sellers may want to assure themselves that the brokerage firm will try diligently to sell the property by advertising in various media, that the property will be put in the local MLS, that the listing agreement is limited to a reasonable period, and that the firm will provide regular reports to the seller about the progress (or lack of it) being made.

The brokerage firm, on the other hand, will want to assure itself that the duration of the listing agreement is long enough to give the firm a reasonable time to sell the property; that the seller understands that a commission will be owed if the firm has found a buyer who is ready, willing, and able to pay the purchase price; that the firm's personnel will have access to the property at all reasonable times; and that the firm is protected for a reasonable time after the listing expires—that is, if a buyer learns about the property through the broker's efforts, but then purchases the property after expiration of the listing, the seller still owes the broker a commission.

Also, the listing contract should specify any items of personal property that are included with the real estate and any items whose status as real estate is questionable (e.g., fireplace tools, drapes, carpets, crystal chandeliers, art objects that are built-in).

Concept Check

19.20 What are five issues on which a seller should be clear before signing a listing agreement?

Termination of a Listing Contract

A listing contract terminates under any of three circumstances: the specified period expires, the property is sold, or one of the parties abrogates the terms of the contract. The first two courses of termination are straightforward, and there is usually little question about the result.

Abrogation of terms is less clear and usually more difficult to prove. On the owners' part, the most clear-cut abrogation would be their unwillingness to sign a sale contract with a ready, willing, and able purchaser. While such a refusal rarely happens, it may result in legal action against the owners by both the broker and the buyers. The owners may be legally compelled to pay the broker's commission, since the broker fulfilled his or her part of the contract. In cases in which the owners abrogate the terms by refusing to show the property or by otherwise discouraging prospective buyers, the broker usually refuses to make any further efforts to sell the property.

The broker may abrogate the terms of the contract by failing to market the property effectively. The broker may not advertise sufficiently or make enough effort to sell the property. While owners may have solid legal grounds for terminating the contract, their usual remedy is to wait for the listing to expire. Such contentions are both difficult to prove and costly to pursue legally.

Splitting the Commission

The commission paid by a seller upon consummation of a transaction can be divided between the listing and selling broker in any way they agree. In most communities, however, members of the Board of Realtors agree to a specified percentage of the total commission that the listing brokerage firm and the selling brokerage firm receive. In many communities this percentage is 50 percent to each, but occasionally it is 60–40 percent (in either direction).

Exhibit 19-6   Typical Commission Split

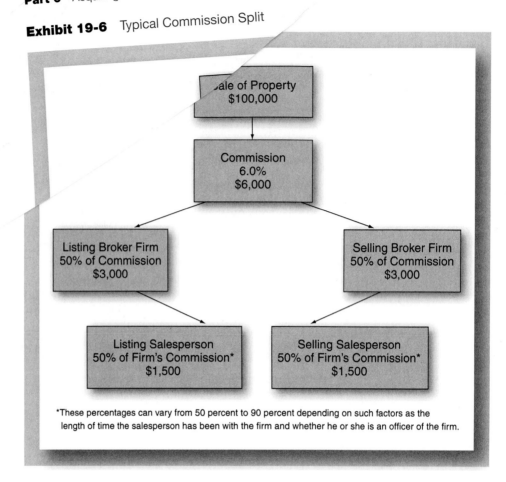

Sale of Property
$100,000

Commission
6.0%
$6,000

Listing Broker Firm
50% of Commission
$3,000

Selling Broker Firm
50% of Commission
$3,000

Listing Salesperson
50% of Firm's Commission*
$1,500

Selling Salesperson
50% of Firm's Commission*
$1,500

*These percentages can vary from 50 percent to 90 percent depending on such factors as the length of time the salesperson has been with the firm and whether he or she is an officer of the firm.

Within each firm the policy may differ as to the percentage the salesman who obtained the listing and the salesman who found the buyer receive, but again, 50 percent each is typical. The split between the salespersons and their broker is more complex. The broker hires most salespersons as independent contractors rather than employees to avoid the responsibility of income tax withholdings, and contributions for workers compensation, unemployment insurance, social security and other benefits. But the broker is responsible for the office expenses and needs to be reimbursed by the salespersons that use it. The most common solution is for the salespersons to split their commission with the broker. Though the split is entirely negotiable, frequently it will give over half to the broker with less experienced salespersons but favors the salesperson more as he or she has more experience. An alternative approach is called a 100 percent commission arrangement; the salesperson gets his or her full commission but is billed by the broker for a share of office expenses plus a fixed management fee. Exhibit 19-6 shows a typical commission split in a transaction involving different listing and selling brokerage firms.

A Listing Situation—Example

Fred and Louise Johnson decide to sell their home in Gainesville, Florida, because Fred's firm has transferred him to Fort Myers. They contact Ben Park, a Realtor with Baden Associates Realty, who sold them the house five years ago. They like Ben—he was courteous and efficient when he helped them find a home, and he has stayed in touch with them since.

Industry Issues

Buyer Brokerage Is Altering the Practice in Residential Real Estate

When a buyer came into Frank T's real estate office in search of a specific Padre Island condominium, the buyer found it was not for sale. So the client hired Frank to find one just like it. With some research, contacts, and phone calls, Frank soon had not only the desired property, but at a price $55,000 less than it had originally listed. He was acting as a buyer's agent—a service that more buyers are using as a way of finding the home they want. "Not enough customers realize that when they talk to a real estate agent, they are talking to someone who represents the interests of the seller," Frank said. That's how it works, unless the buyer enters a contract with the agent to act as a buyer's agent.

The official designation of a person who is representing the buyer is increasing in the consciousness of real estate agents, said the director of the Chicago-based Real Estate Buyers Council, which confers the only official industry designation for buyers' agents—Accredited Buyer Representative. Since the National Association of Realtors adopted the designation in November 1996, the number of Accredited Buyer Representatives has skyrocketed. In March 2000 there were more than 33,000, according to the director, plus more than 900 new members signing up for the designation each month. [In October 2003 there were over 44,000]. "You wouldn't go into court having the other side's attorney represent you," the director pointed out.*

Most commonly, a buyer representative receives a share of the commission from the seller, so the buyer still pays no additional fee. Some buyer brokerages stress the importance of working with an exclusively buyers' brokerage, arguing that a firm doing business for both sellers and buyers never can fully escape a conflict of interest.

Some exclusive buyer agents recommend that persons looking for a buyer agent ask these kinds of questions of prospective agents:

- What percentage of your personal business and what percentage of your company's business is representing buyers? Is the balance of that representing sellers?
- Will you try to sell me one of your listed properties before you show me listings from other real estate companies?
- Do you have information about For Sale by Owner properties?
- How many buyers have you successfully represented in the last six months? May I have the names and phone numbers of three to six of your most recent buyer clients?
- Do you know the six fiduciary, client-level duties you would owe to me if I choose to hire you as my buyer's agent? (Confidentiality, Accountability, Reasonable Skill and Care, Undivided Loyalty, Obedience to Lawful Instructions, Full Disclosure)
- What is your commission? Or do you have hourly rates or a set fee?
- Do you have a list of home inspectors, insurance agents, and reputable lenders for me to consider?
- What clauses will you incorporate in our offer to protect us as buyers?
- Specifically, how will you protect my interests and why should I hire you rather than another agent?

Source: Exerpts from an article by Andrea Jares, "Real Estate Buyers can Hire Agent of their Own," *Corpus Christi Caller-Times*, March 14, 2000.

On May 1, 2003, Ben comes to the Johnsons' home, which is located in Spring Meadow Estates. The Johnsons remind Ben that they paid $132,500 for the house five years ago, but since prices have risen considerably in the meantime, they believe the house is now worth around $165,000. Ben points out some recent sales of similar houses in the neighborhood ranging from $145,000 to $165,000, and he tells them that the house realistically will not sell for more than $155,000. (He suspects this is high and that it will ultimately sell between $145,000 and $155,000 but feels he should give the benefit of the doubt to the client.) After some discussion about the advantages and disadvantages of their house relative to others in the neighborhood, the Johnsons agree the listing price should be $155,000, which will include the kitchen range and refrigerator, two window air conditioners, and one picnic table, as well as the real estate.

514

The property is free of encumbrances except for an existing mortgage with a remaining balance of $82,000. The Johnsons prefer not to give a second mortgage or other financing terms. The existing mortgage has a due-on-sale clause—that is, it cannot be *assumed* (taken over) by the buyer.

The house has four bedrooms, two baths, a living room, dining room, screened porch, double carport, and an outside storage room. It has central heating and central air-conditioning and was built in 1966 with concrete block and stucco (CBS)-on-slab construction. The entire house, except for the kitchen, was carpeted about eight years ago. The house is in reasonably good condition, although the interior and exterior paint is beginning to look dull and the carpet is becoming worn in heavy traffic areas. The lot is approximately one-half acre and is nicely landscaped. The neighborhood contains similar generally well-maintained houses, and property values have increased about 3 percent a year over the past 10 years. According to the Johnsons' deed in the Alachua County Courthouse, the property description is "Parcel No. 3, Block 2 of Spring Meadow Estates, recorded in Plat Book 12, page 28." Ben and the Johnsons agree on a commission rate of 6 percent.

Exhibit 19-7 shows the completed listing form for the Johnsons' property. Not shown is a detailed "profile sheet," referenced in item 2, that accompanies the listing form. This form enables the listing agent to indicate over 200 features of the property, including the presence of the window air conditioners, each appliance, and the picnic table.

Several clauses in the listing contract should be noted: Clause 1 states that it is an exclusive right of sale agreement, covering the real property plus personal property as listed. Note that the default coverage includes all carpets and all light fixtures. Clause 2 addresses the question of latent defects. The seller is held fully responsible for known but undisclosed defects, and the broker is explicitly absolved of any liability for such defects. Clause 4 delineates the seller's responsibility for closing expense items, including responsibility to purchase a title insurance commitment for the prospective buyer. Clause 5 gives the broker the right to incur expenses on behalf of the seller as needed to effect the closing of a sale. Clause 6 gives details of the terms of compensation, including recourses of the seller and broker if the listing is terminated without a sale. Clause 7 explicitly lists the actions that the broker may take during the course of the listing, and provides for the seller's explicit agreement concerning seven particular items. Clause 8 explicitly lists obligations of the seller, including cooperating with the terms of the contract, and to inform the broker prior to taking actions that would affect the broker's capacity to sell the property. Clauses 9 addresses the agency relationship, providing for the possibility of "single agency" or a transaction broker. Clause 12 provides for the distribution of deposits in the event that a buyer fails to complete the transaction.

An issue of growing prominence in residential brokerage is the latent defects problem addressed in clause 2 of the following exhibit. States generally have adopted laws holding the sellers of a residence, *and their agent,* liable for any material defects not plainly evident (e.g., a deteriorated roof or plumbing) if the seller knows about the defects and does not disclose them.

Exhibit 19-7 An Exclusive Right of Sale Listing Agreement

GAINESVILLE MULTIPLE LISTING, INC.
EXCLUSIVE RIGHT OF SALE LISTING AGREEMENT
SINGLE AGENCY

In consideration of the agreement contained here, the sufficiency of which is hereby acknowledged by **Baden Associates Realty**
hereinafter called BROKER, and **Fred and Louise Johnson** hereinafter called SELLER, we hereby jointly agree to the following:

1. AUTHORITY TO SELL PROPERTY: SELLER gives BROKER the EXCLUSIVE RIGHT TO SELL the real and personal property (collectively "Property") described below, at the price and terms described below, beginning the **1st** day of **May** , 20**03** , and terminating at 11:59 p.m. the **30** day of **October** , 20 **03** ("Termination Date"). Upon full execution of a contract for sale and purchase of the Property, all rights and obligations of this Contract will automatically extend through the date of the actual closing of the contract for sale and purchase. SELLER certifies and represents that he/she/it is legally entitled to convey the Property and all improvements.

Price **$155,000.00** Terms **Cash to Owner**

Legal Description **Parcel No 3, Block 2 of Spring Meadow Estates PB 12 PG 28.**

All taxes for the current year, rentals, monthly insurance premiums, hazard insurance premiums and interest on existing mortgages (if any) shall be prorated as of the date of closing. Personal property to be included in the purchase price: All fixed equipment including drapery hardware, light fixtures, carpeting and plants and shrubbery now installed on said property, and such additional personal property as may be listed on the attached profile sheet.

2. SELLER further certifies and represents that the property has no known latent defects and SELLER knows of no facts materially affecting the value or desirability of the property which are not readily observable, except the following: Please Check ☐ **(See Attachment).** SELLER agrees to indemnify and save BROKER harmless of and from any and all loss, damage, suits and claims, including attorney's fees and costs of defense incurred by BROKER on account of any representation made by BROKER in reliance on SELLER'S representation herein. There is attached to this Agreement a GAINESVILLE MULTIPLE LISTING, INC. Profile Sheet and Feature Sheet which are by reference included in and made a part of this Exclusive Right of Sale Listing Agreement.

3. If a lockbox is to be used, the BROKER agrees to use due care in the installation, use, maintenance, and operation of the lockbox. The SELLER agrees to hold the BROKER harmless of and from all claims, demands, costs, judgments and liability which SELLER may suffer as a result of losses or damages arising out of the use, maintenance or operation of the lockbox during the term of this Agreement. Gross negligence on the part of the BROKER or agents acting through him are expressly excluded from this covenant.

SELLER is to initial one of the following: a. SELLER agrees to permit use of lockbox **FJ** . b. SELLER does not agree to permit use of lockbox____ .

4. The SELLER agrees, at his expense, to provide for: (a) preparation of and delivery to the BUYER of a good and sufficient warranty deed (unless otherwise required) conveying an insurable title free and clear of all liens, except encumbrances of record, to be assumed by the BUYER as part of the purchase price and taxes for the year of sale; (b) binder and policy for fee title insurance or abstract from earliest records; (c) state documentary stamps on the deed; (d) SELLER'S attorney fee; (e) recording fees for satisfactions of the liens of record, if same are paid off; (f) certificate of a locally licensed entomologist dated within thirty days prior to closing, showing any improvements on the premises, exclusive of fences, to be apparently free from active infestation (other than infestation by wood destroying fungi) or visible damage (including that caused by wood destroying fungi) by termites or other wood destroying organisms as required to be disclosed by Florida Law.

5. The SELLER agrees that BROKER has the right, at the BROKER'S discretion, to order and obtain on behalf of the SELLER all items necessary to consummate a closing on subject property, such as, but not limited to, pest control report, title insurance, and survey, as may be agreed to in a subsequent purchase and sale agreement and to obtain information relating to the present mortgage(s) on the property. SELLER agrees to reimburse BROKER for any cost incurred in ordering and obtaining such information.

6. (a) For finding a BUYER ready, willing and able to purchase the above described property, SELLER agrees to pay BROKER a compensation of **(6%) six** of the total purchase price, on the terms herein mentioned, or at any price and upon terms acceptable to SELLER, whether the BUYER be secured by BROKER or SELLER, or by ANY OTHER PERSON, or if the property is afterwards sold within **three** months from the termination of this Agreement, or any written extension thereof signed by the BROKER and the SELLER ("The Protection Period") to any person to whom the Property has been shown by the BROKER or his representatives or by cooperating BROKERS, or by the SELLER, or by ANY OTHER PERSON; provided, nevertheless, that the BROKER shall not receive a commission on such a subsequent sale if the SELLER has re-listed the property with another Licensed Real Estate Broker. At SELLER'S request, BROKER may agree to conditionally terminate this Contract as of a date prior to the Termination Date. If BROKER agrees to conditional termination, SELLER must sign a withdrawal agreement and pay a cancellation fee of **$1,000.00** plus applicable sales tax. BROKER may void the conditional termination and SELLER shall pay the fee stated less the cancellation fee in the event SELLER transfers or contracts to transfer the Property during the time period from the date of conditional termination to Termination Date and Protection Period, if applicable.

(b) In the event the property is rented or leased by the SELLER in lieu of sale or in connection with a lease/option agreement, the SELLER will pay the listing BROKER a rental or leasing fee equal to **10** % of the rent to be received, except in cases of occupancy agreements between the SELLER and the BUYER to accommodate the surrender and delivery of possession in connection with closing. Upon exercise of the option to purchase, the owner will pay BROKER compensation in accordance with paragraph 6 (a) hereof.

(c) SELLER **DEFAULT:** In the event a transaction fails to close because of a refusal or failure of SELLER to perform, or Seller refuses to sign a contract for sale and purchase at the price and terms stated in this Contract, SELLER shall pay to BROKER on demand the fee stated in Paragraph 6 (a) hereof.

MLS 012 Page 1 of 3 Rev. 07/00

Exhibit 19-7—continued

7. **BROKER OBLIGATIONS AND AUTHORITY:** BROKER agrees to make diligent and continued efforts to sell the Property until a contract for sale is pending on the Property. SELLER authorizes BROKER to: (SELLER to initial if applicable):

_____ Advertise Property as BROKER deems advisable.

_____ SELLER hereby authorizes BROKER to advertise property on the Internet.

_____ Place For Sale signs on the Property and Sale Pending and/or Sold signs upon full execution of a contract to sell.

_____ Place the Property in a multiple listing service ("MLS"). SELLER authorizes BROKER to cooperate with and compensate buyer agents, transaction brokers and non-representatives as specified in paragraph 10 and 11. SELLER further authorizes BROKER to report to the multiple listing service, in accordance with its rules and regulations, this listing information and price, terms, and financing information on any resulting sale for publication, dissemination and use by authorized Board/Association members, MLS participants and Subscribers.

_____ Utilize SELLER'S name in connection with marketing or advertising the Property, either before or after the sale.

_____ Withhold verbal offers.

_____ Obtain any information relating to the present mortgage(s) on the Property including, but not limited to, existing balance, interest rate, monthly payment, balance in escrow account and payoff amount.

8. **SELLER OBLIGATIONS:** In consideration of the obligations of BROKER, SELLER agrees:
   (a) To cooperate with BROKER in carrying out the purpose of this Contract.
   (b) To refer immediately to BROKER all inquiries regarding the purchase or property lease.
   (c) To provide BROKER with keys to the Property and make the Property available to BROKER to show during reasonable times.
   (d) To inform BROKER prior to leasing, mortgaging or otherwise encumbering the Property.
   (e) To indemnify BROKER and hold BROKER harmless from losses, damages, costs, and expenses of any nature including attorney's fees, and from liability to any person, which BROKER incurs because of SELLER'S negligence, representations, actions, or inactions, or which arise because of use of a lockbox.
   (f) To perform any act reasonably necessary to comply with FIRPTA (Internal Revenue Code Section 1445).

9. **BROKERAGE RELATIONSHIP**

IMPORTANT NOTICE

FLORIDA LAW REQUIRES THAT REAL ESTATE LICENSEES PROVIDE THIS NOTICE TO POTENTIAL SELLERS AND BUYERS OF REAL ESTATE.

You should not assume that any real estate broker or salesperson represents you unless you agree to engage a real estate licensee in an authorized brokerage relationship, either as a single agent or as a transaction broker. You are advised not to disclose any information you want to be held in confidence until you make a decision on representation.

SINGLE AGENT NOTICE

FLORIDA LAW REQUIRES THAT REAL ESTATE LICENSEES OPERATING AS SINGLE AGENTS DISCLOSE TO BUYERS AND SELLERS THEIR DUTIES. As a single agent Baden Associates Realty (insert name of Real Estate entity) and its Associates owe to you the following duties:

1. Dealing honestly and fairly;
2. Loyalty;
3. Confidentiality;
4. Obedience;
5. Full Disclosure;
6. Accounting for all funds;
7. Skill, care and diligence in the transaction;
8. Presenting all offers and counteroffers in a timely manner, unless a party has previously directed the licensee otherwise in writing; and
9. Disclosing all known facts that materially affect the value of residential real property and are not readily observable.

5/1/03	_____	_____
Date	Signature	Signature

IMPORTANT NOTICE

FLORIDA LAW REQUIRES THAT REAL ESTATE LICENSEES PROVIDE THIS NOTICE TO POTENTIAL SELLERS AND BUYERS OF REAL ESTATE.

You should not assume that any real estate broker or salesperson represents you unless you agree to engage a real estate licensee in an authorized brokerage relationship, either as a single agent or as a transaction broker. You are advised not to disclose any information you want to be held in confidence until you make a decision on representation.

Exhibit 19-7—concluded

TRANSACTION BROKER NOTICE

FLORIDA LAW REQUIRES THAT REAL ESTATE LICENSEES OPERATING AS TRANSACTION BROKERS DISCLOSE TO BUYERS AND SELLERS THEIR ROLE AND DUTIES IN PROVIDING A LIMITED FORM OF REPRESENTATION.

As a transaction broker, <u>Baden Associates Realty</u> (insert name of Real Estate entity) and its Associates provides to you a limited form of representation that includes the following duties:

1. Dealing honestly and fairly;
2. Accounting for all funds;
3. Using skill, care and diligence in the transaction;
4. Disclosing all known facts that materially affect the value of residential real property and are not readily observable to the buyer;
5. Presenting all offers and counteroffers in a timely manner, unless a party has previously directed the licensee otherwise in writing;
6. Limited confidentiality, unless waived in writing by a party. This limited confidentiality will prevent disclosure that the seller will accept a price less than the asking or listed price, that the buyer will pay a price greater than the price submitted in a written offer, of the motivation of any party for selling or buying property, that a seller or buyer will agree to financing terms other than those offered, or of any other information requested by a party to remain confidential; and
7. Any additional duties that are entered into by this or by separate written agreement.

Limited representation means that a buyer or seller is not responsible for the acts of the licensee. Additionally, parties are giving up their rights to the undivided loyalty of the licensee. This aspect of limited representation allows a licensee to facilitate a real estate transaction by assisting both the buyer and the seller, but a licensee will not work to represent one party to the detriment of the other party when acting as a transaction broker to both parties.

_5/1/03_	_Fred Johnson_	_Louise Johnson_
Date	Signature	Signature

CONSENT TO TRANSITION TO TRANSACTION BROKER

FLORIDA LAW ALLOWS REAL ESTATE LICENSEES WHO REPRESENT A BUYER OR SELLER AS A SINGLE AGENT TO CHANGE FROM A SINGLE AGENT RELATIONSHIP TO A TRANSACTION BROKERAGE RELATIONSHIP IN ORDER FOR THE LICENSEE TO ASSIST BOTH PARTIES IN A REAL ESTATE TRANSACTION BY PROVIDING A LIMITED FORM OF REPRESENTATION TO BOTH THE BUYER AND THE SELLER. THIS CHANGE IN RELATIONSHIP CANNOT OCCUR WITHOUT YOUR PRIOR WRITTEN CONSENT.

Fred Johnson   _Louise Johnson_ I agree that my agent may assume the role and duties of a transaction broker. (must be initialed or signed)

10. COOPERATION WITH OTHER BROKERS: Broker's office policy is to cooperate with other brokers (check as many as apply):
☒ Buyer's agents ☒ Nonrepresentatives ☒ Transaction brokers ☐ None of the above (if this box is checked, the Property cannot be placed in MLS).

11. COMPENSATION TO OTHER BROKERS: Broker's office policy is to offer compensation to other brokers (check as many as apply):
☒ Buyer's agents ☒ Nonrepresentatives ☒ Transaction brokers ☐ None of the above (if this box is checked, the Property cannot be placed in MLS)

12. SELLER authorizes BROKER or cooperating BROKER to accept in escrow and hold all money paid or deposited as a binder on the subject property and if such deposit is later forfeited by the BUYER to disperse the deposit as follows: (1) all loan application fees, and other costs incurred on behalf of either the BUYER or the SELLER shall be reimbursed to the BROKER; (2) one-half of the remaining net deposit or the total commission the BROKER would have received, whichever is less, shall be disbursed to the BROKER as compensation for his services and marketing expenses; (3) the remainder of the deposit, if any, shall be disbursed to the SELLER as liquidated damages. In the disbursement of any escrowed funds, the BROKER shall be governed and shall comply with the provisions of Chapter 475, Florida Statutes.

13. SELLER and BROKER acknowledge that this Agreement does not guarantee a sale and that there are no other agreements, promises or understandings either expressed or implied between them other than specifically set forth herein and that there can be no alterations or changes to this contract except in writing and signed by each of them. They also agree that this Agreement supersedes any prior agreement regarding the marketing of this property.

14. ATTORNEY'S FEES AND COSTS: In the event any litigation arises out of the Contract, the prevailing party shall be entitled to recover reasonable attorney's fees and costs.

15. THIS IS A LEGAL AND BINDING CONTRACT ON ALL PARTIES HERETO, INCLUDING THEIR HEIRS, LEGAL REPRESENTATIVES, SUCCESSORS AND ASSIGNS. IF THIS CONTRACT IS NOT FULLY UNDERSTOOD SELLER SHOULD SEEK COMPETENT LEGAL ADVICE.

16. THE SELLER AND BROKER ACKNOWLEDGE THAT THIS LISTING SHALL BE WITHDRAWN FROM THE GAINESVILLE MULTIPLE LISTING UPON THE BROKER'S WITHDRAWAL, SUSPENSION OR TERMINATION FROM MLS.

BROKER <u>Baden Associates Realty</u>   SELLER <u>Fred Johnson</u>

By: <u>BEN PARK</u>   SELLER <u>Louise Johnson</u>

Date: <u>MAY 1, 2003</u>   SELLERS' Address <u>1822 NW 40th Avenue</u>

<u>Gainesville FL 32605</u>

PLEASE DO NOT ASK OR EXPECT TO RESTRICT THE SALE OF YOUR PROPERTY ACCORDING TO RACE, COLOR, RELIGION, SEX, HANDICAP, FAMILIAL STATUS, OR NATIONAL ORIGIN. REALTOR POLICY AS WELL AS FEDERAL LAW PROHIBITS REALTORS FROM PLACING ANY SUCH RESTRICTIONS ON SHOWING OR INFORMATION ABOUT THE AVAILABILITY OF HOMES FOR SALE OR RENT.

MLS 012   Page 3 of 3   Rev. 07/00

Summary

Real estate brokerage is an important type of real estate business dealing with marketing. Brokers provide a service for sellers and buyers of properties that involves finding available properties, finding potential buyers, helping buyers identify needs and set priorities, negotiating between buyers and sellers, providing advice about other needs and specialists (e.g., financing, attorneys, architects), making certain all relevant federal and state laws are followed (e.g., those regarding discrimination and disclosure), and arranging for the closing of the transaction. Probably the most important of these functions is helping buyers and sellers determine their needs and enabling them to meet those needs in the best possible manner.

Listing contracts create an agency relationship between a real estate broker and the owners of real estate. This is a fiduciary relationship, binding the broker to a commitment of loyalty, confidentiality, obedience, accounting, disclosure, and skill and care. It requires of the principal a commitment of honesty, openness, and cooperation.

Several forms of special agency relationships arise in real estate brokerage, including listing agent, buying agent, and dual agent. Of particular concern is unintended dual agency. This risk has prompted widespread legislation to either require more extensive disclosures of agency relationships or to prohibit dual agency altogether. Laws have been enacted to create alternative brokerage relationships such as transaction or facilitating brokerage where the broker does not represent either buyer or seller.

There are three types of listing contracts: open, exclusive agency, and exclusive right of sale. The exclusive right of sale listing is the predominant type of contract, especially for residential properties. This contract is required when the property is to be filed with a multiple listing service. A multiple listing service is a cooperative arrangement among brokerage firms in which all member firms pool their listings. All sales personnel of the members can then attempt to sell the listed property. When the property is sold, the commission is split between the listing and selling firms according to a predetermined schedule.

In signing a listing contract, both broker and owner obtain rights and responsibilities. The brokerage firm has the right to collect a commission if the property is sold within a specified or reasonable period and agrees to exert its best efforts to sell the property; the owner can expect the firm to try to sell the property through a marketing program. The owner can also expect an MLS member firm to file the listing with the multiple listing service and for sales personnel of other member firms to work on the sale. The owner is obligated not to impede the selling effort and to pay a commission if the property is sold.

Key Terms

Broker license 500	General agent 494	Principal 494
Buyer agency agreement 495	Internet marketing 506	Real estate commission 500
Commission 492	Law of agency 494	Recovery fund 501
Designated agent 497	Licensing laws 499	Salesperson license 500
Discrimination in housing 505	Listing contract 495	Special agent 494
Dual agency 496	Market segmentation 502	Subagency 496
Errors and omission insurance 501	Multiple listing service (MLS) 496	Submarket 502
Exclusive agency listing 509	National Association of Realtors 502	Transaction broker 499
Exclusive right of sale listing 510	Net listing 492	Universal agent 494
Fiduciary relationship 495	Open listing 509	

Test Problems

Answer the following multiple choice questions:

1. A salesperson who collects a down payment deposit from a potential buyer must place the funds in:
   a. The seller's bank account.
   b. The salesperson's own bank account.
   c. The broker's bank account.
   d. Long-term government bonds.
   e. The hands of his or her broker.

2. One of the most effective ways that salespersons or brokers can distinguish themselves as a preferred agent in a particular specialization of real estate brokerage is to:
   a. Obtain a license to practice.
   b. Take related courses.
   c. Read related books.
   d. Engage in personal advertising.
   e. Obtaining a related industry designation.

3. A broker, acting as the agent of a seller, must deal honestly and fairly with whom?
   a. Only the seller.
   b. The seller and the buyer.
   c. The seller and a lender.
   d. The seller and a title insurance company.
   e. Everyone involved in the transaction.

4. Real estate salespersons can lose their licenses for:
   a. Using aggressive sales techniques.
   b. Not showing buyers all available properties in an area.
   c. Commingling escrow (trust) money with personal funds.
   d. Not using modern sales methods.
   e. All of the above.

5. The state real estate commission is responsible for:
   a. Setting fees for brokerage services.
   b. Marketing data on real estate transactions.
   c. Establishing education requirements for licensees.
   d. Overseeing the activities of mortgage lenders.
   e. Setting up multiple listing systems.

6. Real estate brokers are paid commissions primarily for:
   a. Having an inventory of properties.
   b. Having many contacts.
   c. Providing a service.
   d. Knowing how to close a transaction.
   e. Having specialized education.

7. A real estate broker is what type of agent for his or her principal?
   a. General agent.
   b. Special agent.
   c. Limited agent.
   d. Designated agent.
   e. All of the above.

8. The subagency relationship that traditionally has characterized multiple listing services (MLS) has tended to result in the wide-spread danger of:
   a. Monopoly.
   b. Deliberate dual agency.
   c. Unintended dual agency.
   d. Discrimination.
   e. Price wars.

9. How are commission rates that real estate brokers charge determined?
   a. By agreement among local Realtors.
   b. By rule of the local Board of Realtors.
   c. By state real estate commissions.
   d. By agreement between broker and principal.
   e. By state law.

10. According to most listing contracts, a broker has earned a commission when:
    a. A contract for sale is signed by the buyer.
    b. The transaction closes.
    c. The broker finds a buyer who is ready, willing, and able to buy on the terms specified in the listing contract.
    d. The seller signs a listing contract.
    e. The broker sends a bill for services rendered to the principal (usually the seller).

Study Questions

1. Ted Richardson owns a large industrial building in your city that he wishes to sell. As a real estate broker, you would be delighted to obtain the listing on this property. You have worked with Richardson on two other transactions in which he was the buyer; therefore, you approach Richardson to request that he consider listing his property with you. Richardson agrees to do so, but indicates that he will not give you an exclusive right of sale listing, because he wants to retain the right to sell the property himself without owing a real estate commission. He will, however, give you an exclusive agency listing.
   a. What should you do? Should you accept such a listing from Richardson?
   b. What provisions, if any, would you include in the listing contract to give yourself some protection?

2. You are a real estate salesperson working for Good Earth, Realtors, Inc. You receive 50 percent of all commissions received by the firm (net of MLS fees) for which you were either the listing agent or the selling agent. The firm receives 40 percent of commissions for sales of properties it lists and 45 percent of commissions for sales of properties it sells in cooperation with other firms. Fifteen percent of all commissions for properties sold through the multiple listing service must be paid to the MLS. If you are both the listing and selling agent in a transaction, you receive 60 percent of the firm's proceeds. If you are either the listing agent or the selling agent for a transaction in which another member of Good Earth is the selling agent or the listing agent, your split remains the same as when another firm cooperates in the transaction. Recently, you were the selling agent for a property that sold for $127,250. Another salesperson associated with Good Earth had listed the property two months previously for $135,000. The property was in the MLS, and the commission rate was 6 percent.
   a. How much in total commission, net of the MLS fee, will your firm receive?
   b. What will be your split of the commission?

3. If you owned your own real estate brokerage firm, how could you establish a niche in the market for your firm? How could you set your firm apart from other brokerage firms and create a unique image for your firm?

4. How do you think the real estate marketing function will change in the future? Do you believe that real estate brokers will play a more important or a less important role in the selling and buying process? Why?

5. A friend of yours, Cindy Malvern, is moving to your town. She graduated from college a few years ago and has since been working in another city. Recently, however, she was offered a job at a higher salary in the regional office of a national insurance company located in the city where you attend college. Cindy has decided to buy a condominium, and because you are taking a real estate course, she asks you how to proceed.

You first look at the classified ads in the local newspaper and notice that a number of existing condominiums are for sale. Most of them are advertised by brokers, but some are advertised by the owners. You also notice ads by some local builders for new condominiums. You ask Cindy whether she prefers to buy a previously owned condominium or a new one. She says she doesn't know; it depends on the condominium, the location, the price, and so on.

Next you look in the Yellow Pages of the phone book and find several pages of ads for real estate brokers. You have heard of three or four of the firms, but you have had no direct contact or dealings with any of them.

a. How would you advise Cindy to proceed? Should she call a real estate brokerage firm? Why or why not?

b. If Cindy decides to call a real estate broker, how should she select the broker? What criteria should she use?

c. If Cindy decides to work through a real estate broker, can she look at new condominiums for sale by builders? If she buys a new condominium while working with a broker, would she or the builder have to pay a commission to the broker?

6. You decide to open a real estate office in your community, but you know you would face stiff competition from established firms. You believe that one method of drawing attention to your firm and obtaining clients who would otherwise go to the established brokers is to advertise that you will sell any house in town and charge a commission of only $1,000. Do you believe such a marketing tactic would be successful? Why or why not?

Explore The Web

1. On the World Wide Web go to http://www.realtor.org/ Click on the link "Real Estate Specialties, then look at "Affiliated Institutes, Societies and Councils."
   a. How many societies, institutes, and councils are affiliated with the National Association of Realtors?
   b. Identify each affiliate, and briefly describe its area of specialization.
   c. List the designations offered by each affiliate. What do these designations indicate?

2. On the Realtors' home page, click again on "Realtor Directories." Then click on "Find an Association." Obtain information about your state association of Realtors and write a short report on your findings.

3. One of the best sets of links is found on the home page of the Society of Industrial and Office Realtors (SIOR). Go to www.sior.com and click on "links." Then click on "National Professional Real Estate Associations" and discover more about the various associations listed there. Write a brief report on your findings.

4. Note the other links on the SIOR home page and peruse any that may be of interest to you.

5. Go to www.realtor.com. Select a zip code of interest to you. Determine how many residential listings are available for that zip code. Determine the price range of the listings. Determine how many of the listings have video tours available.

Solutions to Concept Checks

1. The "price of success" in real estate brokerage is educational preparation, dedication to the welfare of customers, and hard work.

2. Without real estate brokers, it would be more difficult and costly to buy and sell property.

3. Five areas of special knowledge of an expert real estate broker are current prices and terms, successful marketing procedures, legal obligations of all parties of the transaction, knowledge of properties in the market, needs of prospective buyers, procedures for a transaction.

4. A cost of selling a property that tends to be overlooked by prospective for-sale-by-owners is the time, inconvenience and risks of handling the sale.

5. A phrase which characterizes an agent's relationship to a principal is that the agent must "stand in the shoes" of the principal.

6. A broker has a fiduciary relationship with the principal and owes the principal the six duties of disclosure, loyalty, confidentiality, accounting, obedience, skill and care.

7. The three basic types of agency relationship are universal, general, and special. A broker is a special agent of the principal (buyer or seller).

8. A very complicated agency relationship that arises when one firm represents both seller and buyer is dual agency.

9. In MLS property listings, the broker selling a listing traditionally was an agent of the seller, in spite of all appearances, by virtue of a required agency relationship called subagency.

10. Brokerage firms are increasingly faced with an unintended internal dual agency problem because of the increase in the practice of buyer brokerage.

11. One attempt to mitigate the dual agency problem occurring within a firm which is both the listing broker and buyer broker is for the broker to appoint designated agents.

12. A broker who represents neither buyer nor seller is called a transaction, facilitating or intermediary broker.

13. Five real estate services which require licensing to be performed for others are buying. auctioning, renting, managing, and selling.

14. Two important functions of a commercial real estate broker are to provide the prospective buyer with information about the property, and to negotiate compromises.

15. Three reasons influencing a customer's choice of brokerage firm include the broker's reputation in the community, recommendations of friends, and familiarity with the broker.

16. Fair housing laws prohibit discrimination on the basis of race, color, religion, age, sex, familial status, and handicap.

17. Discrimination by race is absolutely prohibited in any form or at any level by a 1968 U.S. Supreme Court ruling in the case of *Jones v. Mayer.*

18. Under a listing contract, a broker is entitled to a commission if he or she produces a ready, willing, and able buyer.

19. In an open listing, the broker is entitled to a commission only if the broker procures a ready, willing, and able buyer. In an exclusive agency listing, the broker is entitled to a commission if any broker procures a buyer. In an exclusive right-of-sale listing, the broker is entitled to a commission if any broker or the seller procures a buyer.

20. Five issues on which a seller should be clear before signing a listing agreement are:
    a. What advertising program will be used?
    b. Will the property be placed in the MLS?
    c. How long is the term of the listing?
    d. What progress reports will the broker provide?
    e. What personal property is being listed?

Additional Readings

Reilly, John. *Agency Relationships in Real Estate,* 2nd ed. Chicago: Real Estate Education Company, 1994.

Wilson, Ray. *Bought, Not Sold.* Greenfield, MA: CognaBooks, 1998. An expose-like treatment of real estate agency relationships.

The following periodical is the monthly journal of the National Association of Realtors. It contains articles on both residential and commercial brokerage and runs several special features.

Realtor Magazine (monthly), National Association of Realtors, 430 North Michigan Avenue, Chicago, IL 60611–4049. An online version of the magazine is available through www. realtor.org.

Additionally, several of the affiliates of NAR publish professional journals in specialized areas of brokerage, and many state Boards of Realtors publish monthly magazines containing articles and news features about brokerage issues in those states. You may find information about the publications of the NAR affiliates by using the links on the home page of NAR at http://www.realtor.org/About Us Page down to "Affiliated Institutes, Societies and Councils."

On the same website, under the headings "Products and Services," then "Real Estate Publications," then "Realtor VIP Publications" are listed a variety of publications concerning the real estate brokerage industry.

chapter twenty

Contracts *for* Sale *and* Closing

Learning Objectives

After reading this chapter you will be able to:

1. List the seven requirements for a valid contract for the sale of real estate.

2. Write a simple contract that contains the seven requirements.

3. Complete a standard form contract, given the facts of a property transaction.

4. Identify five expenses typically paid by the seller and five expenses typically paid by the buyer.

5. List three remedies for nonperformance by a buyer and three remedies for nonperformance by a seller.

6. List the steps that must be taken before closing a real estate transaction.

7. Describe the activities that occur at closing.

8. Explain the principal provisions of the Real Estate Settlement Procedures Act (RESPA).

9. Complete a HUD–1 closing statement.

Introduction: The Most Important Document in Real Estate

The value of real estate depends on the rights that a buyer obtains at closing, as conveyed by the deed. The rights and type of deed are determined by the **contract for sale,** the document in which buyers and sellers of real estate specify the details of their agreement. The principal provisions of a contract for sale require the seller to deliver a deed for the property to the buyer in exchange for payment of the purchase price to the seller. The contract is signed when a buyer and seller decide to commit themselves to the transaction under terms and conditions worked out between them. **Contract terms** refers to the arrangements agreed to by the parties, such as price and date of closing, whereas **contract conditions** refers to the circumstances that must prevail, such as mechanical equipment being in good condition and title being unencumbered. Thus, real estate transactions differ from personal property transactions in that realty sales almost always involve a two-step process. The parties reach agreement first; sometime later (e.g., one month) they complete the sale at a meeting called the **closing.** In a personal property transaction, the parties usually close the transaction at the same time they reach agreement.

Like any contract, a contract for sale of real estate is a legal, enforceable document. If its provisions are not carried out, financial penalties (i.e., damages) may be imposed on the party unwilling or unable to fulfill the contract. Because it determines virtually all the important aspects of the transaction—price and terms, property interest conveyed, grantee(s), conditions of the transaction—a contract for sale is the *most important document* in a real estate transaction. Whereas most contracts are legal and enforceable whether they are written or oral, the laws (called statutes of fraud) of every state require that contracts for the sale and purchase of real estate be *in writing* to be enforceable. The many provisions in such a contract leave too much room for both legitimate misunderstandings and purposeful disagreements (fraud) when the agreements are oral. Although disagreements also may arise with written contracts, these contracts contain definite language that the courts can interpret and enforce.

Rights and Obligations of Sellers and Buyers

A contract for the sale of real estate creates certain rights and obligations for both sellers and buyers. Sellers, for example, have the right to receive the sale price on the terms specified in the contract. They are obligated to deliver clear and marketable title to the property to the buyers at closing, to maintain the property in good repair until closing, to allow the buyers to inspect the property just prior to closing, and to pay the agreed upon brokerage commission.

Buyers have the right to obtain clear and marketable title at closing, to receive the property and appliances in the same condition they were when the contract was signed, and usually to back out of the transaction if the property is substantially damaged or destroyed before closing. They are obligated, of course, to pay the price on the terms specified in the contract at closing.

Requirements of a Contract for Sale

A legally binding contract for sale can take many forms. It can be a short handwritten note, a preprinted form containing several standard paragraphs, or a lengthy document prepared by attorneys to cover many points in a complex transaction. Whatever the form, any contract, whether it be for the sale of real estate or for some other purpose (such as a mortgage), must contain the following elements:

1. Competent parties.
2. Legal objective.
3. Offer and acceptance.
4. Consideration.
5. No defects to mutual assent.

Two additional requirements must be part of any contract for the sale of real estate:

1. Written form.
2. Proper description of the property.

Concept Check

20.1 List five essential elements of any valid contract. Name two additional essential elements of a valid contract for sale of real estate.

Competency of the Parties to Act

The principal parties to a transaction must be legally *competent*. In the case of individuals, such parties must have reached a minimum age (18 years in most states) and be of sound mind. Although minors may be legally competent to participate in real estate transactions, a contract with a minor is *voidable:* The minor may legally declare the contract invalid and refuse to carry out its provisions. A contract also may be voidable if one party is under the influence of drugs or alcohol, or is insane at the time the contract is signed. However, the incapacitation must be sufficient that the party is incapable of understanding the nature of the contract. Frequently when an elder parent suffers failing health and mental capacity a child who is caring for the parent may obtain a deed for their home or other real estate, to the exclusion of other sons or daughters. The child may regard the conveyance as compensation for providing care to the parent. However, a court may find the parent incapable of making contracts under the circumstances and set aside the deed.

In the case of corporations, a party acting on behalf of the corporation must be legally empowered to do so. For example, if a corporation sells property, its president or some other officer must be authorized by a resolution of the board of directors or a corporation bylaw to act in this capacity. Similarly, personal representatives (e.g., executors, administrators, agents, and attorneys-in-fact) and trustees must be authorized to act on behalf of their principals by a legal instrument or order, such as a *power of attorney.* Their powers are defined and limited by the instrument. Real estate purchasers or professionals should always assure themselves that personal representatives and trustees have legal authority to sell properties.

Concept Check

20.2 List three aspects of legal competency.

Lawful Intent of the Parties

The objective of a contract must not be illegal or against public policy. For example, a contract to commit a crime for payment is not enforceable in the courts. Similarly, a contract to sell property for the purpose of growing marijuana or for storing illegal weapons is legally invalid. A contract to sell property to members of a certain race, or to exclude members of a certain race, would be counter to public policy against racial discrimination and would be void.

An Offer and an Acceptance

An offer and acceptance indicate that the parties to a contract have a meeting of the minds, or *mutual assent.* The contract binds the parties to specified actions in the future: the seller to deliver *marketable* legal title to the buyer and the buyer to pay the stipulated price for a property. In a real estate contract for sale, the buyer normally offers a specified price under specific terms for specific property rights. The seller has three options: to reject the offer outright, to accept the offer outright, or, as frequently occurs, to reject the offer and present a *counteroffer.* A series of offers and counteroffers often will ensue until an agreement is reached—a successful offer and acceptance—or one party rejects an offer outright.

The basic agreement ultimately reached between buyer and seller may be simple and straightforward. However, it usually creates many other issues on which agreement must be reached, including the closing date, prorating of expenses, type of title evidence, liability for property damage, and condition of the property. The purpose of a contract for sale is to specify these agreements and to make them legally binding.

Concept Check

20.3   What kind of title does a seller implicitly agree to deliver in a contract for sale?

Consideration

The value given up, or promise made, by each party to a contract is the **consideration.** Both parties to a valid and enforceable contract must provide consideration. In a contract for the sale and purchase of real estate, the seller's consideration is the property to be given up. The buyer's consideration is the money or other goods that constitute the purchase price. Mere promise of consideration by one party does not constitute a contract and cannot be enforced. For example, Bill Rich promises to deed a property to his friend B. Weiser, and even writes this promise on a piece of paper. Such a promise cannot be enforced because Mr. Weiser did not promise anything in return. Mutual obligations of the parties are necessary to create a legally binding contract.

No Defects to Mutual Assent

In certain circumstances, mutual assent—the meeting of the minds—between the contracting parties may be broken, thus invalidating the contract. The following constitute defects to mutual assent:

1. One party attempts to perpetrate a fraud on the other party or makes a misrepresentation.[1]
2. A substantial error is made (e.g., the name of one of the parties to a written contract is incorrect).
3. One of the parties is under duress, undue influence, or menace.[2]

In addition to the elements for any contract described above, an enforceable contract for the sale of real estate must fulfill two additional requirements.

Concept Check

20.4   Name three possible defects to mutual assent.

A Written Real Estate Contract

The Statute of Frauds, the old English law that serves as the basis for contract law in most states, imposed the requirement of writing on some types of contracts in order for them to be enforceable.[3] Many agreements involving real estate are subject to this requirement, including contracts for sale, installment sales contracts, option contracts, exchange contracts, and, in many states, leases, listing contracts, and mortgage contracts.[4] In most states, the *parol* evidence rule is in effect, which prohibits the admission of oral evidence in disputes involving written contracts.

---

1. *Fraud* is intentional misrepresentation, whereas a *misrepresentation* per se is unintentional. However, both have the same effect.

2. *Undue influence* involves an abuse of the influence that one person (often a relative) has over another. *Duress* involves compelling a person to act by the use of force, and *menace* is the use of the threat of force to compel a person to act.

3. The *statute of frauds* was intended to prevent fraudulent practices in contracting; thus, the writing requirement was imposed for situations where substantial sums of money would normally be involved.

4. Leases for less than one year normally are not required to be in writing to be enforceable.

As noted, most real estate contracts contain many technicalities and points of agreement. Legitimate misunderstandings could easily arise over any of these points in an oral contract. Even more important, unscrupulous parties to an oral contract could gain an unfair advantage by later claiming they did not agree to protective provisions. For example, most written contracts contain a provision that allows a buyer to back out of a transaction if the building is destroyed by fire or other hazard before the closing. A seller could easily claim such a provision was not part of an oral contract; it would be his or her word against the buyer's.

To satisfy the writing requirement, the contract usually must include adequate identification of the parties, the subject matter, and the terms of agreement, as well as the signatures of the parties or their legally empowered agents. It is essential that both principal parties to a transaction—buyers and sellers—sign the contract. The signatures are legal evidence that the parties understand and agree to the provisions in the contract. They cannot later claim they did not agree to a provision in the contract or did not understand its meaning.

In addition to the principals' signatures, the statute of frauds may require a spouse's signature to release his or her marital rights such as homestead rights, dower rights, or community property rights. Technically, a spouse's signature on a contract indicates his or her agreement to sign the deed, where these rights are actually waived. Also, as noted, legal written authorization must accompany a contract that is signed by an agent, personal representative, or trustee.

Proper Description of the Property

It is essential that the property be properly described so that a court can resolve any controversies about it. If the property is inadequately described, the validity of the contract may be destroyed. Methods for describing property are discussed in Chapter 18, and include the recorded subdivision plat method, the metes and bounds method, and the government rectangular survey system.

Legal Title versus Equitable Title

Legal title means the ownership of a freehold estate. In contrast, **equitable title** is the right to obtain legal title. The importance of this distinction is that when a contract for sale is signed, the buyers immediately obtain equitable title, and the sellers cannot sell the property to someone else. (They could, however, sell the property contingent upon the possibility that the buyers might fail to close the transaction.) In addition, the creation of equitable title gives the buyer a real property interest while converting the seller's interest to personal property. Thus, if the buyer dies the heirs receive the property as part of his or her estate. Also the buyer bears the risk of changing property value before the conveyance of legal title.

Concept Check

20.5 What is legal title? What is equitable title? When does equitable title arise?

The Form of the Contract for Sale

While the contract for sale may take a variety of forms, the important question to be answered is whether all essential ingredients of a valid and enforceable contract for sale are present. Most transactions today, especially residential transactions, are completed with the use of standard forms, which force the parties to consider all of the necessary elements.

Simple Contract

The following statement constitutes a simple real estate contract:

I, Ben Byer, agree to buy and pay $20,000, and I, Cecil Celler, agree to sell the parcel of real estate at 1013 NE Seventh Road in North Platte, Nebraska.

Signed: Ben Byer   Signed: Cecil Celler

For most transactions, such a brief contract would not be sufficient; however, it contains the seven essential elements, and therefore it would be legal. Mr. Byer and Mr. Celler are competent. Mr. Byer offers $20,000, and Mr. Celler accepts by agreeing to sell. Consideration is stated for both: $20,000 for the buyer and the property for the seller. The objective is legal, the property is identified, and there are no defects to mutual assent. The contract is written and is signed by both parties.

But several important points are omitted. These could be subject to disagreement later, and they could cause the transaction to be delayed or even aborted. The missing points are:

- Date of the contract.
- Date and place of closing.
- The marital status of the parties.
- Financing terms, if any.
- Prorating of costs and expenses.
- Inspections of the property for termites, radon, or needed repairs.
- Condition of any buildings.
- Condition of subsystems and appliances.
- Right of occupancy (or rents) until closing.
- Liability for major damage to buildings before closing.
- Remedies by each party for breach of contract by the other party.
- Exact dimensions and location of the property.
- Brokerage commission, if any.
- Earnest money deposit.

Since these points are not covered in the contract, misunderstandings and severe losses for both parties can result. For example, the seller may need the money and count on closing within two weeks. The buyer, however, may be in no hurry and not want to close for three months. Since the contract does not specify the date of closing, the courts will interpret the time between contract and closing as a reasonable time—which could easily be three months. As another example, consider the buyer's problem if the building burns down before closing. Without the contract specifying otherwise, the buyer must complete the transaction even if the building is destroyed. For these reasons, a longer contract form is usually used.

Standard Form Contracts

Since the issues in many transactions are similar, brokers often use standard preprinted contract forms. For most straightforward transactions, these work well. All or most of the normal issues requiring agreement are addressed in a way that protects both buyers and sellers. They are not inherently biased toward one party or the other, as can be the case with contracts drawn up by one of the parties to a transaction. These forms contain ready-made provisions to address issues such as prorations, closing, financing terms, liability for property damage, easements, condition of fixtures and appliances, real estate commission, and so on.

Generally, the best standard form contracts are those prepared and approved by local Boards of Realtors. These usually are superior to a generic contract form obtained from, for example, an office supply firm because they are customized for issues that are especially important in that particular community. For example, they may highlight floodplain risk,

http://moneycentral.msn.com/content/Banking/Homebuyingguide/P37627.asp

Microsoft Money's homebuying guide; usually has sensible advice on rent versus buy and related topics.

www.fool.com/homecenter/homecenter.htm

The Motley Fool is always a good source of ideas in financial and personal planning, and has a rich section on homebuying/financing as well.

Industry Issues

Contract for Sale

A new marketing professor, Dr. David Dennis, was hired by a large midwestern university. After looking at a number of houses, he and his wife, Marie, decided to purchase a large, older home in a pleasant section of town. When they looked at the house, Marie noted that the master bedroom was carpeted, with the carpet fastened to the floor. After the transaction was closed and they began moving in, however, they discovered the carpet in the master bedroom had been removed.

The Dennises immediately protested to the broker who had sold them the house, Ms. Jan Dancy. She contacted the former owners, Mr. and Mrs. Jim Rockledge, who had moved several hundred miles to another city, to inquire why they had removed the carpet. They told Jan they had every right to remove the carpet. It was not part of the house, since it was not tacked to the floor.

When told that Marie had noticed the carpet was fastened to the floor, Mrs. Rockledge replied that the carpet had been tacked down only at the doorway to prevent its being kicked up. It was not fastened down in any other place and was not permanently installed. The contract did not mention the carpet, and it was not intended to be sold as part of the house.

The Dennises were deprived of carpet they believed should have belonged to them, the Rockledges refused to pay, and the broker suffered customer dissatisfaction. To keep their goodwill, Jan bought the Dennises a new bedroom carpet.

---

www.freddiemac.
com/corporate/
homeownership/

www.fanniemae.com/
homebuyers

www.mbaa.org/
consumer/index.html

Three websites that provide information about buying a home, especially concerning credit, qualifying for a mortgage loan, and financing alternatives.

www.hud.gov/
buying/index.cfm

All of these standard websites have a page with resources for persons considering homeownership.

radon inspection, insulation quality, water supply, or other matters of special concern for the local climate and environment. Also, they frequently address local legal and regulatory issues such as state disclosure requirements for real estate transactions, state law concerning evidence of title, or special state or local taxes on real estate transactions.

A standard form real estate contract can be disadvantageous if it is misused. If, for example, parties to the sale of a small commercial or multifamily rental property attempt to adapt a standard residential contract form to the transaction, there is risk that important issues can be overlooked. For example, the standard residential contract form is not likely to clarify rights of the buyer relative to existing tenants of the property, or even to provide for inspection of existing leases, verification and transfer of tenant deposits, or for other landlord and tenant concerns. The same kind of problem could arise in trying to adapt a standard residential contract form to a sale of land for future building or for conversion to another use. The contract form is likely to give inadequate attention to the examination of public land-use controls, private restrictions, or easements that could affect the future use of the property. Local Boards of Realtors, recognizing this risk of the standard contract form, often design a set of different contract forms, each appropriate to one common type of real estate transaction.

Even with standard contract forms and straightforward transactions, buyers and sellers should examine the contract carefully; once they sign a contract, they can be held to its provisions, no matter how deleterious to their interests. Both parties can achieve maximum protection by having a competent attorney examine the document *before* signing. Having an attorney examine a contract after it has been signed is like locking the barn door after the horse has run away. While many buyers and sellers of single-family homes do not hire an attorney to draft or examine the contract and do not suffer severe financial losses, small disagreements and losses are relatively common (see Industry Issues 20-1).

Concept Check

20.6 Name two advantages and one disadvantage of a standard form contract for the sale of real estate.

Contracts for the purchase and sale of larger, more complex, income-producing properties are usually drafted by attorneys. Typically, the sellers or buyers will have their attorneys draft the instrument, sign it, and then submit it to the other parties and their attorneys. The instrument tends to protect the parties that have drafted the instrument, to the detriment of the other side. Thus, it is rare to encounter acceptance of the first draft of a contract drawn by the other parties' attorneys. Usually, objections will be raised, new drafts will be prepared, and a bargaining process will occur before a contract is acceptable to both sides.

A standard form contract for the purchase and sale of real estate is presented in Exhibit 20-1 showing the purchase and sale agreement between the Johnsons and the Joneses from our example in Chapter 19. This form, developed jointly by the Gainesville, Florida/ Alachua County Association of Realtors is relatively comprehensive and fair to both parties. Although our example contract contains all the elements common to purchase and sale agreements, it is important to emphasize that such contracts can vary significantly in form across cities and states within the United States.

Components of a Form Contract

The example contract form is typical in many respects. It has two main sections. The first contains 19 paragraphs or sections with items to be filled in. These concern issues most likely to depend on the specific property and transaction, and thus need to be "customized" or negotiated. The second section of the contract has 20 "Standards for Real Estate Transactions." These are points thought to be less dependent on the specific transaction, and thus are routine. However, these points are no less a part of the contract, no less binding on the parties, and no less negotiable, if the case requires it. An important example of this is clause Q, concerning time. In the example form the "standard" is that failure to perform within specified time limits is not a material breach of the contract. However, if there is time urgency for either party, they may want to replace clause Q with the statement "time is of the essence." In this case, the slightest breach of a specified time limit constitutes "drop dead" default on the contract, and the aggrieved party can take immediate action.

Concept Check

20.7 Distinguish between the two main sections in a standard form contract for the sale of real estate.

Notice that the form contract in Exhibit 20-1 contains the elements of any valid contract. The parties to the transaction are identified at the top of the form. There is an offer and acceptance, stated as an agreement that the seller shall sell and the buyer shall buy. Consideration is stated as the purchase price for the buyer and the property for the seller. The conveyance of title to the property is the legal objective, and the property is identified adequately. The contract is in writing, and the buyers and sellers sign in the spaces provided on page 6 of the form.

In addition to these elements, the contract form also covers other matters. Beginning on page 4, it explicitly incorporates the Standards for Real Estate Transactions, many of which clarify the first set of contract provisions, and are thereby agreed to by the parties. The contract also includes a space on page one to specify items of personal property and questionable items (e.g., the carpet matter from Industry Issues 20-1) as property to which title is being conveyed. The purchase price and form of payment are listed in paragraph 1, and a financing contingency clause is provided in paragraph 5. Buyers normally pay a deposit—known variously as escrow money, earnest money, or a binder—at the time they make an offer to show they are serious and to indemnify the sellers in the event they, the buyers, fail to perform. The broker holds the deposit in a segregated account called an *escrow account* until closing or until other arrangements are made for its disposition.

Exhibit 20-1   Example of a Standard Form Contract for Purchase and Sale of Real Estate

GAINESVILLE-ALACHUA COUNTY ASSOCIATION OF REALTORS®, INC
DEPOSIT RECEIPT AND SALE AND SALE AGREEMENT
CONVENTIONAL FINANCING

Date: May 15, 2003

Receipt is hereby acknowledged by Baden Associates Realty   hereinafter called REALTOR®,

of the sum of   Five Thousand Dollars   (5000.00   ) (by check) from

George and Helen Jones   , hereinafter called BUYER as a deposit and as a part of the

purchase price on account of an offer to purchase the property of   Fred and Louise Johnson

_____hereinafter called SELLER, said property being in Alachua   County, Florida, and described as follows:

     Parcel No. 3 Block 2 of Spring Meadow Estates PB 12 Pg 28

also known as: 1822 NW 40th Avenue, Gainesville, FL   together with
the following personal property:

     2 window air conditioners, 1 picnic table, 1 Kenmore refrigerator,
     1 Hot Point range

The SELLER hereby agrees to sell said property to the BUYER and the BUYER hereby agrees to purchase said property from the SELLER upon the
following terms and conditions:

1. **PURCHASE AND SALES PRICE:** $ ~~152,000.00~~ FJ LJ
    Payable as follows: 147,000.00 GH HJ
    (a) Deposit paid herewith $ 5,000.00
    (b) Additional Deposit within ____ days after Effective Date   ~~24,400.00~~ 25,400 00
    (c) Cash as Closing (US cash, certified or cashiers check)   ~~117,600.00~~ 121,600 00
    (d) Balance payable   see 5A
    (e) _____
         TOTAL PURCHASE AND SALES PRICE FJ LJ
                                          GH HJ $ ~~152,000.00~~ FJ HJ
                                                                  147,000.00 GH HJ

2. **ADDITIONAL TERMS AND CONDITIONS:**

    A. Contingent upon a satisfactory radon and building inspection to be made within 10 days
        of final acceptance of contract, to be paid for by buyers. Failure to notify sellers
        in writing of nonacceptance within this period will automatically remove this
        contingency.

3. **RIDERS:** (check if applicable) ☐
    Additional riders are attached to this agreement and are made a part thereof.

4. **CLOSING DATE:** This transaction shall be closed and the deed and other closing papers delivered on July 1, 2003   or
    such earlier date as may be mutually agreed upon, unless extended by other provisions of this Agreement

5. A. **NEW FINANANCING:** If the purchase price or any part thereof is to be financed by a third party loan, this Agreement is conditioned upon
        the BUYER obtaining a firm commitment for said loan within 30   days from the effective date at an interest rate not to exceed
    six three quarter percent (6.75%), if a fixed rate mortgage, or   N/A   percent (____%) for the initial period of an adjustable
        rate mortgage; term of   30 years
        (____) years; and in the principal amount of not less than one hundred twenty one thousand six hundred
        ($ 121,600.00   ). BUYER shall make application within three   (3   ) days from the effective date, and use
        reasonable diligence to obtain said loan, including furnishing all documents and information required by the Lender, and failure to do so shall
        constitute a breach hereunder. If BUYER fails to obtain same or to waive BUYER'S right hereunder within said time, either party may cancel
        this Agreement and all deposit(s) paid by BUYER shall be refunded to BUYER.

Exhibit 20-1—continued

B. **EXISTING FINANCING:** If the purchase price or any part thereof is to be paid by assumption of existing financing, this Agreement is contingent upon such loan being assumable without qualifying or BUYER qualifying to assume same within _____ days of the effective date if required by the mortgagee. The existing Mortgage has (Check One) ☐ 1) a variable interest rate of _____ or ☐ 2) a fixed interest rate of _____ % per annum. At the time of title transfer some interest rates are subject to increase. If increased, the rate shall

N/A not exceed _____ % per annum. SELLER shall, within ten (10) days from effective date, furnish a copy of the existing note and mortgage to the BUYER. If BUYER has agreed to assume a mortgage which requires approval of BUYER by the Mortgagee for assumption, the BUYER shall promptly obtain all required applications and will diligently complete and return them to the Mortgagee, and failure to do so shall constitute a breach hereunder. If the BUYER is not accepted by the Mortgagee, or the requirements for assumption are not in accordance with the terms of this Agreement, BUYER may rescind this Agreement by prompt written notice to the other party of his/her Agent. Any charges connected with assuming the existing mortgage shall not exceed $_____ and shall be paid by _____. Should such charges exceed this amount, the party responsible to pay the charge may rescind the Agreement unless the other party elects to pay the excess.

C. **PURCHASE MONEY NOTE AND MORTGAGE TO SELLER:** The purchase money note and mortgage, if any, shall provide for a thirty (30) day grace period in the event of default if it is a first mortgage and a fifteen (15) day grace period if it is a second mortgage, shall provide for right of prepayment in whole or in part without penalty, and shall be otherwise in form and content in accordance with covenants established by the Eight Judicial Circuit Bar Association. Said note and mortgage shall provide that in the event any installment is more than

N/A fifteen (15) days delinquent, the holder may assess a late charge of five percent (5%) of the late installment payment, or Ten Dollars ($10) whichever is greater, which late payment shall be due with the late installment payment, and in any event, shall be due no later than the due date of the next installment payment. Failure to pay the late charge when due shall constitute a default under the promissory note and mortgage. Said mortgage shall require all prior liens and encumbrances to be kept in good standing and shall forbid modifications of or future advances under prior mortgage(s).

The purchase money mortgage and note (check one)
☐ shall be fully assumable
☐ shall not be assumable, directly or indirectly, and shall include a standard due on sale clause prohibiting sale or transfer other than by descent and distribution in case of death or for a lease of three years or less not containing an option to purchase
☐ shall be assumable on these conditions: _____

6. **EVIDENCE OF TITLE:** The SELLER shall furnish to BUYER or his ATTORNEY or agent whose name is <u>James Hardy</u>
(Check One)
☐ An abstract from earliest public records, brought current, showing title to be marketable or insurable
☒ ALTA Owner's Title Insurance Commitment in the amount of the purchase price. If BUYER is required to furnish a mortgagee title insurance policy, SELLER agrees to select title agent approved by BUYER'S lender who can provide a simultaneous mortgagee policy.

Title evidence to be furnished within (Check One)
☒ <u>thirty</u>   (<u>30</u>   ) days from the effective date of this Agreement or
☐ _____ (_____) days from _____

7. **EXAMINATION OF TITLE:** The BUYER or his attorney shall have <u>fifteen</u>(<u>15</u>) days within to examine the abstract of title or title insurance and to signify willingness to accept same, whereupon the transaction shall be concluded on the closing date specified above. If title is not acceptable, BUYER shall furnish SELLER a written statement specifying title defects to be cured. If the title is unmarketable, the SELLER shall have <u>sixty</u>   (<u>60</u>) days or a reasonable period of time within which to cure the designated defects in the title that render same unmarketable or uninsurable in the opinion of the BUYER or his said Agent, and the SELLER hereby agrees to use reasonable diligence in curing said defects. Upon the defects being cured and notice of that fact being given to BUYER or his said Agent, this transaction shall then be closed within   <u>five</u>   (<u>5</u>) days of the delivery of the notice. At the option of the BUYER, upon SELLER'S failure or inability to correct the marketability of the title within the time limit or a reasonable period to time, the SELLER shall deliver the title in its existing condition, otherwise the deposit(s) shall be returned to the BUYER upon demand therefore, and all rights and liabilities on the part of the BUYER arising hereunder shall terminate. Provided, however, that in the event of disagreement between the SELLER and the BUYER or his said Agent, as to the marketability of the title, the SELLER may offer a commitment for an ALTA Owner's Title policy issued by a recognized title insurance company doing business in this area, agreeing to insure said title against all exceptions other than those mentioned in this Agreement and the standard printed exceptions, which commitment shall be conclusive evidence that said title is marketable. The commitment and Owner's Title policies pursuant thereto shall be paid for by the BUYER.

8. **TERMITES OR OTHER INFESTATION:** SELLER shall furnish to BUYER or his attorney or his agent at least five (5) days prior to closing a certificate of a locally licensed entomologist dated within thirty (30) days prior to closing, showing any improvements on the premises, exclusive of fences and <u>wood deck</u> to be apparently free from active infestation (other than infestation by wood-destroying fungi) or damage (including that caused by wood-destroying fungi) by termites or other wood-destroying organisms as required to be disclosed by Florida Law. If active infestation or damage is found to be present, the SELLER shall bear the total cost of remedying such active infestation and damage, except BUYER shall be responsible for damage caused by wood-destroying fungi where the cost of repair is less than One Hundred Dollars ($100). Should the cost of such treatment and repair exceed <u>one thousand</u> Dollars ($<u>1,000</u>) the SELLER may elect to terminate this Agreement and all rights and liabilities of all parties shall be an end and the deposit shall be returned to BUYER, unless the BUYER elects to proceed with the transaction having the above amount as a credit at closing.

9. **ASSIGNABILITY:** This Agreement (Check One) ☐ is assignable ☒ is not assignable.

Exhibit 20-1—continued

10. **RESTRICTIONS, EASEMENTS AND LIMITATIONS:** The BUYER shall take title subject to: zoning, restrictions, prohibitions and other requirements imposed by governmental authority, restrictions and matters appearing on the plat or otherwise common to the subdivision, public utility easements of record, taxes for the year of closing and subsequent years, assumed mortgage(s) and purchase money mortgages, if any, other: _____none_____ provided, however, that there exists at closing no violation of the foregoing and that the foregoing do not affect the marketability of title, and they do not prevent the use of the property for _____residential_____ purpose(s).

11. **UTILITIES:** SELLER represents subject property is served by (check if applicable)
    ☒ Central Water system
    ☐ Well
    ☒ Central wastewater system
    ☐ Septic tank
    ☐ None of the above

12. **EXPENSES:**
    SELLER shall pay for the following expenses:
    a. Real estate compensation
    b. State documentary stamps to be affixed to deed
    c. Preparation of instruments required of SELLER
    d. Abstract or title insurance
    e. Termite inspection fee
    f. SELLER'S attorney fee
    g. _____
    h. _____

    BUYER shall pay for the following expenses:
    a. Title examination and title opinion, if any.
    b. Recording of deed
    c. All expenses relative to all notes and mortgages, or a contract for deed, including preparation, recording, documentary stamps, intangible tax, and mortgagee title insurance.
    d. Transfer costs of any existing mortgage(s).
    e. Survey, if any.
    f. BUYER'S attorney fee.
    g. _____
    h. _____

13. **INSPECTION, REPAIR AND MAINTENANCE:** Unless otherwise stated in this Agreement, SELLER warrants that: (a) the ceiling, roof (including fascia and soffit), and exterior and interior walls do not have any visible evidence of leaks, water damage or structural damage. In the event repairs or replacements are required, SELLER shall pay up to _____two thousand_____ Dollars ($ 2,000.00) for such repairs or replacements; (b) SELLER further warrants that the septic tank, pool, all major appliances, heating, cooling, electrical, plumbing systems and machinery are in good working condition. In the event repairs or replacements are required, SELLER shall pay up to _____one thousand_____ Dollars ($ 1,000.00 for such repairs or replacements. However, if the cost for such repairs or replacements for either (a) or (b) above exceeds the stated amount, BUYER or SELLER may elect to pay such excess, failing which either party may cancel this Agreement. BUYER may, at BUYER'S expense, have inspections made of the roof and said items and shall report in writing to SELLER such items that do not meet the above warranty **prior to possession or not less than ten (10) calendar days prior to closing,** whichever date first occurs. All such inspections shall be at the BUYER'S expense, including any utility turn-on charges and costs of electricity and gas if these utilities are not currently on the property. Notwithstanding the provisions hereof, between the effective date of the Agreement and the closing, SELLER shall maintain the real and personal property in the condition herein warranted, reasonable wear and tear excepted, and shall maintain the lawn and shrubbery in substantially the same conditions as exists on the effective date of this Agreement. BUYER'S designee shall be permitted reasonable access for inspection prior to closing in order to confirm the compliance with the maintenance requirements. For the purpose of this provision, all inspections, repairs and replacements shall be made by an appropriately licensed firm or individual, or by a firm or individual specializing in home inspections and holding an appropriate license if required, or other mutually acceptable person. **The items listed above are the only repair items covered by this Agreement unless otherwise specifically provided for in the Agreement.** SELLER makes no warranties as to conformity with current applicable code requirements.

14. **CONVEYANCE:** SELLER shall convey title to the property by statutory warranty, trustee, personal representative or guardian deed, as appropriate to the status of SELLER, free and clear of all encumbrances and liens of whatsoever nature, except taxes for the current year, and except as herein otherwise provided. The SELLER shall also deliver to the BUYER a lien and possession affidavit at closing, sufficient to remove lien and possession exceptions from title insurance coverage. Conveyance of title shall be to: _____George and Helen Jones_____ .

15. **DATE OF POSSESSION:** BUYER shall be given possession _____date of closing_____ .

16. **TIME FOR ACCEPTANCE-FACSIMILE:** If this Agreement is not executed by all parties hereto, or FACT OF EXECUTION communicated in writing between the parties, on or before _____May 18, 2003_____ , the aforesaid deposit(s) shall, at the option of the BUYER, be returned to BUYER and this Agreement shall be null and void. A facsimile copy of this Agreement and any signatures hereon shall be considered for all purposes as originals.

Exhibit 20-1—continued

17. **FLOOD ZONE REPRESENTATION:** Flood Zone "A" is the designation for property that may be subject to more than a minimal risk of flooding. SELLER represents that the improvements (or the effective buildable area of unimproved property) are: (Check One of the Following)
☐ within flood zone "A"
☐ not within flood zone "A"
☐ flood zone status is unknown to SELLER
If SELLER has not represented the improvements (or effective buildable area) to be within Flood Zone "A", and the BUYER produces evidence prior to closing of title that Flood Zone "A" is in fact applicable, the BUYER shall have the option to declare the Agreement terminated and shall thereupon be entitled to a refund of all deposits. Should BUYER close title without obtaining evidence of flood zone status, the BUYER shall be deemed to have waived all objections as to flood zone regardless of the representations set forth in this paragraph.

18. **DISCLOSURES:** BUYER ☒ acknowledges ☐ does not acknowledge receipt of agency and estimated closing costs disclosures
BUYER'S INITIALS _GJ 96Ω_

19. **HOMEOWNER'S ASSOCIATION DISCLOSURE:** If the Property subject to this Agreement lies within a development served by a homeowner's association requiring owners of property to be members in the homeowner's association, a Homeowner's Disclosure Summary is attached hereto and by reference incorporated in and made a part of this Agreement. The BUYER ACKNOWLEDGES having received and read the attached Disclosure Summary required by Section 689.26, Florida Statutes, prior to signing this Agreement.
BUYER'S INITIALS _GJ 9Ω_

STANDARDS FOR REAL ESTATE TRANSACTIONS

A. **EFFECTIVE DATE:** The Effective Date as referred to in this Agreement shall be the date when the last one of the SELLER and the BUYER has signed this Agreement.

B. **VARIANCE IN AMOUNT OF FINANCING TO BE ASSUMED:** Any variance in any amount of financing to be assumed stated herein shall be added to or deducted from purchase money financing if such is contemplated by this Agreement otherwise said variance shall be added or deducted from the cash at closing, provided that if such procedure results in an increase in cash due at closing in excess of Five Hundred Dollars ($500), the BUYER shall not be obligated to perform unless SELLER reduces the purchase price by the amount of the excess over said specified sums.

C. **SURVEY:** If the BUYER desires a survey of the property, he may have the property surveyed as his expense at least five (5) days prior to closing date. If the survey shows an encroachments on the land herein described, or that the improvements located on the land herein described encroach on other lands, or any shortage, written notice to that effect along with a copy of the survey shall be given to the SELLER and the same shall be treated as defects in title to be eliminated by SELLER. SELLER agrees to provide BUYER with copies of existing surveys he has, if any, within five (5) days from the effective date.

D. **PRORATIONS:** All taxes for the current year, rentals, insurance premiums, association assessments and interest on existing mortgages, if any, shall be prorated as of the date of closing with BUYER paying for the day of closing. If part of the purchase price is to be evidenced by the assumption of a mortgage requiring deposit of funds in escrow for payment of taxes, insurance or other charges, the BUYER agrees to reimburse the SELLER for escrowed funds assigned to BUYER at closing. All mortgage payments shall be current at the time of closing.

E. **WARRANTIES:** SELLER warrants that there are not facts or defects known to SELLER materially affecting the value of the real property which are not readily observable by BUYER or which have not been disclosed to BUYER in writing.

F. **DESTRUCTION OF PREMISES:** If any improvements located on the above described premises at the time of execution of this Agreement are damaged by fire or other casualty prior to closing and can be substantially restored within a period not to exceed 45 days after the anticipated closing date, SELLER shall so restore the improvements and the closing date shall be extended accordingly. If such restoration cannot be completed within said period of time, this Agreement, at the option of the BUYER, shall terminate and all deposit(s) shall be returned to BUYER. All risk of loss prior to closing shall be borne by the SELLER.

G. **ESCROW:** Any escrow agent ("Agent") receiving funds or equivalent is authorized and agrees by acceptance of them to deposit them promptly, hold same in escrow and, subject to clearance, disburse them in accordance with the terms and conditions of this Agreement. At SELLER'S option, failure of clearance of funds shall be considered a default. If in doubt as to the Agent's duties or liabilities under the provision of this Agreement, Agent may, at Agent's option, continue to hold the subject matter of the escrow until the parties mutually agree to it disbursement or until a judgment of a court of competent jurisdiction shall determine the right of the parties, or Agent may deposit said escrowed funds with the clerk of the circuit court having jurisdiction of the dispute. Upon notifying all parties concerned of such action, all liability of Agent shall fully terminate, except to the extent of accounting for any items previously delivered out of escrow. If escrow agent is a licensed real estate broker, Agent will comply with provisions of Chapter 475, F.S. (1987), as amended. Any suit between BUYER and SELLER where Agent is made a party because of acting as Agent hereunder, or in any suit wherein Agent interpleads the subject matter of the escrow, Agent shall recover reasonable attorney's fees and costs incurred, with the fees and costs to be charged and assessed in court costs in favor of the prevailing party. Parties agree that Agent shall not be liable to any party or person for misdelivery to BUYER or SELLER of items subject to this escrow, unless such misdelivery is due to willful breach of Agreement or gross negligence of Agent.

H. **DISBURSEMENT OF CLOSING PROCEEDS:** Disbursement of closing proceeds shall be made as soon after closing as final title certification and examination have been made, but which shall be no later than five (5) business days after closing.

Exhibit 20-1—continued

I. FAILURE OF PERFORMANCE: If BUYER fails to perform this Agreement within the time specified (including payment of all deposits hereunder), the deposit(s) paid by BUYER may be retained by or for the account of SELLER as agreed upon liquidated damages, consideration for the execution of this Agreement and in full settlement of any claims; whereupon BUYER and SELLER shall be relieved of all obligations under this Agreement; or SELLER, at SELLER'S option, may proceed in equity to enforce SELLERS right under this Agreement. If, for any reason other than failure of SELLER to make SELLER'S title marketable after diligent effort, SELLER fails, neglects or refuses to perform this Agreement, the BUYER may seek specific performance or elect to receive the return of BUYER'S deposit(s) without thereby waiving any action for damages resulting from SELLER'S breach.

J. OTHER AGREEMENTS: This Agreement constitutes the entire agreement between the parties, and any changes, amendments or modifications hereof shall be null and void unless same are reduced to writing and signed by parties hereto.

K. PERSONS BOUND: The covenants herein contained shall bind and the benefits and advantages shall pass to, the respective heirs, administrators, successors and assigns of the parties hereto. Whenever used, the singular number shall include the plural, and the use of any gender shall include all genders.

L. ATTORNEY'S FEES AND COSTS: In any litigation arising out of this Agreement, the prevailing party in such litigation which, for the purposes of this Standard, shall include SELLER, BUYER, listing broker, BUYER'S broker and any subagents to the listing broker or BUYER'S broker, shall be entitled to recover reasonable attorney's fees and costs, including reasonable attorney's fees and costs incurred in any appeal.

M. PROVISIONS: Typewritten or handwritten provisions inserted in this form shall control all printed provisions in conflict therewith.

N. INSULATION RIDER: If this Agreement is utilized for the sale of a new residence, an Insulation Rider or equivalent shall be attached hereto and become a part hereof.

O. FOREIGN INVESTMENT IN REAL PROPERTY TAX ACT (FIRPTA) RIDER: The parties shall comply with the provisions of FIRPTA and applicable regulations which could require SELLER to provide additional cash at closing to meet withholding requirements, and a FIRPTA Rider or equivalent may be attached to this Agreement.

P. INGRESS AND EGRESS: SELLER warrants and represents that there is ingress and egress to the Real Property sufficient for the intended use as described herein.

Q. TIME: Time periods herein of less than six (6) days shall, in the computation, exclude Saturdays, Sundays and state or national legal holidays, and any time period provided for herein which shall end on a Saturday, Sunday, or legal holiday shall extend to 5:00 p.m. of the next business day. Failure of any party to perform and covenant of this Agreement within the time limits set forth for performance of such covenant shall not be considered a material breach excusing performance unless such failure results in a material loss to the aggrieved party.

R. LEASES: SELLER shall, not less that 15 days before closing, furnish to BUYER copies of all written leases and estoppel letters from each tenant specifying the nature and duration of the tenant's occupancy, rental rates; and advanced rent and security deposits paid by tenant. If SELLER us unable to obtain such letter from each tenant, the same information shall be furnished by SELLER to BUYER writing that time period in the form of a SELLER'S affidavit and BUYER may thereafter contact tenants to confirm such information. SELLER shall, at closing, deliver and assign all original leases to BUYER.

S. SPECIAL ASSESSMENTS:
1. UNIMPROVED PROPERTY: SELLER shall be responsible for payment of all special assessments for improvements whether in place or under construction as of the effective date of this Agreement. BUYER agrees to be responsible for all water and wastewater flow base and connection charges, if any, associated with placing any improvements upon the property.
2. IMPROVED PROPERTY: SELLER shall be responsible for payment of all special assessments for improvements whether in place or under construction as of the effective date of this Agreement. SELLER shall pay (or has paid) all water and wastewater flow base and connection charges.

T. ADDITIONAL INFORMATION

RADON: Radon is a naturally occurring radioactive gas, that when has accumulated in a building in sufficient quantities, may present health risks to persons who are exposed to it over time. Levels of radon that exceed federal and state guidelines have been found in buildings in Florida. Additional information regarding radon and radon testing may be obtained from your county public health unit.

ENERGY-EFFICIENCY RATING DISCLOSURE: Pursuant to 553.996, Florida Statutes, Purchaser may have the energy-efficiency rating of a building being purchased determined. Purchaser acknowledges that this notice as well as a Department of Community Affairs' brochure on the Florida Building Energy-Efficiency Rating System was received at the time of or prior to Purchaser signing this Agreement for Sale and Purchase.

Exhibit 20-1—concluded

THIS IS A LEGALLY BINDING AGREEMENT AND SHALL NOT BE RECORDED UNLESS OTHERWISE AGREED TO BETWEEN THE PARTIES. IF NOT FULLY UNDERSTOOD, SEEK COMPETENT LEGAL ADVICE. DO NOT SIGN UNTIL ALL BLANKS ARE COMPLETED. YOUR REALTOR RECOMMENDS THAT YOU OBTAIN TITLE INSURANCE OR A TITLE OPINION FROM YOUR ATTORNEY.

George Jones	5/15/03	*Fred Johnson*	5/15/03
BUYER	Date	SELLER	Date

Social Security or Tax ID # 122-21-2221   Social Security or Tax ID # 211-12-1112

Helen Jones	5/15/03	*Louise Johnson*	5/15/03
BUYER	Date	SELLER	Date

Social Security or Tax ID # 322-32-2233   Social Security or Tax ID # 233-23-3332

Deposit(s) if other than cash, then subject to clearance Baden Associates Realty
                                        Escrow Agent (REALTOR®)
                        By: *Ben Park*

BROKER'S FEES (CHECK AND COMPLETE THE ONE APPLICABLE)

☒ IF A LISTING AGREEMENT IS CURRENTLY IN EFFECT:
   SELLER agrees to pay the Broker, according to the terms of an existing, separate listing agreement
OR
☐ IF NO LISTING AGREEMENT IS CURRENTLY IN EFFECT:
   SELLER agrees to pay the Broker named below, at time of closing, from the disbursements of the proceeds of the sale, compensation in the amount of (Complete ONLY ONE) _____% of gross purchase price OR $_____ for Broker's services in effecting the sale by finding a BUYER ready, willing and able to purchase pursuant to the foregoing Agreement. If BUYER fails to perform and deposit(s) is retained, 50% thereof, but not exceeding the Broker's fee above provided, shall be paid to the Broker, as full consideration for Broker's services including costs expended by Broker, and the balance shall be paid to SELLER. IF the transaction shall not be closed because of refusal or failure of SELLER to perform, the SELLER shall pay said fees in full to Broker on demand. In any litigation arising out of this Agreement, concerning the Broker's fee, the prevailing party shall be entitled to recover reasonable attorney's fees and costs.

firm name of Broker_____   SELLER_____

By: (authorized signatory) _____   SELLER_____

Firm name of cooperating agent_____

Address of cooperating agent_____

The contract form also covers type of title evidence (section 6); time for acceptance by the parties (16); closing date (4); restrictions, easements, and limitations (10); occupancy date (15); assignability (9); liens (14); special assessments (5); expenses (12); inspections, repair, and maintenance (13); and flood zone representation (17). Spaces are provided for signatures of the principals and the representative of the real estate firm.

A section is provided for a separate agreement between the sellers and the broker if no listing agreement is in effect (see page 6 of the agreement in Exhibit 20-1). The sellers agree to pay the broker a commission at the time of closing from the disbursement of proceeds. If the buyers fail to perform, the broker and sellers agree to split any escrow deposits, with the broker's share not to exceed the amount of the commission. If the sellers fail to perform, they agree to pay the full commission to the broker.

Contract with Contingencies

Contracts for sale may contain sections that cause implementation of the contract to depend on the successful completion of some prior action or condition. These are known as **contracts with contingencies.** Examples are financing contingencies in which the buyer can back out of the transaction if financing cannot be obtained on specified terms, and engineering contingencies in which the buyer can back out if an inspection shows the property is physically deficient. Contingencies appear most often in contracts for properties that are difficult to sell. Unless contingency clauses are worded with great care they can bring unpleasant surprises to either the buyer or seller. They should be written carefully, perhaps with legal guidance, and reviewed with care.

Assignment

In general, most contracts—including real estate contracts—can be assigned. **Assignment** means that one party's contractual rights and obligations are transferred to someone else. If buyers of real estate assign the contract, new buyers, in effect, take their place. The new buyers may pay the agreed upon price and obtain title to the property.

But any type of **personal performance** contracted by one party cannot be assigned without that party's permission. For example, if a seller has agreed to take a purchase money mortgage as part of the payment for the property, the buyer cannot assign this right to someone else unless he or she remains personally liable to the seller for payment of the loan. Similarly, land (installment sale) contracts are not assignable without the owner's permission. In these situations, the seller relies on the buyer's qualifications, and the assignee may not be as well qualified.

Although buyers may assign their rights to someone else, they do not escape liability under the contract. They are still obligated to the seller and, should the assignees not fulfill the requirements of the contract, the seller can look to the assignors for satisfaction. In effect, assignment is an agreement by the assignee to carry out the obligations of the assignor; the assignor's contract with the other party is not affected.

Of course, the other party can agree to an assignment and relieve the assignor of all obligations. When this occurs, a contract is created between the third party and the assignee that absolves the assignor of further responsibility under the contract.

A contract can also prohibit assignment. Such a prohibition would be contained in an *assignment clause.* In the purchase and sale agreement displayed in Exhibit 20-1, paragraph 9 states explicitly that the agreement between the parties to this contract—the Joneses and the Johnsons—is not assignable by either party.

Concept Check

20.8   What is assignment of a contract? Who is liable for a contract that has been assigned?

Remedies for Nonperformance

Buyers and sellers sometimes fail to live up to the provisions of a contract. They may change their minds for a number of reasons. For example, if one spouse dies, the other may not want to move. Or, if their financial circumstances change, they may decide they cannot afford a new home.

When a party fails to perform (e.g., breach of contract, nonperformance, or default), the other party may have one or more remedies. The nondefaulting party may, (1) rescind the contract, (2) sue for specific performance (i.e., require the defaulting party to carry out the contract), (3) or sue for damages. Or, a seller may retain the earnest money deposit as liquidated damages.

Escrow

To lessen the chances for nonperformance, real estate contracts are often placed in **escrow.** An **escrow agent** is a third party who is instructed to carry out the provisions of the contract by means of a separate escrow agreement. The escrow agent must be impartial and may not benefit from the provisions of the purchase and sale contract. The escrow agent is allowed, of course, to collect a fee for services rendered.

Concept Check

20.9 What are three standard remedies to a defaulted contract for sale of real estate? What is one additional remedy commonly available to a seller?

Escrow agents are usually attorneys, financial institutions, or title companies, although in some states they may be separate individuals or companies. They hold the documents and funds relevant to a transaction and distribute them according to the written instructions at the time of closing. For example, a buyer would give a deposit or full purchase price to the escrow agent, while the seller would deliver a deed and evidence of title (e.g., an abstract or a title insurance policy) to the escrow agent. Insurance policies, mortgage financing information, and any other documents would also be provided. When all the documents have been assembled, title has been searched, funds have been obtained, and all other conditions met, the escrow agent delivers the deed to the buyer and the funds to the seller.

When escrow agents are not used, attorneys, title companies, or financial institutions usually provide closing services. Although they assemble the necessary documents and arrange for the title search and evidence of title, the real estate broker may hold the earnest money deposit until closing. The broker, however, must hold the deposit for the benefit of the principal, cannot commingle deposits with personal funds, and must not disburse deposits except as provided in the contract.

Closing and Closing Statements

The first step in a real estate transaction is negotiating and completing the contract for sale. The final step is the closing. Real estate closings, including the roles of the various parties and the documents that are prepared and signed at closing, are the topic of this section.

Role of the Brokers

The selling broker's role may be simply as moral support and facilitator once the contract for sale is signed (if the selling broker is different from the listing broker). The selling broker is normally not an agent of the buyer but, rather, a subagent of the listing broker. Once the contract is signed, therefore, the selling broker has no further *legal* role with the buyers or the listing broker. It is, however, wise business practice and arguably the responsibility of the selling broker to the seller, to assist the buyers toward a smooth and successful closing.

The listing broker's role at closing can vary widely from state to state and community to community. Because real estate brokers are not permitted to give legal advice in many parts of the country, their strictly legal role is largely finished when the contract for sale is signed. Nevertheless, like the selling broker, the wise listing broker continues to counsel the sellers about steps to take before closing. Moreover, as part of the broker's obligation of diligence, the broker is bound to take reasonable steps to assure that the sale is not delayed or aborted due to logistical problems. Therefore, the broker may take care of details such as arranging for title evidence, surveys, termite inspections, and agreed upon repairs. It is in the listing broker's best interest to make certain the closing actually occurs at the time specified in the contract for sale.

Although attorneys, lending institutions, and title companies normally take over a transaction after the contract for sale is signed, the listing broker continues to have *legal* responsibility to the sellers through the closing. In some transactions not financed by a financial institution, the listing broker might actually conduct the closing. Although someone else may prepare the closing statement, the broker is also responsible to the sellers for its accuracy. Thus, real estate brokers must know what happens at closings, as well as all other aspects of a transaction.

Concept Check

20.10   In most closings, who is responsible to see that the closing is completed successfully?

Role of the Lenders

Lenders must protect their security interest in a property involved in a transaction. They want to be certain the buyer is obtaining marketable title to the property. Also, they want to assure that the tax and insurance payments are current so that a tax lien cannot preempt the mortgage lien and that insurance proceeds will cover the property if it is damaged or destroyed. Lenders normally participate in the closing of a real estate transaction by having an attorney present who often conducts the proceedings. The lender normally requires the buyers to have a fire and hazard insurance policy and a title insurance policy, with the lender as the beneficiary. The lender also usually wants an appraisal, a survey, a termite inspection, a certificate of occupancy (for a new building), and establishment of an escrow account for payment of hazard insurance and local property taxes.

Real Estate Settlement Procedures Act

The Real Estate Settlement Procedures Act (RESPA) is a federal law that requires federally chartered or insured lenders (e.g., banks, savings institutions, and credit unions) to provide buyers and sellers of one- to four-family homes, cooperatives, and condominiums with information on all settlement costs. Whenever a buyer obtains a *new* first mortgage loan from one of these lenders, when the loan is insured by the FHA or guaranteed by the VA, or when the loan will be sold to one of the federally related secondary mortgage market agencies (i.e., Fannie Mae or Freddie Mac) the following RESPA requirements must be met:

  1. Special information booklet. A booklet titled *Settlement Costs and You,* written by HUD, must be given to every loan applicant. The booklet contains general information about settlement costs and explains the various RESPA provisions. It also includes a line-by-line explanation of the Uniform Settlement Statement (see item 3 below).

  2. Good-faith estimate of settlement costs. Within three business days of the loan application, a lender must provide the applicant with a good-faith estimate of the settlement costs the borrower is likely to incur. The estimates may be specific figures or a range for each cost, based on recent comparable transactions in the area. Also, if a lender requires the closing to be conducted by a particular attorney or title insurance company, the lender must reveal any business relationship with the attorney or title company and estimate the charges for the service. A detailed example of a good-faith estimate of settlement costs is provided in Exhibit 20-3.

3. Uniform Settlement Statement (HUD-1 Form). Loan closing information must be prepared on a special HUD form, the Uniform Settlement Statement, often referred to as the "HUD-1 Form." All charges imposed by the lender must be listed; charges incurred by the buyer and seller separately and outside the closing are not required to be disclosed. The borrower must be permitted to inspect the statement one business day before the closing to the extent that figures are available. Final figures must be available at the time of closing. An example of a real estate closing using the HUD-1 Form is presented in a following section.

4. Prohibition against kickbacks. Before 1974, when RESPA was enacted, kickbacks were prevalent in real estate transactions and closings. Borrowers, for example, would be charged for title insurance, but part of the title insurance premium would be rebated to the attorney or lender who recommended or required the title insurance. Thus, buyers were faced with hidden costs and were not free to bargain for services on a competitive basis. RESPA explicitly prohibits all such kickbacks or unearned fees. Note, however, that fee splitting between cooperating real estate brokers, members of multiple listing services, or brokers and their salespersons is not prohibited.

Concept Check

20.11   List four ways that the Real Estate Settlement Procedures Act (RESPA) affects most residential real estate closings.

Preparation of Closing Statements

Normally, when a buyer signs an offer to purchase, the broker receives **earnest money** from the purchaser amounting to 5 or 10 percent of the purchase price. This amount should immediately be placed in an account with a title company or financial institution. Most states have laws requiring brokers to maintain a separate account (an escrow account) for earnest money deposits and be able to account for all such moneys at any time. Failure to do so may result in a broker's license being suspended or revoked.

Explore The Web

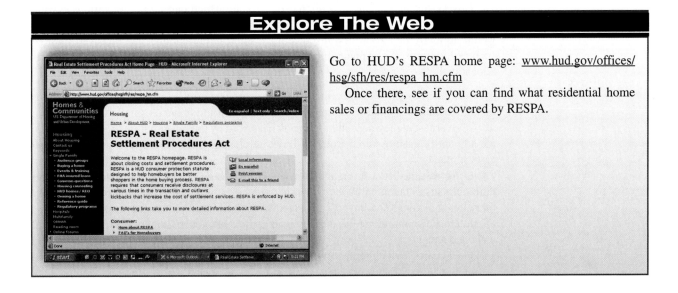

Go to HUD's RESPA home page: www.hud.gov/offices/hsg/sfh/res/respa_hm.cfm

Once there, see if you can find what residential home sales or financings are covered by RESPA.

Exhibit 20-2   Common Closing Expenses and Allocation of Responsibility between Buyer and Seller

Item	Comment
1. Purchase price	Paid from buyer's funds
2. Earnest money deposit	Prepaid by buyer, who requires a credit at closing
3. First mortgage balance (when assumed by buyer)	Assumption is a form of payment to the seller
4. Second mortgage (to seller)	Seller accepts mortgage in lieu of a portion of the sale price
Prorations and prepayments:	
5. Interest on mortgage (existing mortgage)	Paid later by buyer, who is credited at closing
6. Insurance (for unexpired term)	Prepaid by seller, who receives credit at closing
7. Property taxes	Paid after closing by buyer, who receives credit at closing
Expenses:	
8. Title insurance	
Owner's policy	Premium paid by seller
Lender's policy	Premium paid by buyer/borrower
9. Attorney's fee (buyer)	
10. Attorney's fee (seller)	
11. State documentary stamp tax on new mortgage and note	Paid by buyer at closing
12. State documentary stamp tax on deed	Generally paid by seller at closing
13. State intangible tax on new mortgage and note	Paid by buyer at closing
14. Recording of new mortgage	Cost paid by buyer at closing
15. Recording of deed	Cost paid by buyer at closing
16. Brokerage commission	Generally paid by seller at closing

The seller must sign the offer to signify acceptance. The accepted offer is then a contract for sale (and purchase). Expenses incurred by the closing agent for the buyer and seller must be strictly accounted for and accurately disclosed in separate statements prepared for the buyer and seller at closing. The broker must also keep a copy of the closing statement and a summary of receipts and disbursements of all moneys involved in the transaction.

Exhibit 20-2 lists some common expenses paid by the buyer or seller, or prorated between the two. Responsibility for the payment of closing expenses should be governed by the contract for sale; if they are not covered by the contract, local custom should be followed in charging and crediting each expense to the buyer and seller.

Buyers and sellers can (and often do) negotiate which party will pay various closing expenses. In soft markets, buyers can often insist sellers pay all or part of the expenses that would normally be the buyers' responsibility. Substantial amounts can be saved through such negotiations. An explanation of each closing expense listed in Exhibit 20-2 and its allocation between the buyer and seller follows:

1. The purchase price is the principal charge paid from the buyer's funds at closing. It is the ultimate closing cost; without its payment there would be no closing.

2. The earnest money deposit has already been paid by the buyer before the closing. Thus, the amount of cash required from the buyer at closing is reduced by the previously paid earnest money.

3, 4. An assumed first mortgage or a second mortgage provided by the seller are long-term obligations taken on by the buyer that reduce the amount of cash the buyer must pay the seller at closing. The buyer is thus credited at closing for assuming these obligations.

5. Interest on a mortgage is generally paid at the end of each month. Thus, the buyer will make a payment on an assumed mortgage, part of which represents the seller's ownership period and part of which represents the new owner's period. The portion of the buyer's end-of-month payment that represents the period of time during which the seller occupied the house will be credited to the buyer. That is, it will reduce the amount the buyer must pay to the seller at closing.

6. Hazard insurance premiums are typically paid annually. While it is rare for a buyer to continue the existing insurance policy on a residence, it is instructive to consider how that would be accomplished. The seller would have paid for the entire year. Thus, at closing the buyer would need to pay the seller an amount proportionate to the time the buyer will use the insurance.

7. Property taxes are paid in arrears (i.e., after the tax year). Thus, the seller will not have paid the property taxes for the year before transferring ownership to the buyer. As a result, the buyer will be required to pay the entire tax bill at the end of the year. Therefore, the estimated tax bill must be allocated in proportion to the time the property is owned by the respective parties. The buyer receives a credit at closing for the amount the buyer will pay on behalf of the seller's ownership period.

8. The seller must provide assurance of good title to the new owner. Thus, sellers are usually required to pay the full premium at closing for an "owner's" title insurance policy. Lenders also demand assurance of good title and indemnification in the event the title is not good. The borrower generally purchases this title insurance protection on behalf of the lender.

9. Buyers should hire an attorney to examine the seller's evidence of title and to represent them at the closing. These fees are generally paid at closing.

10. Sellers usually hire an attorney to prepare the deed and represent their interests at closing.

11. A state documentary stamp tax on mortgages, notes, and contracts may be required on any new loans used to finance the transaction. This tax is paid by the buyer at closing.

12. A state documentary stamp tax on deeds also may be required. It is considered an expense of delivering title to the buyer and is therefore paid by the seller, unless there is an agreement to the contrary.

13. A state intangible tax on mortgages and notes may be imposed. Since the buyers are obtaining such mortgages to finance the purchase, the tax is usually charged to them.

14, 15. Recording of both the mortgage and the deed is usually the buyer's burden. Recording of the deed is necessary to protect the buyer's interest, whereas the lender requires the borrower (buyer) to pay the mortgage recording charges.

16. Usually the seller has hired the broker and therefore must pay the commission.

Concept Check

20.12   Name two methods of determining which party will be responsible for the various costs of closing.

The procedures for **prorating** should reflect the actual number of days in the period, the number of days during the period the property was owned by the seller, and the number of days it will be owned by the buyer. The date for dividing the financial responsibilities of buyers and sellers is subject to agreement between the parties. Usually the day of closing is said to "belong to the buyer," that is, counted as a day of buyer ownership. However this convention is negotiable. If the contract does not cover this matter, local custom will prevail.

For example, if a transaction is scheduled to close on May 14 of a 365-day year, taxes for the year would be allocated between buyers and sellers as shown below (the day of closing belongs to the buyer):

```
    Jan. 1           May 14          Dec. 31
      |                 |               |
      |    Sellers      |    Buyers     |
      |                 |               |
      |    133 days     |    232 days   |
```

If the estimated tax for the year is $500, the sellers would be responsible for $182.19 [(133 ÷ 365) × $500)]. The buyers would be credited with this amount, since they will pay the entire amount of the tax at year-end.

As another example, consider the hazard insurance proration for a transaction scheduled to close on March 16 of a 365-day year. The premium in the amount of $250 was paid by the sellers for the policy commencing December 15 of the previous year and ending December 14 at midnight of the current year. The premium is prorated between buyers and sellers as shown below, with the day of closing assumed to belong to the buyers:

Dec. 15	March 16	Dec. 14
Sellers	Buyers	
91 days	274 days	

www.alta.org/cnsrinfo/

American Land Title Association website with information for consumers on title insurance and home closings.

Since the sellers paid the premium prior to closing, they are credited with the portion of the policy period the buyers will own the property. Thus, the sellers will receive an additional $187.67 from the buyer at closing [(274 ÷ 365) × $250].

The Continuing Story of a Sale

Recall from Chapter 19 that Fred and Louise Johnson have listed their house with Baden Associates Realty, through Ben Park, a Realtor with the firm. The listing price is $155,000. Another salesperson in the same company, Josh Hairston, shows the Johnson home to George and Helen Jones, who are moving to Gainesville from Ohio.

The Joneses like the house and believe it would suit their needs, but they note several maintenance and replacement items. They believe they would have to paint the interior and exterior, install new carpeting, and purchase drapes. Thus, they decide to make the following offer:

> Price: $147,000
> Financing: New 30-year fixed-rate mortgage at 6.75 percent
> Closing date: July 1, 2003
> Earnest money deposit: $5,000

Ben and Josh present the offer to the Johnsons, who reject it and counter with a price of $152,000. The counteroffer is then presented to the Joneses. They accept this offer contingent on their obtaining a 30-year, 80 percent fixed-rate loan commitment at an initial rate not to exceed 6.75 percent. They also want the sellers to furnish a title insurance policy and a termite inspection report, and they want to have the right to have radon and building inspections made at their own expense. This offer/counteroffer process is reflected in the purchase and sale contract form shown on the first page of Exhibit 20-1. Changes to the original typed offer are initialed by the Johnsons. To accept the counteroffer, the Joneses also initial the changes.

Good-Faith Estimate of Closing Costs

The laws of some states require that real estate brokers provide buyers and sellers with a list of **estimated closing costs** before signing a contract for sale. Also, as previously noted, the Real Estate Settlement Procedures Act (RESPA) requires lenders to provide borrowers with an estimate of the settlement expenses that are likely to occur. Such estimates must be provided when the borrower applies for a loan or within three business days. Exhibit 20-3 shows the buyer's estimated closing expenses, provided by the lender, DownTrust Bank, on the sale of the Johnson property.

The Joneses have applied for a 30-year, 80 percent loan to value ratio, fixed-rate mortgage of $121,600 and must pay several items in connection with the loan at closing. First,

Exhibit 20-3 Good-Faith Estimate of Buyer's Closing Costs

Buyer:	George and Helen Jones		Seller:	Fred and Louise Johnson
Property	1822 N. W. 40th Avenue		Date:	May 25, 2003
Address:	Gainesville, FL		Loan:	$121,600, 6.75% 30-year fixed rate

Estimated Costs		Paid by Borrower
800.	**Items Payable in Connection with Loan**	
801.	Origination fee	$1,216.00
802.	Discount fee	1,216.00
803.	Appraisal fee	275.00
804.	Credit report	16.50
807.	Tax service fee	59.00
811.	Document review	395.00
812.	Flood certification fee	18.00
900.	**Items Required by Lender to Be Paid in Advance**	
901.	Interest for 31 days @ $22.4877 per day	697.12
902.	First-year mortgage insurance premium	
903.	First-year hazard insurance premium	684.00
1000.	**Reserves Deposited with Lender**	
1001.	Hazard insurance: 2 months @ $57.00 per month	114.00
1002.	Mortgage insurance: 2 months @ $ per month	
1003.	City property taxes: 3 months @ $ per month	
1004.	County property taxes: 3 months @ $233.33 per month	699.99
1100.	**Title Charges**	
1102.	Title search	
1105.	Document preparation fee	42.00
1107.	Attorney's fees	250.00
1108.	Title insurance premium:	
1109.	Lender's coverage	200.00
1110.	Owner's coverage	
1111.	Endorsement fees	153.00
1200.	**Government Recording and Transfer Charges**	
1201.	Recording fees	93.00
1202.	City-county tax stamps	
1203.	State tax stamps Deed $ Mtg. $425.60	425.60
1204.	Intangible tax	243.20
1300.	**Additional Settlement Charges**	
1301.	Survey	275.00
1302.	Pest inspection	
1400.	**Total Estimated Closing Costs**	$7,072.41

the lender has quoted a one point loan origination fee (line 801). One point equals 1 percent of the loan amount, in this case $1,216. This fee is meant to cover the lender's administrative costs in processing the loan. The lender is also charging one discount point (line 802). Discount points are a one-time charge imposed by the lender to lower the interest rate that the lender would otherwise offer the loan to the borrowers. The lender estimates that the required appraisal and credit report will cost $275 and $16.50, respectively (lines 803 and 804). The credit report shows the Joneses' credit rating, and was used by DownTrust to decide whether or not to approve the loan. The buyer must also pay a tax service fee of $59 in connection with the loan and pay $18 to certify that the property is not in a flood zone (lines 807 and 812). DownTrust Bank will also charge $395 to prepare and review the loan documents (line 811).

As is typical, DownTrust is requiring the Joneses to prepay certain items at the time of settlement (July 1). In particular, because the first scheduled loan payment will be for August and payable on September 1, the Joneses will be required to prepay 31 days of mortgage interest equal to $697.12 at $22.49 per day, as well as $684 for a one-year hazard insurance policy (lines 901 and 903).[5]

City and county property taxes represent a first lien on mortgaged property. That is, if the property owners fail to pay their taxes in a timely fashion, the local taxing jurisdictions can force a foreclosure sale of the property and use the proceeds to satisfy unpaid property tax debts, including late fees and penalties. Mortgage lenders, who also have a security interest in the property, do not want unpaid property taxes to trigger a foreclosure sale. Thus, lenders often require borrowers to add 1/12 of the borrower's estimated tax bill to their required monthly mortgage payments. These prepaid taxes are held in escrow accounts by the lender until the property tax payments are due, at which time the lender pays the taxes on behalf of the borrower. To help ensure that the property tax reserve account will have a sufficient balance to pay the borrower's taxes when due, lenders generally require that several months of property tax reserves be paid at closing. Similar to property taxes is hazard insurance, for which lenders often require borrowers to create reserves to pay future premiums. These prepaid items are captured in the section under line 1000 titled "Reserves Deposited with Lender" of Exhibit 20-3. Under RESPA the lender is not allowed to collect more than a certain amount of reserves (i.e., escrow deposits) at closing (see Chapter 10). In brief, the lender cannot demand an escrow "cushion" of more that one-sixth of the total charges in the annual escrow cycle. Thus, if total annual payments out of escrow for taxes and insurance are expected to be $1,800, the lender can require excess deposits of no more than $300 above what is needed to meet upcoming expenditures.

With respect to the cost of acquiring title from the seller, the lender estimates that the buyer will need to pay a $42 document preparation fee and a $250 attorney fee (lines 1105 and 1107). The cost to the borrower of obtaining a title insurance policy for the lender is estimated to be $200 (line 1108) plus the cost of an endorsement to extend title coverage for the survey, which is $153 (line 1111). Recording fees, state tax stamps on the mortgage, and the intangible tax are estimated at $93, $425.60, and $243.20, respectively (line 1201–1204). **Recording** documents in the public records provides *constructive notice* of an interest in real property. It informs anyone who may have a potential interest in the property of both the owner and the lender. Finally, the lender will have the property surveyed and charge the borrower the estimated $275 cost (line 1301). The lender estimates that the borrower's closing costs will total $7,072.41.

Buyers must be aware that amounts listed on the Good-Faith Estimate are only estimates. Actual costs may vary. They should keep their estimate so that they may compare it with the final settlement costs and be prepared to ask questions about any changes.

Steps before Closing

Recall that the contract for sale signed by the Johnsons and Joneses specifies that "The transaction shall be concluded on July 1, 2003, or such earlier date as may be mutually agreeable." (See item 4 in Exhibit 20-1.) It is now July 1, 2003. The Johnsons, the sellers; the Joneses, the buyers; the Johnsons' attorney, James Henry; the listing agent, Ben Park; and the selling agent, Josh Hairston, arrive at the offices of DownTrust Bank, where closing is to take place. The Joneses' application for a 6.75 percent, 30-year,

---

5. The $22.4877 per day interest is calculated as $(0.0675 \div 365) \times \$121,600$.

Real Estate Attorney

Lawyers (attorneys) serve multiple roles in real estate. Because of the complexity and value of real estate the contracts that arise can be lengthy, complicated, and diverse, including leases, contracts for sale and purchase, deeds, mortgages, notes, listing agreements, investor agreements, and many others. Attorneys provide important guidance to the parties involved, assisting them in understanding the legal options available and the legal implications of the wording in documents. Attorneys help their clients translate their business goals and requirements into appropriate and effective contract language. Beyond this technical role, attorneys can serve as advisors to their clients on the choices available to them, and frequently represent their client in real estate negotiations.

Attorneys may practice in the area of real estate as part of a broader law practice. Others specialize in real estate, and even in specific aspects of the field such as land use controls, mortgage finance, investments, or a specific type of real estate such as commercial. Those attorneys specializing in real estate may work in various contexts. They may work for a large corporation, handling the corporation's real estate affairs, or they may set up an individual real estate law practice. Especially if they are in a private partnership or individual practice, they may be able to control their work hours. While most attorneys work longer that 40-hour weeks, as they reach retirement age, they often simply reduce the number of clients served, and the number of hours worked. Most of the work of attorneys is in offices. It is less common for them to be involved in public meetings or court proceedings unless they specialize in a field such as land use regulation.

To qualify as an attorney the aspirant generally must complete an undergraduate degree, a graduate law degree, and pass the bar exam in the state where they seek to practice. In the year 2000 attorneys going into private practice earned a starting salary of about $85,000, though attorneys starting into government positions or into advocacy work earned much less. Experienced attorneys in private law firms earned over $120,000.

Source: Based partly on information from Mariwyn Evans, *Real Estate Careers,* McGraw-Hill, New York: 2002, Chapter 7.

---

fixed-rate mortgage was approved by DownTrust. DownTrust's attorney, Joe Jenkins, is there to handle the closing.

After signing the contract for sale on May 15, 2003, and before arriving for closing July 1, 2003, the Joneses and their attorney took the following steps:

1. Surveyed the property for possible encroachments. (The survey was paid for directly by the Joneses as buyers; therefore, this charge does not appear on the settlement statement, Exhibit 20-4.)
2. Reviewed an abstract of documents in the public records to make certain there are no violations of private restrictions.
3. Reviewed the zoning ordinance to make certain the property is used as legally permitted.
4. Examined the list of estimated closing costs to make certain they are correct and reasonable (see Exhibit 20-4).
5. Ordered a lender's title insurance policy from the same company the sellers asked to issue an owner's title policy. When a title company issues a policy to both an owner and a mortgagee, it is termed a *simultaneous issue.*
6. Inspected the property to verify condition and vacancy for possession. (This step is so important that many buyers hire a professional property inspector.)
7. Reviewed the contract to make certain other terms and conditions have been met by the sellers, such as having the property inspected for termites.
8. Arranged to have hazard insurance coverage, utilities, telephone, and other services begin on the date of closing.[6]

---

6. If the Joneses were assuming any mortgages, the attorney would obtain an *estoppel certificate* (or letter) from the lender that would show the amount being assumed, interest rate, length of debt period, periodic payments, and frequency of amortization.

Exhibit 20-4 HUD-1 Form

A. Settlement Statement	U.S. Department of Housing and Urban Development	OMB Approval No. 2502-0265

B. Type of Loan

1. ☐ FHA 2. ☐ FmHA 3. ☑ Conv. Unins.
4. ☐ VA 5. ☐ Conv. Ins.

6. File Number:	7. Loan Number:	8. Mortgage Insurance Case Number:

C. Note: This form is furnished to give you a statement of actual settlement costs. Amounts paid to and by the settlement agent are shown. Items marked "(p.o.c.)" were paid outside the closing; they are shown here for informational purposes and are not included in the totals.

D. Name & Address of Borrower:	E. Name & Address of Seller:	F. Name & Address of Lender:
George and Helen Jones 1228 Omega Avenue Cincinnati, Ohio	Fred and Louise Johnson 1822 NW 40th Avenue Gainesville, FL	DownTrust Bank 232NE 2nd Avenue Gainesville, FL

G. Property Location:	H. Settlement Agent:
1822 NW 40th Avenue Gainesville, FL	DownTrust Bank Place of Settlement: I. Settlement Date: July 1, 2003

J. Summary of Borrower's Transaction		**K. Summary of Seller's Transaction**	
100. Gross Amount Due From Borrower		**400. Gross Amount Due To Seller**	
101. Contract sales price	152,000.00	401. Contract sales price	152,000.00
102. Personal property		402. Personal property	
103. Settlement charges to borrower (line 1400)	7072.41	403.	
104.		404.	
105.		405.	
Adjustments for items paid by seller in advance		Adjustments for items paid by seller in advance	
106. City/town taxes to		406. City/town taxes to	
107. County taxes to		407. County taxes to	
108. Assessments to		408. Assessments to	
109.		409.	
110.		410.	
111.		411.	
112.		412.	
120. Gross Amount Due From Borrower	159,072.41	**420. Gross Amount Due To Seller**	152,000.00
200. Amounts Paid By Or In Behalf Of Borrower		**500. Reductions In Amount Due To Seller**	
201. Deposit or earnest money	5,000.00	501. Excess deposit (see instructions)	
202. Principal amount of new loan(s)	121,600.00	502. Settlement charges to seller (line 1400)	11,420.00
203. Existing loan(s) taken subject to		503. Existing loan(s) taken subject to	
204.		504. Payoff of first mortgage loan	82,000.00
205.		505. Payoff of second mortgage loan	
206.		506.	
207.		507.	
208.		508.	
209.		509.	
Adjustments for items unpaid by seller		Adjustments for items unpaid by seller	
210. City/town taxes to		510. City/town taxes to	
211. County taxes 01/01/03 to 6/30/03	1,400.00	511. County taxes 1/1/03 to 6/30/03	1400.00
212. Assessments to		512. Assessments to	
213.		513.	
214.		514.	
215.		515.	
216.		516.	
217.		517.	
218.		518.	
219.		519.	
220. Total Paid By/For Borrower	128,000.00	**520. Total Reduction Amount Due Seller**	94,820.00
300. Cash At Settlement From/To Borrower		**600. Cash At Settlement To/From Seller**	
301. Gross Amount due from borrower (line 120)	159,072.41	601. Gross amount due to seller (line 420)	152,000.00
302. Less amounts paid by/for borrower (line 220)	128,000.00	602. Less reductions in amt. due seller (line 520)	(94,820.00)
303. Cash ☒ From ☐ To Borrower	31,072.41	**603. Cash** ☒ To ☐ From Seller	57,180.00

Section 5 of the Real Estate Settlement Procedures Act (RESPA) requires the following: • HUD must develop a Special Information Booklet to help persons borrowing money to finance the purchase of residential real estate to better understand the nature and costs of real estate settlement services; • Each lender must provide the booklet to all applicants from whom it receives or for whom it prepares a written application to borrow money to finance the purchase of residential real estate; • Lenders must prepare and distribute with the Booklet a Good Faith Estimate of the settlement costs that the borrower is likely to incur in connection with the settlement. These disclosures are mandatory.

Section 4(a) of RESPA mandates that HUD develop and prescribe this standard form to be used at the time of loan settlement to provide full disclosure of all charges imposed upon the borrower and seller. These are third party disclosures that are designed to provide the borrower with pertinent information during the settlement process in order to be a better shopper.

The Public Reporting Burden for this collection of information is estimated to average one hour per response, including the time for reviewing instructions, searching existing data sources, gathering and maintaining the data needed, and completing and reviewing the collection of information.

This agency may not collect this information, and you are not required to complete this form, unless it displays a currently valid OMB control number.

The information requested does not lend itself to confidentiality.

Exhibit 20-4—concluded

L. Settlement Charges	Paid From Borrowers Funds at Settlement	Paid From Seller's Funds at Settlement
700. Total Sales/Broker's Commission based on price $		
Division of Commission (line 700) as follows:		
701. $9120.00 to Baden Associates Realty		
702. $ to		
703. Commission paid at Settlement		9120.00
704.		
800. Items Payable In Connection With Loan		
801. Loan Origination Fee 1 %	1216.00	
802. Loan Discount 1 %	1216.00	
803. Appraisal Fee to	275.00	
804. Credit Report to Credco	16.50	
805. Lender's Inspection Fee		
806. Mortgage Insurance Application Fee to		
807. Assumption Fee		
808. Tax Service Fee	59.00	
809.		
810. Flood Cerglfication Fee First American Flood Data	18.00	
811. Document Review	395.00	
900. Items Required By Lender To Be Paid In Advance		
901. Interest from July 1 to July 31 @$ 22.49 /day	697.12	
902. Mortgage Insurance Premium for months to		
903. Hazard Insurance Premium for 1 years to	684.00	
904. years to		
905.		
1000. Reserves Deposited With Lender		
1001. Hazard Insurance 2 months @$ 57.00 per month	114.00	
1002. Mortgage Insurance months @$ per month		
1003. City property taxes months @$ per month		
1004. County property taxes 3 months @$233.33 per month	699.99	
1005. Annual assessments months @$ per month		
1006. months @$ per month		
1007. months @$ per month		
1008. months @$ per month		
1100. Title Charges		
1101. Settlement or closing fee to Deed Preparation		100.00
1102. Abstract or title search to		
1103. Title examination to		
1104. Title insurance binder to		
1105. Document preparation to FMDCOM	42.00	
1106. Notary fees to		
1107. Attorney's fees $250 to James Hardy	250.00	
(includes above items numbers:)		
1108. Title Insurance to	200.00	1074.00
(includes above items numbers:)		
1109. Lender's coverage 121,600.00 $ 200.00		
1110. Owner's coverage 152,000.00 $		
1111. Title Endorsement Fees	153.00	
1112.		
1113.		
1200. Government Recording and Transfer Charges		
1201. Recording fees: Deed $ 6.00 ; Mortgage $ 93.00 ; Releases $ 6.00	93.00	12.00
1202. City/county tax/stamps: Deed $; Mortgage $		
1203. State tax/stamps: Deed $ 1064.00 ; Mortgage $ 425.60	425.60	1064.00
1204. Intangible Tax	243.20	
1205.		
1300. Additional Settlement Charges	275.00	
1301. Survey to		50.00
1302. Pest Inspection to		
1303.		
1304.		
1305.		
1400. Total Settlement Charges (enter on lines 103, Section J and 502, Section K)	7072.41	11420.00

As sellers, the Johnsons also took some steps between the signing of the purchase and sale contract and the closing. In particular, they:

1. Ordered an owner's title insurance policy. If the contract for sale had specified that an abstract and attorney's opinion serve as the evidence of title, they would have (*a*) ordered the abstract brought up to date or (*b*) had the abstract delivered to the buyers' attorney, Mr. Henry, for examination.
2. Ordered a termite inspection and had the certificate showing the improvements to be free of active infestation or visible damage delivered to the Joneses' attorney.
3. Ordered their hazard insurance coverage, utilities, and other services to be stopped on the closing date.

As closing agent and representative of DownTrust Bank, Mr. Jenkins has obtained or prepared the following documents and legal instruments:

1. General warranty deed in proper form, to be signed by the Johnsons at closing.
2. Mortgage and note, to be signed by the Joneses at closing.
3. Check from the lender made payable to the seller.
4. HUD-1 form settlement statement showing the expenses and obligations incurred by both parties. Real estate taxes for 2003, as specified in the contract for sale, are prorated between buyers and sellers as of the date of closing.
5. A *satisfaction of mortgage* from the Johnsons' mortgage lender indicating that the remaining balance on their mortgage is $82,000.[7]

Steps at Closing

The Johnsons, the Joneses, Mr. Park, Mr. Hairston, Mr. Henry, and Mr. Jenkins go to a small conference room for the closing. They take seats around a rectangular table, with Mr. Jenkins sitting at the head of the table. He informs everyone that he is closing the transaction on behalf of DownTrust Bank and is also serving as the Joneses' attorney. He introduces Mr. Henry as the Johnsons' attorney. Mr. Jenkins states he has prepared all documents in accordance with the terms of the contract for sale, the loan application and approval, and applicable state and federal laws. He also states that he has coordinated title matters, inspections, and documents with Mr. Henry and Mr. Park.

Mr. Jenkins presents copies of the HUD-1 Form Settlement Statement shown in Exhibit 20-4 to the Johnsons and Joneses and explains it as follows: Settlement charges to be paid by the Joneses total $7,072.41 (second page of HUD-1 Form), as estimated by DownTrust Bank in their good-faith estimate of closing costs. As sellers, the Johnsons will pay the $9,120 (0.06 × $152,000) brokerage commission to Baden Associates Realty (line 701). Other major closing expenses to be paid by the sellers include a $1,074 owner's title insurance policy (line 1108) and $1,064 in state tax stamps to transfer the deed (line 1203). The seller is also responsible for the $50 termite inspection. Total settlement costs paid by the seller equal $11,420 (line 1400).

Moving to the top page of the HUD-1 form, we see in the right-hand column that the sellers are owed the total purchase price of $152,000 (line 401). However, the $152,000 gross amount due the Johnsons is reduced by the $11,240 closing costs (line 502) and the $82,000 that is required to pay off the remaining mortgage balance on their loan (line 504). In addition, because the buyers will be required to pay the entire property tax bill at the end of the year, they must be compensated by the sellers who will have occupied the home for six months. This compensation is accomplished by reducing the amount the buyer must pay the seller at closing by the amount of the sellers' unpaid property taxes (line 511). Reductions in the amount due the sellers at closing total $94,820 (line 520). Thus, the Johnsons will walk away from closing with a $57,180 check ($152,000 − $94,820).

The left-hand column of page 1 the HUD-1 Form summarizes the transaction from the buyers' perspective. In addition to the $152,000 purchase price (line 101), the Joneses are

---

7. If there had been any leases or assignments of interests transferred to the buyers, copies of these documents would also have been obtained.

required to pay $7,072.41 in closing costs (line 103). Thus, the gross amount due from the Joneses is $159,072.41 (line 120). However, the buyers are credited the $5,000 deposit of earnest money (line 201) and the amount of the new mortgage they are obtaining from DownTrust Bank (line 202). In effect, they are responsible for bringing these mortgage funds into the transaction and are committed to paying off the loan, with interest, over the next 30 years.

Property taxes are the only item *prorated* in this transaction. Since property taxes will be paid in arrears (after the period for which they are incurred), the *buyers* will have to pay the tax bill for the entire year of 2003 in November or December of 2003. Therefore, they are given credit for the amount of time the property was occupied by the sellers—181 out of 365 days. Item D in the Standards for Real Estate Transactions (see page 4 of Exhibit 20-1) indicates that the buyer pays for the day of closing. Since the total tax bill for 2003 was estimated to be $2,823.20 (based on the tax bill for the previous year), the adjustment for unpaid property taxes (line 211) is $1,400 [(181 ÷ 365) × $2,823.20].

Including the $1,400 credit for the seller's unpaid property taxes (line 211), a total of $128,000 is either being paid by another party on behalf of the buyer or has already been paid by the buyer (line 220). The total amount collected from the buyer at closing (line 303) is $31,072.41 ($159,022.41 − $128,000). The buyers must write a personal check for this amount which, together with the escrow deposit, borrowed funds, and prorated tax credit, will cover all the amounts owed.

After explaining the various items on the closing statement, Mr. Jenkins asks the Joneses to write a check to DownTrust Bank in the amount of $31,072.41 and to sign the note and mortgage. He asks the Johnsons to sign the deed and to hand it to the Joneses. He then hands a check for $57,180 to the Johnsons and states that all of the expenses have either been paid or will be paid immediately. He gives to Mr. Park a check for $9,120 payable to Baden Associates Realty. The closing is now completed, and all parties in the room rise, shake hands, and leave. Baden Associates Realty will split the commission with Ben and Josh. While commission splits vary within the firm, its agreement with both Ben and Josh is that the firm gets half of any commission they generate. Thus, Ben and Josh will share the other half, receiving a $2,280 commission from the sale [0.50 × (0.50 × $9,120)].

Summary

The contract for sale is the most important document in real estate. It contains the rights and obligations to which the principals in a transaction—buyers and sellers—commit themselves. The contract governs all elements of a transaction; a court can enforce its provisions.

Contracts for sale can be simple or complex. They may be typed, handwritten, or prepared on preprinted forms. No matter what the form, however, an agreement is valid and enforceable if it contains the seven elements required of real estate contracts: (1) competent parties, (2) offer and acceptance, (3) consideration, (4) legal objective, (5) no defects to mutual assent, (6) written form, and (7) a proper description of the property.

Since a contract is a legally binding document, buyers and sellers can protect themselves by having a competent attorney examine the contract before signing; after the contract has been signed is too late and any changes would have to be agreed to by both parties.

When one party breaks the provisions of a contract, the other party may have one or more remedies. Either buyer or seller may (1) rescind the contract, (2) sue for specific performance, or (3) sue for damages. Additionally, some contracts may specify actions that can be taken by one party in the event of default by the other. For example, the seller may be able to retain all or a portion of any deposits if the buyer fails to complete the transaction. Escrow agents often assist in carrying out the provisions of a contract and lessen the chances of default by either party.

Closing is the consummation of a real estate transaction. At closing, title is conveyed and the purchase price is paid. Expenses are paid by each party and prorations between the parties are made. A document summarizing the financial flows that occur at closing is known as the closing (or settlement) statement. The closing statement includes a detailed itemization of the expenses that must be paid by the buyers and sellers at closing.

Prorating is required when an expense has been prepaid by the seller or will be paid subsequently by the buyer, and covers a time period during which both buyer and seller own the property. The procedure involves crediting the party that pays the expense with the proportionate amount covering the period during which the other party owns the property. Typical items to be prorated are prepaid rent, insurance, real estate taxes, mortgage interest (either prepaid or paid in arrears), and prepaid mortgage principal.

Key Terms

Assignment 536
Closing 523
Consideration 525
Contract for sale 522
Contract conditions 523
Contract terms 523

Contracts with contingencies 536
Earnest money 539
Equitable title 526
Escrow 537
Escrow agent 537
Estimated closing costs 542

Legal title 526
Personal performance 536
Prorating 541
Recording 544

Test Problems

Answer the following multiple choice questions:

1. If a buyer defaults on a contract to purchase real property, which of the following is *not* a remedy the seller can pursue?
   a. Rescind the contract.
   b. Sue for damages.
   c. Sue for assignment.
   d. Retain all or part of the binder deposit.
   e. Sue for specific performance.

2. When contracts for the sale of real property are placed with a disinterested third party for executing and closing, they are said to be placed in:
   a. Safekeeping.
   b. A title company or financial institution.
   c. Option.
   d. Escrow.
   e. Assignment.

3. Which of the following conditions would be a defect to mutual assent in a contract for the sale of real property?
   a. One party attempts to perpetrate fraud on the other.
   b. The contract is in written form.
   c. The contract contains an inadequate description of the property.
   d. One of the parties is legally incompetent.
   e. The contract does not specify a time for closing.

4. Oral evidence in contract disputes is prohibited by:
   a. A parol contract.
   b. An executory contract.
   c. An inferred contract.
   d. An unspecified contract.
   e. The parol evidence rule.

5. Which of the following is one of the *terms* of a real estate contract?
   a. Mechanical equipment must be in good condition.
   b. Title must be marketable.
   c. Price to be paid.

   d. Property must be free of termites.
   e. All of the above items are terms.

6. Real estate transactions do not close when the contract for sale is signed by both parties because:
   a. An inspection must be made.
   b. Financing must be arranged.
   c. Title must be checked.
   d. Documents must be prepared.
   e. All of the above.

7. An earnest money deposit is:
   a. A preliminary contract.
   b. A provision in a contract for sale.
   c. A payment of money by a buyer to evidence good faith.
   d. An escrow provision.
   e. A conveyance.

8. In most straightforward transactions involving houses or other relatively small properties, the contract is:
   a. Prepared by the seller's attorney.
   b. Prepared by the buyer's attorney.
   c. Prepared by the broker.
   d. A form, with blanks filled in by the broker.
   e. A form, with blanks filled in by buyer and seller.

9. Equitable title to real estate is:
   a. Legal ownership of property.
   b. Legal title obtained in a court of equity.
   c. Title obtained by adverse possession.
   d. A legal interest in a property conveyed by a listing contract to a broker.
   e. The right to obtain legal title conveyed by the contract for sale.

10. The purpose of a closing statement is to:
    a. Determine who pays the brokerage commission.
    b. Allocate expenses and receipts of buyer and seller.
    c. Prorate expenses between buyer and seller.
    d. Account for moneys in a transaction.
    e. All but **a** above.

Study Questions

1. If a closing occurs on September 1 of a 365-day year, how will the year's property tax of $900 be prorated? (*Note:* The taxes will be due on January 2 of the following year and the day of closing "belongs" to the buyer.)

   Use the following information to answer questions 2 to 5. Rosie Malone sold her house to D.M. Band. The contract was signed June 1, 2004, and closing was set for June 25, 2004. Rosie had prepaid her three-year hazard insurance policy in the amount of $425.00 on April 1, 2003, and D.M. agreed to assume it at closing. Water and sewer are paid the first of each month for the previous month. They are estimated to total $100 for June. D.M. also agrees to assume Rosie's mortgage, which will have a balance of $85,385 on date of closing. Monthly payments are $817.83 payable on the first of the month for the previous month. The seller is responsible for the day of closing.

2. How would the hazard insurance premium be prorated?

3. How would the water and sewer charges be prorated?

4. How will the mortgage assumption be entered?

5. How will the monthly mortgage payment be prorated?

6. The owner of a parcel of land containing approximately 25 acres contracted a debilitating disease and decided to sell his real estate as quickly as possible. Within a week, he received an offer of $12,250. The owner accepted this offer by signing a standard form contract that had been obtained and prepared by the buyer. Soon after, when the owner's family discovered the situation, they convinced him that he had sold the land at much too low a price and he should not complete the transaction.

   The owner commissioned an appraisal that showed the land to be worth $16,000, a difference of $150 per acre between the contract price and the property value. He then refused to attend the closing and to deliver title to the buyer. The buyer sued the owner for damages in the amount of the difference between the property value and the contract price ($3,750). The buyer contended he had a valid contract and he was damaged by the owner's unwillingness to complete the transaction. The seller contended he was not of sound mind when he signed the contract and the price was so ridiculously low, the contract should not be enforced.

   Identify the issues the court probably would consider in deciding whether or not to enforce the contract.

7. A couple decided to sell their house in Washington, D.C., without the aid of a real estate broker. Their asking price was $225,000, which they believed was about $15,000 less than the price they would need to list the property with a broker.

They realized they would probably have to accept an offer as low as $220,000. Another couple looked at the house, liked it, and offered to buy it for $223,500. The sellers were delighted and suggested that they fill in the blanks on a form sales contract used by many of the local real estate brokerage firms, and both parties could sign it. The buyers, however, objected, saying they preferred to write their own contract. The wife was an attorney who worked for the U.S. State Department, specializing in international law.

What advice would you have given the sellers?

8. Given the following situation and facts, complete a closing settlement statement similar to that shown in Exhibit 20-4.

   On May 15, 2004, Eric Martin signed a contract to purchase a rental house for $95,000. Closing is to occur June 8, 2004, with the day of closing to be counted as a day of ownership by the buyer. Eric can assume the seller's first mortgage, which will have a balance of $49,000 on June 8. The seller, Reuben Smith, has agreed to take a second mortgage of $30,000 as part of the payment at closing. Eric paid an escrow deposit of $5,000 when he signed the purchase contract. Other pertinent facts include:

   a. The monthly interest on the first mortgage is $347.08, which must be paid by the 20th day of the month.

   b. Reuben paid a hazard insurance policy for the calendar year 2004. The premium was $550, and Eric has agreed to purchase Reuben's interest in the policy.

   c. The monthly rental of $850 has been collected by Reuben for June.

   d. The total amount of property tax for 2004 is estimated to be $1,200. The tax will be paid by Eric at the end of the year.

   e. The broker will pay the following expenses for Reuben and will be reimbursed at the closing:

Abstract continuation	$ 85.00
Attorney's fee	200.00
Deed stamps (tax)	522.50
Brokerage commission (6%)	5,700.00

   f. The broker will also pay the following expenses for Eric and will be reimbursed at the closing:

Attorney's fee	$150.00
Deed recording fee	6.00
Mortgage recording fee	10.00
Mortgage note stamps (tax)	45.00
Intangible tax on mortgage	60.00

Explore The Web

Examine two or three of the homebuyer websites shown in the text: Motley Fool, Freddie Mac, Fannie Mae, for example, or scout for others. Do they seem to agree on the circumstances in which one should, and should not, buy a home? Do they agree on the up-front costs of home purchase?

Solutions to Concept Checks

1. Essential elements of any contract are competent parties, legal objective, consideration, offer and acceptance, no defects to mutual assent. Two additional essential elements to a contract for sale of real estate are unambiguous description and that the contract be in writing.

2. Three aspects of legal competency are attainment of legal age, not incapacitated, and having authority to enter into a contract.

3. In a contract for sale of real estate, the seller implicitly agrees to deliver marketable title.

4. Three possible defects to mutual assent are fraud, errors, and one party being under duress.

5. Legal title is ownership of a freehold estate. Equitable title is the right to receive legal title. Equitable title results from signing a contract for sale of real estate.

6. Two advantages of a standard form contract for the sale of real estate are that it is relatively easy to complete and that it is likely to be fair to both parties. A disadvantage is that it can fail to address issues important to a particular transaction.

7. Two sections of a standard form contract are the negotiated items that need to be "filled in," and the standard provisions that seldom need to be negotiated.

8. Assignment means to pass all of one's rights and obligations in a contract to a subsequent party. Both the assignor and the assignee are then liable for performance of the contract.

9. Three standard remedies to a defaulted real estate contract are rescission, suit for damages, and suit for specific performance. An additional remedy commonly available to a seller is to retain the buyer's deposit as liquidated damages.

10. In most real estate closings, the listing broker is responsible for the successful completion of the closing.

11. Four effects of RESPA on most residential real estate closings are (1) requires a good-faith estimate of closing costs, (2) requires that the borrower/buyer receive a HUD closing booklet, (3) requires the use of the HUD-1 Form, the Uniform Settlement Statement, and (4) prohibits kickbacks for transaction-related services.

12. Two methods of allocating closing related expenses between buyer and seller are by local custom and by negotiation.

Additional Readings

Gadow, S. *The Complete Guide to Your Real Estate Closing: Answers to All Your Questions-From Opening Escrow, to Negotiating Fees, to Signing the Closing Papers.* New York: McGraw-Hill Trade, August 23, 2002.

Jennings, Marianne. *Real Estate Law,* 6th ed. Cincinnati, OH: West/Thomson Learning, 2002.

Siedel, George J., III; Robert J. Aalberts; Janis K. Cheezem. *Real Estate Law,* 5th ed. Mason, OH: South Western, 2003.

Werner, Raymond J. *Real Estate Law,* 10th ed. Upper Saddle River, NJ: Prentice Hall, 1992.

This quarterly publication contains articles on a wide variety of legal issues in real estate, including contracts and closings:

Real Estate Law Journal, Boston: Warren, Gorham & Lamont.

This monograph presents the fundamentals and many important considerations for attorneys and others (real estate practitioners) who are regularly involved in the writing of real estate contracts:

Holtzschue, Karl B. *Holtzschue on Real Estate Contracts,* 2nd ed. New York: Practicing Law Institute, 1994.

This pamphlet presents a step-by-step analysis of closing procedures and the costs that home buyers must pay:

U.S. Department of Housing and Urban Development. *Settlement Costs: A HUD Guide.*

Advanced Topics

7

Leases *and* Property Types

Learning Objectives

After reading this chapter you will be able to:

1. Identify the essential elements of a valid commercial real estate lease.

2. Describe three common methods by which contract rents are increased over the life of a multiyear lease.

3. Explain the differences among gross, net, net–net, and triple net leases.

4. Explain the difference between lease assignment and subletting.

5. Describe four common options found in commercial leases.

6. Calculate the effective rent of a proposed lease, given appropriate assumptions.

7. Identify the major classes of office properties.

8. Calculate the rentable area of office space, given appropriate assumptions.

9. Identify the four major types of retail shopping centers.

Introduction

The lease is a contract between a property owner (lessor) and tenant (lessee) that transfers exclusive use and possession of space to the tenant. During the term of the lease, the owner possesses a leased fee estate with a reversion interest in the space that allows him or her to retake possession of the property at the expiration of the lease.

Because the lease is the document that sets forth the rights and obligations of each party, every clause and provision can affect the property's net operating income or the riskiness of the income stream. That is why we argued in Chapter 17 that leases are the "engines that drive property values."

This chapter presents an introduction to the important world of commercial real estate leases. We begin by reviewing the essential elements of a valid lease. We then discuss important lease clauses and provisions that are common to all commercial leases. Because the net rent paid by commercial property tenants can be affected by a large number of lease clauses, the quoted rent often conveys limited information about the true cost of a lease. We therefore discuss how to calculate the true, or effective, cost of a commercial lease. We then provide descriptions of the major property types and examine lease clauses that are unique or critical to the understanding and valuation of each property type.

Essential Elements of a Lease

As with any valid contract, parties to a lease must be legally competent, the objective of the lease must be legal, there must be mutual agreement between the tenant and landlord to enter into the lease agreement, and something of value (i.e., consideration) must be given or promised by both parties. The promise to pay rent constitutes the tenant's consideration. Allowing the tenant to occupy the space or property constitutes the landlord's consideration.

Valid and enforceable leases also must include the following elements:

1. The names of the landlord and tenant.
2. An adequate description of the leased premises.
3. An agreement to transfer possession of the property from the landlord to the tenant.
4. The start and end dates of the agreement.
5. A description of the rental payments.
6. The agreement must be in writing.
7. The agreement must be signed by all parties.

The start and end dates of the lease agreement and the agreed upon rental payments are both negotiated items, which we discuss in detail below. The type of description required depends upon the nature of the property, but must be precise about the physical premises being leased. For residential and small commercial properties, a street address and/or apartment number is usually adequate. Descriptions for larger office and retail properties are more detailed and may include items such as floor plans, the total square footage of the leased premises, and descriptions of parking areas.

Concept Check

21.1 List five items that must appear in a lease that do not require negotiation between the owner and tenant.

www.cityfeet.com/
tools/glossary.asp

Comprehensive glossary of
leasing terms.

www.laweasy.com/
llE2.htm

Sample of commercial leases.

Most states require that the owner give the tenant actual possession of the property. Once possession and control are conveyed, the tenant is entitled to **quiet enjoyment** of the property. This does not mean the owner must guarantee the tenant quiet neighbors; rather, it simply means the owner must provide the tenant with uninterrupted use of the property without any interference from the owner, the property manager, or any other person or entity that may threaten or seek to impose upon the tenant's leasehold interest in the property.

Negotiated Lease Provisions

Every clause in a commercial lease can have an impact on the property's operating income and value. Clauses that address rent payments and the responsibilities of owners and tenants for operating expenses have a direct effect on property income. However, numerous clauses that address the operation of the property and the rights of either the tenant or the landlord to change the nature of the contract can also have a significant effect on the economics of a lease and, therefore, its value to an owner. This section discusses the clauses and provisions that are typically part of a commercial lease negotiation.

Use of the Premises

If a lease does not state a specific purpose for which the property may be used or specifically forbid certain uses, the tenant may use the property for any legal purpose. Typically, however, commercial property leases contain a clause that indicates the purpose for which the space may be used. In addition to ensuring that the space is used lawfully, such clauses prevent uses that may damage the building, detract from its image and prestige, disturb other tenants or surrounding neighbors, or expose the owner to potential legal liabilities.

Lease Term

The lease term must be clearly indicated, including the beginning and ending dates. One-year terms for apartment leases are the industry standard. For other commercial property types, however, lease lengths can vary considerably. Longer leases provide more stability for both the tenant and owner and they delay the re-leasing costs faced by tenants and owners when a tenant vacates the premises. For example, owners may face an extended period of vacancy and may incur significant search costs in their attempts to find a new tenant. With the exception of apartment projects, the owner will usually need to pay a leasing commission to the person responsible for securing a new tenant. In addition, the owner will generally need to provide a **tenant improvement ("TI") allowance** to the new tenant. The TI allowance is the amount of funding the owner must give to the tenant, or pay on the tenant's behalf, toward the cost of refurbishing the space to meet the needs of the tenant's business.[1]

When vacating their space upon lease termination, tenants face moving costs, including the possible disruption of their business. In addition, tenants frequently make significant improvements to the space, often in excess of the TI allowance. These improvements are generally lost when they vacate the premises because they have become part of the real estate (see Chapter 4). In short, both tenants and owners are negatively affected by re-leasing costs. As a result, both prefer longer-term leases, all else being the same, in order to minimize such costs.

Although longer-term leases delay re-leasing costs and provide rental rate security for both tenants and owners, a significant cost may be paid in flexibility. If tenants have reason to believe that market rents are likely to fall in the near future, they may prefer to shorten their lease terms. In addition, many tenants are uncertain about what their space needs will be in the future. If tenants expect their business to grow steadily, or if their business is a risky start-up venture, then shorter term leases may be preferred. In general, the more uncertain a tenant's future space needs, the greater the value associated with flexibility.

Flexibility is also valuable to owners. For example, landlords may desire a shorter lease term if they believe that market rents are likely to rise in the near future. In addition, owners may wish to have a small inventory of space to show to potential tenants. Furthermore, owners often desire to alter the mix of tenants to maximize the synergies of the property. This is especially true for shopping center properties, as we discussed in Chapter 17. In short, flexibility considerations suggest shorter-term leases are more valuable to both tenants and owners. Therefore, optimal lease terms reflect the trade-offs between the desire for the flexibility inherent in short-term leases and the reduction in risk and re-leasing costs associated with longer-term leases.

Concept Check

21.2   What is the primary advantage of longer-term leases? What is the primary disadvantage?

---

1. Many leasing decisions are made by property or asset managers on behalf of owners. To simplify terminology, however, we will simply refer in this chapter to tenants and owners with the understanding that managers are often acting as agents for the owner.

Rental Payments

Rent for residential rental units is typically stated as a dollar amount per month. In contrast, rents for commercial properties are quoted on an annual cost per square foot basis; for example, $15 per square foot per year, even though rent is paid monthly.

Because of the short-term nature of most residential leases (generally one-year terms), owners have not found it necessary to include clauses that enable them to adjust rents as local and national economic conditions change. In contrast, many commercial leases have terms of 5, 10, and, in some cases, 25 years or more. Inflation and changing market conditions usually will cause market rental rates to change significantly over such extended periods of time. These changes may result from shifts in supply and demand conditions in the local rental market (see Chapters 5 to 7), changes in property operating costs that must eventually be passed on to tenants, or from rent pressures that result from national economic factors such as inflation.

To maintain the market value of properties subject to long-term leases, commercial leases with durations longer than one year often include clauses that permit the owner to adjust rents over time or require the tenant to reimburse the owner for all or a portion of increased operating expenses. Clearly, the true cost of a commercial lease from the tenant's perspective is a function of both the rental rate and the proportion of operating expenses, if any, that are the responsibility of the tenant. In the remainder of this section, we discuss common methods by which rents are increased over the life of a lease. In the next section we discuss ways that the responsibility for the payment of operating expenses can affect the true cost of a multiyear commercial lease.

Flat Rent. The simplest treatment of rent is to keep it flat for the entire lease term. For example, a five-year office lease might specify a fixed rental rate of $18 per square foot per year. The shorter the lease term, the more a **flat rent** arrangement is likely to be observed. When fixed rental rates are observed, the lease is likely to include a provision that requires the tenant to pay some or all of the property's operating expenses.

Graduated Rent. A **graduated rent** clause provides for prespecified increases in the contract rental rate. For example, a five-year office lease might specify a rental rate of $18 per square foot for the first year, increasing by $1 per square foot each year for the remaining four years of the lease term. These prespecified rent increases are sometimes referred to as "step-ups" or "escalations."

Flat or graduated rent agreements are the simplest methods of specifying rental rates over the term of a lease because the dollar amount of all required lease payments is specified in the lease. The required lease payment is solely a function time—if you know the number of months since the inception of the lease, you know the required lease payment. Thus, the simple two-dimensional graphs presented in Exhibit 21-1 are able to fully capture the magnitude of required lease payments for our flat and graduated office rent examples.

Indexed Lease. Another method for adjusting rents in long-term leases is to create an indexed lease. With an **indexed lease,** rent increases are tied to changes in a regularly reported index, the most common of which is the consumer price index (CPI). For example, assume the rental rate on our five-year office lease example is fully indexed to the CPI, with changes in contract rent made annually. If the CPI indicates that general price inflation was 3 percent during the first year of the lease, then the rental payment for year 2 would increase to $18.54 per square foot ($18.00 × 1.03). This rate would remain fixed for 12 months and then be adjusted again in year 3 based on the actual rate of inflation in year 2.

Note that required lease payments are no longer solely a function of time and therefore cannot be graphed along with the flat and graduated leases in Exhibit 21-1. Instead, future lease payments will depend upon changes in the consumer price index and therefore are not known in advance. Because the inclusion of CPI indexing shifts the risk of unexpected increases in inflation from owners to tenants, owners must expect that tenants in competitive rental markets will require a lower base rental rate in exchange for absorbing the inflation risk.

Exhibit 21-1 Scheduled Rents for a Flat and Graduated Lease

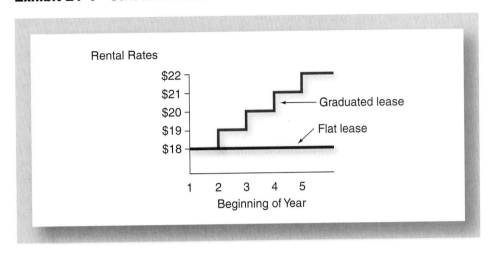

21.3   Which lease clause makes rental payments easier to predict: the graduated rent
clause or the index clause? Why?

Percentage Rent. Shopping center leases often include a clause that ties rent payments to
the tenant's sales revenue. In a percentage lease, there is usually a flat or fixed component
referred to as the **base rent.** In addition, the **percentage rent** clause dictates that the owner
receive a prespecified percentage of tenant sales, or a percentage of tenant sales that exceed
some minimum threshold amount. We will discuss percentage rent clauses in more detail
below. Note, however, that similar to indexed leases, total lease payments in the presence
of a percentage rent clause are no longer solely a function time. An added dimension—
tenant sales—is required to determine the total required rent.

Responsibility for Operating Expenses

Clearly, required rent payments are an important determinant of the tenant's cost of occupancy and the owner's cash flow from the property. However, the *net* rental income generated by a lease also depends on the proportion of property-level operating expenses paid by
the tenant. In Chapter 17 we defined gross and net leases. In a gross lease, the owner pays
all of the property's operating expenses. Thus, owners must fully recover operating expenses in the rent. In a net lease, which is used more frequently than a gross lease in commercial property markets, the tenant is responsible for paying a clearly defined portion of
operating expenses. The standard definitions of "netness" in commercial leases—net,
net-net, and triple net—are displayed in Exhibit 21-2. However, in many situations these
definitions are inadequate to fully describe the responsibilities of the owner and tenant,
and extreme care must be taken by both sides to carefully read and negotiate the operating expense provisions of the lease.

Note that in a gross lease, the *expected* level of operating expenses over the lease
term is built into the rental rate, assuming the lease was negotiated by a knowledgeable
owner and tenant in a competitive rental market. However, the owner still bears all the
risk associated with *unexpected* changes in operating expenses. This risk should therefore be reflected in the agreed upon gross rental rate. In contrast, tenants bear the risk
associated with unexpected changes in operating expenses in a triple net lease. In some
leases, the method used to share responsibility for operating expenses is a hybrid of the

Industry Issues

21-1

Why Office Tenants Are Auditing Their Landlords

Uncle Sam isn't the only one performing audits these days. Many office tenants are taking a closer look at their landlords' books. The goal: to make sure they aren't being overcharged.

What is typically a busy season for the companies that conduct so-called lease audits on behalf of commercial tenants is shaping up to be even more brisk this year. Tenants that have the right to conduct such audits increasingly want to make sure they aren't paying more for building operating expenses and real estate taxes than their lease agreement calls for. "In tough economic times, you'll notice landlords becoming more aggressive in pass-through charges," says Michael Silver, President of Equis Corp., a real estate services firm that represents tenants.

Typically, an office landlord incorporates a building's operating expenses and real estate taxes into the rent tenants pay in the first year of occupancy. In subsequent years, increases in expenses over the base year are passed through to tenants unless they were able to negotiate caps or exclusions.

"Landlords are making more mistakes now because they're under financial pressure and don't have the staff to manage the billings properly," says Marc Betesh, president of KBA Lease Services LLC in Woodbridge, New Jersey. Other auditors contend that the cost of new or replacement equipment, such as energy-efficient systems or elevators, is incorrectly making its way onto tenants' bills. "As things in a building get replaced," says Josh Leonard of Deloitte & Touche LLP, "tenants shouldn't have to pay for it in expenses because they're already paying for it in their base rent." Other miscalculations involve pass-throughs of insurance and security costs, the amount of space for which the tenant is responsible for paying rent and expenses, the expenses included in a tenant's rent for the first year, and increases tied to a consumer price index or other cost-of-living increases. Fees charged to manage the property also are a point of contention.

Source: Adapted from Sheila Muto, "Why Office Tenants Are Auditing Their Landlords," *The Wall Street Journal Online*, March 3, 2002.

Exhibit 21-2 Tenant's Responsibility for Operating Expenses

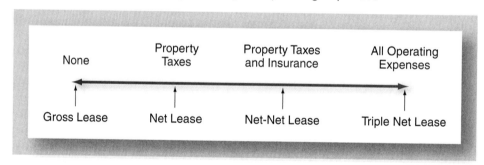

four basic lease types depicted in Exhibit 21-2. For example, with an **operating expense escalation clause,** only *increases* in one or more operating expenses, relative to a base year, become the responsibility of the tenant. The base year is usually the first full calendar year after the tenant moves in.

Operating expenses that are the responsibility of the tenant can be paid directly by the tenant or paid by the landlord and billed back to the tenant(s) for reimbursement. In multitenant properties, the owner will usually pay the expenses and then bill each tenant for his or her pro rata share. For example, if an office tenant occupies 6,000 square feet in a 60,000 square foot property, his or her pro rata share of expenses and other pass-throughs is 10 percent.

Concept Check

21.4 Do tenants pay for expected operating expenses if they sign a gross lease?

Concessions

Once a lease has spelled out how rents are to be determined over the lease term and how owners and tenants are to share the responsibility for operating expenses, the basic economics of the lease have been established. However, lease contracts may also contain one or more **concessions** that reduce the net present value of the lease cash flows. Concessions are usually offered to potential tenants to provide them with an incentive to lease space in the owner's property, but they are not reflected in the quoted rental rate.

A concession often granted to new tenants when the supply of space exceeds demand is a period of free or perhaps reduced rent. The owner also may commit to pay a tenant's moving expenses or penalties incurred by the tenant in breaking an existing lease.

A common concession found in office, industrial, and shopping center leases, are tenant improvement allowances, or TIs. TIs are moneys an owner provides for the modification of leased space before or after a tenant moves in. TIs are usually stated as a per square foot amount and can range as high as $20 per square foot. If a tenant is moving into an existing space that has already been finished out by a prior tenant and requires little in the way of alterations, the negotiated TI allowance may be $5 per square foot or lower. However, if a tenant is moving into newly constructed "shell" space, the owner may be required to provide a significant TI allowance to permit the tenant, or the owner on behalf of the tenant, to build out the space in an appropriate fashion. The magnitude of the tenant improvement allowance is often a heavily negotiated lease item. However, larger TI concessions are more common in overbuilt "renters' markets."

Alterations and Improvements

Landlords will generally not permit tenants to make alterations or improvements to the leased premises without prior approval. This protects the landlord against value-destroying improvements, as well as damage to mechanical, electrical, heating, ventilation, and air-conditioning (HVAC) systems. To the extent the tenant is permitted to alter the leased premises, the lease should clearly state when this may be done, and under what circumstances.

The lease must also be clear about the ownership of such improvements once completed. As discussed in Chapter 4, fixtures are items of personal property permanently attached to the real property and which, after attachment, are real property. As such, they may become the property of the owner when the lease term expires, unless the lease specifically identifies such items as the personal property of the tenant. **Trade fixtures,** in contrast, are usually paid for and installed by the tenant, and may be removed by the tenant at the termination of the lease. However, trade fixtures should be clearly identified to avoid confusion at expiration of the lease.

Explore The Web

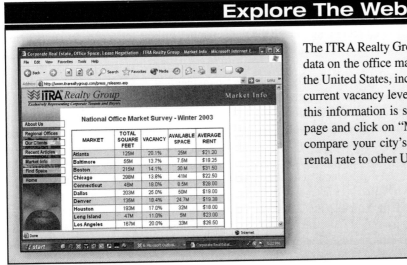

The ITRA Realty Group (www.itrarealtygroup.com) provides data on the office markets of numerous metropolitan areas in the United States, including the total size of the office market, current vacancy levels, and average rental rates. A portion of this information is shown to the left. Go to the ITRA home page and click on "Market Info." Choose a favorite city and compare your city's market size, vacancy rate, and average rental rate to other U.S. cities.

Assignment and Subletting

Tenants, especially those subject to long-term leases, may desire to assign or sublet all, or part, of their leased space. A lease *assignment* occurs when *all* of a tenant's rights and obligations are transferred to another party. However, the assignor remains liable for the promised rent unless relieved in writing of this responsibility by the owner.

A **sublease** occurs when the original tenant transfers only a *subset* of his or her rights to another. For example, the tenant may transfer only a portion of the leased premises or transfer occupancy rights for a period of time less than the remaining lease term. Usually, the sublessee (i.e., the new tenant) pays rent to the original tenant, who in turn pays to the owner the rent stipulated in the original contract. Once again, however, the original tenant remains liable for fulfilling the terms of the original lease.

Unless otherwise prohibited in the lease contract, a tenant may assign the lease or sublet. However, commercial owners, as a condition of the lease, can prohibit assignment and subletting or, alternatively, clearly state the conditions under which one or both strategies may be employed.

There are numerous reasons why a tenant may wish to engage in a sublease or assignment. Perhaps the tenant has sold his or her business and no longer requires the space, or perhaps the tenant's business has grown to the point that more space is required. Conversely, the tenant's business may have encountered financial difficulties and, as a result, he or she is seeking to reduce the firm's leased space.

Assignment and subletting can be major problems in commercial leases. Owners must seek to control who occupies space in their building. Otherwise, unqualified tenants may default on sublease payments, engage in an unsafe or hazardous business, or disrupt the property's tenant mix.

Concept Check

21.5   Contrast lease assignments with subletting.

Lease Options

A lease option is a clause that grants an option holder the right—but not the obligation—to do something. For example, the owner may grant a tenant who is signing a five-year lease the option to renew the lease at the end of its term for an additional five years. Lease options granted by owners to tenants reduce the expected present value of lease cash flows to the owner. Thus, in competitive rental markets, owners will require something of value from the tenant (often a higher base rent) if they grant the tenant an option. Conversely, options granted the owner that may be exercised to the detriment of the tenant require some form of lease concession from the owner. The existence and pricing of options in lease contracts will reflect current conditions in the rental market and the relative negotiating abilities of the two parties.

Renewal Option. **Renewal options** grant the tenant the right, but not the obligation, to renew the lease. Tenants would prefer, all else being equal, the option to renew the lease with the same terms and conditions as the original lease, including the rental rate. Owners, of course, are reluctant to agree to such renewal options for several reasons. First, market rents may increase, perhaps significantly, over the first lease term; thus, owners could be forced to renew the lease at below-market rental rates. This potential loss is not offset by the probability that tenants will renew at above-market rents if market rents decline over the first lease term. Why? Because if rents decline, tenants will not exercise the option to renew at the original contract rental rate. Therefore, this option—like all options—has a one-sided (asymmetric) payoff: If rents decline the payoff to the owner is negative; if rents rise the payoff will be zero because the tenant will not exercise the option to renew. In short, from the owner's perspective this renewal option has a negative net present value. Thus, owners

Exhibit 21-3 Payoffs on the Option to Renew a Five-Year Lease at $18 per sq. ft.

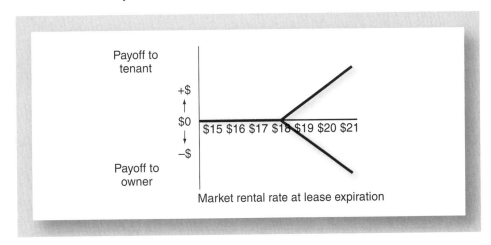

are reluctant to grant such options unless the buyer is willing to pay for it in the form of a higher initial base rent.

An asymmetric payoff associated with options is displayed in Exhibit 21-3. Assume a law firm has negotiated a five-year office lease with a flat rental payment of $18 per square foot. The property owner also has agreed to include an option clause that permits the tenant to renew the lease at expiration for a second five-year term at $18 per square foot. Thus, $18 is referred to as the exercise price of the option.

If market rents in five years are less than $18, the tenant will not exercise her renewal option at the $18 exercise price. Thus, the option payoff to the tenant and cost to the owner would be zero. In option terminology, the option is said to be "out-of-the-money" if prevailing rents are below $18 per square foot. However, if market rents exceed $18 in five years, the option is "in-the-money" and the tenant will likely exercise her option to renew at $18, assuming she still requires the space. The higher market rents are in five years, the greater the payoff or benefit to the tenant from exercising her renewal option. Note that the owner's negative payoff from option exercise mirrors the positive payoff to the tenant.

A more common form of the renewal option gives the tenant the right to renew the lease, but at prevailing market rents. Granting this option is much less costly in present value terms for the owner. However, the expected payoff on the option is still negative. Why? Because the option, if exercised, does not permit the owner to lease the space to an alternative tenant whose business might better match the owner's current marketing and leasing strategy. As previously discussed, the owner's ability to alter the tenant mix is potentially valuable, especially in retail properties and, to a lesser extent, office properties.

Concept Check

21.6 Explain why option payoffs are one-sided, or asymmetric.

Cancelation Option. Tenants may obtain the right to cancel a lease before expiration, usually with a penalty. Owners may also negotiate a **cancelation option.**[2] Although not common in commercial leases, shopping center owners may seek to obtain the right to cancel a lease if the sales of a tenant do not meet or exceed a predetermined minimum amount. Similarly, shopping center tenants may negotiate the right to cancel if their sales, or those of other tenants in the center, do not reach an agreed upon threshold level.

---

2. This clause is also known as a "lease termination clause" or a "kick-out" clause.

Expansion Option. A tenant who expects his or her business to grow may wish to negotiate an **expansion option.** A costly form of this option obligates the property owner to offer the tenant adjacent space, either at the end of the lease term or during some specified time period. Such an option is costly because the owner may have to hold space adjacent to the tenant off the market for an extended period of time to ensure that sufficient space is available should the tenant choose to exercise the expansion option. A less costly alternative for the owner is to offer a **right of first refusal,** which grants the tenant first choice to lease adjacent space should it become available.

Relocation Option. To maintain flexibility, owners of shopping centers and multitenant office buildings often negotiate the right to relocate a tenant to another location within the property. In new office properties, for example, the early leasing of space to small tenants may prevent the owner from leasing larger spaces, or entire floors, to major tenants. Also, existing office and shopping center tenants may wish to expand into a contiguous area that is occupied by a small tenant. If the owner is unable to accommodate the expansion desires of larger tenants, these tenants may move to another property when their leases expire.

Most major tenants will not permit a relocation clause to enter the lease. However, smaller tenants will usually admit such a clause if they are guaranteed the new space will be of similar size and quality and the owner agrees to pay all reasonable moving costs. Obtaining a **relocation option** from as many tenants as possible may make it less costly for the landlord should a particular tenant choose to exercise an option to expand.

Other Common Clauses

Access to Premises. The lease should give owners the right to enter and inspect the leased space without violating a tenant's right to quiet enjoyment. Access to the premises allows the owners to make needed repairs and to show the space to prospective tenants near the end of the current lease term. Inspection also allows owners to monitor whether a tenant's use of the space is allowed under the terms of the lease. However, the lease should specify that, except in emergencies, the owners may inspect only at reasonable times and with sufficient prior notification.

Advertising and Signage. Owners seek to restrict the type, location, and number of signs and graphics that tenants are allowed to display on the property. Large shopping centers, for example, establish uniform graphic images and work to maintain their quality. These restrictions help keep signs and displays consistent with the building's image and the owner's marketing strategy. Shopping center tenants may also be required by their leases to expend a certain portion of their store's sales revenues on advertising to promote their businesses.

www. leasingprofessional.com

Downloadable complete leases and discussions of leasing strategies.

Parking. Shopper access to parking is critical to the success of shopping centers. Thus, retail leases may require that a tenant's employees park only in designated (and less desirable) employee parking areas. Access to suitable parking also is important to office building tenants. The lease should be clear about tenant access to parking, both for customers and employees. The lease also must be clear about the responsibilities of owners and tenants in paying for the lighting and upkeep of the parking area.

Effective Rent

The previous discussion reveals that the net cash flows collected by owners can be affected by a large number of lease clauses and provisions. As a result, the quoted rental rate per square foot often conveys limited information about the true value of a particular lease. In addition, the significant variation often observed in commercial leases makes it difficult to compare lease alternatives, especially long-term leases.

easing agents are real estate sales associates or brokers who specialize in helping landlords find tenants or helping tenants find properties that fit their needs.

Some firms operate much like a traditional brokerage office—representing property owners who are searching for tenants. As agents of the property owner, the job of the leasing agent is to bring tenants to the table and negotiate a transaction that is in the best interests of the owner—even if they claim to be objectively representing the tenant's interests as well.

Leasing Agents

Some leasing agents, often referred to as "tenant reps," work exclusively for corporate tenants. The ITRA Realty Group (www.itrarealtygroup.com) does not believe it is possible to "negotiate from both sides of the table," so ITRA leasing affiliates, located across the country, do not represent owners. As a result, they are able to "work on our (corporate) client's behalf as partner, without conflict of interest and with total objectivity."

Concept Check

21.7 Why is the quoted (i.e., contract) rental rate often not a sufficient measure of the true cost of a lease?

To determine the true cost of a particular lease, it is often useful to calculate its **effective rent.** The effective rent for a monthly payment lease is the level monthly payment over the entire lease term that has the same present value as the lease. Consider, for example a prospective 5,000 square foot, five-year office lease with a quoted rental rate of $20.00, or $1.667 a month, per square foot. The lease is a gross lease; that is, the tenant is not responsible for any of the operating expenses of the property. In addition, the tenant has negotiated eight months of free rent.

The steps in the effective rent calculation are summarized in Exhibit 21-4. First, the owner or tenant must calculate the present value of the promised lease payments. In our example, this can be calculated as the present value of the lease without concessions, minus the present value of the concessions. Assuming an annual discount rate of 10 percent, the present value of the lease without concessions is $395,479.83,[3] while the present value of the eight-month rental concession is $64,769.81.[4] Thus, the present value of the lease *with* concessions is $330,710.

Exhibit 21-4   Steps in the Calculation of Effective Rent

Step 1: Calculate present value of lease (*LPV*) after concessions.

$$LPV = CF_1 + \frac{CF_2}{(1 + k)^1} + \frac{CF_3}{(1 + k)^2} + \frac{CF_T}{(1 + k)^{(T-1)}}$$

Step 2: Calculate equivalent monthly annuity.
Step 3: Calculate annual equivalent level rent per square foot.

3. The calculator keystrokes, assuming beginning of period payments, are $N = 60, I = 10\% \div 12, PV = ?, PMT = \$8,333.33,$ and $FV = 0$.
4. The calculator keystrokes are $N = 8, I = 10\% \div 12, PV = ?, PMT = \$8,333.33,$ and $FV = 0$.

Step 2 in the process is to determine the fixed monthly payment that has the same present value as the lease with concessions. This is referred to as the **equivalent monthly annuity** and is equal to $6,968.54.[5] How is the equivalent monthly annuity to be interpreted? With a 10 percent discount rate, the tenant is exactly indifferent between the following two lease options: (1) making payments of $6,968.54 every month for 60 months and (2) making no payment for eight months followed by 52 monthly payments of $8,333.33.[6]

The final step in the calculation of effective rent is to convert the equivalent monthly annuity into an annual rental rate per square foot. This is know as the **equivalent level rent, (ELR)** and is equal to:

$$ELR = \frac{12 \times Equivalent\ monthly\ annuity}{Rentable\ area} = \frac{12 \times \$6,968.54}{5,000} = \$16.72\ per\ sq.\ ft.$$

Both the prospective tenant and owner can compare the $16.72 *ELR* of the lease to any alternatives they may have.

Broader Lease Considerations

The equivalent level rent calculation captures many of the monetary aspects of the lease—including the time value of money—which allows leases to be compared on a more "apples-to-apples" basis. However, several important dimensions of lease desirability are not captured by the *ELR* calculation.

First, the *ELR* calculation is for a specific lease. Suppose the tenant in the above example expects to need the leased space, or a close substitute, for 10 years. Suppose further that a 10-year lease for highly comparable space is available and that the *ELR* of this alternative lease is $18.00 per square foot. If the choice between these alternatives was based solely on the equivalent level rent the tenant would choose the five-year lease with a $16.72 *ELR*. However, in an uncertain world the tenant may be willing to pay the $1.28 premium ($18.00 − $16.72) associated with the 10-year lease in order to secure appropriate space for 10 years. We label the risk associated with the replacement of one five-year lease with another five-year lease of uncertain terms and conditions as **interlease risk.**

Interlease risk can be significantly mitigated by options embedded in the lease, such as the option to renew. If the 5-year lease above included an option to renew at the rate in effect for the first five years, the tenant's interlease risk would be significantly reduced and would decrease the tenant's incentive to choose the 10-year lease with a higher *ELR*. Even the option to renew the 5-year lease at prevailing market rates in five years reduces interlease risk. In short, options complicate the comparison of lease alternatives and their effects are not included in the *ELR* calculation.

Two other considerations mentioned in our discussion of preferred lease terms are relevant here. First, the significant re-leasing costs faced by both tenants and landlords when a tenant vacates the premises suggests that longer-term leases are preferred by both parties, all else being the same. Thus, another reason the tenant in the example might prefer the 10-year lease with a higher *ELR* is that the longer lease may reduce the present value of future re-leasing costs by allowing the tenant to avoid a costly move at the end of year 5. On the other hand, although longer-term leases reduce re-leasing costs and provide rental rate security for both tenants and owners, a significant cost may be paid in terms of flexibility. If flexibility is deemed to be important, the tenant may rationally choose a shorter-term lease over a longer-term alternative—even if the shorter-term lease has a higher equivalent level rent. The effects of these broader considerations on preferred lease terms are summarized in Exhibit 21-5.

---

5. The calculator keystrokes are $N = 60$, $I = 10\% \div 12$, $PV = 330,710$, $PMT = ?$, and $FV = 0$.

6. The discount rate should equal the rate at which the tenant could borrow money in an unsecured loan with a duration equal to the duration of the lease cash flows

Exhibit 21-5 Summary of Effects of Broader Considerations on Preferred Lease Term

| | Impact on Preferred Lease Term for | |
Consideration	Tenant	Owner
Interlease risk	Longer	Longer
Releasing costs	Longer	Longer
Flexibility	Shorter	Shorter

www.tenantwise.com

Information on topics of interest to tenants and landlords.

Concept Check

21.8 Why is the effective rent of a prospective lease not a definitive measure of its desirability?

We have completed our brief tour of clauses and provisions common to most leases of income properties. However, there is significant variation across property types in the type, number, and complexity of tenants and their businesses. For example, the economics that drive the apartment "business" are much different than the economics of the shopping center "business." Even within the major categories of commercial property—multifamily, office, retail, industrial, and hospitality—there can be substantial variation in the activities and needs of tenants. Contrast, for example, the large department store tenants in a high-end mall with the typical tenants occupying a small, neighborhood shopping center anchored by a grocery store. Not surprisingly, lease clauses have been developed to meet the specific needs of the tenants and owners of the various property types.

We now turn our attention to an examination of the four major types of income-producing properties: residential, office, retail, and industrial. We first define and discuss some of the major property subcategories within each of these major types. We then discuss the lease clauses that are unique, or nearly so, to these property types.

Residential Rental Properties and Leases

The majority of residential rental units in the United States are contained in multifamily structures; that is, apartment buildings that contain five or more housing units. Multifamily structures are often classified by developmental density and architectural style. **High-rise apartment buildings** are popular in many large city centers, where the price of land is at a premium and the intensive use of land is a necessity. Buildings classified as high-rise have at least 10 to 15 stories. Larger structures may have a variety of recreational amenities, a continuously staffed front desk or all-night attendants, and retail establishments such as convenience stores and newsstands.[7] Generally, higher rents are charged for the top floors in high-rise apartment buildings even though the rental services provided by the top floors are no different than the lower floors. Why is this? The consumption of housing is both a necessity and a status symbol. It is assumed that higher floors have better views and they certainly have less street noise.

Midrise apartment buildings range in height from four to nine stories and are found in both cities and suburbs. Midrise apartment buildings in city centers may provide underground parking or no parking at all, whereas their suburban counterparts usually have street-level parking available. Some buildings provide a wide range of amenities, as well as on-site management and service personnel.

---

7. In a few large metropolitan areas such as New York City, units in many high-rise apartment buildings are privately owned, although they are still typically referred to as *apartments*.

Garden apartments have a relatively low density of development and are thus frequently located in suburban and nonurban areas where land is comparatively less expensive. These complexes may consist of numerous low-rise buildings, including a separate building containing a management office and clubhouse. Large garden complexes are also likely to have numerous amenities such as on-site exercise facilities, spacious lawns, extensive landscaping, swimming pools, and tennis courts.

A **condominium** is a multiunit property in which the dwelling units are individually owned and the owner is responsible for the interior of the unit, including the interior walls. The condominium arrangement also provides the owner-investor with joint ownership of the land and all common areas and elements, such as hallways, lobbies, parking areas, and recreational facilities. Similar to apartments, condominiums can be mid- or high-rise structures, or they can look very much like a complex of garden-style apartments. The individually owned units may be occupied by the owner or leased to a tenant. Generally, management control of the complex rests with an owners' association, which has responsibility for maintenance, taxes, insurance, water and sewage, and common-area facilities. Owner-occupied condominiums have served as a bridge from renting to the ownership of single-family detached homes for many families.

www.nmhc.org

National Multi Housing Council, the website of a national association representing the nation's largest apartment firms contains extensive data on the apartment industry.

Common Lease Provisions of Residential Rental Properties

Although we have seen that almost any combination of rights and obligations can be created in a lease, some rights of a tenant cannot be removed or limited in a residential lease. These rights have been created by common law court decisions and by legal statutes to protect tenants who have sometimes been at the mercy of landlords. The essence of these rights is that even if a residential lease stipulated that the tenant waived certain rights, the tenant can still have these rights enforced.

Most important of these nonwaivable rights is to have the property maintained in a safe and habitable condition. Another is the right to protection from unreasonable entry into the premises by the owner or property manager. Apartment owners have a greater right of entry than owners of commercial property because they are obligated to maintain the property in a safe and habitable condition. To do so, they must be able to enter the premises; however, this right is limited to *reasonable* frequency and times. Except in the case of emergencies, landlords must usually provide prior notice of entry. A final nonwaivable right permits residential tenants to cancel the lease if the premises are destroyed by fire or other hazard (a right that is not inherent in commercial leases).

As mentioned in Chapter 17, owners and managers must comply with all applicable landlord-tenant laws. Although such laws vary from state to state, they are intended to protect the tenant's interests in matters relating to the nonwaivable rights discussed above as well as other matters such as application fees, security deposits, and advance rent (e.g., the payment of the last month's rent at lease closing).

Concept Check

21.9 List three nonwaivable rights that are inherent in a residential lease.

Lease Term. The most common lease term for residential rental property is one year, although shorter terms are observed in some markets, such as those heavily influenced by college students.

Condition of Premises. Just prior to moving in, the tenant and property manager will usually inspect the property. The primary purpose of this joint inspection is to uncover existing incidental damage to the property so that the tenant will not be charged for it when vacating the space. The tenant becomes responsible at lease expiration for any damage not listed on the **statement of condition** signed by the tenant after the property inspection.

Utilities. Tenants are usually responsible for the payment of utilities such as gas and electricity. In older buildings where the units are not separately metered, however, utilities may be included in the rent. Responsibility for utility payments must be clearly specified in the lease.

Rules and Regulations. Owners often distribute a set of rules and regulations, in some form or fashion, to new tenants. These rules are designed to protect the property and the rights and safety of tenants. They address issues such as pets, the use of the laundry room and other common areas, and garbage disposal. For these rules and regulations to be enforceable, they must be incorporated into the lease or listed on a separate form, signed by tenants, which indicates they have read and understand the rules.[8]

Office Properties and Leases

While there is no definitive standard for classifying office buildings, the real estate profession commonly refers to office buildings in the following way:

1. *Class A.* These buildings usually command the highest rents because they are the most prestigious in their tenancy, location, and overall desirability. They are usually newer structures and are typically owned by institutional investors such as insurance companies, real estate investment trusts, and pension funds.
2. *Class B.* The rents in these buildings are usually less than those in Class A buildings because of a less desirable location; fewer amenities; less impressive lobbies, elevators, or appearance; or a relatively inefficient layout of the leasable space.
3. *Class C.* These buildings, which were usually once Class A or B, are older and reasonably well maintained but are below current standards for one or more reasons. Rents are set to match the rent-paying ability of lower-income tenants.

The two most important determinants of the classification of an office property are age and obsolescence. However, older buildings can be classified as Class A structures if they accommodate the current needs of potential tenants. Examples include the Chrysler Building in New York and the Sante Fe Railroad Building in Chicago. If the space cannot be improved and updated, the class of the building is likely to decline. For example, many office buildings cannot be easily retrofitted to accommodate technological advances in computer networks and telecommunications.

According to the Institute of Real Estate Management (IREM), there are 12 fundamental criteria for classifying office buildings:

Location	Lobby	Tenant services
Ease of access	Elevators	Mechanical systems
Prestige	Corridors	Management
Appearance	Office interiors	Tenant mix.[9]

www.irem.org

The website of the Institute of Real Estate Management.

www.naiop.org

Website of the National Association of Industrial and Office properties.

Most of these factors are interdependent; for example, highly prestigious buildings are likely to have attractive appearances, an impressive lobby, and quality tenants. The prestige of a building is also a function of its location. For suburban buildings, access to major highways and linkages with places such as restaurants, high-income residential areas, and shopping facilities are extremely important.

---

8. See Institute of Real Estate Management, *Principles of Real Estate Management* (Chicago: IREM, 2001), chap. 9, for an extended discussion of residential leases.

9. See Institute of Real Estate Management, *Principles of Real Estate Management* (Chicago: IREM, 2001), chap. 10.

Exhibit 21-6   A Typical Office Floor Plan

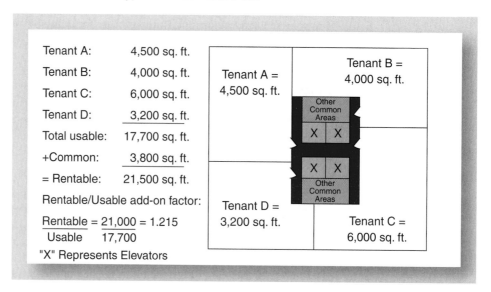

Tenant A: 4,500 sq. ft.

Tenant B: 4,000 sq. ft.

Tenant C: 6,000 sq. ft.

Tenant D: 3,200 sq. ft.

Total usable: 17,700 sq. ft.

+Common: 3,800 sq. ft.

= Rentable: 21,500 sq. ft.

Rentable/Usable add-on factor:

$\dfrac{\text{Rentable}}{\text{Usable}} = \dfrac{21,000}{17,700} = 1.215$

"X" Represents Elevators

Tenant A = 4,500 sq. ft.

Tenant B = 4,000 sq. ft.

Other Common Areas

X X

X X

Other Common Areas

Tenant D = 3,200 sq. ft.

Tenant C = 6,000 sq. ft.

www.boma.org

Website of the Building Owners and Managers Association International.

Defining Rentable Space in Office Properties

Because office rent is usually quoted on a dollar-per-square-foot basis, the accurate measurement of a tenant's square footage is essential. It is also important that square footage be measured in a consistent fashion in a local market so that landlords and tenants can readily compare lease alternatives. The only standard for measuring office space is the one adopted by the Building Owners and Managers Association International (BOMA), although some property owners prefer their own method.

Under BOMA guidelines, the **usable area** is the square footage of the space bounded by the walls that separate one tenant's space from another.[10] Thus, the usable area is the amount of space in the sole possession of the tenant. In the floor plan depicted in Exhibit 21-6, Tenant A occupies 4,500 square feet of usable space while the three remaining tenants control 13,200 square feet. The total usable square footage is 17,700.

The **rentable area** of a tenant's leased office space is equal to the usable area, plus the tenant's prorated share of any common areas. In Exhibit 21-6, the common area (shaded in burgundy) is 3,800 square feet, which includes the open areas and walkways that lead to the elevators (the X's), to the individual office suites, and to other common areas, such as restrooms and storage and utility closets. Thus, the total rentable area of the office floor is 21,500 square feet (17,700 usable plus 3,800 common).[11]

Concept Check

21.10   What is the difference between rentable and usable areas in office leases?

How is the tenant's share of the common area calculated? First, the **rentable/usable ratio** for the entire floor is calculated by dividing the total rentable area by the total usable area. In our example, the R/U ratio, also called the **load factor,** is 1.215 (21,500 ÷ 17,700), indicating the rentable area is 21.5 percent larger than the usable area. To fully allocate the common area among the four tenants, the load factor is multiplied by each tenant's usable area. For example, Tenant A's rentable area is 5,467.5 square feet (4,500 × 1.215).

---

10. Technically, the square footage is measured from the center of the demising walls (the walls between the tenants) and from the inside surface of any exterior walls and common areas walls.

11. The size of the common area does not include the square footage of the elevator shafts (in gray) or other vertical penetrations, such as staircases.

Would it not be simpler to base required rental payments on usable area? Yes, but beginning in the late 1970s some owners, in an apparent attempt make their quoted per square foot rental rates look lower, switched to quoting rents on the basis of rentable square feet. But are owners able to collect more *total* rent because they quote a lower cost per square foot when using the rentable area to measure square footage? Probably not. Prospective tenants looking to rent, for example, the space now occupied by Tenant A will—or at least *should*—be aware of what it would cost on a monthly basis to rent similar space in other properties. Tenants therefore will not be fooled by variations in the quoted cost per square foot, so long as all owners in the market are calculating square footage in a consistent fashion.

Common Lease Provisions of Office Properties

Lease Terms. Office leases involving major tenants may have terms as long as 25 years. However, terms of 5 to 10 years are the most common, with terms shorter than 3 years less frequently observed because they do not provide adequate time for the owner to amortize the cost of initiating the lease, including leasing commissions and required tenant improvements. Renewal options are more prevalent in the office sector than in any other property sector. Tenants generally share in the payment of operating expenses, although the method used to share this responsibility is often a hybrid of the four basic lease types depicted in Exhibit 21-2. Operating expense escalation clauses, which we discussed earlier, have grown in popularity in recent years. Conversely, current practice has moved away from the indexation of rental rates to inflation.

Expense Stops. A clause frequently found in office leases is an **expense stop.** With such a clause, the owner is responsible for reimbursable operating expenses up to a specified ("stop") amount, stated as an amount per square foot of total rentable space in a building. Expenses per square foot beyond the stop are passed through based on each tenant's pro rata share of the building's rentable area.

Assume, for example, that an office building has 60,000 square feet of rentable area, of which Tenant A occupies 6,200 square feet. Assume total reimbursable operating expenses for the office property are $300,000 in the current year, or $5.00 per square foot ($300,000 ÷ 60,000 sq. ft.). Tenant A's pro rata share is $31,000 ($5.00 per sq. ft. × 6,200). However, if Tenant A has a $5.00 per square foot expense stop clause, the landlord is responsible for property operating expenses up to $5.00 per square foot, which is $300,000. However, once expenses exceed $5.00 per square foot, Tenant A pays his pro rata share of the excess amount.

This relation between building expenses and Tenant A's reimbursement to the landlord is displayed in Exhibit 21-7. If total reimbursable expenses are equal to or less than $5.00 per square foot, Tenant A's expense reimbursement is equal to zero. If, for example, total reimbursable expenses in the current year are $350,000, or $5.83 per square foot ($350,000 ÷ 60,000), then $5,146 in operating expenses would be recoverable from Tenant A, calculated as follows:

$$\$5,146 = (\$5.83 - \$5.00) \times 6,200$$

The per square foot expense stop in office leases is often based on the property's total recoverable expenses in the previous calendar year. Thus, tenants in our example who sign leases in the next calendar year will likely be able to negotiate a $5.83 expense stop. Clearly, owners of multitenant properties with expense stops recover a larger percentage of operating expenses from older leases.

Concept Check

21.11 Whose "pain" is capped by an expense stop clause?

Exhibit 21-7   The Relation between Bulding Expenses and Tenant A's
Reimbursement to the Landlord

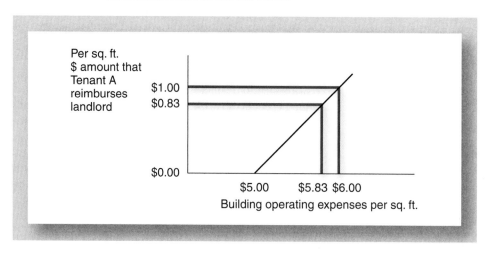

Retail Properties and Leases

Retail establishments are found in a variety of forms. The simplest is a freestanding retail outlet (e.g., a fast-food franchise). Many retail establishments today, however, are found in shopping centers. Shopping centers and, increasingly, freestanding establishments are often popular with individual investors and institutions that invest in commercial real estate. In 2002, according to the National Research Bureau, there were 46,336 shopping centers in the United States. The total leasable retail area was 5.77 billion square feet.

Consider the various types of shopping centers:

1. Neighborhood shopping center. This type of center is located for the convenience of a nearby resident population. It contains retail establishments offering mostly convenience goods (e.g., groceries) and services (e.g., barbershop, video rental, and dry cleaning). These centers, sometimes called a "strip" center, are usually anchored by a large chain grocery store or drugstore. The gross leasable area of the anchor(s) and nonanchored tenant space is approximately 50,000 square feet, but it may be as large as 150,000 square feet. The trade area of a shopping center is the geographic area from which it draws its customers. A strip center's trade area is typically within a two- to three-mile radius of the center. If it is well located, such a center can usually succeed in a trade area with a population of 1,000 to 2,500.

2. Community shopping center. This is a larger version of a neighborhood center. This type of center is often anchored by a discount department store and may include outlets such as clothing stores, banks, furniture stores, lawn and garden stores, fast-food operations, and professional offices (e.g., dentists). The gross leasable area (GLA) is usually three times that of a neighborhood center. A community center's trade area is usually within a three- to six-mile radius of the center.

3. Power shopping center. Power centers have leasable areas ranging from 250,000 to 1,000,000 square feet. The dominating feature of a power center is the high ratio of anchors to ancillary tenants. Typically, power centers contain three or more giants in hard goods retailing (e.g., toys, electronics, home furnishings). Home Depot and Wal-Mart are two prominent "big box" retailers that frequently locate their stores in power centers. These open-air centers are often located near large malls and draw shoppers from a radius of five miles or more.

4. Regional shopping center. Regional centers focus on general merchandise and usually have at least two anchor tenants that are major department stores (e.g., J. C. Penney's) and at least 200,000 square feet of gross leasable area devoted to nonanchor tenants. Major tenants are national chains or well-established local businesses that have high credit ratings and significant net worth. These retailers draw people from a larger area than the neighborhood or community centers, although 80 percent of their sales are typically drawn from within a 10-mile radius. Minor tenants are located between the anchor tenants to capture customers. Often regional centers contain several stores of one type (e.g., shoe stores). Many include small fast-food outlets arranged in food courts.

5. **Superregional malls.** These centers may have as many as five or six major tenants and hundreds of minor tenants. A typical size is 1 million square feet, but many of the larger malls exceed 2 million square feet of leasable area.

6. **Specialty shopping center.** These centers are characterized by a dominant theme or image. Many in downtown areas are located in a rehabilitated historic structure and area. A variation of specialty shopping centers is the **outlet center,** which sells name-brand goods at lower prices by eliminating the wholesale distributor.

Concept Check

21.12 What is the trade area of a shopping center?

www.icsc.org

International Council of Shopping Centers—this website provides a wealth of information on the shopping center industry.

The retail tenant's primary concerns are the availability of adequate space for its business, the volume of consumer traffic generated by the center, and the visibility of the tenant's location within the center. Additional challenges are presented by the special requirements of some tenants. For example, furniture and appliance stores require loading docks, food service providers have garbage disposal problems, and supermarkets need an abundance of close-by short-term parking.[12]

Defining Leasable Area in Retail Properties

In retail, rents are quoted on the basis of **gross leasable area (GLA).** The GLA for a particular tenant captures the amount of space occupied and controlled by the tenant, and is therefore similar to an office tenant's usable area.[13] The GLA of the shopping center is simply the sum of the individual GLAs. The **gross floor area** of a shopping center is equal to the total GLA, plus the square footage of the common areas, which include courtyards, walkways, and escalators.

Common Lease Provisions of Retail Properties

The lease contracts between retail owners and tenants are often extremely complicated and can vary considerably across properties. Many clauses and conditions that are standard in the leases of regional mall department stores are not appropriate for a barbershop or gift store in a strip center. Small retail businesses often lease space for durations as short as one or two years, whereas larger tenants are often willing and able to commit to leases of much longer duration. **Anchor tenants**—the large and generally well-known retailers who draw the majority of customers to the shopping center—may sign leases with terms of 25 to 30 years. Nonanchor tenants often make flat or indexed rental payments plus an additional payment based on some percentage of their gross sales. Tenants also typically share in paying the center's operating expenses. A review of clauses unique to shopping center leases follows.

Percentage Rent Clause. As mentioned previously, shopping center leases often include a clause that ties rent payments to the tenant's sales revenue. In a percentage lease, there is usually a flat or fixed component referred to as the base rent. In addition, the percentage rent clause dictates that the property owner receive a prespecified percentage of tenant sales or a percentage of tenant sales that exceeds some minimum threshold.

---

12. For more detail on the requirements of retail tenants, see Institute of Real Estate Management, *Principles of Real Estate Management* (Chicago: IREM, 2001), chap. 10.

13. The gross leasable area (GLA) is often less than the tenant's "usable" area because most shopping center leases measure space from the inside of the interior walls to the outside of the exterior walls.

Exhibit 21-8 The Payoff to the Owner on a Percentage Rent Clause

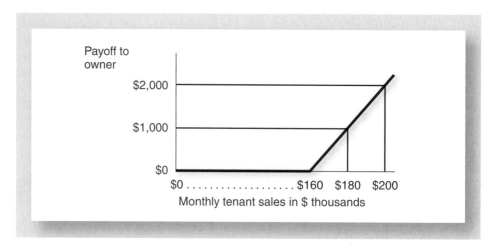

Example 21-1 Percentage Rent

Assume a retail tenant is paying a base rent of $96,000 per year, or $8,000 per month. In addition, the tenant must pay additional monthly rent equal to 5 percent of gross store sales in excess of $160,000 a month. Thus, if the store produces $200,000 in gross sales in a month, total monthly rent is $10,000, calculated as follows:

$$\text{Total rent} = \text{Base rent} + \text{Percentage rent}$$
$$\$10,000 = \$8,000 + 0.05\,(\$200,000 - \$160,000)$$

The percentage rent clause gives the owner an option to claim a portion of tenant sales. If monthly sales exceed the $160,000 threshold amount, the owner exercises her option and claims an additional $2,000 in rent. However, if sales fall short of the $160,000 threshold, the owner collects no percentage rent, but still collects $8,000 in base rent. The payoff to the owner (and cost to the tenant) of this percentage rent clause is depicted in Exhibit 21-8. Note once again that the payoff of this option is one-sided.

Percentage rent clauses are unique to retail and service tenants and offer advantages for both the owner and the tenant. For the tenant, the percentage rental offers a way of leasing space that she might not otherwise be willing to rent because of the uncertainty of her future business success. The percentage rental assures the tenant that increased rental costs will be conditional upon the success of the retail operations.

Perhaps even more important, however, is that the percentage rent clause helps to align the interests of the shopping center owner with those of the tenant. Because the owner's lease cash flows are partially determined by the success of the tenant's business, the owner has an incentive to keep the center clean and attractive, maintain adequate signage, advertise, and ensure that stores with complementary products are located nearby to help drive customers to the tenant's store. From the landlord's perspective, a percentage rental gives the owner an equity like interest in a tenant's business. In a competitive rental market, however, tenants do not freely give away a portion of their firm's upside potential to property owners. To be induced to do so, the base rent must be lower than it would be in the absence of the percentage rent clause. Obviously, a percentage rent clause requires that the shopping center owner have access to the financial records of the tenant.[14]

14. With percentage leases, tenants transfer to the owners some of the risk associated with operating their business. Why do property owners accept this risk? A partial explanation is that, with multiple tenants, owners are able to diversify the risk associated with a "portfolio" of percentage rent clauses. Individual tenants, however, are often exposed to significant firm-specific risk that is difficult, with limited capital, to diversify away. Therefore, both parties can be better off if owners bear some of the tenant-specific risk in their shopping centers.

Concept Check

21.13 How does a percentage rent clause align the incentives of the owner and tenant?

Use Clauses. To help maintain the best mix of tenants in a shopping center, owners frequently specify the merchandise or services that can be sold by the tenant (e.g., "women's shoes" or "costume jewelry"). Conversely, large tenants may seek to restrict the way retail space close to the tenant can be used. Such clauses may be desirable in order to limit the amount of nearby competition or to help ensure that adequate parking is available for potential customers. Some tenants may demand exclusives; that is, the right to be the *only* tenant in the center that provides a certain kind of merchandise or service. Owners of course seek to avoid granting such rights.

Radius Restrictions. When a lease has a percentage rent clause, the owner does not want the tenant to operate a similar store in close proximity for fear such a store would dilute the sales of the tenant's business in the owner's center. A neighborhood shopping center will generally have a radius restriction of 2 to 4 miles, while regional malls often have radius restrictions of 5 to 15 miles.

Hours of Operation. It is important to the success of shopping centers, both large and small, that hours of business operation are consistent across tenants. Most commercial leases allow the owner to set the shopping center's hours of operation or the hours will be specified in the lease.

Common Area Maintenance. This clause specifies exactly what the common areas of the shopping center are, what responsibilities the owner has to maintain and repair the common areas, and what **common area maintenance (CAM)** charges will be billed to the tenants. In addition to maintenance and repair costs, CAM charges typically include the cost of security personnel and alarm systems, as well as fees for the management of the common area. CAM charges, which generally run from $2.00 to $5.00 per square foot per year, are usually prorated among tenants based on the percentage of the center's gross leasable area (GLA) occupied by the tenant.

Other Clauses. Retail leases commonly require the tenant to occupy the space for the entire lease term (continuous occupancy) and to keep his business operating consistently (continuous operation). For the benefit of both the tenant and the owner, retail leases also require the tenant to carry an adequate amount of liability insurance.

Industrial Properties and Leases

Industrial properties include the following:

- Large single-user buildings.
- Warehouses and self storage facilities.
- Multitenant "industrial parks."

Plants and factories are special-use properties not easily converted to other uses. Thus, they are relatively risky and are usually avoided by third-party investors, except those who specialize in the specific production processes employed at the plant (i.e., the companies that use the facilities). In contrast, warehouses and industrial parks have become popular investments in urban areas. Industrial parks are also known as business parks and research parks.

Warehouses provide space for the temporary storage of goods, such as inventory, company records, and excess raw materials. Warehouses are usually built as single-story

Industry Issues

21-2

Retail Lease Negotiation

Ever since the first shopping center leases were negotiated, owners and prospective tenants have been warring over various provisions contained within these documents. Negotiations are often time consuming and even hostile, usually because the drafted forms are so heavily weighted in the owner's favor. To make matters more difficult, more than 50 percent of regional malls are now controlled by real estate investment trusts, which are generally less likely to negotiate favorable lease concessions unless the tenant is deemed to be a low credit risk.

Brokers, tenants, owners, and lawyers cite a variety of retail lease issues—beyond rent—that are difficult to negotiate. These include provisions on the reporting of a tenant's sales; the pass-through of operating expenses; the landlord's financial contributions to tenant improvements as well as the timing of those contributions; provisions that allow tenants to cease operations without being in default; food or retail category exclusives that prohibit similar concepts within the same retail center; the extent of any required personal guarantee on the lease; tenant rights to assign a lease; and common area maintenance costs and tenant rights to audit those charges.

Ultimately, the haggling and fine-tuning of various provisions boil down to the following factors. First, each provision has a legal and economic ramification. Second, the responsibility for operating expenses, including common area maintenance and tenant improvements, are divided between the owner and the tenant depending upon the tenant's perceived financial strength and the participants' lease negotiations skills. Third, the perceived value of the location is based upon the tenant's economic and projected sales modeling specific to the retail location and the supporting demographics. Last, the owner believes that the tenant will contribute positively to the retail center's drawing power, and that the tenant's income stream will contribute positively to the center's overall valuation.

Source: Gretchen Pienta, "Got Space?" *Commercial Investment Real Estate* (CCIM Institute) July–August 2003.

---

structures with fewer design elements than many office building, and shopping centers. They are relatively simple to construct, have long economic lives, and usually require less management effort than other types of commercial property. Generally, warehouse buildings—with their open space for storage—are the least vulnerable of the major property types to functional obsolescence.

Most new space in industrial parks is built as single-story structures that can be configured to accommodate single or multiple tenants. This industrial **flex space** is usually built without fancy lobbies or fixtures and, unlike many office properties, there are no load factors. Rents are lower than traditional office space and there is ample parking. Tenants can be firms that require large amounts of inexpensive space or firms that need their offices in the same building as their manufacturing or warehouse operations.[15]

www.sior.com

Society of Industrial and Office Realtors.

Common Lease Provisions of Industrial Properties

Because of the highly specialized nature of many manufacturing and production processes, manufacturing tenants generally require long-term leases to assure them of possession and control of the space. This is particularly true when the tenant has invested heavily in equipment and other tenant improvements and fixtures that would be expensive to move or replicate in another facility. Most warehouses are single-user buildings leased to tenants on a triple net basis. Most warehouse space is fairly homogenous and, unlike manufacturing and production facilities, few firm-specific tenant improvements are required. Because releasing and moving costs are relatively low and because flexibility is important, warehouse tenants do not usually seek long-term leases—three- to five-year terms are common.

Tenants in multitenant industrial park properties face many of the same leasing issues owners and tenants of multitenant office buildings and shopping centers confront. In par-

---

15. This description of flex space draws from the Institute of Real Estate Management, *Principles of Real Estate Management* (Chicago: IREM, 2001), p. 255.

ticular, leases must be clear about the tenant's responsibility for maintenance and repair. Tenants are generally responsible for their interior space and for the maintenance of mechanical equipment. Owners are usually responsible for the maintenance of the roof and the structural components of the property. Common area maintenance is handled in much the same way as it is in shopping centers; that is, the owner maintains the common area and bills the tenants for the cost based on their pro rata share of the space in the building or park.

Hospitality Properties

Hotels are establishments that provide transient lodging for the public as well as meals and entertainment. Motels are establishments located on or near a highway that are designed to serve the motor traveler. Hotels and motels serve several distinct markets including the traveler (transient market) and the visitor or conventioneer (destination market). Convention hotels cater to meetings of businesses and other organizations and are often located in the downtown areas of major cities. Resort hotels are located near entertainment and vacation-related activities or scenic areas.

Hospitality properties have uncomplicated lease structures. Rooms are usually rented on a daily basis. In addition, hospitality properties are characterized by gross leases; even electric, water, and sewer expenses are included in the "rent."

The success of hospitality property investments is highly dependent on management. A hotel is a service business. Thus, managers should be versed in all aspects of this type of business, not just in collecting room rents and providing maintenance. Because cash flows are dependent on the management of the hospitality business, the ownership of hospitality properties by passive third-party investors is much less common than with the other major property types. As a result, properties often are owned by one of the national corporate chains. Properties owned by third-party investors are typically run by hotel or motel management chains.

Summary

The lease is the document that sets forth the rights and obligations of a tenant and property owner. Thus, from an investor's perspective, leases are the primary determinant of current and future cash flows and, as such, are the engines that drive property value. When investors are contemplating the acquisition of existing multitenant properties subject to long-term leases, their first job is to abstract and to value the "portfolio" of leases that will generate the property's net rental income.

Essential elements of a commercial lease include the term and the amount of rent to be paid by a tenant over the lease term. Because commercial leases often have terms of 5, 10, and, in some cases, 25 years or more, clauses that permit the owner to adjust rents over time are often included. In some cases, rental increases are fully specified in the lease. In other cases, however, the rental increases are tied to changes in a prespecified index, such as the rate of general inflation or, in the case of retail property, to the volume of sales generated by the tenant's business.

Although required rent payments are a fundamental determinant of lease cash flows, the *net* cash flows generated by a lease are also a function of the proportion of property-level operating expenses paid or reimbursed by the tenant. In a gross lease, the tenant makes a single rental payment to the owner, out of which the owner pays for operating expenses. In net leases, however, the tenant is responsible for paying a portion, if not all, of the operating expenses. The degree of expense "netness" must be clearly spelled out in the lease; terms such as "double net" and "triple net" are often inadequate in describing each party's responsibility for operating expenses.

www.mhhe.com/lingarcher1e

Although a tenant's responsibility for rents and operating expenses establishes the basic economics of the lease, other provisions also are potentially important. For example, the owner may grant the tenant concessions that lower the present value of the cash flows collected by the owner. The tenant's ability, described in the lease, to assign or sublease the space may also affect the riskiness and therefore the value of the lease. Options that grant the owner or the tenant the right, but not the obligation, to do something (e.g., the right to renew or cancel) can significantly affect the economics of a lease. The calculation of effective rent is designed to capture many of the monetary aspects of a lease, thereby allowing leases to be compared on a more "apples-to-apples" basis. However, the standard calculation of effective rent ignores many important considerations, such as lease option, releasing costs, and the desire of both parties for flexibility.

Typical lease structures often vary significantly by property type. This chapter provides descriptions of the major property types and examines lease clauses that are unique or critical to the understanding and valuation of each of the major property types: residential rental, office, retail, and industrial.

Key Terms

Anchor tenant 573
Base rent 559
Cancelation option 563
Common area maintenance
   (CAM) 575
Community shopping center 572
Concessions 561
Condominium 568
Effective rent 565
Equivalent monthly annuity 566
Equivalent level rent (*ELR*) 566
Expansion option 564
Expense stop 571
Flat rent 558
Flex space 576
Garden apartments 568

Graduated rent 558
Gross floor area 573
Gross leasable area (GLA) 573
High-rise apartment buildings 567
Indexed lease 558
Interlease risk 566
Load factor 570
Midrise apartment buildings 567
Neighborhood shopping center 572
Operating expense escalation
   clause 560
Outlet center 573
Percentage rent 559
Power shopping center 572
Quiet enjoyment 556
Regional shopping center 572

Relocation option 564
Renewal options 562
Rentable area 570
Right of first refusal 564
R/U ratio 570
Specialty shopping center 573
Statement of condition 568
Sublease 562
Superregional malls 573
Tenant improvement (TI)
   allowance 557
Trade fixtures 561
Usable area 570
Warehouses 575

Test Problems

1. A lease in which the tenant pays a rent based in part on the sales of the tenant's business is known as a:
   a. Percentage lease.
   b. Participation lease.
   c. Net lease.
   d. Gross lease.

2. When the tenant pays a base rent plus some or all of the operating expenses of a property, the result is a:
   a. Gross lease.
   b. Net lease.
   c. Percentage lease.
   d. Graduated lease.

3. Existing leases:
   a. Can be ignored by potential investors when estimating investment value.
   b. Must be considered more carefully when valuing a multi-tenant office building than valuing an apartment complex.

   c. Are more important when estimating market value than estimating investment value.
   d. Should be assumed to have remaining terms of 10 years when estimating investment value.

4. With an expense stop clause:
   a. Operating expenses are borne by the tenant up to a specified level, above which the landlord is responsible for additional expenses.
   b. The landlord is responsible for operating expenses up to a specified level, above which increases in operating expenses become the obligations of the tenant.
   c. Landlords commit to a maximum tenant improvement allowance for new tenants.
   d. Tenants are reimbursed for electric bills in excess of a normal amount.

5. As a tenant, you wish to turn over all rights and responsibilities of your unexpired lease term to a new tenant. By doing so, you are:
   a. Releasing your leasehold interest.
   b. Subleasing your leasehold interest.
   c. Assigning your leasehold interest.
   d. Relieving your leasehold interest.

6. Lease provisions that grant the tenant the right, but not the obligation, to do something generally result in:
   a. A lower base rent.
   b. A higher base rent.
   c. An indexed base rent.
   d. Nothing—a base rent is generally not affected by tenant options.

7. The tenant is responsible for paying property taxes and insurance in a:
   a. Gross lease.
   b. Net lease.
   c. Net-net lease.
   d. Triple net lease.

8. Which of the following statements regarding tenant improvements (TIs) is the least true in the context of commercial real estate leases?
   a. TIs are usually stated as a dollar per square foot amount.
   b. Tenants can generally negotiate higher TIs for existing space than for space in a newly developed project.
   c. Tenants can generally negotiate higher TIs for space in a newly developed project than for space in an existing project.
   d. Smaller TIs are more common in overbuilt renters' markets.

9. In shopping center leases, rents are typically quoted on the basis of what type of area occupied by the tenant?
   a. Gross leasable area.
   b. Net leasable area.
   c. Rentable area.
   d. Usable area.

10. The typical anchor tenant in a neighborhood shopping center is a:
    a. Nationaly known department store.
    b. Regional department store.
    c. "Big box" retailer such as Home Depot and Circuit City.
    d. Grocery store.

Study Questions

1. You have just signed a 10,000 square foot lease. The five-year lease has a base (contract) rent of $18 per square foot per year. Rent payments will be made by you to the landlord at the beginning of each month. The agreement calls for eight months' free rent (at the beginning of the lease). The appropriate discount rate is 10 percent.
   a. What is the present value of the lease with concessions?
   b. What monthly five-year payment/annuity has the same *PV* as the lease with concessions?
   c. What is the per square foot equivalent level annual rent (*ELR*)?

2. Assume the owners of a midsize office building recover all operating expenses from their tenants except management and administrative expenses. The total rentable area of the office building is 100,000 square feet. The total amount of operating expenses recoverable from tenants in the current year is $700,000. Tenant B occupies 10,000 square feet of the building and has an expense stop of $5.50 per square foot. How much of the building's reimbursable operating expenses will the owners recover from Tenant B?

3. Why might a tenant prefer a lease with a higher effective rent than an alternative lease with a lower effective rent?

4. Describe the most common methods used to specify rent changes over time for a commercial lease.

5. What factors tend to make both owners and tenants prefer longer-term leases, all else being equal?

6. Assume a small office building has a total usable area of 40,000 square feet and 5,000 square feet of common area. Tenant Z occupies 6,000 square feet of usable area. What is Tenant Z's rentable area?

7. Assume a retail tenant is paying a base rent of $120,000 per year (or $10,000 per month). In addition, the tenant must pay 7 percent of gross store sales in excess of $143,000 per month as percentage rent. If the store produces $170,000 in gross sales in a month, what is the percentage rent in that month? What is the total rent due?

8. A prospective tenant has presented two lease proposals to the owner of an office building. The first alternative has a five-year term and a contract rental rate $16.00 per square foot in the first year of the lease. The rental rate then steps up 3 percent per year over the remainder of the lease term. So, for example, the rental rate in year 2 (months 13–24) would be $16.48. The second lease alternative is also a five-year lease with an initial contract rate of $16.00 per square foot. However, the rental rate on this lease is indexed to inflation with the adjustment made at the beginning of each year based on the actual rate of inflation in the previous year. The owner of the office property projects that inflation will run at a rate of 3 percent per year over the five-year lease term.
   a. What are the owner's projected payments over the five-year term for the two alternatives?
   b. Which option is the owner likely to prefer and why?

Explore The Web

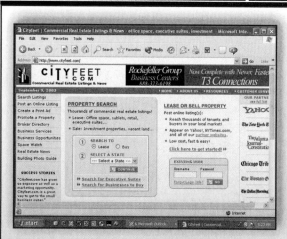

CityFeet.com (www.cityfeet.com) is dedicated to commercial real estate sales and listings. Go to the home page, then click on the "Broker Directory" link in the left margin. Choose a city of your choice and read the profiles of leasing agents working in that city.

Solutions to Concept Checks

1. Five items that must appear in a lease that do not require negotiation between the owner and tenant are (1) the names of the landlord and tenant, (2) an adequate description of the leased premises, and (3) an agreement to transfer possession of the property from the landlord to the tenant, (4) the start and end dates of the agreement, and (5) a description of the rental payments.

2. The primary advantage of longer-term leases is that they delay, and thereby reduce in terms of present value, re-leasing costs. The primary disadvantage is that they reduce flexibility for both the owner and tenant.

3. With a graduated rent clause, the dollar amount of each required lease payment is specified in the lease. If the rental payment is indexed—for example, to inflation—the dollar amount of future rent payments will not be known until the inflation rate for each year is observed. Thus, graduated rents are easy to predict than indexed rents.

4. In competitive rental markets, owners must recover operating expenses from tenants in order to be profitable. With a gross lease, the tenant does not have to reimburse the owner for actual operating expenses because the expected level of operating expenses have already been included in the scheduled lease payments. Tenants win, and owners lose, if actual expenses are greater than expected.

5. A lease assignment conveys all of the tenant's rights and obligations; a sublease conveys only a subset of the original tenant's rights and obligations.

6. The payoffs on lease options are one-sided, or asymmetrical, because they will only be exercised if it benefits the holder of the option. If the option is not in-the-money, it will not be exercised, therefore the payoff is zero.

7. The quoted, or contract, rental rate is often an insufficient measure of the true cost of a lease because from the perspective of the tenant, the cost of the lease is influenced not only by the promised rental payment, but also by the tenant's responsibility for operating expenses and the amount of concessions, including tenant improvements, that the tenant is able to negotiate. The cost of the lease, in present value terms, is also affected by options that the tenant (or owner) may hold, such as the tenant's right to renew or cancel the lease.

8. The effective rent of a prospective lease is not a definitive measure of its desirability because it ignores broader considerations such as re-leasing costs, the desire of both parties for flexibility, and the desire of tenants and owners to avoid the risks associated with having to replace one lease with another.

9. Three nonwaivable rights inherent in a residential lease are (1) the right to have the property maintained in a safe and habitable condition, (2) the right to be protected from unreasonable searches and inspections by the owner, and (3) the right to cancel the lease if the premises are destroyed by fire or other hazards.

10. In office leases, rentable area includes the tenant's usable area plus the tenant's pro rata share of the common areas.

11. The owner's pain is stopped or capped by an expense stop because per square foot operating expenses of the property that exceed the per square foot expense stop are passed through to the tenants. Thus, tenants begin to share the pain once reimbursable expenses, on a per square-foot basis, exceed the stop amount.

12. The trade area of a shopping center is the geographical area from which a shopping center draws it customers. Neighborhood strip centers can survive with a fairly small trade area, needing only to capture those households within a 5- to 10-minute drive of the center. In contrast, regional malls draw from a trade area that can extend for 30 to 45 minutes or more.

13. With a percentage rent clause the owner's lease cash flows are partially determined by the success of the tenant's business. As a result, the owner has an incentive to keep the center clean and attractive, maintain adequate signage, advertise the center and its various stores, and ensure that a proper tenant mix is maintained. All of these efforts by the owners should help to increase the sales of the tenant's business.

Additional Reading

Alexander, Alan A., and Richard F. Muhlebach. *Managing and Leasing Commercial Properties.* Chicago: Institute of Real Estate Management, 1990.

Brueggeman, William B., and Jeffrey Fisher, *Real Estate Finance and Investment,* 11th edition, New York: McGraw-Hill Irwin 2001.

Gelter, D. M., and N. G. Miller. *Commercial Real Estate Analysis and Investments,* 1st ed. Cincinnati, OH: South-Western Publishing 2000.

International Council of Shopping Centers. *Crafting Lease Clauses, Volume III: 1999–2001.* New York: ICSC.

International Council of Shopping Centers. *Essential Factors in Shopping Center Leasing.* Edited by Irving Wolf. New York: ICSC.

Institute of Real Estate Management. *Principles of Real Estate Management,* 14th ed. Chicago: IREM, 2001.

Mitchell, T. G. *The Commercial Lease Guidebook: Learn How to Win the Leasing Game.* MacOre Intl., 1994.

Portman, J., M. Stewart, and R. E. Warner. *Every Landlord's Legal Guide.* Berkeley CA: Nolo Press, 2002.

Society of Industrial and Office Realtors. *Mastering Office Leasing.* Washington, DC: SIOR, 2003.

Society of Industrial and Office Realtors. *Comparative Statistics of Industrial and Office Real Estate Markets.* Washington, DC: SIOR 2003.

Zankel, Martin I. Negotiating Commercial Real Estate Leases, Fort Worth: Mesa House Publishing 2001.

chapter twenty-two

Income Taxation *and* Value

Learning Objectives

After reading this chapter you will be able to:

1. Incorporate income tax considerations into a discounted cash flow analysis, given appropriate assumptions.

2. Distinguish between active, passive, and portfolio income, and explain the tax treatment of each classification.

3. Calculate the after-tax cash flows from annual operations and from sale of the property, given the federal income tax treatment of mortgage financing and depreciation.

4. List and discuss the differential tax treatment of ordinary versus capital gain income and ordinary versus capital assets.

5. List the primary methods employed to defer, reduce, and/or eliminate tax liabilities.

Introduction

The direct ownership of commercial real estate produces cash flows from rental operations and, perhaps, cash flow from the eventual sale of the property. Both of these cash flow components are subject to federal and, in some cases, state income taxation. Moreover, as was noted in Chapter 16, the claims that states and the federal government have on property-level cash flows are substantial; many real estate investors face a combined state and federal tax rate that approaches 50 percent. Consequently, the measure of investment value most relevant to investors is the present value of the *after-tax* cash flows from operations and sale.

In Chapter 16 we extended commercial property discounted cash flow analysis (DCF) to include the effects of federal income taxes. There we saw, using the example of our Centre Point office building, that the effects of federal income taxes on cash flows, discount rates, *NPV*s, and *IRR*s are substantial. However, the estimated tax liabilities incorporated into our DCF analysis in Chapter 16 were presented without explanation. This chapter provides an introduction to the complex tax treatment of real estate.

We begin by identifying the classifications of real estate for tax purposes. A general discussion of the U.S. tax system and how it treats real estate is followed by an analysis of how specific federal income tax provisions affect commercial property investments during both the rental operation phase and the disposition stage.[1] We conclude with a brief discussion of the most important tax rules that affect owner-occupied housing. Because federal income tax laws affecting real estate are extensive and complex, only abbreviated explanations of the most relevant issues are presented here. This information should be considered a starting point for learning about the tax consequences of owning real estate.

Objectives and Implementation of United States Tax Law

The most obvious objective of U.S. tax law is to raise revenues efficiently and equitably for the operations of the federal government. Congress also has designed tax law to promote certain socially desirable real estate–related activities, such as the construction and rehabilitation of housing for low-income households and the rehabilitation of historic structures.

All this is not meant to suggest that everything in the tax code has a strong economic or social rationale. Many tax provisions that apply to real estate are the result of competing political interests, and provisions favoring real estate are more likely to be passed by Congress when the influence of real estate lobbyists is particularly strong.

Tax legislation is combined into a single immense section of the federal statutory law called the Internal Revenue Code. Congress frequently revises this code, and some of these revisions have been extensive. The U.S. Treasury Department issues regulations and rulings interpreting the Internal Revenue Code. Congress also created the **Internal Revenue Service (IRS)** to collect federal taxes and to clarify and interpret regulations.

Comparing the Taxation of Individuals and Corporations

As discussed in Chapter 15, the double taxation of income renders C corporations a less desirable ownership form for real estate investments than alternative ownership forms such as limited partnerships and limited liability companies. This chapter, therefore, focuses attention on the consequences associated with using these unincorporated ownership forms to purchase income property. The advantages and disadvantages of alternative ownership forms, including real estate investment trusts, are discussed in Chapter 15.

Four Classes of Real Property

For purposes of federal income taxes, real property is classified into four categories:

1. Real estate held as a **personal residence.**
2. Real estate held for sale to others: **dealer property.**
3. Real estate held for use in a trade or business activity: **trade or business property.**
4. Real estate held for investment: **investment property.**

These classifications are important because they determine whether the real estate can be depreciated for federal income tax purposes. **Depreciation,** if permitted, allows investors to reduce the amount of taxable income they report by an amount that is intended to reflect the wear and tear that commercial properties experience over time. By reducing taxable income and tax liabilities, depreciation "write-offs" increase the net cash flows taxpayers receive from real property investments. A property's tax classification may also affect the investor's tax liability when the property is sold.

Principal residences are properties used as taxpayers' homes and cannot be depreciated for tax purposes. Commercial real estate, on the other hand, may be classified for tax purposes as dealer, trade or business, or investment property. Real property held for resale

---

1. This chapter focuses on federal tax policies and provisions. State income taxes may also affect after-tax cash flows and returns from real estate investments. However, state income tax provisions often parallel federal provisions. Moreover, several states have no individual income tax (e.g., Florida and Texas).

by a dealer is not depreciable for tax purposes because such property is viewed as inventory, not as a long-term investment. Generally speaking, Congress allows depreciation deductions only on assets intended to be held as long-term investments rather than those held for immediate resale. An example of an individual or firm that would typically be classified as a dealer is a homebuilder who, in the normal course of business, constructs homes for sale to homebuyers. It is important to remember that the dealer versus investor classification is *investment specific,* not *taxpayer specific.* Thus, a taxpayer could be a dealer with respect to one activity (e.g., homebuilding), but an investor with respect to one or more other activities (e.g., investing in small apartment buildings).

A commercial property investment not classified as dealer property is either a trade or business property or an investment property. Consider the operator of a restaurant who owns the building in which the restaurant is located. In this case, the owner acquired the building with the intent to operate, modify, or do whatever is necessary to the structure to maximize the income from the restaurant business. For tax purposes, this real estate investment is classified as trade or business property.

What about a taxpayer who owns an apartment complex? Although this activity would seem to qualify as investment property, it is classified under U.S. tax law as a trade or business property. What about taxpayers who acquire their rental real estate by purchasing an interest in a limited partnership, that, in turn, purchases the real estate? Despite the possible lack of active management, the IRS considers the taxpayers involved in these investments to be operators of a trade or business activity, perhaps if for no other reason than they bear the responsibility for employing the property manager. In short, virtually all rental real estate is included in the trade or business category with the apparent rationale that investors in rental properties are primarily in the "business" of providing rental space to tenants. The tax treatment of trade or business property is determined according to Section 1231 of the federal tax code. Thus, trade or business real estate is often referred to as **Section 1231 property.**

Investment property is held primarily for capital appreciation, not rental income. Raw land and developed lots are prominent real estate examples of investment property. Real estate holdings classified as trade or business (Section 1231) property can be depreciated for tax purposes; in contrast, a depreciation deduction cannot be taken on investment property because the majority of the investment return on such assets is not produced by rental income.

Concept Check

22.1   What is the primary importance of the four income tax classifications for real estate investors?

How else does the tax treatment of trade or business property differ from investment property? The sale of a trade or business property that is held for more than one year is treated as a Section 1231 transaction. Net gains from the sale of Section 1231 assets are taxed at capital gain tax rates—which can be significantly lower than ordinary income tax rates. In addition, net losses from the sale of Section 1231 assets are deductible without limit against other sources of income (including wages and salaries) in the year in which the losses are incurred. In contrast, losses on the sale of investment assets (e.g., undeveloped land, stocks and bonds) may *not* be fully deductible against other income when incurred. (Taxable gains and losses from property dispositions are discussed in more detail below.)

Income Subject to Taxation

There are three types of income subject to federal taxation: active income, portfolio income, and passive income. Income earned from salaries, wages, commissions, and bonuses is classified as **active income.** In contrast, income from investments in securities or unimproved land is classified as **portfolio income** and includes interest and dividend income on investments such as stocks and bonds. Dividends received from the ownership of a real estate investment trust (REIT) are also classified as portfolio income, as is interest earned on a mortgage or mortgage-backed security. Also, gains from the sale of financial securities, such as stocks and bonds, are considered portfolio income.

Passive activity income is defined to include all income generated from rental real estate investments—regardless of how active the investor is in managing the property or properties. For example, owners of small apartment buildings that frequently find themselves doing "light" plumbing repair in the middle of the night probably do not think of themselves as "passive" investors. Nevertheless, in the context of *this* section of the tax code, their rental real estate activities are deemed to be passive in the eyes of the IRS and are therefore subject to **passive activity loss restrictions.** Unfortunately, this "passive" label is confusing because, in a *different* section of the code discussed above, virtually all income property investments are classified for depreciation purposes as trade or business properties—presumably because such investors are actively engaged in the business of providing rental space to tenants. Confused? Well, so are many tax accountants and tax attorneys.

Concept Check

22.2   How is income earned from salaries, wages, and commissions classified? Income from investments in securities? Income generated from rental real estate investments?

What is the significance of the passive activity loss (PAL) restrictions for real estate investors? For individuals and partnerships, tax losses from passive activities can be used to offset positive taxable income from other passive activities, but not active or portfolio income (e.g., wages, interest, and dividends). Consider a real estate investor who owns, through three limited partnerships, an interest in two small apartment buildings and a small neighborhood shopping center. He has no other passive investment activities. Each year, the investor is allocated, by means of the partnership agreements, his share of the taxable gain or loss on each property. Assume in the current tax year he is allocated $3,000 and $5,000, respectively, in positive taxable income from the two apartment investments. However, his shopping center investment produced an allocated taxable loss of $10,000.

What happens? The $10,000 loss can be netted against the $8,000 in positive taxable income from his two other passive investments. However, the net $2,000 in negative taxable income from his passive investment activities cannot be used in the current tax year to offset active or portfolio income. Is this $2,000 tax loss deduction lost forever? No, passive losses that cannot be used in a particular tax year can be carried forward and used to offset positive passive income in future years, including passive income generated by a fully taxable sale.

It is significant that PAL restrictions apply even if the tax losses are caused by decreases in market rental rates, increases in vacancy rates, or both. Even *real* losses—that is, situations in which the before-tax cash flow (*BTCF*) is also negative—are *not* deductible.

Several important exceptions exist to passive activity loss restrictions. First, regular corporations are not subject to the rule. Second, noncorporate taxpayers who actively manage residential rental investments may deduct up to $25,000 in passive losses against nonpassive income if their adjusted gross income (without regard to the losses) is less than $100,000.[2] "Active" management in this context requires the taxpayer to have a 10 percent

---

2. This amount is phased out at $1 for every $2 of income above $100,000. Thus, this exemption is completely phased out when adjusted gross income (*AGI*) reaches $150,000. A taxpayer with modified *AGI* of $120,000 could deduct up to $15,000 [$25,000 − (0.5 × $20,000)] of passive losses against active or portfolio income.

Exhibit 22-1 Single Taxpayers: Ordinary Income Tax Rate Schedule, 2003

If Taxable Income Is Over	But Not Over	Your Tax Liability Is	Of the Amount Over
$ 0	$ 7,000	10%	$ 0
7,000	28,400	$ 700 + 15%	7,000
28,400	68,800	3,910 + 25%	28,400
68,800	143,500	14,010 + 28%	68,800
143,500	311,950	34,926 + 33%	143,500
311,950	—	90,515 + 35%	311,950

Note: To find updated tax rate schedules, visit the IRS website at www.irs.ustreas.gov

www.taxsites.com

Tax and accounting websites directory provides great links to real estate tax sources.

interest in the property (and not be a limited partner) and be involved in the management of the property on a "substantial and continual basis."[3]

Active income is taxed at **ordinary tax rates** (see the next section). Portfolio income generated in the form of interest and dividends is also taxed at ordinary rates. However, if a stock or bond investment appreciates in value during the investment holding period, the appreciation is generally taxed at a lower **capital gain tax rate.** The annual income produced by rental property operations, which is "passive" by definition, is taxed at ordinary rates. Gains from property value appreciation, however, may be eligible for favorable capital gain tax treatment.

Tax Rates

To estimate the tax implications of a noncorporate real estate investment, we must consider the tax rates individuals face, as well as the amount of taxable income the investment generates. In the 2003 tax year, there are six ordinary income tax rates for individuals ranging from 10 percent to 35 percent. Exhibit 22-1 shows these rates and associated ranges of taxable income for single taxpayers in 2003. The corresponding tax rate schedule for married taxpayers (filing jointly with their spouse) is displayed in Exhibit 22-2.

All taxable income of single taxpayers equal to or below $7,000 is taxed at 10 percent. If taxable income exceeds $7,000, but does not exceed $28,400, taxes due will equal $700, plus 15 percent of the amount over $7,000. If taxable income exceeds $28,400, but does not exceed $68,800, the tax liability will equal $3,910, plus 25 percent of the amount over $28,400. Therefore, if a single taxpayer has federal taxable income of $50,000, his or her tax liability is calculated as follows:

$$\text{Tax liability} = \$3,910 + [0.25 \times (\$50,000 - \$28,400)]$$
$$= \$3,910 + [0.25 \times \$21,600]$$
$$= \$9,310$$

The income ranges to which the six rates apply are indexed annually to inflation.[4]

3. Passive activity loss restrictions were further eased for some investors by the Omnibus Budget Reduction Reconciliation Act of 1993. This act relaxed the "automatically passive" status of rental real estate and introduced once again the opportunity to shelter salary or other income with rental losses. The act targets this relaxation to those in the "real estate property business," which includes nearly every type of real estate operation, including development and construction, acquisition, conversion, rental, operation, management, leasing, and brokerage. To be eligible for a waiver of the "automatically passive" rule you must (1) materially participate in the real property businesses, (2) spend more than one-half of your time for the year in those real property businesses, and (3) spend over 750 hours in total in these real property businesses. From an industry perspective, this relief measure provides a more evenhanded treatment of rental real estate than did the prior law.

4. Thus, if general inflation in the U.S. economy averages 3 percent per year from 2003 to 2006, the 15 percent rate would apply to taxable income of up to $31,033 [$28,400 $\times$ $(1.03)^3$] in 2006 for a single taxpayer.

Explore The Web

Download the current tax rate schedule for single taxpayers from the IRS website www.irs.ustreas.gov. What is the maximum statutory tax rate? Calculate the tax liability for a single taxpayer with $50,000 in taxable income. Has the tax liability increased or decreased since 2003?

Exhibit 22-2 Married Taxpayers: Ordinary Income Tax Rate Schedule, 2003

If Taxable Income Is Over	But Not Over	Your Tax Liability Is	Of the Amount Over
$ 0	$ 14,000	10%	$ 0
14,000	56,800	$1,400 + 15%	14,000
56,800	114,650	7,820 + 25%	56,800
114,650	174,700	22,283 + 28%	114,650
174,700	311,950	39,097 + 33%	174,700
311,950	—	84,389 + 35%	311,950

Note: To find updated tax rate schedules, visit the IRS website at www.irs.ustreas.gov

Estimating Tax Liabilities from Operations

In Chapters 9 and 16 we discussed the calculation of net operating income (*NOI*) from direct investments in rental property. The calculation of *NOI* involves deducting from gross rental income (*EGI*) the expenses associated with keeping the property operating and competitive in its market area. These operating expenses include property taxes, management, utilities, maintenance, and insurance. If capital expenditures (*CAPX*) are treated "above line," they also are deducted from *EGI,* resulting in the property's net operating income (*NOI*). Net operating income minus the mortgage payment is equal to the property's estimated before-tax cash flow (BTCF) from operations.[5]

In addition to cash flow, the ownership of income-producing real estate also generates taxable income. If the real estate is held in the form of a corporation or real estate investment trust (REIT), estimating the tax consequences is straightforward. The investor's taxable income usually is increased each year by the amount of dividend income received from the corporation or REIT.[6] However, estimating the tax effects of direct real estate

---

5. As discussed in Chapters 9 and 16, an alternative treatment of *CAPX* in the operating pro forma is a "below-line" treatment; that is, capital expenditures are subtracted *from NOI* to produce what may be called the property's "net cash flow." We continue to use the above-line treatment here to be consistent with our treatment of *CAPX* in previous chapters.

6. Sometimes a portion of the dividend is deemed by the corporation to be "return of capital" and therefore is not taxable. Also, if a portion of the dividend reflects the investor's share of corporate-level capital gains, this portion of the dividend is taxed at the shareholder's applicable capital gain tax rate. Capital gain taxation is discussed later in the chapter.

ownership by individuals and partnerships is more complex. This section discusses the calculation of annual taxable income (*TI*), the ordinary income tax liability (*TAX*), and the after-tax cash flow (*ATCF*) from direct investments in commercial property.

The general forms for calculating *TAX* and *ATCF* are displayed side by side in Exhibit 22-3. In the calculation of before-tax cash flow (*BTCF*), debt service (*DS*) is split into its two components: interest (*INT*) and principal amortization (*PA*). The amount of deductible interest in a given tax year is, generally, equal to total interest paid. The calculation of depreciation (*DEP*) and amortized, up-front, financing costs (*AFC*) are discussed in the following sections.

Cash Calculation versus Tax Calculation

As shown in Exhibit 22-3, two separate calculations are required to estimate after-tax cash flows from annual operations. The "cash" calculation involves a sequence of adjustments to the net operating income the investment is expected to generate. One of these adjustments is for income taxes. A separate tax calculation, however, is required to estimate annual tax effects. Income subject to taxation differs, often significantly, from the actual (before-tax) cash flow generated by the property. As Exhibit 22-3 indicates, one difference between taxable income and before-tax cash flow is that principal amortization is subtracted from net operating income to estimate before-tax cash flow, but it is not tax deductible. Conversely, depreciation and amortized up-front financing costs (discussed below), which are both noncash expenses, *are* subtracted from *NOI* to find taxable income.

Concept Check

22.3 List two cash outflows associated with property operations that are not tax deductible in the year in which they occur. List two deductible expenses that are not associated with a concurrent cash outflow.

Operating Expenses versus Capital Improvements

As discussed in Chapters 9 and 16, operating expenses are defined as expenditures made to operate the property and keep it in good repair; they do not fundamentally alter the value of the property. Repainting the property inside or out, fixing gutters or floors, fixing leaks, plastering, and replacing broken windowpanes are examples of repairs that are classified as operating expenses. A capital expenditure, on the other hand, increases the market value of the property. Examples include the replacement of roofs, gutters, windows, and furnaces. Operating expenses are generally deductible for income tax purposes in the year in which

Exhibit 22-3 Taxable Liability from Operations versus After-Tax Cash Flow

Tax Calculations	**Cash Calculations**
Net operating income (*NOI*)	Net operating income (*NOI*)
+ Capital expenditures (*CAPX*)	
− Depreciation (*DEP*)	
− Interest expense (*INT*)	− Interest expense (*INT*)
− Amortized financing costs (*AFC*)	− Principal amortization (*PA*)
= Taxable income (*TI*)	= Before-tax cash flow (*BTCF*)
× Ordinary Tax rate (*TR*)	− Tax liability (*TAX*)
= Tax liability (*TAX*)	= After-tax cash flow (*ATCF*)

they are paid. Capital expenditures, however, are not immediately deductible in the tax calculation even if they represent an actual cash outflow. Rather, capital expenditures are added to the tax basis of the property and then systematically expensed through annual depreciation deductions, as explained below in the section "Depreciation Deductions." Generally, investors prefer to have expenditures classified for tax purposes as operating expenses rather than capital expenditures because the former are immediately deductible whereas the latter are expensed over time. Tax benefits, like other cash flow benefits, have higher present values when they are received sooner rather than later.

Why, in Exhibit 22-3, are capital expenditures *added* to net operating income in the calculation of taxable income from operations? Because with our above-line treatment of capital expenditures, *CAPX* have been subtracted from *EGI* in the calculation of *NOI*. Because *CAPX* are not tax deductible in the year in which they are paid, they must be added back in the calculation of taxable income.[7]

www.taxprophet.com

The "tax prophet" answers frequently asked questions on real estate taxation.

Costs of Mortgage Financing

The use of mortgage debt, in addition to equity capital, to finance an income property investment has four essential tax consequences. First, the periodic "price" the investor pays for borrowing—that is, the interest—is generally deductible in the year in which it is paid. However, the repayment of principal is not. Second, the annual depreciation deduction is not affected by the mix of debt and equity financing that is used because the entire acquisition price (minus the land) is deductible. Third, mortgage funds, used for purchases or refinancings, are not taxable as income when received.

Finally, **up-front financing costs** (e.g., loan origination fees, discount points, appraisal fees) for investment properties are not fully deductible in the year in which they are paid. Instead, these costs must be amortized over the life of the loan. For example, if up-front financing costs on a 30-year loan total $3,000, the investor may deduct $100 a year when calculating taxable income from operations. If the loan is prepaid before the end of year 30 (perhaps because the property is sold), the remaining up-front financing costs are fully deductible in the year in which the loan obligation is extinguished. If our example loan is prepaid in year 5, then $2,600 [$3,000 − (4 × $100)] can be deducted from taxable income in year 5.

Concept Check

22.4 When does the cash flow effect associated with up-front financing costs occur? When does the tax effect occur?

Depreciation Deductions

Why are investors in trade or business properties permitted a deduction (or "allowance") for depreciation even though it is not associated with an actual cash outflow during the years of operation? Because real estate depreciates or "wears out" as the capital improvements age—the roof shingles become less water resistant, the heating and air-conditioning system is less effective, the wood framing is more susceptible to water and infestation, and so on. As a result, the services and amenities provided by the developed portion of the property will be less valuable to the occupants, in real terms, at the end of a year than at the beginning because of this wear and tear. By allowing a depreciation expense, Congress is effectively permitting investors to deduct an estimate of this wear and tear as a legitimate expense associated with generating the property's rental income.

---

7. Recall from Chapter 9 that investors sometimes set aside money each year in a separate account to accumulate a fund for future capital expenditures, such as replacement of roofs, kitchen equipment, and lobby or reception area furniture. These replacement reserves are not tax deductible. Therefore, if a replacement reserve is included in the calculation of *NOI*, it must be added back when calculating taxable income from operations.

Students may be quick to point out that in many real estate markets and in many time periods, property values often *increase* over time, at least in nominal value. If properties are increasing in nominal (i.e., not adjusted for inflation) value, isn't this evidence that the properties are *not* wearing out? And if the properties are not wearing out, why should investors be allowed to take a deduction that is meant to approximate this aging?

The answers to these questions are found primarily in the distinction between land values and building values. Observable increases in property values may reflect an improvement in the location value of the property (due to changes in supply and demand) and, thus, the value of the land. If the increase in the value of the land exceeds the real loss in the value of the building and other improvements, the *total* value of the property may increase. In addition, increases in nominal values may occur simply because the amount of general inflation (usually measured by the consumer price index) exceeds the loss in the real value of the building and improvements. Nevertheless, the remaining economic life of the property is decreasing over time and this "loss" of economic life should be considered a legitimate cost of providing leasable space to tenants. In a sense, the depreciation allowance is meant to provide for the replacement of the asset (i.e., recovery of initial capital costs) by the end of its economic life.

Concept Check

22.5   What is the "theory" behind depreciation allowances?

The size of the annual depreciation deduction is prescribed by federal law and depends on three factors: the amount of the depreciable basis, the cost recovery period, and the method of depreciation.

Depreciable Basis. The starting point for the calculation of the **depreciable basis** is the **original cost basis,** which is equal to the total acquisition price of the property (land, buildings, and personal property). To this is added any expenses directly associated with acquiring the property, such as brokerage fees (if paid by the buyer) and legal fees.[8]

The land component of the original cost basis is not depreciable because land is assumed not to wear out over time. Therefore, the portion of the total acquisition cost attributed to the land must be separated from the value of the building and its improvements. The IRS does not state how the relative values of the land and building are to be determined. Perhaps the most accurate and defensible method (to the IRS) is to have an independent real estate appraiser separately estimate the market value of each. An alternative approach is to obtain the relative values of the two components from the assessed values placed on the land and buildings by the local property tax assessor. If the property tax assessor concludes that the land constitutes 20 percent of the total taxable value of the property, then the owner can assume with some justification that 20 percent of the total acquisition price represents land value. As a general rule, the value of the land constitutes 10 to 30 percent of the total value of improved commercial properties.

An additional complication is that the depreciable basis may be further segregated into two components: real property (i.e., the building structure) and personal property. For example, hotel acquisitions typically include beds, tables, lobby furniture, and other items. An apartment building may include window air conditioners, refrigerators, and microwaves. Other examples of personal property include wall and floor coverings, swimming pools, and tennis courts. Generally, **personal property** is any tangible property not part of the building's core structure and, in some cases, as much as 40 percent of a property's cost can be classified as personal property.[9]

---

8. The original cost basis of a newly developed project equals the cost of land acquisition, plus land development costs, plus all hard and soft costs of the building and other improvements.

9. In addition to personal property, some land improvements such as grading, filling, roads, and landscaping may be depreciable as land improvements using an accelerated depreciation method over a 15-year depreciation period.

Why is the distinction between real and personal property important? Because personal property (1) may be depreciated over shorter periods than real property and (2) may be depreciated using "accelerated" methods (see below). The combination of these two effects provides significantly larger depreciation deductions in the early years of the investment holding period, which creates an incentive on the acquisition of an existing property to allocate as much of the depreciable cost basis as possible to personal property. However, a word of caution: There are no clear definitions of exactly what constitutes personal in contrast to real property. As a general rule, the allocation of the depreciable basis should be based on each component's fair market value at the time of the acquisition. But what is the value of a 10-year-old heating and air-conditioning system, 5-year-old carpeting, refrigerators, and furniture, or 20-year-old landscaping? Owners who choose to use a **cost segregation** method for separating personal from real property usually choose to hire specialized firms to do most of the work.

Concept Check

22.6   You just purchased a small office building. Why do you have little incentive to attribute as much value as possible to the land? With respect to the nonland component, why have you little incentive to attribute as much value as possible to real property?

Cost Recovery Period. Congressional legislation has repeatedly altered the period of time over which rental real estate may be depreciated. Currently, residential real property (e.g., apartments) may be depreciated over no less than 27½ years.[10] The cost recovery period for nonresidential real property (e.g., shopping centers, industrial warehouses, office buildings) is 39 years.[11] Personal property such as carpeting and draperies may be depreciated over 3 years, office equipment and fixtures over 7 years, and landscaping and sidewalks over 15 years.

Methods of Depreciation. Two basic methods of depreciating capital assets have been allowed: the straight-line method and a variety of "accelerated" methods. Currently, only the straight-line method is permitted for the depreciation of newly acquired or constructed real property. Straight-line depreciation is less generous to investors than accelerated methods—assuming the same cost recovery period—because accelerated methods result in greater depreciation allowances than straight-line depreciation in the early years of the depreciation schedule.

The real property depreciation allowance for a given year can be approximated by multiplying the *depreciable* basis—original cost basis minus the value of the land and personal property—times the appropriate depreciation rate. This rate is a function of the cost recovery period and the method. With a 27½-year recovery period and the straight-line method, the annual depreciation rate is:

$$\textit{Straight-line rate} = \frac{1}{\textit{recovery period}} = \frac{1}{27.5} = 0.03636, \text{ or } 3.636\%$$

---

10. A commercial property is considered a "residential" property for income tax purposes if at least 80 percent of the gross rental income is derived from the leasing of nontransient dwelling units (hotels and motels are not residential property). What about a downtown apartment building that has retail space on the first floor? So long as the rental income from the retail tenants does not exceed 20 percent of total rental income, the property is considered residential and may be depreciated over the shorter 27½-year recovery period.

11. From 1986 until 1993, nonresidential income property could be depreciated (straight-line) over 31½ years. Just prior to 1986, both residential and nonresidential property could be depreciated over 19 years using 175 percent declining balance depreciation. Owners who purchased property prior to 1993 can continue to use these more generous depreciation methods so long as the property is not sold and the cost recovery period has not expired.

If the real property depreciable basis is $100,000, the depreciation allowance is $3,636 (0.03636 × $100,000). With a 39-year recovery period, the annual rate is 0.02564 (i.e., 1/39) and the depreciation allowance, assuming a $100,000 basis, is $2,564.

Determining the real property depreciation allowance is complicated slightly by a tax rule known as the **midmonth convention.** Regardless of the actual date of purchase, the tax law assumes the purchase occurred on the 15th day of the month (i.e., midmonth). For example, if an apartment property is purchased January 10, the depreciation rate in the first year is:

$$11.5 \text{ months} \div 12 \text{ months} \times 0.036363 = 0.03485$$

If the purchase is on April 15, the first-year rate is

$$8.5 \text{ months} \div 12 \text{ months} \times 0.0363636 = 0.02576$$

After the first year of ownership, the depreciation rate for our apartment example is the straight-line rate of 0.03636.

Despite the midmonth convention, the allowable depreciation deduction is easily calculated. Once the depreciable basis is determined, the investor simply refers to the appropriate IRS table to determine the percentage of the original depreciable basis that is deductible in any given year. The midmonth convention is built into these IRS tables. A partial depreciation table for residential property is displayed in Exhibit 22-4. Each year the investor multiplies the original depreciable basis of the real property by the appropriate percentage to determine the depreciation deduction for that year.

Prior to 1986, 175 percent declining balance depreciation and a 19-year cost recovery period was available on commercial real estate. The accelerated depreciation rate in the first year using a 175 percent declining balance depreciation and a 19-year recovery period is:

$$175\% \text{ declining rate} = 1.75 \times \frac{1}{Recovery\ period} = 1.75 \times \frac{1}{19} = 0.09211$$

Thus, if the depreciable basis is $100,000, the accelerated allowance is $9,211, leaving an unrecovered depreciable basis of $90,789 ($100,000 − $9,211). The accelerated rate of 0.09211 is applied to the remaining unrecovered basis to determine the depreciation allowance in a given year, although the IRS supplies taxpayers with depreciation tables similar to those shown in Exhibit 22-4 to simplify the calculations.

Exhibit 22-4 Partial Depreciation Table for Residential Income Property

If Recovery Year Is	Month in the First Recovery Year the Property Is Placed in Service											
	1	2	3	4	5	6	7	8	9	10	11	12
1	3.485	3.182	2.879	2.576	2.273	1.970	1.667	1.364	1.061	0.758	0.455	0.152
2	3.636	3.636	3.636	3.636	3.636	3.636	3.636	3.636	3.636	3.636	3.636	3.636
3	3.636	3.636	3.636	3.636	3.636	3.636	3.636	3.636	3.636	3.636	3.636	3.636
4	3.636	3.636	3.636	3.636	3.636	3.636	3.636	3.636	3.636	3.636	3.636	3.636
5	3.636	3.636	3.636	3.636	3.636	3.636	3.636	3.636	3.636	3.636	3.636	3.636
10	3.637	3.637	3.637	3.637	3.637	3.637	3.636	3.636	3.636	3.636	3.636	3.636
15	3.636	3.636	3.636	3.636	3.636	3.636	3.637	3.637	3.637	3.637	3.637	3.637
20	3.637	3.637	3.637	3.637	3.637	3.637	3.636	3.636	3.636	3.636	3.636	3.636
25	3.636	3.636	3.636	3.636	3.636	3.636	3.637	3.637	3.637	3.637	3.637	3.637
29	0.000	0.000	0.000	0.000	0.000	0.000	0.152	0.455	0.758	1.061	1.364	1.667

Personal property that is eligible for three- and seven-year cost recovery periods can be depreciated using 200 percent declining balance depreciation, with a switch over to straight-line depreciation when it yields a larger deduction. Personal property eligible for a 15-year cost recovery period (e.g., land improvements) can be depreciated using the 150 percent declining balance method. For convenience, the appropriate calculation methods are built into available IRS tables, so it is not necessary to calculate the appropriate percentages.[12]

Example   Calculating Annual Depreciation

On September 21, 2001, Mr. Smith purchased an apartment building for $800,000. Of this amount, $700,000 is allocated to the value of the depreciable real property improvements. Because September is the ninth month of the year, Mr. Smith uses column 9 in Exhibit 22-4. For tax year 1, the percentage is 1.061. Therefore, Mr. Smith is allowed a deduction of $7,427 (0.01061 × $700,000). In tax years 2 through 28, the deduction will be 3.636, or 3.637, percent of $700,000, or $25,452. In tax year 29, if he has not yet disposed of the property, Mr. Smith's depreciation deduction will be $5,306 (0.00758 × $700,000). The 0.758 percent in year 29 is equal to the percent of the original depreciable basis not depreciated in years 1 through 28.

Substantial Improvements. Under current tax rules, capital expenditures made in the years *after* the initial purchase are, effectively, treated as a separate building (if real property) or a separate improvement (if personal property). Thus, total depreciation in a given year will equal the depreciation deductions available on the original depreciable bases for real and personal property, plus the allowable deduction on the subsequent capital expenditures. For example, if the roof on Mr. Smith's $800,000 apartment property is replaced for $30,000 at the end of year 10, the $30,000 roof expenditure would be depreciated on a straight-line basis over the next 27½ years. Thus, in years 11 through 27 of the investment, the total allowable depreciation deduction (*DEP*) would equal the sum of the original annual deduction ($25,452), plus the allowable deduction on the $30,000 roof replacement.

Concept Check

22.7   Assume some office furniture recently purchased by the owner of a small office property can be depreciated over seven years using a 200 percent declining balance depreciation. What percent of the acquisition price of the office furniture can be claimed as a depreciation deduction in year 1?

---

12. In early 2003 President George W. Bush signed legislation that provides a 50 percent depreciation "bonus" for investments in personal property and tenant improvements on commercial (i.e., nonresidential) properties that would normally be depreciated in 20 years or less. For example, assume an owner makes a $10,000 investment in land improvements that would ordinarily be depreciated over 15 years using a 150 percent declining balance depreciation. The accelerated depreciation percentage is 0.10 [1.5 × (1 ÷ 15)]. Thus, the first year deduction would be $1,000 in the absence of the bonus depreciation (0.10 × $10,000). Given that the expenditure would qualify for the new bonus depreciation, the owner could actually claim a $5,500 first-year deduction composed of two parts. First, the owner may deduct 50 percent of the improvements costs in year 1, or $5,000 (0.50 × $10,000). Second, the remaining $5,000 in depreciable basis would be depreciated normally; that is, over 15 years using 150 percent declining balance depreciation. This would generate an additional first-year deduction of $500 (0.10 × $5,000) for a total deduction of $5,500. This new provision increases further the incentive for owners and investors to classify property expenditures as personal property or land improvements. At the time of this writing, however, the bonus depreciation provision was set to expire by year-end 2004.

Tax Credits

Current tax law allows investors to take tax credits for the cost of rehabilitating older or historic structures and for the construction and rehabilitation of qualified low-income housing. It is important to understand the difference between a deduction and a credit. A credit is a dollar-for-dollar reduction of tax liability. Thus, a $1 tax credit reduces the investor's tax liability by one dollar. A deduction, however, is a dollar-for-dollar reduction in taxable income. As a result, a deduction benefits the taxpayer only to the extent of his or her marginal tax bracket. To illustrate, a $1 deduction for an investor in the 30 percent tax bracket, reduces the tax liability by $0.30 ($1 × 0.30).

Why do rehabilitation tax credits exist? Because our elected officials believe that without these tax incentives the private market will not adequately provide for the rehabilitation of older and historic structures and will underproduce housing units for low-income households. The rehabilitation investment tax credit is a subsidy feature of the tax code designed to encourage investment in the preservation of still-useful and historically significant structures.

Provided expenditures meet carefully specified criteria, the rehabilitation investment tax credit may be taken at one of two levels:

1. A 10 percent credit may be taken each year on qualified rehabilitation expenditures on nonresidential structures placed in service before 1936.
2. A 20 percent credit may be taken each year for rehabilitation expenditures on nonresidential structures or residential structures that are rental properties, so long as the property is on the National Register of Historic Places or nominated for placement.[13]

For example, suppose a developer buys a National Register property for $200,000 and spends $500,000 in 2004 on restoration and repairs approved by the Department of the Interior. The developer's 2004 tax credit is $100,000 (0.20 × $500,000).

To qualify for the 10 percent rehabilitation credit, the project must leave at least 50 percent of the building's existing external walls intact and functional. In addition, at least 75 percent of the building's internal structural framework must be kept in place. The historic property tax credit (20 percent) regulations are even more restrictive with respect to the use of materials, construction methods, and building redesign to preserve the historic character of the structures. Thus, redevelopers of nonresidential properties may opt for the 10 percent tax credit because of the less restrictive provisions.

Concept Check

22.8   What is the difference between a tax credit and a tax deduction?

Low-Income Housing. The 1986 Tax Reform Act replaced all previous tax incentives on **low-income housing** with a new system that entitles taxpayers who construct or rehabilitate qualified low-income housing units to benefit from tax credits. Under the Low-Income Housing Tax Credit (LIHTC) program, the present value of these tax credits is determined by several rules, but can be as much as 70 percent of the total acquisition costs (or development costs) over 10 years. Unlike tax credits for rehabilitating older property, low-income housing credits may be used to offset active and portfolio income. To qualify as low-income housing, a project must set aside a certain number of units for lower-income households. The project must also meet a maximum rent restriction, follow special rules for existing housing, and obtain state credit authorization and certification.

---

13. The National Register of Historic Places is a list of properties, areas, and districts that are unique or have some historic significance. The register is maintained by the U.S. Department of the Interior. Placement on the register is made through nomination by a local historic properties committee.

Beyond the important role the LIHTC program has played in providing housing units for low- and moderate-income households, the program has contributed significantly to the overall construction of apartment units. It is estimated, for example, that the LIHTC program accounted for over 25 percent of all multifamily housing permits during the 1987–1999 time period. Nevertheless, critics contend the program is overly complex and not well designed to serve the needs of low-income—as opposed to moderate-income—households. Methods to expand and improve the LIHTC program continue to be debated in academic and public policy forums.

Centre Point Office Building: Taxes from Operations

In order to add the estimated income tax effects to the DCF analysis of our Centre Point office building example, assume the following: 80 percent of the $885,000 Centre Point acquisition price ($708,000) is allocable to depreciable real property; 20 percent ($177,000) is allocated to nondepreciable land (for simplicity we assume no personal property); and the investor's tax rate on ordinary income is 30 percent. The remaining assumptions for the Centre Point example are contained in Exhibit 16-1.

Following the general format displayed in Exhibit 22-3, five-year projections of taxable income and tax liability from operations are reported in Exhibit 22-5. After-tax cash flows (*ATCF*s) from operations are displayed in Exhibit 22-6. Given the assumptions in Exhibit 16-1—(*PGI*) increasing 3 percent per year, 10 percent vacancy and collection losses, operating expenses at 40 percent of (*EGI*), capital expenditures at 5 percent of

Exhibit 22-5 Expected Taxes from Operations

	Year				
	1	**2**	**3**	**4**	**5**
Net operating income (*NOI*)	$89,100	$91,773	$94,526	$97,362	$100,283
+ Capital expenditures (*CAPX*)	8,100	8,343	8,593	8,851	9,117
− Interest (*INT*)	52,900	52,439	51,941	51,401	50,817
− Depreciation (*DEP*)	18,154	18,154	18,154	18,154	18,154
− Amortized financing costs (*AFC*)	664	664	664	664	17,258[†]
= Taxable income (*TI*)	25,483*	28,859	32,361*	35,994	23,171
× Ordinary tax rate (*TR*)	0.30	0.30	0.30	0.30	0.30
= Tax liability (*TAX*)	7,645	8,658	9,708	10,798	6,951

[†]Unamortized up-front financing costs = $19,912.5 − 4 ($663.75) = $17,257.5 or $17,258.

*Subtraction discrepancy due to rounding

Exhibit 22-6 Centre Point Office Building: Expected After-Tax Cash Flow from Operations

	Year				
	1	**2**	**3**	**4**	**5**
Net operating income (*NOI*)	$89,100	$91,773	$94,526	$97,362	$100,283
− Debt service (*DS*)	58,444	58,444	58,444	58,444	58,444
= Before-tax cash flow (*BTCF*)	30,656	33,329	36,082	38,918	41,838*
− Tax liability (*TAX*)	7,645	8,658	9,708	10,798	6,951
= After-tax cash flow (*ATCF*)	23,011	24,671	26,374	28,119*	34,887

*Subtraction discrepancy due to rounding.

EGI—net operating income (*NOI*) is expected to increase from $89,100 in year 1 to $100,283 in year 5. Capital expenditures (*CAPX*) are added back to net operating income because they are not deductible when incurred, even if they represent actual cash expenditures.

The $885,000 Centre Point acquisition price is to be financed with a 75 percent, 30-year, 8 percent monthly payment loan. Total up-front financing costs will equal 3 percent of the $663,750 (0.75 × $885,000) loan amount, or $19,913. The total mortgage payment in each year (*DS*) is $58,444, of which $52,900 is deductible interest in year 1. The amount of deductible interest (INT) decreases each year as the loan balanced is amortized. The $19,913 in up-front financing costs is not immediately deductible; rather, the cost is amortized over the life of the loan. This generates a $664 (*AFC*) deduction each year ($19,913 ÷ 30). If the property is sold in year 5, the unamortized financing costs of $17,258 may be deducted in full. Finally, as real property, the investment can be depreciated over 39 years using straight-line depreciation. Therefore, the annual depreciation allowance (ignoring the midmonth convention) is $18,154 ($708,000 ÷ 39). Taxable income in year 1 is expected to be $25,483; with a 30 percent ordinary tax rate, this produces an estimated tax liability of $7,645. This estimated tax liability is subtracted from the $30,656 *BTCF* to produce a projected *ATCF* of $23,011.[14]

What Is a Tax Shelter?

Sometimes in real estate investments, mortgage interest and depreciation deductions are so large relative to net operating income that taxable income is negative. As discussed previously, commercial real estate investors are able to use negative taxable income from one rental real estate investment to offset positive taxable income from other rental real estate investments.

Suppose a property in its first year of operations after acquisition is expected to generate $20,000 in before-tax cash flow. Also assume the tax calculation yields a negative taxable income of $10,000. Given an assumed 35 percent tax rate, a *negative* $3,500 tax liability is projected. The after-tax cash flow is shown in Exhibit 22-7.

It could be argued that taxable income on a particular project is either positive or zero—if allowable deductions exceed rental income the **excess deductions** are wasted. However, if an investor can use the excess deductions from the project to offset ordinary income from other investments—that is, if the passive activity loss restrictions discussed earlier are not binding—the excess deductions are not wasted because they produce additional tax savings for the investor. Thus, if the investor has $10,000 in negative taxable income from a real estate investment, $10,000 of positive taxable income from other passive investments may be sheltered; for a taxpayer in the 35 percent bracket, $3,500 is saved in

Exhibit 22-7 Taxable Liability versus After-Tax Cash Flow

=	*TI*	$(10,000)	=	*BTCF*	$20,000
×	*TR*	0.35	−	*TAX*	$ (3,500)
=	*TAX*	$ (3,500)	=	*ATCF*	$23,500

14. It should be pointed out that "year 1" in DCF projections should represent the 12 months immediately following the acquisition. Thus, if the property is purchased and placed into service on April 1, 2004, estimated cash flows in year 1 should represent income and expenses received and incurred during the April 2004 through March 2005 time period. However, income taxes are paid on a calendar year (January–December) basis. Thus, the investor's first year of ownership does not usually align perfectly with the tax year. For simplicity, the calculations presented in this chapter assume the tax year and the year of ownership directly correspond; that is, we implicitly assume that cash flows occur on a calendar year basis.

Exhibit 22-8 Calculating Cash Flow from Sale

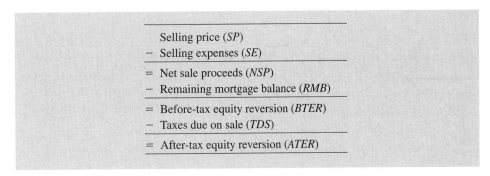

taxes. Note that the additional $3,500 in tax savings occurs only if the property is purchased by the taxpayer; thus, the tax savings are directly attributable to the investment.[15]

Concept Check

22.9   How can the tax liability in a real estate pro forma be negative? Isn't the potential tax liability either positive or zero?

Estimating Tax Liabilities from Sale

The previous sections discuss the calculation of income taxes from annual property operations. This section focuses on the tax liability associated with the disposition of the property. The treatment of gains from property dispositions falls into two general categories:

1. "Fully taxable" sale treatment when the seller receives full payment in the year of sale and taxable gains are fully recognized for tax purposes in the year of sale.
2. Tax-deferred arrangements, including installment sales and like-kind exchanges, in which a portion of the sale proceeds and realized taxable gain is not fully recognized until a later year, if ever.

The calculation of taxable gains from fully taxable sales is discussed first. Two popular tax-deferral strategies—installment sales and like-kind exchanges—are then briefly considered.

Fully Taxable Sale

When sellers of commercial properties effectively receive the full sale price at closing, the sale is treated as a fully taxable sale. This means the realized taxable gain must be fully recognized for tax purposes in the year of the sale, and the associated tax liability must be paid. The estimate of taxes due on sale (*TDS*) is subtracted from the before-tax equity reversion (*BTER*) to produce the projected after-tax equity reversion (*ATER*). The general form for the calculation of the *ATER* is shown in Exhibit 22-8.

Adjusted Basis. The starting point in the calculation of taxes due on sale is the **adjusted basis (*AB*)** of the property at the end of the expected holding period. The *AB* is equal to the original cost basis of the property (*OB*), plus additional real property or personal property capital expenditures (*CAPX*), minus the cumulative amount of tax depreciation that has

---

15. The alternative minimum tax (*AMT*) also may affect the tax consequences of real estate investments. Individuals must pay the higher of their regular tax liability or their minimum tax liability. Discussion of the *AMT* is beyond the scope of this chapter.

Exhibit 22-9   Calculating the Adjusted Basis

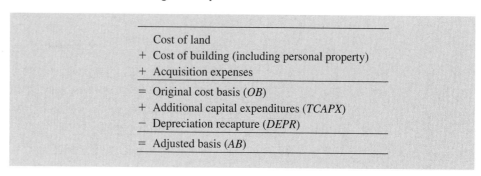

Cost of land
+ Cost of building (including personal property)
+ Acquisition expenses

= Original cost basis (*OB*)
+ Additional capital expenditures (*TCAPX*)
− Depreciation recapture (*DEPR*)

= Adjusted basis (*AB*)

Exhibit 22-10   Calculating Taxable Gain or Loss on Sale

Net sale proceeds (*NSP*)
− Adjusted basis (*AB*)

= Total gain/loss (*TG*)

been taken since the property was placed in service as a rental property, **depreciation recapture** (*DEPR*). The *OB* at acquisition is equal to the original acquisition price—land, building(s), and personal property—plus acquisition expenses (e.g., attorney fees, appraisal fee, and survey costs). Calculation of the adjusted basis, which is sometimes called the "book value" of the property, is summarized in Exhibit 22-9.

Taxable Gain or Loss. For tax purposes, the total gain or loss on the sale of the property is equal to the net sale proceeds minus the adjusted basis. Any excess of the net sale proceeds (*NSP*) over the *AB* results in a taxable gain; any deficit results in a taxable loss, as seen in Exhibit 22-10.

The difference between the before-tax equity reversion (*BTER*) in Exhibit 22-8 and the IRS's definition of the total gain (*TG* in Exhibit 22-10) should be stressed. Similar to taxable income from operations, the total amount of taxable income from the sale is *not* equal to the *BTER*. Thus, multiplying the *BTER* by the capital gain tax rate to determine the taxes due on sale (*TDS*) is incorrect. Separate "tax" and "cash" calculations must be performed.

Concept Check

22.10   Why are taxes due on sale not equal to the before-tax equity reversion times the appropriate tax rate?

Types of Income Generated by a Sale. All taxable income from property sales must eventually be classified as either ordinary income, depreciation recapture income, or capital gain income. The distinctions are important because capital gain income, under the tax rules in place in 2003, is subject to a maximum 15 percent tax rate. Because the maximum statutory tax rate on ordinary income is 35 percent (in 2003), taxpayers can benefit greatly by having income classified as a long-term capital gain instead of ordinary income. As we shall see below, the portion of a positive gain from sale that results from tax depreciation is taxed at a third rate—referred to as the **depreciation recapture rate.** This rate cannot exceed 25 percent.

Exhibit 22-11 Calculating Taxes Due on Sale

Net Sale Proceeds > Original Cost Basis

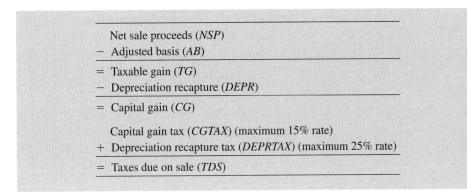

To qualify for the lower capital gain tax rates, the real property being sold must satisfy two criteria. First, the property must be held for more than 12 months to qualify as a long-term investment and thus be subject to favorable capital gain tax rates. The taxable gain on the sale of a property purchased and sold within a single tax year is considered short term and is taxed at the seller's ordinary income tax rate. Second, even if the property is held for at least 12 months, the entire gain on sale could still be taxed at ordinary tax rates if the IRS classifies the asset as dealer property; that is, property held as inventory for sale to others, not as trade or business or investment property. The remainder of this discussion assumes the properties in question are not personal residences, were purchased at least 12 months prior to sale and are not dealer property. The taxation of gains from the sale of a personal residence is discussed at the end of the chapter.

Taxation of Income from a Fully Taxable Sale. As displayed in Exhibit 22-11, if the net sale proceeds exceed the original cost basis, the taxable gain on the sale of depreciable real estate has two components and each is taxed at different rates.

The depreciation recapture component of the taxable gain (*DEPR*) is equal to the total amount of depreciation taken since purchase. The remainder of the taxable gain is the capital gain component ($CG = TG - DEPR$). Note that *CG* is the amount the original acquisition price (and any subsequent capital improvements) has increased in value (net of selling expenses) since acquisition. As summarized in Exhibit 22-11, total taxes due on sale (*TDS*) are equal to the capital gain tax liability, plus the tax on accumulated depreciation ($TDS = CGTAX + DEPRTAX$). (We discuss what happens if the net sale proceeds are *less* than the original cost basis in the section below titled "Section 1231 property.")

But what tax rate do we apply to these two taxable gain components? As of May 6, 2003, there are three possibilities:

1. **10 percent rate.** Individuals who are in the 10 percent ordinary tax bracket (see Exhibits 22-1 and 22-2) pay a rate of 10 percent on any long-term capital gains and on accumulated depreciation. Individuals in the 15 percent ordinary bracket also pay a rate of 10 percent on long-term capital gains.
2. **15 percent rate.** For individuals (not corporations) whose tax rate on ordinary income equals or exceeds 25 percent, the maximum capital gain tax rate is 15 percent.[16] The 15 percent rate also applies to depreciation recapture income if the individuals ordinary rate is 15 percent.
3. **25 percent accumulated depreciation rate.** For individuals whose ordinary tax rate is 25 percent or higher, a 25 percent rate is applied to the portion of the capital gain that results from the use of depreciation over the holding period.

16. From 1997 to May 6, 2003, the maximum capital gain tax rate was 20 percent.

Exhibit 22-12 Tax Rates on Ordinary and Capital Gain Income, and Cumulative Depreciation When Depreciable Real Estate Is Sold

Ordinary rates (*TR*)	10%	15%	25%	28%	33%	35%
Rates on taxable gain from sale if held less than 12 months	10%	15%	25%	28%	33%	35%
Rates on capital gain income (properties held at least 12 months)	10%	10%	15%	15%	15%	15%
Rates applied to the depreciation recapture portion of gain	10%	15%	25%	25%	25%	25%

Why the higher tax rate on the portion of the taxable gain that results from accumulated depreciation? One explanation is that this portion of the gain did not result from appreciation in the market value of the property; rather, it resulted from prior depreciation allowances that have already produced significant tax savings for the investor. At sale, the IRS wants some of these prior tax savings back and therefore assesses a 25 percent tax rate on the depreciation recapture portion of the gain. Most investors still come out ahead, though, because the rate at which they deducted their prior depreciation allowances usually exceeds the depreciation recapture rate. The tax rates that apply to ordinary income, capital gain income, and depreciation recapture income are summarized in Exhibit 22-12.

Example   Taxes Due on Sale

Mary Lucy is selling an industrial warehouse facility for $1,650,000, from which she will net $1,600,000 after deductible selling expenses. She originally purchased the property eight years ago for $1,000,000 (her original cost basis). During her ownership, Mary Lucy claimed a total of $160,000 in depreciation deductions. Therefore, her adjusted basis is $840,000 ($1,000,000 − $160,000). As displayed in Exhibit 22-13, her taxable gain is $760,000. Because her tax rate on ordinary income is 33 percent, Mary Lucy will pay a rate of 25 percent on the depreciation recapture portion of the gain, or $160,000. The capital gain component of $600,000 will be taxed at the 15 percent maximum capital gain rate. Her total taxes due on sale will therefore be $130,000.

Although the accumulated depreciation portion of the total gain is taxed at a higher rate, Mary Lucy benefited substantially from the depreciation allowances. The depreciation she took during her ownership lowered her ordinary taxable income, which was probably being taxed at ordinary rates between 30 and 40 percent.[17] Moreover, her depreciation deductions enabled her to realize those savings earlier, while paying only a portion of the tax savings back much later to the IRS.

Exhibit 22-13 Taxes Due on Sale of Mary Lucy's Industrial Property

	Net sale proceeds (*NSP*)	$1,600,000
−	Adjusted basis (*AB*)	840,000
=	Taxable gain (*TG*)	760,000
−	Depreciation recapture (*DEPR*)	160,000
=	Capital gain (*CG*)	600,000
	Capital gain tax (*CGTAX*) (15%)	90,000
+	Depreciation recapture tax (*DEPRTAX*) (25%)	40,000
=	Taxes due on sale (*TDS*)	$ 130,000

17. Maximum federal tax rates declined in the early 2000s.

22-1

Recapture Rate Catch Trims Tax-Cut Benefits

Real-estate investors beware: Just because the 2003 tax law reduced capital gains taxes, it doesn't mean all gains on property sales will be taxed at the lower rate.

That's because of a quirky concept called depreciation recapture. Under the tax code, when an owner sells a property, the Internal Revenue Service recaptures, through a tax, the deductions that the owner received for depreciation while he or she owned the property. The new law lowered the capital gains tax rate to 15 percent from 20 percent. But, much to the disappointment of the real estate industry, it didn't change the recapture tax rate. It remains at 25 percent.

Consider someone whose tax rate on ordinary income is 35 percent and who buys a commercial property for $100,000 and holds onto it for 10 years. When depreciated on a 39-year schedule, the property's adjusted tax basis is about $75,000. If the owner sells the property for $110,000, that would represent a $35,000 taxable gain. But only $10,000 of that gain would be taxed at the lower 15 percent capital gains rate. The other $25,000, which represents the accumulated depreciation over 10 years, would still be taxed at the 25 percent rate.

While leading real estate organizations welcome the reduction in the capital gains tax rate, they aren't happy the law didn't reduce the recapture tax rate. Stefan F. Tucker, a partner at the law firm Venable LLP, in Washington, says the recapture rate mismatch with capital gains is an issue a lot of his clients are poring over. "It's a major factor in thinking through what you're going to do," he says. "If my gain is all going to be taxed at 15 percent, why not sell, but if a good part of it is going to be taxed at 25 percent, then why sell?"

Source: Adapted from Ray A. Smith "Recapture-Rate Catch Trims Tax-Cut Benefits," *The Wall Street Journal Online*, July 2003.
www.realestatejournal.com

Corporate Tax Rates. We have emphasized numerous times that whenever possible, commercial real estate investors avoid establishing themselves as corporations. Limited liability companies (LLCs), limited partnerships, and subchapter S corporations are preferred to corporate structures because these ownership forms allow investors to obtain limited liability and avoid the double taxation faced by corporations. Although recent tax law changes have reduced the maximum capital gain tax rate paid by individuals from 28 percent to 15 percent, as of 2003 the maximum capital gain tax rate for corporations remains at 35 percent.

Section 1231 Property. As discussed at the beginning of the chapter, virtually all developed commercial real estate is classified as "trade or business" property. Moreover, trade or business property is referred to as a Section 1231 property if it is held by the taxpayer more than one year. Our industrial property example implicitly assumes that Mary Lucy owns just one Section 1231 property. Often, however, investors have a variety of Section 1231 assets, including rental properties, which produce taxable gains and losses when sold. If so, taxes due on sale are not separately calculated for each property and then added up. Instead, at the end of the tax year, all Section 1231 gains are netted against Section 1231 losses. If the netting process produces a net loss, the entire amount is treated as an ordinary loss that is deductible, *without limit,* against the taxpayer's ordinary (wage and salary) income. If the netting process, however, produces a net gain, but a gain that is less than or equal to total accumulated depreciation on all Section 1231 assets, the entire net gain is taxed at the taxpayer's depreciation recapture tax rate. Finally, if the 1231 netting process produces a net gain that is positive and greater than total accumulated depreciation, then the depreciation recapture portion of the net gain is taxed at the recapture rate and the capital gain portion is taxed at the investor's capital gain tax rate, as indicated in Exhibit 22-11 and 22-13.[18]

18. An exception to this rule requires that net Section 1231 gains be treated as ordinary income to the extent that the taxpayer deducted net 1231 losses during the previous five years.

For example, assume Gary receives $87,000 in salary income and has $20,000 of Section 1231 gains and $30,000 of Section 1231 losses in the current year. Gary has no other income, losses, or deductions affecting his adjusted gross income (*AGI*). The net Section 1231 loss of $10,000 is treated as an ordinary loss; thus, Gary's *AGI* is $77,000 ($87,000 salary − $10,000 of ordinary loss). This example illustrates one important advantage to classifying rental property as a Section 1231 asset. Because the net Section 1231 loss is treated as ordinary income, it is fully deductible against active and portfolio income in the current year.

In sharp contrast, if taxpayers realize a loss on the sale of an investment asset, they may use this loss to offset positive capital gains. However, if this nettings procedure produces a net loss on investment asset dispositions, the net loss is deductible to the extent of only $3,000 per year for individual taxpayers. Therefore, if the $20,000 in Section 1231 gains and the $30,000 in losses were treated as investment property gains and losses, Gary would have a $10,000 net long-term capital loss, of which only $3,000 would be deductible against Gary's active and portfolio income in the current year.

In short, Section 1231 assets provide the taxpayer with the best of both worlds: net gains from sales in excess of accumulated depreciation are treated as capital gains, but net losses (if they occur) may be written off without limit against ordinary income.

Centre Point Office Building: Taxes Due on Sale

For the Centre Point Office Building, the net sale proceeds (*NSP*) of the property at the end of the five-year holding period are projected to be $974,700. The remaining mortgage balance (*RMB*) at the end of year 5 will be $631,026. Thus, the projected before-tax equity reversion (*BTER*) is $343,674.

Total estimated capital expenditures over the projected five-year holding period are $43,004 (see Exhibit 22-5). For simplicity, we assume these capital expenditures are not depreciated during the expected holding period, but are simply added to the property's tax basis. Thus, total tax depreciation over the five-year holding period will equal the sum of the annual deductions allowed on the original cost basis ($90,769 = $18,153.8 × 5). The adjusted tax basis of the property (including land), after the fifth year of depreciation, will equal $837,235. This calculation is summarized in Exhibit 22-14.

Assuming depreciation recapture is taxed at 25 percent and the capital gain (*CG* = *TG* − *DEPR*) is taxed at 15 percent, the estimated capital gain and depreciation recapture tax liabilities are $7,004 and $22,692, respectively. Thus, taxes due on sale (*TDS*) and the after-tax equity reversion (*ATER*) are $29,697 and $313,977, respectively. These calculations are summarized in Exhibits 22-15 and 22-16.

Exhibit 22-17 graphically displays the tax consequences associated with the sale of the Centre Point Office Building. The taxable gain (*TG*) of $137,465 is equal to (A − C), where A is the estimated net sale proceeds and C is the adjusted basis at the end of year 5. The undepreciated basis of $928,004 (point B) is equal to the original cost basis of $885,000, plus the total capital expenditures of $43,004. The portion of the taxable gain

Exhibit 22-14 Centre Point Office Building Adjusted Basis

Cost of land	$177,000
+ Cost of building	708,000
+ Acquisition expenses	0
= Original cost basis (*OB*)	885,000
+ Additional capital expenditures (*TCAPX*)	43,004
− Depreciation recapture (*DEPR*)	90,769
= Adjusted basis (*AB*)	$837,235

Exhibit 22-15   Centre Point: Taxes Due on Sale

Net sale proceeds (*NSP*)	$974,700
− Adjusted basis (*AB*)	837,235
= Taxable gain (*TG*)	137,465
− Depreciation recapture (*DEPR*)	90,769
= Capital gain (*CG*)	46,696
Capital gain tax (*CGTAX*) (15%)	7,004
+ Depreciation recapture tax (*DEPRTAX*) (25%)	22,692
= Taxes due on sale (*TDS*)	$ 29,697*

*Adding discrepancy due to rounding.

Exhibit 22-16   Centre Point: Estimated Cash Flow from Sale

Net sale proceeds (*NSP*)	$974,700
− Remaining mortgage balance (*RMB*)	631,026
= Before-tax equity reversion (*BTER*)	343,674
− Taxes due on sale (*TDS*)	29,697
= After-tax equity reversion (*ATER*)	$ 313,977

Exhibit 22-17   Components of Taxable Gain on Sale

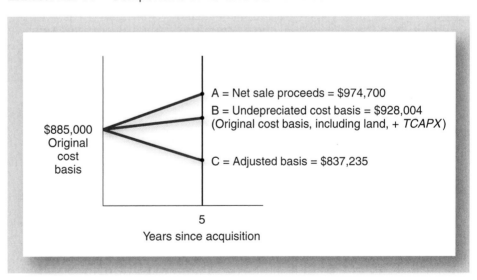

attributable to appreciation in the value of the property (*CG*) is $46,696 (A − B), while the portion due to depreciation recapture (*DEPR*) is $90,769 (B − C).

What would be the total taxable gain if the net sale proceeds were equal to $928,004, which is the original cost basis plus capital expenditures? One might be tempted to conclude that no taxes would be due on sale if the taxpayer invested $928,004 in the property and then netted the same amount from the sale at the end of five years. However, a taxable gain of $90,769 would still be reported, an amount equal to total tax depreciation over the five years.

Net Benefits of Tax Depreciation

Tax depreciation shelters a portion of annual operating income (*NOI*) from taxation. This tax-sheltering ability, perhaps constrained by passive activity loss restrictions, reduces the annual tax liability of investors who own commercial property. However, cumulative tax depreciation (*DEPR*) is taxed only when the property is sold. Thus, the *net* benefit of tax depreciation is reduced by the present value of the increased taxes due on sale that result from depreciation recapture.

Consider, for example, the Centre Point Office Building that will generate an annual depreciation deduction of $18,154. This deduction shelters $18,154 in *NOI* that would otherwise be taxed at a 30 percent rate, thereby saving the taxpayer $5,446 in taxes (0.30 × $18,154) each year for five years, or $27,231 (0.30 × $90,769) over five years.

However, when the property is sold, taxes due on sale will be $22,692 greater (0.25 × $90,769) than if the property had not been depreciated. The net benefit of depreciation over the five-year period, assuming an 11.2 percent discount rate, is therefore:

$$Net\ benefit\ of\ depreciation = \sum_{y=1}^{5} \frac{0.30 \times (\$18,154)}{(1.112)^y} - \frac{\$22,692}{(1.112)^5}$$

$$= \$20,028 - \$13,346 = \$6,682$$

The present value of the annual tax savings is $20,028. The present value of the tax on depreciation recapture is $13,346. The *net* present value of deferring $90,769 in taxable income over five years is therefore $6,682.

This calculation demonstrates that the primary tax advantage of depreciation is that it provides **deferral benefits.** Income that would have been taxed at ordinary rates—$18,154 per year in our example—is, effectively, not taxed until the property is sold. In a sense, the IRS "loans" the investor the $27,231 (0.30 × $18,154 × 5) over the five-year period, and it is not repaid until the property is sold. This amounts to an interest-free loan from the IRS. And because the 25 percent rate on accumulated depreciation is less than the 30 percent ordinary rate (at which the taxpayer deducts annual depreciation), the interest rate on the loan will be negative because the investor will "pay back" in the year of sale an amount ($22,692) that is smaller than what was "borrowed" ($27,231) during the operating years. Said differently, in addition to deferring taxes to the year of sale, depreciation allows the Centre Point investor to "convert" ordinary income (taxed at 30 percent) to income taxed at 25 percent upon sale.[19]

Concept Check

22.11   What are the deferral benefits of depreciation?

Effect of Taxes on Values and Returns

The after-tax cash flows from the Centre Point Office Building are summarized in Exhibit 22-18. The initial equity investment is equal to:

$$E = \$885,000 - (\$663,750 - \$19,913) = \$241,163$$

where $663,750 (0.75 × $885,000) is the face amount of the loan and $19,913 is the amount of the up-front financing costs (0.03 × $663,750).

Given the required equity investment of $241,163, the estimated *ATCF*s from annual operations (Exhibit 22-5), and the estimated *ATER* (Exhibit 22-6), we are now in a position to calculate the levered, after-tax net present value (*NPV*) and internal rate of return (*IRR*) for Centre Point. Recall that in Chapter 16 we discounted the levered, before-tax, cash

---

19. The tax rate on the depreciation portion of the total gain, equal to 25 percent in our example, is referred to in tax publications as the "depreciation recapture" tax rate.

Exhibit 22-18 Cash Flows from Centre Point Office Building

Year	After-Tax Cash Flows	After-Tax Equity Reversion	Total Cash Flow	Present Value Factor @ 11.2%	Present Value
0	($241,163)		$(241,163)	0.000000	$(241,163)
1	23,011		23,011	0.899281	20,693
2	24,671		24,671	0.808706	19,952
3	26,374		26,374	0.727253	19,181
4	28,119		28,119	0.654005	18,390
5	34,887	313,977	348,864	0.588134	205,179
				Net present value =	$ 42,232
				Internal rate of return =	15.5%

Exhibit 22-19 Effect of Debt and Taxes on the Internal Rate of Return and Net Present Value Centre Point Office Building

	IRR	NPV
Unlevered, before-tax cash flows (*NOI*s)	12.2%	$15,181 (with 11.75% discount rate)
Levered, before-tax cash flows (*BTCF*s)	20.3%	$38,191 (with 16.0% discount rate)
Levered, after-tax cash flows (*ATCF*s)	15.5%	$42,232 (with 11.2% discount rate)

flows from Centre Point at a 16 percent rate because we assumed that if an investor did not purchase Centre Point, he or she could invest in an alternative project, of similar risk, and earn a 16 percent before-tax return.

However, as we argued in Chapter 16, the investor is not giving up a 16 percent *after-tax* return by acquiring Centre Point; by not investing in the alternative asset, the investor would be forgoing the 16 percent before-tax return, minus the taxes that would be paid on the 16 percent return. Assuming a tax rate of 30 percent on ordinary income, the investor is giving up an 11.2 percent after-tax return [16% $\times$ (1 − 0.30)] by acquiring Centre Point. Thus, 11.2 percent is an appropriate after-tax discount rate. With these assumptions, the present value of the *ATCF*s and the *ATER* is $283,395, yielding an *NPV* of $42,232 and a going-in *IRR* of 15.5 percent. The project should therefore be accepted.[20]

Exhibit 22-19 summarizes the effects of debt financing and income taxes on the *IRR* associated with our Centre Point office building example. Income taxes reduce the levered going-in *IRR* from 20.3 percent to 15.5 percent. Note that the after-tax *IRR* is not simply 30 percent (the ordinary income tax rate) lower than the before-tax IRR. In fact, the after-tax *IRR* is just 24 percent lower than the before-tax *IRR* [1 − (15.5 ÷ 20.3)]. Twenty-four percent is the **effective tax rate;** that is, the actual percentage amount by which taxes reduce the going-in internal rate of return. The effective tax rate of 24 percent is lower than the 30 percent ordinary tax rate primarily because of the value of tax deferral. As discussed above, depreciation allows the Centre Point investor to defer a portion of operating taxes until the property is sold. Second, depreciation allows the investor to convert ordinary income that would be taxed at a rate of 30 percent into depreciation recapture income that is taxed at 25 percent upon sale. The value of deferral and conversion benefits increase as the length of the assumed holding period increases.

20. The *NPV* and *IRR* also can be solved for using the cash flow (*CF*) keys of a financial calculator.

22.12   The before-tax going-in *IRR* on a shopping center acquisition is 13 percent. The after-tax *IRR* is 10.4 percent. What is the effective tax rate on the investment?

If the inclusion of taxes reduces the going-in internal rate of return by 24 percent to 15.5 percent, why does the net present value *increase* slightly from $38,191 to $42,232? Because we assumed that the appropriate discount rate to apply to these after-tax cash flows is 11.2, or 70 percent of the assumed 16 percent before-tax rate. Thus, although income taxes reduce the investor's cash flows from the Centre Point investment, this reduction is more than offset by the assumed reduction in the opportunity cost of invested equity.

Complications Caused by Alternative Ownership Forms

The calculated 15.5 percent after-tax internal rate of return assumes Centre Point will be purchased by an individual investor facing a 30 percent ordinary tax rate. However, the majority of commercial properties in the United States are owned by multiple investors in the form of partnerships, limited liability companies, and other direct ownership entities. When individuals invest together through partnerships and limited liability companies, all cash flow and income tax consequences "flow through" directly to the individual investors. There is no separate entity that pays corporate income taxes and distributes net cash flows to investors in the form of dividends.

Thus, if we assume that Centre Point were going to be purchased, for example, by a limited partnership, additional assumptions would be required in order to estimate internal rates of return for the general and limited partners. In particular, we would need to know what portion of the before tax cash flows and the before tax equity reversion to allocate to the various investors, what portion of the annual taxable incomes and the taxes due on sale to allocate, as well as the tax rates paid by each partner on ordinary and capital gain income in order to estimate investor specific *NPV*s and *IRR*s.[21] Although a discussion of partnership returns is beyond the scope of this chapter, it is important for the reader to understand that the estimate of property-level taxable income and cash flows is just the first step in determining the tax liability and returns expected by various investors in the ownership entity.

Methods of Deferring Taxes on Disposition

The potentially large amount of taxes due on the sale of commercial property can be a significant deterrent to fully taxable sales. Although taxes on gains from property sales generally cannot be eliminated, two methods—installment sales and like-kind exchanges—can be used in certain situations to *defer* the payment of capital gain taxes.

Installment Sale

A popular method for deferring taxes due on the sale of commercial property is the **installment sale.** Under this method, the seller allows the buyer to pay the purchase price over a number of years. In effect, the seller collects a down payment and then "loans" the buyer the remainder of the purchase price. The buyer then makes periodic payments to the seller, which consist of both interest and principal amortization. Because the seller receives a portion of the sale proceeds (i.e., the principal on the installment loan) over a number of years, the IRS allows the seller to pay the taxable capital gain over a number of years. Es-

---

21. For a detailed example of how cash flows and returns to various investors in a limited partnership investment are calculated, see William B. Brueggeman and Jeffrey D. Fisher, *Real Estate Finance and Investments,* 11th ed. (New York: McGraw-Hill Irwin, 2001), chap. 12.

sentially, the timing of the seller's capital gain tax payments is matched with the receipt of the principal on the installment sale loan. The obvious benefit to sellers is that they are not liable for the full amount of taxes due in the year of the sale, as they are with fully taxable sales. Spreading the recognition of the gain over several years reduces the present value of the tax payments.

Is there a disadvantage to installment sales? Presumably, if the seller were to "cash out" of the property with a fully taxable sale, the entire (net-of-tax) sale proceeds could be immediately reinvested in other assets. However, with an installment sale, the seller must wait to receive a portion of the sale proceeds from the buyer. If the interest rate on the installment loan is at least equal to the rate at which sale proceeds could be invested, the use of an installment sale is clearly beneficial: Taxes are deferred and the seller earns at least his or her opportunity cost on the installment loan.

Like-Kind Exchanges

A second popular option for deferring capital gains taxes is the **like-kind exchange.** Section 1031 of the Internal Revenue Code allows owners of real estate, under certain circumstances, to exchange their properties for other properties and avoid paying taxes at the time of the transaction. The primary motivation for a tax-deferred exchange is to alter property ownership status, yet postpone some or all capital gains taxes.[22] Additionally, an exchange may be the best way to market property in a difficult market setting.

To enter into a like kind exchange, property owners must meet the following requirements:

1. The properties in an exchange must be trade or business properties or investment properties, such as land. This means dealer properties and principal residences cannot be included in the tax-deferred part of exchanges.
2. The properties in an exchange must be *like-kind* properties. To satisfy this requirement, real estate cannot be exchanged for personal property such as mortgages, bonds, stocks, farm animals, and so on. However, apartment buildings can be exchanged for office buildings, office buildings for shopping centers, shopping centers for industrial warehouses, and the like. To qualify, U.S. property must be exchanged for U.S. property.
3. Any cash or personal property (i.e., not like-kind property) received in an exchange is generally fully taxable in the year of the exchange.

Like-kind exchanges have become commonplace in recent years. Therefore, although the execution of an exchange requires the assistance of a tax accountant or attorney, real estate investors need to understand how exchanges work and when they are preferable to a fully taxable sale.

www.irs.gov

Download IRS Publication 537 on installment sales.

www.apiexchange.com

Tax-deferred exchange information.

www.wave.net/ immigration/lawyer/ tax_avoid.html

A layman's guide to tax-deferred exchanges.

Concept Check

22.13   What are the two primary alternatives to fully taxable sales in commercial real estate?

Tax Factors Affecting Homeowners

Homeowners receive preferential tax treatment under current federal income tax laws. The primary benefit is that, in most cases, homeowners do not have to report as income any of the return they earn on the equity capital they have invested in their homes. The nontaxed equity return includes any appreciation in the value of the home that has occurred since they purchased it (i.e., the capital gain).

---

22. Like-kind exchanges postpone, but do not eliminate, capital gain taxes because the investor's tax basis in the old property becomes the starting tax basis in the new property.

As previously discussed, federal income taxes are generally due when appreciated assets such as stocks and rental properties are sold. How do homeowners avoid a similar fate? In most cases, single homeowners are permitted to exclude from taxable income up to $250,000 of the capital gain realized on the sale of property that has been used as a principal residence. The exclusion is $500,000 for married couples filing a joint income tax return. To qualify, the taxpayer must have owned and used the property as his or her principal residence for at least two years during the five-year period immediately preceding the sale. The tax exclusion is allowed each time a taxpayer sells a principal residence and meets the eligibility requirements, but generally no more often than once every two years.

Example   Homeowner Capital Gains

Mr. and Mrs. Jones purchased a home for $170,000 in 2000 and occupied it continuously until the home was sold in 2004 for $250,000. No capital improvements were made to the home subsequent to its acquisition in 2000. Because the home was their personal residence, they were not allowed to depreciate it for tax purposes. Thus, the adjusted basis at the time of sale was $170,000 and the realized capital gain was $80,000. However, this gain did not have to be recognized for tax purposes. The Jones would have owed an additional $12,000 in income taxes if this $80,000 gain had been taxed at 15 percent, their regular capital gain tax rate.

Homeowners receive two significant benefits in addition to the nontaxation of their investment returns. First, homeowners are usually allowed to deduct their mortgage interest expenses on first and second homes when calculating their federal income tax liability.[23] Second, local property taxes are also deductible at the federal level. However, losses on the sale of a personal residence are not recognized.[24] In addition, up-front financing costs on a home acquisition are usually fully deductible in the year paid. In contrast, recall that such costs associated with the acquisition of commercial properties must be amortized over the life of the loan.

Summary

Federal income taxes affect real estate decisions in all of the three major phases of the ownership cycle: acquisition, operation, and disposition. The principal decision to be made during the acquisition phase involves the selection of a form of ownership that offers both tax and nontax advantages (e.g., avoidance of personal liability).

Tax shelter benefits from the direct (i.e., noncorporate) ownership of real estate are realized during the operation phase, mainly through allowances for tax depreciation. Depreciation deductions, as a noncash expense, result in lower taxable incomes, thus saving taxes. Current depreciation rules prescribe a 27½-year cost recovery period for residential rental property and a 39-year recovery period for commercial property. But current tax rules regarding passive activity losses may limit investors from fully utilizing the tax shelter benefits of depreciable real estate.

For projects involving the rehabilitation of older nonresidential structures, tax credits may be taken. If a property has historical significance, 20 percent of all qualifying rehabilitation expenditures may be taken as a tax credit, subject to passive activity loss limits. Tax credits are available to all who invest in low-income housing.

23. If the book value of a married couple's mortgage exceeds $1 million, the interest on this mortgage may not be fully deductible. For more information, see IRS publication 936, *Home Mortgage Interest Deductions*, available on the IRS website, www.irs.ustreas.gov.

24. The IRS website contains answers to frequently asked questions about the taxation of owner-occupied housing. Go to www.irs.ustreas.gov and search for your topic of interest.

Real estate investors have three basic options for tax treatment when they sell property: fully taxable sale treatment, installment sale treatment, and like-kind exchange. In a fully taxable sale, investors receive the entire sale proceeds from the buyer in the year of the sale, but must pay any tax liability in that year. Installment sale treatment allows investors to defer tax payments when only a portion of the sale proceeds are received in the year of the installment sale. Finally, real estate investors may exchange their properties for like kind real estate and defer all or some of the capital gain tax liability, so long as the exchanged properties are used in trade or business or held as investments.

Key Terms

Test Problems

1. Taxable income from the rental of actively managed depreciable real estate is classified as:
   a. Active income.
   b. Passive income.
   c. Portfolio income.
   d. Passive income if taxable income is negative; active income if taxable income is positive.

2. Under current federal income tax law, what is the shortest cost recovery period available to investors purchasing residential rental property?
   a. 15 years. d. 39 years.
   b. 19 years. e. None of the above.
   c. 31½ years.

3. If an investor is a "dealer" with respect to certain real estate, then that real estate is classified (by the IRS) as being held:
   a. As a personal residence.
   b. For sale to others.
   c. For use in trade or business.
   d. As an investment.
   e. None of the above.

4. When a property is sold for less than its remaining book value, its depreciation (wear and tear) was:
   a. Estimated correctly.
   b. Underestimated.
   c. Overestimated.
   d. Determined by the owner.

5. For tax purposes, a substantial real property improvement made after the initial purchase is:
   a. Treated like a separate building.
   b. Added to the adjusted basis.
   c. Depreciated like personal property.
   d. Amortized over five years.

6. What percent of the rental income from residential property must be derived from the leasing of units occupied by tenants as housing?
   a. 20 percent. c. 80 percent.
   b. 50 percent. d. 75 percent.

7. In 2004 you purchase a small office building for $450,000, which you financed with a $337,500, 25-year, fixed-rate mortgage. Up-front financing costs total $6,750. How much of this expense could be written off against ordinary income in 2004?
   a. $6,750.00. c. $270.00.
   b. $173.01. d. $245.45.

8. If the investor is in the 33 percent income tax bracket, how much will a tax credit of $2,000 save the investor in taxes?
   a. $2,000. c. $1,340.
   b. $660. d. None of the above.

9. Which of the following best describes the taxation of gain and losses from the sale of Section 1231 assets?
   a. Net gains and net losses are taxed as ordinary income.
   b. Net gains and net losses are taxed as capital gain income.
   c. Net gains are taxed as ordinary income, net losses are taxed as capital gains.
   d. Net gains are taxed as capital gains, net losses are taxed as ordinary income.

10. Which of the following statements is false?
   a. Tax losses on active income can be used to offset positive portfolio income.
   b. Tax losses on portfolio income can be used to offset positive active income.
   c. A loss on the sale of a REIT stock can be used to offset a positive gain on the sale of a corporate bond.
   d. Net passive losses can be used to offset dividend income from a REIT stock.

Study Questions

1. Why do investors generally care whether the IRS classifies cash expenditures as operating expenses rather than capital expenditures?

2. How are the discount "points" associated with financing an income property handled for tax purposes?

   Use the following information to answer questions 3–5:

   Five years ago you purchased a small apartment complex for $1 million. You borrowed $700,000 at 12 percent for 25 years with annual payments. The original depreciable basis was $750,000 and you have used 27½-year straight-line depreciation over the five-year holding period. Assume no capital expenditures have been made since acquisition. If you sell the property today for $1,270,000 in a fully taxable sale:

3. What will be the taxes due on sale? Assume 6 percent selling costs, 33 percent ordinary tax rate, a 15 percent capital gain tax rate, and a 25 percent recapture rate.

4. What will be the after-tax equity reversion (cash flow) from the sale?

5. Over the entire five-year holding period, how much were your taxes from rental operations reduced by the annual depreciation deductions?

6. What are the four classifications of real estate holdings for tax purposes? Which classifications of property can be depreciated for tax purposes?

   Use the following information to answer questions 7–9:

   You have just purchased an apartment complex that has a $100,000 depreciable basis. You are in the 28 percent ordinary tax bracket and 25 percent depreciation recapture bracket. Capital gains will be taxed at 15 percent. You discount future tax benefits from depreciation at 10 percent. Assume for simplicity that you would depreciate the property on a straight-line basis over 28 (*not* 27½) years.

7. What is your annual depreciation deduction?

8. If you never sold the property, what would be the present value of the annual tax savings from depreciation?

9. If you sold the property at the end of five years, what would be the present value of the depreciation deductions, net of all taxes due on sale?

10. Black Acres Apartment, Inc., needs to compute taxable income (*TI*) for the preceding year and wants your assistance. The effective gross income (*EGI*) was $52,500; operating expenses were $19,000; $2,000 was put into a fund for future replacement of stoves and refrigerators; debt service was $26,662, of which $25,126 was interest; and the depreciation deduction was $17,000. Compute the taxable income from operations.

11. You are considering the purchase of a small apartment complex.
    - The purchase price, including acquisition costs, is $1 million.
    - Gross potential income in the first year is estimated at $175,000 and vacancy and collection losses are estimated to be 12 percent of gross potential income.

    - Operating expenses and capital expenditures are expected to be $36,000 and $2,000, respectively, in year 1.
    - The investor will obtain a $700,000 loan at 8 percent annual interest with annual payments for 25 years.
    - Additional up-front financing expenses will equal $25,000.
    - Assume that 25 percent of the purchase price is payment for land and that the building will be depreciated over 27½ years using straight-line depreciation.
    - Your ordinary and capital gain tax rates are 35 and 15 percent, respectively.
    a. Calculate the mortgage payment, the interest deduction, the depreciation deduction, and the amortized financing costs for the first year of operations.
    b. What will be your net equity investment at "time zero"?
    c. Estimate the after-tax cash flows for the first year of operations. Be sure to set up a "tax" table and a "cash" table.

12. Compute the after-tax cash flow from the sale of the following nonresidential property:
    - The purchase price was $450,000.
    - The investor obtained a $360,000 loan.
    - There were no up-front financing costs.
    - The market value of the property increased to $472,500 over the two-year holding period.
    - Selling costs are 6 percent of the sales price.
    - The investor is in the 35 percent ordinary tax bracket.
    - Capital gains will be taxed at 15 percent.
    - The balance of the loan at the time of sale is $354,276.
    - 15 percent of the initial purchase price represented the value of the land and all improvements have been depreciated using straight-line depreciation and a 39-year cost recovery period.
    - $30,000 in capital expenditures have been incurred since acquisition; for simplicity, however, the capital expenditures have been added to the tax basis but not separately depreciated.
    a. Compute the annual depreciation deduction.
    b. Compute the adjusted basis at the time of sale (after two years).
    c. Compute the tax liability from sale.
    d. Compute the after-tax cash flow (equity reversion) from sale.

13. A real estate investor is considering the purchase of an office building. The following assumptions are made:
    - The purchase price is $775,000.
    - The project is a two-story office building containing a total of 34,000 leasable square feet.
    - Gross rents are expected to be $10 per square foot per year.
    - The vacancy rate is expected to be 15 percent of potential gross income per year.
    - Operating expenses are estimated at 45 percent of effective gross income.
    - 75 percent of the purchase price will be financed with a 20-year, monthly amortized, mortgage at an interest rate of 7.5 percent. There will be no up-front financing costs.

- Of the total acquisition price, 75 percent represents depreciable real property improvements (no personal property).
- The investor's ordinary tax rate is 30 percent and the capital gain tax rate is 15 percent.
- Estimated capital expenditures are projected to be $10,000 per year, but these expenditures will not be separately depreciated, although they will be added to the basis.

Answer the following questions for the first year of operations:

a. What is the equity (cash) down payment required at "time zero"?

b. What is the annual depreciation deduction?

c. What is the total amount of debt service?

d. What is the estimated net operating income?

14. A real estate investor is considering purchasing a warehouse. Analysis has resulted in the following facts:
- The asking price is $450,000.
- There are 10,000 square feet of leasable area.
- The expected rent is $5 per square foot per year; rents are expected to increase 5 percent per year. Since the property is leased to an AAA-grade tenant for 25 more years, no vacancy factor is deducted.
- The tenant will pay all operating expenses except property taxes and insurance. These two expenses will equal 20 percent of the effective gross income (*EGI*) each year.
- The investor can borrow 80 percent of the total cost for 20 years at an interest rate of 7 percent with monthly payments and up-front financing costs equal to 3 percent of the amount borrowed.
- 85 percent of the total acquisition cost is depreciable over the useful life of 39 years using the straight-line method (no personal property).
- The investor expects to sell the investment at the end of year 5.
- The investor's ordinary and capital gain tax rates are 30 and 15 percent, respectively.
- No capital expenditures have been made since acquisition.

Compute the after-tax cash flows from annual rental operations.

15. The property to be analyzed is a two-story, multitenant office building containing 10,000 square feet of rentable space. The building is situated on a 25,000-square-foot site that is partially landscaped and contains 35 parking spaces. The property is being offered for $500,000. The investor's ordinary and capital gain tax rates are 28 and 15 percent, respectively.

Multitenant office buildings are sometimes leased on a gross rental basis. In this case, the property owner pays all operating expenses. Income from the building is $10.51 per square foot of rentable area, for a total of $105,100 per year before vacancy losses. Office buildings in the area experience a vacancy rate of 7 percent, on average, of potential gross income.

Table 1 Reconstructed Income and Expense Statement (First Year Pro Forma)

Potential gross income		$105,100
Less: Vacancy at 7.04%		7,400
Effective gross income		$ 97,700
Less: Operating expenses		
Electricity	$2,000	
Water	400	
Sewer fees	30	
Heating fuel	7,600	
Payroll/contract cleaning	3,600	
Cleaning supplies	700	
Janitorial payroll	4,300	
Janitorial supplies	400	
Heating/air-conditioning	2,100	
Electrical repairs	400	
Plumbing repairs	500	
Exterior repairs	400	
Roof repairs	400	
Parking lot repairs	200	
Decorating (tenant)	1,800	
Decorating (public)	400	
Miscellaneous repairs	1,100	
Management fees	4,500	
Other administrative fees	1,000	
Landscaping maintenance	400	
Trash removal	600	
Window washing	200	
Snow removal	2,200	
Miscellaneous services	500	
Total operating expenses		35,730
Real estate taxes		15,800
Net operating income		$ 46,170

Table 1 contains income and expense information for the property (first year pro forma). Expenses were estimated after studying the building's operating history and that of comparable buildings in the area.

A loan of $375,000 is available at 8 percent interest with a 30-year amortization schedule and annual payments.

The investor will use the straight-line depreciation method over a 39-year period. The expected purchase price of $500,000 is allocated 85 percent to building and 15 percent to the land. This allocation is supported by the local tax assessor's records.

Rental income is expected to grow by 8 percent per year. Operating expenses, are expected to grow by 4 percent per year.

The terminal capitalization rate, of 10.0 percent is applied to expected net operating income in year 3 to determine the future sales price in year 2. Selling expenses are

7 percent of the sale price. All passive activity losses (*PAL*) from the investment will be used to shelter income from passive income generators (*PIGs*), of which the investor has a "barn full." Assuming a two-year holding period, should the investor make this investment given a required levered, after-tax rate of return of 14 percent? Defend your answer with quantitative evidence from the analysis you perform.

Explore The Web

Visit the "tax prophet" (actually Robert L. Sommers, attorney-at-law) by going to www.taxprophet.com. Click on the "Tax Class" link and then choose "Real Estate Taxation." Once there, choose the link "The Sale of a Principal Residence." Read a detailed explanation of the $250,000–$500,000 capital gain exclusion available to homeowners.

Solutions to Concept Checks

1. The primary importance of the four income tax classifications is that they determine whether or not the asset can be depreciated for tax purposes.

2. Income earned from salaries, wages, and commissions is classified as active income, income from investments in securities is classified as portfolio income, and income generated from rental real estate investments is passive activity income.

3. Capital expenditures and the principal amortization portion of the mortgage payment are not tax deductible in the year in which they occur. Depreciation and amortized financing costs are deductible expenses not associated with a concurrent cash outflow.

4. Up-front financing costs increase the amount of cash the investor must bring to the closing table when the property is acquired, so the cash flow effect occurs at time zero. For tax purposes, however, the investor must amortize the up-front financing costs over the life of the loan, so the tax effects associated with the time zero outflow occur in small annual amounts over the investment holding period.

5. The "theory" behind depreciation allowances is that buildings, some land improvements, and personal property such as air conditioners and flooring wear out over time and this wear and tear is an unavoidable cost of providing rental services to tenants. Therefore, like other operating costs it makes sense that investors are able to take a tax deduction that approximates this annual wear and tear.

6. You have little incentive to attribute value to the land because it cannot be depreciated. You also have little incentive to attribute value to real property because personal property generates larger depreciation deductions, all else being equal.

7. The depreciation percentage is calculated as:

$$200\% \ declining \ rate = 2.0 \times \frac{1}{Recovery \ period} =$$

$$2.0 \times \frac{1}{7} = 0.2857, \ or \ 28.6\%$$

8. A $1 tax credit reduces the investor's tax *liability* by a dollar. A $1 tax deduction reduces the investor's taxable *income* by a dollar. Thus, the actual tax savings from a deduction depend on the investor's tax rate (tax savings = deduction × tax rate).

9. To understand why it does make sense to show a negative tax liability if taxable income is negative, the reader must first understand that investment analysis is an *incremental* analysis. That is, investors must decide whether or not to acquire an asset, given what they already hold in their portfolios. So, if a potential real estate investment is expected to produce negative taxable income, the excess deductions are not necessarily wasted. For example, the property owner may have wage or salary income, dividend income from stocks, interest income from Treasury securities, and perhaps even income from other rental properties. If the negative taxable income from the potential real estate investment can be used to reduce the amount of other income the investor must report for tax purposes, the investor's overall tax liability is reduced and the tax savings are expected to result directly from the real estate investment. Thus, it does make sense in a pro forma to show a negative tax liability if taxable income is negative.

10. The tax consequences of a fully taxable sale are not determined by the amount of cash a sale generates. Rather, the taxable gain is a function of the relationship between the net sale proceeds and the adjusted tax basis. Moreover, the *adjusted* basis is not the original cost basis; rather, it is the original cost basis minus total depreciation.

11. A deferral benefit of depreciation is that income from property operations, which would have been taxed at the investor's ordinary tax rate, is sheltered from taxation. For example, if an investor faces a 35 percent tax rate on income generated by the property, each dollar of depreciation saves the investor 35 cents in taxes. However, the investor does not get to keep the 35 cents forever. Why? Because each dollar of depreciation claimed as a deduction reduces the investor's

adjusted tax basis by a dollar. And the taxable gain on a fully taxable sale (if there is a sale) increases by a dollar for every dollar decrease in the adjusted tax basis. Thus, the dollar of property income that is not taxed during, say, year 1 of operations because of the depreciation shield is "recaptured" and taxed at sale. So, even though the investor may eventually "pay the tax man," he or she benefits from the ability to defer the tax payment until sale.

12. The effective tax rate is 20 percent $[1 - (10.4 \div 13)]$.

13. The two primary alternatives to fully taxable sales in commercial real estate are installment sales and tax-deferred exchanges.

Additional Readings

Hoven, V. *The Real Estate Investor's Tax Guide,* 4th ed. Chicago: Dearborn Publishing, 2003.

Irwin, R. *Buy or Sell Real Estate after the 1997 Tax Act: A Guide for Homeowners and Investors.* New York: John Wiley, 1998.

Williamson, R. *Selling Real Estate without Paying Taxes: A Guide to Capital Gains Tax Alternatives.* Chicago: Dearborn Publishing, 2003.

The following journals provide pertinent articles on income taxation and value:

Real Estate Taxation, published quarterly by Warren, Gorham & Lamont, Inc. New York.

Real Estate Issues, published quarterly by the counselors of Real Estate, Chicago.

Real Estate Review, published quarterly by Warren, Gorham and Lamont, Boston.

Risk Management *in* *a* Portfolio Context

Learning Objectives

After reading this chapter you will be able to:

1. Calculate and interpret basic measures of risk for both individual assets and portfolios of assets.

2. Identify and discuss three risk-management tools.

3. Explain the importance of covariance and correlation in investment decisions.

4. Distinguish between systematic and nonsystematic risk.

5. Discuss real estate diversification strategies.

6. Identify the problems with traditional sources of real estate risk and return data, and use this information to address the question, How risky is real estate?

Introduction

Cash flows are said to be risky if their arrival time or their amount is uncertain. If there were no risks, real estate valuation and decision making would be quite simple. Any person with training in basic present value analysis (see Chapter 3) could find the correct answers to real estate valuation questions.

But there is a wide spectrum of cash flow uncertainty in the real estate investment world. As discussed in Chapter 2, among the highest risk levels is investment in raw land. At the lower end of the risk spectrum are "credit deals," that is, investment in a high-quality property leased on a long-term basis to a financially strong tenant. In all cases, however, property valuation requires the specification of the investor's **risk-adjusted discount rate:** the return the investor could earn on an alternative investment of *identical* risk. This discount rate must reflect the degree to which investors are uncertain about their cash flow and value projections.

How should investors measure *and* price risk? Most of the focus of this text is on individual properties and individual real estate transactions, and certainly the assessment of property-level risk is extremely important. However, as first discussed in Chapter 2, one does not own real estate in isolation from other possessions and pursuits. Viewing real estate investments in the context of the owner's other assets and overall situation may be thought of as a **portfolio perspective** on real estate investment. That is, real estate investment is considered in the context of all of the other assets and characteristics of the investor's portfolio, including human capital (i.e., personal capacity or needs). A primary purpose of this chapter is to explain how portfolio considerations affect the required risk premium and, therefore, the appropriate, risk-adjusted, required rate of return on individual real estate investments.

To understand how portfolio considerations affect the measurement and pricing of risk in real estate markets, it is important to understand the diversity of real estate investment risk. Thus, a brief tour of the sources and magnitude of real estate investment risk is provided in the next section. We then turn our attention to the measurement and management of investment risk. Next, we formally introduce the concept of portfolio risk and return. We demonstrate that portfolio diversification is capable of providing the one "free lunch" in investment of which the authors are aware: higher expected returns *and* lower risk. After demonstrating the importance and power of diversification, we turn our attention to "efficient" diversification; that is, choosing portfolios of assets that maximize expected return for a given level of portfolio risk. We then provide a detailed look at the historical investment performance of well-known real estate portfolios relative to the performance of stock and government bond portfolios. We conclude by formally introducing a widely used model for objectively quantifying the appropriate risk-adjusted return for investment assets.

Concept Check

23.1 What is a portfolio perspective on real estate investment?

Sources of Risk

Looking forward, risk is the probability that actual cash flows (i.e., rents) and values, and therefore returns, will vary from expectations. But what causes variations from expectations in real estate cash flows and values? To address this question, it is helpful to refer back to Exhibit 1-6, which is reproduced below as Exhibit 23-1.

In real estate user markets, depicted on the left-hand side of Exhibit 23-1, users compete for physical location and space. As explained in Chapter 5, this competition determines who gains the use of each parcel of land and developed real estate, and how much they must pay in rent for the use of the space.

What causes uncertainty in rental rates and occupancies in user markets? Rental rates result from the interaction of supply and demand in the local market. But market rents may rise or fall if the market area or property type becomes more or less attractive to space users, for whatever reason. For example, the demand for office space depends on the level of office employment, which in turn depends on the demand for services supplied by the occupants of office buildings. Increases in the number of service employees—professional, management, and other white-collar employees—translate into expanded demand for office space. In turn, the demand for the services supplied by the occupants of office space depends on population changes; local, regional, and national economic factors; and changes in the tastes of companies and households.

But supply factors also contribute to market uncertainty. As we know from previous chapters, the effect on rents of change in demand in a particular property market depends critically on the existing supply of space and how quickly supply responds to changes in demand.

Government affects uncertainty in real estate user markets in a host of ways. Local government is perhaps the largest factor. It affects the cost and lead time of real estate supply through zoning codes, planning, and other land use regulations; fees on new land development; and building codes that restrict methods of construction. Further, local

Exhibit 23-1   User Markets, Capital Markets, Government and Real Estate Values

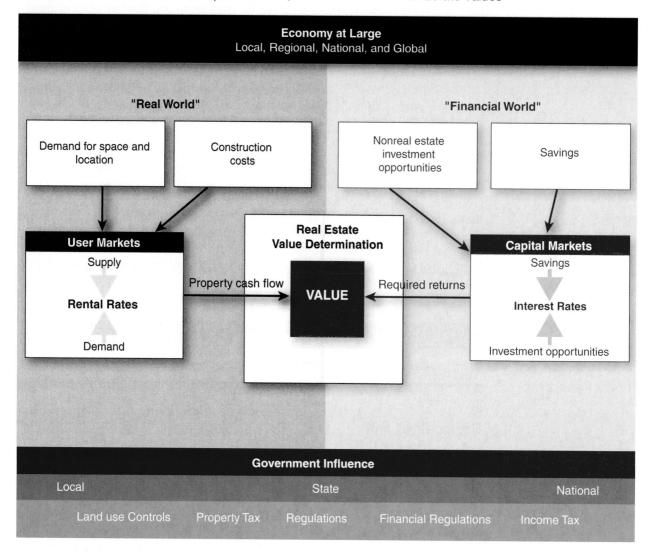

government affects rental rates in user markets through property taxes because increases in these taxes must, eventually, be passed on to tenants in the form of higher rents. In addition, government profoundly affects the supply and quality of real estate by its provision of roads, bridges, mass transit, utilities, flood control, schools, social services, and other infrastructure of the community. Changes in any of these infrastructure components can have dramatic effects on the supply and demand for real estate. We discussed all of these influences in Chapter 6.

The national government influences user markets in many ways. Housing subsidy programs can have enormous effects on the level and type of housing construction in a local market. In addition, laws protecting the environment and endangered species have significantly affected the use of real estate. Finally, national fair housing laws and other civil rights legislation have important influences on rental housing markets.

This brief review of user markets indicates that the sources of real estate risk are numerous and woven throughout the fabric of the economy. User markets never cease to be impacted by change. However, it is difficult to predict the dominant patterns of change and the effects they will have on land use and rental rates. For example, even small changes in the provision of local roads can cause a local market to decline or expand drastically; completion of a new freeway interchange can alter demand for real estate for miles around. But predicting the development of transportation systems within a market is certainly "risky business." As discussed in Chapter 7, real estate market research and analysis seeks to relate the income-producing ability of a property to the user market in which the property is located and, as is stressed in Chapters 5–7, market research and analysis is critically important to the success of real estate investments. Some have argued that risk analysis *is* market analysis!

23.2   What is investment risk?

Microeconomic Risk Factors

Even if rental rates over time were known with certainty, the actual returns earned by investors would still be difficult to predict. As we stressed in Chapter 17, commercial real estate assets are typically held for prolonged periods of time. As a result, they require a high degree of ongoing management. **Management risk** is the risk that the property will not be effectively managed, causing a reduction in net cash flows and returns. In Chapter 14 we demonstrated that the magnitude and variability of returns earned by equity investors are extremely sensitive to the amount and type of debt financing employed by the investor. We term this **capital structure risk.** In Chapters 14 and 15, we also discussed the effects that ownership structure can have on realized returns and risk. For example, we saw that limited partnerships provide limited liability for the limited partners, which reduces investment risk. However, the limited partners usually must give away some of their cash flows to the general partner as compensation for managing the operations of the partnership. **Ownership structure risk** refers to the effects of ownership form on net cash flows and returns. Another major factor in real estate cash flow uncertainty is **liquidity risk,** or the inability to sell quickly at fair market value.

Management, capital structure, ownership structure, and liquidity risk are property specific and, to a large extent, directly controllable by the owner/investor. We refer to these risks as **microeconomic risk factors** because they do not affect the overall, or macro, economy. Rather, they affect only a small (micro) portion of the local economy.

23.3   What are microeconomic risk factors?

Macroeconomic Risk Factors

The capital markets, depicted on the right-hand side of Exhibit 23-1, have their own set of uncertainties. Capital markets serve to allocate financial resources among households and firms requiring funds. Participants in the capital markets invest in financial investment from every corner of the economy—stocks, bonds, mutual funds, private business enterprises, mortgage contracts, real estate, and other opportunities—with the expectation of receiving a financial return on their investment. Funds flow from investors to the investment opportunities yielding the highest going-in internal rates of return, on a risk-adjusted basis, and the flows change quickly with changes in relative expected returns. Thus, real estate competes in a very dynamic and volatile pool against a diverse menu of other investment opportunities.

This competition means that changes or disturbances in the capital market variables can have a significant effect on the pricing of real property. Thus, when Russia defaulted on a portion of its debt obligations in October 1998, U.S. interest rates immediately spiked upward. On the other hand, if interest rates on long-term U.S. Treasury securities decline, required going-in *IRR*s on commercial property investments also will decline, all else being equal. These discount rate declines will increase property values across the country, even if rental rates in local markets are unchanged. **Interest rate risk** is the risk that changes in the general level of interest rates will affect the pricing of all securities and investments. Interest rate risk is an example of a **macroeconomic risk factor**—that is, one that potentially influences all properties in all markets.

Another macroeconomic risk factor is **inflation risk.** If general inflation in the economy is greater than or less than expected, real estate returns are often affected. For example, if an office building owner and tenant agree to a 10-year lease, the owner will generally suffer if general inflation is greater than expected. Why? Because operating and capital expenses will likely increase at the rate of inflation, as will market rents if the property market is not overbuilt. Thus, if the owner is locked into a long-term lease at a fixed rate, unexpected inflation will erode her inflation-adjusted return. Thus, as market fears about inflation change, the relative prices of inflation-protected properties and inflation-vulnerable properties may change as well.

Real estate also is subject to numerous federal laws and regulations that affect all properties. For example, federal financial reporting and disclosure requirements, and government-related financial agencies have profound effects on the operation of the real estate capital markets (see Chapter 13 for details of the government's role in mortgage markets). Another important example is U.S. tax law. If Congress changes the tax treatment of real estate, all property values are affected. For example, in 2002 Congress passed legislation later signed by President George W. Bush that reduced the maximum capital gain tax rate from 20 percent to 15 percent. This change was largely unanticipated and has undoubtedly had a positive, although likely small, impact on all commercial property values. On the downside, the Tax Reform Act of 1986 significantly reduced the allowable depreciation deductions on investment real estate (see Chapter 22). This change had a profound and well-documented negative effect on real estate values, at least in the short run.

In summary, risk is the extent to which actual cash flows and values will vary from expectations. The sources of real estate risk are numerous and varied and as far reaching as the economy itself. Many risk factors affect only specific properties; others affect only small local markets. Still others can affect all U.S. properties. In the next section we formalize the concept of risk as variability in expected, or actual, outcomes.

Concept Check

23.4 Why do changes in the expected internal rates of return, or yields, on U.S. Treasury securities affect real estate pricing?

The Concept of Variability

As argued above, investment risk can be defined as the possibility that future cash flows—and therefore returns and values—will differ from what was expected when the investment was undertaken. Because *risk* refers to the probability of earning a return greater or less than the expected return, **probability distributions** provide the foundation for risk measurement. A probability distribution defines the likelihood of certain events occurring. Probability distributions may be determined after long and rigorous tests, or they may be based on quite logical theorems; for example, the probability of a fair coin coming up heads is one-half. In contrast, **subjective probability distributions** represent an opinion or guess as to the likelihood of particular events occurring. For example, economists may state that there is a 50 percent chance that the national economy will experience average growth over the next five years, a 20 percent chance that there will be either a mild boom or a mild recession, and a 5 percent chance that the economy will experience either a strong boom or a deep recession. These possible states of the economy and their associated probabilities are shown in the first two columns of Exhibit 23-2. Notice that the sum of the probabilities in a distribution must be 100 percent.

Exhibit 23-2 Return Estimates on Three Alternative Investments

Rate of Return if a Certain State of the Economy Occurs

State of the Economy	Probability	Treasury Bond	Office Building	Shopping Center
Deep recession	0.05	7.0%	3.0%	5.0%
Mild recession	0.20	7.0	5.5	8.5
Average economy	0.50	7.0	7.0	11.0
Mild boom	0.20	7.0	8.5	13.5
Strong boom	0.05	7.0	11.0	17.0
Expected return *E(R)*		7.0%	7.0%	11.0%

Assume three investment alternatives are being considered:

1. A U.S. Treasury zero coupon bond with a remaining maturity of five years that offers a 7 percent internal rate of return (*IRR*) if held for the entire five years.[1]
2. A small office building that is expected to produce a 7 percent *IRR* if purchased today and sold at the end of five years.
3. A neighborhood shopping center that is expected to produce an 11 percent *IRR* if held for five years.

The rate of return on the zero coupon Treasury bond is known with certainty—it will yield a 7 percent *IRR* regardless of the state of the economy. Thus, the zero coupon bond has no risk.[2] However, the actual, or realized, rates of return on the two income property investments will not be known until the end of the five-year holding period.

Probability distributions may be either *discrete* or *continuous*. A discrete probability distribution has a finite number of outcomes; Exhibit 23-2 contains a discrete probability distribution with five possible outcomes. By multiplying each outcome by its probability of occurrence, and then summing these products, we can determine a weighted average of the outcomes. The weights are the probabilities, and the weighted average is defined as the **expected value.** The outcomes in the example are holding period *IRR*s. The expected (or most likely) *IRR*, *E(IRR)*, is expressed in equation form as follows:

$$\text{Expected rate of return} = E(IRR) = \sum_{i=1}^{n} o_i p_i \qquad \text{(23-1)}$$

Here o_i is the *i*th possible outcome (state of the economy), p_i is the probability that the *i*th outcome will occur, and *n* is the number of possible outcomes. Using equation 23-1, the expected rate of return on the office building investment is calculated as:

$$
\begin{aligned}
E(IRR) &= o_1(p_1) + o_2(p_2) + o_3(p_3) + o_4(p_4) + o_5(p_5) \\
&= 3.0\% \, (0.05) + 5.5\% \, (0.20) + 7.0\% \, (0.50) + 8.5\% \, (0.20) + 11.0\% \, (0.05) \\
&= 7.0\%
\end{aligned}
$$

1. A zero coupon bond does not pay periodic interest (or principal) to the investor. Instead, "zeros" provide a single cash flow to investors on the maturity date of the bond, and that cash flow is the redemption price (face value) of the bond. Without periodic payments, the zero coupon bond must provide all of its return in the form of price appreciation; that is, a redemption price at the maturity of the bond that is higher than the initial purchase price.

2. Treasury bonds that do pay periodic interest are subject to reinvestment risk, which is the risk that interest rates will fall and the periodic payments will have to be reinvested at lower rates. For zero coupon bonds, no portion of the total return is dependent upon the interest rate at which interim cash flows are reinvested. Thus, a zero coupon bond has zero reinvestment risk if held to maturity. The zero coupon Treasury bond return is riskless in the sense that a *nominal* return of 7 percent is assured. However, the *real* return on a zero coupon bond is risky because it will depend on the rate of general inflation over the investment holding period.

Exhibit 23-3 Discrete Probability Distributions

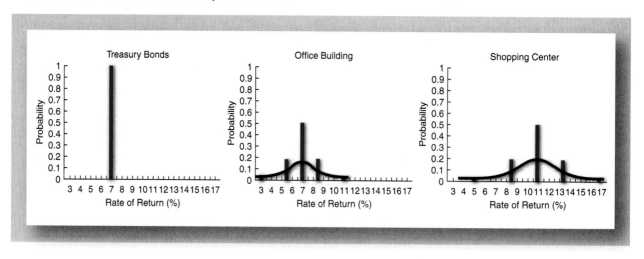

The expected rate of return on the neighborhood shopping center is 11 percent and is calculated similarly.[3]

Future economic conditions may actually be better, in between, or worse than the five discrete probabilities indicate. This situation is represented by a continuous probability distribution. The bar graphs in Exhibit 23-3 represent the discrete probability distributions of Exhibit 23-2. The range of possible discrete returns for the office building investment is from 3 to 11 percent. Note that the height of each bar represents the relative probability of occurrence, and the assumed distribution of rates of return for the office investment is *symmetric* around the 7 percent expected return (i.e., equal on both sides of the expected value). The range of possible IRRs for the shopping center is 5 to 17 percent. The graph for the Treasury bond investment shows the returns represented by a single spike; that is, there is no chance that the actual IRR will differ from 7 percent.

Continuous distributions depicting the three investments that are consistent with the discrete distribution also are contained in Exhibit 23-3. For the office building and shopping center, the area under the probability curve suggests the probability of occurrence. Therefore, the probability investors will earn less than a 5 percent *IRR* on the shopping center investment is quite low, as the area under the curve to the left of 5 percent is quite small. Conversely, the probability that the realized *IRR* will be between 5 and 17 percent is considerably greater. At this point, the problem is to decide which of these investments, if any, investors should choose. In addition to expected returns, the relative attractiveness of the alternatives depends on investor attitudes toward risk.

Concept Check

23.5 What is the primary disadvantage of subjective probability distributions?

Specification of Risk Preferences

Consider first the comparison between the Treasury bond and the office building, both of which are *expected* to produce a 7 percent internal rate of return (*IRR*) over the projected

3. The expected value or mean is not the only statistic available for describing the central value of a probability distribution or the central value of an actual sample from a distribution. The median is the outcome that lies exactly in the middle of the possible or realized outcomes. That is, it is the outcome that exceeds half of the outcomes and is exceeded by the other half. The mode is the outcome with the highest probability of occurrence.

Exhibit 23-4 Investor Attitudes Toward Risk

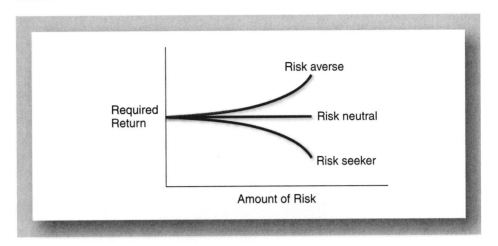

five-year holding period. Assume a full or partial interest in either investment can be purchased for $30,000. Which do you prefer?[4]

A critical element of each investor's investment strategy is the investor's preferences for risk. As Exhibit 23-4 shows, three general states of the relation between risk and return exist. *Risk-seeking* investors are willing to accept lower returns for taking on greater risks, but this response to investment risk is quite uncommon. The *risk-neutral* investor requires the same return regardless of the risk incurred. Again, most investors do not behave in this manner. *Risk-averse* investors must be rewarded—in the form of a higher expected return—for assuming more risk. Thus, to attract risk-averse investors, *expected* returns must increase as the level of investment risk increases.

Virtually all investors are risk averse and would therefore choose the T-bond over the office building. Why? Although both investments are expected to produce a 7 percent return, the actual *IRR* on the office building could vary greatly from 7 percent. Most investors would avoid the office building and its more volatile (less predictable) cash flows and returns. To sell the office building, the current owner would likely be forced to reduce the asking price until the expected rate of return increased enough to convince an investor to forsake the certain 7 percent Treasury return in exchange for undertaking the risky office building investment.[5] We assume in this book that investors are risk averse; that is, rational investors require an expectation of higher return if they are to accept a riskier investment, holding all else constant.

Investors often misunderstand this positive relationship between risk and return. It does not *guarantee* a higher return for undertaking a riskier investment, and there is even some probability that investors will realize *lower* returns on the riskier investments than on the less risky alternatives. Compensation for accepting riskier investments comes in the form of higher *expected* rates of return at the time of purchase.[6]

What about a partial interest in the neighborhood shopping center that also can be purchased for $30,000, and is currently priced to yield an 11 percent rate going-in internal rate of return? Relative to the Treasury bond, the shopping center investment holds out the

4. A full interest would be obtained if the investor became the sole owner of the asset. A partial interest would be obtained if the investor shared ownership of the asset with other investors (e.g., a partnership).

5. Recall that if the expected future cash flows from an investment alternative are held constant, a reduction in the purchase price will increase the expected return (yield).

6. Gamblers who "invest" at casinos and in lotteries may appear to be risk seekers; that is, they appear willing to accept *lower* rates of return in exchange for higher risk. A typical explanation for this behavior is that gambling produces entertainment benefits for these individuals, as well as potential monetary returns. If the entertainment value, or thrill, increases with the level of risk, engaging in gambling does not necessarily indicate that the individual is a risk seeker.

expectation of a higher return. However, the range of possible *IRR*s is 5 to 17 percent. Thus, the higher expected return would be purchased at a cost. Whether the increased *expected* return of 4 percent per year would be sufficient to induce the investor to forsake the safe Treasury bond investment in exchange for the risky shopping center would depend on investor attitudes toward risk.

Specifying risk preference is entirely subjective—there are no easily applied objective measures of risk aversion. For individual investors, the degree of risk aversion is usually related to their age and wealth. Among institutional investors, the degree of risk aversion is often related to the importance of preserving capital and the extent to which investment managers are personally liable for their actions. For example, life insurance companies place a high premium on preserving capital because they *must* pay claims, and managers of pension fund investments are personally liable for their actions as investment managers.

Concept Check

23.6   Are most investors risk averse, risk neutral, or risk seekers? How does this affect the pricing of assets in competitive markets?

Measuring Project-Specific Risk

The concepts of discrete probability distributions and expected values (or rates of return) can be used to quantify risk. We know that risk is present when the estimated distribution of cash flows or returns has more than one possible outcome, but how should risk be measured and quantified? Much of the remainder of this chapter is devoted to answering this question. In this section, we measure the riskiness of an investment held in isolation. Later, we analyze the riskiness of assets held in a portfolio.

Variance and Standard Deviation

Variance is a measure of the dispersion of a distribution around its expected value. The larger the variance, the greater the dispersion. The variance of a distribution is calculated as:

$$Variance = \sigma^2 = \sum_{i-1}^{n} (o_i - E(R))^2 p_i \tag{23-2}$$

where

σ^2 = variance

o_i = outcome (e.g., return, cash flow) for each state of the economy

$E(R)$ = expected outcome (value)

p_i = probability of the *i*th outcome occurring

Equation 23-2 shows that the variance is the sum of the squared deviations from the expected value, weighted by each deviation's probability of occurrence.

To illustrate, we calculate the variance of the *IRR* on the office building investment from Exhibit 23-2. The expected *IRR* on this investment is 7 percent. Using equation (23-2), the variance of the return is calculated as 2.50. These calculations are summarized in Exhibit 23-5.

Another measure, the **standard deviation,** is more frequently used as a measure of dispersion, or risk. The standard deviation, σ, is simply the square root of the variance. Thus, the standard deviation of the office building investment is:

$$Standard\ deviation = \sigma = \sqrt{\sigma^2} = \sqrt{2.50} = 1.58\%$$

Exhibit 23-5 Variance of Return on Office Building Investment

State of the Economy	Probability	Outcome	Deviation from Expected Return	Deviation Squared	Sqaure Deviation Times Probability
Deep recession	0.05	3.0%	−4.0%	16.00	0.80
Mild recession	0.20	5.5	−1.5	2.25	0.45
Average economy	0.50	7.0	0.0	0.00	0.00
Mild boom	0.20	8.5	1.5	2.25	0.45
Strong boom	0.05	11.0	4.0	16.00	0.80
Expected return (outcome)	=	7.0%		Variance =	2.50

Exhibit 23-6 Return and Risk Measures for Exhibit 20-1 Investment Alternatives

Expected Return or Risk Measure	Investment Alternatives		
	Treasury Bond	Office Building	Shopping Center
Expected return	7.00%	7.00%	11.00%
Variance	0.00	2.50	6.10
Standard deviation	0.00	1.58	2.47
Return/risk ratio	∞	4.43	4.45

One standard deviation is the distance of 1.58 percent in either direction from the office building's 7 percent expected return; two standard deviations is double that distance.

The standard deviation in our example comes from a discrete probability distribution with only five possible outcomes. If we assume instead that the 1.58 percent standard deviation came from a distribution of returns that is continuous and approximately normal, then additional interpretations of the standard deviation are possible. For example, we can state that 68.3 percent of the outcomes will fall between plus and minus one standard deviation of the expected value and that 95.4 percent of the outcomes will fall between plus and minus two standard deviations of the expected value. Adding and subtracting the 1.58 percent standard deviation of return on the office building from the 7 percent expected *IRR* results in 8.58 percent and 5.42 percent, respectively. Thus, 68.3 percent of the actual five-year *IRR*s will fall between 5.42 and 8.58 percent. Once the mean and standard deviation are established, it is possible to determine the probability of occurrence of values or returns over any desired interval within the distribution.[7]

Exhibit 23-6 contains the going-in *IRR*s and standard deviations of the three investment alternatives, along with their return/risk ratios that are discussed in the next section. The Treasury bond investment has a zero standard deviation because there will be no dispersion between the actual return and the expected 7 percent return. The shopping center has the largest standard deviation of the three alternatives.

Concept Check

23.7 Does standard deviation measure the risk of a bad outcome?

---

7. Determining the probability of occurrence over a specific interval within the distribution is accomplished by converting distances from the expected value into the number of standard deviations from the expected value. These standardized distances are contained in a reference table, sometimes called a table of Z-values. Such a table shows the portion of the area under the normal distribution lying to the left or right of various specific values.

Return per Unit of Risk

In competitive capital markets, investments with higher expected returns generally have larger standard deviations than investments with smaller expected returns. For example, the expected *IRR* on the neighborhood shopping center is 11 percent, compared with 7 percent on the office building. The corresponding standard deviations are 2.47 and 1.58 percent. Is the community shopping center more risky? In an absolute sense, yes. However, to properly interpret the relative riskiness of two investments, it is sometimes useful to go one step further and to calculate the return per unit of risk, which is the expected return divided by the standard deviation of the return. For the office building investment:

$$Risk\text{-}adjusted\ return = \frac{expected\ return}{standard\ deviation} = \frac{7.0\%}{1.58\%} = 4.43 \qquad \textbf{(23-3)}$$

Investments with higher return/risk ratios are generally preferred to investments with lower returns per unit of risk. On this risk-adjusted basis, there is not much to distinguish the office building and shopping center investments.

The Use of Subjective Probabilities

The challenge in analyzing real estate investment risk lies in the measurement of risk. The ideal process would be to collect data from recent periods on the returns for the property under evaluation (i.e., the subject property). The analyst then would calculate the historical mean and standard deviation of returns as a first measure of the property's risk. This approach is essentially the method of risk analysis used for stock and bond investments.

Unfortunately, data on past returns for subject properties and comparables are not usually available. Unlike the markets for stocks and bonds, one cannot simply leaf through back issues of *The Wall Street Journal* to obtain, for example, past data on the returns from a shopping center investment in Kansas or an office building in Tampa. Moreover, real estate markets are not nearly as active as public securities markets; therefore, data on recent sales are not readily available.

These data constraints mandate that the analysis of real estate investment risks follow alternative—and not altogether satisfactory—courses. One course involves the use of subjective probabilities. This is the course that we have used thus far in our examples of future, or *ex ante*, risk and return measures. Analysts may believe that the assignment of probabilities in this manner is too subjective to be of much use in some situations. In many cases, however, the use of subjective probabilities is the only way to quantify the risk of real estate investments; the unwise alternative is to do no risk analysis at all.

This discussion of subjective probability distributions illustrates an important point. Real estate investors generally face two sources of risk: (1) the risk associated with uncertain outcomes, given a known probability distribution, and (2) the additional risk that results from an assumed probability distribution that may itself be incorrect. Even if historical data on the properties of interest are available, the data may not accurately reflect *current* expectations about future returns and risk. Therefore, this second source of risk is quite important.

www.ppr.info

Property and Portfolio Research—a leading independent provider of portfolio strategy and risk management services.

www.ssrrealty.com

SSR Realty Advisors provides free access to numerous articles on real estate portfolio management.

Risk Management

Thus far we have concentrated on defining and measuring the riskiness of income property investments (as manifested in the expected variability of holding period returns). We also have argued that most investors are risk averse in that, other things being equal, they prefer assets with higher potential mean returns—given comparable levels of risk—and avoid assets with more volatile (i.e., higher standard deviations of returns) cash flows and returns.

Chapter 2 also discussed several strategies that real estate investors can pursue to mitigate cash flow and return uncertainty. For example, a prudent real estate investor should make the study of real estate markets a constant part of his or her activity. The investor may also manage risk by selecting properties of a size and type that appeal to a wide range of investors. Such a strategy will increase the liquidity of the investments when they are subsequently marketed for sale. Risk can also be mitigated by investment patience—that is, by "waiting out" market downturns. A strategy of investing in fully leased existing properties, instead of development projects, can also greatly reduce investment risk. This section discusses four additional tools investors may employ to reduce the variability of their investment returns: (1) avoiding risky projects, (2) using insurance to transfer risk to others, (3) performing due-diligence, and (4) diversification.

Avoiding Risky Projects

One way to reduce the variability of investment returns is to invest in less risky projects or securities—for example, certificates of deposits (CDs) and U.S. Treasury securities. Of course, as we have emphasized previously, risk and expected return are usually correlated. Thus, low-risk investment strategies tend to reduce the chances of achieving higher returns because expected returns in competitive markets tend to increase or decrease along with the risk. Should investment opportunities appear that are priced to yield a return in excess of what market participants require on similar investments of comparable risk, investors in search of positive net present value (*NPV*) projects may quickly enter the market, driving prices *up* and expected returns *down* until they are commensurate with the level of perceived risk. Indeed, the persistent search by well-informed investors competing for positive *NPV* projects tends to reduce the likelihood that such opportunities will be found. If informed market participants perceive that a property is overpriced, a lack of interest in its acquisition will typically force the seller to reduce the asking price until the going-in internal rate of return is comparable to other investment alternatives of similar risk.

Insurance

Losses from fire, flood, and other natural hazards have the potential to devastate investment returns. Indeed, if unprotected, the destruction of the real estate could produce investment returns that are severely negative. Although the prediction of fire and casualty losses is virtually impossible for a *particular* property, it is possible to predict with a reasonable degree of accuracy the percentage of homes in a large market area that will experience, say, fire damage in any particular year. For large insurance firms with many policyholders in diverse locations, the degree of risk associated with providing the insurance is quite small. As a result, real estate investors can, and should, transfer many risks to insurance companies in exchange for a certain insurance premium.

Viewed as an individual investment, buying hazard insurance has a very uncertain and volatile payoff: If the house burns down, the payoff or "return" on the insurance is enormous; if no fire occurs, the payoff will equal zero. Viewed from a portfolio perspective, however, the insurance is a risk-reducing investment because it will provide a positive payoff if the investment in the house, which is often a significant component of household portfolios, performs poorly (i.e., suffers damage). In short, insurance provides a mechanism for real estate investors to replace uncertainty with certainty. This transfer of risk is rational in many situations because very few individuals or firms (presumably only the largest and most wealthy) are in a position to self-insure against catastrophic losses.

Due Diligence

When analyzing investment opportunities, it is important that investors "do their homework." The term due diligence, first mentioned in Chapter 14, is used to describe the process of obtaining, examining, and verifying all pertinent aspects of a commercial property investment opportunity. Typical tasks performed as part of the due diligence process include: a physical inspection of the property, which may include engineering studies; a formal survey of the property's boundary lines, buildings, and other improvements; a review of title/deed documents to determine quality of title and the existence of any liens;

Industry Issues

Source: Lynnette Khalfani, "Why Property Investors Must Learn to Diversify," *The Wall Street Journal Online*, December 4, 2001.

23-1

Why Property Investors Must Learn to Diversify

Anyone who has ever bought or sold a home knows that the right location is the number one rule of real estate. Those purchasing property for investment purposes also would be wise to remember this mantra: Diversification. Diversification. Diversification.

With the stock market gyrating daily, more people are seeking assets that can bring some stability to their investment portfolios. Real estate can act as a hedge against inflation. It offers significant tax benefits and the chance for capital appreciation, and it is not highly correlated with the stock or bond markets. Best of all, though, real estate can generate significant cash flow—often far more than equities. Consider: The average company in the Standard & Poor's 500 Stock Index has an annual dividend yield of 1.1 percent, compared with a 7 percent average yield for real estate stocks.

So, let's assume you are ready to delve into the world of real estate investing. Perhaps the most important thing to keep in mind is the hallmark principle mentioned above: diversification. "Many people think owning a duplex somewhere is doing well," says Leo Wells, president of Wells Real Estate Funds in Atlanta. But Mr. Wells and other real estate pros say that to become a successful real estate investor, you must diversify five ways: geographically, by tenant, by tenant industry, by lease term, and by property sector. Don't make the mistake that most real estate novices commit when they buy a single piece of property and count on that investment to balance out their portfolios.

The idea is to spread out your risk as much as possible, because "no matter how smart you are, you won't be able to predict which areas will remain strong 10 years from now," says Mr. Wells, whose company has $1 billion in real estate investments.

---

an analysis of property tax assessments and liabilities; a review to determine whether the current or intended use of the property is in compliance with current zoning regulations; a review of existing service and maintenance agreements as well as insurance policies; and a thorough analysis of the existing leases and tenants. Clearly, due diligence is an important risk reduction tool for investors.

Diversification as a Risk-Management Tool

Investors can further reduce the variability of investment returns through the use of **diversification.** The intuition behind the concept of diversification is illustrated by the maxim "Don't put all your eggs in one basket." As an example, consider the following two "investment" alternatives:

1. Flip a fair coin once: If heads, you win $10,000; if tails, you lose $9,500.
2. Flip a fair coin 100 times: If heads, you win $100; if tails, you lose $95.

The expected values of the two alternatives, EV_1 and EV_2, are equal to:

$$EV_1 = [(0.50)(\$10,000) + (0.50)(-\$9,500)] = \$250$$
$$EV_2 = [(0.50)(\$100) + (0.50)(-\$95)] \times 100 = [\$2.50] \times 100 = \$250$$

Both investments have an *expected* value or payoff of $250. However, the first alternative is extremely risky in that the actual outcome will be either a positive $10,000 or a negative $9,500. Thus, the actual outcome will vary greatly from the expected outcome of $250. With the second alternative, the investor is, in essence, purchasing a partial interest in 100 different coin flips. This "portfolio" of coin flips will produce a payoff much closer to the $250 expected value. Assuming identical purchase prices, risk-averse investors would choose the second alternative because it allows for a significant reduction in investment risk without sacrificing expected return.

The Portfolio Concept of Risk

The portfolio concept of risk states that investment opportunities should be accepted or rejected on the basis of their effect on the risk and return of the entire portfolio of assets. Most investors do not invest in only one asset, but in many assets. A portfolio may include numerous different stocks, a combination of stocks and bonds, several income property investments, gold, human capital, or combinations of these and other investment alternatives. Combining assets into portfolios reduces risk because those assets that return less than expected will be offset, in whole or in part, by assets whose realized returns are greater than expected. Because of this interaction, the standard deviation of the return on a portfolio is usually less than the average standard deviation of individual investments. This means investors should be concerned with the expected return and variance of their portfolios, rather than the return/risk characteristics of individual assets.

Diversifiable Portfolio Risk

The literature of finance categorizes risk as either diversifiable or nondiversifiable. **Diversifiable risk,** also called **unsystematic risk,** is the term that describes the risk due to the unrealized return expectations of a particular property. It can be eliminated from a portfolio by holding securities and other investments with returns that are less than perfectly correlated. Perfectly **correlated returns** always move exactly together when market conditions change; perfectly negatively correlated returns always move exactly opposite. If one asset in the portfolio reacts negatively to a change in market conditions, losses may be offset through holding another asset that reacts positively to that same change.

To illustrate further the concept of diversification, consider the realized rates of return reported in Exhibit 23-7 for two investments: a common stock and a shopping center. In 1998 the stock produced a positive 14 percent total return; the income property, produced a negative 10 percent return. Over the six-year holding period from 1998 through 2003, the stock and shopping center produced average annual returns of 7.0 percent and 6.2 percent, respectively. The average return on a portfolio invested 50 percent each year in each of the two assets was 6.6 percent. The historical standard deviation of the annual stock return was 12.4 percent. (See Exhibit 23-8.)

Exhibit 23-7 Historical Returns and Risk

Year	Stock	Shopping Center	Equally Weighted Portfolio
1998	14 %	−10%	2.0%
1999	−10	8	−1.0
2000	23	12	17.5
2001	−5	17	6.0
2002	8	25	1.5
2003	12	15	13.5
Mean return	7.0%	6.2%	6.6%
Standard deviation	12.4%	11.1%	7.4%

Exhibit 23-8 Historical Standard Deviation of Stock Return

Year	Realized Return	Deviation from Average	Squared Deviations
1998	14 %	−7.0%	49.0%
1999	−10	−17.0	289.0
2000	23	16.0	256.0
2001	−5	−12.0	144.0
2002	8	1.0	1.0
2003	12	5.0	25.0
Average return	7.0%	Sum of squared deviations	764.0

$$Variance = \sigma^2 = \frac{sum\ of\ squared\ deviations}{n-1} = \frac{764}{5} = 152.8$$

$$Standard\ deviation\ \sigma = \sqrt{\sigma^2} = \sqrt{152.8} = 12.4\%$$

The standard deviation for the shopping center investment over the same time period was 11.1 percent. Computer spreadsheet programs and most financial calculators can be used to perform these calculations more quickly. The procedures are similar to those used for calculating expected returns and risk measures using subjective probabilities (see Exhibit 23-5). The major difference is that each time period (in this case one year) receives an equal weight when using historical data.

Inspection of Exhibit 23-7 shows that if held separately, the two assets produced fairly volatile returns. However, when combined in a portfolio, the return volatility decreased to 7.4 percent, significantly less than the volatility of either asset held separately.

The reason the combination of the stock and shopping center resulted in such a significant reduction in risk at the portfolio level is that their returns tended to move somewhat countercyclically to one another over the sample period. In statistical terms, the returns were negatively correlated over the sample period.

Concept Check

23.9 Is the standard deviation of the return on a portfolio usually more or less than the average standard deviation of the individual assets?

Covariance and Correlation

Covariance (COV) is an absolute measure of how the return on an asset tends to vary with that of another asset over time. The covariance between the stock and shopping center returns was −29.6 during the sample period. This indicates the returns on the two assets tended to move in opposite directions.[8]

Covariance statistics can take on values ranging from minus infinity to positive infinity, making it difficult to know when a covariance is "large" or "small." Therefore, a related statistic, the **correlation coefficient** (ρ), is often used to measure the degree of comovement between two variables. The correlation coefficient is calculated as:

$$Correlation\ coefficient = \rho_{AB} = \frac{COV_{AB}}{\sigma_A \sigma_B} \tag{23-4}$$

8. The covariance for our example was calculated using Microsoft EXCEL by finding the sum of the product of each pair of stock deviation and shopping center deviations from their respective means. This sum is then divided by $n-1$ (i.e., 5).

The correlation coefficient standardizes the covariance by dividing it by the product of the individual standard deviations. This provides a *relative* measure of comovement. If ρ_{AB} is close to zero, the two variables move independently of one another. The correlation coefficient ranges from -1.0 to $+1.0$, making it much easier than using the covariance to interpret the extent to which the two variables are related. In our example:

$$\rho_{AB} = \frac{COV_{AB}}{\sigma_A \sigma_B} = \frac{-29.6}{(12.4)(11.1)} = -0.22$$

The correlation coefficient of -0.22 indicates a negative correlation between the returns on the common stock and shopping center over the sample period.[9]

It should be clear that if the returns on two assets are highly *negatively* correlated, the variance of a portfolio consisting of the two assets will be less than the variance of the return on either asset held in isolation. It should be stressed, however, that although negative correlations occasionally surface in realized returns, it is rarely expected. Moreover, it is not required to achieve risk reduction at the portfolio level. All that is required is for the correlation to be less than $+1.0$ between the returns on an asset and the returns on assets already held in the portfolio. However, the potential for risk reduction at the portfolio level is much greater as the correlation moves further away from $+1.0$.

Examples of Diversifiable Risk

As we mentioned earlier, *diversifiable risk* describes the risk due to the unrealized return expectations of a particular property. Some of this risk is property or site specific; for example, superior management of an apartment complex may lead to lower operating expense levels than expected, increased occupancy, or both. In addition, the relative attractiveness of the property's location may change owing to a new real estate development or road construction in the immediate area. For instance, increased vacancies could result from an inconsistent land use on an adjacent parcel (e.g., a noisy factory next to an office building). The value of a property also may be affected by changes in its environment or the sudden awareness that the existing environment is hazardous or potentially hazardous. For example, developers and investors have become increasingly concerned about the existence of toxic waste buried on a site or an adjacent property. Environmental problems can cause significant losses because investors may be subject to cleanup costs that far exceed the value of properties. Capital structure risk, ownership structure risk, and liquidity risk, all previously discussed, are property or deal specific. In addition, real estate values are often affected positively or negatively by property tax laws, zoning, and other restrictions imposed by local governments.

In addition to property- or site-specific risks, the returns on real estate investments also may vary as a result of changes in the local, state, or regional economy. For example, real estate markets in small public university towns can be significantly affected by sudden changes in the budget of the state that provides the majority of the university's funding. Cities such as Houston and Denver, whose economies had traditionally been linked to the fortunes of the oil industry, suffered high commercial and residential vacancy rates when the price of oil collapsed in 1985. Local real estate markets, less dependent on the oil industry, were not so directly affected. In some cases, regional changes or "shocks" create growth and prosperity in one region, while having a negative effect elsewhere. A classic example has been the shift in U.S. industrial growth from the Midwest to the South and Southwest.

Note that poor management, deteriorating local market conditions, changes in traffic patterns, and the discovery of environmental hazards, as well as other unanticipated

---

9. There are statistical tests that allow the analyst to determine whether the correlation between two series is significant in a statistical sense. For a discussion of correlation and related statistics, see a standard college textbook on elementary statistics.

changes are microeconomic risk factors; that is, they affect individual properties or multiple properties in a local market. Diversification therefore reduces the risk of large variations in portfolio returns due to the performance of an individual investment.

Concept Check

23.10   In what sense is a diversifiable risk "unsystematic"?

Basic Real Estate Diversification Strategies

The examples of diversifiable, or microeconomic, risk discussed above suggest two basic diversification strategies: (1) investing in different property types and (2) investing in different geographical market areas. An additional diversification strategy is to combine investments in public (i.e., securitized) and private (i.e., unsecuritized) real estate markets.

Property Type Diversification. The demand by potential tenants for the various types of leasable space is a **derived demand.** For example, a decrease in the demand for industrial goods causes a decrease in the demand for industrial space. Similarly, the demand for office space is derived from the demand for the services provided by the tenants of office buildings, such as law and accounting firms, banks, insurance companies, real estate brokerage firms, and mortgage banks. The demand for retail space in a market is directly related to the population in the trade area and to the disposable income of the population. However, the demand for some retail space is much more cyclical than others. For example, the demand for the basic products and services sold in a shopping center anchored by a grocery store is much less volatile than the demand for specialty and luxury goods sold in larger shopping malls.

General macroeconomic trends will likely alter the demand for all types of space; for example, the general U.S. recession during the early 1990s had an adverse effect on the return performance of all property types, as did the economic slowdown in the early 2000s. However, because the demand (and supply) for various property types is not driven by the same economic forces, and because the various property types respond differently to changes in the local, regional, or national economy, investors can reduce portfolio risk by holding ownership interests in several or all of the above property categories.

Geographic Diversification. Another popular strategy for diversifying is based on geography. Although national economic trends can have a significant effect on real estate markets, local market conditions are often more important than national economic trends. Indeed, real estate markets are decidedly local in nature. Thus, a portfolio of geographically diverse properties may provide higher risk-adjusted returns than a geographically concentrated real estate portfolio. For example, when the economies of Dallas, Houston, Denver, and other cities in the so-called oil extraction states were rocked by falling oil prices in the mid-1980s, all real estate values were negatively affected, not just office buildings that suffered directly from the demise of numerous oil and oil-related companies that were prime demanders of office space. The across-the-board decline in real estate values in these areas produced low or negative returns for virtually all investors. However, the losses were especially significant for those investors with real estate portfolios concentrated in these areas. Another more recent example is the significant negative effect that the prolonged slump in the airline industry has had on aviation oriented cities such as Seattle and Wichita.

Combining Public and Private Market Investments. The dramatic growth in securitized real estate markets in recent years provides investors with expanded opportunities to purchase interests in real estate that can be traded in public markets. The most prominent example is the growth in the market value of real estate investment trusts, or REITs, that are traded on major stock exchanges. The evidence suggests that the performance of publicly traded real estate securities has differed from the performance of private, direct, property investments, often significantly. Thus, investors may obtain additional diversification benefits by holding a portion of their real estate investments in the form of publicly traded real estate securities, primarily REITs.

Nondiversifiable Risk

What happens when more stocks, bonds, and real estate are added to a portfolio? In general, the riskiness of a portfolio will fall as the number of assets increases. Moreover, the extent to which portfolio risk declines depends on the degree of correlation between the returns on the asset that is added and the returns on assets already included in the portfolio—the smaller the correlation, the greater the risk reduction achieved by adding the asset.

It is difficult to find assets whose expected returns are negatively correlated—most assets tend to do well when the national economy is strong and less well when it is weak. Thus, although diversification can eliminate much of the risk from a portfolio of assets, unanticipated events or macroeconomic "shocks" that affect all, or most, assets will inevitably produce variations in portfolio returns over time, even in large, well-diversified portfolios. Prominent examples of macroeconomic risk factors include inflation rate risk, interest rate risk, and changes in federal income tax provisions. Other nondiversifiable risks that ripple through the entire U.S. economy include events such as September 11, 2001 and the electrical blackout that occurred in the northeast in August of 2003. These nondiversifiable macroeconomic risk factors are frequently referred to as **systematic risk factors** or **market risk factors.**

Concept Check

23.11 What type of risk remains after the investor has constructed a well-diversified portfolio?

Constructing an Efficient Portfolio

The previous discussion of diversification strongly suggests that consideration of only the mean and standard deviation of return for individual investments will not ensure the selection of an optimal portfolio. Investors should base their assessment of an investment's risk (and hence its value) on its contribution to portfolio risk and return. A potential investment is "efficient" in a portfolio context if its acquisition accomplishes one or the other of the following:

- Increases the expected return on a portfolio without increasing portfolio risk.
- Decreases the riskiness of the portfolio without sacrificing the expected rate of return.

A great deal of research has shown that a portfolio can be fully diversified in the sense that its unsystematic risk can be eliminated by choosing as few as 15 or 20 assets at random.

The objective of portfolio risk management is to develop an efficient portfolio by eliminating diversifiable risk. This is achieved by including assets with low return correlations in the portfolio. This so-called *efficient* or *smart diversification* makes it possible to eliminate unsystematic risk with fewer assets.

The expected return and standard deviation for portfolios consisting of various combinations of our sample stock and shopping center are displayed in Exhibit 23-9. Note that if the percentage of the portfolio allocated to the stock had been zero over the sample period, the average return on the portfolio, R_p, and the portfolio standard deviation would have equaled 6.2 percent and 11.1 percent, respectively—the mean return and standard deviation for the shopping center investment. With 20 percent invested in the stock, the average return on the portfolio increases to 6.3 percent while the portfolio standard deviation falls to

Exhibit 23-9   Portfolio Return and Risk under Different Combinations

Proportion of Portfolio in Stock	Proportion of Portfolio in Shopping Center	Portfolio Return	Standard Deviation of Return(s_p)
0.00	1.00	6.2%	11.1%
0.20	0.80	6.3	8.7
0.40	0.60	6.5	7.4
0.50	0.50	6.6	7.4
0.60	0.40	6.7	7.8
0.80	0.20	6.8	9.7
1.00	0.00	7.0	12.4

The standard deviation of the return on a two-asset portfolio is:

$$s_p = \sqrt{w^2 s_i^2 + (1-w)^2 s_j^2 + 2w(1-w)\, COV_{ij}}$$

where w is the share of wealth invested in asset i, $(1-w)$ is the share in asset j, and COV_{ij} is the covariance of their returns.

8.7 percent. With 40 percent of the portfolio invested in the stock, the average return increases slightly to 6.5 percent and the portfolio standard deviation falls still further to 7.4 percent. For stock proportions greater than approximately 0.50, the return on the portfolio continues to increase. However, the standard deviation of the portfolio also increases over this range. That is, for proportions greater than about 0.50, the typical positive relationship holds between risk and return.

What is especially significant about the above example is that for stock proportions less than 0.50, investors could have enhanced the return on their portfolio *and* reduced the volatility of the portfolio return by allocating a larger percentage of the portfolio to the stock. Does this result violate the assertion made earlier in the chapter that increases in expected returns can only be purchased in competitive markets by undertaking more risk? No, the result merely demonstrates the power of diversification. By choosing low or negatively correlated assets, investors can construct portfolios that reduce risk without sacrificing return. So, yes, there is such a thing as a "free lunch" in investment markets. Although estimation of the risk and return on multiple asset portfolios is beyond the scope of this text, the intuition of the two-asset example is directly applicable to the multiple asset case.

www.efficientfrontier.com

Furnishes extensive information on portfolio risk management, including a very interesting reading list.

Concept Check

23.12   What is the one "free lunch" available in financial economics?

Why Are So Many Investors Not Well Diversified?

Despite the use of modern portfolio concepts by many market participants, especially pension funds and other institutional investors, some investors clearly behave in a manner that appears inconsistent with portfolio theory. For example, many homeowning households are very poorly diversified because a large percentage of their wealth is invested in their home. Many readers also can point to individuals, perhaps even parents or other relatives, who have pursued a narrowly focused investment strategy such as investing almost exclusively in local rental houses, small apartments, or some other asset. Are these homeowners and investors irrational? Probably not. Numerous other factors and considerations can constrain or push households to hold undiversified investment portfolios. For example, many households place a great deal of value on home ownership and thus are willing to allocate a significant portion of their monthly income to housing payments.

What about the numerous investors who allocate a substantial portion of their wealth, and often time, to investments in local rental properties? Perhaps their desire to actively manage their rental properties precludes them from diversifying geographically. In addition, their limited resources may not allow them to be active purchasers of more expensive properties such as office buildings and shopping centers. Diversification by property type is therefore problematic. Why not mix more stocks, bonds, and other assets into their rental housing portfolio? Perhaps they consider themselves experts at acquiring, managing, and disposing of rental homes and they want to apply this perceived comparative advantage to as many rental homes as possible. Or perhaps they truly expect returns on their real estate portfolio to far exceed returns on a **mixed-asset portfolio,** one that contains a variety of assets. If their expected returns are high enough, it may be rational for them to "load up" on local real estate because the benefits are expected to offset the increased costs associated with their risky, undiversified portfolio.

How Risky Is Real Estate?

To evaluate the performance of an asset class, such as commercial real estate, it is important to be able to measure both the potential risk and expected return associated with owning the asset. The measurement of portfolio risk and diversification begins with the calculation of historical means and variances, as well as covariances, among the returns from the different assets in the portfolio. For stocks and bonds, this represents little problem because an abundance of historical performance data are available on individual securities and benchmark portfolios. If real estate is held by a *publicly traded* corporation (e.g., a REIT traded on one of the major stock exchanges), accurate historical return data are generally available. However, as we mentioned earlier, past data on returns for *privately held,* individual real estate assets are usually not available.

To obtain evidence on the relative return performance of commercial real estate, two publicly available sources of real estate performance data are analyzed: (1) the National Council of Real Estate Investment Fiduciaries (NCREIF) Property Index, which measures returns on a large portfolio of privately held, institutional-quality real estate, and (2) the National Association of Real Estate Investment Trusts (NAREIT) Index, which measures returns on a large portfolio of publicly traded companies that invest in commercial real estate. A brief description of each index follows.

Appraisal-Based Index of Unsecured Returns

NCREIF (www.NCREIF.com) publishes a quarterly index of value-weighted real estate returns.[10] The **NCREIF Property Index** measures the historical performance of commercial properties held by institutional investors, such as pension funds. The NCREIF returns include both income (*NOI*) and capital appreciation (or depreciation) components that are combined to generate quarterly total returns.

To be included in the index, properties must be existing, investment-grade assets held by tax-exempt institutions. Development projects and agricultural properties are specifically excluded.[11] The universe of properties upon which the total return index is based changes each quarter as new members join NCREIF and existing members alter their holdings through sales and acquisitions. In the first quarter of 2003, there were 3,847 properties

---

10. *Value-weighted* means that the return on each property used to construct the index is weighted by the property's market value as a percentage of the total market value of the properties that the index comprises.

11. The NCREIF Property Index (NPI) contains all equity acquisitions as well as debt-financed properties that have been "unlevered." An unlevered property return is one in which NCREIF has made an attempt to remove the effects of financial leverage on the property's return.

in the NPI, with a combined market value of $124.3 billion. The properties in the NPI are also used to calculate numerous subindexes, including separate indexes for the five major property types: apartment, office, retail, R&D/office, and warehouse. Separate indexes are also calculated by property type and in the aggregate for various geographic regions and subregions of the United States.

One potential weakness with using NCREIF data is that the quarterly increases or decreases in the market value of each property are most often determined by "in-house" adjustments to old appraisals, although each property must be appraised at least once a year by a certified appraiser. However, if the property happens to sell during the quarter, the transaction sale price is used. This methodology for determining the quarterly change in property value has been criticized because the evidence suggests that using appraisal estimates rather than transaction prices to calculate value changes from quarter to quarter may "smooth" the indicated changes in value and therefore bias estimates of the return volatility downward. Nonetheless, the NCREIF Property Index remains a primary source for information on return characteristics of commercial real estate.

REIT-Based Index of Securitized Returns

An alternative source of commercial real estate return information is the National Association of Real Estate Investment Trusts (NAREIT) Index. The **NAREIT Index** is a value-weighted index that tracks the total return (income plus capital appreciation) pattern of all exchange-traded REITs.

NAREIT (www.NAREIT.com) groups all qualified REITs into three main categories for reporting purposes. First, an Equity REIT Index is calculated for those REITs whose primary assets are direct property investments. Second, a Mortgage Index is calculated, based on the performance of those REITs whose primary assets are mortgages, mortgage-backed securities, or both. Third, a Hybrid Index is calculated for those firms that hold a mixture of direct property and mortgage investments. Detailed information regarding the return performance of specific property types (e.g., apartments, warehouses) also is available. As of March 2003, NAREIT covered 151 publicly traded REITs with a total market capitalization of $181.1 billion. Equity REITs accounted for 94 percent of this total market value. In the analysis presented below, we use the Equity REIT Index to measure historical real estate returns.[12]

It is important to realize that NAREIT return data are based on publicly traded securities. To the extent that these security prices represent factors not inherently attributable to the underlying property (e.g., the stock market's opinion of the REIT manager's ability), observed performance patterns may not be representative of the true risk and expected returns associated with investing directly in the underlying real estate.

Historical Returns, Risk, and Correlations

The NCREIF and NAREIT indexes described above provide useful information on the absolute level of risk and expected return associated with portfolios of commercial real estate. What may be more important to potential investors, however, is the riskiness of real estate relative to other assets. Exhibit 23-10 presents the mean returns and standard deviations for five different asset classes over three different time periods. Return and risk measures for a portfolio consisting of an equal fraction of each of the five assets also are included. As mentioned in Chapter 15, the Standard & Poor's (S&P) 500 is a bellwether stock return index that includes 500 of the largest and most important U.S. corporations. As of June 2003, five REITs are contained in the S&P 500 Index. The Russell 2000 is a "small cap" index that tracks the performance of 2,000 publicly traded stocks that rank 1,001 to 3,000 in U.S. stock market capitalization. Bond returns over the three periods are measured by a Lehman Brothers index of returns on a portfolio of long-term government and corporate bonds.

---

12. Other measures of REIT return performance are available—for example, the Wilshire Real Estate Securities Index.

Exhibit 23-10   Average Annual Return and Standard Deviation: Real Estate Compared to Other Asset Classes*

	1979–2003 (Q1)		1979–1992		1993–2003 (Q1)	
	Average	Standard Deviation	Average	Standard Deviation	Average	Standard Deviation
NCREIF[†]	8.3%	4.9%	6.7%	5.9%	10.4%	3.0%
NAREIT	13.7	13.8	15.7	14.0	11.0	13.7
S&P 500	13.8	16.2	16.5	15.7	10.1	16.9
Russell 2000	13.7	22.2	17.6	23.6	8.4	20.2
Lehman Bros. Government/ Corporate Bonds	9.6	7.5	11.1	9.0	7.5	4.6
Equally weighted portfolio	11.8	10.0	13.5	11.0	9.5	8.6

*The reported annualized results are based on quarterly data.

[†]The NCREIF returns have been "unsmoothed" to adjust for appraisal-induced smoothing of quarterly value changes that is inherent in the NCREIF data.

Exhibit 23-10 reveals that equity REITs, unlike direct property investments, have produced average returns similar to those associated with stocks over the full sample period. For example, the average annual return on the NAREIT Index from 1979 through the first quarter of 2003 [2003(Q1)] was 13.7 percent. The corresponding return on the S&P 500 and Russell 2000 were 13.8 and 13.7 percent, respectively. The 13.8 percent annual standard deviation of equity REIT returns, however, is less than the 16.2 percent standard deviation of S&P 500 returns and is significantly less than the 22.2 percent standard deviation of returns on the Russell 2000 Index. Thus, returns to the NAREIT Index have been less volatile than both large and small cap stocks. Said differently, the average return per unit of risk for equity REITs over the 1979–2003 (first quarter) time period was 0.99, which is higher than the return/risk ratio of 0.85 for the S&P 500 and significantly greater than the 0.62 return/risk ratio of the Russell 2000. Over this time period, the NAREIT Index also produced higher average returns than a portfolio consisting of long-term government and corporate bonds, both with and without an adjustment for volatility. A portfolio of privately held, high-quality real estate, as measured by the NCREIF Index produced significantly lower average returns (8.3 percent per year), but with much less volatility ($\sigma =$ 4.9 percent).

During the 1993–2003(first quarter) period, equity REITs produced a higher average return than the S&P 500 and Russell 2000 and, again, had a lower standard deviation of return than both stock indexes. As a result, the 0.80 return/risk ratio for NAREIT exceeds the 0.60 and 0.42 return/risk ratios for the S&P 500 and the Russell 2000, respectively. Direct property investments (as measured by the NPI) produced an average return of 10.4 percent during the 1993–2003(first quarter) period, but with an annualized volatility of just 3.0 percent. Thus, on a return per unit of risk basis, NCREIF appears to have significantly outperformed the other four asset classes.[13]

Concept Check

23.13   How did REITs perform relative to stocks over the 1993–2002 period?

13. The NPI returns have been "unsmoothed" to adjust for the appraisal-induced smoothing of value changes that is inherent in the NPI. However, unsmoothing is a subjective process dependent upon several assumptions. Thus, the standard deviations for the NCREIF NPI Index shown in Exhibit 23-10 should be considered estimates of the true volatility of privately held commercial real estate.

We next examine the return characteristics of an equally weighted portfolio (20 percent each in the NCREIF, NAREIT, S&P 500, Russell 2000, and Lehman Brothers Government/Corporate Bonds Indexes). Compared to the NCREIF, the bottom row of Exhibit 23-10 reveals that an equally weighted portfolio would have produced a higher average return (11.8 percent versus 8.3 percent) and higher standard deviation of return (11.0 percent versus 4.9 percent) during the 1979–2003(first quarter) period. Compared to NAREIT, an equally weighted portfolio would have produced a slightly lower average return over the full sample period (11.8 percent versus 13.7 percent), but with less volatility (10.0 percent versus 13.8 percent standard deviation). On a return per unit of risk basis, the equally weighted portfolio dominated the NAREIT, S&P 500, and the Russell 2000 in each of the three time periods.

The diversification benefits associated with the equally weighted portfolio can be explained by examining the return correlations presented in Exhibit 23-11, 23-12, and 23-13. The first row of Exhibit 23-11 reveals that the NCREIF Index has displayed only a modest correlation with NAREIT (0.18) and a very low correlation with the S&P 500 and the Russell 2000 over the full study period. Moreover, it displayed a negative 21 percent correlation with long-term bonds. The low correlation between NCREIF returns and all three stock categories, coupled with a negative correlation with bonds, produces significant diversification benefits because investors in the equally weighted portfolios are likely to experience quarters with poor direct real estate performance corresponding to quarters of strong returns to other portfolio assets. In effect, diversification allows investors to insulate themselves from potential losses by reducing the volatility of the overall cash flows they receive.

Exhibit 23-11 Return Correlations: 1979 through the First Quarter of 2003

	NCREIF NPI	NAREIT	S&P 500	Russell 2000	Lehman Bros. Government/ Corporate Bonds
NCREIF*	1.00	0.18	0.08	0.09	−0.21
NAREIT		1.00	0.55	0.69	0.30
S&P 500			1.00	0.88	0.17
Russell 2000				1.00	0.13
Lehman Bros. Government/ Corporate bonds					1.00

*The NCREIF returns have been "unsmoothed" to adjust for appraisal-induced smoothing of quarterly value changes that is inherent in the NCREIF data.

Exhibit 23-12 Return Correlations: 1979 through 1992

	NCREIF NPI	NAREIT	S&P 500	Russell 2000	Lehman Bros. Government/ Corporate Bonds
NCREIF*	1.00	0.18	0.05	0.08	−0.22
NAREIT		1.00	0.77	0.84	0.40
S&P 500			1.00	0.89	0.35
Russell 2000				1.00	0.25
Lehman Bros. Government/ Corporate bonds					1.00

*The NCREIF returns have been "unsmoothed" to adjust for appraisal-induced smoothing of quarterly value changes that is inherent in the NCREIF data.

Exhibit 23-13 Return Correlations: 1993 through the First Quarter of 2003

	NCREIF NPI	NAREIT	S&P 500	Russell 2000	Lehman Bros. Government/ Corporate Bonds
NCREIF*	1.00	0.33	0.23	0.20	−0.03
NAREIT		1.00	0.25	0.44	0.07
S&P 500			1.00	0.86	−0.26
Russell 2000				1.00	−0.28
Lehman Bros. Government/ Corporate bonds					1.00

*The NCREIF returns have been "unsmoothed" to adjust for appraisal-induced smoothing of quarterly value changes that is inherent in the NCREIF data.

Equity REITs displayed significant positive correlations with the S&P 500 (0.55) and, especially, the Russell 2000 (0.69). Thus, REITs have provided less significant diversification benefits when added to stock portfolios. However, equity REIT returns were significantly less correlated with bond returns (0.30) than with stock returns over the full study period.

As with average returns and standard deviations, correlations are not constant over time. Most notably, the return correlations between NCREIF and the three stock indexes are much higher in the 1993–2003(first quarter) period than in the earlier years of the study period. Also, the significant negative correlation between NCREIF and long-term bonds for the full sample is clearly the result of the earlier 1979–1992 period. Since 1992 the correlation between NCREIF and bonds is essentially zero (−0.03). Finally, it is important to note that the correlations between NAREIT returns and returns on both the large and small cap stock indexes have been dramatically lower since 1992; the correlation between NAREIT and the S&P 500 fell to just 0.25 in our later time period (compared with 0.77 from 1979 to 1992). The correlation between NAREIT and long-term bonds also decreased from 0.40 in the 1979–1992 period to 0.07 in the later time period. These reduced correlations between NAREIT and the other three asset classes clearly indicate that the diversification benefits of equity REITs have increased substantially in recent years.

www.realera.com and www.handex.com

Two private firms that supply real estate portfolio management services.

Risk-Adjusted Discount Rate

The most frequently used technique for explicitly incorporating risk into a discounted cash flow (DCF) analysis is to *risk-adjust* the discount rate that is (1) used to convert future cash flows into present value and (2) used as the minimum required rate of return in an internal rate of return (*IRR*) analysis. As first discussed in Chapter 2, with a *risk-adjusted* discount-rate approach, investors begin by estimating future cash flows, then make judgments about the riskiness of the cash flows. Algebraically, the required rate of return can be expressed as:

$$E(R_j) = R_f + RP_j$$

where $E(R_j)$ is the expected or required rate of return on the jth investment, R_f is the current return available on a risk-free Treasury security of comparable maturity, and RP_j is the required risk premium.

Investors struggling to determine their required rate of return on a potential investment frequently rely on surveys of other investors, formal and informal, to determine appropriate risk premiums and required rates of return (see Chapters 3 and 16). However, a criticism of the traditional risk-adjusted discount-rate approach to real estate valuation is that the specification of the risk premium relies heavily upon the investor's judgment. The subjectivity of discount-rate specification is perceived by some to be a weakness of the DCF model. At a minimum, it has frequently left investors asking whether more objective quantitative models for specifying the discount rate are available.

Quantifying Required Risk Premiums with Asset-Pricing Models

Can the required risk premium be determined by considering only the riskiness of the investment being evaluated, perhaps as measured by the standard deviation of its expected return? If investors have the ability to diversify away the unsystematic risk of their portfolios, the answer is no. In analyzing the riskiness of the next investment opportunity, they should be interested only in the amount of systematic risk it would bring to their portfolio. The unsystematic risk is of no concern because it can be eliminated through diversification. In a competitive market, investors should not expect to be compensated for bearing unsystematic risk because properties will be priced to yield a going-in internal rate of return that is just sufficient to provide the typical (i.e., well-diversified) investor with an adequate return. Investors seeking additional compensation for unsystematic risk, in the form of a reduced price and larger RP_j, are likely to be outbid by well-diversified investors.

Concept Check

23.14 What kind of risk exposure can investors expect to be compensated for at acquisition?

The consideration of systematic risk requires considerable information about the correlation between returns on the asset in question and the returns on assets currently in the portfolio. This determination of acceptable investment projects in a portfolio context is not unlike many shopping decisions people face in everyday life. For example, consumers do not select neckties solely because of how attractive they appear as they hang on the department store rack. The shopper must consider how the necktie will look with certain combinations of slacks, shirts, and sports jackets. An *efficient* necktie acquisition is one that can be worn with numerous existing combinations. In short, a particular tie may catch the shopper's eye, but if it does not work well with the shopper's current wardrobe, the tie has little value. Similar analogues apply to buying a sofa or a new music CD, adding a basketball player to an existing team, or choosing a wife or husband.[14]

Modern asset-pricing models, developed initially for the valuation of publicly traded stocks, are able to quantify the relationship between systematic risk and required rates of return. A **single-factor asset pricing model** classifies sources of investment risk into two categories: (1) systematic (or macroeconomic) factors and (2) property-specific (microeconomic) factors that are diversifiable. The most widely used version of the single-factor model assumes the macroeconomic risk factors can be captured by a single index of stock market returns, such as the S&P 500. The systematic risk of a portfolio is then measured by determining the sensitivity of the portfolio's return to changes in the macroeconomic risk factor (i.e., stock market index). Because the return on most asset portfolios positively covaries, at least to some extent, with changes in the macroeconomy, systematic risk cannot be diversified away.

In most empirical applications of the single-factor model, the historical risk of a portfolio is measured by the covariance between the returns on the portfolio and the returns on the stock market index that is used as a proxy for systematic risk. This covariance (divided by the variance of the stock market index) is referred to as the portfolio's beta coefficient, or B_j. Historical betas for many stocks, including most publicly traded REITs, are listed in

---

14. However, when making a proposal of marriage, it is probably not advisable to dwell on the "diversification benefits" that your intended would bring to your "portfolio."

Finding REIT Betas Online

Choose a publicly traded REIT and find its ticker symbol. Go to the Multex Investor Website http://yahoo.multexinvestor. com, a financial research and information service provided by Reuters. In the "Quick Quote" box, type in the ticker symbol for your REIT. On your firm's page click on the "ratios" link under "Financial Info" in the left-hand margin. Find your firm's beta, along with an abundance of other data including valuation ratios, recent price performance, institutional holdings of the stock, and earnings estimates from Wall Street firms.

Exhibit 23-14 Selected REIT Betas as of July 2003

Property Type/Company	Beta	Property Type/Company	Beta
Apartment REITs		**Industrial REITs**	
Camden Property Trust	0.24	AMB Properties	0.03
Equity Residential	0.28	CenterPoint Properties	0.10
Avalon Bay	0.31	First Industrial Realty	0.27
Office REITS		**Retail REITs**	
Highwood Properties	0.17	General Growth Properties	0.02
Equity Office Properties	0.27	Federal Realty Investment Trust	0.12
Carr America Realty	0.31	Developers Diversified Realty	0.23

several major financial publications (e.g., *Value Line*) and are also published by such institutions as Merrill Lynch, the Wharton School, and Wells Fargo Bank. Selected betas for nine publicly traded REITs are displayed in Exhibit 23-14. Several websites also provide betas for publicly traded companies. See the example in Explore the Web.[15]

The market risk premium, *MRP,* can be measured as the return on the broad-based stock return index, minus the risk-free rate. The required risk premium on the portfolio being evaluated, RP_j, is calculated as:

$$RP_j = B_j \times MRP \qquad (20\text{-}6)$$

With this formulation, RP_j will be determined by the premium earned by all investors for bearing systematic (macroeconomic) risk, *MRP,* times the sensitivity or exposure of the *j*th portfolio to systematic risk. If the returns on the asset or portfolio being valued have zero

15. Beta can be determined statistically by regressing the historical returns of the asset or portfolio being valued on the historical returns of the stock market index (the proxy for changes in returns due to macroeconomic fluctuations). In the single-factor model, the dependent variable is the actual return on the specific investment or portfolio over a large number of periods. The independent variable is the actual return on the stock market portfolio.

correlation with the proxy for macroeconomic (market) risk, then $B_j = 0$, RP_j will equal zero, and the discount rate will equal the risk-free rate. An asset or portfolio whose return has historically moved one-for-one with the proxy for macroeconomic risk will have a beta equal to one and, therefore, an RP_j equal to the MRP. The intuition here is that if an asset or portfolio is equally as volatile as the macroeconomy (stock market), as determined by a $B_j = 1$, then the required risk premium on the portfolio, RP_j, should equal the risk premium on the market.

Multifactor asset-pricing models assume that there are several sources of macroeconomic risk in the economy, that large subsets of assets respond to fluctuations in these risk factors, and that the influence of these risk factors on asset returns cannot be diversified away—even in large portfolios. That is, these variables or risk factors have been shown to have a systematic effect on portfolio returns. Thus, investors should expect—indeed, demand—compensation in the form of an increased expected return for bearing the risk associated with these factors.

Despite the appeal of a more objective approach to the determination of required risk premiums and discount rates, most investors rely on more informal approaches, such as discussions with other market participants, when seeking to determine appropriate discount rates for commercial properties. Asset pricing models are widely used in the analysis of real estate investment trusts and other publicly traded securities. They are not widely used in private commercial real estate markets. Why? An important explanation is the lack of historical return data on individual properties. Investors simply cannot calculate the historical betas of privately held properties as a first step toward determining the appropriate beta to plug into equation (20-6). And if past data are not available to accurately calculate *historical* betas, investors have little basis for determining the appropriate beta to use in the valuation of *future* cash flows.

Summary

The term *risk* is synonymous with *variability*. Thus, the more variable the returns on an asset, the more risky the asset and the lower its value, all else being the same. Risk in real estate investments can be divided into two broad categories. Systematic risk is the variation in returns caused by macroeconomic events and conditions; unsystematic risk is the variation in returns caused by property-specific sources such as the tenant mix, neighborhood conditions, and property management. In the traditional method for specifying discount rates, known as the risk-adjusted discount-rate approach, risk premiums for systematic and unsystematic risk are subjectively added to a risk-free rate to account for the expected variation in cash flows and returns. These risk premiums are included in the required discount rate to compensate the investor for taking on the systematic and unsystematic risks of the investment.

The incorporation of risk analysis into the overall decision-making process for real estate investments includes the specification of investor risk preferences, identification of major investment risks, and risk management. The most crucial of these elements is risk management because it involves the measurement of risk. Risk measurement is guided by two alternative perspectives: project-specific risk analysis and portfolio risk analysis.

Project-specific risk analysis focuses on measuring the riskiness of one investment at a time. Since past return data are rarely available to calculate the standard deviations of private real estate investments, the analysis of risk depends on the use of forward-looking subjective probability techniques. These techniques require the analyst to estimate the means and standard deviations of estimated returns and thus to quantify the riskiness of an investment.

The portfolio concept of risk considers the riskiness of various assets taken together. It is a more encompassing framework for risk analysis. Two implications arise from the portfolio concept. First, it allows for the virtual elimination of unsystematic risk through asset diversification. Second, it allows analysts to estimate discount rates objectively through the use of asset-pricing models. This extension is of great importance because the subjective specification of discount rates is considered by some to be a shortcoming of real estate investment analysis using discounted cash flow methods.

Key Terms

Test Problems

Answer the following multiple choice questions:

1. Most investors are:
   a. Risk averse.   c. Risk seekers.
   b. Risk neutral.   d. None of the above.

2. When the returns on an asset are more volatile than the returns on the market portfolio (index), the beta of the asset is:
   a. Greater than zero but less than one.
   b. Greater than one.
   c. Less than one.
   d. Less than zero.
   e. None of the above.

3. What type of risk can be eliminated from a portfolio of real estate holdings if the various holdings have returns that are less than perfectly correlated?
   a. Unsystematic risk.
   b. Systematic risk.
   c. Beta risk.
   d. Market risk.

4. Combining assets in a portfolio so that the risk of the portfolio is less than the average risk of each individual asset is called:
   a. Subjective probability analysis.
   b. Risk measurements.
   c. Risk aversion.
   d. Diversification.
   e. Capital asset pricing.

5. Risk management includes all of the following except:
   a. Transferring risks.
   b. Measuring risks.
   c. Diversification.

   d. Purchasing insurance.
   e. Risk management includes all of the above.

6. If the calculated covariance between two assets is positive, the correlation coefficient:
   a. Is always positive.
   b. Is always negative.
   c. Could be positive or negative.

7. Given the following probabilities and their respective outcomes, determine the expected value of the specified distribution of potential returns.

Economy	Probability	Investment Return
Depression	0.05	−5.0%
Recession	0.35	2.5%
Slow Growth	0.40	7.5%
Strong Boom	0.20	14.0%

   a. 4.750 percent.   c. 6.925 percent.
   b. 6.425 percent.   d. 7.250 percent.

8. Calculate the (sample) standard deviation of the following historical return series.

Year	Return
1994	12.0%
1995	11.0
1996	9.0
1997	10.0
1998	12.0

   a. 1.04.   c. 1.30.
   b. 1.17.   d. 1.70.

9. An efficient portfolio is one that:
   a. Minimizes the expected return for a given level of risk.
   b. Minimizes the portfolio management costs.
   c. Minimizes the risk exposure of the portfolio.
   d. Minimizes the risk for a given level of return.

10. Assume β for the subject asset is 0.50, the risk free rate is 6 percent, and the market risk premium is 8 percent. According to the single-factor, asset-pricing model, the expected/required return on the subject asset is:
   a. 8 percent.
   b. 14 percent.
   c. 10 percent.
   d. None of the above.

Study Questions

1. The positive relationship between risk and return is often misunderstood. Does it mean you are guaranteed a higher return when you undertake a riskier investment? Explain.
2. List some examples of diversifiable risk that are site specific.
3. What are the primary tools that investors can employ to reduce the variability of returns on their real estate investments?
4. Distinguish between systematic and unsystematic risk and list some examples of each.
5. Explain "efficient" diversification.
6. In a competitive market, what type of risk can investors expect to be compensated for in the form of a higher expected return?
7. What is an investment's beta coefficient?
8. Distinguish between single-factor asset-pricing models and multifactor asset-pricing models.
9. Define environmental risk and include several examples.
10. Consider the following two investments:

Investment A		Investment B	
Return	**Probability**	**Return**	**Probability**
3%	0.10	4%	0.05
5	0.20	5	0.25
8	0.40	6	0.40
10	0.20	7	0.25
12	0.10	8	0.05

   a. Calculate the expected return on each investment.
   b. Calculate the variance and standard deviation of each.
   c. Calculate the return per unit of risk for each investment. When may it be useful to calculate?
   d. Which investment do you prefer? Explain your choice.

11. You are considering the purchase of a small residential rental property for $200,000 in equity. You feel there are three possible scenarios for future cash flows and appreciation:

Pessimistic—The net operating income (*NOI*) will be $20,000 in the first year, then decrease 3 percent per year over a six-year holding period. The net sale proceeds (*NSP*) will be $180,000.

Most likely—The *NOI* from operations will be $20,000 per year for the next six years and the *NSP* will be $200,000.

Optimistic—The *NOI* will be $20,000 in the first year, then increase 4 percent over the six-year holding period. The *NSP* at the end of year 6 will be $230,000.

You believe there is a 25 percent probability that the pessimistic scenario will occur, a 50 percent probability for the most likely scenario, and a 25 percent probability for the optimistic scenario.
   a. Compute the internal rate of return (*IRR*) for each scenario.
   b. Compute the expected *IRR*.
   c. Compute the variance and standard deviations of the *IRR*s.

12. Consider the following historical returns on two investments:

	Realized Return	
Year	**Investment A**	**Investment B**
1991	3%	27%
1992	10	21
1993	22	10
1994	26	3
1995	15	12

Calculate the following:
   a. Mean return on investment A.
   b. Sample variance of return on investment A.
   c. Sample standard deviation of return on investment A.
   d. Mean return on investment B.
   e. Sample variance of return on investment B.
   f. Sample standard deviation of return on investment B.

Explore The Web

The National Association of Real Estate Investment Trusts (NAREIT), an industry trade organization, collects and disseminates a great deal of information on the public REIT markets. Access to some of the data and information requires membership in NAREIT. However, a significant amount of data, as well as research reports and analysis is freely available. The purpose of this exercise is to use the NAREIT website to download historical return information on both REITs and other asset classes such as stocks and bonds.

1. Go to the NAREIT website (www.nareit.com).
2. Click on the "Investing in REITs" tab and read the informational reports titled "Guide to REIT Investing" and "Diversification Benefits of Investing in REITs."
3. Click on the "Research and Statistics" tab and search for "REIT Watch." Pull up the latest monthly issue of REIT Watch.
4. Find the exhibit titled "Selected Indicators of Equity Market Performance." This exhibit contains annual total returns for the last 10 years on the composite NAREIT Index, the S&P 500, the Russell 2000, and 10-year U.S. Treasury securities. Copy the annual return data for these four indexes into a Microsoft EXCEL spreadsheet.

5. Calculate the following:
   a. Mean annual return on the composite NAREIT Index, the S&P 500, the Russell 2000, and 10-year U.S. Treasury securities.
   b. Standard deviation of the returns on each of the four asset classes.
   c. The average return per unit of risk (i.e., standard deviation) for each of the four asset classes.
   d. Correlation among the total returns on each of the four asset classes.
   e. Discuss the relative return performance of the four asset classes with and without risk adjustments.

Solutions to Concept Checks

1. A portfolio perspective of potential real estate investments considers the other assets already part of the investor's portfolio. In short, investment decisions are not made in isolation.
2. Investment risk is the probability that actual cash flows and returns will vary from expectations. Risk is *not* just the probability that performance will be worse than expected—so-called downside risk. Rather, all potential variation from expectations, positive or negative, is risk.
3. Microeconomic risk factors affect specific properties or markets. They do not affect the overall, or macro, economy.
4. Risk adjusted discount rates for real estate asset must reflect the opportunity cost of investing in real estate. At a minimum, real estate investors give up the opportunity to invest in risk-free Treasury securities if they invest in real estate. Therefore, their minimum, or base, opportunity cost is the rate of return they could earn on a Treasury security with maturity equal to the expected holding period on the real estate. So, real estate investors with 10-year expected holding periods must, at a minimum, expect to earn the return currently available on 10-year Treasury securities.
5. The primary disadvantage of subjective probability distributions is that they are not based on objective facts. Rather, a great deal of judgment by the investor/analyst is required. Unlike a coin flip, where we know the probability of heads is 50 percent, we simply don't know exactly what the probability is, for example, of a mild recession.
6. Most investors are risk averse. This means that, all else being the same, the greater the uncertainty about the future cash flows and returns, the higher must be the going-in *IRR*. Thus, when an asset is priced, there is a positive relation between perceived risk and expected return. Higher returns on riskier investments, however, are not guaranteed.

7. No, standard deviation is a measure of the expected (or actual) variability or dispersion around the expected (or mean) value. It does not measure the probability of just bad outcomes. The basic idea is that all variation from mean or expected values is "bad."
8. Three strategies for managing risk are (1) avoid risky projects, (2) use insurance to transfer risk to others (at a cost to the investor), and (3) diversify the portfolio (at no or little cost to the investor).
9. The standard deviation of the return on a portfolio is usually *less* than the average standard deviation of the individual assets. This is the result of portfolio diversification.
10. A diversifiable risk is unsystematic in the sense that variations in the variable or risk factor do not affect the entire "system" of properties in the United States. Rather, a diversifiable risk factor is one that affects only a single property or a number of properties in a local market. Because the risk is not "systemwide," it is labeled unsystematic.
11. What is left over in an investor's well-diversified portfolio is the "systemwide" risk that affects all assets. We label risk that cannot be diversified away as *systematic risk*.
12. The free lunch in financial economics is the ability to add assets that increase the expected return on the portfolio and decrease (or at least not increase) risk. The addition of all assets does not produce this result, only those that interact with the existing assets in a particular way.
13. Over the 1993–2002 period, REITs outperformed stocks. REITs produced both a slightly higher average return *and* lower standard deviation of return over this time period.
14. In competitive markets, investors can only expect compensation in the form of a higher going-in *IRR,* for exposure to systematic risk.

Additional Readings

The following books contain expanded examples and discussions of commercial real estate risk and portfolio management issues:

Bernstein, Peter L. *Against the Gods: The Remarkable Story of Risk.* New York: John Wiley, 1998.

Bernstein, Peter L. *Capital Ideas: The Improbable Origins of Modern Wall Street.* New York: The Free Press, 1992.

Brueggeman, William B., and Jeffrey D. Fisher. *Real Estate Finance and Investment,* 11th ed. New York: McGraw-Hill Irwin, 2001.

Geltner, David M., and Norman G. Miller. *Commercial Real Estate Analysis and Investments.* Cincinnati, OH: South-Western Publishing, 2001.

Hudson-Wilson, Susan, ed. *Modern Real Estate Portfolio Management.* New Hope, PA: F. J. Fabozzi Associates, 2000.

Many corporate finance and investment textbooks treat risk in more detail than this chapter. See, for example:

Bodie, Zvi, Alex Kane, and Alan J, Marcus. *Investments,* 4th ed. New York: McGraw-Hill Irwin, 1999.

Brealey, Richard A. *Principles of Corporate Finance,* 7th ed. New York: McGraw-Hill Irwin, 2003.

The following journals contain numerous articles on commercial real estate risk and portfolio management issues:

Journal of Real Estate Portfolio Management, published semiannually by the American Real Estate Society, Grand Forks, ND.

Real Estate Issues, published quarterly by the American Society of Real Estate Counselors, Chicago.

Real Estate Review, published quarterly by Warren, Gorham and Lamont, Boston.

chapter twenty-four

Development: The Dynamics *of* Creating Value

Learning Objectives

After reading this chapter you will be able to:

1. List eight stages in the development process.

2. Identify major risks associated with each stage of development.

3. Describe the role of each of these in the development process: market and feasibility consultant, environmental engineer, architect, land planner, landscape architect, general contractor, and construction manager.

4. List three characteristics of the role of developer.

5. List four characteristics generally required of a developer.

Introduction

Development has aptly been defined as the continual reconfiguration of the built environment to meet society's needs.[1] This definition captures the fact that development is a necessity, demanded by society to meet its needs for shelter, working space and other permanent facilities. Developers are in many ways the quarterbacks of the real estate industry. While they are only a tiny fraction of the total industry, their role is central in creating the events that put the industry in motion. Though constrained by available resources and regulations, their decisions still have a dominating effect on what kind and quantity of real estate is available in the marketplace, what jobs are available in construction, architecture, and other related fields, and what real estate investment opportunities are available to the capital markets. Their central and visible role in the process of change and in creating society's structures makes them both a lightning rod for social anxieties and a glamorous form of entrepreneurship.

In this chapter we first view the process of development and the multitude of ingredients involved at each of its several stages. But description cannot capture the dynamics of the opportunities, decisions, challenges, risks, and rewards that "come with the territory."

1. Mike Miles, Gayle Berens, Marc A. Weiss, *Real Estate Development Principles and Process,* 3rd ed. (Washington, DC: Urban Land Institute), 2000, p. 1.

So we use examples to illustrate how the process has played out in several interesting cases. Finally, we consider what the experience of being a developer is about and what it takes to enter the field of development.

In many ways the subject of development is a fitting final chapter for this text because development encompasses virtually every subject covered. The developer must understand the legal nature of real property interests (Chapter 4) as well as the relevant land use regulations and regulatory processes (Chapter 6) in order to know what use is legally feasible with a parcel of land. In addition, the developer must be able to evaluate the market potential for a proposed project in order to determine its economic feasibility (Chapters 5 and 7). Also the developer must understand the relevant cash flow analysis to determine feasibility and profitability (Chapters 3 and 16). Further, the developer must understand financing and investment alternatives to bring together the debt and equity capital for the project (Chapters 10 through 15). If the developer is to obtain financing or expects to sell the property, the appraised value of the project is important (Chapters 8 and 9). If the developer plans to sell the property, he or she must understand the real estate transaction process (Chapters 18 through 20). If the developer is creating income producing property, it is important to understand effective property management, either for his or her own management of the property, or for assuring that the property is designed for effective management (Chapters 17 and Chapter 21). The value created in a development project is potentially influenced by any and all of these many dimensions of real estate.

The Process of Development

Development projects may arise out of a site in search of a use, a use in search of a site, or resources in search of an opportunity.[2] In each case, a specific development concept at a specific site must emerge. The ways that this happens are probably beyond cataloging. At one extreme might be a fast-food giant or an Eckerds, Walgreens, Wal-Mart, or other chain retailer that has evolved a dramatically successful store concept and is committed to replicating it at hundreds of locations. At the other extreme might be a landholder with a single parcel of land who, in the effort to make the land productive, conceives a new plan for use of the site. Mixed into the possibilities are experienced development organizations looking for new engagements and investors looking for high-return uses of their capital. The multitude of specific development ideas springing from these diverse situations no doubt is replete with spontaneity, false starts, amusement, and excitement. Unfortunately, it is little documented except in the "war stories" of individual developers.

We start the process of development at the point where a specific use has been chosen for a specific site. From that point forward, we can think of the process as having eight stages:

1. Establishing site control.
2. Feasibility analysis, refinement, and testing.
3. Obtaining permits.
4. Design.
5. Financing.
6. Construction.
7. Marketing and Leasing.
8. Operation.

Concept Check

24.1 What are three basic perspectives from which development projects arise?

www.nmhc.org

Organization of large-scale apartment owners and developers.

www.uli.org

The Urban land Institute, the principal development organization in the United States (see Explore the Web on page 663).

2. These alternatives were first articulated by James Graaskamp, the legendary professor of real estate and development at the University of Wisconsin. See, for example, *A Guide to Feasibility Analysis* (Chicago: Society of Real Estate Appraisers, 1970).

Establishing Site Control

Site control is the entry ticket to development. Without it, nothing else matters. The problem of site control ranges in the extreme. The dream case for a developer is owning the site outright, with no debt. This is the case when the developer is part of a family or organization owning land that, due to urban growth, has become "ripe" for more intensive use. Many railroad companies, ranches, and paper companies in California and across the "sun belt" have found themselves in this situation. An extreme example is the Irvine Ranch in Orange Country, California. With 93,000 acres on the southern perimeter of greater Los Angeles it has hosted development that ultimately will support a population of over 200,000 in one of the exemplary planned communities of the world. A much smaller example is that of a family whose farm was bisected first by Interstate 75 several decades ago, and subsequently by a major urban arterial of Gainesville, Florida. This created the only case where one owner controlled all four corners of a significant interchange on I-75, a gateway to Florida. At the other extreme of land acquisition is the legendary case of the Disney organization assembling the land for Walt Disney World. The more than 27,000 acres of the prospective site were owned by dozens of different interests. Knowing that any recognition by one of these owners as to who was seeking the land would likely result in a "hostage" situation, Disney devised elaborate blind entities to deftly and successfully acquire all of the pieces that now make up the Walt Disney World site.[3] In urban redevelopment, the problem of gaining control of multiple sites is so great that it early became one of the arguments in support of the use of the public power of eminent domain to assemble land in urban renewal programs.

www.nahb.org

The leading trade association for builders of housing.

Concept Check

24.2   List eight stages of the development process.

A common tool for a developer to gain control of a site is to purchase an **option** on the land which allows the developer, at a predetermined price, to choose by a certain date whether to go through with the purchase. Ideally, it allows the developer sufficient time to conduct feasibility analysis, to run soil and environmental tests, to obtain necessary zoning changes or other permits, and possibly long enough to arrange financing. The terms of an option can be very creative and will depend on the bargaining position of the two parties. It could involve giving the landowner a participation in the development in lieu of cash up front. Further, options can come in disguise, such as a contract for deed.[4] If the developer purchases the land on a contract for deed with a small down payment, then it may be easy to simply abandon the contract if the project turns out to be infeasible.

Yet another way to manage equity for land acquisition is to bring a future tenant into the development as a partner. This arrangement might be the formula that enables a new developer with few resources to enter the industry. For a tenant needing a facility, the arrangement could provide sufficient reward to justify risking involvement with the untested developer, particularly if the tenant can tolerate uncertainty in the date the facility will become available. If the tenant will occupy a large portion of the facility to be built, the risks of the development are further reduced since market uncertainty is resolved.[5]

An important variation on joint venturing with a tenant is **build-to-suit.** The developer preleases to a financially strong, frequently national, tenant to build to the tenant's

---

3. In this strategy of land assembly, Disney was following a time-honored approach in the real estate industry. The prominent New York developer, William Zeckendorf, was well known for similar methods.

4. Often called a land contract. See Chapter 10 for a discussion of a contract for deed.

5. Whatever the option arrangement, it is important for the developer to remember that, if exercised, the option turns into a contract for sale of land, it will govern all aspects of the land purchase. Thus, the option contract needs to be as complete as any contract for sale of land in addressing issues of title examination, arrangement of financing, and other contingencies, which we discussed in Chapter 20.

specifications. This could be, for example, a restaurant for a national fast-food chain, or a freestanding facility for a national retailer.

Still another possible solution to land acquisition is the **ground lease.** Under this arrangement, only the initial land rent must be paid out before development actually gets under way. The ground lease can offer the seller of the land an attractive arrangement since it provides a long-term, inflation-protected income (assuming that rents are reviewed and adjusted periodically) and, in case of default, gives the landowner all of the improvements. One of the most famous examples of development on a ground lease is Rockefeller Center, built during the 1930s on land then owned by Columbia University. This ultimately turned land holdings of marginal value into a fabulous source of wealth for the school.

Concept Check

24.3   List four ways that a developer can finance the establishment of site control.

Feasibility Analysis, Refinement, and Testing

With a site under control the developer has time to evaluate the feasibility of the project. He or she normally will perform a financial feasibility analysis first. In substance, this will compare the present value of the project to its cost, and thus is a classic net present value computation, as presented in Chapter 16. Deriving the value of the project may be very informal, particularly if the *NPV* appears to be so high as to constitute a "slam dunk."[6] On the other hand, if expected *NPV* is marginally positive, then the developer must decide whether to retain additional market research in an effort to narrow the range of the feasibility outcomes. The additional market research also may give the developer useful guides to improve and refine the project concept. Obviously, the cost information of the developer also must be reasonably reliable to conduct the financial feasibility analysis, and the developer may need to order cost estimates on some aspects of the project.

If net present value is negative, then the developer must decide whether a revised plan might be feasible. If not, he or she will abandon the project, allowing any option on the land to elapse.

Even if a development appears financially feasible, it still depends on the land being free of soil problems, environmental concerns, ecological complications, seismic concerns, hydrological concerns, or anthropological or historical sensitivities. Thus, a developer commonly turns to an environmental consultant, a geologist, or other scientific experts at this point. The consultants will examine the site for underlying structural concerns, for any evidence of toxicity, wetlands, and sensitive wildlife habitat that may be protected, for example, under the Endangered Species Act. (See Industry Issues 4-1 for discussion of the Endangered Species Act.) In addition, if there is evidence of ancient ruins, the developer will need to retain an archaeologist or anthropologist to assess the presence of sensitive areas. Local regulatory agencies increasingly require this assessment in the form of an environmental impact statement (EIS) or environmental impact report (EIR) before issuing the necessary development permits. (See Chapter 6 for a discussion of environmental impact statements.)

Concept Check

24.4   What form of financial analysis is at the heart of a feasibility study?

If the consultant reports an underlying structural or environmental complication, the feasibility analysis must be reconsidered. The developer and consultants must determine

---

6. Financial theorists have not yet determined precisely what the threshold *NPV* is for "slam dunk" classification, but developers appear to know.

Exhibit 24-1 The Cycle of Evolving a Project*

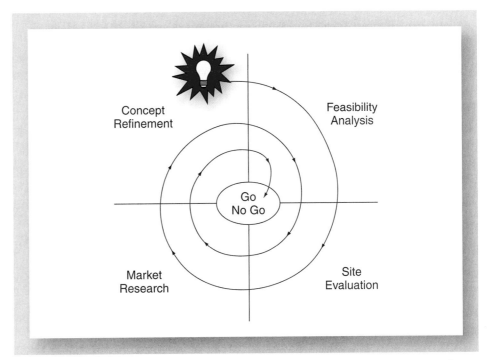

*This diagram borrows from one that addresses a broader perspective on development; see David Geltner and Norman G. Miller, *Commercial Real Estate Analysis and Investments* Prentice Hall, Upper Saddle River NJ: 2001.

whether the problem can be solved through either project redesign or through mitigation, and whether the resulting cost affects feasibility.

If project feasibility survives structural and environmental tests, it must then make it through further hurdles. The land must have marketable title and it would be prudent for the developer to affirm this through title search at this point before significant additional investments in the project begin to occur.

Exhibit 24-1 suggests the evolutionary nature of the project planning and feasibility process. It must cycle or iterate through several dimensions, normally incorporating additional information from each dimension as the process is refined toward a decision. Market research and feasibility tests are crucial components of this process. Since they are much too complex to be treated adequately in this chapter, and since they apply to any real estate valuation or investment, we have given these subjects several separate chapters including 5, 7, and 16. In the cycle depicted in Exhibit 24-1 the sophistication of the market research probably would increase with each "loop." Ultimately, however, many more of these processes will lead to "no go" than to "go."

Concept Check

24.5   Name three concerns for which a developer may retain an environmental consultant.

Obtaining Permits

Virtually all development projects require at least a site plan review. Many others will require a zoning change, possibly coupled with a parallel change in an official land use plan. Large-scale developments are likely to face some form of environmental impact or regional impact review. The cost of these reviews can reach hundreds of thousands of dollars for a large, complex development, and require a year or more to complete.

Exhibit 24-2 Thoughts of an Experienced Developer on Land Use Negotiation

Every successful developer is a good negotiator. The path to a completed project is fraught with perils, and to succeed a developer must deftly wend his or her way through a thicket of obstructions and objections.

One of the most challenging phases of any project is the zoning/site plan process, which usually involves public hearings. The site plan process involves submitting a detailed plan—location of buildings and roads, elevations, landscaping, setbacks, utility tie ins, total square footage—showing exactly how a developer plans to use the land in accordance with an already permitted use. In theory, all the developer must show during the site planning process is that all land use regulations and ordinances have been complied with and then approval is automatic. In real life, gray areas and matters of interpretation always arise. Some requirements are as amorphous as "compatible with the surrounding neighborhood," a stipulation that is probably unconstitutionally vague. But who wants to be the developer who spends five years and a small fortune taking it to the Supreme Court? Easier just to add some buffer or agree to pay for some infrastructure improvements as long as the requested concession is financially tolerable.

With NIMBYism (not in my backyard) virtually a universal response to any development, a successful developer must be prepared to navigate the shoals of opposition. Most challenging during the zoning/site plan process, a developer often must deal with multiparty negotiations, including, at a minimum, the local government planning staff, the hearing body itself, and the citizens and interest groups attending the hearing. Each party has a different agenda, motivations, and positions. Usually people oppose a development because their homes are nearby and they perceive a negative impact on their quality of life or upon the market value of their home, which for many people is their single largest financial investment. These are all jugular emotional issues to which people react strongly. Sometimes people oppose a development for larger environmental issues. There are no magic wands a developer can wave to make opposition go away, but negotiation skills and sincere public relationship efforts can help immensely.

Source: Told by Nathan Collier, principal, Paradigm Properties, Gainesville, Florida.

Concept Check

24.6   Even when a developer does not require a zoning change, the development project still must go through what kind of review?

If even a simple zoning change is required, the time and legal expense can be considerable and can require months, even years, with the ultimate outcome uncertain. It seems to be automatic that a developer who proposes apartments or commercial development near existing single-family neighborhoods will become the target of vigorous political resistance against the change. Even when the developer technically has all necessary permits in hand, preexisting homeowners who perceive the project as an intrusion into their neighborhood and a source of uncertain change often resort to a multitude of political maneuvers to delay and obstruct the project. They may even resort to filing lawsuits that challenge the existing zoning or permits on the slimmest of arguments. (Often a case that fails still delays the developer enough to stop the project.) Since delay is one of the developer's biggest enemies, he or she must attempt to lay the groundwork in advance for neighborhood cooperation, possibly by providing overly generous provisions for buffering (i.e., for providing transition zones that separate surrounding land uses from the development), or by offering gifts to the neighborhood such as, for example, a "vest-pocket" park or other desirable neighborhood improvement. Being prepared for constructive negotiation with both the land use authorities and with neighborhood homeowner groups is an essential component of a developer's resources.[7] (See Exhibits 24-2 and 24-3.) Probably the most dramatic failures (and successes) in the development experience take place in public hearings with land use authorities whose decisions can kill a project instantly (See Industry Issues 24-1 and 24-2). These meetings frequently are dramatized by being packed standing room only with intense and resistant homeowners.

7. Nathan Collier, who combines successful development of multifamily projects with writing, provides excellent firsthand examples of the role of such negotiations in his compact overview of multifamily development: Nathan S. Collier, Courtland A. Collier, and Don Halperin, *Construction Funding, The Process of Real Estate Development, Appraisal and Finance* 3rd ed. (New York: John Wiley, 2002.)

Exhibit 24-3 A Real Story of Developer Negotiation

The "Intruder"

I once was attempting to put together a roughly 300-unit apartment development that involved a rezoning. Due to the build up of the surrounding land, the agricultural zoning was obviously inappropriate and a rezoning was in order. But to what? The adjacent single-family neighborhood association thought single-family zoning was in their best interest and initially fought hard for that position.

A Strategy: Planned Unit Development

We began an education process through a series of meetings with the neighborhood. Our goals were to (1) present information on how extensive the permitted latitude was within the legal definition of "single-family" zoning and (2) present the alternative of a planned unit development. When the neighborhood group thought of single-family zoning, they imagined a development just like theirs: large lots, generous setbacks, expensive homes of 2,000-plus square feet. Through the use of third-party professionals (to add credibility), we were able to show how much of what they liked about their neighborhood came from the quality of the development itself and private deed restrictions and was not a legal requirement of a single-family zoning classification.

The neighborhood group quickly realized that single-family zoning classification alone would not give them the protection they desired. We then introduced the concept of a planned unit development that basically combines the rezoning and the site plan process. The land is rezoned, but it can only be developed according to the site plan submitted at the time of the rezoning. Thus, the site plan is locked into political/regulatory concrete. We offered to submit our rezoning request as a planned unit development that included several concessions: (1) setbacks several times larger than would normally be required under apartment zoning; (2) a berm, (3) extensive landscaping, much greater than the statutory minimum (4) no buildings facing the neighborhood would be higher than two stories nor contain more than eight units, and the roofline would be "complex" (i.e., they would look like large homes), (5) all parking lot lighting would be hooded or shielded so as not to create nighttime "light pollution."

The neighborhood would benefit by knowing exactly what they were getting; the developer would benefit by achieving the approval, or even acquiescence, of the adjacent neighborhood, which virtually assures governmental approval.

So Far, Not So Good

In spite of our concessions and extensive neighborhood meetings, the day of the zoning hearing arrived without endorsement from the neighborhood association. Nonetheless, when our land use attorney inquired if we wanted a postponement, I declined. I knew that a deadline was an excellent motivator during negotiation. We continued to talk with the association, with the last meeting occurring in a crowded conference room outside the main hearing room as the zoning commission finished prior items of its agenda. Citizens, neighborhood association representatives, planning staff, and development professionals bandied about last minute proposals.

Hope?

The upside was that a majority of the neighborhood supported a core group of concessions, although it was not the same majority on every point. The downside was that enough citizens were still in opposition—most hoping for more concessions—that the neighborhood association leaders felt uncomfortable formally supporting any one proposal.

Our development professionals presented our proposal, staff had their say, and then the floor was opened for citizen comments. Requests were made not to allow any rezoning (legally unrealistic) or to have the public buy the land as a park (budget buster extraordinaire!). Requests were made for an even greater buffer or to require that buildings be limited to one story. I waited until the very end and made my presentation speaking as a member of the public.

Last Card

I pointed out that the buffer we offered matched several others in the past and there was no local precedent for a larger buffer. I mentioned that single-family zoning allowed three-story construction and that we were limiting ourselves to two stories in a neighborhood where many homes were also two stories. Also, there were no statutory requirements for the berm we were offering and our landscaping adjacent to the single-family areas vastly exceeded regulatory requirements. I mentioned that we had held a number of meetings attended by well-known and respected professionals. I then played my best card by pointing out that although the neighborhood group was not formally in agreement with us, this was in large measure due to a desire to operate by consensus as an organization. Furthermore, a majority accepted the core of our proposals. I took a bit of a gamble at this point and turned from the podium and gestured toward the president of the neighborhood association who was sitting behind me and asked "Did I state that fairly?" and was rewarded with a nod. We got the rezoning on a 5–0 vote.

Source: Told by Nathan Collier, principal of Paradigm Properties Inc., Gainesville, Florida.

Industry Issues

24-1

Ancient Tequesta Indians Win Over Modern Miami Developer

n 1995 developer Michael Baumann assembled investors and won approval to launch a $100 million, 600-unit apartment and commercial high-rise at the mouth of the Miami River in downtown Miami, Florida. He purchased the 2.2-acre site for $8 million. In the fall of 1998, weeks before he was to launch construction of his Brickell Pointe, archaeologists conducting a routine survey of the site detected an unusual circle formation in the bedrock surface. When experts suggested that the circle of holes might have been carved by Tequesta Indians, a group that disappeared hundreds of years ago, the situation rapidly gained national attention. The focus of the national media, preservation groups, Native Americans, and an endless parade of paranormals, New Age groups, and others spiraled upward, creating an ongoing circus atmosphere at the site for weeks.

By all indications, Baumann had the right to proceed with his development. But the archaeologists involved reported that he made every effort to cooperate with them in evaluating its archaeological significance and in exploring options. He concluded, however, that redesign at that stage was infeasible. An effort to surgically remove and relocate the circle failed in mid-February 1999, and events rapidly led to legal adversarial action by the county, which sought and obtained permission from the court to exercise eminent domain. An injunction against construction was imposed and trial was set for the following October. After a contentious summer, the county and Baumann settled on a purchase price of $26.7 million six days before trial, with Baumann offering to loan the county part of the money for the purchase. The ultimate fate of the site remains to be seen in 2003, but a bill has passed the U.S. Senate to make it part of Biscayne National Park. Baumann, meanwhile, was last seen building another project nearby, where he had to overcome unrelated minor archaeological complications.

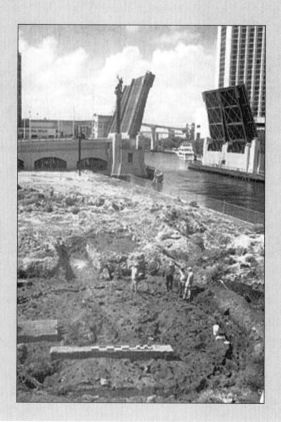

Source: Jim Kelley "Magic Primal," *Miami New Times,* November 16, 2000, miaminewtimes.com

Industry Issues

Gainesville Apartment Developer Haunted by the Ghost of Apartments Past

n 1985, when developer Ken McGurn sought to create the first downtown apartments in Gainesville, Florida, in over a half century, he found himself confronted by the ghost of apartments past. He needed to clear numerous dwellings from his proposed site, among which were the dilapidated shells of four Victorian structures. But a group of local citizens believed that these structures were the "apartments for workers" from an earlier era around 1900. They concluded that the structures were thus historic properties and set about to save them. The result was that McGurn's project was stopped until the issue was resolved with city authorities. Six months later he was obliged to move all four structures a little more than a half mile to four vacant lots. The move was the biggest transportation of houses in the history of the city, and drew suitable press attention. The whole undertaking cost approximately the price of a new small home at the time.

What has become of the "Sad Sisters," as the structures are known locally? They remain exactly as McGurn situated them almost 20 years ago—except for the effect of an additional 20 years of exposure to the elements, drug dealers, vagrants, vandals, and stray animals. In 1994 the city proposed to use them for fire department training, but a very active local historic preservationist stepped up and agreed to take them over by purchasing the lots and receiving the "Sisters" as a gift from McGurn. Unfortunately, she too has been unable to implement a feasible restoration plan for them, and the "Sisters" remain very sad in all respects.

Concept Check

24.7 Other than expense, what is the most common and serious threat to a typical development posed by the permitting process?

Design

When the developer has control of the property, is assured of no undiscovered legal, environmental, and ecological problems, and has the basic zoning required, it is time to turn initial concept drawings into a complete design. Selection of the architect is a vital step in the process, though numerous design professionals and engineers will play important subsidiary roles.

Architect. The architect, while always important, can take on a range of roles. The architect can provide predesign services or schematics, which relate needed building functions to each other and to space, yielding a preliminary indication of the basic building design. From there follows the actual design, which may evolve through several stages of completeness. Design development brings refinement of the interior space and exact specification of building systems such as plumbing, electrical, and HVAC (heating, ventilation, and air conditioning). The design process finally leads to the contract documents, the actual detailed specifications for the components of the building, working drawings, and rules and forms for the bidding process. In addition, the architect can assist or manage the bidding process. Finally, the architect sometimes actually manages the overall project, including the agreement between the developer and the contractor, though this role is infrequent.

Architects also can play another role earlier in the process. Often they are very effective in representing the development in public meetings with land use authorities. This is due in part to their expertise in presentations and perhaps to their comparatively favorable professional image relative to developers and attorneys.

The architect can be compensated according to several methods. Early in the development process, probably during the permitting stage, the architect may be retained on an hourly basis. In the design stage, when the project is much more narrowly defined, the compensation is likely to be based on either a percentage of the construction cost or a fixed fee plus expenses. When a percentage of cost is used, the amount will likely depend on the complexity of the project. For moderately complex designs, compensation can range between 3 and 7 percent; for simple garden apartments, it can range from as low as 1 to 2 percent. Unusual projects might pay 10 percent. Obviously, a potential problem with the percentage compensation is that it rewards the architect for a more costly design. Thus, a fixed fee plus expenses may be used instead.

Concept Check

24.8 During the permitting stage, an architect may be retained and compensated on one basis, while in the design stage the architect would be compensated on another basis. What is each method of compensation?

Selection of the architect for a development is obviously a critical step. The choice will be based on a combination of considerations, including competence and reputation, compatibility of values and goals between developer and architect, and ability of the two to communicate effectively. Since there is, in principal, inherent tension between the design function (i.e., aesthetically oriented) and the developer (i.e., cost and time oriented) communication of views and priorities are vital for a successful outcome.

Land Planner. For land developments the developer gives the key design role to a land planner. In large projects involving multiple structures, extensive grounds, parking areas, and drainage and water retention systems, the developer will rely on a land planner to "solve" the complex land planning puzzle. The developer works closely with the land planner to evolve the basic site plan within which any structures must fit. The **land planner** in turn uses input from a number of specialists, including hydrologists, architects, marketing consultants, engineers, soils engineers, and others. Concerns of the land planner include aesthetics, optimal use and preservation of the site, traffic flows, utility systems, and drainage systems.

Landscape Architect. The landscape architect normally serves in a more detail oriented role than the land planner. The **landscape architect** focuses on the topography, soil, and vegetation that are the context for a structure, with the goal of giving a suitable harmonious and enhancing immediate context for the structure. This involves numerous ingredients, including grading, ground covers, shrubs, trees, flowerbeds, sign character and placement,

www.aia.org

American Institute of Architects, the primary professional organization in the field.

www.planning.org/

The American Planning Association. The primary professional organization of planners.

fountains, benches, or other amenities. The landscape architect's work may also contribute to energy efficiency or drainage needs.

Engineers. The expertise of several types of engineers must be coordinated by the architect in bringing together the final structure design. These engineers commonly work as subcontractors to the architect, but their qualifications need to be reviewed by the developer. A **soils engineer** will determine the sufficient specifications to achieve safety and stability for a structure's foundation. A **structural engineer** will determine the requisite structural skeleton to maintain the building's integrity. A **mechanical engineer** will provide specifications and design for the HVAC system and other building systems. An **electrical engineer** will design the power sources and distribution system. Finally, a **civil engineer** will design on-site utility systems, including sewers, water, streets, parking, and site grading.

Clearly, development involves extremely complex coordination, and this is one of the major challenges of the developer. It is not surprising that one knowledgeable observer has asserted that failure to achieve effective communication between developer, architect, and engineer early in the development process is the single greatest cause of project delays and cost overruns.[8]

Concept Check

24.9   In selecting an architect, a developer will consider design capabilities and experience. What other considerations may be equally important?

Concept Check

24.10   What is the difference between a land planner and a landscape architect?

Financing

Financing of development involves multiple phases of the project, each with a different set of risks and with different combinations of financing. We will consider financing for land acquisition, construction, and postconstruction. Typically, debt financing is involved in each of these stages, but of course there must be equity capital as well. Frequently the combination of debt financing and equity is insufficient to carry the project through the construction stage. Thus, gap financing through mezzanine debt also can play an important role.

Land Acquisition Financing. Usually a developer is reluctant or unable to commit substantial funds in the acquisition of land for development. The period before actual construction could last many months or several years, and the limited capital of a typical developer bears a very high opportunity cost because of its value in providing liquidity in the developer's currently active projects. But institutional lenders, such as banks, thrifts, and insurance companies, are unwilling and largely prohibited from lending on land that generates little or no cash flow. In the rare case when an outside source provides a land loan, the total is likely to be for no more than 50 percent of the value of the land. Thus, a developer must look to other sources. We have already noted the importance of options as a solution. However, when the developer must exercise, or "go hard," on the option, more complete funding must be found. Again, the contract for deed or a purchase money mortgage

---

8. Richard Peiser and Ann Frej, *Professional Real Estate Development: The ULI Guide to the Business,* 2nd ed. (Washington, DC: Urban Land Institute, 2003), p. 41.

from the land seller is a very common solution. Others, as noted, may be to bring the land seller into the development as a joint venture partner, or to acquire use of the land through a ground lease.

But financing the land itself is not sufficient. The developer will incur significant **soft costs** before reaching the stage of construction financing, including the title examination, environmental and ecological evaluation, legal and other costs of the permitting process, and architectural and engineering fees. Thus, the developer must have equity capital. Typically, this will come mainly from outside investors through any of the business entities discussed in Chapter 15, including a subchapter S corporation or, for a large-scale development organization, through a REIT. However, the most common structure used is either a limited partnership or, increasingly, the limited liability company (LLC). Typically the financial investors will contribute funds for their share of the ownership interest, while the developer will contribute mainly expertise for a share of the venture.

Obviously, the financial investors must have confidence in the developer. Thus, the ability of the developer to raise capital depends heavily on his or her relevant track record. Investors are more likely to support a developer with more extensive experience, but it also matters what that experience is. For example, even if the developer has extensive experience in small-scale apartments, investors may be reluctant to invest with the developer in a condominium project, a large-scale apartment project, an office development, or in *any* development outside the developer's "neighborhood." Finally, investors must have confidence in the integrity of the developer since it is difficult or impossible to recover funds from a development that was never completed or from a developer who misappropriates funds.

Concept Check

24.11   What are some expenditures for which a developer may need equity capital?

Construction Financing. Once the developer and architect have completed the design stage, the developer can apply for construction funding. The most common source of construction funding is a bank. Traditionally, the loan had a floating rate over prime; increasingly, it may be tied to a LIBOR rate, floating perhaps 150 to 250 basis points above LIBOR.[9] The construction loan will finance, at most, the cost of land, soft costs and **hard costs,** (i.e. the direct costs of materials, labor and subcontractors for actual construction). The loan will be disbursed to the developer in stages, frequently on the basis of either specific invoices from vendors or as the project reaches various predetermined stages of completion.

The risks of construction lending are less in a number of respects than with the land acquisition stage. Environmental risks, ecological risks, title risks, and especially the permitting risks normally will be in the past. The remaining risks are those that banks can manage effectively, and thus will underwrite. These remaining risks include the ability of the developer to manage and complete the construction process; risks of construction such as weather interruptions, materials shortages, work stoppages, strikes, or construction accidents; and, finally, rent-up following construction. Banks long have had a comparative advantage in managing construction risk because it is similar to working capital risks for any operating business. That is, monitoring the delivery and use of construction materials is similar to monitoring business inventory, while evaluating the capability of the developer to perform is not unlike evaluating other business managers in their ability to perform.

When banks are uncomfortable bearing the postconstruction risk of rent-up, they often will shed it by requiring a *take-out commitment* from a long-term lender which will pay off

---

9. LIBOR is the London Interbank Offering Rate, a floating interest rate among non-U.S. banks for U.S. dollar deposits. While the rate is floating, many lenders provide the option to buy into an interest rate swap that substitutes fixed-rate payments for the actual floating rate on the loan.

the construction loan, as discussed in Chapter 14. Normally, however, the construction lender tends to forgo requiring a take-out commitment with an established developer constructing "mainstream" projects.

Concept Check

24.12 What risks of development already are resolved by the time the construction lender commits to a loan?

Mezzanine Debt. Banks seldom loan 100 percent of construction costs, except on very strong projects with strong developers. More commonly, they may fund 70 to 80 percent of project costs, or less in times of tight money. Frequently, therefore, the developer either needs or prefers to find additional capital to complete the construction stage. Equity capital is one option, but equity money requires a high yield, and funding with more equity dilutes returns to the original equity. Therefore, developers often turn to *mezzanine financing* which can take a range of forms. While it sometimes is second mortgage debt, it often is not mortgage debt at all. Rather, ownership shares in the development entity are pledged to the mezzanine lenders as security. Thus, in the event of default, no foreclosure procedure is necessary for the mezzanine lenders to exercise their recourse. Mezzanine debt is more expensive than normal construction financing. Where construction loans might run 150 basis points to 250 basis points above the LIBOR rate, mezzanine debt might run 300 to 500 basis points above. However, this is considerably lower than the required yield on equity money, and thus is more attractive to the developer.

Concept Check

24.13 Why might a developer need supplemental financing during the construction and leasing stages? Why would mezzanine financing be attractive?

Postconstruction Financing. The construction lender expects his or her loan to be paid off within two to three years, usually shortly after issuance of a **certificate of occupancy** from the local government certifying that the structure is safe for use. The pay off can happen either through financing arranged by the developer as the project nears completion, or through a take-out commitment arranged prior to construction funding. Normally the take-out "permanent" loan will be funded when the certificate of occupancy is issued. However, it may be funded in stages that depend on the level of leasing or occupancy starting with a relatively small **floor loan.** This, again, may necessitate "gap" or mezzanine financing. An alternative to gap financing that sometimes is used is a **subordination agreement** with the construction lender which makes the construction loan lien inferior to the lien securing the take-out loan that follows. If the amount of the take-out loan will not pay off the construction loan completely, the developer may be able to negotiate with a friendly construction lender to subordinate the remaining portion of the loan to the take-out loan. This gets most of their money back to the construction lender while allowing the take-out lender to have a first lien position.

Another approach to postconstruction funding is the *miniperm loan.* This is a construction loan that serves as a "permanent" loan for a few years after the property is completed. The typical term might be five years from inception. The miniperm has served multiple roles in recent years. For example, if current interest rates on permanent financing are higher now than the developer believes will be available for the project in five years, then the miniperm loan is an attractive alternative to the more traditional arrangement.

There is reason to expect that permanent financing normally could be on better terms after two or three years of operating experience since the project then will be regarded as an established property. Exhibit 24-4 suggests the basis for this possibility. The life of the

Exhibit 24-4   Risk Phases of an Income-Producing Property and Four
Alternative Financing Sequences

Construction Period	Lease-up Period	Stable Operations
Construction Loan with Take-out Commitment	Risky Permanent Loan	
Construction Loan with Take-out Commitment	Mezzanine Loan	Safe Permanent Loan
	Floor Loan	
Open-Ended Construction Loan		Safe Permanent Loan
Miniperm Loan		? Safe Permanent Loan

typical income-producing property can be divided into three phases: development and construction, lease-up, and stable operation. This is important because of risk differences between the stages. For the normal income-producing property, risks of the development and construction stage are not only relatively high but quite different from the risks after completion. Quite simply, the dominating risk after construction is market risk, whereas it is not a factor at all until construction is complete. Market risk is greatest in the lease-up stage. Thus, the overall risk level of the property falls progressively from one stage to the next. It is not surprising, therefore, that a developer could get better terms with "permanent" financing for a project that has "graduated" from the lease-up stage and shows two or three years of stable operation. In this case, the miniperm could offer a cost-effective way of deferring permanent financing until more favorable terms are available due to the reduced risk of stable operations.

Concept Check

24.14   Why might a developer be able to obtain more favorable "long-term" financing after a project is leased and operating than when construction has just been completed?

Construction

Even the smallest building project involves a multitude of separate contractors and a still larger number of steps in the process.[10] Thus, construction must be controlled and coordinated by a central authority, the **general contractor,** who in turn is responsible for subcontracting the completion of the various components and systems of the project including excavation, pouring and finishing concrete, components of the structure, building systems such as electrical, plumbing, and HVAC, landscaping, and more. While the general contractor may be fully responsible for selecting the **subcontractors** involved, it is not uncommon for the developer or architect to review, or even prearrange, some of the subcontractors where they provide especially critical elements to the project.

---

10. One of the authors, in adding two rooms to his residence, counted approximately 25 separate subcontractors with over 100 separate tasks.

Construction Manager

n the construction process, a construction manager represents the developer, serving as a monitor, mediator, and advocate of the developer's goals. Because of the construction manager's need to be able to negotiate with the architect, the general contractor, subcontractors, marketing representatives, and possibly the lender, he or she must be mature and experienced enough to have credibility. Although construction managers usually play no direct role in the actual construction of a structure, they may be involved in scheduling and coordinating the design and construction processes, including the selection, hiring, and oversight of specialty trade contractors. They typically need to be very knowledgeable about, and therefore experienced with, the type of project involved.

Construction managers regularly review engineering and architectural drawings and specifications to monitor progress and ensure compliance with plans and schedules. They track and control construction costs against the project budget to avoid cost overruns. They meet regularly with the developer, trade contractors, architects, and others to monitor and coordinate all phases of the construction project. Their background may be that of an architect, contractor, or engineer.

Both the American Institute of Constructors (AIC, www.aicnet.org) and the Construction Management Association of America (CMAA, http://cmaanet.org) have established voluntary certification programs for construction managers. Requirements combine study and written examinations with verification of professional experience. Although certification is not required to work in the construction industry, voluntary certification can be valuable because it provides evidence of competence and experience.

Median annual earnings of construction managers in 2000 were $58,250. The middle 50 percent earned between $44,710 and $76,510. The lowest 10 percent earned less than $34,820; the highest 10 percent earned more than $102,860. According to a 2001 salary survey by the National Association of Colleges and Employers, candidates with a bachelor's degree in construction science/management received job offers averaging $40,740 a year.

Source: Bureau of Labor Statistics, *Occupational Outlook Handbook* (Washington, DC: 2003), http://stats.bls.gov/oco/

The agreement with the general contractor can range on a spectrum from fixed-price bidding to a negotiated agreement at cost plus fee. Government projects usually are made through bidding to meet the requirements of the public for arm's-length, competitive contracts. However, most other construction contracts are completed through negotiation. Often the arrangement will involve a maximum cost plus fee. If the cost runs higher than the maximum, the developer and general contractor split the overrun; if the cost runs less than maximum, they split the savings.

As noted before, effective communication and clear understandings between developer, architect, and the general contractor are vital to keep the project on schedule and on budget. Always a construction project will require change orders in the plans because of materials changes, oversights in the planning, or new market information that dictates modification of the project. These can become extremely costly once the original contracts have been signed. Poor communication or insufficient initial clarity leads to a high incidence of change orders.

No matter what problems arise on the construction project or what agreement exists with the general contractor, the developer bears the brunt of any failure. Therefore, the developer needs to monitor the process and be represented when problems and decisions arise. Often a **construction manager** serves as the developer's liaison and representative on the project site. For example, the construction manager may stand in for the developer in discussions between the general contractor and architect.

Construction often involves a significant number of changes; and resulting renegotiations between the architect, the general contractor, and subcontractors, are very costly. As a result, an alternative arrangement has evolved known as **design-build** where the architect and general contractor are one. In complicated projects this arrangement reduces inherent design-cost conflicts that otherwise must be negotiated due to changed plans. Since the changes will be worked out within one firm, the solutions should be efficient, affording savings for the project.

Sometimes speed of completion is exceptionally important. Then the developer may resort to a procedure called **fast-track construction.** Rather than waiting for the architect to complete the entire project design before construction, the design will be broken into sequential phases, beginning with the site design, footings and foundation, building shell, and so forth. Then construction will begin before the last phases of design are complete. While this procedure can greatly accelerate the process, the procedure has been known to result in dramatic failures where the architect discovered after construction was under way that something in an early phase is incompatible with what must follow.

Concept Check

24.15   Explain fast-track construction and design-build. What problem does each address?

Coordination of Contracting.   The development sequence presented thus far is oversimplified in a number of ways. Commonly, several elements of the process must overlap, and several contracts may need to be negotiated simultaneously. We have noted previously that the architect normally is involved in the permitting stage, providing both initial conceptual renderings and serving as a spokesman for the project. Further, the general contractor often should give input to the design process, and thus must be "on board" before the construction loan is closed. In addition, the construction lender is likely to need cost estimates from the general contractor, which depend on the design as well. Thus, the construction loan commitment may require the general contractor to be under contract. But the construction loan may require a take-out commitment by a "permanent" or long-term lender, who may require preleasing. Thus, it is possible that the developer cannot even close the land purchase (funded by the construction loan) until sufficient preleasing has occurred to satisfy the take-out lender.

Marketing and Leasing

For all but the largest of developers, the marketing and leasing of the project will be through an external broker. The developer must select the broker with care. The broker must be established in the market relevant to the project. Thus, for a locally oriented, general-purpose office building, the broker needs to be familiar with, and be known in, the local business office community in order to have knowledge of prospective tenants who are approaching lease turnover, who must expand to larger facilities, and so forth. Further, the broker should not be simultaneously engaged in marketing competitive projects since this creates conflicts of interest, and dilutes the attention and effort of the broker. In all cases the broker must be genuinely excited about the property.

A good broker not only has valuable connections in the target market, but also has special knowledge of the market regarding what tenants want and respond to in a property. For this reason the developer is wise to bring a broker into the process during the design stage to review and advise on the evolution of the design. Not only does this increase the likelihood of achieving a marketable property, but it allows the broker to have more of a stake in the product and more reason for enthusiasm about it.

Concept Check

24.16   In addition to personal and organizational capability, what are two other important requirements of a marketing agent for a development?

General Contractor

A general contractor is the person, or firm, that executes a contract with the developer to build a project. This must be accomplished according to the plans and specifications developed by the architect and engineers, or the owner, and in line with the prevailing building codes. The general contractor solicits subcontractors who bid or negotiate to perform components of the construction project, including excavation, pouring and finishing concrete, elements of the structure, each of the separate building systems, landscaping, and many more. The general contractor therefore is responsible for coordinating and managing people, materials, and equipment; budgets, schedules, and contracts; and the safety of employees and the general public. The general contractor must maintain the complicated sequencing and timing of all of the subcontractors, and work out solutions when the inevitable disruptions of the schedule occur. He or she is part liaison to the developer and architect, part monitor, and part enforcer.

General contractors are not salaried. The contract with the developer can range between a fixed-price bid and a cost plus fee agreement. Many general contracts involve a maximum price, as discussed in the text. If the cost exceeds the maximum price, the general contractor will share the overrun. If the cost is below, the general contractor will share the savings.

General contractors must hold a state-specific license. Normally there are no technical requirements beyond the license, but general contractors are the persons (or companies) that have gained considerable confidence in their capacity to perform. The individuals involved usually have a voluntary certification from the American Institute of Constructors (AIC, www.aicnet.org) or the Construction Management Association of America (CMAA, http://cmaanet.org). Virtually always the general contractor must be experienced in construction, perhaps having begun as a subcontractor in a construction specialty area. Increasingly, persons serving as general contractors have undergraduate or even graduate degrees in construction science, construction management, or civil engineering.

Developers are increasingly recognizing the value of an advertising and public relations program for a property. Community awareness can be increased through adroit "positioning" of events in the course of the development, including groundbreaking, topping out of a high-rise structure, or announcing of new tenants to the project. Sometimes developments are able to work with community charities and nonprofit organizations to host or sponsor community events. In all cases, an important part of public relations is for the developer to work closely with the press and with public land use authorities. Developers do well to recognize the needs of the press for "copy" to meet deadlines. Providing useful copy can help to foster valuable working relationships.

Similarly, the developer wants to build relationships with regulatory officials early in the process. A "no surprise" policy is advisable wherein the developer anticipates any regulatory problem or issue that may arise with the development and presents it to the regulatory officials—before third parties bring it to their attention—with a recommended solution and a demonstrated willingness to be flexible. Few features in a developer's style appear to engender more goodwill from the public and from officials than an evident willingness to explore alternative courses of action on contentious issues. This approach can be very important in public forums.

Most developments today seem to encounter the NIMBY phenomenon (not in my back yard) and perhaps the BANANA phenomenon (build absolutely nothing anywhere near anything). As noted in Exhibits 24-2 and 24-3, this usually arises from well-intended neighbors, but sometimes stems from well-organized special interest groups who are targeting the development issue merely as a step toward broader political goals. Regardless of the cause of the resistance, it is valuable to have put the project's "best foot forward" through attention to building favorable media coverage, by gaining organizational friends in the community, and by building a relationship of trust with the media and local authorities before the issues arise.

When the actual marketing for the project should begin depends on the type of property. It is not productive to launch advertising for apartments until shortly before the actual units are available. In contrast, as noted earlier, leasing for office buildings and other facilities with long-term tenants not only can begin during the design stage, but needs to start earlier since prospective commercial tenants will contract for space well in advance of their actual move. Similarly, there needs to be preselling of units in a condominium project. Further, preleasing (or preselling) is likely to be required for construction financing. For retail and some office projects, nothing really can go forward until the anchor tenants have been secured. Only then will construction funding be available, which enables closing on the land. Further, where the construction loan depends on a take-out commitment, the take-out commitment is likely to require preleasing to be well under way.

Leasing of commercial space (e.g., retail, office, or industrial) will be through a leasing agent. As explained in Chapter 17, commercial leasing is a particularly challenging and competitive specialty field; the developer wants to be assured that the broker for the project can bring these specialists to the table.

Concept Check

24.17   Why must the marketing program typically begin much sooner for a nonresidential development than for a residential one?

Developers have grown increasingly aware of the need for sophisticated marketing and merchandising programs for their projects. Therefore, they have turned to experienced and qualified outside brokerage and advertising firms rather than using in-house sales staff.

Operation

www.naiop.org

National Association of Industrial and Office Properties. Exceptional resources for commercial development: career information, industry issues, information resources

While marketing and leasing never cease with rental projects, once the project has been largely rented it is then regarded as being in the operating phase. Effective operational management of rental real estate is fundamentally important to maintaining and increasing the value of the property. The function is sufficiently important that it is the subject of two other chapters in this book: Chapter 17, "Enhancing Value through Ongoing Management," and Chapter 21, "Leases and Property Types." We defer to those chapters for discussion of the subject.

Exhibit 24-5 summarizes the phases of development. While there is, in reality, much variation, the arrows are suggestive of the order and which phases might overlap.

Exhibit 24-5   Typical Development Sequence

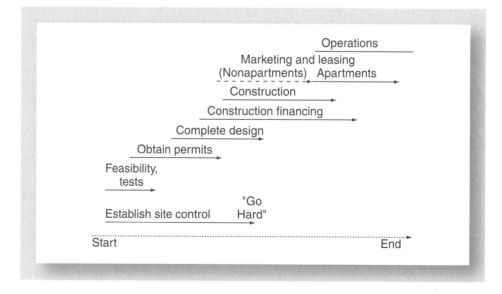

The "Numbers" of Development

Throughout the process of development, the successful developer always keeps the "numbers" in the corner of his or her eye. Even before control of the site is acquired, the developer has a concept of the project, but also will have done back-of-the-envelope calculations (nowadays, probably on a laptop) to "pencil out" the prospects. That is, the developer will not go forward on a project unless the value ultimately to be created appears to exceed its cost sufficiently to justify the venture. At the feasibility stage these numbers normally must be substantially refined, taking into account more of the specifics of the project as they become apparent. Also, the developer not only creates a construction budget in the feasibility stage, but must project the prospective income and operating expenses for one or more years in order to compute, formally or informally, the net present value of the project.

Exhibit 24-6 presents a late stage example of a construction budget such as might be evolved late in the feasibility process. The example is from a quality apartment project, and is fairly typical in its cost breakdown for large-scale suburban development.

The construction budget has six main components: land costs, hard costs, construction soft costs, marketing soft costs, developer's fee and total construction financing costs. Land costs are about 12 percent of the total. They include the acquisition cost, site development in preparation for building, interest or carrying costs, and property taxes on the land. Hard costs which are 66.3 percent of the total, are mainly the actual building construction (57.8 percent). Landscaping and hardscaping (hard surfaces on the grounds) make up another 2.6 percent of total costs, while an always important contingency reserve is 1.4 percent, representing about 2.5 percent of total hard costs.[11] This may be needed, for example, to cover change orders.

Construction soft costs are 9.4 percent of the total. Note that a huge 7.5 percent of this is a fee for utility use. Thus, permitting or impact fees are a very large component of the total cost. The architect's fee is only 0.5 percent, reflecting perhaps that the project is an adaptation of an earlier design, and relatively uncomplicated. Engineering fees are another 0.6 percent.

Other soft costs include marketing and construction financing. While marketing costs comprise 1.6 percent of the budget, construction financing is 10.2 percent, and vies with land cost as the second largest item in the budget.

The last item is the developer's fee, fairly modest at 1.7 percent of the total budget. The project is owned by a financially strong organization which is able to obtain 100 percent construction funding. No equity is required at the outset.

---

11. The hard cost contingency reserve is 1.4 percent out of 66.3 percent. Thus, reserve as a percentage of hard costs it is 2.5 percent (1.4 ÷ 66.3 × 100).

Exhibit 24-6 Construction Budget - Large Apartment Project

	% of Total
Land Costs	
Land acquisition cost	11.7%
Real estate taxes and carry costs	0.2
Total land costs	11.9%
Hard Costs	
Construction hard costs	57.8%
Permits/fees	0.4
Contingency	1.4
Telephone and TV	1.1
Security and water	0.5
Landscape and Hardscape	2.6
Graphics	0.1
Pools	0.7
Other	1.7
Total hard costs	66.3%
Construction Soft Costs	
Architect	0.5%
Engineering	0.6
Geotechnical report and survey	0.1
Testing (soils, environmental assessment, etc.)	0.2
Utility use fees	7.5
Inspections	0.1
Insurance	0.1
Contingency	0.3
Subtotal construction soft costs	9.4%
Marketing Soft Costs	
Furniture, fixtures and equipment	0.7%
Due diligence and legal fees	0.2
Closing cost	0.1
Title policy	0.2
Start-up/advertising	0.5
Subtotal marketing soft costs	1.6%*
Total soft costs	11.0%
Total—Land, Hard, and Soft Costs	89.2%
Developer's fee	1.7
Total Construction Financing Costs	10.2
Positive cash flow from operations during construction	−1.0
Total Basis in Project	100.0%*
Construction loan (100.00%)	100.0%
Equity provided (0.00%)	0.0
Total Capital	100.0%

*Discrepancies in totals are due to rounding.

Exhibit 24-7 Timing of Construction Expenditures

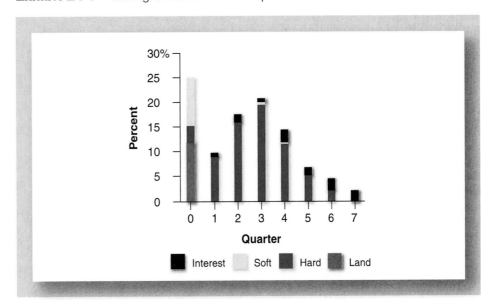

The time distribution of the main construction expenditures is shown in Exhibit 24-7. The entire construction period runs seven quarters. Thus, the first full year of operation is the third year after construction begins.

To determine project feasibility, the developer must, at a minimum, estimate net operating income (*NOI*) for the first full year of operation. Capitalizing this *NOI,* as explained in Chapter 9, will indicate the prospective value of the project when finished and operating, enabling the developer to compute the difference between resulting value and total accumulated construction cost (i.e., the *NPV*) at the time of completion. The developer may take a step further, projecting *NOI* and reversion from sale over perhaps a five-year operating period, as explained in Chapter 16. This would allow for a discounted cash flow analysis for the entire project from the beginning of construction to sale, some seven years later.

What Is It Like to Be a Developer?

Successful development can result in outcomes that are satisfying in the extreme. The developer can have a dramatic and lasting positive impact on a community. Every community has its handful of individuals in the development community whose work is apparent in the character and profile of the community. In the small college city of Gainesville, Florida, for example, the work of one development organization accounts for most of the recently built structures in the downtown, and has been the force behind revitalizing an otherwise languishing central city. (See Industry Issues 24-3). Another developer has transformed neighborhoods around the University of Florida, creating large numbers of quality apartments within walking distance of the campus and alleviating an extremely difficult parking problem for students. Other local developers have contributed heavily to providing quality subdivisions for households on the threshold of housing affordability. Normally, of course, these developers enjoy financial rewards for their successes.

But there is good reason for the financial rewards. The development process depicted above is complex, uncertain, turbulent, and even hostile at times. At best, it is a competitive "sport" with about as many rules and player protections as rugby. As many developers stress, the financial path of a developer usually is best characterized by the roller coaster. Very few developers have not experienced a fall from financial highs to the point where survival is in question—more than one time in their career. As has been observed before, most

Industry Issues

24-3

Can a Developer Affect a Community?

The Gainesville, Florida, MSA is a university, medical, and agricultural center with a population in 2003 of about 220,000. For decades the Gainesville downtown had suffered a steady exodus of businesses in response to the growing influence of I-75 to the west of the city and of the malls and power centers built near its intersections. Few new business buildings and no new residences had been constructed in the downtown for many years prior to 1980 and little remained except a variety of local and federal government facilities (marked Gov. in the photo).

Enter McGurn Investment Company owned and operated by Ken and Linda McGurn. Working with the city, they overcame considerable obstacles to create office, retail, and restaurant space that would surround an old post office which was being converted to house the city's prized regional professional theater group, the Hippodrome (see Hipp). That was the start of a slow but steady resurrection of Gainesville's downtown. In the years that followed, the McGurns engaged in several key projects that others would not touch, and only a lender who trusted the McGurns would finance. These included the first downtown apartments in the modern history of the city, and a dominating mixed-use project (Union Street Station, slightly right of center in the photo). Altogether, in the pivotal southeast quadrant of the downtown, shown in the photo, McGurn Investment Company has built, rehabilitated, or facilitated some 20 projects (indicated by asterisks). The result may be substantial asset accumulation for McGurn Investment Company, but its community effects are the most interesting story. Gainesville now is gaining something that most larger cities strive for, a vibrant 24-hour downtown.

Other developers in other ways have had vital effects on Gainesville. But few development goals are more challenging or more colorful than restoring the heart of a city, as the McGurns have sought to do.

Who are prime developers that have impacted your city?

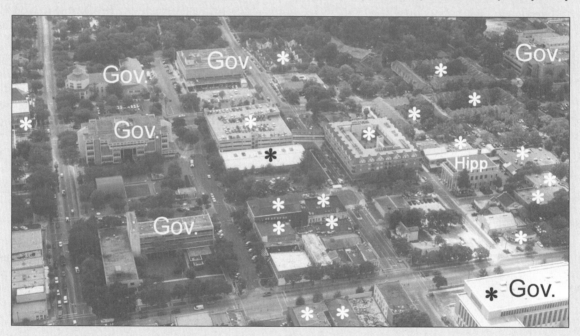

Source: Author's conversations with Ken and Linda McGurn.

developers risk losing everything they have invested in their development two or three times during the process: at the feasibility analysis stage, the permitting stage, and the marketing stage.[12]

While a superficial assessment of development may suggest that the work is for "risk seekers," a more careful assessment is that it is for risk managers, and even crisis managers. A developer also should be detail and plan oriented. It is difficult to believe that a devel-

12. See Piser and Frej, *Professional Real Estate Development*, p. 4.

oper has any chance of surviving the complexities, surprises, and stresses of the development process except by systematic and detailed preparation for a wide range of possible outcomes. Careful preparation also is necessary because virtually all of the problems a developer must solve are in conjunction with other persons whom they do not control. The developer cannot expect to extract assistance or agreement from these individuls without first preparing the situation. As stated before, they must gain the confidence of a host of persons and provide the information, arguments, and incentives to make them friendly toward negotiating the solutions that the developer needs. This holds for land use authorities, lenders, architects, contractors, and ultimately, of course, the "customers."

As if the uncertainties about other players in the development process were not enough, market cycles compound the risks. As noted in Chapter 7, cycles pervade virtually every real estate market. The oscillations of the business cycle appear to be compounded in real estate by the long lead times and the scarcity of signals about immediate conditions. Thus, the developer is condemned to aim a project at a vaguely perceived, oscillating target market. Experts tend to think of real estate cycles as having four phases that might be termed trough, expansion, peak, and decline. With a minimum of perhaps two years between securing control of the land and the completion of construction, the likelihood of entering the market in the most desirable phase, the expansion phase, is little more than 25 percent. Further, the chance of entering a market on the decline may be a little less than 25 percent. While declines are unwelcome to any real estate investor, they are likely to be particularly hazardous to new development since it tends to have the highest cost structure in the market, and thus the highest break-even point.

What Does It Take to Enter Development?

It seems apparent from the demanding nature of development that playing this "quarterback" role requires exceptional capacities. Most observers note the need for strong self-assurance and a capacity to manage under stress and uncertainty. Others have identified creativity, drive, flexibility, and vision as signature characteristics of a successful developer.[13] But the requirements do not appear to stop with this immodest list. The developer also must have credibility and respect to inspire the confidence of those who are betting their work and careers on his or her capacities. James Graaskamp argued that beyond a developer's personal capacities, he or she needs to have control of something to get in the "game." Development requires money, land, knowledge, and tenants—and a would-be developer must have control of at least one of these.[14]

If Graaskamp is correct, then the path for many persons interested in entering development is through gaining knowledge. But how? Rarely, if ever, can one gain the knowledge necessary to have credibility as a developer without experience. As one very successful developer observed, you simply have to pay your dues to have credibility. Historically, the range of experience that serves the purpose has been remarkably diverse: brokerage, property management, income property appraisal, income property finance, construction project management, and construction lending. Some argue that construction lending is particularly valuable because a construction lender is observing the development process very closely and is in a position to ask more questions than most persons can because as the lender they have privileged access to the financial records and business plans of the developer. Attaining credentials as a developer can be accelerated by the right educational background. A degree in civil engineering, construction, and urban planning complemented with business training, or a graduate degree in real estate and development can provide background technical knowledge, and can give access to the jobs that are most effective upon which to build the right experience for entering development.

www.icsc.org

International Council of Shopping Centers, the principal organization of retail developers.

13. Miles, Berens and Weiss, *Real Estate Development Principles and Process,* Chapter 1.

14. As reported in Peiser and Frej, *Professional Real Estate Development,* p. 7.

Summary

Development is the continual reconfiguration of the built environment to meet society's needs. The process of development, done successfully, not only adds great value to the land but also is subject to a myriad of challenges and risks. The development process can be described in roughly eight phases: establishing control of a site; conducting feasibility analysis, refining the development concept, and conducting tests of the site; obtaining necessary permits; design; obtaining financing; construction; marketing and leasing; and operation.

Each of these phases has its particular set of risks and challenges. In the initial stages the risks include the possibility of encountering problems with the site, including title risk, seismic problems, hydrologic problems, toxic substances, the presence of wetlands, endangered species, or archaeologically or historically sensitive matters. Risks for the project often are greatest in the permitting stage, with the threat of delay paramount. Once these risks are resolved, a construction lender is willing to loan funds for the project, The remaining risks, though still substantial, are more in the nature of management and organization, revolving around successful coordination and control of the design, contracting, and construction process. With construction completed, market risk remains as the dominating risk. Successful rent-up and the establishment of a stable operation brings the property risks to their lowest level.

Very different specialists are involved in each phase of the development. Early in the process, market researchers and environmental consultants can be critical. Quickly, the architect becomes important as initial schematic design and concept rendering occur, even as early as the permitting process. Attorneys may also be critical to the permitting process. Once permits are obtained, the architect and all of the design specialists take center stage. Simultaneously, construction lenders become involved and often long-term lenders as well. With design completed, the general contractor, subcontractors, and possibly a construction manager take over the process. For apartments, the marketing and leasing team takes over as soon as construction is completed; for nonresidential or condominium projects, they will have been at work well before completion, and possibly before construction gets under way. Finally, with completion of the project, a property management team steps in. The developer must be able to manage the successful completion of each stage and control the transition from one stage to the next. Errors lead to delays and cost overruns, if not failure.

Many have speculated on what is required to be a developer. Certainly it requires a capacity for risk management, a capacity to work with and engender confidence from people, and a capacity to negotiate conflicting views. Others have observed that creativity, drive, and vision are essential. Breaking into development also requires control of some critical resource such as wealth, land, potential tenants, or unique expertise. Being a developer offers the opportunity to have an exceptional impact on the community and the opportunity to accumulate exceptional wealth. However, the challenges and risks generally are commensurate with that opportunity.

Key Terms

Build-to-suit 647
Civil engineer 655
Certificate of occupancy 657
Construction manager 659
Design-build 659
Electrical engineer 655
Fast-track construction 660

Floor loan 657
General contractor 658
Ground lease 648
Hard costs 656
Land planner 654
Landscape architect 654
Mechanical engineer 655

Option 647
Soft costs 656
Soils engineer 655
Structural engineer 655
Subcontractor 658
Subordination agreement 657

Test Problems

1. The first step in the process of development is to:
   a. Establish site control.
   b. Conduct feasibility analysis.
   c. Conduct environmental tests.
   d. Retain an architect.
   e. Obtain a construction financing commitment.

2. To gain control of a site, a developer may use:
   a. An option.
   b. A ground lease.
   c. A land contract.
   d. A joint venture with a future tenant or purchaser.
   e. All of the above.

3. Which of these phases of the development process comes first?
   a. Feasibility analysis, refinement, and testing.
   b. Design.
   c. Construction financing.
   d. Contracting.
   e. Obtaining permits.

4. All of the following are valuable in facilitating the development permitting process except:
   a. Prior meetings with the neighbors or public.
   b. Establishing a positive relationship with the press.
   c. Demonstrating a willingness to be flexible in solving differences.
   d. Establishing the strength of your legal position early in the process.
   e. Keeping regulatory authorities informed of any "issues" you foresee, and what you propose as a solution.

5. A method of construction where the actual construction begins before the design is finished is known as:
   a. Design-build.
   b. Runaway construction.
   c. Flying design.
   d. Fast-track.
   e. Turnkey.

6. In a *land* development, the primary design professional is a:
   a. Landscape architect.
   b. Civil engineer.
   c. Land planner.
   d. Architect.
   e. Soils engineer.

7. Soft costs include all except:
   a. Permitting costs.
   b. Architectural and engineering fees.
   c. Construction interest.
   d. Environmental and ecological evaluation.
   e. Land improvement costs.

8. Which statement is *incorrect* concerning the typical construction loan?
   a. It is made by a bank.
   b. The interest rate floats over either the prime rate or LIBOR.
   c. The loan typically is for 80 percent or less of total construction costs.
   d. The loan extends a few years after a certificate of occupancy is issued.
   e. The loan is dispersed in stages, based on the level of completion or on actual invoices.

9. The professional responsible for determining adequate specifications for building footings and foundation is a:
   a. Landscape architect.
   b. Land planner.
   c. Civil engineer.
   d. Soils engineer.
   e. Environmental engineer.

10. When construction costs exceed the amount of the construction loan, a developer frequently will seek to cover the "gap" with:
    a. Additional equity
    b. A land contract.
    c. Mezzanine financing.
    d. Advanced rent.
    e. An option.

Study Questions

1. Why is the permitting stage of development often the riskiest stage of the process?

2. List at least five ways that a developer may attempt to reduce the risks of the permitting process.

3. Explain what a construction manager is, and why the role could be important in development.

4. In selecting an architect, what must a developer consider about the architect besides design credentials and relevant experience?

5. Why, in some cases, must a developer begin leasing efforts even before the design is complete?

6. Compare the advantages of competitive bidding for a general contractor with negotiated cost plus fee. What is the argument for using a maximum cost with sharing of overruns or savings between developer and general contractor?

7. Explain the possible advantages of miniperm financing as opposed to traditional construction financing followed by "permanent" financing.

8. Why is property development more vulnerable to business cycle risk than investment in existing property of a similar type?

Explore The Web

Select a city or county of interest to you. Find its official website. From there locate the planning or land use regulation page. What types of maps can you find? What information can you find on the permitting or zoning procedures for a proposed development?

Solutions to Concept Checks

1. Three basic perspectives from which development projects arise are (1) a site in search of a use, (2) a use in search of a site, and (3) capital in search of an opportunity.

2. Eight stages of the development process are to establish site control; feasibility analysis, refinement, and testing; obtaining permits; design; financing; construction; marketing and leasing; and operation.

3. A developer can finance site control by joint venturing with a primary future tenant or owner, purchasing an option, buying a contract for deed, and use of a ground lease.

4. At the heart of feasibility analysis is net present value.

5. Three concerns for which a developer might retain an environmental consultant to investigate are the presence of wetlands, presence of toxic substances and presence of a wildlife habitat.

6. Even without the necessity of a zoning change, a developer almost always must go through a site plan review.

7. Other than expense, the most serious threat to a typical development from the permitting process is delay.

8. In the permitting stage, a developer is likely to retain an architect on an hourly basis. In the design stage, however, the architect will work under a percentage of cost contract or for a fixed fee plus expenses.

9. In selecting an architect, a developer must consider not only the architect's design capacities, but also compatibility of values and goals, and ability to communicate effectively between the two.

10. The land planner has a more macro perspective, concerned with the relationship and arrangement of all components of the project on the land. The landscape architect is responsible for the land and vegetation aesthetics that are the context for each structure.

11. Expenditures for which the developer may need equity capital include any shortfall of construction forecasting; soft costs, which include title examination, environmental and ecological evaluation, legal and other costs of the permitting process, and architectural and engineering fees.

12. By the time a construction lender commits to a loan, these risks normally should be overcome: title flaw, environmental risk, ecological risks, and, above all, the permitting risk.

13. During construction, a developer may need supplemental financing because the construction loan often covers only 70 percent of the financing needs. Mezzanine financing is cheaper than equity capital, and avoids dilution of the equity returns.

14. After a project has been completed and leased for a couple of years, most of the market risk has passed. This makes the project more valuable, facilitating financing at a lower interest rate.

15. Design-build is a construction arrangement that attempts to avoid the problem of conflict of interest between the contractor and the architect by merging the two. Fast-track is a method to improve the speed of construction, which involves beginning actual construction of the footings and cement before the rest of the design is finished.

16. In addition to having personal and organizational capacity, a marketing agent should not be engaged with a competitor and should have genuine enthusiasm for the property.

17. Marketing for a nonresidential development begins earlier because businesses plan moves over a longer period of time and must be sold on the new building beforehand. Further, a lender is likely to key the loan terms to occupancy level, which compels leasing to begin before financing.

Additional Readings

Beyard, Michael D. *Business and Industrial Park Development Handbook.* Washington, DC: Urban Land Institute, 1988.

Bookout, Lloyd W. *Residential Development Handbook.* Washington, DC: Urban Land Institute, 1990.

Collier, Nathan S., Courtland A. Collier, and Don A. Halperin. *Construction Funding: The Process of Real Estate Development, Appraisal and Finance,* 3rd ed. New York: John Wiley, 2002.

Graaskamp, James A. *A Guide to Feasibility Analysis.* Chicago: Society of Real Estate Appraisers, 1972.

McMahan, John. *Property Development,* 2nd ed. New York: McGraw-Hill, 1989.

Miles, Mike E., Gayle Berens, and Marc A. Weiss. *Real Estate Development Principles and Process,* 3rd ed. Washington, DC: Urban Land Institute, 2000.

Peiser, Richard, and Ann Frej. *Professional Real Estate Development: The ULI Guide to the Business,* 2nd ed. Washington, DC: Urban Land Institute, 2003.

Poorvu, William, with Jeffrey L. Cruikshank, *The Real Estate Game: The Intelligent Guide to Decision-Making and Investment.* New York: Free Press, 1999.

Schwanke, Dean. *Mixed-Use Development Handbook.* Washington, DC: Urban Land Institute, 1987.

Stein, J., ed. *Classic Readings in Real Estate Development.* Washington, DC: Urban Land Institute, 1996.

Glossary

Acceleration clause Clause that makes all future payments due upon a single default of a loan. Prevents lender from having to sue for each payment once a single payment is late.

Accretion Growth in size by addition or accumulation of soil to land by gradual, natural deposits.

Accrued depreciation In cost appraisal, the identification and measurement of reductions in the current market value of a property from today's reproduction cost.

Acknowledgment Confirmation that a deed reflects the intention and action of the grantor.

Acre An important measure of land area (containing 43,560 square feet).

Active income In U.S. income tax law, taxable income earned from salaries, wages, commissions, fees, and bonuses.

Actual notice An assertion of real property interests that is open, continuous, and apparent to all who examine the property.

Ad valorem taxes Property taxes that are based on the market value of the property.

Adaptive reuse A conversion where the remodeling produces a creative reuse of the structure that is different from its original purpose.

Adjustable rate mortgage (ARM) Alternative mortgage form where the interest rate is tied to an indexed rate over the life of the loan, allowing interest rate risk to be shared by borrowers and lenders.

Adjusted basis Equal to the original cost basis, plus additional real property or personal property capital expenditures, minus the cumulative amount of tax depreciation taken since the property was placed in service.

Adjustment period The number of initial years in which an ARM remains fixed before the interest rate is allowed to be adjusted.

Adjustments Additions or subtractions from a comparable sale price or cost which are required to make the comparable property more directly comparable to the subject property.

Adverse possession Involuntary conveyance of real property rights by an individual demonstrating a use that is (1) hostile to the interests of the owner, (2) actual, (3) open and notorious, (4) continuous, and (5) exclusive.

Adverse selection Similar to an agency problem, occurs when an advisor may have an incentive to filter the investment opportunities available, keeping the more promising ones and offering the investor the less promising ones.

Affordable housing allocation A requirement that encourages or mandates a "reasonable and fair" component of new housing construction for lower income families.

Affordable housing loans Loan purchase programs offered to primary mortgage market lenders by Fannie Mae and Freddie Mac exclusively for low and moderate-income households.

After-tax cash flow The residual claim on the property's cash flow after the mortgage lender(s) and the state and federal government has collected its share.

After-tax equity reversion The before tax equity reversion, defined as net selling price minus the remaining mortgage balance, at the time of sale less taxes due on sale.

Agency problem Occurs when an investor (principal) relies in an uninformed manner on an adviser (agent) for advice when there may be an incentive for the adviser not to act in the best interest of the investor/principal.

Agency relationship A relationship that empowers the property manager/agent to serve as the owner's fiduciary; thus, the manager's words and actions are binding on the owner.

Age-to-life method Method of estimating improvement value that involves estimating the ratio of the effective age of an improvement to its economic life, and multiplying the resulting age-to-life ratio by the structure's reproduction cost.

Agglomeration economies The emergence of specialized resources in response to demand from multiple industries.

Anchor tenant The large and generally well-known retailers who draw the majority of customers to a shopping center.

Annual percentage rate An approximation of the mortgage loan's annual effective borrowing cost in the absence of early payoff. This measure includes the effect of up-front financing costs on the true cost of borrowing.

Appraisal An unbiased written estimate of the fair market value of a property.

Appraisal report The document the appraiser submits to the client and contains the appraiser's final estimate of market value, the data upon which the estimate is based, and the calculations used to arrive at the estimate.

Appraised value Estimated price or value that the "typical" investor is likely to pay for a property.

Arm's-length transaction A transaction between two parties that have no relationship with each other and who are negotiating on behalf of their own best interests.

Arm's-length transaction A fairly-negotiated transaction and reasonably representative of market value.

Assessed value The value determined as the basis on which an owner's property tax liability is calculated, usually a percentage of market value.

Assessment lien Lien assessment by local governments to ensure that those who receive the primary benefit of neighborhood improvements will be charged their "fair share."

Asset manager The representative of property owners responsible for overseeing property managers and advising owners on important strategic decisions involving properties.

Assignment The transfer of the original lessees' rights under the lease contract to another tenant. The original lessee and the new tenant may be co-liable if rent payments are not made.

Assumability An important characteristic of a loan that permits a subsequent owner of the property to preserve the outstanding loan.

Assumable Loan An existing loan that can be preserved by a buyer instead of being repaid by the seller when title to the mortgaged property changes hands.

Attach To place a lien on real property.

Automated underwriting A loan underwriting approach that exploits the combination of cyber-technology and the vast lending experience imbedded in the giant loan portfolios of Freddie Mac, Fannie Mae and other large mortgage lenders.

Automated valuation models Long-distance, electronic appraisal substitutes used to reduce the cost and time associated with loan underwriting, particularly with refinancing an existing loan. Estimate values are based on statistical techniques.

Balloon loan Loan characterized by an amortization term that is longer than the loan term. Because the loan balance will not be zero at the end of the loan term, a balloon payment is necessary to pay off the remaining loan balance in full.

Balloon mortgage Another name for a balloon loan.

Band-of-investment analysis See mortgage-equity rate analysis.

Bankruptcy There are three types of bankruptcy distinguished by their section in Federal Statutes Chapter 7, liquidation; Chapter 11, court supervised "work-out"; Chapter 13, "wage-earner's proceedings."

Bargain-and-sale deed A deed that conveys the land itself rather than ownership interests through warranties.

Base rent Amount paid by retail tenants in percentage leases regardless of the level of the sales generated by the tenant's business.

Baseline A point of reference that runs east and west and is a feature of government rectangular survey.

Before-tax cash flows Annual net operating income less annual debt service.

Before-tax equity reversion The net sale proceeds less the outstanding balance on the mortgage loan.

Benchmark A reference point used as a standard to quantify the relative performance of a specific asset or manager acting on behalf of an investor.

Bid-rent model Model of how land users bid for location that reveals the influences on how density of land use is determined, how competing urban land uses sort out their locations, how urban land value is determined, and why land uses change over time.

Break-even cash throwoff ratio Another name for the break-even ratio.

Break-even ratio The sum of operating expenses, capital expenditures, and debt service divided by potential gross income, this ratio measures the ability of a property to cover its obligations.

Broker license The authority granted by a state for one to own and operate a real estate brokerage business; the most complete type of real estate license.

Build-to-suit With this arrangement, the developer preleases to a financially strong tenant to build a structure to the tenant's specifications. This arrangement assures the tenant that they will have the space they require when needed and it assures the owner/builder that the space will be fully leased upon completion.

Buydown mortgage A normal level payment mortgage in which the early payments are partially paid out of a lump-sum deposit made at the time of origination. The lump sum deposit/payment is usually made by home builders to lenders, prevalent during periods of high interest rates, to entice them to offer lower-rate mortgages to purchasers of homes in the new development.

Buyer agency agreement A contract for real estate brokerage services between a buyer and a real estate agent. The broker receives compensation for successfully locating a property for the buyer to purchase.

C Corporation Corporate ownership structure that provides limited liability, but suffers from double taxation and does not enable losses to flow through to investors for current use.

Cancellation option Lease clause that gives the tenant or the owner the right, but not the obligation, to cancel the lease before expiration.

Capital expenditures Expenditures for replacements and alterations to a building (or improvement) that materially prolong its life and increase its value.

Capital gain tax rate Rate of tax applied to the portion of the taxable gain on sale that is due to appreciation in the market value of the property.

Capital market The financial sector of the economy that serves to allocate financial resources among households and firms requiring funds.

Capital structure risk The risk associated with the financing package used by the investor. In particular, increased use of mortgage debt (financial leverage) increases the riskiness of the equity investor's return.

Capitalization rate The percentage that is obtained when the income produced by a property (or a specified interest in a property) is divided by the value or sale price of the property (or the specified interest in the property) (Also see *Overall Capitalization Rate*).

Central place pattern A location pattern in which similar economic entities, such as a particular type of convenience service or retail establishment, tend to disperse evenly over the market region.

Certificate of occupancy Issued by the local building inspector certifying that a structure is safe to occupy.

Chain of title A set of deeds and other documents that traces the conveyance of the fee, and any interests that could limit it, down from the earliest time to the current owner.

Change date The date the interest rate on an ARM is recomputed.

Chapter 11 bankruptcy A court supervised "work-out" for a troubled business.

Chapter 13 bankruptcy Similar to Chapter 11, but applies to a household, that allows the petitioner to propose a repayment plan to the court.

Chapter 7 bankruptcy The traditional form of bankruptcy wherein the court simply liquidates the assets of the debtor and distributes the proceeds to creditors in proportion to their share of the total claims.

Checks A component of a grid system, defined as an area of 24 miles by 24 miles, used in a government rectangular survey.

Civil engineer An engineer specializing in the design and construction of public works such as roads, water systems, sewer systems, bridges, dams, and water retention systems.

Closing Event at which possession and title to real estate normally are transferred from seller to buyer.

Closing costs Sometimes called settlement costs, costs in addition to the price of a property, usually including mortgage origination fee, title insurance, attorney's fee, and prepayable items such as taxes and insurance payments collected in advance at closing and held in an escrow account until needed.

Coefficients The calculated relationships between an independent variable and a dependent variable in a regression equation. The coefficient also takes into account the influence of other independent variables and represents the marginal contribution of the explanatory variable to the predicted value.

Collateral Property pledged as security for a debt.

Commercial banks Depository institutions primarily engaged in the business of making short-term loans to businesses for inventory financing and other working capital needs.

Commingled real estate funds A collection of investment capital from various pension funds that are pooled by an investment advisor/fund manager to purchase commercial real estate properties.

Commission Payment a real estate salesperson receives for services rendered, usually expressed as a percentage of the property sale price and not usually paid until the transaction is closed.

Common area maintenance CAM expenses associated with a shopping center typically include maintenance and repair costs, the cost of security personal and alarm systems, as well as fees for the management of the common area.

Community property The automatic right of husband and wife in property acquired by their spouse during the marriage.

Community Reinvestment Act of 1977 A congressional act that encourages mortgage originators to actively lend in their communities and that requires financial institutions to evaluate the "fairness" of their lending practices.

Community shopping center A larger version of a neighborhood shopping center, this type of center is often anchored by a discount department store.

Comparable properties Properties similar to the subject property used in the sales comparison approach to calculate a single indicated value for the subject property.

Comparison activities Good and services whose optimal location pattern is clustering.

Compounding Calculation of future values, given assumptions about the amount or amounts invested and the interest rate that is paid on the invested amounts.

Comprehensive plan A local government's general guide to a community's growth and development based on the community's goals and objectives.

Concentric ring model Model created by E. W. Burgess that offered a concentric ring model of urban form in which the center circle is the central business district. Adjacent to it is a zone of transition which contained warehousing and other industrial land uses. This was followed by a ring of lower income residential land use, followed by a ring of middle and upper income land use.

Concessions Lease clauses, such as free rent, that reduce the cost of the lease to the tenant and therefore provide tenants with an incentive to lease the space from the owner.

Concurrency The requirement that public facilities and services, including roads, sewers, and schools, be available at the same time new development is completed.

Condemnation The legal procedure involved with eminent domain, the right of government to acquire private property, without the owner's consent, for public use in exchange for just compensation.

Condominium An ownership form that combines a fee simple estate for ownership of individual units and tenancy in common for ownership of common areas—describes an ownership form not a type of construction.

Condominium bylaws The official rules and regulations that govern condominium ownership.

Condominium declaration The master deed creating or establishing the condominium corporation.

Conduits Agencies and private companies that pool mortgages and sell mortgage-backed securities, using the pool of mortgages originated or purchased as the collateral for the mortgage-backed security.

Conforming conventional loan A conventional loan that meets the standards required for purchase in the secondary market by Fannie Mae or Freddie Mac.

Consideration Anything of value given to induce another party to enter into a contract.

Constant maturity rate A common index for ARM home loans. The one-year constant maturity rate, for example, is the average of the market yield, found by survey, on any outstanding U. S. Treasury debt having exactly one year remaining to final repayment, regardless of original maturity.

Construction loans Loans used to finance the costs associated with erecting the building or buildings.

Construction manager Person hired by developers to oversee day-to-day construction activities.

Contract conditions Specific requirements that must be satisfied by or for a party to a contract. (See contract conteingencies.)

Contract for deed A sales arrangement in which the actual delivery of the deed conveying ownership will not occur until well after the buyer takes possession of the property. This allows the seller to finance the sale through installment payments and to have recourse to the property in case of default by the buyer/borrower.

Contract for sale The legal document between a buyer and seller that states the purchase price and other details of the transaction, and the detailed manner in which ownership rights are to be transferred. Is generally regarded as the most important contract in real estate.

Contract rent The rent specified in the lease contract.

Contract terms The detailed requirements of a fully enforceable contract, such and the downpayment, any seller financing, provisions for inspections, type evidence of title, type of deed, dates, and other details of the transaction process.

Contract with contingencies An agreement for sale that makes the sale conditional on the buyer's obtaining something such as financing or a favorable engineering report.

Convenience activities Categorization of some types of urban services and products that users seek to obtain the good or service from the closest available source.

Conventional mortgages Mortgage loans that do not enjoy government backing in the form of FHA insurance or a Veterans Administration (VA) guarantee.

Cooperative A form of individual ownership of apartments, the property is owned by a corporation, of which each resident is a shareholder entitled to a proprietory lease for a particular apartment.

Corrective maintenance The ordinary repairs to a building and its equipment on a day-to-day basis.

Correlated returns Returns on one or more assets that generally move together when market conditions change.

Correlation coefficient A relative measure of the tendency of an asset's return to vary with that of another asset over time.

Correspondent relationship A business relationship in which a large lender agrees to purchase loans or to consider loan requests from a mortgage banker or mortgage broker.

Cost segregation An income tax strategy separating personal property from real property. Owners often do this because personal property can be depreciated at accelerated rates if it can be separated from the real property and other personal property.

Cost-of-funds index An index for adjustable rate mortgages based on the weighted average

of interest rates paid for deposits by thrift institutions (savings and loan associations and savings banks).

Covariance An absolute measure of the tendency of an asset's return to vary with that of the returns on another asset over time.

Covenant against encumbrances A promise that the property is not encumbered with liens, easements or other such limitations except as noted in the deed.

Covenant of quiet enjoyment A promise that the property will not be claimed by someone with a better claim to title.

Covenant of seizin A promise that the grantor truly has good title, and that he or she has the right to convey it to the buyer.

Covenants Legally binding promises for which the grantor becomes liable.

Credit scoring The statistical evaluation of borrower creditworthiness that has largely replaced the use of credit reports and the subjective examination of payment punctuality and debt balances.

Credit tenants Companies whose general debt obligations are rated "investment grade" by one or more of the U. S. rating agencies, such as Standard and Poor's and Moody's.

Credit unions Depository institutions that are restricted by their charters to serving a group of people who can show a common bond such as employees of a corporation, government unit, labor union, or trade association.

Custodial maintenance The day-to-day cleaning and upkeep required to maintain property value-and tenants.

Dealer property Under U.S. income tax law, real estate held for sale to others.

Debt coverage ratio (DCR) A measure of the extent to which NOI can decline before it is insufficient to service the debt, defined as net operating income over debt service.

Dedicate To convey certain lands of a subdivision to the local government.

Deed A special form of written contract used to convey a permanent ownership interest in real property.

Deeds-in-lieu of foreclosure A legal instrument issued by defaulting borrowers that transfers all rights they have in a property to the lender. Does not necessarily convey a clean title, just whatever interest the defaulting borrower has at the time of conveyance.

Deed of bargain and sale See bargain and sale deed.

Deed-of-trust An instrument used instead of a mortgage in some states. The borrower conveys a deed of trust to a trustee, who holds the deed on behalf of both borrower and lender. If the loan obligation is paid off in accordance with the note, the trustee returns the deed to the borrower. But if the borrower (trustor) defaults, the trustee exercises his power of sale to dispose of the property on behalf of the lender.

Deed Restrictions Limitations imposed on the use of land and structures by clauses in a deed.

Default The consequence of prolonged delinquency; the failure of a borrower to meet the terms and conditions of a note.

Defeasance prepayment penalty The borrower wishing to prepay must usually offer the lender some combination of U. S. Treasury securities that replace the cash flows of the loan being paid off.

Deferral benefits The gain to the taxpayer from delaying the payment of income taxes until the property is sold. This benefit is produced by the annual depreciation deduction.

Deferred maintenance Ordinary maintenance not performed at the time a problem is detected.

Deficiency judgment The legal right of lenders to file suit against borrowers when the proceeds from a foreclosure sale do not fully pay off an outstanding loan, as well as any late fees and charges.

Delivery An observable, verifiable intent that the deed is to be given by the grantor to the grantee.

Demand clause A right that permits the lender to demand prepayment of the loan.

Dependent variable The variable being "explained" in a regression equation.

Depreciable basis Generally, the value of the acquired property, also called the original cost basis, less the value of the land.

Depreciation Annual deduction that allows investors to reduce the amount of taxable income they report by an amount that is intended to reflect the wear and tear on the property over time.

Depreciation recapture The cumulative amount of depreciation that has been taken since the property was placed into service. This amount is generally taxed at the depreciation recapture tax rate when/if the property is sold.

Depreciation recapture rate The tax rate that is applied to the depreciation recapture portion of the gain on sale when/if the property is sold.

Designated agent In case a brokerage firm is agent for both a seller and a buyer, the firm sometimes designates one salesperson to serve the buyer and one to serve the seller. The two salespersons are presumed to maintain the privacy, and serve the interest of the party they represent.

Design-build An approach to building large structures where the role of architect and general contractor are merged into one.

Devised Conveyance or distribution of a decedent's real property through a will.

Direct capitalization The process of estimating the value of a property by dividing a property's annual net operating income by an overall capitalization rate.

Direct market extraction Method of estimating the appropriate capitalization rate from comparable property sales.

Discount points Upfront financing costs charged by lenders to increase the yield on a loan.

Discounting The process for equating the value of future benefits from a real estate investment to an equivalent current (present) value.

Discrimination in housing Federal and state laws prohibit discrimination in housing on the basis of race, color, religion, national origin, sex, familial status, and handicap.

Disintermediation Reference to the occurrence of conditions when the growth of deposits in banks and savings associations becomes negative, due to other, more attractive, direct investment opportunities.

Diversifiable risk Unsystematic risk that can be eliminated from a portfolio by holding securities and other investments with less than perfectly correlated returns.

Diversification Allocating portfolio resources among alternative investments to reduce the risk of the returns on the portfolio.

Doctrine of constructive notice A common law tradition stating that if a person is capable of knowing about a claim or rule, then he or she can be bound by it.

Dominant parcel A parcel that benefits from a servient parcel in an easement appurtenant.

Dower A common law provision that grants a wife a one-third life estate in all of the real property of a decedent husband.

Dual agency A situation in which a person or firm has an agency and fiduciary relationship to both parties—seller and buyer—of a transaction.

Due diligence After a buyer and seller have agreed on a purchase price, the buyer is provided time to verify the information that has been provided by the seller. For example, the buyer will want to verify the magnitude of certain operating expenses, the current rent charged to tenants, the lack of environmental problems, etc. This process of "kicking the tires" before final closing is the due-diligence process.

Due-on-sale clause The clause in a mortgage document that requires the borrower to pay off the loan in full if the property serving as security for the loan is sold.

Early payment mortgages Loans where the borrower makes additional payments to reduce outstanding principal more quickly than scheduled.

Earnest money A cash deposit by a buyer at the time of the offer to establish credibility of the

offer, and to provide recourse to the seller if the buyer reneges.

Easement A right that the owners of another property may have to use one's land for a specific and limited purpose.

Easement appurtenant A right of use that continues from owner to owner that involves a relationship between two parcels of land: a dominant parcel that benefits from a servient parcel.

Easement by estoppel The right of use created if a landowner gives an adjacent landowner permission to depend on her land.

Easement by prior use An implied right of use that allows owner of a landlocked parcel the right to use a previously existing path across another property for access and egress.

Easement in gross The right to use land for a specific, limited purpose unrelated to any adjacent parcel.

Easement of necessity A created implied right of use that allows owner of a landlocked parcel the right to use path across another property for access and egress.

Economic and environmental impact statements Studies of the effect that a new development will have on the economy or the environment of the region.

Economic base The set of economic activities that a city provides for the world beyond its boundaries.

Effective borrowing cost The true borrowing cost, including the effect of all up-front financing costs. Is similar to the annual percentage rate but allows for the effect of early payoff.

Effective gross income The total annual income the rental property produces after subtracting vacancy losses and adding miscellaneous income.

Effective rent See equivalent level rent

Effective tax rate (income taxes) The percentage amount by which income taxes reduce the going-in IRR on a property acquisition or development.

Effective tax rate (property taxes) The tax liability divided by the property's market value or sale price.

Elective Share Provision that gives a surviving spouse a share of most of the wealth of the decedent.

Electrical engineer An engineer specializing in the design and construction of electrical systems for production and distribution of power, and in electrical circuitry generally.

Elements of comparison The relevant characteristics used to compare and adjust the sale prices of the comparable properties in the sales comparison approach.

Eminent domain The power of government in the United States to take private property for a public purpose by paying the owner just compensation.

Encroachment Unauthorized intrusion of a building or other improvements onto property owned by another.

Equal Credit Opportunity Act (ECOA) This act prohibits discrimination in lending practices on the basis of race, color, religion, national origin, sex, marital status, age, or because all or part of an applicant's income derives from a public assistance program.

Equitable title The right of someone to obtain full, legal title to real estate, provided the terms and conditions of the document creating equitable title (usually a contract for sale) are fulfilled.

Equity Capital invested in the property by the owner. Is generally equal to the current market value of the property minus the value of any outstanding loans.

Equity dividend rate The "capitalization rate" for equity. It is derived by dividing the before-tax cash flow by the value of the invested equity capital. Sometimes referred to as the property's dividend rate/yield.

Equity of redemption A period of time allowed by courts in every state that grants delinquent mortgage borrowers the opportunity to make overdue payments and come current on the mortgage before foreclosure begins.

Equity REITs Real estate investment trusts that invest in and operate income-producing properties.

Equivalent level rent The fixed monthly payment that has the same present value as the actual lease payments after concessions or expenses reimbursement revenue over the same term.

Equivalent monthly annuity The fixed monthly payment that has the same present value as the lease with concessions or expenses reimbursement revenue.

Errors and omission insurance A type of insurance that indemnifies professionals if they make an error in their profession or if they omit something important from their analyses.

Escrow The status of real estate transactions that are closed through the help and intercession of a third party, called an escrow agent. The deed is delivered to the escrow agent for delivery to the buyer on performance of a condition (payment of the purchase price).

Escrow account A segregated account held by brokers for the deposit of earnest money (deposit) funds. Also, a trust account of a lender used to pay for property taxes, hazard insurance or other items on behalf of a borrower.

Escrow agent A person or company that performs the closing function for a fee; escrow agents collect all needed documents and funds for disbursement at the closing.

Escrow clause Requires a mortgage borrower to make monthly deposits into an escrow account.

Estate Interests in real property that include possession.

Estimated closing costs An estimate of all the costs to be incurred at a real estate closing. Most commonly, the estimate is provided by a lender, in accordance with the requirements of the Real Estate Settlement Procedures Act.

Evidence of title Substantiation that demonstrates that good and marketable title is being conveyed as part of a real estate transaction.

Exceptions and reservations clause A clause in a deed that can contain a wide variety of limits on the property interest conveyed.

Excess deductions The amount by which allowable tax deductions (including depreciation) exceed the rental income generated by the property.

Exclusionary zoning Zoning that tends to exclude lower income groups and is prohibited.

Exclusive agency listing An agreement between a seller of property and a broker in which the seller agrees to pay a commission to the broker if anyone other than the owner finds a buyer, during the period of the agreement.

Exclusive right of sale listing An agreement between a seller of property and a broker in which the broker is assured of receiving a commission if the broker or anyone else, including the owner, finds a buyer during the period of the agreement.

Exculpatory clause Loan provision that releases the borrower from liability for fulfillment of the contract.

Expansion option Lease clause that obligates the property owner to find space for the tenant to expand the size of their leased space.

Expected value The weighted average of a series of potential outcomes weighted by their associated probabilities.

Expense stop A clause often found in commercial leases that requires landlords to pay property operating expenses up to a specified amount and tenants to pay the expenses beyond that amount. The expense stop is usually stated in a per square foot amount.

External obsolescence Losses of property value caused by forces or conditions beyond the borders of the property. The losses are deducted from a building's reproduction cost in the cost approach to estimating market value.

Externalities The unaccounted effects that a land use imposes on surrounding parcels.

Extraterritorial jurisdiction Control by a community of an area larger than the community or jurisdiction for planning and zoning purposes, granted by the state legislature, which allows local governments to plan and control

urban development outside their boundaries until annexation can occur.

Fallout risk The potential loss of borrowers from the origination pipeline if mortgage interest rates decline after the loan commitment, but before the closing of the loan, which results in borrowers choosing not to close ("take down") the loan.

Fannie Mae Government-sponsored enterprise; one of the largest purchasers of residential mortgages in the secondary market.

Fast-track construction An approach to construction wherein actual construction begins before design and building specifications are complete.

Federal Housing Administration A government-sponsored housing finance agency that operates in the primary market by providing a default insurance program, as well as other housing programs and initiatives.

Fee simple absolute An estate in land that provides the owner with a complete set of legal rights, limited only by the powers of government.

Fee simple conditional Ownership that is subject to a condition or trigger event.

Fee simple estate The complete ownership of a property, may be either absolute or conditional.

FHA mortgage insurance Government-sponsored mortgage insurance that protects lenders from any loss after foreclosure and conveyance of title to the property to the U. S. Department of Housing and Urban Development (HUD). Insurance premium is paid by the mortgage borrower.

Fiduciary relationship The special duties and obligations to a principal required of an agent, including complete loyalty, confidentiality, obedience, disclosure, accounting, care, skill, and due diligence.

Final adjusted sale price The price paid for a comparable property in the sales comparison approach, adjusted for all conditions and characteristics to approximate the subject property and the current date.

Financial intermediaries Institutions that bring together depositors and mortgage borrowers.

Financial risk The risk NOI will be less than debt service.

Fixtures Personal property that becomes real property by virtue of its permanent attachment to the realty.

Flat rent Describes a lease where the rental rate is fixed for the entire term.

Flex space Industrial space that is often built without fancy lobbies or fixtures that can be used for storage or for simple offices and that can be converted from one use to another relatively inexpensively.

Floating-rate mortgage A debt instrument whose interest rate changes over the life of the loan based on a market index such as the prime rate or LIBOR.

Floor loan In financing of large-scale building construction, a minimum level of loan that is granted until certain progress points in construction and leasing are achieved. Then the loan is increased.

Foreclosure A process to force the public sale of property to satisfy the financial obligations of a delinquent borrower to a lender. The sale forecloses the borrower's equity of redemption.

Forward commitment A contract binding a mortgage lender or investor to purchase or fund a loan on predetermined terms at a future date.

Freddie Mac A government-sponsored enterprise and, along with Fannie Mae, one of the largest purchasers of residential mortgages in the secondary market.

Freehold Estate interests in real estate having unlimited duration, titled interests.

Functional obsolescence Losses in value of a building relative to its reproduction cost because the building is not consistent with modern standards or with current tastes of the market.

Funds from operations (FFO) Net (accounting) income, plus tax depreciation, plus amortization of leasing commissions and tenant improvements, is considered a better measure of a REIT's cash flow than accounting income.

Future value The value of money in some period beyond time zero.

Garden apartments These developments have a relatively low density of development and are located in suburban and nonurban areas where land is less expensive than in urban areas.

General agent One who is empowered to represent a principal, often a business firm, in its business relationships. A general agent can contract and bind the principal within the confines of the business or employment relationship.

General contractor Usually a construction company that has responsibility for seeing that all aspects of construction are completed on time and within budget.

General lien A security interest or lien that arises out of actions unrelated to ownership of the property.

General partnerships An ownership form characterized by multiple owners, unlimited liability for each equity holder, and flow-through taxation of both taxable income and cash distributions.

General warranty deed Highest form of deed in which grantor become liable for all possible covenants, or legal promises, assuring good title.

Geographic information systems (GIS) Computerized methods for analyzing data about communities using various maps and combinations or layers of maps.

Going-in cap rate The overall capitalization rate; the ratio of the first-year net operating income to the overall value (or purchase price) of the property.

Going-out cap rate The ratio of the estimated net operating income in the year following sale to the overall value of the property at the time of sale.

Government National Mortgage Association (GNMA) A federal government agency that promotes affordable housing by buying subsidized mortgages in the secondary market. This agency also guarantees mortgage-backed securities issued by private FHA and VA lenders.

Government-sponsored enterprises A term that refers to Fannie Mae, Freddie Mac, and several other less important government entities created by acts of Congress to promote an active secondary market for home mortgages.

Graduated rent Describes a lease that calls for prespecified increases in the contract rental rate.

Grantee The recipient of a conveyance of a real property interest.

Grantor The person or entity conveying the real property interest to the grantee.

Gross floor area The gross floor area of a shopping center is equal to the total gross leasable area, plus the square footage of the common areas.

Gross income multiplier The ratio of the sale prices to the annual gross income of the income-producing property.

Gross leasable area The standard for measuring retail space, the GLA is simply the sum of the space occupied by the tenant, and is therefore similar to the usable area of office tenants.

Gross lease Lease in which the landlord pays all operating expenses of the property.

Ground lease Leases of vacant land or of the land portion of an improved parcel of real estate.

Growth moratorium A temporary prohibition of further development in a community or jurisdiction.

Habendum clause Clause in a deed that defines or limits the type of interest being conveyed.

Hard costs Amounts of capital committed in development projects to materials, labor, and other tangible or nonservice inputs.

Highest and best use The use of a property found to be (1) legally permissible, (2) physically possible, (3) financially feasible, and (4) maximally productive.

High-rise apartment buildings Buildings of at least 10 to 15 stories.

Holding period Length of time an investment is held prior to sale or disposal.

Home equity loans Second mortgages, used to finance home improvements and other purchases, where homeowners can borrow against the accumulated equity in the home.

Home Mortgage Disclosure Act of 1975 An act of Congress that discourages lenders from avoiding, or redlining, certain neighborhoods in a manner related to minority composition.

Home Ownership and Equity Protection Act An act of Congress that addresses abusive, predatory practices in sub-prime lending and sets a trigger annual percentage rate (APR) and fee levels at which loans become subject to the law's restrictions.

Homestead exemption A provision in some states that allows specified taxpayers (usually owners of their principal, full-time residences) to apply for a deduction of a certain amount from the property's assessed value in calculating the annual property tax liability.

Hospitality property Property classification that includes hotels, motels, and many types of restaurants.

Housing expense ratio A ratio used to assess the ability of a borrower to pay debt; defined as the monthly payment of principal and interest on the loan plus monthly payments into an escrow account toward property taxes and hazard insurance divided by the borrower's gross monthly income.

Hybrid REITs Real estate investment trusts that invest in both properties and mortgages.

Impact fee A fee charged by a community and paid by a developer that is commensurate with the externalities created by a development. Intended to cover the development's impact on such things as roads, sewer systems, schools, and police and fire protection.

Implied easement A right of use not created by an explicit deed, or explicit clause in a deed. It often is created when a subdivision map is placed in the public records.

Improvements on the land Any fixed structures such as buildings, fences, walls, and decks.

Improvements to the land The components necessary to make the land suitable for building construction or other uses and includes infrastructure, such as streets, walkways, utilities, storm water drainage systems and other systems that may be required for land use.

Income capitalization The process of converting periodic income into a value estimate.

Independent variables Variables in a regression equation that are believed to partially explain variations in the dependent variable.

Index rate A market-determined interest rate that is the "moving part" in the adjustable interest rate.

Index rent Describes a lease in which rent increases are tied to changes in a regularly reported index, such as the consumer price index. Because the movements in the index are not know ahead of time, the increases in rental rates are not prespecified.

Indicated value The final value estimate for the subject property resulting from application of one of the major approaches in the appraisal process.

Industrial property Property classification that includes warehouses and structures that house light manufacturing.

Industry economies of scale The growth of an industry within a locality that creates special resources and cost advantages for that industry.

Inflation risk The risk that general inflation in the economy will be greater than or less than expected.

Installment sale Financing arrangement, commonly used to defer taxes due on the sale of commercial property, where the seller allows the buyer to pay the purchase price over a number of years.

Institutional-grade real estate Larger, more valuable commercial properties, generally well over $10 million, targeted by institutional investors, such as pension funds and foreign investors. These investments are generally located in the 50 to 60 largest U. S. metropolitan areas.

Insurance clause Requires the borrower/mortgagor to maintain property casualty insurance acceptable to the lender, giving the lender joint control in the use of the proceeds in case of major damage to the property.

Intangible assets Nonphysical assets such as patents and copyrights.

Intercept The base value estimate in a regression assuming that all of the explanatory variables are set equal to zero.

Interest Rent or a charge paid for the use of money (e. g. , a mortgage loan, a share or right in property). Interest may also refer to the bundle of rights held by owners of real property.

Interest rate risk The risk that changes in the general level of interest rates will affect the pricing of all securities and investments.

Interest-only loans Loan alternative in which borrowers pay only interest over the life of the loan, and then completely repay the principal in one installment at loan maturity.

Interlease risk The risk associated with the replacement of a tenant's first lease with another lease of uncertain terms and conditions.

Internal rate of return (IRR) The rate of interest (discount) that equates the present value of the cash inflows to the present value of the cash outflows; i.e. , it is the rate of discount that makes the net present value equal to zero.

Internal Revenue Service Created by Congress to collect federal income taxes and to clarify and interpret tax rules and regulations.

Internet marketing Use of the Internet to advertise real estate services, to market properties, and to provide information about specific properties. While few properties are sold exclusively through the Internet, it has become a central tool to real estate marketing today.

Intestate Conveyance of a decedent's property without a will.

Inverse condemnation Action, initiated by a property owner against the government, to recover the loss in property value attributed to government activity.

Investment Any decision that involves incurring significant costs in the present for the right to receive future benefits. An outlay of money or something of value for uncertain income or profit.

Investment-grade property Synonymous with institutional-grade real estate, large, relatively new and fully leased, commercial properties located in major metropolitan areas, generally well over $10 million, targeted by institutional investors, such as pension funds and foreign investors.

Investment property Asset, as defined in the U.S. Internal Revenue Code, owned primarily for earning an investment return—especially capital appreciation—as opposed to an asset that is held for use in one's trade or business. Raw land and developed lots are real estate examples of investment properties.

Investment risk The possibility that future cash flows or nonmonetary costs and benefits will differ from expected values.

Investment value The value of the property to a particular investor, based on his or her specific requirements, discount rate, expectations, etc.

Investment yield The growth in the invested dollars of an investment. Usually stated as a percentage growth or return.

Joint tenancy A form of co-ownership in which two or more owners hold equal shares and have equal rights of possession. The surviving partners divide the interests of a deceased partner.

Joint venture Generally, an association of two or more persons or firms in order to carry out a single business project. In real estate, often a business partnership formed between a lender and a developer or investor to develop or purchase a specific property or properties.

Judicial deed A deed issued through a court-ordered proceeding.

Judicial foreclosure The process of bringing the property of delinquent borrowers to public sale that involves court action. Proceeds from the foreclosure sale are used to pay off, to the extent possible, the borrower's creditors.

Jumbo loans Nonconforming loans that exceed the maximum loan amount for purcahse by Fannie Mae or Freddie Mac. Because these loans cannot be purchased by one of the GSEs, they usually carry a slightly higher interest rate.

Just compensation Payment to an owner for property taken in condemnation proceedings, usually the market value of the property taken by the government in its exercise of eminent domain.

Land Commonly used to refer to a parcel that does not include any structures but may include some improvements to the land.

Land acquisition loans Loans to finance the purchase of raw land; perhaps the most risky of real estate loans.

Land development loans Loans to finance the installation of the on-site and off-site improvements to the land that are necessary to ready the land for construction.

Land planner In land development, lays out the basic "map" for use of the land, including location of roads, utilities, structures, water retention areas and other elements.

Landscape architect A an architect specializing in planning the arrangement of trees, other plantings, and placement of other harmonizing objects on land. Usually the focus is designing the grounds for a building or group of buildings.

Late fees Fees assessed for standard home loans when payments are received after the 15th of the month the payment is due. Also found in commercial mortgages.

Law of agency The legal rights, duties, and liabilities of principal, agent, and third parties as a result of the agency relationship between them.

Law of descent The laws and procedures controlling how a state will convey a decedent's estate among the heirs if no will exists.

Leased fee estate The bundle of rights possessed by the landlord in a leased property, made up primarily of the right to receive rental payments during the lease term and ultimately to repossess the property at the end of the lease term.

Leasehold (estate) The interest or rights of a lessee or tenant in a leased property, including the possessory interests that are a temporary conveyance of the rights of exclusion, use, and enjoyment, but not the right of disposition. The tenant receives these rights in exchange for the payment of rent.

Legal life estate A life estate created by the action of law.

Legal title Ownership of property; for real estate, a lawful claim, supported by evidence of ownership.

Lender's yield The implied discount rate, or internal rate of return, on a loan—given all of the cash inflows and outflows on the loan to the lender.

Level-payment mortgage A fully amortizing loan with equal periodic payments.

Leverage The use of mortgage debt to help finance a capital investment.

Levered cash flows The property's net rental income after subtracting any payments due the lender.

LIBOR A common index of interest rates for income producing property, the London Interbank Offering Rate is a short-term interest rate for loans among foreign banks based in London.

License The permission to use another's land for a specific and limited purpose.

Licensing laws State laws that authorize persons who meet specified qualifications to engage in a business or profession.

Lien An interest in real property that serves as security for a loan obligation. In case of default the holder of the lien is entitled to have the property sold to satisfy the debt.

Lien theory Legal theory that interprets a mortgage as a lien rather then a temporary conveyence of title.

Like-kind exchange a popular method of deferring capital gain taxes which allows owners, under certain circumstances, to exchange their properties for another and avoid paying capital gain taxes at the time of the transaction.

Limited liability company A hybrid form of ownership that combines the corporate characteristics of limited liability with the tax characteristics of a partnership.

Limited partnership A partnership in which one party (the general partner) assumes unlimited liability in exchange for control of all material decision making. The limited partners enjoy liability that is, limited to the extent of their equity contributions to the entity. All parties involved benefit from flow-through income and taxation that is the partnership is not taxed.

Linkages The attractions or important access needs that one land use has for other land uses.

Liquidity The ability to sell an asset quickly for fair market value.

Liquidity risk The risk that an owner will not be able to sell an asset quickly for its fair market value.

Listing contract An agreement between an owner of real estate and a real estate broker that obligates the broker to attempt to sell the property under specified conditions and terms. It obligates the property owner to pay a commission to the broker if the broker is successful in obtaining a ready, willing and able buyer for the property on terms specified or on terms acceptable to the seller.

Load factor Another name for the ratio of rentable to usable area in an office building. The factor is multiplied by the tenant's usable area to determine rentable area.

Loan balance The outstanding principal balance on a loan. Will always be equal to the original balance if the loan is an interest-only loan. Declines over time if the loan is self amortizing.

Loan constant The annual debt service on a loan divided by the initial amount of the loan.

Loan commitment A written agreement that commits the lender to make a loan to the borrower provided the borrower satisfies the terms and conditions of the commitment.

Loan servicing All actions and activities associated with administering a mortgage loan, including collection of payments, monitoring insurance and tax obligations, and notification of delinquent borrowers. This function is often provided by an entity different from the entity that owns the mortgage.

Loan underwriting Involves an analysis by the lender of the riskiness of the promised mortgage payments. Requires analysis of the potential borrower's willingness and ability to make scheduled mortgage payments.

Loan underwriting process The process by which a prospective borrower submits a formal loan application and the lender analyzes all relevant information and decides whether or not to commit to the loan.

Local economic activities Activities in a city that serve the local businesses and households.

Location quotient The ratio between the percentage of employees in a certain type of work or job classification in a community and the percentage of employees in that same type of work or job classification nationally. If the ratio exceeds one it indicates the activity is a base economic activity.

Lock-out provision A mortgage clause or provision prohibiting prepayment of the mortgage for a specified period of time after origination.

Low-income housing Housing targeted to households with low or moderate incomes.

Lump sum A one-time receipt or expenditure occurring in a given period.

Macroeconomic risk factors Risk factors or variables that can potentially affect the values and returns on all properties in all markets.

Management agreement The agreement that forms the basis for the relationship between the property owner and the property management firm.

Management risk Risk that a property will not be effectively managed, causing a reduction in net cash flows and returns.

Margin The "markup", typically two to three percentage points, over and above the index rate, which is charged on adjustable rate mortgages.

Market conditions The relationship between supply and demand for a particular type of real estate in a local market at a specified point in time.

Market parameters Critical summary features such as occupancy rates, rental rate growth, or sales rates, that characterize a real estate market.

Market rent The rent that could be obtained by renting a property on the open market.

Market risk factors Risk factors or variables that cannot be diversified away. Also called systematic risk factors.

Market segmentation Identification and delineation of submarkets.

Market value The price a property should sell for in a competitive market when there has been a normal offering time, no coercion, arm's-length bargaining, typical financing, and informed buyers and sellers.

Marketability study An analysis of how best to bring a product or service to the market. It considers characteristics of the product or service in relation to the needs of potential customers and which marketing channels are most likely to produce the desired results.

Marketable title Title to real property that is free of reasonable doubt.

Marketable title laws State laws intended to limit the number of years that title search must "reach back" through the title "chain."

Market-adjusted normal sale price "Normal sale price" adjusted for changes in market conditions between the date of sale and the date of appraisal of the subject property.

Maturity imbalance problem Situation faced by banks, thrifts, and other financial institutions in which long-term assets are funded with short-term liabilities.

Mechanical engineer An engineer specializing in the design and construction of heating, ventilating and air conditioning systems, and in other kinds of mechanical systems.

Mechanics' liens Liens that arise from construction and other improvements to real estate.

Metes and bounds Method of describing real estate in which a *mete* is a unit of measure (foot, mile) and a *bound* is a boundary marker. Essentially, a sequence of directed distances that are the boundaries of the property.

Metropolitan statistical area (MSA) An MSA is comprised of one or more urban counties, identified as a single labor market area, centered around a city with at least 50,000 in population.

Mezzanine financing A method of obtaining additional leverage on top of a traditional first mortgage. This debt is secured by the pledge of an equity interest in the borrower's partnership or business—it usually is not secured by a lien on the property.

Microeconomic risk factors Risk that is specific to a particular property or local market and that is controllable by the owner/investor. This risk can be diversified away in a portfolio.

Midmonth convention Tax rule that assumes the acquisition of an income producing property occurs on the 15th day of the month, regardless of the actual acquisition date.

Mid-rise apartment buildings Apartment buildings that range in height from four to nine stories.

Millage rate The dollars of tax per $1,000 of property value. For example, a millage rate of 20 means that a person owning a property having an assessed value of $100,000 would pay 20 x 100 = $2,000 in tax.

Mills Units used to state amount of property tax assessment; the number of dollars per $1,000. Twenty mills means $20 per each $1,000.

Mineral rights Rights to the subsurface, including rights to oil, gas, coal, and other substances that are mined, and can be separated from land ownership.

Mini-perm loan A loan from an interim lender that provides financing for the construction period, the lease-up period, and for several years beyond the lease-up stage.

Mixed-asset portfolio A portfolio that contains a variety of types of assets; for example, stocks, bonds, and real estate.

Monthly loan constant A loan payment factor used to determine payments on a level payment, fixed rate loan.

Mortgage A lien on real property as security for a debt.

Mortgage assumption When buyers take over payments of mortgages of sellers and become personally liable by creating a note in their name.

Mortgage bankers Full-service mortgage companies that process, close, provide funding, and sell the loans they originate in the secondary mortgage market, and service loans for loan investors.

Mortgage brokers An intermediary between those who demand mortgage funds and those who supply the funds. Brokers arrange mortgage loans for a fee, but do not originate or service the loans.

Mortgage insurance premium (MIP) Up-front insurance premium required by FHA-insured loans.

Mortgage joint venture A relationship between developers and others who supply all or most of the funds in the form of loans to develop properties that will be used in their business or enter their portfolios.

Mortgage menu The many types of residential loans offered by originating lenders to residen-tial borrowers. The menu includes the cost of the various mortgage items, including the contract interest rate and number of up-front discount points and origination fees.

Mortgage pipeline An originating lender's approved, but currently unfunded, loan commitments plus loans funded but unsold.

Mortgage REITs Real estate investment trusts that purchase mortgage obligations and effectively become real estate lenders.

Mortgage A special contract by which the borrower conveys to the lender a security interest in the mortgaged property.

Mortgagee The lender, who receives the mortgage claim.

Mortgage-equity rate analysis Estimation of an overall capitalization rate by calculating a weighted average of the capitalization rate for debt (mortgage constant) and the capitalization rate for equity (equity dividend rate). The weight is determined by the percentage that each component (debt and equity) is of the total investment.

Mortgagor The borrower or grantor of the mortgage claim.

Multifactor asset pricing model Models for determining required discount rates that assume there are several sources of macroeconomic (nondiversifiable) risk in the economy for which investors must be compensated in the form of a higher going-in internal rate of return.

Multifamily Property Residential property classification that includes apartments.

Multi-nuclei City Phrase coined by Harris and Ullman in a landmark study that described the effects of the motor vehicle, combined with new technologies of production, that released the city from its absolute ties to the CBD.

Multiple listing service (MLS) Sharing of property sales listings by a number of real estate brokers with an agreement as to how costs and commissions are to be shared.

Multivariate regression analysis (MRA) A statistical procedure used to examine the relationship between a dependent variable and multiple independent, "explanatory," variables.

Mutual Mortgage Insurance Fund The depository for FHA insurance premiums and the source of reimbursement for lenders in the case of foreclosure losses on FHA-insured properties.

NAREIT index A value-weighted index that tracks the total return patterns of all exchange-listed REITs. Produced by the National Association of Real Estate Investment Trusts.

National Association of Realtors A principal trade or professional organization of real estate brokers. Members agree to abide by a code of ethics.

Natural vacancy rate The proportion of potential gross income not collected when the use (rental) market is in equilibrium.

NCREIF Property Index A measure of the historical performance of income properties held by pension funds and profit-sharing plans. Produced quarterly by the National Council of Real Estate Investment Fiduciaries.

Negative amortization Occurs when the loan payment is not sufficient to cover the interest cost and results in the unpaid interest being added to the original balance, causing the loan amount to increase.

Neighborhood shopping center Located for the convenience of a nearby resident population, this type of center contains retail establishments offering mostly convenience goods. Typically it is "anchored" by a supermarket.

Net asset value Equal to total market value of a REIT's underlying assets, less mortgages and other debt.

Net income multiplier A cash flow multiplier calculated as the acquisition price divided by the net operating income.

Net lease Lease in which the tenant pays some or all of the operating expenses of the property in addition to rent.

Net listing Type of contract in which sellers specify the amount they will accept from the sale, with brokers keeping all proceeds in excess of that amount.

Net operating income (NOI) The type of income to a property used in direct capitalization, calculated by deducting from potential gross income vacancy and collection losses and adding other income to obtain effective gross income. From this amount all operating expenses are subtracted, including management expense and a reserve for replacements and other nonrecurring expenses.

Net present value (NPV) The difference between the present value of the cash inflows and the present value of the cash outflows.

Net sale proceeds The expected selling price less selling expenses.

New urbanism School of planning thought that seeks to revive residential neighborhood features of the pre-automobile era, including sidewalks; houses with front porches located close to streets; narrow, grid pattern streets; and supporting non-residential services interspersed within neighborhoods.

Nonamortizing Loans that require interest payments but no regularly scheduled principal payments.

Nonbasic employment Jobs that are not involved in the production of goods or services that will be exported outside of a community. These are usually jobs involved in serving local residents. Examples are barbers, beauticians, most retail, real estate and insurance salespersons, and local bankers.

Nonconforming conventional loan A conventional loan that does not satisfy one or more underwriting standard required for purchase in the secondary market by Fannie Mae and Freddie Mac.

Nonconforming use A land use inconsistent with current zoning classification, but which is permitted to remain because it predated the current zoning. To be allowed to remain, the use must be uninterrupted, and the property structures cannot be substantially improved.

Nonjudicial foreclosure A process of bringing the property of defaulting borrowers to public sale by the lender or a trustee, outside of the court system. It must follow statutory guidelines, particularly concerning public notices of the sale.

Nonmonetary The nonfinancial costs and benefits of an investment decision.

Nonrealty items Items of personal property.

Nonrecourse Loans that relieve the borrower of personal liability but do not release the property as collateral for the loan.

Normal sale price The transaction price of a comparable property adjusted for nonmarket financing and non-arm's-length bargaining (conditions of sale).

Note The document (contract) defining the exact terms of a debt obligation and the liability of the borrower for the obligation.

Officer's deeds Same as definition of executor's deed.

Open listing Agreement between the seller of property and a broker that provides for the broker to receive a commission if he or she sells the property. No exclusive protection is provided to the broker.

Open-end construction loan A situation in which a forward commitment has not been obtained to repay the construction loan.

Operating expense escalation clause A commercial lease clause in which increases in one or more operating expenses, relative to a base year, become the financial responsibility of the tenant.

Operating expense ratio A measure of annual operating costs, defined as operating expenses divided by effective gross income.

Operating expenses The expenses owners incur in operating their property.

Option The right, but not obligation, to do something, such as buy a property, within a certain time.

Option contract sets a time over which developers may buy property at a specified price

Ordinary annuity A fixed amount of money received every period for some length of time.

Ordinary life estate Estate in which the property owner retains all rights of exclusive posses-sion, use, and enjoyment for life while a subsequent owner holds a remainder interest that follows the life estate.

Ordinary tax rate The rate of tax applied to taxable income that is not deemed to be capital gain income or depreciation recapture income.

Original cost basis The total costs paid to acquire the property including land, building, personal property, and other acquisition costs such as lawyer fees, brokerage commissions, etc.

Outlet center A variation of specialty shopping centers that generally sell name-brand goods at lower prices.

Overall capitalization rate The type of capitalization rate used in direct capitalization, calculated by dividing comparable properties' net operating incomes by their selling prices.

Overall caps Caps on adjustable rate mortgages that limit interest rate changes over the life of the loan.

Overall rate (of return) Another common name for the overall capitalization rate.

Overall rate of direct capitalization An overall capitalization rate estimated directly from actual transactions for comparable properties.

Ownership structure risk The effect that the chosen form of ownership can have on the risk and return ultimately earned by the investors.

Package mortgage Home mortgage loans that include funds for items of personal property such as a range, dishwasher, refrigerator, and furnishings.

Paired sales analysis Method of identifying the incremental market value of a property feature by comparing sale prices of two "nearly-identical" properties, one with and one without the feature.

Par value The remaining balance, or outstanding principal amount of a debt.

Partially amortizing A loan alternative in which the outstanding principal is partially repaid over the life of the loan, then fully retired with a larger lump sum "balloon" payment at maturity.

Participation loan A loan in which the lender receives a specified portion of a property's income or sale proceeds, in addition to interest and principle on the note.

Passive activity income IRS classification of income that includes all income generated from trade and business activities such as rental real estate.

Passive activity loss restrictions IRS rules that, in general, allow losses from passive activities, which includes all rental properties, to be used only to offset income from other passive investments.

Patent Special type of deed that conveys title to real property owned by government to a private party.

Payment caps Protects the borrower against the shock of large payment changes; it is possible for the interest rate to increase enough that the resulting payment increase will not cover the additional interest cost.

Pension funds Retirement savings accounts that now represent a major source of equity capital in commercial real estate markets.

Percentage rent The amount of rent paid by a retail tenant in addition to the base rent. It generally is a percentage of tenant store sales above a prespecified threshold level.

Performance standard An approach to land use control that addresses concerns for urban systems such as traffic, watershed, green space, air quality or other aspects of the environment through limits to detrimental activities.

Periodic caps Provisions in adjustable rate mortgages that limit change in the contract interest rate from one change date to the next.

Periodic tenancy Any lease agreement that has no definite term at the start.

Permanence potential The preference to lease residential units to households whose prior history indicates a probability of a long-term occupancy.

Permanent loan Long-term mortgage financing.

Personal liability Liability assumed by borrowers that allows lenders to sue them personally for fulfillment of the contract.

Personal performance (contract) A contract that requires a service or action on the part of one party. This includes leases and mortgage loans, for example, which require regular payments. Generally, these contracts are not fully assignable in that the lessee or mortgagor remains liable for the obligation.

Personal property Objects that are moveable and not permanently affixed to the land or sturcture, including furniture and tenants fixtures that are often purchased in conjunction with real property acquisitions.

Personal residence An owner-occupied housing unit.

Personal rights Personal freedoms derived primarily from the Bill of Rights and other amendments and clauses of the U. S. Constitution.

Physical deterioration Loss of value of a building from its reproduction cost, resulting from wear and tear over time.

Pipeline risk The time between making a loan commitment and selling the loan. The mortgage banker is exposed to considerable risk during this period.

PITI The monthly payment of principal and interest on a home mortgage loan, plus monthly payments into an escrow account toward annual property taxes and hazard insurance.

Planned unit development (PUD) A development project, often involving a mixture of land uses and densities not permitted by normal zoning. It is allowed because the entire development is viewed as an integrated whole.

Plat books Register of recorded plat maps maintained by a city or county which shows boundaries, shapes, and sizes of land parcels.

Plat lot and block number An unambiguous means to provide a description of property that identifies each parcel in a surveyed map of a subdivision.

Plottage value Value added to land by assembling small parcels into larger tracts.

Police power Right of government to regulate personal activity and the use of property to protect the health, welfare, and safety of the population.

Polychlorinated biphenyls (PCBs) Cancer-causing chemicals formerly used in the manufacture of electrical connectors and equipment.

Portfolio income An IRS classification of income generated from securities such as stocks and bonds. Income directly obtained from rental real estate activities is not considered portfolio income.

Portfolio lenders Financial institutions such as banks that fund mortgage loans and then hold the loans as investments.

Portfolio perspective Viewing real estate investments in the context of an owner's other assets and overall situation.

Potential gross income The total annual income the property would produce if it were fully rented and had no collection losses.

Power of sale Mortgage provision that grants the authority to conduct foreclosure to either the lender or a trustee. Enables non-judicial foreclosure.

Power shopping center These centers typically contain three or more giants in hard goods retailing (for example, Wall Mart and Home Depot). The dominating feature of a power center is the high ratio of anchor tenants to smaller tenants.

Prepayment penalties Charges, designed to discourage prepayment, incurred when a mortgage is repaid before maturity.

Present value The value of future cash flows at time zero.

Preventive maintenance A program of regular inspections and care to avert potential problems.

Primary mortgage market The loan origination market where borrowers and lenders negotiate mortgage terms.

Principal In brokerage, the person giving authority to an agent; in finance, the amount borrowed and owed on a loan.

Principal meridian A line of geographic reference that runs north and south in a government rectangular survey.

Private grants Conveyance of property from one private owner to another.

Private mortgage insurance (PMI) Insurance offered by private companies that reimburses the lender for capital losses in the event of default by the borrower.

Pro forma A cash flow forecast prepared to facilitate discounted cash flow analysis.

Probability distributions The distribution of all potential outcomes and their associated likelihood.

Probate State law that governs the disposition procedure of the conveyance of real property upon the death of a property owner.

Promissory note A note indicating the terms of a financial agreement.

Property Anything that can be owned, or possessed. It can be either a tangible asset or an intangible asset.

Property adjustments Five sale price adjustments made to comparable property transactions prices: location, physical characteristics, legal characteristics, use, and nonrealty items.

Property management Direction of the day-to-day operations of properties.

Property managers Individuals in charge of the day-to-day operations of a property.

Property rights Rights in property that include (exclusive) possession, use (enjoyment) and disposition.

Property tax lien Automatic lien placed by local governments to assure payment of property taxes.

Proprietary lease A lease of indefinite length in which the lessee pays expenses but not rent, associated with a cooperative.

Prorata share An amount proportionate to the ownership interest of an investor.

Prorating Allocation of costs and revenues between buyer and seller of real property at closing, based on the time of ownership by each party.

Psychographics A tool for sophisticated determination of market segmentation.

Public purpose In eminent domain cases, expansion by courts of the public use concept, no longer requiring actual physical use by the condemning agency to take property.

Public use In eminent domain, requirement of actual physical use by the condemning agency to justify condemnation.

Purchase money mortgage Typically, a mortgage loan where the seller lends all or part of the purchase price of a property to the purchaser, and the loan is secured by a mortgage, created simultaneously with conveyance of ownership.

Quiet enjoyment In leasing, once the owner has conveyed possession of the property to the tenant, the owner must provide the tenant with uninterrupted use of the property without any interference that may threaten the tenant's leasehold interest in the property. In conveyance of title, the assurance that no one holds a claim to title superior to that of the grantee, and that the grantor will defend the title claim of the grantee.

Quitclaim deed Deed that conveys an individual's property rights to another but has none of the covenants of the warranty deed.

R^2 statistic Coefficient of multiple determination that measures how well a regression model fits the data.

Radon A naturally occurring radioactive gas found in soils in most parts of the country. In large concentrations, the gas may contribute to or cause cancer.

Range line A feature of a government rectangular survey that separates townships by east and west.

Rate lock agreement An agreement in which a loan applicant pays a non-refundable deposit to protect against an interest rate increase before the loan is closed.

Raw land Land that does not include structures or any improvements.

Real asset Tangible objects that have value because they are useful.

Real estate The tangible assets of land and buildings, the "bundle" of rights associated with the ownership and use of the physical assets, and the industry, or business activities, related to the acquisition, operation, and disposition of the physical assets.

Real estate commission Appointed commission responsible for overseeing the implementation and administration of a state's real estate license law. It usually is empowered to grant, revoke, or suspend licenses, and otherwise discipline real estate brokers operating in the state.

Real estate investment trusts A corporation or trust that uses the pooled capital of many investors to purchase and manage income property (equity REIT) and/or mortgage loans (mortgage REIT).

Real Estate Settlement and Procedures Act (RESPA) A federal law requiring lenders to provide information on all costs associated with closing a residential loan within three business days of the loan application, to use the HUD-1 closing statement, to limit required escrow deposits, and to avoid kick-backs on loan-related services.

Real property Rights associated with ownership of land and all permanent attachments to land.

Reconciliation The process of forming a single point estimate from two or more numbers. It is used widely in the appraisal process. For example, in the sales comparison approach to develop a single indicated value from several final adjusted sale prices of comparables, and in final reconciliation to develop a final estimate of value from two or more indicated values.

Reconstructed operating statement A statement of property income and expenses formatted for the purposes of appraisal and investment analysis. Differs from typical management operating statement in the treatment of certain expenses, including management fees, mortgage payments and vacancy and collection losses.

Recorded plat map See Plat books.

Recording Filing of a document with the appropriate public official or office in order to provide constructive notice to the public of a sales transaction or legal contract.

Recording statutes State laws requiring documents that convey an interest in real property to be placed in the public records in order to be binding on the public.

Recourse loans Loans in which the borrower has personal liability and the lender has legal recourse against the borrower in case of default.

Recovery fund Reserve of funds collected from real estate license fees to pay for losses to clients legally judged to have been caused by a licensed salesperson or broker. The existence of such funds varies from state to state.

Redlining Term used to describe when mortgage lenders avoid certain neighborhoods without regard to the merits of the individual loan applications.

Regional shopping center These centers are focused on apparel and discretionary merchandise, and have at least two anchor tenants that are major department stores.

Regulatory taking Under precedents of the U. S. Supreme Court, the degree of land regulation that is considered to constitute effective taking of the property. If this degree of regulation is reached, the government must compensate the property owner for loss of value.

Rehabilitation The restoration of a property to satisfactory condition without changing the floor plan, form, or style of the structure.

Reinvestment risk The risk that lenders will need to reinvest the remaining loan balance at a lower rate when borrowers prepay mortgages with above-market rates.

Release of liability A document by which a lender releases a borrower from personal liability on a note.

Reliction Receding water line that leaves dry land to be added to an adjacent landowner's property.

Relocation option Generally a lease clause that gives the property owner the option to relocate a tenant within a shopping center or office building, provided the new space is of similar size

and quality and provided the owner agrees to pay all reasonable moving costs.

Remainder estate The ownership interest subsequent to a life estate which, upon the death of life estate owner, becomes a fee simple absolute interest.

Remodeling Actions resulting in changes to the floor plan, form, or style of a structure to correct functional or economic deficiencies.

Renewal option Lease clause that gives the tenant the right, but not the obligation to renew the lease.

Rentable area The office tenant's usable area, plus his or her prorated share of the common areas.

Rentable/usable (R/U) ratio The ratio of total rentable area to total usable area. Will be greater than one in office buildings.

Repeat-sale analysis Estimation of the rate of property appreciation through statistical examination of properties that have sold twice during the sample period. Normally the analysis is by statistical regression.

Replacement cost The cost to build a new building of equal utility to an existing building that is not an exact physical replica of the existing building.

Reproduction cost The cost to build a new building that is exactly like an existing building in every physical detail.

Rescind The termination of a contract by cancellation. Under the Truth-in-lending Act, a borrower's right to cancel a loan contract within three days that is secured by his or her principal residence.

Reserve for replacements an allowance in a cash flow forecast to reflect an annual allocation for periodic replacements, releasing expenses, or tenant improvements.

Restrictive covenant See deed restriction.

Reverse mortgage An arrangement where the lender agrees to pay money to an elderly homeowner, either regularly or occasionally, and to be repaid from the homeowner's equity when he or she sells the home or obtains other financing.

Reversion The cash proceeds from sale.

Reverter An uncertain interest held by the previous owner (or heirs) associated with a conditional fee.

Right of first refusal Commercial lease clause that grants the tenant first choice to lease space in a property should it become available.

Right of prepayment The right to retire a mortgage before maturity. The right of prepayment will depend on the law of the state where the property is located and on the particular mortgage contract.

Right of survivorship The rights of surviving partners in a joint tenancy to divide the interests of a deceased partner.

Riparian rights The rights of adjacent landowners to bodies of non-navigable waters.

Risk The possibility that actual outcomes will vary from what was expected when the asset was purchased.

Risk-adjusted discount rate The discount rate used by potential investors to value risky cash flows. Must reflect the relative riskiness of the asset/property being valued.

Risk-weighted assets The sum of an institution's portfolio assets weighted by their appropriate risk classification, used to determine regulatory capital requirements for depository institutions.

Rule of capture The owner of an oil or gas well could claim all that is pumped from it, regardless of whether the oil or gas migrated from adjacent property.

S corporation Corporate ownership structure that provides limited liability. It is not, however, a separate taxable entity; hence, income and losses flow through taxation to stockholders.

Sale-leasebacks Agreements in which a property owner simultaneously sells the property to a buyer and leases the property back from the buyer.

Salesperson license Authority granted by a state to engage in the real estate brokerage business as an employee or agent of a real estate broker.

Sandwich lease A sublet arrangement in which the initial lessee collects rent from the new lessee and pays rent to the landlord under the original lease agreement.

Savings and loan associations (S&Ls) Historically, a highly specialized home mortgage lending depository institution. Today, S&Ls range in character from mortgage lending specialists to being very similar to commercial banks.

Savings banks Historically empowered with wider investment powers than S&Ls, the two institutional forms are virtually indistinguishable today.

Secondary mortgage market The market where mortgage originators can divest their holdings, and existing mortgages are resold.

Section 1231 property Trade or business property held for more than one year, as classified in Section 1231 of the Internal Revenue Code.

Section 203 loan The most widely used FHA program, covering single-family home mortgages insured by the FHA under Title II, section 203 of the National Housing Act.

Section A specifically surveyed and identified square mile within the framework of the rectangular survey system.

Sector model Model of urban form proposed by Homer Hoyt that is characterized by radial corridors or wedges, particularly for higher income residential land use.

Securitized investments Investment instruments that pool investment assets, enabling investors to purchase a share in the pool of assets.

Selling expenses Costs associated with the disposition of a property.

Separate property In community property states, property that the husband or wife acquired prior to the marriage, or gifts or inheritance received during the marriage.

Servient parcel A parcel that is constrained or diminished by an easement appurtenant.

Sheriff's deed Same as definition of executor's deed.

Single-factor asset pricing model A model for determining required risk-adjusted rates of return that classifies investment risk into only two categories, systematic (or macroeconomic) and property-specific (or microeconomic).

Sinking fund factor The amount that must be deposited periodically at a specified interest rate, for a specified time period, to accumulate to $1.00 and the end of the period.

Site plan Map showing the arrangement of structures, parking, streets and other features of a development or subdivision project.

Smart growth Planning concept similar to new urbanism, and also emphasizing "compact" urban development.

Soft costs A component of construction cost including the cost of permits, legal fees, financing and insurance fees, architectural and design costs, other professional fees, and the cost of marketing.

Soils engineer An engineer specializing in the analysis of soils and soil load-bearing capacity, and in determining adequate footing and foundation requirements for a structure.

Sole proprietorship Ownership structure where all cash flow and income tax consequences flow through directly to the individual's income tax return, thereby avoiding taxation at the entity level.

Special agent A person to whom a principal has granted authority to handle a specific business transaction or to perform a specific function. Real estate brokers and salespersons are special agents.

Special assessments Property taxes levied to finance special improvements to benefit adjacent property owners. For example, property owners in a subdivision could be forced to pay for the installation of sanitary sewers.

Special warranty deed Identical to a general warranty deed except that the covenant against encumbrances applies only to the time that the grantor owned the property.

Specialty shopping center These centers are characterized by a dominant theme or image and many are located in downtown areas or rehabilitated historic structures. Outlet centers are a variation of this theme.

Specific lien An interest that derives directly from events related to a property, such as property tax and assessment liens, mortgages, and mechanics' liens.

Sprawl A term applied pejoratively to many aspects of suburban development. A relatively restrictive use of the term refers to unregulated real estate development outside of central urban areas, and to "leap-frog" development.

Spread The difference between the expected yield on an investment and the yield on a riskless Treasury security with a comparable maturity.

Standard deduction The amount of deductible expenses, specified by Congress, that a taxpayer may claim in lieu of itemizing allowable personal expenditures.

Standard deviation A measure of the dispersion of a distribution around its expected value, defined as the square root of the variance.

Standard error (SE) The standard deviation of the sampling distribution of a statistic, such as an estimated mean value, or a regression coefficient.

Standby forward commitment In mortgage lending, forward commitments where the mortgage banker has the right, but not the obligation, to sell a prespecified dollar amount of a certain loan type at a prespecified price to the seller of the commitment.

Statement of condition A document signed by the tenant of a residential property before moving in that lists any prior damage to the unit.

Statute of Frauds Provision adopted by all states requiring that all deeds, long-term leases and mortgages must be in writing to be enforceable. Derives from the original Statute of Frauds on 1677.

Statutory redemption Law in some states that provides time to borrowers of foreclosed properties to regain title after the foreclosure sale.

Structural engineer An engineer specializing in the design of buildings and other structures that are efficient for their purpose, while meeting standards of sturdiness and safety.

Subagency The agency role of a broker is extended to one or more additional brokers, who also become a fiduciary of the principal and are empowered to act on his or her behalf. The sub-agent shares any commission with the original broker. This agency chain can extend through multiple agents in the case of multiple-list services.

Subchapter S corporation Corporate ownership structure that is a federal tax election made with the unanimous consent of the shareholders. An S corporation possesses the same limited liability benefits for its shareholders as do C corporations but it is not a separate taxable entity.

Subcontractor Companies or individuals who provide specialized construction activities, such as installation of heating, ventilating and air conditioning systems, elevator systems, paint-ing, carpet installation, and a multitude of other building components.

Subject property The property for which an appraisal of fair market value is produced.

Subject to When a buyer acquires a property having an existing mortgage loan and begins making the required payments without assuming personal responsibility for the note.

Subjective probability distribution For a set of possible outcomes of an uncertain event, an opinion or guess as to the likelihood of each possible outcome.

Sublease Occurs when the original tenant transfers a subset of his or her rights under the lease to another tenant, although the original tenant (lessee) continues to be obligated for payments.

Submarket Segment or portion of a market in which all of the properties are considered to be close substitutes by a relatively homogeneous group of potential buyers; properties that provide similar utility or satisfaction.

Subordination agreement A contract by which a party holding a superior claim agrees to make it subject to a previously inferior claim. Commonly used to reverse the priority of mortgage liens.

Sub-prime loans Loans made to homeowners who do not qualify for standard home loans. Sub-prime loans can have high fees, and costly prepayment penalties that "lock in" the borrower to a high interest rate.

Superregional malls These shopping centers have as many as five to six major tenants and hundreds of minor tenants.

Survey (of land) Process of accurately establishing the boundaries of a parcel of real estate.

Syndicate A group of persons or legal entities who come together to carry out a particular investment activity.

Systematic risk Risk that cannot be diversified away—even in a large portfolio. This type of risk results from exposure to macroeconomic risk factors.

Take-out commitment Agreement, issued by a long-term lender, to disburse the permanent loan proceeds when construction of a project has been completed according to specifications.

Tangible assets Physical things, such as automobiles, clothing, land, or buildings.

Tax assessor The local public official in charge of determining the taxable value of property in the jurisdiction as the basis for property taxation. In some states this official is called the county property appraiser.

Tax base All of the taxable properties in a jurisdiction.

Tax certificates Obligations for unpaid taxes sold by taxing jurisdictions in order to collect the amount of unpaid taxes. The property owner, in order to redeem (take back) the property, or any future purchaser of the property, must pay off the tax certificates to obtain title to the property.

Tax depreciation The reduction in annual taxable income, in accordance with IRS rules, intended to reflect the wear and tear that income properties experience over time.

Tax rate (property tax) The number of dollars of property tax divided by the taxable value of the properties. The percentage that, when multiplied by a property's taxable value, will yield the tax liability.

Taxable value The assessed value less any applicable exemptions, to determine the amount of property tax owed.

Tax-exempt properties Properties against which local jurisdictions may not levy taxes, usually including churches, synagogues, public schools, and government property.

Teaser rate The initial interest rate on an adjustable rate mortgage if it is less than the index rate plus the margin at the time of origination.

Tenancy at sufferance A tenancy that occurs when a tenant that is supposed to vacate does not, but continues to pay rent, and the landlord accepts it.

Tenancy at will A tenancy granted by landlords to tenants allowing them to remain in possession without written agreement.

Tenancy by the entireties A form of joint tenancy ownership for husband and wife.

Tenancy for years A leasehold interest for a definite period of time exceeding one year.

Tenancy in common The "normal" form of direct co-ownership, which is as close to the fee simple absolute estate as is possible, subject to the provision that one owner cannot use the property in a manner that infringes on the rights of co-owners.

Tenant improvement allowance The amount of funding the owner of commercial property must provide toward the cost of refurbishing the space to meet the tenant's needs.

Tenant mix The synergism created by the right grouping of tenants that results in the right mix of tenants that "makes the whole greater than the sum of its parts."

Tenant reps Brokers or agents that specialize in helping tenants find suitable space to lease.

Term for amortization Time period that determines the payment, and the schedule of interest and principal payments on a mortgage.

Term to maturity Term found in a balloon loan that determines when the entire remaining balance on the loan must be paid in full.

Terminal capitalization rate Rate used to convert annual net cash at the end of an expected holding period into an estimate of future sale price.

Terminal value The sale price at the end of the expected holding period.

Terms Arrangements of a sale agreed to by the parties, for example, the transaction price, the date of closing, and condition of the property upon closing.

Testate Conveyance of real property upon the death of a property owner in accordance with a will.

Tier line A feature of government rectangular survey that serves to number townships south or north from the base line.

Timesharing Property occupancy arrangement in which multiple individuals have use of property but, unlike traditional forms of co-ownership, the interests are at different time intervals rather than simultaneous. A timesharing arrangement may involve true co-ownership, leasehold interests, or simply permission to occupy (i. e. license).

Time-value-of-money (TVM) techniques Standard techniques for quantifying the effects of time and risk on value.

Title abstract with attorney's opinion Traditional evidence of title.

Title abstract The compilation of all documents summarizing the chain of title into a chronological volume and then given to an attorney for final interpretation.

Title insurance commitment A commitment to issue a title insurance policy.

Title insurance Insurance paying monetary damages for loss of property from unexpected superior legal claims or for litigation to protect title. Deemed superior to the traditional abstract with opinion since it offers insurance, in addition.

Title search The task of examining the evidence of title in the public records.

Title theory Lender receives title to the mortgaged property that ripens upon default.

Torrens certificate A rarely used means of providing evidence of title.

Total debt ratio One of two common ratios used by home mortgage lenders to determine a borrower's ability to pay a debt; defined at PITI and other long-term obligations divided by the borrower's gross monthly income.

Township A unit within the government rectangular survey system having an area of six miles by six miles, and containing 36 fully described, one square mile sections.

Toxic waste Hazardous materials such as asbestos, fiberglass, lead paint, radon, PCBs, leaking underground storage tanks, and the like.

Trade fixtures Personal property usually paid for by the tenant that may be removed by the tenant at lease expiration.

Trade or business property Under Section 1231 of the Internal Revenue Code, real estate held for more than one year in a trade or business activity, including most income-producing property.

Transaction broker One who facilitates a real estate transaction but who is not an agent of either buyer or seller. A transaction broker is required to deal honestly and fairly with both parties and to exercise skill, care, and diligence in carrying out his or her duties.

Transaction price The prices observed on sold properties.

Transactional adjustments In an appraisal, adjustments to comparable property transaction prices that concern the nature and terms of the deal.

Trustee In mortgage lending, person who holds the deed on behalf of both the borrower and lender in a deed of trust.

Trustee's deed A deed issued by the trustee in a court-supervised disposition of property, for example by an executor and administrator of an estate, a guardian of a minor, a bankruptcy trustee, or possibly by an attorney in divorce proceedings.

Truth-in-Lending Act (TILA) A federal law requiring lenders to provide residential loan applicants with estimates of the total finance charges and the annual percentage rate (APR).

Turnkey Refers to a project where the owner or builder makes a property ready for the occupant to immediately move in and begin business.

Umbrella partnership REIT (UPREIT) An organizational structure in which a publicly traded REIT owns a fractional interest in an Operating Partnership, which in turn, owns all or part of individual property partnerships.

Uniform Standards of Professional Appraisal Practice Rules governing the appraisal process and reporting of appraisals that are developed by the Appraisal Standards Board of the Appraisal Foundation. Appraisers are obligated by law to follow these rules and guidelines.

Universal agent One to whom a principal delegates the power to act in all matters that can be delegated in place of the principal.

Unlevered cash flows The expected stream of NOIs and the expected net sale proceeds (NSP). This represents the income producing ability of the property before subtracting the portion of the cash flows that must be paid to the lender to service or retire the debt.

Unsystematic risk The variation in portfolio returns that can be eliminated by holding securities and other investments with less than perfectly correlated returns. Results from exposure to microeconomic risk factors.

Up-front financing costs Cost incurred by the property owner to obtain mortgage financing, including loan origination fees, discount points, appraisal fees, and survey. On a rental property investment, these costs are amortized over the life of the loan for tax purposes.

Urban service area An area delineated around a community within which the local government plans to provide public services and facilities and beyond which urban development is discouraged or prohibited.

Usable area The area of an office building that is in the sole possession of the tenant.

User markets Potential occupants, both owner occupants and tenants, or renters competing for physical location and space.

VA-guaranteed loan A Government guaranteed loan designed to help veterans obtain home mortgage loans for which they might not otherwise qualify.

Variance (statistics) A measure of the dispersion of an ex ante distribution probability around its expected value or the dispersion of historical (realized) cash flows or returns around the mean value.

Variance (zoning) A permitted deviation for a particular property from the applicable zoning requirements. To be granted only when the zoning ordinance imposes undue hardship to the property owner.

Veterans Affairs A United States government Department whose purpose is to help veterans readjust to civilian life.

Warehouses Provide space for the temporary storage of goods.

Warehousing The provision by commercial banks of short-term funds to mortgage banking companies to enable them to originate and fund mortgage loans until they can be sold in the secondary mortgage market.

Words of conveyance Early in the deed will be words such as "does hereby grant, bargain, sell, and convey unto...." that serve to assure the grantor clearly intends to convey an interest in real property and indicate the type of deed offered by the grantor.

Wrap-around mortgage Financing, usually from the seller, in which a new loan is created around an existing loan that the seller keeps in place.

Yield maintenance penalty Provision requiring a borrower who wishes to prepay the mortgage to pay the principal balance, plus the present value (as defined in the note) of the interest income that will be lost by the lender due to prepayment.

Zoning Regulation of land use, population density, and building size by district. May be viewed as a phase of comprehensive planning in which the plan's implementation is enforced through the police power of local governments.

Photo Credits

Chapter 1

Photo 1-1, page 7, Copyright University of Cincinnati.

Photo 1-2, page 14, Copyright *The Economist* Newspaper, Limited, 2003.

Photo 1-3, page 18, Copyright US Department of Housing and Urban Development.

Chapter 2

Photo 2-1, page 25, Copyright US Department of Housing and Urban Development.

Photo 2-2, page 32, Copyright *Palm Beach Post,* June 7, 2002.

Photo 2-3, page 32, Copyright *Palm Beach Post,* June 7, 2002.

Chapter 4

Photo 4-1, page 73, Reprinted with permission from http://www.egghof.com/NewYork/metlife.htm.

Photo 4-2, page 73, Reprinted with permission from www.chicagoneweastside.com/index2.html.

Photo 4-3, page 74, Copyright Cable News Network, LP, LLLP (CNN).

Photo 4-4, page 74, Copyright Cable News Network, LP, LLLP (CNN).

Photo 4-5, page 90, Copyright The State of Texas.

Photo 4-6, page 95, Copyright The State of New York Senate.

Chapter 5

Photo 5-1, page 105, Reprinted with permission from Marshall, Texas Chamber of Commerce.

Photo 5-2, page 105, Kelley Bergstrom, Marshall Mall L.L.C./Kelley Bergstrom Investment Management, L.L.C.

Photo 5-3, page 106, Copyright U.S. Census Bureau.

Photo 5-4, page 106, Copyright U.S. Census Bureau.

Photo 5-5, page 107, Copyright U.S. Census Bureau.

Photo 5-6, page 107, Copyright U.S. Census Bureau.

Photo 5-7, page 107, Copyright U.S. Census Bureau.

Photo 5-8, page 107, Copyright U.S. Census Bureau.

Photo 5-9, page 120, Copyright BellSouth.

Photo 5-10, page 120, Copyright from BellSouth.

Photo 5-11, page 121, Author photo.

Photo 5-12, page 121, Author photo.

Photo 5-13, page 123, Reprinted with permission from www.taylorsvillenc.com/projects.htm.

Chapter 6

Photo 6-1, page 134, Reprinted with permission from Planetizen.

Photo 6-2, page 137, Reprinted with permission from The National Geographic Society.

Photo 6-3, page 137, Author photo.

Photo 6-4, page 155, Reprinted with permission from Gainesville-Alachua County, Florida.

Chapter 7

Photo 7-1, page 175, Copyright U.S. Bureau of Labor Statistics.

Photo 7-2, page 183, Copyright Metropolitan Washington Airports Authority.

Chapter 8

Photo 8-1, page 211, Copyright The Electronic Appraiser.

Chapter 9

Photo 9-1, page 235, Copyright LoopNet.

Photo 9-2, page 242, Copyright The CoStar Group.

Chapter 10

Photo 10-1, page 256, Copyright Freddie Mac.

Photo 10-2, page 256, Copyright Freddie Mac.

Chapter 11
Photo 11-1, page 295, Copyright Freddie Mac.

Chapter 12
Photo 12-1, page 319, Copyright Mortgage Select.com.

Chapter 13
Photo 13-1, page 349, Copyright Freddie Mac.

Chapter 15
Photo 15-1, page 385, Copyright National Association of Real Estate Investment Trusts (NAREIT).
Photo 15-2, page 396, Copyright National Association of Industrial and Office Properties (NAIOP).

Chapter 16
Photo 16-1, page 416, Reprinted with permission from The National Council of Real Estate Investment Fiduciaries (NCREIF).

Chapter 18
Photo 18-1, page 472, Reprinted with permission from Douglas County, Colorado.
Photo 18-2, page 482, Reprinted with permission from www.tngenweb.org.
Photo 18-3, page 484, Copyright Baseline Meridian California State Office.
Photo 18-4, page 486, Author photo.

Chapter 19
Photo 19-1, page 499, Copyright Association of Real Estate License Law Officials (ARELLO).
Photo 19-2, page 515, Copyright Gainesville-Alachua County Association of Realtors, Inc.

Chapter 20
Photo 20-1, page 530, Copyright Gainesville-Alachua County Association of Realtors, Inc.
Photo 20-2, page 539, Copyright U.S. Department of Housing and Urban Development.
Photo 20-3, page 546, Copyright U.S. Department of Housing and Urban Development.

Chapter 21
Photo 21-1, page 559, Copyright ITRA Realty Group.
Photo 21-2, page 578, Copyright CityFeet.com.

Chapter 22
Photo 22-1, page 585, Copyright Internal Revenue Service, U.S. Department of the Treasury.

Chapter 23
Photo 23-1, page 637, Copyright Reuters Research Inc.

Chapter 24
Photo 24-1, page 650, Copyright *St. Petersburg Times*.
Photo 24-2, page 650, Mark Diamond/Diamond Images.
Photo 24-3, page 651, Author photo.
Photo 24-4, page 651, Author photo.
Photo 24-5, page 661, Copyright Urban Land Institute.
Photo 24-6, page 664, Author photo.

Index

Chapter Eight

www.appraisalinstitute.org

www.rics.org

www.iaao.org

www.masterappraiser.org

www.appraisalfoundation.org

www.realestate.yahoo.com/realestate/homevalues

www.cswcasa.com

www.marshallswift.com

www.rsmeans.com

www.appraisal_network.com

www.electronicappraiser.com

www.realestate.yahoo.com/re/homevalues

www.appraisalinstitute.com

Chapter Nine

www.appraisalinstitute.org/publications/
periodicals/ano/default.asp

www.reis.com

www.cpnrenet.com

www.appraise.com

www.blacksguide.com

www.tortowheatonresearch.com

www.cushmanwakefield.com

www.grubb-ellis.com

www.economy.com

www.nreionline.com

www.loopnet.com

www.costar.com

Chapter Ten

www.fhfb.gov/MIRS/MIRS_rates.htm

www.research.stlouisfed.org/fred2/series/DGS1/22

www.federalreserve.gov/releases/h15/update

www.freddiemac.com/pmms/pmmsarm.htm

www.federalreserve.gov/pubs/brochures/
arms/arms.pdf

www.freddiemac.com

www.foreclosures.com'pages/statelaws.asp

www.foreclosuresassistance.com/states.html

www.hud.gov/offices/hsg/sfh/res/
respa_hm.cfm

www.aba/com/Consumer+Connection/
CNC_pred2.htm

www.ftc.gov/bcp/con_line/pubs/homes/eqscams.pdf

www.ffiec.gov/hmda/default.htm

www.ffiec.gov/cra/default.htm

www.freddiemac.com/uniform/

Chapter Eleven

www.federalreserve.gov/regulations/regref.htm#z

www.hud.gov/offices/hsg/sfh/res/respa_hm.cfm

www.freddiemac.com/calculators

www.fanniemae.com/homebuyers/calculators

www.mbaa.org/consumer/index.html

www.fanniemae.com

www.freddiemac.com

Chapter Twelve

www.freddiemac.com

www.fanniemae.com

www.mgic.com

www.mgic.com/pdf/71-6704.pdf/

www.hud.gov/offices/hsg/sfh/insured.cfm

www.entp.hud.gov/idapp/html:hicostlook

www.homeloans.va.gov/veteran.htm

www.reversemortgage.org/index.html

www.aarp.org/revmort/

www.hud.gov/offices/hsg/sfh/hecm/hecmhome.cfm

www.fanniemae.com/homebuyers/
fundamortgate/mortgages

www.mortgageselect.com/cales/
refinance.asp?referrer=162

Chapter Thirteen

www.fdic.gov/bank/historical/index.html

www.mortgagebankers.org/resident

www.namb.org

www.ginniemae.gov

www.fanniemae.com/index.jhtml

www.freddiemac.com/singlefamily/

www.freddiemac.com/mbs

www.freddiemac.com/lp

www.freddiemac.com/sell/expmkts/affprod.html

www.hud.gov/offices/hsg/pred/predlnd1.cfm

www.mbaa.org/resources/predlend

www.myfico.com

Chapter Fourteen

www.mbaa.org

www.namb.org

www.malert.com

www.property.com

www.globest.com

www.lmres.com/ourbusinesses/financing/
    mortgagecalculator.asp

www.looplender.com

www.ired.com

www.freddiemac.com

www.freddiemac.com/multifamily/product.htm

Chapter Fifteen

www.nareit.com

www.mbaaorg

www.prea.org

www.irei.com

www.ncreif.org

www.cmba.org

www.realwebfunds.com

www.naiop.org

www.crewnetwork.org

www.nmhc.org

www.icsc.org

www.reits.com

Chapter Sixteen

www.realstateindex.com

www.wellsref.com

www.grubb-ellis.com

www.boma.org

www.icsc.org

www.nmhc.org

www.reis.com

www.pikenet.com

www.ncreif.com

www.ncreif.org

www.nationalreia.com

www.ccim.com

Chapter Seventeen

www.nreionline.com

www.recenter.tamu.edu

www.naiop.org

www.irem.org

www.boma.org

www.narpm.org

www.ifma.org

www.ncreif.com

www.nareit.com

www.wilshire.com/indexes.realestate

www.corenetglobal.com

www.caplease.com

www.wpcarey.com

www.cnlreit.com

www.usrealtyadvisors.com

www.law.cornell.edu/topics.landlord_tenant.html

Chapter Eighteen

www.nccusl.org/ncusl/uniformactsalphabetically.asp

www.alta.org/cnsrinfo/educabtli/

Chapter Nineteen

www.realtor.org

www.realtor.org/mempolweb.nsf/pages/code/
    opendocument

www.arello.com/site/ruleslans.jsp#USrules-laws

www.dos.state.ny.us/lcns/realest.html

www.dre.ca.gov/

www.obre/state.il.us/realest/realest.htm

www.arello.com/site/ruleslaws.jsp

www.realtor.org

www.sior.com

www.cre.org

www.ired.com

www.realtor.com